Tony Billinghurst,
33 Christchurch Rd,
TILBURY,
Essex. 1961.

THE BOOK OF
CRICKET RECORDS

ROY WEBBER

The Book of

Cricket

Records

Completely Revised and
Reset Edition 1961

PHOENIX HOUSE

LONDON

Contents

PAGE

Introduction 9

TEST CRICKET RECORDS

TABLE OF RESULTS AND INNINGS TOTALS OF ALL TEST
    MATCHES 12
PART I. THE SIDES 23
PART II. BATTING 33
PART III. WICKET PARTNERSHIPS 45
PART IV. BOWLING 49
PART V. ALL-ROUND CRICKET 53
PART VI. FIELDING AND WICKET-KEEPING . . . 54
PART VII. CAREER RECORDS 56
PART VIII. MEMORABILIA 61
APPENDIX A. COMPLETE CAREER RECORD IN TESTS FOR
    ALL PLAYERS 75
APPENDIX B. CENTURIES IN TEST CRICKET . . . 105
APPENDIX C. BOWLERS TAKING TEN WICKETS IN A TEST
    MATCH 117
APPENDIX D. CENTURY WICKET PARTNERSHIPS IN TEST
    CRICKET 120
APPENDIX E. TEST MATCH CAPTAINS 136
APPENDIX F. RECORDS OF INDIVIDUAL TEST SERIES . 141
APPENDIX G. COUNTIES PROVIDING ENGLAND PLAYERS 156

FIRST-CLASS CRICKET RECORDS

PART I. THE SIDES 162
PART II. BATTING 183
PART III. WICKET PARTNERSHIPS 271
PART IV. BOWLING 312
PART V. ALL-ROUND CRICKET 366
PART VI. FIELDING AND WICKET-KEEPING . . 376
PART VII. CAREER RECORDS 388
PART VIII. COMPETITION RECORDS, ETC. . . . 403
PART IX. MISCELLANEOUS 455

Note.—An alphabetical index of the more important items in the book can be found on pages 473 to 480.

Contents

PAGE

Introduction

TEST CRICKET RECORDS

Table of Results and Innings Totals of all Test Matches ... 13
Part I. The Sides ... 19
Part II. Batting ... 31
Part III. Wicket Partnerships ... 45
Part IV. Bowling ... 48
Part V. All-Round Cricket ... 63
Part VI. Fielding and Wicket-keeping ... 69
Part VII. Career Records ... 75
Part VIII. Memorabilia ... 81
Appendix A. Complete Career Record in Tests for all Players ... 75
Appendix B. Centuries in Test Cricket ... 105
Appendix C. Bowlers taking Ten Wickets in a Test Match ... 117
Appendix D. Century Wicket Partnerships in Test Cricket ... 120
Appendix E. Test Match Captains ... 126
Appendix F. Records of Individual Test Series ... 141
Appendix G. Complete Provincial England Players ... 156

FIRST-CLASS CRICKET RECORDS

Part I. The Sides ... 165
Part II. Batting ... 187
Part III. Wicket Partnerships ... 221
Part IV. Bowling ... 243
Part V. All-Round Cricket ... 366
Part VI. Fielding and Wicket-keeping ... 376
Part VII. Career Records ... 384
Part VIII. Competition Records, etc. ... 403
Part IX. Miscellaneous ... 414

Note. An alphabetical index of the more important items in the book can be found on pages 474 to 480.

Introduction

TEN YEARS ago my collection of Cricket Records was published for the first time under the title of *The Playfair Book of Cricket Records*, but so much has happened in the past decade that a new and completely recompiled book appears to have become an urgent necessity. If one wished to give a title to the 1950s it would obviously have to be the 'decade of the slow scorer', as a glance at the pages of fast and slow scoring will confirm.

When this book was first published ten years ago two things quickly became obvious from the correspondence received. The first was that a number of items worthy of inclusion had not been recorded in various reference books and could only be traced by going back to source material in the form of scorebooks. This proved to be the case with J. C. Laker's first hat-trick at Hastings in 1947, which had not been mentioned in the reports of the match and thus escaped the notice of all those who were not actually at the match.

The second conclusion was that a reliable list of all first-class matches was a necessity before revision of the book could begin. Quite obviously a list compiled by one person would be liable both to inaccuracy and suspicion of personal views over the status of matches. To this end I asked Mr N. S. Curnow and Mr A. H. Wagg if they would assist, and a couple of hard years' work followed before we did finally emerge from a mass of data with two lists, one of first-class matches in England, the other of first-class matches overseas. It would be surprising if these lists were accepted without query, but we would need a very good case put forward before any more matches were added, or any there deleted. For the overseas list one had to go back only to 1855–56, but the problem of when to start the list in England could be settled only by compromise, and we decided on the year 1800 as an arbitrary date. This would mean that all Gentlemen v. Players and University matches would be included—to go much later would mean the exclusion of some of these early fixtures. For the pre-1864 period in England the demarcation line of first-class cricket has been given a very strict view, but as few items of record interest are involved this is a small matter.

Over the past ten years I have been involved in a continual check and recheck of the Cricket Records, and those included in this book are complete to the end of the 1960 cricket season. It would be wishful thinking to feel that this work could be free of errors of omission and commission, but much work has been done to ensure as high a standard of accuracy as possible.

I would be pleased to receive letters from readers who spot errors, as it is hoped that in future an appendix volume will be issued every few years, and any items omitted can be included in the first appendix volume.

I should like to conclude by thanking the many people, too numerous to mention, who wrote to me after the publication of the first book ten years ago and whose letters have helped to make this edition more complete—also those to whom I have written with queries and have been kind enough to take the time and trouble to deal with queries raised—and finally to my main helpers, Messrs N. S. Curnow and A. H. Wagg, for whose assistance it is impossible to find the words to thank them adequately. Last, but not least, to Mr M. Fordham, who read through the proofs at the final stage and I hope unearthed the errors which I had overlooked.

In this work the sign * denotes a not-out innings or unfinished partnership, and 'd' an innings declared closed. Other signs are explained in their correct place in the text.

ROY WEBBER

TEST CRICKET RECORDS

Results and Scores of all Test Matches

ENGLAND v. AUSTRALIA

Venue and Result	England 1st inns	England 2nd inns	Australia 1st inns	Australia 2nd inns
1876–77 in Australia				
Melbourne—Australia 45 runs	196	108	245	104
Melbourne—England 4 wkts	261	122–6	122	259
1878–79 in Australia				
Melbourne—Australia 10 wkts	113	160	256	19–0
1880 in England				
Oval—England 5 wkts	420	57–5	149	327
1881–82 in Australia				
Melbourne—Drawn	294	308	320	127–3
Sydney—Australia 5 wkts	133	232	197	169–5
Sydney—Australia 6 wkts	188	134	260	66–4
Melbourne—Drawn	309	234–2	300	—
1882 in England				
Oval—Australia 7 runs	101	77	63	122
1882–83 in Australia				
Melbourne—Australia 9 wkts	177	169	291	58–1
Melbourne—England Inns & 27 runs	294	—	114	153
Sydney—England 69 runs	247	123	218	83
Sydney—Australia 4 wkts	263	197	262	199–6
1884 in England				
Manchester—Drawn	95	180–9	182	—
Lord's—England Inns & 5 runs	379	—	229	145
Oval—Drawn	346	85–2	551	—
1884–85 in Australia				
Adelaide—England 8 wkts	369	67–2	243	191
Melbourne—England 10 wkts	401	7–0	279	126
Sydney—Australia 6 runs	133	207	181	165
Sydney—Australia 8 wkts	269	77	309	38–2
Melbourne—England Inns & 98 runs	386	—	163	125
1886 in England				
Manchester—England 4 wkts	223	107–6	205	123
Lord's—England Inns & 106 runs	353	—	121	126
Oval—England Inns & 217 runs	434	—	68	149
1886–87 in Australia				
Sydney—England 13 runs	45	184	119	97
Sydney—England 71 runs	151	154	84	150
1887–88 in Australia				
Sydney—England 126 runs	113	137	42	82
1888 in England				
Lord's—Australia 61 runs	53	62	116	60
Oval—England Inns & 137 runs	317	—	80	100
Manchester—England Inns & 21 runs	172	—	81	70
1890 in England				
Lord's—England 7 wkts	173	137–3	132	176
Oval—England 2 wkts	100	95–8	92	102
Manchester—Abandoned	—	—	—	—
1891–92 Australia				
Melbourne—Australia 54 runs	264	158	240	236
Sydney—Australia 73 runs	307	156	145	391
Adelaide—England Inns & 230 runs	499	—	100	169
1893 in England				
Lord's—Drawn	334	234–8d	269	—
Oval—England Inns & 43 runs	483	—	91	349
Manchester—Drawn	243	118–4	204	236

Venue and Result	England		Australia	
	1st inns	*2nd inns*	*1st inns*	*2nd inns*
1894–95 in Australia				
Sydney—England 10 runs	325	437	586	166
Melbourne—England 94 runs	75	475	123	333
Adelaide—Australia 382 runs	124	143	238	411
Sydney—Australia Inns & 147 runs	65	72	284	—
Melbourne—England 6 wkts	385	298–4	414	267
1896 in England				
Lord's—England 6 wkts	292	111–4	53	347
Manchester—Australia 3 wkts	231	305	412	125–7
Oval—England 66 runs	145	84	119	44
1897–98 in Australia				
Sydney—England 9 wkts	551	96–1	237	408
Melbourne—Australia Inns & 55 runs	315	150	520	—
Adelaide—Australia Inns & 13 runs	278	282	573	—
Melbourne—Australia 8 wkts	174	263	323	115–2
Sydney—Australia 6 wkts	335	178	239	276–4
1899 in England				
Nottingham—Drawn	193	155–7	252	230–8d
Lord's—Australia 10 wkts	206	240	421	28–0
Leeds—Drawn	220	19–0	172	224
Manchester—Drawn	372	94–3	196	346–7d
Oval—Drawn	576	—	352	254–5
1901–02 in Australia				
Sydney—England Inns & 124 runs	464	—	168	172
Melbourne—Australia 229 runs	61	175	112	353
Adelaide—Australia 4 wkts	388	247	321	315–6
Sydney—Australia 7 wkts	317	99	299	121–3
Melbourne—Australia 32 runs	189	178	144	255
1902 in England				
Birmingham—Drawn	376–9d	—	36	46–2
Lord's—Drawn	102–2	—	—	—
Sheffield—Australia 143 runs	145	195	194	289
Manchester—Australia 3 runs	262	120	299	86
Oval—England 1 wkt	183	263–9	324	121
1903–04 in Australia				
Sydney—England 5 wkts	577	194–5	285	485
Melbourne—England 185 runs	315	103	122	111
Adelaide—Australia 216 runs	245	278	388	351
Sydney—England 157 runs	249	210	131	171
Melbourne—Australia 218 runs	61	101	247	133
1905 in England				
Nottingham—England 213 runs	196	426–5d	221	188
Lord's—Drawn	282	151–5	181	—
Leeds—Drawn	301	295–5d	195	224–7
Manchester—England Inns & 80 runs	446	—	197	169
Oval—Drawn	430	261–6d	363	124–4
1907–08 in Australia				
Sydney—Australia 2 wkts	273	300	300	275–8
Melbourne—England 1 wkt	382	282–9	266	397
Adelaide—Australia 245 runs	363	183	285	506
Melbourne—Australia 308 runs	105	186	214	385
Sydney—Australia 49 runs	281	229	137	422
1909 in England				
Birmingham—England 10 wkts	121	105–0	74	151
Lord's—Australia 9 wkts	269	121	350	41–1
Leeds—Australia 126 runs	182	87	188	207
Manchester—Drawn	119	108–3	147	279–9d
Oval—Drawn	352	104–3	325	339–5d
1911–12 in Australia				
Sydney—Australia 146 runs	318	291	447	308
Melbourne—England 8 wkts	265	219–2	184	299
Adelaide—England 7 wkts	501	112–3	133	476
Melbourne—England Inns & 225 runs	589	—	191	173
Sydney—England 70 runs	324	214	176	292

Venue and Result	England 1st inns	2nd inns	Australia 1st inns	2nd inns
1912 in England				
Lord's—Drawn	310–7d	—	282–7	—
Manchester—Drawn	203	—	14–0	—
Oval—England 244 runs	245	175	111	65
1920–21 in Australia				
Sydney—Australia 377 runs	190	281	267	581
Melbourne—Australia Inns & 91 runs	251	157	499	—
Adelaide—Australia 119 runs	447	370	354	582
Melbourne—Australia 8 wkts	284	315	389	211–2
Sydney—Australia 9 wkts	204	280	392	93–1
1921 in England				
Nottingham—Australia 10 wkts	112	147	232	30–0
Lord's—Australia 8 wkts	187	283	342	131–2
Leeds—Australia 219 runs	259	202	407	273–7d
Manchester—Drawn	362–4d	44–1	175	—
Oval—Drawn	403–8d	244–2	389	—
1924–25 in Australia				
Sydney—Australia 193 runs	298	411	450	452
Melbourne—Australia 81 runs	479	290	600	250
Adelaide—Australia 11 runs	365	363	489	250
Melbourne—England Inns & 29 runs	548	—	269	250
Sydney—Australia 307 runs	167	146	295	325
1926 in England				
Nottingham—Drawn	32–0	—	—	—
Lord's—Drawn	475–3d	—	383	194–5
Leeds—Drawn	294	254–3	494	—
Manchester—Drawn	305–5	—	335	—
Oval—England 289 runs	280	436	302	125
1928–29 in Australia				
Brisbane—England 675 runs	521	342–8d	122	66
Sydney—England 8 wkts	636	16–2	253	397
Melbourne—England 3 wkts	417	332–7	397	351
Adelaide—England 12 runs	334	383	369	336
Melbourne—Australia 5 wkts	519	257	491	287–5
1930 in England				
Nottingham—England 93 runs	270	302	144	335
Lord's—Australia 7 wkts	425	375	729–6d	72–3
Leeds—Drawn	391	95–3	566	—
Manchester—Drawn	251–8	—	345	—
Oval—Australia Inns & 39 runs	405	251	695	—
1932–33 in Australia				
Sydney—England 10 wkts	524	1–0	360	164
Melbourne—Australia 111 runs	169	139	228	191
Adelaide—England 338 runs	341	412	222	193
Brisbane—England 6 wkts	356	162–4	340	175
Sydney—England 8 wkts	454	168–2	435	182
1934 in England				
Nottingham—Australia 238 runs	268	141	374	273–8d
Lord's—England Inns & 38 runs	440	—	284	118
Manchester—Drawn	627–9d	123–0d	491	66–1
Leeds—Drawn	200	229–6	584	—
Oval—Australia 562 runs	321	145	701	327
1936–37 in Australia				
Brisbane—England 322 runs	358	256	234	58
Sydney—England Inns & 22 runs	426–6d	—	80	324
Melbourne—Australia 365 runs	76–9d	323	200–9d	564
Adelaide—Australia 148 runs	330	243	288	433
Melbourne—Australia Inns & 200 runs	239	165	604	—
1938 in England				
Nottingham—Drawn	658–8d	—	411	427–6
Lord's—Drawn	494	242–8d	422	204–6
Manchester—Abandoned	—	—	—	—
Leeds—Australia 5 wkts	223	123	242	107–5
Oval—England Inns & 579 runs	903–7d	—	201	123

Venue and Result	England 1st inns	2nd inns	Australia 1st inns	2nd inns
1946–47 in Australia				
Brisbane—Australia Inns & 332 runs	141	172	645	—
Sydney—Australia Inns & 33 runs	255	371	659–8d	—
Melbourne—Drawn	351	310–7	365	536
Adelaide—Drawn	460	340–8d	487	215–1
Sydney—Australia 5 wkts	280	186	253	214–5
1948 in England				
Nottingham—Australia 8 wkts	165	441	509	98–2
Lord's—Australia 409 runs	215	186	350	460–7d
Manchester—Drawn	363	174–3d	221	92–1
Leeds—Australia 7 wkts	496	365–8d	458	404–3
Oval—Australia Inns & 149 runs	52	188	389	—
1950–51 in Australia				
Brisbane—Australia 70 runs	68–7d	122	228	32–7d
Melbourne—Australia 28 runs	197	150	194	181
Sydney—Australia Inns & 13 runs	290	123	426	—
Adelaide—Australia 274 runs	272	228	371	403–8d
Melbourne—England 8 wkts	320	95–2	217	197
1953 in England				
Nottingham—Drawn	144	120–1	249	123
Lord's—Drawn	372	282–7	346	368
Manchester—Drawn	276	—	318	35–8
Leeds—Drawn	167	275	266	147–4
Oval—England 8 wkts	306	132–2	275	162
1954–55 in Australia				
Brisbane—Australia Inns & 154 runs	190	257	601–8d	—
Sydney—England 38 runs	154	296	228	184
Melbourne—England 128 runs	191	279	231	111
Adelaide—England 5 wkts	341	97–5	323	111
Sydney—Drawn	371–7d	—	221	118–6
1956 in England				
Nottingham—Drawn	217–8d	188–3d	148	120–3
Lord's—Australia 185 runs	171	186	285	257
Leeds—England Inns & 42 runs	325	—	143	140
Manchester—England Inns & 170 runs	459	—	84	205
Oval—Drawn	247	182–3d	202	27–5
1958–59 in Australia				
Brisbane—Australia 8 wkts	134	198	186	147–2
Melbourne—Australia 8 wkts	259	87	308	42–2
Sydney—Drawn	219	287–7d	357	54–2
Adelaide—Australia 10 wkts	240	270	476	36–0
Melbourne—Australia 9 wkts	205	214	351	70–1

ENGLAND v. SOUTH AFRICA

Venue and Result	England 1st inns	2nd inns	South Africa 1st inns	2nd inns
1888–89 in South Africa				
Port Elizabeth—England 8 wkts	148	67–2	84	129
Cape Town—England Inns & 202 runs	292	—	47	43
1891–92 in South Africa				
Cape Town—England Inns & 189 runs	369	—	97	83
1895–96 in South Africa				
Port Elizabeth—England 288 runs	185	226	93	30
Johannesburg—England Inns & 197 runs	482	—	151	134
Cape Town—England Inns & 33 runs	265	—	115	117
1898–99 in South Africa				
Johannesburg—England 32 runs	145	237	251	99
Cape Town—England 210 runs	92	330	177	35
1905–06 in South Africa				
Johannesburg—South Africa 1 wkt	184	190	91	287–9
Johannesburg—South Africa 9 wkts	148	160	277	33–1
Johannesburg—South Africa 243 runs	295	196	385	349–5d
Cape Town—England 4 wkts	198	160–6	218	138
Cape Town—South Africa Inns & 16 runs	187	130	333	—

	England		South Africa	
Venue and Result	*1st inns*	*2nd inns*	*1st inns*	*2nd inns*
1907 in England				
Lord's—Drawn	428	—	140	185–3
Leeds—England 53 runs	76	162	110	75
Oval—Drawn	295	138	178	159–5
1909–10 in South Africa				
Johannesburg—South Africa 19 runs	310	224	208	345
Durban—South Africa 95 runs	199	252	199	347
Johannesburg—England 3 wkts	322	221–7	305	237
Cape Town—South Africa 4 wkts	203	178	207	175–6
Cape Town—England 9 wkts	417	16–1	103	327
1912 in England				
Lord's—England Inns & 62 runs	337	—	58	217
Leeds—England 174 runs	242	238	147	159
Oval—England 10 wkts	176	14–0	95	93
1913–14 in South Africa				
Durban—England Inns & 157 runs	450	—	182	111
Johannesburg—England Inns & 12 runs	403	—	160	231
Johannesburg—England 91 runs	238	308	151	304
Durban—Drawn	163	154–5	170	305–9d
Port Elizabeth—England 10 wkts	411	11–0	193	228
1922–23 in South Africa				
Johannesburg—South Africa 168 runs	182	218	148	420
Cape Town—England 1 wkt	183	173–9	113	242
Durban—Drawn	428	11–1	368	—
Johannesburg—Drawn	244	376–6d	295	247–4
Durban—England 109 runs	281	241	179	234
1924 in England				
Birmingham—England Inns & 18 runs	438	—	30	390
Lord's—England Inns & 18 runs	531–2d	—	273	240
Leeds—England 9 wkts	396	60–1	132	323
Manchester—Drawn	—	—	116–4	—
Oval—Drawn	421–8	—	342	—
1927–28 in South Africa				
Johannesburg—England 10 wkts	313	57–0	196	170
Cape Town—England 87 runs	133	428	250	224
Durban—Drawn	430	132–2	246	464–8d
Johannesburg—South Africa 4 wkts	265	215	328	156–6
Durban—South Africa 8 wkts	282	118	332–7d	69–2
1929 in England				
Birmingham—Drawn	245	308–4d	250	171–1
Lord's—Drawn	302	312–8d	322	90–5
Leeds—England 5 wkts	328	186–5	236	275
Manchester—England Inns & 32 runs	427–7d	—	130	265
Oval—Drawn	258	264–1	492–8d	—
1930–31 in South Africa				
Johannesburg—South Africa 28 runs	193	211	126	306
Cape Town—Drawn	350	252	513–8d	—
Durban—Drawn	223–1d		177	145–8
Johannesburg—Drawn	442	169–9d	295	280–7
Durban—Drawn	230	72–4	252	219–7d
1935 in England				
Nottingham—Drawn	384–7d	—	220	17–1
Lord's—South Africa 157 runs	198	151	228	278–7d
Leeds—Drawn	216	294–7d	171	194–5
Manchester—Drawn	357	231–6d	318	169–2
Oval—Drawn	534–6d	—	476	287–6
1938–39 in South Africa				
Johannesburg—Drawn	422	291–4d	390	108–1
Cape Town—Drawn	559–9d	—	286	201–2
Durban—England Inns & 13 runs	469–4d	—	103	353
Johannesburg—Drawn	215	203–4	349–8d	—
Durban—Drawn	316	654–5	530	481

	England 1st inns	2nd inns	South Africa 1st inns	2nd inns
Venue and Result				
1947 in England				
Nottingham—Drawn	208	551	533	166–1
Lord's—England 10 wkts	554–8d	26–0	327	252
Manchester—England 7 wkts	478	130–3	339	267
Leeds—England 10 wkts	317–7d	47–0	175	184
Oval—Drawn	427	325–6d	302	423–7
1948–49 in South Africa				
Durban—England 2 wkts	253	128–8	161	219
Johannesburg—Drawn	608	—	315	270–2
Cape Town—Drawn	308	276–3d	356	142–4
Johannesburg—Drawn	379	253–7d	257–9d	194–4
Port Elizabeth—England 3 wkts	395	174–7	379	187–3d
1951 in England				
Nottingham—South Africa 71 runs	419–9d	114	483–9d	121
Lord's—England 10 wkts	311	16–0	115	211
Manchester—England 9 wkts	211	142–1	158	191
Leeds—Drawn	505	—	538	87–0
Oval—England 4 wkts	194	164–6	202	154
1955 in England				
Nottingham—England Inns & 5 runs	334	—	181	148
Lord's—England 71 runs	133	353	304	111
Manchester—South Africa 3 wkts	284	381	521–8d	145–7
Leeds—South Africa 224 runs	191	256	171	500
Oval—England 92 runs	151	204	112	151
1956–57 in South Africa				
Johannesburg—England 131 runs	268	150	215	72
Cape Town—England 312 runs	369	220–6d	205	72
Durban—Drawn	218	254	283	142–6
Johannesburg—South Africa 17 runs	251	214	340	142
Port Elizabeth—South Africa 58 runs	110	130	164	134
1960 in England				
Birmingham—England 100 runs	292	203	186	209
Lord's—England Inns & 73 runs	362–8d	—	152	137
Nottingham—England 8 wkts	287	49–2	88	247
Manchester—Drawn	260	153–7d	229	46–0
Oval—Drawn	155	479–7d	419	97–4

ENGLAND v. WEST INDIES

	England 1st inns	2nd inns	West Indies 1st inns	2nd inns
Venue and Result				
1928 in England				
Lord's—England Inns & 58 runs	401	—	177	166
Manchester—England Inns & 30 runs	351	—	206	115
Oval—England Inns & 71 runs	438	—	238	129
1929–30 in West Indies				
Barbados—Drawn	467	167–3	369	384
Trinidad—England 167 runs	208	425–8d	254	212
Georgetown—West Indies 289 runs	145	327	471	290
Kingston—Drawn	849	272–9d	286	408–5
1933 in England				
Lord's—England Inns & 27 runs	296	—	97	172
Manchester—Drawn	374	—	375	225
Oval—England Inns & 17 runs	312	—	100	195
1934–35 in West Indies				
Barbados—England 4 wkts	81–7d	75–6	102	51–6d
Trinidad—West Indies 217 runs	258	107	302	280–6d
Georgetown—Drawn	226	160–6d	184	104–5
Kingston—West Indies Inns & 161 runs	271	103	535–7d	—
1939 in England				
Lord's—England 8 wkts	404–5d	100–2	277	225
Manchester—Drawn	164–7d	128–6d	133	43–4
Oval—Drawn	352	366–3	498	—
1947–48 in West Indies				
Barbados—Drawn	253	86–4	296	351–9d
Trinidad—Drawn	362	275	497	72–3
Georgetown—West Indies 7 wkts	111	263	297–8d	78–3
Kingston—West Indies 10 wkts	227	336	490	76–0

Venue and Result	England 1st inns	2nd inns	West Indies 1st inns	2nd inns
1950 in England				
Manchester—England 202 runs	312	288	215	183
Lord's—West Indies 326 runs	151	274	326	425–6d
Nottingham—West Indies 10 wkts	223	436	558	103–0
Oval—West Indies Inns & 56 runs	344	103	503	—
1953–54 in West Indies				
Kingston—West Indies 140 runs	170	316	417	209–6d
Barbados—West Indies 181 runs	181	313	383	292–2d
Georgetown—England 9 wkts	435	75–1	251	256
Trinidad—Drawn	537	98–3	681–8d	212–4d
Kingston—England 9 wkts	414	72–1	139	346
1957 in England				
Birmingham—Drawn	186	583–4d	474	72–7
Lord's—England Inns & 36 runs	424	—	127	261
Nottingham—Drawn	619–6d	64–1	372	367
Leeds—England Inns & 5 runs	279	—	142	132
Oval—England Inns & 237 runs	412	—	89	86
1959–60 in West Indies				
Barbados—Drawn	482	71–0	563–8d	—
Trinidad—England 256 runs	382	230–9d	112	244
Kingston—Drawn	277	305	353	175–6
Georgetown—Drawn	295	334–8	402–8d	—
Trinidad—Drawn	393	350–7d	338–8d	209–5

ENGLAND v. NEW ZEALAND

Venue and Result	England 1st inns	2nd inns	New Zealand 1st inns	2nd inns
1929–30 in New Zealand				
Christchurch—England 8 wkts	181	66–2	112	131
Wellington—Drawn	320	107–4	440	164–4d
Auckland—Drawn	330–4d	—	96–1	—
Auckland—Drawn	540	22–3	387	—
1931 in England				
Lord's—Drawn	454	146–5	224	469–9d
Oval—England Inns & 26 runs	416–4d	—	193	197
Manchester—Drawn	224–3	—	—	—
1932–33 in New Zealand				
Christchurch—Drawn	560–8d	—	223	35–0
Auckland—Drawn	548–7d	—	158	16–0
1937 in England				
Lord's—Drawn	424	226–4d	295	175–8
Manchester—England 130 runs	358–9d	187	281	134
Oval—Drawn	254–7d	31–1	249	187
1946–47 in New Zealand				
Christchurch—Drawn	265–7d	—	345–9d	—
1949 in England				
Leeds—Drawn	372	267–4d	341	195–2
Lord's—Drawn	313–9d	306–5	484	—
Manchester—Drawn	440–9d	—	293	348–7
Oval—Drawn	482	—	345	308–9d
1950–51 in New Zealand				
Christchurch—Drawn	550	—	417–8d	46–3
Wellington—England 6 wkts	227	91–4	125	189
1954–55 in New Zealand				
Dunedin—England 8 wkts	209–8d	49–2	125	132
Auckland—England Inns & 20 runs	246	—	200	26
1958 in England				
Birmingham—England 205 runs	221	215–6d	94	137
Lord's—England Inns & 148 runs	269	—	47	74
Leeds—England Inns & 71 runs	267–2d	—	67	129
Manchester—England Inns & 13 runs	365–9d	—	267	85
Oval—Drawn	219–9d	—	161	91–3

Venue and Result	England 1st inns	2nd inns	New Zealand 1st inns	2nd inns
1958–59 in New Zealand				
Christchurch—England Inns & 99 runs	374	—	142	133
Auckland—Drawn	311–7	—	181	—

ENGLAND v. INDIA

Venue and Result	England 1st inns	2nd inns	India 1st inns	2nd inns
1932 in England				
Lord's—England 158 runs	259	275–8d	189	187
1933–34 in India				
Bombay—England 9 wkts	438	40–1	219	258
Calcutta—Drawn	403	7–2	247	237
Madras—England 202 runs	335	261–7d	145	249
1936 in England				
Lord's—England 9 wkts	134	108–1	147	93
Manchester—Drawn	571–8d	—	203	390–5
Oval—England 9 wkts	471–8d	64–1	222	312
1946 in England				
Lord's—England 10 wkts	428	48–0	200	275
Manchester—Drawn	294	153–5d	170	152–9
Oval—Drawn	95–3	—	331	—
1951–52 in India				
New Delhi—Drawn	203	368–6	418–6d	—
Bombay—Drawn	456	55–2	485–9d	208
Calcutta—Drawn	342	252–5d	344	103–0
Kanpur—England 8 wkts	203	76–2	121	157
Madras—India Inns & 8 runs	266	183	457–9d	—
1952 in England				
Leeds—England 7 wkts	334	128–3	293	165
Lord's—England 8 wkts	537	79–2	235	378
Manchester—England Inns & 207 runs	347–9d	—	58	82
Oval—Drawn	326–6d	—	98	—
1959 in England				
Nottingham—England Inns & 59 runs	422	—	206	157
Lord's—England 8 wkts	226	108–2	168	165
Leeds—England Inns & 173 runs	483–8d	—	161	149
Manchester—England 171 runs	490	265–8d	208	376
Oval—England Inns & 27 runs	361	—	140	194

ENGLAND v. PAKISTAN

Venue and Result	England 1st inns	2nd inns	Pakistan 1st inns	2nd inns
1954 in England				
Lord's—Drawn	117–9d	—	87	121–3
Nottingham—England Inns & 129 runs	558–6d	—	157	272
Manchester—Drawn	359–8d	—	90	25–4
Oval—Pakistan 24 runs	130	143	133	164

AUSTRALIA v. SOUTH AFRICA

Venue and Result	Australia 1st inns	2nd inns	South Africa 1st inns	2nd inns
1902–03 in South Africa				
Johannesburg—Drawn	296	372–7d	454	101–4
Johannesburg—Australia 159 runs	175	309	240	85
Cape Town—Australia 10 wkts	252	59–0	85	225
1910–11 in Australia				
Sydney—Australia Inns & 114 runs	528	—	174	240
Melbourne—Australia 89 runs	348	327	506	80
Adelaide—South Africa 38 runs	465	339	482	360
Melbourne—Australia 530 runs	328	578	205	171
Sydney—Australia 7 wkts	364	198–3	160	401

Venue and Result	Australia 1st inns	2nd inns	South Africa 1st inns	2nd inns
1912 in England				
Manchester—Australia Inns & 88 runs	448	—	265	95
Lord's—Australia 10 wkts	390	48–0	263	173
Nottingham—Drawn	219	—	329	—
1921–22 in South Africa				
Durban—Drawn	299	324–7d	232	184–7
Johannesburg—Drawn	450	7–0	243	472–8d
Cape Town—Australia 10 wkts	396	1–0	180	216
1931–32 in Australia				
Brisbane—Australia Inns & 163 runs	450	—	170	117
Sydney—Australia Inns & 155 runs	469	—	153	161
Melbourne—Australia 169 runs	198	554	358	225
Adelaide—Australia 10 wkts	513	73–0	308	274
Melbourne—Australia Inns & 72 runs	153	—	36	45
1935–36 in South Africa				
Durban—Australia 9 wkts	429	102–1	248	282
Johannesburg—Drawn	250	274–2	157	491
Cape Town—Australia Inns & 78 runs	362–8d	—	102	182
Johannesburg—Australia Inns & 184 runs	439	—	157	98
Durban—Australia Inns & 6 runs	455	—	222	227
1949–50 in South Africa				
Johannesburg—Australia Inns & 85 runs	413	—	137	191
Cape Town—Australia 8 wkts	526–7d	87–2	278	333
Durban—Australia 5 wkts	75	336–5	311	99
Johannesburg—Drawn	465–8d	259–2	352	—
Port Elizabeth—Australia Inns & 259 runs	549–7d	—	158	132
1952–53 in Australia				
Brisbane—Australia 96 runs	280	277	221	240
Melbourne—South Africa 82 runs	243	290	227	388
Sydney—Australia Inns & 38 runs	443	—	173	232
Adelaide—Drawn	530	233–3d	387	177–6
Melbourne—South Africa 6 wkts	520	209	435	297–4
1957–58 in South Africa				
Johannesburg—Drawn	368	162–3	470–9d	201
Cape Town—Australia Inns & 141 runs	449	—	209	99
Durban—Drawn	163	292–7	384	—
Johannesburg—Australia 10 wkts	401	1–0	203	198
Port Elizabeth—Australia 8 wkts	291	68–2	214	144

AUSTRALIA v. WEST INDIES

Venue and Result	Australia 1st inns	2nd inns	West Indies 1st inns	2nd inns
1930–31 in Australia				
Adelaide—Australia 10 wkts	376	172–0	296	249
Sydney—Australia Inns & 172 runs	369	—	107	90
Brisbane—Australia Inns & 217 runs	558	—	193	148
Melbourne—Australia Inns & 122 runs	328–8d	—	99	107
Sydney—West Indies 30 runs	224	220	350–6d	124–5d
1951–52 in Australia				
Brisbane—Australia 3 wkts	226	236–7	216	245
Sydney—Australia 7 wkts	517	137–3	362	290
Adelaide—West Indies 6 wkts	82	255	105	233–4
Melbourne—Australia 1 wkt	216	260–9	272	203
Sydney—Australia 202 runs	116	377	78	213
1954–55 in West Indies				
Kingston—Australia 9 wkts	515–9d	20–1	259	275
Trinidad—Drawn	600–9d	—	382	273–4
Georgetown—Australia 8 wkts	257	133–2	182	207
Barbados—Drawn	668	249	510	234–6
Kingston—Australia Inns & 82 runs	758–8d	—	357	319

AUSTRALIA v. NEW ZEALAND

Venue and Result	Australia 1st inns	2nd inns	New Zealand 1st inns	2nd inns
1945–46 in New Zealand				
Wellington—Australia Inns & 103 runs	199–8d	—	42	54

AUSTRALIA v. INDIA

Venue and Result	Australia 1st inns	2nd inns	India 1st inns	2nd inns
1947–48 in Australia				
Brisbane—Australia Inns & 226 runs	382–8d	—	58	98
Sydney—Drawn	107	—	188	61–7
Melbourne—Australia 233 runs	394	255–4d	291–9d	125
Adelaide—Australia Inns & 16 runs	674	—	381	277
Melbourne—Australia Inns & 177 runs	575–8d	—	331	67
1956–57 in India				
Madras—Australia Inns & 5 runs	319	—	161	153
Bombay—Drawn	523–7d	—	251	250–5
Calcutta—Australia 94 runs	177	189–9d	136	136
1959–60 in India				
New Delhi—Australia Inns & 127 runs	468	—	135	206
Kanpur—India 119 runs	219	105	152	291
Bombay—Drawn	387–8d	34–1	289	226–5d
Madras—Australia Inns & 55 runs	342	—	149	138
Calcutta—Drawn	331	121–2	194	339

AUSTRALIA v. PAKISTAN

Venue and Result	Australia 1st inns	2nd inns	Pakistan 1st inns	2nd inns
1956–57 in Pakistan				
Karachi—Pakistan 9 wkts	80	187	199	69–1
1959–60 in Pakistan				
Dacca—Australia 8 wkts	225	112–2	200	134
Lahore—Australia 7 wkts	391–9d	123–3	146	366
Karachi—Drawn	257	83–2	287	194–8d

SOUTH AFRICA v. NEW ZEALAND

Venue and Result	South Africa 1st inns	2nd inns	New Zealand 1st inns	2nd inns
1931–32 in New Zealand				
Christchurch—South Africa Inns & 12 runs	451	—	293	146
Wellington—South Africa 8 wkts	410	150–2	364	193
1952–53 in New Zealand				
Wellington—South Africa Inns & 180 runs	524–8d		172	172
Auckland—Drawn	377	200–5d	245	31–2
1953–54 in South Africa				
Durban—South Africa Inns & 58 runs	437–9d	—	230	149
Johannesburg—South Africa 132 runs	271	148	187	100
Cape Town—Drawn	326	159–3	505	—
Johannesburg—South Africa 9 wkts	243	25–1	79	188
Port Elizabeth—South Africa 5 wkts	237	215–5	226	222

WEST INDIES v. NEW ZEALAND

Venue and Result	West Indies 1st inns	2nd inns	New Zealand 1st inns	2nd inns
1951–52 in New Zealand				
Christchurch—West Indies 5 wkts	287	142–5	236	189
Auckland—Drawn	546–6d	—	160	17–1
1955–56 in New Zealand				
Dunedin—West Indies Inns & 71 runs	353	—	74	208
Christchurch—West Indies Inns & 64 runs	386	—	158	164
Wellington—West Indies 9 wkts	404	13–1	208	208
Auckland—New Zealand 190 runs	145	77	255	157–9d

WEST INDIES v. INDIA

Venue and Result	West Indies 1st inns	2nd inns	India 1st inns	2nd inns
1948–49 in India				
New Delhi—Drawn	631	—	454	220–6
Bombay—Drawn	629–6d	—	273	333–3
Calcutta—Drawn	366	336–9d	272	325–3
Madras—West Indies Inns & 193 runs	582	—	245	144
Bombay—Drawn	286	267	193	355–8

Venue and Result	West Indies 1st inns	2nd inns	India 1st inns	2nd inns
1952–53 in West Indies				
Trinidad—Drawn	438	142–0	417	294
Barbados—West Indies 142 runs	296	228	253	129
Trinidad—Drawn	315	192–2	279	362–7d
Georgetown—Drawn	364	—	262	190–5
Kingston—Drawn	576	92–4	312	444
1958–59 in India				
Bombay—Drawn	227	323–4d	152	289–5
Kanpur—West Indies 203 runs	222	443–7d	222	240
Calcutta—West Indies Inns & 336 runs	614–5d	—	124	154
Madras—West Indies 295 runs	500	168–5d	222	151
New Delhi—Drawn	644–8d	—	415	275

WEST INDIES v. PAKISTAN

Venue and Result	West Indies 1st inns	2nd inns	Pakistan 1st inns	2nd inns
1957–58 in West Indies				
Barbados—Drawn	579–9d	28–0	106	657–8d
Trinidad—West Indies 120 runs	325	312	282	235
Kingston—West Indies Inns & 174 runs	790–3d	—	328	288
Georgetown—West Indies 8 wkts	410	317–2	408	318
Trinidad—Pakistan Inns & 1 run	268	227	496	—
1958–59 in Pakistan				
Karachi—Pakistan 10 wkts	146	245	304	88–0
Dacca—Pakistan 41 runs	76	172	145	144
Lahore—West Indies Inns & 156 runs	469	—	209	104

NEW ZEALAND v. INDIA

Venue and Result	New Zealand 1st inns	2nd inns	India 1st inns	2nd inns
1955–56 in India				
Hyderabad—Drawn	326	212–2	498–4d	—
Bombay—India Inns & 27 runs	258	136	421–8d	—
New Delhi—Drawn	450–2d	112–1	531–7d	—
Calcutta—Drawn	336	74–6	132	438–7d
Madras—India Inns & 109 runs	209	219	537–3d	—

NEW ZEALAND v. PAKISTAN

Venue and Result	New Zealand 1st inns	2nd inns	Pakistan 1st inns	2nd inns
1955–56 in Pakistan				
Karachi—Pakistan Inns & 1 run	164	124	289	—
Lahore—Pakistan 4 wkts	348	328	561	117–6
Dacca—Drawn	70	69–6	195–6d	—

INDIA v. PAKISTAN

Venue and Result	India 1st inns	2nd inns	Pakistan 1st inns	2nd inns
1952–53 in India				
New Delhi—India Inns & 70 runs	372	—	150	152
Lucknow—Pakistan Inns & 43 runs	106	182	331	—
Bombay—India 10 wkts	387–4d	45–0	186	242
Madras—Drawn	175–6	—	344	—
Calcutta—Drawn	397	28–0	257	236–7d
1954–55 in Pakistan				
Dacca—Drawn	148	147–2	257	158
Bahawalpur—Drawn	235	209–5	312–9d	—
Lahore—Drawn	251	74–2	328	136–5d
Peshawar—Drawn	245	23–1	188	182
Karachi—Drawn	145	69–2	162	241–5d

Test Cricket Records, 1876–77 to 1960

Part I—The Sides

HIGHEST INNINGS TOTALS

903—7d	England v. Australia (Oval)	1938
849	England v. West Indies (Kingston)	1929–30
790—3d	West Indies v. Pakistan (Kingston)	1957–58
758—8d	Australia v. West Indies (Kingston)	1954–55
729—6d	Australia v. England (Lord's)	1930
701	Australia v. England (Oval)	1934
695	Australia v. England (Oval)	1930
681—8d	West Indies v. England (Trinidad)	1953–54
674	Australia v. India (Adelaide)	1947–48
668	Australia v. West Indies (Barbados)	1954–55
659—8d	Australia v. England (Sydney)	1946–47
658—8d	England v. Australia (Nottingham)	1938
657—8d	Pakistan v. West Indies (Barbados)	1957–58
654—5	England v. South Africa (Durban)	1938–39
645	Australia v. England (Brisbane)	1946–47
644—8d	West Indies v. India (New Delhi)	1958–59
636	England v. Australia (Sydney)	1928–29
631	West Indies v. India (New Delhi)	1948–49
629—6d	West Indies v. India (Bombay)	1948–49
627—9d	England v. Australia (Manchester)	1934
619—6d	England v. West Indies (Nottingham)	1957
614—5d	West Indies v. India (Calcutta)	1958–59
608	England v. South Africa (Johannesburg)	1948–49
604	Australia v. England (Melbourne)	1936–37
601—8d	Australia v. England (Brisbane)	1954–55
600—9d	Australia v. West Indies (Trinidad)	1954–55
600	Australia v. England (Melbourne)	1924–25
589	England v. Australia (Melbourne)	1911–12
586	Australia v. England (Sydney)	1894–95
584	Australia v. England (Leeds)	1934
583—4d	England v. West Indies (Birmingham)	1957
582	Australia v. England (Adelaide)	1920–21
582	West Indies v. India (Madras)	1948–49
581	Australia v. England (Sydney)	1920–21
579—9d	West Indies v. Pakistan (Barbados)	1957–58
578	Australia v. South Africa (Melbourne)	1910–11
577	England v. Australia (Sydney)	1903–04
576	England v. Australia (Oval)	1899
576	West Indies v. India (Kingston)	1952–53
575—8d	Australia v. India (Melbourne)	1947–48
573	Australia v. England (Adelaide)	1897–98
571—8d	England v. India (Manchester)	1936
566	Australia v. England (Leeds)	1930
564	Australia v. England (Melbourne)	1936–37
563—8d	West Indies v. England (Barbados)	1959–60
561	Pakistan v. New Zealand (Lahore)	1955–56
560—8d	England v. New Zealand (Christchurch)	1932–33
559—9d	England v. South Africa (Cape Town)	1938–39
558	Australia v. West Indies (Brisbane)	1930–31
558	West Indies v. England (Nottingham)	1950
558—6d	England v. Pakistan (Nottingham)	1954
554	Australia v. South Africa (Melbourne)	1931–32
554—8d	England v. South Africa (Lord's)	1947
551	Australia v. England (Oval)	1884
551	England v. Australia (Sydney)	1897–98
551	England v. South Africa (Nottingham)	1947
550	England v. New Zealand (Christchurch)	1950–51

The highest innings totals by the other countries are:

538	South Africa v. England (Leeds)	1951
505	New Zealand v. South Africa (Cape Town)	1953–54
537—3d	India v. New Zealand (Madras)	1955–56

HIGHEST SECOND INNINGS TOTALS (First innings in brackets)

657—8d	(106)	Pakistan v. West Indies (Barbados)	1957–58
654—5	(316)	England v. South Africa (Durban)	1938–39
583—4d	(186)	England v. West Indies (Birmingham)	1957
582	(354)	Australia v. England (Adelaide)	1920–21
581	(267)	Australia v. England (Sydney)	1920–21
578	(328)	Australia v. South Africa (Melbourne)	1910–11
564	(200—9d)	Australia v. England (Melbourne)	1936–37
554	(198)	Australia v. South Africa (Melbourne)	1931–32
551	(208)	England v. South Africa (Nottingham)	1947

LOWEST INNINGS TOTALS

26	New Zealand v. England (Auckland)...	1954–55
30	South Africa v. England (Port Elizabeth)	1895–96
30	South Africa v. England (Birmingham)	1924
35	South Africa v. England (Cape Town)	1898–99
36	Australia v. England (Birmingham)	1902
36	South Africa v. Australia (Melbourne)	1931–32
42	Australia v. England (Sydney)	1887–88
42	New Zealand v. Australia (Wellington)	1945–46
43	South Africa v. England (Cape Town)..	1888–89
44	Australia v. England (Oval)	1896
45	England v. Australia (Sydney)	1886–87
45	South Africa v. Australia (Melbourne)	1931–32
47	South Africa v. England (Cape Town)	1888–89
47	New Zealand v. England (Lord's)	1958
52	England v. Australia (Oval)	1948
53	England v. Australia (Lord's)	1888
53	Australia v. England (Lord's)	1896
54	New Zealand v. Australia (Wellington)	1945–46
58	South Africa v. England (Lord's)	1912
58	Australia v. England (Brisbane)	1936–37
58	India v. Australia (Brisbane)	1947–48
58	India v. England (Manchester)	1952
60	Australia v. England (Lord's)	1888

The lowest innings totals by the other countries are:

87	Pakistan v. England (Lord's)...	1954
76	West Indies v. Pakistan (Dacca)	1958–59

The following innings closed at a low total:

32—7d	Australia v. England (Brisbane)	1950–51
35—8	Australia v. England (Manchester)	1953
51—6d	West Indies v. England (Barbados)	1934–35

On the following occasions a country was dismissed for totals of less than 100 in both innings of the match:

42 & 82	Australia v. England (Sydney)	1887–88
53 & 62	England v. Australia (Lord's)	1888
81 & 70	Australia v. England (Manchester)	1888
47 & 43	South Africa v. England (Cape Town)	1888–89
97 & 83	South Africa v. England (Cape Town)	1891–92
65 & 72	England v. Australia (Sydney)	1894–95
93 & 30	South Africa v. England (Port Elizabeth)	1895–96
95 & 93	South Africa v. England (Oval)	1912
36 & 45	South Africa v. Australia (Melbourne)	1931–32
42 & 54	New Zealand v. Australia (Wellington)	1945–46
58 & 98	India v. Australia (Brisbane)	1947–48
58 & 82	India v. England (Manchester)	1952
89 & 86	West Indies v. England (Oval)	1957
47 & 74	New Zealand v. England (Lord's)	1958

HIGHEST FOURTH INNINGS TOTALS

654—5	(set 696 runs)	England v. South Africa (Durban)	1938–39
423—7	(set 451 runs)	South Africa v. England (Oval)	1947
411	(lost 193 runs)	England v. Australia (Sydney)	1924–25

408—5	(set 836 runs)	West Indies v. England (Kingston)	1929–30
404—3	(and won)	Australia v. England (Leeds)	1948
376	(lost 171 runs)	India v. England (Manchester)	1959
370	(lost 119 runs)	England v. Australia (Adelaide)	1920–21
363	(lost 11 runs)	England v. Australia (Adelaide)	1924–25
355—8	(set 361 runs)	India v. West Indies (Bombay)	1948–49
339	(lost 38 runs)	Australia v. South Africa (Adelaide)	1910–11
336—5	(and won)	Australia v. South Africa (Durban)	1949–50
336	(lost 12 runs)	Australia v. England (Adelaide)	1928–29
335	(lost 93 runs)	Australia v. England (Nottingham)	1930
333	(lost 94 runs)	Australia v. England (Melbourne)	1894–95
332—7	(and won)	England v. Australia (Melbourne)	1928–29
327	(lost 289 runs)	England v. West Indies (Georgetown)	1929–30
325—3	(set 431 runs)	India v. West Indies (Calcutta)	1948–49
323	(lost 365 runs)	England v. Australia (Melbourne)	1936–37
317—2	(and won)	West Indies v. Pakistan (Georgetown)	1957–58
316	(lost 140 runs)	England v. West Indies (Kingston)	1953–54
315—6	(and won)	Australia v. England (Adelaide)	1901–02
313	(lost 181 runs)	England v. West Indies (Barbados)	1953–54
310—7	(set 551 runs)	England v. Australia (Melbourne)	1946–47
304	(lost 91 runs)	South Africa v. England (Johannesburg)	1913–14

RECORD INNINGS TOTALS FOR EACH TEST GROUND

Highest innings totals			*Lowest innings totals*		
Birmingham	583–4d	England 1957	30	South Africa	1924
Leeds	584	Australia 1934	67	New Zealand	1958
Lord's	729–6d	Australia 1930	47	New Zealand	1958
Manchester	627–9d	England 1934	58	India	1952
Nottingham	658–8d	England 1938	88	South Africa	1960
Oval	903–7d	England 1938	44	Australia	1896
Sheffield	289	Australia 1902	145	England	1902
Adelaide	674	Australia 1947–48	82	Australia	1951–52
Brisbane	645	Australia 1946–47	58	Australia & India	—
Melbourne	604	Australia 1936–37	36	South Africa	1931–32
Sydney	659–8d	Australia 1946–47	42	Australia	1887–88
Cape Town	559–8d	England 1938–39	35	South Africa	1898–99
Durban	654–5	England 1938–39	75	South Africa	1949–50
Johannesburg	608	England 1948–49	72	South Africa	1956–57
Port Elizabeth	549–7d	Australia 1949–50	30	South Africa	1895–96
Barbados	668	Australia 1954–55	102	West Indies	1934–35
Georgetown	471	West Indies 1929–30	111	England	1947–48
Kingston	849	England 1929–30	103	England	1934–35
Trinidad	681–8d	West Indies 1953–54	107	England	1947–48
Auckland	548–7d	England 1932–33	26	New Zealand	1954–55
Christchurch	560–8d	England 1932–33	112	New Zealand	1929–30
Dunedin	353	West Indies 1955–56	74	New Zealand	1955–56
Wellington	524–8d	South Africa 1952–53	42	New Zealand	1945–46
Bombay	629–6d	West Indies 1948–49	136	New Zealand	1955–56
Calcutta	614–5d	West Indies 1958–59	124	India	1958–59
Hyderabad	498–4d	India 1955–56	326	New Zealand	1955–56
Kanpur	443–7d	West Indies 1958–59	105	Australia	1959–60
Lucknow	331	Pakistan 1952–53	106	India	1952–53
Madras	582	West Indies 1948–49	138	India	1959–60
New Delhi	644–8d	West Indies 1958–59	135	India	1959–60
Bahawalpur	312–9d	Pakistan 1954–55	235	India	1954–55
Dacca	257	Pakistan 1954–55	70	New Zealand	1955–56
Karachi	304	Pakistan 1958–59	80	Australia	1956–57
Lahore	561	Pakistan 1955–56	104	Pakistan	1958–59
Peshawar	245	India 1954–55	182	Pakistan	1954–55

HIGHEST MATCH AGGREGATES

1981—35 wkts	South Africa v. England (Durban)	1938–39
1815—34 wkts	West Indies v. England (Kingston)	1929–30
1753—40 wkts	England v. Australia (Adelaide)	1920–21
1723—31 wkts	England v. Australia (Leeds)	1948
1661—36 wkts	West Indies v. Australia (Barbados)	1954–55
1646—40 wkts	Australia v. South Africa (Adelaide)	1910–11

1619—40 wkts	Australia v. England (Melbourne)	1924–25
1611—40 wkts	Australia v. England (Sydney)	1924–25
1601—29 wkts	England v. Australia (Lord's)	1930
1562—37 wkts	Australia v. England (Melbourne)	1946–47
1554—35 wkts	Australia v. England (Melbourne)	1928–29
1541—35 wkts	Australia v. England (Sydney)	1903–04
1528—24 wkts	West Indies v. England (Trinidad)	1953–54
1514—40 wkts	Australia v. England (Sydney)	1894–95
1502—29 wkts	Australia v. England (Adelaide)	1946–47
1497—37 wkts	Australia v. England (Melbourne)	1928–29
1496—24 wkts	England v. Australia (Nottingham)	1938
1494—37 wkts	England v. Australia (Oval)	1934
1477—33 wkts	England v. South Africa (Oval)	1947
1467—40 wkts	Australia v. England (Adelaide)	1924–25
1461—34 wkts	Australia v. South Africa (Melbourne)	1952–53
1458—31 wkts	England v. South Africa (Nottingham)	1947
1453—32 wkts	West Indies v. Pakistan (Georgetown)	1957–58
1434—28 wkts	West Indies v. Australia (Kingston)	1954–55
1424—33 wkts	West Indies v. India (Kingston)	1952–53
1422—40 wkts	Australia v. England (Adelaide)	1928–29
1422—27 wkts	England v. West Indies (Nottingham)	1957
1406—21 wkts	West Indies v. Pakistan (Kingston)	1957–58

LOWEST MATCH AGGREGATES—COMPLETED MATCHES

234—29 wkts	Australia v. South Africa (Melbourne)	1931–32
291—40 wkts	England v. Australia (Lord's)	1888
295—28 wkts	New Zealand v. Australia (Wellington)	1945–46
309—29 wkts	West Indies v. England (Barbados)	1934–35
323—30 wkts	England v. Australia (Manchester)	1888
363—40 wkts	England v. Australia (Oval)	1882
374—40 wkts	Australia v. England (Sydney)	1887–88
378—30 wkts	England v. South Africa (Oval)	1912
382—30 wkts	South Africa v. England (Cape Town)	1888–89
389—38 wkts	England v. Australia (Oval)	1890
390—30 wkts	England v. New Zealand (Lord's)	1958
392—40 wkts	England v. Australia (Oval)	1896

GREATEST VICTORIES

Innings & 579 runs	England v. Australia (Oval)	1938
Innings & 336 runs	West Indies v. India (Calcutta)	1958–59
Innings & 332 runs	Australia v. England (Brisbane)	1946–47
Innings & 259 runs	Australia v. South Africa (Port Elizabeth)	1949–50
Innings & 237 runs	England v. West Indies (Oval)	1957
Innings & 230 runs	England v. Australia (Adelaide)	1891–92
Innings & 226 runs	Australia v. India (Brisbane)	1947–48
Innings & 225 runs	England v. Australia (Melbourne)	1911–12
Innings & 217 runs	England v. Australia (Oval)	1886
Innings & 217 runs	Australia v. West Indies (Brisbane)	1930–31
Innings & 207 runs	England v. India (Manchester)	1952
Innings & 202 runs	England v. South Africa (Cape Town)	1888–89
675 runs	England v. Australia (Brisbane)	1928–29
562 runs	Australia v. England (Oval)	1934
530 runs	Australia v. South Africa (Melbourne)	1910–11
409 runs	Australia v. England (Lord's)	1948
382 runs	Australia v. England (Adelaide)	1894–95
377 runs	Australia v. England (Sydney)	1920–21
365 runs	Australia v. England (Melbourne)	1936–37
338 runs	England v. Australia (Adelaide)	1932–33
326 runs	West Indies v. England (Lord's)	1950
322 runs	England v. Australia (Brisbane)	1936–37
312 runs	England v. South Africa (Cape Town)	1956–57
308 runs	Australia v. England (Melbourne)	1907–08
307 runs	Australia v. England (Sydney)	1924–25

CLOSEST VICTORIES

1 wkt	England v. Australia (Oval)	1902
1 wkt	South Africa v. England (Johannesburg)	1905–06
1 wkt	England v. Australia (Melbourne)	1907–08

1 wkt   England v. South Africa (Cape Town) 1922–23
1 wkt   Australia v. West Indies (Melbourne) 1951–52

3 runs Australia v. England (Manchester) 1902
6 runs Australia v. England (Sydney) 1884–85
7 runs Australia v. England (Oval) 1882
10 runs England v. Australia (Sydney) 1894–95
11 runs Australia v. England (Adelaide) 1924–25
12 runs England v. Australia (Adelaide) 1928–29
13 runs England v. Australia (Sydney) 1886–87

England lost by 217 runs v. West Indies (Trinidad) 1934–35—the last wicket falling to the fifth ball of the last possible over of the match.

England beat South Africa by two wickets off the last possible ball of the match at Durban 1948–49.

LONGEST MATCHES

10 days South Africa v. England (Durban) 1938–39
9 days   West Indies v. England (Kingston) 1929–30
8 days   Australia v. England (Melbourne)......................................1928–29

MATCHES COMPLETED IN TWO DAYS

England (101 & 77) v. Australia (63 & 122) at Oval 1882
England (53 & 62) v. Australia (116 & 60) at Lord's 1888
England (317) v. Australia (80 & 100) at Oval 1888
England (172) v. Australia (81 & 70) at Manchester......................................1888
South Africa (84 & 129) v. England (148 & 67—2) at Port Elizabeth 1888–89
South Africa (47 & 43) v. England (292) at Cape Town......................................1888–89
England (100 & 95—8) v. Australia (92 & 102) at Oval 1890
South Africa (93 & 30) v. England (185 & 226) at Port Elizabeth......................................1895–96
South Africa (115 & 117) v. England (265) at Cape Town 1895–96
England (176 & 14—0) v. South Africa (95 & 93) at Oval 1912
Australia (448) v. South Africa (265 & 95) at Manchester 1912
England (112 & 147) v. Australia (232 & 30—0) at Nottingham 1921
Australia (328—8d) v. West Indies (99 & 107) at Melbourne......................................1930–31
South Africa (157 & 98) v. Australia (439) at Johannesburg......................................1935–36
New Zealand (42 & 54) v. Australia (199—8d) at Wellington 1945–46

COMPLETE SIDE DISMISSED TWICE IN A DAY'S PLAY

England (65 & 72) v. Australia at Sydney on third day 1894–95
India (58 & 82) v. England at Manchester on third day 1952

MOST RUNS SCORED IN A DAY'S PLAY BY ONE SIDE

503—2 England (531—2d) v. South Africa at Lord's on second day 1924
494—6 Australia (528) v. South Africa at Sydney at on first day 1910–11
475—2 Australia (701) v. England at the Oval on first day......................................1934
471—8 England (471—8d) v. India at the Oval on first day 1936
458—3 Australia (566) v. England at Leeds on first day 1930
455—1 Australia (584) v. England at Leeds on second day 1934

MOST RUNS SCORED IN A DAY'S PLAY BY BOTH SIDES

588—6   England (398—6) v. India (190—0) at Manchester on second day 1936
522—2   England (503—2) v. South Africa (19—0) at Lord's on second day 1924
508—8   England (221—2) v. South Africa (287—6) at the Oval on third day 1935
496—4   England (437—4) v. Pakistan (59—0) at Nottingham on second day......................................1954
473—4   England (264—1) v. South Africa (209—8) at the Oval on third day......................................1929
469—7   England (366—3) v. West Indies (103—4) at the Oval on third day 1939
464—11 Australia (448) v. South Africa (16—1) at Manchester on first day 1912

England scored 437 runs for four wickets in 290 minutes (11.30 a.m. to 5.20 p.m.) on the second day v. Pakistan (Nottingham) 1954. Starting the day at 121—2, the score advanced as follows: 200 in 210, 250 in 240, 300 in 275, 350 in 300, 400 in 335, 450 in 360, 500 in 382, 550 in 413 and 558 in 425 minutes. The score was taken from 262—3 to 495—4 in 125 minutes between lunch and tea, 233 runs of which D. C. S. Compton's share was 173.

MATCHES DOMINATED BY BATTING (over 50 runs per wicket)

109·3 India (531—7d) v. New Zealand (450—2d & 112—1) at New Delhi 1955–56
66·9 West Indies (790—3d) v. Pakistan (328 & 288) at Kingston 1957–58
65·3 England (627—9d & 123—0d) v. Australia (491 & 66—1) at Manchester 1934
65·0 India (273 & 333—3) v. West Indies (629—6d) at Bombay 1948–49
64·7 India (498—4d) v. New Zealand (326 & 212—2) at Hyderabad 1955–56
63·6 West Indies (681—8d & 212—4d) v. England (537 & 98—3) at Trinidad 1953–54
62·3 England (658—8d) v. Australia (411 & 427—6) at Nottingham......................1938
62·0 West Indies (563—8d) v. England (482 & 71—0) at Barbados......................1959–60
58·9 England (534—6d) v. South Africa (476 & 287—6) at Oval 1935
58·4 England (475—3d) v. Australia (383 & 194—5) at Lord's 1926
56·6 South Africa (530 & 481) v. England (316 & 654—5) at Durban 1938–39
56·5 England (505) v. South Africa (538 & 87—0) at Leeds 1951
55·5 England (496 & 365—8d) v. Australia (458 & 404—3) at Leeds 1948
55·2 England (425 & 375) v. Australia (729—6d & 72—3) at Lord's....................1930

ECLECTIC SCORE CARD

No. 1......L. Hutton: England v. Australia (Oval) 1938..............................364
No. 2......A. Sandham: England v. West Indies (Kingston) 1929–30 325
No. 3......G. Sobers: West Indies v. Pakistan (Kingston) 1957–58 ....365*
No. 4......P. B. H. May: England v. West Indies (Nottingham) 1957 ....285*
No. 5......D. G. Bradman: Australia v. England (Leeds) 1934...................304
No. 6......D. G. Bradman: Australia v. England (Sydney) 1946–47 234
No. 7......D. G. Bradman: Australia v. England (Melbourne) 1936–37 270
No. 8......Imtiaz Ahmed: Pakistan v. New Zealand (Lahore) 1955–56 ....209*
No. 9......G. O. Allen: England v. New Zealand (Lord's) 1931 122
No. 10......W. W. Read: England v. Australia (Oval) 1884.......................117
No. 11......A. E. E. Vogler: South Africa v. England (Cape Town) 1905–06.........62*
Extras......New Zealand v. England (Auckland) 1929–30 57
                                                                            ‾‾‾‾
                                                              Total................ 2714

FIVE CENTURIES IN ONE INNINGS

Australia (758—8d) v. West Indies (Kingston) 1954–55
    (C. C. McDonald 127, R. N. Harvey 204, K. R. Miller 109, R. G. Archer 128, R. Benaud 121).

FOUR CENTURIES IN ONE INNINGS

England (658—8d) v. Australia (Nottingham) 1938
    (L. Hutton 100, C. J. Barnett 126, E. Paynter 216*, D. C. S. Compton 102).
West Indies (631) v. India (New Delhi) 1948–49
    (C. L. Walcott 152, G. E. Gomez 101, E. D. Weekes 128, R. J. Christiani 107).

THREE CENTURIES IN ONE INNINGS

Australia (551) v. England (Oval) 1884
    (P. S. McDonnell 103, W. L. Murdoch 211, H. J. H. Scott 102).
Australia (582) v. England (Adelaide) 1920–21
    (C. Kelleway 147, W. W. Armstrong 121, C. E. Pellew 104).
England (531—2d) v. South Africa (Lord's) 1924
    (J. B. Hobbs 211, H. Sutcliffe 122, F. E. Woolley 134*).
Australia (494) v. England (Leeds) 1926
    (W. M. Woodfull 141, C. G. Macartney 151, A. J. Richardson 100).
South Africa (513—8d) v. England (Cape Town) 1930–31
    (I. J. Siedle 141, B. Mitchell 123, H. W. Taylor 117).
England (416—4d) v. New Zealand (Oval) 1931
    (H. Sutcliffe 117, K. S. Duleepsinhji 109, W. R. Hammond 100*).
England (524) v. Australia (Sydney) 1932–33
    (H. Sutcliffe 194, W. R. Hammond 112, Nawab of Pataudi 102).
Australia (604) v. England (Melbourne) 1936–37
    (D. G. Bradman 169, C. L. Badcock 118, S. J. McCabe, 112).
England (903—7d) v. Australia (Oval) 1938
    (L. Hutton 364, M. Leyland 187, J. Hardstaff jun. 169*).
England (559—9d) v. South Africa (Cape Town) 1938–39
    (W. R. Hammond 181, L. E. G. Ames 115, B. H. Valentine 112).
England (654—5) v. South Africa (Durban) 1938–39
    (P. A. Gibb 120, W. J. Edrich 219, W. R. Hammond 140).

Australia (674) v. India (Adelaide) 1947–48
    (S. G. Barnes 112, D. G. Bradman 201, A. L. Hassett 198*).
England (608) v. South Africa (Johannesburg) 1948–49
    (L. Hutton 158, C. Washbrook 195, D. C. S. Compton 114).
Australia (549—7d) v. South Africa (Port Elizabeth) 1949–50
    (A. R. Morris 157, R. N. Harvey 116, A. L. Hassett 167).
West Indies (546—6d) v. New Zealand (Auckland) 1951–52
    (J. B. Stollmeyer 152, F. M. Worrell 100, C. L. Walcott 115).
West Indies (576) v. India (Kingston) 1952–53
    (F. M. Worrell 237, E. D. Weekes 109, C. L. Walcott 118).
West Indies (681—8d) v. England (Trinidad) 1953–54
    (E. D. Weekes 206, F. M. Worrell 167, C. L. Walcott 124).
Australia (600—9d) v. West Indies (Trinidad) 1954–55
    (C. C. McDonald 110, A. R. Morris 111, R. N. Harvey 133).
South Africa (521—8d) v. England (Manchester) 1955
    (D. J. McGlew 104*, J. H. B. Waite 113, P. L. Winslow 108).
India (498—4d) v. New Zealand (Hyderabad) 1955–56
    (P. R. Umrigar 223, V. L. Manjrekar 118, A. G. Kripal Singh 100*).
England (619—6d) v. West Indies (Nottingham), 1957
    (P. E. Richardson 126, T. W. Graveney 258, P. B. H. May 104).
West Indies (614—5d) v. India (Calcutta) 1958–59
    (R. Kanhai 256, B. F. Butcher 103, G. Sobers 106*).
West Indies (644—8d) v. India (New Delhi) 1958–59
    (J. K. Holt 123, O. G. Smith 100, J. Solomon 100*).

MOST CENTURIES SCORED IN ONE TEST MATCH

7	England v. Australia (Nottingham)	1938
7	West Indies v. Australia (Kingston)	1954–55
6	Australia v. England (Adelaide)	1920–21
6	Australia v. England (Sydney)	1924–25
6	Australia v. England (Melbourne)	1928–29
6	South Africa v. England (Durban)	1938–39
6	Australia v. India (Adelaide)	1947–48
6	West Indies v. India (Kingston)	1952–53
6	West Indies v. Australia (Trinidad)	1954–55

MOST CENTURIES SCORED IN ONE TEST RUBBER

21	West Indies v. Australia in West Indies	1954–55
17	Australia v. England in Australia	1928–29
17	South Africa v. England in South Africa	1938–39
16	India v. West Indies in India	1948–49
15	Australia v. England in Australia	1946–47

MOST CENTURIES SCORED BY ONE SIDE IN A TEST RUBBER

12	Australia v. West Indies in West Indies	1954–55
11	England v. South Africa in South Africa	1938–39
11	West Indies v. India in India	1948–49
11	Australia v. South Africa in South Africa	1949–50
10	Australia v. England in Australia	1920–21
10	England v. South Africa in England	1929
10	Australia v. England in Australia	1946–47

TEST TEAM UNCHANGED FOR COMPLETE TEST RUBBER

4 Tests.	England v. Australia in Australia	1881–82
3 Tests.	Australia v. England in England	1884
5 Tests.	England v. Australia in Australia	1884–85
3 Tests.	Australia v. England in England	1893
5 Tests.	South Africa v. England in South Africa	1905–06

MOST PLAYERS ENGAGED BY ONE SIDE IN COMPLETE RUBBER

20 in 3 Tests.	South Africa v. England in South Africa	1895–96
28 in 4 Tests.	West Indies v. England in West Indies	1929–30
25 in 4 Tests.	England v. West Indies in England	1950
30 in 5 Tests.	England v. Australia in England	1921
28 in 5 Tests.	Australia v. England in Australia	1884–85

MOST CONSECUTIVE VICTORIES IN ALL TEST CRICKET

8 Australia: Sydney 1920–21 to Leeds 1921.
7 England: Melbourne 1884–85 to Sydney 1887–88.
7 England: Lord's 1928 to Adelaide 1928–29.
6 England: Oval 1888 to Oval 1890.

MOST CONSECUTIVE MATCHES WITHOUT DEFEAT

25 Australia: Wellington 1945–46 to Adelaide 1950–51.
17 Australia: Madras 1956–57 to New Delhi 1959–60.
17 England: Christchurch 1958–59 to date.
16 Australia: Sydney 1920–21 to Adelaide 1924–25.
15 England: Melbourne 1910–11 to Port Elizabeth 1913–14.
13 India: Trinidad 1952–53 to Madras 1955–56.
12 England: Oval 1938 to Oval 1946.
12 Pakistan: Manchester 1954 to Barbados 1957–58.

MOST CONSECUTIVE MATCHES WITHOUT VICTORY

44 New Zealand: Christchurch 1929–30 to Wellington 1955–56.
28 South Africa: Leeds 1935 to Port Elizabeth 1949–50.
24 India: Lord's 1932 to Kanpur 1951–52.
16 South Africa: Melbourne 1910–11 to Cape Town 1921–22.
13 India: Madras 1952–53 to Hyderabad 1955–56.
12 South Africa: Cape Town 1922–23 to Durban 1927–28.

MOST CONSECUTIVE DEFEATS IN ALL TEST CRICKET

8 South Africa: Port Elizabeth 1888–89 to Cape Town 1898–99.
8 England: Sydney 1920–21 to Leeds 1921.
7 Australia: Melbourne 1884–85 to Sydney 1887–88.
6 South Africa: Melbourne 1910–11 to Lord's 1912.
6 New Zealand: Johannesburg 1953–54 to Lahore 1955–56.
6 India: Nottingham 1959 to New Delhi 1959–60.

MOST CONSECUTIVE VICTORIES IN A SERIES

8 Australia v. England: Sydney 1920–21 to Leeds 1921.
8 England v. South Africa: Port Elizabeth 1888–89 to Cape Town 1898–99.
7 England v. Australia: Melbourne 1884–85 to Sydney 1887–88.
7 England v. South Africa: Cape Town 1909–10 to Johannesburg 1913–14.
7 Australia v. South Africa: Cape Town 1921–22 to Durban 1935–36.
7 England v. New Zealand: Wellington 1950–51 to Manchester 1958.
6 Australia v. South Africa: Cape Town 1935–36 to Durban 1949–50.

MOST CONSECUTIVE MATCHES WITHOUT DEFEAT IN A SERIES

28 England v. New Zealand: Christchurch 1929–30 to date.
24 Australia v. South Africa: Melbourne 1910–11 to Brisbane 1952–53.
18 England v. South Africa: Leeds 1935 to Port Elizabeth 1948–49.
15 West Indies v. India: New Delhi 1948–49 to date.
14 Australia v. England: Brisbane 1946–47 to Adelaide 1950–51.
14 England v. India: Lord's 1932 to Kanpur 1951–52.
13 Australia v. England: Sydney 1920–21 to Adelaide 1924–25.
13 England v. West Indies: Georgetown 1953–54 to date.
12 England v. South Africa: Cape Town 1922–23 to Durban 1927–28.

DOUBLE FIGURES BY ALL ELEVEN BATSMEN IN AN INNINGS

475	England v. Australia (Melbourne)	1894–95
385	South Africa v. England (Johannesburg)	1905–06
636	England v. Australia (Sydney)	1928–29
358	South Africa v. Australia (Melbourne)	1931–32
575—9d	Australia v. India (Melbourne)	1947–48
397	India v. Pakistan (Calcutta)	1952–53

COMPLETE INNINGS WITHOUT A SCORE OF DOUBLE FIGURES

30 (inc. 11 extras)   South Africa v. England (Birmingham) 1924

OUTSTANDING COLLAPSES

215—3 to 260 all out	Australia v. England (Sydney)	1881–82
130—2 to 166 all out	Australia v. England (Sydney)	1894–95
58—0 to 105 all out	England v. Australia (Melbourne)......................................	1907–08
90—2 to 111 all out	Australia v. England (Oval)	1912
46—0 to 65 all out	Australia v. England (Oval)	1912
270—4 to 284 all out	England v. Australia (Melbourne)......................................	1920–21
240—3 to 282 all out	England v. South Africa (Durban)	1927–28
385—3 to 440 all out	New Zealand v. England (Wellington)	1929–30
400—2 to 471 all out	West Indies v. England (Georgetown)	1929–30
519—3 to 554 all out	Australia v. South Africa (Melbourne)	1931–32
470—4 to 524 all out	England v. Australia (Sydney)	1932–33
207—2 to 258 all out	India v. England (Bombay)	1933–34
202—4 to 234 all out	Australia v. England (Brisbane)..	1936–37
236—5 to 239 all out	England v. Australia (Melbourne)	1936–37
190—4 to 225 all out	West Indies v. England (Lord's)	1939
291—3 to 336 all out	England v. West Indies (Kingston)	1947–48
423—2 to 496 all out	England v. Australia (Leeds)	1948
516—2 to 608 all out	England v. South Africa (Johannesburg)	1948–49
521—3 to 558 all out	West Indies v. England (Nottingham)	1950
264—3 to 293 all out	India v. England (Leeds)	1952
543—3 to 576 all out	West Indies v. India (Kingston)..	1952–53
237—3 to 249 all out	Australia v. England (Nottingham)....................................	1953
277—2 to 316 all out	England v. West Indies (Kingston)	1953–54
116—1 to 158 all out	Pakistan v. India (Dacca)...	1954–55
108—2 to 140 all out	Australia v. England (Leeds)..	1956
62—2 to 84 all out	Australia v. England (Manchester)	1956
222—3 to 247 all out	England v. Australia (Oval)	1956
112—3 to 142 all out	West Indies v. England (Leeds)	1957
255—2 to 308 all out	Australia v. England (Melbourne)	1958–59
182—2 to 222 all out	India v. West Indies (Kanpur)..	1958–59
243—3 to 275 all out	India v. West Indies (New Delhi)	1958–59
172—3 to 206 all out	India v. Australia (New Delhi)	1959–60
299—2 to 353 all out	West Indies v. England (Kingston).....................................	1959–60

Australia (35—8) lost eight second innings wickets for only 35 runs in the last hour of the match v. England (Manchester) 1953, the match then being left drawn.

Australia's score changed from 59—1 to 61—5 in fifteen minutes, the batsmen being G. B. Hole, R. N. Harvey, K. R. Miller, and A. R. Morris, v. England (Oval) 1953.

England lost seven wickets for only eight runs v. West Indies (Kingston) 1953–54, the score changing from 277—2 to 285—9—six wickets fell for three runs and five for only a single (282—3 to 283—8).

OUTSTANDING RECOVERIES

26—7 to 113 all out	England v. Australia (Melbourne)	1878–79
187—8 to 327 all out	Australia v. England (Oval)	1880
181—8 to 346 all out	England v. Australia (Oval)	1884
254—8 to 401 all out	England v. Australia (Melbourne)	1884–85
134—7 to 309 all out	Australia v. England (Sydney)	1884–85
144—6 to 369 all out	England v. South Africa (Cape Town)	1891–92
58—6 to 323 all out	Australia v. England (Melbourne)	1897–98
154—6 to 372 all out	England v. Australia (Manchester)	1899
167—8 to 353 all out	Australia v. England (Melbourne)	1901–02
44—5 to 262 all out	England v. Australia (Manchester)	1902
175—7 to 324 all out	Australia v. England (Oval)	1902
48—5 to 263—9 (won)	England v. Australia (Oval)	1902
332—8 to 577 all out	England v. Australia (Sydney)..	1903–04
180—7 to 506 all out	Australia v. England (Adelaide)	1907–08
332—5 to 581 all out	Australia v. England (Sydney)	1920–21
282—7 to 499 all out	Australia v. England (Melbourne)	1920–21
191—5 to 403—8d	England v. Australia (Oval)	1921
276—8 to 411 all out	England v. Australia (Sydney)..	1924–25
119—6 to 489 all out	Australia v. England (Adelaide)	1924–25
217—5 to 521 all out	England v. Australia (Brisbane)	1928–29
21—7 to 112 all out	New Zealand v. England (Christchurch)	1929–30

133—4 to 560—8d	England v. New Zealand (Christchurch)	1932–33
182—5 to 440 all out	England v. Australia (Lord's)	1934
97—5 to 564 all out	Australia v. England (Melbourne)	1936–37
281—4 to 658—8d	England v. Australia (Nottingham)	1938
164—4 to 498 all out	West Indies v. England (Oval)	1939
70—4 to 428 all out	England v. India (Lord's)	1946
170—4 to 551 all out	England v. South Africa (Nottingham)	1947
185—4 to 509 all out	Australia v. England (Nottingham)	1948
141—6 to 363 all out	England v. Australia (Manchester)	1948
27—3 to 631 all out	West Indies v. India (New Delhi)	1948–49
95—4 to 336—5 (won)	Australia v. South Africa (Durban)	1949–50
110—5 to 372 all out	India v. Pakistan (New Delhi)	1952–53
115—5 to 344 all out	Pakistan v. India (Madras)	1952–53
12—3 to 282—7 (draw)	England v. Australia (Lord's)	1953
147—6 to 510 all out	West Indies v. Australia (Barbados)	1954–55
245—5 to 521—8d	South Africa v. England (Manchester)	1955
111—6 to 561 all out	Pakistan v. New Zealand (Lahore)	1955–56
197—5 to 474 all out	West Indies v. England (Birmingham)	1957
113—3 to 583—4d	England v. West Indies (Birmingham)	1957
134—5 to 424 all out	England v. West Indies (Lord's)	1957
89—5 to 367 all out	West Indies v. England (Nottingham)	1957

Part II—Batting

HIGHEST INDIVIDUAL INNINGS

365* G. Sobers: West Indies v. Pakistan (Kingston) 1957–58
364 L. Hutton: England v. Australia (Oval) 1938
337 Hanif Mohammed: Pakistan v. West Indies (Barbados) 1957–58
336* W. R. Hammond: England v. New Zealand (Auckland) 1932–33
334 D. G. Bradman: Australia v. England (Leeds) 1930
325 A. Sandham: England v. West Indies (Kingston) 1929–30
304 D. G. Bradman: Australia v. England (Leeds) 1934
299* D. G. Bradman: Australia v. South Africa (Adelaide) 1931–32
287 R. E. Foster: England v. Australia (Sydney) 1903–04
285* P. B. H. May: England v. West Indies (Birmingham) 1957
278 D. C. S. Compton: England v. Pakistan (Nottingham) 1954
270* G. Headley: West Indies v. England (Kingston) 1934–35
270 D. G. Bradman: Australia v. England (Melbourne) 1936–37
266 W. H. Ponsford: Australia v. England (Oval) 1934
261 F. M. Worrell: West Indies v. England (Nottingham) 1950
260 C. C. Hunte: West Indies v. Pakistan (Kingston) 1957–58
258 T. W. Graveney: England v. West Indies (Nottingham) 1957
256 R. Kanhai: West Indies v. India (Calcutta) 1958–59
255* D. J. McGlew: South Africa v. New Zealand (Wellington) 1952–53
254 D. G. Bradman: Australia v. England (Lord's) 1930
251 W. R. Hammond: England v. Australia (Sydney) 1928–29
244 D. G. Bradman: Australia v. England (Oval) 1934
243 E. Paynter: England v. South Africa (Durban) 1938 39
240 W. R. Hammond: England v. Australia (Lord's) 1938
237 F. M. Worrell: West Indies v. India (Kingston) 1952–53
236 E. A. B. Rowan: South Africa v. England (Leeds) 1951
234 D. G. Bradman: Australia v. England (Sydney) 1946–47
234 S. G. Barnes: Australia v. England (Sydney) 1946–47
232 D. G. Bradman: Australia v. England (Oval) 1930
232 S. J. McCabe: Australia v. England (Nottingham) 1938
231 A. D. Nourse jun.: South Africa v. Australia (Johannesburg) 1935–36
231* W. R. Hammond: England v. Australia (Sydney) 1936–37
231 V. Mankad: India v. New Zealand (Madras) 1955–56
230* B. Sutcliffe: New Zealand v. India (New Delhi) 1955–56
227 W. R. Hammond: England v. New Zealand (Christchurch) 1932–33
226 D. G. Bradman: Australia v. South Africa (Brisbane) 1931–32
226 G. Sobers: West Indies v. England (Barbados) 1959–60
223 G. Headley: West Indies v. England (Kingston) 1929–30
223 D. G. Bradman: Australia v. West Indies (Brisbane) 1930–31
223 P. R. Umrigar: India v. New Zealand (Hyderabad) 1955–56
223 V. Mankad: India v. New Zealand (Bombay) 1955–56
220 C. L. Walcott: West Indies v. England (Barbados) 1953–54
219 W. J. Edrich: England v. South Africa (Durban) 1938–39
219 D. Atkinson: West Indies v. Australia (Barbados) 1954–55
217 W. R. Hammond: England v. India (Oval) 1936
217 R. Kanhai: West Indies v. Pakistan (Lahore) 1958–59
216* E. Paynter: England v. Australia (Nottingham) 1938
214* V. T. Trumper: Australia v. South Africa (Adelaide) 1910–11
212 D. G. Bradman: Australia v. England (Adelaide) 1936–37
211 W. L. Murdoch: Australia v. England (Oval) 1884
211 J. B. Hobbs: England v. South Africa (Lord's) 1924
209 C. A. Roach: West Indies v. England (Georgetown) 1929–30
209 Imtiaz Ahmed: Pakistan v. New Zealand (Lahore) 1955–56
208 D. C. S. Compton: England v. South Africa (Lord's) 1947
208 A. D. Nourse jun.: South Africa v. England (Nottingham) 1951
207 E. D. Weekes: West Indies v. India (Trinidad) 1952–53
206* W. A. Brown: Australia v. England (Lord's) 1938
206 M. P. Donnelly: New Zealand v. England (Lord's) 1949
206 L. Hutton: England v. New Zealand (Oval) 1949
206 A. R. Morris: Australia v. England (Adelaide) 1950–51
206 E. D. Weekes: West Indies v. England (Trinidad) 1953–54

B   33

205* E. Hendren: England v. West Indies (Trinidad) 1929–30
205* J. Hardstaff jun.: England v. India (Lord's)..................................1946
205 R. N. Harvey: Australia v. South Africa (Melbourne) 1952–53
205 L. Hutton: England v. West Indies (Kingston)..........................1953–54
204 G. A. Faulkner: South Africa v. Australia (Melbourne)................1910–11
204 R. N. Harvey: Australia v. West Indies (Kingston)....................1954–55
203 H. L. Collins: Australia v. South Africa (Johannesburg) 1921–22
202* L. Hutton: England v. West Indies (Oval) 1950
201 S. E. Gregory: Australia v. England (Sydney) 1894–95
201* J. Ryder: Australia v. England (Adelaide) 1924–25
201 D. G. Bradman: Australia v. India (Adelaide) 1947–48
200 W. R. Hammond: England v. Australia (Melbourne) 1928–29

A CENTURY ON DÉBUT IN TEST CRICKET

118 L. Amarnath: India v. England (Bombay)...............................1933–34
112 A. A. Baig: India v. England (Manchester)..............................1959
165* C. Bannerman: Australia v. England (Melbourne) 1876–77
101* J. W. Burke: Australia v. England (Adelaide) 1950–51
104 H. L. Collins: Australia v. England (Sydney) 1920–21
104 R. A. Duff: Australia v. England (Melbourne) 1901–02
287 R. E. Foster: England v. Australia (Sydney) 1903–04
112 A. G. Ganteaume: West Indies v. England (Trinidad) 1947–48
106 P. A. Gibb: England v. South Africa (Johannesburg) 1938–39
152 W. G. Grace: England v. Australia (Oval) 1880
107 H. Graham: Australia v. England (Lord's) 1893
140 S. C. Griffith: England v. West Indies (Trinidad) 1947–48
119 G. Gunn: England v. Australia (Sydney) 1907–08
116 R. J. Hartigan: Australia v. England (Adelaide) 1907–08
176 G. Headley: West Indies v. England (Barbados) 1929–30
142 C. C. Hunte: West Indies v. Pakistan (Barbados) 1957–58
164 A. A. Jackson: Australia v. England (Adelaide) 1928–29
100* A. G. Kripal Singh: India v. New Zealand (Hyderabad) 1955–56
138 P. B. H. May: England v. South Africa (Leeds) 1951
117 J. W. E. Mills: New Zealand v. England (Wellington)................1929–30
104* C. A. Milton: England v. New Zealand (Leeds) 1958
115 B. H. Pairaudeau: West Indies v. India (Trinidad) 1952–53
102 Nawab of Pataudi: England v. Australia (Sydney) 1932–33
110 W. H. Ponsford: Australia v. England (Sydney) 1924–25
154* K. S. Ranjitsinhji: England v. Australia (Manchester) 1896
110 D. H. Shodhan: India v. Pakistan (Calcutta) 1952–53
104 O. G. Smith: West Indies v. Australia (Kingston) 1954–55
136 B. H. Valentine: England v. India (Bombay) 1933–34
132* P. F. Warner: England v. South Africa (Johannesburg) 1898–99

In addition, the following batsmen scored a century on début in a series against an individual country, although they had previously appeared in Test cricket:

114* H. R. Adhikari: India v. West Indies (New Delhi) 1948–49
122 G. O. Allen: England v. New Zealand (Lord's) 1931
137 L. E. G. Ames: England v. New Zealand (Lord's) 1931
107 A. H. Bakewell: England v. West Indies (Oval) 1933
132 W. Bardsley: Australia v. South Africa (Sydney) 1910–11
128 K. F. Barrington: England v. West Indies (Barbados) 1959–60
226 D. G. Bradman: Australia v. South Africa (Brisbane) 1931–32
185 D. G. Bradman: Australia v. India (Brisbane) 1947–48
104 L. C. Braund: England v. South Africa (Lord's) 1907
109 A. G. Chipperfield: Australia v. South Africa (Durban) 1935–36
107 R. J. Christiani: West Indies v. India (New Delhi) 1948–49
103 J. A. J. Christy: South Africa v. New Zealand (Christchurch) 1931–32
102 D. C. S. Compton: England v. Australia (Nottingham)...............1938
120 D. C. S. Compton: England v. West Indies (Lord's) 1939
163 D. C. S. Compton: England v. South Africa (Nottingham) 1947
154 M. C. Cowdrey: England v. West Indies (Birmingham)..............1957
136* E. R. Dexter: England v. West Indies (Barbados)......................1959–60
119 J. W. H. T. Douglas: England v. South Africa (Durban) 1913–14
173 K. S. Duleepsinhji: England v. Australia (Lord's) 1930
101 G. E. Gomez: West Indies v. India (New Delhi) 1948–49
175 T. W. Graveney: England v. India (Bombay) 1951–52
102 J. W. Guy—New Zealand v. India (Hyderabad) 1955–56
337 Hanif Mohammed: Pakistan v. West Indies (Barbados) 1957–58
114 J. Hardstaff jun.: England v. New Zealand (Lord's) 1937

112   R. N. Harvey: Australia v. England (Leeds) 1948
112   A. L. Hassett: Australia v. South Africa (Johannesburg) 1949–50
142   C. Hill: Australia v. South Africa (Johannesburg) 1902–03
100   L. Hutton: England v. Australia (Nottingham) 1938
196   L. Hutton: England v. West Indies (Lord's) 1939
146   A. F. Kippax: Australia v. West Indies (Adelaide) 1930–31
137   M. Leyland: England v. Australia (Melbourne) 1928–29
101   S. J. E. Loxton: Australia v. South Africa (Johannesburg) 1949–50
118   V. L. Manjrekar: India v. New Zealand (Hyderabad) 1955–56
255* D. J. McGlew: South Africa v. New Zealand (Wellington)..........................1952–53
113   B. Mitchell: South Africa v. New Zealand (Christchurch) 1931–32
109   A. R. A. Murray: South Africa v. New Zealand (Wellington) 1952–53
106   Mushtaq Ali: India v. West Indies (Calcutta) 1948–49
101* J. M. Parks: England v. West Indies (Trinidad) 1959–60
117 & 100   E. Paynter: England v. South Africa (Johannesburg) 1938–39
117   P. E. Richardson: England v. South Africa (Johannesburg) 1956–57
100   P. E. Richardson: England v. New Zealand (Birmingham) 1958
127   K. E. Rigg: Australia v. South Africa (Sydney) 1931–32
121   J. D. Robertson—England v. New Zealand (Lord's) 1949
152   A. Sandham: England v. West Indies (Barbados) 1929–30
103   R. T. Simpson: England v. New Zealand (Manchester)...................................1949
100   M. J. K. Smith: England v. India (Manchester) 1959
161   O. G. Smith: West Indies v. England (Birmingham) 1957
142* G. Sobers: West Indies v. India (Bombay) 1958–59
119   R. H. Spooner: England v. South Africa (Lord's) 1912
100   R. Subba Row: England v. West Indies (Georgetown) 1959–60
137* B. Sutcliffe: New Zealand v. India (Hyderabad) 1955–56
115   H. Sutcliffe: England v. Australia (Sydney) 1924–25
117   H. Sutcliffe: England v. New Zealand (Oval) 1931
122   E. Tyldesley: England v. West Indies (Lord's) 1928
223   P. R. Umrigar: India v. New Zealand (Hyderabad) 1955–56
152   C. L. Walcott: West Indies v. India (New Delhi) 1948–49
114   C. Washbrook: England v. West Indies (Lord's)...1950
138* A. J. Watkins: England v. India (New Delhi) 1951–52
109   W. Watson: England v. Australia (Lord's) 1953
116   W. Watson: England v. West Indies (Kingston) 1953–54
128   E. D. Weekes: West Indies v. India (New Delhi) 1948–49
197   E. D. Weekes: West Indies v. Pakistan (Barbados) 1957–58

A CENTURY IN EACH INNINGS OF A MATCH

136   130   W. Bardsley: Australia v. England (Oval) 1909
140   111   A. C. Russell: England v. South Africa (Durban) 1922–23
176   127   H. Sutcliffe: England v. Australia (Melbourne) 1924–25
119* 177   W. R. Hammond: England v. Australia (Adelaide) 1928–29
104   109* H. Sutcliffe: England v. South Africa (Oval) 1929
114   112   G. Headley: West Indies v. England (Georgetown) 1929–30
117   100   E. Paynter: England v. South Africa (Johannesburg) 1938–39
106   107   G. Headley: West Indies v. England (Lord's) 1939
147   103* D. C. S. Compton: England v. Australia (Adelaide) 1946–47
122   124* A. R. Morris: Australia v. England (Adelaide) 1946–47
189   104* A. Melville: South Africa v. England (Nottingham) 1947
120   189* B. Mitchell: South Africa v. England (Oval) 1947
132   127* D. G. Bradman: Australia v. India (Melbourne)....................................1947–48
116   145   V. S. Hazare: India v. Australia (Adelaide) 1947–48
162   101   E. D. Weekes: West Indies v. India (Calcutta) 1948–49
118   101* J. A. R. Moroney: Australia v. South Africa (Johannesburg) 1949–50
126   110   C. L. Walcott: West Indies v. Australia (Trinidad) 1954–55
155   110   C. L. Walcott: West Indies v. Australia (Kingston) 1954–55
125   109* G. Sobers: West Indies v. Pakistan (Georgetown) 1957–58

The following batsmen just missed the distinction:

124   83   P. S. McDonnell: Australia v. England (Adelaide) 1884–85
106   81   A. Shrewsbury: England v. Australia (Lord's) 1893
98   97   C. Hill: Australia v. England (Adelaide) 1901–02
95   93   F. E. Woolley: England v. Australia (Lord's) 1921
201* 88   J. Ryder: Australia v. England (Adelaide) 1924–25
83   95*   F. E. Woolley: England v. South Africa (Leeds) 1929
136   80*   C. S. Dempster: New Zealand v. England (Wellington)..........................1929–30
93   86   E. Hendren: England v. South Africa (Cape Town) 1930–31
93   106   P. A. Gibb: England v. South Africa (Johannesburg) 1938–39

125	97	P. G. Van der Byl: South Africa v. England (Durban)	1938–39
80	87	R. S. Modi: India v. West Indies (Calcutta)	1948–49
84	116	R. N. Harvey: Australia v. South Africa (Adelaide)	1952–53
85	150	P. Roy: India v. West Indies (Kingston)	1952–53
139	87*	E. D. Weekes: West Indies v. Australia (Trinidad)	1954–55
109	96	C. G. Borde: India v. West Indies (New Delhi)	1958–59
114	97	M. C. Cowdrey: England v. West Indies (Kingston)	1959–60

FIVE CENTURIES IN CONSECUTIVE INNINGS

E. D. Weekes (West Indies): 141 (Kingston) v. England in 1947–48, 128 (New Delhi), 194 (Bombay) 162 & 101 (Calcutta) v. India in 1948–49.

FOUR CENTURIES IN CONSECUTIVE INNINGS

J. H. Fingleton (Australia): 112 (Cape Town), 108 (Johannesburg), 118 (Durban) v. South Africa in 1935–36, 100 (Brisbane) v. England in 1936–37.
A. Melville (South Africa): 103 (Durban) v. England in 1938–39, 189 & 104* (Nottingham), 117 (Lord's) v. England in 1947.

THREE CENTURIES IN CONSECUTIVE INNINGS

W. Bardsley (Australia): 136 & 130 (Oval) v. England in 1909, 132 (Sydney) v. South Africa in 1910–11.
H. Sutcliffe (England): 115 (Sydney), 176 & 127 (Melbourne) v. Australia in 1924–25.
C. G. Macartney (Australia): 133* (Lord's), 151 (Leeds), 109 (Manchester) v. England in 1926.
G. Headley (West Indies): 270* (Kingston) v. England in 1934–35, 106 & 107 (Lord's) v. England in 1939.
A. R. Morris (Australia): 155 (Melbourne), 122 & 124* (Adelaide) v. England in 1946–47.
D. C. S. Compton (England): 163 (Nottingham), 208 (Lord's), 115 (Manchester) v. South Africa in 1947.
D. G. Bradman (Australia): 132 & 127* (Melbourne), 201 (Adelaide) v. India in 1947–48.
V. S. Hazare (India): 122 (Bombay) v. West Indies in 1948–49, 164* (New Delhi), 155 (Bombay) v. England in 1951–52.
E. D. Weekes (West Indies): 123 (Dunedin), 103 (Christchurch), 156 (Wellington) v. New Zealand in 1955–56.
G. Sobers (West Indies): 365* (Kingston), 125 & 109* (Georgetown) v. Pakistan in 1957–58.

MOST FIFTIES IN CONSECUTIVE INNINGS

7   E. D. Weekes (West Indies): 141 (1947–48), 128, 194, 162, 101, 90, 56 (1948–49)
6   G. Headley (West Indies): 93, 53, 270* (1934–35), 106, 107, 51 (1939).
6   E. Hendren (England): 77, 205*, 56, 123, 61, 55 (1929–30).
6   A. Melville (South Africa): 67, 78, 103 (1938–39), 189, 104*, 117 (1947).
6   J. Ryder (Australia): 78*, 58, 56, 142 (1920–21), 201*, 88 (1924–25).
6   G. Sobers (West Indies): 52, 52, 80, 365*, 125, 109* (1957–58).

HIGHEST RUN AGGREGATES IN A TEST RUBBER

	Season	Tests	Inns.	N.O.	Runs	H.S.	Avge.	100s	50s
D. G. Bradman (A. v. E.)	1930	5	7	0	974	334	139·14	4	—
W. R. Hammond (E. v. A.)	1928–29	5	9	1	905	251	113·12	4	—
R. N. Harvey (A. v. SA.)	1952–53	5	9	0	834	205	92·66	4	3
C. L. Walcott (WI. v. A.)	1954–55	5	10	0	827	155	82·70	5	2
G. Sobers (WI. v. P.)	1957–58	5	8	2	824	365*	137·33	3	3
D. G. Bradman (A. v. E.)	1936–37	5	9	0	810	270	90·00	3	1
D. G. Bradman (A. v. SA.)	1931–32	5	5	1	806	299*	201·50	4	—
E. D. Weekes (WI. v. I.)	1948–49	5	7	0	779	194	111·28	4	2
D. G. Bradman (A. v. E.)	1934	5	8	0	758	304	94·75	2	1
D. C. S. Compton (E. v. SA.)	1947	5	8	0	753	208	94·12	4	2
H. Sutcliffe (E. v. A.)	1924–25	5	9	0	734	176	81·55	4	2
G. A. Faulkner (SA. v. A.)	1910–11	5	10	0	732	204	73·20	2	5
E. D. Weekes (WI. v. I.)	1952–53	5	8	1	716	207	102·28	3	2
D. G. Bradman (A. v. I.)	1947–48	5	6	2	715	201	178·75	4	1
G. Sobers (WI. v. E.)	1959–60	5	8	1	709	226	101·28	3	1
G. Headley (WI. v. E.)	1929–30	4	8	0	703	223	87·87	4	—
C. L. Walcott (WI. v. E.)	1953–54	5	10	2	698	220	87·25	3	3
A. R. Morris (A. v. E.)	1948	5	9	1	696	196	87·00	3	3
E. Hendren (E. v. WI.)	1929–30	4	8	2	693	205*	115·50	2	5
D. G. Bradman (A. v. E.)	1946–47	5	8	1	680	234	97·14	2	3

	Season	Tests	Inns.	N.O.	Runs	H.S.	Avge.	100s	50s
L. Hutton (E. v. WI.)	1953–54	5	8	1	677	205	96·71	2	3
J. B. Hobbs (E. v. A.)	1911–12	5	9	1	662	187	82·75	3	1
V. T. Trumper (A. v. SA.)	1910–11	5	9	2	661	214*	94·42	2	2
R. N. Harvey (A. v. SA.)	1949–50	5	8	3	660	178	132·00	4	1
E. Paynter (E. v. SA.)	1938–39	5	8	0	653	243	81·62	3	2
R. N. Harvey (A. v. WI.)	1954–55	5	7	1	650	204	108·33	3	1
Hanif Mohammed (P. v. WI.)	1957–58	5	9	0	628	337	69·77	1	3
C. C. Hunte (WI. v. P.)	1957–58	5	9	1	622	260	77·75	3	—
A. D. Nourse jun. (SA. v. E.)	1947	5	9	0	621	149	69·00	2	5
B. Sutcliffe (NZ. v. I.)	1955–56	5	9	2	611	230*	87·28	2	1
W. R. Hammond (E. v. SA.)	1938–39	5	8	1	609	181	87·00	3	2

FIVE CENTURIES IN ONE TEST RUBBER

C. L. Walcott (108, 126 & 110, 155 & 110): West Indies v. Australia 1954–55

FOUR CENTURIES IN ONE TEST RUBBER

D. G. Bradman (131, 254, 334, 232): Australia v. England 1930
D. G. Bradman (226, 112, 167, 299*): Australia v. South Africa 1931–32
D. G. Bradman (185, 132 & 127*, 201): Australia v. India 1947–48
D. C. S. Compton (163, 208, 115, 113): England v. South Africa 1947
W. R. Hammond (251, 200, 119* & 177): England v. Australia 1928–29
R. N. Harvey (178, 151*, 100, 116): Australia v. South Africa 1949–50
R. N. Harvey (109, 190, 116, 205): Australia v. South Africa 1952–53
G. Headley (176, 114 & 112, 223): West Indies v. England 1929–30
H. Sutcliffe (115, 176 & 127, 143): England v. Australia 1924–25
H. Sutcliffe (114, 100, 104 & 109*): England v. South Africa 1929
E. D. Weekes (128, 194, 162 & 101): West Indies v. India 1948–49

HIGHEST INDIVIDUAL INNINGS SCORED ON EACH TEST GROUND

Birmingham ....285* P. B. H. May: England v. West Indies 1957
Leeds ....334 D. G. Bradman: Australia v. England 1930
Lord's ....254 D. G. Bradman: Australia v. England 1930
Manchester ....191 W. J. Edrich: England v. South Africa 1947
Nottingham ....278 D. C. S. Compton: England v. Pakistan 1954
Oval ....364 L. Hutton: England v. Australia 1938
Sheffield ....119 C. Hill: Australia v. England 1902
Adelaide ....299* D. G. Bradman: Australia v. South Africa 1931–32
Brisbane ....226 D. G. Bradman: Australia v. South Africa 1931–32
Melbourne ....270 D. G. Bradman: Australia v. England 1936–37
Sydney ....287 R. E. Foster: England v. Australia 1903–04
Cape Town ....189 J. W. Burke: Australia v. South Africa 1957–58
Durban ....243 E. Paynter: England v. South Africa 1938–39
Johannesburg ....231 A. D. Nourse jun.: South Africa v. Australia 1935–36
Port Elizabeth ....167 A. L. Hassett: Australia v. South Africa 1949–50
Barbados ....337 Hanif Mohammed: Pakistan v. West Indies 1957–58
Georgetown ....209 C. A. Roach: West Indies v. England 1929–30
Kingston ....365* G. Sobers: West Indies v. Pakistan 1957–58
Trinidad ....207 E. D. Weekes: West Indies v. India 1952–53
Auckland ....336* W. R. Hammond: England v. New Zealand 1932–33
Christchurch.................227 W. R. Hammond: England v. New Zealand 1932–33
Dunedin ....123 E. D. Weekes: West Indies v. New Zealand 1955–56
Wellington ....255* D. J. McGlew: South Africa v. New Zealand 1952–53
Bombay.........................223 V. Mankad: India v. New Zealand 1955–56
Calcutta ....256 R. Kanhai: West Indies v. India 1958–59
Hyderabad ....223 P. R. Umrigar: India v. New Zealand 1955–56
Kanpur..........................198 G. Sobers: West Indies v. India 1958–59
Lucknow ....124* Nazar Mohammed: Pakistan v. India 1952–53
Madras ....231 V. Mankad: India v. New Zealand 1955–56
New Delhi ....230* B. Sutcliffe: New Zealand v. India 1955–56
Bahawalpur ....142 Hanif Mohammed: Pakistan v. India 1954–55
Dacca ....103 Hanif Mohammed: Pakistan v. New Zealand 1955–56
Karachi ....103* Alimuddin: Pakistan v. India 1954–55
Karachi ....103 Hanif Mohammed: Pakistan v. West Indies 1958–59
Lahore ....217 R. Kanhai: West Indies v. Pakistan 1958–59
Peshawar ....108 P. R. Umrigar: India v. Pakistan 1954–55

MOST RUNS SCORED BY A BATSMAN IN A DAY'S PLAY

```
309   D. G. Bradman (334): Australia v. England (Leeds) ...................................1930
295   W. R. Hammond (336*): England v. New Zealand (Auckland) ...............1932–33
273   D. C. S. Compton (278): England v. Pakistan (Nottingham) ..................1954
271   D. G. Bradman (304): Australia v. England (Leeds) ...............................1934
244   D. G. Bradman (244): Australia v. England (Oval) .................................1934
239   F. M. Worrell (261): West Indies v. England (Nottingham) ....................1950
223   W. R. Hammond (227): England v. New Zealand (Christchurch) .............1932–33
223   D. G. Bradman (223): Australia v. West Indies (Brisbane)  ...................1930–31
217   W. R. Hammond (217): England v. India (Oval)  ..................................1936
214   R. E. Foster (287): England v. Australia (Sydney) ...............................1903–04
213   S. J. McCabe (232): Australia v. England (Nottingham) ........................1938
210   W. R. Hammond (240): England v. Australia (Lord's) ...........................1938
209   C. A. Roach (209): West Indies v. England (Georgetown) .....................1929–30
208   G. Sobers (365*): West Indies v. Pakistan (Kingston) ..........................1957–58
206   V. T. Trumper (214*): Australia v. South Africa (Adelaide) ..................1910–11
206   L. Hutton (206): England v. New Zealand (Oval) .................................1949
205   W. H. Ponsford (266): Australia v. England (Oval) .............................1934
203   H. L. Collins (203): Australia v. South Africa (Johannesburg) ..............1921–22
203   R. Kanhai (256): West Indies v. India (Calcutta) .................................1958–59
201   D. G. Bradman (201): Australia v. India (Adelaide) .............................1947–48
200   D. G. Bradman (226): Australia v. South Africa (Brisbane) ...................1931–32
```

MOST RUNS ADDED DURING A BATSMAN'S INNINGS

```
770   L. Hutton (364): England v. Australia (Oval) .....................................1938
720   A. Sandham (325): England v. West Indies (Kingston)  ........................1929–30
703   G. Sobers (365*): West Indies v. Pakistan (Kingston) ..........................1957–58
628   Hanif Mohammed (337): Pakistan v. West Indies (Barbados)  ...............1957–58
574   W. H. Ponsford (266): Australia v. England (Oval)  ...........................1934
564   S. G. Barnes (234): Australia v. England (Sydney) .............................1946–47
530   G Headley (270*): West Indies v. England (Kingston) ..........................1934–35
518   F. M. Worrell (237): West Indies v. India (Kingston) ..........................1952–53
518   P. B. H. May (285*): England v. West Indies (Birmingham)  .................1957
511   D. G. Bradman (304): Australia v. England (Leeds)  ..........................1934
506   D. G. Bradman (334): Australia v. England (Leeds)  ..........................1930
504   R. E. Foster (287): England v. Australia (Sydney) .............................1903–04
504   D. G. Bradman (299*): Australia v. South Africa (Adelaide)  ...............1931–32
```

BATSMEN SCORING A HIGH PERCENTAGE OF INNINGS TOTAL

```
67·3% (165*–245)   C. Bannerman: Australia v. England (Melbourne) ...................1876–77
60·6% ( 74 –122)   V. T. Trumper: Australia v. England (Melbourne) .................1903–04
60·1% ( 62 –103)   J. T. Tyldesley: England v. Australia (Melbourne) ................1903–04
59·8% (106 –177)   J. H. Sinclair: South Africa v. England (Cape Town) ...........1898–99
59·8% (109 –182)   H. W. Taylor: South Africa v. England (Durban) ................1913–14
59·2% ( 74 –125)   B. Sutcliffe: New Zealand v. England (Dunedin) ................1954–55
59·0% (334 –566)   D. G. Bradman: Australia v. England (Leeds)  ..................1930
58·7% (202*–344)   L. Hutton: England v. West Indies (Oval) ........................1950
58·2% (188 –323)   C. Hill: Australia v. England (Melbourne) .......................1897–98
58·2% (299*–513)   D. G. Bradman: Australia v. South Africa (Adelaide) ..........1931–32
57·6% ( 30 – 52)   L. Hutton: England v. Australia (Oval) ..........................1948
57·4% (220 –383)   C. L. Walcott: West Indies v. England (Barbados) .............1953–54
57·3% (156*–272)   L. Hutton: England v. Australia (Adelaide) .....................1950–51
56·5% (147 –260)   P. S. McDonnell: Australia v. England (Sydney) ...............1881–82
56·5% ( 56*– 99)   T. L. Goddard: South Africa v. Australia (Cape Town)........1957–58
56·4% (232 –411)   S. J. McCabe: Australia v. England (Nottingham) .............1938
55·6% (132*–237)   P. F. Warner: England v. South Africa (Johannesburg)  .......1898–99
55·6% (158 –284)   D. C. S. Compton: England v. South Africa (Manchester) ....1955
55·5% (206 –371)   A. R. Morris: Australia v. England (Adelaide) ................1950–51
55·3% ( 26 – 47)   A. B. Tancred: South Africa v. England (Cape Town) .........1888–89
```

OPENING BATSMAN CARRYING BAT THROUGH INNINGS

```
 26*   (47)    A. B. Tancred: South Africa v. England (Cape Town) ...................1888–89
 67*   (176)   J. E. Barrett: Australia v. England (Lord's) ............................1890
132*   (307)   R. Abel: England v. Australia (Sydney) ................................1891–92
132*   (237)   P. F. Warner: England v. South Africa (Johannesburg) ...............1898–99
159*   (309)   W. W. Armstrong: Australia v. South Africa (Johannesburg) .........1902–03
```

43*	(103)	J. W. Zulch: South Africa v. England (Cape Town)	1909–10
193*	(383)	W. Bardsley: Australia v. England (Lord's)	1926
30*	(66)	W. M. Woodfull: Australia v. England (Brisbane)	1928–29
73*	(193)	W. M. Woodfull: Australia v. England (Adelaide)	1932–33
206*	(422)	W. A. Brown: Australia v. England (Lord's)	1938
202*	(344)	L. Hutton: England v. West Indies (Oval)	1950
156*	(272)	L. Hutton: England v. Australia (Adelaide)	1950–51
124*	(331)	Nazar Mohammed: Pakistan v. India (Lucknow)	1952–53
191*	(372)	F. M. Worrell: West Indies v. England (Nottingham)	1957
56*	(99)	T. L. Goddard: South Africa v. Australia (Cape Town)	1957–58

BATSMEN WHO SCORED MAIDEN CENTURY IN A TEST MATCH

165*	†C. Bannerman: Australia v. England (Melbourne)	1876–77
153*	W. L. Murdoch: Australia v. England (Oval)	1880
147	P. S. McDonnell: Australia v. England (Sydney)	1881–82
102	H. J. H. Scott: Australia v. England (Oval)	1884
134*	H. Wood: England v. South Africa (Cape Town)	1891–92
107	†H. Graham: Australia v. England (Lord's)	1893
124	A. J. L. Hill: England v. South Africa (Cape Town)	1895–96
106	J. H. Sinclair: South Africa v. England (Cape Town)	1898–99
115	P. W. Sherwell: South Africa v. England (Lord's)	1907
116	†R. J. Hartigan: Australia v. England (Adelaide)	1907–08
129	H. G. Owen-Smith: South Africa v. England (Leeds)	1929
122	C. A. Roach: West Indies v. England (Barbados)	1929–30
140	†S. C. Griffith: England v. West Indies (Trinidad)	1947–48
133	V. L. Manjrekar: India v. England (Leeds)	1952
122	C. Depeiza: West Indies v. Australia (Barbados)	1954–55
108	P. L. Winslow: South Africa v. England (Manchester)	1955
111	S. N. McGregor: New Zealand v. Pakistan (Lahore)	1955–56

† *The player was making his début in Test cricket.*

A CENTURY AND 'DUCK' IN THE SAME TEST

0 & 163*	M. L. Apte: India v. West Indies (Trinidad)	1952–53
0 & 141	S. G. Barnes: Australia v. England (Lord's)	1948
105 & 0	I. Barrow: West Indies v. England (Manchester)	1933
0 & 103*	D. G. Bradman: Australia v. England (Melbourne)	1932–33
138 & 0	D. G. Bradman: Australia v. England (Nottingham)	1948
102 & 0	L. C. Braund: England v. Australia (Sydney)	1903–04
0 & 120	R. H. Catterall: South Africa v. England (Birmingham)	1924
145* & 0	D. C. S. Compton: England v. Australia (Manchester)	1948
119 & 0	M. C. Cowdrey: England v. West Indies (Trinidad)	1959–60
122* & 0	G. A. Faulkner: South Africa v. Australia (Manchester)	1912
100 & 0	J. H. Fingleton: Australia v. England (Brisbane)	1936–37
122* & 0	G. Gunn: England v. Australia (Sydney)	1907–08
122 & 0	R. N. Harvey: Australia v. England (Manchester)	1953
188 & 0	C. Hill: Australia v. England (Melbourne)	1897–98
101 & 0	L. Hutton: England v. New Zealand (Leeds)	1949
209 & 0	Imtiaz Ahmed: Pakistan v. New Zealand (Lahore)	1955–56
122 & 0	Imtiaz Ahmed: Pakistan v. West Indies (Kingston)	1957–58
196 & 0	G. B. Legge: England v. New Zealand (Auckland)	1929–30
133 & 0	V. L. Manjrekar: India v. England (Leeds)	1952
111 & 0	V. Mankad: India v. Australia (Melbourne)	1947–48
0 & 112	P. B. H. May: England v. South Africa (Lord's)	1955
0 & 153*	W. L. Murdoch: Australia v. England (Oval)	1880
0 & 231	A. D. Nourse jun.: South Africa v. Australia (Johannesburg)	1935–36
140 & 0	P. Roy: India v. England (Bombay)	1951–52
0 & 104	J. H. Sinclair: South Africa v. Australia (Cape Town)	1902–03
0 & 143	G. H. S. Trott: Australia v. England (Lord's)	1896
0 & 100	J. T. Tyldesley: England v. Australia (Leeds)	1905
0 & 123	F. E. Woolley: England v. Australia (Sydney)	1924–25

BATSMEN REGISTERING A 'PAIR OF SPECTACLES'

R. Peel (England) was dismissed three times for a 'pair': v. Australia in consecutive matches at Adelaide and Sydney in 1894–95 and at the Oval in 1896.

The following batsmen have been dismissed twice for a 'pair':

A. V. Bedser (England): v. Australia (Oval) 1948 and v. West Indies (Oval) 1950.
R. J. Crisp (South Africa): v. Australia (Cape Town and Durban) 1935–36.

K. Mackay (Australia): v. England (Manchester) 1956 and v. India (Kanpur) 1959–60.
Q. McMillan (South Africa): v. Australia (Brisbane and Melbourne) 1931–32.
C. A. Roach (West Indies): v. England (Trinidad) 1929–30 and (Lord's) 1933.
L. J. Tancred (South Africa): v. England (Leeds) 1907 and (Oval) 1912.
A. L. Valentine (West Indies): v. England (Manchester) 1950 and (Georgetown) 1953–54.

The following batsmen have collected one 'pair':

England: G. F. Grace (1880), W. Attewell (1891–92), G. A. Lohmann (1895–96), E. G. Arnold (1903–04), A. E. Knight (1903–04), E. G. Hayes (1905–06), M. C. Bird (1909–10), H. Strudwick (1921), P. Holmes (1927–28), C. I. J. Smith (1934–35), J. T. Ikin (1946–47), J. J. Warr (1950–51), F. Ridgway (1951–52), R. T. Spooner (1955), J. H. Wardle (1956), F. S. Trueman (1958–59), T. E. Bailey (1958–59).
Australia: P. S. McDonnell (1882–83), T. W. Garrett (1882–83), E. Evans (1886), P. G. McShane (1887–88), A. C. Bannerman (1888), M. A. Noble (1899), S. E. Gregory (1899), C. E. McLeod (1901–02), J. Darling (1902), J. J. Kelly (1902), H. Trumble (1903–04), J. V. Saunders (1907–08), V. T. Trumper (1907–08), C. V. Grimmett (1930), W. A. Oldfield (1931–32), J. H. Fingleton (1932–33), V. Y. Richardson (1932–33), C. L. Badcock (1938), I. W. Johnson (1946–47), J. Iverson (1950–51), J. A. R. Moroney (1950–51), L. Maddocks (1956), R. N. Harvey (1956).
South Africa: C. Wimble (1891–92), J. T. Willoughby (1895–96), P. S. T. Jones (1902–03), J. J. Kotze (1902–03), A. E. E. Vogler (1910–11), C. B. Llewellyn (1912), T. A. Ward (1912), J. L. Cox (1913–14), C. E. Dixon (1913–14), P. T. Lewis (1913–14), A. E. Hall (1922–23), G. A. L. Hearne (1922–23), X. C. Balaskas (1935–36), F. Nicholson (1935–36), C. N. McCarthy (1948–49), D. J. McGlew (1955), W. R. Endean (1955), P. S. Heine (1956–57).
West Indies: C. R. Browne (1929–30), H. C. Griffith (1933), E. Achong (1934–35), J. Trim (1951–52), A. P. Binns (1954–55), O. G. Smith (1954–55), K. T. Ramadhin (1957), E. D. Weekes (1957), F. C. M. Alexander (1957), L. Gibbs (1958–59).
New Zealand: F. T. Badcock (1929–30), K. C. James (1929–30), J. A. Cowie (1937), L. A. Butterfield (1945–46), C. G. Rowe (1945–46), L. S. M. Miller (1953–54), M. B. Poore (1954–55), I. A. Colquhoun (1954–55), J. A. Hayes (1954–55), A. R. MacGibbon (1955–56), H. B. Cave (1955–56), R. W. Blair (1955–56), N. S. Harford (1958).
India: V. S. Hazare (1951–52), P. Roy (1952), G. S. Ramchand (1952), P. G. Joshi (1952–53), C. V. Gadkari (1952–53), N. S. Tamhane (1958–59), Surendra Nath (1959), R. B. Desai (1959–60).
Pakistan: M. E. Z. Ghazali (1954), Nasimul Ghani (1957–58), Wazir Mohammed (1957–58).

The following batsmen who registered 'spectacles' were dismissed by the same fielding combination in each innings:

R. Peel, st Jarvis b Turner: England v. Australia (Sydney) 1894–95
J. Darling, c Braund b Barnes: Australia v. England (Sheffield).................................1902
P. T. Lewis, c Woolley b Barnes: South Africa v. England (Durban) 1913–14
P. G. Joshi, c Worrell b Valentine: India v. West Indies (Barbados) 1952–53
K. Mackay, c Oakman b Laker: Australia v. England (Manchester) 1956

F. E. Woolley (England) totalled thirteen 'ducks' in his ninety-eight Test innings for England, but was never dismissed for 'spectacles.'
V. T. Trumper (Australia) recorded three consecutive 'ducks' in the 1907–08 rubber against England.
P. Roy (India) recorded four consecutive 'ducks' v. England in 1952—he failed to score in five of his seven innings during the rubber.
L. S. M. Miller (New Zealand) recorded four consecutive 'ducks' in the 1953–54 rubber against South Africa.
Three batsmen were dismissed for 'spectacles' in the match for New Zealand v. England (Auckland) 1954–55—M. B. Poore, I. A. Colquhoun and J. A. Hayes.
N. A. T. Adcock (South Africa) was '0 not out' in each innings v. England (Lord's) 1955, but did not receive a ball in either innings.

FASTEST TIMES TO CERTAIN SCORES

Fastest fifties:

35 min.   J. H. Sinclair (104): South Africa v. Australia (Cape Town) 1902–03
35 min.   C. G. Macartney (56): Australia v. South Africa (Sydney).............................1910–11
35 min.   J. M. Gregory (119): Australia v. South Africa (Johannesburg) 1921–22
38 min.   R. Benaud (121): Australia v. West Indies (Kingston) 1954–55
42 min.   S. J. McCabe (189*): Australia v. South Africa (Johannesburg) 1935–36
45 min.   J. J. Lyons (55): Australia v. England (Lord's) 1890
45 min.   V. T. Trumper (63): Australia v. South Africa (Johannesburg) 1902–03
45 min.   G. L. Jessop (93): England v. South Africa (Lord's) 1907
45 min.   P. W. Sherwell (115): South Africa v. England (Lord's) 1907
45 min.   F. B. Smith (54*): New Zealand v. England (Leeds) 1949
45 min.   R. R. Lindwall (50): Australia v. England (Lord's) 1953

Fastest centuries:

70 min.	J. M. Gregory (119): Australia v. South Africa (Johannesburg) 1921–22
75 min.	G. L. Jessop (104): England v. Australia (Oval)...1902
78 min.	R. Benaud (121): Australia v. West Indies (Kingston) 1954–55
80 min.	J. H. Sinclair (104): South Africa v. Australia (Cape Town) 1902–03
90 min.	D. G. Bradman (334): Australia v. England (Leeds) 1930
91 min.	S. J. McCabe (189*): Australia v. South Africa (Johannesburg) 1935–36
95 min.	P. W. Sherwell (115): South Africa v. England (Lord's) 1907
97 min.	C. G. Macartney (116): Australia v. South Africa (Durban) 1921–22
98 min.	D. Denton (104): England v. South Africa (Johannesburg) 1909–10
98 min.	C. Hill (191): Australia v. South Africa (Sydney) 1910–11
98 min.	D. G. Bradman (167): Australia v. South Africa (Melbourne) 1931–32

Fastest double-centuries:

225 min.	S. J. McCabe (232): Australia v. England (Nottingham) 1938
226 min.	V. T. Trumper (214*): Australia v. South Africa (Adelaide) 1910–11
240 min.	W. R. Hammond (336*): England v. New Zealand (Auckland) 1932–33
245 min.	D. C. S. Compton (278): England v. Pakistan (Nottingham) 1954
254 min.	D. G. Bradman (226): Australia v. South Africa (Brisbane) 1931–32
265 min.	H. L. Collins (203): Australia v. South Africa (Johannesburg) 1921–22
270 min.	J. B. Hobbs (211): England v. South Africa (Lord's) 1924

FAST SCORING IN A COMPLETE INNINGS

Min.

25 — 10	C. I. J. Smith: England v. West Indies (Georgetown) 1934–35
35 — 14	W. P. Howell: Australia v. England (Sydney) 1901–02
42*— 18	A. P. F. Chapman: England v. Australia (Leeds) 1926
38 — 23	M. W. Tate: England v. South Africa (Johannesburg) 1930–31
37 — 24	L. Hutton: England v. Australia (Sydney) 1946–47
49*— 25	F. G. Mann: England v. New Zealand (Leeds) 1949
41*— 27	W. Voce: England v. South Africa (Johannesburg) 1930–31
44 — 30	Amar Singh: India v. England (Manchester) 1936
56 — 40	C. G. Macartney: Australia v. South Africa (Sydney) 1910–11
62 — 50	V. T. Trumper: Australia v. England (Sheffield) 1902
63 — 50	V. T. Trumper: Australia v. South Africa (Johannesburg) 1902–03
62*— 55	G. A. Lohmann: England v. Australia (Oval) 1888
72 — 63	E. A. V. Williams: West Indies v. England (Barbados) 1947–48
104*— 75	G. L. Jessop: England v. Australia (Oval) 1902
104 — 80	J. H. Sinclair: South Africa v. Australia (Cape Town)...................1902–03
119 — 87	J. M. Gregory: Australia v. South Africa (Johannesburg) 1921–22
115 —105	P. W. Sherwell: South Africa v. England (Lord's) 1907
113 —110	D. C. S. Compton: England v. South Africa (Oval) 1947
161 —130	M. Leyland: England v. South Africa (Oval) 1935
137 —135	K. H. Weekes: West Indies v. England (Oval)...........................1939
160 —165	J. Darling: Australia v. England (Sydney) 1897–98
154 —165	F. E. Woolley: England v. South Africa (Manchester) 1929
159 —171	V. T. Trumper: Australia v. South Africa (Melbourne) 1910–11
189*—165	S. J. McCabe: Australia v. South Africa (Johannesburg) 1935–36
191 —202	C. Hill: Australia v. South Africa (Sydney) 1910–11
232 230	S. J. McCabe: Australia v. England (Nottingham) 1938
278 —290	D. C. S. Compton: England v. Pakistan (Nottingham) 1954
336*—315	W. R. Hammond: England v. New Zealand (Auckland) 1932–33

W. P. Howell (above 1901–02) scored 23 runs in five minutes.

W. R. Hammond (336*)—England v. New Zealand (Auckland) 1932–33—scored as follows: 50* in 72 minutes, 100* in 130, 150* in 168, 200* in 240 and 300* in 287.

W. R. Hammond (140)—England v. New Zealand (Lord's) 1937—moved from 50* to 140 in 80 minutes.

R. T. Simpson (103)—England v. New Zealand (Manchester) 1949—moved from 53* to 103 in 27 minutes.

FAST PARTNERSHIPS

Runs	Wkt.	Min.	
33	10th	10	B. Sutcliffe & R. W. Blair: New Zealand v. South Africa (Johannesburg) 1953–54
42*	9th	15	F. W. Freer & G. Tribe: Australia v. England (Sydney) 1946–47
44*	4th	18	E. Hendren & A. P. F. Chapman: England v. Australia (Leeds) 1926
61	8th	25	M. W. Tate & H. Larwood: England v. West Indies (Oval) 1928
57	10th	27	M. W. Tate & W. Voce: England v. South Africa (Johannesburg) 1930–31
63	7th	30	L. E. G. Ames & R. W. V. Robins: England v. India (Lord's) 1932

* B

Runs	Wkt.	Min.		
74	8th	40	Amar Singh & Lall Singh: India v. England (Lord's)	1932
77	1st	40	C. A. Roach & I. Barrow: West Indies v. England (Oval)	1933
76*	6th	45	F. E. Woolley & M. W. Tate: England v. South Africa (Leeds)	1929
108	7th	45	F. R. Brown & W. Voce: England v. New Zealand (Christchurch)	1932–33
121*	3rd	55	F. E. Woolley & E. Hendren: England v. South Africa (Lord's)	1924
104	1st	60	B. Mitchell & J. A. J. Christy: South Africa v. New Zealand (Christchurch)	1931–32
105	5th	60	R. T. Simpson & T. E. Bailey: England v. New Zealand (Manchester)	1949
109	6th	65	F. S. Jackson & G. L. Jessop: England v. Australia (Oval)	1902
102	5th	65	J. Ryder & O. E. Nothling: Australia v. England (Sydney)	1928–29
103	10th	65	H. G. Owen-Smith & A. J. Bell: South Africa v. England (Leeds)	1929
137	9th	70	E. L. Dalton & A. B. C. Langton: South Africa v. England (Oval)	1935
138	8th	70	R. W. V. Robins & H. Verity: England v. India (Manchester)	1936
154	9th	73	S. E. Gregory & J. McC. Blackham: Australia v. England (Sydney)	1894–95
145	6th	75	L. C. Braund & G. L. Jessop: England v. South Africa (Lord's)	1907
154	8th	87	D. Tallon & R. R. Lindwall: Australia v. England (Melbourne)	1946–47
154	4th	89	D. C. S. Compton & T. W. Graveney: England v. Pakistan (Nottingham)	1954
158	6th	90	J. T. Tyldesley & R. H. Spooner: England v. Australia (Oval)	1905
192	5th	108	D. C. S. Compton & T. E. Bailey: England v. Pakistan (Nottingham)	1954
224	2nd	115	W. Bardsley & C. Hill: Australia v. South Africa (Sydney)	1910–11
196	1st	120	B. Mitchell & J. A. J. Christy: South Africa v. New Zealand (Wellington)	1931–32
202	3rd	130	C. Kelleway & W. Bardsley: Australia v. South Africa (Manchester)	1912
206	5th	140	E. Paynter & D. C. S. Compton: England v. Australia (Nottingham)	1938
248	4th	140	L. Hutton & D. C. S. Compton: England v. West Indies (Lord's)	1939
242	5th	145	W. R. Hammond & L. E. G. Ames: England v. New Zealand (Christchurch)	1932–33
231	2nd	150	W. M. Woodfull & D. G. Bradman: Australia v. England (Lord's)	1930
218	2nd	160	L. Hutton & W. J. Edrich: England v. New Zealand (Oval)	1949
221	4th	165	G. H. S. Trott & S. E. Gregory: Australia v. England (Lord's)	1896
245	3rd	165	R. E. S. Wyatt & F. E. Woolley: England v. South Africa (Manchester)	1929
229	3rd	165	D. G. Bradman & A. F. Kippax: Australia v. England (Leeds)	1930
246	8th	165	L. E. G. Ames & G. O. Allen: England v. New Zealand (Lord's)	1931
264	3rd	180	L. Hutton & W. R. Hammond: England v. West Indies (Oval)	1939
301	2nd	225	A. R. Morris & D. G. Bradman: Australia v. England (Leeds)	1948
319	3rd	240	A. Melville & A. D. Nourse jun.: South Africa v. England (Nottingham)	1947

J. B. Hobbs and H. Sutcliffe—England v. South Africa (Lord's) 1924—took an overnight score of 28–0 to 228–0 in 150 minutes before lunch on the second day of match.

W. R. Hammond and L. E. G. Ames—England v. New Zealand (Christchurch) 1932–33—added 100 in 65 minutes and 200 in 110 minutes during their stand of 242 (above).

L. Hutton and C. J. Barnett—England v. Australia (Nottingham) 1938—scored 169 runs without loss before lunch on the first day of the match.

E. Paynter and W. R. Hammond—England v. South Africa (Durban) 1938–39—took the score from 215 to 315 in 42 minutes.

MOST RUNS SCORED OFF A SINGLE OVER

25 (66061600) B. Sutcliffe off H. J. Tayfield: New Zealand v. South Africa (Johannesburg) (the fourth six was by R. W. Blair) 1953–54

22 (116626) M. W. Tate off A. E. Hall: England v. South Africa (Johannesburg) (the second single was scored by W. Voce) 1930–31

22 (42444004) P. G. Van der Byl off D. V. P. Wright: South Africa v. England (Durban) 1938–39

21 (124464) J. H. Sinclair off A. J. Hopkins: South Africa v. Australia (Cape Town) (the first single was scored by M. Hathorn) 1902–03

21 (122466) S. G. Barnes off J. C. Laker: Australia v. England (Lord's) (the first single was scored by D. G. Bradman) 1948

20 (6644) E. A. V. Williams off J. C. Laker: West Indies v. England (Barbados) 1947–48

J. M. Gregory (119)—Australia v. South Africa (Johannesburg) 1921–22—scored 34 runs off two consecutive overs, 18 off W. F. E. Marx and 16 off E. P. Nupen. Later in his innings he scored 16 runs off an over from A. D. Nourse sen.

W. R. Hammond (336*)—England v. New Zealand (Auckland) 1932–33—hit three consecutive balls bowled by J. Newman for six each.

D. V. P. Wright—England v. Australia (Nottingham) 1938—conceded 44 runs off three consecutive overs bowled in the closing stages of S. J. McCabe's innings of 232.

V. H. Stollmeyer and K. H. Weekes—West Indies v. England (Oval) 1939—scored 43 runs off the first four overs bowled by M. S. Nichols and R. T. D. Perks with the new ball taken at 200.

N. B. F. Mann (41)—South Africa v. Australia (Port Elizabeth) 1949–50—scored 31 off two consecutive overs, 19 off I. W. Johnson and 12 off C. L. McCool.

J. H. Wardle (38)—England v. Australia (Melbourne) 1954–55—scored 30 runs off two consecutive overs—16 (00444004) off W. A. Johnston and 14 (40204400) off I. W. Johnson.

F. S. Trueman (36*)—England v. West Indies (Lord's) 1957—hit three sixes (060606) in one over bowled by K. T. Ramadhin.

MOST BOUNDARY STROKES IN AN INNINGS

6s. 4s.

6s	4s					
10	33	(192)	336*	W. R. Hammond: England v. New Zealand (Auckland)	1932–33
—	46	(184)	334	D. G. Bradman: Australia v. England (Leeds)	1930
2	43	(184)	304	D. G. Bradman: Australia v. England (Leeds)	1934
—	38	(152)	287	R. E. Foster: England v. Australia (Sydney)	1903–04
2	35	(152)	261	F. M. Worrell: West Indies v. England (Nottingham)	1950
—	38	(152)	365*	G. Sobers: West Indies v. Pakistan (Kingston)	1957–58
—	36	(144)	231	A. D. Nourse jun.: South Africa v. Australia (Johannesburg)	1935–36
1	34	(142)	232	S. J. McCabe: Australia v. England (Nottingham)	1938
1	34	(142)	278	D. C. S. Compton: England v. Pakistan (Nottingham)	1954
—	35	(140)	364	L. Hutton: England v. Australia (Oval)	1938
—	35	(140)	237	F. M. Worrell: West Indies v. India (Kingston)	1952–53

MONOPOLY OF RUN SCORING DURING INNINGS

(Batsman's score given first, runs scored during innings second.)

32 — 34	P. S. McDonnell: Australia v. England (Oval)	1888
34 — 38	G. J. Bonnor: Australia v. England (Melbourne)	1882–83
48 — 57	J. C. Laker: England v. Australia (Leeds)	1953
50 — 63	R. R. Lindwall: Australia v. England (Lord's)	1953
50 — 64	G. Headley: West Indies v. England (Lord's)	1933
55 — 66	H. H. Massie: Australia v. England (Oval)	1882
55 — 66	J. J. Lyons: Australia v. England (Lord's)	1890
60 — 81	A. R. Morris: Australia v. England (Nottingham)	1953
60 — 84	Yuvraj of Patiala: India v. England (Madras)	1933–34
62 — 81	J. N. Crawford: England v. Australia (Adelaide)	1907–08
72 — 96	E. A. V. Williams: West Indies v. England (Barbados)	1947–48
80*—105	B. Sutcliffe: New Zealand v. South Africa (Johannesburg)	1953–54
76 —106	A. K. Davidson: Australia v. England (Lord's)	1953
76 —108	W. R. Hammond: England v. Australia (Leeds)	1938
79 —109	L. N. Constantine: West Indies v. England (Oval)	1939
84 —114	E. L. Bartlett: West Indies v. Australia (Adelaide)	1930–31
74 —115	H. Sutcliffe: England v. Australia (Manchester)	1930
90 —126	H. B. Cameron: South Africa v. England (Lord's)	1935
90 —128	L. N. Constantine: West Indies v. England (Trinidad)	1934–35
94 —133	E. D. Weekes: West Indies v. England (Georgetown)	1953–54
91 —135	P. B. H. May: England v. Australia (Melbourne)	1954–55
93 —137	W. A. Hadlee: New Zealand v. England (Manchester)	1937
104 —139	G. L. Jessop: England v. Australia (Oval)	1902
103 —141	E. D. Weekes: West Indies v. New Zealand (Christchurch)	1955–56
91 —146	M. Leyland: England v. South Africa (Johannesburg)	1930–31
115 —153	P. W. Sherwell: South Africa v. England (Lord's)	1907
121 —161	R. Benaud: Australia v. West Indies (Kingston)	1954–55
117 —165	W. W. Read: England v. Australia (Oval)	1884
134 —175	J. J. Lyons: Australia v. England (Sydney)	1891–92
170 —216	W. G. Grace: England v. Australia (Oval)	1886
232 —300	S. J. McCabe: Australia v. England (Nottingham)	1938
278 —429	D. C. S. Compton: England v. Pakistan (Nottingham)	1954
336*—492	W. R. Hammond: England v. New Zealand (Auckland)	1932–33

P. S. McDonnell (147) and A. C. Bannerman (70) scored 217 out of the 246 runs from the bat in Australia's innings of 260 v. England (Sydney) 1881–82.

H. H. Massie (43)—Australia v. England (Melbourne) 1882–83—scored all the first 26 runs from the bat in the first 13 minutes of Australia's innings.

F. R. Spofforth (50)—Australia v. England (Melbourne)—1884–85—scored 50 of the 64 runs added for the tenth wicket with J. W. Trumble.

J. J. Lyons (55)—Australia v. England (Lord's) 1890—scored his runs out of a first wicket stand of 66 which lasted 45 minutes.

J. H. Sinclair (106)—South Africa v. England (Cape Town) 1898–99—scored 47 of the 51 runs added by the last three wickets on the second morning of the match.

J. Worrall (76)—Australia v. England (Leeds) 1899—scored his runs out of 95 in 85 minutes. He scored all the first 28 runs and 47 out of the first 52.

K. L. Hutchings (126)—England v. Australia (Melbourne) 1907–08—scored 71 out of 90 in an hour at one stage of his innings.

G. A. Faulkner (76)—South Africa v. England (Johannesburg) 1909–10—scored 76 of the 114 runs added for the fourth wicket with G. C. White.

D. G. Bradman (334)—Australia v. England (Leeds) 1930—scored his first 102 runs out of 127 in 95 minutes before lunch.

S. J. McCabe (187)—Australia v. England (Brisbane) 1932–33—scored 60 out of the last 70 runs scored in the first innings and added 55 in 30 minutes for the tenth wicket with T. W. Wall (4).

C. F. Walters—England v. Australia (Manchester) 1934—scored 52 of the 68 runs added with H. Sutcliffe for the first wicket.

C. I. J. Smith (25)—England v. West Indies (Trinidad) 1934–35—scored all 25 runs added with R. E. S. Wyatt for the second wicket in 10 minutes (3 sixes were included in the scoring strokes).

W. R. Hammond (167)—England v. India (Manchester) 1936—completed his century out of 138 in 100 minutes.

S. J. McCabe (232)—Australia v. England (Nottingham) 1938—scored 72 of the 77 runs added for the tenth wicket with L. O.'B. Fleetwood-Smith (5).

R. T. Simpson (156*)—England v. Australia (Melbourne) 1950–51—scored 64 of the 74 runs added for the tenth wicket with R. Tattersall (10).

R. A. McLean—South Africa v. Australia (Melbourne) 1952–53—scored 81 out of 101 in the first innings and 76* out of 106 in the second.

B. Sutcliffe (80*)—New Zealand v. South Africa (Johannesburg) 1953–54—retired hurt before he had scored, but returned later to score 80* out of 105 in 98 minutes, hitting 7 sixes and 4 fours.

D. C. S. Compton (278)—England v. Pakistan (Nottingham) 1954—scored his runs out of 429 in 290 minutes. He scored 173 out of the 233 runs added between lunch and tea in 125 minutes, and 164 of the 192 runs added for the fifth wicket with T. E. Bailey (36*). He moved from 100 to 278 in 122 minutes.

Part III—Wicket Partnerships

RECORD WICKET PARTNERSHIPS—ALL TEST CRICKET

1st 413 V. Mankad & P. Roy: India v. New Zealand (Madras) 1955–56
2nd 451 W. H. Ponsford & D. G. Bradman: Australia v. England (Oval) 1934
3rd 370 W. J. Edrich & D. C. S. Compton: England v. South Africa (Lord's) 1947
4th 411 P. B. H. May & M. C. Cowdrey: England v. West Indies (Birmingham)..............1957
5th 405 S. G. Barnes & D. G. Bradman: Australia v. England (Sydney) 1946–47
6th 346 J. H. Fingleton & D. G. Bradman: Australia v. England (Melbourne) 1936–37
7th 347 D. Atkinson & C. Depeiza: West Indies v. Australia (Barbados) 1954–55
8th 246 L. E. G. Ames & G. O. Allen: England v. New Zealand (Lord's)...................1931
9th 154 S. E. Gregory & J. McC. Blackham: Australia v. England (Sydney) 1894–95
10th 130 R. E. Foster & W. Rhodes: England v. Australia (Sydney) 1903–04

RECORD WICKET PARTNERSHIPS—ENGLAND

1st 359 L. Hutton & C. Washbrook v. South Africa (Johannesburg) 1948–49
2nd 382 L. Hutton & M. Leyland v. Australia (Oval)...1938
3rd 370 W. J. Edrich & D. C. S. Compton v. South Africa (Lord's) 1947
4th 411 P. B. H. May & M. C. Cowdrey v. West Indies (Birmingham) 1957
5th 242 W. R. Hammond & L. E. G. Ames v. New Zealand (Christchurch) 1932–33
6th 215 L. Hutton & J. Hardstaff jun. v. Australia (Oval) 1938
7th 197 M. J. K. Smith & J. M. Parks v. West Indies (Trinidad) 1959–60
8th 246 L. E. G. Ames & G. O. Allen v. New Zealand (Lord's) 1931
9th 151 W. H. Scotton & W. W. Read v. Australia (Oval) 1884
10th 130 R. E. Foster & W. Rhodes v. Australia (Sydney) 1903–04

RECORD WICKET PARTNERSHIPS—AUSTRALIA

1st 233 J. H. Fingleton & W. A. Brown v. South Africa (Cape Town) 1935–36
2nd 451 W. H. Ponsford & D. G. Bradman v. England (Oval)...............................1934
3rd 295 C. C. McDonald & R. N. Harvey v. West Indies (Kingston) 1954–55
4th 388 W. H. Ponsford & D. G. Bradman v. England (Leeds) 1934
5th 405 S. G. Barnes & D. G. Bradman v. England (Sydney) 1946–47
6th 346 J. H. Fingleton & D. G. Bradman v. England (Melbourne) 1936–37
7th 165 C. Hill & H. Trumble v. England (Melbourne) 1897–98
8th 243 C. Hill & R. J. Hartigan v. England (Adelaide) 1907–08
9th 154 S. E. Gregory & J. McC. Blackham v. England (Sydney) 1894–95
10th 127 J. M. Taylor & A. A. Mailey v. England (Sydney) 1920–21

RECORD WICKET PARTNERSHIPS—SOUTH AFRICA

1st 260 B. Mitchell & I. J. Siedle v. England (Cape Town) 1930–31
2nd 198 E. A. B. Rowan & C. B. Van Ryneveld v. England (Leeds) 1951
3rd 319 A. Melville & A. D. Nourse jun. v. England (Nottingham) 1947
4th 214 H. W. Taylor & H. G. Deane v. England (Oval) 1929
5th 135 R. H. Catterall & H. B. Cameron v. England (Durban) 1927–28
6th 171 J. H. B. Waite & P. L. Winslow v. England (Manchester) 1955
7th 246 D. J. McGlew & A. R. A. Murray v. New Zealand (Wellington) 1952–53
8th 124 A. D. Nourse sen. & E. A. Halliwell v. Australia (Johannesburg) 1902–03
9th 137 E. L. Dalton & A. B. C. Langton v. England (Oval) 1935
10th 103 H. G. Owen-Smith & A. J. Bell v. England (Leeds) 1929

RECORD WICKET PARTNERSHIPS—WEST INDIES

1st 239 J. B. Stollmeyer & A. F. Rae v. India (Madras) 1948–49
2nd 446 C. C. Hunte & G. Sobers v. Pakistan (Kingston) 1957–58
3rd 338 E. D. Weekes & F. M. Worrell v. England (Trinidad) 1953–54
4th 399 G. Sobers & F. M. Worrell v. England (Barbados) 1959–60
5th 219 E. D. Weekes & B. H. Pairaudeau v. India (Trinidad) 1952–53
6th 211 C. L. Walcott & G. E. Gomez v. England (Lord's) 1950
7th 347 D. Atkinson & C. Depeiza v. Australia (Barbados) 1954–55

45

8th   99   C. A. McWatt & J. K. Holt v. England (Georgetown) 1953–54
9th   106   R. J. Christiani & D. Atkinson v. India (New Delhi) 1948–49
10th   55   F. M. Worrell & K. T. Ramadhin v. England (Nottingham) 1957

RECORD WICKET PARTNERSHIPS—NEW ZEALAND

1st   276   C. S. Dempster & J. W. E. Mills v. England (Wellington) 1929–30
2nd   131   B. Sutcliffe & J. R. Reid v. England (Christchurch) 1950–51
3rd   222*   B. Sutcliffe & J. R. Reid v. India (New Delhi) 1955–56
4th   142   M. L. Page & R. C. Blunt v. England (Lord's) 1931
5th   174   J. R. Reid & J. E. F. Beck v. South Africa (Cape Town) 1953–54
6th   100   H. G. Vivian & F. T. Badcock v. South Africa (Wellington) 1931–32
7th   100   T. C. Lowry & H. M. McGirr v. England (Auckland) 1929–30
8th   104   D. A. R. Moloney & A. W. Roberts v. England (Lord's) 1937
9th   69   C. F. W. Alliott & I. B. Cromb v. South Africa (Wellington) 1931–32
10th   57   F. L. H. Mooney & J. A. Cowie v. England (Leeds) 1949

RECORD WICKET PARTNERSHIPS—INDIA

1st   413   V. Mankad & P. Roy v. New Zealand (Madras) 1955–56
2nd   237   P. Roy & V. L. Manjrekar v. West Indies (Kingston) 1952–53
3rd   238   P. R. Umrigar & V. L. Manjrekar v. New Zealand (Hyderabad) 1955–56
4th   222   V. S. Hazare & V. L. Manjrekar v. England (Leeds) 1952
5th   131   P. R. Umrigar & D. G. Phadkar v. West Indies (Trinidad) 1952–53
6th   188   V. S. Hazare & D. G. Phadkar v. Australia (Adelaide) 1947–48
7th   153   M. L. Apte & V. Mankad v. West Indies (Trinidad) 1952–53
8th   82   G. S. Ramchand & N. S. Tamhane v. Pakistan (Bahawalpur) 1954–55
9th   54   G. S. Ramchand & S. G. Shinde v. England (Lord's) 1952
10th   109   H. R. Adhikari & Ghulam Ahmed v. Pakistan (New Delhi) 1952–53

RECORD WICKET PARTNERSHIPS—PAKISTAN

1st   152   Hanif Mohammed & Imtiaz Ahmed v. West Indies (Barbados) 1957–58
2nd   178   Hanif Mohammed & Saeed Ahmed v. West Indies (Karachi) 1958–59
3rd   169   Saeed Ahmed & Wazir Mohammed v. West Indies (Trinidad) 1957–58
4th   154   Wazir Mohammed & Hanif Mohammed v. West Indies (Trinidad) ...1957–58
5th   155   Alimuddin & A. H. Kardar v. India (Karachi) 1954–55
6th   166   Waqar Hasan & Wazir Mohammed v. West Indies (Kingston) 1957–58
7th   308   Waqar Hasan & Imtiaz Ahmed v. New Zealand (Lahore) 1955–56
8th   {63   Nazar Mohammed & Zulfiqar Ahmed v. India (Lucknow).........1952–53
       {63   Imtiaz Ahmed & Maqsood Ahmed v. New Zealand (Lahore) 1955–56
9th   71   Wallis Mathias & Fazal Mahmood v. West Indies (Trinidad) 1957–58
10th   104   Zulfiqar Ahmed & Amir Elahi v. India (Madras) 1952–53

HIGHEST SCORE REACHED AT THE FALL OF EACH WICKET

1st   413   India (537—3d) v. New Zealand (Madras) 1955–56
2nd   533   West Indies (790—3d) v. Pakistan (Kingston) 1957–58
3rd   602   West Indies (790—3d) v. Pakistan (Kingston) 1957–58
4th   667   England (849) v. West Indies (Kingston) 1929–30
5th   720   England (849) v. West Indies (Kingston) 1929–30
6th   770   England (903—7d) v. Australia (Oval) 1938
7th   876   England (903—7d) v. Australia (Oval) 1938
8th   813   England (849) v. West Indies (Kingston) 1929–30
9th   821   England (849) v. West Indies (Kingston) 1929–30
10th   849   England (849) v. West Indies (Kingston) 1929–30

LOWEST SCORE REACHED AT THE FALL OF EACH WICKET

1st   0   On several occasions.
2nd   0   On several occasions.
3rd   0   {Australia (32—7d) v. England (Brisbane) 1950–51
              {India (165) v. England (Leeds) 1952
4th   0   India (165) v. England (Leeds) 1952
5th   6   India (98) v. England (Oval) 1952
6th   7   Australia (70) v. England (Manchester) 1888
7th   18   Australia (60) v. England (Lord's) 1888
8th   22   New Zealand (26) v. England (Auckland) 1954–55
9th   26   New Zealand (26) v. England (Auckland) 1945–55
10th   26   New Zealand (26) v. England (Auckland) 1954–55

WICKET PARTNERSHIPS OF OVER 300

451   2nd   W. H. Ponsford & D. G. Bradman: Australia v. England (Oval) 1934
446   2nd   C. C. Hunte & G. Sobers: West Indies v. Pakistan (Kingston) 1957–58
413   1st   V. Mankad & P. Roy: India v. New Zealand (Madras) 1955–56
411   4th   P. B. H. May & M. C. Cowdrey: England v. West Indies (Birmingham)..............1957
405   5th   S. G. Barnes & D. G. Bradman: Australia v. England (Sydney).....................1946–47
399   4th   G. Sobers & F. M. Worrell: West Indies v. England (Barbados).................1959–60
388   4th   W. H. Ponsford & D. G. Bradman: Australia v. England (Leeds) 1934
382   2nd   L. Hutton & M. Leyland: England v. Australia (Oval) 1938
370   3rd   W. J. Edrich & D. C. S. Compton: England v. South Africa (Lord's) 1947
359   1st   L. Hutton & C. Washbrook: England v. South Africa (Johannesburg) 1948–49
347   7th   D. Atkinson & C. Depeiza: West Indies v. Australia (Barbados) 1954–55
346   6th   J. H. Fingleton & D. G. Bradman: Australia v. England (Melbourne) 1936–37
338   3rd   E. D. Weekes & F. M. Worrell: West Indies v. England (Trinidad)   1953–54
323   1st   J. B. Hobbs & W. Rhodes: England v. Australia (Melbourne) 1911–12
319   3rd   A. Melville & A. D. Nourse jun.: South Africa v. England (Nottingham) 1947
308   7th   Waqar Hasan & Imtiaz Ahmed: Pakistan v. New Zealand (Lahore) 1955–56
301   2nd   A. R. Morris & D. G. Bradman: Australia v. England (Leeds) 1948

FOUR CENTURY STANDS IN ONE INNINGS

England (382—2, 135—3, 215—6, 106—7) v. Australia (Oval) 1938
West Indies (267—4, 101—6, 118—7, 106—9) v. India (New Delhi) 1948–49
Pakistan (152—1, 112—2, 154—3, 121—4) v. West Indies (Barbados) 1957–58

THREE CENTURY STANDS IN ONE INNINGS

England (151—1, 103—4, 131—6) v. Australia (Oval) 1893
Australia (171—4, 139—5, 154—9) v. England (Sydney) 1894–95
England (119—3, 122—4, 154—8) v. South Africa (Johannesburg) 1895–96
England (185—1, 131—2, 110—4) v. Australia (Oval) 1899
England (192—5, 115—9, 130—10) v. Australia (Sydney) 1903–04
Australia (123—1, 111—2, 187—6) v. England (Sydney) 1920–21
England (268—1, 142—2, 121*—3) v. South Africa (Lord's) 1924
Australia (161—1, 123—6, 100—9) v. England (Melbourne)....................................1924–25
England (126—1, 106—2, 133—7) v. Australia (Melbourne) 1924–25
England (182—1, 140—3, 116*—4) v. Australia (Lord's)..1926
England (173—1, 148—2, 249—4) v. West Indies (Kingston) 1929–30
Australia (162—1, 231—2, 192—3) v. England (Lord's) 1930
England (112—1, 188—2, 123—3) v. Australia (Sydney) 1932–33
England (134—2, 127—3, 138—8) v. India (Manchester).......................................1936
Australia (276—3, 106—4, 131—6) v. England (Brisbane) 1946–47
Australia (236—2, 105—3, 142—4) v. India (Adelaide) 1947–48
England (168—1, 100—2, 155—3) v. Australia (Leeds) 1948
West Indies (197—1, 115—3, 189—5) v. New Zealand (Auckland) 1951–52
Australia (122—1, 103—3, 148—4) v. South Africa (Melbourne) 1952–53
Australia (108—1, 100—3, 206—6) v. West Indies (Barbados) 1954–55
Australia (295—3, 220—5, 137—8) v. West Indies (Kingston) 1954–55
West Indies (108—3, 217—4, 160*—6) v. India (Calcutta) 1958–59

CENTURY STAND FOR SAME WICKET IN EACH INNINGS

1st Wicket

157 & 110   J. B. Hobbs & H. Sutcliffe: England v. Australia (Sydney)........................1924–25
119 & 171   R. H. Catterall & B. Mitchell: South Africa v. England (Birmingham) 1929
131 & 191   P. G. Van der Byl with A. Melville (1st inns) & B. Mitchell (2nd inns): South
                  Africa v. England (Durban) 1938–39
137 & 100   L. Hutton & C. Washbrook: England v. Australia (Adelaide) 1946–47
168 & 129   L. Hutton & C. Washbrook: England v. Australia (Leeds) 1948

2nd Wicket

127 & 108   W. Rhodes & J. W. Hearne (1st inns), J. B. Hobbs & G. Gunn (2nd inns):
                  England v. Australia (Melbourne) 1911–12
184 & 168   P. A. Gibb & E. Paynter: England v. South Africa (Johannesburg) 1938–39
275 & 157   C. C. McDonald & A. L. Hassett (1st inns) and A. R. Morris & R. N. Harvey
                  (2nd inns): Australia v. South Africa (Adelaide) 1952–53

125 & 165   A. L. Hassett & R. N. Harvey (1st inns) and A. R. Morris & K. R. Miller (2nd inns): Australia v. England (Lord's) 1953
269 & 135   G. Sobers with C. L. Walcott (1st inns) & C. C. Hunte (2nd inns): West Indies v. Pakistan (Georgetown) 1957–58

3rd Wicket

120 & 121   B. Mitchell & H. W. Taylor: South Africa v. Australia (Adelaide) 1931–32
245 & 104   J. Hardstaff with W. R. Hammond (1st inns) & C. J. Barnett (2nd inns): England v. New Zealand (Lord's) 1937
155 & 103   W. J. Edrich with A. V. Bedser (1st inns) & D. C. S. Compton (2nd inns): England v. Australia (Leeds) 1948
129 & 108   R. S. Modi & V. S. Hazare: India v. West Indies (Calcutta) 1948–49
242 & 127   C. L. Walcott & E. D. Weekes: West Indies v. Australia (Trinidad)...............1954–55

4th Wicket

117 & 113   G. Gunn with L. C. Braund (1st inns) & J. Hardstaff sen. (2nd inns): England v. Australia (Sydney) 1907–08
126 & 137   J. Ryder with A. A. Jackson (1st inns) & A. F. Kippax (2nd inns): Australia v. England (Adelaide) 1928–29
110 & 179   C. L. Walcott with F. M. Worrell (1st inns) & G. Sobers (2nd inns): West Indies v. Australia (Kingston) 1954–55
121 & 104   M. C. Cowdrey with P. B. H. May (1st inns) & P. E. Richardson (2nd inns): England v. New Zealand (Birmingham) 1958

BATSMEN WITH MOST CENTURY STANDS

The following batsmen have shared in the most century stands:

	Total	1st	2nd	3rd	4th	5th	6th	7th	8th	9th	10th
L. Hutton (E.)	41	17	13	7	1	—	2	1	—	—	—
D. G. Bradman (A.)	36	—	15	11	3	6	1	—	—	—	—
W. R. Hammond (E.)	33	1	6	12	11	2	1	—	—	—	—
H. Sutcliffe (E.)	33	21	10	1	—	1	—	—	—	—	—
J. B. Hobbs (E.)	32	24	6	1	—	—	—	1	—	—	—
D. C. S. Compton (E.)	30	—	—	14	7	7	1	—	1	—	—
R. N. Harvey (A.)	29	—	6	11	8	3	1	—	—	—	—
B. Mitchell (SA.)	24	9	3	8	2	—	—	1	1	—	—
P. B. H. May (E.)	22	—	6	7	8	1	—	—	—	—	—
A. L. Hassett (A.)	21	—	4	8	7	1	—	—	1	—	—
E. D. Weekes (WI.)	21	—	—	8	4	6	2	1	—	—	—
A. R. Morris (A.)	19	8	4	5	1	1	—	—	—	—	—
C. Hill (A.)	17	—	8	3	3	1	—	1	1	—	—
W. Rhodes (E.)	17	9	4	2	—	—	1	—	—	—	1
C. L. Walcott (WI.)	17	—	1	2	10	2	2	—	—	—	—
W. M. Woodfull (A.)	17	4	11	—	1	1	—	—	—	—	—
M. C. Cowdrey (E.)	16	4	2	—	8	1	—	1	—	—	—
K. R. Miller (A.)	16	—	2	1	9	2	1	1	—	—	—
G. Sobers (WI.)	16	—	3	3	3	5	2	—	—	—	—
E. Hendren (E.)	15	—	—	5	4	2	1	2	1	—	—
A. D. Nourse jun. (SA.)	15	—	—	8	4	1	1	1	—	—	—
F. M. Worrell (WI.)	15	—	2	4	6	2	1	—	—	—	—

Part IV—Bowling

'HAT-TRICKS'

F. R. Spofforth	Australia v. England (Melbourne)	1878–79
W. Bates	England v. Australia (Melbourne)	1882–83
J. Briggs	England v. Australia (Sydney)	1891–92
G. A. Lohmann	England v. South Africa (Port Elizabeth)	1895–96
J. T. Hearne	England v. Australia (Leeds)	1899
H. Trumble	Australia v. England (Melbourne)	1901–02
H. Trumble	Australia v. England (Melbourne)	1903–04
T. J. Matthews†	Australia v. South Africa (Manchester)	1912
T. J. Matthews†	Australia v. South Africa (Manchester)	1912
M. J. C. Allom‡	England v. New Zealand (Christchurch)	1929–30
T. W. Goddard	England v. South Africa (Johannesburg)	1938–39
P. J. Loader	England v. West Indies (Leeds)	1957
L. Kline	Australia v. South Africa (Cape Town)	1957–58
W. Hall	West Indies v. Pakistan (Lahore)	1958–59
G. Griffin	South Africa v. England (Lord's)	1960

(†Matthews achieved the 'hat-trick' in each innings)
(‡Allom took four wickets with five consecutive balls)

THREE WICKETS WITH FOUR CONSECUTIVE BALLS

F. R. Spofforth	Australia v. England (Oval)	1882
F. R. Spofforth	Australia v. England (Sydney)	1884–85
J. Briggs	England v. South Africa (Cape Town)	1888–89
E. P. Nupen	South Africa v. England (Johannesburg)	1930–31
W. J. O'Reilly	Australia v. England (Manchester)	1934
W. Voce	England v. Australia (Sydney)	1936–37
R. R. Lindwall	Australia v. England (Adelaide)	1946–47
K. Cranston†	England v. South Africa (Leeds)	1947
R. Appleyard	England v. New Zealand (Auckland)	1954–55
R. Benaud	Australia v. West Indies (Georgetown)	1954–55

(†Cranston took four wickets in a six-ball over)

EIGHT OR MORE WICKETS IN AN INNINGS

10—53	J. C. Laker: England v. Australia (Manchester)	1956
9—28	G. A. Lohmann: England v. South Africa (Johannesburg)	1895–96
9—37	J. C. Laker: England v. Australia (Manchester)	1956
9—69	J. S. Patel: India v. Australia (Kanpur)	1959–60
9—102	S. P. Gupte: India v. West Indies (Kanpur)	1958–59
9—103	S. F. Barnes: England v. South Africa (Johannesburg)	1913–14
9—113	H. J. Tayfield: South Africa v. England (Johannesburg)	1956–57
9—121	A. A. Mailey: Australia v. England (Melbourne)	1920–21
8—7	G. A. Lohmann: England v. South Africa (Port Elizabeth)	1895–96
8—11	J. Briggs: England v. South Africa (Cape Town)	1888–89
8—29	S. F. Barnes: England v. South Africa (Oval)	1912
8—31	F. Laver: Australia v. England (Manchester)	1909
8—31	F. S. Trueman: England v. India (Manchester)	1952
8—35	G. A. Lohmann: England v. Australia (Sydney)	1886–87
8—43	A. E. Trott: Australia v. England (Adelaide)	1894–95
8—43	H. Verity: England v. Australia (Lord's)	1934
8—52	V. Mankad: India v. Pakistan (New Delhi)	1952–53
8—55	V. Mankad: India v. England (Madras)	1951–52
8—56	S. F. Barnes: England v. South Africa (Johannesburg)	1913–14
8—58	G. A. Lohmann: England v. Australia (Sydney)	1891–92
8—59	C. Blythe: England v. South Africa (Leeds)	1907
8—65	H. Trumble: Australia v. England (Oval)	1902
8—68	W. Rhodes: England v. Australia (Melbourne)	1903–04
8—69	H. J. Tayfield: South Africa v. England (Durban)	1956–57
8—70	S. J. Snooke: South Africa v. England (Johannesburg)	1905–06

8—81   L. C. Braund: England v. Australia (Melbourne) 1903–04
8—94   T. Richardson: England v. Australia (Sydney) 1897–98
8—104   A. L. Valentine: West Indies v. England (Manchester) 1950
8—107   B. J. T. Bosanquet: England v. Australia (Nottingham) 1905
8—126   J. C. White: England v. Australia (Adelaide) 1928–29

FOURTEEN OR MORE WICKETS IN A MATCH

19—90   J. C. Laker: England v. Australia (Manchester) 1956
17—159   S. F. Barnes: England v. South Africa (Johannesburg) 1913–14

15—28   J. Briggs: England v. South Africa (Cape Town) 1888–89
15—45   G. A. Lohmann: England v. South Africa (Port Elizabeth) 1895–96
15—99   C. Blythe: England v. South Africa (Leeds) 1907
15—104   H. Verity: England v. Australia (Lord's) 1934
15—124   W. Rhodes: England v. Australia (Melbourne) 1903–04

14—90   F. R. Spofforth: Australia v. England (Oval) 1882
14—99   A. V. Bedser: England v. Australia (Nottingham) 1953
14—124   J. S. Patel: India v. Australia (Kanpur) 1959–60
14—144   S. F. Barnes: England v. South Africa (Durban) 1913–14
14—199   C. V. Grimmett: Australia v. South Africa (Adelaide) 1931–32

OUTSTANDING INNINGS BOWLING ANALYSES

O.   M.   R.   W.
51·2—23—53—10   J. C. Laker: England v. Australia (Manchester) 1956
14·2— 6—28— 9   G. A. Lohmann: England v. South Africa (Johannesburg) 1895–96
16·4— 4—37— 9   J. C. Laker: England v. Australia (Manchester) 1956
9·4— 5— 7— 8   G. A. Lohmann: England v. South Africa (Port Elizabeth) 1895–96
14·2— 5—11— 8   J. Briggs: England v. South Africa (Cape Town) 1888–89
19·1—11—17— 7   J. Briggs: England v. South Africa (Cape Town) 1888–89
7·4— 2—17— 7   M. A. Noble: Australia v. England (Melbourne) 1901–02
11 — 3—17— 7   W. Rhodes: England v. Australia (Birmingham) 1902
6·3— 4— 7— 6   A. E. R. Gilligan: England v. South Africa (Birmingham) 1924
11·4— 6—11— 6   S. Haigh: England v. South Africa (Cape Town) 1898–99
14 — 7—13— 6   H. J. Tayfield: South Africa v. New Zealand (Johannesburg) 1953–54
18 —11—15— 6   C. T. B. Turner: Australia v. England (Sydney) 1886–87
2·3— 1— 2— 5   E. R. H. Toshack: Australia v. India (Brisbane) 1947–48
7·2— 5— 6— 5   H. Ironmonger: Australia v. South Africa (Melbourne) 1931–32
6·3— 2— 7— 4   J. C. White: England v. Australia (Brisbane) 1928–29
5 — 2— 7— 4   J. H. Wardle: England v. Australia (Manchester) 1953
6 — 3— 7— 4   R. Appleyard: England v. New Zealand (Auckland) 1954–55
3·4— 3— 0— 3   R. Benaud: Australia v. India (New Delhi) 1959–60

OUTSTANDING MATCH BOWLING ANALYSES

19—90 (9—37 & 10—53)   J. C. Laker: England v. Australia (Manchester) 1956
15—28 (7—17 &   8—11)   J. Briggs: England v. South Africa (Cape Town) 1888–89
15—45 (7—38 &   8— 7)   G. A. Lohmann: England v. South Africa (Port Elizabeth) 1895–96
13—57 (5—29 &   8—28)   S. F. Barnes: England v. South Africa (Oval) 1912
11—24 (5—   6 &   6—18)   H. Ironmonger: Australia v. South Africa (Melbourne)...........1931–32
11—31 (5—   2 &   6—29)   E. R. H. Toshack: Australia v. India (Brisbane) 1947–48
11—48 (5—28 &   6—20)   G. A. R. Lock: England v. West Indies (Oval) 1957
10—49 (5—29 &   5—20)   F. E. Woolley: England v. Australia (Oval) 1912

MOST WICKETS TAKEN BY A BOWLER IN A DAY

15—28   J. Briggs: England v. South Africa (Cape Town) 1888–89
         (He bowled one maiden over on the first evening)
14—80   H. Verity: England v. Australia (Lord's) 1934
         (His complete match figures were 15—104)

BOWLERS TAKING TEN OR MORE WICKETS ON DÉBUT

12—102   F. Martin: England v. Australia (Oval) 1890
10—156   T. Richardson: England v. Australia (Manchester)...............................1893
11—112   A. E. Hall: South Africa v. England (Cape Town) 1922–23

11— 82   C. V. Grimmett: Australia v. England (Sydney) 1924–25
11— 96   C. S. Marriott: England v. West Indies (Oval) 1933
10—179   K. Farnes: England v. Australia (Nottingham) 1934
11—145   A. V. Bedser: England v. India (Lord's) 1946
10— 96   H. H. Johnson: West Indies v. England (Kingston) 1947–48
11—204   A. L. Valentine: West Indies v. England (Manchester) 1950

BOWLERS TAKING A WICKET WITH FIRST BALL IN TEST CRICKET

A. Coningham ....Australia v. England (Melbourne) 1894–95
G. G. Macaulay ....England v. South Africa (Cape Town) 1922–23
M. W. Tate ....England v. South Africa (Birmingham)......................1924
T. Johnson ....West Indies v. England (Oval) 1939
R. Howorth ....England v. South Africa (Oval) 1947
Intikhab Alam ....Pakistan v. Australia (Karachi) 1959–60

HIGHEST WICKET AGGREGATES IN A TEST RUBBER

	Season	Tests	Balls	Mdns.	Runs	Wkts.	Avge.	5wI.	10wM.
S. F. Barnes (E. v. SA.)	1913–14	4	1356	56	536	49	10·93	7	3
J. C. Laker (E. v. A.)	1956	5	1703	127	442	46	9·60	4	2
C. V. Grimmett (A. v. SA.)	1935–36	5	2077	140	642	44	14·59	5	3
A. V. Bedser (E. v. A.)	1953	5	1591	58	682	39	17·48	5	1
M. W. Tate (E. v. A.)	1924–25	5	2528	62	881	38	23·18	5	1
W. J. Whitty (A. v. SA.)	1910–11	5	1395	55	632	37	17·08	2	—
H. J. Tayfield (SA. v. E.)	1956–57	5	2280	105	636	37	17·18	4	1
A. E. E. Vogler (SA. v. E.)	1909–10	5	1349	33	783	36	21·75	4	1
A. A. Mailey (A. v. E.)	1920–21	5	1463	27	946	36	26·27	4	2
G. A. Lohmann (E. v. SA.)	1895–96	3	520	38	203	35	5·80	4	2
G. Giffen (A. v. E.)	1894–95	5	2060	111	820	34	24·11	3	—
S. F. Barnes (E. v. A.)	1911–12	5	1782	64	778	34	22·88	3	—
S. F. Barnes (E. v. SA.)	1912	3	768	38	282	34	8·29	5	3
V. Mankad (I. v. E.)	1951–52	5	2224	151	571	34	16·79	1	1
S. P. Gupte (I. v. NZ.)	1955–56	5	2140	153	669	34	19·67	4	—
G. A. R. Lock (E. v. NZ.)	1958	5	1056	93	254	34	7·47	3	1
C. V. Grimmett (A. v. WI.)................	1930–31	5	1433	60	593	33	17·96	2	1
C. V. Grimmett (A. v. SA.)	1931–32	5	1836	108	557	33	16·87	3	1
H. Larwood (E. v. A.)	1932–33	5	1322	42	644	33	19·51	2	1
A. L. Valentine (WI. v. E.)	1950	4	2535	197	674	33	20·42	2	2
T. Richardson (E. v. A.)	1894–95	5	1855	63	849	32	26·53	4	—
M. A. Noble (A. v. E.).......................	1901–02	5	1380	68	608	32	19·00	4	1
H. V. Hordern (A. v. E.)	1911–12	5	1664	43	780	32	24·37	4	2
F. R. Foster (E. v. A.)	1911–12	5	1654	58	692	32	21·62	3	—
W. Rhodes (E. v. A.)	1903–04	5	1032	36	488	31	15·74	3	1
J. V. Saunders (A. v. E.)	1907–08	5	1603	52	716	31	23·09	3	—
A. S. Kennedy (E. v. SA.)	1922–23	5	1683	91	599	31	19·32	2	—
H. Ironmonger (A. v. SA.)	1931–32	4	1319	112	296	31	9·54	3	1
R. Benaud (A. v. E.)	1958–59	5	1866	65	584	31	18·83	1	—
J. N. Crawford (E. v. A.)...................	1907–08	5	1426	36	742	30	24·73	3	—
A. V. Bedser (E. v. A.)	1950–51	5	1560	34	482	30	16·06	2	1
A. V. Bedser (E. v. SA.)	1951	5	1655	84	517	30	17·23	3	1
H. J. Tayfield (SA. v. A.)...................	1952–53	5	2228	58	843	30	28·10	2	1
R. Benaud (A. v. SA.)	1957–58	5	1937	56	658	30	21·93	4	—
W. Hall (WI. v. I)	1958–59	5	1330	65	530	30	17·66	2	1

MOST RUNS CONCEDED IN AN INNINGS

O.   M.   R.   W.
87 —11—298—1   L. O'B. Fleetwood-Smith: Australia v. England (Oval) 1938
80·2—13—266—5   O. C. Scott: West Indies v. England (Kingston) 1929–30
54 — 5—259—0   Khan Mohammed: Pakistan v. West Indies (Kingston) 1957–58
85·2—20—247—2   Fazal Mahmood: Pakistan v. West Indies (Kingston) 1957–58
82 —17—228—5   V. Mankad: India v. West Indies (Kingston) 1952–53
71 — 8—204—6   I. A. R. Peebles: England v. Australia (Oval) 1930
75 —16—202—3   V. Mankad: India v. West Indies (Bombay) 1948–49
73 —24—196—5   V. Mankad: India v. England (Lord's) 1952
64 —14—191—2   C. V. Grimmett: Australia v. England (Sydney) 1928–29
59 — 9—189—7   W. J. O'Reilly: Australia v. England (Manchester) 1934

42 — 5—188—2   C. L. Vincent: South Africa v. England (Oval) 1935
43·6— 2—186—4   A. A. Mailey: Australia v. England (Melbourne)............................1924–25
53·3—13—181—5   T. Richardson: England v. Australia (Sydney) 1894–95
65·1—14—180—5   S. P. Gupte: India v. West Indies (Kingston) 1952–53
32 — 0—179—3   A. A. Mailey: Australia v. England (Sydney) 1924–25
98 —35—179—2   K. T. Ramadhin: West Indies v. England (Birmingham) 1957
85 —26—178—3   W. J. O'Reilly: Australia v. England (Oval) 1938
59 —14—178—2   G. A. R. Lock: England v. West Indies (Trinidad) 1953–54
34·3— 4—176—3   A. V. Bedser: England v. Australia (Melbourne) 1946–47
58 — 7—176—2   V. Mankad: India v. West Indies (New Delhi) 1948–49
61·3—18—176—3   M. J. Hilton: England v. South Africa (Leeds) 1951

MOST RUNS CONCEDED IN A MATCH

O.   M.   R.   W.

105·2—13—374— 9   O. C. Scott: West Indies v. England (Kingston) 1929–30
63 — 3—308— 7   A. A. Mailey: Australia v. England (Sydney) 1924–25
61·3— 6—302—10   A. A. Mailey: Australia v. England (Adelaide) 1920–21
84·1—10—298— 9   C. V. Grimmett: Australia v. England (Brisbane) 1928–29
87 —11—298— 1   L. O'B. Fleetwood-Smith: Australia v. England (Oval) 1938
94·2—19—290— 9   R. O. Jenkins: England v. West Indies (Lord's) 1950
69 —13—288— 5   D. V. P. Wright: England v. South Africa (Durban) 1938–39
69 — 3—282— 7   D. W. Carr: England v. Australia (Oval) 1909
65·3— 8—275— 6   A. V. Bedser: England v. Australia (Melbourne) 1946–47
85 —17—275— 3   Haseeb Ahsan: Pakistan v. West Indies (Georgetown) 1957–58
86 —17—272— 8   C. V. Grimmett: Australia v. England (Lord's) 1930
76·4— 9—266— 9   A. A. Mailey: Australia v. England (Oval) 1926
84 —15—266— 7   W. A. Johnston: Australia v. South Africa (Melbourne) 1952–53
73 —10—260— 4   Mahmood Hussain: Pakistan v. West Indies (Trinidad) 1957–58
74·2— 9—259— 6   A. A. Mailey: Australia v. England (Adelaide) 1924–25
54 — 5—259— 0   Khan Mohammed: Pakistan v. West Indies (Kingston) 1957–58
86 —15—258— 5   A. P. Freeman: England v. Australia (Sydney) 1924–25
124·5—37—256—13   J. C. White: England v. Australia (Adelaide) 1928–29
92·2—17—256— 1   N. Gordon: South Africa v. England (Durban) 1938–39
58 — 5—255— 5   D. V. P. Wright: England v. Australia (Melbourne) 1946–47
104 —28—254— 6   V. Mankad: India v. West Indies (Kingston) 1952–53
108·3—36—253— 8   S. G. Shinde: India v. England (New Delhi)......................1951–52

BOWLERS UNCHANGED IN A COMPLETED INNINGS

England:

F. Morley (2—34) & R. G. Barlow (7—40) v. Australia (Sydney) 1882–83
G. A. Lohmann (7—36) & J. Briggs (3—28) v. Australia (Oval) 1886
G. A. Lohmann (5—17) & R. Peel (5—18) v. Australia (Sydney) 1887–88
J. Briggs (8—11) & A. J. Fothergill (1—30) v. South Africa (Cape Town) 1888–89
J. J. Ferris (7—37) & F. Martin (2—39) v. South Africa (Cape Town) 1891–92
J. Briggs (6—19) & G. A. Lohmann (3—46) v. Australia (Adelaide) 1891–92
T. Richardson (6—39) & G. A. Lohmann (3—13) v. Australia (Lord's) 1896
S. Haigh (6—11) & A. E. Trott (4—19) v. South Africa (Cape Town) 1898–99
S. F. Barnes (6—42) & C. Blythe (4—64) v. Australia (Melbourne) 1901–02
G. H. Hirst (4—28) & C. Blythe (6—44) v. Australia (Birmingham) 1909
F. R. Foster (5—16) & S. F. Barnes (5—25) v. South Africa (Lord's) 1912
A. E. R. Gilligan (6—7) & M. W. Tate (4—12) v. South Africa (Birmingham) 1924

Australia:

G. E. Palmer (7—68) & E. Evans (3—64) v. England (Sydney) 1881–82
F. R. Spofforth (5—30) & G. E. Palmer (4—32) v. England (Sydney) 1884–85
C. T. B. Turner (6—15) & J. J. Ferris (4—27) v. England (Sydney) 1886–87
C. T. B. Turner (5—36) & J. J. Ferris (5—26) v. England (Lord's) 1888
G. Giffen (5—26) & C. T. B. Turner (4—33) v. England (Sydney) 1894–95
H. Trumble (3—38) & M. A. Noble (7—17) v. England (Melbourne)............1901–02
M. A. Noble (5—54) & J. V. Saunders (5—43) v. England (Sydney) 1901–02

Part V—All-round Cricket

ALL-ROUND PERFORMANCES—100 runs and 8 wickets in a match

G. Giffen (161 & 41, 8—239): Australia v. England (Sydney) 1894–95
A. E. Trott (38* & 72*, 8—52): Australia v. England (Adelaide)....................................1894–95
J. H. Sinclair (106 & 4, 9—89): South Africa v. England (Cape Town) 1898–99
G. A. Faulkner (78 & 123, 8—160): South Africa v. England (Johannesburg) 1909–10
J. M. Gregory (100, 8—101): Australia v. England (Melbourne) 1920–21
H. Larwood (70 & 37, 8—62): England v. Australia (Brisbane) 1928–29
G. O. Allen (35 & 68, 8—107): England v. Australia (Brisbane) 1936–37
W. J. Edrich (191 & 22*, 8—172): England v. South Africa (Manchester) 1947
K. R. Miller (109, 8—165): Australia v. West Indies (Kingston) 1954–55
R. Benaud (100, 9—154): Australia v. South Africa (Johannesburg) 1957–58

A. E. Trott (above) was making his début in Test cricket.

W. Bates—England v. Australia (Melbourne) 1882–83—scored 55 and took 13 wickets for 102 runs, including the 'hat-trick'.

J. Briggs (England) is the only player to have scored a century (121 v. Australia at Melbourne in 1884–85) and achieved the 'hat-trick' (v. Australia at Sydney in 1891–92) in Test cricket.

V. Mankad—India v. England (Lord's) 1952—scored 72 and 184 and bowled 73—24—196—5 and 24—12—35—0. On the fourth morning he took an overnight score of 84* to 179* by the lunch interval.

BEST ALL-ROUND RECORDS IN A TEST RUBBER

Runs	Avge.	Wkts.	Avge.		
475	(52·77)	34	(24·11)	G. Giffen: Australia v. England	1894–95
256	(36·57)	21	(35·14)	L. C. Braund: England v. Australia	1901–02
267	(33·37)	23	(26·91)	G. J. Thompson: England v. South Africa	1909–10
545	(60·55)	29	(21·89)	G. A. Faulkner: South Africa v. England	1909–10
226	(32·28)	32	(21·62)	F. R. Foster: England v. Australia	1911–12
442	(73·66)	23	(24·17)	J. M. Gregory: Australia v. England	1920–21
224	(28·00)	22	(37·09)	J. M. Gregory: Australia v. England	1924–25
223	(31·85)	34	(16·79)	V. Mankad: India v. England	1951–52
362	(40·22)	20	(19·90)	K. R. Miller: Australia v. West Indies	1951–52
211	(26·37)	21	(23·04)	R. R. Lindwall: Australia v. West Indies	1951–52
439	(73·16)	20	(32·00)	K. R. Miller: Australia v. West Indies	1954–55
235	(23·50)	25	(21·12)	T. L. Goddard: South Africa v. England	1955
203	(22·55)	21	(22·23)	K. R. Miller: Australia v. England	1956
329	(54·83)	30	(21·93)	R. Benaud: Australia v. South Africa	1957–58

In addition to the above figures J. M. Gregory held 15 catches in 1920–21 and L. C. Braund 12 in 1901–02.

Part VI—Fielding and Wicket-keeping

FIELDERS—MOST CATCHES IN AN INNINGS

5 V. Y. Richardson: Australia v. South Africa (Durban) 1935–36

FIELDERS—MOST CATCHES IN A MATCH

6 A. Shrewsbury: England v. Australia (Sydney) 1887–88
6 A. E. E. Vogler: South Africa v. England (Durban)..1909–10
6 F. E. Woolley: England v. Australia (Sydney) 1911–12
6 J. M. Gregory: Australia v. England (Sydney) 1920–21
6 B. Mitchell: South Africa v. Australia (Melbourne) 1931–32
6 V. Y. Richardson: Australia v. South Africa (Durban) 1935–36

MOST CATCHES BY A FIELDER IN A TEST RUBBER

15 (5 Tests) J. M. Gregory: Australia v. England in Australia 1920–21
13 (5 Tests) R. Simpson: Australia v. South Africa in South Africa 1957–58
12 (5 Tests) L. C. Braund: England v. Australia in Australia 1901–02
12 (5 Tests) A. E. E. Vogler: South Africa v. England in South Africa 1909–10
12 (5 Tests) B. Mitchell: South Africa v. England in South Africa 1930–31
12 (5 Tests) W. R. Hammond: England v. Australia in England 1934
12 (3 Tests) J. T. Ikin: England v. South Africa in England 1951
12 (5 Tests) T. L. Goddard: South Africa v. England in South Africa 1956–57

WICKET-KEEPERS—MOST DISMISSALS IN AN INNINGS

6 (6ct. 0st.) A. W. Grout: Australia v. South Africa (Johannesburg) 1957–58
5 (1ct. 4st.) W. A. Oldfield: Australia v. England (Melbourne) 1924–25
5 (2ct. 3st.) G. R. Langley: Australia v. West Indies (Georgetown) 1954–55
5 (5ct. 0st.) G. R. Langley: Australia v. West Indies (Kingston)............................1954–55
5 (5ct. 0st.) G. R. Langley: Australia v. England (Lord's) 1956
5 (3ct. 2st.) A. W. Grout: Australia v. South Africa (Durban) 1957–58
5 (5ct. 0st.) A. W. Grout: Australia v. Pakistan (Lahore) 1959–60
5 (4ct. 1st.) Imtiaz Ahmed: Pakistan v. Australia (Lahore) 1959–60
5 (5ct. 0st.) F. C. M. Alexander: West Indies v. England (Barbados)....................1959–60

WICKET-KEEPERS—MOST DISMISSALS IN A MATCH

9 (8ct. 1st.) G. R. Langley: Australia v. England (Lord's) 1956
8 (8ct. 0st.) J. J. Kelly: Australia v. England (Sydney) 1901–02
8 (6ct. 2st.) L. E. G. Ames: England v. West Indies (Oval) 1933
8 (8ct. 0st.) G. R. Langley: Australia v. West Indies (Kingston)............................1954–55
8 (6ct. 2st.) A. W. Grout: Australia v. Pakistan (Lahore) 1959–60
7 (4ct. 3st.) H. Strudwick: England v. South Africa (Johannesburg) 1913–14
7 (4ct. 3st.) C. L. Walcott: West Indies v. England (Kingston) 1947–48
7 (4ct. 3st.) R. A. Saggers: Australia v. South Africa (Cape Town) 1949–50
7 (3ct. 4st.) G. R. Langley: Australia v. West Indies (Brisbane) 1951–52
7 (5ct. 2st.) J. H. B. Waite: South Africa v. New Zealand (Port Elizabeth) 1953–54
7 (7ct. 0st.) Imtiaz Ahmed: Pakistan v. England (Oval) 1954
7 (6ct. 1st.) T. G. Evans: England v. South Africa (Lord's) 1955
7 (6ct. 1st.) T. G. Evans: England v. Australia (Lord's) 1956
7 (7ct. 0st.) T. G. Evans: England v. West Indies (Nottingham) 1957

MOST DISMISSALS BY A WICKET-KEEPER IN A TEST RUBBER

Ttl. Ct. St. Tests
23 16 7 (5) J. H. B. Waite: South Africa v. New Zealand in South Africa 1953–54
23 22 1 (5) F. C. M. Alexander: West Indies v. England in West Indies 1959–60

Ttl. Ct. St. Tests

21	15	6	(5)	H. Strudwick: England v. South Africa in South Africa	1913–14
21	13	8	(5)	R. A. Saggers: Australia v. South Africa in South Africa	1949–50
21	16	5	(5)	G. R. Langley: Australia v. West Indies in Australia	1951–52
20	16	4	(5)	D. Tallon: Australia v. England in Australia	1946–47
20	16	4	(4)	G. R. Langley: Australia v. West Indies in West Indies	1954–55
20	18	2	(5)	T. G. Evans: England v. South Africa in South Africa	1956–57
20	17	3	(5)	A. W. Grout: Australia v. England in Australia	1958–59
19	12	7	(5)	N. S. Tamhane: India v. Pakistan in Pakistan	1954–55
19	18	1	(3)	G. R. Langley: Australia v. England in England	1956
19	15	4	(5)	A. W. Grout: Australia v. South Africa in South Africa	1957–58
19	16	3	(5)	F. C. M. Alexander: West Indies v. Pakistan in West Indies	1957–58
18	16	2	(5)	H. Strudwick: England v. Australia in Australia	1924–25
18	10	8	(5)	W. A. Oldfield: Australia v. England in Australia	1924–25
18	18	0	(5)	F. C. M. Alexander: West Indies v. India in India	1958–59

NO BYES CONCEDED IN A HIGH INNINGS TOTAL

659—8d	T. G. Evans: England v. Australia (Sydney)	1946–47
559—9d	W. W. Wade: South Africa v. England (Cape Town)	1938–39
551	J. J. Kelly: Australia v. England (Sydney)	1897–98
521	W. A. Oldfield: Australia v. England (Brisbane)	1928–29
520	J. H. B. Waite: South Africa v. Australia (Melbourne)	1952–53
498	A. Wood: England v. West Indies (Oval)	1939
489	H. Strudwick: England v. Australia (Adelaide)	1924–25
485—9d	R. T. Spooner: England v. India (Bombay)	1951–52
471—8d	D. Hussain: India v. England (Oval)	1936
443—7d	N. S. Tamhane: India v. West Indies (Kanpur)	1958–59
440	W. A. Oldfield: Australia v. England (Lord's)	1934
425—6d	T. G. Evans: England v. West Indies (Lord's)	1950
421	A. A. Lilley: England v. Australia (Lord's)	1899
421—8d	E. C. Petrie: New Zealand v. India (Bombay)	1955–56
417	A. P. Binns: West Indies v. India (Trinidad)	1952–53
414	C. A. McWatt: West Indies v. England (Kingston)	1953–54
405	W. A. Oldfield: Australia v. England (Oval)	1930
403—8d	W. A. Oldfield: Australia v. England (Oval)	1921
401	J. H. B. Waite: South Africa v. Australia (Johannesburg)	1957–58

Part VII—Career Records

HIGHEST RUN AGGREGATES

	Tests	Inns.	N.O.	Runs	H.S.	Avge.	100s	50s
W. R. Hammond (England)	85	140	16	7249	336*	58·45	22	24
D. G. Bradman (Australia)	52	80	10	6996	334	99·94	29	13
L. Hutton (England)	79	138	15	6971	364	56·67	19	33
D. C. S. Compton (England)	78	131	15	5807	278	50·06	17	28
J. B. Hobbs (England)	61	102	7	5410	211	56·94	15	28
R. N. Harvey (Australia)	65	111	10	5273	205	52·20	19	19
H. Sutcliffe (England)	54	84	9	4555	194	60·73	16	23
E. D. Weekes (West Indies)	48	81	5	4455	207	58·61	15	19
P. B. H. May (England)	62	98	8	4265	285*	47·38	13	20
C. L. Walcott (West Indies)	44	74	7	3798	220	56·68	15	14
A. R. Morris (Australia)	46	79	3	3533	206	46·48	12	12
E. Hendren (England)	51	83	9	3525	205*	47·63	7	21
B. Mitchell (South Africa)	42	80	9	3471	189*	48·88	8	21
C. Hill (Australia)	49	89	2	3412	191	39·21	7	19
F. E. Woolley (England)	64	98	7	3283	154	36·07	5	23
M. C. Cowdrey (England)	49	80	4	3243	160	42·67	9	19
V. T. Trumper (Australia)	48	89	8	3164	214*	39·06	8	13
A. L. Hassett (Australia)	43	69	3	3073	198*	46·56	10	11
F. M. Worrell (West Indies)	36	63	6	3011	261	52·82	9	12
A. D. Nourse jun. (South Africa)	34	62	7	2960	231	53·81	9	14
K. R. Miller (Australia)	55	87	7	2958	147	36·97	7	13
H. W. Taylor (South Africa)	42	76	4	2936	176	40·77	7	17
G. Sobers (West Indies)	32	54	8	2922	365*	63·52	9	8
W. W. Armstrong (Australia)	50	84	10	2863	159*	38·68	6	8
M. Leyland (England)	41	65	5	2764	187	46·06	9	10
S. J. McCabe (Australia)	39	62	5	2748	232	48·21	6	13
C. C. McDonald (Australia)	39	68	4	2674	170	41·78	5	13
T. W. Graveney (England)	48	76	10	2590	258	39·24	4	11
C. Washbrook (England)	37	66	6	2569	195	42·81	6	12
P. R. Umrigar (India)	45	72	6	2550	223	38·63	7	11
W. Bardsley (Australia)	41	66	5	2469	193*	40·47	6	14
W. J. Edrich (England)	39	63	2	2440	219	40·00	6	13
T. G. Evans (England)	91	133	14	2439	104	20·49	2	8
L. E. G. Ames (England)	47	72	12	2434	149	40·56	8	7
P. Roy (India)	42	78	4	2418	173	32·67	5	9
B. Sutcliffe (New Zealand)	34	62	5	2335	230*	40·96	4	12
W. Rhodes (England)	58	98	21	2325	179	30·19	2	11
W. M. Woodfull (Australia)	35	54	4	2300	161	46·00	7	13
T. E. Bailey (England)	61	91	14	2290	134*	29·74	1	10
S. E. Gregory (Australia)	58	100	7	2282	201	24·53	4	8
A. D. Nourse sen. (South Africa)	45	83	8	2234	111	29·78	1	15
V. S. Hazare (India)	30	52	6	2192	164*	47·65	7	9
G. Headley (West Indies)	22	40	4	2190	270*	60·83	10	5
J. B. Stollmeyer (West Indies)	32	56	5	2159	160	42·33	4	12
C. G. Macartney (Australia)	35	55	4	2131	170	41·78	7	9
W. H. Ponsford (Australia)	29	48	4	2122	266	48·22	7	6
V. Mankad (India)	44	72	5	2109	231	31·47	5	6
D. J. McGlew (South Africa)	29	55	4	2014	255*	39·49	5	9

BEST BATTING AVERAGES—Qualification 15 innings

	Tests	Inns.	N.O.	Runs	H.S.	Avge.	100s	50s
D. G. Bradman (Australia)	52	80	10	6996	334	99·94	29	13
C. S. Dempster (New Zealand)	10	15	4	723	136	65·72	2	5
G. Sobers (West Indies)	32	54	8	2922	365*	63·52	9	8
S. G. Barnes (Australia)	13	19	2	1072	234	63·05	3	5
N. O'Neill (Australia)	13	19	5	876	163	62·57	3	3
G. Headley (West Indies)	22	40	4	2190	270*	60·83	10	5
H. Sutcliffe (England)	54	84	9	4555	194	60·73	16	23
E. Paynter (England)	20	31	5	1540	243	59·23	4	7

	Tests	Inns.	N.O.	Runs	H.S.	Avge.	100s	50s
E. D. Weekes (West Indies) 48	81	5	4455	207	58·61	15	19
K. S. Duleepsinhji (England) 12	19	2	995	173	58·52	3	5
W. R. Hammond (England) 85	140	16	7249	336*	58·45	22	24
J. B. Hobbs (England) 61	102	7	5410	211	56·94	15	28
A. C. Russell (England) 10	18	2	911	140	56·93	5	2
C. L. Walcott (West Indies) 44	74	7	3798	220	56·68	15	14
L. Hutton (England) 79	138	15	6971	364	56·67	19	33
E. Tyldesley (England) 14	20	2	990	122	55·00	3	6
A. D. Nourse jun. (South Africa)............34	62	7	2960	231	53·81	9	14
F. M. Worrell (West Indies) 36	63	6	3011	261	52·82	9	12
A. Melville (South Africa) 11	19	2	894	189	52·58	4	3
C. F. Walters (England) 11	18	3	784	102	52·26	1	7
R. N. Harvey (Australia) 65	111	10	5273	205	52·20	19	19
Saeed Ahmed (Pakistan) 11	21	1	1041	166	52·05	2	6
J. Ryder (Australia) 20	32	5	1394	201*	51·62	3	9
G. Pullar (England)........................11	20	2	920	175	51·11	2	5
D. C. S. Compton (England)................78	131	15	5807	278	50·06	17	28

BATSMEN SCORING MOST CENTURIES

	100s	H.S.	Eng.	Aust.	S.A.	W.I.	N.Z.	India	Pak.
					Scored v.				
D. G. Bradman (Australia) 29	334	19	—	4	2	0	4	0
W. R. Hammond (England) 22	336*	—	9	6	1	4	2	0
R. N. Harvey (Australia) 19	205	4	—	8	3	0	4	0
L. Hutton (England) 19	364	—	5	4	5	3	2	0
D. C. S. Compton (England) 17	278	—	5	7	2	2	0	1
H. Sutcliffe (England)...........................16	194	—	8	6	0	2	0	0
J. B. Hobbs (England) 15	211	—	12	2	1	0	0	0
C. L. Walcott (West Indies) 15	220	4	5	0	—	1	4	1
E. D. Weekes (West Indies) 15	207	3	1	0	—	3	7	1
P. B. H. May (England) 13	285*	—	3	3	3	3	1	0
A. R. Morris (Australia) 12	206	8	—	2	1	0	1	0
A. L. Hassett (Australia) 10	198*	4	—	3	2	0	1	0
G. Headley (West Indies) 10	270*	8	2	0	—	0	0	0

HIGHEST WICKET AGGREGATES

	Tests	Balls	Mdns.	Runs	Wkts.	Avge.	5wI.	10wM.
A. V. Bedser (England) 51	15941	572	5876	236	24·89	15	5
R. R. Lindwall (Australia) 61	13666	418	5257	228	23·05	12	—
C. V. Grimmett (Australia) 37	14573	734	5231	216	24·21	21	7
J. B. Statham (England) 55	11967	472	4510	196	23·01	7	1
J. C. Laker (England) 46	12009	673	4099	193	21·23	9	3
S. F. Barnes (England) 27	7873	358	3106	189	16·43	24	7
R. Benaud (Australia) 45	12454	579	4300	181	23·75	11	1
F. S. Trueman (England) 41	8606	325	3742	174	21·50	7	—
K. R. Miller (Australia) 55	10474	338	3905	170	22·97	7	1
H. J. Tayfield (South Africa) 37	13565	602	4405	170	25·91	14	2
V. Mankad (India) 44	14686	777	5235	162	32·31	8	2
W. A. Johnston (Australia) 40	11048	370	3825	160	23·90	7	—
K. T. Ramadhin (West Indies) 42	13643	809	4439	155	28·63	10	1
M. W. Tate (England) 39	12571	579	4051	155	26·13	7	1
W. J. O'Reilly (Australia) 27	10024	585	3254	144	22·59	11	3
H. Verity (England) 40	11143	604	3510	144	24·37	5	2
H. Trumble (Australia) 32	8099	452	3072	141	21·78	9	3
S. P. Gupte (India) 31	9882	513	3902	134	29·11	11	1
T. E. Bailey (England) 61	9712	379	3856	132	29·21	5	1
W. Rhodes (England) 58	8220	368	3425	127	26·96	6	1
Fazal Mahmood (Pakistan) 26	7851	440	2768	125	22·14	12	4
G. A. R. Lock (England) 31	8033	511	2554	123	20·76	8	3
A. L. Valentine (West Indies) 29	11165	708	3568	123	29·00	8	2
M. A. Noble (Australia) 42	7109	361	3027	121	25·01	9	2
J. Briggs (England) 33	5332	389	2094	118	17·74	9	4
G. A. Lohmann (England) 18	3821	364	1205	112	10·75	9	5
I. W. Johnson (Australia) 45	8773	328	3182	109	29·19	3	—
D. V. P. Wright (England) 34	8141	176	4224	108	39·11	6	1
A. K. Davidson (Australia) 30	7182	291	2164	106	20·41	5	1
G. Giffen (Australia) 31	6325	434	2791	103	27·09	7	1

	Tests	Balls	Mdns.	Runs	Wkts.	Avge.	5wI.	10wM.
R. Peel (England) 20		5216	444	1715	102	16·81	6	2
J. H. Wardle (England) 28		6597	404	2080	102	20·39	5	1
C. T. B. Turner (Australia) 17		5179	457	1670	101	16·53	11	2
C. Blythe (England) 19		4438	231	1863	100	18·63	9	4
A. A. Mailey (Australia) 21		6117	116	3358	99	33·91	6	2
W. Voce (England) 27		6360	209	2733	98	27·88	3	2
N. A. T. Adcock (South Africa)....24		5931	179	2047	95	21·54	5	—
F. R. Spofforth (Australia) 18		4185	416	1731	94	18·41	7	4
A. Cotter (Australia) 21		4633	86	2549	89	28·64	7	—
T. Richardson (England) 14		4485	191	2220	88	25·22	11	4
W. W. Armstrong (Australia) 50		8052	403	2923	87	33·59	3	—
J. M. Gregory (Australia)...............24		5581	138	2648	85	31·15	4	—
C. L. Vincent (South Africa) 25		5863	194	2631	84	31·32	3	—
W. R. Hammond (England) 85		7967	299	3140	83	37·83	2	—
F. E. Woolley (England) 64		6495	251	2815	83	33·91	4	1
G. A. Faulkner (South Africa) 25		4227	124	2180	82	26·58	4	—
G. O. Allen (England) 25		4392	116	2379	81	29·37	5	1

BEST BOWLING AVERAGES—Qualification 25 wickets

	Tests	Balls	Mdns.	Runs	Wkts.	Avge.	5wI.	10wM.
G. A. Lohmann (England) 18		3821	364	1205	112	10·75	9	5
J. J. Ferris (Australia & England) ... 9		2302	251	775	61	12·70	6	1
W. Barnes (England) 21		2285	271	793	51	15·54	3	—
S. F. Barnes (England) 27		7873	358	3106	189	16·43	24	7
C. T. B. Turner (Australia) 17		5179	457	1670	101	16·53	11	2
W. Bates (England) 15		2362	282	821	49	16·75	4	1
R. Peel (England) 20		5216	444	1715	102	16·81	6	2
J. Briggs (England) 33		5332	389	2094	118	17·74	9	4
L. Kline (Australia) 11		1947	101	553	31	17·83	1	—
R. Appleyard (England) 9		1596	70	554	31	17·87	1	—
W. S. Lees (England) 5		1256	69	467	26	17·96	2	—
H. Ironmonger (Australia) 14		4699	328	1330	74	17·97	4	2
F. R. Spofforth (Australia) 18		4185	416	1731	94	18·41	7	4
F. H. Tyson (England) 17		3452	98	1411	76	18·56	4	1
C. Blythe (England) 19		4438	231	1863	100	18·63	9	4
G. F. Bissett (South Africa) 4		989	28	469	25	18·76	2	—
A. S. Kennedy (England) 5		1683	91	599	31	19·32	2	—
G. Ulyett (England) 25		2623	299	1011	51	19·82	1	—

MOST FREQUENT WICKET-TAKERS—Qualification 25 wickets

	Balls p.w.	Tests	Balls	Mdns.	Runs	Wkts.	Avge.
G. A. Lohmann (England)	34·11	18	3821	364	1205	112	10·75
J. J. Ferris (Australia & England)	37·73	9	2302	251	775	61	12·70
G. F. Bissett (South Africa)	39·56	4	989	28	469	25	18·76
B. J. T. Bosanquet (England)	39·56	7	989	10	604	25	24·16
S. F. Barnes (England)	41·65	27	7873	358	3106	189	16·43

MOST ECONOMICAL BOWLING FIGURES—Qualification 1800 balls

	Runs per 100 balls	Tests	Balls	Mdns.	Runs	Wkts.	Avge.
W. Attewell (England)	21·96	10	2850	326	626	27	23·18
K. Mackay (Australia)	25·14	24	2712	145	682	24	28·41
C. Gladwin (England)	26·82	8	2129	89	571	15	38·06
T. L. Goddard (South Africa)	27·43	20	6305	377	1729	64	27·01
H. Ironmonger (Australia)	28·30	14	4699	328	1330	74	17·97
L. Kline (Australia)	28·40	11	1947	101	553	31	17·83
A. J. Richardson (Australia)	28·75	9	1812	91	521	12	43·41
J. C. Watkins (South Africa)	29·09	15	2805	134	816	29	28·13
R. Illingworth (England)	29·44	12	2418	144	712	17	41·88
A. K. Davidson (Australia)	30·13	30	7182	291	2164	106	20·41
G. E. Gomez (West Indies)	30·36	27	5236	284	1590	58	27·41
R. Kilner (England)	30·99	9	2368	82	734	24	30·58
R. G. Barlow (England)	31·22	17	2456	315	767	35	21·91
D. Atkinson (West Indies)	31·49	22	5201	312	1647	47	35·04
E. R. H. Toshack (Australia)	31·49	12	3140	155	989	47	21·04

	Runs per 100 balls	Tests	Balls	Mdns.	Runs	Wkts.	Avge.
H. Verity (England)	31·49	40	11143	604	3510	144	24·37
J. H. Wardle (England)	31·52	28	6597	404	2080	102	20·39
G. A. Lohmann (England)	31·53	18	3821	364	1205	112	10·75

MOST DISMISSALS BY A WICKET-KEEPER

	Total	Ct.	St.	Tests	Runs	Batting H.S.	Avge.	100s
T. G. Evans (England)	219	173	46	91	2439	104	20·49	2
W. A. Oldfield (Australia)	130	78	52	54	1427	65*	22·65	—
J. H. B. Waite (South Africa)	101	87	14	36	1785	134	30·25	3
L. E. G. Ames (England)	98	75	23	47	2434	149	40·56	8
G. R. Langley (Australia)	98	83	15	26	374	53	14·96	—
A. A. Lilley (England)	92	70	22	35	903	84	20·52	—
F. C. M. Alexander (West Indies)	74	69	5	20	477	70	19·87	—
Imtiaz Ahmed (Pakistan)	73	61	12	29	1320	209	27·50	2
H. Strudwick (England)	72	60	12	28	230	24	7·93	—
H. Carter (Australia)	65	44	21	28	873	72	22·97	—
A. W. Grout (Australia)	65	52	13	17	457	74	26·88	—
J. J. Kelly (Australia)	63	43	20	36	664	46*	17·02	—
J. McC. Blackham (Australia)	60	36	24	35	800	74	15·68	—
G. Duckworth (England)	60	45	15	24	234	39*	14·62	—
D. Tallon (Australia)	58	50	8	21	394	92	17·13	—
H. B. Cameron (South Africa)	51	39	12	26	1239	90	30·21	—

MOST CATCHES BY A FIELDER

	Catches	Tests	Avge. per Test
W. R. Hammond (England)	110	85	1·29
F. E. Woolley (England)	64	64	1·00
W. Rhodes (England)	60	58	1·03
L. Hutton (England)	57	79	0·72
B. Mitchell (South Africa)	56	42	1·33
M. C. Cowdrey (England)	56	49	1·14
D. C. S. Compton (England)	49	78	0·62
E. D. Weekes (West Indies)	49	48	1·02
R. N. Harvey (Australia)	48	65	0·73
H. Trumble (Australia)	45	32	1·40
W. W. Armstrong (Australia)	44	50	0·88
T. W. Graveney (England)	44	48	0·91
R. Benaud (Australia)	43	45	0·95
A. D. Nourse sen. (South Africa)	43	45	0·95
P. B. H. May (England)	42	62	0·67
S. J. McCabe (Australia)	42	39	1·07
F. S. Trueman (England)	42	41	1·02
W. R. Endean (South Africa)	41	28	1·46
L. C. Braund (England)	39	23	1·69
W. J. Edrich (England)	39	39	1·00
W. G. Grace (England)	39	22	1·77
K. R. Miller (Australia)	38	55	0·69
J. M. Gregory (Australia)	37	24	1·54
G. A. R. Lock (England)	37	31	1·19

BEST ALL-ROUND RECORDS

Over 1000 runs & 100 wickets:

	Tests	Runs	H.S.	Avge.	100s	Wkts.	Avge.
T. E. Bailey (England)	61	2290	134*	29·74	1	132	29·21
R. Benaud (Australia)	45	1504	122	24·25	3	181	23·75
G. Giffen (Australia)	31	1238	161	23·35	1	103	27·09
I. W. Johnson (Australia)	45	1000	77	18·51	—	109	29·19
R. R. Lindwall (Australia)	61	1502	118	21·15	2	228	23·05
V. Mankad (India)	44	2109	231	31·47	5	162	32·31
K. R. Miller (Australia)	55	2958	147	36·97	7	170	22·97
M. A. Noble (Australia)	42	1997	133	30·25	1	121	25·01
W. Rhodes (England)	58	2325	179	30·19	2	127	26·96
M. W. Tate (England)	39	1198	100*	25·48	1	155	26·13

Over 750 runs & 50 wickets:

	Tests	Runs	H.S.	Avge.	100s	Wkts.	Avge.
G. O. Allen (England)	25	750	122	24·19	1	81	29·37
W. W. Armstrong (Australia)	50	2863	159*	38·68	6	87	33·59
J. Briggs (England)	33	815	121	18·11	1	118	17·74
A. K. Davidson (Australia)	30	807	76	23·05	—	106	20·41
G. A. Faulkner (South Africa)	25	1754	204	40·79	4	82	26·58
T. L. Goddard (South Africa)	20	1072	99	28·97	—	64	27·01
G. E. Gomez (West Indies)	29	1243	101	30·31	1	58	27·41
J. M. Gregory (Australia)	24	1146	119	36·96	2	85	31·15
W. R. Hammond (England)	85	7249	336*	58·45	22	83	37·83
G. H. Hirst (England)	24	790	85	22·57	—	59	30·00
C. Kelleway (Australia)	26	1422	147	37·42	3	52	32·36
A. R. MacGibbon (New Zealand)	26	814	66	19·85	—	70	30·65
D. G. Phadkar (India)	31	1229	123	32·34	2	62	36·85
J. H. Sinclair (South Africa)	25	1069	106	23·23	3	63	31·68
H. J. Tayfield (South Africa)	37	562	75	16·90	—	170	25·91
H. Trumble (Australia)	32	851	70	19·79	—	141	21·78
G. Ulyett (England)	25	949	149	24·33	1	51	19·82
F. E. Woolley (England)	64	3283	154	36·07	5	83	33·91
F. M. Worrell (West Indies)	36	3011	261	52·82	9	54	38·72

The ten players to complete the Test 'double' of 1000 runs and 100 wickets reached the figures as follows—V. Mankad (23rd Test), M. A. Noble (27th), G. Giffen (30th), R. Benaud (32nd), K. R. Miller and M. W. Tate (33rd), R. R. Lindwall (38th), W. Rhodes (44th), I. W. Johnson (45th) and T. E. Bailey (47th).

Part VIII—Memorabilia

ABANDONED WITHOUT A BALL BOWLED

Two Test matches have been abandoned without a ball being bowled, those due to be played at Manchester in 1890 and 1938. Details of the team selections were as follows:

1890—England: W. G. Grace (captain), A. E. Stoddart, W. W. Read, G. MacGregor, G. A. Lohmann, J. M. Read, W. Attewell, W. Gunn, A. Shrewsbury, J. Briggs, and either A. Mold or F. H. Sugg, Australia: W. L. Murdoch (captain), G. H. S. Trott, J. E. Barrett, C. T. B. Turner, J. J. Ferris, J. J. Lyons, J. McC. Blackham, P. C. Charlton, S. E. Gregory, K. E. Burn, H. Trumble.

1938—England: (from) W. R. Hammond (captain), C. J. Barnett, L. Hutton, W. J. Edrich, E. Paynter, J. Hardstaff jun., M. S. Nichols, T. F. Smailes, P. A. Gibb, D. V. P. Wright, T. W. Goddard, H. Verity, D. C. S. Compton. Australia: not selected.

ACCIDENTS

G. L. Jessop strained a back muscle when returning the ball from the outfield to the wicket-keeper and was unable to play again that season—England v. Australia (Leeds) 1909.

Hon. L. H. Tennyson—England v. Australia (Leeds) 1921—split his left hand when fielding and had four stitches inserted. Batting literally with one hand, he scored 63 in 75 minutes in the first innings and 36 in the second.

ATTENDANCE RECORDS IN ENGLAND

159,000	£34,000	England v. Australia (Leeds)	1948
151,000	£48,313	England v. Australia (Leeds)	1953
137,915	£57,716	England v. Australia (Lord's)	1953
134,875		England v. Australia (Lord's)	1956
133,740	£30,593	England v. Australia (Manchester)	1948
132,000	£43,000	England v. Australia (Lord's)	1948
116,000	£26,000	England v. South Africa (Leeds)	1951
115,000	£14,500	England v. Australia (Lord's)	1930
115,000	£37,000	England v. Australia (Oval)	1953
113,500	£31,032	England v. South Africa (Leeds)	1955
112,000		England v. West Indies (Lord's)	1950
110,775	£21,785	England v. West Indies (Nottingham)	1950
108,000	£13,000	England v. Australia (Oval)	1930
103,000	£11,470	England v. Australia (Oval)	1938
103,000		England v. South Africa (Lord's)	1955
100,933	£28,164	England v. Australia (Lord's)	1938
100,011		England v. India (Lord's)	1952
100,000	£23,500	England v. West Indies (Oval)	1950
100,000	£11,361	England v. South Africa (Nottingham)	1951
100,000	£36,179	England v. Australia (Leeds)	1956

The record attendance at Birmingham is 64,968 (£29,426) for the England v. West Indies match in 1957.

The total receipts for the 1953 England v. Australia rubber were £200,194 for the five Tests—a record.

ATTENDANCE RECORDS IN AUSTRALIA

350,534	£30,124	Australia v. England (Melbourne—3rd Test)	1936–37
343,675	£44,063	Australia v. England (Melbourne—3rd Test)	1946–47
300,270	£38,344	Australia v. England (Melbourne—3rd Test)	1954–55
262,487	£22,561	Australia v. England (Melbourne—3rd Test)	1928–29
239,175	£22,628	Australia v. England (Melbourne—2nd Test)	1924–25
230,948	£A46,791	Australia v. England (Melbourne—2nd Test)	1958–59
218,064	£15,745	Australia v. England (Melbourne—5th Test)	1928–29
200,635	£16,722	Australia v. England (Melbourne—2nd Test)	1932–33
172,858	£A33,151	Australia v. England (Sydney—3rd Test)	1958–59
172,346	£16,241	Australia v. England (Adelaide—3rd Test)	1932–33

169,537 £17,128 Australia v. England (Sydney—2nd Test) 1928–29
165,038 £25,816 Australia v. England (Adelaide—4th Test) 1954–55
163,453 £16,205 Australia v. England (Sydney—1st Test) 1932–33

The record at Brisbane is 93,143 (£10,909) for the Australia v. England match (4th Test) in 1932–33. The record receipts are £21,000 (gate 77,008) for the Australia v. England match in 1958–59.

The record attendance for one day is 87,798 (£7,405) on January 4th, 1937, the third day of the third Australia v. England Test in 1936–37.

ATTENDANCE RECORDS IN SOUTH AFRICA

112,000   South Africa v. Australia (Johannesburg) 1957–58
 83,000 £16,700 South Africa v. Australia (Johannesburg) 1949–50
 79,000 £15,325 South Africa v. England (Johannesburg) 1948–49

The record attendance for one day is 35,000 on December 27th, 1948—South Africa v. England (Johannesburg) 1948–49 (this was the day on which L. Hutton and C. Washbrook established the first wicket record stand of 359).

BATTING CURIOSITIES

A. C. Bannerman (91)—Australia v. England (Sydney)—scored off only 5 of the 208 balls he received from W. Attewell.

W. Rhodes (England) played the following consecutive innings v. Australia between 1899 and 1903–04—8*, 38*, 7*, 7*, 5, 4*, 0*, 6*, 40*. He thus scored 115 runs in nine innings for only once out.

C. Kelleway (147)—Australia v. England (Adelaide) 1920–21—played a minor part during his innings, scoring only 147 of the 420 runs added while he was at the wicket.

H. L. Collins (40)—Australia v. England (Manchester) 1921—scored his 40 out of 161 runs added during his innings.

C. F. Root holds the unique record in playing in three Test matches for England without batting —all v. Australia in 1926.

G. C. Grant (West Indies) was the first batsman to score a not-out innings of fifty in each innings of a Test match—53* & 71* v. Australia (Adelaide) 1930–31.

G. O. Allen—England v. Australia (Adelaide) 1932–33—was 'l.b.w. b C. V. Grimmett 15' in each innings.

W. M. Woodfull (Australia) carried his bat through a completed innings against England on two occasions—at Brisbane in 1928–29 and Adelaide in 1932–33 but on each occasion Australia batted short and all the wickets did not fall.

H. Larwood (98)—England v. Australia (Sydney) 1932–33—went in to bat as 'night-watchman' on the second evening when England were 153 for two. He was not dismissed until the score had reached 310 on the following day, his innings lasting 135 minutes.

H. Sutcliffe and W. R. Hammond each scored 440 runs (av. 55.00) for England in the 1932–33 rubber v. Australia.

C. S. Nayudu (15)—India v. England (Calcutta) 1933–34—made only four scoring strokes (6441) in a stay of 145 minutes.

The 1938 rubber between England and Australia provided five double-centuries—E. Paynter (216*), W. R. Hammond (240) and L. Hutton (364) for England and S. J. McCabe (232) and W. A. Brown (206*) for Australia.

W. J. Edrich—England v. South Africa (Nottingham) 1947—had the unusual experience of playing two innings in the pre-lunch session on the third day. Not out at the start of play, he had started his innings in the follow-on before the adjournment.

In Australia's second innings against England at Manchester in 1948, A. R. Morris batted at one end and I. W. Johnson and D. G. Bradman at the other for 100 minutes before the first single was scored and the batsmen changed ends for the first time.

The first four England batsmen reached fifty in each innings v. Australia (Leeds) 1948—L. Hutton (81 & 57), C. Washbrook (143 & 65), W. J. Edrich (111 & 54) and A. V. Bedser (79) in the first innings and D. C. S. Compton (66) in the second innings.

Three batsmen—A. R. Morris (67), A. L. Hassett (115) and K. R. Miller (55)—scored 237 of the 244 runs from the bat in Australia's first innings total of 249 v. England (Nottingham) 1953. There were two century stands in the innings, Hassett adding 122 for the second wicket with Morris and 109 for the fourth with Miller.

G. Headley (16)—West Indies v. England (Kingston) 1953–54—was allowed a single to 'get off the mark' on his return to Test cricket after an absence of five years.

Each batsman to start an innings in the India v. New Zealand Test at New Delhi in 1955–56 reached double figures.

BATTING THROUGH COMPLETE DAY'S PLAY

J. B. Hobbs (154) and H. Sutcliffe (176)—England v. Australia (Melbourne) 1924–25—batted for the whole of the third day in an opening partnership of 283. This was the first occasion on which two batsmen batted through a complete day's play without the loss of a wicket.

D. Atkinson (219) and C. Depeiza (122)—West Indies v. Australia (Barbados) 1954–55—batted through the fourth day, taking an overnight total of 187 for six wickets to 494 for six wickets.

G. Sobers (226) and F. M. Worrell (197*)—West Indies v. England (Barbados) 1959–60—. batted right through two consecutive days' play, the fourth and fifth, taking an overnight score of 114 for three wickets on to 279 and then to 486 for three wickets.

BENEFITS AND COLLECTIONS

A collection for Charles Bannerman on the occasion of the first century in Test cricket—165* for Australia v. England (Melbourne) 1876–77 realized £165.

A collection for W. Bates when he scored 55 in his only innings and took 13 wickets, including the 'hat-trick',—England v. Australia (Melbourne) 1882–83—realized £31.

J. M. Read (Surrey) was allocated the 1893 Test match between England and Australia at the Oval as his benefit match.

A collection for S. E. Gregory on the occasion of the first Test double-century in Australia—201 for Australia v. England (Sydney) 1894–95—realized £103 10s. 0d.

A collection for T. Hayward on the occasion of his first Test century on his home ground—137 for England v. Australia (Oval) 1899—realized £131 3s. 6d.

There were two collections during the South Africa v. England match at Johannesburg in 1909–1910. D. Denton received £88 for scoring 104 out of 161 in 100 minutes and A. E. E. Vogler £60 for his bowling.

BOUNDARIES

A. Cotter—Australia v. England (Manchester) 1909—made a straight drive out of the ground off the bowling of C. Blythe.

E. Hendren (169)—England v. Australia (Brisbane) 1928–29—hit one ball for 8 (including 4 overthrows) from the bowling of P. M. Hornibrook.

England won two consecutive Test matches in 1932–33 by means of hits for six—by E. Paynter at Brisbane and by W. R. Hammond at Sydney.

K. H. Weekes (137)—West Indies v. England (Oval) 1939—hit the bowling of R. T. D. Perks for 4 consecutive fours.

Australia's innings of 404–3 v. England (Leeds) 1948, included 66 fours—33 by A. R. Morris, 29 by D. G. Bradman, 2 by K. R. Miller and one each by A. L. Hassett and R. N. Harvey.

G. Sobers (43)—West Indies v. Australia (Barbados) 1954–55— included 10 fours in his innings, the other three runs being singles.

BOWLING AGGREGATES

M. W. Tate (England) took 65 wickets (av. 20·07) in a year—27 (av. 15·70) v. South Africa 1924 and 38 (av. 23·18) v. Australia 1924–25.

C. V. Grimmett (Australia) is the only bowler to have conceded over 1,000 runs in a Test rubber—he took 23 wickets at a cost of 1024 runs (av. 44·52) v. England in 1928–29.

C. V. Grimmett (Australia) took 62 wickets (av. 24·48) in a year—29 (av. 31·89) v. England 1930 and 33 (av. 17·96) v. West Indies 1930–31.

A. V. Bedser (England took 62 wickets (av. 18·33) in a year—30 (av. 16·06) v. Australia 1950–51, 2 (av. 69.00) v. New Zealand 1950–51 and 30 (av. 17·23) v. South Africa 1951.

BOWLING CURIOSITIES

J. Briggs (15–28)—England v. South Africa (Cape Town) 1888–89—took his wickets without assistance from the field, 14 batsmen being bowled and one l.b.w.

Hon. F. S. Jackson—England v. Australia (Nottingham) 1905—took three wickets in a six-ball over (woowow), his victims being M. A. Noble, C. Hill and J. Darling.

W. W. Armstrong—Australia v. England (Nottingham) 1905—bowled off-breaks outside the leg-stump in an attempt to slow down the scoring. Only 25 out of 204 consecutive balls were scored from, and 160 of the remaining 179 balls were allowed to go straight through to the wicket-keeper.

T. J. Matthews achieved the 'hat-trick' in each innings of the Australia v. South Africa match at Manchester in 1912. These six wickets were, oddly enough, the only ones he took in the match.

W. W. Armstrong—Australia v. England (Manchester) 1921—bowled two consecutive overs. Hon. L. H. Tennyson, the England captain, closed the innings on the second day, and, as no play had been possible on the first day, did not leave Australia sufficient batting time in accordance with the Laws. After some discussion in the pavilion the Australians returned to the field and Armstrong, who had bowled the last over before the incident, bowled the first over on the resumption.

W. J. O'Reilly—Australia v. England (Manchester) 1934—took three wickets in four balls (C. F. Walters, R. E. S. Wyatt and W. R. Hammond). The original ball had gone out of shape and this feat was achieved in the first over of the replacement ball.

G. O. Allen opened the bowling for England v. Australia (Manchester) 1934, with a thirteen-ball over, three wides and four no-balls being included.

H. Verity—England v. South Africa (Leeds) 1935—had the remarkable match bowling analysis of 25–20–9–2.

E. L. McCormick (Australia) took a wicket (that of T. S. Worthington) with the first ball he bowled in a Test match against England—at Brisbane 1936–37.

England's innings total of 469—7d v. South Africa (Durban) 1938–39 did not include a single maiden over (eight-ball overs).

A. V. Bedser (England) took 22 wickets in his first two Test matches—11–145 at Lord's and 11–93 at Manchester, both v. India in 1946.

K. R. Miller (Australia) bowled 11 eight-ball overs in each of the first four England second innings of the 1946–47 rubber.

N. B. F. Mann, making his debut in Test cricket for South Africa v. England (Nottingham) 1947, bowled eight consecutive maiden overs before conceding his first run.

K. Cranston—England v. South Africa (Leeds) 1947—took four wickets in a six-ball over (wowoww).

A. M. Moir—New Zealand v. England (Wellington) 1950–51—bowled two consecutive overs on the last day of the match, the last before the tea interval and the first after.

H. J. Tayfield—South Africa v. New Zealand (Johannesburg) 1953–54—had an innings bowling analysis of 14–7–13–6, his ball by ball figures being as follows: 10001000—000W0000—0000W000—0000W0W0 — 00000000 — 00W00010 — 00000000 — 00000400 — 00000000 — 00100002 — 00001000 — 00100000 — 00000W00 — 01000000.

K. R. Miller—Australia v. England (Melbourne) 1954–55—bowled unchanged before lunch on the first day, sending down nine overs for the following analysis: 9–8–5–3. The five runs were all scored in the fourth over.

BOWLING MILESTONES REACHED QUICKLY

The following bowlers reached 100 wickets in Test cricket in the shortest space of time:

A. L. Valentine (West Indies) in 3 years 263 days in his 19th Test.
W. A. Johnston (Australia) in 4 years 21 days in his 22nd Test.
A. V. Bedser (England) in 4 years 51 days in his 26th Test.
W. J. O'Reilly (Australia) in 4 years 342 days in his 20th Test.

Bowlers to reach other milestones quickly in the number of Tests played are:

200 wickets ... C. V. Grimmett (Australia) in his 36th Test.
150 wickets ... S. F. Barnes (England) in his 24th Test.
100 wickets ... G. A. Lohmann (England) in his 16th Test. S. F. Barnes, C. V. Grimmett and C. T. B. Turner each reached this mark in their 17th Test.
50 wickets ... C. T. B. Turner (Australia) in his 6th Test and T. Richardson (England) in his 7th Test.

BOWLING SPELLS

T. Richardson—England v. Australia (Manchester) 1896—bowled unchanged for three hours in the second innings and returned the following analysis—42·3–16–76–6.

H. Trumble—Australia v. England (Oval) 1902—bowled unchanged from the Pavilion end throughout the match, his full analysis being 64·5–17–173–12.

S. F. Barnes—England v. Australia (Melbourne) 1911–12—took five wickets for six runs in 11 overs (including 7 maidens). In his first five overs he took four wickets at the cost of a single.

A. M. B. Rowan—South Africa v. England (Leeds) 1947—had an unchanged spell of 46 six-ball overs, his figures being 46–12–89–1.

Ghulam Ahmed—India v. Pakistan (Dacca) 1954–55—had an unchanged bowling spell of 40 overs (40–8–84–4) on the first day of the match.

T. L. Goddard—South Africa v. England (Leeds) 1955—had an unchanged spell of 46 overs (46–27–45–4) on the last day of the match.

H. J. Tayfield—South Africa v. England (Oval) 1955—had an unchanged spell of 53·4 overs (53·4–29–60–5) in England's second innings.

CAPTAINCY CURIOSITIES

The rival captains in 1905—Hon. F. S. Jackson (England) and J. Darling (Australia)—were both born on the same day—November 21st, 1870.

In the period between 1887–88 (when amateur England captains became the rule) and 1952 (when L. Hutton was appointed) only one professional led England in the field—J. B. Hobbs assuming the captaincy after A. W. Carr had been taken ill during the match v. Australia (Manchester) 1926.

A. P. F. Chapman won the first nine Tests in which he was England captain—v. Australia 1926 (1), 1928–29 (4), and 1930 (1) and v. West Indies 1928 (3). Although he captained England in eight more Tests, he was never again on the winning side.

F. R. Brown, the then Chairman of the England Test Selection Committee, played for England v. Australia under the captaincy of L. Hutton at Lord's in 1953.

CENTURIES AND FIFTIES

C. Hill (Australia) scored consecutive innings of 99 (Melbourne) 98 & 97 (Adelaide) v. England in 1901–02.

Hon. F. S. Jackson (England) scored five centuries against Australia in England—he never toured Australia.

C. Hill (Australia) scored four Test centuries against England and was dismissed in the 'nineties' on five occasions—96 in 1897–98, 99, 98 & 97 in 1901–02 and 98 in 1911–12. He scored three centuries against South Africa and was 91* at Cape Town in 1902–03.

CENTURY BEFORE LUNCH ON FIRST DAY

V. T. Trumper (104): Australia v. England (Manchester) 1902
C. G. Macartney (151): Australia v. England (Leeds) 1926
D. G. Bradman (334): Australia v. England (Leeds) 1930

C. J. Barnett (126)—completed his century off the first ball after lunch—England v. Australia (Nottingham) 1938.

CENTURY BEFORE LUNCH ON OTHER DAYS

C. Hill (142): Australia v. South Africa (Johannesburg) 1902–03
(Score taken from 22* to 138* on third day)
J. B. Hobbs (211): England v. South Africa (Lord's) 1924
(Score taken from 12* to 114* on second day)
H. G. Owen-Smith (129): South Africa v. England (Leeds) 1929
(Score taken from 27* to 129 on third day)
W. R. Hammond (336*): England v. New Zealand (Auckland) 1932–33
(Score taken from 41* to 152* on second day)
S. J. McCabe (189*): Australia v. South Africa (Johannesburg) 1935–36
(Score taken from 59* to 159* on fourth day)

T. G. Evans, starting his innings on the third morning, was 98* at lunch—England v. India (Lord's), 1952.

CENTURIES BY BATSMAN LOWER THAN No. 8 IN ORDER

117 W. W. Read (No. 10): England v. Australia (Oval) 1884
116 R. J. Hartigan (No. 9): Australia v. England (Adelaide) 1907–08
100 J. M. Gregory (No. 9): Australia v. England (Melbourne) 1924–25
122 G. O. Allen (No. 9): England v. New Zealand (Lord's)............................1931
100 R. R. Lindwall (No. 9): Australia v. England (Melbourne).........................1946–47

DÉBUT IN TEST CRICKET

Two batsmen have had the misfortune to be dismissed with their score at 99 in their first Test match—A. G. Chipperfield for Australia v. England (Nottingham) 1934 and R. J. Christiani for West Indies v. England (Barbados) 1947–48.

Each of the three Indian players to appear for England v. Australia scored a century on début in the series—K. S. Ranjitsinhji (154*) at Manchester in 1896, K. S. Duleepsinhji (173) at Lord's in 1930 and Nawab of Pataudi (102) at Sydney in 1932–33.

G. Gunn was playing in his first innings in Australia when he scored 119 on début in Test cricket —England v. Australia (Sydney) 1907–08.

H. L. Collins scored 70 & 104 (Sydney), 64 (Melbourne) and 162 (Adelaide) v. England in 1920–21 in his first four innings in Test cricket.

P. A. Gibb (England) opened his Test career with three consecutive fifties—93 and 106 at Johannesburg and 58 at Cape Town v. South Africa in 1938–39.

A. L. Valentine—West Indies v. England (Manchester) 1950—claimed the first eight wickets which fell in the first Test innings in which he bowled.

R. Appleyard—England v. Pakistan (Nottingham) 1954—took a wicket (that of Waqar Hasan) with his second ball in Test cricket and took four wickets in 27 balls (4·3–2–6–4).

DECLARATIONS

G. C. Grant—West Indies v. Australia (Sydney) 1930–31 declared both innings closed and won the match by 30 runs.

England were the first team to win after a declaration by their opponents—West Indies declared their second innings at 51—6 at Barbados in 1934–35 and lost by four wickets.

C

Both captains declared their first innings closed in the Australia v. England Test at Melbourne in 1936–37—D. G. Bradman (Australia) at 200—9d and G. O. Allen (England) at 76—9d.

F. G. Mann, the England captain, declared the innings closed at 6 p.m. on the first day of the Test v. New Zealand at Lord's in 1949. Although an experimental Law was in force which allowed a first day declaration after 300 runs had been scored, this did not apply to Test cricket and the declaration was not in order. No query being raised at the time, the match was continued on the second day and the state of affairs allowed to remain.

DISMISSALS

Australia lost five batsmen run out, including three in the first innings, v. England (Sydney) 1920–21. During the rubber of five Test matches they lost nine batsmen run out.

A total of 34 batsmen were dismissed l.b.w. during the five South Africa v. England Test matches in 1927–28—20 for England and 14 for South Africa.

India lost six batsmen l.b.w. against England at Bombay in 1933–34.

There were six l.b.w.(n) dismissals in the England v. South Africa Test match at Lord's in 1935.

England lost six batsmen l.b.w. in their first innings against South Africa at Leeds in 1955—there were ten l.b.w. dismissals in the match.

DISMISSAL—ESCAPES FROM

H. Wood (59) was clean bowled at 6 by C. H. Vintcent—England v. South Africa (Cape Town) 1888–89—but was allowed to continue batting as he had not been ready. He had held up his bat as a signal, but the bowler was unable to stop the delivery.

W. G. Grace (16)—England v. Australia (Oval) 1890—was dropped by G. H. S. Trott at point off the first ball he received in the second innings. He had registered a 'duck' in the first innings and thus missed a 'pair', a fate which he escaped in his first-class career.

C. B. Fry (54)—England v. South Africa (Leeds) 1907—played a ball from G. A. Faulkner into his own wicket without removing a bail when his score was 10.

E. A. McDonald (36)—Australia v. England (Oval) 1921—retired from the wicket thinking he had been bowled. He was recalled and continued his innings, as the bail had been removed by G. Brown, the wicket-keeper.

F. E. Woolley (115*)—England v. South Africa (Johannesburg) 1922–23—played the first ball he received, from A. E. Hall, into his wicket without dislodging a bail.

R. H. Catterall (17)—South Africa v. England (Durban) 1922–23—had his stumps hit by A. S. Kennedy, when his score was 9, without a bail being dislodged.

H. L. Collins (61)—Australia v. England (Oval) 1926—caught a ball from M. W. Tate which had rebounded forward off the wicket-keeping pads of H. Strudwick. No appeal was made and Collins continued his innings, but he was technically out 'handled ball'.

W. M. Woodfull (111)—Australia v. England (Sydney) 1928–29—played a ball from M. W. Tate into his wicket without dislodging a bail when his score was 10.

A. F. Kippax (51)—Australia v. England (Manchester) 1930—survived l.b.w. appeals to each of the first three balls he received from I. A. R. Peebles.

H. Sutcliffe (194)—England v. Australia (Sydney) 1932–33—played a ball into his wicket without dislodging the bails when his score was 43.

H. B. Cameron (49)—South Africa v. England (Leeds) 1935—had his stumps hit by a ball from W. R. Hammond early in his innings without the bails being dislodged.

J. Hardstaff jun. (26)—England v. Australia (Sydney) 1936–37—hit his wicket early in his innings, but as neither umpire saw the incident was permitted to continue his innings.

L. Hutton (100)—England v. Australia (Nottingham) 1938—played a ball into his wicket without dislodging a bail in the first few minutes of his innings.

C. Washbrook (58)—England v. New Zealand (Christchurch) 1950–51—was given out l.b.w. to the bowling of G. F. Cresswell when he was 13 and the total 27. W. A. Hadlee, the New Zealand captain, felt certain that Washbrook had hit the ball on to his pad, and after a few words with the umpire, recalled Washbrook to continue his innings.

DISMISSALS—UNUSUAL

A. Cotter—Australia v. England (Sydney) 1907–08—broke the off-stump in clean bowling S. F. Barnes.

S. J. Snooke (53)—South Africa v. England (Durban) 1909–10—was stumped by a substitute, N. C. Tufnell, keeping wicket in place of H. Strudwick (injured).

F. R. Foster—England v. Australia (Adelaide) 1911–12—broke the middle stump in clean bowling R. B. Minnett.

E. Tyldesley (7)—England v. Australia (Nottingham) 1921—was clean bowled by a ball from J. M. Gregory which hit the wicket via the batsman's face—the batsman was assisted from the wicket in a state of collapse.

A. Ducat (3)—England v. Australia (Leeds) 1921—had the shoulder of his bat broken by a ball from E. A. McDonald, the broken piece of the bat disturbed the bails and the ball was caught by J. M. Gregory.

W. H. Brann (4)—South Africa v. England (Cape Town) 1922–23—was given 'not out' for a catch at the wicket off the bowling of G. C. Macaulay, but was given out l.b.w. to the same ball.

Mushtaq Ali (13)—India v. England (Manchester) 1936—was run out in an unusual manner. A ball hit by his partner, V. M. Merchant, struck the back of Mushtaq Ali's bat and was deflected to A. E. Fagg, fielding at mid-on, the fielder putting down the bowler's wicket before Mushtaq Ali could regain his ground.

D. C. S. Compton (65)—England v. New Zealand (Oval) 1937—was run out by a straight drive by J. Hardstaff jun. which the bowler, H. G. Vivian, deflected on to the wicket while Compton was backing up.

D. G. Bradman (185)—Australia v. India (Brisbane) 1947–48—was out 'hit wkt., b Amarnath' —he played back to such an extent that he broke the wicket from behind on the downward swing of the bat.

W. A. Brown (18)—Australia v. India (Sydney) 1947–48—was run out by the bowler, V. Mankad, when backing up too far before the ball was delivered. Mankad did not warn Brown, as the players had been concerned in a similar incident a month before in the match between an Australian XI and the Indians on the same ground.

D. J. Insole (21)—England v. West Indies (Nottingham) 1950—was given out l.b.w. to a ball from K. T. Ramadhin, the ball going on to the wicket and bowling him off his pads.

W. G. A. Parkhouse (2)—England v. New Zealand (Wellington) 1950–51—was given out l.b.w. to a ball which hit his pads and then trickled into the wicket and dislodged a bail, the bowler being T. B. Burtt. The umpires later ruled the dismissal to be bowled, but l.b.w. has been retained in reference books.

L. Hutton (27)—England v. South Africa (Oval) 1951—was dismissed 'obstructing the field'. A ball from A. M. B. Rowan rose into the air off Hutton's bat handle or hand and the batsman hit it away as it fell, with the intention of preventing the ball hitting the wicket. The wicket-keeper, W. R. Endean, was preparing to take the catch and appealed for the obstruction.

W. R. Endean (3)—South Africa v. England (Cape Town) 1956–57—was given out 'handled ball'—a ball from J. C. Laker rose sharply and Endean palmed the ball away in the style of hockey players.

DISPUTES

W. L. Murdoch, the Australian captain, protested against the bowling of R. G. Barlow (England) at Sydney in 1882–83, on the grounds that the long spikes in Barlow's boots were cutting up the wicket. Hon. Ivo Bligh, the England captain, requested Barlow to remove his spikes, but pointed out that F. R. Spofforth (Australia) had been doing just as much damage with spikes of equal length.

W. Barnes did not bowl for England v. Australia (Sydney) 1884–85—it was stated at the time that 'owing to some unpleasantness between Shrewsbury and Barnes the latter refused to bowl when asked to do so'.

J. J. Ferris—Australia v. England (Oval) 1888—was stopped from bowling under Law 14 as he had changed ends more than twice in the innings.

P. Holmes and H. Sutcliffe—England v. South Africa (Cape Town) 1927–28—made a unique protest, objecting to the colour of the ball being too dark. The appeal was dismissed as the ball had been approved by the captains.

D. R. Jardine—England v. Australia (Sydney) 1932–33—registered a protest over H. H. Alexander cutting up the wicket in his follow-through when bowling.

'DUCKS'

The England v. Australia match at Manchester in 1888 provided eleven 'ducks' in three completed innings.

J. Trim—West Indies v. Australia (Melbourne) 1951–52—was 'run out 0' in each innings of the match.

ENGLAND TEST SELECTORS

1899 (Australia)—Lord Hawke, W. G. Grace, H. W. Bainbridge.
1902 (Australia)—Lord Hawke, G. MacGregor, H. W. Bainbridge.
1905 (Australia)—Lord Hawke, J. A. Dixon, P. F. Warner.
1907 (South Africa)—Lord Hawke, H. K. Foster, C. H. B. Marsham.
1909 (Australia)—Lord Hawke, C. B. Fry, H. D. G. Leveson-Gower.
1911 (Trials)—Lord Hawke, P. F. Warner, G. L. Jessop.
1912 (Triangular Tournament)—J. Shuter, C. B. Fry, H. K. Foster.
1921 (Australia)—H. K. Foster, R. H. Spooner, J. Daniell.
1924 (South Africa)—H. D. G. Leveson-Gower, J. Sharp, J. Daniell.
1926 (Australia)—P. F. Warner, P. A. Perrin, A. E. R. Gilligan, J. B. Hobbs and W. Rhodes were
          co-opted as professional members.
1927 (Trials)—H. D. G. Leveson-Gower, J. W. H. T. Douglas, A. W. Carr.
1928 (West Indies)—H. D. G. Leveson-Gower, J. W. H. T. Douglas, A. W. Carr.

1929 (South Africa)—H. G. D. Leveson-Gower, J. C. White, N. E. Haig.
1930 (Australia)—H. D. G. Leveson-Gower, J. C. White, F. T. Mann.
1931 (New Zealand)—P. F. Warner, P. A. Perrin, T. A. Higson.
1932 (India)—P. F. Warner, P. A. Perrin, T. A. Higson.
1933 (West Indies)—Lord Hawke, P. A. Perrin, T. A. Higson.
1934 (Australia)—Hon. F. S. Jackson, P. A. Perrin, T. A. Higson.
1935 (South Africa)—P. F. Warner, P. A. Perrin, T. A. Higson.
1936 (India)—P. F. Warner, P. A. Perrin, T. A. Higson.
1937 (New Zealand)—Sir Pelham Warner, P. A. Perrin, T. A. Higson, E. R. T. Holmes was a
    co-opted member.
1938 (Australia)—Sir Pelham Warner, P. A. Perrin, A. B. Sellers, M. J. Turnbull.
1939 (West Indies)—P. A. Perrin, A. B. Sellers, M. J. Turnbull, A. J. Holmes.
1946 (India)—Sir F. S. Jackson, A. B. Sellers, A. J. Holmes, R. W. V. Robins.
1947 (South Africa)—A. J. Holmes, R. W. V. Robins, J. C. Clay.
1948 (Australia)—A. J. Holmes, R. W. V. Robins, J. C. Clay.
1949 (New Zealand)—A. J. Holmes, A. B. Sellers, R. W. V. Robins, T. N. Pearce.
1950 (West Indies)—R. E. S. Wyatt, A. B. Sellers, T. N. Pearce, L. E. G. Ames.
1951 (South Africa)—N. W. D. Yardley, R. E. S. Wyatt, F. R. Brown, L. E. G. Ames.
1952 (India)—N. W. D. Yardley, R. E. S. Wyatt, F. R. Brown, L. E. G. Ames.
1953 (Australia)—F. R. Brown, N. W. D. Yardley, R. E. S. Wyatt, L. E. G. Ames.
1954 (Pakistan)—H. S. Altham, R. W. V. Robins, R. E. S. Wyatt, L. E. G. Ames.
1955 (South Africa)—G. O. Allen, W. Wooller, A. B. Sellers, L. E. G. Ames.
1956 (Australia)—G. O. Allen, W. Wooller, C. Washbrook, L. E. G. Ames.
1957 (West Indies)—G. O. Allen, W. Wooller, C. Washbrook, H. E. Dollery.
1958 (New Zealand)—G. O. Allen, W. Wooller, L. E. G. Ames, H. E. Dollery.
1959 (India)—G. O. Allen, W. Wooller, D. J. Insole, H. Sutcliffe.
1960 (South Africa)—G. O. Allen, W. Wooller, D. J. Insole, H. Sutcliffe.

(*The name of the chairman is given first. The captain is normally a co-opted member. L. E. G. Ames, in 1950, was the first professional member.*)

EXTRAS

Neither wicket-keeper—G. MacGregor (England) and J. McC. Blackham (Australia)—conceded a single bye in the Test match at Lord's in 1890—the only extras conceded in a match aggregate of 618 runs were seven leg byes.

W. A. Oldfield did not concede a single bye in either innings of 521 and 342—8d—for Australia v. England (Brisbane) 1928–29. He conceded only three byes in the first five innings played by England in the series while 1,932 runs were scored.

The highest number of extras conceded in a single Test Innings is 57 (31 byes, 16 leg-byes, 10 no-balls)—by W. F. Cornford for England v. New Zealand (Auckland) 1929–30.

England conceded 50 extras (37 byes, 8 leg-byes, 4 no-balls) in Australia's second innings total of 327 at the Oval in 1934—F. E. Woolley was keeping wicket in place of L. E. G. Ames (injured).

The England v. Australia match at the Oval in 1934 provided a total of 94 extras, England conceding 83 of them.

L. E. G. Ames conceded only a single bye in Australia's innings of 604—England v. Australia (Melbourne) 1936–37.

B. A. Barnett conceded only a single bye in England's innings of 658—8d—Australia v. England (Nottingham) 1938.

Australia conceded 50 extras (22 byes, 19 leg-byes, 1 wide, 8 no-balls) in England's innings of 903—7d at the Oval in 1938—B. A. Barnett was the Australian wicket-keeper.

T. G. Evans did not concede a single bye in the first two innings in which he kept wicket for England v. Australia—659–8d at Sydney and 365 at Melbourne in 1946–47.

Extras totalled 35 (30 byes, 2 leg-byes, 3 no-balls) in New Zealand's total of 189 v. England (Wellington) 1950–51.

FAMILY RELATIONSHIPS IN TEST CRICKET

Father and son:

E. J. and S. E. Gregory—D. W. was a brother of E. J. and J. M. a cousin of S. E.
J. Hardstaff sen. and jun. (England).
F. and G. A. L. Hearne (South Africa)—F. also played for England.
F. T. and F. G. Mann (England)—both captained England in Test cricket.
A. D. Nourse sen. and jun. (South Africa).
J. H. and J. M. Parks (England).
F. W. and M. W. Tate (England).
C. L. and D. C. H. Townsend (England).
L. R. and L. Tuckett (South Africa).
S. Wazir Ali (India) and Khalid Wazir (Pakistan).

Three brothers:

E. M., W. G. and G. F. Grace (England)—all three played at the Oval in 1880.
Alec., Frank and G. G. Hearne (England)—J. T. was a cousin.
Hanif, Mushtaq and Wazir Mohammed (Pakistan).
A. B., L. J. and V. M. Tancred (South Africa).

There are a considerable number of instances of two brothers playing for their country, two pairs of whom both acted as Test captains—A. E. R. and A. H. H. Gilligan (England) and G. C. and R. S. Grant (West Indies).

E. J. Gregory and S. E. Gregory, father and son, both registered 'ducks' on their début for Australia in Test cricket. J. M. Gregory, another member of the family, also registered a 'duck' on his Test début in 1920–21.

FAVOURITE GROUNDS OF BATSMEN

W. R. Hammond's record in Test matches at Sydney was as follows: 251 (1928–29), 112, 101, 75* (1932–33), 231* (1936–37), 1, 37 (1946–47)—a total of 808 runs (av. 161·60).

L. Hutton's favourite Test ground was the Oval and in consecutive matches on the ground he scored: 12 (1937), 364 (1938), 73 & 165* (1939), 25 (1946), 83 & 36 (1947), 30 & 64 (1948), 206 (1949), 202* & 2 (1950), 28 & 27 (1951), 86 (1952), 82 & 17 (1953), and 14 & 5 (1954)—a total of 1,521 runs (av. 89·47).

D. C. S. Compton scored a century on each of his first four Test appearances at Nottingham— 102 v. Australia in 1938, 65 & 163 v. South Africa in 1947, 19 & 184 v. Australia in 1948 and 112 & 5 v. South Africa in 1951. He followed with 0 v. Australia in 1953, 278 v. Pakistan in 1954 and 27 v. South Africa in 1955—a total of 955 runs (av. 95·50).

FIELDING

G. F. Grace caught G. J. Bonnor off a catch which had gone so high in the air that the batsmen had completed their second run and commenced their third before the ball came to rest in the fieldsman's hands—England v. Australia (Oval) 1880.

W. G. Grace fielded in every position in the field during Australia's innings of 551 and held a catch while keeping wicket—England v. Australia (Oval) 1884.

Two Australian players have held 'sub' catches for England—W. L. Murdoch at Lord's in 1884 and A. H. Jarvis at Melbourne in 1884–85.

England won the match against Australia at the Oval in 1890 by means of an overthrow by J. E. Barrett.

C. Hill returned a ball from the deep field which broke the wicket at one end and went on and broke the wicket at the other end—Australia v. England (Sheffield) 1902.

A. O. Jones (twelfth man) was allowed to keep wicket in place of A. A. Lilley (injured)—England v. Australia (Oval) 1905.

N. C. Tufnell (twelfth man) was allowed to keep wicket in place of H. Strudwick (injured)— England v. South Africa (Durban) 1909–10. He stumped the South African captain (S. J. Snooke) later in the innings.

H. F. Wade, the fielding captain, appealed against the light—South Africa v. Australia (Johannesburg) 1935–36.

V. Y. Richardson Australia v. South Africa (Durban) 1935–36—caught five of the last six batsmen to be dismissed in the innings, including each of the last four.

L. Hutton kicked the ball over the boundary to prevent the more experienced batsman (W. A. Brown) retaining the strike off the last ball of an over. Under the Laws five runs were scored, a single for the hit, and Brown retained the bowling—England v. Australia (Oval) 1938.

FIGURE CURIOSITIES

A. J. Richardson's batting and bowling averages were identical at 31·00 for Australia v. England in 1924–25—he scored 248 runs in 8 innings and took 8 wickets for 248 runs.

J. B. Hobbs and H. Sutcliffe each scored 1529 runs in three consecutive Test series v. Australia in Australia—Hobbs, 505 (1920–21), 573 (1924–25) and 451 (1928–29) and Sutcliffe, 734 (1924–25), 355 (1928–29), and 440 (1932–33).

C. Kelleway's batting and bowling averages in all Test matches v. England were identical at 31·21—he scored 874 runs in 28 completed innings and took 37 wickets for 1155 runs.

FOUR BOWLERS ONLY IN A LONG INNINGS

England—while Australia totalled 349 (Oval) 1893
Australia—while England totalled 403—8d (Oval) 1921
South Africa—while England totalled 421—8 (Oval) 1924
Australia—while England totalled 342—8d (Brisbane) 1928–29

New Zealand—while England totalled 372 (Leeds) 1949
New Zealand—while England totalled 482 (Oval) 1949
England—while Australia totalled 426 (Sydney) 1950–51
England—while Australia totalled 318 (Manchester) 1953
Pakistan—while West Indies totalled 325 and 312 (Trinidad) 1957–58
India—while England totalled 361 (Oval) 1959

All eleven England players, including the wicket-keeper, went on to bowl during Australia's innings of 551 at the Oval in 1884. The wicket-keeper (Hon. A. Lyttelton) returned the best bowling figures by taking four wickets at a cost of 19 runs.

GOOD BATTING SEQUENCES

W. R. Hammond (England) scored consecutive innings of 251, 200 and 32, 119* and 177 v. Australia in 1928–29.

D. G. Bradman (Australia) scored 1421 runs (av. 109·30) in Test cricket in less than nine months in 1930 and 1930–31—974 runs (av. 139·14) v. England in 1930 and 447 runs (av. 74·50) v. West Indies in 1930–31.

W. R. Hammond (England) scored 1003 runs (av. 111·44) between December 3rd, 1932, and April 1st, 1933—440 runs (av. 55·00) v. Australia and 563 runs (av. 563·00) v. New Zealand.

W. R. Hammond (England) scored 739 runs in four consecutive Test innings in 1932–33—101 and 75* v. Australia (Sydney) and 227 v. New Zealand (Christchurch) and 336* v. New Zealand (Auckland).

W. R. Hammond (England) scored three consecutive centuries against New Zealand—227 at Christchurch and 336* at Auckland in 1932–33 and 140 at Lord's in 1937.

D. G. Bradman (Australia) scored centuries in eight consecutive Test matches, all against England, in which he batted—270, 212 and 169 in 1936–37, 144, 102* and 103 in 1938 and 187 and 234 in 1946–47.

D. G. Bradman (Australia) had a batting average of over 50 in each of his eight Test rubbers v. England—66·85 in 1928–29, 139·14 in 1930, 56·57 in 1932–33, 94·75 in 1934, 90·00 in 1936–37, 108·50 in 1938, 97·14 in 1946–47 and 72·57 in 1948.

GOOD BOWLING SEQUENCES

3 consecutive innings:

25—145 J. C. Laker (6—55, 9—37, 10—53) 1956
24—73   G. A. Lohmann (7—38, 8—7, 9—28) 1895–96
22—207 S. F. Barnes (5—48, 8—56, 9—103)..1913–14
21—261 H. J. Tayfield (8—69, 4—79, 9—113) 1956–57
20—160 C. Blythe (8—59, 7—40, 5—61) 1907
20—213 C. V. Grimmett (7—40, 7—100, 6—73) 1935–36
20—218 W. Rhodes (5—94, 7—56, 8—68)..1903–04
20—291 C. V. Grimmett (6—92, 7—116, 7—83) 1931–32

4 consecutive innings:

30—203 J. C. Laker (5—58, 6—55, 9—37, 10—53) 1956
27—116 G. A. Lohmann (7—38, 8—7, 9—28, 3—43) 1895–96
27—264 S. F. Barnes (5—57, 5—48, 8—56, 9—103) 1913–14

5 consecutive innings:

34—283 J. C. Laker (5—58, 6—55, 9—37, 10—53, 4—80) 1956
34—158 G. A. Lohmann (7—38, 8—7, 9—28, 3—43, 7—42) 1895–96
32—343 S. F. Barnes (8—56, 9—103, 3—26, 5—102, 7—56) 1913–14
30—521 T. Richardson (6—104, 6—39, 5—134, 7—168, 6—76) ....1894–95 & 1896
30—290 S. F. Barnes (5—57, 5—48, 8—56, 9—103, 3—26) 1913–14

6 consecutive innings:

39—431 S. F. Barnes (8—56, 9—103, 3—26, 5—102, 7—56, 7—88) 1913–14
37—291 J. C. Laker (5—58, 6—55, 9—37, 10—53, 4—80, 3—8) 1956
35—203 G. A. Lohmann (7—38, 8—7, 9—28, 3—43, 7—42, 1—45)....................1895–96
35—392 S. F. Barnes (5—57, 5—48, 8—56, 9—103, 3—26, 5—102) 1913–14

GOOD BOWLING SPELLS

6—6 in 45 balls S. Haigh: England v. South Africa (Cape Town) 1898–99
7—17 in 46 balls M. A. Noble: Australia v. England (Melbourne) 1901–02

6—7   in 29 balls   S. J. **Pegler**: South Africa v. England (Lord's) 1912
5—1   in 17 balls   G. R. **Hazlitt**: Australia v. England (Oval) 1912
5—7   in 31 balls   E. P. **Nupen**: South Africa v. England (Durban) 1927–28
6—11 in 24 balls   E. P. **Nupen**: South Africa v. England (Johannesburg) 1930–31
5—18 in 59 balls   I. A. R. **Peebles**: England v. South Africa (Johannesburg) 1930–31
                    (*including 3 in 5 balls*)
6—8   in 36 balls   H. **Ironmonger**: Australia v. South Africa (Melbourne) 1931–32
                    (*including 4 in 11 balls*)
6—9   in 56 balls   C. V. **Grimmett**: Australia v. South Africa (Adelaide) 1931–32
5—13 in 47 balls   M. S. **Nichols**: England v. South Africa (Nottingham) 1935
4—6   in 32 balls   H. J. **Tayfield**: South Africa v. Australia (Durban) 1949–50
                    (*including 3 in 5 balls and 4 in 9 balls*)
4—2   in 26 balls   A. V. **Bedser**: England v. Australia (Nottingham) 1953
4—4   in 11 balls   J. H. **Wardle**: England v. Australia (Manchester) 1953
5—0   in 32 balls   H. J. **Tayfield**: South Africa v. New Zealand (Johannesburg) 1953–54
4—6   in 26 balls   R. **Appleyard**: England v. Pakistan (Nottingham) 1954
5—5   in 45 balls   F. H. **Tyson**: England v. South Africa (Nottingham) 1955

W. P. **Howell**—Australia v. South Africa (Cape Town) 1902–03—took 3 wickets in 5 balls and 4 wickets in 12 balls.

J. W. H. T. **Douglas**—England v. South Africa (Port Elizabeth) 1913–14—took 3 wickets in 5 balls and 4 wickets in 13 balls.

A. E. R. **Gilligan** (4 in 12 balls) and M. W. **Tate** (4 in 13 balls) both had good spells in the innings of 30—England v. South Africa (Birmingham) 1924.

B. **Mitchell**—South Africa v. Australia (Johannesburg) 1935–36—took 3 wickets in 5 balls and 4 wickets in 8 balls.

INNINGS TOTALS

The following teams eventually lost the match after they had started with an innings of over 500 at the opening of the game:

Australia (586) v. England (Sydney) 1894–95
England (519) v. Australia (Melbourne) 1928–29
Australia (520) v. South Africa (Melbourne) 1952–53

Australia were dismissed by England for consecutive innings totals of 119 & 97, 84 & 150, 42 & 82, 116 & 60, 80 & 100 and 81 & 70 between January 1887 and August 1888.

England (325 & 437) defeated Australia (586 & 166) by 10 runs after being 261 runs behind on first innings and following-on, at Sydney 1894–95.

There was a variation of 426 between the first innings (506) and second innings (80) by South Africa v. Australia (Melbourne) 1910–11.

Australia scored second innings totals of 250 in three consecutive Test matches v. England in 1924–25.

Australia did not reach a total of 200 in any of their five second innings v. England in 1932–33.

Australia (201 & 123) followed-on 702 runs behind against England at the Oval in 1938.

The England v. Pakistan match at the Oval in 1954 was the first Test match in which a new ball had not been available to the fielding side since the passing of the 'new ball after 200 runs law' in 1907.

Australia (601—8d) recorded the highest innings total after being sent in to bat by the captain winning the toss—Australia v. England (Brisbane) 1954–55.

The England v. South Africa Test match at the Oval in 1955 was also played through without a new ball being taken.

India scored an innings total of over 400 in each of the five Test matches v. New Zealand in 1955–56, the first team to achieve this record in Test cricket.

MOST CONSECUTIVE TEST APPEARANCES

52   F. E. **Woolley** (England): Oval 1909 to Oval 1926
52   P. B. H. **May** (England): Oval 1953 to Leeds 1959.
48   V. T. **Trumper** (Australia): Nottingham 1899 to Sydney 1911–12.
46   R. N. **Harvey** (Australia): Leeds 1948 to Calcutta 1956–57.
45   A. D. **Nourse** sen (South Africa): Johannesburg 1902–03 to Oval 1924.
42   M. A. **Noble** (Australia): Melbourne 1897–98 to Oval 1909.
42   B. **Mitchell** (South Africa): Birmingham 1929 to Port Elizabeth 1948–49.
41   P. R. **Umrigar** (India): New Delhi 1951–52 to Manchester 1959.
39   S. E. **Gregory** (Australia): Adelaide 1891–92 to Sydney 1903–04.
39   S. J. **McCabe** (Australia): Nottingham 1930 to Oval 1938.
37   R. **Benaud** (Australia): Brisbane 1954–55 to date.
36   J. J. **Kelly** (Australia): Lord's 1896 to Oval 1905.
35   K. R. **Miller** (Australia): Wellington 1945–46 to Adelaide 1952–53.
35   W. M. **Woodfull** (Australia): Nottingham 1926 to Oval 1934.
34   J. R. **Reid** (New Zealand): Manchester 1949 to date.

33   W. A. Oldfield (Australia): Sydney 1924–25 to Adelaide 1932–33.
32   A. D. Nourse jun. (South Africa): Manchester 1935 to Oval 1951.
32   H. J. Tayfield (South Africa): Brisbane 1952–53 to date.
32   J. H. B. Waite (South Africa): Brisbane 1952–53 to date.
31   G. Sobers (West Indies): Trinidad 1954–55 to date.
30   W. Rhodes (England): Leeds 1909 to Nottingham 1921.
30   H. W. Taylor (South Africa): Manchester 1912 to Birmingham 1929.

MOST TEST APPEARANCES

England

T. G. Evans 91
W. R. Hammond 85
L. Hutton 79
D. C. S. Compton 78
F. E. Woolley 64
P. B. H. May 62
T. E. Bailey 61
J. B. Hobbs 61
W. Rhodes 58
J. B. Statham 55
H. Sutcliffe 54
A. V. Bedser 51
E. Hendren 51
M. C. Cowdrey 49
T. W. Graveney 48
L. E. G. Ames 47

Australia

R. N. Harvey 65
R. R. Lindwall 61
S. E. Gregory 58
K. R. Miller 55
W. A. Oldfield 54
D. G. Bradman 52
W. W. Armstrong 50
C. Hill 49
V. T. Trumper 48
A. R. Morris 46
R. Benaud 45
I. W. Johnson 45
A. L. Hassett 43
M. A. Noble 42
W. Bardsley 41
W. A. Johnston 40

South Africa

A. D. Nourse sen. 45
B. Mitchell 42
H. W. Taylor 42
H. J. Tayfield 37
J. H. B. Waite...............36
A. D. Nourse jun. 34
R. A. McLean 33

West Indies

E. D. Weekes 48
C. L. Walcott 44
K. T. Ramadhin 41
F. M. Worrell 36
G. Sobers 32
J. B. Stollmeyer 32

New Zealand

B. Sutcliffe 34
J. R. Reid 34
A. R. MacGibbon 26
H. B. Cave...................19
A. M. Moir 17
J. A. Hayes...................15
S. N. McGregor 15

India

P. R. Umrigar 45
V. Mankad 44
P. Roy 42
G. S. Ramchand 33
V. L. Manjrekar 32
D. G. Phadkar 31
S. P. Gupte...................31

Pakistan

Imtiaz Ahmed 29
Hanif Mohammed...........27
Fazal Mahmood 26
A. H. Kardar 23
Waqar Hasan 21
Wazir Mohammed 20

OLDEST PLAYERS TO MAKE DÉBUT IN TEST CRICKET

Years	Days		
49	119	J. Southerton: England v. Australia (Melbourne) 1876–77
47	275	Miran Bux: Pakistan v. India (Lahore) 1954–55
46	273	D. D. J. Blackie: Australia v. England (Sydney).............................1928–29
41	337	E. R. Wilson: England v. Australia (Sydney) 1920–21
41	275	H. Ironmonger: Australia v. England (Brisbane) 1928–29
41	28	R. J. Jamshedji: India v. England (Bombay) 1933–34
40	346	C. A. Wiles: West Indies v. England (Manchester) 1933
40	110	H. W. Lee: England v. South Africa (Johannesburg) 1930–31
40	56	G. W. A. Chubb: South Africa v. England (Nottingham) 1951
40	37	C. Ramaswami: India v. England (Manchester) 1936
39	361	G. Challenor: West Indies v. England (Lord's) 1928
39	360	A. Wood: England v. Australia (Oval)..1938

J. Southerton and G. Challenor (above) were playing in the first Test match in which their country appeared.

ON FIELD FOR WHOLE OF MATCH

W. A. Brown—Australia v. England (Lord's) 1938—was on the field continuously from the start of the match until 5 p.m. on the fourth day (he carried his bat for 206* through the first Australian innings).

B. Mitchell was on the field for the whole of the four-day Test between South Africa and England at the Oval in 1947, with the exception of 8 minutes during which 12 balls were bowled at the end of the first South African innings. He batted 801 minutes to score 309 runs (120 in 381 minutes in the first innings and 189* in 420 in the second).

D. J. McGlew—South Africa v. New Zealand (Wellington) 1952–53—scored an innings of 255* and was on the field for the whole of all four days of the match, the first player to achieve this feat in Test cricket.

PARTNERSHIP MEMORABILIA

H. Sutcliffe—England v. Australia (Sydney) 1932–33—shared in century stands for each of the first three wickets—112—1st with R. E. S. Wyatt, 188—2nd with W. R. Hammond and 123—3rd with Nawab of Pataudi.

The following opening pairs have shared in the greatest number of century opening stands in Test cricket:

J. B. Hobbs & H. Sutcliffe (England)	15
J. B. Hobbs & W. Rhodes (England)	8
L. Hutton & C. Washbrook (England)	8

J. B. Hobbs and H. Sutcliffe recorded four century opening stands for England v. Australia in 1924–25—157 & 110 at Sydney, 283 at Melbourne (2nd Test) and 126 at Melbourne (4th Test). The first three stands were recorded in the first three innings the pair opened against Australia.

L. Hutton and C. Washbrook recorded three consecutive century opening stands for England v. Australia in 1946–47—138 at Melbourne and 137 & 110 at Adelaide.

R. S. Modi and V. S. Hazare recorded three consecutive century partnerships for the third wicket for India v. West Indies in 1948–49—156 at Bombay and 129 and 108 at Calcutta.

Four century stands for the same wicket during the course of a rubber have been recorded for:

England v. Australia in Australia (4th)	1907–08
Australia v. South Africa in Australia (2nd)	1931–32
England v. South Africa in South Africa (2nd)	1938–39

A total of 18 century stands were recorded in the 1920–21 rubber in Australia, 7 for England and 11 for Australia.

A total of 18 century stands were recorded in the 1938–39 rubber in South Africa, 8 for England and 10 for South Africa.

At least one century stand for each of the first seven wickets was recorded for England v. Australia in England in 1938.

PLAYERS WHO HAVE REPRESENTED TWO COUNTRIES

Amir Elahi	India (1947–48) and Pakistan (1952–53)
J. J. Ferris	Australia (1886–87 to 1890) and England (1891–92)
S. C. Guillen	West Indies (1951–52) and New Zealand (1955–56)
Gul Mahomed	India (1946 to 1952–53) and Pakistan (1956–57)
F. Hearne	England (1888–89) and South Africa (1891 to 1895–96)
A. H. Kardar	India (1946) and Pakistan (1952–53 to 1957–58)
W. E. Midwinter	Australia (1876–77 to 1886–87) and England (1881–82)
F. Mitchell	England (1898–99) and South Africa (1912)
W. L. Murdoch	Australia (1876–77 to 1890) and England (1891–92)
Nawab of Pataudi	England (1932–33 to 1934) and India (1946)
A. E. Trott	Australia (1894–95) and England (1898–99)
S. M. J. Woods	Australia (1888) and England (1895–96)

UMPIRES

F. Chester made his first appearance as a Test match umpire at Lord's in 1924, and by the time of his retirement in 1955 had officiated in 48 Tests.

R. W. Crockett officiated in 33 Test matches in Australia between 1901–02 and 1924–25, missing only two of 35 consecutive Tests in Australia.

J. Phillips, an Australian, officiated in 29 Tests—13 in Australia (1884–85 to 1897–98), 11 in England (1893 to 1905) and 5 in South Africa (1905–06).

The two umpires in the third Test match between South Africa and New Zealand at Cape Town in 1953–54 were brothers—Dalkeith Collins and Stanley Collins.

WEATHER

The England v. Australia match at Adelaide in 1907–08 was played under heat-wave conditions. The temperatures on the third day were 102·2 in the shade and 150 in the sun, while figures of 106·7 and 151·7 were recorded on the fourth day and 107·6 and 151·9 on the sixth.

The England v. Australia match at the Oval in 1912 was arranged to be played to a finish—the first 'timeless' Test in England. The match was completed on the fourth day, but as the next two days were wet it would have continued into the seventh day if a result had not been reached on the fourth afternoon.

The wicket was dried by artificial means on the second day of the England v. India match at Lord's in 1936—the first time that this course had been adopted in a Test match in England.

Rain caused a record number of blank days during the England v. Pakistan rubber in 1954, play being impossible on seven days owing to rain—the first second and third days at Lord's, the second fourth and fifth at Manchester and the second at the Oval. Rain was so unfriendly at Lord's that the first ball of the match could not be bowled until 3.45 p.m. on the fourth day.

* C

YOUNGEST PLAYERS TO MAKE DÉBUT IN TEST CRICKET

Years Days
16	70	Mushtaq Mohammed: Pakistan v. West Indies (Lahore)	1958–59
16	248	Nasimul Ghani: Pakistan v. West Indies (Barbados)	1957–58
16	352	Khalid Hassan: Pakistan v. England (Nottingham)	1954
17	122	J. E. D. Sealey: West Indies v. England (Barbados)	1929–30
17	239	I. D. Craig: Australia v. South Africa (Melbourne)	1952–53
17	245	G. Sobers: West Indies v. England (Kingston)	1953–54
17	265	V. Mehra: India v. New Zealand (Bombay)	1955–56
17	300	Hanif Mohammed: Pakistan v. India (New Delhi)	1952–53
18	31	M. R. Bynoe: West Indies v. Pakistan (Lahore)	1958–59
18	44	Khalid Wazir: Pakistan v. England (Lord's)	1954
18	105	J. B. Stollmeyer: West Indies v. England (Lord's)	1939
18	149	D. B. Close: England v. New Zealand (Manchester)	1949
18	186	Haseeb Ahsan: Pakistan v. West Indies (Barbados)	1957–58
18	197	D. L. Freeman: New Zealand v. England (Christchurch)	1932–33
18	232	T. W. Garrett: Australia v. England (Melbourne)	1876–77
18	267	H. G. Vivian: New Zealand v. England (Oval)	1931

D. L. Freeman (above) was still at Nelson College when he made his début for New Zealand v. England at Christchurch in 1932–33.

YOUNGEST PLAYERS TO SCORE A CENTURY IN TEST CRICKET

Years Days
19	121	H. G. Vivian (100): New Zealand v. South Africa (Wellington)	1931–32
19	121	R. N. Harvey (153): Australia v. India (Melbourne)	1947–48
19	152	A. A. Jackson (164): Australia v. England (Adelaide)	1928–29
20	19	D. C. S. Compton (102): England v. Australia (Nottingham)	1938
20	58	Hanif Mohammed (142): Pakistan v. India (Bahawalpur)	1954–55
20	130	D. G. Bradman (112): Australia v. England (Melbourne)	1928–29
20	131	A. A. Baig (112): India v. England (Manchester)	1959
20	148	H. G. Owen-Smith (129): South Africa v. England (Leeds)	1929
20	230	G. Headley (176): West Indies v. England (Barbados)	1929–30
20	253	V. L. Manjrekar (133): India v. England (Leeds)	1952
20	317	C. Hill (188): Australia v. England (Melbourne)	1897–98
20	323	J. W. Hearne (114): England v. Australia (Melbourne)	1911–12
20	325	Hanif Mohammed (103): Pakistan v. New Zealand (Dacca)	1955–56
20	330	O. G. Smith (104): West Indies v. Australia (Kingston)	1954–55

MISCELLANEOUS

Charles Bannerman—Australia v. England (Melbourne) 1876–77—received the first ball bowled in Test cricket and scored the first Test run, a single, off the second ball of the match. The bowler was A. Shaw. By a strange coincidence, his brother, A. C. Bannerman, scored the first Test run in England for Australia in 1880.

Sussex postponed their fixture with the 1880 Australian touring team in order that the first Test match in England could be played. Sussex were granted £100 from the profits of the match. Surrey took £1470 and the Australians' share was £1110.

The closing stages of the England v. Australia match at the Oval in 1882 proved so exciting that one spectator dropped dead with heart failure and another chewed away the top of his umbrella.

S. F. Barnes (Staffordshire) is the only Minor County cricketer to be regarded as a 'first-choice' for England. During his years with the county he played against Australia in 1907–08, 1909, 1911–12 and 1912 and South Africa in 1912 and 1913–14.

W. Rhodes made his last appearance for England v. Australia at the Oval in 1926. He made his debut in the series between the two countries in 1899, before three of the members of the 1926 side had been born—A. P. F. Chapman (captain), G. T. S. Stevens and H. Larwood.

The first Test match to be the subject of a radio running commentary was England v. Australia at Nottingham in 1930.

R. A. Duff and W. H. Ponsford (both Australians) are the only batsmen to have scored centuries in both their first and last Test matches.

M. Leyland (England) scored centuries in his first and last Test innings against Australia—137 at Melbourne in 1928–29 and 187 at the Oval in 1938.

At least one century was scored in each of the six innings commenced by England in the 1949 rubber against New Zealand.

India played 19 Test matches between November 1951 and April 1953 (17 months). England played 18 Test matches between June 1929 and August 1930 (14½ months).

Five Yorkshire players were included in the England team against Australia at the Oval in 1938—L. Hutton, M. Leyland, A. Wood, H. Verity and W. E. Bowes.

Appendix A
Test Career Records, 1876–77 to 1960
Batting and Fielding

ENGLAND

	M.	I.	N.O.	Runs	H.S.	Avge.	100s	50s	Ct.	St.
Abel, R.	13	22	2	744	132*	37·20	2	2	13	—
Absolom, C. A.	1	2	0	58	52	29·00	—	1	—	—
Allen, D. A.	7	13	6	197	55	28·14	—	1	2	—
Allen, G. O.	25	33	2	750	122	24·19	1	3	20	—
Allom, M. J. C.	5	3	2	14	8*	14·00	—	—	—	—
Ames, L. E. G.	47	72	12	2434	149	40·56	8	7	75	23
Andrew, K. V.	1	2	0	11	6	5·50	—	—	—	—
Appleyard, R.	9	9	6	51	19*	17·00	—	—	4	—
Archer, A. G.	1	2	1	31	24*	31·00	—	—	—	—
Armitage, T.	2	3	0	33	21	11·00	—	—	—	—
Arnold, E. G.	10	15	3	160	40	13·33	—	—	8	—
Arnold, J.	1	2	0	34	34	17·00	—	—	—	—
Astill, W. E.	9	15	0	190	40	12·66	—	—	7	—
Attewell, W.	10	15	6	150	43*	16·66	—	—	9	—
Bailey, T. E.	61	91	14	2290	134*	29·74	1	10	32	—
Bakewell, A. H.	6	9	0	409	107	45·44	1	3	3	—
Barber, R. W.	1	2	0	9	5	4·50	—	—	—	—
Barber, W.	2	4	0	83	44	20·75	—	—	1	—
Barlow, R. G.	17	30	4	591	62	22·73	—	2	14	—
Barnes, S. F.	27	39	9	242	38*	8·06	—	—	12	—
Barnes, W.	21	33	2	725	134	23·38	1	5	19	—
Barnett, C. J.	20	35	4	1098	129	35·41	2	5	14	—
Barratt, F.	5	4	1	28	17	9·33	—	—	2	—
Barrington, K. F.	16	25	1	1056	128	42·00	2	7	7	—
Barton, V. A.	1	1	0	23	23	23·00	—	—	—	—
Bates, W.	15	26	2	656	64	27·33	—	5	9	—
Bean, G.	3	5	0	92	50	18·40	—	1	4	—
Bedser, A. V.	51	71	15	714	79	12·75	—	1	26	—
Berry, R.	2	4	2	6	4*	3·00	—	—	2	—
Bird, M. C.	10	16	1	280	61	18·66	—	2	5	—
Bligh, Hon. Ivo	4	7	1	62	19	10·33	—	—	7	—
Blythe, C.	19	31	12	183	27	9·63	—	—	6	—
Board, J. H.	6	12	2	108	29	10·80	—	—	8	3
Booth, M. W.	2	2	0	46	32	23·00	—	—	—	—
Bosanquet, B. J. T.	7	14	3	147	27	13·36	—	—	9	—
Bowden, M. P.	2	2	0	25	25	12·50	—	—	1	—
Bowes, W. E.	15	11	5	28	10*	4·66	—	—	2	—
Bowley, E. H.	5	7	0	252	109	36·00	1	—	2	—
Bradley, W. M.	2	2	1	23	23*	23·00	—	—	—	—
Braund, L. C.	23	41	3	987	104	25·97	3	2	39	—
Brearley, W.	4	5	2	21	11*	7·00	—	—	—	—
Brennan, D. V.	2	2	0	16	16	8·00	—	—	—	—
Briggs, J.	33	50	5	815	121	18·11	1	2	12	—
Brockwell, W.	7	12	0	202	49	16·83	—	—	6	—
Brookes, D.	1	2	0	17	10	8·50	—	—	1	—
Brown, F. R.	22	30	1	734	79	25·31	—	5	22	—
Brown, G.	7	12	2	299	84	29·90	—	2	9	3
Brown, J. T.	8	16	3	470	140	36·15	1	1	7	—
Buckenham, C. P.	4	7	0	43	17	6·14	—	—	2	—
Butler, H. J.	2	2	1	15	15*	15·00	—	—	1	—
Butt, H. R.	3	4	1	22	13	7·33	—	—	1	1
Calthorpe, Hon. F. S. G.	4	7	0	129	49	18·42	—	—	2	—
Carr, A. W.	11	13	1	237	63	19·75	—	1	3	—
Carr, D. B.	2	4	0	135	76	33·75	—	1	—	—
Carr, D. W.	1	1	0	0	0	0·00	—	—	—	—
Chapman, A. P. F.	26	36	4	925	121	28·90	1	5	32	—
Charlwood, H.	2	4	0	63	36	15·75	—	—	—	—

	M.	I.	N.O.	Runs	H.S.	Avge.	100s	50s	Ct.	St.
Chatterton, W.	1	1	0	48	48	48·00	—	—	—	—
Christopherson, S.	1	1	0	17	17	17·00	—	—	—	—
Clark, E. W.	8	9	5	36	10	9·00	—	—	—	—
Clay, J. C.	1	—	—	—	—	—	—	—	1	—
Close, D. B.	6	9	0	164	42	18·22	—	—	7	—
Compton, D. C. S.	78	131	15	5807	278	50·06	17	28	49	—
Cook, C.	1	2	0	4	4	2·00	—	—	—	—
Copson, W. H.	3	1	0	6	6	6·00	—	—	1	—
Cornford, W. F.	4	4	0	36	18	9·00	—	—	5	3
Coventry, Hon. C. J.	2	2	1	13	12	13·00	—	—	—	—
Cowdrey, M. C.	49	80	4	3243	160	42·67	9	19	56	—
Coxon, A.	1	2	0	19	19	9·50	—	—	—	—
Cranston, J.	1	2	0	31	16	15·50	—	—	1	—
Cranston, K.	8	14	0	209	45	14·92	—	—	3	—
Crapp, J. F.	7	13	2	319	56	29·00	—	3	7	—
Crawford, J. N.	12	23	2	469	74	22·33	—	2	13	—
Cuttell, W. R.	2	4	0	65	21	16·25	—	—	2	—
Davenport, H. R. B.	4	6	0	128	84	21·33	—	1	1	—
Dawson, E. W.	5	9	0	175	55	19·44	—	1	—	—
Dean, H.	3	4	2	10	8	5·00	—	—	2	—
Denton, D.	11	22	1	424	104	20·19	1	1	8	—
Dewes, J. G.	5	10	0	121	67	12·10	—	1	—	—
Dexter, E. R.	17	28	1	1037	141	38·40	3	5	1	—
Dipper, A. E.	1	2	0	51	40	25·50	—	—	—	—
Doggart, G. H. G.	2	4	0	76	29	19·00	—	—	3	—
Dollery, H. E.	4	7	0	72	37	10·28	—	—	1	—
Dolphin, A.	1	2	0	1	1	0·50	—	—	1	—
Douglas, J. W. H. T.	23	35	2	962	119	29·15	1	6	9	—
Druce, N, F,	5	9	0	252	64	28·00	—	1	5	—
Ducat, A.	1	2	0	5	3	2·50	—	—	1	—
Duckworth, G.	24	28	12	234	39*	14·62	—	—	45	15
Duleepsinhji, K. S.	12	19	2	995	173	58·52	3	5	10	—
Durston, T. J.	1	2	1	8	6*	8·00	—	—	—	—
Edrich, W. J.	39	63	2	2440	219	40·00	6	13	39	—
Elliott, H.	4	5	1	61	37*	15·25	—	—	8	3
Emmett, G. M.	1	2	0	10	10	5·00	—	—	—	—
Emmett, T.	7	13	1	160	48	13·33	—	—	9	—
Evans, A. J.	1	2	0	18	14	9·00	—	—	—	—
Evans, T. G.	91	133	14	2439	104	20·49	2	8	173	46
Fagg, A. E.	5	8	0	150	39	18·75	—	—	5	—
Fane, F. L.	14	27	1	682	143	26·23	1	3	6	—
Farnes, K.	15	17	5	58	20	4·83	—	—	1	—
Farrimond, W. F.	4	7	0	116	35	16·57	—	—	6	2
Fender, P. G. H.	13	21	1	380	60	19·00	—	2	14	—
Ferris, J. J.	1	1	0	16	16	16·00	—	—	—	—
Fielder, A.	6	12	5	78	20	11·14	—	—	4	—
Fishlock, L. B.	4	5	1	47	19*	11·75	—	—	1	—
Flowers, W.	8	14	0	254	56	18·14	—	1	2	—
Ford, F. G. J.	5	9	0	168	48	18·66	—	—	5	—
Foster, F. R.	11	15	1	330	71	23·57	—	3	11	—
Foster, R. E.	8	14	1	602	287	46·30	1	1	13	—
Fothergill, A.J.	2	2	0	33	32	16·50	—	—	—	—
Freeman, A. P.	12	16	5	154	50*	14·00	—	1	4	—
Fry, C. B.	26	41	3	1223	144	32·18	2	7	17	—
Gay, L. H.	1	2	0	37	33	18·50	—	—	3	1
Geary, G.	14	20	4	249	66	15·56	—	2	13	—
Gibb, P. A.	8	13	0	581	120	44·69	2	3	3	1
Gilligan, A. E. R.	11	16	3	209	39*	16·07	—	—	3	—
Gilligan, A. H. H.	4	4	0	71	32	17·75	—	—	—	—
Gimblett, H.	3	5	1	129	67*	32·25	—	1	1	—
Gladwin, C.	8	11	5	170	51*	28·33	—	1	2	—
Goddard, T. W.	8	5	3	13	8	6·50	—	—	3	—
Gover, A. R.	4	1	1	2	2*	—	—	—	1	—
Grace, E. M.	1	2	0	36	36	18·00	—	—	1	—
Grace, G. F.	1	2	0	0	0	0·00	—	—	2	—
Grace, W. G.	22	36	2	1098	170	32·29	2	5	39	—
Graveney, T. W.	48	76	10	2590	258	39·24	4	11	44	—
Greenhough, T.	4	4	1	4	2	1·33	—	—	1	—
Greenwood, A.	2	4	0	77	49	19·25	—	—	2	—
Grieve, B. A. F.	2	3	2	40	14*	40·00	—	—	—	—
Griffith, S. C.	3	5	0	157	140	31·40	1	—	5	—

	M.	I.	N.O.	Runs	H.S.	Avge.	100s	50s	Ct.	St.
Gunn, G.	15	29	1	1120	122*	40·00	2	7	15	—
Gunn, J.	6	10	2	85	24	10·62	—	—	3	—
Gunn, W.	11	20	2	392	102*	21·77	1	1	5	—
Haig, N. E.	5	9	0	126	47	14·00	—	—	4	—
Haigh, S.	11	18	3	113	25	7·53	—	—	8	—
Hallows, C.	2	2	1	42	26	42·00	—	—	—	—
Hammond, W. R.	85	140	16	7249	336*	58·45	22	24	110	—
Hardinge, H. T. W.	1	2	0	30	25	15·00	—	—	—	—
Hardstaff, J. sen.	5	10	0	311	72	31·10	—	3	1	—
Hardstaff, J. jun.	23	38	3	1636	205*	46·74	4	10	9	—
Harris, Lord	4	6	1	145	52	29·00	—	1	2	—
Hartley, J. C.	2	4	0	15	9	3·75	—	—	2	—
Hawke, Lord	5	8	1	55	30	7·85	—	—	3	—
Hayes, E. G.	5	9	1	86	35	10·75	—	—	2	—
Hayward, T.	35	60	2	1999	137	34·45	3	12	19	—
Hearne, A.	1	1	0	9	9	9·00	—	—	1	—
Hearne, F.	2	2	0	47	27	23·50	—	—	1	—
Hearne, G. G.	1	1	0	0	0	0·00	—	—	—	—
Hearne, J. T.	12	18	4	126	40	9·00	—	—	4	—
Hearne, J. W.	24	36	5	806	114	26·00	1	2	13	—
Hendren, E.	51	83	9	3525	205*	47·63	7	21	33	—
Heseltine, C.	2	2	0	18	18	9·00	—	—	3	—
Hill, A.	2	4	2	101	49	50·50	—	—	1	—
Hill, A. J. L.	3	4	0	251	124	62·75	1	1	1	—
Hilton, M. J.	4	6	1	37	15	7·40	—	—	1	—
Hirst, G. H.	24	38	3	790	85	22·57	—	5	18	—
Hitch, J. W.	7	10	3	103	51*	14·71	—	1	4	—
Hobbs, J. B.	61	102	7	5410	211	56·94	15	28	17	—
Hollies, W. E.	13	15	8	37	18*	5·28	—	—	2	—
Holmes, E. R. T.	5	9	2	114	85*	16·28	—	1	3	—
Holmes, P.	7	14	1	357	88	27·36	—	4	3	—
Hone, L.	1	2	0	13	7	6·50	—	—	2	—
Hopwood, J. L.	2	3	1	12	8	6·00	—	—	—	—
Hornby, A. N.	3	6	0	21	9	3·50	—	—	—	—
Horton, M. J.	2	2	0	60	58	30·00	—	1	2	—
Howard, N. D.	4	6	1	86	23	17·20	—	—	4	—
Howell, H.	5	8	6	15	5	7·50	—	—	—	—
Howorth, R.	5	10	2	145	45*	18·12	—	—	2	—
Humphries, J.	3	6	1	44	16	8·80	—	—	7	—
Hunter, J.	5	7	2	93	39*	18·60	—	—	8	3
Hutchings, K. L.	7	12	0	341	126	28·41	1	1	9	—
Hutton, L.	79	138	15	6971	364	56·67	19	33	57	—
Iddon, J.	5	7	1	170	73	28·33	—	2	—	—
Ikin, J. T.	18	31	2	606	60	20·89	—	3	31	—
Illingworth, R.	12	18	5	294	50	22·61	—	1	7	—
Insole, D. J.	9	17	2	408	110*	27·20	1	1	8	—
Jackson, L.	1	1	1	7	7*	—	—	—	—	—
Jackson, Hon. F. S.	20	33	4	1415	144*	48·79	5	6	10	—
Jardine, D. R.	22	33	6	1296	127	48·00	1	10	26	—
Jenkins, R. O.	9	12	1	198	39	18·00	—	—	4	—
Jessop, G. L.	18	26	0	569	104	21·88	1	3	11	—
Jones, A. O.	12	21	0	291	34	13·85	—	—	15	—
Jupp, H.	2	4	0	68	63	17·00	—	1	2	—
Jupp, V. W. C.	8	13	1	208	38	17·33	—	—	5	—
Keeton, W. W.	2	4	0	57	25	14·25	—	—	—	—
Kennedy, A. S.	5	8	2	93	41*	15·50	—	—	5	—
Kenyon, D.	8	15	0	192	87	12·80	—	1	5	—
Killick, E. T.	2	4	0	81	31	20·25	—	—	2	—
Kilner, R.	9	8	1	233	74	33·28	—	2	6	—
King, J. H.	1	2	0	64	60	32·00	—	1	—	—
Kinneir, S. P.	1	2	0	52	30	26·00	—	—	—	—
Knight, A. E.	3	6	1	81	70*	16·20	—	1	1	—
Knight, D. J.	2	4	0	54	38	13·50	—	—	1	—
Knox, N. A.	2	4	1	24	8*	8·00	—	—	—	—
Laker, J. C.	46	63	15	676	63	14·08	—	2	12	—
Langridge, James	8	9	0	242	70	26·88	—	1	6	—
Larwood, H.	21	28	3	485	98	19·40	—	2	15	—
Leadbeater, E.	2	2	0	40	38	20·00	—	—	3	—
Lee, H. W.	1	2	0	19	18	9·50	—	—	—	—
Lees, W. S.	5	9	3	66	25*	11·00	—	—	2	—
Legge, G. B.	5	7	1	299	196	49·83	1	—	1	—

	M.	I.	N.O.	Runs	H.S.	Avge.	100s	50s	Ct.	St.
Leslie, C. F. H.	4	7	0	106	54	15·14	—	1	1	—
Leveson-Gower, H. D. G.	3	6	2	95	31	23·75	—	—	1	—
Levett, W. H. V.	1	2	1	7	5	7·00	—	—	3	—
Leyland, M.	41	65	5	2764	187	46·06	9	10	13	—
Lilley, A. A.	35	52	8	903	84	20·52	—	4	70	22
Lillywhite, James	2	3	1	16	10	8·00	—	—	1	—
Loader, P. J.	13	19	6	76	17	5·84	—	—	2	—
Lock, G. A. R.	31	39	6	375	25*	11·36	—	—	37	—
Lockwood, W. H.	12	16	3	231	52*	17·76	—	1	4	—
Lohmann, G. A.	18	26	2	213	62*	8·87	—	1	28	—
Lowson, F. A.	7	13	0	245	68	18·84	—	2	5	—
Lucas, A. P.	5	9	1	157	55	19·62	—	1	1	—
Lyttelton, Hon. A.	4	7	1	94	31	15·66	—	—	2	—
Macaulay, G. G.	8	10	4	112	76	18·66	—	1	5	—
MacBryan, J. C. W.	1	—	—	—	—	—	—	—	—	—
MacGregor, G.	8	11	3	96	31	12·00	—	—	14	2
Mackinnon, F. A.	1	2	0	5	5	2·50	—	—	—	—
MacLaren, A. C.	35	61	4	1931	140	33·87	5	8	29	—
Makepeace, H.	4	8	0	279	117	34·87	1	2	—	—
Mann, F. G.	7	12	2	376	136*	37·60	1	—	3	—
Mann, F. T.	5	9	1	281	84	35·12	—	2	4	—
Marriott, C. S.	1	1	0	0	0	0·00	—	—	1	—
Martin, F.	2	2	0	14	13	7·00	—	—	2	—
Martin, J. W.	1	2	0	26	26	13·00	—	—	—	—
Mason, J. R.	5	10	0	129	32	12·90	—	—	3	—
Matthews, A. D. G.	1	1	1	2	2*	—	—	—	1	—
May, P. B. H.	62	98	8	4265	285*	47·38	13	20	42	—
McConnon, J. E.	2	3	1	18	11	9·00	—	—	4	—
McGahey, C. P.	2	4	0	38	18	9·50	—	—	1	—
McIntyre, A. J.	3	6	0	19	7	3·16	—	—	8	—
McMaster, J. E. P.	1	1	0	0	0	0·00	—	—	—	—
Mead, C. P.	17	26	2	1185	182*	49·37	4	3	4	—
Mead, W.	1	2	0	7	7	3·50	—	—	1	—
Midwinter, W. E.	4	7	0	95	36	13·57	—	—	5	—
Miller, A. M.	1	2	2	24	20*	—	—	—	—	—
Milligan, F. W.	2	4	0	58	38	14·50	—	—	1	—
Milton. C. A.	6	9	1	204	104*	15·50	1	—	5	—
Mitchell, A.	6	10	0	298	72	29·80	—	2	9	—
Mitchell, F.	2	4	0	88	41	22·00	—	—	2	—
Mitchell, T. B.	5	6	2	20	9	5·00	—	—	1	—
Mitchell-Innes, N. S.	1	1	0	5	5	5·00	—	—	—	—
Mold, A.	3	3	1	0	0*	0·00	—	—	1	—
Moon, L. J.	4	8	0	182	36	22·75	—	—	4	—
Morley, F.	4	6	2	6	2*	1·50	—	—	4	—
Mortimore, J. B.	5	7	1	118	44*	19·66	—	—	—	—
Moss, A. E.	9	7	1	61	26	10·16	—	—	1	—
Murdoch, W. L.	1	1	0	12	12	12·00	—	—	—	1
Newham, W.	1	2	0	26	17	13·00	—	—	—	—
Nichols, M. S.	14	19	7	355	78*	29·58	—	2	12	—
Oakman, A. S. M.	2	2	0	14	10	7·00	—	—	7	—
O'Brien, T. C.	5	8	0	59	20	7·37	—	—	4	—
O'Connor, J.	4	7	0	153	51	21·85	—	1	2	—
Oldfield, N.	1	2	0	99	80	49·50	—	1	—	—
Padgett, D. E. V.	2	4	0	51	31	12·75	—	—	—	—
Paine, G. A. E.	4	7	1	97	49	16·16	—	—	5	—
Palairet, L. C. H.	2	4	0	49	20	12·25	—	—	2	—
Palmer, C. H.	1	2	0	22	22	11·00	—	—	—	—
Parker, C. W. L.	1	1	1	3	3*	—	—	—	—	—
Parkhouse, W. G. A.	7	13	0	373	78	28·69	—	2	3	—
Parkin, C. H.	10	16	3	160	36	12·30	—	—	3	—
Parks, J. H.	1	2	0	29	22	14·50	—	—	—	—
Parks, J. M.	7	11	1	313	101*	31·30	1	—	18	2
Pataudi, Nawab of	3	5	0	144	102	28·80	1	—	—	—
Paynter, E.	20	31	5	1540	243	59·23	4	7	7	—
Peate, E.	9	14	8	70	13	11·66	—	—	2	—
Peebles, I. A. R.	13	17	8	98	26	10·88	—	—	5	—
Peel, R.	20	33	4	427	83	14·72	—	3	17	—
Penn, F.	1	2	1	50	27*	50·00	—	—	—	—
Perks, R. T. D.	2	2	2	3	2*	—	—	—	1	—
Philipson, H.	5	8	1	63	30	9·00	—	—	8	3
Pilling, R.	8	13	1	91	23	7·58	—	—	10	4

	M.	I.	N.O.	Runs	H.S.	Avge.	100s	50s	Ct.	St.
Place, W.	3	6	1	144	107	28·80	1	—	—	—
Pollard, R.	4	3	2	13	10*	13·00	—	—	3	—
Poole, C. J.	3	5	1	161	69*	40·25	—	2	1	—
Pope, G. H.	1	1	1	8	8*	—	—	—	—	—
Pougher, A. D.	1	1	0	17	17	17·00	—	—	2	—
Price, W. F.	1	2	0	6	6	3·00	—	—	2	—
Pullar, G.	11	20	2	920	175	51·11	2	5	—	—
Quaife, W. G.	7	13	1	228	68	19·00	—	1	4	—
Ranjitsinhji, K. S.	15	26	4	989	175	44·95	2	6	13	—
Read, H. D.	1	—	—	—	—	—	—	—	—	—
Read, J. M.	17	29	2	463	57	17·14	—	2	8	—
Read, W. W.	18	27	1	720	117	27·69	1	5	16	—
Relf, A. E.	13	21	3	416	63	23·11	—	1	14	—
Rhodes, H. J.	2	1	1	0	0*	—	—	—	—	—
Rhodes, W.	58	98	21	2325	179	30·19	2	11	60	—
Richardson, D. W.	1	1	0	33	33	33·00	—	—	1	—
Richardson, P. E.	25	40	0	1623	126	40·57	5	7	1	—
Richardson, T.	14	24	8	177	25*	11·06	—	—	5	—
Richmond, T. L.	1	2	0	6	4	3·00	—	—	—	—
Ridgway, F.	5	6	0	49	24	8·16	—	—	3	—
Robertson, J. D.	11	21	2	881	133	46·36	2	6	6	—
Robins, R. W. V.	19	27	4	612	108	26·60	1	4	12	—
Root, C. F.	3	—	—	—	—	—	—	—	1	—
Royle, V. P. F. A.	1	2	0	21	18	10·50	—	—	2	—
Russell, A. C.	10	18	2	911	140	56·93	5	2	8	—
Sandham, A.	14	23	0	878	325	38·17	2	3	4	—
Schultz, S. S.	1	2	1	20	20	20·00	—	—	—	—
Scotton, W. H.	15	25	2	510	90	22·17	—	3	4	—
Selby, J.	6	12	1	256	70	23·27	—	2	1	—
Shackleton, D.	3	6	2	92	42	23·00	—	—	—	—
Sharp, J.	3	6	2	188	105	47·00	1	1	1	—
Sharpe, J. W.	3	6	4	44	26	22·00	—	—	2	—
Shaw, A.	7	12	1	111	40	10·09	—	—	4	—
Sheppard, D. S.	12	16	1	608	119	40·53	2	2	8	—
Sherwin, M.	3	6	4	30	21*	15·00	—	—	5	2
Shrewsbury, A.	23	40	4	1277	164	35·47	3	4	29	—
Shuter, J.	1	1	0	28	28	28·00	—	—	—	—
Simpson, R. T.	27	45	3	1401	156*	33·35	4	6	5	—
Simpson-Hayward, G. H.	5	8	1	105	29*	15·00	—	—	1	—
Sims, J. M.	4	4	0	16	12	4·00	—	—	6	—
Sinfield, R. A.	1	1	0	6	6	6·00	—	—	—	—
Smailes, T. F.	1	1	0	25	25	25·00	—	—	—	—
Smith, C. A.	1	1	0	3	3	3·00	—	—	—	—
Smith, C. I. J.	5	10	0	102	27	10·20	—	—	1	—
Smith, D.	2	4	0	128	57	32·00	—	1	1	—
Smith, D. V.	3	4	1	25	16*	8·33	—	—	—	—
Smith, E. J.	11	14	1	113	22	8·69	—	—	17	3
Smith, H.	1	1	0	7	7	7·00	—	—	1	—
Smith, M. J. K.	14	22	0	764	108	34·72	2	4	11	—
Smith, T. P. B.	4	5	0	33	24	6·60	—	—	1	—
Smithson, G. A.	2	3	0	70	35	23·33	—	—	—	—
Southerton, J.	2	3	1	7	6	3·50	—	—	2	—
Spooner, R. H.	10	15	0	481	119	32·06	1	4	4	—
Spooner, R. T.	7	14	1	354	92	27·23	—	3	10	2
Stanyforth, R. T.	4	6	1	13	6*	2·60	—	—	7	2
Staples, S. J.	3	5	0	65	39	13·00	—	—	—	—
Statham, J. B.	55	68	21	532	38	11·31	—	—	21	—
Steel, A. G.	13	20	3	600	148	35·29	2	—	5	—
Stevens, G. T. S.	10	17	0	263	69	15·47	—	1	9	—
Stoddart, A. E.	16	30	2	996	173	35·57	2	3	6	—
Storer, W.	6	11	0	215	51	19·54	—	1	11	—
Street, G.	1	2	1	11	7*	11·00	—	—	—	1
Strudwick, H.	28	42	13	230	24	7·93	—	—	60	12
Studd, C. T.	5	9	1	160	48	20·00	—	—	5	—
Studd, G. B.	4	7	0	31	9	4·42	—	—	8	—
Subba Row, R.	8	12	1	516	100	46·90	1	3	3	—
Sugg, F. H.	2	2	0	55	31	27·50	—	—	—	—
Sutcliffe, H.	54	84	9	4555	194	60·73	16	23	23	—
Swetman, R.	11	17	2	254	65	16·93	—	1	24	2
Tate, F. W.	1	2	1	9	5*	9·00	—	—	2	—
Tate, M. W.	39	52	5	1198	100*	25·48	1	5	11	—

	M.	I.	N.O.	Runs	H.S.	Avge.	100s	50s	Ct.	St.
Tattersall, R.	16	17	7	50	10*	5·00	—	—	8	—
Taylor, K.	2	3	0	33	24	11·00	—	—	1	—
Tennyson, Hon. L. H.	9	12	1	345	74*	31·36	—	4	6	—
Thompson, G. J.	6	10	1	273	63	30·33	—	2	5	—
Titmus, F. J.	2	4	0	39	19	9·75	—	—	2	—
Townsend, C. L.	2	3	0	51	38	17·00	—	—	—	—
Townsend, D. C. H.	3	6	0	77	36	12·83	—	—	1	—
Townsend, L. F.	4	6	0	97	40	16·16	—	—	1	—
Tremlett, M. F.	3	5	2	20	18*	6·66	—	—	—	—
Trott, A. E.	2	4	0	23	16	5·75	—	—	—	—
Trueman, F. S.	41	50	12	586	39*	15·42	—	—	42	—
Tufnell, N. C.	1	1	0	14	14	14·00	—	—	—	1
Turnbull, M. J.	9	13	2	224	61	20·36	—	1	1	—
Tyldesley, E.	14	20	2	990	122	55·00	3	6	2	—
Tyldesley, J. T.	31	55	1	1661	138	30·75	4	9	16	—
Tyldesley, R.	7	7	1	47	29	7·83	—	—	1	—
Tylecote, E. F. S.	6	9	1	152	66	19·00	—	1	5	5
Tyler, E. J.	1	1	0	0	0	0·00	—	—	—	—
Tyson, F. H.	17	24	3	230	37*	10·95	—	—	4	—
Ulyett, G.	25	39	0	949	149	24·33	1	7	19	—
Valentine, B. H.	7	9	2	454	136	64·85	2	1	2	—
Verity, H.	40	44	12	669	66*	20·90	—	3	30	—
Vernon, G. F.	1	2	1	14	11*	14·00	—	—	—	—
Vine, J.	2	3	2	46	36	46·00	—	—	—	—
Voce, W.	27	38	15	308	66	13·39	—	1	16	—
Waddington, A.	2	4	0	16	7	4·00	—	—	1	—
Wainwright, E.	5	9	0	132	49	14·66	—	—	2	—
Walker, P. M.	3	4	0	128	52	32·00	—	1	5	—
Walters, C. F.	11	18	3	784	102	52·26	1	7	6	—
Ward, A.	7	13	0	487	117	37·46	1	3	1	—
Wardle, J. H.	28	41	8	653	66	19·78	—	2	12	—
Warner, P. F.	15	28	2	622	132*	23·92	1	3	3	—
Warr, J. J.	2	4	0	4	4	1·00	—	—	—	—
Warren, A. R.	1	1	0	7	7	7·00	—	—	1	—
Washbrook, C.	37	66	6	2569	195	42·81	6	12	12	—
Watkins, A. J.	15	24	4	811	138*	40·55	2	4	17	—
Watson, W.	23	37	3	879	116	25·85	2	3	8	—
Webbe, A. J.	1	2	0	4	4	2·00	—	—	2	—
Wellard, A. W.	2	4	0	47	38	11·75	—	—	2	—
Wharton, A.	1	2	0	20	13	10·00	—	—	—	—
White, J. C.	15	22	9	239	29	18·38	—	—	6	—
Whysall, W. W.	4	7	0	209	76	29·85	—	2	7	—
Wilkinson, L. L.	3	2	1	3	2	3·00	—	—	—	—
Wilson, C. E. M.	2	4	1	42	18	14·00	—	—	—	—
Wilson, E. R.	1	2	0	10	5	5·00	—	—	—	—
Wood, A.	4	5	1	80	53	20·00	—	1	10	1
Wood, G. E. C.	3	2	0	7	6	3·50	—	—	5	1
Wood, H.	4	4	1	204	134*	68·00	1	1	2	1
Wood, R.	1	2	0	6	6	3·00	—	—	—	—
Woods, S. M. J.	3	4	0	122	53	30·50	—	1	4	—
Woolley, F. E.	64	98	7	3283	154	36·07	5	23	64	—
Worthington, T. S.	9	11	0	321	128	29·18	1	1	8	—
Wright, C. W.	3	4	0	125	71	31·25	—	1	—	—
Wright, D. V. P.	34	39	13	289	45	11·11	—	—	10	—
Wyatt, R. E. S.	40	64	6	1839	149	31·70	2	12	17	—
Wynyard, E. G.	3	6	0	72	30	12·00	—	—	—	—
Yardley, N. W. D.	20	34	2	812	99	25·37	—	4	14	—
Young, H.	2	2	0	43	43	21·50	—	—	1	—
Young, J. A.	8	10	5	28	10*	5·60	—	—	5	—
Young, R. A.	2	4	0	27	13	6·75	—	—	6	—
Extras, etc.	—	—	—	7795	—	—	—	—	37	1
Total	4048	6256	819	168010	364	30·90	295	714	3024	172

AUSTRALIA

	M.	I.	N.O.	Runs	H.S.	Avge.	100s	50s	Ct.	St.
a'Beckett, E. L.	4	7	0	143	41	20·42	—	—	4	—
Alexander, G.	2	4	0	52	33	13·00	—	—	2	—
Alexander, H. H.	1	2	1	17	17*	17·00	—	—	—	—
Allan, F. E.	1	1	0	5	5	5·00	—	—	—	—
Allen, R.	1	2	0	44	30	22·00	—	—	2	—

	M.	I.	N.O.	Runs	H.S.	Avge.	100s	50s	Ct.	St.
Andrews, T. J. E.	16	23	1	592	94	26·90	—	4	12	—
Archer, K. M.	5	9	0	234	48	26·00	—	—	—	—
Archer, R. G.	19	30	1	713	128	24·58	1	2	20	—
Armstrong, W. W.	50	84	10	2863	159*	38·68	6	8	44	—
Badcock, C. L.	7	12	1	160	118	14·54	1	—	3	—
Bannerman, A. C.	28	50	2	1108	94	23·08	—	8	21	—
Bannerman, C.	3	6	2	239	165*	59·75	1	—	—	—
Bardsley, W.	41	66	5	2469	193*	40·47	6	14	12	—
Barnes, S. G.	13	19	2	1072	234*	63·05	3	5	14	—
Barnett, B. A.	4	8	1	195	57	27·85	—	1	3	2
Barrett, J. E.	2	4	1	80	67*	26·66	—	1	1	—
Benaud, R.	45	68	6	1504	122	24·25	3	4	43	—
Blackham, J. McC.	35	62	11	800	74	15·68	—	4	36	24
Blackie, D. D. J.	3	6	3	24	11*	8·00	—	—	2	—
Bonnor, G. J.	17	30	0	512	128	17·06	1	2	16	—
Boyle, H. F.	12	16	4	153	36*	12·75	—	—	10	—
Bradman, D. G.	52	80	10	6996	334	99·94	29	13	32	—
Bromley, E. H.	2	4	0	38	26	9·50	—	—	2	—
Brown, W. A.	22	35	1	1592	206*	46·82	4	9	14	—
Bruce, W.	14	26	2	702	80	29·25	—	5	12	—
Burn, K. E.	2	4	0	41	19	10·25	—	—	—	—
Burge, P.	14	20	2	454	83	25·22	—	3	10	—
Burke, J. W.	24	44	7	1280	189	34·59	3	5	18	—
Burton, F. J.	2	4	2	4	2*	2·00	—	—	1	1
Callaway, S. T.	3	6	1	87	41	17·40	—	—	—	—
Carkeek, W.	6	5	2	16	6*	5·33	—	—	6	—
Carter, H.	28	47	9	873	72	22·97	—	4	44	21
Charlton, P. C.	2	4	0	29	11	7·25	—	—	—	—
Chipperfield, A. G.	14	20	3	552	109	32·47	1	2	15	—
Collins, H. L.	19	31	1	1352	203	45·06	4	6	13	—
Coningham, A.	1	2	0	13	10	6·50	—	—	—	—
Cooper, B. B.	1	2	0	18	15	9·00	—	—	2	—
Cooper, W. H.	2	3	1	13	7	6·50	—	—	1	—
Cottam, W. J.	1	2	0	4	3	2·00	—	—	1	—
Cotter, A.	21	37	2	457	45	13·05	—	—	8	—
Coulthard, G.	1	1	1	6	6*	—	—	—	—	—
Craig, I. D.	11	18	0	358	53	19·88	—	2	2	—
Crawford, P.	4	5	2	53	34	17·66	—	—	1	—
Darling, J.	34	60	2	1657	178	28·56	3	8	27	—
Darling, L. S.	12	18	1	474	85	27·88	—	3	8	—
Davidson, A. K.	30	39	4	807	76	23·05	—	3	32	—
de Courcy, J. H.	3	6	1	81	41	16·20	—	—	3	—
Donnan, H.	5	10	1	75	15	8·33	—	—	1	—
Dooland, B.	3	5	1	76	29	19·00	—	—	3	—
Duff, R. A.	22	40	3	1316	146	35·56	2	6	14	—
Eady, C. J.	2	4	1	20	10*	6·66	—	—	2	—
Ebeling, H. I.	1	2	0	43	41	21·50	—	—	—	—
Edwards, J. D.	3	6	1	48	26	9·60	—	—	1	—
Emery, S. H.	4	2	0	6	5	3·00	—	—	2	—
Evans, E.	6	10	2	82	33	10·25	—	—	5	—
Fairfax, A. G.	10	12	4	410	65	51·25	—	4	15	—
Favell, L.	15	23	2	608	101	28·95	1	4	8	—
Ferris, J. J.	8	16	4	98	20*	8·16	—	—	4	—
Fingleton, J. H.	18	29	1	1189	136	42·46	5	3	13	—
Fleetwood-Smith, L. O'B.	10	11	5	54	16*	9·00	—	—	—	—
Freer, F. W.	1	1	1	28	28*	—	—	—	—	—
Garrett, T. W.	19	33	6	339	51*	12·55	—	1	7	—
Gaunt, R. A.	1	1	1	0	0*	—	—	—	—	—
Gehrs, D. R. A.	6	11	0	221	67	20·09	—	2	6	—
Giffen, G.	31	53	0	1238	161	23·35	1	6	24	—
Giffen, W. F.	3	6	0	11	3	1·83	—	—	1	—
Graham, H.	6	10	0	301	107	30·10	2	—	3	—
Gregory, D. W.	3	5	2	60	43	20·00	—	—	—	—
Gregory, E. J.	1	2	0	11	11	5·50	—	—	1	—
Gregory, J. M.	24	34	3	1146	119	36·96	2	7	37	—
Gregory, R. G.	2	3	0	153	80	51·00	—	2	1	—
Gregory, S. E.	58	100	7	2282	201	24·53	4	8	25	—
Grimmett, C. V.	37	50	10	557	50	13·92	—	1	17	—
Groube, T. U.	1	2	0	11	11	5·50	—	—	—	—
Grout, A. W.	17	21	4	457	74	26·88	—	3	52	13
Hamence, R. A.	3	4	1	81	30*	27·00	—	—	1	—

	M.	I.	N.O.	Runs	H.S.	Avge.	100s	50s	Ct.	St.
Harry, J.	1	2	0	8	6	4·00	—	—	1	—
Hartigan, R. J.	2	4	0	170	116	42·50	1	—	1	—
Hartkopf, A. E. V.	1	2	0	80	80	40·00	—	1	—	—
Harvey, M.	1	2	0	43	31	21·50	—	—	—	—
Harvey, R. N.	65	111	10	5273	205	52·20	19	19	48	—
Hassett, A. L.	43	69	3	3073	198*	46·56	10	11	30	—
Hazlitt, G. R.	9	12	4	89	34*	11·12	—	—	4	—
Hendry, H. L.	11	18	2	335	112	20·93	1	—	10	—
Hill, C.	49	89	2	3412	191	39·21	7	19	33	—
Hill, J. C.	3	6	3	21	8*	7·00	—	—	2	—
Hodges, J.	2	4	1	10	8	3·33	—	—	—	—
Hole, G. B.	18	33	2	789	66	25·45	—	6	21	—
Hopkins, A. J.	20	33	2	509	43	16·42	—	—	11	—
Horan, T.	15	27	2	471	124	18·84	1	1	6	—
Hordern, H. V.	7	13	2	254	50	23·09	—	1	6	—
Hornibrook, P. M.	6	7	1	60	26	10·00	—	—	7	—
Howell, W. P.	18	27	6	158	35	7·52	—	—	12	—
Hunt, W. A.	1	1	0	0	0	0·00	—	—	1	—
Hurwood, A.	2	2	0	5	5	2·50	—	—	2	—
Iredale, F. A.	14	23	1	807	140	36·68	2	4	16	—
Ironmonger, H.	14	21	5	42	12	2·62	—	—	3	—
Iverson, J.	5	7	3	3	1*	0·75	—	—	2	—
Jackson, A. A.	8	11	1	474	164	47·40	1	2	7	—
Jarman, B.	1	2	0	1	1	0·50	—	—	2	—
Jarvis, A. H.	11	21	3	303	82	16·83	—	1	9	8
Jennings, C. B.	6	8	2	107	32	17·83	—	—	5	—
Johnson, I. W.	45	66	12	1000	77	18·51	—	6	30	—
Johnson, L.	1	1	1	25	25*	—	—	—	2	—
Johnston, W. A.	40	49	25	273	29	11·37	—	—	16	—
Jones, E.	19	26	1	126	20	5·04	—	—	21	—
Jones, S. P.	12	24	4	432	87	21·60	—	1	12	—
Kelleway, C.	26	42	4	1422	147	37·42	3	6	24	—
Kelly, J. J.	36	56	17	664	46*	17·02	—	—	43	20
Kelly, T. J. D.	2	3	0	64	35	21·33	—	—	1	—
Kendall, T.	2	4	1	39	17*	13·00	—	—	2	—
Kippax, A. F.	22	34	1	1192	146	36·12	2	8	13	—
Kline, L.	11	12	5	40	14	5·71	—	—	8	—
Langley, G. R.	26	37	12	374	53	14·96	—	1	83	15
Laver, F.	15	23	6	196	45	11·52	—	—	8	—
Lee, P. K.	2	3	0	57	42	19·00	—	—	1	—
Lindwall, R. R.	61	84	13	1502	118	21·15	2	5	26	—
Love, H. S. B.	1	2	0	8	5	4·00	—	—	3	—
Loxton, S. J. E.	12	15	0	554	101	36·93	1	3	7	—
Lyons, J. J.	14	27	0	731	134	27·07	1	3	3	—
Macartney, C. G.	35	55	4	2131	170	41·78	7	9	17	—
Mackay, K.	24	31	4	912	89	33·77	—	8	12	—
Maddocks, L.	7	12	2	177	69	17·70	—	1	18	1
Mailey, A. A.	21	29	9	222	46*	11·10	—	—	14	—
Marr, A. P.	1	2	0	5	5	2·50	—	—	—	—
Massie, H. H.	9	16	0	249	55	15·56	—	1	5	—
Matthews, T. J.	8	10	1	153	53	17·00	—	1	7	—
Mayne, E. R.	4	4	1	64	25*	21·33	—	—	2	—
McAlister, P. A.	8	16	1	252	41	16·80	—	—	10	—
McCabe, S. J.	39	62	5	2748	232	48·21	6	13	42	—
McCool, C. L.	14	17	4	459	104*	35·30	1	1	14	—
McCormick, E. L.	12	14	5	54	17*	6·00	—	—	8	—
McDonald, C. C.	39	68	4	2674	170	41·78	5	13	12	—
McDonald, E. A.	11	12	5	116	36	16·57	—	—	3	—
McDonnell, P. S.	19	34	1	950	147	28·78	3	2	6	—
McIlwraith, J.	1	2	0	9	7	4·50	—	—	1	—
McKibbin, T. R.	5	8	2	88	28*	14·66	—	—	4	—
McLaren, J. W.	1	2	2	0	0*	—	—	—	—	—
McLeod, C. E.	17	29	5	573	112	23·87	1	4	9	—
McLeod, R. W.	6	11	0	146	31	13·27	—	—	3	—
McShane, P. G.	3	6	1	26	12*	5·20	—	—	2	—
Meckiff, I.	15	15	5	135	45*	13·50	—	—	7	—
Meuleman, K.	1	1	0	0	0	0·00	—	—	1	—
Midwinter, W. E.	8	14	1	174	37	13·38	—	—	5	—
Miller, K. R.	55	87	7	2958	147	36·97	7	13	38	—
Minnett, R. B.	9	15	0	391	90	26·06	—	3	—	—
Moroney, J. A. R.	7	12	1	383	118	34·81	2	1	—	—

	M.	I.	N.O.	Runs	H.S.	Avge.	100s	50s	Ct.	St.
Morris, A. R.	46	79	3	3533	206	46·48	12	12	15	—
Morris, S.	1	2	1	14	10*	14·00	—	—	—	—
Moses, H.	6	10	0	198	33	19·80	—	—	1	—
Moule, W. H.	1	2	0	40	34	20·00	—	—	1	—
Murdoch, W. L.	18	33	5	896	211	32·00	2	1	12	1
Musgrove, H.	1	2	0	13	9	6·50	—	—	—	—
Nagel, L. E.	1	2	1	21	21*	21·00	—	—	—	—
Nash, L. J.	2	2	0	30	17	15·00	—	—	6	—
Nitschke, H. C.	2	2	0	53	47	26·50	—	—	3	—
Noble, M. A.	42	73	7	1997	133	30·25	1	16	26	—
Noblet, G. J.	3	4	1	22	13*	7·33	—	—	1	—
Nothling, O. E.	1	2	0	52	44	26·00	—	—	—	—
O'Brien, L. P.	5	8	0	211	61	26·37	—	2	3	—
O'Connor, J. A.	4	8	1	86	20	12·28	—	—	3	—
Oldfield, W. A.	54	80	17	1427	65*	22·65	—	4	78	52
O'Neill, N.	13	19	5	876	163	62·57	3	3	6	—
O'Reilly, W. J.	27	39	7	410	56*	12·81	—	1	7	—
Oxenham, R. K.	7	10	0	151	48	15·10	—	—	4	—
Palmer, G. E.	17	25	4	296	48	14·09	—	—	13	—
Park, R. L.	1	1	0	0	0	0·00	—	—	—	—
Pellew, C. E.	10	14	1	484	116	37·23	2	1	4	—
Ponsford, W. H.	29	48	4	2122	226	48·22	7	6	21	—
Pope, R. J.	1	2	0	3	3	1·50	—	—	—	—
Ransford, V. S.	20	38	6	1211	143*	37·84	1	7	10	—
Reedman, J. C.	1	2	0	21	17	10·50	—	—	1	—
Richardson, A. J.	9	13	0	403	100	31·00	1	2	1	—
Richardson, V. Y.	19	30	0	706	138	23·53	1	1	24	—
Rigg, K. E.	8	12	0	401	127	33·41	1	1	5	—
Ring, D. T.	13	21	2	426	67	22·42	—	4	5	—
Robertson, W. R.	1	2	0	2	2	1·00	—	—	—	—
Robinson, R. H.	1	2	0	5	3	2·50	—	—	1	—
Rorke, G.	4	4	2	9	7	4·50	—	—	1	—
Rutherford, J.	1	1	0	30	30	30·00	—	—	—	—
Ryder, J.	20	32	5	1394	201*	51·62	3	9	17	—
Saggers, R. A.	6	5	2	30	14	10·00	—	—	16	8
Saunders, J. V.	14	23	6	39	11*	2·29	—	—	5	—
Scott, H. J. H.	8	14	1	359	102	27·61	1	1	8	—
Sievers, M. W.	3	6	1	67	25*	13·40	—	—	4	—
Simpson, R.	6	8	1	136	60	19·42	—	1	13	—
Slater, K.	1	1	1	1	1*	—	—	—	—	—
Slight, J.	1	2	0	11	11	5·50	—	—	—	—
Smith, D.	2	3	1	30	24*	15·00	—	—	—	—
Spofforth, F. R.	18	29	6	217	50	9·43	—	1	11	—
Stevens, G.	4	7	0	112	28	16·00	—	—	2	—
Tallon, D.	21	26	3	394	92	17·13	—	2	50	8
Taylor, J. M.	20	28	0	997	108	35·60	1	8	11	—
Thompson, N.	2	4	0	67	41	16·75	—	—	3	—
Thoms, G.	1	2	0	44	28	22·00	—	—	—	—
Thurlow, H. M.	1	1	0	0	0	0·00	—	—	—	—
Toshack, E. R. H.	12	11	6	73	20*	14·60	—	—	4	—
Travers, J.	1	2	0	10	9	5·00	—	—	1	—
Tribe, G.	3	3	1	35	25*	17·50	—	—	—	—
Trott, A. E.	3	5	3	205	85*	102·50	—	2	4	—
Trott, G. H. S.	24	42	0	921	143	21·92	1	4	21	—
Trumble, H.	32	57	14	851	70	19·79	—	4	45	—
Trumble, J. W.	7	13	1	243	59	20·25	—	1	3	—
Trumper, V. T.	48	89	8	3164	214*	39·06	8	13	31	—
Turner, C. T. B.	17	32	4	323	29	11·53	—	—	8	—
Waite, M. G.	2	3	0	11	8	3·66	—	—	1	—
Wall, T. W.	18	24	5	121	20	6·36	—	—	11	—
Walters, F. H.	1	2	0	12	7	6·00	—	—	2	—
Ward, F. A.	4	8	2	36	18	6·00	—	—	1	—
Watson, W.	4	7	1	106	30	17·66	—	—	2	—
Whitty, W. J.	14	19	7	161	39*	13·41	—	—	4	—
Wilson, J.	1	—	—	—	—	—	—	—	—	—
Woodfull, W. M.	35	54	4	2300	161	46·00	7	13	7	—
Woods, S. M. J.	3	6	0	32	18	5·33	—	—	1	—
Worrall, J.	11	22	3	478	76	25·15	—	5	13	—
Extras, etc.				4804					32	
Total	2750	4367	545	117035	334	30·62	218	456	2105	174

SOUTH AFRICA

	M.	I.	N.O.	Runs	H.S.	Avge.	100s	50s	Ct.	St.
Adcock, N. A. T.	24	36	12	100	17	4·16	—	—	3	—
Anderson, J. H.	1	2	0	43	32	21·50	—	—	1	—
Ashley, W. H.	1	2	0	1	1	0·50	—	—	—	—
Balaskas, X. C.	9	13	1	174	122*	14·50	1	—	5	—
Baumgartner, H. V.	1	2	0	19	16	9·50	—	—	1	—
Beaumont, R.	5	9	0	70	31	7·77	—	—	2	—
Begbie, D. W.	5	7	0	138	48	19·71	—	—	2	—
Bell, A. J.	16	23	12	69	26*	6·27	—	—	6	—
Bisset, M.	3	6	2	103	35	25·75	—	—	2	1
Bissett, G. F.	4	4	2	38	23	19·00	—	—	—	—
Blanckenberg, J. M.	18	30	6	455	59	18·95	—	2	9	—
Bock, G. E.	1	2	2	11	9*	—	—	—	—	—
Bond, G. E.	1	1	0	0	0	0·00	—	—	—	—
Brann, W. H.	3	5	0	71	50	14·20	—	1	2	—
Briscoe, A. W.	2	3	0	33	16	11·00	—	—	1	—
Brown, L. S.	2	3	0	17	8	5·66	—	—	—	—
Burger, C. G.	2	4	1	62	37*	20·66	—	—	1	—
Buys, I. D.	1	2	1	4	4*	4·00	—	—	—	—
Cameron, H. B.	26	45	4	1239	90	30·21	—	10	39	12
Campbell, T.	5	9	3	90	48	15·00	—	—	7	1
Carlstein, P. R.	6	11	0	152	42	13·81	—	—	2	—
Carter, C. P.	10	15	5	181	45	18·10	—	—	2	—
Catterall, R. H.	24	43	2	1555	120	37·92	3	11	12	—
Chapman, H. W.	2	4	1	39	17	13·00	—	—	1	—
Cheetham, J. E.	24	43	6	883	89	23·86	—	5	13	—
Christy, J. A. J.	10	18	0	618	103	34·33	1	5	3	—
Chubb, G. W. A.	5	9	3	63	15*	10·50	—	—	—	—
Cochran, J. A. K.	1	1	0	4	4	4·00	—	—	—	—
Coen, S. K.	2	4	2	101	41*	50·50	—	—	1	—
Commaille, J. M. M.	12	22	1	355	47	16·90	—	—	1	—
Conyngham, D. P.	1	2	2	6	3*	—	—	—	1	—
Cook, F. J.	1	2	0	7	7	3·50	—	—	—	—
Cooper, A. H. C.	1	2	0	6	6	3·00	—	—	1	—
Cox, J. L.	3	6	2	17	12*	4·25	—	—	1	—
Cripps, G.	1	2	0	21	18	10·50	—	—	—	—
Crisp, R. J.	9	13	1	123	35	10·25	—	—	3	—
Curnow, S. H.	7	14	0	168	47	12·00	—	—	5	—
Dalton, E. L.	15	24	2	698	117	31·72	2	3	5	—
Davies, E. Q.	5	8	3	9	3	1·80	—	—	—	—
Dawson, O. C.	9	15	1	293	55	20·92	—	1	10	—
Deane, H. G.	17	27	2	628	93	25·12	—	3	8	—
Dixon, C. D.	1	2	0	0	0	0·00	—	—	1	—
Dower, R. R.	1	2	0	9	9	4·50	—	—	2	—
Draper, R. G.	2	3	0	25	15	8·33	—	—	—	—
Duckworth, C. A. R.	2	4	0	28	13	7·00	—	—	3	—
Duminy, J. P.	3	6	0	30	12	5·00	—	—	2	—
Dunell, O. R.	2	4	1	42	26*	14·00	—	—	1	—
Du Toit, J. F.	1	2	2	2	2*	—	—	—	1	—
Dyer, D. V.	3	6	0	96	62	16·00	—	1	—	—
Endean, W. R.	28	52	4	1630	162*	33·95	3	8	41	—
Faulkner, G. A.	25	47	4	1754	204	40·79	4	8	20	—
Fellows-Smith, J. P.	4	8	2	166	35	27·66	—	—	2	—
Fichardt, C. G.	2	4	0	15	10	3·75	—	—	2	—
Finlason, C. E.	1	2	0	6	6	3·00	—	—	—	—
Floquet, C. E.	1	2	1	12	11*	12·00	—	—	—	—
Francis, H. H.	2	4	0	39	29	9·75	—	—	1	—
Francois, C. M.	5	9	1	252	72	31·50	—	1	5	—
Frank, C. N.	3	6	0	236	152	39·33	1	—	—	—
Frank, W. H. B.	1	2	0	7	5	3·50	—	—	—	—
Fuller, E. R. H.	7	9	1	64	17	8·00	—	—	3	—
Fullerton, G. M.	7	13	0	325	88	25·00	—	3	10	2
Funston, K. J.	18	33	1	824	92	25·75	—	5	7	—
Gleeson, R. A.	1	2	1	4	3	4·00	—	—	2	—
Glover, C. K.	1	2	1	21	18*	21·00	—	—	—	—
Goddard, T. L.	20	39	2	1072	99	28·97	—	7	29	—
Gordon, N.	5	6	2	8	7*	2·00	—	—	1	—
Graham, R.	2	4	0	6	4	1·50	—	—	2	—
Grieveson, R. E.	2	2	0	114	75	57·00	—	1	8	2
Griffin, G.	2	4	0	25	14	6·25	—	—	—	—

	M.	I.	N.O.	Runs	H.S.	Avge.	100s	50s	Ct.	St.
Hall, A. E.	7	8	2	11	5	1·83	—	—	4	—
Halliwell, E. A.	8	15	0	188	57	12·55	—	1	9	2
Hands, P. A. M.	7	12	0	300	83	25·00	—	2	3	—
Hands, R. II. M.	1	2	0	7	7	3·50	—	—	—	—
Hanley, M. A.	1	1	0	0	0	0·00	—	—	—	—
Harris, T. A.	3	5	1	100	60	25·00	—	1	1	—
Hartigan, G. P. D.	5	10	0	114	51	11·40	—	1	—	—
Harvey, R. L.	2	4	0	51	28	12·75	—	—	—	—
Hathorn, M.	12	20	1	325	102	17·10	1	—	5	—
Hearne, F.	4	8	0	121	30	15·12	—	—	2	—
Hearne, G. A. L.	3	5	0	59	28	11·80	—	—	3	—
Heine, P. S.	13	23	3	178	24	8·90	—	—	8	—
Hime, C. F. W.	1	2	0	8	8	4·00	—	—	—	—
Hutchinson, P.	2	4	0	14	11	3·50	—	—	3	—
Innes, A. R.	2	4	0	14	13	3·50	—	—	2	—
Ironside, D. E. J.	3	4	2	37	13	18·50	—	—	1	—
Johnson, C. L.	1	2	0	10	7	5·00	—	—	1	—
Jones, P. S. T.	1	2	0	0	0	0·00	—	—	—	—
Keith, H. J.	8	16	1	318	73	21·20	—	2	9	—
Kempis, G. A.	1	2	1	0	0*	0·00	—	—	—	—
Kotze, J. J.	3	5	0	2	2	0·40	—	—	3	—
Kuys, F.	1	2	0	26	26	13·00	—	—	—	—
Langton, A. B. C.	15	23	4	298	73*	15·68	—	2	8	—
Le Roux, F. L.	1	2	0	1	1	0·50	—	—	—	—
Lewis, P. T.	1	2	0	0	0	0·00	—	—	—	—
Lindsay, J. D.	3	5	2	21	9*	7·00	—	—	4	1
Lindsay, N. V.	1	2	0	35	29	17·50	—	—	1	—
Ling, W. V. S.	6	10	0	168	38	16·80	—	—	1	—
Llewellyn, C. B.	15	28	1	544	90	20·14	—	4	7	—
Lundie, E. B.	1	2	1	1	1	1·00	—	—	—	—
Mann, N. B. F.	19	31	1	400	52	13·33	—	1	3	—
Mansell, P. N. F.	13	22	2	355	90	17·75	—	2	15	—
Markham, L. A.	1	1	0	20	20	20 00	—	—	—	—
Marx, W. F. E.	3	6	0	125	36	20·83	—	—	—	—
McCarthy, C. N.	15	24	15	28	5	3·11	—	—	6	—
McGlew, D. J.	29	55	4	2014	255*	39·49	5	9	15	—
McKinnon, A. H.	1	1	0	22	22	22·00	—	—	—	—
McLean, R. A.	33	60	3	1689	142	29·63	4	8	19	—
McMillan, Q.	13	21	4	306	50*	18·00	—	1	8	—
Meintjes, D. J.	2	3	0	43	21	14·33	—	—	3	—
Melle, M. G.	7	12	4	68	17	8·50	—	—	4	—
Melville, A.	11	19	2	894	189	52·58	4	3	8	—
Middleton, J.	6	12	5	52	22	7·42	—	—	1	—
Mills, C.	1	2	0	25	21	12·50	—	—	2	—
Milton, W. H.	3	6	0	68	21	11·33	—	—	1	—
Mitchell, B.	42	80	9	3471	189*	48·88	8	21	56	—
Mitchell, F.	3	6	0	28	12	4·66	—	—	—	—
Morkel, D. P. B.	16	28	1	663	88	24·55	—	4	13	—
Murray, A. R. A.	10	14	1	289	109	22·23	1	1	3	—
Nel, J. D.	6	11	0	150	38	13·63	—	—	1	—
Newberry, C.	4	8	0	62	16	7·75	—	—	3	—
Newson, E. S.	3	5	1	30	16	7·50	—	—	3	—
Nicholson, F.	4	8	1	76	29	10·85	—	—	3	—
Nicolson, J. F. W.	3	5	0	179	78	35·80	—	1	—	—
Norton, N. O.	1	2	0	9	7	4·50	—	—	—	—
Nourse, A. D. sen.	45	83	8	2234	111	29·78	1	15	43	—
Nourse, A. D. jun.	34	62	7	2960	231	53·81	9	14	12	—
Nupen, E. P.	17	31	7	348	69	14·50	—	2	9	—
Ochse, A. E.	2	4	0	16	8	4·00	—	—	1	—
Ochse, A. L.	3	4	1	11	4*	3·66	—	—	1	—
O'Linn, S.	5	8	0	261	98	32·62	—	2	3	—
Owen-Smith, H. G.	5	8	2	252	129	42·00	1	1	4	—
Palm, A. W.	1	2	0	15	13	7·50	—	—	1	—
Parker, G. M.	2	4	2	3	2*	1·50	—	—	—	—
Parkin, D. C.	1	2	0	6	6	3·00	—	—	1	—
Pearse, C. O. C.	3	6	0	55	31	9·16	—	—	1	—
Pegler, S. J.	16	28	5	356	35*	15·47	—	—	5	—
Pithey, A. J.	5	9	0	104	25	11·55	—	—	1	—
Plimsoll, J. B.	1	2	1	16	8*	16·00	—	—	—	—
Poore, R. M.	3	6	0	76	20	12·66	—	—	3	—
Pothecary, J. E.	3	4	0	26	12	6·50	—	—	2	—

	M.	I.	N.O.	Runs	H.S.	Avge.	100s	50s	Ct.	St.
Powell, A. W.	1	2	0	16	11	8·00	—	—	2	—
Prince, C. F.	1	2	0	6	5	3·00	—	—	—	—
Promnitz, H. L. E.	2	4	0	14	5	3·50	—	—	2	—
Quinn, N. A.	12	18	3	90	28	6·00	—	—	1	—
Reid, N.	1	2	0	17	11	8·50	—	—	—	—
Richards, A.	1	2	0	6	6	3·00	—	—	—	—
Richards, W. H.	1	2	0	4	4	2·00	—	—	—	—
Robertson, J. B.	3	6	1	51	17	10·20	—	—	2	—
Routledge, T.	4	8	0	72	24	9·00	—	—	2	—
Rowan, A. M. B.	15	23	6	290	41	17·05	—	—	7	—
Rowan, E. A. B.	26	50	5	1965	236	43·66	3	12	14	—
Rowe, G. A.	5	9	3	26	13*	4·33	—	—	4	—
Samuelson, H. V.	1	2	0	22	15	11·00	—	—	1	—
Schwarz, R. O.	20	35	8	374	61	13·85	—	1	18	—
Seccull, A. W.	1	2	1	23	17*	23·00	—	—	1	—
Shalders, W. A.	12	23	1	355	42	16·13	—	—	3	—
Shepstone, G. H.	2	4	0	38	21	9·50	—	—	2	—
Sherwell, P. W.	13	22	4	427	115	23·72	1	1	20	16
Siedle, I. J.	18	34	0	977	141	28·73	1	5	7	—
Sinclair, J. H.	25	47	1	1069	106	23·23	3	3	9	—
Smith, C. J. E.	3	6	1	106	45	21·20	—	—	2	—
Smith, F. W.	3	6	1	45	12	9·00	—	—	2	—
Smith, V. I.	9	16	6	39	11*	3·90	—	—	3	—
Snooke, S. D.	1	1	0	0	0	0·00	—	—	2	—
Snooke, S. J.	26	46	1	1008	103	22·40	1	5	24	—
Solomon, W. R.	1	2	0	4	2	2·00	—	—	1	—
Stewart, R. B.	1	2	0	13	9	6·50	—	—	2	—
Stricker, L. A.	13	24	0	342	48	14·25	—	—	3	—
Susskind, M. J.	5	8	0	268	65	33·50	—	4	1	—
Taberer, H. M.	1	1	0	2	2	2·00	—	—	—	—
Tancred, A. B.	2	4	1	87	29	29·00	—	—	2	—
Tancred, L. J.	14	26	1	530	97	21·20	—	2	3	—
Tancred, V. M.	1	2	0	25	18	12·50	—	—	—	—
Tapscott, G. L.	1	2	0	5	4	2·50	—	—	1	—
Tapscott, L. E.	2	3	1	58	50*	29·00	—	1	—	—
Tayfield, H. J.	37	60	9	862	75	16·90	—	2	26	—
Taylor, A. I.	1	2	0	18	12	9·00	—	—	—	—
Taylor, D.	2	4	0	85	36	21·25	—	—	—	—
Taylor, H. W.	42	76	4	2936	176	40·77	7	17	19	—
Theunissen, N.	1	2	1	2	2*	2·00	—	—	1	—
Thornton, G.	1	1	1	1	1*	—	—	—	1	—
Tomlinson, D. S.	1	1	0	9	9	9·00	—	—	—	—
Tuckett, L.	9	14	3	131	40*	11·90	—	—	9	—
Tuckett, L. R.	1	2	1	0	0*	0·00	—	—	2	—
Van der Byl, P. G.	5	9	0	460	125	51·11	1	2	1	—
Van der Merwe, E. A.	2	4	1	27	19	9·00	—	—	3	—
Van Ryneveld, C. B.	19	33	6	724	83	26·81	—	3	14	—
Viljoen, K. G.	27	50	2	1365	124	28·43	2	9	5	—
Vincent, C. L.	25	38	12	526	60	20·23	—	2	27	—
Vintcent, C. H.	3	6	0	26	9	4·33	—	—	1	—
Vogler, A. E. E.	15	26	6	340	65	17·00	—	2	20	—
Wade, H. F.	10	18	2	327	40*	20·43	—	—	4	—
Wade, W. W.	11	19	1	511	125	28·38	1	3	14	3
Waite, J. H. B.	36	66	7	1785	134	30·25	3	12	87	14
Ward, T. A.	23	42	9	459	64	13·90	—	2	19	12
Watkins, J. C.	15	27	1	612	92	23·53	—	3	12	—
Wesley, C.	3	5	0	49	35	9·80	—	—	1	—
Westcott, R. J.	5	9	0	166	62	18·44	—	1	—	—
White, G. C.	17	31	2	872	147	30·06	2	4	10	—
Willoughby, J. T.	2	4	0	8	5	2·00	—	—	—	—
Wimble, C. S.	1	2	0	0	0	0·00	—	—	—	—
Winslow, P. L.	5	9	0	186	108	20·66	1	—	1	—
Wynne, O. E.	6	12	0	219	50	18·25	—	1	3	—
Zulch, J. W.	16	32	2	985	150	32·83	2	4	4	—
Extras, etc.				3161					14	
Total	1562	2757	322	61458	255*	25·23	77	274	1059	66

WEST INDIES

	M.	I.	N.O.	Runs	H.S.	Avge.	100s	50s	Ct.	St.
Achong, E.	6	11	1	81	22	8·10	—	—	6	—
Alexander, F. C. M.	20	28	4	477	70	19·87	—	2	69	5
Asgarali, N.	2	4	0	62	29	15·50	—	—	—	—
Atkinson, D.	22	35	6	922	219	31·79	1	5	11	—
Atkinson, E.	8	9	1	126	37	15·75	—	—	2	—
Barrow, I.	11	19	2	276	105	16·23	1	—	17	5
Bartlett, E. L.	5	8	1	131	84	18·71	—	1	2	—
Betancourt, N.	1	2	0	46	33	23·00	—	—	—	—
Binns, A. P.	5	8	1	64	27	9·14	—	—	14	3
Birkett, L. S.	4	8	0	136	64	17·00	—	1	4	—
Browne, C. R.	4	8	1	176	70*	25·14	—	1	1	—
Butcher, B. F.	10	16	2	650	142	46·42	2	4	1	—
Butler, L.	1	1	0	16	16	16·00	—	—	—	—
Bynoe, R.	1	1	0	1	1	1·00	—	—	1	—
Caires, F. I. de	3	6	0	232	80	38·66	—	2	1	—
Cameron, F. J.	5	7	1	151	75*	25·16	—	1	—	—
Cameron, J. H.	2	3	0	6	5	2·00	—	—	—	—
Carew, G.	4	7	1	170	107	28·33	1	—	1	—
Challenor, G.	3	6	0	101	46	16·83	—	—	—	—
Christiani, C. M.	4	7	2	98	32*	19·60	—	—	6	1
Christiani, R. J.	22	37	3	896	107	26·35	1	4	19	2
Clarke, C. B.	3	4	1	3	2	1·00	—	—	—	—
Constantine, L. N.	18	33	0	641	90	19·42	—	4	28	—
Costa, O. C. da	5	9	1	153	39	19·12	—	—	5	—
Depeiza, C.	5	8	2	187	122	31·16	1	—	6	4
Dewdney, T.	9	12	5	17	5*	2·42	—	—	—	—
Ferguson, W.	8	10	3	200	75	28·57	—	2	11	—
Fernandes, M. P.	2	4	0	49	22	12·25	—	—	—	—
Francis, G. N.	10	18	4	81	19*	5·78	—	—	7	—
Frederick, M.	1	2	0	30	30	15·00	—	—	—	—
Fuller, A.	1	1	0	1	1	1·00	—	—	—	—
Furlonge, H.	3	5	0	99	64	19·80	—	1	—	—
Ganteaume, A. G.	1	1	0	112	112	112·00	1	—	—	—
Gaskin, B. M.	2	3	0	17	10	5·66	—	—	1	—
Gibbs, G.	1	2	0	12	12	6·00	—	—	1	—
Gibbs, L.	8	11	0	111	22	10·09	—	—	6	—
Gilchrist, R.	13	14	3	60	12	5·45	—	—	4	—
Gladstone, G.	1	1	1	12	12*	—	—	—	—	—
Goddard, J. D. C.	27	39	11	859	83*	30·67	—	4	22	—
Gomez, G. E.	29	46	5	1243	101	30·31	1	8	18	—
Grant, G. C.	12	21	5	413	71*	25·81	—	3	10	—
Grant, R. S.	7	11	1	220	77	22·00	—	1	13	—
Grell, M. I.	1	2	0	34	21	17·00	—	—	1	—
Griffith, C.	1	1	1	5	5*	—	—	—	—	—
Griffith, H. C.	13	23	5	91	18	5·05	—	—	4	—
Guillen, S. C.	5	6	2	104	54	26·00	—	1	9	2
Hall, W.	13	15	5	102	29	10·20	—	—	4	—
Headley, G.	22	40	4	2190	270*	60·83	10	5	14	—
Hoad, E. L. G.	4	8	0	98	36	12·25	—	—	1	—
Holt, J. K.	17	31	2	1066	166	36·75	2	5	8	—
Hunte, C. C.	16	27	2	1150	260	46·00	3	2	6	—
Hunte, E.	2	4	1	78	53	26·00	—	1	5	—
Hunte, R. L.	1	2	0	88	58	44·00	—	1	—	—
Hylton, L. G.	6	8	2	70	19	11·66	—	—	1	—
Johnson, H. H.	3	4	0	38	22	9·50	—	—	—	—
Johnson, T.	1	1	0	9	9*	—	—	—	1	—
Jones, C. M.	4	7	0	63	19	9·00	—	—	3	—
Jones, P. E.	9	11	2	47	10*	5·22	—	—	4	—
Kanhai, R.	23	40	2	1642	256	43·21	3	6	11	—
Kentish, E. S. M.	2	2	1	1	1*	1·00	—	—	1	—
King, F.	14	17	3	116	21	8·28	—	—	5	—
Legall, R.	4	5	0	50	23	10·00	—	—	8	1
Madray, I.	2	3	0	3	2	1·00	—	—	1	—
Marshall, N.	1	2	0	8	8	4·00	—	—	—	—
Marshall, R. E.	4	7	0	143	30	20·42	—	—	1	—
Martin, F. R.	9	18	1	486	123*	28·58	1	—	2	—
Martindale, E. A.	10	14	3	58	22	5·27	—	—	4	—
McMorris, E.	5	8	0	153	73	19·12	—	1	1	—
McWatt, C. A.	6	9	2	202	54	28·85	—	2	9	1

	M.	I.	N.O.	Runs	H.S.	Avge.	100s	50s	Ct.	St.
Merry, C. A.	2	4	0	34	13	8·50	—	—	1	—
Miller, R.	1	1	0	23	23	23·00	—	—	—	—
Moodie, C. H.	1	1	0	5	5	5·00	—	—	—	—
Neblett, J. M.	1	2	1	16	11*	16·00	—	—	—	—
Nunes, R. K.	4	8	0	245	92	30·62	—	2	2	—
Nurse, S.	1	2	0	81	70	40·50	—	1	—	—
Pairaudeau, B. H.	13	21	0	454	115	21·61	1	3	6	—
Passailaigue, C. C.	1	2	1	46	44	46·00	—	—	3	—
Pierre, L. R.	1	—	—	—	—	—	—	—	—	—
Rae, A. F.	15	24	2	1016	109	46·18	4	4	9	—
Ramadhin, K. T.	41	54	14	340	44	8·50	—	—	9	—
Rickards, K.	2	3	0	104	67	34·66	—	1	—	—
Roach, C. A.	16	32	1	952	209	30·70	2	6	5	—
Roberts, A.	1	2	0	28	28	14·00	—	—	—	—
St Hill, E.	2	4	0	18	12	4·50	—	—	—	—
St Hill, W. H.	3	6	0	117	38	19·50	—	—	1	—
Scarlett, R.	3	4	1	54	29*	18·00	—	—	2	—
Scott, A. P. H.	1	1	0	5	5	5·00	—	—	—	—
Scott, O. C.	8	13	3	171	35	17·10	—	—	—	—
Sealey, B. J.	1	2	0	41	29	20·50	—	—	—	—
Sealey, J. E. D.	11	19	2	478	92	28·11	—	3	6	1
Singh, C.	2	3	0	11	11	3·66	—	—	2	—
Small, J. A.	3	6	0	79	52	13·16	—	1	3	—
Smith, O. G.	26	42	0	1331	168	31·69	4	6	9	—
Sobers, G.	32	54	8	2922	365*	63·52	9	8	23	—
Solomon, J.	9	15	4	545	100*	49·54	1	4	4	—
Stollmeyer, J. B.	32	56	5	2159	160	42·33	4	12	20	—
Stollmeyer, V. H.	1	1	0	96	96	96·00	—	1	—	—
Taylor, J.	3	5	3	4	4*	2·00	—	—	—	—
Trim, J.	4	5	1	21	12	5·25	—	—	2	—
Valentine, A. L.	29	39	12	102	14	3·77	—	—	9	—
Valentine, V. A.	2	4	1	35	19*	11·66	—	—	—	—
Walcott, C. L.	44	74	7	3798	220	56·68	15	14	54	11
Walcott, L. A.	1	2	1	40	24	40·00	—	—	—	—
Watson, C.	5	3	1	3	3	1·50	—	—	—	—
Weekes, E. D.	48	81	5	4455	207	58·61	15	19	49	—
Weekes, K. H.	2	3	0	173	137	57·66	1	—	—	—
Wight, C. V.	2	4	1	67	23	22·33	—	—	—	—
Wight, L.	1	1	0	21	21	21·00	—	—	—	—
Wiles, C. A.	1	2	0	2	2	1·00	—	—	—	—
Williams, E. A. V.	4	6	0	113	72	18·83	—	1	2	—
Wishart, K. L.	1	2	0	52	52	26·00	—	1	—	—
Worrell, F. M.	36	63	6	3011	261	52·82	9	12	31	—
Extras, etc.				1652					17	
Total	924	1477	187	42353	365*	32·81	93	167	660	36

NEW ZEALAND

	M.	I.	N.O.	Runs	H.S.	Avge.	100s	50s	Ct.	St.
Alabaster, J. C.	8	12	1	102	18	9·27	—	—	4	—
Allcott, C. F. W.	6	7	2	113	33	22·60	—	—	3	—
Anderson, W. McD.	1	2	0	5	4	2·50	—	—	1	—
Badcock, F. T.	7	9	2	137	64	19·57	—	2	1	—
Barber, R. T.	1	2	0	17	12	8·50	—	—	1	—
Beard, D. D.	4	7	2	101	31	20·20	—	—	2	—
Beck, J. E. F.	8	15	0	394	99	26·26	—	3	—	—
Bell, W.	2	3	3	21	21*		—	—	1	—
Blair, R. W.	14	25	4	89	22	4·23	—	—	5	—
Blunt, R. C.	9	13	1	330	96	27·50	—	1	5	—
Bolton, B. A.	2	3	0	59	33	19·66	—	—	1	—
Burke, C. C.	1	2	0	4	3	2·00	—	—	—	—
Burtt, T. B.	10	15	3	252	42	21·00	—	—	2	—
Butterfield, L. A.	1	2	0	0	0	0·00	—	—	—	—
Cave, H. B.	19	31	5	229	22*	8·80	—	—	8	—
Chapple, M. E.	8	15	0	233	76	15·53	—	1	6	—
Cleverley, D. C.	2	4	3	19	10*	19·00	—	—	—	—
Colquhoun, I. A.	2	4	2	1	1*	0·50	—	—	4	—
Cowie, J. A.	9	13	4	90	45	10·00	—	—	3	—
Cresswell, G. F.	3	5	3	14	12*	7·00	—	—	—	—
Cromb, I. B.	5	8	2	123	51*	20·50	—	1	1	—
D'Arcy, J. W.	5	10	0	136	33	13·60	—	—	—	—

	M.	I.	N.O.	Runs	H.S.	Avge.	100s	50s	Ct.	St.
Dempster, C. S.	10	15	4	723	136	65·72	2	5	2	—
Dempster, E. W.	5	8	2	106	47	17·66	—	—	1	—
Dickinson, G. R.	3	5	0	31	11	6·20	—	—	3	—
Donnelly, M. P.	7	12	1	582	206	52·90	1	4	7	—
Dunning, J. A.	4	6	1	38	19	7·60	—	—	2	—
Emery, R. W. G.	2	4	0	46	28	11·50	—	—	—	—
Fisher, F. E.	1	2	0	23	14	11·50	—	—	—	—
Foley, H.	1	2	0	4	2	2·00	—	—	—	—
Freeman, D. L.	2	2	0	2	1	1·00	—	—	—	—
Gallichan, N. M.	1	2	0	32	30	16·00	—	· —	—	—
Guillen, S. C.	3	6	0	98	41	16·33	—	—	4	1
Guy, J. W.	10	19	2	422	102	24·82	1	3	1	—
Hadlee, W. A.	11	19	1	543	116	30·16	1	2	6	—
Harford, N. S.	8	15	0	229	93	15·26	—	2	—	—
Harris, P. G. Z.	3	6	0	93	28	15·50	—	—	1	—
Harris, R. M.	2	3	0	31	13	10·33	—	—	—	—
Hayes, J. A.	15	22	7	73	19	4·86	—	—	3	—
Henderson, M.	1	2	1	8	6	8·00	—	—	1	—
Hough, K. W.	2	3	2	62	31*	62·00	—	—	1	—
James, K. C.	11	13	2	52	14	4·72	—	—	11	5
Kerr, J. L.	7	12	1	212	59	19·27	—	1	4	—
Leggat, I. B.	1	1	0	0	0	0·00	—	—	2	—
Leggat, J. G.	9	18	2	351	61	21·93	—	2	—	—
Lissette, A. F.	2	4	2	2	1*	1·00	—	—	1	—
Lowry, T. C.	7	8	0	223	80	27·87	—	2	8	—
MacGibbon, A. R.	26	46	5	814	66	19·85	—	3	13	—
Matheson, A. M.	2	1	0	7	7	7·00	—	—	2	—
McGirr, H. M.	2	1	0	51	51	51·00	—	1	—	—
McGregor, S. N.	15	27	1	433	111	16·65	1	—	5	—
McLeod, E. A.	1	2	1	18	16	18·00	—	—	—	—
McMahon, T. G.	5	7	4	8	4*	2·66	—	—	7	1
McRae, D. A. N.	1	2	0	8	8	4·00	—	—	—	—
Meale, T.	2	4	0	21	10	5·25	—	—	—	—
Merritt, W. E.	6	8	1	73	19	10·42	—	—	2	—
Meuli, E. M.	1	2	0	38	23	19·00	—	—	—	—
Miller, L. S. M.	13	25	0	346	47	13·84	—	—	1	—
Mills, J. W. E.	7	10	1	241	117	26·77	1	—	1	—
Moir, A. M.	17	30	8	326	41*	14·81	—	—	2	—
Moloney, D. A. R.	3	6	0	156	64	26·00	—	1	3	—
Mooney, F. L. H.	14	22	2	343	46	17·15	—	—	22	8
Newman, J.	3	4	0	33	19	8·25	—	—	—	—
Overton, G. W. F.	3	6	1	8	3*	1·60	—	—	1	—
Page, M. L.	14	20	0	492	104	24·60	1	2	6	—
Petrie, E. C.	11	19	4	143	45*	9·53	—	—	21	—
Playle, W. R.	5	9	0	56	18	6·22	—	—	3	—
Poore, M. B.	14	24	1	354	45	15·39	—	—	1	—
Rabone, G. O.	12	20	2	562	107	31·22	1	2	5	—
Reid, J. R.	34	62	3	1663	135	28·18	3	10	27	1
Roberts, A. W.	5	10	1	248	66*	27·55	—	3	4	—
Rowe, C. G.	1	2	0	0	0	0·00	—	—	1	—
Scott, R. H.	1	1	0	18	18	18·00	—	—	—	—
Scott, V. J.	10	17	1	458	84	28·62	—	3	7	—
Sinclair, I. M.	2	4	1	25	18*	8·33	—	—	1	—
Smith, D.	1	1	0	4	4	4·00	—	—	—	—
Smith, F. B.	4	6	1	237	96	47·40	—	2	1	—
Snedden, C. A.	1	—	—	—	—	—	—	—	—	—
Sparling, J. T.	5	8	2	116	50	19·33	—	1	1	—
Sutcliffe, B.	34	62	5	2335	230*	40·96	4	12	18	—
Taylor, D. D.	3	5	0	159	77	31·80	—	1	2	—
Tindill, E. W.	5	9	1	73	37*	9·12	—	—	6	1
Vivian, H. G.	7	10	0	421	100	42·10	1	5	4	—
Wallace, W. M.	13	21	0	439	66	20·90	—	5	5	—
Watt, L. A.	1	2	0	2	2	1·00	—	—	—	—
Weir, G. L.	11	16	2	416	74*	29·71	—	3	3	—
Whitelaw, P. E.	2	4	2	64	30	32·00	—	—	—	—
Extras, etc.				1096					6	
Total	572	951	115	18760	230*	21·24	17	83	287	17

INDIA

	M.	I.	N.O.	Runs	H.S.	Avge.	100s	50s	Ct.	St.
Adhikari, H. R.	21	36	8	872	114*	31·14	1	4	8	—
Ali, S. Nazir	2	4	0	30	13	7·50	—	—	—	—
Ali, S. Wazir	7	14	0	237	42	16·92	—	—	1	—
Amarnath, L.	24	40	4	878	118	24·38	1	4	13	—
Amar Singh	7	14	1	292	51	22·46	—	1	3	—
Amir Elahi	1	2	0	17	13	8·50	—	—	—	—
Apte, A. L.	1	2	0	15	8	7·50	—	—	—	—
Apte, M. L.	7	13	2	542	163*	49·27	1	3	2	—
Baig, A. A.	5	10	0	342	112	34·20	1	2	4	—
Banerjee, S.	1	1	0	0	0	0·00	—	—	3	—
Banerjee, S. N.	1	2	0	13	8	6·50	—	—	—	—
Bhandari, P.	3	4	0	77	39	19·25	—	—	1	—
Borde, C. G.	13	24	1	586	109	25·47	1	4	8	—
Chowdhury, N. R.	2	2	1	3	3*	3·00	—	—	—	—
Colah, S. H. M.	2	4	0	69	31	17·25	—	—	2	—
Contractor, N. J.	19	34	1	1086	108	32·90	1	7	7	—
Dani, H. T.	1	—	—	—	—	—	—	—	1	—
Desai, R. B.	9	18	7	79	17*	7·18	—	—	3	—
Divecha, R. V.	5	5	0	60	26	12·00	—	—	5	—
Durani, A. S.	1	1	0	18	18	18·00	—	—	—	—
Gadkari, C. V.	6	10	4	132	50*	22·00	—	1	6	—
Gaekwad, D. K.	10	19	1	341	52	18·94	—	1	5	—
Gaekwad, H. G.	1	2	0	22	14	11·00	—	—	—	—
Ghorpade, J. M.	8	15	0	229	41	15·26	—	—	4	—
Ghulam Ahmed	22	31	9	192	50	8·72	—	1	11	—
Gopalan, M. J.	1	2	1	18	11*	18·00	—	—	3	—
Gopinath, C. D.	8	12	1	242	50*	22·00	—	1	2	—
Guard, G.	2	2	0	11	11	5·50	—	—	2	—
Gul Mahomed	8	15	0	166	34	11·06	—	—	3	—
Gupte, S. P.	31	39	12	182	21	6·74	—	—	12	—
Hardikar, M. S.	2	4	1	56	32*	18·66	—	—	3	—
Hazare, V. S.	30	52	6	2192	164*	47·65	7	9	11	—
Hindlekar, D. D.	4	7	2	71	26	14·20	—	—	3	—
Hussain, Dilawar	3	6	0	254	59	42·33	—	3	6	1
Ibrahim, K. C.	4	8	0	169	85	21·12	—	1	—	—
Irani, J. K.	2	3	2	3	2*	3·00	—	—	2	1
Jahangir Khan, M.	4	7	0	39	13	5·57	—	—	4	—
Jai, L. P.	1	2	0	19	19	9·50	—	—	—	—
Jaisimha, M. L.	2	4	1	103	74	34·33	—	1	1	—
Jamshedji, R. J.	1	2	2	5	4*	—	—	—	2	—
Jilani, M. Baqa	1	2	1	16	12	16·00	—	—	—	—
Joshi, P. G.	11	19	0	155	32	8·15	—	—	16	8
Kardar, A. H.	3	5	0	80	43	16·00	—	—	1	—
Kenny, R. B.	5	10	1	245	62	27·22	—	3	1	—
Kishenchand, G.	5	10	0	89	44	8·90	—	—	1	—
Kripal Singh, A. G.	8	11	2	349	100*	38·77	1	2	1	—
Kunderam, B. K.	3	6	0	137	71	22·83	—	1	2	2
Lall Singh	1	2	0	44	29	22·00	—	—	1	—
Maka, E. S.	2	1	1	2	2*	—	—	—	2	1
Manjrekar, V. L.	32	54	6	1683	177	35·06	4	7	9	2
Mankad, V.	44	72	5	2109	231	31·47	5	6	33	—
Mantri, M. K.	4	8	1	67	39	9·57	—	—	8	1
Meherhomji, K. R.	1	1	1	0	0*	—	—	—	1	—
Mehra, V.	2	2	0	42	32	21·00	—	—	1	—
Merchant, V. M.	10	18	0	859	154	47·72	3	3	7	—
Milkha Singh, A. G.	1	2	0	25	16	12·50	—	—	1	—
Modi, R. S.	10	17	1	736	112	46·00	1	6	3	—
Muddiah, V. M.	1	2	1	0	0*	0·00	—	—	—	—
Mushtaq Ali	11	20	1	612	112	32·21	2	3	7	—
Nadkarni, R. G.	11	21	3	422	76	23·44	—	2	6	—
Naoomal Jeoomal	3	5	1	108	43	27·00	—	—	—	—
Navle, J. G.	2	4	0	42	13	10·50	—	—	1	—
Nayudu, C. K.	7	14	0	350	81	25·00	—	2	4	—
Nayudu, C. S.	11	19	3	147	36	9·18	—	—	3	—
Nissar, M.	6	11	3	55	14	6·87	—	—	2	—
Nyalchand, K.	1	2	1	7	6*	7·00	—	—	—	—
Palia, P. E.	2	4	1	29	16	9·66	—	—	—	—
Patankar, C. T.	1	2	1	14	13	14·00	—	—	3	1
Pataudi, Nawab of	3	5	0	55	22	11·00	—	—	—	—

	M.	I.	N.O.	Runs	H.S.	Avge.	100s	50s	Ct.	St.
Patel, J. S.	7	10	1	25	12	2·77	—	—	2	—
Patil, S. R.	1	1	1	14	14*	—	—	—	1	—
Patiala, Yuvraj of	1	2	0	84	60	42·00	—	1	2	—
Phadkar, D. G.	31	45	7	1229	123	32·34	2	8	21	—
Punjabi, P. L.	5	10	0	164	33	16·40	—	—	5	—
Rai Singh	1	2	0	26	24	13·00	—	—	—	—
Rajindernath, V.	1	—	—	—	—	—	—	—	—	4
Ramaswami, C.	2	4	1	170	60	56·66	—	1	—	—
Ramchand, G. S.	33	53	5	1180	109	24·58	2	5	20	—
Ramji, L.	1	2	0	1	1	0·50	—	—	1	—
Rangachari, C. R.	4	6	3	8	8*	2·66	—	—	—	—
Rangnekar, K. M.	3	6	0	33	18	5·50	—	—	1	—
Ranjane, V.	1	2	0	15	12	7·50	—	—	—	—
Rege, M. R.	1	2	0	15	15	7·50	—	—	1	—
Roy, P.	42	78	4	2418	173	32·67	5	9	15	—
Sarwate, C. T.	9	17	1	208	37	13·00	—	—	—	—
Sen, P.	14	18	4	165	25	11·78	—	—	20	11
Sengupta, A. K.	1	2	0	9	8	4·50	—	—	—	—
Shinde, S. G.	7	11	5	85	14	14·16	—	—	—	—
Shodhan, D. H.	3	4	1	181	110	60·33	1	—	1	—
Sohoni, S. W.	4	7	2	83	29*	16·60	—	—	2	—
Sood, M. M.	1	2	0	3	3	1·50	—	—	—	—
Sunderram, G.	2	1	1	3	3*	—	—	—	—	—
Surendra Nath	9	18	6	125	27	10·41	—	—	4	—
Swamy, N. V.	1	—	—	—	—	—	—	—	—	—
Tamhane, N. S.	19	25	5	219	54*	10·95	—	1	32	16
Tarapore, K. K.	1	1	0	2	2	2·00	—	—	—	—
Umrigar, P. R.	45	72	6	2550	223	38·63	7	11	22	—
Vizianagram, M. of	3	6	2	33	19*	8·25	—	—	1	—
Extras, etc.				1441					15	
Total	737	1228	156	28630	231*	26·70	46	114	421	48

PAKISTAN

	M.	I.	N.O.	Runs	H.S.	Avge.	100s	50s	Ct.	St.
Agha Saadat Ali	1	1	1	8	8*	—	—	—	3	—
Alimuddin	19	34	2	708	103*	22·12	1	3	6	—
Amir Elahi	5	7	1	65	47	10·83	—	—	—	—
Anwar Hussain	4	6	0	42	17	7·00	—	—	—	—
Antao D'souza	1	1	1	3	3*	—	—	—	—	—
Duncan Sharpe	3	6	0	134	56	22·33	—	1	2	—
Fazal Mahmood	26	39	6	541	60	16·39	—	1	7	—
Ghazali, M. E. Z.	2	4	0	32	18	8·00	—	—	—	—
Gul Mahomed	1	2	1	39	27*	39·00	—	—	—	—
Hanif Mohammed	27	48	3	1937	337	43·04	5	9	14	—
Haseeb Ahsan	5	8	4	11	4*	2·75	—	—	—	—
Ijaz Butt	5	10	2	213	58	26·62	—	1	2	—
Imtiaz Ahmed	29	48	0	1320	209	27·50	2	7	61	12
Intikhab Alam	1	2	0	6	6	3·00	—	—	1	—
Israr Ali	4	8	1	33	10	4·71	—	—	1	—
Kardar, A. H.	23	37	3	847	93	24·91	—	5	15	—
Khalid Hassan	1	2	1	17	10	17·00	—	—	—	—
Khalid Wazir	2	3	1	14	9*	7·00	—	—	—	—
Khan Mohammed	13	17	7	100	26*	10·00	—	—	4	—
Mahmood Hussain	18	26	5	183	32	8·71	—	—	3	—
Maqsood Ahmed	16	27	1	507	99	19·50	—	2	13	—
Miran Bux	2	3	2	1	1*	1·00	—	—	—	—
Mohammed Aslam	1	2	0	34	18	17·00	—	—	—	—
Mohammed Munaf	2	4	2	32	19	16·00	—	—	—	—
Munir Malik	1	1	0	0	0	0·00	—	—	—	—
Mushtaq Mohammed	1	2	0	18	14	9·00	—	—	—	—
Nasimul Ghani	10	17	1	116	22	7·25	—	—	1	—
Nazar Mohammed	5	8	1	277	124*	39·57	1	1	7	—
Rehman, S. F.	1	2	0	10	8	5·00	—	—	1	—
Saeed Ahmed	11	21	1	1041	166	52·05	2	6	1	—
Shujauddin	17	29	6	375	47	16·30	—	—	7	—
Wallis Mathias	12	20	1	501	77	26·36	—	3	17	—
Waqar Hasan	21	35	1	1071	189	31·50	1	6	10	—
Wazir Mohammed	20	33	4	801	189	27·62	2	3	5	—
Zulfiqar Ahmed	9	10	4	200	63*	33·33	—	1	5	—
Extras, etc.				543					4	
Total	319	523	63	11780	337	25·60	14	49	190	12

Bowling

ENGLAND

	M.	Balls	Mdns.	Runs	Wkts.	Avge.	5wI.	10wM.
Allen, D. A.	7	1523	79	518	13	39·84	—	—
Allen, G. O.	25	4392	116	2379	81	29·37	5	1
Allom, M. J. C.	5	810	28	265	14	18·92	1	—
Appleyard, R.	9	1596	70	554	31	17·87	1	—
Armitage, T.	2	12	0	15	0	—	—	—
Arnold, E. G.	10	1677	64	788	31	25·41	1	—
Astill, W. E.	9	2181	98	856	25	34·24	—	—
Attewell, W.	10	2850	326	626	27	23·18	—	—
Bailey, T. E.	61	9712	379	3856	132	29·21	5	1
Bakewell, A. H.	6	18	0	8	0	—	—	—
Barber, R. W.	1	96	2	55	1	55·00	—	—
Barber, W.	2	2	0	0	1	—	—	—
Barlow, R. G.	17	2456	315	767	35	21·91	3	—
Barnes, S. F.	27	7873	358	3106	189	16·43	24	7
Barnes, W.	21	2285	271	793	51	15·54	3	—
Barnett, C. J.	20	256	11	93	0	—	—	—
Barratt, F.	5	750	33	235	5	47·00	—	—
Barrington, K. F.	16	941	49	357	10	35·70	—	—
Bates, W.	15	2362	282	821	49	16·75	4	1
Bedser, A. V.	51	15941	572	5876	236	24·89	15	5
Berry, R.	2	653	47	228	9	25·33	1	—
Bird, M. C.	10	264	12	120	8	15·00	—	—
Blythe, C.	19	4438	231	1863	100	18·63	9	4
Booth, M. W.	2	312	8	130	7	18·57	—	—
Bosanquet, B. J. T.	7	989	10	604	25	24·16	2	—
Bowes, W. E.	15	3655	131	1519	68	22·33	6	—
Bowley, E. H.	5	252	7	116	0	—	—	—
Bradley, W. M.	2	625	49	233	6	38·83	1	—
Braund, L. C.	23	3693	144	1810	47	38·51	3	—
Brearley, W.	4	705	25	359	17	21·11	1	—
Briggs, J.	33	5332	389	2094	118	17·74	9	4
Brockwell, W.	7	582	31	309	5	61·80	—	—
Brown, F. R.	22	3260	117	1398	45	31·06	1	—
Brown, J. T.	8	35	0	22	0	—	—	—
Buckenham, C. P.	4	1182	25	593	21	28·23	1	—
Butler, H. J.	2	552	30	215	12	17·91	—	—
Calthorpe, Hon. F. S. G.	4	204	8	91	1	91·00	—	—
Carr, D. B.	2	210	6	140	2	70·00	—	—
Carr, D. W.	1	414	3	282	7	40·28	1	—
Chapman, A. P. F.	26	40	1	20	0	—	—	—
Christopherson, S.	1	136	13	69	1	69·00	—	—
Clark, E. W.	8	1931	71	899	32	28·09	1	—
Clay, J. C.	1	192	7	75	0	—	—	—
Close, D. B.	6	416	17	174	7	24·85	—	—
Compton, D. C. S.	78	2722	70	1410	25	56·40	1	—
Cook, C.	1	180	4	127	0	—	—	—
Copson, W. H.	3	762	31	297	15	19·80	1	—
Cowdrey, M. C.	49	29	0	32	0	—	—	—
Coxon, A.	1	378	13	172	3	57·33	—	—
Cranston, K.	8	1010	37	461	18	25·61	—	—
Crawford, J. N.	12	2203	61	1150	39	29·48	3	—
Cuttell, W. R.	2	285	32	73	6	12·16	—	—
Davenport, H. R. B.	4	155	6	98	4	24·50	—	—
Dean, H.	3	447	23	153	11	13·90	—	—
Dexter, E. R.	17	1152	52	447	16	27·93	—	—
Douglas, J. W. H. T.	23	2812	66	1486	45	33·02	1	—
Duleepsinhji, K. S.	12	6	0	7	0	—	—	—
Durston, T. J.	1	202	2	136	5	27·20	—	—
Edrich, W. J.	39	3234	80	1693	41	41·29	—	—
Emmett, T.	7	804	92	293	9	32·55	1	—
Farnes, K.	15	3932	103	1718	60	28·63	3	1
Fender, P. G. H.	13	2178	67	1185	29	40·86	2	—
Ferris, J. J.	1	272	27	91	13	7·00	2	1

	M.	Balls	Mdns.	Runs	Wkts.	Avge.	5wI.	10wM.
Fielder, A.	6	1485	42	711	26	27·34	1	—
Flowers, W.	8	858	92	296	14	21·14	1	—
Ford, F. G. J.	5	210	6	129	1	129·00	—	—
Foster, F. R.	11	2441	108	926	45	20·57	4	—
Fothergill, A. J.	2	321	42	90	8	11·25	—	—
Freeman, A. P.	12	3732	142	1707	66	25·86	5	3
Fry, C. B.	26	10	1	3	0	—	—	—
Geary, G.	14	3810	181	1353	46	29·41	4	1
Gilligan, A. E. R.	11	2405	74	1046	36	29·05	2	1
Gladwin, C.	8	2129	89	571	15	38·06	—	—
Goddard, T. W.	8	1563	62	588	22	26·72	1	—
Gover, A. R.	4	816	26	359	8	44·87	—	—
Grace, W. G.	22	663	65	236	9	26·22	—	—
Graveney, T. W.	48	168	5	122	1	122·00	—	—
Greenhough, T.	4	1129	66	357	16	22·31	1	—
Gunn, G.	15	12	0	8	0	—	—	—
Gunn, J.	6	903	54	387	18	21·50	1	—
Haig, N. E.	5	1026	54	448	13	34·46	—	—
Haigh, S.	11	1294	61	622	24	25·91	1	—
Hammond, W. R.	85	7967	299	3140	83	37·83	2	—
Harris, Lord	4	32	1	29	0	—	—	—
Hartley, J. C.	2	192	2	115	1	115·00	—	—
Hayes, E. G.	5	90	1	52	1	52·00	—	—
Hayward, T.	35	869	42	514	14	36·71	—	—
Hearne, J. T.	12	2976	211	1082	49	22·08	4	1
Hearne, J. W.	24	2955	59	1462	30	48·73	1	—
Hendren, E.	51	47	0	31	1	31·00	—	—
Heseltine, C.	2	157	3	84	5	16·80	1	—
Hill, A.	2	340	37	130	6	21·66	—	—
Hill, A. J. L.	3	40	4	8	4	2·00	—	—
Hilton, M. J.	4	1238	69	471	14	33·64	1	—
Hirst, G. H.	24	3979	146	1770	59	30·00	3	—
Hitch, J. W.	7	462	5	325	7	46·42	—	—
Hobbs, J. B.	61	376	15	165	1	165·00	—	—
Hollies, W. E.	13	3554	176	1332	44	30·27	5	—
Holmes, E. R. T.	5	108	4	76	2	38·00	—	—
Hopwood, J. L.	2	462	32	155	0	—	—	—
Hornby, A. N.	3	28	7	0	1		—	—
Horton, M. J.	2	238	18	59	2	29·50	—	—
Howorth, R.	5	1523	61	637	19	33·52	1	—
Howell, H.	5	918	23	559	7	79·85	—	—
Hutchings, K. L.	7	90	1	81	1	81·00	—	—
Hutton, L.	79	260	4	232	3	77·33	—	—
Iddon, J.	5	66	3	27	0	—	—	—
Ikin, J. T.	18	572	12	354	3	118·00	—	—
Illingworth, R.	12	2418	144	712	17	41·88	—	—
Jackson, L.	1	234	14	72	3	24·00	—	—
Jackson, Hon. F. S.	20	1587	77	799	24	33·29	1	—
Jardine, D. R.	22	6	0	10	0	—	—	—
Jenkins, R. O.	9	2118	51	1098	32	34·31	1	—
Jessop, G. L.	18	672	28	354	10	35·40	—	—
Jones, A. O.	12	228	14	133	3	44·33	—	—
Jupp, V. W. C.	8	1301	55	616	28	22·00	—	—
Kennedy, A. S.	5	1683	91	599	31	19·32	2	—
Kilner, R.	9	2368	82	734	24	30·58	—	—
King, J. H.	1	162	5	99	1	99·00	—	—
Knox, N. A.	2	132	2	105	3	35·00	—	—
Laker, J. C.	46	12009	673	4099	193	21·23	9	3
Langridge, James	8	1074	51	413	19	21·73	2	—
Larwood, H.	21	4969	167	2216	78	28·41	4	1
Leadbeater, E.	2	289	9	218	2	109·00	—	—
Lees, W. S.	5	1256	69	467	26	17·96	2	—
Legge, G. B.	5	30	0	34	0	—	—	—
Leslie, C. F. H.	4	96	10	44	4	11·00	—	—
Leyland, M.	41	1103	35	585	6	97·50	—	—
Lilley, A. A.	35	25	1	23	1	23·00	—	—
Lillywhite, James	2	340	37	126	8	15·75	—	—
Loader, P. J.	13	2662	117	878	39	22·51	1	—
Lock, G. A. R.	31	8033	511	2554	123	20·76	8	3
Lockwood, W. H.	12	1973	100	884	43	20·55	5	1
Lohmann, G. A	18	3821	364	1205	112	10·75	9	5

	M.	Balls	Mdns.	Runs	Wkts.	Avge.	5wI.	10wM.
Lucas, A. P.	5	120	13	54	0	—	—	—
Lyttelton, Hon. A.	4	48	5	19	4	4·75	—	—
Macaulay, G. G.	8	1701	79	662	24	27·58	1	—
Marriott, C. S.	1	247	8	96	11	8·72	2	1
Martin, F.	2	410	30	141	14	10·07	2	1
Martin, J. W.	1	270	6	129	1	129·00	—	—
Mason, J. R.	5	324	13	149	2	74·50	—	—
Matthews, A. D. G.	1	180	8	65	2	32·50	—	—
McConnon, J. E.	2	216	12	74	4	18·50	—	—
Mead, W.	1	265	24	91	1	91·00	—	—
Midwinter, W. E.	4	776	79	272	10	27·20	—	—
Milligan, F. W.	2	45	2	29	0	—	—	—
Milton, C. A.	6	24	2	12	0	—	—	—
Mitchell, A.	6	6	0	4	0	—	—	—
Mitchell, T. B.	5	894	21	498	8	62·25	—	—
Mold, A.	3	491	32	234	7	33·42	—	—
Morley, F.	4	972	124	296	16	18·50	1	—
Mortimore, J. B.	5	704	41	267	7	38·14	—	—
Moss, A. E.	9	1657	79	626	21	29·80	—	—
Nichols, M. S.	14	2565	98	1152	41	28·09	2	—
Oakman, A. S. M.	2	48	3	21	0	—	—	—
O'Connor, J.	4	162	6	72	1	72·00	—	—
Padgett, D. E. V.	2	12	0	8	0	—	—	—
Paine, G. A. E.	4	1044	39	467	17	27·47	1	—
Palmer, C. H.	1	30	1	15	0	—	—	—
Parker, C. W. L.	1	168	16	32	2	16·00	—	—
Parkin, C. H.	10	2095	55	1128	32	35·25	2	—
Parks, J. H.	1	126	9	36	3	12·00	—	—
Peate, E.	9	2096	260	682	31	22·00	2	—
Peebles, I. A. R.	13	2882	78	1391	45	30·91	3	—
Peel, R.	20	5216	444	1715	102	16·81	6	2
Penn, F.	1	12	1	2	0	—	—	—
Perks, R. T. D.	2	829	17	355	11	32·27	2	—
Pollard, R.	4	1102	64	378	15	25·20	1	—
Poole, C. J.	3	30	1	9	0	—	—	—
Pope, G. H.	1	218	12	85	1	85·00	—	—
Pougher, A. D.	1	105	8	26	3	8·66	—	—
Pullar, G.	11	12	0	7	1	7·00	—	—
Quaife, W. G.	7	15	1	6	0	—	—	—
Ranjitsinhji, K. S.	15	97	6	39	1	39·00	—	—
Read, H. D.	1	270	14	200	6	33·33	—	—
Read, W. W.	18	60	2	63	0	—	—	—
Relf, A. E.	13	1764	91	624	25	24·96	—	—
Rhodes, H. J.	2	449	10	244	9	27·11	—	—
Rhodes, W.	58	8220	368	3425	127	26·96	6	1
Richardson, T.	14	4485	191	2220	88	25·22	11	4
Richmond, T. L.	1	114	3	86	2	43·00	—	—
Ridgway, F.	5	793	23	379	7	54·14	—	—
Robertson, J. D.	11	138	4	58	2	29·00	—	—
Robins, R. W. V.	19	3318	77	1758	64	27·46	1	—
Root, C. F.	3	642	47	194	8	24·25	—	—
Royle, V. P. F. A.	1	16	1	6	0	—	—	—
Schultz, S. S.	1	35	3	26	1	26·00	—	—
Scotton, W. H.	15	20	1	20	0	—	—	—
Shackleton, D.	3	618	23	250	3	83·33	—	—
Sharp, J.	3	183	3	111	3	37·00	—	—
Sharpe, J. W.	3	975	61	305	11	27·72	1	—
Shaw, A.	7	1099	155	285	12	23·75	1	—
Shrewsbury, A.	23	12	2	2	0	—	—	—
Simpson, R. T.	27	45	2	22	2	11·00	—	—
Simpson-Hayward, G. H.	5	898	18	420	23	18·26	2	—
Sims, J.	4	887	21	480	11	43·63	1	—
Sinfield, R. A.	1	378	16	123	2	61·50	—	—
Smailes, T. F.	1	120	3	62	3	20·66	—	—
Smith, C. A.	1	154	16	61	7	8·71	1	—
Smith, C. I. J.	5	930	40	392	15	26·13	1	—
Smith, D. V.	3	270	13	97	1	97·00	—	—
Smith, M. J. K.	14	6	0	15	0	—	—	—
Smith, T. P. B.	4	538	5	319	3	106·33	—	—
Southerton, J.	2	263	24	107	7	15·28	—	—
Staples, S. J.	3	1149	50	435	15	29·00	—	—

	M.	Balls	Mdns.	Runs	Wkts.	Avge.	5wI.	10wM.
Statham, J. B.	55	11967	473	4510	196	23·01	7	1
Steel, A. G.	13	1404	108	605	29	20·86	—	—
Stevens, G. T. S.	10	1186	24	648	20	32·40	2	1
Stoddart, A. E.	16	162	7	94	2	47·00	—	—
Storer, W.	6	168	5	108	2	54·00	—	—
Studd, C. T.	5	384	60	98	3	32·66	—	—
Subba Row, R.	8	6	0	2	0	—	—	—
Tate, F. W.	1	96	4	51	2	25·50	—	—
Tate, M. W.	39	12571	579	4051	155	26·13	7	1
Tattersall, R.	16	4186	208	1523	58	26·26	4	1
Tennyson, Hon. L. H.	9	6	0	1	0	—	—	—
Thompson, G. J.	6	1367	66	638	23	27·73	—	—
Titmus, F. J.	2	198	10	101	1	101·00	—	—
Townsend, C. L.	2	140	5	75	3	25·00	—	—
Townsend, D. C. H.	3	6	0	9	0	—	—	—
Townsend, L. F.	4	399	22	205	6	34·16	—	—
Tremlett, M. F.	3	492	13	226	4	56·50	—	—
Trott, A. E.	2	474	37	198	17	11·64	1	—
Trueman, F. S.	41	8606	325	3742	174	21·50	7	—
Tyldesley, E.	14	3	0	2	0	—	—	—
Tyldesley, R.	7	1615	76	619	19	32·57	—	—
Tyler, E. J.	1	145	6	65	4	16·25	—	—
Tyson, F. H.	17	3452	98	1411	76	18·56	4	1
Ulyett, G.	25	2623	299	1011	51	19·82	1	—
Verity, H.	40	11143	604	3510	144	24·37	5	2
Voce, W.	27	6360	209	2733	98	27·88	3	2
Waddington, A.	2	276	7	119	1	119·00	—	—
Wainwright, E.	5	127	6	73	0	—	—	—
Walker, P. M.	3	78	3	34	0	—	—	—
Wardle, J. H.	28	6597	404	2080	102	20·39	5	1
Warr, J. J.	2	584	6	281	1	281·00	—	—
Warren, A. R.	1	236	9	113	6	18·83	1	—
Washbrook, C.	37	36	0	33	1	33·00	—	—
Watkins, A. J.	15	1364	45	554	11	50·36	—	—
Wellard, A. W.	2	456	9	237	7	33·85	—	—
White, J. C.	15	4819	253	1581	49	32·26	3	1
Whysall, W. W.	4	16	0	9	0	—	—	—
Wilkinson, L. L.	3	573	9	271	7	38·71	—	—
Wilson, E. R.	1	126	5	36	3	12·00	—	—
Woods, S. M. J.	3	195	8	129	5	25·80	—	—
Woolley, F. E.	64	6495	251	2815	83	33·91	4	1
Worthington, T. S.	9	633	18	316	8	39·50	—	—
Wright, D. V. P.	34	8141	176	4224	108	39·11	6	1
Wyatt, R. E. S.	40	1392	67	642	18	35·66	—	—
Wynyard, E. G.	3	24	0	17	0	—	—	—
Yardley, N. W. D.	20	1662	41	707	21	33·66	—	—
Young, H.	2	551	39	262	12	21·83	—	—
Young, J. A.	8	2368	119	757	17	44·52	—	—
Extras, etc.				7823	237			
Total		378642	18010	161768	6042	26·75	306	66

AUSTRALIA

	M.	Balls	Mdns.	Runs	Wkts.	Avge.	5wI.	10wM.
a'Beckett, E. L.	4	1062	47	317	3	105·66	—	—
Alexander, G.	2	168	13	93	2	46·50	—	—
Alexander, H. H.	1	276	3	154	1	154·00	—	—
Allan, F. E.	1	180	15	80	4	20·00	—	—
Andrews, T. J. E.	16	156	5	116	1	116·00	—	—
Archer, R. G.	19	3570	160	1313	48	27·35	1	—
Armstrong, W. W.	50	8052	403	2923	87	33·59	3	—
Bannerman, A. C.	28	292	17	163	4	40·75	—	—
Barnes, S. G.	13	594	11	218	4	54·50	—	—
Benaud, R.	45	12454	579	4300	181	23·75	12	1
Blackie, D. D. J.	3	1260	51	444	14	31·71	1	—
Bonnor, G. J.	17	164	16	84	2	42·00	—	—
Boyle, H. F.	12	1732	173	641	32	20·03	1	—
Bradman, D. G.	52	164	4	72	2	36·00	—	—
Bromley, E. H.	2	60	4	19	0	—	—	—
Bruce, W.	14	954	71	440	12	36·66	—	—
Burke, J. W.	24	814	41	230	8	28·75	—	—

	M.	Balls	Mdns.	Runs	Wkts.	Avge.	5wI.	10wM.
Callaway, S. T.	3	471	33	142	6	23·66	1	—
Charlton, P. C.	2	45	1	24	3	8·00	—	—
Chipperfield, A. G.	14	926	28	437	5	87·40	—	—
Collins, H. L.	19	654	31	252	4	63·00	—	—
Coningham, A.	1	186	9	76	2	38·00	—	—
Cooper, W. H.	2	466	31	226	9	25·11	1	—
Cotter, A.	21	4633	86	2549	89	28·64	7	—
Crawford, P.	4	438	27	107	7	15·28	—	—
Darling, L. S.	12	162	7	65	0	—	—	—
Davidson, A. K.	30	7182	291	2164	106	20·41	5	1
Donnan, H.	5	54	2	22	0	—	—	—
Dooland, B.	3	880	9	419	9	46·55	—	—
Duff, R. A.	22	180	8	85	4	21·25	—	—
Eady, C. J.	2	223	14	112	7	16·00	—	—
Ebeling, H. I.	1	186	9	89	3	29·66	—	—
Emery, S. H.	4	462	13	249	5	49·80	—	—
Evans, E.	6	1266	166	332	7	47·42	—	—
Fairfax, A. G.	10	1520	54	645	21	30·71	—	—
Ferris, J. J.	8	2030	224	684	48	14·25	4	—
Fleetwood-Smith, L. O'B.	10	3093	78	1570	42	37·38	2	1
Freer, F. W.	1	160	3	74	3	24·66	—	—
Garrett, T. W.	19	2708	297	970	36	26·94	2	—
Gaunt, R. A.	1	216	2	87	2	43·50	—	—
Gehrs, D. R. A.	6	6	0	4	0	—	—	—
Giffen, G.	31	6325	434	2791	103	27·09	7	1
Gregory, D. W.	3	20	1	9	0	—	—	—
Gregory, J. M.	24	5581	138	2648	85	31·15	4	—
Gregory, R. G.	2	24	0	14	0	—	—	—
Gregory, S. E.	58	30	0	33	0	—	—	—
Grimmett, C. V.	37	14573	734	5231	216	24·21	21	7
Hartigan, R. J.	2	12	0	7	0	—	—	—
Hartkopf, A. E. V.	1	240	2	134	1	134·00	—	—
Harvey, R. N.	65	376	21	107	3	35·66	—	—
Hassett, A. L.	43	111	2	78	0	—	—	—
Hazlitt, G. R.	9	1563	73	623	23	27·08	1	—
Hendry, H. L.	11	1706	73	640	16	40·00	—	—
Hill, J. C.	3	606	29	273	8	34·12	—	—
Hodges, J.	2	136	9	84	6	14·00	—	—
Hole, G. B.	18	398	14	126	3	42·00	—	—
Hopkins, A. J.	20	1327	49	696	26	26·76	—	—
Horan, T.	15	373	45	143	11	13·00	1	—
Hordern, H. V.	7	2150	50	1075	46	23·36	5	2
Hornibrook, P. M.	6	1579	63	664	17	39·05	1	—
Howell, W. P.	18	3892	245	1409	49	28·75	1	—
Hunt, W. A.	1	96	2	39	0	—	—	—
Hurwood, A.	2	517	28	170	11	15·45	—	—
Iredale, F. A.	14	12	0	3	0	—	—	—
Ironmonger, H.	14	4699	328	1330	74	17·97	4	2
Iverson, J.	5	1108	29	320	21	15·23	1	—
Johnson, I. W.	45	8773	328	3182	109	29·19	3	—
Johnson, L.	1	282	10	74	6	12·33	—	—
Johnston, W. A.	40	11048	370	3825	160	23·90	7	—
Jones, E.	19	3754	161	1857	64	29·01	3	1
Jones, S. P.	12	262	26	112	6	18·66	—	—
Kelleway, C.	26	4363	141	1683	52	32·36	1	—
Kendall, T.	2	563	56	215	14	15·35	1	—
Kippax, A. F.	22	72	5	19	0	—	—	—
Kline, L.	11	1947	101	553	31	17·93	1	—
Laver, F.	15	2367	122	961	37	25·97	2	—
Lee, P. K.	2	436	18	212	5	42·40	—	—
Lindwall, R. R.	61	13666	418	5257	228	23·05	12	—
Loxton, S. J. E.	12	906	19	349	8	43·62	—	—
Lyons, J. J.	14	316	17	149	6	24·83	1	—
Macartney, C. G.	35	3615	175	1240	45	27·55	2	1
Mackay, K.	24	2712	145	682	24	28·41	1	—
Mailey, A. A.	21	6117	116	3358	99	33·91	6	2
Marr, A. P.	1	48	6	14	0	—	—	—
Matthews, T. J.	8	1081	46	419	16	26·18	—	—
Mayne, E. R.	4	6	0	1	0	—	—	—
McCabe, S. J.	39	3746	127	1543	36	42·86	—	—
McCool, C. L.	14	2512	45	958	36	26·61	3	—

	M.	Balls	Mdns.	Runs	Wkts.	Avge.	5wI.	10wM.
McCormick, E. L.	12	2107	50	1079	36	29·97	—	—
McDonald, C. C.	39	8	0	3	0	—	—	—
McDonald, E. A.	11	2885	90	1431	43	33·27	2	—
McDonnell, P. S.	19	52	1	53	0	—	—	—
McKibbin, T. R.	5	1032	41	496	17	29·17	—	—
McLaren, J. W.	1	144	3	70	1	70·00	—	—
McLeod, C. E.	17	3374	172	1325	33	40·15	2	—
McLeod, R. W.	6	1089	67	384	12	32·00	1	—
McShane, P. G.	3	108	9	48	1	48·00	—	—
Meckiff, I.	15	3452	115	1173	43	27·27	2	—
Midwinter, W. E.	8	949	102	333	14	23·78	1	—
Miller, K. R.	55	10474	338	3905	170	22·97	7	1
Minnett, R. B.	9	589	26	290	11	26·36	—	—
Morris, A. R.	46	111	1	50	2	25·00	—	—
Morris, S.	1	136	14	73	2	36·50	—	—
Moule, W. H.	1	51	4	23	3	7·66	—	—
Nagel, L. E.	1	262	9	110	2	55·00	—	—
Nash, L. J.	2	311	12	126	10	12·60	—	—
Noble, M. A.	42	7109	361	3027	121	25·01	9	2
Noblet, G. J.	3	774	25	183	7	26·14	—	—
Nothling, O. E.	1	276	15	72	0	—	—	—
O'Connor, J. A.	4	692	24	340	13	26·15	1	—
O'Neill, N.	13	184	9	100	1	100·00	—	—
O'Reilly, W. J.	27	10024	585	3254	144	22·59	11	3
Oxenham, R. K.	7	1796	112	522	14	37·28	—	—
Palmer, G. E.	17	4519	452	1678	78	21·51	6	2
Park, R. L.	1	6	0	9	0	—	—	—
Pellew, C. E.	10	78	3	34	0	—	—	—
Ransford, V. S.	20	43	3	28	1	28·00	—	—
Reedman, J. C.	1	57	2	24	1	24·00	—	—
Richardson, A. J.	9	1812	91	521	12	43·41	—	—
Ring, D. T.	13	3024	69	1305	35	37·28	2	—
Robertson, W. R.	1	44	3	24	0	—	—	—
Rorke, G.	4	703	27	203	10	20·30	—	—
Rutherford, J.	1	36	2	15	1	15·00	—	—
Ryder, J.	20	1897	73	743	17	43·70	—	—
Saunders, J. V.	14	3565	116	1797	79	22·74	6	—
Scott, H. J. H.	8	28	1	26	0	—	—	—
Sievers, M. W.	3	602	25	161	9	17·88	1	—
Slater, K.	1	256	9	101	2	50·50	—	—
Spofforth, F. R.	18	4185	416	1731	94	18·41	7	4
Taylor, J. M.	20	114	5	45	1	45·00	—	—
Thompson, N.	2	112	16	31	1	31·00	—	—
Thurlow, H. M.	1	234	7	86	0	—	—	—
Toshack, E. R. H.	12	3140	155	989	47	21·04	4	1
Travers, J.	1	48	2	14	1	14·00	—	—
Tribe, G.	3	760	9	330	2	165·00	—	—
Trott, A. E.	3	474	17	192	9	21·33	1	—
Trott, G. H. S.	24	1890	47	1019	29	35·13	—	—
Trumble, H.	32	8099	452	3072	141	21·78	9	3
Trumble, J. W.	7	600	59	222	10	22·20	—	—
Trumper, V. T.	48	546	19	315	8	39·37	—	—
Turner, C. T. B.	17	5179	457	1670	101	16·53	11	2
Waite, M. G.	2	552	23	190	1	190·00	—	—
Wall, T. W.	18	4752	154	2010	56	35·89	3	—
Ward, F. A.	4	1268	30	574	11	52·18	1	—
Watson, W.	4	6	0	5	0	—	—	—
Whitty, W. J.	14	3357	163	1373	65	21·12	3	—
Wilson, J.	1	216	17	64	1	64·00	—	—
Woods, S. M. J.	3	217	18	121	5	24·20	—	—
Worrall, J.	11	255	29	127	1	127·00	—	—
Extras, etc.				5127	138			
Total		276808	13013	112747	4191	26·90	219	37

SOUTH AFRICA

	M.	Balls	Mdns.	Runs	Wkts.	Avge.	5wI.	10wM.
Adcock, N. A. T.	24	5931	179	2047	95	21·54	5	—
Ashley, W. H.	1	173	18	95	7	13·57	1	—
Balaskas, X. C.	9	1584	28	806	22	36·63	1	—
Baumgartner, H. V.	1	166	3	99	2	49·50	—	—

D

	M.	Balls	Mdns.	Runs	Wkts.	Avge.	5wI.	10wM.
Beaumont, R.	5	6	1	0	0	—	—	—
Begbie, D. W.	5	160	0	130	1	130·00	—	—
Bell, A. J.	16	3342	89	1567	48	32·64	4	—
Bissett, G. F.	4	989	28	469	25	18·76	2	—
Blanckenberg, J. M.	18	3888	132	1817	60	30·28	4	—
Bock, G. E.	1	138	2	91	0	—	—	—
Bond, G. E.	1	16	0	16	0	—	—	—
Brown, L. S.	2	318	7	189	3	63·00	—	—
Buys, I. D.	1	144	4	52	0	—	—	—
Carter, C. P.	10	1475	47	694	28	24·78	2	—
Catterall, R. H.	24	342	7	162	7	23·14	—	—
Chapman, H. W.	2	126	1	104	1	104·00	—	—
Cheetham, J. E.	24	6	0	2	0	—	—	—
Christy, J. A. J.	10	138	4	92	2	46·00	—	—
Chubb, G. W. A.	5	1424	63	577	21	26·47	2	—
Cochran, J. A. K.	1	138	5	47	0	—	—	—
Coen, S. K.	2	12	0	7	0	—	—	—
Conyngham, D. P.	1	366	22	103	2	51·50	—	—
Cox, J. L.	3	576	24	245	4	61·25	—	—
Cripps, G.	1	15	0	23	0	—	—	—
Crisp, R. J.	9	1428	30	747	20	37·35	1	—
Dalton, E. L.	15	864	7	500	12	41·66	—	—
Davies, E. Q.	5	768	7	481	7	68·71	—	—
Dawson, O. C.	9	1294	41	578	10	57·80	—	—
Dixon, C. D.	1	240	6	118	3	39·33	—	—
Duminy, J. P.	3	60	0	39	1	39·00	—	—
Du Toit, J. F.	1	85	5	47	1	47·00	—	—
Faulkner, G. A.	25	4227	124	2180	82	26·58	4	—
Fellows-Smith, J. P.	4	114	1	61	0	—	—	—
Finlason, C. E.	1	12	0	7	0	—	—	—
Floquet, C. E.	1	48	2	24	0	—	—	—
Francois, C. M.	5	684	36	225	6	37·50	—	—
Frank, W. H. B.	1	58	3	52	1	52·00	—	—
Fuller, E. R. H.	7	1898	61	668	22	30·36	1	—
Glover, G. K.	1	65	4	28	1	28·00	—	—
Goddard, T. L.	20	6305	377	1729	64	27·01	3	—
Gordon, N.	5	1966	28	807	20	40·35	2	—
Graham, R.	2	240	13	127	3	42·33	—	—
Griffin, G.	2	432	14	192	8	24·00	—	—
Hall, A. E.	7	2361	107	886	40	22·15	3	1
Hands, P. A. M.	7	37	0	18	0	—	—	—
Hanley, M. A.	1	232	7	88	1	88·00	—	—
Hartigan, G. P. D.	5	252	7	141	1	141·00	—	—
Hearne, F.	4	62	0	40	2	20·00	—	—
Heine, P. S.	13	3674	99	1332	56	23·78	4	—
Hime, C. F. W.	1	55	4	31	1	31·00	—	—
Innes, A. R.	2	128	8	89	5	17·80	1	—
Ironside, D. E. J.	3	985	41	275	15	18·33	1	—
Johnson, C. L.	1	140	12	57	0	—	—	—
Keith, H. J.	8	108	1	63	0	—	—	—
Kempis, G. A.	1	168	17	76	4	19·00	—	—
Kotze, J. J.	3	413	8	243	6	40·50	—	—
Kuys, F.	1	60	4	31	2	15·50	—	—
Langton, A. B. C.	15	4199	104	1818	40	45·45	1	—
Le Roux, F. L.	1	54	3	24	0	—	—	—
Ling, W. V. S.	6	18	0	20	0	—	—	1
Llewellyn, C. B.	15	2292	55	1421	48	29·60	4	1
Lundie, E. B.	1	286	9	107	4	26·75	—	—
Mann, N. B. F.	19	5796	260	1920	58	33·10	1	—
Mansell, P. N. F.	13	1506	31	736	11	66·90	—	—
Markham, L. A.	1	104	1	72	1	72·00	—	—
Marx, W. F. E.	3	228	1	144	4	36·00	—	—
McCarthy, C. N.	15	3499	63	1510	36	41·94	2	—
McGlew, D. J.	29	32	0	23	0	—	—	—
McKinnon, A. H.	1	156	8	64	2	32·00	—	—
McLean, R. A.	33	4	0	1	0	—	—	—
McMillan, Q.	13	2021	38	1243	36	34·52	2	—
Meintjes, D. J.	2	246	7	115	6	19·16	—	—
Melle, M. G.	7	1667	20	851	26	32·73	2	—
Middleton, J.	6	1064	61	442	24	18·41	2	—
Mills, C.	1	140	7	83	2	41·50	—	—

	M.	Balls	Mdns.	Runs	Wkts.	Avge.	5wI.	10wM.
Milton, W. H.	3	79	5	48	2	24·00	—	—
Mitchell, B.	42	2519	26	1379	27	51·07	1	—
Morkel, D. P. B.	16	1704	55	821	18	45·61	—	—
Murray, A. R. A.	10	2374	111	710	18	39·44	—	—
Newberry, C.	4	558	15	268	11	24·36	—	—
Newson, E. S.	3	874	18	265	4	66·25	—	—
Nicolson, J. F. W.	3	24	0	17	0	—	—	—
Norton, N. O.	1	90	4	47	4	11·75	—	—
Nourse, A. D., sen.	45	3234	120	1553	41	37·87	—	—
Nourse, A. D., jun.	34	20	1	9	0	—	—	—
Nupen, E. P.	17	4159	133	1788	50	35·76	5	1
Ochse, A. L.	3	649	10	362	10	36·20	—	—
Owen-Smith, H. G.	5	156	0	113	0	—	—	—
Parker, G. M.	2	366	2	273	8	34·12	1	—
Parkin, D. C.	1	130	4	82	3	27·33	—	—
Pearse, C. O. C.	3	144	0	106	3	35·33	—	—
Pegler, S. J.	16	2989	84	1572	47	33·44	2	—
Plimsoll, J. B.	1	237	9	143	3	47·66	—	—
Poore, R. M.	3	9	0	4	1	4·00	—	—
Pothecary, J. E.	3	828	32	354	9	39·33	—	—
Powell, A. W.	1	20	1	10	1	10·00	—	—
Promnitz, H. L. E	2	528	30	161	8	20·12	1	—
Quinn, N. A.	12	2922	103	1145	35	32·71	1	—
Reid, N.	1	126	3	63	2	31·50	—	—
Robertson, J. B.	3	738	26	321	6	53·50	—	—
Rowan, A. M. B.	15	5193	136	2084	54	38·59	4	—
Rowan, E. A. B.	26	19	1	7	0	—	—	—
Rowe, G. A.	5	998	50	456	15	30·40	1	—
Samuelson, H. V.	1	108	2	64	0	—	—	—
Schwarz, R. O.	20	2639	66	1417	55	25·76	2	—
Seccull, A. W.	1	60	2	37	2	18·50	—	—
Shalders, W. A.	12	48	3	6	1	6·00	—	—
Shepstone, G. H.	2	115	9	47	0	—	—	—
Siedle, I. J.	18	19	1	7	1	7·00	—	—
Sinclair, J. H.	25	3598	110	1996	63	31·68	1	—
Smith, V. I.	9	1655	55	769	12	64·08	—	—
Snooke, S. J.	26	1620	62	702	35	20·05	1	1
Stricker, L. A.	13	174	3	105	1	105·00	—	—
Taberer, H. M.	1	60	2	48	1	48·00	—	—
Tapscott, L. E.	2	12	1	2	0	—	—	—
Tayfield, H. J.	37	13565	602	4405	170	25·91	14	2
Taylor, H. W.	42	342	18	156	5	31·20	—	—
Theunissen, N.	1	80	5	51	0	—	—	—
Thornton, G.	1	24	0	20	1	20·00	—	—
Tomlinson, D. S.	1	60	0	38	0	—	—	—
Tuckett, L.	9	2104	46	980	19	51·57	2	—
Tuckett, L. R.	1	120	4	69	0	—	—	—
Van Ryneveld, C. B.	19	1554	27	671	17	39·47	—	—
Viljoen, K. G.	27	48	1	23	0	—	—	—
Vincent, C. L.	25	5863	194	2631	84	31·32	3	—
Vintcent, C. H.	3	369	23	193	4	48·25	—	—
Vogler, A. E. E.	15	2764	96	1455	64	22·73	5	1
Watkins, J. C.	15	2805	134	816	29	28·13	—	—
Westcott, R. J.	5	32	0	22	0	—	—	—
White, G. C.	17	498	14	301	9	33·44	—	—
Willoughby, J. T.	2	275	12	159	6	26·50	—	—
Zulch, J. W.	16	24	0	28	0	—	—	—
Extras, etc.				3004	63			
Total		146570	4877	66391	2042	32·51	99	7

WEST INDIES

	M.	Balls	Mdns.	Runs	Wkts.	Avge.	5wI.	10wM.
Achong, E.	6	918	34	378	8	47·25	—	—
Atkinson, D.	22	5201	312	1647	47	35·04	3	—
Atkinson, E.	8	1634	77	589	25	23·56	1	—
Birkett, L. S.	4	126	1	71	1	71·00	—	—
Browne, C. R.	4	840	38	288	6	48·00	—	—
Butcher, B. F.	10	36	1	17	0	—	—	—
Butler, L.	1	240	7	151	2	75·50	—	—

	M.	Balls	Mdns.	Runs	Wkts.	Avge.	5wI.	10wM.
Caires, F. I. de	3	12	0	9	0	—	—	—
Cameron, F. J.	5	786	34	278	3	92·66	—	—
Cameron, J. H.	2	232	6	88	3	29·33	—	—
Carew, G.	4	18	2	2	0	—	—	—
Christiani, R. J.	22	234	1	108	3	36·00	—	—
Clarke, C. B.	3	456	2	261	6	43·50	—	—
Constantine, L. N.	18	3553	125	1746	58	30·10	2	—
Costa, O. C. da	5	372	13	175	3	58·33	—	—
Depeiza, C.	5	30	0	15	0	—	—	—
Dewdney, T.	9	1641	67	807	21	38·42	1	—
Ferguson, W.	8	2556	90	1165	34	34·26	3	1
Francis, G. N.	10	1619	54	763	23	33·17	—	—
Fuller, A.	1	48	2	12	0	—	—	—
Gaskin, B. M.	2	474	24	158	2	79·00	—	—
Gibbs, G.	1	24	1	7	0	—	—	—
Gibbs, L.	8	1746	91	633	25	25·32	1	—
Gilchrist, R.	13	3227	124	1521	57	26·68	1	—
Gladstone, G.	1	300	5	189	1	189·00	—	—
Goddard, J. D. C.	27	2931	148	1050	33	31·81	1	—
Gomez, G. E.	29	5236	284	1590	58	27·41	1	1
Grant, G. C.	12	24	0	18	0	—	—	—
Grant, R. S.	7	986	32	353	11	32·09	—	—
Grell, M. I.	1	30	1	17	0	—	—	—
Griffith, C.	1	144	3	102	1	102·00	—	—
Griffith, H. C.	13	2663	89	1243	44	28·25	2	—
Hall, W.	13	3347	132	1496	68	22·00	5	1
Headley, G.	22	398	7	230	0	—	—	—
Holt, J. K.	17	30	2	20	1	20·00	—	—
Hunte, C. C.	16	96	5	30	1	30·00	—	—
Hylton, L. G.	6	966	32	418	16	26·12	—	—
Johnson, H. H.	3	789	37	238	13	18·30	2	1
Johnson, T.	1	240	3	129	3	43·00	—	—
Jones, C. M.	4	102	11	11	0	—	—	—
Jones, P. E.	9	1842	64	751	25	30·04	1	—
Kanhai, R.	23	24	3	2	0	—	—	—
Kentish, E. S. M.	2	540	30	178	8	22·25	1	—
King, F.	14	2869	139	1159	29	39·96	1	—
Madray, I.	2	210	6	108	0	—	—	—
Marshall, N.	1	279	21	63	2	31·50	—	—
Marshall, R. E.	4	52	2	15	0	—	—	—
Martin, F. R.	9	1346	27	619	8	77·37	—	—
Martindale, E. A.	10	1605	40	804	37	21·72	3	—
McWatt, C. A.	6	24	1	16	1	16·00	—	—
Miller, R.	1	96	8	28	0	—	—	—
Moodie, C. H.	1	174	12	40	3	13·33	—	—
Neblett, J. M.	1	216	11	75	1	75·00	—	—
Pairaudeau, B. H.	13	6	0	3	0	—	—	—
Passailaigue, C. C.	1	12	0	15	0	—	—	—
Pierre, L. R.	1	42	0	28	0	—	—	—
Ramadhin, K. T.	41	13643	809	4439	155	28·63	10	1
Roach, C. A.	16	222	5	103	2	51·50	—	—
St Hill, E.	2	558	29	221	3	73·66	—	—
St Hill, W. H.	3	18	0	9	0	—	—	—
Scarlett, R.	3	804	53	209	2	104·50	—	—
Scott, A. P. H.	1	264	9	140	0	—	—	—
Scott, O. C.	8	1405	17	925	22	42·04	1	—
Sealey, B. J.	1	30	1	10	1	10·00	—	—
Sealey, J. E. D.	11	156	4	94	3	31·33	—	—
Singh, C.	2	506	35	165	5	33·00	—	—
Small, J. A.	3	366	11	184	3	61·33	—	—
Smith, O. G.	26	4431	227	1625	48	33·85	1	—
Sobers, G.	32	4651	232	1800	40	45·00	—	—
Solomon, J.	9	324	17	135	1	135·00	—	—
Stollmeyer, J. B.	32	990	32	507	13	39·00	—	—
Taylor, J.	3	672	33	273	10	27·30	1	—
Trim, J.	4	794	28	291	18	16·16	1	—
Valentine, A. L.	29	11165	708	3568	123	29·00	8	2
Valentine, V. A.	2	288	14	104	1	104·00	—	—
Walcott, C. L.	44	1194	72	408	11	37·09	—	—
Walcott, L. A.	1	48	1	32	1	32·00	—	—
Watson, C.	5	1194	39	593	16	37·06	—	—

	M.	Balls	Mdns.	Runs	Wkts.	Avge.	5wI.	10wM.
Weekes, E. D.	48	128	3	77	1	77·00	—	—
Wight, C. V.	2	30	1	6	0	—	—	—
Williams, E. A. V.	4	796	34	241	9	26·77	—	—
Worrell, F. M.	36	5390	200	2091	54	38·72	2	—
Extras, etc.				2006	70			
Total		103709	4875	42183	1303	32·37	53	7

NEW ZEALAND

	M.	Balls	Mdns.	Runs	Wkts.	Avge.	5wI.	10wM.
Alabaster, J. C.	8	980	47	464	9	51·55	—	—
Allcott, C. F. W.	6	1206	41	541	6	90·16	—	—
Badcock, F. T.	7	1608	66	610	16	38·12	—	—
Beard, D. D.	4	812	38	302	9	33·55	—	—
Bell, W.	2	491	13	235	2	117·50	—	—
Blair, R. W.	14	2361	64	1031	26	39·65	—	—
Blunt, R. C.	9	933	34	472	12	39·33	—	—
Burke, C. C.	1	66	2	30	2	15·00	—	—
Burtt, T. B.	10	2611	119	1170	33	35·45	3	—
Butterfield, L. A.	1	78	6	24	0	—	—	—
Cave, H. B.	19	4080	244	1467	34	43·14	—	—
Chapple, M. E.	8	8	0	1	0	—	—	—
Cleverley, D. C.	2	222	3	130	0	—	—	—
Cowie, J. A.	9	2028	65	969	45	21·53	4	1
Cresswell, G. F.	3	644	30	292	13	22·46	1	—
Cromb, I. B.	5	960	36	442	8	55·25	—	—
Dempster, C. S.	10	5	0	10	0	—	—	—
Dempster, E. W.	5	544	17	219	2	109·50	—	—
Dickinson, G. R.	3	451	13	245	8	30·62	—	—
Donnelly, M. P.	7	30	0	20	0	—	—	—
Dunning, J. A.	4	830	20	493	5	98·60	—	—
Emery, R. W. G.	2	46	0	52	2	26·00	—	—
Fisher, F. E.	1	204	6	78	1	78·00	—	—
Freeman, D. L.	2	240	3	169	1	169·00	—	—
Gallichan, N. M.	1	264	11	113	3	37·66	—	—
Hayes, J. A.	15	2681	87	1217	30	45·66	—	—
Henderson, M.	1	90	3	64	2	32·00	—	—
Hough, K. W.	2	462	22	175	6	29·16	—	—
Leggat, I. B.	1	24	0	6	0	—	—	—
Lissette, A. F.	2	288	16	124	3	41·33	—	—
Lowry, T. C.	7	12	1	5	0	—	—	—
MacGibbon, A. R.	26	5605	230	2160	70	30·85	1	—
Matheson, A. M.	2	282	9	136	2	68·00	—	—
McGirr, H. M.	2	180	5	115	1	115·00	—	—
McLeod, E. A.	1	12	0	5	0	—	—	—
McRae, D. A. N.	1	84	3	44	0	—	—	—
Merritt, W. E.	6	936	10	617	12	51·41	—	—
Miller, L. S. M.	13	2	0	1	0	—	—	—
Moir, A. M.	17	2638	92	1418	28	50·64	2	—
Moloney, D. A. R.	3	12	1	9	0	—	—	—
Mooney, F. L. H.	14	8	1	0	0	—	—	—
Newman, J.	3	425	11	254	2	127·00	—	—
Overton, G. W. F.	3	730	23	258	9	28·66	—	—
Page, M. L.	14	381	11	231	5	46·20	—	—
Poore, M. B.	14	788	24	367	9	40·77	—	—
Rabone, G. O.	12	1385	48	633	16	39·56	1	—
Reid, J. R.	34	4642	243	1665	47	35·42	—	—
Roberts, A. W.	5	459	19	209	7	29·85	—	—
Scott, R. H.	1	138	3	74	1	74·00	—	—
Scott, V. J.	10	18	0	14	0	—	—	—
Sinclair, I. M.	2	233	9	120	1	120·00	—	—
Smith, D.	1	120	0	113	1	113·00	—	—
Snedden, C. A.	1	96	4	46	0	—	—	—
Sparling, J. T.	5	480	22	210	2	105·00	—	—
Sutcliffe, B.	34	435	4	260	2	130·00	—	—
Vivian, H. G.	7	1311	44	633	17	37·23	—	—
Wallace, W. M.	13	6	0	5	0	—	—	—
Weir, G. L.	11	342	7	209	7	29·85	—	—
Extras, etc.				920	28			
Total		47007	1830	21896	545	40·17	12	1

INDIA

	M.	Balls	Mdns.	Runs	Wkts.	Avge.	5wI.	10wM.
Adhikari, H. R.	21	170	2	82	3	27·33	—	—
Ali, S. Nazir	2	138	0	83	4	20·75	—	—
Ali, S. Wazir	7	30	1	25	0	—	—	—
Amarnath, L.	24	4121	195	1481	45	32·91	2	—
Amar Singh	7	2182	95	858	28	30·64	2	—
Apte, M. L.	7	6	0	3	0	—	—	—
Baig, A. A.	5	12	0	13	0	—	—	—
Banerjee, S.	1	306	3	181	5	36·20	—	—
Banerjee, S. N.	1	273	8	127	5	25·40	—	—
Bhandari, P.	3	78	2	39	0	—	—	—
Borde, C. G.	13	1531	43	786	14	56·14	—	—
Chowdhury, N. R.	2	516	21	205	1	205·00	—	—
Contractor, N. J.	19	102	4	44	1	44·00	—	—
Dani, H. T.	1	60	5	19	1	19·00	—	—
Desai, R. B.	9	2161	70	1117	25	44·68	1	—
Divecha, R. V.	5	1044	44	361	11	32·81	—	—
Durani, A. S.	1	6	0	9	0	—	—	—
Gadkari, C. V.	6	102	4	45	0	—	—	—
Gaekwad, D. K.	10	12	0	12	0	—	—	—
Gaekwad, H. G.	1	222	21	47	0	—	—	—
Ghorpade, J. M.	8	150	1	131	0	—	—	—
Ghulam Ahmed	22	5650	253	2052	68	30·17	4	1
Gopalan, M. J.	1	114	7	39	1	39·00	—	—
Gopinath, C. D.	8	48	2	11	1	11·00	—	—
Gul Mahomed	8	77	4	24	2	12·00	—	—
Guard, G.	2	396	16	182	3	60·66	—	—
Gupte, S. P.	31	9882	513	3902	134	29·11	11	1
Hardikar, M. S.	2	108	7	55	1	55·00	—	—
Hazare, V. S.	30	2840	97	1220	20	61·00	—	—
Jahangir Khan, M.	4	606	28	255	4	63·75	—	—
Jaisimha, M. L.	2	66	2	38	0	—	—	—
Jamshedji, R. J.	1	210	4	137	3	45·66	—	—
Jilani, M. Baqa	1	90	4	55	0	—	—	—
Kripal Singh, A. G.	8	84	5	35	0	—	—	—
Manjrekar, V. L.	32	132	13	21	1	21·00	—	—
Mankad, V.	44	14686	777	5235	162	32·31	8	2
Mehra, V.	2	18	0	3	0	—	—	—
Merchant, V. M.	10	54	0	40	0	—	—	—
Modi, R. S.	10	30	1	14	0	—	—	—
Muddiah, V. M.	1	72	3	32	0	—	—	—
Mushtaq Ali	11	378	9	202	3	67·33	—	—
Nadkarni, R. G.	11	2234	119	811	21	38·61	1	—
Naoomal Jeoomal	3	108	0	68	2	34·00	—	—
Nayudu, C. K.	7	858	24	386	9	42·88	—	—
Nayudu, C. S.	11	522	6	359	2	179·50	—	—
Nissar, M.	6	1211	34	707	25	28·28	3	—
Nyalchand, K.	1	384	33	97	3	32·33	—	—
Palia, P. E.	2	42	3	13	0	—	—	—
Patel, J. S.	7	1665	94	636	29	21·93	2	1
Patil, S. R.	1	138	7	51	2	25·50	—	—
Phadkar, D. G.	31	5975	275	2285	62	36·85	3	—
Ramchand, G. S.	33	4976	258	1900	41	46·34	2	—
Ramji, L.	1	138	5	64	0	—	—	—
Rangachari, C. R.	4	846	11	493	9	54·77	1	—
Ranjane, V.	1	108	6	35	1	35·00	—	—
Roy, P.	42	98	4	62	1	62·00	—	—
Sarwate, C. T.	9	658	5	374	3	124·66	—	—
Shinde, S. G.	7	1515	60	717	12	59·75	1	—
Shodhan, D. H.	3	60	3	26	0	—	—	—
Sohoni, S. W.	4	532	20	202	2	101·00	—	—
Sunderram, G.	2	396	12	164	3	54·66	—	—
Surendra Nath	9	1972	111	802	20	40·10	2	—
Swamy, N. V.	1	108	5	45	0	—	—	—
Tarapore, K. K.	1	114	2	72	0	—	—	—
Umrigar, P. R.	45	2446	111	848	18	47·11	1	—
Extras, etc.				1134	37			
Total		75867	3472	31571	848	37·24	43	5

PAKISTAN

	M.	Balls	Mdns.	Runs	Wkts.	Avge.	5wI.	10wM.
Alimuddin	19	84	0	76	1	76·00	—	—
Amir Elahi	5	400	5	248	7	35·42	—	—
Anwar Hussain	4	36	1	29	1	29·00	—	—
Antao Dsouza	1	162	5	78	2	39·00	—	—
Fazal Mahmood	26	7851	440	2768	125	22·14	12	4
Ghazali, M. E. Z.	2	48	1	18	0	—	—	—
Hanif Mohammed	27	156	6	73	1	73·00	—	—
Haseeb Ashan	5	1101	30	635	8	79·37	—	—
Imtiaz Ahmed	29	6	1	0	0	—	—	—
Intikhab Alam	1	150	5	62	3	20·66	—	—
Israr Ali	4	318	12	165	6	27·50	—	—
Kardar, A. H.	23	2712	147	953	21	45·38	—	—
Khalid Hassan	1	126	1	116	2	58·00	—	—
Khan Mohammed	13	3169	152	1294	54	23·96	4	—
Mahmood Hussain	18	3826	133	1737	48	36·18	1	—
Maqsood Ahmed	16	462	21	191	3	63·66	—	—
Miran Bux	2	348	22	115	2	57·50	—	—
Mohammed Munaf	2	312	10	190	5	38·00	—	—
Munir Malik	1	186	4	100	3	33·33	—	—
Mushtaq Mohammed	1	36	0	34	0	—	—	—
Nasimul Ghani	10	2068	91	878	34	25·82	2	—
Nazar Mohammed	5	12	1	4	0	—	—	—
Rehman, S. F.	1	204	3	99	1	99·00	—	—
Saeed Ahmed	11	139	3	54	1	54·00	—	—
Shujauddin	17	2004	113	665	17	39·11	—	—
Wallis Mathias	12	24	0	20	0	—	—	—
Waqar Hasan	21	6	0	10	0	—	—	—
Wazir Mohammed	20	24	0	15	0	—	—	—
Zulfiqar Ahmed	9	1285	84	365	20	18·25	2	1
Extras, etc.				478	16			
Total		27255	1291	11470	381	30·10	21	5

CONSOLIDATED RECORD OF PLAYERS WHO APPEARED FOR TWO COUNTRIES

BATTING AND FIELDING

	M.	I.	N.O.	Runs	H.S.	Avge.	100s	50s	Ct.	St.
Amir Elahi	6	9	1	82	47	10·25	—	—	—	—
J. J. Ferris	9	17	4	114	20*	8·76	—	—	4	—
S. C. Guillen	8	12	2	202	54	20·20	—	1	13	3
Gul Mahomed	9	17	1	205	34	12·81	—	—	3	—
F. Hearne	6	10	0	168	30	16·80	—	—	3	—
A. H. Kardar	26	42	3	927	93	23·76	—	5	16	—
W. E. Midwinter	12	21	1	269	37	13·45	—	—	10	—
F. Mitchell	5	10	0	116	41	11·60	—	—	2	—
W. L. Murdoch	19	34	5	908	211	31·31	2	1	12	2
Nawab of Pataudi	6	10	0	199	102	19·90	1	—	—	—
A. E. Trott	5	9	3	228	85*	38·00	—	2	4	—
S. M. J. Woods	6	10	0	154	53	15·40	—	1	5	—

BOWLING

	M.	Balls	Mdns.	Runs	Wkts.	Avge.	5wI.	10wM.
Amir Elahi	6	400	5	248	7	35·42	—	—
J. J. Ferris	9	2302	251	775	61	12·70	6	1
Gul Mahomed	9	77	4	24	2	12·00	—	—
F. Hearne	6	62	0	40	2	20·00	—	—
A. H. Kardar	26	2712	147	953	21	45·38	—	—
W. E. Midwinter	12	1725	181	605	24	25·20	1	—
A. E. Trott	5	948	54	390	26	15·00	2	—
S. M. J. Woods	6	412	26	250	10	25·00	—	—

Summary of Averages

BATTING AND FIELDING

	M.	I.	N.O.	Runs	H.S.	Avge.	100s	50s	Ct.	St.
England	368	6256	819	168010	364	30·90	295	714	3024	172
Australia	250	4367	545	117035	334	30·62	218	456	2105	174
South Africa	142	2757	322	61458	255*	25·23	77	274	1059	66
West Indies	84	1477	187	42353	365*	32·81	93	167	660	36
New Zealand	52	951	115	18760	230*	21·24	17	83	287	17
India	67	1228	156	28630	231*	26·70	46	114	421	48
Pakistan	29	523	63	11780	337	25·60	14	49	190	12
Total	992	17559	2207	448026	365*	29·18	760	1857	7746	525

BOWLING

	Balls	Mdns.	Runs	Wkts.	Avge.	5wI.	10wM.
England	378642	18010	161768	6042	26·75	306	66
Australia	276808	13013	112747	4191	26·90	219	37
South Africa	146570	4877	66391	2042	32·51	99	7
West Indies	103709	4875	42183	1303	32·37	53	7
New Zealand	47007	1830	21896	545	40·17	12	1
India	75867	3472	31571	848	37·24	43	5
Pakistan	27255	1291	11470	381	30·10	21	5
Total	1055858	47368	448026	15352	29·18	753	128

MISCELLANEOUS

	Extras Rec'd	Extras Conc'd	Run Out	Ct. Sub.	St. Sub.	Ob. Field	Hand' Ball	Toss Won	Toss Lost
England	7795	7823	236	37	1	—	1	192	176
Australia	4804	5127	138	32	—	—	—	120	130
South Africa	3161	3004	62	14	—	1	—	66	76
West Indies	1652	2006	70	17	—	—	—	43	41
New Zealand	1096	920	28	6	—	—	—	29	23
India	1441	1134	37	15	—	—	—	33	34
Pakistan	543	478	16	4	—	—	—	13	16
Total	20492	20492	587	125	1	1	1	496	496

Appendix B
Centuries in Test Cricket

ENGLAND (295)

Abel, R. ....(2)	120	v. South Africa (Cape Town)	1888–89
	132*	v. Australia (Sydney)	1891–92
Allen, G. O. ....(1)	122	v. New Zealand (Lord's)	1931
Ames, L. E. G. ....(8)	105	v. West Indies (Trinidad)	1929–30
	149	v. West Indies (Kingston)	1929–30
	137	v. New Zealand (Lord's)	1931
	103	v. New Zealand (Christchurch)	1932–33
	120	v. Australia (Lord's)	1934
	126	v. West Indies (Kingston)	1934–35
	148*	v. South Africa (Oval)	1935
	115	v. South Africa (Cape Town)	1938–39
Bailey, T. E. ....(1)	134*	v. New Zealand (Christchurch)	1950–51
Bakewell, A. H. ....(1)	107	v. West Indies (Oval)	1933
Barnes, W. ....(1)	134	v. Australia (Adelaide)	1884–85
Barnett, C. J. ....(2)	129	v. Australia (Adelaide)	1936–37
	126	v. Australia (Nottingham)	1938
Barrington, K. F. ....(2)	128	v. West Indies (Barbados)	1959–60
	121	v. West Indies (Trinidad)	1959–60
Bowley, E. H. ....(1)	109	v. New Zealand (Auckland)	1929–30
Braund, L. C. ....(3)	103*	v. Australia (Adelaide)	1901–02
	102	v. Australia (Sydney)	1903–04
	104	v. South Africa (Lord's)	1907
Briggs, J. ....(1)	121	v. Australia (Melbourne)	1884–85
Brown, J. T. ....(1)	140	v. Australia (Melbourne)	1894–95
Chapman, A. P. F. ....(1)	121	v. Australia (Lord's)	1930
Compton, D. C. S. ....(17)	102	v. Australia (Nottingham)	1938
	120	v. West Indies (Lord's)	1939
	147 103* }	v. Australia (Adelaide)	1946–47
	163	v. South Africa (Nottingham)	1947
	208	v. South Africa (Lord's)	1947
	115	v. South Africa (Manchester)	1947
	113	v. South Africa (Oval)	1947
	184	v. Australia (Nottingham)	1948
	145*	v. Australia (Manchester)	1948
	114	v. South Africa (Johannesburg)	1948–49
	114	v. New Zealand (Leeds)	1949
	116	v. New Zealand (Lord's)	1949
	112	v. South Africa (Nottingham)	1951
	133	v. West Indies (Trinidad)	1953–54
	278	v. Pakistan (Nottingham)	1954
	158	v. South Africa (Manchester)	1955
Cowdrey, M. C. ....(9)	102	v. Australia (Melbourne)	1954–55
	101	v. South Africa (Cape Town)	1956–57
	154	v. West Indies (Birmingham)	1957
	152	v. West Indies (Lord's)	1957
	100*	v. Australia (Sydney)	1958–59
	160	v. India (Leeds)	1959
	114	v. West Indies (Kingston)	1959–60
	119	v. West Indies (Trinidad)	1959–60
	155	v. South Africa (Oval)	1960
Denton, D. ....(1)	104	v. South Africa (Johannesburg)	1909–10
Dexter, E. R. ....(3)	141	v. New Zealand (Christchurch)	1958–59
	136*	v. West Indies (Barbados)	1959–60
	110	v. West Indies (Georgetown)	1959–60
Douglas, J. W. H. T. ....(1)	119	v. South Africa (Durban)	1913–14
Duleepsinhji, K. S. ....(3)	117	v. New Zealand (Auckland)...	1929–30

*D

Duleepsinhji, K. S. (*cont.*)	173	v. Australia (Lord's)	1930
	109	v. New Zealand (Oval)	1931
Edrich, W. J. ....(6)	219	v. South Africa (Durban)	1938–39
	119	v. Australia (Sydney)	1946–47
	189	v. South Africa (Lord's)	1947
	191	v. South Africa (Manchester)	1947
	111	v. Australia (Leeds)	1948
	100	v. New Zealand (Oval)	1949
Evans, T. G...................(2)	104	v. West Indies (Manchester)	1950
	104	v. India (Lord's)	1952
Fane, F. L. ....(1)	143	v. South Africa (Johannesburg)	1905–06
Foster, R. E. ....(1)	287	v. Australia (Sydney)	1903–04
Fry, C. B. ....(2)	144	v. Australia (Oval)	1905
	129	v. South Africa (Oval)	1907
Gibb, P. A. ....(2)	106	v. South Africa (Johannesburg)	1938–39
	120	v. South Africa (Durban)	1938–39
Grace, W. G. ....(2)	152	v. Australia (Oval)	1880
	170	v. Australia (Oval)	1886
Graveney, T. W. ....(4)	175	v. India (Bombay)	1951–52
	111	v. Australia (Sydney)	1954–55
	258	v. West Indies (Nottingham)	1957
	164	v. West Indies (Oval)	1957
Griffith, S. C. ....(1)	140	v. West Indies (Trinidad)	1947–48
Gunn, G. ....(2)	119	v. Australia (Sydney)	1907–08
	122*	v. Australia (Sydney)	1907–08
Gunn, W. ....(1)	102*	v. Australia (Manchester)	1893
Hammond, W. R. ....(22)	251	v. Australia (Sydney)	1928–29
	200	v. Australia (Melbourne)	1928–29
	119* 177 }	v. Australia (Adelaide)	1928–29
	138*	v. South Africa (Birmingham)	1929
	101*	v. South Africa (Oval)	1929
	113	v. Australia (Leeds)	1930
	136*	v. South Africa (Durban)	1930–31
	100*	v. New Zealand (Oval)	1931
	112	v. Australia (Sydney)	1932–33
	101	v. Australia (Sydney)	1932–33
	227	v. New Zealand (Christchurch)	1932–33
	336*	v. New Zealand (Auckland)	1932–33
	167	v. India (Manchester)	1936
	217	v. India (Oval)	1936
	231*	v. Australia (Sydney)	1936–37
	140	v. New Zealand (Lord's)	1937
	240	v. Australia (Lord's)	1938
	181	v. South Africa (Cape Town)	1938–39
	120	v. South Africa (Durban)	1938–39
	140	v. South Africa (Durban)	1938–39
	138	v. West Indies (Oval)	1939
Hardstaff, J., jun. ....(4)	114	v. New Zealand (Lord's)	1937
	103	v. New Zealand (Oval)	1937
	169*	v. Australia (Oval)	1938
	205*	v. India (Lord's)	1946
Hayward, T. ....(3)	122	v. South Africa (Johannesburg)	1895–96
	130	v. Australia (Manchester)	1899
	137	v. Australia (Oval)	1899
Hearne, J. W. ....(1)	114	v. Australia (Melbourne)	1911–12
Hendren, E. ....(7)	132	v. South Africa (Leeds)	1924
	142	v. South Africa (Oval)	1924
	127*	v. Australia (Lord's)	1926
	169	v. Australia (Brisbane)	1928–29
	205*	v. West Indies (Trinidad)	1929–30
	123	v. West Indies (Georgetown)	1929–30
	132	v. Australia (Manchester)	1934
Hill, A. J. L. ....(1)	124	v. South Africa (Cape Town)	1895–96
Hobbs, J. B. ....(15)	187	v. South Africa (Cape Town)	1909–10
	126*	v. Australia (Melbourne)	1911–12
	187	v. Australia (Adelaide)	1911–12
	178	v. Australia (Melbourne)	1911–12
	107	v. Australia (Lord's)	1912
	122	v. Australia (Melbourne)	1920–21
	123	v. Australia (Adelaide)	1920–21
	211	v. South Africa (Lord's)	1924

Hobbs, J. B. (*cont*.)	115	v. Australia (Sydney)	1924–25
	154	v. Australia (Melbourne)	1924–25
	119	v. Australia (Adelaide)	1924–25
	119	v. Australia (Lord's)	1926
	100	v. Australia (Oval)	1926
	159	v. West Indies (Oval)	1928
	142	v. Australia (Melbourne)	1928–29
Hutchings, K. L. ....(1)	126	v. Australia (Melbourne)	1907–08
Hutton, L. ....(19)	100	v. New Zealand (Manchester)	1937
	100	v. Australia (Nottingham)	1938
	364	v. Australia (Oval)	1938
	196	v. West Indies (Lord's)	1939
	165*	v. West Indies (Oval)	1939
	122*	v. Australia (Sydney)	1946–47
	100	v. South Africa (Leeds)	1947
	158	v. South Africa (Johannesburg)	1948–49
	123	v. South Africa (Johannesburg)	1948–49
	101	v. New Zealand (Leeds)	1949
	206	v. New Zealand (Oval)	1949
	202*	v. West Indies (Oval)	1950
	156*	v. Australia (Adelaide)	1950–51
	100	v. South Africa (Leeds)	1951
	150	v. India (Lord's)	1952
	104	v. India (Manchester)	1952
	145	v. Australia (Lord's)	1953
	169	v. West Indies (Georgetown)	1953–54
	205	v. West Indies (Kingston)	1953–54
Insole, D. J. ....(1)	110*	v. South Africa (Durban)	1956–57
Jackson, F. S. ....(5)	103	v. Australia (Oval)	1893
	118	v. Australia (Oval)	1899
	128	v. Australia (Manchester)	1902
	144*	v. Australia (Leeds)	1905
	113	v. Australia (Manchester)	1905
Jardine, D. R. ....(1)	127	v. West Indies (Manchester)	1933
Jessop, G. L. ....(1)	104	v. Australia (Oval)	1902
Legge, G. B. ....(1)	196	v. New Zealand (Auckland)	1929–30
Leyland, M. ....(9)	137	v. Australia (Melbourne)	1928–29
	102	v. South Africa (Lord's)	1929
	109	v. Australia (Lord's)	1934
	153	v. Australia (Manchester)	1934
	110	v. Australia (Oval)	1934
	161	v. South Africa (Oval)	1935
	126	v. Australia (Brisbane)	1936–37
	111*	v. Australia (Melbourne)	1936–37
	187	v. Australia (Oval)	1938
MacLaren, A. C. ....(5)	120	v. Australia (Melbourne)	1894–95
	109	v. Australia (Sydney)	1897–98
	124	v. Australia (Adelaide)	1897–98
	116	v. Australia (Sydney)	1901–02
	140	v. Australia (Nottingham)	1905
Makepeace, H...............(1)	117	v. Australia (Melbourne)	1920–21
Mann, F. G...................(1)	136*	v. South Africa (Port Elizabeth)	1948–49
May, P. B. H. ....(13)	138	v. South Africa (Leeds)	1951
	135	v. West Indies (Trinidad)	1953–54
	104	v. Australia (Sydney)	1954–55
	112	v. South Africa (Lord's)	1955
	117	v. South Africa (Manchester)	1955
	101	v. Australia (Leeds)	1956
	285*	v. West Indies (Birmingham)	1957
	104	v. West Indies (Nottingham)	1957
	113*	v. New Zealand (Leeds)	1958
	101	v. New Zealand (Manchester)	1958
	113	v. Australia (Melbourne)	1958–59
	124*	v. New Zealand (Auckland)	1958–59
	106	v. India (Nottingham)	1959
Mead, C. P. ....(4)	102	v. South Africa (Johannesburg)	1913–14
	117	v. South Africa (Port Elizabeth)	1913–14
	182*	v. Australia (Oval)	1921
	181	v. South Africa (Durban)	1922–23
Milton, C. A. ....(1)	104*	v. New Zealand (Leeds)	1958
Parks, J. M...................(1)	101*	v. West Indies (Trinidad)	1959–60
Pataudi, Nawab of ....(1)	102	v. Australia (Sydney)	1932–33

Paynter, E. ....(4)	216*	v. Australia (Nottingham) 1938
	117 100 }	v. South Africa (Johannesburg) 1938–39
	243	v. South Africa (Durban) 1938–39
Place, W. ....(1)	107	v. West Indies (Kingston) 1947–48
Pullar, G. ....(2)	131	v. India (Manchester) 1959
	175	v. South Africa (Oval) 1960
Ranjitsinhji, K. S. ......(2)	154*	v. Australia (Manchester) 1896
	175	v. Australia (Sydney) 1897–98
Read, W. W. ....(1)	117	v. Australia (Oval) 1884
Rhodes, W. ....(2)	179	v. Australia (Melbourne) 1911–12
	152	v. South Africa (Johannesburg) 1913–14
Richardson, P. E. ......(5)	104	v. Australia (Manchester) 1956
	117	v. South Africa (Johannesburg) 1956–57
	126	v. West Indies (Nottingham) 1957
	107	v. West Indies (Oval) 1957
	100	v. New Zealand (Birmingham) 1958
Robertson, J. D. ....(2)	133	v. West Indies (Trinidad) 1947–48
	121	v. New Zealand (Lord's) 1949
Robins, R. W. V. ....(1)	108	v. South Africa (Manchester) 1935
Russell, A. C. ....(5)	135*	v. Australia (Adelaide) 1920–21
	101	v. Australia (Manchester) 1921
	102*	v. Australia (Oval) 1921
	140 111 }	v. South Africa (Durban) 1922–23
Sandham, A. ....(2)	152	v. West Indies (Barbados) 1929–30
	325	v. West Indies (Kingston) 1929–30
Sharp, J. ....(1)	105	v. Australia (Oval) 1909
Sheppard, D. S. ....(2)	119	v. India (Oval) 1952
	113	v. Australia (Manchester) 1956
Shrewsbury, A. ....(3)	105*	v. Australia (Melbourne) 1884–85
	164	v. Australia (Lord's) 1886
	106	v. Australia (Lord's) 1893
Simpson, R. T. ....(4)	103	v. New Zealand (Manchester) 1949
	156*	v. Australia (Melbourne) 1950–51
	137	v. South Africa (Nottingham) 1951
	101	v. Pakistan (Nottingham) 1954
Smith, M. J. K. ....(2)	100	v. India (Manchester) 1959
	108	v. West Indies (Trinidad) 1959–60
Spooner, R. H. ....(1)	119	v. South Africa (Lord's) 1912
Steel, A. G. ....(2)	135*	v. Australia (Sydney) 1882–83
	148	v. Australia (Lord's) 1884
Stoddart, A. E. ....(2)	134	v. Australia (Adelaide) 1891–92
	173	v. Australia (Melbourne) 1894–95
Subba Row, R...............(1)	100	v. West Indies (Georgetown) 1959–60
Sutcliffe, H. ....(16)	122	v. South Africa (Lord's) 1924
	115	v. Australia (Sydney) 1924–25
	176 127 }	v. Australia (Melbourne) 1924–25
	143	v. Australia (Melbourne) 1924–25
	161	v. Australia (Oval) 1926
	102	v. South Africa (Johannesburg) 1927–28
	135	v. Australia (Melbourne) 1928–29
	114	v. South Africa (Birmingham) 1929
	100	v. South Africa (Lord's) 1929
	104 109* }	v. South Africa (Oval) 1929
	161	v. Australia (Oval) 1930
	117	v. New Zealand (Oval) 1931
	109*	v. New Zealand (Manchester) 1931
	194	v. Australia (Sydney) 1932–33
Tate, M. W. ....(1)	100*	v. South Africa (Lord's) 1929
Tyldesley, E...............(3)	122	v. South Africa (Johannesburg) 1927–28
	100	v. South Africa (Durban) 1927–28
	122	v. West Indies (Lord's) 1928
Tyldesley, J. T. ....(4)	112	v. South Africa (Cape Town) 1898–99
	138	v. Australia (Birmingham) 1902
	100	v. Australia (Leeds) 1905
	112*	v. Australia (Oval) 1905
Ulyett, G. ....(1)	149	v. Australia (Melbourne) 1881–82
Valentine, B. H. ....(2)	136	v. India (Bombay) 1933–34
	112	v. South Africa (Cape Town) 1938–39

Walters, C. F.	(1)	102	v. India (Madras)	1933–34
Ward, A.	(1)	117	v. Australia (Sydney)	1894–95
Warner, P. F.	(1)	132*	v. South Africa (Johannesburg)	1898–99
Washbrook, C.	(6)	112	v. Australia (Melbourne)	1946–47
		143	v. Australia (Leeds)	1948
		195	v. South Africa (Johannesburg)	1948–49
		103*	v. New Zealand (Leeds)	1949
		114	v. West Indies (Lord's)	1950
		102	v. West Indies (Nottingham)	1950
Watkins, A. J.	(2)	111	v. South Africa (Johannesburg)	1948–49
		138*	v. India (New Delhi)	1951–52
Watson, W.	(2)	109	v. Australia (Lord's)	1953
		116	v. West Indies (Kingston)	1953–54
Wood, H.	(1)	134*	v. South Africa (Cape Town)	1891–92
Woolley, F. E.	(5)	133*	v. Australia (Sydney)	1911–12
		115*	v. South Africa (Johannesburg)	1922–23
		134*	v. South Africa (Lord's)	1924
		123	v. Australia (Sydney)	1924–25
		154	v. South Africa (Manchester)	1929
Worthington, T. S.	(1)	128	v. India (Oval)	1936
Wyatt, R. E. S.	(2)	113	v. South Africa (Manchester)	1929
		149	v. South Africa (Nottingham)	1935

AUSTRALIA (218)

Archer, R. G.	(1)	128	v. West Indies (Kingston)	1954–55
Armstrong, W. W.	(6)	159*	v. South Africa (Johannesburg)	1902–03
		133*	v. England (Melbourne)	1907–08
		132	v. South Africa (Melbourne)	1910–11
		158	v. England (Sydney)	1920–21
		121	v. England (Adelaide)	1920–21
		123*	v. England (Melbourne)	1920–21
Badcock, C. L.	(1)	118	v. England (Melbourne)	1936–37
Bannerman, C.	(1)	165*	v. England (Melbourne)	1876–77
Bardsley, W.	(6)	136 130 }	v. England (Oval)	1909
		132	v. South Africa (Sydney)	1910–11
		121	v. South Africa (Manchester)	1912
		164	v. South Africa (Lord's)	1912
		193*	v. England (Lord's)	1926
Barnes, S. G.	(3)	234	v. England (Sydney)	1946–47
		112	v. India (Adelaide)	1947–48
		141	v. England (Lord's)	1948
Benaud, R.	(3)	121	v. West Indies (Kingston)	1954–55
		122	v. South Africa (Johannesburg)	1957–58
		100	v. South Africa (Johannesburg)	1957–58
Bonnor, G. J.	(1)	128	v. England (Sydney)	1884–85
Bradman, D. G.	(29)	112	v. England (Melbourne)	1928–29
		123	v. England (Melbourne)	1928–29
		131	v. England (Nottingham)	1930
		254	v. England (Lord's)	1930
		334	v. England (Leeds)	1930
		232	v. England (Oval)	1930
		223	v. West Indies (Brisbane)	1930–31
		152	v. West Indies (Melbourne)	1930–31
		226	v. South Africa (Brisbane)	1931–32
		112	v. South Africa (Sydney)	1931–32
		167	v. South Africa (Melbourne)	1931–32
		299*	v. South Africa (Adelaide)	1931–32
		103*	v. England (Melbourne)	1932–33
		304	v. England (Leeds)	1934
		244	v. England (Oval)	1934
		270	v. England (Melbourne)	1936–37
		212	v. England (Adelaide)	1936–37
		169	v. England (Melbourne)	1936–37
		144*	v. England (Nottingham)	1938
		102*	v. England (Lord's)	1938
		103	v. England (Leeds)	1938
		187	v. England (Brisbane)	1946–47
		234	v. England (Sydney)	1946–47
		185	v. India (Brisbane)	1947–48

110

Bradman, D. G. (cont.)	132 127*	} v. India (Melbourne)	1947–48
	201	v. India (Adelaide)	1947–48
	138	v. England (Nottingham)	1948
	173*	v. England (Leeds)	1948
Brown, W. A. ....(4)	105	v. England (Lord's)	1934
	121	v. South Africa (Cape Town)	1935–36
	133	v. England (Nottingham)	1938
	206*	v. England (Lord's)	1938
Burke, J. W. ....(3)	101*	v. England (Adelaide)	1950–51
	161	v. India (Bombay)	1956–57
	189	v. South Africa (Cape Town)	1957–58
Chipperfield, A. G. ......(1)	109	v. South Africa (Durban)	1935–36
Collins, H. L. ....(4)	104	v. England (Sydney)	1920–21
	162	v. England (Adelaide)	1920–21
	203	v. South Africa (Johannesburg)	1921–22
	114	v. England (Sydney)	1924–25
Darling, J. ....(3)	101	v. England (Sydney)	1897–98
	178	v. England (Adelaide)	1897–98
	160	v. England (Sydney)	1897–98
Duff, R. A. ....(2)	104	v. England (Melbourne)	1901–02
	146	v. England (Oval)	1905
Favell, L. ....(1)	101	v. India (Madras)	1959–60
Fingleton, J. H. ....(5)	112	v. South Africa (Cape Town)	1935–36
	108	v. South Africa (Johannesburg)	1935–36
	118	v. South Africa (Durban)	1935–36
	100	v. England (Brisbane)	1936–37
	136	v. England (Melbourne)	1936–37
Giffen, G. ....(1)	161	v. England (Sydney)	1894–95
Graham, H. ....(2)	107	v. England (Lord's)	1893
	105	v. England (Sydney)	1894–95
Gregory, J. M. ....(2)	100	v. England (Melbourne)	1920–21
	119	v. South Africa (Johannesburg)	1921–22
Gregory, S. E. ....(4)	201	v. England (Sydney)	1894–95
	103	v. England (Lord's)	1896
	117	v. England (Oval)	1899
	112	v. England (Adelaide)	1903–04
Hartigan, R. J. ....(1)	116	v. England (Adelaide)	1907–08
Harvey, R. N. ....(19)	153	v. India (Melbourne)	1947–48
	112	v. England (Leeds)	1948
	178	v. South Africa (Cape Town)	1949–50
	151*	v. South Africa (Durban)	1949–50
	100	v. South Africa (Johannesburg)	1949–50
	116	v. South Africa (Port Elizabeth)	1949–50
	109	v. South Africa (Brisbane)	1952–53
	190	v. South Africa (Sydney)	1952–53
	116	v. South Africa (Adelaide)	1952–53
	205	v. South Africa (Melbourne)	1952–53
	122	v. England (Manchester)	1953
	162	v. England (Brisbane)	1954–55
	133	v. West Indies (Kingston)	1954–55
	133	v. West Indies (Trinidad)	1954–55
	204	v. West Indies (Kingston)	1954–55
	140	v. India (Bombay)	1956–57
	167	v. England (Melbourne)	1958–59
	114	v. India (New Delhi)	1959–60
	102	v. India (Bombay)	1959–60
Hassett, A. L. ....(10)	128	v. England (Brisbane)	1946–47
	198*	v. India (Adelaide)	1947–48
	137	v. England (Nottingham)	1948
	112	v. South Africa (Johannesburg)	1949–50
	167	v. South Africa (Port Elizabeth)	1949–50
	132	v. West Indies (Sydney)	1951–52
	102	v. West Indies (Melbourne)	1951–52
	163	v. South Africa (Adelaide)	1952–53
	115	v. England (Nottingham)	1953
	104	v. England (Lord's)	1953
Hendry, H. L. ....(1)	112	v. England (Sydney)	1928–29
Hill, C. ....(7)	188	v. England (Melbourne)	1897–98
	135	v. England (Lord's)	1899
	119	v. England (Sheffield)	1902
	142	v. South Africa (Johannesburg)	1902–03

Hill, C. (*cont.*)	160	v. England (Adelaide)	1907–08
	191	v. South Africa (Sydney)	1910–11
	100	v. South Africa (Melbourne)	1910–11
Horan, T. ....(1)	124	v. England (Melbourne)	1881–82
Iredale, F. A. ....(2)	140	v. England (Adelaide)	1894–95
	108	v. England (Manchester)	1896
Jackson, A. A. ....(1)	164	v. England (Adelaide)	1928–29
Kelleway, C...................(3)	114	v. South Africa (Manchester)	1912
	102	v. South Africa (Lord's)	1912
	147	v. England (Adelaide)	1920–21
Kippax, A. F. ....(2)	100	v. England (Melbourne)	1928–29
	146	v. West Indies (Adelaide)	1930–31
Lindwall, R. R. ....(2)	100	v. England (Melbourne)	1946–47
	118	v. West Indies (Barbados)	1954–55
Loxton, S. J. E. ....(1)	101	v. South Africa (Johannesburg)	1949–50
Lyons, J. J. ....(1)	134	v. England (Sydney)	1891–92
Macartney, C. G. ....(7)	137	v. South Africa (Sydney)	1910–11
	170	v. England (Sydney)	1920–21
	115	v. England (Leeds)	1921
	116	v. South Africa (Durban)	1921–22
	133*	v. England (Lord's)	1926
	151	v. England (Leeds)	1926
	109	v. England (Manchester)	1926
McCabe, S. J. ....(6)	187*	v. England (Sydney)	1932–33
	137	v. England (Manchester)	1934
	149	v. South Africa (Durban)	1935–36
	189*	v. South Africa (Johannesburg)	1935–36
	112	v. England (Melbourne)	1936–37
	232	v. England (Nottingham)	1938
McCool, C. L. ....(1)	104*	v. England (Melbourne)	1946–47
McDonald, C. C. ....(5)	154	v. South Africa (Adelaide)	1952–53
	110	v. West Indies (Trinidad)	1954–55
	127	v. West Indies (Kingston)	1954–55
	170	v. England (Adelaide)	1958–59
	133	v. England (Melbourne)	1958–59
McDonnell, P. S..............(3)	147	v. England (Sydney)	1881–82
	103	v. England (Oval)	1884
	124	v. England (Adelaide)	1884–85
McLeod, C. E. ....(1)	112	v. England (Melbourne)	1897–98
Miller, K. R. ....(7)	141*	v. England (Adelaide)	1946–47
	145*	v. England (Sydney)	1950–51
	129	v. West Indies (Sydney)	1951–52
	109	v. England (Lord's)	1953
	147	v. West Indies (Kingston)	1954–55
	137	v. West Indies (Barbados)	1954–55
	109	v. West Indies (Kingston)	1954–55
Moroney, J. A. R. ....(2)	118 } 101* }	v. South Africa (Johannesburg)	1949–50
Morris, A. R. ....(12)	155	v. England (Melbourne)	1946–47
	122 } 124* }	v. England (Adelaide)	1946–47
	100*	v. India (Melbourne)	1947–48
	105	v. England (Lord's)	1948
	182	v. England (Leeds)	1948
	196	v. England (Oval)	1948
	111	v. South Africa (Johannesburg)	1949–50
	157	v. South Africa (Port Elizabeth)	1949–50
	206	v. England (Adelaide)	1950–51
	153	v. England (Brisbane)	1954–55
	111	v. West Indies (Trinidad)	1954–55
Murdoch, W. L. ....(2)	153*	v. England (Oval)	1880
	211	v. England (Oval)	1884
Noble, M. A. ....(1)	133	v. England (Sydney)	1903–04
O'Neill, N. ....(3)	134	v. Pakistan (Lahore)	1959–60
	163	v. India (Bombay)	1959–60
	113	v. India (Calcutta)	1959–60
Pellew, C. E. ....(2)	116	v. England (Melbourne)	1920–21
	104	v. England (Adelaide)	1920–21
Ponsford, W. H. ....(7)	110	v. England (Sydney)	1924–25
	128	v. England (Melbourne)	1924–25
	110	v. England (Oval)	1930
	183	v. West Indies (Sydney)	1930–31

Ponsford, W. H. (*cont.*)	109	v. West Indies (Brisbane) 1930–31
	181	v. England (Leeds) 1934
	266	v. England (Oval) 1934
Ransford, V. S. ....(1)	143*	v. England (Lord's) 1909
Richardson, A. J. ....(1)	100	v. England (Leeds) 1926
Richardson, V. Y. ....(1)	138	v. England (Melbourne).................................1924–25
Rigg, K. E. ....(1)	127	v. South Africa (Sydney) 1931–32
Ryder, J. ....(3)	142	v. South Africa (Cape Town) 1921–22
	201*	v. England (Adelaide) 1924–25
	112	v. England (Melbourne).................................1928–29
Scott, H. J. H. ....(1)	102	v. England (Oval) 1884
Taylor, J. M. ....(1)	108	v. England (Sydney) 1924–25
Trott, G. H. S...............(1)	143	v. England (Lord's) 1896
Trumper, V. T. ....(8)	135*	v. England (Lord's) 1899
	104	v. England (Manchester) 1902
	185*	v. England (Sydney) 1903–04
	113	v. England (Adelaide) 1903–04
	166	v. England (Sydney) 1907–08
	159	v. South Africa (Melbourne).........................1910–11
	214*	v. South Africa (Adelaide) 1910–11
	113	v. England (Sydney) 1911–12
Woodfull, W. M.............(7)	141	v. England (Leeds) 1926
	117	v. England (Manchester) 1926
	111	v. England (Sydney) 1928–29
	107	v. England (Melbourne).................................1928–29
	102	v. England (Melbourne).................................1928–29
	155	v. England (Lord's) 1930
	161	v. South Africa (Melbourne).........................1931–32

SOUTH AFRICA (77)

Balaskas, X. C. ....(1)	122*	v. New Zealand (Wellington) 1931–32
Catterall, R. H. ....(3)	120	v. England (Birmingham) 1924
	120	v. England (Lord's) 1924
	119	v. England (Durban) 1927–28
Christy, J. A. J. ....(1)	103	v. New Zealand (Christchurch) 1931–32
Dalton, E. L. ....(2)	117	v. England (Oval) 1935
	102	v. England (Johannesburg) 1938–39
Endean, W. R. ....(3)	162*	v. Australia (Melbourne) 1952–53
	116	v. New Zealand (Auckland) 1952–53
	116*	v. England (Leeds) 1955
Faulkner, G. A. ....(4)	123	v. England (Johannesburg) 1909–10
	204	v. Australia (Melbourne) 1910–11
	115	v. Australia (Adelaide) 1910–11
	122*	v. Australia (Manchester) 1912
Frank, C. N. ....(1)	152	v. Australia (Johannesburg) 1921–22
Hathorn, M...................(1)	102	v. England (Johannesburg) 1905–06
McGlew, D. J. ....(5)	255*	v. New Zealand (Wellington) 1952–53
	104*	v. England (Manchester) 1955
	133	v. England (Leeds) 1955
	108	v. Australia (Johannesburg) 1957–58
	105	v. Australia (Durban).....................................1957–58
McLean, R. A. ....(4)	101	v. New Zealand (Durban) 1953–54
	142	v. England (Lord's) 1955
	100	v. England (Durban) 1956–57
	109	v. England (Manchester) 1960
Melville, A. ....(4)	103	v. England (Durban) 1938–39
	189 104* }	v. England (Nottingham).....................................1947
	117	v. England (Lord's) 1947
Mitchell, B. ....(8)	123	v. England (Cape Town) 1930–31
	113	v. New Zealand (Christchurch) 1931–32
	164*	v. England (Lord's) 1935
	128	v. England (Oval) 1935
	109	v. England (Durban) 1938–39
	120 189* }	v. England (Oval) 1947
	120	v. England (Cape Town) 1948–49
Murray, A. R. A. ....(1)	109	v. New Zealand (Wellington) 1952–53
Nourse, A. D., sen..........(1)	111	v. Australia (Johannesburg) 1921–22

Nourse, A. D., jun.........(9)	231	v. Australia (Johannesburg)	1935–36
	120	v. England (Cape Town)	1938–39
	103	v. England (Durban)	1938–39
	149	v. England (Nottingham)	1947
	115	v. England (Manchester)	1947
	112	v. England (Cape Town)	1948–49
	129*	v. England (Johannesburg)	1948–49
	114	v. Australia (Cape Town)	1949–50
	208	v. England (Nottingham)	1951
Owen-Smith, H. G. ......(1)	129	v. England (Leeds)	1929
Rowan, E. A. B. ....(3)	156*	v. England (Johannesburg)	1948–49
	143	v. Australia (Durban)	1949–50
	236	v. England (Leeds)	1951
Sherwell, P. W. ....(1)	115	v. England (Lord's)	1907
Siedle, I. J. ....(1)	141	v. England (Cape Town)	1930–31
Sinclair, J. H. ....(3)	106	v. England (Cape Town)	1898–99
	101	v. Australia (Johannesburg)	1902–03
	104	v. Australia (Cape Town)	1902–03
Snooke, S. J. ....(1)	103	v. Australia (Adelaide)	1910–11
Taylor, H. W. ....(7)	109	v. England (Durban)	1913–14
	176	v. England (Johannesburg)	1922–23
	101	v. England (Johannesburg)	1922–23
	102	v. England (Durban)	1922–23
	101	v. England (Johannesburg)	1927–28
	121	v. England (Oval)	1929
	117	v. England (Cape Town)	1930–31
Van der Byl, P. G. ....(1)	125	v. England (Durban)	1938–39
Viljoen, K. G. ....(2)	111	v. Australia (Melbourne)	1931–32
	124	v. England (Manchester)	1935
Wade, W. W. ....(1)	125	v. England (Port Elizabeth)	1948–49
Waite, J. H. B...............(3)	113	v. England (Manchester)	1955
	115	v. Australia (Johannesburg)	1957–58
	134	v. Australia (Durban)	1957–58
White, G. C. ....(2)	147	v. England (Johannesburg)	1905–06
	118	v. England (Durban)	1909–10
Winslow, P. L. ....(1)	108	v. England (Manchester)	1955
Zulch, J. W. ....(2)	105	v. Australia (Adelaide)	1910–11
	150	v. Australia (Sydney)	1910–11

WEST INDIES (93)

Atkinson, D. ....(1)	219	v. Australia (Barbados)	1954–55
Barrow, I. ....(1)	105	v. England (Manchester)	1933
Butcher, B. F. ....(2)	103	v. India (Calcutta)	1958–59
	142	v. India (Madras)	1958–59
Carew, G. ....(1)	107	v. England (Trinidad)	1947–48
Christiani, R. J. ....(1)	107	v. India (New Delhi)	1948–49
Depeiza, C. ....(1)	122	v. Australia (Barbados)	1954–55
Ganteaume, A. G. ....(1)	112	v. England (Trinidad)	1947–48
Gomez, G. E. ....(1)	101	v. India (New Delhi)	1948–49
Headley, G. ....(10)	176	v. England (Barbados)	1929–30
	114 ⎫ 112 ⎬	v. England (Georgetown)	1929–30
	223	v. England (Kingston)	1929–30
	102*	v. Australia (Brisbane)	1930–31
	105	v. Australia (Sydney)	1930–31
	169*	v. England (Manchester)	1933
	270*	v. England (Kingston)	1934–35
	106 ⎫ 107 ⎬	v. England (Lord's)	1939
Holt, J. K. ....(2)	166	v. England (Barbados)	1953–54
	123	v. India (New Delhi)	1958–59
Hunte, C. C. ....(3)	142	v. Pakistan (Barbados)	1957–58
	260	v. Pakistan (Kingston)	1957–58
	114	v. Pakistan (Georgetown)	1957–58
Kanhai, R. ....(3)	256	v. India (Calcutta)	1958–59
	217	v. Pakistan (Lahore)	1958–59
	110	v. England (Trinidad)	1959–60
Martin, F. R. ....(1)	123*	v. Australia (Sydney)	1930–31
Pairaudeau, B. H. ....(1)	115	v. India (Trinidad)	1952–53

Rae, A. F.	...............(4)	104	v. India (Bombay) 1948–49
		109	v. India (Madras) 1948–49
		106	v. England (Lord's) 1950
		109	v. England (Oval) 1950
Roach, C. A.	..............(2)	122	v. England (Barbados) 1929–30
		209	v. England (Georgetown) 1929–30
Smith, O. G.	..............(4)	104	v. Australia (Kingston) 1954–55
		161	v. England (Birmingham) 1957
		168	v. England (Nottingham)...1957
		100	v. India (New Delhi) 1958–59
Sobers, G.	....................(9)	365*	v. Pakistan (Kingston) 1957–58
		125 109* }	v. Pakistan (Georgetown) 1957–58
		142*	v. India (Bombay) 1958–59
		198	v. India (Kanpur) 1958–59
		106*	v. India (Calcutta) 1958–59
		226	v. England (Barbados) 1959–60
		147	v. England (Kingston) 1959–60
		145	v. England (Georgetown) 1959–60
Solomon, J.	.................(1)	100*	v. India (New Delhi) 1958–59
Stollmeyer, J. B.	............(4)	160	v. India (Madras) 1948–49
		104	v. Australia (Sydney) 1951–52
		152	v. New Zealand (Auckland) 1951–52
		104*	v. India (Trinidad) 1952–53
Walcott, C. L.	...........(15)	152	v. India (New Delhi) 1948–49
		108	v. India (Calcutta) 1948–49
		168*	v. England (Lord's) 1950
		115	v. New Zealand (Auckland) 1951–52
		125	v. India (Georgetown) 1952–53
		118	v. India (Kingston) 1952–53
		220	v. England (Barbados) 1953–54
		124	v. England (Trinidad)..1953–54
		116	v. England (Kingston) 1953–54
		108	v. Australia (Kingston) 1954–55
		126 110 }	v. Australia (Trinidad) 1954–55
		155 110 }	v. Australia (Kingston) 1954–55
		145	v. Pakistan (Georgetown) 1957–58
Weekes, E. D.	...........(15)	141	v. England (Kingston) 1947–48
		128	v. India (New Delhi) 1948–49
		194	v. India (Bombay) 1948–49
		162 101 }	v. India (Calcutta) 1948–49
		129	v. England (Nottingham)..1950
		207	v. India (Trinidad) 1952–53
		161	v. India (Trinidad) 1952–53
		109	v. India (Kingston) 1952–53
		206	v. England (Trinidad)..1953–54
		139	v. Australia (Trinidad) 1954–55
		123	v. New Zealand (Dunedin) 1955–56
		103	v. New Zealand (Christchurch)............................1955–56
		156	v. New Zealand (Wellington) 1955–56
		197	v. Pakistan (Barbados) 1957–58
Weekes, K. H.	............(1)	137	v. England (Oval) 1939
Worrell, F. M.	............(9)	131*	v. England (Georgetown) 1947–48
		261	v. England (Nottingham)..1950
		138	v. England (Oval) 1950
		108	v. Australia (Melbourne) 1951–52
		100	v. New Zealand (Auckland) 1951–52
		237	v. India (Kingston) 1952–53
		167	v. England (Trinidad)..1953–54
		191*	v. England (Nottingham)...1957
		197*	v. England (Barbados) 1959–60

NEW ZEALAND (17)

Dempster, C. S.	............(2)	136	v. England (Wellington)......................................1929–30
		120	v. England (Lord's) 1931
Donnelly, M. P.	............(1)	206	v. England (Lord's) 1949
Guy, J. W.	..................(1)	102	v. India (Hyderabad) 1955–56

Hadlee, W. A.	(1)	116	v. England (Christchurch) 1946–47
McGregor, S. N.	(1)	111	v. Pakistan (Lahore) 1955–56
Mills, J. W. E.	(1)	117	v. England (Wellington)..............................1929–30
Page, M. L.	(1)	104	v. England (Lord's) 1931
Rabone, G. O.	(1)	107	v. South Africa (Durban) 1953–54
Reid, J. R.	(3)	135	v. South Africa (Cape Town) 1953–54
		119*	v. India (New Delhi) 1955–56
		120	v. India (Calcutta) 1955–56
Sutcliffe, B.	(4)	101	v. England (Manchester) 1949
		116	v. England (Christchurch) 1950–51
		137*	v. India (Hyderabad) 1955–56
		230*	v. India (New Delhi) 1955–56
Vivian, H. G.	(1)	100	v. South Africa (Wellington)........................1931–32

INDIA (46)

Adhikari, H. R.	(1)	114*	v. West Indies (New Delhi) 1948–49
Amarnath, L.	(1)	118	v. England (Bombay) 1933–34
Apte, M. L.	(1)	163*	v. West Indies (Trinidad) 1952–53
Baig, A. A.	(1)	112	v. England (Manchester) 1959
Borde, C. G.	(1)	109	v. West Indies (New Delhi) 1958–59
Contractor, N. J.	(1)	108	v. Australia (Bombay) 1959–60
Hazare, V. S.	(7)	116 145 }	v. Australia (Adelaide) 1947–48
		134*	v. West Indies (Bombay) 1948–49
		122	v. West Indies (Bombay) 1948–49
		164*	v. England (New Delhi) 1951–52
		155	v. England (Bombay) 1951–52
		146*	v. Pakistan (Bombay) 1952–53
Kripal Singh, A. G.	(1)	100*	v. New Zealand (Hyderabad) 1955–56
Manjrekar, V. L.	(4)	133	v. England (Leeds) 1952
		118	v. West Indies (Kingston) 1952–53
		118	v. New Zealand (Hyderabad) 1955–56
		177	v. New Zealand (New Delhi) 1955–56
Mankad, V.	(5)	116	v. Australia (Melbourne) 1947–48
		111	v. Australia (Melbourne) 1947–48
		184	v. England (Lord's) 1952
		223	v. New Zealand (Bombay) 1955–56
		231	v. New Zealand (Madras) 1955–56
Merchant, V. M.	(3)	114	v. England (Manchester) 1936
		128	v. England (Oval) 1946
		154	v. England (New Delhi) 1951–52
Modi, R. S.	(1)	112	v. West Indies (Bombay) 1948–49
Mushtaq Ali	(2)	112	v. England (Manchester) 1936
		106	v. West Indies (Calcutta) 1948–49
Phadkar, D. G.	(2)	123	v. Australia (Adelaide) 1947–48
		115	v. England (Calcutta) 1951–52
Ramchand, G. S.	(2)	106*	v. New Zealand (Calcutta) 1955–56
		109	v. Australia (Bombay) 1956–57
Roy, P.	(5)	140	v. England (Bombay) 1951–52
		111	v. England (Madras) 1951–52
		150	v. West Indies (Kingston) 1952–53
		100	v. New Zealand (Calcutta) 1955–56
		173	v. New Zealand (Madras) 1955–56
Shodhan, D. H.	(1)	110	v. Pakistan (Calcutta)..................................1952–53
Umrigar, P. R.	(7)	130*	v. England (Madras) 1951–52
		102	v. Pakistan (Bombay) 1952–53
		130	v. West Indies (Trinidad) 1952–53
		117	v. West Indies (Kingston) 1952–53
		108	v. Pakistan (Peshawar) 1954–55
		223	v. New Zealand (Hyderabad) 1955–56
		118	v. England (Manchester) 1959

PAKISTAN (14)

Alimuddin	(1)	103*	v. India (Karachi) 1954–55
Hanif Mohammed	(5)	142	v. India (Bahawalpur) 1954–55
		103	v. New Zealand (Dacca) 1955–56
		337	v. West Indies (Barbados) 1957–58
		103	v. West Indies (Karachi) 1958–59
		101*	v. Australia (Karachi) 1959–60

Imtiaz Ahmed ....(2)	209	v. New Zealand (Lahore) 1955–56
	122	v. West Indies (Kingston) 1957–58
Nazar Mohammed ....(1)	124*	v. India (Lucknow) 1952–53
Saeed Ahmed ....(2)	150	v. West Indies (Georgetown) 1957–58
	166	v. Australia (Lahore) 1959–60
Waqar Hasan ....(1)	189	v. New Zealand (Lahore) 1955–56
Wazir Mohammed ....(2)	106	v. West Indies (Kingston) 1957–58
	189	v. West Indies (Trinidad) 1957–58

Appendix C
Bowlers taking Ten Wickets in a Test Match

ENGLAND (66)

Allen, G. O.	(1) 10—78	v. India (Lord's)	1936
Barnes, S. F.	(7) 13—163	v. Australia (Melbourne)	1901–02
	11—110	v. South Africa (Lord's)	1912
	10—115	v. South Africa (Leeds)	1912
	13—57	v. South Africa (Oval)	1912
	10—105	v. South Africa (Durban)	1913–14
	17—159	v. South Africa (Johannesburg)	1913–14
	14—144	v. South Africa (Durban)	1913–14
Bailey, T. E.	(1) 11—98	v. West Indies (Lord's)	1957
Bates, W.	(1) 13—102	v. Australia (Melbourne)	1882–83
Bedser, A. V.	(5) 11—145	v. India (Lord's)	1946
	11—93	v. India (Manchester)	1946
	10—105	v. Australia (Melbourne)	1950–51
	12—112	v. South Africa (Manchester)	1951
	14—99	v. Australia (Nottingham)	1953
Blythe, C.	(4) 11—118	v. South Africa (Cape Town)	1905–06
	15—99	v. South Africa (Leeds)	1907
	11—102	v. Australia (Birmingham)	1909
	10—104	v. South Africa (Cape Town)	1909–10
Briggs, J	(4) 11—74	v. Australia (Lord's)	1886
	15—28	v. South Africa (Cape Town)	1888–89
	12—136	v. Australia (Adelaide)	1891–92
	10—148	v. Australia (Oval)	1893
Farnes, K.	(1) 10—179	v. Australia (Nottingham)	1934
Ferris, J. J.	(1) 13—91	v. South Africa (Cape Town)	1891–92
Freeman, A. P.	(3) 10—93	v. West Indies (Manchester)	1928
	10—207	v. South Africa (Leeds)	1929
	12—171	v. South Africa (Manchester)	1929
Geary, G.	(1) 12—130	v. South Africa (Johannesburg)	1927–28
Gilligan, A. E. R.	(1) 11—90	v. South Africa (Birmingham)	1924
Hearne, J. T.	(1) 10—60	v. Australia (Oval)	1896
Laker, J. C.	(3) 10—119	v. South Africa (Oval)	1951
	11—113	v. Australia (Leeds)	1956
	19—90	v. Australia (Manchester)	1956
Larwood, H.	(1) 10—124	v. Australia (Sydney)	1932–33
Lock, G. A. R.	(3) 11—48	v. West Indies (Oval)	1957
	11—65	v. New Zealand (Leeds)	1958
	11—84	v. New Zealand (Christchurch)	1958–59
Lockwood, W. H.	(1) 11—76	v. Australia (Manchester)	1902
Lohmann, G. A.	(5) 12—104	v. Australia (Oval)	1886
	10—87	v. Australia (Sydney)	1886–87
	10—142	v. Australia (Sydney)	1891–92
	15—45	v. South Africa (Port Elizabeth)	1895–96
	12—71	v. South Africa (Johannesburg)	1895–96
Marriott, C. S.	(1) 11—96	v. West Indies (Oval)	1933
Martin, F.	(1) 12—102	v. Australia (Oval)	1890
Peel, R.	(2) 10—58	v. Australia (Sydney)	1887–88
	11—68	v. Australia (Manchester)	1888
Rhodes, W.	(1) 15—124	v. Australia (Melbourne)	1903–04
Richardson, T.	(4) 10—156	v. Australia (Manchester)	1893
	11—173	v. Australia (Lord's)	1896
	13—244	v. Australia (Manchester)	1896
	10—204	v. Australia (Sydney)	1897–98
Statham, J. B.	(1) 11—97	v. South Africa (Lord's)	1960
Stevens, G. T. S.	(1) 10—195	v. West Indies (Barbados)	1929–30
Tate, M. W.	(1) 11—228	v. Australia (Sydney)	1924–25
Tattersall, R.	(1) 12—101	v. South Africa (Lord's)	1951
Tyson, F. H.	(1) 10—130	v. Australia (Sydney)	1954–55

Verity, H. ....(2) 11—153 v. India (Madras) 1933–34
                                     15—104 v. Australia (Lord's) 1934
Voce, W. ....(2) 11—149 v. West Indies (Trinidad)................................1929–30
                                     10—57   v. Australia (Brisbane) 1936–37
Wardle, J. H. ....(1) 12—89   v. South Africa (Cape Town) 1956–57
White, J. C. ....(1) 13—256 v. Australia (Adelaide) 1928–29
Woolley, F. E. ....(1) 10—49   v. Australia (Oval) 1912
Wright, D. V. P. ....(1) 10—175 v. South Africa (Lord's) 1947

AUSTRALIA (37)

Benaud, R. ....(1) 11—105 v. India (Calcutta) 1956–57
Davidson, A. K. ....(1) 12—124 v. India (Kanpur) 1959–60
Fleetwood-Smith, L. O'B. (1) 10—239 v. England (Adelaide) 1936–37
Giffen, G. ....(1) 10—160 v. England (Sydney) 1891–92
Grimmett, C. V. ....(7) 11—82   v. England (Sydney) 1924–25
                                     10—201 v. England (Nottingham) 1930
                                     11—183 v. West Indies (Adelaide) 1930–31
                                     14—199 v. South Africa (Adelaide) 1931–32
                                     10—88   v. South Africa (Cape Town) 1935–36
                                     10—110 v. South Africa (Johannesburg) 1935–36
                                     13—173 v. South Africa (Durban) 1935–36
Hordern, H. V. ....(2) 12—175 v. England (Sydney) 1911–12
                                     10—161 v. England (Sydney) 1911–12
Ironmonger, H. ....(2) 11—79   v. West Indies (Melbourne)............................1930–31
                                     11—24   v. South Africa (Melbourne) 1931–32
Jones, E. ....(1) 10—164 v. England (Lord's) 1899
Macartney, C. G.............(1) 11—85   v. England (Leeds) 1909
Mailey, A. A. ....(2) 10—302 v. England (Adelaide) 1920–21
                                     13—236 v. England (Melbourne) 1920–21
Miller, K. R. ....(1) 10—152 v. England (Lord's) 1956
Noble, M. A. ....(2) 13—77   v. England (Melbourne) 1901–02
                                     11—103 v. England (Sheffield) 1902
O'Reilly, W. J. ....(3) 10—129 v. England (Melbourne) 1932–33
                                     11—129 v. England (Nottingham) 1934
                                     10—122 v. England (Leeds) 1938
Palmer, G. E. ....(2) 11—165 v. England (Sydney) 1881–82
                                     10—126 v. England (Melbourne) 1882–83
Spofforth, F. R. ....(4) 13—110 v. England (Melbourne) 1878–79
                                     14—90   v. England (Oval) 1882
                                     11—117 v. England (Sydney) 1882–83
                                     10—144 v. England (Sydney) 1884–85
Toshack, E. R. H. ....(1) 11—31   v. India (Brisbane) 1947–48
Trumble, H. ....(3) 12—89   v. England (Oval) 1896
                                     10—128 v. England (Manchester) 1902
                                     12—173 v. England (Oval) 1902
Turner, C. T. B. ....(2) 12—87   v. England (Sydney) 1887–88
                                     10—63   v. England (Lord's) 1888

SOUTH AFRICA (7)

Hall, A. E. ....(1) 11—112 v. England (Cape Town) 1922–23
Llewellyn, C. B. ....(1) 10—116 v. Australia (Johannesburg) 1902–03
Nupen, E. P. ....(1) 11—150 v. England (Johannesburg) 1930–31
Snooke, S. J. ....(1) 12—127 v. England (Johannesburg) 1905–06
Tayfield, H. J. ....(2) 13—165 v. Australia (Melbourne) 1952–53
                                     13—192 v. England (Joahannesburg) 1956–57
Vogler, A. E. E. ....(1) 12—181 v. England (Johannesburg) 1909–10

WEST INDIES (7)

Ferguson, W. ....(1) 11—229 v. England (Trinidad) 1947–48
Gomez, G. E. ....(1) 10—113 v. Australia (Sydney) 1951–52
Hall, W. ....(1) 11—126 v. India (Kanpur) 1958–59
Johnson, H. H. ....(1) 10—96   v. England (Kingston) 1947–48
Ramadhin, K. T. ....(1) 11—152 v. England (Lord's) 1950
Valentine, A. L. ....(2) 11—204 v. England (Manchester) 1950
                                     10—160 v. England (Oval) 1950

NEW ZEALAND (1)

Cowie, J. A. ....(1) 10—140   v. England (Manchester) 1937

INDIA (5)

Ghulam Ahmed ....(1) 10—130   v. Australia (Calcutta) 1956–57
Gupte, S. P. ....(1) 10—223   v. West Indies (Kanpur) 1958–59
Mankad, V. ....(2) 12—108   v. England (Madras) 1951–52
                                 13—131   v. Pakistan (New Delhi) 1952–53
Patel, J. S. ....(1) 14—124   v. Australia (Kanpur) 1959–60

PAKISTAN (5)

Fazal Mahmood ....(4) 12—94   v. India (Lucknow) 1952–53
                                 12—99   v. England (Oval) 1954
                                 13—114   v. Australia (Karachi) 1956–57
                                 12—100   v. West Indies (Dacca) 1958–59
Zulfiqar Ahmed ....(1) 11—79   v. New Zealand (Karachi) 1955–56

Appendix D
Century Wicket Partnerships

A complete list of all century wicket partnerships in Test cricket is given in this appendix.
Where a century stand has not been recorded for the wicket the highest stand is given.

ENGLAND

FIRST WICKET (72)

359	L. Hutton & C. Washbrook v. South Africa (Johannesburg)	1948–49
323	J. B. Hobbs & W. Rhodes v. Australia (Melbourne)	1911–12
290	G. Pullar & M. C. Cowdrey v. South Africa (Oval)	1960
283	J. B. Hobbs & H. Sutcliffe v. Australia (Melbourne)	1924–25
268	J. B. Hobbs & H. Sutcliffe v. South Africa (Lord's)	1924
221	J. B. Hobbs & W. Rhodes v. South Africa (Cape Town)	1909–10
219	L. Hutton & C. J. Barnett v. Australia (Nottingham)	1938
212	C. Washbrook & R. T. Simpson v. West Indies (Nottingham)	1950
185	T. Hayward & F. S. Jackson v. Australia (Oval)	1899
182	J. B. Hobbs & H. Sutcliffe v. Australia (Lord's)	1926
177	G. Pullar & M. C. Cowdrey v. West Indies (Kingston)	1959–60
174	P. E. Richardson & M. C. Cowdrey v. Australia (Manchester)	1956
173	G. Gunn & A. Sandham v. West Indies (Kingston)	1929–30
172	J. B. Hobbs & H. Sutcliffe v. Australia (Oval)	1926
170	W. G. Grace & W. H. Scotton v. Australia (Oval)	1886
168	L. Hutton & C. Washbrook v. Australia (Leeds)	1948
160	R. E. S. Wyatt & W. R. Hammond v. South Africa (Durban)	1930–31
159	J. B. Hobbs & W. Rhodes v. South Africa (Johannesburg)	1909–10
158	A. C. Russell & G. Brown v. Australia (Oval)	1921
157	J. B. Hobbs & H. Sutcliffe v. Australia (Sydney)	1924–25
156	J. B. Hobbs & H. Sutcliffe v. Australia (Leeds)	1926
155	J. B. Hobbs & H. Sutcliffe v. West Indies (Oval)	1928
154	T. Hayward & A. C. MacLaren v. Australia (Sydney)	1901–02
153	A. Sandham & A. C. Russell v. South Africa (Johannesburg)	1922–23
151	W. G. Grace & A. E. Stoddart v. Australia (Oval)	1893
151	P. E. Richardson & M. C. Cowdrey v. Australia (Nottingham)	1956
149	T. Hayward & A. C. MacLaren v. Australia (Adelaide)	1901–02
148	T. Hayward & P. F. Warner v. Australia (Adelaide)	1903–04
147	J. B. Hobbs & W. Rhodes v. Australia (Adelaide)	1911–12
147	L. Hutton & R. T. Simpson v. New Zealand (Oval)	1949
146	W. G. A. Parkhouse & G. Pullar v. India (Leeds)	1959
145	T. Hayward & A. C. MacLaren v. Australia (Nottingham)	1905
143	J. B. Hobbs & H. Sutcliffe v. Australia (Adelaide)	1928–29
143	L. Hutton & J. D. Robertson v. New Zealand (Lord's)	1949
143	L. Hutton & D. S. Sheppard v. India (Oval)	1952
141	W. Rhodes & A. E. Relf v. South Africa (Johannesburg)	1913–14
141	L. Hutton & C. Washbrook v. South Africa (Leeds)	1947
140	P. Holmes & H. Sutcliffe v. South Africa (Cape Town)	1927–28
138	L. Hutton & C. Washbrook v. Australia (Melbourne)	1946–47
137	L. Hutton & C. Washbrook v. Australia (Adelaide)	1946–47
136	J. B. Hobbs & H. Sutcliffe v. South Africa (Birmingham)	1924
133	J. B. Hobbs & W. Rhodes v. South Africa (Durban)	1913–14
130	L. Hutton & W. Watson v. West Indies (Kingston)	1953–54
129	L. Hutton & J. D. Robertson v. West Indies (Kingston)	1947–48
129	L. Hutton & C. Washbrook v. Australia (Leeds)	1948
128	D. Smith & A. Mitchell v. South Africa (Leeds)	1935
126	J. B. Hobbs & H. Sutcliffe v. Australia (Melbourne)	1924–25
126	P. E. Richardson & W. Watson v. New Zealand (Manchester)	1958
125	J. B. Hobbs & H. Sutcliffe v. Australia (Nottingham)	1930
123*	C. F. Walters & H. Sutcliffe v. Australia (Manchester)	1934
122	G. Ulyett & R. G. Barlow v. Australia (Sydney)	1881–82
122	T. Hayward & P. F. Warner v. Australia (Melbourne)	1903–04
121	L. Hutton & J. T. Ikin v. South Africa (Manchester)	1951
119	J. B. Hobbs & H. Sutcliffe v. West Indies (Manchester)	1928
118	H. Sutcliffe & R. E. S. Wyatt v. South Africa (Nottingham)	1935

115 P. E. Richardson & T. E. Bailey v. South Africa (Durban)....................................1956–57
114 H. Sutcliffe & D. R. Jardine v. Australia (Brisbane)..1932–33
112 J. B. Hobbs and W. Rhodes v. Australia (Lord's) 1912
112 H. Sutcliffe & R. E. S. Wyatt v. Australia (Sydney) 1932–33
111 A. C. MacLaren & E. Wainwright v. Australia (Sydney)..1897–98
111 A. H. Bakewell & C. F. Walters v. India (Madras) 1933–34
110 J. B. Hobbs & H. Sutcliffe v. Australia (Sydney) 1924–25
108 J. B. Hobbs & H. Sutcliffe v. Australia (Manchester)...1930
107 J. B. Hobbs & W. Rhodes v. Australia (Oval) 1912
106 L. Hutton & R. T. Simpson v. India (Lord's) 1952
105* J. B. Hobbs & C. B. Fry v. Australia (Birmingham) 1909
105 J. B. Hobbs & H. Sutcliffe v. Australia (Melbourne) 1928–29
104 H. Sutcliffe & C. F. Walters v. Australia (Oval) 1934
103 L. Hutton & C. Washbrook v. New Zealand (Manchester) 1949
100 J. B. Hobbs & W. Rhodes v. South Africa (Johannesburg)......................................1913–14
100 L. Hutton & C. J. Barnett v. New Zealand (Manchester) 1937
100 L. Hutton & C. Washbrook v. Australia (Adelaide) 1946–47

SECOND WICKET (65)

382 L. Hutton & M. Leyland v. Australia (Oval) 1938
280 P. A. Gibb & W. J. Edrich v. South Africa (Durban)...1938–39
266 P. E. Richardson & T. W. Graveney v. West Indies (Nottingham) 1957
230 H. Sutcliffe & E. Tyldesley v. South Africa (Johannesburg) 1927–28
221 H. Sutcliffe & W. R. Hammond v. South Africa (Birmingham) 1929
218 L. Hutton & W. J. Edrich v. New Zealand (Oval) 1949
191 M. C. Cowdrey & E. R. Dexter v. West Indies (Trinidad) 1959–60
188 H. Sutcliffe & W. R. Hammond v. Australia (Sydney)..1932–33
187* H. Sutcliffe & W. R. Hammond v. South Africa (Oval) 1929
184 P. A. Gibb & E. Paynter v. South Africa (Johannesburg) 1938–39
182 T. W. Graveney & P. B. H. May v. Australia (Sydney) 1954–55
178 H. Sutcliffe & K. S. Duleepsinhji v. New Zealand (Oval) 1931
168 P. A. Gibb & E. Paynter v. South Africa (Johannesburg) 1938–39
168 L. Hutton & T. W. Graveney v. Australia (Lord's) 1953
158 L. Hutton & P. B. H. May v. India (Lord's) 1952
152 A. Shrewsbury & W. Gunn v. Australia (Lord's) 1893
150 L. Hutton & W. J. Edrich v. Australia (Sydney) 1946–47
148 A. Sandham & R. E. S. Wyatt v. West Indies (Kingston) 1929–30
147 C. Washbrook & W. J. Edrich v. Australia (Melbourne)...................................1946–47
146 P. E. Richardson & T. W. Graveney v. West Indies (Oval) 1957
144 L. Hutton & R. T. Simpson v. South Africa (Nottingham) 1951
142 A. C. MacLaren & K. S. Ranjitsinhji v. Australia (Adelaide)...........................1897–98
142 J. B. Hobbs & F. E. Woolley v. South Africa (Lord's) 1924
137 G. Ulyett & J. Selby v. Australia (Melbourne) 1881–82
137 A. C. MacLaren & T. Hayward v. Australia (Sydney) 1897–98
134 J. B. Hobbs & G. Gunn v. Australia (Sydney) 1907–08
134 A. E. Fagg & W. R. Hammond v. India (Manchester) 1936
134 L. Hutton & J. F. Crapp v. South Africa (Cape Town) 1948–49
133 H. Sutcliffe & W. R. Hammond v. Australia (Melbourne) 1928–29
132 T. W. Graveney & P. B. H. May v. South Africa (Lord's) 1955
131 T. Hayward & K. S. Ranjitsinhji v. Australia (Oval) 1899
131 L. Hutton & N. Oldfield v. West Indies (Oval) 1939
131 L. Hutton & R. T. Simpson v. Australia (Melbourne) 1950–51
131 G. Pullar & M. C. Cowdrey v. India (Manchester)................................1959
130 H. Sutcliffe & E. Tyldesley v. South Africa (Durban) 1927–28
129 J. B. Hobbs & E. Tyldesley v. West Indies (Oval) 1928
129 L. Hutton & P. B. H. May v. South Africa (Leeds) 1951
128 L. Hutton & J. Hardstaff jun. v. New Zealand (Manchester) 1937
127 W. Rhodes & J. W. Hearne v. Australia (Melbourne) 1911–12
126 H. Sutcliffe & K. S. Duleepsinhji v. New Zealand (Manchester) 1931
124 W. Rhodes & R. H. Spooner v. South Africa (Lord's) 1912
124 C. Washbrook & W. J. Edrich v. Australia (Manchester) 1948
122 H. Sutcliffe & W. R. Hammond v. Australia (Sydney)....................1932–33
120 W. G. Grace & A. P. Lucas v. Australia (Oval) 1880
120 C. Washbrook & J. F. Crapp v. South Africa (Johannesburg) 1948–49
118 C. Washbrook & W. J. Edrich v. New Zealand (Leeds) 1949
118 D. S. Sheppard & J. T. Ikin v. India (Oval) 1952
116 A. Shrewsbury & W. Barnes v. Australia (Melbourne) 1884–85
115 P. A. Gibb & E. Paynter v. South Africa (Durban)..............1938–39
113 W. Rhodes & H. Makepeace v. Australia (Melbourne) 1920–21
112 J. B. Hobbs & G. Gunn v. Australia (Melbourne) 1911–12
111 E. H. Bowley & K. S. Duleepsinhji v. New Zealand (Auckland) ...1929–30

108* H. Gimblett & M. J. Turnbull v. India (Lord's) 1936
107 L. Hutton & P. B. H. May v. West Indies (Barbados) 1953–54
106 A. C. MacLaren & J. T. Tyldesley v. Australia (Sydney)......................1901–02
106 H. Sutcliffe & J. W. Hearne v. Australia (Melbourne) 1924–25
105 W. G. Grace & R. Abel v. Australia (Lord's) 1896
105 J. B. Hobbs & H. Makepeace v. Australia (Adelaide) 1920–21
104 A. Ward & A. E. Stoddart v. Australia (Melbourne) 1894–95
103 G. Pullar & K. F. Barrington v. West Indies (Barbados)......................1959–60
102 W. Rhodes & G. Gunn v. Australia (Melbourne) 1911–12
102 P. Holmes & E. Tyldesley v. South Africa (Durban) 1927–28
100 J. B. Hobbs & J. W. Hearne v. Australia (Sydney) 1920–21
100 C. Washbrook & W. J. Edrich v. Australia (Leeds) 1948
100 L. Hutton & P. B. H. May v. Australia (Oval) 1953

THIRD WICKET (55)

370 W. J. Edrich & D. C. S. Compton v. South Africa (Lord's) 1947
264 L. Hutton & W. R. Hammond v. West Indies (Oval) 1939
262 W. R. Hammond & D. R. Jardine v. Australia (Adelaide) 1928–29
245 R. E. S. Wyatt & F. E. Woolley v. South Africa (Manchester) 1929
245 J. Hardstaff jun. & W. R. Hammond v. New Zealand (Lord's) 1937
242 E. Paynter & W. R. Hammond v. South Africa (Durban) 1938–39
228 W. J. Edrich & D. C. S. Compton v. South Africa (Manchester) 1947
210 A. Ward & J. T. Brown v. Australia (Melbourne) 1894–95
207 T. W. Graveney & P. B. H. May v. West Indies (Nottingham) 1957
194* C. A. Milton & P. B. H. May v. New Zealand (Leeds) 1958
175 W. H. Scotton & W. Barnes v. Australia (Adelaide) 1884–85
169 R. Subba Row & M. J. K. Smith v. India (Oval) 1959
168 A. Sandham & E. Hendren v. West Indies (Barbados).........................1929–30
166 P. B. H. May & D. C. S. Compton v. West Indies (Trinidad) 1953–54
155 W. J. Edrich & A. V. Bedser v. Australia (Leeds) 1948
152 W. Rhodes & C. P. Mead v. South Africa (Johannesburg) 1913–14
150 J. F. Crapp & D. C. S. Compton v. South Africa (Johannesburg).........1948–49
150 L. Hutton & D. C. S. Compton v. West Indies (Georgetown) 1953–54
149 W. R. Hammond & E. Paynter v. New Zealand (Auckland) 1932–33
148 E. R. Dexter & R. Subba Row v. West Indies (Georgetown) 1959–60
145 J. T. Tyldesley & R. E. Foster & L. C. Braund v. Australia (Melbourne) ...1903–04
     (Foster retired hurt after 89 had been added)
142 J. B. Hobbs & E. Hendren v. Australia (Melbourne) 1920–21
140 F. E. Woolley & E. Hendren v. Australia (Lord's) 1926
139 A. C. Russell & C. P. Mead v. South Africa (Durban) 1922–23
137 A. Shrewsbury & F. S. Jackson v. Australia (Lord's) 1893
135 L. Hutton & W. R. Hammond v. Australia (Oval) 1938
129 W. R. Hammond & M. Leyland v. Australia (Sydney) 1936–37
129 R. T. Simpson & D. C. S. Compton v. New Zealand (Christchurch) ...1950–51
127 E. Tyldesley & W. R. Hammond v. South Africa (Durban) 1927–28
127 W. R. Hammond & T. S. Worthington v. India (Manchester) 1936
125* W. R. Hammond & R. E. S. Wyatt v. Australia (Sydney) 1932–33
124 W. J. Edrich & P. B. H. May v. Australia (Brisbane) 1954–55
124 P. B. H. May & D. C. S. Compton v. South Africa (Manchester) 1955
123 H. Sutcliffe & Nawab of Pataudi v. Australia (Sydney) 1932–33
121* F. E. Woolley & E. Hendren v. South Africa (Lord's) 1924
119 T. Hayward & C. B. Fry v. South Africa (Johannesburg) 1895–96
119 W. R. Hammond & E. Hendren v. South Africa (Johannesburg) 1930–31
113 W. Place & J. Hardstaff jun. v. West Indies (Kingston) 1947–48
111 L. Hutton & D. C. S. Compton v. Australia (Nottingham) 1948
109 P. A. Gibb & W. R. Hammond v. South Africa (Cape Town) 1938–39
109 L. Hutton & D. C. S. Compton v. West Indies (Oval) 1950
108 P. E. Richardson & P. B. H. May v. Australia (Nottingham) 1956
106 J. T. Tyldesley & J. Sharp v. Australia (Leeds) 1909
106 W. J. Edrich & D. C. S. Compton v. South Africa (Nottingham) 1947
106 J. G. Dewes & W. G. A. Parkhouse v. West Indies (Nottingham) 1950
104 W. Rhodes & C. B. Fry v. Australia (Oval) 1909
104 J. Hardstaff jun. & C. J. Barnett v. New Zealand (Lord's) 1937
103 W. J. Edrich & D. C. S. Compton v. Australia (Leeds) 1948
102* A. C. MacLaren & F. S. Jackson v. Australia (Lord's) 1902
102 J. T. Brown & A. Ward v. Australia (Sydney) 1894–95
102 W. J. Edrich & D. C. S. Compton v. Australia (Sydney)......................1946–47
102 L. Hutton & D. C. S. Compton v. New Zealand (Leeds) 1949
102 L. Hutton & D. C. S. Compton v. Australia (Lord's)...........................1953
101 P. B. H. May & D. J. Insole v. South Africa (Leeds) 1955
100 T. Hayward & C. B. Fry v. Australia (Oval) 1905

FOURTH WICKET (45)

411	P. B. H. May & M. C. Cowdrey v. West Indies (Birmingham)	1957
266	W. R. Hammond & T. S. Worthington v. India (Oval)	1936
249	A. Sandham & L. E. G. Ames v. West Indies (Kingston)	1929–30
248	L. Hutton & D. C. S. Compton v. West Indies (Lord's)	1939
237	E. Hendren & L. E. G. Ames v. West Indies (Trinidad)	1929–30
222	W. R. Hammond & E. Paynter v. Australia (Lord's)	1938
197	W. R. Hammond & L. E. G. Ames v. South Africa (Cape Town)	1938–39
193	M. C. Cowdrey & K. F. Barrington v. India (Leeds)	1959
187	P. B. H. May & C. Washbrook v. Australia (Leeds)	1956
182	P. B. H. May & M. C. Cowdrey v. Australia (Sydney)	1958–59
164	W. R. Hammond & E. Paynter v. South Africa (Durban)	1938–39
158	D. B. Carr & A. J. Watkins v. India (New Delhi)	1951–52
156	P. B. H. May & D. C. S. Compton v. Australia (Oval)	1956
154	D. C. S. Compton & T. W. Graveney v. Pakistan (Nottingham)	1954
151	C. B. Fry & F. S. Jackson v. Australia (Oval)	1905
151	W. R. Hammond & M. Leyland v. South Africa (Oval)	1935
145	W. R. Hammond & E. Hendren v. Australia (Sydney)	1928–29
142	K. F. Barrington & E. R. Dexter v. West Indies (Trinidad)	1959–60
141	D. C. S. Compton & W. Watson v. South Africa (Nottingham)	1951
139	R. E. S. Wyatt & M. Leyland v. South Africa (Nottingham)	1935
130	W. R. Hammond & L. E. G. Ames v. New Zealand (Oval)	1931
129	W. R. Hammond & R. E. S. Wyatt v. South Africa (Leeds)	1935
125	D. C. S. Compton & J. Hardstaff jun. v. New Zealand (Oval)	1937
125	P. B. H. May & K. F. Barrington v. India (Nottingham)	1959
122	T. Hayward & A. J. L. Hill v. South Africa (Johannesburg)	1895–96
122	D. C. S. Compton & W. Watson v. South Africa (Lord's)	1951
121	P. E. Richardson & M. C. Cowdrey v. South Africa (Johannesburg)	1956–57
121	P. B. H. May & M. C. Cowdrey v. New Zealand (Birmingham)	1958
120	W. R. Hammond & D. R. Jardine v. West Indies (Manchester)	1928
117	G. Gunn & L. C. Braund v. Australia (Sydney)	1907–08
116*	E. Hendren & A. P. F. Chapman v. Australia (Lord's)	1926
116	P. B. H. May & M. C. Cowdrey v. Australia (Sydney)	1954–55
113	G. Gunn & J. Hardstaff sen. v. Australia (Sydney)	1907–08
113	L. C. Braund & J. Hardstaff sen. v. Australia (Adelaide)	1907–08
111*	D. C. S. Compton & A. J. Watkins v. South Africa (Cape Town)	1948–49
110	C. B. Fry & A. C. MacLaren v. Australia (Oval)	1899
109	M. J. K. Smith & K. F. Barrington v. India (Manchester)	1959
108	L. C. Braund & K. L. Hutchings v. Australia (Melbourne)	1907–08
108	P. B. H. May & M. C. Cowdrey v. South Africa (Manchester)	1955
104	K. S. Duleepsinhji & E. Hendren v. Australia (Lord's)	1930
104	W. R. Hammond & L. E. G. Ames v. Australia (Sydney)	1936–37
104	P. E. Richardson & M. C. Cowdrey v. New Zealand (Birmingham)	1958
103	A. Shrewsbury & A. Ward v. Australia (Oval)	1893
101	M. J. Turnbull & W. R. Hammond v. South Africa (Johannesburg)	1930–31
100	F. L. Fane & F. E. Woolley v. South Africa (Cape Town)	1909–10

FIFTH WICKET (34)

242	W. R. Hammond & L. E. G. Ames v. New Zealand (Christchurch)	1932–33
237	D. C. S. Compton & N. W. D. Yardley v. South Africa (Nottingham)	1947
206	E. Paynter & D. C. S. Compton v. Australia (Nottingham)	1938
192	R. E. Foster & L. C. Braund v. Australia (Sydney)	1903–04
192	D. C. S. Compton & T. E. Bailey v. Pakistan (Nottingham)	1954
191	E. Hendren & M. Leyland v. Australia (Manchester)	1934
184	G. B. Legge & M. S. Nichols v. New Zealand (Auckland)	1929–30
182	J. Hardstaff jun. & P. A. Gibb v. India (Lord's)	1946
179	M. Leyland & L. E. G. Ames v. South Africa (Oval)	1935
163	W. Watson & T. E. Bailey v. Australia (Lord's)	1953
162	A. C. MacLaren & R. Peel v. Australia (Melbourne)	1894–95
161	A. Shrewsbury & W. Barnes v. Australia (Lord's)	1886
156	M. Leyland & R. E. S. Wyatt v. Australia (Adelaide)	1932–33
154	C. P. Mead & P. G. H. Fender v. South Africa (Durban)	1922–23
148	T. W. Graveney & A. J. Watkins v. India (Bombay)	1951–52
145	D. R. Jardine & B. H. Valentine v. India (Bombay)	1933–34
144	D. C. S. Compton & T. E. Bailey v. South Africa (Manchester)	1955
134	D. C. S. Compton & T. E. Bailey v. Australia (Sydney)	1954–55
126	W. R. Hammond & D. R. Jardine v. Australia (Melbourne)	1928–29
125	F. S. Jackson & R. H. Spooner v. Australia (Manchester)	1905
118	D. C. S. Compton & J. Hardstaff jun. v. Australia (Adelaide)	1946–47
118	P. B. H. May & M. C. Cowdrey v. Australia (Melbourne)	1958–59

115   A. Shrewsbury & W. Bates & W. Flowers v. Australia (Melbourne) 1884–85
113   P. F. Warner & F. E. Woolley v. South Africa (Lord's) 1912
112   R. Abel & W. Barnes v. Australia (Oval) 1888
111   J. W. Hearne & F. E. Woolley v. South Africa (Leeds) 1912
110   D. C. S. Compton & T. W. Graveney v. West Indies (Trinidad) 1953–54
107   A. J. Watkins & C. J. Poole v. India (Calcutta) 1951–52
106   H. Makepeace & J. W. H. T. Douglas v. Australia (Melbourne) 1920–21
105   R. Abel & H. Wood v. South Africa (Cape Town) 1888–89
105   R. T. Simpson & T. E. Bailey v. New Zealand (Manchester) 1949
104   C. P. Mead & F. E. Woolley v. South Africa (Port Elizabeth) 1913–14
102* E. Tyldesley & P. G. H. Fender v. Australia (Manchester) 1921
101   A. Sandham & E. Hendren v. South Africa (Oval) 1924

SIXTH WICKET (34)

215   L. Hutton & J. Hardstaff jun. v. Australia (Oval) 1938
189   D. C. S. Compton & T. E. Bailey v. New Zealand (Lord's) 1949
186   W. R. Hammond & L. E. G. Ames v. Australia (Lord's) 1938
170   H. Sutcliffe & R. E. S. Wyatt v. Australia (Oval) 1930
161   T. E. Bailey & T. G. Evans v. West Indies (Manchester) 1950
159   T. W. Graveney & T. G. Evans v. India (Lord's) 1952
158   J. T. Tyldesley & R. H. Spooner v. Australia (Oval) 1905
157   L. E. G. Ames & J. Iddon v. West Indies (Kingston) 1934–35
156   C. P. Mead & F. T. Mann v. South Africa (Durban) 1922–23
145   L. C. Braund & G. L. Jessop v. South Africa (Lord's) 1907
142   M. Leyland & L. E. G. Ames v. Australia (Manchester) 1934
141   F. S. Jackson & L. C. Braund v. Australia (Manchester) 1902
140   E. Hendren & M. Leyland v. Australia (Melbourne) 1928–29
131   W. W. Read & F. S. Jackson v. Australia (Oval) 1893
129   M. Leyland & M. W. Tate v. South Africa (Lord's) 1929
129   M. Leyland & L. E. G. Ames v. Australia (Lord's) 1934
125   A. P. F. Chapman & G. O. Allen v. Australia (Lord's) 1930
124   G. H. Hirst & K. S. Ranjitsinhji v. Australia (Sydney) 1897–98
124   J. W. H. T. Douglas & A. C. Russell v. Australia (Adelaide) 1920–21
124   F. E. Woolley & F. T. Mann v. South Africa (Johannesburg) 1922–23
121   C. P. Mead & Hon. L. H. Tennyson v. Australia (Oval) 1921
121   M. Leyland & L. E. G. Ames & G. O. Allen v. Australia (Oval)........1934
120   M. J. K. Smith & P. M. Walker v. South Africa (Lord's) 1960
115   W. W. Read & E. F. S. Tylecote v. Australia (Sydney) 1882–83
113* F. S. Jackson & W. Rhodes v. Australia (Nottingham) 1905
113   J. T. Ikin and N. W. D. Yardley v. Australia (Melbourne) 1946–47
109   F. S. Jackson & G. L. Jessop v. Australia (Oval) 1902
108   W. G. Quaife & L. C. Braund v. Australia (Adelaide) 1901–02
108   L. Hutton & T. G. Evans v. West Indies (Kingston) 1953–54
106   F. E. Woolley & M. Leyland v. South Africa (Leeds) 1929
106   M. J. Horton & T. G. Evans v. India (Nottingham) 1959
105   M. Leyland & R. W. V. Robins v. South Africa (Manchester)........1935
104   J. W. H. T. Douglas & P. G. H. Fender v. Australia (Melbourne) 1920–21
100   F. G. Mann & R. O. Jenkins v. South Africa (Port Elizabeth) 1948–49

SEVENTH WICKET (18)

197   M. J. K. Smith & J. M. Parks v. West Indies (Trinidad) 1959–60
174   M. C. Cowdrey & T. G. Evans v. West Indies (Lord's) 1957
143   F. E. Woolley & J. Vine v. Australia (Sydney) 1911–12
142   J. Sharp & K. L. Hutchings v. Australia (Oval) 1909
140   D. R. Jardine & R. W. V. Robins v. West Indies (Manchester) 1933
133   W. W. Whysall & R. Kilner v. Australia (Melbourne) 1924–25
124   A. A. Lilley & L. C. Braund v. Australia (Sydney) 1901–02
123   E. R. Dexter & R. Swetman v. West Indies (Barbados) 1959–60
117   J. B. Hobbs & E. Hendren v. Australia (Adelaide) 1924–25
115   J. W. H. T. Douglas & M. C. Bird v. South Africa (Durban) 1913–14
113   T. Hayward & A. A. Lilley v. Australia (Manchester) 1899
111   M. Leyland & R. W. V. Robins v. Australia (Melbourne) 1936–37
108   F. R. Brown & W. Voce v. New Zealand (Christchurch) 1932–33
106   J. Hardstaff jun. & A. Wood v. Australia (Oval) 1938
105   L. Hutton & J. H. Wardle v. West Indies (Kingston) 1953–54
102   W. Flowers & J. M. Read v. Australia (Sydney) 1884–85
102   R. Illingworth & R. Swetman v. India (Oval) 1959
101   E. Hendren & G. Geary v. Australia (Nottingham) 1934

EIGHTH WICKET (5)

246 L. E. G. Ames & G. O. Allen v. New Zealand (Lord's) 1931
154 C. W. Wright & H. R. B. Davenport v. South Africa (Johannesburg) 1895–96
138 R. W. V. Robins & H. Verity v. India (Manchester) 1936
124 E. Hendren & H. Larwood v. Australia (Brisbane) 1928–29
121 D. C. S. Compton & A. V. Bedser v. Australia (Manchester) 1948

NINTH WICKET (5)

151 W. H. Scotton & W. W. Read v. Australia (Oval) 1884
128 F. E. Woolley & A. P. Freeman v. Australia (Sydney)..1924–25
117 T. E. Bailey & D. V. P. Wright v. New Zealand (Christchurch)...........................1950–51
115 R. E. Foster & A. E. Relf v. Australia (Sydney) 1903–04
108 G. Geary & G. G. Macaulay v. Australia (Leeds) 1926

TENTH WICKET (1)

130 R. E. Foster & W. Rhodes v. Australia (Sydney) 1903–04

AUSTRALIA

FIRST WICKET (31)

233 J. H. Fingleton & W. A. Brown v. South Africa (Cape Town) 1935–36
214 A. R. Morris & J. A. R. Moroney v. South Africa (Johannesburg) 1949–50
191 C. C. McDonald & A. R. Morris v. West Indies (Trinidad) 1954–55
190 C. C. McDonald & J. W. Burke v. South Africa (Cape Town) 1957–58
180 W. Bardsley & S. E. Gregory v. England (Oval) 1909
172* W. H. Ponsford & A. A. Jackson v. West Indies (Adelaide) 1930–31
171 C. C. McDonald & J. W. Burke v. England (Adelaide) 1958–59
162 W. M. Woodfull & W. H. Ponsford v. England (Lord's) 1930
162 J. H. Fingleton & W. A. Brown v. South Africa (Durban) 1935–36
159 W. M. Woodfull & W. H. Ponsford v. England (Oval) 1930
137 C. C. McDonald & J. W. Burke v. England (Lord's) 1956
135 V. T. Trumper & R. A. Duff v. England (Manchester) 1902
133 W. M. Woodfull & V. Y. Richardson v. England (Brisbane) 1932–33
129 V. T. Trumper & R. A. Duff v. England (Adelaide) 1903–04
126 V. T. Trumper & M. A. Noble v. England (Melbourne) 1907–08
126 S. G. Barnes & A. R. Morris v. England (Sydney) 1946–47
123 H. L. Collins & C. G. Macartney v. England (Sydney) 1920–21
122 S. G. Barnes & A. R. Morris v. England (Lord's) 1948
122 C. C. McDonald & A. R. Morris v. South Africa (Melbourne) 1952–53
117 H. L. Collins & W. Bardsley v. England (Melbourne) 1920–21
117 S. G. Barnes & A. R. Morris v. England (Oval) 1948
116 C. E. McLeod & J. Worrall v. England (Oval) 1899
116 H. L. Collins & W. Bardsley v. England (Melbourne) 1920–21
116 A. R. Morris & M. Harvey v. England (Adelaide) 1946–47
110 A. C. Bannerman & W. L. Murdoch v. England (Melbourne) 1881–82
108 C. C. McDonald & L. Favell v. West Indies (Barbados) 1954–55
106 W. M. Woodfull & W. H. Ponsford v. England (Manchester) 1930
105 J. H. Fingleton & W. A. Brown v. South Africa (Johannesburg) 1935–36
103 W. Bardsley & T. J. E. Andrews v. England (Lord's).....................................1921
102 C. C. McDonald & A. R. Morris v. West Indies (Kingston) 1954–55
100 V. T. Trumper & R. A. Duff v. South Africa (Cape Town) 1902–03

SECOND WICKET (51)

451 W. H. Ponsford & D. G. Bradman v. England (Oval) 1934
301 A. R. Morris & D. G. Bradman v. England (Leeds) 1948
275 C. C. McDonald & A. L. Hassett v. South Africa (Adelaide) 1952–53
274 W. M. Woodfull & D. G. Bradman v. South Africa (Melbourne) 1931–32
236 S. G. Barnes & D. G. Bradman v. India (Adelaide) 1947–48
235 W. M. Woodfull & C. G. Macartney v. England (Leeds) 1926
231 W. M. Woodfull & D. G. Bradman v. England (Lord's) 1930
229 W. H. Ponsford & D. G. Bradman v. West Indies (Brisbane) 1930–31
224 W. Bardsley & C. Hill v. South Africa (Sydney) 1910–11
215 W. M. Woodfull & H. L. Hendry v. England (Sydney) 1928–29
204 J. W. Burke & R. N. Harvey v. India (Bombay) 1956–57
196 W. A. Brown & S. J. McCabe v. England (Manchester) 1934
192 W. M. Woodfull & C. G. Macartney v. England (Manchester) 1926

192   W. M. Woodfull & D. G. Bradman v. England (Leeds) 1930
190   H. L. Collins & W. H. Ponsford v. England (Sydney) 1924–25
177   J. H. Fingleton & D. J. McCabe v. South Africa (Johannesburg) 1935–36
176   W. M. Woodfull & D. G. Bradman v. South Africa (Adelaide) 1931–32
174   A. C. Bannerman & J. J. Lyons v. England (Sydney) 1891–92
174   S. G. Barnes & D. G. Bradman v. England (Lord's) 1948
170   W. A. Brown & D. G. Bradman v. England (Nottingham) 1938
170   J. A. R. Moroney & R. N. Harvey v. South Africa (Johannesburg) 1949–50
165   A. R. Morris & K. R. Miller v. England (Lord's) 1953
163   W. M. Woodfull & D. G. Bradman v. South Africa (Brisbane) 1931–32
162   W. M. Woodfull & D. G. Bradman v. West Indies (Melbourne) 1930–31
161   W. A. Brown & S. J. McCabe v. South Africa (Durban) 1935–36
157   A. R. Morris & R. N. Harvey v. South Africa (Adelaide) 1952–53
148   J. Darling & C. Hill v. England (Adelaide) 1897–98
146   C. Kelleway & C. G. Macartney v. England (Lord's)..............................1912
143   P. S. McDonnell & W. L. Murdoch v. England (Oval) 1884
143   V. T. Trumper & C. Hill v. England (Adelaide) 1903–04
137   W. M. Woodfull & K. E. Rigg v. South Africa (Sydney) 1931–32
136   V. T. Trumper & C. Hill v. England (Adelaide) 1901–02
134   W. A. Brown & D. G. Bradman & K. R. Miller v. India (Melbourne) 1947–48
131   F. A. Iredale & G. Giffen v. England (Manchester) 1896
128   V. T. Trumper & C. Hill & M. A. Noble v. England (Nottingham) 1905
        (Hill and Noble added 106 after Trumper had retired hurt)
126   C. C. McDonald & R. N. Harvey v. England (Melbourne) 1958–59
125   A. L. Hassett & R. N. Harvey v. England (Lord's) 1953
124   C. E. McLeod & C. Hill v. England (Melbourne) 1897–98
124   C. G. Macartney & H. V. Hordern v. South Africa (Sydney) 1910–11
124   J. H. Fingleton & D. G. Bradman v. England (Sydney) 1936–37
123   H. L. Collins & C. G. Macartney v. England (Lord's) 1926
122   A. R. Morris & A. L. Hassett v. England (Nottingham) 1953
121   C. Kelleway & C. Hill v. England (Sydney) 1911–12
121   K. M. Archer & A. L. Hassett v. England (Sydney) 1950–51
115   W. M. Woodfull & D. G. Bradman v. England (Sydney) 1932–33
113   H. L. Collins & J. Ryder v. South Africa (Johannesburg) 1921–22
111   H. L. Collins & W. Bardsley v. England (Sydney) 1920–21
109   S. G. Barnes & W. A. Brown v. New Zealand (Wellington) 1945–46
105   C. C. McDonald & R. N. Harvey & N. O'Neill v. England (Adelaide) 1958–59
104   J. A. R. Moroney & K. R. Miller v. South Africa (Cape Town) 1949–50
101   W. Bardsley & C. Hill v. South Africa (Melbourne)..............................1910–11

THIRD WICKET (41)

295   C. C. McDonald & R. N. Harvey v. West Indies (Kingston) 1954–55
276   D. G. Bradman & A. L. Hassett v. England (Brisbane) 1946–47
249   D. G. Bradman & S. J. McCabe v. England (Melbourne) 1936–37
242   W. Bardsley & C. Kelleway v. South Africa (Lord's) 1912
229   D. G. Bradman & A. F. Kippax v. England (Leeds) 1930
224   R. N. Harvey & K. R. Miller v. West Indies (Kingston) 1954–55
209   H. L. Collins & J. M. Gregory v. South Africa (Johannesburg) 1921–22
207   W. L. Murdoch & H. J. H. Scott v. England (Oval) 1884
207   R. N. Harvey & N. O'Neill v. India (Bombay) 1959–60
202   W. Bardsley & C. Kelleway v. South Africa (Manchester) 1912
202   A. R. Morris & R. N. Harvey v. England (Brisbane) 1954–55
193   J. Darling & J. Worrall v. England (Sydney) 1897–98
193   D. G. Bradman & A. F. Kippax v. West Indies (Brisbane) 1930–31
192   D. G. Bradman & A. F. Kippax v. England (Lord's) 1930
189   A. R. Morris & A. L. Hassett v. England (Adelaide) 1946–47
187   A. R. Morris & R. N. Harvey v. South Africa (Port Elizabeth) 1949–50
169   D. G. Bradman & A. L. Hassett v. India (Melbourne) 1947–48
164   W. W. Armstrong & C. Hill v. South Africa (Johannesburg) 1902–03
158   J. W. Burke & R. Benaud v. South Africa (Johannesburg) 1957–58
157   C. Hill & H. Carter v. England (Adelaide) 1911–12
155   R. N. Harvey & A. L. Hassett v. South Africa (Brisbane) 1952–53
150   D. G. Bradman & S. J. McCabe v. England (Oval) 1934
145   C. G. Macartney & W. Bardsley v. South Africa (Sydney) 1910–11
144   C. Hill & D. R. A. Gehrs v. South Africa (Sydney) 1910–11
137   J. W. Burke & P. Burge v. India (Bombay) 1956–57
128* J. Ryder & J. M. Gregory v. England (Melbourne) 1920–21
118   R. N. Harvey & N. O'Neill v. England (Melbourne) 1958–59
115   R. A. Duff & M. A. Noble v. England (Oval) 1905
114   V. T. Trumper & S. E. Gregory v. England (Sydney) 1907–08
113   C. C. McDonald & R. N. Harvey v. South Africa (Sydney) 1952–53

111 K. E. Rigg & D. G. Bradman v. South Africa (Sydney) 1931–32
110 A. R. Morris & R. N. Harvey v. England (Adelaide) 1950–51
109 D. G. Bradman & S. J. McCabe v. England (Adelaide) 1936–37
109 A. R. Morris & A. L. Hassett v. England (Oval) 1948
108 C. G. Macartney & T. J. E. Andrews v. England (Oval) 1921
105 D. G. Bradman & A. L. Hassett v. India (Adelaide) 1947–48
103 R. N. Harvey & A. L. Hassett v. South Africa (Melbourne) 1952–53
102 W. Bardsley & W. W. Armstrong v. South Africa (Melbourne) 1910–11
101 C. G. Macartney & C. E. Pellew v. England (Leeds) 1921
101 D. G. Bradman & A. L. Hassett v. India (Brisbane) 1947–48
100 R. N. Harvey & W. Watson v. West Indies (Barbados) 1954–55

FOURTH WICKET (42)

388 W. H. Ponsford & D. G. Bradman v. England (Leeds) 1934
243 D. G. Bradman & A. A. Jackson v. England (Oval) 1930
235 A. L. Hassett & K. R. Miller v. West Indies (Sydney) 1951–52
221 G. H. S. Trott & S. E. Gregory v. England (Lord's) 1896
198 C. G. Macartney & J. M. Gregory v. England (Sydney) 1920–21
194 C. Kelleway & W. W. Armstrong v. England (Adelaide)..1920–21
191 A. C. Bannerman & P. S. McDonnell v. England (Sydney) 1881–82
182 A. F. Kippax & S. J. McCabe v. West Indies (Adelaide)..1930–31
173 R. N. Harvey & G. B. Hole v. England (Manchester) 1953
171 F. A. Iredale & G. Giffen v. England (Sydney) 1894–95
168 R. N. Harvey & K. R. Miller v. South Africa (Sydney) 1952–53
162 M. A. Noble & S. E. Gregory v. England (Adelaide) 1903–04
161 W. H. Ponsford & J. M. Taylor v. England (Melbourne) 1924–25
161 A. F. Kippax & J. Ryder v. England (Melbourne) 1928–29
159 R. N. Harvey & S. J. E. Loxton v. India (Melbourne)..1947–48
154 W. W. Armstrong & C. Hill v. South Africa (Melbourne) 1910–11
150 N. O'Neill & P. Burge v. India (Calcutta) 1959–60
148 R. N. Harvey & I. D. Craig v. South Africa (Melbourne) 1952–53
142 A. L. Hassett & K. R. Miller v. India (Adelaide) 1947–48
137 J. Ryder & A. F. Kippax v. England (Adelaide) 1928–29
132 R. N. Harvey & K. Mackay v. India (New Delhi) 1959–60
131 R. N. Harvey & G. B. Hole v. England (Brisbane) 1954–55
130 C. Hill & M. A. Noble v. England (Lord's) 1899
130 J. W. Burke & K. Mackay v. South Africa (Cape Town) 1957–58
129 W. M. Woodfull & A. J. Richardson v. England (Leeds) 1926
126 A. A. Jackson & J. Ryder v. England (Adelaide) 1928–29
124 W. A. Brown & A. L. Hassett v. England (Lord's) 1938
124 R. N. Harvey & K. R. Miller v. West Indies (Melbourne) 1951–52
121 K. R. Miller & R. N. Harvey v. England (Leeds) 1948
120 D. G. Bradman & K. R. Miller v. India (Brisbane) 1947–48
118 W. Bardsley & V. T. Trumper v. South Africa (Adelaide) 1910–11
114 A. F. Kippax & S. J. McCabe v. South Africa (Melbourne) 1931–32
114 A. R. Morris & A. L. Hassett v. South Africa (Port Elizabeth) 1949–50
112 W. A. Brown & S. J. McCabe v. England (Nottingham) 1934
110 N. O'Neill & L. Favell v. England (Sydney) 1958–59
109 C. G. Macartney & J. M. Taylor v. England (Leeds) 1921
109 K. R. Miller & A. L. Hassett v. South Africa (Johannesburg) 1949–50
109 A. L. Hassett & K. R. Miller v. England (Nottingham) 1953
107 S. E. Gregory & C. Hill v. England (Sheffield) 1902
106 M. A. Noble & W. W. Armstrong v. England (Sydney) 1903–04
106 C. G. Macartney & J. Ryder v. South Africa (Durban) 1921–22
106 A. L. Hassett & K. R. Miller v. England (Brisbane)..1946–47

FIFTH WICKET (25)

405 S. G. Barnes & D. G. Bradman v. England (Sydney) 1946–47
223* A. R. Morris & D. G. Bradman v. India (Melbourne)...1947–48
220 K. R. Miller & R. G. Archer v. West Indies (Kingston) 1954–55
183 D. G. Bradman & A. G. Fairfax v. England (Melbourne) 1928–29
183 W. H. Ponsford & W. M. Woodfull v. West Indies (Sydney) 1930–31
161 C. L. Badcock & R. G. Gregory v. England (Melbourne) 1936–37
150 K. R. Miller & I. W. Johnson v. England (Adelaide) 1946–47
143 W. W. Armstrong & V. T. Trumper v. South Africa (Melbourne).........................1910–11
142 S. E. Gregory & J. Darling v. England (Melbourne) 1894–95
140 R. N. Harvey & S. J. E. Loxton v. South Africa (Cape Town) 1949–50
139 G. Giffen & S. E. Gregory v. England (Sydney) 1894–95
135 D. G. Bradman & R. G. Gregory v. England (Adelaide) 1936–37
135 R. N. Harvey & S. J. E. Loxton v. South Africa (Durban) 1949–50

129 S. J. McCabe & V. Y. Richardson v. England (Sydney) 1932–33
124 F. A. Iredale & G. H. S. Trott v. England (Melbourne) 1897–98
120 D. G. Bradman & A. L. Hassett v. England (Nottingham) 1948
118 W. Bardsley & V. T. Trumper v. England (Oval) 1909
114 D. G. Bradman & K. E. Rigg v. South Africa (Adelaide) 1931–32
108 V. T. Trumper & C. Hill v. England (Sydney) 1907–08
107 T. Horan & G. Giffen v. England (Melbourne) 1881–82
106 G. H. S. Trott & H. Graham v. England (Oval) 1893
106 C. G. Macartney & W. W. Armstrong v. England (Melbourne) 1907–08
105 R. N. Harvey & S. J. E. Loxton v. England (Leeds) 1948
101 J. Ryder & O. E. Nothling v. England (Sydney) 1928–29
100 J. Darling & S. E. Gregory v. England (Oval) 1899

SIXTH WICKET (12)

346 J. H. Fingleton & D. G. Bradman v. England (Melbourne) 1936–37
206 K. R. Miller & R. G. Archer v. West Indies (Barbados) 1954–55
187 W. W. Armstrong and C. Kelleway v. England (Sydney) 1920–21
145 J. M. Gregory & W. W. Armstrong v. England (Melbourne) 1920–21
142 S. E. Gregory & H. Graham v. England (Lord's) 1893
131 C. L. McCool & I. W. Johnson v. England (Brisbane)..............................1946–47
126 C. E. Pellew & C. Kelleway v. England (Adelaide) 1920–21
123 V. Y. Richardson & C. Kelleway v. England (Melbourne) 1924–25
109 V. T. Trumper & R. B. Minnett v. England (Sydney) 1911–12
107 C. Kelleway & V. S. Ransford v. South Africa (Melbourne) 1910–11
106* R. N. Harvey & C. L. McCool v. South Africa (Durban) 1949–50
105 W. H. Ponsford & A. F. Kippax v. England (Sydney) 1924–25

SEVENTH WICKET (7)

165 C. Hill & H. Trumble v. England (Melbourne) 1897–98
150 K. R. Miller & I. W. Johnson v. England (Sydney) 1950–51
134 J. Ryder & T. J. E. Andrews v. England (Adelaide) 1924–25
117 K. Mackay & R. Benaud v. England (Lord's) 1956
115 K. Mackay & A. K. Davidson v. England (Sydney) 1958–59
115 R. Benaud & A. W. Grout v. England (Melbourne)................................1958–59
107 H. L. Collins & J. M. Gregory v. England (Oval) 1926

EIGHTH WICKET (9)

243 C. Hill & R. J. Hartigan v. England (Adelaide) 1907–08
173 C. E. Pellew & J. M. Gregory v. England (Melbourne) 1920–21
154 G. J. Bonnor & S. P. Jones v. England (Sydney) 1884–85
154 D. Tallon & R. R. Lindwall v. England (Melbourne) 1946–47
137 R. Benaud & I. W. Johnson v. West Indies (Kingston) 1954–55
116 C. Kelleway & W. A. Oldfield v. England (Sydney) 1924–25
112 H. Graham & A. E. Trott v. England (Sydney) 1894–95
112 W. W. Armstrong & H. Carter v. England (Melbourne) 1907–08
107 A. L. Hassett & R. R. Lindwall v. England (Nottingham) 1948

NINTH WICKET (3)

154 S. E. Gregory & J. McC. Blackham v. England (Sydney) 1894–95
108 J. Ryder & W. A. Oldfield v. England (Adelaide) 1924–25
100 A. E. V. Hartkopf & W. A. Oldfield v. England (Melbourne) 1924–25

TENTH WICKET (2)

127 J. M. Taylor & A. A. Mailey v. England (Sydney) 1924–25
120 R. A. Duff & W. W. Armstrong v. England (Melbourne) 1901–02

SOUTH AFRICA

FIRST WICKET (20)

260 B. Mitchell & I. J. Siedle v. England (Cape Town) 1930–31
196 B. Mitchell & J. A. J. Christy v. New Zealand (Christchurch) 1931–32
191 B. Mitchell & P. G. Van der Byl v. England (Durban) 1938–39
176 D. J. McGlew & T. L. Goddard v. England (Leeds) 1955
176 D. J. McGlew & T. L. Goddard v. Australia (Johannesburg).................1957–58

171	B. Mitchell & R. H. Catterall v. England (Birmingham)	1929
153	H. W. Taylor & J. W. Zulch v. England (Johannesburg)	1913–14
147	D. J. McGlew & T. L. Goddard v. England (Manchester)	1955
131	A. Melville & P. G. Van der Byl v. England (Durban)	1938–39
129	H. W. Taylor & J. W. Zulch v. England (Port Elizabeth)	1913–14
127	B. Mitchell & I. J. Siedle v. England (Durban)	1930–31
119	B. Mitchell & R. H. Catterall v. England (Birmingham)	1929
116	B. Mitchell & I. J. Siedle v. England (Oval)	1935
115	H. W. Taylor & J. M. M. Commaille v. England (Cape Town)	1927–28
113	D. J. McGlew & J. H. B. Waite v. New Zealand (Durban)	1953–54
110	H. W. Taylor & R. H. Catterall v. England (Durban)	1922–23
108	A. Melville & P. G. Van der Byl v. England (Johannesburg)	1938–39
104	B. Mitchell & J. A. J. Christy v. New Zealand (Wellington)	1931–32
104	D. J. McGlew & R. J. Westcott v. New Zealand (Johannesburg)	1953–54
101	B. Mitchell & E. A. B. Rowan v. England (Port Elizabeth)	1948–49

SECOND WICKET (15)

198	E. A. B. Rowan & C. B. Van Ryneveld v. England (Leeds)	1951
173	L. J. Tancred & C. B. Llewellyn v. Australia (Johannesburg)	1902–03
155	R. H. Catterall & H. W. Taylor v. England (Cape Town)	1922–23
147	P. G. Van der Byl & E. A. B. Rowan v. England (Cape Town)	1938–39
145*	A. Melville & K. G. Viljoen v. England (Nottingham)	1947
139	P. W. Sherwell & M. Hathorn v. England (Lord's)	1907
135	J. W. Zulch & G. A. Faulkner v. Australia (Adelaide)	1910–11
119	B. Mitchell & E. A. B. Rowan v. England (Durban)	1938–39
113	E. A. B. Rowan & K. G. Viljoen v. England (Johannesburg)	1948–49
112	T. L. Goddard & J. H. B. Waite v. England (Johannesburg)	1956–57
111	J. H. B. Waite & W. R. Endean v. Australia (Melbourne)	1952–53
110	L. J. Tancred & G. C. White v. England (Johannesburg)	1905–06
107	J. W. Zulch & G. A. Faulkner v. Australia (Melbourne)	1910–11
104	B. Mitchell & E. A. B. Rowan v. England (Lord's)	1935
102	B. Mitchell & J. A. J. Christy v. Australia (Melbourne)	1931–32

THIRD WICKET (20)

319	A. Melville & A. D. Nourse jun. v. England (Nottingham)	1947
231	D. J. McGlew & J. H. B. Waite v. Australia (Durban)	1957–58
190	B. Mitchell & A. D. Nourse jun. v. England (Cape Town)	1948–49
184	B. Mitchell & A. D. Nourse jun. v. England (Oval)	1947
167	E. A. B. Rowan & A. D. Nourse jun. v. Australia (Durban)	1949–50
162*	E. A. B. Rowan & A. D. Nourse jun. v. England (Johannesburg)	1948–49
143	J. W. Zulch & G. A. Faulkner v. Australia (Sydney)	1910–11
134	H. W. Taylor & A. D. Nourse sen. v. England (Johannesburg)	1922–23
122	R. H. Catterall & B. Mitchell v. England (Johannesburg)	1930–31
121	B. Mitchell & H. W. Taylor v. Australia (Adelaide)	1931–32
120	G. C. White & A. D. Nourse sen. v. England (Johannesburg)	1905–06
120	B. Mitchell & H. W. Taylor v. Australia (Adelaide)	1931–32
118	A. Melville & A. D. Nourse jun. v. England (Lord's)	1947
116	B. Mitchell & A. D. Nourse jun. v. England (Johannesburg)	1938–39
116	B. Mitchell & E. A. B. Rowan v. England (Johannesburg)	1938–39
110	G. A. Faulkner & A. D. Nourse sen. v. Australia (Melbourne)	1910–11
105	C. N. Frank & H. W. Taylor v. Australia (Johannesburg)	1921–22
101	B. Mitchell & A. D. Nourse jun. v. England (Port Elizabeth)	1948–49
100	G. A. Faulkner & A. D. Nourse sen. v. England (Johannesburg)	1909–10
100	H. W. Taylor & A. D. Nourse sen. v. England (Durban)	1922–23

FOURTH WICKET (19)

214	H. W. Taylor & H. G. Deane v. England (Oval)	1929
206	C. N. Frank & A. D. Nourse sen. v. Australia (Johannesburg)	1921–22
150	B. Mitchell & W. W. Wade v. England (Port Elizabeth)	1948–49
148	H. W. Taylor & R. H. Catterall v. England (Cape Town)	1930–31
143	A. D. Nourse sen. & G. C. White v. England (Durban)	1909–10
135	K. J. Funston & R. A. McLean v. New Zealand (Durban)	1953–54
129	B. Mitchell & A. D. Nourse jun. v. Australia (Johannesburg)	1935–36
121	A. D. Nourse jun. & K. G. Viljoen v. England (Manchester)	1947
120	S. J. Snooke & G. A. Faulkner v. England (Cape Town)	1909–10
118	E. A. B. Rowan & A. D. Nourse jun. v. Australia (Durban)	1935–36
115	T. L. Goddard & J. H. B. Waite v. England (Oval)	1960
114	G. C. White & G. A. Faulkner v. England (Johannesburg)	1909–10

E

112   M. J. Susskind & R. H. Catterall v. England (Lord's) 1924
111   H. W. Taylor & W. V. S. Ling v. England (Johannesburg) 1922–23
108   J. H. B. Waite & K. J. Funston v. Australia (Adelaide) 1952–53
107   J. F. W. Nicolson & R. H. Catterall v. England (Durban) 1927–28
107   W. R. Endean & J. C. Watkins v. New Zealand (Port Elizabeth) 1953–54
106   A. D. Nourse jun. & W. W. Wade v. England (Johannesburg) 1948–49
104   J. H. B. Waite & W. R. Endean v. Australia (Johannesburg) 1957–58

FIFTH WICKET (9)

135   R. H. Catterall & H. B. Cameron v. England (Durban) 1927–28
130   W. R. Endean & J. E. Cheetham v. New Zealand (Auckland) 1952–53
129   J. H. B. Waite & W. R. Endean v. Australia (Johannesburg) 1957–58
121   A. D. Nourse jun. & G. M. Fullerton v. England (Nottingham) 1951
114   R. H. Catterall & J. M. Blanckenberg v. England (Birmingham) 1924
109   G. A. Faulkner & C. B. Llewellyn v. Australia (Adelaide) 1910–11
108   E. A. B. Rowan & R. A. McLean v. England (Leeds) 1951
106* H. J. Keith & R. A. McLean v. Australia (Melbourne) 1952–53
104   A. Melville & K. G. Viljoen v. England (Durban) 1938–39

SIXTH WICKET (4)

171   J. H. B. Waite & P. L. Winslow v. England (Manchester) 1955
109   R. A. McLean & H. J. Keith v. England (Lord's) 1955
106   A. D. Nourse jun. & F. Nicholson v. Australia (Johannesburg)............1935–36
102   R. A. McLean & S. O'Linn v. England (Manchester) 1960

SEVENTH WICKET (9)

246   D. J. McGlew & A. R. A. Murray v. New Zealand (Wellington) 1952–53
123   H. G. Deane & E. P. Nupen v. England (Durban) 1927–28
121   G. C. White & A. D. Nourse sen. v. England (Johannesburg) 1905–06
111   J. E. Cheetham & P. N. F. Mansell v. Australia (Melbourne) 1952–53
109   S. O'Linn & J. H. B. Waite v. England (Nottingham) 1960
108   K. G. Viljoen & E. L. Dalton v. England (Johannesburg) 1938–39
107   A. D. Nourse jun. & R. E. Grieveson v. England (Durban) 1938–39
105   X. C. Balaskas & C. L. Vincent v. New Zealand (Wellington) 1931–32
101   B. Mitchell & A. B. C. Langton v. England (Lord's) 1935

EIGHTH WICKET (5)

124   A. D. Nourse sen. & E. A. Halliwell v. Australia (Johannesburg) 1902–03
109* B. Mitchell & L. Tuckett v. England (Oval) 1947
104   K. G. Viljoen & Q. McMillan v. Australia (Melbourne) 1931–32
100   G. A. Faulkner & R. O. Schwarz v. Australia (Sydney) 1910–11
100   H. J. Tayfield & N. B. F. Mann v. Australia (Cape Town) 1949–50

NINTH WICKET (1)

137   E. L. Dalton & A. B. C. Langton v. England (Oval) 1935

TENTH WICKET (1)

103   H. G. Owen-Smith & A. J. Bell v. England (Leeds) 1929

WEST INDIES

FIRST WICKET (10)

239   J. B. Stollmeyer & A. F. Rae v. India (Madras) 1948–49
197   J. B. Stollmeyer & A. F. Rae v. New Zealand (Auckland) 1951–52
173   G. Carew & A. G. Ganteaume v. England (Trinidad) 1947–48
159   C. C. Hunte & J. K. Holt v. India (New Delhi) 1958–59
144   C. A. Roach & E. Hunte v. England (Georgetown) 1929–30
142* J. B. Stollmeyer & A. F. Rae v. India (Trinidad) 1952–53
134   J. B. Stollmeyer & A. F. Rae v. India (Bombay) 1948–49
125   C. C. Hunte & R. Kanhai v. Pakistan (Georgetown) 1957–58
122   C. C. Hunte & R. Kanhai v. Pakistan (Barbados) 1957–58
103* J. B. Stollmeyer & A. F. Rae v. England (Nottingham) 1950

SECOND WICKET (14)

446 C. C. Hunte & G. Sobers v. Pakistan (Kingston) 1957–58
269 G. Sobers & C. L. Walcott v. Pakistan (Georgetown) 1957–58
228 R. K. Nunes & G. Headley v. England (Kingston) 1929–30
222 J. K. Holt & F. M. Worrell v. England (Barbados) 1953–54
200 I. Barrow & G. Headley v. England (Manchester) 1933
192 C. A. Roach & G. Headley v. England (Georgetown) 1929–30
172 A. F. Rae & F. M. Worrell v. England (Oval) 1950
156 C. A. Roach & G. Headley v. England (Barbados) 1929–30
152 F. R. Martin & G. Headley v. Australia (Sydney) 1930–31
135 C. C. Hunte & G. Sobers v. Pakistan (Georgetown) 1957–58
134 J. B. Stollmeyer & J. K. Holt v. England (Kingston) 1953–54
118 J. B. Stollmeyer & G. Headley v. England (Lord's) 1939
113 J. B. Stollmeyer & G. Headley v. England (Oval) 1939
102 J. K. Holt & O. G. Smith v. Australia (Kingston) 1954–55

THIRD WICKET (18)

338 E. D. Weekes & F. M. Worrell v. England (Trinidad) 1953–54
243 E. McMorris & G. Sobers & S. Nurse v. England (Kingston) 1959–60
242 C. L. Walcott & E. D. Weekes v. Australia (Trinidad) 1954–55
202 G. Headley & J. E. D. Sealey v. England (Kingston) 1934–35
197 F. M. Worrell & E. D. Weekes v. India (Kingston) 1952–53
162 R. Kanhai & G. Sobers v. Pakistan (Lahore) 1958–59
143 A. F. Rae & F. M. Worrell v. England (Nottingham) 1950
142 G. Headley & F. I. de Caires v. England (Barbados) 1929–30
127* J. B. Stollmeyer & E. D. Weekes v. India (Trinidad) 1952–53
127 C. L. Walcott & E. D. Weekes v. Australia (Trinidad) 1954–55
115 J. B. Stollmeyer & E. D. Weekes v. New Zealand (Auckland) 1951–52
115 R. Kanhai & G. Sobers v. England (Georgetown) 1959–60
110 G. Headley & G. C. Grant v. Australia (Sydney) 1930–31
110 J. B. Stollmeyer & E. D. Weekes v. India (Bombay) 1948–49
109 F. M. Worrell & R. Kanhai v. England (Nottingham) 1957
108 R. Kanhai & O. G. Smith v. India (Calcutta) 1958–59
105 A. F. Rae & E. D. Weekes v. England (Lord's) 1950
104 J. B. Stollmeyer & G. E. Gomez v. England (Barbados) 1947–48

FOURTH WICKET (17)

399 G. Sobers & F. M. Worrell v. England (Barbados) 1959–60
283 F. M. Worrell & E. D. Weekes v. England (Nottingham) 1950
267 C. L. Walcott & G. E. Gomez v. India (New Delhi) 1948–49
217 R. Kanhai & B. F. Butcher v. India (Calcutta) 1958–59
213 F. M. Worrell & C. L. Walcott v. India (Kingston) 1952–53
188* G. Sobers & C. L. Walcott v. Pakistan (Kingston) 1957–58
179 C. L. Walcott & G. Sobers v. Australia (Kingston) 1954–55
165 C. L. Walcott & B. H. Pairaudeau v. England (Barbados) 1953–54
162 E. D. Weekes & O. G. Smith v. New Zealand (Dunedin) 1955–56
130 E. D. Weekes & C. L. Walcott v. India (Georgetown) 1952–53
129 F. M. Worrell & C. L. Walcott v. New Zealand (Christchurch) 1951–52
127 B. F. Butcher & O. G. Smith v. India (New Delhi) 1958–59
125 C. L. Walcott & F. M. Worrell v. Australia (Georgetown) 1954–55
124 F. I. de Caires & J. E. D. Sealey v. England (Barbados) 1929–30
119 G. Sobers & O. G. Smith v. India (Bombay) 1958–59
110 C. L. Walcott & F. M. Worrell v. Australia (Kingston) 1954–55
101 E. D. Weekes & C. L. Walcott v. India (Trinidad) 1952–53

FIFTH WICKET (14)

219 E. D. Weekes & B. H. Pairaudeau v. India (Trinidad) 1952–53
189 F. M. Worrell & C. L. Walcott v. New Zealand (Auckland) 1951–52
185 E. D. Weekes & O. G. Smith v. Pakistan (Barbados) 1957–58
170 E. D. Weekes & R. J. Christiani v. India (Bombay) 1948–49
163 V. H. Stollmeyer & K. H. Weekes v. England (Oval) 1939
134* G. Sobers & B. F. Butcher v. India (Bombay) 1958–59
121 G. Sobers & F. M. Worrell v. England (Georgetown) 1959–60
120 E. D. Weekes & D. Atkinson v. New Zealand (Wellington) 1955–56
116 E. D. Weekes & K. Rickards v. England (Kingston) 1947–48
114 G. Sobers & B. F. Butcher v. India (Kanpur) 1958–59
101* C. L. Walcott & D. Atkinson v. England (Trinidad) 1953–54

101 G. Sobers & O. G. Smith v. Pakistan (Trinidad) 1957–58
100 F. M. Worrell & G. E. Gomez v. England (Trinidad) 1947–48
100 G. Sobers & E. D. Weekes v. England (Lord's) 1957

SIXTH WICKET (12)

211 C. L. Walcott & G. E. Gomez v. England (Lord's) 1950
190 O. G. Smith & F. M. Worrell v. England (Birmingham) 1957
163 G. Sobers & J. Solomon v. India (Kanpur) 1958–59
160* G. Sobers & J. Solomon v. India (Calcutta) 1958–59
138 C. L. Walcott & O. G. Smith v. Australia (Kingston) 1954–55
114 G. C. Grant & E. L. Bartlett v. Australia (Adelaide) 1930–31
109 G. E. Gomez & J. D. C. Goddard v. England (Oval) 1950
106 E. D. Weekes & A. P. Binns v. New Zealand (Wellington) 1955–56
105 O. G. Smith & D. Atkinson v. England (Nottingham) 1957
101 J. D. C. Goddard & E. D. Weekes v. India (New Delhi) 1948–49
101 B. F. Butcher & J. Solomon v. India (Madras) 1958–59
100 R. Kanhai & J. Solomon v. Pakistan (Lahore) 1958–59

SEVENTH WICKET (6)

347 D. Atkinson & C. Depeiza v. Australia (Barbados) 1954–55
154 O. G. Smith & J. D. C. Goddard v. England (Nottingham) 1957
147 G. Headley & R. S. Grant v. England (Kingston) 1934–35
143 D. Atkinson & J. D. C. Goddard v. New Zealand (Christchurch) 1955–56
118 E. D. Weekes & R. J. Christiani v. India (New Delhi) 1948–49
100 J. Solomon & F. C. M. Alexander v. India (Kanpur) 1958–59

EIGHTH WICKET (0)

99 C. A. McWatt & J. K. Holt v. England (Georgetown) 1953–54

NINTH WICKET (1)

106 R. J. Christiani & D. Atkinson v. India (New Delhi) 1948–49

TENTH WICKET (0)

55 F. M. Worrell & K. T. Ramadhin v. England (Nottingham) 1957

NEW ZEALAND

FIRST WICKET (6)

276 C. S. Dempster & J. W. E. Mills v. England (Wellington) 1929–30
133 B. Sutcliffe & W. A. Hadlee v. England (Christchurch) 1946–47
126 G. O. Rabone & M. E. Chapple v. South Africa (Cape Town) 1953–54
121 B. Sutcliffe & V. J. Scott v. England (Oval) 1949
112 B. Sutcliffe & V. J. Scott v. England (Leeds) 1949
101 J. G. Leggat & S. N. McGregor v. India (New Delhi) 1955–56

SECOND WICKET (2)

131 B. Sutcliffe & J. R. Reid v. England (Christchurch) 1950–51
130 B. Sutcliffe & J. W. Guy v. India (New Delhi) 1955–56

THIRD WICKET (4)

222* B. Sutcliffe & J. R. Reid v. India (New Delhi) 1955–56
184 J. W. Guy & J. R. Reid v. India (Calcutta) 1955–56
118 C. S. Dempster & M. L. Page v. England (Lord's) 1931
108* B. Sutcliffe & J. R. Reid v. India (Hyderabad) 1955–56

FOURTH WICKET (1)

142 M. L. Page & R. C. Blunt v. England (Lord's) 1931

FIFTH WICKET (5)

174 J. R. Reid & J. E. F. Beck v. South Africa (Cape Town) 1953–54
150 S. N. McGregor & N. S. Harford v. Pakistan (Lahore) 1955–56
120 M. P. Donnelly & F. B. Smith v. England (Leeds) 1949
116 M. P. Donnelly & J. R. Reid v. England (Manchester) 1949
104 J. R. Reid & J. E. F. Beck v. West Indies (Auckland) 1955–56

SIXTH WICKET (1)

100 H. G. Vivian & F. T. Badcock v. South Africa (Wellington) 1931–32

SEVENTH WICKET (1)

100 T. C. Lowry & H. M. McGirr v. England (Auckland)...1929–30

EIGHTH WICKET (1)

104 D. A. R. Moloney & A. W. Roberts v. England (Lord's) 1937

NINTH WICKET (0)

 69 C. F. W. Allcott & I. B. Cromb v. South Africa (Wellington) 1931–32

TENTH WICKET (0)

 57 F. L. H. Mooney & J. A. Cowie v. England (Leeds) 1949

INDIA

FIRST WICKET (7)

413 V. Mankad & P. Roy v. New Zealand (Madras) 1955–56
203 V. M. Merchant & Mushtaq Ali v. England (Manchester) 1936
124 V. M. Merchant & Mushtaq Ali v. England (Manchester) 1946
124 V. Mankad & C. T. Sarwate v. Australia (Melbourne) 1947–48
121 P. Roy & N. J. Contractor v. New Delhi (New Delhi) 1959–60
106 V. Mankad & P. Roy v. England (Lord's) 1952
103* P. Roy & V. Mankad v. England (Calcutta) 1951–52

SECOND WICKET (5)

237 P. Roy & V. L. Manjrekar v. West Indies (Kingston) 1952–53
137 N. J. Contractor & P. R. Umrigar v. West Indies (New Delhi) 1958–59
124 V. Mankad & H. R. Adhikari v. Australia (Melbourne) 1947–48
121 K. C. Ibrahim & R. S. Modi v. West Indies (New Delhi) 1948–49
109 N. J. Contractor & A. A. Baig v. England (Manchester) 1959

THIRD WICKET (13)

238 P. R. Umrigar & V. L. Manjrekar v. New Zealand (Hyderabad) 1955–56
211 V. M. Merchant & V. S. Hazare v. England (New Delhi) 1951–52
211 V. Mankad & V. S. Hazare v. England (Lord's) 1952
187 P. Roy & V. S. Hazare v. England (Bombay) 1951–52
186 L. Amarnath & C. K. Nayudu v. England (Bombay) 1933–34
156 R. S. Modi & V. S. Hazare v. West Indies (Bombay) 1948–49
143 P. Roy & V. L. Manjrekar v. New Zealand (Calcutta).......................................1955–56
133 N. J. Contractor & A. A. Baig v. Australia (Bombay) 1959–60
130* P. Roy & V. L. Manjrekar v. Pakistan (Dacca)..1954–55
129 R. S. Modi & V. S. Hazare v. West Indies (Calcutta) 1948–49
123 P. Roy & V. L. Manjrekar v. Pakistan (Bahawalpur) 1954–55
112 M. L. Apte & V. S. Hazare v. West Indies (Barbados) 1952–53
108 R. S. Modi & V. S. Hazare v. West Indies (Calcutta) 1948–49

FOURTH WICKET (9)

222 V. S. Hazare & V. L. Manjrekar v. England (Leeds) 1952
183 V. S. Hazare & P. R. Umrigar v. Pakistan (Bombay) 1952–53
171 P. R. Umrigar & A. G. Kripal Singh v. New Zealand (Hyderabad) 1955–56
167 V. Mankad & A. G. Kripal Singh v. New Zealand (Bombay) 1955–56
150 P. Roy & P. R. Umrigar v. West Indies (Kingston) 1952–53

144* V. S. Hazare & L. Amarnath v. West Indies (Bombay) 1948–49
139 R. S. Modi & V. S. Hazare v. West Indies (Bombay) 1948–49
135 M. L. Apte & P. R. Umrigar v. West Indies (Trinidad) 1952–53
108 C. G. Borde & H. R. Adhikari v. West Indies (New Delhi) 1958–59

FIFTH WICKET (3)

131 P. R. Umrigar & D. G. Phadkar v. West Indies (Trinidad) 1952–53
127 V. L. Manjrekar & G. S. Ramchand v. New Zealand (New Delhi) 1955–56
109 A. A. Baig & R. B. Kenny v. Australia (Bombay) 1959–60

SIXTH WICKET (6)

188 V. S. Hazare & D. G. Phadkar v. Australia (Adelaide) 1947–48
134 C. G. Borde & H. R. Adhikari v. West Indies (New Delhi) 1958–59
123 V. L. Manjrekar & R. G. Nadkarni v. New Zealand (New Delhi) 1955–56
118 P. R. Umrigar & D. K. Gaekwad v. West Indies (Trinidad) 1952–53
105 V. S. Hazare & D. G. Phadkar v. England (Leeds) 1952
104 D. G. Phadkar & P. R. Umrigar v. England (Madras) 1951–52

SEVENTH WICKET (2)

153 M. L. Apte & V. Mankad v. West Indies (Trinidad) 1952–53
132 V. S. Hazare & H. R. Adhikari v. Australia (Adelaide) 1947–48

EIGHTH WICKET (0)

82 G. S. Ramchand & N. S. Tamhane v. Pakistan (Bahawalpur) 1954–55

NINTH WICKET (0)

54 G. S. Ramchand & S. G. Shinde v. England (Lord's) 1952

TENTH WICKET (1)

109 H. R. Adhikari & Ghulam Ahmed v. Pakistan (New Delhi) 1952–53

PAKISTAN
FIRST WICKET (2)

152 Hanif Mohammed & Imtiaz Ahmed v. West Indies (Barbados) 1957–58
127 Hanif Mohammed & Alimuddin v. India (Bahawalpur) 1954–55

SECOND WICKET (5)

178 Hanif Mohammed & Saeed Ahmed v. West Indies (Karachi)............................1958–59
165 Hanif Mohammed & Waqar Hasan v. India (Bombay) 1952–53
130 Hanif Mohammed & Saeed Ahmed v. West Indies (Trinidad) 1957–58
118 Imtiaz Ahmed & Saeed Ahmed v. West Indies (Kingston) 1957–58
112 Hanif Mohammed & Alimuddin v. West Indies (Barbados) 1957–58

THIRD WICKET (5)

169 Saeed Ahmed & Wazir Mohammed v. West Indies (Trinidad) 1957–58
169 Saeed Ahmed & Shujauddin v. Australia (Lahore) 1959–60
154 Hanif Mohammed & Saeed Ahmed v. West Indies (Barbados) 1957–58
136 Saeed Ahmed & Hanif Mohammed v. West Indies (Georgetown) 1957–58
101 Imtiaz Ahmed & Wallis Mathias v. West Indies (Kingston) 1957–58

FOURTH WICKET (3)

154 Wazir Mohammed & Hanif Mohammed v. West Indies (Trinidad) 1957–58
136 Maqsood Ahmed & A. H. Kardar v. India (Lahore) 1954–55
121 Hanif Mohammed & Wazir Mohammed v. West Indies (Barbados) 1957–58

FIFTH WICKET (1)

155 Alimuddin & A. H. Kardar v. India (Karachi) 1954–55

SIXTH WICKET (2)

166   Wazir Mohammed & A. H. Kardar v. West Indies (Kingston 1957–58
104   Wazir Mohammed & A. H. Kardar v. Australia (Karachi) 1956–57

SEVENTH WICKET (1)

308   Waqar Hasan & Imtiaz Ahmed v. New Zealand (Lahore) 1955–56

EIGHTH WICKET (0)

63   Nazar Mohammed & Zulfiqar Ahmed v. India (Lucknow) 1952–53
63   Imtiaz Ahmed & Maqsood Ahmed v. New Zealand (Lahore) 1955–56

NINTH WICKET (0)

71   Wallis Mathias & Fazal Mahmood v. West Indies (Trinidad) 1957–58

TENTH WICKET (1)

104   Zulfiqar Ahmed & Amir Elahi v. India (Madras) 1952–53

SUMMARY OF CENTURY WICKET PARTNERSHIPS

Country	Total	1st	2nd	3rd	4th	5th	6th	7th	8th	9th	10th
England	334	72	65	55	45	34	34	18	5	5	1
Australia	223	31	51	41	42	25	12	7	9	3	2
South Africa	103	20	15	20	19	9	4	9	5	1	1
West Indies................	92	10	14	18	17	14	12	6	0	1	0
New Zealand	21	6	2	4	1	5	1	1	1	0	0
India	46	7	5	13	9	3	6	2	0	0	1
Pakistan	20	2	5	5	3	1	2	1	0	0	1
TOTAL	839	148	157	156	136	91	71	44	20	10	6

Appendix E
Test Match Captains, 1876–1960

ENGLAND

Allen, G. O. ....(11) 3 v. India 1936, 5 v. Australia 1936–37, 3 v. West Indies 1947–48.
Bligh, Hon. Ivo ....(4) 4 v. Australia 1882–83.
Bowden, M. P...................(1) 1 v. South Africa 1888–89.
Brown, F. R. ....(15) 2 v. New Zealand 1949, 1 v. West Indies 1950, 5 v. Australia and 2 v. New Zealand 1950–51, 5 v. South Africa 1951.
Calthorpe, Hon. F. S. G. ...(4) 4 v. West Indies 1929–30.
Carr, A. W. ....(6) 4 v. Australia 1926, 2 v. South Africa 1929.
Carr, D. B. ....(1) 1 v. India 1951–52.
Chapman, A. P. F. ....(17) 1 v. Australia 1926, 3 v. West Indies 1928, 4 v. Australia 1928–29, 4 v. Australia 1930, 5 v. South Africa 1930–31.
Cowdrey, M. C. ....(9) 2 v. India 1959, 2 v. West Indies 1959–60, 5 v. South Africa 1960.
Cranston, K. ....(1) 1 v. West Indies 1947–48.
Douglas, J. W. H. T. ......(18) 5 v. Australia 1911–12, 5 v. South Africa 1913–14, 5 v. Australia 1920–21, 2 v. Australia 1921, 1 v. South Africa 1924.
Fane, F. L. ....(5) 3 v. Australia 1907–08, 2 v. South Africa 1909–10.
Foster, R. E. ....(3) 3 v. South Africa 1907.
Fry, C. B. ....(6) 3 v. Australia and 3 v. South Africa 1912.
Gilligan, A. E. R. ....(9) 4 v. South Africa 1924, 5 v. Australia 1924–25.
Gilligan, A. H. H. ....(4) 4 v. New Zealand 1929–30.
Grace, W. G. ....(13) 2 v. Australia 1888, 2 v. Australia 1890, 3 v. Australia 1891–92, 2 v. Australia 1893, 3 v. Australia 1896, 1 v. Australia 1899.
Hammond, W. R. ....(20) 4 v. Australia 1938, 5 v. South Africa 1938–39, 3 v. West Indies 1939, 3 v. India 1946, 4 v. Australia and 1 v. New Zealand 1946–47.
Harris, Lord ....(4) 1 v. Australia 1878–79, 1 v. Australia 1880, 2 v. Australia 1884.
Hawke, Lord ....(4) 2 v. South Africa 1895–96, 2 v. South Africa 1899–99.
Hornby, A. N. ....(2) 1 v. Australia 1882, 1 v. Australia 1884.
Howard, N. D. ....(4) 4 v. India 1951–52.
Hutton, L. ....(23) 4 v. India 1952, 5 v. Australia 1953, 5 v. West Indies 1953–54, 2 v. Pakistan 1954, 5 v. Australia and 2 v. New Zealand 1954–55.
Jackson, Hon. F. S. ....(5) 5 v. Australia 1905.
Jardine, D. R. ....(15) 3 v. New Zealand 1931, 1 v. India 1932, 5 v. Australia and 1 v. New Zealand 1932–33, 2 v. West Indies 1933, 3 v. India 1933–34.
Jones, A. O. ....(2) 2 v. Australia 1907–08.
Leveson Gower, H. D. G. ...(3) 3 v. South Africa 1909–10.
Lillywhite, James ....(2) 2 v. Australia 1876–77.
MacLaren, A. C. ....(22) 3 v. Australia 1897–98, 4 v. Australia 1899, 5 v. Australia 1901–02, 5 v. Australia 1902, 5 v. Australia 1909.
Mann, F. G......................(7) 5 v. South Africa 1948–49, 2 v. New Zealand 1949.
Mann, F. T. ....(5) 5 v. South Africa 1922–23.
May, P. B. H. ....(38) 5 v. South Africa 1955, 5 v. Australia 1956, 5 v. South Africa 1956–57, 5 v. West Indies 1957, 5 v. New Zealand 1958, 5 v. Australia and 2 v. New Zealand 1958–59, 3 v. India 1959, 3 v. West Indies 1959–60.
O'Brien, T. C. ....(1) 1 v. South Africa 1895–96.
Read, W. W. ....(2) 1 v. Australia 1887–88, 1 v. South Africa 1891–92.
Robins, R. W. V. ....(3) 3 v. New Zealand 1937.
Shaw, A. ....(4) 4 v. Australia 1881–82.
Sheppard, D. S. ....(2) 2 v. Pakistan 1954.
Shrewsbury, A. ....(7) 5 v. Australia 1884–85, 2 v. Australia 1886–87.
Smith, C. A. ....(1) 1 v. South Africa 1888–89.
Stanyforth, R. T. ....(4) 4 v. South Africa 1927–28.
Steel, A. G. ....(4) 3 v. Australia 1886, 1 v. Australia 1888.
Stevens, G. T. S...............(1) 1 v. South Africa 1927–28.
Stoddart, A. E. ....(8) 1 v. Australia 1893, 5 v. Australia 1894–95, 2 v. Australia 1897–98.
Tennyson, Hon. L. H. ......(3) 3 v. Australia 1921.
Walters, C. F. ....(1) 1 v. Australia 1934.

Warner, P. F. ....(10)   5 v. Australia 1903–04, 5 v. South Africa 1905–06.
White, J. C. ....(4)   1 v. Australia 1928–29, 3 v. South Africa 1929.
Wyatt, R. E. S. ....(16)   1 v. Australia 1930, 1 v. New Zealand 1932–33, 1 v. West Indies 1933, 4 v. Australia 1934, 4 v. West Indies 1934–35, 5 v. South Africa 1935.
Yardley, N. W. D. ....(14)   1 v. Australia 1946–47, 5 v. South Africa 1947, 5 v. Australia 1948, 3 v. West Indies 1950.

AUSTRALIA

Armstrong, W. W. ....(10)   5 v. England 1920–21, 5 v. England 1921.
Bardsley, W...................(2)   2 v. England 1926.
Benaud, R. ....(13)   5 v. England 1958–59, 3 v. Pakistan and 5 v. India 1959–60.
Blackham, J. McC. ....(8)   1 v. England 1884–85, 3 v. England 1891–92, 3 v. England 1893, 1 v. England 1894–95.
Bradman, D. G. ....(24)   5 v. England 1936–37, 4 v. England 1938, 5 v. England 1946–47, 5 v. India 1947–48, 5 v. England 1948.
Brown, W. A. ....(1)   1 v. New Zealand 1945–46.
Collins, H. L. ....(11)   3 v. South Africa 1921–22, 5 v. England 1924–25, 3 v. England 1926.
Craig, I. D. ....(5)   5 v. South Africa 1957–58.
Darling, J. ....(21)   5 v. England 1899, 3 v. England 1901–02, 5 v. England 1902, 3 v. South Africa 1902–03, 5 v. England 1905.
Giffen, G.......................(4)   4 v. England 1894–95.
Gregory, D. W. ....(3)   2 v. England 1876–77, 1 v. England 1878–79.
Gregory, S. E. ....(6)   3 v. England and 3 v. South Africa 1912.
Hassett, A. L. ....(24)   5 v. South Africa 1949–50, 5 v. England 1950–51, 4 v. West Indies 1951–52, 5 v. South Africa 1952–53, 5 v. England 1953.
Hill, C. ....(10)   5 v. South Africa 1910–11, 5 v. England 1911–12.
Horan, T.........................(2)   2 v. England 1884–85.
Johnson, I. W. ....(17)   4 v. England 1954–55, 5 v. West Indies 1954–55, 5 v. England 1956, 1 v. Pakistan and 2 v. India 1956–57.
Lindwall, R. R. ....(1)   1 v. India 1956–57
Massie, H. H. ....(1)   1 v. England 1884–85.
McDonnell, P. S.............(6)   2 v. England 1886–87, 1 v. England 1887–88, 3 v. England 1888.
Morris, A. R. ....(2)   1 v. West Indies 1951–52, 1 v. England 1954–55.
Murdoch, W. L. ....(16)   1 v. England 1880, 4 v. England 1881–82, 1 v. England 1882, 4 v. England, 1882–83, 3 v. England 1884, 1 v. England 1884–85, 2 v. England 1890.
Noble, M. A. ....(15)   5 v. England 1903–04, 5 v. England 1907–08, 5 v. England 1909.
Richardson, V. Y. ....(5)   5 v. South Africa 1935–36.
Ryder, J. ....(5)   5 v. England 1928–29.
Scott, H. J. H. ....(3)   3 v. England 1886.
Trott, G. H. S..................(8)   3 v. England 1896, 5 v. England 1897–98.
Trumble, H. ....(2)   2 v. England 1901–02.
Woodfull, W. M. ....(25)   5 v. England 1930, 5 v. West Indies 1930–31, 5 v. South Africa 1931–32, 5 v. England 1932–33, 5 v. England 1934.

SOUTH AFRICA

Anderson, J. H. ....(1)   1 v. Australia 1902–03.
Bisset, M. ....(2)   2 v. England 1898–99.
Cameron, H. B. ....(9)   2 v. England 1930–31, 5 v. Australia and 2 v. New Zealand 1931–32.
Cheetham, J. E. ....(15)   5 v. Australia and 2 v. New Zealand 1952–53, 5 v. New Zealand 1953–54, 3 v. England 1955.
Deane, H. G. ....(12)   5 v. England 1927–28, 5 v. England 1929, 2 v. England 1930–31.
Dunell, O. R. ....(1)   1 v. England 1888–89.
Halliwell, E. A. ....(3)   2 v. England 1895–96, 1 v. Australia 1902–03.
McGlew, D. J. ....(9)   2 v. England 1955, 1 v. England 1956–57, 1 v. Australia 1957–58, 5 v. England 1960.
Melville, A. ....(10)   5 v. England 1938–39, 5 v. England 1947.
Milton, W. H. ....(2)   1 v. England 1888–89, 1 v. England 1891–92.
Mitchell, F. ....(3)   1 v. England and 2 v. Australia 1912.
Nourse, A. D., jun. ....(15)   5 v. England 1948–49, 5 v. Australia 1949–50, 5 v. England 1951.
Nupen, E. P. ....(1)   1 v. England 1930–31.
Richards, A. ....(1)   1 v. England 1895–96.
Sherwell, P. W. ....(13)   5 v. England 1905–06, 3 v. England 1907, 5 v. Australia 1910–11.
Snooke, S. J. ....(5)   5 v. England 1909–10.
Taberer, H. M. ....(1)   1 v. Australia 1902–03.
Tancred, L. J. ....(3)   2 v. England and 1 v. Australia 1912.

*E

Taylor, H. W. ....(18)   5 v. England 1913–14, 3 v. Australia 1921–22, 5 v. England 1922–23, 5 v. England 1924.
Van Ryneveld, C. B. ....(8)   4 v. England 1956–57, 4 v. Australia 1957–58.
Wade, H. F. ....(10)   5 v. England 1935, 5 v. Australia 1935–36.

WEST INDIES

Alexander, F. C. M. ....(18)   5 v. Pakistan 1957–58, 5 v. India and 3 v. Pakistan 1958–59, 5 v. England 1959–60.
Atkinson, D. ....(7)   3 v. Australia 1954–55, 4 v. New Zealand 1955–56.
Fernandes, M. P................(1)   1 v. England 1929–30.
Goddard, J. D. C. ....(22)   2 v. England 1947–48, 5 v. India 1948–49, 4 v. England 1950, 4 v. Australia and 2 v. New Zealand 1951–52, 5 v. England 1957.
Gomez, G. E. ....(1)   1 v. England 1947–48.
Grant, G. C. ....(12)   5 v. Australia 1930–31, 3 v. England 1933, 4 v. England 1934–35.
Grant, R. S. ....(3)   3 v. England 1939.
Grell, M. I. ....(1)   1 v. England 1929–30.
Headley, G. ....(1)   1 v. England 1947–48.
Hoad, E. L. G. ....(1)   1 v. England 1929–30.
Nunes, R. K. ....(4)   3 v. England 1928, 1 v. England 1929–30.
Stollmeyer, J. B...............(13)   1 v. Australia 1951–52, 5 v. India 1952–53, 5 v. England 1953–54, 2 v. Australia 1954–55.

NEW ZEALAND

Cave, H. B. ....(9)   3 v. Pakistan, 5 v. India and 1 v. West Indies 1955–56.
Hadlee, W. A. ....(8)   1 v. Australia 1945–46, 1 v. England 1946–47, 4 v. England 1949, 2 v. England 1950–51.
Lowry, T. C. ....(7)   4 v. England 1929–30, 3 v. England 1931.
Page, M. L. ....(7)   2 v. South Africa 1931–32, 2 v. England 1932–33, 3 v. England 1937.
Rabone, G. O. ....(5)   3 v. South Africa 1953–54, 2 v. England 1954–55.
Reid, J. R. ....(10)   3 v. West Indies 1955–56, 5 v. England 1958, 2 v. England 1958–59.
Sutcliffe, B. ....(4)   2 v. West Indies 1951–52, 2 v. South Africa 1953–54.
Wallace, W. M. ....(2)   2 v. South Africa 1952–53.

INDIA

Adhikari, H. R. ....(1)   1 v. West Indies 1958–59.
Amarnath, L. ....(15)   5 v. Australia 1947–48, 5 v. West Indies 1948–49, 5 v. Pakistan 1952–53.
Gaekwad, D. K. ....(4)   4 v. England 1959.
Ghulam Ahmed ....(3)   1 v. New Zealand 1955–56, 2 v. West Indies 1958–59.
Hazare, V. S. ....(14)   5 v. England 1951–52, 4 v. England 1952, 5 v. West Indies 1952–53.
Mankad, V. ....(6)   5 v. Pakistan 1954–55, 1 v. West Indies 1958–59.
Nayudu, C. K. ....(4)   1 v. England 1932, 3 v. England 1933–34.
Pataudi, Nawab of ....(3)   3 v. England 1946.
Ramchand, G. S................(5)   5 v. Australia 1959–60.
Roy, P................(1)   1 v. England 1959.
Umrigar, P. R..................(8)   4 v. New Zealand 1955–56, 3 v. Australia 1956–57, 1 v. West Indies 1958–59.
Vizianagram, M. of............(3)   3 v. England 1936.

PAKISTAN

Fazal Mahmood ....(5)   3 v. West Indies 1958–59, 2 v. Australia 1959–60.
Imtiaz Ahmed ....(1)   1 v. Australia 1959–60.
Kardar, A. H. ....(23)   5 v. India 1952–53, 4 v. England 1954, 5 v. India 1954–55, 3 v. New Zealand 1955–56, 1 v. Australia 1956–57, 5 v. West Indies 1957–58.

TEST MATCH CAPTAINS ON MOST OCCASIONS

38   P. B. H. May (England): from 1955 to 1959–60.
25   W. M. Woodfull (Australia): from 1930 to 1934.
24   D. G. Bradman (Australia): from 1936–37 to 1948.
24   A. L. Hassett (Australia): from 1949–50 to 1953.

23   L. Hutton (England): from 1952 to 1954–55.
23   A. H. Kardar (Pakistan): from 1952–53 to 1957–58.
22   J. D. C. Goddard (West Indies): from 1947–48 to 1957.
22   A. C. MacLaren (England): from 1897–98 to 1909.
21   J. Darling (Australia): from 1899 to 1905.
20   W. R. Hammond (England): from 1938 to 1946–47.

LONGEST RUNS AS CAPTAIN IN CONSECUTIVE MATCHES

35   P. B. H. May (England): from Nottingham 1955 to Leeds 1959.
25   W. M. Woodfull (Australia): from Nottingham 1930 to Oval 1934.
23   A. H. Kardar (Pakistan): from New Delhi 1952–53 to Trinidad 1957–58.
19   W. R. Hammond (England): from Nottingham 1938 to Adelaide 1946–47.
18   F. C. M. Alexander (West Indies): from Barbados 1957–58 to Trinidad 1959–60.
18   H. W. Taylor (South Africa): from Durban 1913–14 to Oval 1924.
15   D. G. Bradman (Australia): from Brisbane 1946–47 to Oval 1948.
15   J. D. C. Goddard (West Indies): from Georgetown 1947–48 to Melbourne 1951–52.
15   L. Hutton (England): from Leeds 1952 to Lord's 1954.
15   I. W. Johnson (Australia): from Melbourne 1954–55 to Madras 1956–57.
15   A. D. Nourse jun. (South Africa): from Durban 1948–49 to Oval 1951.

CAPTAINS WHO WON TOSS IN ALL FIVE TESTS OF A RUBBER

Hon. F. S. Jackson: England v. Australia in England 1905
M. A. Noble: Australia v. England in England 1909
H. G. Deane: South Africa v. England in South Africa 1927–28
J. D. C. Goddard: West Indies v. India in India.......................................1948–49
A. L. Hassett: Australia v. England in England 1953
M. C. Cowdrey: England v. West Indies in West Indies 1959–60

    England won all five tosses v. West Indies in 1959–60—P. B. H. May was captain in the first three Tests and M. C. Cowdrey in the fourth and fifth.

CAPTAINS WHO SENT OPPONENTS IN ON WINNING THE TOSS

G. Giffen (Lost): Australia v. England (Melbourne) 1894–95
A. E. Stoddart (Lost): England v. Australia (Sydney) 1894–95
E. A. Halliwell (Lost): South Africa v. England (Port Elizabeth) 1895–96
Lord Hawke (Won): England v. South Africa (Cape Town)......................1895–96
A. C. MacLaren (Lost): England v. Australia (Melbourne) 1901–02
A. O. Jones (Lost): England v. Australia (Sydney) 1907–08
M. A. Noble (Won): Australia v. England (Lord's) 1909
P. W. Sherwell (Lost): South Africa v. Australia (Melbourne) 1910–11
P. W. Sherwell (Lost): South Africa v. Australia (Sydney) 1910–11
J. W. H. T. Douglas (Won): England v. Australia (Melbourne) 1911–12
H. W. Taylor (Lost): South Africa v. England (Birmingham) 1924
A. W. Carr (Drawn): England v. Australia (Leeds) 1926
H. G. Deane (Lost): South Africa v. England (Cape Town) 1927–28
H. G. Deane (Won): South Africa v. England (Johannesburg) 1927–28
H. G. Deane (Won): South Africa v. England (Durban) 1927–28
H. G. Deane (Drawn): South Africa v. England (Oval) 1929
A. P. F. Chapman (Lost): England v. South Africa (Johannesburg) 1930–31
A. P. F. Chapman (Drawn): England v. South Africa (Durban) 1930–31
T. C. Lowry (Drawn): New Zealand v. England (Manchester) 1931
R. E. S. Wyatt (Won): England v. West Indies (Barbados) 1934–35
R. E. S. Wyatt (Lost): England v. West Indies (Trinidad).......................1934–35
R. E. S. Wyatt (Drawn): England v. South Africa (Oval): 1935
G. O. Allen (Won): England v. India (Lord's) 1936
R. S. Grant (Drawn): West Indies v. England (Manchester) 1939
Nawab of Pataudi (Drawn): India v. England (Manchester) 1946
F. R. Brown (Drawn): England v. New Zealand (Manchester) 1949
A. L. Hassett (Won): Australia v. West Indies (Sydney) 1951–52
B. Sutcliffe (Drawn): New Zealand v. West Indies (Auckland)...............1951–52
L. Amarnath (Drawn): India v. Pakistan (Calcutta) 1952–53
A. L. Hassett (Drawn): Australia v. England (Leeds) 1953
B. Sutcliffe (Lost): New Zealand v. South Africa (Johannesburg) 1953–54
L. Hutton (Drawn): England v. Pakistan (Lord's) 1954
L. Hutton (Lost): England v. Australia (Brisbane) 1954–55
A. R. Morris (Lost): Australia v. England (Sydney) 1954–55
I. W. Johnson (Drawn): Australia v. England (Sydney).......................1954–55

L. Hutton (Won): England v. New Zealand (Dunedin) 1954–55
P. R. Umrigar (Lost): India v. Australia (Calcutta) 1956–57
P. B. H. May (Lost): England v. Australia (Adelaide) 1958–59
R. Benaud (Won): Australia v. England (Melbourne) 1958–59
Fazal Mahmood (Won): Pakistan v. West Indies (Karachi) 1958–59
F. C. M. Alexander (Lost): West Indies v. Pakistan (Dacca) 1958–59
R. Benaud (Won): Australia v. Pakistan (Dacca) 1959–60

A total of 42 captains have sent their opponents in to bat—12 have followed by winning the match, 17 have lost and 13 matches were drawn.

MATCH RESULTS RECORD OF LEADING CAPTAINS (12 or more Tests)

The following percentages are worked out on a basis of two points for a win and one point for a draw:

	Played	Won	Drawn	Lost	Per cent	Toss Won	Toss Lost
R. Benaud (Australia)	13	8	4	1	76·92	3	10
D. R. Jardine (England)	15	9	5	1	76·66	7	8
D. G. Bradman (Australia)	24	15	6	3	75·00	10	14
A. L. Hassett (Australia)	24	14	6	4	70·83	18	6
A. P. F. Chapman (England)	17	9	6	2	70·58	9	8
W. G. Grace (England)	13	8	2	3	69·23	4	9
L. Hutton (England)	23	11	8	4	65·21	7	16
W. M. Woodfull (Australia)	25	14	4	7	64·00	12	13
P. B. H. May (England)	38	19	10	9	63·15	25	13
M. A. Noble (Australia)	15	8	2	5	60·00	11	4
F. C. M. Alexander (West Indies)	18	7	7	4	58·33	9	9
J. Darling (Australia)	21	7	10	4	57·14	7	14
J. E. Cheetham (South Africa)	15	7	3	5	56·66	6	9
I. W. Johnson (Australia)	17	7	5	5	55·88	6	11
W. R. Hammond (England)	20	4	13	3	52·50	11	9
J. D. C. Goddard (West Indies)	22	8	7	7	52·27	12	10
J. W. H. T. Douglas (England)	18	8	2	8	50·00	7	11
A. H. Kardar (Pakistan)	23	6	11	6	50·00	10	13
J. B. Stollmeyer (West Indies)	13	3	6	4	50·00	7	6
F. R. Brown (England)	15	5	4	6	46·66	3	12
P. W. Sherwell (South Africa)	13	5	2	6	46·15	5	8
R. E. S. Wyatt (England)	16	3	8	5	43·75	12	4
W. L. Murdoch (Australia)	16	5	4	7	43·75	7	9
H. G. Deane (South Africa)	12	2	6	4	41·66	9	3
N. W. D. Yardley (England)	14	4	3	7	39·28	9	5
L. Amarnath (India)	15	2	7	6	36·66	4	11
V. S. Hazare (India)	14	1	8	5	35·71	8	6
A. C. MacLaren (England)	22	4	7	11	34·09	11	11
G. C. Grant (West Indies)	12	3	2	7	33·33	5	7
H. W. Taylor (South Africa)	18	1	7	10	25·00	11	7
A. D. Nourse jun. (South Africa)	15	1	5	9	23·33	7	8

Appendix F
Records of Individual Test Series

ENGLAND v. AUSTRALIA

Series	Pl.	Eng. won	Aust. won	Dr.
1876–77 in Australia	2	1	1	0
1878–79 in Australia	1	0	1	0
1880 in England	1	1	0	0
1881–82 in Australia	4	0	2	2
1882 in England	1	0	1	0
1882–83 in Australia	4	2	2	0
1884 in England	3	1	0	2
1884–85 in Australia	5	3	2	0
1886 in England	3	3	0	0
1886–87 in Australia	2	2	0	0
1887–88 in Australia	1	1	0	0
1888 in England	3	2	1	0
1890 in England	2	2	0	0
1891–92 in Australia	3	1	2	0
1893 in England	3	1	0	2
1894–95 in Australia	5	3	2	0
1896 in England	3	2	1	0
1897–98 in Australia	5	1	4	0
1899 in England	5	0	1	4
1901–02 in Australia	5	1	4	0
1902 in England	5	1	2	2
1903–04 in Australia	5	3	2	0
1905 in England	5	2	0	3
1907–08 in Australia	5	1	4	0
1909 in England	5	1	2	2
1911–12 in Australia	5	4	1	0
1912 in England	3	1	0	2
1920–21 in Australia	5	0	5	0
1921 in England	5	0	3	2
1924–25 in Australia	5	1	4	0
1926 in England	5	1	0	4
1928–29 in Australia	5	4	1	0
1930 in England	5	1	2	2
1932–33 in Australia	5	4	1	0
1934 in England	5	1	2	2
1936–37 in Australia	5	2	3	0
1938 in England	4	1	1	2
1946–47 in Australia	5	0	3	2
1948 in England	5	0	4	1
1950–51 in Australia	5	1	4	0
1953 in England	5	1	0	4
1954–55 in Australia	5	3	1	1
1956 in England	5	2	1	2
1958–59 in Australia	5	0	4	1
At Lord's	19	5	7	7
At the Oval	21	11	4	6
At Manchester	17	4	2	11
At Nottingham	10	2	3	5
At Leeds	11	1	4	6
At Birmingham	2	1	0	1
At Sheffield	1	0	1	0
At Melbourne	37	14	20	3
At Sydney	36	15	19	2
At Adelaide	17	6	10	1
At Brisbane	7	3	4	0
In England	81	24	21	36
In Australia	97	38	53	6
Total	178	62	74	42

ENGLAND v. SOUTH AFRICA

Series	Pl.	Eng. won	S.A. won	Dr.
1888–89 in South Africa	2	2	0	0
1891–92 in South Africa	1	1	0	0
1895–96 in South Africa	3	3	0	0
1898–99 in South Africa	2	2	0	0
1905–06 in South Africa	5	1	4	0
1907 in England	3	1	0	2
1909–10 in South Africa	5	2	3	0
1912 in England	3	3	0	0
1913–14 in South Africa	5	4	0	1
1922–23 in South Africa	5	2	1	2
1924 in England	5	3	0	2
1927–28 in South Africa	5	2	2	1
1929 in England	5	2	0	3
1930–31 in South Africa	5	0	1	4
1935 in England	5	0	1	4
1938–39 in South Africa	5	1	0	4
1947 in England	5	3	0	2
1948–49 in South Africa	5	2	0	3
1951 in England	5	3	1	1
1955 in England	5	3	2	0
1956–57 in South Africa	5	2	2	1
1960 in England	5	3	0	2
At Lord's	9	6	1	2
At Leeds	8	5	1	2
At the Oval	9	3	0	6
At Birmingham	3	2	0	1
At Manchester	7	3	1	3
At Nottingham	5	2	1	2
At Port Elizabeth	5	4	1	0
At Cape Town	14	9	2	3
At Johannesburg	21	7	8	6
At Durban	13	4	2	7
In England	41	21	4	16
In South Africa	53	24	13	16
Total	94	45	17	32

ENGLAND v. WEST INDIES

Series	Pl.	Eng. won	W.I. won	Dr.
1928 in England............	3	3	0	0
1929–30 in West Indies	4	1	1	2
1933 in England............	3	2	0	1
1934–35 in West Indies	4	1	2	1
1939 in England............	3	1	0	2
1947–48 in West Indies	4	0	2	2
1950 in England............	4	1	3	0
1953–54 in West Indies	5	2	2	1
1957 in England............	5	3	0	2
1959–60 in West Indies	5	1	0	4
At Lord's	5	4	1	0
At Manchester	4	2	0	2
At the Oval	5	3	1	1
At Nottingham	2	0	1	1
At Birmingham	1	0	0	1
At Leeds	1	1	0	0
At Barbados	5	1	1	3
At Trinidad	6	2	1	3
At Georgetown	5	1	2	2
At Kingston	6	1	3	2
In England	18	10	3	5
In West Indies	22	5	7	10
Total	40	15	10	15

ENGLAND v. INDIA

Series	Pl.	Eng. won	Ind. won	Dr.
1932 in England............	1	1	0	0
1933–34 In India	3	2	0	1
1936 in England............	3	2	0	1
1946 in England............	3	1	0	2
1951–52 in India	5	1	1	3
1952 in England............	4	3	0	1
1959 in England............	5	5	0	0
At Lord's	5	5	0	0
At Manchester	4	2	0	2
At the Oval	4	2	0	2
At Leeds	2	2	0	0
At Nottingham	1	1	0	0
At Bombay	2	1	0	1
At Calcutta	2	0	0	2
At Madras	2	1	1	0
At New Delhi	1	0	0	1
At Kanpur	1	1	0	0
In England	16	12	0	4
In India	8	3	1	4
Total	24	15	1	8

ENGLAND v. PAKISTAN

Series	Pl.	Eng. won	Pak. won	Dr.
1954 in England	4	1	1	2

ENGLAND v. NEW ZEALAND

Series	Pl.	Eng. won	N.Z. won	Dr.
1929–30 in New Zealand ...	4	1	0	3
1931 in England............	3	1	0	2
1932–33 in New Zealand ...	2	0	0	2
1937 in England............	3	1	0	2
1946–47 in New Zealand ...	1	0	0	1
1949 in England............	4	0	0	4
1950–51 in New Zealand ...	2	1	0	1
1954–55 in New Zealand ...	2	2	0	0
1958 in England............	5	4	0	1
1958–59 in New Zealand ...	2	1	0	1
At Lords	4	1	0	3
At the Oval	4	1	0	3
At Manchester	4	2	0	2
At Leeds	2	1	0	1
At Birmingham	1	1	0	0
At Christchurch	5	2	0	3
At Wellington	2	1	0	1
At Auckland	5	1	0	4
At Dunedin	1	1	0	0
In England	15	6	0	9
In New Zealand	13	5	0	8
Total	28	11	0	17

AUSTRALIA v. SOUTH AFRICA

Series	Pl.	Aust. won	S.A. won	Dr.
1902–03 in South Africa......	3	2	0	1
1910–11 in Australia	5	4	1	0
1912 in England............	3	2	0	1
1921–22 in South Africa......	3	1	0	2
1931–32 in Australia	5	5	0	0
1935–36 in South Africa......	5	4	0	1
1949–50 in South Africa......	5	4	0	1
1952–53 in Australia	5	2	2	1
1957–58 in South Africa......	5	3	0	2
At Melbourne	6	4	2	0
At Sydney	4	4	0	0
At Adelaide	3	1	1	1
At Brisbane	2	2	0	0
At Johannesburg	9	4	0	5
At Cape Town	5	5	0	0
At Durban	5	3	0	2
At Port Elizabeth	2	2	0	0
At Lord's	1	1	0	0
At Manchester	1	1	0	0
At Nottingham	1	0	0	1
In Australia	15	11	3	1
In South Africa	21	14	0	7
In England	3	2	0	1
Total	39	27	3	9

AUSTRALIA v. WEST INDIES

Series	Pl.	Aust. won	W.I. won	Dr.
1930–31 in Australia 5		4	1	0
1951–52 in Australia 5		4	1	0
1954–55 in West Indies 5		3	0	2
Total 15		11	2	2

AUSTRALIA v. NEW ZEALAND

Series	Pl.	Aust. won	N.Z. won	Dr.
1945–46 in New Zealand ... 1		1	0	0

AUSTRALIA v. INDIA

Series	Pl.	Aust. won	I. won	Dr.
1947–48 in Australia 5		4	0	1
1956–57 in India 3		2	0	1
1959–60 in India 5		2	1	2
Total 13		8	1	4

AUSTRALIA v. PAKISTAN

Series	Pl.	Aust. won	Pak. won	Dr.
1956–57 in Pakistan 1		0	1	0
1959–60 in Pakistan 3		2	0	1
Total 4		2	1	1

SOUTH AFRICA v. NEW ZEALAND

Series	Pl.	S.A. won	N.Z. won	Dr.
1931–32 in New Zealand ... 2		2	0	0
1952–53 in New Zealand ... 2		1	0	1
1953–54 in South Africa...... 5		4	0	1
Total 9		7	0	2

WEST INDIES v. NEW ZEALAND

Series	Pl.	W.I. won	N.Z. won	Dr.
1951–52 in New Zealand ... 2		1	0	1
1955–56 in New Zealand ... 4		3	1	0
Total 6		4	1	1

WEST INDIES v. INDIA

Series	Pl.	W.I. won	Ind. won	Dr.
1948–49 in India 5		1	0	4
1952–53 in West Indies 5		1	0	4
1958–59 in India 5		3	0	2
Total 15		5	0	10

WEST INDIES v. PAKISTAN

Series	Pl.	W.I. won	Pak. won	Dr.
1957–58 in West Indies 5		3	1	1
1958–59 in Pakistan 3		1	2	0
Total 8		4	3	1

NEW ZEALAND v. INDIA

Series	Pl.	N.Z. won	Ind. won	Dr.
1955–56 in India 5		0	2	3

NEW ZEALAND v. PAKISTAN

Series	Pl.	N.Z. won	Pak. won	Dr.
1955–56 in Pakistan 3		0	2	1

INDIA v. PAKISTAN

Series	Pl	Ind. won	Pak. won	Dr.
1952–53 in India 5		2	1	2
1954–55 in Pakistan 5		0	0	5
Total 10		2	1	7

Highest Run Aggregates in each Series

ENGLAND v. AUSTRALIA

	Tests	Inns.	N.O.	Runs	H.S.	Avge.	100s	50s
D. G. Bradman (Australia)	37	63	7	5028	334	89·78	19	13
J. B. Hobbs (England)	41	71	4	3636	187	54·26	12	15
W. R. Hammond (England)	33	58	3	2852	251	51·85	9	7
H. Sutcliffe (England)	27	46	5	2741	194	66·85	8	16
C. Hill (Australia)	41	76	1	2660	188	35·46	4	16
L. Hutton (England)	27	49	6	2428	364	56·46	5	14
V. T. Trumper (Australia)	40	74	5	2264	185*	32·81	6	9
S. E. Gregory (Australia)	52	92	7	2193	201	25·80	4	8
W. W. Armstrong (Australia)	42	71	9	2172	158	35·03	4	5
A. R. Morris (Australia)	24	43	2	2080	206	50·73	8	8
A. C. MacLaren (England)	35	61	4	1931	140	33·87	5	8
S. J. McCabe (Australia)	24	43	3	1931	232	48·27	4	9
M. A. Noble (Australia)	39	68	6	1905	133	30·72	1	15
D. C. S. Compton (England)	28	51	8	1842	184	42·83	5	9
T. Hayward (England)	29	51	2	1747	137	35·65	2	12
E. Hendren (England)	28	48	4	1740	169	39·54	3	10
W. Rhodes (England)	41	69	14	1706	179	31·01	1	9
M. Leyland (England)	20	34	4	1705	187	56·83	7	3

ENGLAND v. SOUTH AFRICA

	Tests	Inns.	N.O.	Runs	H.S.	Avge.	100s	50s
B. Mitchell (South Africa)	30	57	7	2732	189*	54·64	7	16
H. W. Taylor (South Africa)	30	54	3	2287	176	44·84	7	12
D. C. S. Compton (England)	24	42	1	2205	208	53·78	7	11
W. R. Hammond (England)	24	42	7	2188	181	62·51	6	14
A. D. Nourse jun. (South Africa)	24	43	6	2037	208	55·05	7	9
L. Hutton (England)	19	34	4	1564	158	56·13	4	7
J. B. Hobbs (England)	18	29	3	1562	211	60·07	2	12
R. H. Catterall (South Africa)	24	43	2	1555	120	37·92	3	—
A. D. Nourse sen. (South Africa)	31	57	4	1415	93*	26·69	—	10

ENGLAND v. WEST INDIES

	Tests	Inns.	N.O.	Runs	H.S.	Avge.	100s	50s
G. Headley (West Indies)	16	29	3	1852	270*	71·23	8	5
F. M. Worrell (West Indies)	20	34	5	1837	261	63·34	6	6
L. Hutton (England)	13	24	3	1661	205	79·09	5	6
C. L. Walcott (West Indies)	20	36	5	1391	220	44·87	4	5
E. D. Weekes (West Indies)	17	30	1	1313	206	45·27	3	7
G. Sobers (West Indies)	11	20	2	1069	226	59·38	3	3
P. B. H. May (England)	13	21	2	986	285*	51·89	3	3
M. C. Cowdrey (England)	10	16	1	926	154	61·73	4	4
E. Hendren (England)	9	17	3	909	205*	64·92	2	5
J. B. Stollmeyer (West Indies)	14	25	2	858	78	37·30	—	7
C. A. Roach (West Indies)	11	22	1	758	209	36·09	2	5
L. E. G. Ames (England)	11	18	3	748	149	49·86	3	1
T. W. Graveney (England)	9	15	4	737	258	67·00	2	2

ENGLAND v. NEW ZEALAND

	Tests	Inns.	N.O.	Runs	H.S.	Avge.	100s	50s
W. R. Hammond (England)	9	11	2	1015	336*	112·77	4	1
B. Sutcliffe (New Zealand)	15	26	1	992	116	39·92	2	7
L. Hutton (England)	11	17	0	767	206	45·11	3	4
C. S. Dempster (New Zealand)	8	11	4	619	136	58·42	2	4
P. B. H. May (England)	9	11	2	603	124*	67·00	3	2
M. P. Donnelly (New Zealand)	7	12	1	582	206	52·90	1	4
K. S. Duleepsinhji (England)	7	10	2	566	117	70·75	2	3
J. R. Reid (New Zealand)	13	24	1	542	93	23·56	—	5
W. A. Hadlee (New Zealand)	10	17	1	534	116	33·37	1	2
D. C. S. Compton (England)	8	11	0	510	116	46·36	2	2

ENGLAND v. INDIA

	Tests	Inns.	N.O.	Runs	H.S.	Avge.	100s	50s
V. M. Merchant (India)	10	18	0	859	154	47·72	3	3
V. S. Hazare (India)	12	19	2	803	164*	47·23	2	3
P. Roy (India)	14	25	1	620	140*	25·83	2	1
V. Mankad (India)	11	18	1	618	184	36·35	1	4
W. R. Hammond (England)	6	9	2	555	217	79·28	2	1
T. W. Graveney (England)	8	13	3	554	175	55·40	1	2
L. Hutton (England)	7	11	2	522	150	58·00	2	2
P. R. Umrigar (India)	13	22	1	516	130*	24·57	2	—
A. J. Watkins (England)	8	11	1	503	138*	50·30	1	3

AUSTRALIA v. SOUTH AFRICA

	Tests	Inns.	N.O.	Runs	H.S.	Avge.	100s	50s
R. N. Harvey (Australia)	15	23	3	1625	205	81·25	8	5
W. Bardsley (Australia)	11	17	1	982	164	61·37	3	6
A. D. Nourse jun. (South Africa)	10	19	1	923	231	51·27	2	5
V. T. Trumper (Australia)	8	15	3	900	214*	75·00	2	4
G. A. Faulkner (South Africa)	8	15	1	880	204	62·85	3	5
A. D. Nourse sen. (South Africa)	14	26	4	819	111	37·22	1	5
D. G. Bradman (Australia)	5	5	1	806	299*	201·50	4	—
A. R. Morris (Australia)	10	17	0	792	157	46·58	2	3
C. C. McDonald (Australia)	10	18	1	786	154	46·23	1	5
C. Hill (Australia)	8	13	1	752	191	62·66	3	3

AUSTRALIA v. WEST INDIES

	Tests	Inns.	N.O.	Runs	H.S.	Avge.	100s	50s
C. L. Walcott (West Indies)	8	16	0	914	155	57·12	5	3
R. N. Harvey (Australia)	10	17	1	911	204	56·88	3	2
K. R. Miller (Australia)	10	16	1	801	147	53·40	4	1
E. D. Weekes (West Indies)	10	20	2	714	139	39·66	1	5
C. C. McDonald (Australia)	6	10	1	543	127	60·33	2	3
F. M. Worrell (West Indies)	9	18	0	543	108	30·16	1	3

WEST INDIES v. INDIA

	Tests	Inns.	N.O.	Runs	H.S.	Avge.	100s	50s
E. D. Weekes (West Indies)	10	15	1	1495	207	106·78	7	4
P. R. Umrigar (India)	11	20	2	927	130	51·50	2	7
C. L. Walcott (West Indies)	10	14	1	909	152	69·92	4	3
V. S. Hazare (India)	10	20	2	736	134*	40·88	2	4
P. Roy (India)	9	18	0	717	150	39·83	1	3
J. B. Stollmeyer (West Indies)	9	14	3	696	160	63·27	2	4

Highest Wicket Aggregates in each Series

ENGLAND v. AUSTRALIA

	Tests	Balls	Mdns.	Runs	Wkts.	Avge.	5wI.	10wM.
H. Trumble (Australia)	31	7895	448	2945	141	20·88	9	3
M. A. Noble (Australia)	39	6845	353	2862	115	24·88	9	2
R. R. Lindwall (Australia)	29	6590	217	2559	114	22·44	6	—
W. Rhodes (England)	41	5785	237	2616	109	24·00	6	1
S. F. Barnes (England)	20	5749	264	2288	106	21·58	12	1
C. V. Grimmett (Australia)	22	9224	426	3439	106	32·44	11	2
A. V. Bedser (England)	21	7125	208	2859	104	27·49	7	2
G. Giffen (Australia)	31	6325	434	2791	103	27·09	7	1
W. J. O'Reilly (Australia)	19	7864	439	2587	102	25·36	8	3
R. Peel (England)	20	5216	444	1715	102	16·81	6	2
C. T. B. Turner (Australia)	17	5179	457	1670	101	16·53	11	2
J. Briggs (England)	31	4918	338	1993	97	20·54	6	3
F. R. Spofforth (Australia)	18	4185	416	1731	94	18·41	7	4
T. Richardson (England)	14	4485	191	2200	88	25·22	11	4
K. R. Miller (Australia)	29	5717	225	1949	87	22·40	3	1
A. A. Mailey (Australia)	18	5199	91	2935	86	34·12	6	2
M. W. Tate (England)	20	7686	330	2536	83	30·55	6	1

ENGLAND v. SOUTH AFRICA

	Tests	Balls	Mdns.	Runs	Wkts.	Avge.	5wI.	10wM.
S. F. Barnes (England)	7	2124	94	818	83	9·85	12	6
H. J. Tayfield (South Africa)	15	5286	297	1658	75	22·10	7	1
J. B. Statham (England)	15	3611	142	1281	62	20·66	3	1
C. L. Vincent (South Africa)	18	4441	154	1967	72	27·31	3	—
G. A. Faulkner (South Africa)	17	3086	104	1472	68	21·64	4	—
A. E. E. Vogler (South Africa)	13	2736	91	1279	60	21·31	5	1
C. Blythe (England)	10	1261	132	986	59	16·71	6	3
N. A. T. Adcock (South Africa)	14	3488	137	1152	57	20·21	2	—
A. V. Bedser (England)	13	3814	148	1457	54	26·98	3	1
A. M. B. Rowan (South Africa)	15	5193	136	2084	54	38·59	4	—
M. W. Tate (England)	14	3649	174	1185	53	22·37	1	—

ENGLAND v. WEST INDIES

	Tests	Balls	Mdns.	Runs	Wkts.	Avge.	5wI.	10wM.
K. T. Ramadhin (West Indies)	18	7154	464	2201	80	27·51	5	1
F. S. Trueman (England)	13	3164	123	1424	52	27·38	2	—
J. C. Laker (England)	13	4090	239	1549	51	30·37	1	—
L. N. Constantine (West Indies)	13	2788	110	1339	50	26·78	2	—
A. L. Valentine (West Indies)	9	3836	282	1140	40	28·50	2	2
J. B. Statham (England)	10	2639	105	1179	39	30·23	1	—
E. A. Martindale (West Indies)	10	1605	40	804	37	21·72	3	—
H. C. Griffith (West Indies)	8	1860	69	850	30	28·33	2	—

ENGLAND v. NEW ZEALAND

	Tests	Balls	Mdns.	Runs	Wkts.	Avge.	5wI.	10wM.
G. A. R. Lock (England)	7	1505	122	367	47	7·80	5	2
J. A. Cowie (New Zealand)	8	1902	57	929	39	23·82	3	1
T. E. Bailey (England)	12	1876	70	866	32	27·06	2	—

ENGLAND v. INDIA

	Tests	Balls	Mdns.	Runs	Wkts.	Avge.	5wI.	10wM.
V. Mankad (India)	11	4101	259	1249	54	23·12	3	1
F. S. Trueman (England)	9	1784	78	787	53	14·84	2	—
A. V. Bedser (England)	7	1867	90	577	44	13·11	4	2
H. Verity (England)	6	1601	105	615	38	16·18	1	1

AUSTRALIA v. SOUTH AFRICA

	Tests	Balls	Mdns.	Runs	Wkts.	Avge.	5wI.	10wM.
C. V. Grimmett (Australia)	10	3913	248	1199	77	15·57	8	4
H. J. Tayfield (South Africa)	15	6027	181	2208	64	34·50	4	1
W. J. Whitty (Australia)	8	2055	89	875	50	17·50	3	—
W. A. Johnston (Australia)	10	3420	90	1129	44	25·65	3	—
C. B. Llewellyn (South Africa)	10	1838	34	1138	42	27·09	4	1
R. Benaud (Australia)	9	2783	78	964	40	24·10	4	—

AUSTRALIA v. WEST INDIES

	Tests	Balls	Mdns.	Runs	Wkts.	Avge.	5wI.	10wM.
R. R. Lindwall (Australia)	10	1980	44	1127	41	27·48	2	—
K. R. Miller (Australia)	10	1907	53	1028	40	25·70	3	—
C. V. Grimmett (Australia)	5	1433	60	593	33	17·96	2	1
A. L. Valentine (West Indies)	8	2143	84	1040	29	35·85	3	—

WEST INDIES v. INDIA

	Tests	Balls	Mdns.	Runs	Wkts.	Avge.	5wI.	10wM.
S. P. Gupte (India)	10	3852	158	1716	49	35·02	4	1
V. Mankad (India)	12	4257	169	1802	36	50·05	1	—
W. Hall (West Indies)	5	1330	65	530	30	17·66	2	1
A. L. Valentine (West Indies)	5	2580	179	828	28	29·57	2	—
G. E. Gomez (West Indies)	9	2860	184	805	27	29·81	—	—
R. Gilchrist (West Indies)	4	1189	73	419	26	16·11	1	—

England v. Australia

HIGHEST INNINGS TOTALS BY:

England in England ....903—7d at the Oval 1938
England in Australia.........................636 at Sydney 1928–29
Australia in England........................729—6d at Lord's 1930
Australia in Australia ....659—8d at Sydney 1946–47

LOWEST INNINGS TOTALS BY:

England in England ....52 at the Oval 1948
England in Australia.........................45 at Sydney 1886–87
Australia in England........................36 at Birmingham 1902
Australia in Australia ....42 at Sydney 1887–88

Highest Match Aggregate.....................1753—40 wkts at Adelaide 1920–21
Lowest Match Aggregate ....291—40 wkts at Lord's 1888

HIGHEST INDIVIDUAL INNINGS FOR:

England in England ....364 L. Hutton (Oval) 1938
England in Australia.........................287 R. E. Foster (Sydney) 1903–04
Australia in England........................334 D. G. Bradman (Leeds) 1930
Australia in Australia ....270 D. G. Bradman (Melbourne) 1936–37

BEST INNINGS BOWLING FIGURES FOR:

England in England ....10—53 J. C. Laker (Manchester) 1956
England in Australia......................... 8—35 G. A. Lohmann (Sydney)........................1886–87
Australia in England........................ 8—31 F. Laver (Manchester) 1909
Australia in Australia ....: 9—121 A. A. Mailey (Melbourne) 1920–21

HIGHEST RUN AGGREGATE BY A BATSMAN IN A RUBBER:

England in England ....562 (av. 62·44) D. C. S. Compton 1948
England in Australia.........................905 (av. 113·12) W. R. Hammond 1928–29
Australia in England........................974 (av. 139·14) D. G. Bradman 1930
Australia in Australia ....810 (av. 90·00) D. G. Bradman 1936–37

HIGHEST WICKET AGGREGATE BY A BOWLER IN A RUBBER:

England in England ....46 (av. 9·60) J. C. Laker 1956
England in Australia.........................38 (av. 23·18) M. W. Tate 1924–25
Australia in England........................29 (av. 31·89) C. V. Grimmett 1930
Australia in Australia ....36 (av. 26·27) A. A. Mailey............................1920–21

RECORD WICKET PARTNERSHIPS—ENGLAND

1st	323	J. B. Hobbs & W. Rhodes at Melbourne	1911–12
2nd	382	L. Hutton & M. Leyland at the Oval	1938
3rd	262	W. R. Hammond & D. R. Jardine at Adelaide	1928–29
4th	222	W. R. Hammond & E. Paynter at Lord's	1938
5th	206	E. Paynter & D. C. S. Compton at Nottingham	1938
6th	215	L. Hutton & J. Hardstaff jun. at the Oval	1938
7th	143	F. E. Woolley & J. Vine at Sydney	1911–12
8th	124	E. Hendren & H. Larwood at Brisbane	1928–29
9th	151	W. H. Scotton & W. W. Read at the Oval	1884
10th	130	R. E. Foster & W. Rhodes at Sydney	1903–04

RECORD WICKET PARTNERSHIPS—AUSTRALIA

1st	180	W. Bardsley & S. E. Gregory at the Oval	1909
2nd	451	W. H. Ponsford & D. G. Bradman at the Oval	1934
3rd	276	D. G. Bradman & A. L. Hassett at Brisbane	1946–47
4th	388	W. H. Ponsford & D. G. Bradman at Leeds	1934
5th	405	S. G. Barnes & D. G. Bradman at Sydney	1946–47
6th	346	J. H. Fingleton & D. G. Bradman at Melbourne	1936–37
7th	165	C. Hill & H. Trumble at Melbourne	1897–98
8th	243	C. Hill & R. J. Hartigan at Adelaide	1907–08
9th	154	S. E. Gregory & J. McC. Blackham at Sydney	1894–95
10th	127	J. M. Taylor & A. A. Mailey at Sydney	1924–25

England v. South Africa

HIGHEST INNINGS TOTALS BY:
England in England ....554—8d at Lord's 1947
England in South Africa ....654—5 at Durban 1938–39
South Africa in England ....538 at Leeds..1951
South Africa in South Africa ....530 at Durban 1938–39

LOWEST INNINGS TOTALS BY:
England in England ....76 at Leeds 1907
England in South Africa ....92 at Cape Town 1898–99
South Africa in England ....30 at Birmingham 1924
South Africa in South Africa ....30 at Port Elizabeth 1895–96

Highest Match Aggregate....................1981—35 wkts at Durban 1938–39
Lowest Match Aggregate ....378—30 wkts at the Oval 1912

HIGHEST INDIVIDUAL INNINGS FOR:
England in England ....211 J. B. Hobbs (Lord's) 1924
England in South Africa ....243 E. Paynter (Durban) 1938–39
South Africa in England ....236 E. A. B. Rowan (Leeds) 1951
South Africa in South Africa ....176 H. W. Taylor (Johannesburg) 1922–23

BEST INNINGS BOWLING FIGURES FOR:
England in England ....8—29 S. F. Barnes (Oval) 1912
England in South Africa ....9—28 G. A. Lohmann (Johannesburg) 1895–96
South Africa in England ....7—65 S. J. Pegler (Lord's) 1912
South Africa in South Africa ....9—113 H. J. Tayfield (Johannesburg) 1956–57

HIGHEST RUN AGGREGATE BY A BATSMAN IN A RUBBER:
England in England ....753 (av. 94·12) D. C. S. Compton 1947
Fngland in South Africa ....653 (av. 81·62) E. Paynter 1938–39
South Africa in England ....621 (av. 69·00) A. D. Nourse jun. 1947
South Africa in South Africa ....582 (av. 64·66) H. W. Taylor 1922–23

HIGHEST WICKET AGGREGATE BY A BOWLER IN A RUBBER:
England in England ....34 (av. 8·29) S. F. Barnes 1912
Fngland in South Africa ....49 (av. 10·93) S. F. Barnes 1913–14
South Africa in England .... { 26 (av. 21·84) H. J. Tayfield 1955
                                        { 26 (av. 22·57) N. A. T. Adcock 1960
South Africa in South Africa ....37 (av. 17·18) H. J. Tayfield 1956–57

RECORD WICKET PARTNERSHIPS—ENGLAND
1st	359	L. Hutton & C. Washbrook at Johannesburg	1948–49
2nd	280	P. A. Gibb & W. J. Edrich at Durban	1938–39
3rd	370	W. J. Edrich & D. C. S. Compton at Lord's	1947
4th	197	W. R. Hammond & L. E. G. Ames at Cape Town	1938–39
5th	237	D. C. S. Compton & N. W. D. Yardley at Nottingham	1947
6th	156	C. P. Mead & F. T. Mann at Durban	1922–23
7th	115	J. W. H. T. Douglas & M. C. Bird at Durban	1913–14
8th	154	C. W. Wright & H. R. B. Davenport at Johannesburg	1895–96
9th	71	H. Wood & J. T. Hearne at Cape Town	1891–92
10th	92	A. C. Russell & A. E. R. Gilligan at Durban	1922–23

RECORD WICKET PARTNERSHIPS—SOUTH AFRICA
1st	260	I. J. Siedle & B. Mitchell at Cape Town	1930–31
2nd	198	E. A. B. Rowan & C. B. Van Ryneveld at Leeds	1951
3rd	319	A. Melville & A. D. Nourse jun. at Nottingham	1947
4th	214	H. W. Taylor & H. G. Deane at the Oval	1929
5th	135	R. H. Catterall & H. B. Cameron at Durban	1927–28
6th	171	J. H. B. Waite & P. L. Winslow at Manchester	1955
7th	123	H. G. Deane & E. P. Nupen at Durban	1927–28
8th	109*	B. Mitchell & L. Tuckett at the Oval	1947
9th	137	E. L. Dalton & A. B. C. Langton at the Oval	1935
10th	103	H. G. Owen-Smith & A. J. Bell at Leeds	1929

England v. West Indies

HIGHEST INNINGS TOTALS BY:
England in England ....619—6d at Nottingham 1957
England in West Indies ....849 at Kingston.................................1929—30
West Indies in England ....558 at Nottingham 1950
West Indies in West Indies ....681—8d at Trinidad ....1953—54

LOWEST INNINGS TOTALS BY:
England in England ....103 at the Oval 1950
England in West Indies ....103 at Kingston.................................1934—35
West Indies in England ....86 at the Oval 1957
West Indies in West Indies ....102 at Barbados ....1934—35

Highest Match Aggregate...................1815—34 wkts at Kingston ....1929—30
Lowest Match Aggregate ....309—29 wkts at Barbados ....1934—35

HIGHEST INDIVIDUAL INNINGS FOR:
England in England ....285* P. B. H. May (Birmingham) 1957
England in West Indies ....325 A. Sandham (Kingston) ....1929—30
West Indies in England ....261 F. M. Worrell (Nottingham) 1950
West Indies in West Indies ....270* G. Headley (Kingston) ....1934—35

BEST INNINGS BOWLING FIGURES FOR:
England in England ....7—44 T. E. Bailey (Lord's) 1957
England in West Indies ....7—34 T. E. Bailey (Kingston) ....1953—54
West Indies in England ....8—104 A. L. Valentine (Manchester) 1950
West Indies in West Indies ....7—69 W. Hall (Kingston) ....1959—60

HIGHEST RUN AGGREGATE BY A BATSMAN IN A RUBBER:
England in England ....489 (av. 97·80) P. B. H. May 1957
England in West Indies ....693 (av. 115·50) E. Hendren ....1929—30
West Indies in England ....539 (av. 89·83) F. M. Worrell 1950
West Indies in West Indies ....709 (av. 101·28) G. Sobers ....1959—60

HIGHEST WICKET AGGREGATE BY A BOWLER IN A RUBBER:
England in England ....{ 22 (av. 13·72) A. P. Freeman 1928
....{ 22 (av. 20·68) F. S. Trueman 1957
England in West Indies ....21 (av. 26·14) F. S. Trueman ....1959—60
West Indies in England ....33 (av. 20·42) A. L. Valentine 1950
West Indies in West Indies ....23 (av. 24·65) W. Ferguson ....1947—48

RECORD WICKET PARTNERSHIPS—ENGLAND
1st	212	C. Washbrook & R. T. Simpson at Nottingham	1950
2nd	266	P. E. Richardson & T. W. Graveney at Nottingham	1957
3rd	264	L. Hutton & W. R. Hammond at the Oval	1939
4th	411	P. B. H. May & M. C. Cowdrey at Birmingham	1957
5th	110	D. C. S. Compton & T. W. Graveney at Trinidad	1953—54
6th	161	T. E. Bailey & T. G. Evans at Manchester	1950
7th	197	M. J. K. Smith & J. M. Parks at Trinidad	1959—60
8th	95	C. J. Barnett & M. S. Nichols at the Oval	1933
9th	62	E. R. T. Holmes & W. F. Farrimond at Trinidad	1934—35
10th	56	J. C. Laker & H. J. Butler at Trinidad	1947—48

RECORD WICKET PARTNERSHIPS—WEST INDIES
1st	173	G. Carew & A. G. Ganteaume at Trinidad	1947—48
2nd	228	R. K. Nunes & G. Headley at Kingston	1929—30
3rd	338	E. D. Weekes & F. M. Worrell at Trinidad	1953—54
4th	399	G. Sobers & F. M. Worrell at Barbados	1959—60
5th	163	V. H. Stollmeyer & K. H. Weekes at the Oval	1939
6th	211	C. L. Walcott & G. E. Gomez at Lord's	1950
7th	154	O. G. Smith & J. D. C. Goddard at Nottingham	1957
8th	99	C. A. McWatt & J. K. Holt at Georgetown	1953—54
9th	33	C. R. Browne & E. St Hill at Georgetown	1929—30
10th	55	F. M. Worrell & K. T. Ramadhin at Nottingham	1957

England v. New Zealand

HIGHEST INNINGS TOTALS BY:
England in England ....482 at the Oval 1949
England in New Zealand ....560—8d at Christchurch 1932–33
New Zealand in England ....484 at Lord's 1949
New Zealand in New Zealand ....440 at Wellington 1929–30

LOWEST INNINGS TOTALS BY:
England in England ....187 at Manchester 1937
England in New Zealand ....181 at Christchurch 1929–30
New Zealand in England .... 47 at Lord's 1958
New Zealand in New Zealand .... 26 at Auckland 1954–55

Highest Match Aggregate ....1293—34 wkts at Lord's 1931
Lowest Match Aggregate ....390—30 wkts at Lord's 1958

HIGHEST INDIVIDUAL INNINGS FOR:
England in England ....206 L. Hutton (Oval) 1949
England in New Zealand ....336* W. R. Hammond (Auckland) 1932–33
New Zealand in England ....206 M. P. Donnelly (Lord's) 1949
New Zealand in New Zealand ....136 C. S. Dempster (Wellington) 1929–30

BEST INNINGS BOWLING FIGURES FOR:
England in England ....7—35 G. A. R. Lock (Manchester) 1958
England in New Zealand ....7—76 F. E. Woolley (Wellington) 1929–30
New Zealand in England ....6—67 J. A. Cowie (Manchester) 1937
New Zealand in New Zealand ....6—83 J. A. Cowie (Christchurch) 1946–47

HIGHEST RUN AGGREGATE BY A BATSMAN IN A RUBBER:
England in England ....469 (av. 78·16) L. Hutton 1949
England in New Zealand ....563 (av. 563·00) W. R. Hammond 1932–33
New Zealand in England ....462 (av. 77·00) M. P. Donnelly 1949
New Zealand in New Zealand ....341 (av. 85·25) C. S. Dempster 1929–30

HIGHEST WICKET AGGREGATE BY A BOWLER IN A RUBBER:
England in England ....34 (av. 7·47) G. A. R. Lock 1958
England in New Zealand .... {13 (av. 14·92) M. J. C. Allom.............................1929–30
                                       {13 (av. 8·69) G. A. R. Lock 1958–59
New Zealand in England ....20 (av. 19·45) A. R. MacGibbon 1958
New Zealand in New Zealand .... 9 (av. 19·00) R. C. Blunt 1929–30

RECORD WICKET PARTNERSHIPS—ENGLAND
1st	147	L. Hutton & R. T. Simpson at the Oval	1949
2nd	218	L. Hutton & W. J. Edrich at the Oval	1949
3rd	245	J. Hardstaff jun. & W. R. Hammond at Lord's	1937
4th	130	W. R. Hammond & L. E. G. Ames at the Oval	1931
5th	242	W. R. Hammond & L. E. G. Ames at Christchurch	1932–33
6th	189	D. C. S. Compton & T. E. Bailey at Lord's	1949
7th	108	F. R. Brown & W. Voce at Christchurch	1932–33
8th	246	L. E. G. Ames & G. O. Allen at Lord's	1931
9th	117	T. E. Bailey & D. V. P. Wright at Christchurch	1950–51
10th	30	J. C. Laker & P. J. Loader at Birmingham	1958

RECORD WICKET PARTNERSHIPS—NEW ZEALAND
1st	276	C. S. Dempster & J. W. E. Mills at Wellington	1929–30
2nd	131	B. Sutcliffe & J. R. Reid at Christchurch	1950–51
3rd	118	C. S. Dempster & M. L. Page at Lord's	1931
4th	142	M. L. Page & R. C. Blunt at Lord's	1931
5th	120	M. P. Donnelly & F. B. Smith at Leeds	1949
6th	99	W. A. Hadlee & H. G. Vivian at Manchester	1937
7th	100	T. C. Lowry & H. M. McGirr at Auckland	1929–30
8th	104	D. A. R. Moloney & A. W. Roberts at Lord's	1937
9th	63	M. L. Page & C. F. W. Allcott at Lord's	1931
10th	57	F. L. H. Mooney & J. A. Cowie at Leeds	1949

England v. India

HIGHEST INNINGS TOTALS BY:

England in England ....571—8d at Manchester 1936
England in India ....456 at Bombay 1951–52
India in England ....390—5 at Manchester 1936
India in India ....485—9d at Bombay 1951–52

LOWEST INNINGS TOTALS BY:

England in England ....134 at Lord's 1936
England in India ....183 at Madras 1951–52
India in England .... 58 at Manchester 1952
India in India ....121 at Kanpur 1951–52

Highest Match Aggregate ....1339—38 wkts at Manchester 1959
Lowest Match Aggregate ....482—31 wkts at Lord's 1936

HIGHEST INDIVIDUAL INNINGS FOR:

England in England ....217 W. R. Hammond (Oval) 1936
England in India ....175 T. W. Graveney (Bombay)..........................1951–52
India in England ....184 V. Mankad (Lord's) 1952
India in India ....164* V. S. Hazare (New Delhi) 1951–52

BEST INNINGS BOWLING FIGURES FOR:

England in England ....8—31 F. S. Trueman (Manchester) 1952
England in India ....7—49 H. Verity (Madras) 1933–34
India in England ....6—35 Amar Singh (Lord's) 1936
India in India ....8—55 V. Mankad (Madras) 1951–52

HIGHEST RUN AGGREGATE BY A BATSMAN IN A RUBBER:

England in England ....399 (av. 79·80) L. Hutton 1952
England in India ....451 (av. 64·42) A. J. Watkins 1951–52
India in England ....333 (av. 55·50) V. S. Hazare 1952
India in India ....387 (av. 55·28) P. Roy 1951–52

HIGHEST WICKET AGGREGATE BY A BOWLER IN A RUBBER:

England in England ....29 (av. 13·31) F. S. Trueman 1952
England in India ....23 (av. 16·82) H. Verity 1933–34
India in England ....17 (av. 34·64) S. P. Gupte 1959
India in India ....34 (av. 16·79) V. Mankad 1951–52

RECORD WICKET PARTNERSHIPS—ENGLAND

1st	146	W. G. A. Parkhouse & G. Pullar at Leeds	1959
2nd	158	L. Hutton & P. B. H. May at Lord's	1952
3rd	169	R. Subba Row & M. J. K. Smith at the Oval	1959
4th	266	W. R. Hammond & T. S. Worthington at the Oval	1936
5th	182	J. Hardstaff jun & P. A. Gibb at Lord's	1946
6th	159	T. W. Graveney & T. G. Evans at Lord's	1952
7th	102	R. Illingworth & R. Swetman at the Oval	1959
8th	138	R. W. V. Robins & H. Verity at Manchester	1936
9th	70	H. Verity & L. F. Townsend at Calcutta	1933–34
10th	32	H. Verity & E. W. Clark at Calcutta	1933–34
	32	J. B. Statham & A. E. Moss at Nottingham	1959

RECORD WICKET PARTNERSHIPS—INDIA

1st	203	V. M. Merchant & Mushtaq Ali at Manchester	1936
2nd	109	N. J. Contractor & A. A. Baig at Manchester	1959
3rd	211	V. M. Merchant & V. S. Hazare at New Delhi	1951–52
		V. Mankad & V. S. Hazare at Lord's	1952
4th	222	V. S. Hazare & V. L. Manjrekar at Leeds	1952
5th	89	V. L. Manjrekar & A. G. Kripal Singh at Lords	1959
6th	105	V. S. Hazare & D. G. Phadkar at Leeds	1952
7th	93	P. R. Umrigar & C. D. Gopinath at Madras	1951–52
8th	74	Amar Singh & Lall Singh at Lord's	1932
9th	54	G. S. Ramchand & S. G. Shinde at Lord's	1952
10th	43	R. S. Modi & S. G. Shinde at Lord's	1946

Australia v. South Africa

HIGHEST INNINGS TOTALS BY:
Australia in Australia ....578 at Melbourne 1910–11
Australia in South Africa...............:..549—7d at Port Elizabeth 1949–50
South Africa in Australia.................506 at Melbourne 1910–11
South Africa in South Africa ....491 at Johannesburg..1935–36

LOWEST INNINGS TOTALS BY:
Australia in Australia ....153 at Melbourne 1931–32
Australia in South Africa............... 76 at Durban 1949–50
South Africa in Australia................. 36 at Melbourne 1931–32
South Africa in South Africa .... 85 at Johannesburg and Cape Town 1902–03

Highest Match Aggregate.....................1646—40 wkts at Adelaide 1910–11
Lowest Match Aggregate ....234—29 wkts at Melbourne 1931–32

HIGHEST INDIVIDUAL INNINGS FOR:
Australia in Australia ....299* D. G. Bradman (Adelaide) 1931–32
Australia in South Africa................203 H. L. Collins (Johannesburg) 1921–22
South Africa in Australia.................204 G. A. Faulkner (Melbourne) 1910–11
South Africa in South Africa ....231 A. D. Nourse jun. (Johannesburg) 1935–36

BEST INNINGS BOWLING FIGURES FOR:
Australia in Australia ....7—83 C. V. Grimmett (Adelaide) 1931–32
Australia in South Africa................7—34 J. V. Saunders (Johannesburg) 1902–03
South Africa in Australia.................7—81 H. J. Tayfield (Melbourne) 1952–53
South Africa in South Africa ....7—23 H. J. Tayfield (Durban) 1949–50

HIGHEST RUN AGGREGATE BY A BATSMAN IN A RUBBER:
Australia in Australia ....834 (av. 92·66) R. N. Harvey 1952–53
Australia in South Africa................660 (av. 132·00) R. N. Harvey 1949–50
South Africa in Australia.................732 (av. 73·20) G. A. Faulkner 1910–11
South Africa in South Africa ....518 (av. 57·55) A. D. Nourse jun. 1935–36

HIGHEST WICKET AGGREGATE BY A BOWLER IN A RUBBER:
Australia in Australia ....37 (av. 17·08) W. J. Whitty 1910–11
Australia in South Africa................44 (av. 14·59) C. V. Grimmett 1935–36
South Africa in Australia.................30 (av. 28·10) H. J. Tayfield 1952–53
South Africa in South Africa ....25 (av. 17·92) C. B. Llewellyn........................1902–03

RECORD WICKET PARTNERSHIPS—AUSTRALIA

1st	233	J. H. Fingleton & W. A. Brown at Cape Town	1935–36
2nd	275	C. C. McDonald & A. L. Hassett at Adelaide	1952–53
3rd	242	W. Bardsley & C. Kelleway at Lord's	1912
4th	168	R. N. Harvey & K. R. Miller at Sydney	1952–53
5th	143	W. W. Armstrong & V. T. Trumper at Melbourne	1910–11
6th	107	C. Kelleway & V. S. Ransford at Melbourne	1910–11
7th	67	R. Benaud & A. K. Davidson at Johannesburg	1957–58
8th	83	A. G. Chipperfield & C. V. Grimmett at Durban	1935–36
9th {	78	D. G. Bradman & W. J. O'Reilly at Adelaide	1931–32
	78	K. Mackay & I. Meckiff at Johannesburg	1957–58
10th	82	V. S. Ransford & W. J. Whitty at Melbourne	1910–11

RECORD WICKET PARTNERSHIPS—SOUTH AFRICA

1st	176	D. J. McGlew & T. L. Goddard at Johannesburg	1957–58
2nd	173	L. J. Tancred & C. B. Llewellyn at Johannesburg	1902–03
3rd	231	D. J. McGlew & J. H. B. Waite at Durban	1957–58
4th	206	C. N. Frank & A. D. Nourse sen. at Johannesburg	1921–22
5th	129	J. H. B. Waite & W. R. Endean at Johannesburg	1957–58
6th	106	A. D. Nourse jun. & F. Nicholson at Johannesburg	1935–36
7th	111	J. E. Cheetham & P. N. F. Mansell at Melbourne	1952–53
8th	124	A. D. Nourse sen. & E. A. Halliwell at Johannesburg	1902–03
9th	54	J. M. Blanckenberg & E. P. Nupen at Johannesburg	1921–22
10th	53	S. J. Pegler & L. A. Stricker at Adelaide	1910–11

Australia v. West Indies

HIGHEST INNINGS TOTALS BY:

Australia in Australia ....558 at Brisbane 1930–31
Australia in West Indies ....758—8d at Kingston 1954–55
West Indies in Australia ....362 at Sydney 1951–52
West Indies in West Indies ....510 at Barbados 1954–55

LOWEST INNINGS TOTALS BY:

Australia in Australia .... 82 at Adelaide 1951–52
Australia in West Indies ....249 at Barbados 1954–55
West Indies in Australia .... 78 at Sydney 1951–52
West Indies in West Indies ....182 at Georgetown 1954–55

Highest Match Aggregate......................1661—36 wkts at Barbados 1954–55
Lowest Match Aggregate ....534—28 wkts at Melbourne 1930–31

HIGHEST INDIVIDUAL INNINGS FOR:

Australia in Australia ....223 D. G. Bradman (Brisbane) 1930–31
Australia in West Indies ....204 R. N. Harvey (Kingston) 1954–55
West Indies in Australia ....123* F. R. Martin (Sydney) 1930–31
West Indies in West Indies ....219 D. Atkinson (Barbados) 1954–55

BEST INNINGS BOWLING FIGURES FOR:

Australia in Australia ....7—23 H. Ironmonger (Melbourne) 1930–31
Australia in West Indies ....7—44 I. W. Johnson (Georgetown) 1954–55
West Indies in Australia ....7—55 G. E. Gomez (Sydney) 1951–52
West Indies in West Indies ....5—56 D. Atkinson (Barbados) 1954–55

HIGHEST RUN AGGREGATE BY A BATSMAN IN A RUBBER:

Australia in Australia ....467 (av. 77·83) W. H. Ponsford 1930–31
Australia in West Indies ....650 (av. 108·33) R. N. Harvey 1954–55
West Indies in Australia ....337 (av. 33·70) F. M. Worrell 1951–52
West Indies in West Indies ....827 (av. 82·70) C. L. Walcott 1954–55

HIGHEST WICKET AGGREGATE BY A BOWLER IN A RUBBER:

Australia in Australia .... 33 (av. 17·96) C. V. Grimmett 1930–31
Australia in West Indies .... { 20 (av. 32·15) R. R. Lindwall 1954–55
.... { 20 (av. 32·00) K. R. Miller 1954–55
West Indies in Australia .... 24 (av. 28·79) A. L. Valentine......................1951–52
West Indies in West Indies .... 13 (av. 35·30) D. Atkinson 1954–55

RECORD WICKET PARTNERSHIPS—AUSTRALIA

1st   191   C. C. McDonald & A. R. Morris at Trinidad 1954–55
2nd 229   W. H. Ponsford & D. G. Bradman at Brisbane 1930–31
3rd   295   C. C. McDonald & R. N. Harvey at Kingston 1954–55
4th   235   A. L. Hassett & K. R. Miller at Sydney 1951–52
5th   220   K. R. Miller & R. G. Archer at Kingston 1954–55
6th   206   K. R. Miller & R. G. Archer at Barbados 1954–55
7th   70   R. G. Archer & I. W. Johnson at Trinidad 1954–55
8th   137   R. Benaud & I. W. Johnson at Kingston 1954–55
9th   64   I. W. Johnson & G. R. Langley at Barbados 1954–55
10th   45   G. R. Langley & J. C. Hill at Barbados 1954–55

RECORD WICKET PARTNERSHIPS—WEST INDIES

1st   72   R. E. Marshall & J. B. Stollmeyer at Adelaide 1951–52
2nd 152   F. R. Martin & G. Headley at Sydney 1930–31
3rd   242   C. L. Walcott & E. D. Weekes at Trinidad 1954–55
4th   179   C. L. Walcott & G. Sobers at Kingston 1954–55
5th   92* G. E. Gomez & R. J. Christiani at Melbourne 1951–52
6th   138   C. L. Walcott & O. G. Smith at Kingston 1954–55
7th   347   D. Atkinson & C. Depeiza at Barbados 1954–55
8th   45   G. E. Gomez & R. E. Marshall at Brisbane 1951–52
9th   37   J. D. C. Goddard & K. T. Ramadhin at Brisbane 1951–52
10th   29   G. C. Grant & H. C. Griffith at Adelaide 1930–31

West Indies v. India

HIGHEST INNINGS TOTALS BY:

West Indies in West Indies ....576 at Kingston...............................1952–53
West Indies in India ....644—8d at New Delhi 1958–59
India in West Indies ....444 at Kingston...............................1952–53
India in India ....454 at New Delhi 1948–49

LOWEST INNINGS TOTALS BY:

West Indies in West Indies ....228 at Barbados 1952–53
West Indies in India ....222 at Kanpur 1958–59
India in West Indies ....129 at Barbados 1952–53
India in India ....124 at Calcutta 1958–59

Highest Match Aggregate.....................1424—33 wkts at Kingston 1952–53
Lowest Match Aggregate ....892—25 wkts at Calcutta....................1958–59

HIGHEST INDIVIDUAL INNINGS FOR:

West Indies in West Indies ....237 F. M. Worrell (Kingston) 1958–59
West Indies in India ....256 R. Kanhai (Calcutta) 1958–59
India in West Indies ....163* M. L. Apte (Trinidad) 1952–53
India in India ....134* V. S. Hazare (Bombay) 1948–49

BEST INNINGS BOWLING FIGURES FOR:

West Indies in West Indies ....5—26 K. T. Ramadhin (Barbados) 1952–53
West Indies in India ....6—50 W. Hall (Kanpur) 1958–59
India in West Indies ....7—162 S. P. Gupte (Trinidad) 1952–53
India in India ....9—102 S. P. Gupte (Kanpur) 1958–59

HIGHEST RUN AGGREGATE BY A BATSMAN IN A RUBBER:

West Indies in West Indies ....716 (av. 102·28) E. D. Weekes 1952–53
West Indies in India ....779 (av. 111·28) E. D. Weekes 1948–49
India in West Indies ....560 (av. 62·22) P. R. Umrigar....................1952–53
India in India ....560 (av. 56·00) R. S. Modi 1948–49

HIGHEST WICKET AGGREGATE BY A BOWLER IN A RUBBER :

West Indies in West Indies ....28 (av. 29·57) A. L. Valentine............................1952–53
West Indies in India ....30 (av. 17·66) W. Hall 1958–59
India in West Indies ....27 (av. 29·22) S. P. Gupte 1952–53
India in India ....22 (av. 42·13) S. P. Gupte 1958–59

RECORD WICKET PARTNERSHIPS—WEST INDIES

1st	239	J. B. Stollmeyer & A. F. Rae at Madras	1948–49
2nd	97	B. H. Pairaudeau and F. M. Worrell at Kingston	1952–53
3rd	197	F. M. Worrell & E. D. Weekes at Kingston	1952–53
4th	267	C. L. Walcott & G. E. Gomez at New Delhi	1948–49
5th	219	E. D. Weekes & B. H. Pairaudeau at Trinidad	1952–53
6th	163	G. Sobers & J. Solomon at Kanpur	1958–59
7th	118	E. D. Weekes & R. J. Christiani at New Delhi	1948–49
8th	70	J. Solomon & E. Atkinson at New Delhi	1958–59
9th	106	R. J. Christiani & D. Atkinson at New Delhi	1948–49
10th	27	J. D. C. Goddard & J. Trim at Bombay	1948–49

RECORD WICKET PARTNERSHIPS—INDIA

1st	99	P. Roy & N. J. Contractor at Kanpur	1958–59
2nd	237	P. Roy & V. L. Manjrekar at Kingston	1952–53
3rd	156	R. S. Modi & V. S. Hazare at Bombay	1948–49
4th	150	P. Roy & P. R. Umrigar at Kingston	1952–53
5th	131	P. R. Umrigar & D. G. Phadkar at Trinidad	1952–53
6th	134	C. G. Borde & H. R. Adhikari at New Delhi	1958–59
7th	153	M. L. Apte & V. Mankad at Trinidad	1952–53
8th	74	A. G. Kripal Singh & G. S. Ramchand at Madras	1958–59
9th	54	J. M. Ghorpade & E. S. Maka & S. P. Gupte at Trinidad	1952–53
10th	26	C. V. Gadkari & S. P. Gupte at Georgetown	1952–53

Appendix 'G'
Counties Providing England Players

The cricketers that have represented England in Test cricket have been drawn from the various counties as follows (* signifies that the player gained England caps with two counties):

DERBYSHIRE (15—52 caps)

D. B. Carr 2	J. Humphries 3	D. Smith 2
W. Chatterton 1	L. Jackson 1	W. Storer 6
W. H. Copson 3	T. B. Mitchell 5	L. F. Townsend 4
H. Elliott 4	G. H. Pope 1	A. R. Warren 1
C. Gladwin 8	H. J. Rhodes 2	T. S. Worthington 9

ESSEX (14—164 caps)

T. E. Bailey 61	D. J. Insole................ 9	H. D. Read 1
C. P. Buckenham 4	C. P. McGahey 2	A. C. Russell 10
J. W. H. T. Douglas 23	W. Mead................ 1	T. P. B. Smith 4
F. L. Fane 14	M. S. Nichols................14	H. Young 2
K. Farnes 15	J. O'Connor 4	

GLAMORGAN (7—38 caps)

J. C. Clay 1	W. G. A. Parkhouse 7	P. M. Walker 3
A. D. G. Matthews 1	M. J. Turnbull 9	A. J. Watkins 15
J. E. McConnon 2		

GLOUCESTERSHIRE (23—248 caps)

D. A. Allen 7	J. J. Ferris 1	W. E. Midwinter 4
C. J. Barnett 20	T. W. Goddard 8	C. A. Milton 6
J. H. Board 6	E. M. Grace 1	J. B. Mortimore................ 5
C. Cook 1	G. F. Grace 1	C. W. L. Parker................ 1
J. Cranston 1	W. G. Grace 22	R. A. Sinfield 1
J. F. Crapp 7	T. W. Graveney 48	H. Smith 1
A. E. Dipper 1	W. R. Hammond 85	C. L. Townsend 2
G. M. Emmett 1	G. L. Jessop 18	

HAMPSHIRE (11—57 caps)

J. Arnold 1	C. Heseltine 2	D. Shackleton 3
V. A. Barton 1	A. J. L. Hill 3	Hon. L. H. Tennyson 9
G. Brown 7	A. S. Kennedy 5	E. G. Wynyard 3
C. B. Fry* 6	C. P. Mead 17	

KENT (34—417 caps)

C. A. Absolom 1	A. Fielder 6	C. S. Marriott 1
L. E. G. Ames 47	A. P. Freeman 12	F. Martin 2
Hon. Ivo Bligh 4	H. T. W. Hardinge 1	J. W. Martin 1
C. Blythe 19	Lord Harris 4	J. R. Mason 5
W. M. Bradley 2	A. Hearne 1	F. Penn 1
D. W. Carr 1	F. Hearne 2	F. Ridgway................ 5
A. P. F. Chapman............26	G. G. Hearne 1	E. F. S. Tylecote 6
S. Christopherson 1	K. L. Hutchings 7	B. H. Valentine 7
M. C. Cowdrey 49	G. B. Legge 5	G. E. C. Wood 3
A. J. Evans 1	W. H. V. Levett 1	F. E. Woolley 64
T. G. Evans 91	F. A. Mackinnon 1	D. V. P. Wright 34
A. E. Fagg 5		

LANCASHIRE (45—445 caps)

R. W. Barber	1	A. N. Hornby	3	S. S. Schultz	1
R. G. Barlow	17	N. D. Howard	4	J. Sharp	3
S. F. Barnes*	4	J. Iddon	5	R. H. Spooner	10
R. Berry	2	J. T. Ikin	18	J. B. Statham	55
W. Brearley	4	A. C. MacLaren	35	A. G. Steel	13
J. Briggs	33	H. Makepeace	4	F. H. Sugg	2
K. Cranston	8	A. Mold	3	R. Tattersall	16
W. R. Cuttell	2	N. Oldfield	1	E. Tyldesley	14
H. Dean	3	C. H. Parkin	10	J. T. Tyldesley	31
G. Duckworth	24	E. Paynter	20	R. Tyldesley	7
W. F. Farrimond	4	R. Pilling	8	A. Ward	7
T. Greenhough	4	W. Place	3	C. Washbrook	37
C. Hallows	2	R. Pollard	4	A. Wharton	1
M. J. Hilton	4	G. Pullar	11	L. L. Wilkinson	3
J. L. Hopwood	2	V. P. F. A. Royle	1	R. Wood	1

LEICESTERSHIRE (8—40 caps)

W. E. Astill	9	J. H. King	1	A. D. Pougher	1
E. W. Dawson	5	A. E. Knight	3	W. Watson*	6
G. Geary	14	C. H. Palmer	1		

MIDDLESEX (40—429 caps)

G. O. Allen	25	C. F. H. Leslie	4	J. M. Sims	4
B. J. T. Bosanquet	7	Hon. A. Lyttelton	4	C. I. J. Smith	5
D. C. S. Compton	78	G. MacGregor	8	G. T. S. Stevens	10
H. R. B. Davenport	4	F. G. Mann	7	A. E. Stoddart	16
J. G. Dewes	5	F. T. Mann	5	C. T. Studd	5
T. J. Durston	1	L. J. Moon	4	G. B. Studd	4
W. J. Edrich	39	A. E. Moss	9	F. J. Titmus	2
F. G. J. Ford	5	T. C. O'Brien	5	A. E. Trott	2
N. E. Haig	5	I. A. R. Peebles	13	G. F. Vernon	1
J. T. Hearne	12	H. Philipson	5	P. F. Warner	15
J. W. Hearne	24	W. F. Price	1	J. J. Warr	2
E. Hendren	51	J. D. Robertson	11	A. J. Webbe	1
E. T. Killick	2	R. W. V. Robins	19	J. A. Young	8
H. W. Lee	1				

NORTHAMPTONSHIRE (9—69 caps)

K. V. Andrew	1	F. R. Brown*	16	R. Subba Row	8
A. H. Bakewell	6	E. W. Clark	8	G. J. Thompson	6
D. Brookes	1	V. W. C. Jupp*	6	F. H. Tyson	17

NOTTINGHAMSHIRE (27—278 caps)

W. Attewell	10	J. Hardstaff sen.	5	J. Selby	6
W. Barnes	21	J. Hardstaff jun.	23	A. Shaw	7
F. Barratt	5	A. O. Jones	12	M. Sherwin	3
H. J. Butler	2	W. W. Keeton	2	A. Shrewsbury	23
A. W. Carr	11	H. Larwood	21	R. T. Simpson	27
W. Flowers	8	F. Morley	4	S. J. Staples	3
G. Gunn	15	C. J. Poole	3	W. Voce	27
J. Gunn	6	T. L. Richmond	1	W. W. Whysall	4
W. Gunn	11	W. H. Scotton	15	C. W. Wright	3

SOMERSET (12—57 caps)

L. C. Braund	23	J. C. W. MacBryan	1	E. J. Tyler	1
A. J. Fothergill	2	N. S. Mitchell-Innes	1	A. W. Wellard	2
L. H. Gay	1	L. C. H. Palairet	2	J. C. White	15
H. Gimblett	3	M. F. Tremlett	3	S. M. J. Woods	3

SURREY (44—601 caps)

R. Abel 13	T. Hayward 35	A. P. Lucas 5
M. J. C. Allom 5	J. W. Hitch 7	P. B. H. May 62
K. F. Barrington 16	J. B. Hobbs 61	A. J. McIntyre 3
A. V. Bedser 51	E. R. T. Holmes 5	J. M. Read 17
M. C. Bird 10	D. R. Jardine 22	W. W. Read 18
M. P. Bowden 2	H. Jupp 2	T. Richardson 14
W. Brockwell 7	D. J. Knight 2	A. Sandham 14
F. R. Brown* 6	N. A. Knox 2	J. W. Sharpe 3
J. N. Crawford 12	J. C. Laker 46	J. Shuter 1
N. F. Druce 5	W. S. Lees 5	J. Southerton 2
A. Ducat 1	H. D. G. Leveson-Gower... 3	H. Strudwick 28
P. G. H. Fender 13	P. J. Loader 13	R. Swetman 11
L. B. Fishlock 4	G. A. R. Lock 31	N. C. Tufnell 1
A. R. Gover 4	W. H. Lockwood 12	H. Wood.................... 4
E. G. Hayes 5	G. A. Lohmann 18	

SUSSEX (31—201 caps)

G. Bean 3	S. C. Griffith 3	K. S. Ranjitsinhji 15
E. H. Bowley 5	J. C. Hartley 2	A. E. Relf 13
H. R. Butt 3	V. W. C. Jupp* 2	D. S. Sheppard 12
H. Charlwood 2	James Langridge 8	C. A. Smith 1
W. F. Cornford 4	James Lillywhite 2	D. V. Smith 3
E. R. Dexter 17	W. L. Murdoch 1	G. Street 1
G. H. G. Doggart 2	W. Newham 1	F. W. Tate 1
K. S. Duleepsinhji 12	A. S. M. Oakman 2	M. W. Tate 39
C. B. Fry* 20	J. H. Parks 1	J. Vine 2
A. E. R. Gilligan 11	J. M. Parks.................... 7	R. A. Young 2
A. H. H. Gilligan 4		

WARWICKSHIRE (13—156 caps)

Hon. F. S. G. Calthorpe ... 4	S. P. Kinneir 1	E. J. Smith 11
H. E. Dollery 4	A. A. Lilley 35	M. J. K. Smith 14
F. R. Foster 11	G. A. E. Paine 4	R. T. Spooner 7
W. E. Hollies 13	W. G. Quaife 7	R. E. S. Wyatt 40
H. Howell 5		

WORCESTERSHIRE (13—92 caps)

E. G. Arnold 10	D. Kenyon 8	P. E. Richardson 25
R. E. Foster 8	Nawab of Pataudi 3	C. F. Root 3
M. J. Horton 2	R. T. D. Perks 2	G. H. Simpson-Hayward ... 5
R. Howorth 5	D. W. Richardson 1	C. F. Walters 11
R. O. Jenkins 9		

YORKSHIRE (52—670 caps)

R. Appleyard 9	G. H. Hirst.....................24	W. Rhodes 58
T. Armitage 2	P. Holmes 7	T. F. Smailes 1
W. Barber 2	J. Hunter 5	G. A. Smithson 2
W. Bates 15	L. Hutton 79	R. T. Stanyforth 4
M. W. Booth 2	R. Illingworth 12	H. Sutcliffe 54
W. E. Bowes 15	Hon. F. S. Jackson 20	K. Taylor 2
D. V. Brennan 2	R. Kilner 9	F. S. Trueman 41
J. T. Brown 8	E. Leadbeater.................... 2	G. Ulyett 25
D. B. Close.................... 6	M. Leyland 41	H. Verity...............40
A. Coxon 1	F. A. Lowson 7	A. Waddington 2
D. Denton 11	G. G. Macaulay 8	E. Wainwright 5
A. Dolphin 1	F. W. Milligan 2	J. H. Wardle 28
T. Emmett 7	A. Mitchell 6	W. Watson* 17
P. A. Gibb 8	F. Mitchell 2	C. E. M. Wilson 2
A. Greenwood 2	D. E. V. Padgett 2	E. R. Wilson 1
S. Haigh 11	E. Peate 9	A. Wood 4
Lord Hawke 5	R. Peel 20	N. W. D. Yardley 20
A. Hill 2		

MISCELLANEOUS (8—34 caps)

A. G. Archer 1
S. F. Barnes* 23
Hon. C. J. Coventry 2

B. A. F. Grieve 2
L. Hone 1
J. E. P. McMaster 1

A. M. Miller 1
D. C. H. Townsend 3

ENGLAND CAPTAINS WERE PROVIDED AS FOLLOWS:

Derbyshire .... (1)   D. B. Carr (1)
Essex ....(23)   J. W. H. T. Douglas (18), F. L. Fane (5)
Gloucestershire ......(33)   W. G. Grace (13), W. R. Hammond (20)
Hampshire .... (9)   C. B. Fry (6), Hon. L. H. Tennyson (3)
Kent ....(34)   Hon. Ivo Bligh (4), A. P. F. Chapman (17), M. C. Cowdrey (9), Lord
                                        Harris (4)
Lancashire ....(33)   K. Cranston (1), A. N. Hornby (2), N. D. Howard (4), A. C. MacLaren
                                        (22), A. G. Steel (4)
Middlesex ....(46)   G. O. Allen (11), F. G. Mann (7), F. T. Mann (5), T. C. O'Brien (1),
                                        R. W. V. Robins (3), G. T. S. Stevens (1), A. E. Stoddart (8), P. F.
                                        Warner (10)
Northamptonshire ...(15)   F. R. Brown (15)
Nottinghamshire ......(19)   A. W. Carr (6), A. O. Jones (2), A. Shaw (4), A. Shrewsbury (7)
Somerset .... (4)   J. C. White (4)
Surrey ....(59)   M. P. Bowden (1), D. R. Jardine (15), H. D. G. Leveson-Gower (3),
                                        P. B. H. May (38), W. W. Read (2)
Sussex ....(18)   A. E. R. Gilligan (9), A. H. H. Gilligan (4), James Lillywhite (2), D. S.
                                        Sheppard (2), C. A. Smith (1)
Warwickshire ....(20)   Hon. F. S. G. Calthorpe (4), R. E. S. Wyatt (16)
Worcestershire ...... (4)   R. E. Foster (3), C. F. Walters (1)
Yorkshire ....(50)   Lord Hawke (4), L. Hutton (23), Hon. F. S. Jackson (5), R. T. Stany-
                                        forth (4), N. W. D. Yardley (14)

FIRST-CLASS CRICKET
RECORDS

Part I—The Sides

Large Innings Totals

1107	Victoria v. New South Wales (Melbourne)	1926–27
1059	Victoria v. Tasmania (Melbourne)	1922–23
918	New South Wales v. South Australia (Sydney)	1900–01
912—8d	Holkar v. Mysore (Indore)	1945–46
903—7d	England v. Australia (Oval)	1938
887	Yorkshire v. Warwickshire (Birmingham)	1896
849	England v. West Indies (Kingston)	1929–30
843	Australians v. Oxford & Cambridge Univs. P. & P. (Portsmouth)	1893
839	New South Wales v. Tasmania (Sydney)	1898–99
826—4	Maharashtra v. Western India States (Poona)	1948–49
821—7d	South Australia v. Queensland (Adelaide)	1939–40
815	New South Wales v. Victoria (Sydney)	1908–09
811	Surrey v. Somerset (Oval)	1899
807	New South Wales v. South Australia (Adelaide)	1899–00
805	New South Wales v. Victoria (Melbourne)	1905–06
803—4d	Kent v. Essex (Brentwood)	1934
803	Non-Smokers v. Smokers (East Melbourne)	1886–87
802	New South Wales v. South Australia (Sydney)	1920–21
801	Lancashire v. Somerset (Taunton)	1895

Innings Totals of over 600

Innings of over 600 in England and Australia are listed under the respective teams. In cases where an innings total of over 600 has yet to be scored, the highest innings to date is given.

IN ENGLAND

Derbyshire	645	v. Hampshire (Derby)	1898
Essex	692	v. Somerset (Taunton)	1895
	673	v. Leicestershire (Leicester)	1899
	616—5d	v. Surrey (Oval)	1904
	609—4d	v. Derbyshire (Leyton)	1912
	604—7d	v. Northamptonshire (Northampton)	1921
Glamorgan	587—8d	v. Derbyshire (Cardiff)	1951
Gloucestershire	653—6d	v. Glamorgan (Bristol)	1928
	643—5d	v. Nottinghamshire (Bristol)	1946
	636	v. Nottinghamshire (Nottingham)	1904
	634	v. Nottinghamshire (Bristol)	1898
	627—2d	v. Oxford U. (Oxford)	1930
	625—6d	v. Worcestershire (Dudley)	1934
	608—7d	v. Sussex (Cheltenham)	1934
	603—6d	v. Glamorgan (Bristol)	1934
Hampshire	672—7d	v. Somerset (Taunton)	1899
	642—9d	v. Somerset (Taunton)	1901
	616—7d	v. Warwickshire (Portsmouth)	1920
Kent	803—4d	v. Essex (Brentwood)	1934
	621—6d	v. Essex (Tonbridge)	1922
	615	v. Derbyshire (Derby)	1908
	610	v. Hampshire (Bournemouth)	1906
	607—6d	v. Gloucestershire (Cheltenham)	1910
	602—7d	v. Worcestershire (Dudley)	1938
	601—8d	v. Somerset (Taunton)	1908
Lancashire	801	v. Somerset (Taunton)	1895
	676—7d	v. Hampshire (Manchester)	1911
	640—8d	v. Sussex (Hove)	1937
	627	v. Nottinghamshire (Nottingham)	1905
	601—8d	v. Sussex (Hove)	1905

Leicestershire	701—4d	v. Worcestershire (Worcester)	1906
	609—8d	v. Sussex (Leicester)	1900
	603	v. Sir Julien Cahn's XI (Nottingham)	1935
Middlesex	642—3d	v. Hampshire (Southampton)	1923
	637—4d	v. Leicestershire (Leicester)	1947
	632—8d	v. Sussex (Hove)	1937
	623—5d	v. Worcestershire (Worcester)	1949
	621—9d	v. Nottinghamshire (Nottingham)	1931
	612—8d	v. Nottinghamshire (Lord's)	1921
	608—7d	v. Hampshire (Lord's)	1919
Northamptonshire	557—6d	v. Sussex (Hove)	1914
Nottinghamshire	739—7d	v. Leicestershire (Nottingham)	1903
	726	v. Sussex (Nottingham)	1895
	674	v. Sussex (Hove)	1893
	662—8d	v. Essex (Nottingham)	1947
	661	v. Derbyshire (Derby)	1901
	656—3d	v. Warwickshire (Coventry)	1928
	642—7d	v. Sussex (Hove)	1901
	607	v. Gloucestershire (Bristol)	1899
	602	v. Kent (Nottingham)	1904
Somerset	675—9d	v. Hampshire (Bath)	1924
	630	v. Yorkshire (Leeds)	1901
Surrey	811	v. Somerset (Oval)	1899
	742	v. Hampshire (Oval)	1909
	706—4d	v. Nottinghamshire (Nottingham)	1947
	698	v. Sussex (Oval)	1888
	650	v. Oxford U. (Oval)	1888
	645—9d	v. New Zealanders (Oval)	1949
	634	v. Lancashire (Oval)	1898
	634	v. Warwickshire (Oval)	1906
	631	v. Sussex (Oval)	1885
	619—5d	v. Northamptonshire (Northampton)	1920
	617—6d	v. Oxford U. (Oval)	1928
	617	v. Kent (Oval)	1897
	616—5d	v. Northamptonshire (Oval)	1921
	614	v. Oxford U. (Oval)	1889
	611—9d	v. Derbyshire (Derby)	1904
	609	v. Warwickshire (Oval)	1898
	602	v. Warwickshire (Oval)	1897
Sussex	705—8d	v. Surrey (Hastings)	1902
	686—8	v. Leicestershire (Leicester)	1900
	670—9d	v. Northamptonshire (Hove)	1921
	631—4d	v. Northamptonshire (Northampton)	1938
	611	v. Essex (Leyton)	1905
	600—7d	v. Surrey (Oval)	1903
Warwickshire	657—6d	v. Hampshire (Birmingham)	1899
	645—7d	v. Worcestershire (Dudley)	1914
	635	v. Derbyshire (Birmingham)	1900
	614—8d	v. Essex (Birmingham)	1904
	605	v. Leicestershire (Leicester)	1899
	603—9d	v. Worcestershire (Birmingham)	1920
Worcestershire	633	v. Warwickshire (Worcester)	1906
	627—9d	v. Kent (Worcester)	1905
Yorkshire	887	v. Warwickshire (Birmingham)	1896
	704	v. Surrey (Oval)	1899
	681—5d	v. Sussex (Sheffield)	1897
	662	v. Derby (Chesterfield)	1898
	660	v. Leicestershire (Leicester)	1896
Oxford University	651	v. Sussex (Hove)	1895
	644—8d	v. H. D. G. Leveson-Gower's XI (Eastbourne)	1921
	612	v. Middlesex (Princes)	1876
Cambridge University	703—9d	v. Sussex (Hove)	1890
	611	v. Sussex (Hove)	1919
	609—8d	v. M.C.C. (Lord's)	1913
M.C.C.	607	v. Cambridge U. (Lord's)	1902
England (Test matches)	903—7d	v. Australia (Oval)	1938
	658—8d	v. Australia (Nottingham)	1938
	627—9d	v. Australia (Manchester)	1934
	619—6d	v. West Indies (Nottingham)	1957

Australians	843	v. Oxford and Cambridge U. P. & P. (Portsmouth)	...1893
	774—7d	v. Gloucestershire (Bristol)	1948
	729—6d	v. England (Lord's)	1930
	721	v. Essex (Southend)	1948
	708—5d	v. Cambridge U. (Cambridge)	1938
	708—7d	v. Hampshire (Southampton)	1921
	701	v. England (Oval)	1934
	695	v. England (Oval)	1930
	694—6	v. Leicestershire (Leicester)	1956
	679—7d	v. Oxford U. (Oxford)	1938
	676	v. Kent (Canterbury)	1921
	675	v. Nottinghamshire (Nottingham)	1921
	650—8d	v. Cambridge U. (Cambridge)	1919
	643	v. Sussex (Hove)	1882
	632	v. Surrey (Oval)	1948
	629	v. Surrey (Oval)	1934
	625	v. Derbyshire (Derby)	1896
	624—4d	v. Sussex (Hove)	1899
	621	v. Northamptonshire (Northampton)	1921
	620	v. Hampshire (Southampton)	1905
	610—5d	v. Gentlemen of England (Lord's)	1948
	609—4d	v. Somerset (Bath)	1905
	609—6d	v. Essex (Leyton)	1909
	609	v. Northamptonshire (Northampton)	1905
South Africans	692	v. Cambridge U. (Cambridge)	1901
	611	v. Nottinghamshire (Nottingham)	1904
West Indians	730—3	v. Cambridge U. (Cambridge)	1950
	682—2d	v. Leicestershire (Leicester)	1950
	665	v. Middlesex (Lord's)	1939
New Zealanders	546	v. Sussex (Hove)	1937
Indians	533—3d	v. Sussex (Hove)	1946
Pakistan	428	v. Worcestershire (Worcester)	1954
Gentlemen	578	v. Players (Oval)	1904
Players	651—7d	v. Gentlemen (Oval)	1934
	647	v. Gentlemen (Oval)	1899
	608—8d	v. Gentlemen (Oval)	1921

Other innings totals of over 600 in England are:

676—8d	Oxford Harlequins v. West Indians (Eastbourne)	1928
636—7d	Free Foresters v. Cambridge U. (Cambridge)	1938
633	London County v. M.C.C. (Crystal Palace)	1901
631—5d	Rest of England v. Warwickshire (Champion County) (Oval)	1911
603—5d	Rest of England v. Middlesex (Champion County) (Oval)	1920
603—8d	Rest of England v. Lancashire (Champion County) (Oval)	1928

IN AUSTRALIA

New South Wales	918	v. South Australia (Sydney)	1900–01
	839	v. Tasmania (Sydney)	1898–99
	815	v. Victoria (Sydney)	1908–09
	807	v. South Australia (Adelaide)	1899–00
	805	v. Victoria (Melbourne)	1905–06
	802	v. South Australia (Sydney)	1920–21
	786	v. South Australia (Adelaide)	1922–23
	775	v. Victoria (Sydney)	1881–82
	770	v. South Australia (Adelaide)	1920–21
	763	v. Queensland (Brisbane)	1906–07
	761—8d	v. Queensland (Sydney)	1929–30
	713—6d	v. Victoria (Sydney)	1928–29
	713	v. South Australia (Adelaide)	1908–09
	708	v. Victoria (Sydney)	1925–26
	705	v. Victoria (Melbourne)	1925–26
	691	v. Queensland (Brisbane)	1905–06
	690	v. South Australia (Adelaide)	1919–20
	686	v. Queensland (Sydney)	1904–05
	684	v. South Australia (Sydney)	1923–24
	681	v. South Australia (Sydney)	1903–04
	675	v. Victoria (Sydney)	1913–14
	672—8d	v. Victoria (Sydney)	1933–34

New South Wales (*cont.*)	645	v. Rest (except Victoria) (Sydney)	1924–25
	642	v. South Australia (Sydney)	1925–26
	640	v. Queensland (Sydney)	1899–00
	639	v. Western Australia (Sydney)	1925–26
	639	v. Queensland (Sydney)	1927–28
	629—8d	v. M.C.C. (Sydney)	1929–30
	624	v. South Australia (Adelaide)	1903–04
	619	v. M.C.C. (Sydney)	1924–25
	614—5d	v. Tasmania (Hobart)	1912–13
	614—6d	v. Queensland (Sydney)	1933–34
	614	v. Victoria (Sydney)	1924–25
	610	v. South Australia (Adelaide)	1930–31
Queensland	687	v. New South Wales (Brisbane)	1930–31
South Australia	821—7d	v. Queensland (Adelaide)	1939–40
	688	v. Tasmania (Adelaide)	1935–36
	644—7d	v. Queensland (Adelaide)	1934–35
	642—8d	v. Queensland (Adelaide)	1935–36
	614—8d	v. Western Australia (Adelaide)	1929–30
	612	v. Western Australia (Adelaide)	1925–26
	610	v. Victoria (Melbourne)	1939–40
	603	v. New South Wales (Adelaide)	1946–47
	600—8d	v. New South Wales (Adelaide)	1938–39
Tasmania	458	v. Indians (Launceston)	1947–48
Victoria	1107	v. New South Wales (Melbourne)	1926–27
	1059	v. Tasmania (Melbourne)	1922–23
	793	v. Queensland (Melbourne)	1927–28
	724	v. South Australia (Melbourne)	1920–21
	699	v. South Australia (Melbourne)	1907–08
	697	v. South Australia (Adelaide)	1945–46
	660	v. Tasmania (Melbourne)	1909–10
	649	v. South Australia (Melbourne)	1926–27
	647	v. Tasmania (Melbourne)	1951–52
	646—8d	v. South Australia (Adelaide)	1927–28
	639	v. South Australia (Adelaide)	1920–21
	637	v. South Australia (Melbourne)	1927–28
	626	v. Tasmania (Launceston)	1908–09
	620	v. South Australia (Adelaide)	1921–22
	617—6d	v. M.C.C. (Melbourne)	1922–23
	614	v. South Australia (Melbourne)	1910–11
	605	v. South Australia (Melbourne)	1919–20
	604	v. South Australia (Melbourne)	1925–26
	602	v. New Zealanders (Melbourne)	1898–99
Western Australia	532—8d	v. New South Wales (Perth)	1957–58
M.C.C.	734—7d	v. New South Wales (Sydney)	1928–29
	660—8d	v. South Australia (Adelaide)	1907–08
	634—9d	v. South Australia (Adelaide)	1932–33
	627	v. South Australia (Adelaide)	1920–21
	626	v. New South Wales (Sydney)	1924–25
England	636	v. Australia (Sydney)	1928–29
Australia	674	v. India (Adelaide)	1947–48
	659—8d	v. England (Sydney)	1946–47
	645	v. England (Brisbane)	1946–47
	604	v. England (Melbourne)	1936–37
	601—8d	v. England (Brisbane)	1954–55
	600	v. England (Melbourne)	1924–25
South Africans	512	v. South Australia (Adelaide)	1931–32
West Indians	495	v. Victoria (Melbourne)	1930–31
New Zealanders	459	v. South Australia (Adelaide)	1953–54
Indians	475—7d	v. Tasmania (Launceston)	1947–48

Other innings totals of over 600 in Australia are:

803	Non Smokers v. Smokers (East Melbourne)	1886–87
769	A. C. MacLaren's XI v. New South Wales (Sydney)	1901–02
663	J. Ryder's XI v. W. M. Woodfull's XI (Sydney)	1929–30
648	Australian XI v. Rest of Australia (Melbourne)	1908–09
624	A. Shrewsbury's XI v. Victoria (Melbourne)	1887–88
619	Australian XI v. Rest of Australia (Melbourne)	1883–84
609	A. E. Stoddart's XI v. South Australia (Adelaide)	1894–95

IN SOUTH AFRICA

676	M.C.C. v. Griqualand West (Kimberley)	1938–39
664—6d	Natal v. Western Province (Durban)	1936–37
654—5	England v. South Africa (Durban)	1938–39
609	Transvaal v. Orange Free State (Johannesburg)	1934–35
608—6d	Transvaal v. Natal (Johannesburg)	1939–40
608	England v. South Africa (Johannesburg)	1948–49
603	Griqualand West v. Western Province (Kimberley)	1929–30
602	Griqualand West v. Rhodesia (Kimberley)	1929–30
601	Western Province v. Border (Cape Town)	1929–30

IN THE WEST INDIES

849	England v. West Indies (Kingston)	1929–30
790—3d	West Indies v. Pakistan (Kingston)	1957–58
758—8d	Australia v. West Indies (Kingston)	1954–55
753	Barbados v. Jamaica (Barbados)	1951–52
750—8d	Trinidad v. British Guiana (Trinidad)	1946–47
726—7d	Barbados v. Trinidad (Barbados)	1926–27
715—9d	Barbados v. British Guiana (Barbados)	1926–27
702—5d	Jamaica v. Lord Tennyson's XI (Kingston)	1931–32
698	Barbados v. Trinidad (Barbados)	1948–49
692—9d	British Guiana v. Barbados (Georgetown)	1951–52
686—6d	Barbados v. British Guiana (Barbados)	1949–50
681—8d	West Indies v. England (Trinidad)	1953–54
673	Barbados v. Trinidad (Georgetown)	1922–23
668	Australia v. West Indies (Barbados)	1954–55
657—8d	Pakistan v. West Indies (Barbados)	1957–58
650—3d	Barbados v. Trinidad (Barbados)	1943–44
641—6	M.C.C. v. Berbice (Blairmont)	1959–60
629	British Guiana v. Barbados (Georgetown)	1937–38
627	British Guiana v. Trinidad (Georgetown)	1937–38
623—5d	Barbados v. Trinidad (Barbados)	1919–20
619—3d	Barbados v. Trinidad (Trinidad)	1945–46
610	British Guiana v. Barbados (Georgetown)	1929–30
609	Jamaica v. Hon L. H. Tennyson's XI (Kingston)	1927–28
609	British Guiana v. Jamaica (Georgetown)	1952–53
607	M.C.C. v. British Guiana (Georgetown)	1953–54
606—7d	Barbados v. Indians (Barbados)	1952–53
605—5d	M.C.C. v. British Guiana (Georgetown)	1929–30
601—5d	British Guiana v. Jamaica (Georgetown)	1956–57
601—9d	Barbados v. British Guiana (Georgetown)	1946–47
601	M.C.C. v. Barbados (Barbados)	1934–35
600—9d	Australia v. West Indies (Trinidad)	1954–55

IN NEW ZEALAND

752—8d	New South Wales v. Otago (Dunedin)	1923–24
693—9d	Auckland v. Canterbury (Auckland)	1939–40
663	Australians v. New Zealand XI (Auckland)	1920–21
658	Australians v. Auckland (Auckland)	1913–14
653—5d	M.C.C. v. New Zealand XI (Dunedin)	1935–36
653	Australians v. Canterbury (Christchurch)	1913–14
643	Auckland v. Canterbury (Auckland)	1919–20
610—6d	Australians v. New Zealand XI (Auckland)	1913–14
602—8d	Otago v. Canterbury (Dunedin)	1928–29

IN INDIA

912—8d	Holkar v. Mysore (Indore)	1945–46
826—4	Maharashtra v. Western India States (Poona)	1948–49
798	Maharashtra v. Northern India (Poona)	1940–41
784	Baroda v. Holkar (Baroda)	1946–47
764	Bombay v. Holkar (Bombay)	1944–45
760	Bengal v. Assam (Calcutta)	1951–52
757	Holkar v. Hyderabad (Indore)	1950–51
735	Bombay v. Maharashtra (Bombay)	1943–44
725—8d	Bombay v. Maharashtra (Bombay)	1950–51
714—8d	Bombay v. Maharashtra (Poona)	1948–49

703	Bengal Cyclone XI v. Bijapur Famine XI (Bombay)	1942–43
675	Maharashtra v. Bombay (Poona)	1940–41
673	Bijapur Famine XI v. Bengal Cyclone XI (Bombay)	1942–43
658—8d	Southern Punjab v. Northern India (Patiala)	1945–46
657—9d	Bombay v. Maharashtra (Bombay)	1956–57
654	Cricket Club of India v. C. K. Nayudu's XI (Bombay)	1944–45
652	Bombay v. Hyderabad (Bombay)	1947–48
651	Bombay v. Maharashtra (Poona)	1948–49
650—9d	Maharashtra v. Baroda (Poona)	1939–40
650	Bombay v. Maharashtra (Poona)	1940–41
645	Bombay v. Baroda (Bombay)	1945–46
644—8d	West Indies v. India (New Delhi)	1958–59
638—8d	Bombay v. Sind (Bombay)	1947–48
634—9d	Bombay v. Madras (Bombay)	1956–57
632—7d	Bombay v. Maharashtra (Bombay)	1947–48
631	West Indies v. India (New Delhi)	1948–49
629—6d	West Indies v. India (Bombay)	1948–49
629	Gujerat v. Maharashtra (Kolaphur)	1951–52
620	Bombay v. Northern India (Bombay)	1944–45
620	Bombay v. Baroda (Bombay)	1948–49
618	Holkar v. Bengal (Indore)	1942–43
615—4d	Cricket Club of India v. Services XI (Bombay)	1944–45
615	Holkar v. Delhi and District (Delhi)	1949–50
615	Rajasthan v. Vidarbha (Udaipur)	1957–58
614—5d	West Indies v. India (Calcutta)	1958–59
613—7d	Northern India v. N.W.F.P. (Lahore)	1941–42
613—7d	Commonwealth XI v. North Zone (Patiala)	1949–50
612—6d	India in England 1946 v. Rest of India (Calcutta)	1946–47
611	Commonwealth XI v. West Zone (Poona)	1949–50
608—8d	Commonwealth XI v. Indian XI (New Delhi)	1949–50
604	Maharashtra v. Bombay (Poona)	1948–49
603	M.C.C. v. Madras (Madras)	1933–34

IN PAKISTAN

772—7d	Karachi v. Bahawalpar (Karachi)	1958–59
762	Karachi Whites v. Karachi Blues (Karachi)	1956–57
702	Punjab Univ. v. Sind Univ. (Karachi)	1958–59

Somerset conceded innings totals of 692 v. Essex and 801 v. Lancashire, both at Taunton, in consecutive innings in the 1895 season.

South Australia conceded the following innings totals in their matches during the 1920–21 season—639 by Victoria (Adelaide), 512—5d by M.C.C. (Adelaide), 310 & 724 by Victoria (Melbourne), 802 by New South Wales (Sydney), 304 & 770 by New South Wales (Adelaide) and 627 by M.C.C. (Adelaide).

Australians scored the following innings totals in succession during their 1921 tour of England— 621 v. Northamptonshire (Northampton), 675 v. Nottinghamshire (Nottingham) and 506 v. Warwickshire (Birmingham).

Northamptonshire conceded the following innings totals in succession during the 1921 season— 616—5d by Surrey (Oval), 604—7d by Essex (Northampton), 621 by Australians (Northampton) and 545—9d by Essex (Leyton).

New South Wales scored a first innings total of 614 v. Victoria (Sydney) 1924–25, but were dismissed for a second innings total of 152 and lost the match by seven wickets.

New South Wales totalled 642 and 592 v. South Australia (Sydney) 1925–26.

Bombay totalled 651 and 714—8d v. Maharashtra (Poona) 1948–49, the home team replying with totals of 407 and 604—the highest scoring match on record.

Large Second Innings Totals

770	New South Wales v. South Australia (Adelaide)	1920–21
764	Bombay v. Holkar (Bombay)	1944–45
761—8d	New South Wales v. Queensland (Sydney)	1929–30
726—7d	Barbados v. Trinidad (Barbados)	1926–27
724	Victoria v. South Australia (Melbourne)	1920–21
714—8d	Bombay v. Maharashtra (Poona)	1948–49
703—9d	Cambridge University v. Sussex (Hove)	1890

Small Innings Totals

12	Oxford University v. M.C.C. (Oxford)	(a) 1877
12	Northamptonshire v. Gloucestershire (Gloucester)	1907
13	Wellington v. Nelson (Nelson)	1862–63
13	Auckland v. Canterbury (Auckland)	(b) 1877–78
13	Nottinghamshire v. Yorkshire (Nottingham)	1901
15	M.C.C. v. Surrey (Lord's)	1839
15	Victoria v. M.C.C. (Melbourne)	1903–04
15	Northamptonshire v. Yorkshire (Northampton)	(c) 1908
15	Hampshire v. Warwickshire (Birmingham)	(d) 1922
16	M.C.C. v. Surrey (Lord's)	(e) 1872
16	Derbyshire v. Nottinghamshire (Nottingham)	1879
16	Surrey v. Nottinghamshire (Oval)	1880
16	Warwickshire v. Kent (Tonbridge)	1913
16	Trinidad v. Barbados (Barbados)	1941–42
16	Border v. Natal (East London) 1st innings	1959–60
17	Gentlemen of Kent v. Gentlemen of England (Lord's)	1850
17	Gloucestershire v. Australians (Cheltenham)	1896
18	The B's v. England (Lord's)	1831
18	Kent v. Sussex (Gravesend)	1867
18	Tasmania v. Victoria (Melbourne)	1868–69
18	Australians v. M.C.C. (Lord's)	1896
18	Border v. Natal (East London) 2nd innings	1959–60
19	Sussex v. Surrey (Godalming)	1830
19	Sussex v. Nottinghamshire (Hove)	1873
19	M.C.C. v. Australians (Lord's)	1878
19	Wellington v. Nelson (Nelson)	1885–86

(a) Oxford University were dismissed for 35 in their second innings, batting one short in each innings.

(b) There were 8 extras, the highest individual score being 2.

(c) Northamptonshire were dismissed for 27 in their first innings, their match aggregate of 42 being the lowest on record until 1959–60, when Border totalled 34 in two innings.

(d) Hampshire followed-on, scored 521 and won the match by 155 runs.

(e) Seven wickets fell before the first run was scored, the 8th wicket fell at 2, and the 9th wicket at 8.

IN ENGLAND

Derbyshire	16	v. Nottinghamshire (Nottingham)	1879
	20	v. Yorkshire (Sheffield)	1939
	23	v. Yorkshire (Hull)	1921
	26	v. M.C.C. (Lord's)	1880
	26	v. Yorkshire (Derby)	1880
	30	v. Nottinghamshire (Chesterfield)	1913
Essex	30	v. Yorkshire (Leyton)	1901
Glamorgan	22	v. Lancashire (Liverpool)	1924
	26	v. Lancashire (Cardiff)	1958
Gloucestershire	17	v. Australians (Cheltenham)	1896
	22	v. Somerset (Bristol)	1920
	25	v. Somerset (Cheltenham)	1891
Hampshire	15	v. Warwickshire (Birmingham)	1922
	23	v. Derbyshire (Burton-upon-Trent)	1958
	30	v. Worcestershire (Worcester)	1903
	30	v. Nottinghamshire (Southampton)	1932
Kent	18	v. Sussex (Gravesend)	1867
	20	v. Surrey (Oval)	1870
	21	v. England (Lord's)	1834
	23	v. Sussex (Brighton)	1828
	23	v. England (Bromley)	1840
	25	v. Derbyshire (Wirksworth)	1874
	25	v. M.C.C. (Lord's)	1879
	27	v. Sussex (Town Malling)	1836
	27	v. M.C.C. (Lord's)	1856
	28	v. Gloucestershire (Moreton in the Marsh)	1888
	30	v. England (Bromley)	1840
Lancashire	25	v. Derbyshire (Manchester)	1871
	27	v. Surrey (Manchester)	1958

Lancashire *(cont.)*   28   v. Australians (Liverpool) 1896
                         30   v. Yorkshire (Holbeck) 1868

Leicestershire 25   v. Kent (Leicester) 1912
                         26   v. Kent (Leicester) 1911
                         28   v. Australians (Leicester) 1899

Middlesex 20   v. M.C.C. (Lord's) 1864
                         24   v. M.C.C. (Lord's) 1815
                         25   v. Surrey (Oval) 1885
                         29   v. Derbyshire (Chesterfield) 1957

Northamptonshire 12   v. Gloucestershire (Gloucester)........................1907
                         15   v. Yorkshire (Northampton) 1908
                         27   v. Yorkshire (Northampton) 1908
                         27   v. Yorkshire (Kettering) 1933

Nottinghamshire 13   v. Yorkshire (Nottingham) 1901
                         21   v. M.C.C. (Lord's) 1891
                         23   v. M.C.C. (Nottingham) 1883
                         24   v. Yorkshire (Sheffield) 1888

Somerset 25   v. Gloucestershire (Bristol) 1947

Surrey 16   v. Nottinghamshire (Oval)................................1880
                         26   v. Nottinghamshire (Nottingham) 1876
                         27   v. Gloucestershire (Cheltenham) 1874

Sussex 19   v. Surrey (Godalming) 1830
                         19   v. Nottinghamshire (Hove) 1873
                         20   v. Yorkshire (Hull) 1922
                         22   v. Kent (Sevenoaks) 1828
                         23   v. M.C.C. (Lord's) 1838
                         24   v. Yorkshire (Hove) 1878
                         24   v. Lancashire (Manchester) 1890
                         25   v. M.C.C. (Lord's) 1843
                         25   v. M.C.C. (Lord's) 1856
                         29   v. M.C.C. (Lord's)..1861
                         29   v. Gloucestershire (Cheltenham) 1878
                         29   v. Lancashire (Liverpool) 1907

Warwickshire 16   v. Kent (Tonbridge) 1913
                         28   v. Derbyshire (Derby) 1937

Worcestershire 24   v. Yorkshire (Huddersfield) 1903
                         25   v. Yorkshire (Hull) 1906
                         25   v. Surrey (Oval) 1954
                         25   v. Kent (Tunbridge Wells)..............................1960
                         28   v. Yorkshire (Bradford) 1907

Yorkshire 26   v. Surrey (Oval) 1909
                         30   v. Kent (Sheffield) 1865

Oxford University 12   v. M.C.C. (Oxford)..1877

Cambridge University 28   v. M.C.C. (Lord's) 1845
                         30   v. Yorkshire (Cambridge) 1928

M.C.C. 15   v. Surrey (Lord's) 1839
                         16   v. Surrey (Lord's) 1872
                         19   v. Australians (Lord's) 1878
                         24   v. Oxford U. (Lord's)....................................1846
                         27   v. Yorkshire (Lord's) 1902
                         29   v. The B's (Lord's) 1832
                         29   v. North (Lord's) 1848
                         30   v. Lancashire (Lord's) 1886

Other totals of less than 30 in England are as follows:

17   Gentlemen of Kent v. Gentlemen of England (Lord's).....................1850
18   The B's v. England (Lord's) 1831
18   Australians v. M.C.C. (Lord's) 1896
23   Australians v. Yorkshire (Leeds) 1902
24   Players v. Gentlemen (Lord's) 1829
26   Slow Bowlers v. Fast Bowlers (Lord's) 1849
26   England v. M.C.C. (Lord's) 1877
26   England XI v. Australians (Aston, Birmingham) 1884
27   England v. Sussex (Brighton) 1827
27   Lord Sheffield's XI v. Australians (Sheffield Park) 1890
27   Rest v. England (Bradford—Test Trial) 1950
28   England XI v. Australians (Stoke) 1888

* F

29	Gentlemen of Kent v. Gentlemen of England (Lord's)	1848
30	England v. Sussex (Brighton)	1833
30	England v. Kent (Bromley)	1841
30	Gentlemen of England v. Gentlemen of Kent (Canterbury)	1859
30	United North of England XI v. United South of England XI (Northampton)	1872
30	South Africa v. England (Birmingham)	1924
30	Ireland v. New Zealanders (Dublin)	1937

IN AUSTRALIA

15	Victoria v. M.C.C. (Melbourne)	1903–04
18	Tasmania v. Victoria (Melbourne)	1868–69
23	South Australia v. Victoria (Melbourne)	1882–83
27	South Australia v. New South Wales (Sydney)	1955–56
28	Victoria v. New South Wales (Melbourne)	1855–56
31	Victoria v. New South Wales (Melbourne)	1906–07
32	Australian XI v. G. F. Vernon's XI (Sydney)	1887–88
34	Victoria v. New South Wales (Melbourne)	1875–76
35	Victoria v. New South Wales (Melbourne)	1887–88
35	Victoria v. New South Wales (Sydney)	1926–27
36	Tasmania v. Victoria (Melbourne)	1870–71
36	South Africa v. Australia (Melbourne)	1931–32
37	New South Wales v. Victoria (Sydney)	1868–69
37	Victoria v. New South Wales (Sydney)	1875–76
38	Victoria v. New South Wales (Sydney)	1856–57
38	Victoria v. New South Wales (Sydney)	1858–59
38	Rest of Australia v. Australian XI (Sydney)	1888–89
38	Western Australia v. Victoria (Melbourne)	1892–93
39	Tasmania v. Victoria (Hobart)	1889–90
40	Queensland v. Victoria (Brisbane)	1902–03

IN SOUTH AFRICA

16	Border v. Natal (East London) 1st innings	1959–60
18	Border v. Natal (East London) 2nd innings	1959–60
23	Border v. Natal (East London)	1920–21
29	Griqualand West v. Transvaal (Johannesburg)	1950–51
30	South Africa v. England (Port Elizabeth)	1895–96
31	Griqualand West v. Natal (Johannesburg)	1906–07
34	Griqualand West v. Transvaal (Port Elizabeth)	1902–03
34	Border v. Eastern Province (East London)	1946–47
35	South Africa v. England (Cape Town)	1898–99
36	Eastern Province v. Transvaal (Port Elizabeth)	1937–38
37	Orange Free State v. Transvaal (Bloemfontein)	1936–37
37	Eastern Province v. Western Province (Port Elizabeth)	1933–34
40	Eastern Province v. Orange Free State (Durban)	1910–11

IN WEST INDIES

16	Trinidad v. Barbados (Barbados)	1941–42
22	British Guiana v. Barbados (Barbados)	1864–65
33	British Guiana v. Barbados (Barbados)	1864–65
33	A. Priestley's XI v. Trinidad (Trinidad)	1896–97
33	Jamaica v. R. A. Bennett's XI (Kingston)	1901–02
33	West Indian XI v. R. A. Bennett's XI (Georgetown)	1901–02
35	Trinidad v. Barbados (Trinidad)	1892–93

IN NEW ZEALAND

13	Wellington v. Nelson (Nelson)	1862–63
13	Auckland v. Canterbury (Auckland)	1877–78
19	Wellington v. Nelson (Nelson)	1885–86
22	1st inns	Wellington v. Auckland (Auckland)	1862–63
22	2nd inns		
22	Wellington v. Canterbury (Wellington)	1903–04
25	Canterbury v. Otago (Christchurch)	1866–67
26	New Zealand v. England (Auckland)	1954–55
27	Canterbury v. Otago (Dunedin)	1896–97

28	Hawke's Bay v. Auckland (Auckland)	1910–11
29	Wellington v. Nelson (Nelson)	1879–80
30	Wellington v. Nelson (Nelson)	1883–84
31	Wellington v. Nelson (Nelson)	1862–63
31	Wellington v. Nelson (Nelson)	1887–88
32	Canterbury v. Otago (Dunedin)	1863–64
32	Canterbury v. Otago (Christchurch)	1866–67
32	Nelson v. Wellington (Wellington)	1866–67
32	Nelson v. Wellington (Wellington)	1870–71
32	Wellington v. Canterbury (Wellington)	1877–78
32	Hawke's Bay v. Wellington (Wellington)	1883–84
33	Nelson v. Wellington (Wellington)	1866–67
33	Nelson v. Auckland (Nelson)	1882–83
34	Wellington v. Canterbury (Wellington)	1886–87
34	Otago v. Wellington (Dunedin)	1956–57
35	Nelson v. Wellington (Nelson)	1862–63
35	Wellington v. Auckland (Wellington)	1873–74
35	Otago v. Auckland (Christchurch)	1884–85
36	Wellington v. Nelson (Nelson)	1885–86
36	Otago v. New South Wales (Dunedin)	1889–90
37	Nelson v. Wellington (Wellington)	1863–64
37	Wellington v. Nelson (Nelson)	1876–77
37	Canterbury v. Southland (Invercargill)	1920–21
37	Canterbury v. Wellington (Wellington)	1925–26
38	Canterbury v. Otago (Christchurch)	1873–74
39	Wellington v. Auckland (Wellington)	1859–60
39	Taranaki v. Hawke's Bay (Napier)	1891–92
40	Otago v. Canterbury (Dunedin)	1869–70
40	Nelson v. Auckland (Nelson)	1873–74
40	Tasmania v. Otago (Dunedin)	1883–84

IN INDIA

21	Muslims v. Europeans (Poona)	1915–16
22	Southern Punjab v. Northern India (Amritsar)	1934–35
23	Sind v. Southern Punjab (Patiala)	1938–39
24	Europeans v. Parsis (Bombay)	1894–95
25	Saurashtra v. Bombay (Bombay)	1951–52
28	Mysore v. Bombay (Bangalore)	1951–52
30	Europeans v. Parsis (Poona)	1895–96
31	East Punjab v. Railways (Jullundur)	1958–59
32	Rajputana v. M.C.C. (Ajmer)	1933–34
33	Parsis v. Europeans (Poona)	1918–19
33	Railways v. Services (New Delhi)	1958–59
35	Orissa v. Bihar (Patna)	1958–59
35	Patiala v. Services (New Delhi)	1958–59
36	Europeans v. Parsis (Poona)	1913–14
37	Parsis v. Europeans (Poona)	1898–99
37	Parsis v. Europeans (Poona)	1909–10
37	Delhi v. United Provinces (Agra)	1934–35
37	Baroda v. Nawanagar (Jamnagar)	1937–38
37	Jammu & Kashmir v. Services (New Delhi)	1959–60
38	Mysore v. Madras (Madras)	1936–37
39	Muslims v. Europeans (Poona)	1915–16
39	Maharashtra v. Nawanagar (Jamnagar)	1941–42
39	East Zone v. West Indians (Jorhat)	1958–59
40	Europeans v. Parsis (Bombay)	1904–05
40	Delhi and District v. N.W.F.P. (Peshawar)	1938–39

IN PAKISTAN

30	Quetta v. Karachi B (Karachi)	1957–58
33	East Pakistan Whites v. Services (Dacca)	1956–57
39	Dacca University v. Bahawalpur (Bahawalpur)	1957–58

Wellington scored only 184 runs in their six completed innings of the 1862–63 seasons—13 & 51 v. Nelson (Nelson), 22 & 22 v. Auckland (Auckland) and 31 & 45 v. Nelson (Nelson).

Canterbury dismissed Auckland for an innings total of 13 at Auckland in 1877–78—the highest score by a batsman was 2, extras contributing 8 runs to the total.

Middlesex totalled only 86 v. Somerset (Lord's) 1899, but dismissed the visitors for totals of 35 and 44, winning the match by an innings and seven runs after about three hours' actual play.

Derbyshire (0—1d) declared their second innings closed after only two balls had been bowled v. Essex (Leyton) 1900—Derbyshire wished to forgo their second innings as little time remained for play, but the umpires ordered Derbyshire to bat again.

Worcestershire (155 in their first innings) were dismissed for a second innings total of 28 by Yorkshire (62 & 91) at Bradford in 1907, but won the match by 30 runs.

Yorkshire needed only 58 runs to win v. Lancashire (Leeds) 1924, but were dismissed for 33 and lost the match by 24 runs—this is the smallest task that has been set a defeated team in a County Championship match.

Derbyshire (1—0d) declared their second innings closed after only one ball had been bowled v. Somerset (Derby) 1935—the visitors were then dismissed for 35 and Derbyshire won by 114 runs.

Glamorgan (4—2d) declared their second innings closed after only four balls had been bowled v. Worcestershire (Worcester) 1935.

Border needed only 42 runs to win v. Eastern Province (East London) 1946–47, but were dismissed for 34 and lost the match by 7 runs—this is the lowest task set a defeated team in first-class cricket.

Essex were 13 for seven wickets in the second innings when the match ended v. Kent (Blackheath) 1951.

Lancashire (0—1d) declared their second innings closed after only one ball had been bowled v. Nottinghamshire (Liverpool) 1956; the visitors saved the match, the score being 93—7 when stumps were drawn.

LOWEST AGGREGATES BY ONE TEAM IN A MATCH

34	(16 & 18)	Border v. Natal (East London)	1959–60
42	(27 & 15)	Northamptonshire v. Yorkshire (Northampton)	1908
44	(22 & 22)	Wellington v. Auckland (Auckland)	1862–63
47	(12 & 35)	Oxford U. v. M.C.C. (Oxford)	1877
52	(33 & 19)	M.C.C. v. Australians (Lord's)	1878
53	(18 & 35)	The B's v. England (Lord's)	1831
53	(23 & 30)	Kent v. England (Bromley)	1840
57	(35 & 22)	Sussex v. Kent (Sevenoaks)	1828
59	(35 & 24)	Sussex v. Yorkshire (Hove)	1878
59	(35 & 24)	Sussex v. Lancashire (Manchester)	1890

Large Fourth Innings Totals

The following innings totals of 400 or over have been recorded:

654—5	(set 696 runs)	England v. South Africa (Durban)	1938–39
604	(lost 354 runs)	Maharashtra v. Bombay (Poona)	1948–49
576—8	(set 672 runs)	Trinidad v. Barbados (Trinidad)	1945–46
572	(lost 20 runs)	New South Wales v. South Australia (Sydney)	1907–08
518	(lost 234 runs)	Victoria v. Queensland (Brisbane)	1926–27
507—7	(and won)	Cambridge U. v. M.C.C. (Lord's)	1896
502—6	(and won)	Middlesex v. Nottinghamshire (Nottingham)	1925
502—8	(and won)	Players v. Gentlemen (Lord's)	1900
495	(lost 145 runs)	Otago v. Wellington (Dunedin)	1923–24
492	(lost 374 runs)	Holkar v. Bombay (Bombay)	1944–45
473—6	(and won)	Canterbury v. Auckland (Christchurch)	1930–31
472	(lost 79 runs)	New South Wales v. Australian XI (Sydney)	1905–06
466	(lost 86 runs)	New South Wales v. West Indians (Sydney)	1930–31
463—8	(set 568 runs)	Hampshire v. Kent (Southampton)	1911
460	(lost 5 runs)	Surrey v. M.C.C. (Lord's)	1938
458	(lost 276 runs)	Auckland v. Wellington (Canterbury)	1927–28
456	(lost 50 runs)	Queensland v. Victoria (Melbourne)	1928–29
447	(lost 111 runs)	Orange Free State v. Transvaal (Bloemfontein)	1926–27
446—6	(and won)	New South Wales v. South Australia (Adelaide)	1926–27
442	(lost 45 runs)	South Africans v. New South Wales (Sydney)	1910–11
435—7	(and won)	Victoria v. New South Wales (Melbourne)	1931–32
430—3	(set 448 runs)	New South Wales v. South Africans (Sydney)	1931–32
428—5	(and won)	Sussex v. Northamptonshire (Kettering)	1939
428—6	(and won)	Surrey & Kent v. Middlesex & Essex (Kingston)	1947
427—4	(and won)	Cambridge U. v. Surrey (Oval)	1925
425	(lost 121 runs)	A. L. Hassett's XI v. A. R. Morris's XI (Melbourne)	1952–53
424—4	(set 508 runs)	Hampshire v. Worcestershire (Worcester)	1926
423—7	(set 451 runs)	South Africa v. England (Oval)	1947
422—9	(set 499 runs)	M.C.C. v. Victoria (Melbourne)	1907–08
420—5	(and won)	Free Foresters v. Oxford U. (Oxford)	1921
419—6	(and won)	Nottinghamshire v. Leicestershire (Nottingham)	1926
416—6	(and won)	Kent v. Surrey (Blackheath)	1934
415	(lost 26 runs)	Victoria v. New South Wales (Sydney)	1935–36

412—4	(and won)	I. Zingari v. Gentlemen of England (Lord's)	1904
412—5	(and won)	M.C.C. v. Oxford U. (Lord's)	1923
412—8	(and won)	Gentlemen v. Players (Lord's)	1904
412	(lost 84 runs)	South Australia v. New South Wales (Sydney)	1912–13
411	(lost 193 runs)	England v. Australia (Sydney)	1924–25
409—7	(and won)	Victoria v. South Australia (Adelaide)	1924–25
409—8	(and won)	Rest of Australia v. New South Wales (Sydney)	1933–34
408—5	(set 836 runs)	West Indies v. England (Kingston)	1929–30
406	(lost 17 runs)	South Australia v. New South Wales (Adelaide)	1921–22
404—3	(and won)	Australia v. England (Leeds)	1948
404—5	(and won)	Lancashire v. Hampshire (Southampton)	1910
404	(lost 50 runs)	M.C.C. v. Cambridge U. (Lord's)	1959
403—7	(and won)	Oxford U. v. Worcestershire (Worcester)	1904
403—8	(and won)	Lancashire v. Nottinghamshire (Manchester)	1910
403	(lost 385 runs)	South Australia v. Victoria (Melbourne)	1920–21
402—9	(set 403 runs)	D. G. Bradman's XI v. A. L. Hassett's XI (Melbourne)	1948–49
401—4	(and won)	New South Wales v. Queensland (Brisbane)	1928–29
401—6	(and won)	Gentlemen of England v. Cambridge U. (Eastbourne)	1908

Variation of Innings Totals

On six occasions there have been cases of the two innings of a side in a match varying by over 500 runs—a very great reversal of form.

551	Barbados (175 & 726—7d) v. Trinidad (Barbados)	1926–27
551	Pakistan (106 & 657—8d) v. West Indies (Barbados)	1957–58
543	Somerset (87 & 630) v. Yorkshire (Leeds)	1901
531	Free Foresters (65 & 596—8d) v. Cambridge U. (Cambridge)	1919
524	Cambridge U. (179 & 703—9d) v. Sussex (Hove)	1890
506	Hampshire (15 & 521) v. Warwickshire (Birmingham)	1922
500	Essex (597 & 97) v. Derbyshire (Chesterfield)	1904

Victories by Vast Margins

The following are the greatest innings victories:

Inns & 666 runs	Victoria (1059) v. Tasmania (Melbourne)	1922–23
Inns & 656 runs	Victoria (1107) v. New South Wales (Melbourne)	1926–27
Inns & 605 runs	New South Wales (918) v. South Australia (Sydney)	1900–01
Inns & 579 runs	England (903—7d) v. Australia (Oval)	1938
Inns & 527 runs	New South Wales (713) v. South Australia (Adelaide)	1908–09
Inns & 517 runs	Australians (675) v. Nottinghamshire (Nottingham)	1921
Inns & 487 runs	New South Wales (839) v. Tasmania (Sydney)	1898–99
Inns & 487 runs	Australians (679—7d) v. Oxford U. (Oxford)	1938
Inns & 485 runs	Surrey (698) v. Sussex (Oval)	1888
Inns & 484 runs	Australians (621) v. Northamptonshire (Northampton)	1921
Inns & 479 runs	Karachi (772—7d) v. Bahawalpur (Karachi)	1958–59
Inns & 468 runs	Surrey (742) v. Hampshire (Oval)	1909
Inns & 456 runs	A. Shrewsbury's XI (634) v. Victoria (Melbourne)	1887–88
Inns & 455 runs	Lancashire (676—7d) v. Hampshire (Manchester)	1911
Inns & 453 runs	Bombay (638—8d) v. Sind (Bombay)	1947–48
Inns & 452 runs	Lancashire (801) v. Somerset (Taunton)	1895
Inns & 451 runs	Australians (721) v. Essex (Southend)	1948

The following are the greatest victories by runs margins:

685 runs	New South Wales (235 & 761—8d) v. Queensland (Sydney)	1929–30
675 runs	England (521 & 342—8d) v. Australia (Brisbane)	1928–29
638 runs	New South Wales (304 & 770) v. South Australia (Adelaide)	1920–21
571 runs	Victoria (304 & 649) v. South Australia (Adelaide)	1926–27
562 runs	Australia (701 & 327) v. England (Oval)	1934
541 runs	New South Wales (642 & 593) v. South Australia (Sydney)	1925–26
540 runs	Bengal (479 & 321—9d) v. Orissa (Cuttack)	1953–54
531 runs	Bombay (596 & 442—5d) v. Holkar (Bombay)	1951–52
530 runs	Australia (328 & 578) v. South Africa (Melbourne)	1910–11
512 runs	Wellington (447 & 374) v. Auckland (Wellington)	1926–27

Yorkshire (555—1d) defeated Essex (78 & 164) by an innings and 313 runs at Leyton in 1932, after losing only one wicket in their innings.

Lancashire (166—0d & 66—0) defeated Leicestershire (108 & 122) by ten wickets at Manchester in 1956, not losing a single wicket in the match.

Highest Match Aggregates

Runs Wkts.

2376—38	Bombay v. Maharashtra (Poona) 1948–49
2078—40	Bombay v. Holkar (Bombay) 1944–45
1981—35	South Africa v. England (Durban) 1938–39
1929—39	New South Wales v. South Australia (Sydney) 1925–26
1911—34	New South Wales v. Victoria (Sydney) 1908–09
1905—40	Otago v. Wellington (Dunedin) 1923–24
1815—34	West Indies v. England (Kingston) 1929–30
1801—40	A. L. Hassett's XI v. A. R. Morris's XI (Melbourne) 1953–54
1753—40	Australia v. England (Adelaide) 1920–21
1752—34	New South Wales v. Queensland (Sydney) 1926–27
1744—40	New South Wales v. South Africans (Sydney) 1910–11
1739—40	New South Wales v. A. E. Stoddart's XI (Sydney) 1897–98
1723—31	England v. Australia (Leeds) 1948
1716—40	New South Wales v. South Australia (Sydney) 1907–08
1704—39	J. Ryder's XI v. W. M. Woodfull's XI (Sydney) 1929–30
1683—40	Victoria v. South Australia (Melbourne) 1920–21
1677—37	Barbados v. Trinidad (Barbados) 1926–27
1672—39	D. G. Bradman's XI v. A. L. Hassett's XI (Melbourne) 1948–49
1661—36	West Indies v. Australia (Barbados) 1954–55
1647—30	Bengal Cyclone XI v. Bijapur Famine XI (Bombay) 1942–43
1646—40	Australia v. South Africa (Adelaide) 1910–11
1635—31	Trinidad v. Barbados (Trinidad)..1945–46
1619—40	Australia v. England (Melbourne) 1924–25
1615—40	New South Wales v. Victoria (Sydney) 1907–08
1611—40	Australia v. England (Sydney) 1924–25
1611—24	Holkar v. Mysore (Indore) 1945–46
1607—22	New South Wales v. M.C.C. (Sydney) 1929–30
1605—38	New South Wales v. Queensland (Sydney) 1927–28
1601—29	England v. Australia (Lord's) 1930
1587—40	British Guiana v. Barbados (Georgetown) 1929–30
1581—39	South Australia v. New South Wales (Adelaide) 1921–22
1573—36	South Australia v. New South Wales (Adelaide) 1926–27
1571—38	British Guiana v. Trinidad (Georgetown) 1937–38
1570—40	New South Wales v. South Australia (Sydney) 1912–13
1567—37	Auckland v. Wellington (Auckland) 1936–37
1562—37	Australia v. England (Melbourne) 1946–47
1560—37	New South Wales v. Queensland (Sydney) 1928–29
1558—30	Victoria v. New South Wales (Melbourne) 1926–27
1555—40	Holkar v. Gujerat (Indore) 1950–51
1554—35	Australia v. England (Melbourne) 1928–29
1554—40	Wellington v. Auckland (Wellington) 1922–23
1553—33	Australian XI v. Rest of Australia (Sydney)..........................1898–99
1545—34	Bombay v. Holkar (Bombay) 1951–52
1541—35	Australia v. England (Sydney) 1903–04
1541—28	New South Wales v. M.C.C. (Sydney) 1924–25
1533—33	New South Wales v. Victoria (Sydney) 1924–25
1531—39	Wellington v. Auckland (Wellington) 1923–24
1528—24	West Indies v. England (Trinidad) 1953–54
1516—37	Barbados v. British Guiana (Barbados) 1949–50
1514—40	Australia v. England (Sydney) 1894–95
1513—29	New South Wales v. Victoria (Sydney) 1927–28
1510—38	South Australia v. New South Wales (Adelaide) 1920–21
1504—39	Victoria v. Tasmania (Melbourne) 1912–13
1503—37	South Australia v. Victoria (Adelaide) 1924–25
1502—40	Queensland v. New South Wales (Brisbane)..........................1926–27
1502—28	M.C.C. v. New Zealanders (Lord's).....................................1927
1502—29	Australia v. England (Adelaide) 1946–47
1501—37	Canterbury v. Otago (Christchurch) 1931–32
1500—35	South Australia v. New South Wales (Adelaide) 1929–30

Matches of over 1400 runs in England are:

1723—31	England v. Australia (Leeds), 5-day match 1948
1601—29	England v. Australia (Lord's), 4-day match 1930
1502—28	M.C.C. v. New Zealanders (Lord's).....................................1927
1496—24	England v. Australia (Nottingham).......................................1938
1494—37	England v. Australia (Oval) 1934
1492—33	Worcestershire v. Oxford U. (Worcester) 1904
1477—32	Hampshire v. Oxford U. (Southampton) 1913

Runs Wkts.
1477—33	England v. South Africa (Oval)	1947
1475—27	Northamptonshire v. Surrey (Northampton)	1920
1469—30	Surrey v. Cambridge U. (Oval)	1921
1458—31	England v. South Africa (Nottingham)	1947
1451—36	Sussex v. Kent (Hastings)	1929
1446—33	Hampshire v. Kent (Southampton)	1911
1443—34	Middlesex v. Gloucestershire (Lord's)	1938
1427—21	Sussex v. Surrey (Hastings)	1902
1426—30	Cambridge U. v. Free Foresters (Cambridge)	1934
1425—16	Worcestershire v. Leicestershire (Worcester)	1906
1424—30	Hampshire v. Worcestershire (Bournemouth)	1905
1423—37	North v. South (Torquay)	1955
1422—34	Kent v. Essex (Gravesend)	1938
1422—27	England v. West Indies (Nottingham)	1957
1417—32	North v. South (Kingston)	1947
1414—24	Essex v. Kent (Brentwood)	1934
1410—28	Sussex v. Oxford U. (Hove)	1895
1409—25	Surrey v. Middlesex (Oval)	1919
1409—29	Oxford U. v. M.C.C. (Oxford)	1919
1406—37	Navy & Army v. Oxford & Cambridge U. (Portsmouth)	1911
1405—24	Leicestershire v. Middlesex (Leicester)	1947
1402—40	Sussex v. Cambridge U. (Hove)	1891

Lowest Match Aggregates

The lowest aggregates for a completed match are:

Runs Wkts.
105—31	M.C.C. v. Australians (Lord's)	1878
134—30	England v. The B's (Lord's)	1831
147—40	Kent v. Sussex (Sevenoaks)	1828
149—30	England v. Kent (Lord's)	1858
151—30	Canterbury v. Otago (Christchurch)	1866–67
153—37	M.C.C. v. Sussex (Lord's)	1843
153—31	Otago v. Canterbury (Dunedin)	1896–97
158—22	Surrey v. Worcestershire (Oval)	1954
165—30	Yorkshire v. Nottinghamshire (Sheffield)	1888
165—30	Middlesex v. Somerset (Lord's)	1899
171—29	Oxford U. v. M.C.C. (Oxford)	1877
175—35	M.C.C. v. Surrey (Lord's)	1872
175—29	Essex v. Yorkshire (Leyton)	1901
176—32	Otago v. Tasmania (Dunedin)	1883–84
181—33	M.C.C. v. North (Lord's)	1848
183—33	Gentlemen of Kent v. M.C.C. (Chislehurst)	1838
183—37	Victoria v. New South Wales (Melbourne)	1855–56
183—30	Lancashire v. Derbyshire (Manchester)	1871
184—40	Fast Bowlers v. Slow Bowlers (Lord's)	1849
184—30	Gentlemen of England v. Gentlemen of Kent (Lord's)	1850
185—30	Kent v. England (Canterbury)	1846
187—36	M.C.C. v. Sussex (Lord's)	1890
188—32	England v. Kent (Lord's)	1834
188—30	Gentlemen v. Players (Lord's)	1837
188—30	M.C.C. v. Sussex (Lord's)	1838
188—30	M.C.C. v. Oxford U. (Lord's)	1863
188—32	Orissa v. Bihar (Patna)	1958–59
191—40	Oxford U. v. Australians (Oxford)	1886
193—31	Oxford U. v. M.C.C. (Oxford)	1868
193—29	Yorkshire v. Worcestershire (Bradford)	1900
195—40	Wellington v. Auckland (Wellington)	1862–63
197—30	England v. Surrey (Lord's)	1805
197—31	M.C.C. v. Sussex (Lord's)	1856
198—30	Kent v. England (Bromley)	1841
198—22	Eastern Province v. Transvaal (Port Elizabeth)	1937–38

The lowest aggregates for a match in which all 40 wickets fell are:

147—40	Kent v. Sussex (Sevenoaks)	1828
184—40	Fast Bowlers v. Slow Bowlers (Lord's)	1849
191—40	Oxford U. v. Australians (Oxford)	1886
195—40	Wellington v. Auckland (Wellington)	1862–63

Runs Wkts.
210—40   M.C.C. v. Middlesex (Lord's) 1815
210—40   England v. Kent (Lord's) 1841
210—40   M.C.C. v. Kent (Lord's) 1856
210—40   M.C.C. v. Kent (Lord's) 1879
223—40   Lancashire v. Yorkshire (Manchester) 1893
226—40   Otago v. Canterbury (Dunedin) 1863–64

Tie Matches

The first recorded tie match was played at Hambledon in 1783, Hambledon (with Lumpy) 'tie-ing' with Kent (with Bedster and Yalden). Kent actually won the match, as it was discovered later that one of the scorers had cut a deep notch after the eleventh run on one occasion, instead of after the tenth as was the usual practice. Pratt, the scorer, later produced his stick, but the other scorer either could not, or would not, produce his.

The tie law was amended in 1948 to the effect that the match must have been played out, a decision which would have severely cut the number of tie matches in earlier years.

M.C.C. (69 & 107) v. Oxford & Cambridge U. (115 & 61) at Lord's 1839
Surrey (112 & 160) v. Kent (127 & 145) at the Oval 1847
Kent lost their last three wickets when scores were level.
Surrey (204 & 93) v. M.C.C. (175 & 122) at the Oval 1868
Surrey (93 & 186) v. Middlesex (112 & 167) at the Oval 1868
Wellington (63 & 118) v. Nelson (111 & 70) at Wellington 1873–74
Surrey (215 & 245) v. Middlesex (138 & 322) at the Oval 1876
When the game ended it was announced that Middlesex had won by one run, but when the scorers balanced their figures they found another single, altered Surrey's second innings total to 245 and made the result a tie.
Gentlemen (235 & 149) v. Players (203 & 181) at the Oval 1883
The only representative match to end in a tie.
Surrey (97 & 124) v. Lancashire (147 & 74) at the Oval 1894
Worcestershire (224 & 209) v. South Africans (293 & 140) at Worcester 1901
Middlesex (272 & 225) v. South Africans (287 & 210) at Lord's 1904
Surrey (125 & 161) v. Kent (202 & 84) at the Oval 1905
Lancashire (253 & 168—7) v. England XI (193 & 228—6d) at Blackpool.............................1905
Lancashire had three wickets to fall with two balls to go, but insufficient time remained for another batsman to go in.
M.C.C. (371 & 69) v. Leicestershire (239 & 201) at Lord's 1907
Jamaica (173 & 227) v. M.C.C. (269 & 131) at Kingston 1910–11
Somerset (243 & 103) v. Sussex (242 & 104) at Taunton 1919
The last Sussex batsman, H. J. Heygate, was not allowed to bat under Law 45. He had retired ill earlier in the match, and as it was assumed he would not bat, one of the Somerset players invoked the 'two-minute' rule.
Orange Free State (100 & 349) v. Eastern Province (225 & 224—8) at Bloemfontein 1925–26
Eastern Province had two wickets in hand. The match was ruled as an Eastern Province win for the Currie Cup table.
Essex (178 & 137—9) v. Somerset (208 & 107) at Chelmsford 1926
The ninth Essex wicket fell half a minute before time, and M.C.C. ruled that the match ranked as a tie.
Gloucestershire (72 & 202) v. Australians (157 & 117) at Bristol 1930
Victoria (327 & 177—3) v. M.C.C. (321 & 183—9d) at Melbourne 1932–33
The third Victorian wicket fell to the last ball of the match with one run needed for victory.
Worcestershire (130 & 142) v. Somerset (131 & 141) at Kidderminster 1939
Southern Punjab (167 & 146) v. Baroda (106 & 207) at Patiala 1945–46
Baroda won the spin of a coin to decide the right to enter the final of the Ranji Trophy.
Essex (267 & 239) v. Northamptonshire (215 & 291) at Ilford 1947
Hampshire (363 & 224—7d) v. Lancashire (367—9d & 220) at Bournemouth 1947
D. G. Bradman's XI (434 & 402—9) v. A. L. Hassett's XI (406 & 430) at Melbourne 1948–49
Hampshire (180 & 152) v. Kent (162 & 170) at Southampton 1950
By a strange coincidence, the bowlers of both sides delivered 137 overs in the match, but Hampshire were credited with 11 no-balls by the Kent bowlers.
Sussex (123 & 131) v. Warwickshire (138 & 116) at Hove 1952
Essex (261 & 231) v. Lancashire (266 & 226—7d) at Brentwood 1952
Northamptonshire (182 & 226) v. Middlesex (96 & 312) at Peterborough 1953
Yorkshire (351—4d & 113) v. Leicestershire (328 & 136) at Huddersfield 1954
Sussex (172 & 120) v. Hampshire (153 & 139) at Eastbourne 1955
Victoria (244 & 197) v. New South Wales (281 & 160) at Sydney 1956–57
T. N. Pearce's XI (313—7d & 258) v. New Zealanders (268 & 303—8d) at Scarborough 1958
Essex (364—6d & 176—8d) v. Gloucestershire (329 & 211) at Leyton 1959

The Middlesex v. Yorkshire match at Prince's in 1873 ended on an unusual note, the scorers announcing that Middlesex had won, when in fact the score was a tie and one run still needed for victory. Stumps were drawn, but the mistake was then noticed, the stumps re-erected, and the necessary run scored to give Middlesex a ten-wickets victory.

The Players (204 & 112) beat the Gentlemen (204 & 111) by one run at Hove in 1881, after there had been a tie on first innings.

Warwickshire (201) and Nottinghamshire (87 & 114—9) played a drawn match at Birmingham in 1926, the game ending with scores level and the last two Nottinghamshire batsmen together.

Essex (261 & 327—8) and Nottinghamshire (371 & 217—8d) had a drawn match at Southend in 1948, which would have been recorded as a tie under the old laws.

The nearest approach to a tie match in Test cricket was recorded at Durban in 1948–49, when England needed one run to win off the last ball of the match. A leg-bye off C. Gladwin gave England a two-wickets victory off the last possible ball.

Cambridge U. (359—6d & 205—3d) and Middlesex (244 & 320—9) played a drawn match at Cambridge in 1951, the game ending with the last two county batsmen together and one run needed for victory.

Sussex (332 & 199—6d) and Worcestershire (323 & 208—5) played a drawn match at Eastbourne in 1957, the visitors needing one run for victory when the match ended—under the old laws the result would have been a tie.

First-Class Matches Completed in One Day

A number of first-class matches have been started and completed in the course of a single day's cricket, excluding the famous 'freak declaration' matches of the 1930's. Possibly the most dismal experience was that of Somerset in 1894. Losing a match to Lancashire on July 17th in a day, they went on to Huddersfield, only to lose again in the course of a day's play on July 19th.

The complete list of matches completed in one day is as follows:

1831	The B's (18 & 35) v. England (81) at Lord's on June 13th.
1837	Cambridge U. (81 & 54—2) v. M.C.C. (70 & 64) at Cambridge on May 18th.
1840	M.C.C. (125) v. Oxford U. (34 & 86) at Lord's on July 9th.
1848	M.C.C. (54 & 81—8) v. Cambridge U. (70 & 64) at Lord's on June 19th.
1848	M.C.C. (167 & 19—3) v. Surrey (56 & 128) at Lord's on July 17th.
1849	Gentlemen of Kent (87 & 29) v. Gentlemen of England (85 & 32—5) at Lord's on July 2nd.
1850	Gentlemen of Kent (59 & 17) v. Gentlemen of England (108) at Lord's on July 1st.
1850	North (131) v. South (36 & 76) at Lord's on July 15th.
1853	Gentlemen of Kent (69 & 65) v. Gentlemen of England (184) at Lord's on July 4th.
1854	M.C.C. (154) v. Surrey (60 & 47) at Lord's on June 12th.
1856	M.C.C. (88 & 11—1) v. Sussex (75 & 23) at Lord's on June 2nd.
1857	Surrey (166) v. Sussex (35 & 31) at the Oval on July 16th.
1858	Kent (33 & 41) v. England (73 & 2—0) at Lord's on July 5th.
1862–63	Auckland (82 & 69) v. Wellington (22 & 22) at Auckland on December 6th.
1863	M.C.C. (31 & 53) v. Oxford U. (104) at Lord's on June 18th.
1866–67	Canterbury (25 & 32) v. Otago (94) at Christchurch on February 7th.
1868	North of Thames (73 & 56) v. South of Thames (106 & 25—1) at Lord's on June 8th.
1872	M.C.C. (16 & 71) v. Surrey (49 & 39—5) at Lord's on May 14th.
1874	Middlesex (61 & 47) v. Oxford U. (123) at Princes on June 18th.
1875	North (90 & 72) v. South (123 & 41—0) at Lord's on May 17th.
1877	Oxford U. (12 & 35) v. M.C.C. (124) at Oxford on May 24th.
1878	M.C.C. (33 & 19) v. Australians (41 & 12—1) at Lord's on May 27th.
1880	Oxford U. (53 & 75) v. M.C.C. (85 & 41—9) at Oxford on May 28th.
1884	England XI (82 & 26) v. Australians (76 & 33—6) at Aston, Birmingham on May 26th.
1886	M.C.C. (30 & 92) v. Lancashire (53 & 71—4) at Lord's on May 18th.
1887	North (99 & 46—4) v. South (61 & 82) at Lord's on May 30th.
1888	Lancashire (35 & 63) v. Surrey (123) at Manchester on August 2nd.
1889–90	Auckland (62 & 68) v. Otago (48 & 83—2) at Auckland on December 26th.
1891	M.C.C. (127) v. Nottinghamshire (21 & 69) at Lord's on June 1st.
1892	Lancashire (116 & 32—2) v. Somerset (88 & 58) at Manchester on August 9th.
1893–94	Auckland (93 & 102) v. New South Wales (185 & 14—1) at Auckland on January 20th.
1894	M.C.C. (103) v. Sussex (42 & 59) at Lord's on May 2nd.
1894	Lancashire (231) v. Somerset (31 & 132) at Manchester on July 17th.
1894	Yorkshire (173) v. Somerset (74 & 94) at Huddersfield on July 19th.
1897	Leicestershire (35 & 35) v. Surrey (164) at Leicester on June 10th.
1898	(a) Hampshire (42 & 36) v. Yorkshire (157) at Southampton on May 27th.
1899	(b) Middlesex (86) v. Somerset (35 & 44) at Lord's on May 23rd.
1900	Yorkshire (99) v. Worcestershire (43 & 51) at Bradford on May 7th.
1903	M.C.C. (150 & 10—1) v. London County (72 & 87) at Lord's on May 20th.
1906–07	Transvaal (180 & 4—0) v. Orange Free State (118 & 64) at Johannesburg on December 30th.

1908   Middlesex (92 & 24—3) v. Philadelphians (58 & 55) at Lord's on July 20th.
1909   Gloucestershire (33 & 81) v. Middlesex (145) at Bristol on August 26th.
1912–13 Eastern Province (209) v. Orange Free State (57 & 121) at Port Elizabeth on December 26th.
1919   Kent (261—6d) v. Sussex (60 & 78) at Tonbridge on June 21st.
1925   Lancashire (130 & 20—1) v. Somerset (74 & 73) at Manchester on May 21st.
1934–35 Madras (130) v. Mysore (48 & 59) at Madras on November 4th.
1937   Ireland (79 & 30) v. New Zealanders (64 & 46—2) at Dublin on September 11th.
1947   Derbyshire (231) v. Somerset (68 & 38) at Chesterfield on June 11th.
1950   Lancashire (239) v. Sussex (101 & 51) at Manchester on July 12th.
1953   Surrey (146) v. Warwickshire (45 & 52) at the Oval on May 16th.
1953   (c) Somerset (55 & 79) v. Lancashire (158) at Bath on June 6th.
1960   Kent (187) v. Worcestershire (25 & 61) at Tunbridge Wells on June 15th.

(a) Match awarded to H. Baldwin as a benefit.
(b) Match awarded to W. Flowers as a benefit.
(c) Match awarded to H. T. F. Buse as a benefit.

Teams Scoring Four or More Centuries in an Innings

SIX

HOLKAR (912—8d) v. MYSORE (Indore) 1945–46
  K. V. Bhandarkar 142, C. T. Sarwate 101, M. M. Jagdale 164, C. K. Nayudu 101, B. B. Nimbalkar 172, R. Pratapsingh 100.

FIVE

NEW SOUTH WALES (918) v. SOUTH AUSTRALIA (Sydney) 1900–01
  F. A. Iredale 118, M. A. Noble 153, S. E. Gregory 168, R. A. Duff 119, L. O. S. Poidevin 140*.
AUSTRALIA (758—8d) v. WEST INDIES (Kingston) 1954–55
  C. C. McDonald 127, R. N. Harvey 204, K. R. Miller 109, R. G. Archer 128, R. Benaud 121.

FOUR

YORKSHIRE (887) v. WARWICKSHIRE (Birmingham) 1896
  R. Peel 210*, F. S. Jackson 117, E. Wainwright 126, Lord Hawke 166.
DERBYSHIRE (645) v. HAMPSHIRE (Derby) 1898
  L. G. Wright 134, W. Storer 100, W. Chatterton 142, G. Davidson 108.
LANCASHIRE (580) v. SOMERSET (Manchester) 1904
  A. C. MacLaren 151, J. T. Tyldesley 103, A. H. Hornby 114, W. R. Cuttell 101.
M.C.C. (660—8d) v. SOUTH AUSTRALIA (Sydney) 1907–08
  A. O. Jones 119, J. Hardstaff sen. 135, L. C. Braund 160, J. N. Crawford 114.
KENT (601—8d) v. SOMERSET (Taunton) 1908
  James Seymour 129, F. E. Woolley 105, A. P. Day 118, E. Humphreys 149.
AUSTRALIAN XI (610—6d) v. NEW ZEALAND XI (Auckland) 1913–14
  E. L. Waddy 140, C. E. Dolling 104, W. W. Armstrong 110*, J. N. Crawford 134.
NEW SOUTH WALES (690) v. SOUTH AUSTRALIA (Adelaide) 1919–20
  W. Bardsley 106, J. Bogle 200, T. J. E. Andrews 103, C. Kelleway 121*.
MIDDLESEX (543—4d) v. SUSSEX (Lord's) 1920
  P. F. Warner 139, H. W. Lee 119, J. W. Hearne 116*, N. E. Haig 131. The first four batsmen on the side.
NEW SOUTH WALES (786) v. SOUTH AUSTRALIA (Adelaide) 1922–23
  J. M. Taylor 159, A. F. Kippax 170, H. L. Hendry 146, W. A. Oldfield 118.
VICTORIA (617—6d) v. M.C.C. (Melbourne) 1922–23
  H. S. B. Love 192, R. L. Park 101, V. S. Ransford 118*, A. E. Liddicut 102.
MIDDLESEX (642—3d) v. HAMPSHIRE (Southampton) 1923
  H. L. Dales 103, H. W. Lee 107, J. W. Hearne 232, E. Hendren 177*. The first four batsmen on the side.
NEW SOUTH WALES (645) v. REST OF AUSTRALIA (except Victoria) (Sydney) 1924–25
  H. L. Collins 105, J. M. Taylor 111, A. F. Kippax 115, C. Kelleway 101.
VICTORIA (1107) v. NEW SOUTH WALES (Melbourne) 1926–27
  W. M. Woodfull 133, W. H. Ponsford 352, H. L. Hendry 100, J. Ryder 295. The first four batsmen on the side.
BARBADOS (715—9d) v. BRITISH GUIANA (Barbados) 1926–27
  P. H. Tarilton 120, G. Challenor 104, E. L. G. Hoad 115, C. A. Browne 131*.
NEW SOUTH WALES (571) v. NEW ZEALANDERS (Sydney) 1927–28
  J. M. Gregory 152, T. J. E. Andrews 134, A. F. Kippax 119, A. A. Jackson 104.

NEW SOUTH WALES (533) v. VICTORIA (Sydney) 1927–28
    A. F. Kippax 134, J. G. Morgan 110, W. A. Oldfield 101, C. O. Nicholls 110.
NOTTINGHAMSHIRE (656—3d) v. WARWICKSHIRE (Coventry) 1928
    G. Gunn 148, W. W. Whysall 132, W. Walker 146*, F. Barratt 139*.
M.C.C. (502) v. TASMANIA (Launceston) 1932–33
    H. Sutcliffe 101, Nawab of Pataudi 109, L. E. G. Ames 107, E. Paynter 102.
VICTORIA (558) v. NEW SOUTH WALES (Melbourne) 1934–35
    L. P. O'Brien 126, K. E. Rigg 111, L. S. Darling 106, E. H. Bromley 102.
SOUTH AUSTRALIA (644—7d) v. QUEENSLAND (Adelaide) 1934–35
    V. Y. Richardson 185, H. C. Nitschke 116, A. R. Lonergan 137, C. L. Badcock 137. The first
    four batsmen on the side.
AUCKLAND (590) v. CANTERBURY (Auckland) 1937–38
    P. E. Whitelaw 108, A. J. Postles 103, V. J. Scott 122, A. M. Matheson 112.
AUSTRALIANS (708—5d) v. CAMBRIDGE UNIVERSITY (Cambridge) 1938
    J. H. Fingleton 111, D. G. Bradman 137, C. L. Badcock 186, A. L. Hassett 220*.
ENGLAND (658—8d) v. AUSTRALIA (Nottingham) 1938
    L. Hutton 100, C. J. Barnett 126, E. Paynter 216*, D. C. S. Compton 102.
SUSSEX (631—4d) v. NORTHAMPTONSHIRE (Northampton) 1938
    John Langridge 227, J. H. Parks 106, G. Cox 101, H. T. Bartlett 101*.
M.C.C. (676) v. GRIQUALAND WEST (Kimberley) 1938–39
    L. Hutton 149, W. J. Edrich 109, E. Paynter 158, N. W. D. Yardley 142.
SOUTH AUSTRALIA (821—7d) v. QUEENSLAND (Adelaide) 1939–40
    K. L. Ridings 151, D. G. Bradman 138, C. L. Badcock 236, M. G. Waite 137.
CRICKET CLUB OF INDIA (654) v. C. K. NAYUDU'S XI (Bombay) 1944–45
    V. Mankad 121, V. M. Merchant 130, V. S. Hazare 168, R. S. Cooper 127*.
BOMBAY (645) v. BARODA (Bombay) 1945–46
    K. C. Ibrahim 132, V. M. Merchant 171, U. M. Merchant 136, K. M. Rangnekar 113.
INDIANS (533—3d) v. SUSSEX (Hove) 1946
    V. M. Merchant 205, V. Mankad 105, Nawab of Pataudi 110*, L. Amarnath 106. The only
    four batsmen to go to the wicket.
SURREY (706—4d) v. NOTTINGHAMSHIRE (Nottingham) 1947
    D. G. W. Fletcher 194, H. S. Squires 154, J. F. Parker 108*, E. R. T. Holmes 122*.
BOMBAY (632—7d) v. MAHARASHTRA (Bombay) 1947–48
    K. C. Ibrahim 159, P. J. Dickinson 122, M. M. Dalvi 143, M. N. Raiji 130.
AUSTRALIANS (721) v. ESSEX (Southend) 1948
    W. A. Brown 153, D. G. Bradman 187, S. J. E. Loxton 120, R. A. Saggers 104*.
WEST INDIES (631) v. INDIA (New Delhi) 1948–49
    C. L. Walcott 152, G. E. Gomez 101, E. D. Weekes 128, R. J. Christiani 107.
BENGAL (760) v. ASSAM (Cuttack) 1951–52
    P. Roy 146, S. Bose 145, A. D. Gupte 117, C. S. Nayudu 119.
BRITISH GUIANA (601—3d) v. JAMAICA (Georgetown) 1956–57
    B. H. Pairaudeau 111, R. Kanhai 129, B. F. Butcher 154*, J. Solomon 114*.
PUNJAB UNIVERSITY (702) v. SIND UNIVERSITY (Karachi) 1958–59
    Saeed Ahmed 140, Khalid Aziz 106, Mohammed Yusuf 115, Zafar Altaf 111.

Each of the seven Australian batsmen to be dismissed in an innings of 679—7d v. Oxford U. (Oxford) 1938 completed fifty—J. H. Fingleton 124, W. A. Brown 72, D. G. Bradman 58, S. J. McCabe 110, A. G. Chipperfield 53, A. L. Hassett 146 and M. G. Waite 54. C. W. Walker, the 'not out' batsman, was 31*.

Matches Dominated by Batting

For the purpose of this record only matches in which 1,200 runs were scored have been included.

Avge.

189	Cambridge U. (594—4d) v. West Indians (730—3) at Cambridge	1950
89	Worcs. (380 & 344—2) v. Leics. (701—4d) at Worcester	1906
81	Leics. (609—8d) v. Sussex (686—8) at Leicester	1900
75	Glos. (643—5d) v. Notts. (467 & 168—2) at Bristol	1946
73	Surrey (551—7) v. Yorkshire (704) at the Oval	1899
72	N.S.W. (349 & 364—3) v. M.C.C. (734—7d) at Sydney	1928–29
72	N.S.W. (629—8d & 305—3d) v. M.C.C. (469 & 204—2) at Sydney	1929–30
72	Notts. (401 & 201—4) v. Surrey (706—4d) at Nottingham	1947
70	British Guiana (601—5d & 60—1) v. Jamaica (469) at Georgetown	1956–57
67	Sussex (705—8d & 170—4) v. Surrey (552) at Hastings	1902
67	O.F.S. (552) v. Natal (402 & 452—1) at Bloemfontein	1926–27
67	Glamorgan (196 & 577—4) v. Glos. (505—5d) at Newport	1939
67	Holkar (912—8d) v. Mysore (190 & 509—6) at Indore	1945–46
67	Notts (191 & 519—5) v. Derby (496—3d) at Nottingham	1947
66	Somerset (560—8d) v. Sussex (236 & 466—1) at Taunton	1901

Avge.

66	Surrey (475—9d & 162—2) v. Australians (629) at the Oval	1934
66	Maharashtra (675) v. Bombay (650) at Poona	1940–41
65	England (627—9d & 123—0d) v. Australia (491 & 66—1) at Manchester	1934
65	India (273 & 333—3) v. West Indies (629—6d) at Bombay	1948–49
64	N.S.W. (713—6d) v. Victoria (265 & 510—7) at Sydney	1928–29
63	West Indies (681–8d & 212–4d) v. England (537 & 98–3) at Trinidad	1953–54
62	Essex (453 & 242–1) v. Sussex (611) at Leyton	1905
62	England (658—8d) v. Australia (411 & 427—6) at Nottingham	1938
62	Hants. (594—6d) v. Glos. (317 & 403—5) at Southampton	1911
62	Maharashtra (798) v. Western India States (442) at Poona	1940–41
62	Bombay (651 & 714—8d) v. Maharashtra (407 & 604) at Poona	1948–49
61	Sussex (415—5d & 281) v. South Africans (555—6d & 45—0) at Hove	1947
60	Cambridge U. (533) v. Free Foresters (636—7d & 223—6) at Cambridge	1938

Collapses and Recoveries

During the history of cricket there have been many cases of sudden changes in the fortunes of a team in the course of a match, and a list of the outstanding cases is given.

VICTORY AFTER LARGE ARREARS ON FIRST INNINGS

Lancashire (205 & 172) beat Oxford U. (315 & 42) by 20 runs after following-on and losing eight second innings wickets before clearing the arrears—at Manchester in 1888.

England (325 & 437) beat Australia (586 & 166) by 10 runs after being 261 runs behind on first innings—at Sydney in 1894–95.

Somerset (87 & 630) beat Yorkshire (325 & 113) by 279 runs after being 238 runs behind on first innings—at Leeds in 1901.

South Australia (304 & 454) beat Lord Hawke's XI (553 & 108) by 97 runs after being 249 runs behind on first innings and following-on under the compulsory law in effect at the time—at Adelaide in 1902–03.

Derbyshire (548 & 149—1) beat Essex (597 & 97) by nine wickets after Essex had scored 597 (P. A. Perrin 343*) in their first innings—at Chesterfield in 1904.

England XI (43 & 326) beat Australians (174 & 167) by 28 runs after a first innings collapse, thus inflicting the first defeat to the touring team—at Eastbourne in 1921.

Hampshire (15 & 521) beat Warwickshire (223 & 158) by 155 runs, after being 208 runs behind on first innings and losing six second innings wickets before clearing off the arrears—at Birmingham in 1922.

Victoria (502 & 265—3) beat New South Wales (614 & 152) by seven wickets after New South Wales had scored 614 runs in their first innings—at Sydney in 1924–25.

Barbados (175 & 726—7d) beat Trinidad (559 & 217) by 125 runs after being 364 runs behind on first innings—at Barbados in 1926–27.

Natal (115 & 458) beat Transvaal (370 & 190) by 13 runs after being 255 runs behind on first innings and following-on—at Cape Town in 1932–33.

COLLAPSES

The following are some of the outstanding collapses:

Surrey (76 all out) lost their last nine wickets for six runs v. Yorkshire (Sheffield) 1867—the second wicket fell at 70.

M.C.C. (16 all out) lost their first seven wickets before a run was scored v. Surrey at Lords in 1872—the eighth wicket fell at 2, the ninth wicket fell at 8 and the last wicket partnership doubling the score.

Australia (70 all out) lost their first six wickets for seven runs v. England (Manchester) 1888.

Leicestershire (28 all out) lost their first seven wickets for four runs v. Australians (Leicester) 1899.

M.C.C. (139 all out) lost their first seven wickets for only eight runs, v. Lancashire (Lord's) 1890.

The Middlesex v. Somerset match at Lord's in 1899 was completed in a little over three hours' play. Somerset collapsed in their first innings, their first eight wickets falling for eight runs in four overs, the total eventually reaching 35. In their second innings they lost five wickets for five runs, the eighth at 18 and were all out for 44. Middlesex scored 86 and won the match by an innings and seven runs.

Surrey (59 all out) lost their last nine wickets for four runs v. Kent (Canterbury) 1902. R. Abel was out immediately the innings started but T. Hayward and E. G. Hayes took the score to 55 before they were parted.

Gloucestershire (36 all out) lost their first five wickets for three runs—all overthrows—their seventh wicket at 6 and eighth at 11 v. Yorkshire (Sheffield) 1903.

Nottinghamshire (393 all out) collapsed and lost their ten wickets for 90 runs after A. O. Jones (187) and J. Iremonger (138) had opened with a first wicket stand of 303, v. Gloucestershire (Nottingham) 1904.

Northamptonshire (60 all out) lost their first seven wickets to the bowling of C. Blythe for 4 runs (including 2 extras) v. Kent (Northampton) 1907. Blythe (10—30 & 7—18) went on to take seventeen wickets in a day.

Natal lost their first six wickets for five runs v. M.C.C. (Pietermaritzburg) 1909–10. After a stand of 36 for the seventh wicket, the score changed from 41—6 to 50 all out.

Sussex were all out for 237 v. Somerset (Hove) 1919, after J. Vine (91) and R. R. Relf (111) had made an opening stand of 204 runs.

Hampshire were left to score 66 runs to win by Lancashire (Liverpool) 1921. They reached 54—5 but were all out for 64, losing the match by one run.

Leicestershire were left to score 37 runs to win by Gloucestershire (Ashby-de-la-Zouch) 1922. They lost their first five wickets for five runs, the seventh at eight, Geary and Sidwell then making a stand to bring victory by two wickets.

Worcestershire needed only four runs to win v. Glamorgan (Worcester) 1923, but lost three wickets without a run scored, the winning hit being made off the tenth ball.

H. D. G. Leveson-Gower's XI needed 28 runs to win v. West Indians (Scarborough) 1923. The tourists' bowling proved so effective that six wickets—J. B. Hobbs, G. T. S. Stevens, E. Tyldesley, W. Rhodes, A. P. F. Chapman and F. T. Mann—fell for 19 runs before J. W. H. T. Douglas and P. G. H. Fender hit off the remaining runs to secure a four wickets victory.

Gloucestershire (92 all out) lost their first five wickets for three runs v. Hampshire (Southampton) 1924. The total of 92 was due almost entirely to the batting of F. G. Rogers, who scored 69 out of the 91 runs from the bat, his first 50 being scored out of 60 in 45 minutes.

Surrey (77 all out) lost seven wickets for three runs at one point of their innings—the second at 52, third, fourth and fifth at 54 and sixth, seventh and eighth at 55—v. Glamorgan (Cardiff) 1926.

Gloucestershire were all out for 133 v. Glamorgan (Cheltenham) 1926, after the opening pair—A. E. Dipper (77) and C. S. Barrett (39)—had added 116 runs.

Kent collapsed from 221—4 to 223 all out (both no-balls) v. Gloucestershire (Folkestone) 1928.

Warwickshire (69 all out) lost their first four wickets before a run had been scored, v. Middlesex (Lord's) 1932.

Derbyshire (47 all out) lost their last nine wickets for six runs v. Hampshire (Portsmouth) 1933, the scoreboard changing from 41—1 to 47 all out. G. S. Boyes (9·1-6-5-6) went on to bowl at 41.

Glamorgan (245—9) lost their first five wickets for 10 runs, and their ninth at 114, before the last pair added 131 runs in an hour without being parted, v. South Africans (Cardiff) 1935.

A probable collapse was checked by a declaration at Worcester in 1935. Glamorgan lost two wickets for four runs off the first four balls of their second innings and immediately declared.

Muslims (246 all out) lost their last eight wickets for 40 runs, the score changing from 206—2 to 246 all out, v. Europeans (Bombay) 1938–39.

Derbyshire needed to score 208 runs for victory v. Sussex (Derby) 1939, and reached 185—2, but their last eight wickets fell for only nine runs and they lost by 14 runs.

Queensland (133 all out) lost their last five wickets for only one run, the score changing from 132—5 to 133 all out, v. South Australia (Brisbane) 1939–40.

New Zealand (42 all out) lost their last eight wickets for five runs in their first Test match with Australia, at Wellington in 1945–46.

Lancashire (91 all out) lost their last seven wickets for only two runs (both leg-byes) in 50 minutes, the score changing from 89—3 to 91, v. Leicestershire (Leicester) 1951.

Gloucestershire (198 all out) lost their last six wickets for one run, the score changing from 197—4 to 198 all out, v. Leicestershire (Bristol) 1953.

Glamorgan lost 16 wickets for 37 runs v. Surrey (Oval) 1957, a first innings score of 56—2 changing to 62 all out and a second innings total of 31 all out (one man absent in each innings).

Leicestershire (214 all out) reached 198 before their first wicket fell, but then lost ten wickets for sixteen runs, v. Middlesex (Lord's) 1960.

RECOVERIES

The following are some of the best recoveries in an innings after a small total had seemed likely:

24—7 to 160 all out	Sussex v. Kent (Hove)	1877
48—7 to 188 all out	M.C.C. v. Yorks. (Scarborough)	1881
21—6 to 298 all out	Gentlemen of England v. Cambridge U (Cambridge)	1886
7—5 to 116 all out	Somerset v. Surrey (Oval)	1896
55—9 to 285 all out	Middx. v. Kent (Lord's)	1899
67—5 to 507—9d	Essex v. Derby (Leyton)	1905
105—6 to 287—9 and won	South Africa v. England (Johannesburg)	1905–06
31—5 to 335 all out	Players v. Gentlemen (Oval)	1906
58—8 to 206 all out	Canterbury v. Otago (Dunedin)	1908–09
118—7 to 653	Australians v. Canterbury (Christchurch)	1913–14
55—6 to 286—8 and won	Notts. v. Hants. (Southampton)	1921
197—7 to 430 all out	Notts. v. Essex (Nottingham)	1923
79—7 to 367 all out	Australians v. Sussex (Hove)	1930
34—5 to 375 all out	Surrey v. Kent (Blackheath)	1930
21—5, 110—9 to 249 all out	Indians v. Scotland (Dundee)	1932
60—5 to 365 all out	Worcs. v. Northants. (Worcester)	1935
150—8 to 326 all out	Sind v. Nawanagar (Karachi)	1938–39

99—8 to 266 all out	Western India States v. Sind (Karachi)	1939–40
63—5 to 387 all out	Rest v. Hindus (Bombay)	1942–43
111—8 to 351 all out	Wellington v. Auckland (Wellington)	1943–44
66—5 to 349 all out	Essex v. Lancs. (Manchester)	1946
39—6 to 308 all out	Northants. v. Surrey (Oval)	1947
44—6 to 247 all out	Maharashtra v. Rest of India (Poona)	1947–48
71—5 to 425—9d	Essex v. Leics. (Westcliff)	1948
59—6 to 249 all out	Maharashtra v. M.C.C. (Poona)	1951–52
30—8 to 148 all out	Oxford U. v. Derby (Oxford)	1958
49—7 to 210 all out	Northants. v. Derby (Derby)	1959

Part II—Batting

Highest Individual Innings

499	Hanif Mohammed: Karachi v. Bahawalpur (Karachi)	1958–59
452*	D. G. Bradman: New South Wales v. Queensland (Sydney)	1929–30
443*	B. B. Nimbalkar: Maharashtra v. Western India States (Poona)	1948–49
437	W. H. Ponsford: Victoria v. Queensland (Melbourne)	1927–28
429	W. H. Ponsford: Victoria v. Tasmania (Melbourne)	1922–23
424	A. C. MacLaren: Lancashire v. Somerset (Taunton)	1895
385	B. Sutcliffe: Otago v. Canterbury (Christchurch)	1952–53
383	C. W. Gregory: New South Wales v. Queensland (Brisbane)	1906–07
369	D. G. Bradman: South Australia v. Tasmania (Adelaide)	1935–36
365*	C. Hill: South Australia v. New South Wales (Adelaide)	1900–01
365*	G. Sobers: West Indies v. Pakistan (Kingston)	1957–58
364	L. Hutton: England v. Australia (Oval)	1938
359*	V. M. Merchant: Bombay v. Maharashtra (Bombay)	1943–44
357*	R. Abel: Surrey v. Somerset (Oval)	1899
357	D. G. Bradman: South Australia v. Victoria (Melbourne)	1935–36
355	B. Sutcliffe: Otago v. Auckland (Dunedin)	1949–50
352	W. H. Ponsford: Victoria v. New South Wales (Melbourne)	1926–27
345	C. G. Macartney: Australians v. Nottinghamshire (Nottingham)	1921
344*	G. Headley: Jamaica v. Lord Tennyson's XI (Kingston)	1931–32
344	W. G. Grace: M.C.C. v. Kent (Canterbury)	1876
343*	P. A. Perrin: Essex v. Derbyshire (Chesterfield)	1904
341	G. H. Hirst: Yorkshire v. Leicestershire (Leicester)	1905
340*	D. G. Bradman: New South Wales v. Victoria (Sydney)	1928–29
338*	R. C. Blunt: Otago v. Canterbury (Christchurch)	1931–32
338	W. W. Read: Surrey v. Oxford U. (Oval)	1888
337	Hanif Mohammed: Pakistan v. West Indies (Barbados)	1957–58
336*	W. R. Hammond: England v. New Zealand (Auckland)	1932–33
336	W. H. Ponsford: Victoria v. South Australia (Melbourne)	1927–28
334	D. G. Bradman: Australia v. England (Leeds)	1930
333	K. S. Duleepsinhji: Sussex v. Northamptonshire (Hove)	1930
332	W. H. Ashdown: Kent v. Essex (Brentwood)	1934
331*	J. D. Robertson: Middlesex v. Worcestershire (Worcester)	1949
325*	H. L. Hendry: Victoria v. New Zealanders (Melbourne)	1925–26
325	C. L. Badcock: South Australia v. Victoria (Adelaide)	1935–36
325	A. Sandham: England v. West Indies (Kingston)	1929–30
324	J. B. Stollmeyer: Trinidad v. British Guiana (Trinidad)	1946–47
322	E. Paynter: Lancashire v. Sussex (Hove)	1937
321	W. L. Murdoch: New South Wales v. Victoria (Sydney)	1881–82
319	Gul Mahomed: Baroda v. Holkar (Baroda)	1946–47
318*	W. G. Grace: Gloucestershire v. Yorkshire (Cheltenham)	1876
317	W. R. Hammond: Gloucestershire v. Nottinghamshire (Gloucester)	1936
316*	V. S. Hazare: Maharashtra v. Baroda (Poona)	1939–40
316*	J. B. Hobbs: Surrey v. Middlesex (Lord's)	1926
316	R. H. Moore: Hampshire v. Warwickshire (Bournemouth)	1937
315*	T. Hayward: Surrey v. Lancashire (Oval)	1898
315*	P. Holmes: Yorkshire v. Middlesex (Lord's)	1925
315*	A. F. Kippax: New South Wales v. Queensland (Sydney)	1927–28
314*	C. L. Walcott: Barbados v. Trinidad (Trinidad)	1945–46
313	H. Sutcliffe: Yorkshire v. Essex (Leyton)	1932
312*	W. W. Keeton: Nottinghamshire v. Middlesex (Oval)	1939
311	J. T. Brown: Yorkshire v. Sussex (Sheffield)	1897
310	H. Gimblett: Somerset v. Sussex (Eastbourne)	1948
309	V. S. Hazare: Rest v. Hindus (Bombay)	1943–44
308*	F. M. Worrell: Barbados v. Trinidad (Barbados)	1943–44
306*	A. Ducat: Surrey v. Oxford U. (Oval)	1919
306*	E. A. B. Rowan: Transvaal v. Natal (Johannesburg)	1939–40
305*	F. E. Woolley: M.C.C. v. Tasmania (Hobart)	1911–12

305* F. R. Foster: Warwickshire v. Worcestershire (Dudley) 1914
305* W. H. Ashdown: Kent v. Derbyshire (Dover) 1935
304* P. H. Tarilton: Barbados v. Trinidad (Barbados) 1919–20
304* A. D. Nourse sen.: Natal v. Transvaal (Johannesburg) 1919–20
304* E. D. Weekes: West Indians v. Cambridge U. (Cambridge) 1950
304 R. M. Poore: Hampshire v. Somerset (Taunton) 1899
304 D. G. Bradman: Australia v. England (Leeds) 1934
303* W. W. Armstrong: Australians v. Somerset (Bath) 1905
302* P. Holmes: Yorkshire v. Hampshire (Portsmouth) 1920
302* W. R. Hammond: Gloucestershire v. Glamorgan (Bristol) 1934
302 W. R. Hammond: Gloucestershire v. Glamorgan (Newport) 1939
301 W. G. Grace: Gloucestershire v. Sussex (Bristol) 1896
301* E. Hendren: Middlesex v. Worcestershire (Dudley) 1933
300* V. T. Trumper: Australians v. Sussex (Hove) 1899
300* F. Watson: Lancashire v. Surrey (Manchester) 1928
300* Imtiaz Ahmed: Prime Minister's XI v. Commonwealth (Bombay) 1950–51
300 J. T. Brown: Yorkshire v. Derbyshire (Chesterfield) 1898
300 D. C. S. Compton: M.C.C. v. North-Eastern Transvaal (Benoni) 1948–49
300 R. Subba Row: Northamptonshire v. Surrey (Oval) 1958
299* D. G. Bradman: Australia v. South Africa (Adelaide) 1931–32
297* H. Moses: New South Wales v. Victoria (Sydney) 1887–88
296 A. O. Jones: Nottinghamshire v. Gloucestershire (Nottingham) 1903
295* J. T. Tyldesley: Lancashire v. Kent (Manchester) 1906
295 L. E. G. Ames: Kent v. Gloucestershire (Folkestone) 1933
295 J. Ryder: Victoria v. New South Wales (Melbourne) 1926–27
294 J. Gunn: Nottinghamshire v. Leicestershire (Nottingham) 1903
293 V. T. Trumper: Australians v. Canterbury (Christchurch) 1913–14
292* V. T. Trumper: New South Wales v. Tasmania (Sydney) 1898–99
292* A. Sandham: Surrey v. Northamptonshire (Oval) 1921
292 L. C. H. Palairet: Somerset v. Hampshire (Southampton) 1896
291 E. Paynter: Lancashire v. Hampshire (Southampton) 1938
290* A. Ducat: Surrey v. Essex (Leyton) 1921
290 W. N. Carson: Auckland v. Otago (Dunedin) 1936–37
290 W. R. Hammond: Gloucestershire v. Kent (Tunbridge Wells) 1934
290 A. R. Morris: Australians v. Gloucestershire (Bristol) 1948

HIGHEST INDIVIDUAL INNINGS FOR AND AGAINST EACH TEAM

(Complete details of each innings over 200 can be found by reference to the list of double centuries.

England:

		For		Against
Derbyshire	274	G. Davidson	343*	P. A. Perrin (Essex)
Essex	343*	P. A. Perrin	332	W. H. Ashdown (Kent)
Glamorgan	287*	E. Davies	302*	W. R. Hammond (Glos.)
Gloucestershire	318*	W. G. Grace	296	A. O. Jones (Notts.)
Hampshire	316	R. H. Moore	302*	P. Holmes (Yorks.)
Kent	332	W. H. Ashdown	344	W. G. Grace (M.C.C.)
Lancashire	424	A. C. MacLaren	315*	T. Hayward (Surrey)
Leicestershire	252*	S. Coe	341	G. H. Hirst (Yorks.)
Middlesex	331*	J. D. Robertson	316*	J. B. Hobbs (Surrey)
Northamptonshire	300	R. Subba Row	333	K. S. Duleepsinhji (Sussex)
Nottinghamshire	312*	W. W. Keeton	345	C. G. Macartney (Australians)
Somerset	310	H. Gimblett	424	A. C. MacLaren (Lancs).
Surrey	357*	R. Abel	300*	F. Watson (Lancs.)
			300	R. Subba Row (Northants.)
Sussex	333	K. S. Duleepsinhji	322	E. Paynter (Lancs.)
Warwickshire	305*	F. R. Foster	316	R. H. Moore (Hants.)
Worcestershire	276	F. L. Bowley	331*	J. D. Robertson (Middx.)
Yorkshire	341	G. H. Hirst	318*	W. G. Grace (Glos.)
M.C.C.	344	W. G. Grace	281*	W. H. Ponsford (Australia)
Oxford U.	281	K. J. Key	338	W. W. Read (Surrey)
Cambridge U.	254*	K. S. Duleepsinhji	304*	E. D. Weekes (West Indians)
Gentlemen	232*	C. B. Fry	266*	J. B. Hobbs (Players)
England (Tests)	364	L. Hutton	334	D. G. Bradman (Australia)
Australians	345	C. G. Macartney	364	L. Hutton (England)
South Africans	239	M. Hathorn	229	G. J. Bryan (Combined Services)
West Indians	304*	E. D. Weekes	285*	P. B. H. May (England)
New Zealanders	243	B. Sutcliffe	255	J. F. Parker (Surrey)
Indians	252*	P. R. Umrigar	234*	G. Cox (Sussex)
Pakistan	142*	Hanif Mohammed	278	D. C. S. Compton (England)
	142	Alimuddin		

Australia:

For		Against	
New South Wales	452* D. G. Bradman	365*	C. Hill (South Australia)
Queensland	275* F. C. Thompson	452*	D. G. Bradman (N.S.W.)
South Australia	369 D. G. Bradman	336	W. H. Ponsford (Victoria)
Tasmania	274 C. L. Badcock	429	W. H. Ponsford (Victoria)
Victoria	437 W. H. Ponsford	357	D. G. Bradman (South Australia)
Western Australia	236* R. B. Simpson	227	A. J. Richardson (South Australia)
M.C.C.	305* F. E. Woolley	280	A. J. Richardson (South Australia)
Australia (Tests)	299* D. G. Bradman	287	R. E. Foster (England)
South Africans	204 G. A. Faulkner	299*	D. G. Bradman (Australia)
West Indians	186 C. L. Walcott	223	D. G. Bradman (Australia)
New Zealanders	160 J. R. Reid	325*	H. L. Hendry (Victoria)
Indians	228* L. Amarnath	201	D. G. Bradman (Australia)

South Africa:

For		Against	
Border	206* A. J. Clarke	261*	S. S. L. Steyn (Western Province)
Eastern Province	284 E. A. B. Rowan	247	W. R. Endean (Transvaal)
Griqualand West	215 K. G. Viljoen	284	E. A. B. Rowan (Eastern Province)
Natal	304* A. D. Nourse sen.	306*	E. A. B. Rowan (Transvaal)
North-Eastern Transvaal	220 P. C. Davies	300	D. C. S. Compton (M.C.C.)
Orange Free State	258 C. Richardson	279*	P. Holmes (M.C.C.)
Rhodesia	179 B. J. Carew	206 / 206	X. C. Balaskas (Griqualand West) / P. B. H. May (M.C.C.)
Transvaal	306* E. A. B. Rowan	304*	A. D. Nourse sen. (Natal)
Western Province	271* J. E. Cheetham	240	A. D. Nourse jun. (Natal)
M.C.C.	300 D. C. S. Compton	176* / 176	J. W. Zulch (Transvaal) / H. W. Taylor (South Africa)
Australians	235 H. L. Collins	231	A. D. Nourse jun. (South Africa)
New Zealanders	175 J. R. Reid	120	R. A. McLean (Natal)

West Indies:

For		Against	
Barbados	314* C. L. Walcott	281*	W. R. Hammond (M.C.C.)
Berbice	201* J. Solomon	183	J. M. Parks (M.C.C.)
British Guiana	268 H. P. Bayley	324	J. B. Stollmeyer (Trinidad)
Jamaica	344* G. Headley	261*	J. B. Stollmeyer (Trinidad)
Leeward Islands	100 O. Williams	127*	C. Headlam (Jamaica)
Trinidad	324 J. B. Stollmeyer	314*	C. L. Walcott (Barbados)
Windward Islands	25 O. Jackson	38	P. B. H. May (M.C.C.)
M.C.C.	325 A. Sandham	344*	G. Headley (Jamaica)
Australians	204 R. N. Harvey	219	D. Atkinson (West Indies)
Indians	169 V. L. Manjrekar	253	E. D. Weekes (Barbados)
Pakistan	337 Hanif Mohammed	365*	G. Sobers (West Indies)

New Zealand:

For		Against	
Auckland	290 W. N. Carson	355	B. Sutcliffe (Otago)
Canterbury	206 M. L. Page	385	B. Sutcliffe (Otago)
Central Districts	154 E. M. Meuli	264	B. Sutcliffe (Otago)
Northern Districts	136 E. C. Petrie	191*	J. R. Reid (Wellington)
Otago	385 B. Sutcliffe	290	W. N. Carson (Auckland)
Wellington	283 J. R. Reid	206	M. L. Page (Canterbury)
M.C.C.	336* W. R. Hammond	197	B. Sutcliffe (Otago)
Australians	293 V. T. Trumper	198	W. A. Hadlee (Otago)
South Africans	255* D. J. McGlew	165	M. E. Chapple (Canterbury)
West Indies	156 E. D. Weekes	114	L. S. M. Miller (Wellington)

NOTE. So many changes of title have been made by teams in India and Pakistan that records for these countries have been omitted.

HIGHEST MAIDEN CENTURIES

The following batsmen have hit a score of over 250 when recording their maiden century in first-class cricket:

292* V. T. Trumper: New South Wales v. Tasmania (Sydney) 1898–99
290 W. N. Carson: Auckland v. Otago (Dunedin) 1936–37
282 H. L. Collins: New South Wales v. Tasmania (Hobart) 1912–13
275 W. A. Farmer: Barbados v. Jamaica (Barbados) 1951–52
274 G. Davidson: Derbyshire v. Lancashire (Manchester) 1896
271 R. Maddocks: Victoria v. Tasmania (Melbourne)..1951–52
268 C. R. Maxwell: Cahn's XI v. Leicestershire (Nottingham) 1935
268 H. P. Bayley: British Guiana v. Barbados (Georgetown)...1937–38

264   P. Vaulkhard: Derbyshire v. Nottinghamshire (Nottingham) 1946
264* R. Flockton: New South Wales v. South Australia (Sydney) 1959–60
262* L. Wight: British Guiana v. Barbados (Georgetown) 1951–52
261* S. S. L. Steyn: Western Province v. Border (Cape Town) 1929–30
253   L. S. Birkett: Trinidad v. British Guiana (Georgetown) 1929–30

Double Centuries

The following batsmen have scored four or more double centuries during a season:

Six	D. G. Bradman 1930	334	254	252*	236	232	205*
Five	K. S. Ranjitsinhji 1900	275	222	220	215*	202	
	E. D. Weekes 1950	232	304*	279	246*	200*	
Four	C. B. Fry 1901	244	241	219*	209		
	E. Hendren 1929–30	254*	223*	211*	205* (West Indies)		
	W. R. Hammond 1933	264	239	231	206		
	W. R. Hammond 1934	302*	290	265*	217		
	V. M. Merchant 1944–45	221*	217	278	201 (India)		

The following batsmen have scored two double centuries in successive innings:
W. W. Read (Surrey) in 1887—247 and 244*.
K. S. Ranjitsinhji (Sussex) in 1900—222 and 215*.
K. S. Ranjitsinhji (Sussex) in 1901—285* and 204.
F. A. Tarrant (Middlesex) in 1914—250* and 200.
T. F. Shepherd (Surrey) in 1921—212 and 210*.
W. H. Ponsford (Victoria) in 1927–28—437 and 202.
W. R. Hammond (England) in 1928–29—251 and 200 (both in Test matches).
E. Hendren (M.C.C. in West Indies) in 1929–30—223* and 211*.
E. Hendren (M.C.C. in West Indies) in 1929–30—205* and 254*.
D. G. Bradman (New South Wales) in 1931–32—226 and 219.
W. R. Hammond (England) in 1932–33—227 and 336* (both in Test matches).
A. H. Bakewell (Northamptonshire) in 1933—246 and 257.
Nawab of Pataudi (Worcestershire) in 1933—231* and 222.
D. G. Bradman (Australia) in 1934—304 and 244 (both in Test matches).
W. H. Ponsford (Australians) in 1934—229* and 281*.
D. G. Bradman (South Australia) in 1935–36—233 and 357.
W. R. Hammond (Gloucestershire) in 1933—231 and 264.
D. G. Bradman (South Australia) in 1935–36 and 1936–37—369 and 212.
A. E. Fagg (Kent) in 1938—244 and 202* (both in same match).
V. M. Merchant (Hindus) in 1941–42—243* and 221.
V. M. Merchant (Hindus & Bombay) in 1944–45—221* and 217.
R. S. Modi (Bombay) in 1944–45—210 and 245*.
E. D. Weekes (West Indians) in 1950—232 and 304*.
E. D. Weekes (West Indians) in 1950—246* and 200*.
F. M. Worrell (West Indians) in 1950—241* and 261.
E. D. Weekes (Barbados) in 1952–53—207 and 253.
R. B. Simpson (Western Australia) in 1959–60—236* and 230*.

The following batsmen have come the nearest to scoring three double centuries in successive innings:
W. G. Grace (Gloucestershire) in 1876—344, 177 and 318*.
C. Hill (South Australia) in 1909–10—176, 205 and 185.
E. Hendren (M.C.C. in West Indies) in 1929–30—205*, 254* and 171.
V. M. Merchant (Hindus) in 1941–42—170*, 243*, 221 and 153*.

The complete list of double centuries recorded in first-class cricket is as follows:

Abel, R. ....(9)	217	Surrey v. Essex (Oval) 1895
	231	Surrey v. Essex (Oval) 1896
	250	Surrey v. Warwickshire (Oval) 1897
	215	Surrey v. Nottinghamshire (Oval) 1897
	219	Surrey v. Kent (Oval)..1898
	357*	Surrey v. Somerset (Oval) 1899
	221	Surrey v. Worcestershire (Oval) 1900
	247	Players v. Gentlemen (Oval) 1901
	205*	Surrey v. Middlesex (Oval) 1901
Abell, G. E. B...............(1)	210	Northern India v. Army (Lahore) 1934–35
Adhikari, H. R. ....(1)	230*	Services v. Rajasthan (Ajmer).................................1951–52
Allen, B. O. ....(1)	220	Gloucestershire v. Hampshire (Bournemouth) 1947
Alley, W. E..................(2)	209*	Commonwealth v. West Zone (Patiala) 1949–50
	206*	Commonwealth v. Cricket Club of India (Bombay) ...1949–50
Amarnath, L. ....(4)	241	Hindus v. Rest (Bombay) 1938–39

Amarnath, L. (*cont.*)	262	India in England v. Rest of India (Calcutta) 1946–47
	228*	Indians v. Victoria (Melbourne) 1947–48
	223*	North Zone v. West Indians (Patiala) 1948–49
Ames, L. E. G. ....(9)	200	Kent v. Surrey (Blackheath) 1928
	210	Kent v. Warwickshire (Tonbridge) 1933
	295	Kent v. Gloucestershire (Folkestone) 1933
	201	Players v. Gentlemen (Folkestone) 1933
	202*	Kent v. Essex (Brentwood) 1934
	201*	Kent v. Worcestershire (Gillingham) 1937
	201	Kent v. Worcestershire (Worcester) 1939
	212*	Kent v. Nottinghamshire (Gravesend) 1947
	212	Kent v. Gloucestershire (Dover) 1948
Andrews, C. W. ....(1)	253	Queensland v. New South Wales (Sydney) 1934–35
Andrews, T. J. E. ....(2)	247*	New South Wales v. Victoria (Sydney) 1919–20
	224	New South Wales v. M.C.C. (Sydney) 1924–25
Armstrong, W. W. ....(7)	200	Victoria v. Queensland (Melbourne) 1904–05
	303*	Australians v. Somerset (Bath) 1905
	248*	Australians v. Gentlemen (Lord's) 1905
	231	Victoria v. South Australia (Melbourne) 1907–08
	250	Victoria v. South Australia (Melbourne) 1911–12
	202*	Victoria v. Queensland (Melbourne) 1913–14
	245	Victoria v. South Australia (Melbourne) 1920–21
Arnold, E. G. ....(2)	200*	Worcestershire v. Warwickshire (Birmingham) 1909
	215	Worcestershire v. Oxford U. (Oxford) 1910
Arnold, J. ....(1)	227	Hampshire v. Glamorgan (Cardiff) 1932
Ashdown, W. H. ....(2)	332	Kent v. Essex (Brentwood) 1934
	305*	Kent v. Derbyshire (Dover) 1935
Ashton, H. ....(1)	236*	Cambridge U. v. Free Foresters (Cambridge) 1920
Atkinson, D. ....(1)	219	West Indies v. Australia (Barbados) 1954–55
Avery, A. V..................(4)	210	Essex v. Surrey (Oval) 1946
	214*	Essex v. Worcestershire (Clacton) 1948
	224	Essex v. Northamponshire (Northampton) 1952
	208*	Essex v. Glamorgan (Westcliff) 1953
Badcock, C. L................(4)	274	Tasmania v. Victoria (Launceston) 1933–34
	325	South Australia v. Victoria (Adelaide) 1935–36
	271*	South Australia v. New South Wales (Adelaide)..........1938–39
	236	South Australia v. Queensland (Adelaide) 1939–40
Baig, A. A. ....(1)	221*	Oxford U. v. Free Foresters (Oxford) 1959
Bailey, T. E. ....(1)	205	Essex v. Sussex (Eastbourne) 1947
Bakewell, A. H. ....(4)	204	Northamptonshire v. Somerset (Bath).......................1930
	246	Northamptonshire v. Nottinghamshire (Northampton) ...1933
	257	Northamptonshire v. Glamorgan (Swansea) 1933
	241*	Northamptonshire v. Derbyshire (Chesterfield) 1936
Balaskas, X. C. ....(2)	206	Griqualand West v. Rhodesia (Kimberley) 1929–30
	200*	Rest of South Africa v. Western Province (Cape Town) 1932–33
Baldwin, C. ....(1)	234	Surrey v. Kent (Oval).....................................1897
Barber, W. ....(2)	248	Yorkshire v. Kent (Leeds) 1934
	255	Yorkshire v. Surrey (Sheffield) 1935
Bardsley, W..................(7)	264	Australian XI v. Rest (Melbourne) 1908–09
	219	Australians v. Essex (Leyton) 1909
	211	Australians v. Gloucestershire (Bristol) 1909
	235	New South Wales v. South Australia (Sydney) 1920–21
	235	New South Wales v. South Australia (Adelaide)..........1920–21
	209	Australians v. Hampshire (Southampton) 1921
	200*	New South Wales v. Auckland (Auckland) 1923–24
Barling, T. H. ....(2)	269	Surrey v. Hampshire (Southampton) 1933
	233*	Surrey v. Nottinghamshire (Oval) 1946
Barnes, S. G. ....(2)	200	New South Wales v. Queensland (Sydney) 1945–46
	234	Australia v. England (Sydney) 1946–47
Barnett, C. J. ....(4)	204*	Gloucestershire v. Leicestershire (Leicester) 1936
	259	M.C.C. v. Queensland (Brisbane) 1936–37
	232	Gloucestershire v. Lancashire (Gloucester) 1937
	228*	Gloucestershire v. Leicestershire (Gloucester) 1947
Barrett, E. I. M. ....(1)	215	Hampshire v. Gloucestershire (Southampton) 1920
Barrick, D. ....(1)	211	Northamptonshire v. Essex (Northampton) 1952
Barton, V. A. ....(1)	205	Hampshire v. Sussex (Hove) 1900
Bates, L. A. ....(2)	200	Warwickshire v. Worcestershire (Birmingham) 1928
	211	Warwickshire v. Gloucestershire (Gloucester) 1932
Bates, W. E. ....(1)	200*	Glamorgan v. Worcestershire (Kidderminster) 1927
Bayley, H. P. ....(1)	268	British Guiana v. Barbados (Georgetown) 1937–38
Beames, P. J. ....(1)	226*	Victoria v. Tasmania (Launceston) 1938–39
Begbie, D. W. ....(1)	207*	Transvaal v. Orange Free State (Johannesburg).........1937–38

Bell, J. T. ....(2)   225 Glamorgan v. Worcestershire (Dudley) 1926
                                      209* Wales v. M.C.C. (Lord's) 1927
Berry, L. G. ....(2)   207 Leicestershire v. Worcestershire (Ashby de la Zouch) 1928
                                      232 Leicestershire v. Sussex (Leicester) 1930
Bhandari, P. ....(1)   227 Delhi v. Patiala (Patiala) 1957–58
Bhandarkar, K. V. ....(1)   205 Maharashtra v. Western India States (Poona) 1948–49
Bird, M. C. ....(1)   200 M.C.C. v. Orange Free State (Bloemfontein) 1913–14
Birkett, L. S. ....(1)   253 Trinidad v. British Guiana (Georgetown)...................1929–30
Blunt, R. C. ....(3)   221 Otago v. Canterbury (Dunedin) 1928–29
                                      225* New Zealanders v. Gentlemen (Eastbourne) 1931
                                      338* Otago v. Canterbury (Christchurch) 1931–32
Board, J. H. ....(1)   214 Gloucestershire v. Somerset (Bristol) 1900
Bogle, J. ....(1)   200 New South Wales v. South Australia (Adelaide).........1919–20
Bonitto, N. ....(1)   207* Jamaica v. British Guiana (Georgetown) 1952–53
Booth, M. W. ....(1)   210 Yorkshire v. Worcestershire (Worcester) 1911
Bosanquet, B. J. T. ....(1)   214 Rest of England v. Yorkshire (Oval) 1908
Bowell, A......................(1)   204 Hampshire v. Lancashire (Bournemouth) 1914
Bowley, E. H. ....(4)   228 Sussex v. Northamptonshire (Hove) 1921
                                      220 Sussex v. Gloucestershire (Hove) 1927
                                      280* Sussex v. Gloucestershire (Hove) 1929
                                      283 Sussex v. Middlesex (Hove) 1933
Bowley, F. L. ....(3)   217 Worcestershire v. Leicestershire (Stourbridge) 1905
                                      201 Worcestershire v. Gloucestershire (Worcester) 1913
                                      276 Worcestershire v. Hampshire (Dudley) 1914
Bowring, T. ....(1)   228 Oxford U. v. Gentlemen of England (Oxford) 1908
Bradman, D. G. ....(37)   340* New South Wales v. Victoria (Sydney) 1928–29
                                      228 Woodfull's XI v. Ryder's XI (Sydney) 1929–30
                                      452* New South Wales v. Queensland (Sydney) 1929–30
                                      236 Australians v. Worcestershire (Worcester) 1930
                                      252* Australians v. Surrey (Oval) 1930
                                      254 Australia v. England (Lord's) 1930
                                      334 Australia v. England (Leeds) 1930
                                      232 Australia v. England (Oval) 1930
                                      205* Australians v. Kent (Canterbury)................................1930
                                      258 New South Wales v. South Australia (Adelaide).........1930–31
                                      223 Australia v. West Indies (Brisbane) 1930–31
                                      220 New South Wales v. Victoria (Sydney) 1930–31
                                      226 Australia v. South Africa (Brisbane) 1931–32
                                      219 New South Wales v. South Africans (Sydney) 1931–32
                                      299* Australia v. South Africa (Adelaide) 1931–32
                                      238 New South Wales v. Victoria (Sydney) 1932–33
                                      200 New South Wales v. Queensland (Brisbane) 1933–34
                                      253 New South Wales v. Queensland (Sydney) 1933–34
                                      206 Australians v. Worcestershire (Worcester) 1934
                                      304 Australia v. England (Leeds) 1934
                                      244 Australia v. England (Oval) 1934
                                      233 South Australia v. Queensland (Adelaide) 1935–36
                                      357 South Australia v. Victoria (Melbourne) 1935–36
                                      369 South Australia v. Tasmania (Adelaide) 1935–36
                                      212 Bradman's XI v. Richardson's XI (Sydney) 1936–37
                                      270 Australia v. England (Melbourne) 1936–37
                                      212 Australia v. England (Adelaide) 1936–37
                                      246 South Australia v. Queensland (Adelaide) 1937–38
                                      258 Australians v. Worcestershire (Worcester) 1938
                                      278 Australians v. M.C.C. (Lord's)....................................1938
                                      202 Australians v. Somerset (Taunton) 1938
                                      225 South Australia v. Queensland (Adelaide) 1938–39
                                      251* South Australia v. New South Wales (Adelaide).........1939–40
                                      267 South Australia v. Victoria (Melbourne) 1939–40
                                      209* South Australia v. Western Australia (Perth) 1939–40
                                      234 Australia v. England (Sydney) 1946–47
                                      201 Australia v. India (Adelaide) 1947–48
Braund, L. C. ....(1)   257* Somerset v. Worcestershire (Worcester) 1913
Brockwell, W. ....(1)   225 Surrey v. Hampshire (Oval) 1897
Brookes, D. ....(6)   200 Northamptonshire v. Worcestershire (Kidderminster) 1946
                                      210 Northamptonshire v. Leicestershire (Leicester) 1947
                                      257 Northamptonshire v. Gloucestershire (Bristol) 1949
                                      204* Northamptonshire v. Essex (Northampton) 1952
                                      210* Northamptonshire v. Somerset (Northampton) 1954
                                      203* Northamptonshire v. Somerset (Taunton) 1956
Brown, F. R. ....(1)   212 Surrey v. Middlesex (Oval) 1932
Brown, G......................(3)   232* Hampshire v. Yorkshire (Leeds) 1920

Brown, G. (*cont.*)	230	Hampshire v. Essex (Bournemouth) 1920
	204	Hampshire v. Yorkshire (Portsmouth) 1927
Brown, J. T. ....(3)	203	Yorkshire v. Middlesex (Lord's) 1896
	311	Yorkshire v. Sussex (Sheffield) 1897
	300	Yorkshire v. Derbyshire (Chesterfield) 1898
Brown, S. M. ....(2)	200	Middlesex v. Kent (Canterbury) 1949
	232*	Middlesex v. Somerset (Lord's) 1951
Brown, W. A. ....(5)	205	New South Wales v. Victoria (Sydney).....................1933–34
	206*	Australia v. England (Lord's) 1938
	265*	Australians v. Derbyshire (Chesterfield).........1938
	215	Queensland v. Victoria (Brisbane) 1938–39
	200	Australians v. Cambridge U. (Cambridge) 1948
Bryan, G. J. ....(1)	229	Combined Services v. South Africans (Portsmouth) 1924
Bryan, J. L. ....(2)	231	Cambridge U. v. Surrey (Oval) 1921
	236	Kent v. Hampshire (Canterbury) 1923
Burge, P. ....(1)	210	Queensland v. Victoria (Brisbane) 1956–57
Burke, J. W. ....(1)	220	New South Wales v. South Australia (Adelaide).........1956–57
Burnup, C. J. ....(1)	200	Kent v. Lancashire (Manchester) 1900
Byrne, J. F. ....(1)	222	Warwickshire v. Lancashire (Birmingham)................1905
Callaway, N. ....(1)	207	New South Wales v. Queensland (Sydney) 1914–15
Calthorpe, Hon. F. S. G. (1)	209	Warwickshire v. Hampshire (Birmingham) 1921
Carr, A. W. ....(2)	204	Nottinghamshire v. Essex (Leyton) 1921
	206	Nottinghamshire v. Leicestershire (Leicester)................1925
Carson, W. N. ....(1)	290	Auckland v. Otago (Dunedin) 1936–37
Challenor, G. ....(2)	237*	Barbados v. Jamaica (Barbados) 1924–25
	220	Barbados v. Trinidad (Barbados) 1926–27
Chaplin, H. P...............(1)	213*	Sussex v. Nottinghamshire (Hove) 1914
Chapman, A. P. F. ....(1)	260	Kent v. Lancashire (Maidstone) 1927
Charlesworth, C. ....(2)	216	Warwickshire v. Derbyshire (Blackwell) 1910
	206	Warwickshire v. Yorkshire (Dewsbury) 1914
Cheetham, J. E. ....(1)	271*	Western Province v. Orange Free State (Bloemfontein) 1950–51
Chowdhari, Y. M. ....(1)	211	Delhi v. Patiala (New Delhi) 1955–56
Clarke, A. J...................(1)	206*	Border v. Eastern Province (Port Elizabeth) 1925–26
Coe, S. ....(1)	252*	Leicestershire v. Northamptonshire (Leicester) 1914
Collins, H. L. ....(3)	282	New South Wales v. Tasmania (Hobart) 1912–13
	235	A.I.F. v. South African XI (Johannesburg) 1919–20
	203	Australia v. South Africa (Johannesburg) 1921–22
Compton, D. C. S. ....(9)	214*	Middlesex v. Derbyshire (Lord's)............................1939
	249*	Holkar v. Bombay (Bombay) 1944–45
	202	Middlesex v. Cambridge U. (Cambridge) 1946
	235	Middlesex v. Surrey (Lord's) 1946
	208	England v. South Africa (Lord's)............................1947
	246	Middlesex v. Rest (Oval) 1947
	252*	Middlesex v. Somerset (Lord's) 1948
	300	M.C.C. v. North-Eastern Transvaal (Benoni) 1948–49
	278	England v. Pakistan (Nottingham) 1954
Constable, B. ....(1)	205*	Surrey v. Somerset (Oval) 1952
Cook, T. E. ....(3)	278	Sussex v. Hampshire (Hove) 1930
	214	Sussex v. Worcestershire (Eastbourne) 1933
	220	Sussex v. Worcestershire (Worcester) 1934
Cooper, E. ....(1)	216*	Worcestershire v. Warwickshire (Dudley) 1938
Cowdrey, M. C. ....(2)	204*	Kent v. Cambridge U. (Cambridge) 1956
	250	Kent v. Essex (Blackheath) 1959
Cox, A. ....(1)	204	Canterbury v. Otago (Christchurch) 1925–26
Cox, G. ....(4)	232	Sussex v. Northamptonshire (Kettering) 1939
	234*	Sussex v. Indians (Hove) 1946
	205*	Sussex v. Glamorgan (Hove) 1947
	212*	Sussex v. Yorkshire (Leeds) 1949
Craig, I. D. ....(1)	213*	New South Wales v. South Africans (Sydney) 1952–53
Crawford, J. N. ....(1)	232	Surrey v. Somerset (Oval) 1908
Crawley, A. M. ....(1)	204	Oxford U. v. Northamptonshire (Wellingborough) 1929
Crawley, L. G. ....(1)	222	Essex v. Glamorgan (Swansea) 1928
Creese, W. L. ....(1)	241	Hampshire v. Northamptonshire (Northampton) 1939
Croom, A. J. ....(1)	211	Warwickshire v. Worcestershire (Birmingham) 1934
Curnow, S. H. ....(1)	224	North v. South (Cape Town) 1932–33
Cutmore, J. A. ....(1)	238*	Essex v. Gloucestershire (Bristol) 1927
Dacre, C. C. ....(1)	223	Gloucestershire v. Worcestershire (Worcester) 1930
Darling, J. ....(1)	210	South Australia v. Queensland (Brisbane) 1898–99
Davidson, G. ....(1)	274	Derbyshire v. Lancashire (Manchester) 1896
Davies, D. ....(1)	216	Glamorgan v. Somerset (Newport) 1939
Davies, E. ....(2)	287*	Glamorgan v. Gloucestershire (Newport) 1939
	215	Glamorgan v. Essex (Brentwood) 1948

Davies, P. C. ....(1) 220 N.-E.Transvaal v. Orange Free State (Bloemfontein)...1955–56
Davis, P. ....(1) 237 Northamptonshire v. Somerset (Northampton) 1947
de Courcy, J. H. ....(1) 204 Australians v. Combined Services (Kingston) 1953
de Saram, F. C. ....(1) 208 Oxford U. v. Leveson-Gower's XI (Reigate) 1934
de Villiers, D. I. ....(1) 200* Orange Free State v. Border (Johannesburg) 1923–24
Dempster, C. S. ....(2) 212 New Zealanders v. Essex (Leyton) 1931
                              207* Leicestershire v. Sir J. Cahn's XI (Nottingham) 1935
Denton, D. ....(3) 200* Yorkshire v. Warwickshire (Birmingham) 1912
                              221 Yorkshire v. Kent (Tunbridge Wells) 1912
                              209* Yorkshire v. Worcestershire (Worcester) 1920
Denton, W. H..............(1) 230* Northamptonshire v. Essex (Leyton) 1913
Deodhar, D. B. ....(1) 246 Maharashtra v. Bombay (Poona) 1940–41
Devey, J. ....(1) 246 Warwickshire v. Derbyshire (Birmingham) 1900
Dewes, J. G................(2) 204* Cambridge U. v. Essex (Cambridge) 1949
                              212 Cambridge U. v. Sussex (Hove) 1950
Diamond, A. ....(1) 210* New South Wales v. Victoria (Sydney) 1906–07
Dipper, A. E. ....(3) 252* Gloucestershire v. Glamorgan (Cheltenham) 1923
                              247 Gloucestershire v. Oxford U. (Bristol) 1924
                              212 Gloucestershire v. Worcestershire (Bristol)................1927
Dixon, J. A. ....(1) 268* Nottinghamshire v. Sussex (Nottingham) 1897
Doggart, G. H. G. ....(2) 215* Cambridge U. v. Lancashire (Cambridge) 1948
                              219* Cambridge U. v. Essex (Cambridge) 1949
Doll, C. C. T. ....(1) 224* M.C.C. v. London County (Crystal Palace) 1901
Dollery, H. E. ....(2) 200 Warwickshire v. Gloucestershire (Gloucester) 1949
                              212 Warwickshire v. Leicestershire (Birmingham) 1952
Donnelly, M. P. ....(2) 208* M.C.C. v. Yorkshire (Scarborough) 1948
                              206 New Zealand v. England (Lord's) 1949
Douglas, J. ....(1) 204 Middlesex v. Gloucestershire (Bristol)......................1903
Douglas, J. W. H. T. ......(1) 210* Essex v. Derbyshire (Leyton) 1921
Druce, N. F. ....(1) 227* Cambridge U. v. Thornton's XI (Cambridge) 1897
Ducat, A. ....(8) 306* Surrey v. Oxford U. (Oval) 1919
                              271 Surrey v. Hampshire (Southampton) 1919
                              203 Surrey v. Sussex (Oval) 1920
                              290* Surrey v. Essex (Leyton) 1921
                              204* Surrey v. Northamptonshire (Northampton) 1921
                              235 Surrey v. Leicestershire (Oval) 1926
                              208 Surrey v. Essex (Leyton) 1928
                              218 Surrey v. Nottinghamshire (Nottingham) 1930
Duckfield, R. ....(1) 280* Glamorgan v. Surrey (Oval) 1936
Duff, R. A. ....(1) 271 New South Wales v. South Australia (Sydney) 1903–04
Duleepsinhji, K. S. ....(4) 254* Cambridge U. v. Middlesex (Cambridge) 1927
                              202 Sussex v. Essex (Leyton) 1929
                              246 Sussex v. Kent (Hastings) 1929
                              333 Sussex v. Northamptonshire (Hove) 1930
Dyson, A. H. ....(1) 208 Glamorgan v. Surrey (Oval) 1932
Edrich, W. J. ....(9) 245 Middlesex v. Nottinghamshire (Lord's) 1938
                              219 England v. South Africa (Durban) 1938–39
                              222* Middlesex v. Northamptonshire (Northampton) 1946
                              225 Middlesex v. Warwickshire (Birmingham) 1947
                              257 Middlesex v. Leicestershire (Leicester) 1947
                              267* Middlesex v. Northamptonshire (Northampton) 1947
                              239 Middlesex v. Oxford U. (Oxford) 1952
                              211 Middlesex v. Essex (Lord's) 1953
                              208* Middlesex v. Derbyshire (Chesterfield) 1956
Eggar, J. D. ....(1) 219 Derbyshire v. Yorkshire (Bradford)..........................1949
Elliott, C. S. ....(1) 215 Derbyshire v. Nottinghamshire (Nottingham) 1947
Endean, W. R. ....(3) 235 Transvaal v. Orange Free State (Johannesburg) 1954–55
                              247 Transvaal v. Eastern Province (Johannesburg) 1955–56
                              204* Transvaal A v. Border (Johannesburg) 1959–60
Fagg, A. E. ....(6) 257 Kent v. Hampshire (Southampton) 1936
                              244 Kent v. Essex (Colchester) 1st innings 1938
                              202* Kent v. Essex (Colchester) 2nd innings 1938
                              203 Kent v. Middlesex (Dover) 1948
                              221 Kent v. Nottinghamshire (Nottingham) 1951
                              269* Kent v. Nottinghamshire (Nottingham) 1953
Fane, F. L. ....(2) 207 Essex v. Leicestershire (Leicester) 1899
                              217 Essex v. Surrey (Oval) 1911
Farmer, W. A. ....(1) 275 Barbados v. Jamaica (Barbados) 1951–52
Faulkner, G. A. ....(1) 204 South Africa v. Australia (Melbourne) 1910–11
Fishlock, L. B. ....(2) 253 Surrey v. Leicestershire (Leicester) 1948
                              210 Surrey v. Somerset (Oval) 1949
Flockton ,R..................(1) 264* New South Wales v. South Australia (Adelaide) 1959–60

Foster, F. R. ....(2)	200	Warwickshire v. Surrey (Birmingham) 1911	
	305*	Warwickshire v. Worcestershire (Dudley) 1914	
Foster, H. K. ....(2)	216	Worcestershire v. Somerset (Worcester) 1903	
	215	Worcestershire v. Warwickshire (Worcester) 1908	
Foster, R. E. ....(2)	287	England v. Australia (Sydney) 1903–04	
	246*	Worcestershire v. Kent (Worcester) 1905	
Freeman, J. R. ....(1)	286	Essex v. Northamptonshire (Northampton) 1921	
Fry, C. B. ....(16)	229	Sussex v. Surrey (Oval) 1900	
	241	Sussex v. Cambridge U. (Hove) 1901	
	219*	Sussex v. Oxford U. (Eastbourne) 1901	
	244	Sussex v. Leicestershire (Leicester) 1901	
	209	Sussex v. Yorkshire (Hove) 1901	
	234	Sussex v. Yorkshire (Bradford) 1903	
	232*	Gentlemen v. Players (Lord's) 1903	
	200	Sussex v. Surrey (Hove) 1903	
	226	Sussex v. Derbyshire (Hove) 1904	
	211	Sussex v. Hampshire (Hove). 1904	
	229	Sussex v. Yorkshire (Hove). 1904	
	201*	Sussex v. Nottinghamshire (Hove) 1905	
	233	Sussex v. Nottinghamshire (Nottingham) 1905	
	214	Sussex v. Worcestershire (Hove) 1908	
	258*	Hampshire v. Gloucestershire (Southampton) 1911	
	203*	Hampshire v. Oxford U. (Southampton) 1912	
Gaekwad, D. K. ....(2)	218	Baroda v. Bombay (Sholapur) 1957–58	
	249*	Baroda v. Maharashtra (Poona).....................1959–60	
Gardner, F. C. ....(1)	215*	Warwickshire v. Somerset (Taunton) 1950	
Gibb, P. A. ....(1)	204	Cambridge U. v. Free Foresters (Cambridge) 1938	
Gibb, P. J. M..............(1)	203	Transvaal v. North-Eastern Transvaal (Johannesburg) 1952–53	
Gibbons, H. H. ....(2)	200*	Worcestershire v. West Indians (Worcester)... 1928	
	212*	Worcestershire v. Northamptonshire (Dudley) 1939	
Gibbs, G. ....(1)	216	British Guiana v. Barbados (Georgetown) 1951–52	
Giffen, G. ....(4)	203	South Australia v. Vernon's XI (Adelaide) 1887–88	
	237	South Australia v. Victoria (Melbourne) 1890–91	
	271	South Australia v. Victoria (Adelaide) 1891–92	
	205	South Australia v. New South Wales (Adelaide).........1893–94	
Gilbert, W. R. ....(1)	205*	England XI v. Cambridge U. (Cambridge) 1876	
Gillingham, F. H. ....(1)	201	Essex v. Middlesex (Lord's) 1904	
Gimblett, H.................(2)	231	Somerset v. Middlesex (Taunton) 1946	
	310	Somerset v. Sussex (Eastbourne) 1948	
Girdhari, S. K. ....(1)	229*	Assam v. Orissa (Cuttack) 1957–58	
Goddard, J. D. C. ....(1)	218*	Barbados v. Trinidad (Barbados) 1943–44	
Goddard, T. L. ....(1)	200	Natal v. Rhodesia (Durban) 1959–60	
Gomez, G. E. ....(2)	216*	Trinidad v. Barbados (Trinidad) 1942–43	
	213*	Trinidad v. Barbados (Trinidad) 1945–46	
Goonesena, G. ....(1)	211	Cambridge U. v. Oxford U. (Lord's) 1957	
Gopinath, C. D. ....(1)	234	Madras v. Mysore (Coimbatore) 1958–59	
Grace, W. G. ....(13)	224*	England v. Surrey (Oval) 1866	
	215	Gentlemen v. Players (Oval) 1870	
	268	South v. North (Oval) 1871	
	217	Gentlemen v. Players (Brighton) 1871	
	344	M.C.C. v. Kent (Canterbury) 1876	
	318*	Gloucestershire v. Yorkshire (Cheltenham) 1876	
	261	South v. North (Princes) 1877	
	221*	Gloucestershire v. Middlesex (Clifton) 1885	
	215	Gloucestershire v. Sussex (Hove) 1888	
	288	Gloucestershire v. Somerset (Bristol) 1895	
	257	Gloucestershire v. Kent (Gravesend) 1895	
	243*	Gloucestershire v. Sussex (Hove) 1896	
	301	Gloucestershire v. Sussex (Bristol) 1896	
Graveney, T. W. ....(7)	201	Gloucestershire v. Sussex (Worthing) 1950	
	201	Gloucestershire v. Oxford U. (Oxford) 1951	
	211	Gloucestershire v. Kent (Gillingham) 1953	
	231	M.C.C. v. British Guiana (Georgetown) 1953–54	
	222	Gloucestershire v. Derbyshire (Chesterfield) 1954	
	200	Gloucestershire v. Glamorgan (Newport) 1956	
	258	England v. West Indies (Nottingham) 1957	
Gregory, C. W. ....(1)	383	New South Wales v. Queensland (Brisbane) 1906–07	
Gregory, R. J. ....(1)	243	Surrey v. Somerset (Oval) 1938	
Gregory, S. E. ....(2)	201	Australia v. England (Sydney) 1894–95	
	201	New South Wales v. Victoria (Sydney) 1907–08	
Greig, J. G. ....(2)	249*	Hampshire v. Lancashire (Liverpool) 1901	
	216	England XII v. Indian XII (Bombay) 1915–16	

Grewal, S. S.	...............(1)	211	Services v. Southern Punjab (Patiala) 1950–51
Grieves, K.	...................(3)	224	Lancashire v. Cambridge U. (Cambridge) 1957
		202*	Lancashire v. Indians (Blackpool) 1959
		216	Lancashire v. Cambridge U. (Manchester) 1960
Gul Mahomed	.............(1)	319	Baroda v. Holkar (Baroda) 1946–47
Gunasekara, C. I.	.........(1)	212	Ceylon v. Madras (Colombo) 1958–59
Gunn, G.	.....................(1)	220	Nottinghamshire v. Derbyshire (Nottingham) 1923
Gunn, J.	......................(1)	294	Nottinghamshire v. Leicestershire (Nottingham) 1903
Gunn, W.	.....................(8)	203	M.C.C. v. Yorkshire (Lord's) 1885
		205*	Nottinghamshire v. Sussex (Nottingham) 1887
		228	Players v. Australians (Lord's) 1890
		219	Nottinghamshire v. Sussex (Nottingham) 1895
		207*	Nottinghamshire v. Derbyshire (Derby) 1896
		230	Nottinghamshire v. Derbyshire (Nottingham) 1897
		236*	Nottinghamshire v. Surrey (Oval) 1898
		273	Nottinghamshire v. Derbyshire (Derby) 1901
Hadow, W. H.	............(1)	217	Middlesex v. M.C.C. (Lord's) 1871
Hallam, M. R.	............(2)	200	Leicestershire v. Derbyshire (Leicester) 1959
		210*	Leicestershire v. Glamorgan (Leicester) 1959
Hallebone, J.	...............(1)	202	Victoria v. Tasmania (Melbourne) 1951–52
Hallows, C.	.................(3)	227	Lancashire v. Warwickshire (Manchester) 1921
		233*	Lancashire v. Hampshire (Liverpool) 1927
		232	Lancashire v. Sussex (Manchester) 1928
Hamer, A.	....................(1)	227	Derbyshire v. Nottinghamshire (Nottingham) 1955
Hammond, W. R.	......(36)	250*	Gloucestershire v. Lancashire (Manchester) 1925
		238*	M.C.C. v. West Indian XI (Barbados) 1925–26
		205*	Gloucestershire v. Surrey (Oval) 1928
		218*	Gloucestershire v. Glamorgan (Bristol) 1928
		244	Gloucestershire v. Essex (Chelmsford) 1928
		225	M.C.C. v. New South Wales (Sydney) 1928–29
		251	England v. Australia (Sydney) 1928–29
		200	England v. Australia (Melbourne) 1928–29
		238*	Gloucestershire v. Warwickshire (Birmingham)................1929
		211*	Gloucestershire v. Oxford U. (Oxford) 1930
		264	Gloucestershire v. Lancashire (Liverpool) 1932
		203	M.C.C. v. Victoria (Melbourne)...........................1932–33
		227	England v. New Zealand (Christchurch) 1932–33
		336*	England v. New Zealand (Auckland) 1932–33
		206	Gloucestershire v. Leicestershire (Leicester) 1933
		239	Gloucestershire v. Glamorgan (Gloucester) 1933
		231	Gloucestershire v. Derbyshire (Cheltenham) 1933
		264	Gloucestershire v. West Indians (Bristol) 1933
		290	Gloucestershire v. Kent (Tunbridge Wells) 1934
		217	Gloucestershire v. Nottinghamshire (Bristol) 1934
		265*	Gloucestershire v. Worcestershire (Dudley) 1934
		302*	Gloucestershire v. Glamorgan (Bristol) 1934
		281*	M.C.C. v. Barbados (Barbados) 1934–35
		252	Gloucestershire v. Leicestershire (Leicester) 1935
		217	England v. India (Oval) 1936
		317	Gloucestershire v. Nottinghamshire (Gloucester) 1936
		231*	England v. Australia (Sydney) 1936–37
		217	Gloucestershire v. Leicestershire (Gloucester) 1937
		237	Gloucestershire v. Derbyshire (Bristol) 1938
		240	England v. Australia (Lord's) 1938
		271	Gloucestershire v. Lancashire (Bristol) 1938
		302	Gloucestershire v. Glamorgan (Newport) 1939
		207	Gloucestershire v. Essex (Westcliff) 1939
		211*	Gloucestershire v. Nottinghamshire (Bristol) 1946
		214	Gloucestershire v. Somerset (Bristol) 1946
		208	M.C.C. v. Western Australia (Perth) 1946–47
Hanif Mohammed	.........(5)	203*	Pakistan v. Bombay (Bombay) 1952–53
		230*	Karachi v. Sind (Karachi) 1954–55
		228	Karachi Whites v. Karachi Blues (Karachi) 1956–57
		337	Pakistan v. West Indies (Barbados) 1957–58
		499	Karachi v. Bahawalpur (Karachi) 1958–59
Hardikar, M. S.	............(1)	204	Bombay v. Gujerat (Bombay) 1956–57
Hardinge, H. T. W.	......(4)	207	Kent v. Surrey (Blackheath) 1921
		249*	Kent v. Leicestershire (Leicester) 1922
		263*	Kent v. Gloucestershire (Gloucester) 1928
		205	Kent v. Warwickshire (Tunbridge Wells) 1928
Hardstaff, J., sen.	............(1)	213*	Nottinghamshire v. Sussex (Hove) 1914
Hardstaff, J., jun.	.........(10)	230*	M.C.C. v. Australian XI (Sydney) 1935–36

Hardstaff, J., jun. (*cont.*)	214*	Nottinghamshire v. Somerset (Nottingham)	1937
	266	Nottinghamshire v. Leicestershire (Leicester)	1937
	243	Nottinghamshire v. Middlesex (Nottingham)	1937
	213	Tennyson's XI v. Madras (Madras)	1937–38
	205*	England v. India (Lord's)	1946
	200*	Nottinghamshire v. Somerset (Nottingham)	1947
	202	Nottinghamshire v. Worcestershire (Dudley)	1947
	221*	Nottinghamshire v. Warwickshire (Nottingham)	1947
	247	Nottinghamshire v. Northamptonshire (Nottingham)	1951
Harris, C. B. ....(2)	234	Nottinghamshire v. Middlesex (Nottingham)	1933
	239*	Nottinghamshire v. Hampshire (Nottingham)	1950
Hartley, A. ....(1)	234	Lancashire v. Somerset (Manchester)	1910
Harvey, R. N. ....(5)	205	Australia v. South Africa (Melbourne)	1952–53
	202*	Australians v. Leicestershire (Leicester)	1953
	204	Australia v. West Indies (Kingston)	1954–55
	225	Australians v. M.C.C. (Lord's)	1956
	209	Victoria v. New South Wales (Sydney)	1956–57
Hassett, A. L. ....(8)	220*	Australians v. Cambridge U. (Cambridge)	1938
	211*	Victoria v. South Australia (Melbourne)	1938–39
	200	Victoria v. Queensland (Brisbane)	1946–47
	204	Victoria v. Queensland (Brisbane)	1947–48
	200*	Australians v. Gentlemen (Lord's)	1948
	205	Victoria v. Queensland (Brisbane)	1948–49
	232	Victoria v. M.C.C. (Melbourne)	1950–51
	229	Victoria v. South Australia (Adelaide)	1951–52
Hathorn, M...................(1)	239	South Africans v. Cambridge U. (Cambridge)	1901
Hayes, E. G. ....(4)	273*	Surrey v. Derbyshire (Derby)	1904
	218	Surrey v. Oxford U. (Oval)	1906
	202	Surrey v. Middlesex (Oval)	1907
	276	Surrey v. Hampshire (Oval)	1909
Hayward, T. ....(8)	229*	Surrey v. Derbyshire (Derby)	1896
	315*	Surrey v. Lancashire (Oval)	1898
	273	Surrey v. Yorkshire (Oval)	1899
	203	Players v. Gentlemen (Oval)	1904
	219	Surrey v. Northamptonshire (Oval)	1906
	208	Surrey v. Warwickshire (Oval)	1906
	204*	Surrey v. Warwickshire (Oval)	1909
	202	Surrey v. Derbyshire (Derby)	1911
Hazare, V. S. ....(10)	316*	Maharashtra v. Baroda (Poona)	1939–40
	309	Rest v. Hindus (Bombay)	1942–43
	264	Bengal Cyclone XI v. Bijapur Famine XI (Bombay)	1942–43
	248	Rest v. Muslims (Bombay)	1943–44
	223	India States v. Rest of India (Poona)	1943–44
	200*	Cricket Club of India v. Services XI (Bombay)	1944–45
	244*	Indians v. Yorkshire (Sheffield)	1946
	288	Baroda v. Holkar (Baroda)	1946–47
	204	Baroda v. Gujerat (Ahmedabad)	1954–55
	203	Baroda v. Services (Baroda)	1957–58
Headley, G. ....(9)	211	Jamaica v. Tennyson's XI (Kingston)	1927–28
	223	West Indies v. England (Kingston)	1929–30
	344*	Jamaica v. Tennyson's XI (Kingston)	1931–32
	224*	West Indians v. Somerset (Taunton)	1933
	200*	West Indians v. Derbyshire (Derby)	1933
	270*	West Indies v. England (Kingston)	1934–35
	227	West Indians v. Middlesex (Lord's)	1939
	234*	West Indians v. Nottinghamshire (Nottingham)	1939
	203*	Jamaica v. Barbados (Kingston)	1946–47
Healy, G. E. ....(1)	218	Victoria v. Tasmania (Melbourne)	1909–10
Hearne, J. W...............(11)	234*	Middlesex v. Somerset (Lord's)	1911
	204	Middlesex v. Lancashire (Lord's)	1914
	218*	Middlesex v. Hampshire (Lord's)	1919
	215*	Middlesex v. Warwickshire (Birmingham)	1920
	202	Middlesex v. Warwickshire (Birmingham)	1921
	201	Middlesex v. Gloucestershire (Gloucester)	1922
	221*	Middlesex v. Warwickshire (Birmingham)	1922
	232	Middlesex v. Hampshire (Southampton)	1923
	245*	Middlesex v. Gloucestershire (Bristol)	1927
	223*	Middlesex v. Somerset (Taunton)	1928
	285*	Middlesex v. Essex (Leyton)	1929
Hendren, E. ....(22)	214	M.C.C. v. Yorkshire (Lord's)	1919
	201	Middlesex v. Hampshire (Lord's)	1919
	232	Middlesex v. Nottinghamshire (Lord's)	1920

Hendren, E. (*cont.*)

271	M.C.C. v. Victoria (Melbourne)	1920–21
277*	Middlesex v. Kent (Lord's)	1922
200*	Middlesex v. Essex (Leyton)	1923
234	Middlesex v. Worcestershire (Lord's)	1925
240	Middlesex v. Kent (Tonbridge)	1925
206*	Middlesex v. Nottinghamshire (Nottingham)	1925
213	Middlesex v. Yorkshire (Lord's)	1926
201*	Middlesex v. Essex (Leyton)	1927
200	Middlesex v. Hampshire (Lord's)	1928
209*	Middlesex v. Warwickshire (Birmingham)	1928
223*	M.C.C. v. Barbados (Barbados)	1929–30
211*	M.C.C. v. Barbados (Barbados)	1929–30
205*	England v. West Indies (Trinidad)	1929–30
254*	M.C.C. v. British Guiana (Georgetown)	1929–30
232	Middlesex v. Nottinghamshire (Nottingham)	1931
203	Middlesex v. Northamptonshire (Lord's)	1931
301*	Middlesex v. Worcestershire (Dudley)	1933
222*	Middlesex v. Essex (Leyton)	1933
202	M.C.C. v. Surrey (Lord's)	1936

Hendry, H. L. ....(1) 325* Victoria v. New Zealanders (Melbourne) 1925–26
Hewett, H. T. ....(1) 201 Somerset v. Yorkshire (Taunton) 1892
Hiddleston, J. S. ....(2) 212 Wellington v. Canterbury (Wellington) 1925–26
                                 204 Wellington v. Auckland (Wellington) 1925–26
Hill, C. ....(4) 206* South Australia v. New South Wales (Sydney) 1895–96
                                 200 South Australia v. Stoddart's XI (Adelaide) 1897–98
                                 365* South Australia v. New South Wales (Adelaide) 1900–01
                                 205 South Australia v. New South Wales (Adelaide) 1909–10
Hirst, G. H. ....(4) 214 Yorkshire v. Worcestershire (Worcester) 1901
                                 341 Yorkshire v. Leicestershire (Leicester) 1905
                                 232* Yorkshire v. Surrey (Oval) 1905
                                 218 Yorkshire v. Sussex (Hastings) 1911
Hobbs, J. B. ....(16) 205 Surrey v. Hampshire (Oval) 1909
                                 215* Surrey v. Essex (Leyton) 1914
                                 226 Surrey v. Nottinghamshire (Oval) 1914
                                 202 Surrey v. Yorkshire (Lord's) 1914
                                 205* Surrey v. A.I.F. (Oval) 1919
                                 215 Rest v. Middlesex (Oval) 1920
                                 211 England v. South Africa (Lord's) 1924
                                 203* Surrey v. Nottinghamshire (Nottingham) 1924
                                 215 Surrey v. Warwickshire (Birmingham) 1925
                                 266* Players v. Gentlemen (Scarborough) 1925
                                 261 Surrey v. Oxford U. (Oval) 1926
                                 200 Surrey v. Hampshire (Southampton) 1926
                                 316* Surrey v. Middlesex (Lord's) 1926
                                 200* Surrey v. Warwickshire (Birmingham) 1928
                                 204 Surrey v. Somerset (Oval) 1929
                                 221 Surrey v. West Indians (Oval) 1933
Holdsworth, R. L. ....(1) 202 Oxford U. v. Free Foresters (Oxford) 1921
Hole, G. B. ....(1) 226 South Australia v. Queensland (Adelaide) 1953–54
Holmes, E. R. T. ....(2) 236 Oxford U. v. Free Foresters (Oxford) 1927
                                 206 Surrey v. Derbyshire (Chesterfield) 1935
Holmes, P. ....(12) 302* Yorkshire v. Hampshire (Portsmouth) 1920
                                 277* Yorkshire v. Northamptonshire (Harrogate) 1921
                                 209 Yorkshire v. Warwickshire (Birmingham) 1922
                                 220* Yorkshire v. Warwickshire (Huddersfield) 1922
                                 202* Thornton's XI v. South Africans (Scarborough) 1924
                                 315* Yorkshire v. Middlesex (Lord's) 1925
                                 244 M.C.C. v. Jamaica (Kingston) 1925–26
                                 279* M.C.C. v. Orange Free State (Bloemfontein) 1927–28
                                 275 Yorkshire v. Warwickshire (Bradford) 1928
                                 285 Yorkshire v. Nottinghamshire (Nottingham) 1929
                                 250 Yorkshire v. Warwickshire (Birmingham) 1931
                                 224* Yorkshire v. Essex (Leyton) 1932
Hopkins, A. J. ....(1) 218 New South Wales v. South Australia (Adelaide) 1908–09
Hopwood, J. L. ....(1) 220 Lancashire v. Gloucestershire (Bristol) 1934
Horner, N. F. ....(1) 203* Warwickshire v. Surrey (Oval) 1960
Horsfall, R. ....(1) 206 Essex v. Kent (Blackheath) 1951
Horton, M. J. ....(1) 212 Worcestershire v. Essex (Leyton) 1959
Hosie, A. L. ....(1) 200 Europeans v. Hindus (Bombay) 1924–25
Hudson, R. E. H. ....(1) 217 Army v. R.A.F. (Oval) 1932
Humphreys, E. ....(2) 208 Kent v. Gloucestershire (Catford) 1909
                                 200* Kent v. Lancashire (Tunbridge Wells) 1910

Hunte, C. C.	(1)	260	West Indies v. Pakistan (Kingston)	1957–58
Hutton, L.	(11)	271*	Yorkshire v. Derbyshire (Sheffield)	1937
		364	England v. Australia (Oval)	1938
		202	M.C.C. v. Eastern Province (Port Elizabeth)	1938–39
		280*	Yorkshire v. Hampshire (Sheffield)	1939
		270*	Yorkshire v. Hampshire (Bournemouth)	1947
		201	Yorkshire, v. Lancashire (Manchester)	1949
		269*	Yorkshire v. Northamptonshire (Wellingborough)	1949
		206	England v. New Zealand (Oval)	1949
		202*	England v. West Indies (Oval)	1950
		241	Players v. Gentlemen (Scarborough)	1953
		205	England v. West Indies (Kingston)	1953–54
Ibrahim, K. C.	(5)	230*	Bombay v. Western India States (Bombay)	1941–42
		250	Bijapur Famine XI v. Bengal Cyclone XI (Bombay)	1942–43
		218*	Ibrahim's XI v. Raiji's XI (Bombay)	1947–48
		234*	Ibrahim's XI v. Mantri's XI (Bombay)	1947–48
		219	Bombay v. Baroda (Bombay)	1948–49
Iddon, J.	(5)	222	Lancashire v. Leicestershire (Liverpool)	1929
		201	Lancashire v. Sussex (Manchester)	1932
		204*	Lancashire v. Warwickshire (Birmingham)	1933
		200*	Lancashire v. Nottinghamshire (Manchester)	1934
		217*	Lancashire v. Worcestershire (Manchester)	1939
Imtiaz Ahmed	(3)	300*	Prime Minister's XI v. Commonwealth (Bombay)	1950–51
		213*	Pakistan v. Central Zone (Nagpur)	1952–53
		209	Pakistan v. New Zealand (Lahore)	1955–56
Insole, D. J.	(1)	219*	Essex v. Yorkshire (Colchester)	1949
Iremonger, J.	(4)	210	Nottinghamshire v. Kent (Nottingham)	1903
		272	Nottinghamshire v. Kent (Nottingham)	1904
		239	Nottinghamshire v. Essex (Nottingham)	1905
		200*	Nottinghamshire v. Gloucestershire (Nottingham)	1906
Jakeman, F.	(1)	258*	Northamptonshire v. Essex (Northampton)	1951
James, R.	(1)	210	South Australia v. Queensland (Adelaide)	1947–48
Jardine, D. R.	(1)	214	M.C.C. v. Tasmania (Launceston)	1928–29
Jeacocke, A.	(1)	201*	Surrey v. Sussex (Oval)	1922
Jephson, D. L. A.	(1)	213	Surrey v. Derbyshire (Oval)	1900
Jessop, G. L.	(5)	233	Rest of England v. Yorkshire (Lord's)	1901
		286	Gloucestershire v. Sussex (Hove)	1903
		206	Gloucestershire v. Nottinghamshire (Nottingham)	1904
		234	Gloucestershire v. Somerset (Bristol)	1905
		240	Gloucestershire v. Sussex (Bristol)	1907
Jones, A. O.	(4)	250	Nottinghamshire v. Gloucestershire (Bristol)	1899
		249	Nottinghamshire v. Sussex (Hove)	1901
		296	Nottinghamshire v. Gloucestershire (Nottingham)	1903
		274	Nottinghamshire v. Essex (Leyton)	1905
Jones, W. E.	(2)	207	Glamorgan v. Kent (Gravesend)	1948
		212*	Glamorgan v. Essex (Brentwood)	1948
Jupp, V. W. C.	(1)	217*	Sussex v. Worcestershire (Worcester)	1914
Kanga, H. D.	(1)	233	Parsis v. Europeans (Poona)	1905–06
Kanhai, R.	(2)	256	West Indies v. India (Calcutta)	1958–59
		217	West Indies v. Pakistan (Lahore)	1958–59
Keeton, W. W.	(7)	200*	Nottinghamshire v. Cambridge U. (Cambridge)	1932
		242	Nottinghamshire v. Glamorgan (Nottingham)	1932
		261	Nottinghamshire v. Gloucestershire (Nottingham)	1934
		233	Nottinghamshire v. Worcestershire (Worksop)	1934
		312*	Nottinghamshire v. Middlesex (Oval)	1939
		210	Nottinghamshire v. Yorkshire (Sheffield)	1949
		208	Nottinghamshire v. Glamorgan (Nottingham)	1949
Kenny, R. B.	(1)	218	Bombay v. Madras (Bombay)	1956–57
Kenyon, D.	(7)	238*	Worcestershire v. Yorkshire (Worcester)	1953
		202*	Worcestershire v. Hampshire (Portsmouth)	1954
		253*	Worcestershire v. Leicestershire (Worcester)	1954
		259	Worcestershire v. Yorkshire (Kidderminster)	1956
		200*	Worcestershire v. Nottinghamshire (Worcester)	1957
		229	Worcestershire v. Hampshire (Portsmouth)	1959
		201	Worcestershire v. Glamorgan (Stourbridge)	1960
Key, K. J.	(1)	281	Oxford U. v. Middlesex (Chiswick Park)	1887
Khanna, A. K.	(1)	218	Services v. Delhi (New Delhi)	1952–53
Killick, E. H.	(1)	200	Sussex v. Yorkshire (Hove)	1901
Killick, E. T.	(3)	200*	Cambridge U. v. Glamorgan (Cambridge)	1929
		201	Cambridge U. v. Essex (Cambridge)	1929
		206	Middlesex v. Warwickshire (Lord's)	1931
Kilner, N.	(1)	228	Warwickshire v. Worcestershire (Worcester)	1935

Kilner, R.	............(1)	206*	Yorkshire v. Derbyshire (Sheffield)	1920
King, J. H.	............(2)	227*	Leicestershire v. Worcestershire (Coalville)	1914
		205	Leicestershire v. Hampshire (Leicester)	1923
Kinneir, S. P.	.........(2)	215*	Warwickshire v. Lancashire (Birmingham).........	1901
		268*	Warwickshire v. Hampshire (Birmingham)	1911
Kippax, A. F.	.........(7)	248	New South Wales v. South Australia (Sydney) 1923–24	
		212*	New South Wales v. Victoria (Sydney) 1924–25	
		271*	New South Wales v. Victoria (Sydney) 1925–26	
		217*	New South Wales v. Victoria (Sydney) 1926–27	
		315*	New South Wales v. Queensland (Sydney) 1927–28	
		260*	New South Wales v. Victoria (Melbourne) 1928–29	
		250	Australians v. Sussex (Hove)	1934
Kishenchand, G.	............(1)	218	North Zone v. South Zone (Bombay) 1946–47	
Knight, A. E.	.........(2)	229*	Leicestershire v. Worcestershire (Worcester)	1903
		203	Leicestershire v. M.C.C. (Lord's)	1904
Knott, C. H.	.........(1)	261*	Harlequins v. West Indians (Eastbourne)	1928
Koch, L. B.	.........(1)	216*	Orange Free State v. Natal (Bloemfontein) 1952–53	
Kortlang, B. J.	.........(1)	214*	Wellington v. Auckland (Wellington) 1925–26	
Kripal Singh, A. G.	......(1)	208	Madras v. Travancore-Cochin (Ernakulam) 1954–55	
Kunderam, B. K.	.........(1)	205	Railways v. Jammu & Kashmir (New Delhi) 1959–60	
Langridge, John	.........(8)	250*	Sussex v. Glamorgan (Hove)	1933
		232*	Sussex v. Northamptonshire (Peterborough)	1934
		227	Sussex v. Northamptonshire (Northampton)	1938
		215	Sussex v. Glamorgan (Eastbourne)	1938
		202	Sussex v. Leicestershire (Hastings)	1939
		234*	Sussex v. Derbyshire (Ilkeston)	1949
		241	Sussex v. Somerset (Worthing)	1950
		200*	Sussex v. Derbyshire (Derby)	1951
Lashley, P.	.........(1)	200*	Barbados v. British Guiana (Barbados) 1958–59	
Lee, G. M.	.........(1)	200*	Nottinghamshire v. Leicestershire (Nottingham)	1913
Lee, H. W.	.........(4)	221*	Middlesex v. Hampshire (Southampton)	1920
		243*	Middlesex v. Nottinghamshire (Lord's)	1921
		200	Middlesex v. Oxford U. (Oxford)	1929
		225	Middlesex v. Surrey (Oval)	1929
Lee, I. S.	.........(1)	268	Victoria v. Tasmania (Melbourne) 1933–34	
Lewis, A. E.	.........(1)	201*	Somerset v. Kent (Taunton)	1909
Leyland, M.	.........(5)	204*	Yorkshire v. Middlesex (Sheffield)	1927
		247	Yorkshire v. Worcestershire (Worcester)	1928
		211*	Yorkshire v. Lancashire (Leeds)	1930
		210*	Yorkshire v. Kent (Dover)	1933
		263	Yorkshire v. Essex (Hull)	1936
Livingston, T. L.	.........(4)	201*	Northamptonshire v. South Africans (Northampton) 1951	
		210	Northamptonshire v. Somerset (Weston-super-Mare) 1951	
		200	Northamptonshire v. Kent (Maidstone)	1954
		207*	Northamptonshire v. Nottinghamshire (Nottingham) 1954	
Llewellyn, C. B.	.........(1)	216	Hampshire v. South Africans (Southampton)	1901
Lockwood, E.	.........(1)	208	Yorkshire v. Kent (Gravesend)	1883
Longrigg, E. F.	.........(1)	205	Somerset v. Leicestershire (Taunton)	1930
Lowndes, W. G. L. F.	...(1)	216	Oxford U. v. Leveson-Gower's XI (Eastbourne) 1921	
Lowson, F. A.	.........(1)	259*	Yorkshire v. Worcestershire (Worcester)	1953
Loxton, S. J. E.	.........(1)	232*	Victoria v. Queensland (Melbourne) 1946–47	
Lucas, F. M.	.........(1)	215*	Sussex v. Gloucestershire (Hove)	1885
Lucas, J. H.	.........(1)	216*	Barbados v. Trinidad (Barbados) 1948–49	
Lyon, M. D.	.........(2)	219	Somerset v. Derbyshire (Burton upon Trent).........	1924
		210	Somerset v. Gloucestershire (Taunton)	1930
Macartney, C. G.	.........(4)	208	Australians v. Essex (Leyton)	1912
		201	New South Wales v. Victoria (Sydney) 1913–14	
		345	Australians v. Nottinghamshire (Nottingham)	1921
		221	New South Wales v. Canterbury (Christchurch) 1923–24	
Mackay, J. R. M.	.........(1)	203	New South Wales v. Queensland (Brisbane) 1905–06	
Mackay, K.	.........(2)	223	Queensland v. Victoria (Brisbane) 1953–54	
		203	Queensland v. New South Wales (Sydney) 1955–56	
MacLaren, A. C.	.........(6)	228	Stoddart's XI v. Victoria (Melbourne) 1894–95	
		424	Lancashire v. Somerset (Taunton)	1895
		226*	Lancashire v. Kent (Canterbury)	1896
		244	Lancashire v. Kent (Canterbury)	1897
		204	Lancashire v. Gloucestershire (Liverpool)	1903
		200*	M.C.C. v. New Zealand XI (Wellington) 1922–23	
Maddocks, R.	.........(1)	271	Victoria v. Tasmania (Melbourne) 1951–52	
Makepeace, H.	.........(2)	203	Lancashire v. Worcestershire (Worcester)	1923
		200*	Lancashire v. Northamptonshire (Liverpool)	1923
Manjrekar, V. L.	.........(1)	204*	Indians v. Oxford U. (Oxford)	1959

Mankad, V.	.................(3)	223 India v. New Zealand (Bombay)	1955–56
		231 India v. New Zealand (Madras)	1955–56
		221 Rajasthan v. Vidarbha (Udaipur)	1957–58
Mantri, M. K.	................(1)	200 Bombay v. Maharashtra (Poona)	1948–49
Marks, A. E.	................(1)	201 New South Wales v. Queensland (Sydney)	1935–36
Martin, F. R.	................(1)	204* Jamaica v. Tennyson's XI (Kingston)	1926–27
Marx, W. F. E.	................(1)	240 Transvaal v. Griqualand West (Johannesburg)	1920–21
Massie, H. H.	................(1)	206 Australians v. Oxford U. (Oxford)	1882
Matthews, T. G.	................(1)	201 Gloucestershire v. Surrey (Clifton)	1871
Maxwell, C. R.	................(1)	268 Cahn's XI v. Leicestershire (Nottingham)	1935
May, P. B. H.	................(5)	227* Cambridge U. v. Hampshire (Cambridge)	1950
		211* Surrey v. Nottinghamshire (Nottingham)	1954
		207 Surrey v. Cambridge U. (Oval)	1954
		206 M.C.C. v. Rhodesia (Salisbury)	1956–57
		285* England v. West Indies (Birmingham)	1957
Maynard, A.	................(1)	200* Trinidad v. M.C.C. (Trinidad)	1934–35
Mayne, E. R.	................(1)	209 Victoria v. Queensland (Melbourne)	1923–24
McAlister, P. A.	................(1)	224 Victoria v. New Zealanders (Melbourne)	1898–99
McCabe, S. J.	................(3)	229* New South Wales v. Queensland (Brisbane)	1931–32
		240 Australians v. Surrey (Oval)	1934
		232 Australia v. England (Nottingham)	1938
McCorkell, N.	................(1)	203 Hampshire v. Gloucestershire (Gloucester)	1951
McDonald, C. C.	.........(2)	207 Victoria v. New South Wales (Melbourne)	1951–52
		229 Victoria v. South Australia (Adelaide)	1952–53
McDonnell, P. S.	.............(1)	239 New South Wales v. Victoria (Melbourne)	1886–87
McGahey, C. P.	.............(3)	225 Essex v. Nottinghamshire (Leyton)	1904
		277 Essex v. Derbyshire (Leyton)	1905
		230 Essex v. Northamptonshire (Northampton)	1908
McGlew, D. J.	.........(2)	255* South Africa v. New Zealand (Wellington)	1952–53
		213* Natal v. Border (Durban)	1957–58
McKenzie, C.	................(1)	211 Victoria v. Western Australia (Perth)	1909–10
McLean, A. R.	.............(1)	213 South Australia v. Queensland (Adelaide)	1949–50
McLean, R. A.	................(1)	207 South Africans v. Worcestershire (Worcester)	1960
Mead, C. P.	................(13)	207* Hampshire v. Warwickshire (Southampton)	1911
		223 Players v. Gentlemen (Scarborough)	1911
		213 Hampshire v. Yorkshire (Southampton)	1914
		207 Hampshire v. Essex (Leyton)	1919
		280* Hampshire v. Nottinghamshire (Southampton)	1921
		224 Hampshire v. Sussex (Horsham)	1921
		235 Hampshire v. Worcestershire (Worcester)	1922
		211* Hampshire v. Warwickshire (Southampton)	1922
		222 Hampshire v. Warwickshire (Birmingham)	1923
		213* Hampshire v. Worcestershire (Bournemouth)	1925
		200* Hampshire v. Essex (Southampton)	1927
		233 M.C.C. Australian XI v. Hawke's XI (Scarborough)	1929
		227 Hampshire v. Derbyshire (Ilkeston)	1933
Merchant, U. M.	.... (1)	217 Bombay v. Hyderabad (Bombay)	1947–48
Merchant, V. M.	.........(11)	243* Hindus v. Muslims (Bombay)	1941–42
		221 Hindus v. Parsis (Bombay)	1941–42
		250* Hindus v. Rest (Bombay)	1942–43
		359* Bombay v. Maharashtra (Bombay)	1943–44
		221* Hindus v. Parsis (Bombay)	1944–45
		217 Bombay v. Western India States (Bombay)	1944–45
		278 Bombay v. Holkar (Bombay)	1944–45
		201 Cricket Club of India v. Services XI (Bombay)	1944–45
		234* Bombay v. Sind (Bombay)	1945–46
		242* Indians v. Lancashire (Manchester)	1946
		205 Indians v. Sussex (Hove)	1946
Meuleman, K.	................(2)	206 Victoria v. Tasmania (Melbourne)	1947–48
		234* Western Australia v. South Australia (Perth)	1956–57
Meyer, R. J. O.	............(1)	202* Somerset v. Lancashire (Taunton)	1936
Midlane, F. A.	............(1)	222* Wellington v. Otago (Wellington)	1914–15
Miller, K. R.	................(7)	206* Victoria v. New South Wales (Sydney)	1946–47
		202* Australians v. Leicestershire (Leicester)	1948
		201* New South Wales v. Queensland (Brisbane)	1950–51
		214* New South Wales v. M.C.C. (Sydney)	1950–51
		220* Australians v. Worcestershire (Worcester)	1953
		262* Australians v. Combined Services (Kingston)	1953
		281* Australians v. Leicestershire (Leicester)	1956
Minnett, R. B.	............(1)	216* New South Wales v. Victoria (Sydney)	1911–12
Mitchell, N. F.	...............(1)	220 Victoria v. Tasmania (Melbourne)	1926–27
Mitchell-Innes, N. S.	(1)	207 Oxford U. v. Leveson-Gower's XI (Reigate)	1936

Modi, R. S. ....(4) 215 Parsis v. Europeans (Bombay) 1944–45
                             210 Bombay v. Western India States (Bombay) 1944–45
                             245* Bombay v. Baroda (Baroda) 1944–45
                             203 Indian XI v. Australian Services (Madras) 1945–46
Moore, D. N. ....(1) 206 Gloucestershire v. Oxford U. (Oxford) 1930
Moore, R. H. ....(1) 316 Hampshire v. Warwickshire (Bournemouth) 1937
Mordaunt, G. J.   ....(1) 264* Oxford U. v. Sussex (Hove) 1895
Morkel, D. P. B.   ....(2) 208* Western Province v. Natal (Cape Town) 1929–30
                             251 Sir J. Cahn's XI v. South Americans (Nottingham) 1932
Moroney, J. A. R. ....(1) 217 Morris' XI v. Hassett's XI (Sydney) 1948–49
Morris, A. R. ....(4) 290 Australians v. Gloucestershire (Bristol) 1948
                             206 Australia v. England (Adelaide) 1950–51
                             253 New South Wales v. Queensland (Brisbane) 1951–52
                             210 New South Wales v. Victoria (Melbourne) 1951–52
Morrison, J. S. F. ....(1) 233* Cambridge U. v. M.C.C. (Cambridge) 1914
Moses, H. ....(1) 297* New South Wales v. Victoria (Sydney) 1887–88
Murdoch, W. L. ....(5) 321 New South Wales v. Victoria (Sydney) 1881–82
                             286* Australians v. Sussex (Hove) 1882
                             279* Australian XI v. Rest (Melbourne) 1883–84
                             211 Australia v. England (Oval) 1884
                             226 Sussex v. Cambridge U. (Hove) 1895
Mushtaq Ali ....(1) 233 Holkar v. United Provinces (Indore) 1947–48
Nadkarni, R. G. ....(1) 201* Maharashtra v. Saurashtra (Poona) 1957–58
Naoomal Jeoomal ....(1) 203* Sind v. Nawanagar (Karachi) 1938–39
Nayudu, C. K. ....(1) 200 Holkar v. Baroda (Indore) 1945–46
Nel, J. D. ....(1) 217* Western Province v. Eastern Province (Port Elizabeth) 1952–53
Newham, W. ....(1) 201* Sussex v. Somerset (Hove) 1896
Nichol, M. ....(1) 262* Worcestershire v. Hampshire (Bournemouth) 1930
Nichols, M. S. ....(1) 205 Essex v. Hampshire (Southend) 1936
Nicolson, J. F. W. ....(1) 252* Natal v. Orange Free State (Bloemfontein) 1926–27
Nimbalkar, B. B. ....(2) 443* Maharashtra v. Western India States (Poona) 1948–49
                             219 Holkar v. Bengal (Calcutta) 1952–53
Noble, M. A. ....(7) 200 New South Wales v. South Australia (Adelaide)........1899–00
                             284 Australians v. Sussex (Hove) 1902
                             230 New South Wales v. South Australia (Sydney) 1903–04
                             267 Australians v. Sussex (Hove) 1905
                             281 New South Wales v. Victoria (Melbourne) 1905–06
                             213 New South Wales v. South Australia (Adelaide)........1908–09
                             213 New South Wales v. Victoria (Sydney) 1908–09
Nourse, A. D., sen. ....(7) 212 Natal v. Griqualand West (Johannesburg) 1906–07
                             200* Natal v. Western Province (Cape Town) 1907–08
                             201* South Africans v. South Australia (Adelaide) 1910–11
                             213* South Africans v. Hampshire (Bournemouth) 1912
                             304* Natal v. Transvaal (Johannesburg) 1919–20
                             204 Transvaal v. Griqualand West (Johannesburg) 1925–26
                             219* Western Province v. Natal (Cape Town) 1932–33
Nourse, A. D., jun. ....(6) 231 South Africa v. Australia (Johannesburg) 1935–36
                             260* Natal v. Transvaal (Johannesburg) 1936–37
                             240 Natal v. Western Province (Durban) 1936–37
                             205* South Africans v. Warwickshire (Birmingham) 1947
                             214* Natal v. Griqualand West (Durban) 1947–48
                             208 South Africa v. England (Nottingham) 1951
Nunes, R. K. ....(1) 200* Jamaica v. Tennyson's XI (Kingston) 1926–27
Nurse, S. ....(1) 213 Barbados v. M.C.C. (Barbados) 1959–60
O'Brien, T. C. ....(1) 202 Middlesex v. Sussex (Hove) 1895
O'Connor, J. ....(2) 237 Essex v. Somerset (Leyton) 1933
                             248 Essex v. Surrey (Brentwood) 1934
Ollivierre, C. A. ....(1) 229 Derbyshire v. Essex (Chesterfield) 1904
O'Neill, N. ....(2) 233 New South Wales v. Victoria (Sydney) 1957–58
                             284 Australians v. President's XI (Ahmedabad) 1959–60
Outschoorn, L. ....(2) 215* Worcestershire v. Northamptonshire (Worcester) 1949
                             200* Worcestershire v. Scotland (Dundee) 1951
Page, M. L. ....(1) 206 Canterbury v. Wellington (Wellington) 1931–32
Paine, A. I. ....(1) 220 Western Province v. Griqualand West (Johannesburg) 1896–97
Palairet, L. C. H. ....(2) 292 Somerset v. Hampshire (Southampton) 1896
                             203 Somerset v. Worcestershire (Worcester) 1904
Palia, P. E. ....(1) 216 United Provinces v. Maharashtra (Poona) 1939–40
Palmer, C. H. ....(1) 201 Leicestershire v. Northamptonshire (Northampton) 1953
Pandit, B. ....(1) 262* Kerala v. Andhra (Pulghat) 1959–60
Park, R. L. ....(1) 228 Victoria v. South Australia (Melbourne) 1919–20
Parker, G. W. ....(1) 210 Gloucestershire v. Kent (Dover) 1937
Parker, J. F. ....(2) 204* Surrey v. Derbyshire (Oval) 1947

Parker, J. F. (*cont.*)
255 Surrey v. New Zealanders (Oval) 1949
Parkhouse, W. G. A. ......(1)
201 Glamorgan v. Kent (Swansea) 1956
Parks, H. W. ....(1)
200* Sussex v. Essex (Chelmsford) 1931
Parks, J. M. ....(1)
205* Sussex v. Somerset (Hove) 1955
Parsons, J. H. ....(1)
225 Warwickshire v. Glamorgan (Birmingham) 1927
Passailaigue, C. C. ....(1)
261* Jamaica v. Tennyson's XI (Kingston) 1931–32
Pataudi, Nawab of ....(5)
238* Oxford U. v. Cambridge U. (Lord's) 1931
224* Worcestershire v. Kent (Worcester) 1933
231* Worcestershire v. Essex (Worcester) 1933
222 Worcestershire v. Somerset (Weston-super-Mare) 1933
214* Worcestershire v. Glamorgan (Worcester) 1934
Paynter, E. ....(7)
208* Lancashire v. Northamptonshire (Northampton) 1935
266 Lancashire v. Essex (Manchester) 1937
322 Lancashire v. Sussex (Hove) 1937
291 Lancashire v. Hampshire (Southampton) 1938
216* England v. Australia (Nottingham) 1938
243 England v. South Africa (Durban) 1938–39
222 Lancashire v. Derbyshire (Manchester) 1939
Peach, H. A. ....(1)
200* Surrey v. Northamptonshire (Northampton) 1920
Pearce, T. N. ....(1)
211* Essex v. Leicestershire (Westcliff) 1948
Peel, R. ....(1)
210* Yorkshire v. Warwickshire (Birmingham) 1896
Pellew, C. E. ....(1)
271 South Australia v. Victoria (Adelaide) 1919–20
Perrin, P. A. ....(3)
205 Essex v. Kent (Leyton) 1900
343* Essex v. Derbyshire (Chesterfield) 1904
245 Essex v. Derbyshire (Leyton) 1912
Phadkar, D. G. ....(1)
217 Bombay v. Maharashtra (Bombay) 1950–51
Place, W. ....(3)
266* Lancashire v. Oxford U. (Oxford) 1947
200 Lancashire v. Somerset (Taunton) 1948
226* Lancashire v. Nottinghamshire (Nottingham) 1949
Ponsford, W. H. ....(13)
429 Victoria v. Tasmania (Melbourne) 1922–23
248 Victoria v. Queensland (Melbourne) 1923–24
214 Victoria v. South Australia (Adelaide) 1926–27
352 Victoria v. New South Wales (Melbourne) 1926–27
437 Victoria v. Queensland (Melbourne) 1927–28
202 Victoria v. New South Wales (Melbourne) 1927–28
336 Victoria v. South Australia (Melbourne) 1927–28
275* Victoria v. South Australia (Melbourne) 1928–29
220* Australians v. Oxford U. (Oxford) 1930
200 Victoria v. New South Wales (Sydney) 1932–33
229* Australians v. Cambridge U. (Cambridge) 1934
281* Australians v. M.C.C. (Lord's) 1934
266 Australia v. England (Oval) 1934
Poole, C. J. ....(2)
222* Nottinghamshire v. Indians (Nottingham) 1952
219 Nottinghamshire v. Derbyshire (Ilkeston) 1952
Poore, R. M. ....(1)
304 Hampshire v. Somerset (Taunton) 1899
Pope, G. H. ....(1)
207* Derbyshire v. Hampshire (Portsmouth) 1948
Pretty, H. C. ....(1)
200 Northamptonshire v. Derbyshire (Chesterfield) 1906
Punjabi, P. H. ....(1)
224* Gujerat v. Saurashtra (Rajkot) 1959–60
Quaife, W. G. ....(4)
207* Warwickshire v. Hampshire (Birmingham) 1899
223* Warwickshire v. Essex (Leyton) 1900
200* Warwickshire v. Essex (Birmingham) 1904
255* Warwickshire v. Surrey (Oval) 1905
Quin, S. O. ....(1)
210 Victoria v. Tasmania (Melbourne) 1933–34
Ram Prakash ....(1)
209* Northern India v. Maharashtra (Poona) 1940–41
Ramchand, G. S............(1)
230* Bombay v. Maharashtra (Bombay) 1950–51
Rangnekar, K. M. ....(3)
202 Bombay v. Maharashtra (Poona) 1940–41
200* West Zone v. East Zone (Bombay) 1946–47
217 Holkar v. Hyderabad (Indore) 1950–51
Ranjitsinhji, K. S. ....(14)
260 Sussex v. M.C.C. (Lord's) 1897
222 Sussex v. Somerset (Hove) 1900
215* Sussex v. Cambridge U. (Cambridge) 1900
202 Sussex v. Middlesex (Hove) 1900
275 Sussex v. Leicestershire (Leicester) 1900
220 Sussex v. Kent (Hove) 1900
285* Sussex v. Somerset (Taunton) 1901
204 Sussex v. Lancashire (Hove) 1901
219 Sussex v. Essex (Hove) 1901
230 Sussex v. Essex (Leyton) 1902
234* Sussex v. Surrey (Hastings) 1902
204 Sussex v. Surrey (Oval) 1903
207* Sussex v. Lancashire (Hove) 1904
200 Sussex v. Surrey (Oval) 1908

Raphael, J. E.	(1)	201	Oxford U. v. Yorkshire (Oxford) 1904
Ratcliffe, A.	(1)	201	Cambridge U. v. Oxford U. (Lord's) 1931
Read, W. W.	(3)	247	Surrey v. Lancashire (Manchester) 1887
		244*	Surrey v. Cambridge U. (Oval) 1887
		338	Surrey v. Oxford U. (Oval) 1888
Reid, J. R.	(2)	283	Wellington v. Otago (Wellington) 1951–52
		201	Otago v. Canterbury (Dunedin) 1957–58
Relf, R. R.	(3)	210	Sussex v. Kent (Canterbury) 1907
		272*	Sussex v. Worcestershire (Eastbourne) 1909
		225	Sussex v. Lancashire (Eastbourne) 1920
Reynolds, R.	(1)	203*	Queensland v. South Australia (Adelaide) 1957–58
Rhodes, W.	(3)	201	Yorkshire v. Somerset (Taunton) 1905
		210	M.C.C. v. South Australia (Adelaide) 1920–21
		267*	Yorkshire v. Leicestershire (Leeds) 1921
Richardson, A. J.	(4)	280	South Australia v. M.C.C. (Adelaide) 1922–23
		200*	South Australia v. M.C.C. (Adelaide) 1924–25
		227	South Australia v. Western Australia (Adelaide) 1925–26
		232	South Australia v. Queensland (Adelaide) 1926–27
Richardson, C.	(1)	258	Orange Free State v. Transvaal B (Johannesburg) 1959–60
Richardson, V. Y.	(2)	231	South Australia v. M.C.C. (Adelaide) 1928–29
		203	South Australia v. Victoria (Adelaide) 1932–33
Riches, N. V. H.	(1)	239*	Wales v. Ireland (Belfast) 1926
Roach, C. A.	(1)	209	West Indies v. England (Georgetown) 1929–30
Robertson, J. D.	(4)	229	Middlesex v. Hampshire (Lord's) 1947
		331*	Middlesex v. Worcestershire (Worcester) 1949
		201*	Middlesex v. Somerset (Taunton) 1951
		201*	Middlesex v. Essex (Lord's) 1957
Rock, H. O.	(1)	235	New South Wales v. Victoria (Sydney) 1924–25
Roller, W. E.	(1)	204	Surrey v. Sussex (Oval) 1885
Rowan, E. A. B.	(5)	306*	Transvaal v. Natal (Johannesburg) 1939–40
		284	Eastern Province v. Griqualand West (Port Elizabeth) 1945–46
		277*	Transvaal v. Griqualand West (Johannesburg) 1950–51
		202*	South Africans v. Northamptonshire (Northampton) 1951
		236	South Africa v. England (Leeds) 1951
Russell, A. C.	(2)	201	M.C.C. v. South Australia (Adelaide) 1920–21
		273	Essex v. Northamptonshire (Leyton) 1921
Ryder, J.	(3)	242	Victoria v. South Australia (Melbourne) 1921–22
		201*	Australia v. England (Adelaide) 1924–25
		295	Victoria v. New South Wales (Melbourne) 1926–27
Sandham, A.	(11)	292*	Surrey v. Northamptonshire (Oval) 1921
		209*	Surrey v. Somerset (Oval) 1921
		200	Surrey v. Essex (Leyton) 1923
		230	Surrey v. Essex (Oval) 1927
		282*	Surrey v. Lancashire (Manchester) 1928
		248*	Surrey v. Glamorgan (Cardiff) 1928
		325	England v. West Indies (Kingston) 1929–30
		204	Surrey v. Warwickshire (Birmingham) 1930
		215	Surrey v. Somerset (Taunton) 1932
		219	Surrey v. Australians (Oval) 1934
		239	Surrey v. Glamorgan (Oval) 1937
Santall, F. R.	(1)	201*	Warwickshire v. Northamptonshire (Northampton) 1933
Sarwate, C. T.	(3)	235	Holkar v. Delhi (Delhi) 1949–50
		246	Holkar v. Bengal (Calcutta) 1950–51
		234	Holkar v. Gujerat (Indore) 1950–51
Sathasivam, M.	(1)	215	All Ceylon v. South India (Madras) 1946–47
Scott, S. W.	(1)	224	Middlesex v. Gloucestershire (Lord's) 1892
Scott, V. J.	(2)	204	Auckland v. Otago (Dunedin) 1947–48
		203	New Zealanders v. Combined Services (Gillingham) 1949
Sellers, A. B.	(1)	204	Yorkshire v. Cambridge U. (Cambridge) 1936
Seymour, James	(3)	204	Kent v. Hampshire (Tonbridge) 1907
		218*	Kent v. Essex (Leyton) 1911
		214	Kent v. Essex (Tunbridge Wells) 1914
Shahid Mahmood	(1)	220	Karachi U. v. Peshawar U. (Karachi) 1958–59
Sharp, A. T.	(1)	216	Leicestershire v. Derbyshire (Chesterfield) 1911
Sharp, J.	(1)	211	Lancashire v. Leicestershire (Manchester) 1912
Sharpe, P. J.	(2)	202	Minor Counties v. Indians (Stoke) 1959
		203*	Yorkshire v. Cambridge U. (Cambridge) 1960
Shepherd, T. F.	(5)	212	Surrey v. Lancashire (Oval) 1921
		210*	Surrey v. Kent (Blackheath) 1921
		207*	Surrey v. Kent (Blackheath) 1925
		277*	Surrey v. Gloucestershire (Oval) 1927
		234	Surrey v. Cambridge U. (Oval) 1930

Sheppard, D. S.	.........(3)	204	Sussex v. Glamorgan (Eastbourne) 1949
		227	Cambridge U. v. West Indies (Cambridge) 1950
		239*	Cambridge U. v. Worcestershire (Worcester)..................1952
Shipman, A.	..............(1)	226	Leicestershire v. Kent (Tonbridge) 1928
Shodhan, D. H.	..........(1)	261	Baroda v. Maharashtra (Ahmedabad) 1957–58
Shrewsbury, A.	..........(10)	207	Nottinghamshire v. Surrey (Oval) 1882
		209	Nottinghamshire v. Sussex (Hove) 1884
		224*	Nottinghamshire v. Middlesex (Lord's) 1885
		227*	Nottinghamshire v. Gloucestershire (Moreton-in-theMarsh) 1886
		236	Non-Smokers v. Smokers (East Melbourne) 1886–87
		267	Nottinghamshire v. Middlesex (Nottingham) 1887
		232	Shrewsbury's XI v. Victoria (Melbourne) 1887–88
		206	Shrewsbury's XI v. Australian XI (Sydney) 1887–88
		267	Nottinghamshire v. Sussex (Nottingham) 1890
		212	Nottinghamshire v. Middlesex (Lord's) 1892
Siedle, I. J.	..............(3)	212*	Natal v. Border (Durban) 1928–29
		265*	Natal v. Orange Free State (Durban) 1929–30
		207	Natal v. Western Province (Durban) 1936–37
Simpson, R. B.	..........(2)	236*	Western Australia v. New South Wales (Perth) 1959–60
		230	Western Australia v. Queensland (Perth) 1959–60
Simpson, R. T.	..........(10)	201	Nottinghamshire v. Warwickshire (Nottingham) 1946
		200*	Nottinghamshire v. Surrey (Nottingham) 1949
		238	Nottinghamshire v. Lancashire (Manchester) 1949
		230*	Nottinghamshire v. Glamorgan (Swansea) 1950
		243*	Nottinghamshire v. Worcestershire (Nottingham)..................1950
		259	M.C.C. v. New South Wales (Sydney) 1950–51
		201	Nottinghamshire v. Oxford U. (Oxford) 1951
		212	Nottinghamshire v. Essex (Clacton) 1951
		216	Nottinghamshire v. Sussex (Nottingham) 1952
		200	Nottinghamshire v. Warwickshire (Nottingham) 1952
Sinfield, R. A.	..............(1)	209*	Gloucestershire v. Glamorgan (Cardiff) 1935
Smith, D.	..................(2)	225	Derbyshire v. Hampshire (Chesterfield) 1935
		202*	Derbyshire v. Nottinghamshire (Nottingham) 1937
Smith, D. V.	..................(1)	206*	Sussex v. Nottinghamshire (Nottingham) 1950
Smith, M. J. K.	..........(2)	201*	Oxford U. v. Cambridge U. (Lord's) 1954
		200*	Warwickshire v. Worcestershire (Birmingham) 1959
Smith, S. G.	..................(2)	204	Northamptonshire v. Gloucestershire (Northampton) 1910
		256	Auckland v. Canterbury (Auckland) 1919–20
Sobers, G.	..................(3)	219*	West Indians v. Nottinghamshire (Nottingham) 1957
		365*	West Indies v. Pakistan (Kingston) 1957–58
		226	West Indies v. England (Barbados) 1959–60
Sohoni, S. W.	..............(1)	218*	Maharashtra v. Northern India (Poona) 1940–41
Solomon, J.	..................(1)	201*	Berbice v. M.C.C. (Blairmont) 1959–60
Spooner, R. H.	..........(5)	247	Lancashire v. Nottinghamshire (Nottingham) 1903
		215	Lancashire v. Essex (Leyton) 1904
		240	Lancashire v. Somerset (Bath) 1906
		200*	Lancashire v. Yorkshire (Manchester) 1910
		224	Lancashire v. Surrey (Oval) 1911
Squires, H. S.	..............(3)	200*	Surrey v. Cambridge U. (Oval) 1931
		236	Surrey v. Lancashire (Oval) 1933
		210	Surrey v. Derbyshire (Oval) 1949
Stevens, G.	..................(1)	259*	South Australia v. New South Wales (Sydney) 1958–59
Steyn, S. S. L.	..............(1)	261*	Western Province v. Border (Cape Town) 1929–30
Stoddart, A. E.	..........(2)	215*	Middlesex v. Lancashire (Manchester) 1891
		221	Middlesex v. Somerset (Lord's) 1900
Stollmeyer, J. B.	..........(5)	210	Trinidad v. Barbados (Barbados) 1943–44
		324	Trinidad v. British Guiana (Trinidad) 1946–47
		244*	West Indians v. South Zone (Madras) 1948–49
		261	Trinidad v. Jamaica (Trinidad) 1949–50
		208	Trinidad v. Barbados (Barbados) 1950–51
Storer, H.	..................(2)	209	Derbyshire v. Essex (Derby) 1929
		232	Derbyshire v. Essex (Derby) 1933
Storer, W.	..................(1)	216*	Derbyshire v. Leicestershire (Chesterfield) 1899
Subba Row, R.	..........(2)	260*	Northamptonshire v. Lancashire (Northampton) 1955
		300	Northamptonshire v. Surrey (Oval) 1958
Sudhir Das	..................(1)	221*	Bihar v. Assam (Jamshedpur) 1957–58
Sugg, F. H.	..................(1)	220	Lancashire v. Gloucestershire (Bristol) 1896
Surti, R.	..................(1)	246*	Rajasthan v. Uttar Pradesh (Udaipur) 1959–60
Sutcliffe, B.	..................(7)	208*	North Island v. South Island (Dunedin) 1947–48
		243	New Zealanders v. Essex (Southend) 1949
		355	Otago v. Auckland (Dunedin) 1949–50
		275	Otago v. Auckland (Auckland) 1950–51

Sutcliffe, B. *(cont.)*	385	Otago v. Canterbury (Christchurch) 1952–53	
	230*	New Zealand v. India (New Delhi) 1955–56	
	264	Otago v. Central Districts (Dunedin) 1959–60	
Sutcliffe, H. ....(17)	232	Yorkshire v. Surrey (Oval) 1922	
	213	Yorkshire v. Somerset (Dewsbury) 1924	
	255*	Yorkshire v. Essex (Southend) 1924	
	235	Yorkshire v. Middlesex (Leeds) 1925	
	206	Yorkshire v. Warwickshire (Dewsbury) 1925	
	200	Yorkshire v. Leicestershire (Leicester).........................1926	
	227	England v. Rest (Bristol) 1927	
	228	Yorkshire v. Sussex (Eastbourne) 1928	
	230	Yorkshire v. Kent (Folkestone) 1931	
	313	Yorkshire v. Essex (Leyton) 1932	
	270	Yorkshire v. Sussex (Leeds) 1932	
	205	Yorkshire v. Warwickshire (Birmignham) 1933	
	203	Yorkshire v. Surrey (Oval) 1934	
	200*	Yorkshire v. Worcestershire (Sheffield) 1935	
	212	Yorkshire v. Leicestershire (Leicester)........................1935	
	202	Yorkshire v. Middlesex (Scarborough) 1936	
	234*	Yorkshire v. Leicestershire (Hull) 1939	
Tarilton, P. H. ....(1)	304*	Barbados v. Trinidad (Barbados) 1919–20	
Tarrant, F. A. ....(4)	206	Victoria v. New South Wales (Sydney) 1907–08	
	207*	Middlesex v. Yorkshire (Bradford) 1911	
	250*	Middlesex v. Essex (Leyton) 1914	
	200	Middlesex v. Worcestershire (Lord's) 1914	
Tate, M. W. ....(1)	203	Sussex v. Northamptonshire (Hove) 1921	
Taylor, H. W. ....(1)	250*	Natal v. Transvaal (Johannesburg) 1912–13	
Tennyson, Lord ....(1)	217	Hampshire v. West Indians (Southampton) 1928	
Thompson, F. C. ....(1)	275*	Queensland v. New South Wales (Brisbane) 1930–31	
Timms, J. E. ....(1)	213	Northamptonshire v. Worcestershire (Stourbridge) 1934	
Townsend, C. L. ....(2)	224*	Glocestershire v. Essex (Clifton) 1899	
	214	Gloucestershire v. Worcestershire (Cheltenham) 1906	
Townsend, L. F. ....(1)	233	Derbyshire v. Leicestershire (Loughborough) 1933	
Trumper, V. T. ....(8)	292*	New South Wales v. Tasmania (Sydney) 1898–99	
	253	New South Wales v. New Zealanders (Sydney) 1898–99	
	300*	Australians v. Sussex (Hove) 1899	
	208	New South Wales v. Queensland (Sydney) 1899–00	
	230	New South Wales v. Victoria (Sydney) 1900–01	
	214*	Australia v. South Africa (Adelaide) 1910–11	
	201*	New South Wales v. South Australia (Sydney) 1912–13	
	293	Australians v. Canterbury (Christchurch) 1913–14	
Tunnicliffe, J. ....(1)	243	Yorkshire v. Derbyshire (Chesterfield) 1898	
Turnbull, M. J. ....(3)	205	Glamorgan v. Nottinghamshire (Cardiff) 1932	
	200*	Glamorgan v. Northamptonshire (Swansea) 1933	
	233	Glamorgan v. Worcestershire (Swansea).......................1937	
Tyldesley, E.................(7)	244	Lancashire v. Warwickshire (Birmingham)...................1920	
	236	Lancashire v. Surrey (Oval) 1923	
	226	Lancashire v. Sussex (Manchester) 1926	
	242	Lancashire v. Leicestershire (Leicester) 1928	
	256*	Lancashire v. Warwickshire (Manchester) 1930	
	225*	Lancashire v. Worcestershire (Worcester) 1932	
	239	Lancashire v. Glamorgan (Cardiff) 1934	
Tyldesley, J. T. ....(13)	200	Lancashire v. Derbyshire (Manchester) 1898	
	249	Lancashire v. Leicestershire (Leicester) 1899	
	221	Lancashire v. Nottinghamshire (Nottingham) 1901	
	248	Lancashire v. Worcestershire (Liverpool) 1903	
	210	Lancashire v. Somerset (Bath) 1904	
	225	Lancashire v. Nottinghamshire (Nottingham) 1904	
	250	Lancashire v. Nottinghamshire (Nottingham) 1905	
	295*	Lancashire v. Kent (Manchester) 1906	
	209	Lancashire v. Warwickshire (Birmingham)...................1907	
	243	Lancashire v. Leicestershire (Leicester) 1908	
	210	Lancashire v. Surrey (Oval) 1913	
	253	Lancashire v. Kent (Canterbury) 1914	
	272	Lancashire v. Derbyshire (Chesterfield) 1919	
Umrigar, P. R................(9)	229*	Indians v. Oxford U. (Oxford) 1952	
	204	Indians v. Lancashire (Manchester) 1952	
	204	Indians v. Kent (Canterbury) 1952	
	223	India v. New Zealand (Hyderabad) 1955–56	
	245	Bombay v. Saurashtra (Poona) 1957–58	
	213	Bombay v. Gujerat (Khadakvasla) 1957–58	
	252*	Indians v. Cambridge U. (Cambridge) 1959	

Umrigar, P. R. (*cont.*)	203	Indians v. Somerset (Taunton)	1959
	202*	Indians v. Northamptonshire (Northampton)	1959
Valentine, B. H. ....(2)	242	Kent v. Leicestershire (Oakham)	1938
	201	Kent v. Nottinghamshire (Nottingham)	1939
Vaulkhard, P. ....(1)	264	Derbyshire v. Nottinghamshire (Nottingham)	1946
Viljoen, K. G. ....(3)	215	Griqualand West v. Western Province (Kimberley)	1929–30
	200*	Orange Free State v. Transvaal (Bloemfontein)	1933–34
	201*	South Africans v. Sussex (Hove)	1947
Vine, J. ....(1)	202	Sussex v. Northamptonshire (Hastings)	1920
Wade, W. W. ....(1)	208	Natal v. Eastern Province (Pietermaritzburg)	1939–40
Wainwright, E. ....(1)	228	Yorkshire v. Surrey (Oval)	1899
Waite, J. H. B...............(1)	219	Eastern Province v. Griqualand West (Kimberley)	1950–51
Walcott, C. L. ....(4)	314*	Barbados v. Trinidad (Trinidad)	1945–46
	211*	Barbados v. British Guiana (Barbados)	1949–50
	209	Barbados v. Trinidad (Barbados)	1950–51
	220	West Indies v. England (Barbados)	1953–54
Walford, M. M. ....(2)	201*	Oxford U. v. M.C.C. (Lord's)	1938
	264	Somerset v. Hampshire (Weston-super-Mare)	1947
Walker, L. ....(1)	222	London County v. M.C.C. (Crystal Palace)	1901
Wallace, W. M. ....(1)	211	Auckland v. Canterbury (Auckland)	1939–40
Walters, C. F. ....(1)	226	Worcestershire v. Kent (Gravesend)	1933
Waqar Hasan ....(1)	201*	Cannon's XI v. Hasan Mahmood's XI (Karachi)	1953–54
Ward, A. ....(1)	219	Stoddart's XI v. South Australia (Adelaide)	1894–95
Warner, P. F. ....(3)	211	Hawke's XI v. Otago (Dunedin)	1902–03
	204	M.C.C. v. Sussex (Lord's)	1905
	244	Rest of England v. Warwickshire (Oval)	1911
Washbrook, C. ....(7)	228	Lancashire v. Oxford U. (Oxford)	1935
	219*	Lancashire v. Gloucestershire (Bristol)	1938
	204*	Lancashire v. Sussex (Manchester)	1947
	251*	Lancashire v. Surrey (Manchester)	1947
	200	Lancashire v. Hampshire (Manchester)	1948
	209*	Lancashire v. Warwickshire (Birmingham)	1951
	211*	Lancashire v. Somerset (Manchester)	1952
Watson, F. ....(4)	223	Lancashire v. Northamptonshire (Manchester)	1928
	300*	Lancashire v. Surrey (Manchester)	1928
	236	Lancashire v. Sussex (Hove)	1928
	207	Lancashire v. Worcestershire (Worcester)	1929
Watson, W. ....(2)	257	M.C.C. v. British Guiana (Georgetown)	1953–54
	214*	Yorkshire v. Worcestershire (Worcester)	1955
Watson, W. ....(1)	206	New South Wales v. Western Australia (Perth)	1956–57
Wazir Ali, S. ....(1)	222*	Southern Punjab v. Bengal (Calcutta)	1938–39
Webbe, A. J. ....(1)	243*	Middlesex v. Yorkshire (Huddersfield)	1887
Weekes, E. D. ....(9)	236*	Barbados v. British Guiana (Barbados)	1949–50
	232	West Indians v. Surrey (Oval)	1950
	304*	West Indians v. Cambridge U. (Cambridge)	1950
	279	West Indians v. Nottinghamshire (Nottingham)	1950
	246*	West Indians v. Hampshire (Southampton)	1950
	200*	West Indians v. Leicestershire (Leicester)	1950
	207	West Indies v. India (Trinidad)	1952–53
	253	Barbados v. Indians (Barbados)	1952–53
	206	West Indies v. England (Trinidad)	1953–54
Wells, C. M...................(1)	244	Middlesex v. Nottinghamshire (Nottingham)	1899
Whysall, W. W. ....(3)	209	Nottinghamshire v. Essex (Leyton)	1926
	244	Nottinghamshire v. Gloucestershire (Nottingham)	1929
	248	Nottinghamshire v. Northamptonshire (Nottingham)	1930
Wight, L. ....(1)	262*	British Guiana v. Barbados (Georgetown)	1951–52
Wight, P. B. ....(1)	222*	Somerset v. Kent (Taunton)	1959
Williams, E. S. B. ....(2)	209	Army v. Oxford U. (Oxford)	1925
	228	Army v. Royal Navy (Lord's)	1928
Wilson, B. B. ....(1)	208	Yorkshire v. Sussex (Bradford)	1914
Wilson, J. V. ....(2)	223*	Yorkshire v. Scotland (Edinburgh)	1951
	230	Yorkshire v. Derbyshire (Sheffield)	1952
Winrow, H. ....(1)	204*	Nottinghamshire v. Derbyshire (Nottingham)	1947
Wood, C. J. B...............(2)	200*	Leicestershire v. Hampshire (Leicester)	1905
	225	Leicestershire v. Worcestershire (Worcester)	1906
Woodfull, W. M............(7)	212*	Victoria v. Canterbury (Christchurch)	1924–25
	236	Victoria v. South Australia (Melbourne)	1925–26
	201	Australians v. Essex (Leyton)	1926
	284	Australians v. New Zealand XI (Auckland)	1927–28
	275*	Victoria v. M.C.C. (Melbourne)	1928–29
	216	Australians v. Cambridge U. (Cambridge)	1930
	228*	Australians v. Glamorgan (Swansea)	1934

Woods, S. M. J.	............(1)	215	Somerset v. Sussex (Hove) 1895
Woolley, C. N.	............(1)	204*	Northamptonshire v. Worcestershire (Northampton) 1921
Woolley, F. E.	............(9)	305*	M.C.C. v. Tasmania (Hobart) 1911–12
		224*	Kent v. Oxford U. (Oxford) 1913
		270	Kent v. Middlesex (Canterbury) 1923
		202	Rest of England v. Yorkshire (Oval) 1924
		215	Kent v. Somerset (Gravesend) 1925
		217	Kent v. Northamptonshire (Northampton) 1926
		219	M.C.C. v. New South Wales (Sydney) 1929–30
		224	Kent v. New Zealanders (Canterbury) 1931
		229	Kent v. Surrey (Oval) 1935
Worrell, F. M.	...............(7)	308*	Barbados v. Trinidad (Barbados) 1943–44
		255*	Barbados v. Trinidad (Trinidad) 1945–46
		223*	Commonwealth v. Indian XI (Cawnpore) 1949–50
		241*	West Indians v. Leicestershire (Leicester) 1950
		261	West Indies v. England (Nottingham) 1950
		285	Commonwealth v. Ceylon (Colombo) 1950–51
		237	West Indies v. India (Kingston) 1952–53
Worthington, T. S.	.........(2)	200*	Derbyshire v. Worcestershire (Chesterfield) 1933
		238*	Derbyshire v. Sussex (Derby) 1937
Wyatt, R. E. S.	............(2)	232	Warwickshire v. Derbyshire (Birmingham) 1937
		201*	Warwickshire v. Lancashire (Birmingham)..................1937
Wynne, O. E.	...............(1)	200*	Transvaal v. Border (Johannesburg) 1946–47
Wynyard, E. G.	............(2)	268	Hampshire v. Yorkshire (Southampton) 1896
		225	Hampshire v. Somerset (Taunton) 1899
Young, R. A.	...............(1)	220	Sussex v. Essex (Leyton) 1905

A Century on Début in First-class Cricket

Allsopp, A.	117	New South Wales v. M.C.C. (Sydney) 1929–30
Asif Ahmed	148	Combined Universities v. East Pakistan (Karachi) 1959–60
Barker, G. E.	...................107*	Essex v. Canadians (Clacton) 1954
Bernau, E. H. L.	117	Wellington v. Auckland (Wellington) 1922–23
Biggs, M.	108	Queensland v. South Australia (Brisbane) 1930–31
Bill, O. W.	115	New South Wales v. Tasmania (Sydney) 1929–30
Bisgood, B. L.	...................116*	Somerset v. Worcestershire (Worcester) 1907
Bloomfield, H. O.	.........107*	Surrey v. Northamptonshire (Northampton) 1921
Bogle, J.	145	New South Wales v. Victoria (Sydney) 1918–19
Bradman, D. G.	118	New South Wales v. South Australia (Adelaide)..............1927–28
Briggs, R.	121	New South Wales v. Western Australia (Perth) 1952–53
Brook-Smith, W.	...................112*	Auckland v. Hawke's Bay (Auckland) 1904–05
Bryan, G. J.	124	Kent v. Nottinghamshire (Nottingham) 1920
Byrne, J. F.	100	Warwickshire v. Leicestershire (Birmingham) 1897
Callaway, N.	207	New South Wales v. Queensland (Sydney) 1914–15
Chambers, J. L.	132	Victoria v. Tasmania (Melbourne) 1949–50
Chapman, A. P. F.	118	Cambridge U. v. Essex (Cambridge) 1920
Cheshire, F. W.	107	Border v. Orange Free State (Johannesburg) 1923–24
Clark, E. A.	...................100*	Middlesex v. Cambridge U. (Cambridge) 1959
Contractor, N. J.	152 & 102*	Gujerat v. Baroda (Baroda) 1952–53
Day, S. H.	...................101*	Kent v. Gloucestershire (Cheltenham) 1897
de Saram, F. C.	176	Oxford U. v. Gloucestershire (Oxford) 1934
Dillon, E. W.	108	London County v. Worcestershire (Crystal Palace) 1900
Doggart, G. H. G.	.........215*	Cambridge U. v. Lancashire (Cambridge) 1948
Draper, R. G.	114	Eastern Province v. Orange Free State (Port Elizabeth) ...1945–46
Dyer, D. V.	185	Natal v. Eastern Province (Pietermaritzburg) 1939–40
Ebden, C. H. M.	137	Cambridge U. v. Leveson-Gower's XI (Cambridge) 1902
Ellis, M.	118	Victoria v. South Australia (Melbourne) 1902–03
Fairbairn, A.	108	Middlesex v. Somerset (Taunton) 1947
Favell, L.	164	South Australia v. New South Wales (Adelaide)..........1951–52
Fernley, D. L.	106	Eastern Province v. North Eastern Transvaal (Pretoria) ...1954–55
Forssberg, E. B.	143	New South Wales v. Queensland (Sydney) 1920–21
Francis, J.	135	Victoria v. Tasmania (Launceston) 1932–33
Frank, C. N.	108	Transvaal v. A.I.F. (Johannesburg) 1919–20
Freakes, H. D.	...................122*	Eastern Province v. Natal (Johannesburg) 1931–32
Gill, J. R.	106	Ireland v. M.C.C. (Dublin) 1948
Gimblett, H.	123	Somerset v. Essex (Frome) 1935
Gooden, N. L.	102	South Australia v. Western Australia (Adelaide) 1912–13
Gordon-Stewart, C. S.	...121	Victoria v. New South Wales (Melbourne) 1869–70

Grangel, H.	108	Victoria v. Tasmania (Melbourne)	1935–36
Gwynne, L.	138	New South Wales v. South Australia (Adelaide)	1924–25
Hall, P. M.	101	Oxford U. v. Free Foresters (Oxford)	1919
Hallebone, J.	202	Victoria v. Tasmania (Melbourne)	1951–52
Hamence, R. A.	121	South Australia v. Tasmania (Adelaide)	1935–36
Hamilton, C. P.	121	Army v. West Indians (Aldershot)	1933
Harbottle, M. N.	156	Army v. Oxford U. (Camberley)	1938
Harris, T. A.	114*	Griqualand West v. Orange Free State (Kimberley)	1933–34
Hearn, P.	124	Kent v. Warwickshire (Gillingham)	1947
Higgs, K. A.	101	Sussex v. Worcestershire (Hove)	1920
Hilder, A. L.	103*	Kent v. Essex (Gravesend)	1924
Hone, B. W.	137	South Australia v. Victoria (Adelaide)	1928–29
Human, J. H.	158*	Cambridge U. v. Leveson-Gower's XI (Eastbourne)	1932
Hyett, F.	108*	Victoria v. Tasmania (Melbourne)	1914–15
Kerr, C.	122	Auckland v. Wellington (Auckland)	1941–42
Kerr, E. A. D.	112	Victoria v. Tasmania (Launceston)	1946–47
Khurshid Ahmed	101	Pakistan v. Central Zone (Nagpur)	1952–53
King, C. H.	135	British Guiana v. Trinidad (Georgetown)	1895–96
Lacey, S.	102	Transvaal v. Rhodesia (Salisbury)	1945–46
Leadbeater, L.	128	New South Wales v. Tasmania (Sydney)	1929–30
Leslie, C. F. H.	111*	Oxford U. v. M.C.C. (Oxford)	1881
Levy, R. M.	129	Queensland v. Victoria (Brisbane)	1928–29
Loxton, S. J. E.	232*	Victoria v. Queensland (Melbourne)	1946–47
Lukeman, E.	118	New South Wales v. South Australia (Adelaide)	1946–47
Lyons, E.	102	Queensland v. Victoria (Brisbane)	1955–56
MacLaren, A. C.	108	Lancashire v. Sussex (Hove)	1890
Maqsood Ahmed	144	Southern Punjab v. Northern India (Lahore)	1944–45
Marks, N.	180	New South Wales v. South Australia (Sydney)	1958–59
Marlow, F. W.	144	Sussex v. M.C.C. (Lord's)	1891
Martin, F. C.	145	Western Province v. Eastern Province (Cape Town)	1929–30
Martin, F. R.	195	Jamaica v. Barbados (Barbados)	1925–26
Marx, W. F. E.	240	Transvaal v. Griqualand West (Johannesburg)	1920–21
Maynard, A.	200*	Trinidad v. M.C.C. (Trinidad)	1934–35
Mollwraith, J.	133	Victoria v. New South Wales (Melbourne)	1885–86
McLeod, D.	107	Victoria v. Tasmania (Hobart)	1894–95
McLeod, D. N.	117	Central Districts v. Wellington (Wanganui)	1956–57
McPetrie, W.	123	Victoria v. Tasmania (Melbourne)	1904–05
Miller, K. R.	181	Victoria v. Tasmania (Melbourne)	1937–38
Miller, N.	124	Surrey v. Sussex (Hove)	1899
Morris, A. R.	148 & 111	New South Wales v. Queensland (Sydney)	1940–41
Morton, H. G. S	135*	Queensland v. Victoria (Melbourne)	1904–05
Moyes, A. G.	104	South Australia v. Western Australia (Adelaide)	1912–13
Mullarkey, D.	130	New South Wales v. Queensland (Brisbane)	1923–24
Murray-Wood, W.	106*	Oxford U. v. Gloucestershire (Oxford)	1936
Nichol, M.	104	Worcestershire v. West Indians (Worcester)	1928
Nicholson, W. G.	101	Scotland v. Ireland (Dublin)	1929
Nutt, R. H.	102	New South Wales v. South Australia (Adelaide)	1931–32
Oakley, H. H.	108	Victoria v. South Australia (Melbourne)	1930–31
O'Halloran, J.	128*	Victoria v. New South Wales (Melbourne)	1896–97
Ongley, J. A.	110	Wellington v. Otago (Wellington)	1938–39
Parija, L.	103	Orissa v. Assam (Cuttack)	1952–53
Passailaigue, C. C.	183	Jamaica v. M.C.C. (Kingston)	1929–30
Payne, C. A. L.	101	M.C.C. v. Derbyshire (Lord's)	1905
Persaud, C. S.	174	British Guiana v. Barbados (Georgetown)	1937–38
Pinch, F. B.	138*	Glamorgan v. Worcestershire (Swansea)	1921
Poidevin, L. O. S.	140*	New South Wales v. South Australia (Sydney)	1900–01
Pretty, H. C.	124	Surrey v. Nottinghamshire (Oval)	1899
Pye, L. W.	166	New South Wales v. Queensland (Brisbane)	1896–97
Rhys, H. R. J.	149	Free Foresters v. Cambridge U. (Cambridge)	1929
Ricketts, J.	195*	Lancashire v. Surrey (Oval)	1867
Rock, C. W.	102	Tasmania v. Victoria (Melbourne)	1888–89
Rock, H. O.	127	New South Wales v. South Australia (Sydney)	1924–25
Roy, P.	112*	Bengal v. United Provinces (Calcutta)	1946–47
Sampath, C.	123	Barbados v. Trinidad (Barbados)	1948–49
Scott, J. G. C.	137	Sussex v. Oxford U. (Eastbourne)	1907
Scott, V. J.	122	Auckland v. Canterbury (Auckland)	1937–38
Sealey, J. E. D.	100	Barbados v. M.C.C. (Barbados)	1929–30
Sen Gupta, A. K.	100*	Services v. West Indians (Poona)	1958–59
Shepherd, B.	103*	Western Australia v. Queensland (Perth)	1955–56
Siedle, J. R.	127	Western Province v. Eastern Province (Cape Town)	1955–56
Slack, J. K. E.	135	Cambridge U. v. Middlesex (Cambridge)	1954
Smith, K. F. H.	141*	Wellington v. Central Districts (Wellington)	1954–55

Snedden, N. R.	119	Auckland v. Hawke's Bay (Auckland)	1920–21
Stocks, F. W.	114	Nottinghamshire v. Kent (Nottingham)	1946
Talbot, R. O.	105	Canterbury v. Otago (Dunedin)	1922–23
Tennyson, Hon. L. H.	...110	M.C.C. v. Oxford U. (Lord's)	1913
Tindill, E. W.	106	Wellington v. Auckland (Auckland)	1932–33
Trevor, A. H.	103	Sussex v. Kent (Hove)	1880
Tuck, G. S.	125	Royal Navy v. New Zealanders (Portsmouth)	1927
Tyson, C.	................100*	Yorkshire v. Hampshire (Southampton)	1921
Waddy, E. F.	...............129*	New South Wales v. South Australia (Adelaide)	1904–05
Walker I. D.	102	Middlesex v. Surrey (Oval)	1862
Watson, G.	175	Canterbury v. Otago (Christchurch)	1880–81
Watt, D. G.	105	Otago v. Canterbury (Christchurch)	1943–44
Weekes, K. H.	106	Jamaica v. Oxford & Cambridge Us. (Kingston)	1938–39
Whitehead, R.	...............131*	Lancashire v. Nottinghamshire (Manchester)	1908
Whitehead, T. H.	.........107*	Eastern Province v. Orange Free State (Port Elizabeth)	...1921–22
Williams, O.	100	Leeward Islands v. Jamaica (Kingston)	1958–59
Wilson, E. R.	...............117*	Webbe's XI v. Cambridge U. (Cambridge)	1899
Winslow, L.	124	Sussex v. Gloucestershire (Hove)	1875
Wood, B. B.	108	Canterbury v. Wellington (Wellington)	1907–08
Wootton, S. C.	105	Victoria v. Tasmania (Hobart)	1923–24

F. C. Holland's first four innings for Surrey in 1894 and 1895 were: 76 in 1894; 123, 62, 171, in 1895.

J. J. Broughton, playing in his first match for Leicestershire, scored 99 v. Essex (Leyton) 1901.

Hon. L. H. Tennyson (Hampshire) played the following first eight innings in first-class cricket: 20 and 110, 28, 38 and 116, 111 and 4, 96, in 1913.

W. H. Ponsford (Victoria) played the following first five innings in first-class cricket: 6 and 19, 162, 429, 108, in 1921–22 and 1922–23.

E. F. Wilson, making his debut in first-class cricket for Surrey v. Northamptonshire (Northampton) 1928, was dismissed at 99.

W. N. Carson (Auckland) played the following first three innings in first-class cricket in 1936–37: 12, 290, 194.

J. R. Thompson, making his debut in first-class cricket for Cambridge U. v. Northamptonshire (Cambridge) 1938, scored 96 and shared in a first-wicket partnership of 241 with P. A. Gibb.

N. H. Rogers, making his debut in first-class cricket for Hampshire v. Worcestershire (Southampton) 1946, scored 90 and shared in a fifth-wicket stand of 209 with J. Bailey.

P. F. Harvey (Nottinghamshire) did not bat in his first match, but scored 5 and 125* v. Derbyshire (Nottingham) 1947 in his second match in first-class cricket. In the second innings he shared in a sixth-wicket stand of 303 with H. Winrow.

C. G. Burger, after one match for Free Foresters in 1955, scored 94* for Natal v. Eastern Province (Durban) 1955–56, his first first-class match in South Africa, but then run out of partners.

N. Marks (New South Wales) scored 180 v. South Australia (Sydney) and 103 v. Victoria (Melbourne) in his first two innings in first-class cricket in 1958–59.

The following batsmen scored a century in their only match in first-class cricket: N. Callaway (1914–15), H. Grangel (1935–36), M. N. Harbottle (1938), S. C. Wootton (1923–24), and J. R. Gill (1948).

A Century on Début for First-class County

The following batsmen scored a century on début for a first-class county, but had previously played in first-class cricket:

Abercrombie, C. H.	126	Hampshire v. Oxford U. (Southampton)	1913
Baldry, D. O.	151	Hampshire v. Glamorgan (Portsmouth)	1959
Bartlett, H. T.	122	Sussex v. Cambridge U. (Worthing)	1937
Barton, M. R.	124	Surrey v. M.C.C. (Lord's)	1948
Dixon, E. J. H.	123	Northamptonshire v. Somerset (Northampton)	1939
Evans, A. J.	102	Kent v. Northamptonshire (Northampton)	1921
Fiddian-Green, C. A.	108	Worcestershire v. Essex (Worcester)	1931
Gibb, P. A.	..................157*	Yorkshire v. Nottinghamshire (Sheffield)	1935
Miller, K. R.	...............102*	Nottinghamshire v. Cambridge U. (Nottingham)	1959
Moore, D. N.	206	Gloucestershire v. Oxford U. (Oxford)	1930
Ranjitsinhji, K. S.	150	Sussex v. M.C.C. (Lord's)	1895
Sarel, W. G. M.	103	Sussex v. Oxford U. (Hove)	1919
Walford, M. M.	...........141*	Somerset v. Indians (Taunton)	1946
Wight, P. B.	...............109*	Somerset v. Australians (Taunton)	1953

E. G. Hayes, after playing for Surrey from 1896 to 1919, scored 5 and 99 v. Nottinghamshire (Nottingham) in his first match for Leicestershire in 1926.

A Century on Début for a Touring Team

Several batsmen have succeeded in scoring a century in their first match for a touring team on their first visit to that country. Details of these performances are as follows:

ENGLAND TEAMS IN AUSTRALIA

J. T. Brown	115	Stoddart's XI v. South Australia (Adelaide)	1894–95
A. C. MacLaren	228	Stoddart's XI v. Victoria (Melbourne)	1894–95
K. S. Ranjitsinhji	189	Stoddart's XI v. South Australia (Adelaide)	1897–98
G. Gunn	119	England v. Australia (Sydney)	1907–08
F. R. Foster	158	M.C.C. v. South Australia (Adelaide)	1911–12
A. C. Russell	156	M.C.C. v. South Australia (Adelaide)	1920–21
R. Kilner	103	M.C.C. v. Western Australia (Perth)	1924–25
D. R Jardine	109	M.C.C. v. Western Australia (Perth)	1928–29
Nawab of Pataudi	166	M.C.C. v. Western Australia (Perth)	1932–33
D. B. Close	108*	M.C.C. v. Western Australia (Perth)	1950–51

ENGLAND TEAMS IN SOUTH AFRICA

J. B. Hobbs	114	M.C.C. v. Western Province (Cape Town)	1909–10
G. B. Legge	120	M.C.C. v. Orange Free State (Bloemfontein)	1927–28
E. Paynter	158	M.C.C. v. Griqualand West (Kimberley)	1938–39
N. W. D. Yardley	142	M.C.C. v. Griqualand West (Kimberley)	1938–39
F. G. Mann	112	M.C.C. v. Western Province (Cape Town)	1948–49
P. B. H. May	162	M.C.C. v. Western Province (Cape Town)	1956–57

ENGLAND TEAMS IN WEST INDIES

E. Humphreys	106	M.C.C. v. Barbados (Barbados)	1912–13
E. Tyldesley	101	Tennyson's XI v. Jamaica (Kingston)	1926–27
C. P. Mead	103*	Tennyson's XI v. Jamaica (Kingston)	1927–28
E. Hendren	223*	M.C.C. v. Barbados (Barbados)	1929–30
A. Mitchell	101*	Yorkshire v. Jamaica (Kingston)	1935–36
R. C. M. Kimpton	113	Oxford & Cambridge Us. v. Jamaica (Kingston)	1938–39
W. Watson	161	M.C.C. v. Jamaica (Kingston)	1953–54

ENGLAND TEAMS IN NEW ZEALAND

C. H. Titchmarsh	154	M.C.C. v. Auckland (Auckland)	1922–23
L. E. G. Ames	103	England v. New Zealand (Christchurch)	1932–33
W. R. Hammond	227	England v. New Zealand (Christchurch)	1932–33
C. Washbrook	133	M.C.C. v. Wellington (Wellington)	1946–47
N. W. D. Yardley	126	M.C.C. v. Otago (Dunedin)	1946–47
T. W. Graveney	101	M.C.C. v. Canterbury (Christchurch)	1954–55

ENGLAND TEAMS IN INDIA

C. J. Barnett	122	M.C.C. v. Sind (Karachi)	1933–34
D. R. Jardine	101*	M.C.C. v. Sind (Karachi)	1933–34
W. J. Edrich	140*	Tennyson's XI v. Sind (Karachi)	1937–38
Lord Tennyson	118	Tennyson's XI v. Sind (Karachi)	1937–38
G. M. Emmett	104	Commonwealth v. Cricket Club of India (Bombay)	1950–51
T. W. Graveney	101	M.C.C. v. Combined Universities (Bombay)	1951–52

AUSTRALIAN TEAMS IN ENGLAND

H. H. Massie	206	Australians v. Oxford U. (Oxford)	1882
M. A. Noble	116*	Australians v. South of England (Crystal Palace)	1899
W. M. Woodfull	201	Australians v. Essex (Leyton)	1926
D. G. Bradman	236	Australians v. Worcestershire (Worcester)	1930
A. G. Chipperfield	175	Australians v. Essex (Chelmsford)	1934
A. R. Morris	138	Australians v. Worcestershire (Worcester)	1948
G. B. Hole	112	Australians v. Worcestershire (Worcester)	1953
R. G. Archer	108	Australians v. Worcestershire (Worcester)	1953

AUSTRALIAN TEAMS IN SOUTH AFRICA

C. Hill	142	Australia v. South Africa (Johannesburg)	1902–03
W. A. Brown	148	Australians v. Natal (Durban)	1935–36
J. H. Fingleton	121	Australians v. Natal (Durban)	1935–36
J. A. R. Moroney	106	Australians v. Natal (Durban)	1949–50
A. R. Morris	153	Australians v. Natal (Durban)	1949–50
I. D. Craig	113	Australians v. Rhodesia (Salisbury)	1957–58
R. Benaud	117*	Australians v. Rhodesia (Salisbury)	1957–58
A. K. Davidson	100*	Australians v. Rhodesia (Salisbury)	1957–58

AUSTRALIAN TEAMS IN WEST INDIES

A. R. Morris	157	Australians v. Jamaica (Kingston)	1954–55

AUSTRALIAN TEAMS IN NEW ZEALAND

S. R. Walford	102	New South Wales v. Canterbury (Christchurch)	1895–96
E. R. Mayne	102	Australians v. Canterbury (Christchurch)	1909–10
E. L. Waddy	130	Australians v. Auckland (Auckland)	1913–14
V. S. Ransford	159	Australians v. Auckland (Auckland)	1913–14
J. L. Ellis	103	Victoria v. Otago (Dunedin)	1924–25
S. G. Barnes	107	Australians v. Auckland (Auckland)	1945–46
K. R. Miller	139	Australians v. Auckland (Auckland)	1945–46
A. L. Hassett	121	Australians v. Auckland (Auckland)	1945–46

AUSTRALIAN TEAMS IN INDIA

O. W. Bill	101	Australians v. Ceylon (Colombo)	1935–36
E. A. Williams	100*	Australians v. Prince's XI (New Delhi)	1945–46

SOUTH AFRICAN TEAMS IN ENGLAND

M. Hathorn	103	South Africans v. Hampshire (Southampton)	1901
H. B. Cameron	102	South Africans v. Worcestershire (Worcester)	1929

SOUTH AFRICAN TEAMS IN AUSTRALIA

A. D. Nourse sen.	201*	South Africans v. South Australia (Adelaide)	1910–11
L. A. Stricker	146	South Africans v. South Australia (Adelaide)	1910–11
J. A. J. Christy	102	South Africans v. Western Australia (Perth)	1931–32
D. J. McGlew	182	South Africans v. Western Australia (Perth)	1952–53

SOUTH AFRICAN TEAMS IN NEW ZEALAND

B. Mitchell	123	South Africans v. Auckland (Auckland)	1931–32
H. W. Taylor	113	South Africans v. Auckland (Auckland)	1931–32
D. J. McGlew	255*	South Africa v. New Zealand (Wellington)	1952–53
A. R. A. Murray	100*	South Africans v. Canterbury (Christchurch)	1952–53

WEST INDIAN TEAMS IN NEW ZEALAND

R. E. Marshall	102*	West Indians v. Otago (Dunedin)	1951–52

WEST INDIAN TEAMS IN INDIA

E. D. Weekes	172*	West Indians v. North Zone (Patiala)	1948–49

NEW ZEALAND TEAMS IN ENGLAND

C. C. Dacre	107	New Zealanders v. M.C.C. (Lord's)	1927
T. C. Lowry	106	New Zealanders v. M.C.C. (Lord's)	1927

NEW ZEALAND TEAMS IN AUSTRALIA

B. Sutcliffe ....142 New Zealanders v. Western Australia (Perth) 1953–54
L. S. M. Miller ....142 New Zealanders v. South Australia (Adelaide) 1953–54

NEW ZEALAND TEAMS IN SOUTH AFRICA

J. R. Reid ....111 New Zealanders v. Western Province (Cape Town) 1953–54

NEW ZEALAND TEAMS IN PAKISTAN

J. R. Reid ....150* New Zealanders v. Chief Commissioner's XI (Karachi) ...1955–56

INDIAN TEAMS IN ENGLAND

S. Wazir Ali ....108* Indians v. Glamorgan (Cardiff) 1932
A. A. Baig ....102 Indians v. Middlesex (Lord's) 1959

INDIAN TEAMS IN WEST INDIES

V. S. Hazare.............153* Indians v. Trinidad (Trinidad) ....,.............1952–53

PAKISTAN TEAMS IN ENGLAND

Alimuddin ....142 Pakistan v. Worcestershire (Worcester) 1954
Maqsood Ahmed...........111 Pakistan v. Worcestershire (Worcester) 1954

A. R. Morris is the only player to have scored a century in his first match in each of the four countries in which he played: Australia, England, South Africa and West Indies. Morris did not visit either New Zealand or India.

A Century in Each Innings of a Match

Adhikari, H. R. ....(1)	128	151*	Baroda v. Nawanagar (Jamnagar) 1945–46	
Allan, J. M. ....(1)	121*	105	Kent v. Northamptonshire (Northampton) 1955	
Amarnath, L. ....(1)	130	107	Indians v. Essex (Brentwood) 1936	
Ames, L. E. G. ....(3)	132	145*	Kent v. Northamptonshire (Dover) 1933	
	119	127	Kent v. Surrey (Blackheath) 1937	
	112	119	Kent v. Gloucestershire (Bristol) 1950	
Armstrong, W. W. ....(1)	157*	245	Victoria v. South Australia (Melbourne) 1920–21	
Arnold, E. G. ....(1)	101*	128	Worcestershire v. Cambridge U. (Cambridge) 1903	
Ashdown, W. H. ....(1)	121	103	Kent v. Middlesex (Lord's) 1931	
Avery, A. V.................(1)	117	100	Essex v. Glamorgan (Ebbw Vale) 1949	
Badcock, C. L................(1)	120	102	South Australia v. Victoria (Melbourne) 1940–41	
Bardsley, W.................(1)	136	130	Australia v. England (Oval) 1909	
Barrington, K. F. ....(1)	186	118*	Surrey v. Warwickshire (Birmingham) 1959	
Bates, L. A. ....(1)	116	144	Warwickshire v. Kent (Coventry) 1927	
Bates, W. E. ....(1)	105	111	Glamorgan v. Essex (Leyton) 1927	
Berry, L. G..................(1)	165	111*	Leicestershire v. Essex (Clacton) 1947	
Bosanquet, B. J. T. ......(2)	136	139	Middlesex v. Leicestershire (Lord's) 1900	
	103	100*	Middlesex v. Sussex (Lord's) 1905	
Bradman, D. G. ....(4)	131	133*	New South Wales v. Queensland (Brisbane) 1928–29	
	124	225	Woodfull's XI v. Ryder's XI (Sydney) 1929–30	
	107	113	South Australia v. Queensland (Brisbane) 1937–38	
	132	127*	Australia v. India (Melbourne).........................1947–48	
Brann, G.....................(1)	105	101	Sussex v. Kent (Hove) 1892	
Brookes, D. ....(1)	112	154*	Northamptonshire v. Sussex (Eastbourne) 1946	
Burke, J. W. ....(1)	138	125*	Australians v. Somerset (Taunton) 1956	
Burki, J. ....(1)	144*	109*	Oxford U. v. Essex (Brentwood) 1960	
Carpenter, H. ....(1)	127	104	Essex v. Kent (Leyton) 1901	
Carr, D. B. ....(1)	156*	109	Derbyshire v. Kent (Canterbury) 1959	
Charlesworth, C. ....(1)	100	101*	Warwickshire v. Surrey (Birmingham) 1913	
Chinnery, H. B. ....(1)	105	165	M.C.C. v. Oxford U. (Oxford) 1901	
Christiani, R. J. ....(1)	131*	100*	West Indians v. Middlesex (Lord's) 1950	

Compton, D. C. S.	.........(3)	124	100	Middlesex v. Lancashire (Manchester) 1946
		147	103*	England v. Australia (Adelaide) 1946–47
		135	125*	M.C.C. S.A. XI v. Leveson-Gower's XI (Scarborough)1948
Contractor, N. J.	.........(1)	152	102*	Gujerat v. Baroda (Baroda) 1952–53
Cooper, E.	...................(1)	191	106*	Worcestershire v. Northamptonshire (Kidderminster) 1946
Cowdrey, M. C.	...........(2)	110	103	M.C.C. v. New South Wales (Sydney) 1954–55
		115*	103*	Kent v. Essex (Gillingham) 1955
Dacre, C. C.	...............(2)	127*	101*	Auckland v. Victoria (Auckland) 1924–25
		119	125*	Gloucestershire v. Worcestershire (Worcester).........1933
Dalton, E. L.	...........(1)	157	116*	South Africans v. Kent (Canterbury) 1929
Daniell, J.	...............(1)	174*	108	Somerset v. Essex (Taunton) 1925
Dempster, C. S.	.........(1)	133	154*	Leicestershire v. Gloucestershire (Gloucester) 1937
Denton, D.	...................(3)	107	109*	Yorkshire v. Nottinghamshire (Nottingham) 1906
		133	121	Yorkshire v. M.C.C. (Scarborough) 1908
		139	138	M.C.C. v. Transvaal (Johannesburg) 1909–10
Deodhar, D. B.	...........(1)	105	141	Maharashtra v. Nawanagar (Poona) 1944–45
Dewes, J. G.	...............(1)	128	101	Middlesex v. Sussex (Hove) 1950
Dipper, A. E.	...............(1)	117	103	Gloucestershire v. Sussex (Horsham) 1922
Doggart, G. H. G.	.........(1)	140	105	Sussex v. Oxford U. (Oxford)...........................1954
Draper, R. G.	...............(1)	129	177	Griqualand West v. Border (Kimberley)............1952–53
Duleepsinhji, K. S.	.........(3)	115	246	Sussex v. Kent (Hastings) 1929
		116	102*	Sussex v. Middlesex (Lord's) 1930
		125	103*	Gentlemen v. Players (Lord's) 1930
Eady, C. J.	...................(1)	116	112*	Tasmania v. Victoria (Hobart) 1894–95
Edrich, J. H.	...............(1)	112	124	Surrey v. Nottinghamshire (Nottingham) 1959
Edwards, A.	...............(1)	103	105	Western Australia v. Queensland (Perth) 1950–51
Emmett, G. M.	............(2)	115	103*	Gloucestershire v. Leicestershire (Leicester) 1947
		110	102*	Gloucestershire v. Somerset (Bristol)....................1951
Enthoven, H. J.	...........(1)	123	115	Middlesex v. Sussex (Lord's) 1930
Fagg, A. E.	...................(2)	244	202*	Kent v. Essex (Colchester) 1938
		136	117*	Kent v. Essex (Maidstone) 1948
Favell, L.	.....................(2)	112	114	South Australia v. New South Wales (Sydney) ...1956–57
		104	145	South Australia v. Western Australia (Adelaide) 1958–59
Fellows-Smith, J. P.	.......(1)	100*	102*	Transvaal v. Commonwealth (Johannesburg) ...1959–60
Fishlock, L. B.	.............(4)	131*	100*	Surrey v. Sussex (Oval) 1936
		113	105	Surrey v. Yorkshire (Oval) 1937
		129	112	Surrey v. Leicestershire (Leicester).........................1946
		111	118	Surrey v. Nottinghamshire (Nottingham) 1949
Fordham, C. B.	.............(1)	140	100*	Minor Counties v. Oxford U. (Oxford) 1933
Foster, M. K.	...............(1)	141	106	Worcestershire v. Hampshire (Worcester) 1926
Foster, R. E.	...................(3)	134	101*	Worcestershire v. Hampshire (Worcester) 1899
		128	100*	Oxford U. v. Webbe's XI (Oxford) 1900
		102*	136	Gentlemen v. Players (Lord's) 1900
Foster, W. L.	...............(1)	140	172*	Worcestershire v. Hampshire (Worcester) 1899
Fry, C. B.	.....................(5)	108	123*	Sussex v. Middlesex (Hove) 1898
		125	229	Sussex v. Surrey (Hove) 1900
		138	101*	Sussex v. Kent (Hove) 1903
		156	106	Sussex v. M.C.C. (Lord's) 1905
		123	112	Hampshire v. Kent (Canterbury) 1911
Gaekwad, D. K.	.............(1)	128	101*	Baroda v. Gujerat (Baroda) 1949–50
Gardner, F. C.	.............(1)	113	101*	Warwickshire v. Essex (Ilford) 1950
Gehrs, D. R. A.	.............(1)	148*	100*	South Australia v. Western Australia (Fremantle) 1905–06
Gibbons, H. H.	.............(1)	111*	100*	Worcestershire v. Hampshire (Worcester) 1939
Gimblett, H.	...................(2)	115	127*	Somerset v. Hampshire (Taunton) 1949
		146	116	Somerset v. Derbyshire (Taunton) 1952
Gomez, G. E.	...............(1)	148	108*	Trinidad v. British Guiana (Georgetown) 1953–54
Grace, W. G.	...............(3)	130	102*	South of Thames v. North of Thames (Canterbury)...1868
		101	103*	Gloucestershire v. Kent (Clifton) 1887
		148	153	Gloucestershire v. Yorkshire (Clifton) 1888
Graveney, T. W.	............(3)	103	105*	Gloucestershire v. Northamptonshire (Bristol) 1951
		153	120	Howard's XI v. President's XI (Bombay) 1956–57
		106	101*	Gloucestershire v. Warwickshire (Birmingham) 1957
Gregory, J. M.	.............(1)	122	102	A.I.F. v. New South Wales (Sydney) 1919–20
Greig, J. G.	...................(1)	115	130	Hampshire v. Worcestershire (Worcester) 1905
Gunn, G.	.....................(3)	132	109*	Nottinghamshire v. Yorkshire (Nottingham) 1913
		169	185*	Nottinghamshire v. Surrey (Nottingham) 1919
		100	110	Nottinghamshire v. Warwickshire (Nottingham)......1927
Hallam, M. R.	............(1)	210	157*	Leicestershire v. Glamorgan (Leicester) 1959
Hallows, C.	...................(2)	112*	103*	Lancashire v. Leicestershire (Ashby de la Zouch) ...1924
		123	101*	Lancashire v. Warwickshire (Birmingham) 1928
Hamence, R. A.	............(2)	130	103*	South Australia v. Victoria (Melbourne) 1940–41
		132	101*	South Australia v. New South Wales (Adelaide) 1946–47

Hammond, W. R.	.........(7)	108	128	Gloucestershire v. Surrey (Oval) 1927
		139	143	Gloucestershire v. Surrey (Cheltenham) 1928
		119*	177	England v. Australia (Adelaide) 1928–29
		122	111*	Gloucestershire v. Worcestershire (Worcester).........1933
		104	136	M.C.C. v. South Australia (Adelaide) 1936–37
		110	123	Gloucestershire v. Derbyshire (Burton-upon-Trent) 1938
		121	102	England XI v. Dominions XI (Lord's) 1945
Hanif Mohammed	.........(1)	121	109*	Pakistan v. North Zone (Amritsar) 1952–53
Harbinson, W. K.	.....,..(1)	130	109*	Cambridge U. v. Glamorgan (Cambridge) 1929
Hardinge, H. T. W.	......(4)	153	126	Kent v. Essex (Leyton) 1908
		175	109	Kent v. Hampshire (Southampton) 1911
		117	105*	Kent v. Hampshire (Dover) 1913
		207	102*	Kent v. Surrey (Blackheath) 1921
Hardstaff, J., sen.	.........(1)	118	106*	Nottinghamshire v. Derbyshire (Nottingham) 1911
Hardstaff, J., jun.	.........(1)	100*	114*	Nottinghamshire v. Northamptonshire (Nottingham) 1949
Hassett, A. L.	...............(2)	122	122	Victoria v. New South Wales (Sydney) 1939–40
		187	124*	Australian Services v. Prince's XI (New Delhi) ...1945–46
Hayward, T.	...............(3)	106	112	Surrey v. Sussex (Hove) 1904
		144*	100	Surrey v. Nottinghamshire (Nottingham) 1906
		143	125	Surrey v. Leicestershire (Leicester)....................1906
Hazare, V. S.	...............(3)	127	162*	Baroda v. Maharashtra (Poona) 1944–45
		116	145	India v. Australia (Adelaide) 1947–48
		130	101	Baroda v. Holkar (Baroda) 1949–50
Headley, G.	.................(2)	114	112	West Indies v. England (Georgetown)...............1929–30
		106	107	West Indies v. England (Lord's)....................1939
Hearne, J. W.	...............(1)	104	101*	Middlesex v. Glamorgan (Lord's) 1931
Hendren, E.	...............(4)	119	102	M.C.C. v. Kent (Folkestone) 1927
		189	100*	Middlesex v. Warwickshire (Birmingham) 1931
		101	101	Middlesex v. Kent (Lord's) 1933
		104	101	Middlesex v. Surrey (Lord's) 1936
Hill, A. J. L.	...............(1)	124	118*	Hampshire v. Somerset (Southampton) 1905
Hill, N.	.....................(1)	101	102	Nottinghamshire v. Lancashire (Nottingham) 1959
Hirst, G. H.	.................(1)	111	117*	Yorkshire v. Somerset (Bath) 1906
Hobbs, J. B.	...............(6)	160	100	Surrey v. Warwickshire (Birmingham) 1909
		104	143*	Surrey v. Cambridge U. (Oval) 1925
		101	101*	Surrey v. Somerset (Taunton) 1925
		112	104	Surrey v. Hampshire (Oval) 1927
		137	111*	Surrey v. Glamorgan (Oval) 1930
		113	119*	Surrey v. Essex (Oval) 1932
Holmes, P.	...................(1)	126	111*	Yorkshire v. Lancashire (Manchester) 1920
Howell, M.	...................(1)	115	102	Oxford U. v. Leveson-Gower's XI (Eastbourne) ...1919
Human, J. H.	.................(1)	110	122	Cambridge U. v. Surrey (Oval) 1933
Hutchings, K. L.	.........(1)	109	109*	Kent v. Worcestershire (Worcester) 1907
Hutton, L.	...................(3)	197	104	Yorkshire v. Essex (Southend) 1947
		165	100	Yorkshire v. Sussex (Hove) 1949
		103	137	Yorkshire v. M.C.C. (Scarborough) 1952
Ingle, R. A.	...................(1)	117	100*	Somerset v. Middlesex (Taunton) 1928
Insole, D. J.	...................(1)	111	118	Essex v. Kent (Gillingham) 1955
Jackson, A. A.	.............(1)	131	122	New South Wales v. South Australia (Sydney) ...1927–28
Jessop, G. L.	.................(4)	104	139	Gloucestershire v. Yorkshire (Bradford) 1900
		143	133*	Gloucestershire v. Somerset (Bath) 1908
		161	129	Gloucestershire v. Hampshire (Bristol) 1909
		153	123*	Gloucestershire v. Hampshire (Southampton) 1911
Johnson, P. R.	...........(1)	164	131	Somerset v. Middlesex (Taunton) 1908
Johnston, A. C.	.............(1)	175	100*	Hampshire v. Warwickshire (Coventry) 1912
Jones, A. O.	.................(1)	137	100	Nottinghamshire v. Lancashire (Nottingham) 1900
Kadri, S. M.	...................(1)	105	114	Bombay v. Western India States (Poona) 1935–36
Keith, H. J.	...................(1)	111	113*	South Africans v. Victoria (Melbourne) 1952–53
Kenny, A.	.....................(1)	164	100*	Victoria v. Queensland (Brisbane) 1909–10
Kimpton, R. C. M.	......(1)	101	106	Oxford U. v. Gloucestershire (Oxford) 1936
King, J. H.	...................(2)	104	109*	Players v. Gentlemen (Lord's) 1904
		111	100*	Leicestershire v. Northamptonshire (Leicester) 1913
Kinneir, S. P.	.................(1)	124	110	Warwickshire v. Sussex (Chichester) 1911
Kippax, A. F.	.................(2)	127	131	New South Wales v. Queensland (Brisbane) 1926–27
		158	102*	Australians v. Sussex (Hove) 1930
Knight, D. J.	...............(1)	114	101	Surrey v. Yorkshire (Oval) 1919
Lambert, W.	...................(1)	107*	157	Sussex v. Epsom (Lord's) 1817
Langridge, John	............(2)	115	129	Sussex v. Lancashire (Manchester) 1949
		146	146*	Sussex v. Derbyshire (Worthing) 1949
Lee, F. S.	.....................(1)	109*	107	Somerset v. Worcestershire (Worcester) 1938
Lee, H. W.	...................(2)	163	126	Middlesex v. Surrey (Oval) 1919
		124	105*	Middlesex v. Lancashire (Lord's) 1929

Lester, E. ....(2)	126	142	Yorkshire v. Northamptonshire (Northampton) 1947
	125*	132	Yorkshire v. Lancashire (Manchester) 1948
Llewellyn, C. B. ....(2)	102	100	Hampshire v. Derbyshire (Derby) 1905
	130	101*	Hampshire v. Sussex (Hove) 1909
Lonergan, A. R. ....(1)	115	100	South Australia v. Victoria (Melbourne) 1933–34
Lyon, B. H. ....(1)	115	101*	Gloucestershire v. Essex (Bristol) 1930
Macartney, C. G. ....(2)	119	126	New South Wales v. South Africans (Sydney) ...1910–11
	142	121	Australians v. Sussex (Hove) 1912
Mackay, J. R. M. ....(1)	105	102*	New South Wales v. South Australia (Sydney) ...1905–06
MacLaren, A. C. ....(1)	142	100	Stoddart's XI v. New South Wales (Sydney) ...1897–98
May, P. B. H. ....(3)	167	103*	Surrey v. Essex (Southend) 1951
	174	100*	M.C.C. v. Yorkshire (Scarborough) 1952
	140	114	M.C.C. v. Australian XI (Sydney) 1958–59
McCabe, S. J. ....(1)	106	103*	New South Wales v. Victoria (Sydney) 1931–32
McGahey, C. P. ....(1)	114	145*	Essex v. Gloucestershire (Leyton) 1901
Mead, C. P. ....(3)	109	100*	Hampshire v. Leicestershire (Leicester) 1911
	102	113*	Hampshire v. Leicestershire (Southampton)............1913
	113	224	Hampshire v. Sussex (Horsham) 1921
Melville, A. ....(1)	189	104*	South Africa v. England (Nottingham) 1947
Merchant, U. M. ....(1)	143	156	Bombay v. Maharashtra (Poona) 1948–49
Miller, K. R. ....(1)	100	101	Hassett's XI v. Morris's XI (Melbourne) 1953–54
Mitchell, A. ....(1)	100*	100*	Leveson-Gower's XI v. M.C.C. Australian XI
			(Scarborough)............1933
Mitchell, B. ....(1)	120	189*	South Africa v. England (Oval) 1947
Moroney, J. A. R. ....(1)	118	101*	Australia v. South Africa (Johannesburg) 1949–50
Morris, A. R. ....(2)	148	111	New South Wales v. Queensland (Sydney) 1940–41
	122	124*	Australia v. England (Adelaide) 1946–47
Mushtaq Ali ....(1)	109	130	Holkar v. Bombay (Bombay) 1944–45
Needham, E. ....(1)	107*	104	Derbyshire v. Essex (Leyton) 1908
Newman, J. A................(1)	102	102*	Hampshire v. Surrey (Oval) 1927
Noble, M. A. ....(1)	176	123	New South Wales v. Victoria (Sydney) 1907–08
Nourse, A. D., jun........(1)	147	108*	South Africans v. Surrey (Oval) 1935
O'Connor, J. ....(1)	138	120*	Essex v. Gloucestershire (Bristol) 1930
O'Connor, L. P. D..........(1)	103	143*	Queensland v. New South Wales (Sydney) 1926–27
O'Keefe, F. A. ....(1)	177	141	Rest v. Australian XI (Sydney) 1921–22
Onyons, B. A. ....(1)	105	127	Victoria v. Queensland (Brisbane) 1928–29
Ord, J. D. ....(1)	107*	101	Warwickshire v. Nottinghamshire (Nottingham)......1948
Parkhouse, W. G. A. ......(1)	121	148	Glamorgan v. Somerset (Cardiff) 1950
Parks, H. W. ....(1)	114*	105*	Sussex v. Essex (Leyton) 1933
Parks, J. M. ....(1)	101	100*	Sussex v. Worcestershire (Worcester) 1957
Pataudi, Nawab of ....(1)	165	100	Oxford U. v. Surrey (Oval) 1931
Paynter, E. ....(2)	125	113*	Lancashire v. Warwickshire (Birmingham) 1938
	117	100	England v. South Africa (Johannesburg) 1938–39
Perrin, P. A. ....(4)	170	102*	Essex v. Nottinghamshire (Nottingham) 1903
	140	103*	Essex v. Middlesex (Lord's) 1905
	112	100*	Essex v. Nottinghamshire (Nottingham) 1911
	126	101*	Essex v. Kent (Leyton) 1919
Phadkar, D. G. ....(1)	131	160	Bombay v. Maharashtra (Poona) 1948–49
Pinch, C. ....(2)	110	100	South Australia v. Western Australia (Perth) ...1956–57
	102	102	South Australia v. Victoria (Melbourne) 1957–58
Place, W. ....(1)	105	132*	Lancashire v. Nottinghamshire (Manchester) 1947
Ponsford, W. H. ....(1)	110	110*	Victoria v. New South Wales (Sydney) 1923–24
Poore, R. M. ....(1)	104	119*	Hampshire v. Somerset (Portsmouth) 1899
Prideaux, R. M. ....(1)	102	106	Cambridge U. v. Somerset (Taunton) 1960
Quaife, W. G. ....(1)	124	109	Warwickshire v. Surrey (Oval) 1913
Rae, A. F. ....(1)	111	128	Jamaica v. Barbados (Kingston) 1946–47
Ranjitsinhji, K. S. ....(1)	100	125*	Sussex v. Yorkshire (Hove) 1896
Ransford, V. S. ....(1)	182	110	Victoria v. New South Wales (Sydney) 1908–09
Ratcliffe, A. ....(1)	130	104*	Cambridge U. v. Surrey (Oval) 1932
Rege, M. R. ....(1)	133	100	Maharashtra v. Bombay (Poona) 1948–49
Rhodes, W. ....(2)	128	115	Yorkshire v. M.C.C. (Scarborough) 1911
	119	109	M.C.C. v. New South Wales (Sydney) 1911–12
Richardson, V. Y. ....(1)	100	125	South Australia v. New South Wales (Sydney) ...1924–25
Rigg, K. E. ....(1)	100	167*	Victoria v. New South Wales (Melbourne) 1936–37
Robertson, J. D. ....(1)	147	137	Middlesex v. Sussex (Lord's) 1948
Roy, P. ....(1)	170*	143	Bengal v. Orissa (Cuttack) 1953–54
Russell, A. C. ....(3)	115	118	Essex v. Surrey (Oval) 1922
	140	111	England v. South Africa (Durban) 1922–23
	131	104	Essex v. Lancashire (Liverpool) 1928
Sandham, A. ....(1)	137	104	M.C.C. v. New South Wales (Sydney) 1924–25
Seymour, James ....(2)	108	136*	Kent v. Worcestershire (Maidstone) 1904
	143	105*	Kent v. Essex (Leyton) 1923

Shepherd, T. F.	...........(1)	121	101*	Surrey v. Leicestershire (Oval) 1926
Sheppard, D. S.	...........(1)	143	126	Cambridge U. v. Middlesex (Cambridge) 1951
Shrewsbury, A.	...........(1)	101	127*	Nottinghamshire v. Gloucestershire (Nottingham) ...1902
Simpson, R. T.	...........(1)	143	102*	Nottinghamshire v. Leicestershire (Nottingham) ...1949
Smith, A. C.	...............(1)	145	124	Oxford U. v. Hampshire (Bournemouth) 1959
Smith, H.	......................(1)	120	102*	Gloucestershire v. Hampshire (Southampton) 1919
Sobers, G.	.....................(1)	125	109*	West Indies v. Pakistan (Georgetown) 1957-58
Squires, H. S.	..............(1)	131	102	Surrey v. Oxford U. (Oval) 1932
Stephens, S.	..................(1)	108	181	Victoria v. Tasmania (Launceston) 1913-14
Stevens, G.	...................(1)	164	111	South Australia v. New South Wales (Sydney) ...1957-58
Stewart, W. J.	...............(1)	155	125	Warwickshire v. Lancashire (Blackpool) 1959
Stoddart, A. E.	...........(1)	195*	124	Middlesex v. Nottinghamshire (Lord's) 1893
Storer, H.	.....................(1)	119	100	Derbyshire v. Sussex (Derby) 1929
Storer, W.	....................(1)	100	100*	Derbyshire v. Yorkshire (Derby) 1896
Sutcliffe, B.	..................(4)	197	128	Otago v. M.C.C. (Dunedin) 1946-47
		118	125	Otago v. Canterbury (Dunedin) 1947-48
		141	135	Auckland v. Canterbury (Auckland) 1948-49
		243	100*	New Zealanders v. Essex (Southend) 1949
Sutcliffe, H.	..................(4)	176	127	England v. Australia (Melbourne) 1924-25
		107	109*	Yorkshire v. M.C.C. (Scarborough) 1926
		111	100*	Yorkshire v. Nottinghamshire (Nottingham) 1928
		104	109*	England v. South Africa (Oval) 1929
Timms, J. E.	..................(1)	101	114*	Northamptonshire v. Sussex (Kettering) 1939
Tompkin, M.	................(1)	156	107*	Leicestershire v. Middlesex (Leicester) 1952
Trumper, V. T.	...........(1)	109	119	Australians v. Essex (Leyton) 1902
Tyldesley, E.	.................(2)	165	123*	Lancashire v. Essex (Leyton) 1921
		109	108*	Lancashire v. Glamorgan (Cardiff) 1930
Tyldesley, J. T.	............(3)	106	100*	Lancashire v. Warwickshire (Birmingham) 1897
		121	100*	North v. South (Hastings) 1900
		136	101	Lancashire v. Hampshire (Manchester)..................1910
Uttley, K. F. M.	............(1)	132	138	Otago v. Auckland (Auckland) 1937-38
Waite, J. H. B.	...............(1)	159*	134*	Transvaal v. Natal (Durban) 1959-60
Warner, P. F.	.................(1)	116	113*	Rest v. Nottinghamshire (Oval) 1907
Washbrook, C.	..............(1)	176	121*	Lancashire v. Sussex (Eastbourne) 1947
Weekes, E. D.	................(1)	162	101	West Indies v. India (Calcutta).......................1948-49
Whitelaw, P. E.	............(1)	115	155	Auckland v. Wellington (Auckland) 1934-35
Whysall, W. W.	............(2)	100	167*	Nottinghamshire v. Gloucestershire (Nottingham) ...1926
		117	101*	Nottinghamshire v. Hampshire (Nottingham) 1930
Wilcox, D. R.	.................(1)	104	129	Essex v. Kent (Westcliff) 1937
Winlaw, R. de W. K.	.......(1)	108	109*	Cambridge U. v. Glamorgan (Cardiff) 1934
Wood, C. J. B.	................(1)	107*	117*	Leicestershire v. Yorkshire (Bradford) 1911
Woolley, F. E.	.................(1)	104	148*	Kent v. Somerset (Tunbridge Wells) 1911
Worthington, T. S.	.........(1)	103	110*	Derbyshire v. Nottinghamshire (Ilkeston) 1938
Wright, L. G.	..................(1)	176	122	Derbyshire v. Warwickshire (Birmingham) 1905
Young, D. M.	................(1)	121	117*	Gloucestershire v. Northamptonshire (Kettering) ...1955
Zulch, J. W.	................(1)	185	125	Transvaal v. Orange Free State (Bloemfontein)...1920-21

K. S. Ranjitsinhji (Sussex) scored 100 and 125* v. Yorkshire (Hove) 1896, both centuries being scored on the same day (22nd August), a unique feat. His first innings was started late on the second afternoon, but when stumps were drawn for the day Ranjitsinhji still had to open his score.

T. Hayward (Surrey) performed the feat twice in six days in 1906, his scores being made in two successive matches.

In addition to performing the feat five times, C. B. Fry (Sussex) missed by a single run on three occasions: 99 & 123 v. Hampshire (Hove), 1898, 99 & 127* v. Leicestershire (Hove) 1903, and 125 & 99* v. Worcestershire (Hove) 1907.

C. J. B. Wood (Leicestershire) carried his bat through each innings in performing the feat v. Yorkshire (Bradford) 1911—a unique feat.

J. B. Hobbs (Surrey) scored 101 & 101* v. Somerset (Taunton) 1925, his 126th and 127th centuries—thus first equalling and then beating W. G. Grace's record of 126 centuries in the same match.

D. G. Bradman in 1929–30 came near to equalling K. S. Ranjitsinhji's feat. Playing for W. M. Woodfull's XI v. J. Ryder's XI at Sydney, he took an overnight score of 54* to 124, and, when his side followed on, opened the second innings with W. M. Woodfull and scored 205* before stumps were drawn, his innings ending early on the next day for 225. He thus scored 275 runs during the day's play.

A. H. Dyson, playing for Glamorgan v. Essex (Neath) 1934, scored 96 & 104*—he was dismissed in the first innings off a ball he had cut to the boundary to complete his century, it then being found that he had hit his wicket in completing the stroke.

The only batsman to score a double-century in each innings of the same match is A. E. Fagg—244 & 202* for Kent v. Essex (Colchester) 1938.

A. R. Morris (1940–41) and N. J. Contractor (1952–53) both scored a century in each innings of their début matches in first-class cricket—a unique feat.

Three batsmen performed the feat in the match Bombay v. Maharashtra (Poona) in 1948–49—U. M. Merchant, D. G. Phadkar and M. R. Rege.

Batsmen Scoring Over 350 Runs in a Match

A number of batsmen have succeeded in scoring over 350 runs in the course of a match. There are, strangely enough, two cases where the batsman's side lost the match after he had scored 350 runs for them, P. A. Perrin in 1904 and V. S. Hazare in 1943–44. Batsmen whose only innings was of 350 or over are omitted.

455	(3 & 452*)	D. G. Bradman: N.S.W. v. Queensland (Sydney)	1929–30
446	(244* & 202*)	A. E. Fagg: Kent v. Essex (Colchester)	1938
402	(157* & 245)	W. W. Armstrong: Victoria v. South Australia (Melbourne)	1920–21
375	(325 & 50)	A. Sandham: England v. West Indies (Kingston)	1929–30
370	(32 & 338*)	R. C. Blunt: Otago v. Canterbury (Christchurch)	1931–32
368	(59 & 309)	V. S. Hazare: Rest v. Hindus (Bombay)	1943–44
367	(210* & 157)	M. R. Hallam: Leics. v. Glamorgan (Leicester)	1959
361	(17 & 344)	W. G. Grace: M.C.C. v. Kent (Canterbury)	1876
361	(115 & 246)	K. S. Duleepsinhji: Sussex v. Kent (Hastings)	1929
358	(78 & 280*)	E. H. Bowley: Sussex v. Glos. (Hove)	1929
354	(125 & 229)	C. B. Fry: Sussex v. Surrey (Oval)	1900
354	(169 & 185*)	G. Gunn: Notts. v. Surrey (Nottingham)	1919
351	(343* & 8)	P. A. Perrin: Essex v. Derby (Chesterfield)	1904

Three or More Centuries in Successive Innings

SIX CENTURIES

Bradman, D. G. (South Australia) in 1938–39—118 Bradman's XI v. Rigg's XI (Melbourne), 143 v. N.S.W. (Adelaide), 225 v. Queensland (Adelaide), 107 v. Victoria (Melbourne), 186 v. Queensland (Brisbane), 135 v. N.S.W. (Sydney).

Fry, C. B. (Sussex) in 1901—106 v. Hants. (Portsmouth), 209 v. Yorks. (Hove), 149 v. Middx. (Hove), 105 v. Surrey (Oval), 140 v. Essex (Hove), 105 Rest of England v. Yorks. (Lords).

FIVE CENTURIES

Weekes, E. D. (West Indians) in 1955–56—156 v. Auckland (Auckland), 148 v. Canterbury (Christchurch), 123 v. New Zealand (Dunedin), 119* v. Wellington (Wellington), 103 v. New Zealand (Christchurch).

FOUR CENTURIES

Bradman, D. G. (N.S.W.) in 1931–32—135 for N.S.W. (Sydney), 226 for Australia (Brisbane), 219 for N.S.W. (Sydney), 112 for Australia (Sydney): all v. South Africa.

Bradman, D. G. (Australians) in 1948 and 1948–49—150 v. Gentlemen of England (Lord's), 143 v. South of England (Hastings), 153 v. Leveson-Gower's XI (Scarborough). (His last three innings in England.) 123 Bradman's XI v. Hassett's XI (Melbourne) 1948–49.

Compton, D. C. S. (Middx.) in 1946–47—124 M.C.C. v. Combined XI (Hobart), 163 M.C.C. v. Tasmania (Launceston), 147 & 103* England v. Australia (Adelaide).

Contractor, N. J. (Gujerat) in 1957–58—102 v. Bombay (Khadakvasla), 135 v. Saurashtra (Poona), 167 v Baroda (Sangli), 110 v. Maharashtra (Poona).

Duleepsinhji, K. S. (Sussex) in 1931—161* v. Worcs. (Dudley), 109 England v. New Zealand (Oval), 103 v. Middx. (Hove), 127 v. Hants. (Hastings).

Fry, C. B. (Hants.) in 1911—123 & 112 v. Kent (Canterbury), 258* v. Glos. (Southampton), 102* Rest of England v. Warwicks. (Oval).

Hammond, W. R. (M.C.C.) in 1936–37—141 v. Western Australia (Perth), 107 v. Combined XI (Perth), 104 & 136 v. South Australia (Adelaide).

Hammond, W. R. (Glos.) in 1945 and 1946—121 & 102 England XI v. Dominions XI (Lord's) 1945, 132 v. Oxford U. (Oxford), 134 v. Lancs. (Gloucester) 1946.

Hardinge, H. T. W. (Kent) in 1913—154* v. Leics. (Canterbury), 117 & 105* v. Hants. (Dover), 107 v. Northants. (Dover).

Hayward, T. (Surrey) in 1906—144* & 100 v. Notts. (Nottingham), 143 & 125 v. Leics. (Leicester). All scored within six days.

Hobbs, J. B. (Surrey) in 1920—110 v. Sussex (Oval), 134 v. Leics. (Leicester), 101 v. Warwicks. (Birmingham), 112 v. Yorks. (Sheffield).

Hobbs, J. B. (Surrey) in 1925—104 & 143* v. Cambridge U. (Oval), 111 v. Somerset (Oval), 215 v. Warwicks. (Birmingham). (His two previous innings were 107 & 87 v. Essex (Oval).)

Langridge, John (Sussex) in 1949—115* v. Cambridge U. (Cambridge), 115 & 129 v. Lancs. (Manchester), 120 v. Glos. (Chichester).

Macartney, C. G. (Australians) in 1921—105 v. Hants. (Southampton), 193 v. Northants. (Northampton), 345 v. Notts. (Nottingham), 115 v. England (Leeds).

May, P. B. H. (M.C.C.) in 1956–57—162 v. Western Province (Cape Town), 118 v. Eastern Province (Port Elizabeth), 124* v. Rhodesia (Bulawayo), 206 v. Rhodesia (Salisbury).

Merchant, V. M. (Bombay & India) in 1941–42—170* Bombay v. Nawanagar (Jamnagar), 243* Hindus v. Rest (Bombay), 221 Hindus v. Parsis (Bombay), 153* Bombay v. Sind (Bombay).

Mitchell, A. (Yorks.) in 1933—150* v. Worcs. (Worcester), 107 v. M.C.C. (Scarborough), 100* & 100* Leveson-Gower's XI v. M.C.C. Australian XI (Scarborough).

Nawab of Pataudi (Oxford U.) in 1931—183* v. Army (Folkestone), 165 & 100 v. Surrey (Oval), 138 v. Leveson-Gower's XI (Eastbourne).

Sutcliffe, H. (Yorks.) in 1931—120* v. Middx. (Lord's), 107 v. Hants. (Portsmouth), 230 v. Kent (Folkestone), 183 v. Somerset (Dewsbury).

Sutcliffe, H. (Yorks.) in 1939—163 v. Lancs. (Manchester), 116 v. Hants. (Sheffield), 234* v. Leics. (Hull), 175 v. Middx. (Lord's).

Tyldesley, E. (Lancs.) in 1926—131 v. Surrey (Oval), 131 Players v. Gentlemen (Lord's), 106 v. Essex (Nelson), 126 v. Somerset (Taunton).

Whysall, W. W. (Notts.) in 1930—117 & 101* v. Hants. (Nottingham), 120 v. Australians (Nottingham), 158 v. Warwicks. (Birmingham).

Woolley, F. E. (Kent) in 1929—155 v. Derby (Chesterfield), 108 v. Somerset (Tonbridge), 131 v. Yorks. (Tonbridge), 117 v. Hants. (Folkestone).

THREE CENTURIES

Abel, R. (Surrey) in 1896—138 v. Warwicks. (Oval), 152 v. Leics. (Oval), 231 v. Essex (Oval).

Ames, L. E. G. (Kent) in 1932—130 v. Middx. (Tunbridge Wells), 149 v. Northants. (Tunbridge Wells), 120 v. Surrey (Blackheath).

Ames, L. E. G. (Kent) in 1937—125 v. Worcs. (Worcester), 119 & 127 v. Surrey (Blackheath).

Balaskas, X. C. (Griqualand West) in 1929–30—206 v. Rhodesia (Kimberley), 132 v. Eastern Province (Kimberley), 101 v. Western Province (Kimberley).

Bardsley, W. (N.S.W.) in 1910–11—191* v. South Australia (Sydney), 132 Australia v. South Africa (Sydney), 124 v. Victoria (Melbourne).

Bardsley, W. (Australians) in 1926—127 v. Derby (Chesterfield), 193* v. England (Lord's), 112 v. Northants. (Northampton).

Bradman, D. G. (N.S.W.) in 1929–30—157 v. M.C.C. (Sydney), 124 & 225 Woodfull's XI v. Ryder's XI (Sydney).

Bradman, D. G. (N.S.W.) in 1933–34 and 1934—253 v. Queensland (Sydney), 128 v. Victoria (Sydney) in 1933–34, 206 Australians v. Worcs. (Worcester) in 1934.

Bradman, D. G. (Australians) in 1934—140 v. Yorks. (Sheffield), 304 v. England (Leeds), 244 v. England (Oval).

Bradman, D. G. (South Australia) in 1935–36—117 v. N.S.W. (Adelaide), 233 v. Queensland (Adelaide), 357 v. Victoria (Melbourne).

Bradman, D. G. (Australians) in 1937–38 and 1938—144 v. Tasmania (Hobart), 102 v. Western Australia (Perth) 1937–38, 258 v. Worcs. (Worcester) 1938.

Bradman, D. G. (South Australia) in 1946–47—119 v. Victoria (Adelaide), 187 Australia v. England (Brisbane), 234 Australia v. England (Sydney).

Bradman, D. G. (Australia) in 1947–48—132 & 127* v. India (Melbourne), 201 v. India (Adelaide).

Brown, W. A. (Australians) in 1948—200 v. Cambridge U. (Cambridge), 153 v. Essex (Southend), 108 v. Oxford U. (Oxford).

Cameron, H. B. (Transvaal) in 1933–34 and 1934–35—110 v. Western Province (Cape Town) 1933–34, 182 v. Griqualand West (Johannesburg), 112 v. Natal (Durban) 1934–35.

Chinnery, H. B. (Middx.) in 1901—105 & 165 M.C.C. v. Oxford U. (Oxford), 100 v. Glos. (Lord's).

Christy, J. A. J. (Transvaal) in 1927–28 and 1928–29—103 v. Rhodesia (Bulawayo), 175 v. Rhodesia (Salisbury) 1927–28, 141 v. Natal (Durban) 1928–29.

Compton, D. C. S. (Middx.) in 1947—112 v. Worcs. (Lord's), 110 v. Sussex (Lord's), 154 v. South Africans (Lord's).

Compton, D. C. S. (M.C.C.) in 1948–49—121 v. Cape Province (Cape Town), 150* v. Griqualand West (Kimberley), 106 v. Natal (Durban).

Cox, G. (Sussex) in 1947—103 v. Lancs. (Eastbourne), 142 v. Glos. (Hove), 132 v. South Africans (Hove).

Croom, A. J. (Warwicks.) in 1931—109 v. Kent (Birmingham), 105 v. Northants. (Peterborough), 159 v. Notts. (Birmingham).

Dalton, E. L. (South Africans) in 1929—157 & 116* v. Kent (Canterbury), 102 v. Sussex (Hove).

Davies, D. (Glamorgan) in 1928—126* v. Sussex (Swansea), 103 v. Northants. (Northampton), 165* v. Sussex (Eastbourne).

Dempster, C. S. (Leics.) in 1937—110 v. Sussex (Leicester), 133 & 154* v. Glos. (Gloucester).

Dempster, C. S. (Leics.) in 1938—105 v. Australians (Leicester), 110 v. Hants. (Southampton), 187 v. Oxford U. (Oxford).

Denton, D. (M.C.C.) in 1909–10—139 & 138 v. Transvaal (Johannesburg), 104 England v. South Africa (Johannesburg).

Ducat, A. (Surrey) in 1921—290* v. Essex (Leyton), 134 v. Northants. (Oval), 120 v. Warwicks. (Birmingham).

Ducat, A. (Surrey) in 1928—179* v. Warwicks. (Oval), 101* v. Sussex (Horsham), 208 v. Essex (Leyton).

Duleepsinhji, K. S. (Sussex) in 1932—116 v. Worcs. (Horsham), 126 v. Surrey (Hove), 128 South v. North (Manchester).

Fiddian-Green, C. A. (Cambridge U.) in 1922—103 v. Essex (Colchester), 113 v. Sussex (Hove), 120 v. Leveson-Gower's XI (Eastbourne).
Fishlock, L. B. (Surrey) in 1937—113 & 105 v. Yorks. (Oval), 127 v. Middx. (Lord's).
Foster, R. E. (Oxford U.) in 1900—128 & 100* v. Webbe's XI (Oxford), 169 v. London County (Oxford).
Fry, C. B. (Sussex) in 1900—125 & 229 v. Surrey (Hove), 110 v. Middx. (Hove).
Grace, W. G. (Glos.) in 1871—118 Gentlemen of South v. Gentlemen of North (West Brompton), 178 South v. North (Lord's), 162 Gentlemen of England v. Cambridge U. (Cambridge).
Grace, W. G. (Glos.) in 1872—112 Gentlemen v. Players (Lord's), 117 Gentlemen v. Players (Oval), 170* England v. Notts. & Yorks. (Lord's).
Grace, W. G. (Glos.) in 1873—134 Gentlemen of South v. Players of South (Oval), 163 Gentlemen v. Players (Lord's), 158 Gentlemen v. Players (Oval).
Grace, W. G. (Glos.) in 1874—121 Kent & Glos. v. England (Canterbury), 123 M.C.C. v. Kent (Canterbury), 127 v. Yorks. (Clifton).
Grace, W. G. (Glos.) in 1876—344 M.C.C. v. Kent (Canterbury), 177 v. Notts. (Clifton), 318* v. Yorks. (Cheltenham).
Hallows, C. (Lancs.) in 1927 and 1928—120 v. Rest of England (Oval) 1927, 100 v. Northants. (Manchester), 101 v. Glamorgan (Manchester) 1928.
Hamence, R. A. (South Australia) in 1946–47—116 v. Victoria (Adelaide), 132 & 101* v. N.S.W. (Adelaide).
Hammond, W. R. (Glos.) in 1927—135 v. Yorks. (Gloucester), 108 & 128 v. Surrey (Oval).
Hammond, W. R. (M.C.C.) in 1928–29—119* & 177 England v. Australia (Adelaide), 114 v. Victoria (Melbourne).
Hammond, W. R. (Glos.) in 1937—140 England v. New Zealand (Lord's), 108 v. New Zealanders (Bristol), 112 v. Hants. (Bristol).
Hammond, W. R. (Glos.) in 1938—110 & 123 v. Derby (Burton-on-Trent), 240 England v. Australia (Lord's).
Harvey, R. N. (Australians) in 1953—141 v. Glos. (Bristol), 118 v. Northants. (Northampton), 122 v. England (Manchester).
Hassett, A. L. (Australians) in 1938—146 v. Oxford U. (Oxford), 148 v. Leics. (Leicester), 220* v. Cambridge U. (Cambridge).
Hassett, A. L. (Victoria) in 1939–40—122 & 122 v. N.S.W. (Sydney), 136 Rest of Australia v. N.S.W. (Sydney).
Hassett, A. L. (Australians) in 1948—200* v. Gentlemen of England (Lord's), 103 v. Somerset (Taunton), 151 v. South of England (Hastings).
Hayward, T. (Surrey) in 1899—273 v. Yorks. (Oval), 137 England v. Australia (Oval), 158 v. Somerset (Taunton).
Hazare, V. S. (India) in 1943–44—309 Rest v. Hindus (Bombay), 101 Baroda v. Bombay (Bombay), 233 Indian States v. Rest of India (Poona).
Hazare, V. S. (India) in 1949–50 and 1950—130 & 101 Baroda v. Holkar (Baroda) 1949–50, 114 Commonwealth XI v. England XI (Kingston) 1950.
Headley, G. (West Indians) in 1939—106 & 107 v. England (Lord's), 234* v. Notts. (Nottingham).
Hendren, E. (M.C.C.) in 1929–30—205 England v. West Indies (Trinidad), 254* M.C.C. v. British Guiana (Georgetown), 171 M.C.C. v. British Guiana (Georgetown).
Hendren, E. (Middx.) in 1931—232 v. Notts. (Nottingham), 189 & 100* v. Warwicks. (Birmingham).
Hendren, E. (Middx.) in 1933—111 v. Surrey (Lord's), 101 & 101 v. Kent (Lord's),
Hendry, H. L. (Victoria) in 1926–27—177 v. South Australia (Adelaide), 140 v. Queensland (Melbourne), 100 v. N.S.W. (Melbourne).
Hill, C. (South Australia) in 1909–10—176 v. Victoria (Adelaide), 205 v. N.S.W. (Adelaide), 185 v. Victoria (Melbourne).
Hirst, G. H. (Yorks.) in 1899—186 v. Surrey (Oval), 131 v. Hants. (Bradford), 138 v. Notts. (Nottingham).
Hobbs, J. B. (Surrey) in 1914—122 v. Kent (Blackheath), 226 v. Notts. (Oval), 126 v. Worcs. (Worcester).
Hobbs, J. B. (Surrey) in 1926—261 v. Oxford U. (Oval), 119 England v. Australia (Lord's), 200 v. Hants. (Southampton).
Hobbs, J. B. (Surrey) in 1932—113 & 119* v. Essex (Oval), 123 v. Somerset (Taunton).
Howell, M. (Oxford U.) in 1919—115 & 102 v. Leveson-Gower's XI (Eastbourne), 170 v. Cambridge U. (Lord's).
Hutton, L. (Yorks.) in 1937—136 v. Kent (Tonbridge), 271* v. Derby (Sheffield), 153 v. Leics. (Hull).
Hutton, L. (Yorks.) in 1947—197 & 104 v. Essex (Southend), 270* v. Hants. (Bournemouth).
Hutton, L. (Yorks.) in 1952—120 v. Kent (Canterbury), 103 & 137 v. M.C.C. (Scarborough).
Iremonger, J. (Notts.) in 1904—189* v. Middx. (Lord's), 272 v. Kent (Nottingham), 142 v. Derby (Chesterfield).
Jardine, D. R. (Surrey) in 1927—120 Oxford Harlequins v. Oxford U. (Oxford), 147 v. Leics. (Leicester), 143 v. Lancs. (Manchester).
Jardine, D. R. (M.C.C.) in 1928–29—109 v. Western Australia (Perth), 104 v. Victoria (Melbourne), 140 v. N.S.W. (Sydney).
Johnson, P. R. (Somerset) in 1908—164 & 131 v. Middx. (Taunton), 117 v. Hants. (Southampton).
Keeton, W. W. (Notts.) in 1933—110 v. Hants. (Southampton), 168 v. Middx. (Nottingham), 110 v. Yorks. (Bradford).
Keeton, W. W. (Notts.) in 1949—109* v. Hants. (Nottingham), 208 v. Glamorgan (Nottingham), 134 v. Lancs. (Manchester).

Kippax, A. F. (N.S.W.) in 1925–26 and 1926–27—271* v. Victoria (Sydney) 1925–26, 127 & 131 v. Queensland (Brisbane) 1926–27.

Knight, D. J. (Surrey) in 1919—114 & 101 v. Yorks. (Oval), 146 v. Lancs. (Manchester).

Lee, F. S. (Somerset) in 1938—109* & 107 v. Worcs. (Worcester), 141 v. Surrey (Taunton).

Lester, E. (Yorks.) in 1947—127 v. Derby (Scarborough), 126 & 142 v. Northants. (Northampton).

Leyland, M. (Yorks.) in 1934—104* v. M.C.C. (Lord's), 100 v. Oxford U. (Oxford), 126 v. Glamorgan (Swansea).

Macartney, C. G. (N.S.W.) in 1910–11—119 & 126 v. South Africans (Sydney), 137 Australia v. South Africa (Sydney).

Macartney, C. G. (Australians) in 1912—127 v. Northants. (Northampton), 208 v. Essex (Leyton), 123 v. Surrey (Oval).

Macartney, C. G. (N.S.W.) in 1923–24—120 v. Wellington (Wellington), 120 v. Otago (Dunedin), 221 v. Canterbury (Christchurch).

Mackay, J. R. M. (N.S.W.) in 1905–06—194 v. Victoria (Melbourne), 105 & 102* v. South Australia (Sydney).

MacLaren, A. C. (Lancs.) in 1895—152 v. Notts. (Manchester), 108 v. Middx. (Lord's), 135 v. Leics. (Leicester).

MacLaren, A. C. (A. E. Stoddart's XI) in 1897–98—142 & 100 v. N.S.W. (Sydney), 109 England v. Australia (Sydney).

Mason, J. R. (Kent) in 1904—138 v. Yorks. (Tunbridge Wells), 126 v. Somerset (Beckenham), 133 v. Essex (Colchester).

Mason, J. R. (Kent) in 1909—179* v. Sussex (Hove), 111 v. Somerset (Taunton), 152* v. Surrey (Oval).

May, P. B. H. (Surrey) in 1952—197 v. Leics. (Leicester), 174 & 100* M.C.C. v. Yorks. (Scarborough).

May, P. B. H. (Surrey) in 1958—155 v. Yorks. (Oval), 101 England v. New Zealand (Manchester), 112* v. New Zealanders (Oval).

McCabe, S. J. (N.S.W.) in 1931–32—229* v. Queensland (Brisbane), 106 & 103* v. Victoria (Sydney).

Mead, C. P. (Hants.) in 1921—280* v. Notts. (Southampton), 113 & 224 v. Sussex (Horsham).

Mead, C. P. (Hants.) in 1922—152 v. Kent (Southampton), 235 v. Worcs. (Worcester), 105 v. Leics. (Southampton).

Mead, C. P. (Hants.) in 1923—132 v. Worcs. (Worcester), 222 v. Warwicks. (Birmingham), 147 v. Sussex (Hove).

Mead, C. P. (Hants.) in 1933—135 v. Kent (Canterbury), 152 v. Notts. (Southampton), 113* v. Lancs. (Manchester).

Melville, A. (South Africans) in 1947—189 & 104* v. England (Nottingham), 117 v. England (Lord's).

Merchant, V. M. (India) in 1943–44—250* Hindus v. Rest (Bombay), 141 Bombay v. Baroda (Bombay), 359* Bombay v. Maharashtra (Bombay).

Mitchell, B. (South Africans) in 1947—131 v. Lancs. (Manchester), 120 & 189* v. England (Oval).

Moroney, J. A. R. (Australians) in 1949–50—118 & 101* v. South Africa (Johannesburg), 133 v. Natal (Pietermaritzburg).

Morris, A. R. (Australians) in 1949–50—102* v. Griqualand West (Kimberley), 157 v. South Africa (Port Elizabeth), 103 v. Western Province (Cape Town).

Nichol, M. (Worcs.) in 1933—116 v. Hants. (Bournemouth), 165* v. Glamorgan (Worcester), 154 v. Yorks. (Worcester).

Noble, M. A. (N.S.W.) in 1898–99—101 v. South Australia (Sydney), 100 v. Victoria (Sydney), 111 Australian XI v. Rest of Australia (Adelaide).

Nourse, A. D., jun. (South Africans) in 1935—147 & 108* v. Surrey (Oval), 148 v. Oxford U. (Oxford).

Nourse, A. D., jun. (Natal) in 1950–51—124 v. Border (Pietermaritzburg), 121 v. O.F.S. (Bloemfontein), 114 v. Western Province (Durban).

O'Connor, L. P. D. (Queensland) in 1926–27—196 v. N.S.W. (Brisbane), 103 & 143* v. N.S.W. (Sydney).

O'Keefe, F. A. (Victoria) in 1921–22—180 v. South Australia (Adelaide), 177 & 141 Rest of Australia v. Australian XI (Sydney).

Onyons, B. A. (Victoria) in 1928–29—131 v. N.S.W. (Sydney), 105 & 127 v. Queensland (Brisbane).

Pairaudeau, B. H. (British Guiana) in 1952–53—101 v. Jamaica (Georgetown), 126 v. Jamaica (Georgetown), 115 West Indies v. India (Trinidad).

Parkhouse, W. G. A. (Glamorgan) in 1950—121 & 148 v. Somerset (Cardiff), 127 v. Combined Services (Cardiff).

Paynter, E. (Lancs.) in 1936—123* v. Notts. (Nottingham), 177 v. Glamorgan (Manchester), 119 v. Northants. (Manchester).

Perrin, P. A. (Essex) in 1903—170 & 102* v. Notts. (Nottingham), 102* v. Derby (Leyton).

Phadkar, D. G. (Bombay), in 1948–49—134* v. Madras (Madras), 131 & 160 v. Maharashtra (Poona).

Place, W. (Lancs.) in 1947—171 v. Essex (Clacton), 105 & 132* v. Notts. (Manchester).

Ponsford, W. H. (Victoria) in 1921–22 and 1922–23—162 v. Tasmania (Melbourne) 1921–22, 429 v. Tasmania (Melbourne), 108 v. South Australia (Adelaide) 1922–23. (His 3rd, 4th and 5th innings in first-class cricket.)

Ponsford, W. H. (Victoria) in 1923–24—159 v. South Australia (Melbourne), 110 & 110* v. N.S.W. (Sydney).

Ponsford, W. H. (Victoria) in 1926–27—151 v. Queensland (Melbourne), 352 v. N.S.W. (Melbourne), 108 v. South Australia (Melbourne).

Ponsford, W. H. (Victoria) in 1927–28—133 v. South Australia (Adelaide), 437 v. Queensland (Melbourne), 202 v. N.S.W. (Melbourne).

Ponsford, W. H. (Victoria) in 1930–31—109* v. N.S.W. (Melbourne), 183 Australia v. West Indies (Sydney), 109 v. West Indies (Brisbane).
Poore, R. M. (Hants.) in 1899—104 & 119* v. Somerset (Portsmouth), 111 v. Lancs. (Southampton).
Quaife, W. G. (Warwicks.) in 1901—118* v. Yorks. (Birmingham), 108 London County v. Cambridge U. (Crystal Palace), 117* v. Derby (Derby).
Quaife, W. G. (Warwicks.) in 1913—124 & 109 v. Surrey (Oval), 107 v. Northants. (Birmingham).
Ranjitsinhji, K. S. (Sussex) in 1896—165 v. Lancs. (Hove), 100 & 125* v. Yorks. (Hove).
Ranjitsinhji, K. S. (Sussex) in 1900—127 v. Glos. (Hove), 222 v. Somerset (Hove), 215* v. Cambridge U. (Cambridge).
Rhodes, W. (M.C.C.) in 1911–12—179 England v. Australia (Melbourne), 119 & 109 v. N.S.W. (Sydney).
Richardson, P. E. (Worcs.) in 1956—134 v. Notts. (Worcester), 104 England v. Australia (Manchester), 147 v. Essex (Worcester).
Robertson, J. D. (Middx.) in 1947—140 v. Kent (Canterbury), 127 v. Surrey (Oval), 110 v. Kent (Lord's).
Robertson, J. D. (Middx.) in 1954—123 v. Glamorgan (Lord's), 101 v. Northants. (Northampton), 101 v. Worcs. (Worcester).
Rowan, E. A. B. (Transvaal) in 1952–53—157 v. Border (Johannesburg), 196 v. N.-E. Transvaal (Johannesburg), 102 v. Griqualand West (Kimberley).
Roy, P. (Bengal) in 1957–58—154 v. Assam (Calcutta), 114 v. Orissa (Cuttack), 114 v. Bihar (Patna).
Siedle, I. J. (Natal) in 1936–37—105 v. Border (Durban), 111 v. Eastern Province (Pietermaritzburg), 207 v. Western Province (Durban).
Simpson, R. T. (Notts.) in 1959—108* v. Surrey (Oval), 132 v. Sussex (Nottingham), 100 v. Indians (Nottingham).
Squires, H. S. (Surrey) in 1932—103 v. Cambridge U. (Oval), 131 & 102 v. Oxford U. (Oval).
Stevens, G. (South Australia) in 1957–58—164 & 111 v. N.S.W. (Sydney), 143 v. Queensland (Brisbane).
Stewart, W. J. (Warwicks.) in 1959—156 v. Essex (Coventry), 155 & 125 v. Lancs. (Blackpool).
Storer, W. (Derby) in 1896—100 & 100* v. Yorks. (Derby), 142* v. Leics. (Leicester).
Sutcliffe, B. (Otago) in 1947–48—103 v. Auckland (Auckland), 118 & 135 v. Canterbury (Dunedin).
Sutcliffe, B. (Auckland) in 1948–49—141 & 135 v. Canterbury (Auckland), 140 New Zealand v. Rest (Wellington).
Sutcliffe, H. (M.C.C.) in 1924–25—115 England v. Australia (Sydney), 176 & 127 England v. Australia (Melbourne).
Sutcliffe, H. (Yorks.) in 1928—111 v. Derby (Derby), 111 & 100* v. Notts (Nottingham).
Sutcliffe, H. (Yorks.) in 1931—117 England v. New Zealand (Oval), 195 v. Lancs. (Sheffield), 187 v. Leics. (Leicester).
Tate, M. W. (Sussex) in 1927—113 v. Cambridge U. (Cambridge), 122 v. Worcs. (Hove), 101 v. Hants. (Portsmouth).
Tyldesley, E. (Lancs.) in 1928—159 v. Kent (Manchester), 242 v. Leics. (Leicester), 118 v. Sussex (Hove).
Tyldesley, E. (Lancs.) in 1934—239 v. Glamorgan (Cardiff), 107 v. Australians (Manchester), 134 v. Glos. (Bristol).
Tyldesley, J. T. (Lancs.) in 1897—106 & 100* v. Warwicks. (Birmingham), 174 v. Sussex (Manchester).
Tyldesley, J. T. (Lancs.) in 1904—103 v. Somerset (Manchester), 225 v. Notts. (Nottingham), 196 v. Worcs. (Worcester).
Weekes, E. D. (West Indians) in 1950—246* v. Hants. (Southampton), 200* v. Leics. (Leicester), 129 v. England (Nottingham).
Wilson, J. V. (Yorks.) in 1955—109* v. Somerset (Taunton), 132* v. Warwicks. (Birmingham), 132 v. Essex (Bradford).
Wright, L. G. (Derby) in 1905—195 v. Northants. (Derby), 176 & 122 v. Warwicks. (Birmingham).
Zulch, J. W. (Transvaal) in 1920–21—124 v. Eastern Province (Port Elizabeth), 185 & 125 v. O.F.S. (Bloemfontein).

Sequences of Centuries in Successive Innings

In addition to the above runs of successive centuries, the following runs of success are worthy of note, but each run is broken by scores of less than the hundred.

5 CENTURIES IN 6 INNINGS

H. T. W. Hardinge—154*–117–105*–107–3–110 1913
J. B. Hobbs—107–87–104–143*–111–215 1925
E. Tyldesley—144*–226–51–131–131–106 1926
C. Hallows—120–100–101–51*–123–101* ....1927 & 1928
Nawab of Pataudi—183*–165–100–138–68–238* 1931
D. G. Bradman—135–226–219–112–2–167 1931–32
E. Hendren—111–101–101–12–105–154 1933
D. G. Bradman—144–102–258–58–137–278 ....1937–38 & 1938
V. M. Merchant—109–137–12–170*–243*–221 ....1940–41 & 1941–42
W. R. Hammond—121–102–132–134–59*–143 ....1945 & 1946

6 CENTURIES IN 7 INNINGS

E. Tyldesley—144*–226–51–131–131–106–126 1926
V. M. Merchant—109–137–12–170*–243*–221–153 ....1940–41 & 1941–42
W. R. Hammond—121–102–132–134–59*–143–104 ....1945 & 1946

7 CENTURIES IN 9 INNINGS

C. B. Fry—119*–36–88–106–209–149–105–140–105 1901
E. Tyldesley—144–69–144*–226–51–131–131–106–126 1926
D. G. Bradman—135–226–219–112–2–167–23–167–299* 1931–32
D. G. Bradman—144–102–258–58–137–278–2–143–145* ....1937–38 & 1938
D. G. Bradman—202–17–67–118–143–225–107–186–135* ....1938 & 1938–39
D. G. Bradman—132–127*–201–57–115–107–81–146–117 ....1947–48 & 1948

8 CENTURIES IN 11 INNINGS

D. G. Bradman—103–16–202–17–67–118–143–225–107–186–135* ....1938 & 1938–39

8 CENTURIES IN 12 INNINGS

E. Tyldesley—144–69–144*–226–51–131–131–106–126–81–44–139 1926
W. H. Ponsford—214–54–151–352–108–84–12–116–131–7–133–437 ....1926–27 & 1927–28
D. G. Bradman—140–304–244–77–19–149*–132–15–50–117–233–357 ....1934 & 1935–36
D. G. Bradman—118–143–225–107–186–135*–5–76–64–251*–90*–138 ....1938–39 & 1939–40
V. M. Merchant—140–192–4–32–88*–109–137–12–170*–243*–221–153* ....1939 to 1942

Most Fifties in Successive Innings

10 CONSECUTIVE FIFTIES

E. Tyldesley—144–69–144*–226–51–131–131–126–106–81 1926
D. G. Bradman—132–127*–201–57*–115–107–81–146–187–98 1947–48

9 CONSECUTIVE FIFTIES

T. Hayward—61*–70*–63–144*–100–143–125–54–69* 1906
V. S. Hazare—264–81–97–248–59–309–101–223–87................1942–43 & 1943–44
R. B. Simpson—98–236*–230*–79–98–161*–67–80–52 1959–60

8 CONSECUTIVE FIFTIES

C. B. Fry—135–68–72–125–229–110–96–105 1900
C. B. Fry—88–106–209–149–105–140–105–82 ....1901 & 1902
C. P. Mead—162–78–62*–132–222–147–58–80* 1923
W. R. Hammond—101–75*–59–64–227–336*–55–51 ....1932–33 & 1933
D. G. Bradman—85–79–144–102–258–58–137–278 ....1937–38 & 1938
B. Sutcliffe—71–74–111–62*–197–128–58–75 ....1946–47 & 1947–48

7 CONSECUTIVE FIFTIES

E. Tyldesley—96–174*–66–58–65–82–67 1919
W. W. Whysall—54–117–101*–120–158–60–64 1930
W. R. Hammond—84*–54–81–100–53–75–70 1930–31
D. G. Bradman—67–118–143–225–107–186–135* 1938–39
S. G. Barnes—137–132–55–185–79–51–200 ....1940–41 & 1945–46
R. S. Cooper—73–58*–62–68–127*–52–104 1944–45
W. R. Hammond—121–102–132–134–59*–143–104 ....1945 & 1946
A. R. Morris—60–105–62–290–51*–54–109 1948
L. Hutton—125–62*–134–61–78–174–83 1948–49

R. T. Simpson—54–143–102*–96–63*–80–54 1949
L. Hutton—147–52–54–101–54–75–52 ....1949 & 1950
D. J. McGlew—85–66–53–118–68–51–69 1955
G. Pullar—62–57*–107–51–76*–76–105 1959
R. E. Marshall—51–56–104–63–63–75–63 1959

Other good runs are as follows but a score of less than 50 is included in each sequence:
H. Sutcliffe—59–119–176–127–33–59–188–88–143 1924–25
D. R. Jardine—91–157–86–40–83–109–104–140 ....1928 & 1928–29
H. H. Gibbons—43–93–7–88–104–157–70*–100–129 1934
H. Gimblett—53–108–93–103–108–23–108–57–129 1939
W. A. Brown—99–12–174*–95–168–1–81–215–87–137 1939–40
S. G. Barnes—137–132–55–185–79–51–200–25–115–146–34–154–102 ....1940–41 & 1945–46
V. M. Merchant—109–137–12–170*–243*–221–153 1941–42
B. Sutcliffe—21–71–74–111–62*–197–128–58–75–12–98–103–118–125–7–108*......1946–47 & 1947–48
D. C. S. Compton—123*–84–82–135–125*–34–30*–121–150*–106–9–300–84–72–28–114–1–151*–
                                                            108.................1948 & 1948–49

Most Runs Before Being Dismissed

The following are the most runs that have been recorded by one batsman in a series of not-out innings before being finally dismissed:

709 K. C. Ibrahim (Bombay) in 1947–48 ....218*, 36*, 234*, 77*, 144
634 V. M. Merchant (Hindus) in 1941–42 ....170*, 243*, 221
630 E. Hendren (M.C.C.) in 1929–30 ....205*, 254*, 171
575 E. D. Weekes (West Indians) in 1950.............246*, 200*, 129
558 F. Jakeman (Northants.) n 1951 .... 80*, 258*, 176*, 44
545 R. B. Simpson (Western Australia) in 1959–60...236*, 230*, 79
517 D. G. Bradman (N.S.W.) in 1933–34.............187*, 77*, 253
514 E. Hendren (M.C.C.) in 1929–30 ....223*, 211*, 80
510 W. H. Ponsford (Australians) in 1934 ....229*, 281*, 0
502 F. M. Worrell (West Indians) in 1950 ....241*, 261
474 W. G. Quaife (Warwicks.) in 1898 .... 60*, 117*, 157*, 24*, 52*, 61*, 3

High Aggregate of Runs in a Season

The following batsmen have scored 3000 runs in an English season:

	Season	Inns.	N.O.	Runs	H.S.	Avge.	100s
D. C. S. Compton (Middx.)	1947	50	8	3816	246	90·85	18
W. J. Edrich (Middx.)	1947	52	8	3539	267*	80·43	12
T. Hayward (Surrey)	1906	61	8	3518	219	66·37	13
L. Hutton (Yorks.)	1949	56	6	3429	269*	68·58	12
F. E. Woolley (Kent)	1928	59	4	3352	198	60·94	12
H. Sutcliffe (Yorks.)	1932	52	7	3336	313	74·13	14
W. R. Hammond (Glos.)	1933	54	5	3323	264	67·81	13
E. Hendren (Middx.)	1928	54	7	3311	209*	70·44	13
R. Abel (Surrey)	1901	68	8	3309	247	55·15	7
W. R. Hammond (Glos.)	1937	55	5	3252	217	65·04	13
M. J. K. Smith (Warwicks.)	1959	67	11	3245	200*	57·94	8
E. Hendren (Middx.)	1933	65	9	3186	301*	56·89	11
C. P. Mead (Hants.)	1921	52	6	3179	280*	69·10	10
T. Hayward (Surrey)	1904	63	5	3170	203	54·65	11
K. S. Ranjitsinhji (Sussex)	1899	58	8	3159	197	63·18	8
C. B. Fry (Sussex)	1901	43	3	3147	244	78·67	13
K. S. Ranjitsinhji (Sussex)	1900	40	5	3065	275	87·57	11
L. E. G. Ames (Kent)	1933	57	5	3058	295	58·80	9
J. T. Tyldesley (Lancs.)	1901	60	5	3041	221	55·29	9
C. P. Mead (Hants.)	1928	50	10	3027	180	75·67	13
J. B. Hobbs (Surrey)	1925	48	5	3024	266*	70·32	16
E. Tyldesley (Lancs.)	1928	48	10	3024	242	79·57	10
W. R. Hammond (Glos.)	1938	42	2	3011	271	75·27	15
E. Hendren (Middx.)	1923	51	12	3010	200*	77·17	13
H. Sutcliffe (Yorks.)	1931	42	11	3006	230	96·96	13
J. H. Parks (Sussex)	1937	63	4	3003	168	50·89	11
H. Sutcliffe (Yorks.)	1928	44	5	3002	228	76·97	13

2000 Runs in an English Season

	Season	Inns.	N.O.	Runs	H.S.	Avge.	100s
Abel, R. (Surrey) ....(8)	1895	50	4	2057	217	44·71	5
	1896	55	3	2218	231	42·65	5
	1897	50	3	2099	250	44·65	6
	1898	45	3	2053	219	48·88	7
	1899	53	3	2685	357*	53·70	7
	1900	49	3	2592	221	56·34	12
	1901	68	8	3309	247	55·15	7
	1902	64	8	2299	179	41·05	9
Ames, L. E. G. (Kent) ....(6)	1932	50	7	2482	180	57·72	9
	1933	57	5	3058	295	58·80	9
	1934	43	6	2113	202*	57·10	5
	1937	52	4	2347	201*	48·89	7
	1947	42	7	2272	212*	64·91	7
	1949	47	2	2125	160	47·22	7
Armstrong, N. F. (Leics.) ....(1)	1933	54	5	2113	164	43·12	4
Arnold, J. (Hants.) ....(1)	1934	52	5	2261	160	48·10	7
Ashdown, W. H. (Kent)............(2)	1928	55	3	2247	178	43·21	3
	1934	51	2	2030	332	41·42	6
Bailey, T. E. (Essex) ....(1)	1959	55	12	2011	146	46·76	6
Bakewell, A. H. (Northants.) ....(1)	1933	47	1	2149	257	46·71	7
Barber, W. (Yorks.) ....(1)	1935	55	4	2147	255	42·09	4
Bardsley, W. (Australians) ....(3)	1909	49	4	2072	219	46·04	6
	1912	52	6	2365	184*	51·41	8
	1921	41	4	2005	209	54·18	8
Barling, T. H. (Surrey) ....(1)	1946	52	6	2014	233*	43·78	6
Barnett, C. J. (Glos.) ....(4)	1933	59	3	2280	154	40·71	6
	1934	58	4	2348	194	43·48	6
	1936	58	3	2098	204*	38·14	6
	1937	65	3	2489	232	40·14	5
Barrington, K. F. (Surrey) ....(1)	1959	52	6	2499	186	54·32	6
Berry, L. G. (Leics.) ....(1)	1937	51	4	2446	184*	52·04	7
Bowley, E. H. (Sussex) ....(4)	1923	66	5	2180	120	35·73	2
	1927	41	3	2062	220	54·26	4
	1928	53	1	2359	188	45·36	6
	1929	57	3	2360	280*	43·70	5
Bradman, D. G. (Australians) ....(4)	1930	36	6	2960	334	98·66	10
	1934	27	3	2020	304	84·16	7
	1938	26	5	2429	278	115·66	13
	1948	31	4	2428	187	89·92	11
Brookes, D. (Northants.) ....(6)	1946	48	5	2191	200	50·95	7
	1947	55	2	2217	210	41·83	6
	1949	54	5	2163	257	44·14	7
	1950	45	6	2000	171	51·28	5
	1952	54	7	2229	204*	47·42	6
	1955	58	5	2012	177	37·96	3
Brown, G. (Hants.) ....(1)	1926	53	2	2040	146	40·00	6
Brown, S. M. (Middx.) ....(1)	1947	60	5	2078	155	37·78	4
Burnup, C. J. (Kent) ....(1)	1902	55	3	2048	161	39·38	6
Carr, A. W. (Notts.) ....(1)	1925	49	4	2338	206	51·95	8
Carr, D. B. (Derby) ....(1)	1959	60	8	2292	156*	44·07	5
Compton, D. C. S. (Middx.) ....(6)	1939	50	6	2468	214*	56·09	8
	1946	45	6	2403	235	61·61	10
	1947	50	8	3816	246	90·85	18
	1948	47	7	2451	252*	61·27	9
	1949	56	4	2530	182	48·65	9
	1951	40	6	2193	172	64·50	8
Cook, T. E. (Sussex) ....(1)	1934	45	6	2132	220	54·66	4
Cowdrey, M. C. (Kent) ....(1)	1959	44	4	2008	250	50·20	6
Cox, G. (Sussex) ....(2)	1947	56	2	2032	205*	37·62	8
	1950	55	7	2369	165*	49·35	6
Crapp, J. F. (Glos.) ....(1)	1949	48	4	2014	140	45·77	7
Davies, E. (Glamorgan) ....(1)	1937	52	2	2012	140	40·24	3
Denton, D. (Yorks.) ....(5)	1904	55	3	2088	119	40·15	3
	1905	60	3	2405	172	42·19	8
	1906	60	4	2287	157*	40·83	7
	1911	57	4	2232	137*	42·11	6
	1912	54	4	2127	221	42·54	6

	Season	Inns.	N.O.	Runs	H.S.	Avge.	100s
Dewes, J. G. (Middx.) ....(1)	1950	45	4	2432	212	59·31	9
Dexter, E. R. (Sussex) ....(2)	1959	53	8	2055	127	45·66	7
	1960	53	2	2217	157	43·47	7
Dipper, A. E. (Glos.) ....(5)	1923	57	6	2048	252*	40·15	3
	1926	63	6	2147	135	37·66	2
	1927	53	8	2246	212	49·91	7
	1928	49	6	2365	188	55·00	7
	1929	50	3	2218	153	47·19	3
Dodds, T. C. (Essex) ....(1)	1947	58	2	2147	157	38·33	1
Doggart, G. H. G. (Sussex) ....(1)	1949	51	6	2063	219*	45·84	5
Dollery, H. E. (Warwicks.) ....(2)	1949	48	4	2084	200	47·36	6
	1952	51	2	2073	212	42·30	4
Donnelly, M. P. (New Zealanders) ......(1)	1949	45	8	2287	206	61·81	5
Ducat, A. (Surrey) ....(1)	1930	48	6	2067	218	49·21	5
Duleepsinhji, K. S. (Sussex) ....(3)	1929	51	3	2545	246	53·02	8
	1930	48	3	2562	333	56·93	9
	1931	51	2	2684	162	54·79	12
Edrich, G. A. (Lancs.) ....(1)	1952	53	3	2067	162	41·34	4
Edrich, W. J. (Middx.) ....(9)	1937	53	5	2154	175	44·87	3
	1938	51	6	2378	245	52·84	6
	1939	45	1	2186	161	49·68	7
	1947	52	8	3539	267*	80·43	12
	1948	55	6	2428	168*	49·55	9
	1949	62	5	2253	182	39·52	5
	1951	58	4	2086	118	38·62	2
	1952	63	4	2281	239	38·66	6
	1953	60	2	2557	211	47·35	5
Emmett, G. M. (Glos.) ....(3)	1949	51	2	2005	116	40·91	3
	1951	56	5	2019	146	39·58	3
	1953	62	2	2115	141	35·25	4
Fagg, A. E. (Kent) ....(5)	1938	53	6	2456	244	52·25	9
	1947	56	5	2203	184	43·19	5
	1948	48	3	2423	203	53·84	8
	1950	54	3	2034	156	39·88	6
	1951	51	1	2081	221	41·62	6
Fishlock, L. B. (Surrey) ....(6)	1936	53	13	2129	133*	53·22	5
	1938	53	1	2121	165	40·78	4
	1946	46	2	2221	172	50·47	5
	1948	56	2	2106	253	39·00	5
	1949	56	3	2426	210	45·77	7
	1950	59	5	2417	147	44·75	6
Foster, R. E. (Worcs.) ....(1)	1901	44	2	2128	136	50·66	6
Fry, C. B. (Sussex) ....(6)	1899	55	1	2366	181	43·81	5
	1900	41	3	2325	229	61·18	9
	1901	43	3	3147	244	78·67	13
	1903	40	7	2683	234	81·30	9
	1904	42	2	2824	229	70·60	10
	1905	44	4	2801	233	70·02	10
Gibbons, H. H. (Worcs.) ....(3)	1933	57	4	2008	155	37·88	4
	1934	57	6	2654	157	52·03	8
	1938	55	6	2120	178	43·26	6
Gimblett, H. (Somerset) ....(2)	1949	52	4	2093	156	43·60	5
	1952	55	1	2134	169	39·51	5
Grace, W. G. (Glos.) ....(5)	1871	39	4	2739	268	78·25	10
	1876	46	4	2622	344	62·42	7
	1887	46	8	2062	183*	54·26	6
	1895	48	2	2346	288	51·00	9
	1896	54	4	2135	301	42·70	4
Graveney, T. W. (Glos.) ....(5)	1951	50	3	2291	201	48·74	8
	1952	51	7	2066	171	48·04	6
	1955	51	2	2117	159	43·20	5
	1956	54	6	2397	200	49·93	9
	1957	53	5	2361	258	49·18	8
Gray, J. R. (Hants.) ....(1)	1959	57	5	2170	176*	41·73	6
Gregory, R. J. (Surrey) ....(2)	1934	49	3	2379	180	51·71	8
	1937	50	3	2166	154	46·08	7
Grieves, K. (Lancs.) ....(1)	1959	58	4	2253	202*	41·72	4
Gunn, W. (Notts.) ....(1)	1893	51	3	2057	156	42·85	7
Hallam, M. R. (Leics.) ....(2)	1957	62	2	2068	176	34·46	6
	1959	62	1	2070	210*	33·93	4
Hallows, C. (Lancs.) ....(3)	1925	51	6	2354	163	52·31	8

	Season	Inns.	N.O.	Runs	H.S.	Avge.	100s
Hallows, C. (*cont.*)	1927	44	13	2343	233*	75·58	7
	1928	46	5	2645	232	64·51	11
Hammond, W. R. (Glos.) ....(12)	1927	47	4	2969	197	69·04	12
	1928	48	5	2825	244	65·69	9
	1929	47	9	2456	238*	64·63	10
	1930	44	6	2032	211*	53·47	5
	1932	49	4	2528	264	56·17	8
	1933	54	5	3323	264	67·81	13
	1934	35	4	2366	302*	76·32	8
	1935	58	5	2616	252	49·35	7
	1936	42	5	2107	317	56·94	5
	1937	55	5	3252	217	65·04	13
	1938	42	2	3011	271	75·27	15
	1939	46	7	2479	302	63·56	7
Hardinge, H. T. W. (Kent) ....(5)	1913	56	7	2037	168	41·57	7
	1921	52	7	2339	207	51·97	9
	1922	48	8	2207	249*	55·17	7
	1926	52	5	2234	176	47·53	7
	1928	46	5	2446	263*	59·65	5
Hardstaff, J., jun. (Notts.) ....(4)	1937	46	2	2540	266	57·72	8
	1939	46	7	2129	159	54·58	5
	1947	44	7	2396	221*	64·75	7
	1949	40	9	2251	162*	72·61	8
Harvey, R. N. (Australians) ....(1)	1953	35	4	2040	202*	65·80	10
Hayes, E. G. (Surrey) ....(2)	1906	56	5	2309	218	45·27	7
	1909	65	5	2161	276	36·01	3
Hayward, T. (Surrey) ....(10)	1899	49	4	2647	273	58·82	7
	1900	57	7	2693	193	53·86	10
	1901	58	8	2535	181	50·70	2
	1903	64	3	2177	156*	35·68	3
	1904	63	5	3170	203	54·65	11
	1905	64	6	2592	129*	44·68	5
	1906	61	8	3518	219	66·37	13
	1907	58	6	2353	161	45·25	7
	1908	52	1	2337	175	45·82	5
	1911	51	6	2149	202	47·75	5
Headley, G. (West Indians) ....(1)	1933	38	3	2320	224*	66·28	7
Hearne, J. W. (Middx.) ....(4)	1913	49	3	2036	189	44·26	6
	1914	43	8	2116	204	60·45	8
	1920	46	7	2148	215*	55·07	6
	1932	52	3	2151	176	43·89	6
Hendren, E. (Middx.) ....(15)	1920	47	6	2520	232	61·46	6
	1921	53	5	2013	113	41·93	7
	1922	38	7	2072	277*	66·83	7
	1923	51	12	3010	200*	77·17	13
	1924	48	11	2100	142	56·75	5
	1925	50	6	2601	240	59·11	8
	1926	53	11	2643	213	62·92	9
	1927	43	5	2784	201*	73·26	13
	1928	54	7	3311	209*	70·44	13
	1929	63	9	2213	156	40·98	5
	1931	54	9	2548	232	56·62	7
	1932	47	7	2041	194	51·02	5
	1933	65	9	3186	301*	56·89	11
	1934	55	6	2213	135	45·16	7
	1936	58	2	2654	202	47·39	9
Hill, N. (Notts.) ....(1)	1959	57	2	2129	167	38·70	6
Hirst, G. H. (Yorks.) ....(3)	1904	50	4	2501	157	54·36	9
	1905	52	10	2266	341	53·95	6
	1906	58	6	2385	169	45·86	6
Hobbs, J. B. (Surrey) ....(17)	1907	63	6	2135	166*	37·45	4
	1909	54	2	2114	205	40·65	6
	1911	60	3	2376	154*	41·68	4
	1912	60	6	2042	111	37·81	3
	1913	57	5	2605	184	50·09	9
	1914	48	2	2697	226	58·63	11
	1919	49	6	2594	205*	60·32	8
	1920	50	2	2827	215	58·89	11
	1922	46	5	2552	168	62·24	10
	1923	59	4	2087	136	37·94	5
	1924	43	7	2094	211	58·16	6

Player	Season	Inns.	N.O.	Runs	H.S.	Avge.	100s
Hobbs, J. B. (*cont.*)	1925	48	5	3024	266*	70·32	16
	1926	41	3	2949	316*	77·60	10
	1928	38	7	2542	200*	82·00	12
	1929	39	5	2263	204	66·55	10
	1930	43	2	2103	146*	51·29	5
	1931	49	6	2418	153	56·23	10
Holmes, P. (Yorks.) ....(7)	1920	51	6	2254	302*	50·08	7
	1923	54	3	2001	199	39·23	3
	1925	52	9	2453	315*	57·04	6
	1926	50	4	2006	143	43·60	4
	1927	47	9	2174	180	57·21	6
	1928	43	5	2220	275	58·42	6
	1930	52	6	2003	132*	43·54	4
Horton, H. (Hants.) ....(2)	1959	59	8	2428	140*	47·60	4
	1960	59	9	2170	131	43·40	7
Horton, M. J. (Worcs.) ....(1)	1959	58	3	2468	212	44·87	4
Hutton, L. (Yorks.) ....(9)	1937	58	7	2888	271*	56·62	10
	1939	52	6	2883	280*	62·67	12
	1947	44	4	2585	270*	64·62	11
	1948	48	7	2654	176*	64·73	10
	1949	56	6	3429	269*	68·58	12
	1950	40	3	2128	202*	57·51	6
	1951	47	8	2145	194*	55·00	7
	1952	45	3	2567	189	61·11	11
	1953	44	5	2458	241	63·02	8
Iddon, J. (Lancs.) ....(1)	1934	51	6	2381	200*	52·91	6
Insole, D. J. (Essex) ....(3)	1951	57	9	2032	186*	42·33	3
	1955	62	5	2427	142	42·57	9
	1959	50	5	2045	180	45·44	5
Jessop, G. L. (Glos.) ....(2)	1900	58	3	2210	179	40·18	6
	1901	58	1	2323	233	40·75	5
Jones, A. O. (Notts.) ....(1)	1901	51	2	2292	249	46·77	5
Jupp, V. W. C. (Sussex) ....(1)	1921	60	4	2169	179	38·73	7
Keeton, W. W. (Notts.) ....(6)	1932	51	3	2062	242	42·95	7
	1933	56	3	2258	168	42·60	6
	1934	46	0	2006	261	43·60	3
	1937	52	8	2004	136	45·54	4
	1946	48	2	2021	160	43·93	5
	1949	38	1	2049	210	55·37	6
Kenyon, D. (Worcs.) ....(7)	1950	58	3	2351	163	42·74	6
	1951	59	6	2145	145	40·47	6
	1952	60	2	2489	171	42·91	7
	1953	58	3	2439	238*	44·38	6
	1954	58	7	2636	253*	51·68	6
	1955	64	3	2296	131	37·63	5
	1957	62	3	2231	200*	37·81	6
Kilner, N. (Warwicks.) ....(1)	1933	50	2	2159	197	44·97	6
Langridge, James (Sussex) ....(1)	1937	58	7	2082	150*	40·82	1
Langridge, John (Sussex) ....(11)	1933	51	6	2056	250*	45·68	4
	1934	52	6	2256	232*	49·04	4
	1935	56	4	2035	195	39·13	4
	1937	63	3	2514	175	41·90	10
	1938	54	4	2347	227	46·94	5
	1939	51	0	2106	202	41·29	6
	1947	57	5	2023	138*	38·90	3
	1949	53	5	2914	234*	60·70	12
	1950	65	5	2412	241	40·20	5
	1951	53	3	2041	200*	40·82	5
	1952	60	4	2082	140	37·17	6
Lee, F. S. (Somerset) ....(1)	1938	51	6	2019	162	44·86	7
Leyland, M. (Yorks.) ....(3)	1930	50	7	2175	211*	50·58	6
	1933	50	4	2317	210*	50·36	7
	1934	44	4	2142	182	53·55	7
Livingston, T. L. (Northants.) ....(3)	1954	48	7	2269	207*	55·34	6
	1955	58	5	2172	172*	40·98	5
	1956	47	6	2006	188*	48·92	2
Lowson, F. A. (Yorks.) ....(1)	1950	56	5	2152	141*	42·19	5
Macartney, C. G. (Australians) ....(2)	1912	49	1	2187	208	45·56	6
	1921	41	2	2317	345	59·41	8
Makepeace, H. (Lancs.) ....(2)	1923	53	6	2310	203	49·14	6
	1926	54	5	2340	180	48·75	5

Player	Season	Inns.	N.O.	Runs	H.S.	Avge.	100s
Marshall, R. E. (Hants.) ....(4)	1955	60	4	2115	110*	37·76	3
	1958	57	3	2118	193	39·22	5
	1959	63	1	2532	150	40·83	4
	1960	62	5	2380	168	41·75	5
May, P. B. H. (Surrey) ....(5)	1951	43	9	2339	178*	68·79	9
	1952	47	7	2498	197	62·45	10
	1953	59	9	2554	159	51·08	8
	1957	41	3	2347	285*	61·76	7
	1958	41	6	2231	174	63·74	8
McCabe, S. J. (Australians) ....(1)	1934	37	7	2078	240	69·26	8
Mead, C. P. (Hants.) ....(11)	1911	52	5	2562	223	54·51	9
	1913	60	8	2627	171*	50·51	9
	1914	53	5	2476	213	51·58	7
	1921	52	6	3179	280*	69·10	10
	1922	50	10	2391	235	59·77	8
	1923	52	8	2604	222	59·18	7
	1926	45	8	2326	177*	62·86	10
	1927	41	9	2385	200*	74·53	8
	1928	50	10	3027	180	75·67	13
	1933	44	6	2576	227	67·78	10
	1934	46	8	2011	198	52·92	6
Merchant, V. M. (Indians) ....(1)	1946	41	9	2385	242*	74·53	7
Mitchell, A. (Yorks.) ....(1)	1933	51	12	2300	158	58·97	8
Mitchell, B. (South Africans) ....(1)	1947	37	4	2014	189*	61·03	8
Nichol, M. (Worcs.) ....(1)	1933	54	5	2154	165*	43·95	8
Noble, M. A. (Australians) ....(1)	1905	46	2	2053	267	46·65	6
O'Connor, J. (Essex) ....(4)	1928	53	4	2325	157	47·44	6
	1929	54	3	2288	168*	44·86	9
	1933	52	5	2077	237	44·19	6
	1934	49	7	2350	248	55·95	9
Oldfield, N. (Northants.) ....(1)	1949	47	3	2192	168	49·81	4
Padgett, D. E. V. (Yorks.) ....(1)	1959	61	8	2181	161*	41·15	4
Palmer, C. H. (Leics.)....................(1)	1952	56	4	2071	127	39·82	4
Parkhouse, W. G. A. (Glamorgan) ......(1)	1959	49	3	2243	154	48·76	6
Parks, H. W. (Sussex).....................(1)	1947	57	2	2122	170	38·58	5
Parks, J. H. (Sussex) ....(1)	1937	63	4	3003	168	50·89	11
Parks, J. M. (Sussex) ....(3)	1955	63	8	2314	205*	42·07	5
	1957	55	6	2171	132*	44·30	4
	1959	56	11	2313	157*	51·40	6
Paynter, E. (Lancs.) ....(4)	1932	55	1	2035	159	37·68	5
	1936	54	10	2016	177	45·81	4
	1937	58	4	2904	322	53·77	5
	1938	52	6	2691	291	58·50	8
Place, W. (Lancs.) ....(1)	1947	47	7	2501	266*	62·52	10
Pullar, G. (Lancs.) ....(1)	1959	55	7	2647	161	55·14	8
Quaife, W. G. (Warwicks.) ....(1)	1905	52	14	2060	255*	54·21	6
Ranjitsinhji, K. S. (Sussex) ....(5)	1896	55	7	2780	171*	57·91	10
	1899	58	8	3159	197	63·18	8
	1900	40	5	3065	275	87·57	11
	1901	40	5	2468	285*	70·51	8
	1904	34	6	2077	207*	74·17	8
Rhodes, W. (Yorks.) ....(2)	1909	59	7	2094	199	40·26	5
	1911	64	5	2261	128	38·32	5
Richardson, P. E. (Worcs.) ....(1)	1953	61	3	2294	171	39·55	3
Robertson, J. D. (Middx.) ....(9)	1946	58	3	2114	128	38·43	5
	1947	57	4	2760	229	52·07	12
	1948	54	7	2366	154	50·34	7
	1949	57	1	2244	331*	40·07	7
	1950	59	3	2093	138*	37·37	4
	1951	56	4	2917	201*	56·09	7
	1952	64	2	2337	162	37·69	2
	1955	64	0	2070	137	32·34	1
	1957	59	2	2155	201*	37·80	4
Rogers, N. H. (Somerset) ....(1)	1952	58	3	2244	164	40·80	3
Russell, A. C. (Essex) ....(5)	1920	56	1	2432	197	44·21	3
	1921	44	3	2236	273	54·53	8
	1922	50	3	2575	172	54·78	9
	1925	47	4	2081	150	48·39	7
	1928	42	7	2243	182	64·08	8
Russell, W. E. (Middx.) ....(1)	1960	63	9	2051	182	37·98	2
Sandham, A. (Surrey) ....(8)	1921	48	5	2117	292*	49·23	5

H

	Season	Inns.	N.O.	Runs	H.S.	Avge.	100s
Sandham, A. (*cont.*)	1924	37	2	2082	169	59·48	7
	1925	47	6	2255	181	55·00	5
	1927	46	6	2315	230	57·87	7
	1928	47	4	2532	282*	58·88	8
	1929	52	2	2565	187	51·30	6
	1930	50	4	2295	204	49·89	6
	1931	50	8	2209	175	52·59	9
Seymour, James (Kent) ....(1)	1913	60	6	2088	124	38·66	5
Sharp, J. (Lancs.) ....(1)	1911	55	3	2099	184*	40·36	4
Shepherd, T. F. (Surrey) ....(1)	1927	45	6	2145	277*	55·00	8
Sheppard, D. S. (Sussex) ....(3)	1951	43	3	2014	183	52·60	7
	1952	39	4	2262	239*	64·62	10
	1953	57	7	2270	186*	45·40	7
Simpson, R. T. (Notts.) ....(5)	1949	46	6	2525	238	63·12	6
	1950	47	6	2576	243*	62·82	8
	1952	54	1	2222	216	41·92	5
	1953	60	5	2505	157	45·54	7
	1959	55	5	2033	132	40·66	5
Smith, D. (Derby) ....(1)	1935	61	6	2175	225	39·54	2
Smith, D. V. (Sussex) ....(1)	1957	54	5	2088	166	42·61	5
Smith, M. J. K. (Warwicks.) ....(4)	1957	63	5	2125	127	36·63	3
	1958	51	3	2126	160	44·29	3
	1959	67	11	3245	200*	57·94	8
	1960	63	7	2551	169*	45·55	4
Spooner, R. H. (Lancs.) ....(1)	1911	45	0	2312	224	51·37	7
Stoddart, A. E. (Middx.) ....(1)	1893	50	1	2072	195*	42·28	4
Stott, W. B. (Yorks.) ....(1)	1959	56	2	2034	144*	37·66	3
Sutcliffe, B. (New Zealanders) ....(1)	1949	49	5	2627	243	59·70	7
Sutcliffe, H. (Yorks.) ....(15)	1922	48	5	2020	232	46·97	4
	1923	60	6	2220	139	41·11	3
	1924	52	8	2142	255*	48·68	6
	1925	51	8	2308	235	53·67	7
	1926	47	9	2528	200	66·52	8
	1927	49	6	2414	227	56·13	6
	1928	44	5	3002	228	76·97	13
	1929	46	4	2189	150	52·11	9
	1930	44	8	2312	173	64·22	6
	1931	42	11	3006	230	96·96	13
	1932	52	7	3336	313	74·13	14
	1933	52	5	2211	205	47·04	7
	1934	44	3	2023	203	49·34	4
	1935	54	3	2494	212	48·90	8
	1937	54	5	2162	189	44·12	4
Tarrant, F. A. (Middx.) ....(1)	1911	48	4	2030	207*	46·13	5
Todd, L. J. (Kent) ....(1)	1947	55	5	2312	173	46·24	7
Tompkin, M. (Leics.) ....(1)	1955	62	3	2190	131	37·11	3
Townsend, C. L. (Glos.) ....(1)	1899	54	7	2440	224*	51·91	9
Townsend, L. F. (Derby) ....(1)	1933	59	8	2268	233	44·47	6
Tremlett, M. F. (Somerset) ....(1)	1951	59	0	2101	185	35·61	2
Trumper, V. T. (Australians) ....(1)	1902	53	0	2570	128	48·49	11
Tyldesley, E. (Lancs.) ....(6)	1922	57	5	2168	178	41·69	4
	1923	60	6	2040	236	37·77	4
	1926	51	7	2826	226	64·22	10
	1928	48	10	3024	242	79·57	10
	1932	48	7	2420	225*	59·02	8
	1934	51	8	2487	239	57·83	8
Tyldesley, J. T. (Lancs.) ....(5)	1901	60	5	3041	221	55·29	9
	1904	44	5	2439	225	62·53	8
	1906	52	3	2270	295*	46·32	4
	1907	63	5	2132	209	36·75	5
	1910	51	2	2265	158	46·22	7
Walters, C. F. (Worcs.) ....(2)	1933	52	3	2404	226	50·08	9
	1934	48	4	2048	178	46·54	4
Warner, P. F. (Middx.) ....(1)	1911	51	5	2123	244	46·15	5
Washbrook, C. (Lancs.) ....(2)	1946	43	8	2400	182	68·57	9
	1947	47	8	2662	251*	68·25	11
Watson, F. (Lancs.) ....(3)	1928	46	4	2583	300*	61·05	9
	1929	50	4	2137	207	46·45	6
	1930	47	2	2031	135	45·13	3
Watson, W. (Leics.) ....(1)	1959	50	10	2212	173	55·30	7
Weekes, E. D. (West Indians) ....(1)	1950	33	4	2310	304*	79·65	7

	Season	Inns.	N.O.	Runs	H.S.	Avge.	100s
Wharton, A. (Lancs.) ....(1)	1959	59	6	2157	199	40·69	4
Whysall, W. W. (Notts.) ....(5)	1926	56	5	2138	209	41·92	6
	1927	50	5	2069	184	45·97	5
	1928	51	2	2573	166	52·51	9
	1929	56	3	2716	244	51·24	7
	1930	47	3	2174	248	49·40	8
Wight, P. B. (Somerset) ....(1)	1960	62	5	2375	155*	41·66	7
Wilson, J. V. (Yorks.) ....(1)	1951	51	9	2027	223*	48·26	6
Wood, C. J. B. (Leics.) ....(1)	1901	52	3	2033	156	41·48	3
Woolley, F. E. (Kent) ....(13)	1914	52	2	2272	160*	45·44	6
	1921	50	1	2101	174	42·87	6
	1922	47	3	2022	188	45·95	5
	1923	56	5	2091	270	41·00	5
	1924	49	2	2344	202	49·87	8
	1925	43	4	2190	215	56·15	5
	1926	50	3	2183	217	46·44	6
	1928	59	4	3352	198	60·94	12
	1929	55	5	2804	176	56·08	11
	1930	50	5	2023	120	44·95	5
	1931	51	4	2301	224	48·95	5
	1934	56	1	2643	176	48·05	10
	1935	56	0	2339	229	41·76	6
Wyatt, R. E. S. (Warwicks.) ....(5)	1928	52	10	2408	177	57·33	6
	1929	55	6	2630	161*	53·67	10
	1933	50	10	2379	187*	59·47	8
	1935	55	9	2019	149	43·89	4
	1937	54	5	2625	232	53·57	9
Young, D. M. (Glos.).........................(2)	1955	63	1	2106	170	33·96	4
	1959	57	4	2179	148	41·11	6

1000 Runs in a Season in Australia

	Season	Inns.	N.O.	Runs	H.S.	Avge.	100s
Amarnath, L. (Indians) ....(1)	1947–48	23	3	1162	228*	58·10	5
Armstrong, W. W. (Victoria) ....(2)	1907–08	16	2	1033	231	73·78	5
	1920–21	15	3	1069	245	89·08	5
Bardsley, W. (N.S.W.) ....(1)	1910–11	19	1	1233	191*	68·50	3
Barnes, S. G. (N.S.W.) ....(1)	1940–41	14	0	1050	185	75·00	6
Barnett, C. J. (M.C.C.) ....(1)	1936–37	25	0	1375	259	55·00	5
Bradman, D. G. (N.S.W. and (12)	1928–29	24	6	1690	340*	93·88	7
South Australia)	1929–30	16	2	1586	452*	113·28	5
	1930–31	18	0	1422	258	79·00	5
	1931–32	13	1	1403	299*	116·91	7
	1932–33	21	2	1171	238	61·63	3
	1933–34	11	2	1192	253	132·44	5
	1935–36	9	0	1173	369	130·33	4
	1936–37	19	1	1552	270	86·22	6
	1937–38	18	2	1437	246	89·81	7
	1939–40	15	3	1475	267	122·91	5
	1946–47	14	1	1032	234	79·38	4
	1947–48	12	2	1296	201	129·60	8
Brown, W. A. (Queensland) ....(1)	1938–39	11	1	1057	215	105·70	3
Compton, D. C. S. (M.C.C.) ....(1)	1946–47	25	3	1432	163	65·09	5
Endean, W. R. (South Africans)......(1)	1952–53	27	3	1281	181*	53·37	2
Faulkner, G. A. (South Africans) ...(1)	1910–11	27	1	1534	204	59·00	3
Hammond, W. R. (M.C.C.) ....(2)	1928–29	18	1	1553	251	91·35	7
	1936–37	20	2	1206	231*	67·00	5
Hardstaff, J. sen. (M.C.C.) ....(1)	1907–08	28	2	1360	135	52·30	3
Harvey, R. N. (Victoria) ....(3)	1950–51	25	1	1099	146	45·79	3
	1952–53	27	1	1659	205	63·80	5
	1954–55	24	2	1009	162	45·86	1
Hassett, A. L. (Victoria) ....(2)	1946–47	18	1	1213	200	71·35	5
	1950–51	25	3	1423	232	64·68	4
Hazare, V. S. (Indians)...................(1)	1947–48	23	1	1056	145	48·00	4
Headley, G. (West Indians) ....(1)	1930–31	25	1	1066	131	44·41	4

	Season	Inns.	N.O.	Runs	H.S.	Avge.	100s
Hendren, E. (M.C.C.) ....(3)	1920–21	20	1	1178	271	62·00	4
	1924–25	22	3	1233	168	64·89	4
	1928–29	17	1	1033	169	64·56	3
Hill, C. (South Australia) ....(2)	1897–98	19	1	1186	200	65·89	5
	1901–02	20	0	1035	107	50·17	1
Hutton, L. (M.C.C.) ....(2)	1946–47	21	3	1267	151*	70·38	3
	1950–51	21	4	1199	156*	70·52	5
Jardine, D. R. (M.C.C.) ....(1)	1928–29	19	1	1168	214	64·88	6
Kippax, A. F. (N.S.W.) ....(2)	1926–27	13	1	1039	217*	86·58	5
	1928–29	19	2	1079	260*	63·47	4
MacLaren, A. C. ....(1)	1897–98	20	1	1037	142	54·57	5
May, P. B. H. (M.C.C.) ....(1)	1958–59	22	1	1197	140	57·00	5
Miller, K. R. (Victoria and N.S.W.) (2)	1946–47	19	3	1202	206*	75·12	4
	1950–51	20	3	1332	214	78·35	5
Morris, A. R. (N.S.W.) ....(3)	1946–47	20	2	1234	155	68·55	5
	1948–49	17	1	1069	177	66·81	6
	1950–51	22	1	1221	206	58·14	6
Noble, M. A. (N.S.W.) ....(1)	1907–08	19	1	1071	176	59·50	3
Nourse, A. D. sen. (South Africans) (1)	1910–11	29	5	1454	201*	60·58	5
O'Neill, N. (N.S.W.) ....(1)	1957–58	14	2	1005	233	83·75	4
Ponsford, W. H. (Victoria) ....(2)	1926–27	10	0	1229	352	122·90	6
	1927–28	8	0	1217	437	152·12	4
Ranjitsinhji, K. S. ....(1)	1897–98	22	3	1157	189	60·89	3
Rhodes, W. (M.C.C.) ....(1)	1911–12	24	4	1098	179	54·90	4
Ryder, J. (Victoria) ....(1)	1928–29	17	2	1045	175	69·66	3
Sutcliffe, H. (M.C.C.) ....(2)	1924–25	18	0	1250	188	69·44	5
	1932–33	19	1	1318	194	73·22	5
Trumper, V. T. (N.S.W.) ....(1)	1910–11	20	2	1246	214*	69·22	3

The only Australian batsmen to score 1000 runs in a purely domestic season are: S. G. Barnes, D. G. Bradman, W. A. Brown, A. F. Kippax, A. R. Morris, N. O'Neill and W. H. Ponsford.

1000 Runs in a Season in South Africa

	Season	Inns.	N.O.	Runs	H.S.	Avge.	100s
D. C. S. Compton (M.C.C.) 1948–49	1948–49	26	5	1781	300	84·80	8
R. N. Harvey (Australians) 1949–50	1949–50	25	5	1526	178	76·30	8
J. B. Hobbs (M.C.C.) 1913–14	1913–14	22	2	1489	170	74·45	5
L. Hutton (M.C.C.) 1948–49	1948–49	21	1	1477	174	73·85	5
A. R. Morris (Australians) 1949–50	1949–50	27	3	1411	157	58·79	8
J. A. R. Moroney (Australians) 1949–50	1949–50	27	3	1331	160*	55·45	6
P. B. H. May (M.C.C.) 1956–57	1956–57	24	1	1270	206	55·21	6
J. B. Hobbs (M.C.C.) 1909–10	1909–10	20	1	1194	187	62·84	3
J. H. Fingleton (Australians)..................1935–36	1935–36	19	4	1192	167	79·46	6
L. Hutton (M.C.C.) 1938–39	1938–39	19	1	1168	202	64·88	5
B. Sutcliffe (New Zealanders) 1953–54	1953–54	27	2	1155	196	46·20	1
E. Tyldesley (M.C.C.)..........................1927–28	1927–28	21	2	1130	161	59·47	4
C. Washbrook (M.C.C.) 1948–49	1948–49	23	2	1124	195	53·52	3
P. Holmes (M.C.C.) 1927–28	1927–28	22	3	1112	279*	58·52	3
E. Paynter (M.C.C.) 1938–39	1938–39	14	0	1072	243	76·57	5
W. A. Brown (Australians) 1935–36	1935–36	19	2	1065	148	62·64	2
W. R. Hammond (M.C.C.) 1930–31	1930–31	19	2	1045	136*	61·47	3
J. W. Burke (Australians) 1957–58	1957–58	19	3	1041	189	65·06	4
M. C. Cowdrey (M.C.C.) 1956–57	1956–57	27	1	1035	173	39·80	2
H. Sutcliffe (M.C.C.) 1927–28	1927–28	23	3	1030	102	51·50	2
W. R. Hammond (M.C.C.) 1938–39	1938–39	18	1	1025	181	60·29	4
J. R. Reid (New Zealanders) 1953–54	1953–54	27	0	1012	175	37·48	3

Highest aggregates by home batsmen:

	Season	Inns.	N.O.	Runs	H.S.	Avge.	100s
D. J. McGlew (Natal) 1957–58	1957–58	21	2	953	213*	50·16	3
E. A. B. Rowan (Transvaal) 1952–53	1952–53	12	0	899	196	74·91	3
A. D. Nourse jun. (Natal) 1948–49	1948–49	16	3	877	129*	67·46	3
A. D. Nourse jun. (Natal) 1947–48	1947–48	11	2	864	214*	96·00	4
A. D. Nourse jun. (Natal) 1936–37	1936–37	6	1	846	260*	169·20	4
H. W. Taylor (Natal) 1913–14	1913–14	14	2	824	109	68·66	2

	Season	Inns.	N.O.	Runs	H.S.	Avge.	100s
A. D. Nourse jun. (Natal)	1946–47	12	0	775	192	64·58	2
M. J. Susskind (Transvaal)	1931–32	13	1	769	124	64·08	4
A. D. Nourse sen. (Natal)	1921–22	16	2	768	143	54·85	3
E. A. B. Rowan (Transvaal)	1950–51	9	2	765	277*	109·28	3
G. A. Faulkner (Transvaal)	1909–10	13	2	748	148*	68·00	2
K. G. Viljoen (Transvaal)	1936–37	11	3	743	124	92·87	3
S. K. Coen (O.F.S.)	1926–27	11	1	737	172	73·70	3
B. Mitchell (Transvaal)	1938–39	12	1	720	133	65·45	2
W. W. Wade (Natal)	1947–48	10	0	716	158	71·60	3

Over 700 Runs in the West Indies

	Season	Inns.	N.O.	Runs	H.S.	Avge.	100s
E. Hendren (M.C.C.)	1929–30	18	5	1765	254	135·76	6
A. Sandham (M.C.C.)	1929–30	20	0	1281	325	64·05	6
M. C. Cowdrey (M.C.C.)	1959–60	18	2	1014	173	63·37	5
G. Sobers (Barbados)	1957–58	10	3	1007	365*	143·85	4
E. D. Weekes (Barbados)	1952–53	9	1	969	253	121·12	4
C. L. Walcott (Barbados)	1954–55	13	0	945	155	72·69	5
E. R. Dexter (M.C.C.)	1959–60	18	2	908	136*	56·75	3
W. Watson (M.C.C.)	1953–54	16	3	892	257	68·61	4
G. Headley (Jamaica)	1929–30	11	0	891	223	81·00	4
Hanif Mohammed (Pakistan)	1957–58	16	1	867	337	57·80	2
G. Sobers (Barbados)	1959–60	9	1	863	226	107·87	4
Wazir Mohammed (Pakistan)	1957–58	16	4	850	189	70·83	4
K. F. Barrington (M.C.C.)	1959–60	19	1	830	128	46·11	3
L. E. G. Ames (M.C.C.)	1929–30	19	2	818	149	48·11	4
P. R. Umrigar (Indians)	1952–53	16	3	813	130	62·53	2
P. Holmes (M.C.C.)	1925–26	17	0	797	244	46·88	1
W. R. Hammond (M.C.C.)	1934–35	17	3	789	281*	56·35	3
R. N. Harvey (Australians)	1954–55	12	2	789	204	78·90	3
Saeed Ahmed (Pakistan)	1957–58	16	0	784	150	49·00	1
L. Hutton (M.C.C.)	1953–54	12	2	780	205	78·00	2
G. Pullar (M.C.C.)	1959–60	18	2	777	141	48·56	1
W. R. Hammond (M.C.C.)	1925–26	18	3	732	238*	48·80	2
G. Headley (Jamaica)	1931–32	4	2	723	344*	361·50	3
C. L. Walcott (Barbados)	1953–54	12	2	723	220	72·30	3
G. Gunn (M.C.C.)	1929–30	17	0	707	178	41·59	1
C. C. Hunte (Barbados)	1957–58	11	1	706	260	70·60	3

Over 600 Runs in New Zealand

	Season	Inns.	N.O.	Runs	H.S.	Avge.	100s
E. D. Weekes (West Indians)	1955–56	10	1	940	156	104·44	6
B. Sutcliffe (Otago)	1952–53	13	0	859	385	66·07	1
B. Sutcliffe (Otago)	1950–51	12	0	798	275	66·50	4
W. M. Woodfull (Australians)	1927–28	9	3	781	284	130·16	3
B. Sutcliffe (Otago)	1947–48	8	1	747	208*	106·71	4
B. Sutcliffe (Otago)	1959–60	17	1	747	264	46·88	2
J. R. Reid (Wellington)	1959–60	16	1	724	165*	48·26	2
B. Sutcliffe (Auckland & Otago)	1946–47	8	1	722	197	103·14	3
W. M. Woodfull (Victoria)	1924–25	9	5	710	212*	177·50	3
J. T. Sparling (Auckland)	1959–60	20	1	705	105	37·11	1
B. Sutcliffe (Otago)	1949–50	9	0	698	355	77·55	2
L. S. M. Miller (Wellington)	1955–56	16	1	679	144	45·26	2
J. L. Kerr (Canterbury)	1935–36	13	2	655	146*	59·54	3
C. G. Macartney (Australians)	1923–24	8	1	641	221	91·57	3
V. T. Trumper (Australians)	1913–14	9	0	628	293	89·51	1
W. Bardsley (N.S.W.)	1923–24	7	2	623	200*	124·00	1
J. S. Hiddleston (Wellington)	1923–24	12	0	619	163	51·58	2
C. S. Dempster (Wellington)	1927–28	12	1	616	145	56·00	1
P. F. Warner (Hawke's XI)	1902–03	10	1	615	211	68·33	2
R. V. de W. Worker (Otago)	1923–24	12	0	606	172	50·50	2

1000 Runs in a Season in India, Pakistan and Ceylon

	Season	Inns.	N.O.	Runs	H.S.	Avge.	100s
F. M. Worrell (Commonwealth)	1950–51	33	3	1900	285	63·33	5
A. Sandham (M.C.C.)	1926–27	30	2	1756	150	62·71	7
R. E. S. Wyatt (M.C.C.)	1926–27	37	4	1747	138	52·93	5
F. M. Worrell (Commonwealth)	1949–50	26	4	1640	223*	74·54	5
R. Kanhai (West Indians)	1958–59	28	2	1518	256	58·38	4
G. Sobers (West Indians)	1958–59	26	5	1419	198	67·57	5
T. W. Graveney (M.C.C.)	1951–52	32	7	1393	175	55·72	6
R. S. Modi	1944–45	15	3	1386	245*	115·50	6
C. L. Walcott (West Indians)	1948–49	22	4	1366	152	75·88	5
V. S. Hazare	1949–50	19	3	1364	195	85·24	5
E. D. Weekes (West Indians)	1948–49	19	4	1350	194	90·00	6
V. M. Merchant	1944–45	15	3	1323	275	110·25	5
V. S. Hazare	1948–49	21	3	1310	146	72·77	6
G. M. Emmett (Commonwealth)	1950–51	37	5	1296	104	40·50	2
J. T. Ikin (Commonwealth)	1950–51	33	5	1292	111	46·14	2
J. H. Parsons (M.C.C.)	1926–27	28	2	1289	160	49·58	2
H. Gimblett (Commonwealth)	1950–51	38	6	1269	111	39·65	1
W. E. Alley (Commonwealth)	1949–50	28	9	1255	209*	66·05	3
M. W. Tate (M.C.C.)	1926–27	33	0	1193	133	36·15	3
K. Grieves (Commonwealth)	1950–51	32	4	1193	155	42·60	2
J. D. Robertson (M.C.C.)	1951–52	31	3	1173	183	41·89	3
K. C. Ibrahim	1947–48	11	4	1171	234*	167·28	4
K. Meuleman (Commonwealth)	1953–54	26	4	1158	131	52·63	3
A. F. Rae (West Indians)	1948–49	25	0	1150	160	46·00	6
V. S. Hazare	1950–51	20	3	1140	186	67·05	5
B. F. Butcher (West Indians)	1958–59	29	5	1133	142	47·20	2
C. C. Hunte (West Indians)	1958–59	32	3	1127	137	38·86	1
L. B. Fishlock (Commonwealth)	1950–51	32	2	1123	138	37·43	3
J. B. Stollmeyer (West Indians)	1948–49	22	5	1091	244*	64·17	2
V. S. Hazare	1943–44	7	0	1066	309	152·28	4
B. Sutcliffe (New Zealanders)	1955–56	28	4	1031	230*	42·95	3
P. R. Umrigar	1955–56	14	2	1028	223	85·66	3
J. R. Reid (New Zealanders)	1955–56	25	6	1024	150*	53·89	3
T. L. Livingston (Commonwealth)	1949–50	25	5	1020	123	51·00	3
F. A. Lowson (M.C.C.)	1951–52	28	5	1016	138	44·17	1
J. K. Holt jun. (West Indians)	1958–59	27	4	1001	123	43·52	3

Twelve or More Centuries in a Season

The first batsman to score ten centuries in the course of an English season was W. G. Grace in 1871. Since that date the progressive records have been: 12 by R. Abel in 1900, 13 by C. B. Fry in 1901, 16 by J. B. Hobbs in 1925, and 18 by D. C. S. Compton in 1947.

18	D. C. S. Compton (Middx.)	1947	13	H. Sutcliffe (Yorks.)	1928
16	J. B. Hobbs (Surrey)	1925	13	H. Sutcliffe (Yorks.)	1931
15	W. R. Hammond (Glos.)	1938	12	R. Abel (Surrey)	1900
14	H. Sutcliffe (Yorks.)	1932	12	K. S. Duleepsinhji (Sussex)	1931
13	D. G. Bradman (Australians)	1938	12	W. J. Edrich (Middx.)	1947
13	C. B. Fry (Sussex)	1901	12	W. R. Hammond (Glos.)	1927
13	W. R. Hammond (Glos.)	1933	12	J. B. Hobbs (Surrey)	1928
13	W. R. Hammond (Glos.)	1937	12	L. Hutton (Yorks.)	1939
13	T. Hayward (Surrey)	1906	12	L. Hutton (Yorks.)	1949
13	E. Hendren (Middx.)	1923	12	John Langridge (Sussex)	1949
13	E. Hendren (Middx.)	1927	12	J. D. Robertson (Middx.)	1947
13	E. Hendren (Middx.)	1928	12	F. E. Woolley (Kent)	1928
13	C. P. Mead (Hants.)	1928			

Owing to the restricted fixture lists overseas no batsman has reached a season's aggregate of ten centuries, the records being as follows:

Australia ....8—D.G. Bradman (1947–48), 7—D. G. Bradman (1928–29, 1931–32 and 1937–38), W. R. Hammond (1928–29).

South Africa..................8—D. C. S. Compton (1948–49), R. N. Harvey, A. R. Morris (1949–50).

West Indies ....6—E. Hendren (1929–30), A. Sandham (1929-30).

New Zealand ....6—E. D. Weekes (1955–56).

India ....7—A. Sandham (1926–27).

Leading Batsmen of the Season

For each season since 1894 the batsman with the highest average, qualification 20 innings, is listed.

Season		Inns.	N.O.	Runs	H.S.	Avge.	100s
1894	W. Brockwell (Surrey)	45	6	1491	128	38·23	5
1895	A. C. MacLaren (Lancs.)	24	0	1229	424	51·20	4
1896	K. S. Ranjitsinhji (Sussex)	55	7	2780	171*	57·91	10
1897	N. F. Druce (Cambridge U. & Surrey)	20	2	928	227*	51·55	3
1898	W. G. Quaife (Warwicks.)	28	8	1219	157*	60·95	3
1899	R. M. Poore (Hants.)	21	4	1551	304	91·23	7
1900	K. S. Ranjitsinhji (Sussex)	40	5	3065	275	87·57	11
1901	C. B. Fry (Sussex)	43	3	3147	244	78·67	13
1902	A. Shrewsbury (Notts.)	32	7	1250	127*	50·00	4
1903	C. B. Fry (Sussex)	40	7	2683	234	81·30	9
1904	K. S. Ranjitsinhji (Sussex)	34	6	2077	207*	74·17	8
1905	C. B. Fry (Sussex)	44	4	2801	233	70·02	10
1906	C. J. Burnup (Kent)	21	3	1207	179	67·05	4
1907	C. B. Fry (Sussex)	34	3	1449	187	46·74	4
1908	B. J. T. Bosanquet (Middx.)	22	2	1081	214	54·05	3
1909	A. P. Day (Kent)	24	1	1014	177	44·08	3
1910	J. T. Tyldesley (Lancs.)	51	2	2265	158	46·22	7
1911	C. B. Fry (Hants.)	26	2	1728	258*	72·00	7
1912	C. B. Fry (Hants.)	31	3	1592	203*	56·85	5
1913	C. P. Mead (Hants.)	60	8	2627	171*	50·51	9
1914	J. W. Hearne (Middx.)	43	8	2116	204	60·45	8
1919	G. Gunn (Notts.)	25	2	1451	185*	63·08	5
1920	E. Hendren (Middx.)	47	6	2520	232	61·46	6
1921	C. P. Mead (Hants.)	52	6	3179	280*	69·10	10
1922	E. Hendren (Middx.)	38	7	2072	277	66·83	7
1923	E. Hendren (Middx.)	51	12	3010	200*	77·17	13
1924	A. Sandham (Surrey)	37	2	2082	169	59·48	7
1925	J. B. Hobbs (Surrey)	48	5	3024	266*	70·32	16
1926	J. B. Hobbs (Surrey)	41	3	2949	316*	77·60	10
1927	C. Hallows (Lancs.)	44	13	2343	233*	75·58	7
1928	J. B. Hobbs (Surrey)	38	7	2542	200*	82·00	12
1929	J. B. Hobbs (Surrey)	39	5	2263	204	66·55	10
1930	H. Sutcliffe (Yorks.)	44	8	2312	173	64·22	6
1931	H. Sutcliffe (Yorks.)	42	11	3006	230	96·96	13
1932	H. Sutcliffe (Yorks.)	52	7	3336	313	74·13	14
1933	W. R. Hammond (Glos.)	54	5	3323	264	67·81	13
1934	W. R. Hammond (Glos.)	35	4	2366	302*	76·32	8
1935	W. R. Hammond (Glos.)	58	5	2616	252	49·35	7
1936	W. R. Hammond (Glos.)	42	5	2107	317	56·94	5
1937	W. R. Hammond (Glos.)	55	5	3252	217	65·04	13
1938	W. R. Hammond (Glos.)	42	2	3011	271	75·27	15
1939	W. R. Hammond (Glos.)	46	7	2479	302	63·56	8
1946	W. R. Hammond (Glos.)	26	5	1783	214	84·90	7
1947	D. C. S. Compton (Middx.)	50	8	3816	246	90·85	18
1948	C. Washbrook (Lancs.)	31	4	1900	200	70·37	7
1949	J. Hardstaff jun. (Notts.)	40	9	2251	162*	72·61	8
1950	R. T. Simpson (Notts.)	47	6	2576	243*	62·82	8
1951	P. B. H. May (Cambridge U. & Surrey)	43	9	2339	178*	68·79	9
1952	D. S. Sheppard (Cambridge U. & Sussex)	39	4	2262	239*	64·62	10
1953	L. Hutton (Yorks.)	44	5	2458	241	63·02	8
1954	D. C. S. Compton (Middx.)	28	2	1524	278	58·62	4
1955	P. B. H. May (Surrey)	42	5	1902	125	51·40	5
1956	T. W. Graveney (Glos.)	54	6	2397	200	49·93	9
1957	P. B. H. May (Surrey)	41	3	2347	285*	61·76	7
1958	P. B. H. May (Surrey)	41	6	2231	174	63·74	8
1959	M. J. K. Smith (Warwicks.)	67	11	3245	200*	57·94	8
1960	R. Subba Row (Northants.)	32	5	1503	147*	55·66	4

In the following seasons batsmen of the touring team finished with a better average than the leading English batsmen:

Season		Inns.	N.O.	Runs	H.S.	Avge.	100s
1909	W. Bardsley (Australians)	49	4	2072	219	46·04	6
1930	D. G. Bradman (Australians)	36	6	2960	334	98·66	10
1934	D. G. Bradman (Australians)	27	3	2020	304	84·16	7

		Inns.	N.O.	Runs	H.S.	Avge.	100s
1934	W. H. Ponsford (Australians)	27	4	1784	281*	77·56	5
1938	D. G. Bradman (Australians)	26	5	2429	278	115·66	13
1939	G. Headley (West Indians)	30	6	1745	234*	72·70	6
1948	D. G. Bradman (Australians)	31	4	2428	187	89·92	11
1948	A. L. Hassett (Australians)	27	6	1563	200*	74·42	7
1948	A. R. Morris (Australians)	29	2	1922	290	71·18	7
1950	E. D. Weekes (West Indians)	33	4	2310	304*	79·65	7
1950	F. M. Worrell (West Indians)	31	5	1775	261	68·26	6
1953	R. N. Harvey (Australians)	35	4	2040	202*	65·80	10
1955	D. J. McGlew (South Africans)	34	2	1871	161	58·46	5
1956	K. Mackay (Australians)	28	7	1103	163*	52·52	3

Outstanding Batting Averages

A complete list of all batting averages of over 70 in an English season is given, the only qualification being the playing of at least 12 innings. D. G. Bradman's record is without parallel, 98·66 in 1930, 84·16 in 1934, 115·66 in 1938 and 89·92 in 1948—his only four seasons in English cricket.

	Season	Inns.	N.O.	Runs	H.S.	Avge.	100s
D. G. Bradman (Australians)	1938	26	5	2429	278	115·66	13
W. A. Johnston (Australians)	1953	17	16	102	28*	102·00	—
D. G. Bradman (Australians)	1930	36	6	2960	334	98·66	10
H. Sutcliffe (Yorks.)	1931	42	11	3006	230	96·96	13
R. M. Poore (Hants.)	1899	21	4	1551	304	91·23	7
D. R. Jardine (Surrey)	1927	14	3	1002	147	91·09	5
D. C. S. Compton (Middx.)	1947	50	8	3816	246	90·85	18
D. G. Bradman (Australians)	1948	31	4	2428	187	89·92	11
K. S. Ranjitsinhji (Sussex)	1900	40	5	3065	275	87·57	11
D. R. Jardine (Surrey)	1928	17	4	1133	193	87·15	3
W. R. Hammond (Glos.)	1946	26	5	1783	214	84·90	7
D. G. Bradman (Australians)	1934	27	3	2020	304	84·16	7
J. B. Hobbs (Surrey)	1928	38	7	2542	200*	82·00	12
C. B. Fry (Sussex)	1903	40	7	2683	234	81·30	9
W. J. Edrich (Middx.)	1947	52	8	3539	267*	80·43	12
E. D. Weekes (West Indians)	1950	33	4	2310	304*	79·65	7
E. Tyldesley (Lancs.)	1928	48	10	3024	242	79·57	10
Nawab of Pataudi (Worcs.)	1934	15	3	945	214*	78·75	3
A. Shrewsbury (Notts.)	1887	23	2	1653	267	78·71	8
C. B. Fry (Sussex)	1901	43	3	3147	244	78·67	13
W. G. Grace (Glos.)	1871	39	4	2739	268	78·25	10
J. B. Hobbs (Surrey)	1926	41	3	2949	316*	77·60	10
W. H. Ponsford (Australians)	1934	27	4	1784	281*	77·56	5
E. Hendren (Middx.)	1923	51	12	3010	200*	77·17	13
H. Sutcliffe (Yorks.)	1928	44	5	3002	228	76·97	13
W. R. Hammond (Glos.)	1934	35	4	2366	302*	76·32	8
C. P. Mead (Hants.)	1928	50	10	3027	180	75·67	13
C. Hallows (Lancs.)	1927	44	13	2343	233*	75·58	7
W. R. Hammond (Glos.)	1938	42	2	3011	271	75·27	15
C. P. Mead (Hants.)	1927	41	9	2385	200*	74·53	8
V. M. Merchant (Indians)	1946	41	9	2385	242*	74·53	7
A. L. Hassett (Australians)	1948	27	6	1563	200*	74·42	7
K. S. Ranjitsinhji (Sussex)	1904	34	6	2077	207*	74·17	8
H. Sutcliffe (Yorks.)	1932	52	7	3336	313	74·13	14
E. Hendren (Middx.)	1927	43	5	2784	201*	73·26	13
G. Headley (West Indians)	1939	30	6	1745	234*	72·70	6
J. Hardstaff jun. (Notts.)	1949	40	9	2251	162*	72·61	8
K. R. Miller (Australians)	1945	13	3	725	185	72·50	3
W. G. Grace (Glos.)	1873	32	7	1805	192*	72·20	6
C. B. Fry (Hants.)	1911	26	2	1728	258*	72·00	7
A. R. Morris (Australians)	1948	29	2	1922	290	71·18	7
C. B. Fry (Sussex)	1904	42	2	2824	229	70·60	10
K. S. Ranjitsinhji (Sussex)	1901	40	5	2468	285*	70·51	8
E. Hendren (Middx.)	1928	54	7	3311	209*	70·44	13
C. Washbrook (Lancs.)	1948	31	4	1900	200	70·37	7
J. B. Hobbs (Surrey)	1925	48	5	3024	266*	70·32	16
C. B. Fry (Sussex)	1905	44	4	2801	233	70·02	10

1000 Runs with Average of less than 20

A few batsmen have passed the 1000-runs aggregate in an English season and failed to reach a batting average of 20.

	Season	Inns.	N.O.	Runs	H.S.	Avge.
A. H. H. Gilligan (Sussex)	1923	70	3	1186	68	17·70
J. J. Lyons (Australians)	1890	59	1	1029	99	17·74
G. H. S. Trott (Australians)	1888	61	2	1081	73	18·32
A. W. Wellard (Somerset)	1937	60	4	1049	91*	18·73
J. E. Timms (Northants.)	1932	55	1	1032	97	19·11
A. F. T. White (Worcs.)	1947	54	2	1001	79	19·25
W. E. Bates (Glamorgan)	1931	52	0	1001	74	19·25
G. Ulyett (Yorks.)	1886	52	0	1005	78	19·32
M. W. Tate (Sussex)	1922	56	2	1050	88	19·44
J. T. Murray (Middx.)	1957	57	5	1025	120	19·71
C. H. Bull (Worcs.)	1936	54	0	1066	108	19·74
J. Lawrence (Somerset)	1953	52	1	1015	89	19·90
F. J. Titmus (Middx.)	1957	56	3	1056	70	19·92

Batsmen Scoring 1000 Runs in a Month

Month	Season		Inns.	N.O.	Runs	H.S.	Avge.
May	1895	W. G. Grace (Glos)	10	1	1016	288	112·88
	1927	W. R. Hammond (Glos.)	14	0	1042	192	74·42
	1928	C. Hallows (Lancs.)	11	3	1000	232	125·00
June	1899	K. S. Ranjitsinhji (Sussex)	15	2	1037	197	79·76
	1901	C. B. Fry (Sussex)	11	2	1130	244	125·55
	1904	J. Iremonger (Notts.)	11	1	1010	272	101·00
	1921	C. P. Mead (Hants.)	13	1	1159	280*	96·58
	1925	E. Hendren (Middx.)	12	2	1122	240	112·20
	1925	J. B. Hobbs (Surrey)	14	1	1112	215	85·53
	1925	P. Holmes (Yorks.)	12	2	1021	315*	102·10
	1932	H. Sutcliffe (Yorks.)	14	3	1193	313	108·45
	1949	L. Hutton (Yorks.)	16	2	1294	201	92·42
July	1900	K. S. Ranjitsinhji (Sussex)	12	1	1059	275	96·27
	1912	D. Denton (Yorks.)	14	2	1023	221	85·25
	1923	C. P. Mead (Hants.)	13	6	1070	222	152·85
	1926	E. Tyldesley (Lancs.)	9	1	1024	226	128·00
	1938	A. E. Fagg (Kent)	15	1	1016	244	72·57
	1946	C. Washbrook (Lancs.)	14	3	1079	162	98·09
	1947	W. J. Edrich (Middx.)	11	3	1047	267*	130·87
	1959	M. J. K. Smith (Warwicks.)	15	2	1209	200*	93·00
August	1871	W. G. Grace (Glos.)	11	0	1024	268	93·09
	1876	W. G. Grace (Glos.)	11	1	1278	344	127·80
	1899	K. S. Ranjitsinhji (Sussex)	14	1	1011	161	77·76
	1901	C. B. Fry (Sussex)	12	1	1116	209	101·45
	1932	H. Sutcliffe (Yorks.)	13	1	1006	194	83·83
	1932	M. Leyland (Yorks.)	13	1	1013	166	84·41
	1933	E. Hendren (Middx.)	18	2	1110	222*	69·37
	1933	W. R. Hammond (Glos.)	13	3	1060	264	106·00
	1933	W. W. Keeton (Notts.)	15	2	1102	136*	84·76
	1936	W. R. Hammond (Glos.)	16	3	1281	317	98·53
	1936	E. Hendren (Middx.)	14	0	1026	156	73·28
	1937	J. Hardstaff jun. (Notts.)	11	1	1150	266	115·00
	1947	D. C. S. Compton (Middx.)	12	3	1039	178	115·44
	1949	L. Hutton (Yorks.)	15	1	1050	269*	75·00
December	1927	W. H. Ponsford (Victoria)	5	0	1146	437	229·20

The following batsmen performed the feat twice in the same season: K. S. Ranjitsinhji in 1899 (June and August), C. B. Fry in 1901 (June and August), H. Sutcliffe in 1932 (June and August), and L. Hutton in 1949 (June and August).

* H

1000 Runs During May

Only three batsmen have succeeded in scoring 1000 during the month of May, although three others have scored 1000 runs by the end of May, helped by some runs scored in April. The first batsman to perform the feat was W. G. Grace in his marvellous season of 1895. It was during this month that Grace also scored his 100th century, so that it was indeed a 'golden' month for him. His record remained unequalled until 1927.

W. G. Grace (Gloucestershire) in 1895. (May 9th to May 30th, 22 days)—13, 103, 18, 25, 288, 52, 257, 73*, 18, 169—1016 runs.

W. R. Hammond (Gloucestershire) in 1927. (May 7th to May 31st, 25 days)—27, 135, 108, 128, 17, 11, 99, 187, 4, 30, 83, 7, 192, 14—1042 runs. Hammond scored his 1000th run on May 28th, equalling Grace's record of 22 days.

C. Hallows (Lancashire) in 1928. (May 5th to May 31st, 27 days)—100, 101, 51*, 123, 101*, 22, 74, 104, 58, 34*, 232—1000 runs.

The following batsmen have scored 1000 runs by the end of May, but they were assisted by some runs scored in April.

T. Hayward (Surrey) in 1900. (April 16th to May 31st)—120*, 55, 108, 131*, 55, 193, 120, 5, 6, 3, 40, 146, 92—1074 runs.

D. G. Bradman (Australians) in 1930. (April 30th to May 31st)—236, 185*, 78, 9, 48*, 66, 4, 44, 252*, 32, 47*—1001 runs.

D. G. Bradman (Australians) in 1938. (April 30th to May 31st)—258, 58, 137, 278, 2, 143, 145*, 5, 30*—1056 runs. Bradman actually scored his 1000th run on May 27th.

W. J. Edrich (Middlesex) in 1938. (April 30th to May 31st)—104, 37, 115, 63, 20*, 182, 71, 31, 53*, 45, 15, 245, 0, 9, 20*—1010 runs. Edrich scored all his runs at Lord's.

Earliest Dates for Reaching Run Aggregates

1000 runs	27 May 1938	D. G. Bradman (Australians).
	28 May 1927	W. R. Hammond (Gloucestershire).
	30 May 1895	W. G. Grace (Gloucestershire).
	31 May 1900	T. Hayward (Surrey)
	31 May 1928	C. Hallows (Lancashire).
	31 May 1930	D. G. Bradman (Australians).
	31 May 1938	W. J. Edrich (Middlesex)
2000 runs	5 July 1906	T. Hayward (Surrey)
	6 July 1927	W. R. Hammond (Gloucestershire)
	11 July 1930	D. G. Bradman (Australians)
	11 July 1949	John Langridge (Sussex)
	12 July 1921	C. P. Mead (Hampshire)
	14 July 1937	W. R. Hammond (Gloucestershire).
3000 runs	20 August 1906	T. Hayward (Surrey).
	20 August 1937	W. R. Hammond (Gloucestershire)
	21 August 1959	M. J. K. Smith (Warwickshire).
	26 August 1921	C. P. Mead (Hampshire).
	27 August 1947	D. C. S. Compton (Middlesex).
	28 August 1947	W. J. Edrich (Middlesex)

Most Runs Added During a Batsman's Innings

The following batsmen have assisted in adding over 700 runs during the course of an innings in first-class cricket. R. Abel, when setting the record, carried his bat through the innings.

811	R. Abel (357*): Surrey v. Somerset (Oval)	1899
801	W. H. Ponsford (429): Victoria v. Tasmania (Melbourne)	1922–23
792	A. C. MacLaren (424): Lancashire v. Somerset (Taunton)	1895
792	W. H. Ponsford (437): Victoria v. Queensland (Melbourne)	1927–28
770	L. Hutton (364): England v. Australia (Oval)	1938
745	B. B. Nimbalkar (443*): Maharashtra v. Western India States (Poona)	1948–49
739	D. G. Bradman (452*): New South Wales v. Queensland (Sydney)	1929–30
720	A. Sandham (325): England v. West Indies (Kingston)	1929–30

Successful First Season's Batting

A few batsmen have marked their first season in first-class cricket by passing the 1000 run aggregate. The age given is that at the start of the season. Several other batsmen have enjoyed a really outstanding second season after an odd appearance in their debut year, and a note of the outstanding cases is given.

	Age	Season	Inns.	N.O.	Runs	H.S.	Avge.	100s
A. E. Relf (Sussex)	25	1900	48	3	1059	96	23·53	—
J. G. Greig† (Hants.)	29	1901	35	4	1277	249*	41·19	5
A. P. Day (Kent)	20	1905	39	4	1149	107*	32·82	2
J. B. Hobbs (Surrey)	22	1905	54	3	1317	155	25·82	2
R. A. Young (Sussex)	19	1905	33	0	1170	220	35·45	3
H. L. Wilson (Sussex)	31	1913	47	1	1352	109	29·39	1
H. Sutcliffe (Yorks.)	24	1919	45	4	1839	174	44·85	5
H. L. V. Day (Hants.)	23	1922	27	0	1062	107	39·33	1
D. N. Moore (Glos.)	19	1930	34	2	1317	206	41·15	3
F. C. de Saram (Oxford U.)	21	1934	23	1	1119	208	50·86	3
N. Oldfield (Lancs.)	24	1935	40	7	1066	111*	32·30	2
D. C. S. Compton (Middx.)	17	1936	32	3	1004	100*	34·62	1
J. F. Crapp (Glos.)	23	1936	48	8	1052	168	26·30	1
T. C. Dodds† (Essex)	26	1946	42	1	1050	111	25·60	2
K. Cranston (Lancs.)	29	1947	41	4	1228	155*	33·18	1
D. J. Insole (Essex)	21	1947	41	5	1237	161*	34·36	2
G. H. G. Doggart (Sussex)	23	1948	37	3	1169	215*	34·38	3
W. G. A. Parkhouse (Glamorgan)	22	1948	49	1	1204	117	25·08	2
D. B. Close (Yorks.)	18	1949	50	10	1098	88*	27·45	—
F. A. Lowson (Yorks.)	23	1949	55	5	1799	104	35·98	1
D. M. Green (Lancs.)	19	1959	45	3	1049	125	24·97	1
D. Kirby (Leics.)	20	1959	53	2	1102	109	21·60	1
P. J. Watts (Northants.)	18	1959	41	2	1118	113	28·66	2
B. S. Crump (Northants.)	22	1960	36	7	1000	90	34·48	—
S. E. J. Russell (Middx.)	22	1960	39	3	1119	129	31·08	1

† *Greig had played several matches in India after 1893–94 and Dodds had played one match in India in 1943–44.*

C. P. Mead (Hampshire) scored 1014 runs (av. 26·68) in 1906, after playing only one match in 1905.

Hon. L. H. Tennyson (Hampshire) scored 832 runs (av. 46·22) in 1913, scoring a century—110 for M.C.C. v. Oxford U. (Lord's)—in his debut match.

T. F. Shepherd (Surrey) scored 1907 runs (av. 52·97) in 1921, his first full season, after playing 18 innings in 1919 and 1920.

W. J. Edrich (Middlesex) scored 2154 runs (av. 44·87) in 1937, his first full season, after playing 15 innings in 1934, 1935 and 1936.

J. R. Thompson (Cambridge U.) scored 858 runs (av. 50·47) in 1938, his debut season in first-class cricket.

J. M. Lomas (Oxford U.) scored 908 runs (av. 45·40) in 1938, his debut season in first-class cricket.

D. G. W. Fletcher (Surrey) scored 1857 runs (av. 43·18) in 1947, after playing only one match in 1946.

Carrying Bat through a Completed Innings

The feat of an opening batsman staying at the wickets throughout a completed innings and seeing all ten of his partners dismissed in turn is now more unusual than in earlier years. Many batsmen have achieved the feat at least once and a large number have several instances to their credit.

On four occasions a batsman has carried his bat through both completed innings of a match:

H. Jupp	43*	(95)	109*	(193)	Surrey v. Yorks. (Oval)	1874
S. P. Kinneir	70*	(239)	69*	(166)	Warwicks. v. Leics. (Leicester)	1907
C. J. B. Wood	107*	(309)	117*	(296)	Leics. v. Yorks. (Bradford)	1911
V. M. Merchant	135*	(271)	77*	(161)	Indians v. Lancs. (Liverpool)	1936

The following batsmen just missed the distinction, carrying their bats through one innings and being last man out in the other:

H. Jupp	 53	(102)	51*	(113)	Surrey v. Notts. (Oval) 1873
R. G. Barlow	.... 44*	(93)	49	(188)	Lancs. v. Notts. (Liverpool) 1882
F. S. Lee	.................109*	(196)	107	(205)	Somerset v. Worcs. (Worcester) 1938

The following is a complete list of batsmen carrying their bat through a completed innings († denotes completed innings in which ten wickets did not fall):

Abel, R.	......................(8)	88*	(198)	Surrey v. Gloucestershire (Cheltenham) 1885
		151*	(425)	Surrey v. Middlesex (Lord's) 1890
		132*	(307)	England v. Australia (Sydney) 1891–92
		136*	(300)	Surrey v. Middlesex (Oval) 1894
		168*	(363)	Players v. Gentlemen (Oval) 1894
		357*	(811)	Surrey v. Somerset (Oval) 1899
		153*	(302)	Players v. Gentlemen (Oval) 1900
		151*	(265)	Surrey v. Sussex (Oval) 1902
Adams, W. W.	............(1)	14*	(40)	Northamptonshire v. Yorkshire (Northampton) ...1920
Alderman, A. E.	.........(1)	124*	(291)	Derbyshire v. Hampshire (Portsmouth) 1934
Anson, T. A.	................(1)	22*	(54)	M.C.C. v. North (Burton-on-Trent) 1840
Anstruther, W.	............(1)	23*	(93)	Sussex v. Surrey (Oval) 1878
Armstrong, W. W.	......(1)	159*	(309)	Australia v. South Africa (Johannesburg) 1902–03
Ashdown, W. H.	.........(4)	150*	(303)	Kent v. Surrey (Oval)...................................1926
		100*	(236)	Kent v. Sussex (Tunbridge Wells) 1928
		83*	(223)	Kent v. Gloucestershire (Maidstone) 1930
		305*	(560)	Kent v. Derbyshire (Dover) 1935
Ashton, H.	...................(1)	236*	(484)	Cambridge U. v. Free Foresters (Cambridge) 1920
Atkinson, G.	...............(1)	30*	(73)	Yorkshire v. Nottinghamshire (Bradford) 1865
Avery, A. V.	...............(3)	84*	(180)	Essex v. Derbyshire (Southend) 1939
		83*	(165)	Essex v. Gloucestershire (Brentwood) 1946
		92*	(154)	Essex v. Nottinghamshire (Nottingham) 1954
Bagshaw, H.	...............(1)	114*	(218)	Derbyshire v. Surrey (Oval) 1897
Bailey, J.	....................(1)	70*	(139)	Hampshire v. West Indians (Bournemouth) 1939
Bainbridge, H. W.	......(1)	65*	(113)	Warwickshire v. Kent (Birmingham) 1894
Baker, A.	...................(1)	55*	(110)	Surrey v. Gloucestershire (Bristol) 1905
Bakewell, A. H.	.........(3)	83*	(166)	Northamptonshire v. New Zealanders (Peterboro') 1931
		90*	(169)	Northamptonshire v. Essex (Leyton) 1931
		120*	(211)	Northamptonshire v. Leicestershire (Leicester) ...1936
Bannerman, A. C.	......(7)	71*	(171)	Australians v. Orleans Club (Twickenham) 1878
		45*	(83)	Australians XI v. Shrewsbury's XI (Sydney) ...1887–98
		93*	(319)	Australians v. Cambridge U. P. &. P. (Leyton)......1888
		39*	(168)	Australians v. England XI (Harrogate) 1888
		45*	(151)	New South Wales v. Victoria (Melbourne) 1890–91
		7*	(60)	Australians v. Kent (Canterbury)......................1893
		79*	(258)	Australians v. Philadelphians (Philadelphia) ...1893–94
Bardsley, W.	..............(5)	143*	(271)	Australians v. Cochrane's XI (Bray) 1909
		191*	(361)	New South Wales v. South Australia (Sydney) 1910–11
		50*	(213)	New South Wales v. Victoria (Sydney) 1914–15
		200*	(352)	New South Wales v. Auckland (Auckland) 1923–24
		193*	(383)	Australia v. England (Lord's) 1926
Barlow, R. G.	............(11)	26*	(116)	Lancashire v. Kent (Maidstone) 1874
		34*	(187)	Lancashire v. Nottinghamshire (Nottingham) 1876
		34*	(99)	Lancashire v. M.C.C. (Lord's) 1878
		10*	(47)	Lancashire v. Yorkshire (Manchester) 1880
		66*	(269)	Lancashire v. Australians (Manchester) 1882
		5*	(69)	Lancashire v. Nottinghamshire (Nottingham) 1882
		44*	(93)	Lancashire v. Nottinghamshire (Liverpool) 1882
		58*	(240)	Lancashire v. Gloucestershire (Clifton) 1882
		62*	(183)	Lancashire v. Gloucestershire (Clifton) 1885
		51*	(215)	Lancashire v. Kent (Maidstone) 1889
		29*	(131)	Lancashire v. Surrey (Oval) 1890
Barnes, W.	...................(1)	118*	(236)	M.C.C. v. Oxford U. (Lord's) 1880
Barnett, C. J.	...............(1)	228*	(363)	Gloucestershire v. Leicestershire (Gloucester) 1947
Barnett, C. S.	...............(1)	62*	(235)	Gloucestershire v. Worcestershire (Cheltenham) 1913
Barnett, E. P.	............(1)	52*	(141)	Gloucestershire v. Yorkshire (Bradford) 1905
Barrett, J. E.	...............(2)	67*	(176)	Australia v. England (Lord's) 1890
		61*	(134)	Australians v. C. I. Thornton's XI (Barnes) 1890
Barton, W. E.	..............(1)	76*	(150)	Auckland v. Otago (Dunedin) 1882–83
Bates, L. A.	................(2)	96*	(207)	Warwickshire v. Surrey (Oval) 1921
		50*	(125)	Warwickshire v. Yorkshire (Huddersfield) 1922
Bates, W. E.	...............(2)	200*	(390)	Glamorgan v. Worcestershire (Kidderminster) 1927
		73*	(160)	Glamorgan v. Northamptonshire (Swansea) 1928

Bean, G.	(1)	145*	(264)	Sussex v. Nottinghamshire (Hove) 1891
Beldam, G. W.	(1)	12*	(51)	Middlesex v. Sussex (Lord's) 1902
Bell, J. T.	(2)	72*	(164)	Glamorgan v. Essex (Cardiff) 1926
		209*	(395)	Wales v. M.C.C. (Lord's) 1927
Berry, A.	(1)	23*	(147)†	Cambridgeshire v. Nottinghamshire (Nottingham) 1862
Berry, L. G.	(4)	75*	(177)	Leicestershire v. Nottinghamshire (Leicester).........1932
		58*	(126)	Leicestershire v. Derbyshire (Chesterfield) 1939
		45*	(121)	Leicestershire v. South Africans (Leicester) 1947
		109*	(236)	Leicestershire v. Somerset (Leicester) 1949
Blacklock, R. V.	(1)	84*	(202)	Wellington v. Canterbury (Christchurch) 1883–84
Blunt, R. C.	(2)	137*	(336)	Canterbury v. Wellington (Wellington) 1919–20
		131*	(204)	Otago v. Canterbury (Dunedin) 1926–27
Bokul, M. H.	(1)	90*	(159)	East Pakistan v. Combined Us. (Karachi) 1959–60
Bowley, E. H.	(4)	110*	(245)	Sussex v. Glamorgan (Swansea) 1922
		93*	(188)	Sussex v. Hampshire (Hove) 1923
		71*	(119)	Sussex v. Worcestershire (Hove) 1926
		94*	(206)	Sussex v. Nottinghamshire (Hastings) 1926
Bowley, F. L.	(1)	104*	(267)	Worcestershire v. Middlesex (Lord's) 1911
Braund, L. C.	(4)	28*	(97)	Somerset v. Middlesex (Lord's) 1907
		42*	(113)	Somerset v. Yorkshire (Taunton) 1907
		67*	(226)	Somerset v. Middlesex (Taunton) 1907
		58*	(148)	Somerset v. Worcestershire (Taunton) 1914
Brockwell, W.	(1)	76*	(158)	Surrey v. Leicestershire (Leicester) 1898
Brookes D.	(5)	80*	(170)	Northamptonshire v. Leicestershire (Northampton) 1946
		166*	(347)	Northamptonshire v. Kent (Northampton) 1950
		102*	(185)	Northamptonshire v. Kent (Northampton) 1952
		139*	(300)	Rest v. South (Hastings) 1953
		113*	(252)	Northamptonshire v. Glamorgan (Ebbw Vale) ...1958
Brown, G.	(2)	103*	(188)	Hampshire v. Middlesex (Bournemouth) 1926
		150*	(294)	Hampshire v. Surrey (Oval) 1933
Brown, S. M.	(1)	96*	(153)	Middlesex v. Cambridge U. (Cambridge) 1948
Brown, W. A.	(2)	206*	(422)	Australia v. England (Lord's) 1938
		174*	(311)	Queensland v. South Australia (Adelaide) 1938–39
Bruce, Hon. C. N.	(1)	64*	(120)	Oxford U. v. Worcestershire (Oxford) 1907
Bryan, J. L.	(2)	82*	(157)	Kent v. Yorkshire (Tunbridge Wells) 1921
		93*	(186)	Kent v. Middlesex (Lord's) 1929
Bull, C. H.	(1)	57*	(156)	Worcestershire v. Lancashire (Kidderminster) 1935
Burke, J. W.	(2)	162*	(360)	New South Wales v. Victoria (Melbourne) 1949–50
		132*	(281)	New South Wales v. Victoria (Melbourne) 1956–57
Burnup, C. J.	(1)	103*	(209)	Kent v. Surrey (Oval)................................1899
Bush, J. E.	(1)	52*	(146)	Oxford U. v. Surrey (Guildford) 1952
Cadman, S.	(3)	36*	(71)	Derbyshire v. Hampshire (Derby) 1912
		73*	(155)	Derbyshire v. Leicestershire (Leicester) 1914
		19*	(53)	Derbyshire v. Leicestershire (Leicester) 1920
Carris, H. E.	(1)	35*	(92)	Middlesex v. Yorkshire (Bradford) 1929
Chalk, F. G. H.	(1)	115*	(215)	Kent v. Yorkshire (Dover) 1939
Challenor, G.	(1)	155*	(305)	West Indians v. Surrey (Oval) 1923
Chatterton, W.	(1)	109*	(238)	M.C.C. v. Lancashire (Lord's) 1892
Clark, T. H.	(1)	81*	(135)	Surrey v. Yorkshire (Oval) 1956
Claxton, N.	(1)	199*	(378)	South Australia v. Victoria (Melbourne) 1905–06
Cobcroft, L. T.	(1)	85*	(239)	New South Wales v. Wellington (Wellington) 1895–96
Collins, D. C.	(1)	53*	(131)	Wellington v. Canterbury (Christchurch) 1906–07
Collins, G. G.	(1)	18*	(67)	Kent v. Northamptonshire (Gravesend) 1924
Cook, G. G.	(1)	36*	(74)	Queensland v. Victoria (Melbourne) 1932–33
Cook, G. W.	(1)	61*	(134)	Cambridge U. v. Yorkshire (Cambridge) 1957
Cooper, E.	(2)	104*	(273)	Worcestershire v. Lancashire (Manchester) 1939
		69*	(154)	Worcestershire v. Warwickshire (Dudley) 1951
Cowdrey, M. C.	(1)	65*	(169)	Kent v. Gloucestershire (Cheltenham) 1956
Croom, A. J.	(4)	131*	(311)	Warwickshire v. Northamptonshire (Birmingham) 1929
		58*	(120)	Warwickshire v. Gloucestershire (Cheltenham) ...1930
		102*	(204)	Warwickshire v. Lancashire (Manchester) 1931
		69*	(133)	Warwickshire v. Leicestershire (Hinckley) 1936
Cutmore, J. A.	(1)	31*	(64)	Essex v. Yorkshire (Dewsbury) 1933
Dadu Sattar	(1)	48*	(88)	East Pakistan B. v. Dacca U. (Dacca) 1957–58
Daft, H. B.	(1)	77*	(240)	Nottinghamshire v. Surrey (Oval) 1896
Daft, R.	(1)	12*	(48)	Nottinghamshire v. Lancashire (Nottingham) 1877
Daniell, J.	(3)	24*	(82)	Somerset v. Kent (Gravesend) 1903
		129*	(312)	Somerset v. Hampshire (Southampton) 1911
		174*	(318)	Somerset v. Essex (Taunton)..........................1925
Darnton, T.	(1)	81*	(144)	Yorkshire v. All England XI (Sheffield) 1865
Davey, D. C.	(1)	62*	(106)	Natal v. Griqualand West (Kimberley) 1888–89
Davies, D.	(1)	100*	(161)	Glamorgan v. Worcestershire (Worcester) 1923

Davies, D. D.	(1)	40*	(95)	Border v. Transvaal (Port Elizabeth)...............1902–03
Davies, E.	(3)	75*	(142)	Glamorgan v. South Africans (Cardiff) 1935
		155*	(340)	Glamorgan v. Somerset (Weston-super-mare) 1935
		107*	(180)	Over 32 v. Under 32 (Hastings) 1950
Dawson, E. W.	(1)	126*	(256)	Leicestershire v. Essex (Leyton) 1928
Dean, J.	(1)	46*	(102)	Sussex v. M.C.C. (Brighton) 1850
Dempster, C. S.	(2)	167*	(345)	New Zealanders v. Glamorgan (Cardiff)...............1927
		28*	(62)	Leicestershire v. Yorkshire (Bradford) 1938
Denton, W. H.	(2)	230*	(476)	Northamptonshire v. Essex (Leyton) 1913
		108*	(305)	Northamptonshire v. Gloucestershire (Northampton)1914
Dewes, J. G.	(1)	101*	(203)	Middlesex v. Surrey (Oval) 1955
Dillon, E. W.	(1)	38*	(86)	Kent v. Nottinghamshire (Gravesend) 1902
Dipper, A. E.	(11)	168*	(343)	Gloucestershire v. Somerset (Taunton) 1914
		37*	(104)	Gloucestershire v. Lancashire (Manchester) 1919
		99*	(185)	Gloucestershire v. Worcestershire (Cheltenham) ...1919
		120*	(175)	Gloucestershire v. Warwickshire (Birmingham)......1920
		22*	(72)	Gloucestershire v. Leicestershire (Ashby) 1922
		37*	(138)	Gloucestershire v. Kent (Cheltenham) 1922
		87*	(192)	Gloucestershire v. Warwickshire (Bristol) 1923
		126*	(211)	Gloucestershire v. West Indians (Bristol) 1923
		85*	(210)	Gloucestershire v. Northamptonshire (Northampton) 1926
		66*	(119)	Gloucestershire v. Kent (Bristol) 1929
		64*	(192)	Gloucestershire v. Glamorgan (Swansea) 1930
Donnan, H.	(1)	160*	(374)	New South Wales v. South Australia (Adelaide)1898–99
Dunn, A.	(1)	42*	(136)	Griqualand West v. Western Province (Kimberley)1946–47
Dyer, D. V.	(1)	49*	(96)	Natal v. Transvaal (Durban) 1945–46
Dyson, A. H.	(5)	75*	(156)	Glamorgan v. Northamptonshire (Kettering) 1931
		109*	(204)	Glamorgan v. Middlesex (Cardiff) 1932
		191*	(352)	Glamorgan v. Lancashire (Cardiff) 1934
		110*	(210)	Glamorgan v. J. Cahn's XI (Newport) 1938
		99*	(196)	Glamorgan v. Gloucestershire (Newport) 1939
Edrich, W. J.	(1)	140*	(303)	Lord Tennyson's XI v. Sind (Karachi) 1937–38
Elliott, C. S.	(1)	51*	(126)	Derbyshire v. Leicestershire (Ashby) 1948
Ellis, R. T.	(1)	50*	(107)	Sussex v. Australians (Hove) 1880
Emmett, G. M.	(1)	104*	(156)	Gloucestershire v. Oxford U. (Oxford) 1948
Fagg, A. E.	(3)	37*	(127)	Kent v. Gloucestershire (Gillingham) 1938
		117*	(230)	Kent v. Essex (Maidstone) 1948
		71*	(134)	Kent v. Surrey (Oval)......................................1950
Ferris, J. J.	(2)	62*	(170)	Gentlemen v. Players (Scarborough) 1892
		34*	(77)	Gloucestershire v. Sussex (Bristol) 1894
Fiddian-Green, C. A.	(1)	60*	(123)	†Warwickshire v. Hampshire (Southampton) 1922
Fingleton, J. H.	(1)	119*	(361)	New South Wales v. M.C.C. (Sydney) 1932–33
Fishlock, L. B.	(1)	81*	(141)	Surrey v. Australians (Oval) 1948
Fishwick, T. S.	(1)	85*	(181)	Warwickshire v. Lancashire (Manchester) 1907
Fletcher, D. G. W.	(1)	127*	(271)	Surrey v. Yorkshire (Bradford) 1947
Freakes, H. D.	(1)	122*	(190)	Eastern Province v. Natal (Johannesburg) 1931–32
Freeman, J. R.	(2)	67*	(206)	Essex v. Lancashire (Colchester) 1922
		113*	(283)	Essex v. Oxford U. (Chelmsford) 1926
Fry, C. B.	(3)	104*	(197)	Sussex v. Middlesex (Lord's) 1898
		179*	(311)	Sussex v. Yorkshire (Hove) 1898
		170*	(254)	Sussex v. Nottinghamshire (Nottingham) 1901
Gardner, F. C.	(4)	140*	(283)	Warwickshire v. Worcestershire (Birmingham) 1949
		73*	(133)	Warwickshire v. Glamorgan (Swansea) 1950
		184*	(286)	Warwickshire v. Lancashire (Liverpool) 1952
		62*	(149)	Warwickshire v. Glamorgan (Birmingham) 1954
Gehrs, D. R. A.	(1)	148*	(235)	South Australia v. Western Australia (Fremantle)1905–06
Gibb, P. A.	(1)	80*	(163)	Cambridge U. v. Australians (Cambridge) 1938
Gibbes, W. R. L.	(1)	75*	(193)	Wellington v. Canterbury (Christchurch) 1911–12
Gibbons, H. H.	(2)	70*	(165)	Worcestershire v. Warwickshire (Kidderminster) ...1934
		83*	(148)	Worcestershire v. Lancashire (Kidderminster) 1935
Gilbert, W. R.	(2)	205*	(383)	England XI v. Cambridge U. (Cambridge) 1876
		40*	(110)	Gloucestershire v. Lancashire (Clifton) 1885
Goddard, T. L.	(1)	56*	(99)	South Africa v. Australia (Cape Town) 1957–58
Godsell, R. T.	(1)	98*	(269)	Gloucestershire v. Nottinghamshire (Bristol) 1905
Grace, E. M.	(1)	192*	(344)	M.C.C. v. Gentlemen of Kent (Canterbury) 1862
Grace, W. G.	(17)	138*	(215)	M.C.C. v. Surrey (Oval) 1869
		117*	(183)	M.C.C. v. Nottinghamshire (Lord's) 1870
		189*	(310)	Single v. Married (Lord's) 1871
		81*	(141)	W. G. Grace's XI v. Kent (Maidstone) 1871
		170*	(290)	England v. Nottinghamshire & Yorkshire (Lord's) 1872
		192*	(311)	South v. North (Oval) 1873

Grace, W. G. (*cont.*)	318* (528)	Gloucestershire v. Yorkshire (Cheltenham)	1876
	221* (348)	Gloucestershire v. Middlesex (Clifton)	1885
	81* (128)	M.C.C. v. Sussex (Lord's)	1887
	113* (186)	Gloucestershire v. Nottinghamshire (Clifton)	1887
	37* (87)	Gloucestershire v. Lancashire (Bristol)	1889
	127* (282)	Gloucestershire v. Middlesex (Cheltenham)	1889
	190* (231)	Gloucestershire v. Kent (Maidstone)	1890
	159* (284)	Sheffield's XI v. Victoria (Melbourne)	1891–92
	61* (105)	Gloucestershire v. Surrey (Oval)	1893
	243* (463)	Gloucestershire v. Sussex (Hove)	1896
	102* (238)	Gloucestershire v. Lancashire (Bristol)	1896
Gray, J. R. ....(1)	118* (208)	Hampshire v. Essex (Portsmouth)	1956
Greig, J. G. ....(2)	79* (170)	Europeans v. Parsis (Bombay)	1894–95
	249* (487)	Hampshire v. Lancashire (Liverpool)	1901
Griffiths, E. L. ....(1)	24* (123)	Gloucestershire v. Nottinghamshire (Nottingham)	1885
Grimshaw, I. ....(1)	36* (182)	Yorkshire v. Kent (Maidstone)	1881
Gunn, G. ....(8)	91* (188)	Nottinghamshire v. Yorkshire (Nottingham)	1909
	52* (146)	Nottinghamshire v. Essex (Leyton)	1911
	62* (176)	Nottinghamshire v. Yorkshire (Dewsbury)	1913
	64* (144)	Nottinghamshire v. Middlesex (Lord's)	1913
	117* (283)	Nottinghamshire v. Middlesex (Lord's)	1921
	67* (155)	Nottinghamshire v. Gloucestershire (Cheltenham)	1926
	109* (267)	Nottinghamshire v. Sussex (Eastbourne)	1929
	85* (186)	Nottinghamshire v. Kent (Nottingham)	1931
Gwynne, L. H. ....(1)	153* (274)	Dublin U. v. Leicestershire (Leicester)	1895
Hall, L. ....(15)	31* (94)	Yorkshire v. Sussex (Hove)	1878
	124* (331)	Yorkshire v. Sussex (Hove)	1883
	128* (285)	Yorkshire v. Sussex (Sheffield)	1884
	32* (81)	Yorkshire v. Kent (Sheffield)	1885
	79* (285)	Yorkshire v. Surrey (Sheffield)	1885
	37* (96)	Yorkshire v. Derbyshire (Derby)	1885
	50* (173)	Yorkshire v. Sussex (Huddersfield)	1886
	74* (172)	Yorkshire v. Kent (Canterbury)	1886
	119* (334)	Yorkshire v. Gloucestershire (Dewsbury)	1887
	82* (218)	Yorkshire v. Sussex (Hove)	1887
	105* (261)	North v. South (Scarborough)	1887
	34* (104)	Yorkshire v. Surrey (Oval)	1888
	129* (461)	Yorkshire v. Gloucestershire (Clifton)	1888
	85* (259)	Yorkshire v. Middlesex (Lord's)	1889
	41* (106)	Yorkshire v. Nottinghamshire (Sheffield)	1891
Hallows, C. ....(6)	109* (230)	Lancashire v. Sussex (Manchester)	1921
	110* (183)	Lancashire v. Leicestershire (Manchester)	1921
	179* (393)	Lancashire v. Essex (Southend)	1923
	158* (297)	Lancashire v. Leicestershire (Leicester)	1925
	65* (103)	Lancashire v. Derbyshire (Nelson)	1925
	152* (305)	Lancashire v. Yorkshire (Manchester)	1929
Hamer, A. ....(4)	35* (90)	Derbyshire v. Gloucestershire (Bristol)	1950
	147* (272)	Derbyshire v. Yorkshire (Leeds)	1954
	112* (208)	Derbyshire v. Surrey (Oval)	1957
	57* (105)	Derbyshire v. Gloucestershire (Bristol)	1958
Hamilton, L. A.............(1)	117* (205)	Kent v. Australians (Canterbury)......................1890
Hanif Mohammed........(2)	147* (252)	Bahawalpur v. Sind (Bahawalpur)	1953–54
	142* (241)	Pakistan v. Essex (Southend)	1954
Hardinge, H. T. W. ...(11)	113* (220)	Rest v. England (Lord's)	1911
	123* (203)	Kent v. Essex (Tonbridge)..............................1911
	79* (169)	Kent v. Yorkshire (Leeds)	1919
	172* (339)	Kent v. Essex (Canterbury)	1919
	62* (163)	Kent v. Hampshire (Canterbury)	1920
	118* (196)	Kent v. M.C.C. (Lord's)	1921
	249* (440)	Kent v. Leicestershire (Leicester)	1932
	71* (161)	Kent v. Gloucestershire (Tunbridge Wells)	1923
	54* (96)	Kent v. Oxford U. (Oxford)	1924
	30* (55)	Kent v. Somerset (Tonbridge)	1926
	49* (122)	Kent v. Essex (Southend)	1930
Harris, C. B. ....(2)	117* (246)	Nottinghamshire v. Yorkshire (Leeds)	1934
	239* (401)	Nottinghamshire v. Hampshire (Nottingham)	1950
Harris, Lord ....(1)	80* (148)	Kent v. Yorkshire (Gravesend)	1883
Harris, L. M. ....(1)	41* (65)	Otago v. Tasmania (Dunedin)	1883–84
Hawke, Lord ....(1)	107* (229)	M.C.C. v. Oxford U. (Lord's)	1902
Hayman, H. B. ....(1)	104* (213)	Middlesex v. Kent (Catford)	1898
Hayward, T. ....(8)	156* (287)	Surrey v. Philadelphians (Oval)	1903
	188* (321)	Surrey v. Kent (Canterbury)	1904

Hayward, T. (*cont.*)	129*	(286)	Surrey v. Australians (Oval)	1905
	144*	(225)	Surrey v. Nottinghamshire (Nottingham)	1906
	114*	(190)	Surrey v. Lancashire (Oval)	1907
	146*	(278)	Players v. Gentlemen (Lord's)	1907
	90*	(156)	Surrey v. Somerset (Taunton)	1909
	96*	(178)	Surrey v. Australians (Oval)	1909
Haywood, R. ....(1)	131*	(251)	Northamptonshire v. Sussex (Hove)	1921
Hearn, P. ....(1)	12*	(32)	Kent v. Hampshire (Southampton)	1952
Hearne, A. ....(6)	43*	(189)	Kent v. Somerset (Catford)	1892
	116*	(256)	Kent v. Gloucestershire (Canterbury)	1892
	22*	(76)	Kent v. Gloucestershire (Gravesend)	1895
	55*	(114)	Kent v. Sussex (Tonbridge)	1899
	79*	(172)	Kent v. Worcestershire (Canterbury)	1903
	90*	(294)	Kent v. Gloucestershire (Tonbridge)	1904
Hearne, J. W.............(1)	152*	(390)	Middlesex v. Leicestershire (Leicester)	1931
Hearne, W. ....(1)	58*	(126)	M.C.C. v. Oxford U. (Oxford)	1879
Henty, E. ....(1)	32*	(81)	Kent v. Yorkshire (Dewsbury)	1870
Hillyer, W ....(1)	11*	(67)	Players v Gentlemen (Lord's)	1842
Hobbs, J. B. ....(7)	60*	(155)	Surrey v. Warwickshire (Birmingham)	1907
	154*	(292)	Players v. Gentlemen (Lord's)	1911
	117*	(190)	M.C.C. v. Londesborough's XI (Scarborough)	1911
	205*	(344)	Surrey v. A. I. F. (Oval)	1919
	172*	(294)	Surrey v. Yorkshire (Leeds)	1921
	153*	(300)	Surrey v. Yorkshire (Oval)	1931
	161*	(320)	Players v. Gentlemen (Lord's)	1932
Hofmeyr, M. B. ....(2)	95*	(247)	Oxford U. v. New Zealanders (Oxford)	1949
	64*	(169)	Oxford U. v. Cambridge U. (Lord's)	1949
Holdsworth, R. L.........(1)	100*	(227)	N.W. Frontier Province v. South Punjab (Patiala)	1938–39
Holland, J. ....(1)	46*	(95)	Leicestershire v. Surrey (Leicester)	1894
Holmes, P. ....(3)	145*	(270)	Yorkshire v. Northamptonshire (Northampton)	...1920
	175*	(377)	Yorkshire v. New Zealanders (Bradford)	1927
	110*	(219)	Yorkshire v. Northamptonshire (Bradford)	1929
Holt, J. K. jun...........(1)	103*	(196)	West Indians v. Cricket Club of India (Bombay)	1958–59
Hopkins, A. J. ....(1)	91*	(159)	Rest v. Australian XI (Sydney)	1908–09
Hopkins, H. O. ....(1)	142*	(314)	Oxford U. v. Army (Oxford)	1922
Hopwood, J. L. ....(2)	60*	(153)	Lancashire v. Somerset (Nelson)	1931
	73*	(128)	Lancashire v. South Africans (Manchester)	1935
Hornby, A. N. ....(2)	23*	(56)	Lancashire v. Yorkshire (Manchester)	1876
	121*	(194)	M.C.C. v. Cambridge U. (Lord's)	1882
Howard, T...................(1)	47*	(202)	Western Australia v. South Australia (Fremantle)	1905–06
Howell, M. ....(1)	15*	(73)	Surrey v. Kent (Blackheath)	1920
Humphrey, R. ....(1)	30*	(60)	Surrey v. Nottinghamshire (Oval)	1872
Humphrey, T. ....(1)	43*	(95)	Surrey v. Sussex (Brighton)	1867
Hussain, Dilawas ....(1)	101*	(249)	Indians v. Warwickshire (Birmingham)	1936
Hutton, L. ....(4)	99*	(200)	Yorkshire v. Leicestershire (Sheffield)	1948
	78*	(153)	Yorkshire v. Worcestershire (Sheffield)	1949
	202*	(344)	England v. West Indies (Oval)	1950
	156*	(272)	England v. Australia (Adelaide)	1950–51
Ibrahim, K. C. ....(2)	218*	(380)	Ibrahim's XI v. Raiji's XI (Bombay)	1947–48
	234*	(398)	Ibrahim's XI v. Mantri's XI (Bombay)	1947–48
Ikin, J. T. ....(3)	119*	(261)	†Lancashire v. Middlesex (Manchester)	1949
	96*	(227)	Commonwealth v. Indian XI (Calcutta)	1950–51
	125*	(197)	Lancashire v. Surrey (Oval)	1951
Iremonger, J. ....(1)	189*	(377)	Nottinghamshire v. Middlesex (Lord's)	1904
Jackson, F. S. ....(1)	59*	(162)	Yorkshire v. Cambridge U. (Cambridge)	1897
Johnstone, C. P. ....(1)	78*	(206)	M.C.C. v. Cambridge U. (Lord's)	1939
Jones, A. O. ....(1)	125*	(239)	Nottinghamshire v. Australians (Nottingham)	1909
Jones, S. P. ....(1)	134*	(266)	Australian XI v. Shrewsbury's XI (Sydney)	...1887–88
Jordaan, H. ....(1)	83*	(183)	N.E. Transvaal v. Western Province (Cape Town)	1946–47
Jupp, H. ....(11)	90*	(222)	Surrey v. Yorkshire (Sheffield)	1868
	27*	(95)	Surrey v. Lancashire (Manchester)	1870
	50*	(88)	Surrey v. Gloucestershire (Clifton)	1870
	50*	(98)	South v. North (Lord's)	1873
	51*	(113)	Surrey v. Nottinghamshire (Oval)	1873
	43*	(95)	Surrey v. Yorkshire (Oval) 1st innings	1874
	109*	(193)	Surrey v. Yorkshire (Oval) 2nd innings	1874
	37*	(74)	Surrey v. Yorkshire (Sheffield)	1876
	73*	(268)	Surrey v. Kent (Oval)	1876
	91*	(264)	Surrey v. Kent (Oval)	1877
	117*	(284)	Surrey v. Yorkshire (Sheffield)	1880
Keeton, W. W. ....(1)	99*	(190)	Nottinghamshire v. Kent (Nottingham)	1937
Kennedy, A. S. ....(1)	152*	(344)	Hampshire v. Nottinghamshire (Nottingham)	1921

Kenyon, D. ....(1)	103*	(215)	Worcestershire v. Hampshire (Bournemouth) 1955
Kerr, J. L. ....(1)	146*	(243)	Canterbury v. M.C.C. (Christchurch) 1935–36
Kilner, N. ....(1)	40*	(119)	Warwickshire v. Kent (Tunbridge Wells) 1928
Kinneir, S. P. ....(3)	70*	(239)	Warwickshire v. Leicestershire (Leicester) 1st inns. 1907
	69*	(166)	Warwickshire v. Leicestershire (Leicester) 2nd inns. 1907
	65*	(164)	Warwickshire v. Somerset (Taunton) 1908
Kitcat, S. A. P. ....(1)	18*	(70)	Gloucester v. Yorkshire (Hull) 1901
Knapp, ...(1)	9*	(52)	Nelson v. Wellington (Wellington) 1870–71
Knight, A. E. ....(5)	91*	(155)	†Leicestershire v. Surrey (Oval) 1903
	61*	(131)	Leicestershire v. Nottinghamshire (Nottingham) ...1908
	137*	(345)	Leicestershire v. Warwickshire (Birmingham) 1909
	66*	(182)	Leicestershire v. Hampshire (Portsmouth) 1911
	74*	(182)	Leicestershire v. Surrey (Leicester) 1911
Langdon, T. ....(1)	78*	(151)	Gloucestershire v. South Africans (Bristol) 1907
Langridge, John.............(3)	108*	(218)	Sussex v. Nottinghamshire (Hove) 1948
	48*	(101)	Sussex v. Lancashire (Manchester) 1950
	111*	(191)	Sussex v. Somerset (Hove) 1952
Lee, C. ....(1)	96*	(211)	Derbyshire v. Middlesex (Chesterfield) 1956
Lee, F. S. ....(3)	134*	(236)	Somerset v. Sussex (Taunton) 1931
	59*	(116)	Somerset v. Australians (Taunton) 1934
	109*	(196)	Somerset v. Worcestershire (Worcester) 1938
Lee, H. W. ....(1)	80*	(212)	Middlesex v. Essex (Leyton) 1920
Lee, J. W. ....(2)	135*	(352)	Somerset v. Kent (Taunton) 1934
	54*	(160)	Somerset v. Cambridge U. (Cambridge) 1935
Lenham, L. J. ....(2)	66*	(147)	Sussex v. Surrey (Hove) 1957
	51*	(161)	Sussex v. Glamorgan (Margam) 1960
Lillywhite, W. ....(2)	42*	(89)	Sussex v. M.C.C. (Lord's) 1839
	18*	(38)	M.C.C. v. Cambridge U. (Cambridge) 1845
Lockwood, E. ....(2)	67*	(115)	Players v. Gentlemen (Oval) 1874
	68*	(121)	England XI v. Cambridge U. (Cambridge) 1879
Lowson, F. A. ....(1)	76*	(218)	Yorkshire v. M.C.C. (Lord's) 1951
Lucas, A. P. ....(3)	36*	(121)	Surrey v. Gloucestershire (Clifton) 1877
	43*	(126)	M.C.C. v. Lancashire (Lord's) 1881
	47*	(149)	Gentlemen v. Players (Oval) 1883
Lusk, H. B. ....(1)	65*	(163)	Hawke's Bay v. M.C.C. (Napier) 1906–07
Mackinnon, F. A. ....(1)	33*	(64)	Kent v. Yorkshire (Bradford) 1881
Makepeace, H. ....(4)	39*	(88)	Lancashire v. Kent (Maidstone) 1913
	71*	(185)	Lancashire v. Cambridge U. (Cambridge) 1921
	106*	(208)	Lancashire v. Nottinghamshire (Nottingham) 1923
	92*	(159)	Lancashire v. Nottinghamshire (Nottingham) 1926
Marlow, F. W. ....(2)	43*	(123)	Sussex v. Surrey (Oval) 1891
	144*	(268)	Sussex v. M.C.C. (Lord's) 1891
Marshal, A. ....(1)	66*	(114)	Queensland v. New Zealanders (Brisbane) 1913–14
Maynard, E. A. J. ....(1)	28*	(55)	Derbyshire v. Lancashire (Derby) 1882
Mayne, E. R. ....(1)	154*	(345)	Victoria v. New South Wales (Sydney) 1923–24
McGlew, D. J. ....(3)	114*	(251)	South Africans v. Hampshire (Southampton) 1951
	64*	(95)	South Africans v. Pearce's XI (Scarborough) 1951
	54*	(147)	Natal v. Australians (Durban) 1957–58
McKenzie, U. M. ....(1)	115*	(292)	British Guiana v. Trinidad (Trinidad) 1943–44
Mead, C. P. ....(3)	88*	(223)	Hampshire v. Warwickshire (Leamington) 1909
	120*	(234)	Hampshire v. Yorkshire (Huddersfield) 1911
	117*	(221)	Hampshire v. Nottinghamshire (Nottingham) 1935
Merchant, V. M. ....(4)	135*	(271)	Indians v. Lancashire (Liverpool) 1st innings 1936
	77*	(161)	Indians v. Lancashire (Liverpool) 2nd innings 1936
	86*	(197)	Indians v. Warwickshire (Birmingham) 1946
	184*	(317)	Bombay v. Commonwealth (Bombay) 1950–51
Midlane, F. A. ....(2)	14*	(60)	Wellington v. Canterbury (Christchurch) 1910–11
	222*	(498)	Wellington v. Otago (Wellington) 1914–15
Midwinter, W. E. ....(1)	16*	(76)	Australians v. Nottinghamshire (Nottingham) 1878
Mills, G. ....(1)	106*	(235)	Auckland v. Wellington (Auckland) 1895–96
Mills, I. ....(1)	88*	(156)	Auckland v. Otago (Dunedin) 1893–94
Millyard, G. ....(1)	10*	(47)	Sussex v. Kent (Brighton) 1841
Milton, C. A. ....(2)	51*	(117)	Gloucestershire v. Lancashire (Bristol) 1955
	28*	(69)	Gloucestershire v. Middlesex (Gloucester) 1956
Miller, L. S. M. ....(1)	81*	(154)	Wellington v. Otago (Dunedin) 1956–57
Mitchell, B. ....(1)	103*	(198)	South Africans v. M.C.C. (Lord's) 1947
Mitchell, R. A. H..........(1)	125*	(204)	M.C.C. v. Kent (Canterbury) 1872
Mitford, ...(1)	65*	(97)	Army v. M.C.C. (Pretoria) 1905–06
Moon, L. J. ....(1)	62*	(136)	Middlesex v. Essex (Leyton) 1903
Moore, D. N. ....(1)	101*	(217)	South of England v. M.C.C. (Folkestone) 1930
Morgan, T. R. ....(4)	22*	(68)	†Glamorgan v. Yorkshire (Cardiff) 1922
	14*	(47)	Glamorgan v. Nottinghamshire (Cardiff) 1922

Morgan, T. R. (*cont.*)   13*   (42)   Glamorgan v. Lancashire (Swansea) 1922
   87*   (188)   †Glamorgan v. Leicestershire (Leicester) 1923
Morris, E. B. ....(1)   106*   (297)   Natal v. Orange Free State (Johannesburg) ...1906–07
Morton, A. ....(2)   28*   (62)   Derbyshire v. Yorkshire (Bradford).....................1910
   105*   (204)   Derbyshire v. Leicestershire (Derby) 1920
Moulder, E. R. D. ...(1)   104*   (264)   West Indian XI v. M.C.C. (Georgetown) 1912–13
Murdoch, W. L. ....(2)   82*   (177)   New South Wales v. Harris's XI (Sydney) ...1878–79
   107*   (240)   Australians v. Orleans Club (Twickenham) 1882
Nazar Mohammed ......(1)   124*   (331)   Pakistan v. India (Lucknow) 1952–53
Needham, E. ....(2)   58*   (111)   Derbyshire v. Surrey (Derby) 1908
   107*   (195)   Derbyshire v. Essex (Leyton) 1908
Newham, W. ....(1)   110*   (174)   Sussex v. Lancashire (Manchester) 1894
Nicholson, W. G. ....(1)   63*   (143)   Gentlemen of South v. Gentlemen of North (Lord's) 1862
Nitschke, H. C. ....(1)   130*   (246)   South Australia v. New South Wales (Sydney) 1933–34
North, M. K. ....(1)   32*   (73)   British Guiana v. Lucas's XI (Georgetown) ...1894–95
Northway, R. P. ....(1)   21*   (43)   Somerset v. Yorkshire (Bradford) 1930
Norton, W. S. ....(1)   64*   (143)   Gentlemen of Kent & Sussex v. Gentlemen of
                        England (Canterbury) 1857
Oakman, A. S. M. ......(1)   137*   (238)   Sussex v. Lancashire (Hove) 1956
Oliver, L. ....(1)   75*   (146)   Derbyshire v. Warwickshire (Birmingham) 1912
Oscroft, E. ....(1)   53*   (94)   Nottinghamshire v. Surrey (Nottingham) 1865
Palairet, L. C. H. ....(4)   75*   (197)   Oxford U. v. Sussex (Hove) 1892
   22*   (58)   Somerset v. Lancashire (Manchester) 1892
   51*   (122)   Somerset v. Kent (Taunton) 1893
   113*   (172)   Somerset v. Middlesex (Taunton) 1895
Parkhouse, W. G. A. ...(1)   60*   (152)   Glamorgan v. Lancashire (Swansea) 1954
Parks, H. W. ....(2)   49*   (105)   Sussex v. Yorkshire (Eastbourne) 1946
   119*   (221)   Sussex v. Lancashire (Eastbourne) 1947
Parks, J. H. ....(2)   33*   (137)   Sussex v. Glamorgan (Swansea) 1936
   144*   (262)   Sussex v. Cambridge U. (Cambridge) 1937
Parsons, J. H. ....(1)   161*   (347)   Warwickshire v. Gloucestershire (Nuneaton) 1913
Patterson, G. S. ....(1)   109*   (234)   Philadelphians v. Mitchell's XI (Philadelphia) 1895–96
Patterson, W. H. ....(1)   107*   (306)   Oxford U. v. Cambridge U. (Lord's) 1881
Payne, C. ....(3)   53*   (165)   Sussex v. Kent (Brighton) 1865
   135*   (367)   Kent v. Surrey (Gravesend) 1866
   37*   (79)   Sussex v. Middlesex (Brighton) 1868
Payton, W. E. G. ....(1)   33*   (84)   Combined Services v. Oxford U. (Oxford) 1947
Pearson, F. ....(4)   154*   (342)   Worcestershire v. Surrey (Dudley) 1912
   67*   (152)   Worcestershire v. Sussex (Eastbourne) 1914
   151*   (275)   Worcestershire v. Warwickshire (Worcester) 1921
   68*   (123)   Worcestershire v. Hampshire (Southampton) 1923
Phebey, A. H. ....(4)   89*   (209)   Kent v. Worcestershire (Kidderminster) 1951
   54*   (126)   Kent v. Middlesex (Lord's) 1951
   85*   (181)   Kent v. Australians (Canterbury)........................1953
   50*   (127)   Kent v. Northamptonshire (Northampton) 1954
Phillips, G. ....(1)   8*   (13)   Wellington v. Nelson (Nelson) 1862–63
Picknell, G. ....(1)   27*   (64)   Sussex v. Surrey (Oval) 1850
Pilkington, H. C. ....(1)   77*   (169)   Oxford U. v. M.C.C. (Lord's) 1899
Pinch, C. ....(1)   146*   (259)   South Australia v. Victoria (Melbourne) 1950–51
Place, W. ....(1)   101*   (244)   Lancashire v. Warwickshire (Manchester) 1950
Ponsford, W. H. ....(2)   143*   (283)   Australians v. Glamorgan (Swansea) 1926
   109*   (185)   Victoria v. New South Wales (Melbourne) 1930–31
Poore, R. M. ....(1)   49*   (97)   Hampshire v. Somerset (Bath) 1898
Prentice, F. T. ....(1)   36*   (89)   Leicestershire v. Worcestershire (Hinckley) 1937
Quaife, B. W. ....(1)   31*   (112)   Warwickshire v. Kent (Stourbridge) 1931
Quaife, W. ....(1)   40*   (81)   Sussex v. Lancashire (Manchester) 1887
Quaife, W. G. ....(1)   178*   (475)   †Warwickshire v. Hampshire (Southampton) 1897
Radcliffe, O. G. ....(2)   104*   (207)   Gloucestershire v. Middlesex (Lord's) 1886
   101*   (214)   Gloucestershire v. Kent (Canterbury) 1889
Raghinath, R. ....(1)   68*   (169)   Kerala v. Mysore (Palghat) 1958–59
Ram, D. ....(1)   31*   (79)   Kerala v. Madras (Madurai) 1957–58
Rawlin, J. T. ....(1)   122*   (290)   M.C.C. v. London County (Crystal Palace) 1902
Read, W. W. ....(2)   196*   (413)   Surrey v. Sussex (Oval) 1892
   142*   (368)   Vernon's XI v. Victoria (Melbourne) 1887–88
Rees, J. S. ....(1)   21*   (54)   South Australia v. Western Australia (Perth) ...1905–06
Relf, R. R. ....(1)   272*   (433)   Sussex v. Worcestershire (Eastbourne) 1909
Rhodes, W. ....(3)   98*   (184)   Yorkshire v. M.C.C. (Lord's) 1903
   85*   (152)   Yorkshire v. Essex (Leyton) 1910
   79*   (165)   Capped v. Uncapped (Hastings) 1923
Rice, R. W. ....(2)   38*   (101)   Gloucestershire v. Yorkshire (Cheltenham) 1900
   58*   (147)   Gloucestershire v. Essex (Clifton) 1901

Richardson, P. E.	.........(2)	91*	(155)	Worcestershire v. Hampshire (Worcester) 1955
		59*	(105)	M.C.C. v. Pakistan XI (Dacca) 1955–56
Riches, N. V. H.	.........(2)	177*	(347)	Glamorgan v. Leicestershire (Leicester) 1921
		85*	(161)	Glamorgan v. Yorkshire (Leeds) 1922
Ricketts, J.	...............(1)	195*	(429)	Lancashire v. Surrey (Oval) 1867
Rippon, A. D. E.	.........(1)	87*	(194)	Somerset v. Kent (Taunton) 1914
Rippon, A. E. S.	.........(2)	19*	(66)	†Somerset v. Sussex (Bath) 1920
		90*	(165)	Somerset v. Hampshire (Southampton) 1921
Robertson, G. J.	.........(1)	83*	(249)	Otago v. Canterbury (Christchurch) 1939–40
Roderigo, M.	...........(1)	135*	(318)	Ceylon v. West Indians (Colombo) 1948–49
Rogers, N. H.	...........(5)	32*	(68)	†Hampshire v. Leicestershire (Loughborough) 1953
		56*	(126)	M.C.C. v. Surrey (Lord's) 1954
		172*	(327)	Hampshire v. Gloucestershire (Bristol) 1954
		125*	(221)	Hampshire v. Somerset (Glastonbury) 1954
		101*	(182)	England XI v. Pakistan (Hastings) 1954
Rothery, J. W.	...........(1)	53*	(258)	Yorkshire v. Worcestershire (Worcester) 1907
Roy, P.	...................(1)	170*	(479)	Bengal v. Orissa (Cuttack) 1953–54
Russell, A. C.	...............(1)	89*	(161)	Essex v. Northamptonshire (Northampton) 1913
Ryder, J.	...................(1)	93*	(188)	Victoria v. New South Wales (Sydney) 1914–15
Sandham, A.	...............(7)	123*	(323)	Surrey v. Hampshire (Portsmouth) 1922
		155*	(330)	Surrey v. Somerset (Oval) 1923
		96*	(158)	Surrey v. Cambridge U. (Oval) 1924
		159*	(271)	Cahn's XI v. Jamaica (Kingston) 1928–29
		125*	(282)	Surrey v. Northamptonshire (Northampton) 1930
		113*	(221)	Surrey v. Hampshire (Bournemouth) 1931
		169*	(333)	Surrey v. Hampshire (Oval) 1933
Scotton, W. H.	...........(4)	110*	(223)	Nottinghamshire v. Surrey (Nottingham) 1886
		35*	(92)	Nottinghamshire v. Lancashire (Manchester) 1887
		17*	(58)	Nottinghamshire v. Yorkshire (Sheffield) 1888
		9*	(28)	England XI v. Australians (Stoke) 1888
Serrurier, L. R.	...........(1)	74*	(162)	Western Province v. M.C.C. (Cape Town) 1927–28
Sewell, C. O. H.	.........(1)	88*	(127)	Gloucestershire v. Yorkshire (Sheffield) 1898
Shaw, E. D.	...............(1)	78*	(189)	Oxford U. v. Australians (Oxford) 1882
Shipman, A.	...............(1)	100*	(212)	Leicestershire v. Lancashire (Manchester) 1935
Shrewsbury, A.	...........(8)	224*	(415)	Nottinghamshire v. Middlesex (Lord's) 1885
		227*	(430)	Nottinghamshire v. Gloucestershire (Moreton-in-the-Marsh...............1886
		54*	(90)	North v. South (Lord's)...............................1890
		81*	(167)	Players v. Gentlemen (Lord's) 1891
		151*	(345)	Sherwin's XI v. Hall's XI (Bradford) 1891
		111*	(226)	Nottinghamshire v. Kent (Canterbury) 1892
		151*	(325)	Players v. Gentlemen (Oval) 1892
		125*	(277)	Nottinghamshire v. Gloucestershire (Nottingham) 1896
Shuter, J.	...................(1)	45*	(92)	Surrey v. Nottinghamshire (Oval) 1878
Siedle, I. J.	...................(1)	132*	(297)	South Africans v. M.C.C. (Lord's) 1935
Simpson, R. B.	...........(1)	161*	(294)	Western Australia v. New South Wales (Sydney) 1959–60
Simpson, R. T.	...........(2)	119*	(237)	M.C.C. v. Natal (Durban) 1948–49
		230*	(352)	Nottinghamshire v. Glamorgan (Swansea) 1950
Sinfield, R. A.	...........(5)	161*	(374)	Gloucestershire v. Oxford U. (Oxford) 1931
		39*	(104)	Gloucestershire v. Sussex (Cheltenham) 1931
		100*	(290)	Gloucestershire v. Sussex (Bristol) 1935
		38*	(106)	Gloucestershire v. Derbyshire (Buxton) 1937
		69*	(165)	Gloucestershire v. Worcestershire (Bristol)............1939
Smith, C. H.	...............(1)	47*	(128)	Sussex v. Surrey (Oval) 1868
Smith, D.	...................(2)	140*	(265)	Derbyshire v. Hampshire (Chesterfield) 1937
		57*	(112)	Derbyshire v. Kent (Ilkeston) 1939
Smith, D. V.	...............(1)	147*	(256)	Sussex v. West Indians (Hove) 1957
Smith, H. O.	...............(1)	124*	(264)	Tasmania v. South Africans (Launceston) 1910–11
Smith, M. J. K.	.........(1)	76*	(137)	Oxford U. v. Hampshire (Bournemouth) 1955
Snary, H. C.	...............(1)	124*	(291)	Leicestershire v. Indians (Leicester) 1932
Spooner, R. T.	...........(1)	98*	(210)	Warwickshire v. Worcestershire (Worcester) 1952
Stoddart, A. E.	...........(2)	216*	(372)	Middlesex v. Lancashire (Manchester) 1891
		195*	(327)	Middlesex v. Nottinghamshire (Lord's) 1893
Stollmeyer, J. B.	.........(1)	45*	(84)	West Indians v. Somerset (Taunton) 1939
Stott, W. B.	...............(1)	144*	(262)	Yorkshire v. Worcestershire (Worcester) 1959
Studd, G. B.	...............(1)	106*	(187)	Cambridge U. v. Lancashire (Liverpool) 1881
Sutcliffe, H.	...............(7)	125*	(307)	Yorkshire v. Essex (Southend) 1920
		104*	(170)	†Yorkshire v. Hampshire (Leeds) 1932
		110*	(307)	†North v. South (Manchester) 1932
		114*	(202)	Yorkshire v. Rest of England (Oval) 1933
		187*	(401)	Yorkshire v. Worcestershire (Bradford) 1934
		135*	(262)	Yorkshire v. Glamorgan (Neath) 1935

Name		Score	()	Match	Year
Sutcliffe, H. (*cont.*)		125*	(322)	Yorkshire v. Oxford U. (Oxford)	1939
Tancred, A. B.	(1)	26*	(47)	South Africa v. England (Cape Town)	1888–89
Tancred, L. J.	(1)	61*	(135)	South Africans v. M.C.C. (Lord's)	1907
Tarrant, F. A.	(6)	51*	(114)	M.C.C. v. Kent (Lord's)	1907
		48*	(162)	M.C.C. v. Oxford U. (Oxford)	1908
		55*	(145)	Middlesex v. Gloucestershire (Bristol)	1909
		140*	(262)	Middlesex v. Sussex (Lord's)	1910
		207*	(378)	Middlesex v. Yorkshire (Bradford)	1911
		81*	(159)	Middlesex v. Lancashire (Liverpool)	1913
Tayfield, A.	(1)	133*	(261)	Transvaal v. Eastern Province (Port Elizabeth)	1955–56
Taylor, C. H.	(1)	105*	(274)	Oxford U. v. Worcestershire (Oxford)	1925
Taylor, H. W.	(1)	83*	(124)	Natal v. M.C.C. (Pietermaritzburg)	1913–14
Taylor, K. A.	(1)	81*	(222)	Warwickshire v. Yorkshire (Birmingham)	1948
Thompson, G. J.	(1)	103*	(270)	Northamptonshire v. Cambridge U. (Cambridge)	1906
Thompson, W. K.	(1)	74*	(225)	Natal v. Transvaal (Durban)	1904–05
Timms, J. E.	(1)	82*	(156)	Northamptonshire v. Derbyshire (Chesterfield)	1935
Tindill, E. W.	(1)	47*	(111)	Wellington v. Otago (Dunedin)	1946–47
Todd, L. J.	(1)	133*	(265)	Kent v. Leicestershire (Tunbridge Wells)	1946
Townsend, A. F.	(1)	102*	(228)	Derbyshire v. Lancashire (Manchester)	1948
Troup, W.	(1)	127*	(388)	Gloucestershire v. Worcestershire (Bristol)	1902
Ulyett, G.	(2)	146*	(248)	Yorkshire v. M.C.C. (Scarborough)	1884
		199*	(399)	Yorkshire v. Derbyshire (Sheffield)	1887
Van Der Berg, J. H.	(1)	55*	(188)	Eastern Province v. Transvaal (Johannesburg)	1926–27
Varnals, G. D.	(1)	151*	(267)	Eastern Province v. Border (East London)	1957–58
Vials, G. A. T.	(1)	62*	(105)	Northamptonshire v. Surrey (Northampton)	1910
Vine, J.	(9)	75*	(178)	Sussex v. Middlesex (Eastbourne)	1902
		62*	(241)	Sussex v. Somerset (Hove)	1906
		80*	(218)	Sussex v. Somerset (Bath)	1906
		78*	(222)	Sussex v. Middlesex (Lord's)	1907
		67*	(186)	Sussex v. Essex (Hove)	1907
		37*	(160)	Sussex v. Gloucestershire (Bristol)	1909
		19*	(100)	Sussex v. Lancashire (Liverpool)	1910
		23*	(98)	Sussex v. Kent (Tonbridge)	1910
		72*	(153)	Sussex v. Worcestershire (Hove)	1910
Walker, D. F.	(1)	107*	(236)	Oxford U. v. Gloucestershire (Oxford)	1933
Walker, I. D.	(1)	47*	(126)	Middlesex v. Surrey (Lord's)	1884
Walters, C. F.	(1)	53*	(100)	Worcestershire v. Glamorgan (Pontypridd)	1931
Ward, A.	(5)	140*	(281)	Lancashire v. Gloucestershire (Bristol)	1893
		45*	(97)	Lancashire v. Australians (Manchester)	1893
		75*	(168)	Lancashire v. Leicestershire (Manchester)	1895
		109*	(337)	Lancashire v. Hampshire (Southampton)	1899
		83*	(262)	Lancashire v. Middlesex (Lord's)	1899
Warne, F.	(1)	43*	(153)	Worcestershire v. Middlesex (Lord's)	1937
Warne, T.	(1)	61*	(129)	Victoria v. MacLaren's XI (Melbourne)	1901–02
Warner, E. W.	(3)	141*	(279)	Orange Free State v. Griqualand West (Kimberley)	1936–37
		102*	(210)	Orange Free State v. Border (Bethlehem)	1936–37
		87*	(235)	Orange Free State v. Eastern Province (Bloemfontein)	1937–38
Warner, P. F.	(10)	46*	(75)	Middlesex v. Gloucestershire (Lord's)	1898
		132*	(237)	England v. South Africa (Johannesburg)	1898–99
		197*	(400)	Middlesex v. Somerset (Lord's)	1901
		73*	(168)	Middlesex v. Yorkshire (Lord's)	1901
		65*	(130)	Middlesex v. Nottinghamshire (Nottingham)	1907
		59*	(139)	Middlesex v. Nottinghamshire (Lord's)	1907
		64*	(95)	M.C.C. v. Yorkshire (Lord's)	1908
		64*	(124)	M.C.C. v. Kent (Lord's)	1908
		102*	(201)	Middlesex v. Surrey (Lord's)	1909
		145*	(279)	Middlesex v. Hampshire (Lord's)	1910
Washbrook, C.	(1)	49*	(124)	Lancashire v. Worcestershire (Manchester)	1935
Watson, W.	(1)	79*	(132)	Leicestershire v. Yorkshire (Leicester)	1959
Webbe, A. J.	(8)	62*	(118)	Middlesex v. Yorkshire (Sheffield)	1882
		97*	(201)	Middlesex v. Nottinghamshire (Prince's)	1875
		44*	(134)	Middlesex v. Nottinghamshire (Nottingham)	1876
		83*	(196)	Middlesex v. Surrey (Oval)	1884
		63*	(119)	Middlesex v. Oxford U. (Chiswick Park)	1887
		243*	(527)	Middlesex v. Yorkshire (Huddersfield)	1887
		192*	(412)	Middlesex v. Kent (Canterbury)	1887
		37*	(82)	M.C.C. v. Kent (Lord's)	1888
Wells, G.	(2)	38*	(81)	Sussex v. Kent (Brighton)	1858
		55*	(73)	Sussex v. M.C.C. (Lord's)	1860
Whitehead, H.	(1)	130*	(271)	Leicestershire v. Lancashire (Leicester)	1907
Whitelaw, P. E.	(1)	99*	(183)	Auckland v. M.C.C. (Auckland)	1936–37

Whitfield, H. J.	...........(1)	41*	(109)	Sussex v. Surrey (Oval) 1884
Whysall, W. W.	.........(2)	109*	(242)	Nottinghamshire v. Kent (Canterbury) 1924
		111*	(238)	Nottinghamshire v. Essex (Nottingham) 1929
Wight, P. B.	................(1)	222*	(450)	Somerset v. Kent (Taunton) 1959
Wilkinson, A. J.	.........(1)	84*	(209)	Gents of Middlesex v. Gents of England (Islington) 1865
Wilson, H. L.	............(2)	42*	(104)	†Sussex v. Somerset (Taunton) 1919
		108*	(215)	Sussex v. Warwickshire (Hove) 1924
Wood, A. M.	............(1)	73*	(149)	Philadelphians v. Cambridge U. (Cambridge) 1897
Wood, C. J. B.	............(17)	21*	(98)	Leicestershire v. Yorkshire (Dewsbury) 1898
		46*	(262)	Leicestershire v. Sussex (Leicester) 1903
		118*	(322)	Leicestershire v. Yorkshire (Leicester)................1903
		160*	(419)	Leicestershire v. Yorkshire (Leicester)................1905
		200*	(507)	Leicestershire v. Hampshire (Leicester) 1905
		56*	(112)	Leicestershire v. Lancashire (Leicester) 1906
		105*	(303)	Leicestershire v. Essex (Southend) 1906
		110*	(220)	Leicestershire v. Northamptonshire (Northampton) 1906
		84*	(159)	Leicestershire v. Lancashire (Leicester) 1908
		38*	(116)	Leicestershire v. Derbyshire (Derby) 1910
		78*	(270)	Leicestershire v. Kent (Leicester) 1911
		54*	(151)	Leicestershire v. Northamptonshire (Leicester) 1911
		54*	(164)	Leicestershire v. Warwickshire (Hinckley) 1911
		107*	(309)	Leicestershire v. Yorkshire (Bradford) 1st innings 1911
		117*	(296)	Leicestershire v. Yorkshire (Bradford) 2nd innings 1911
		38*	(179)	Leicestershire v. Lancashire (Leicester) 1913
		164*	(392)	Leicestershire v. Warwickshire (Hinckley) 1913
Woodfull, W. M.	.........(4)	116*	(281)	Australians v. England XI (Blackpool) 1926
		30*	(66)	†Australia v. England (Brisbane) 1928–29
		67*	(164)	Victoria v. M.C.C. (Melbourne)..................1928–29
		73*	(193)	†Australia v. England (Adelaide) 1932–33
Woolley, C. N.	............(3)	62*	(113)	Northamptonshire v. Sussex (Hove) 1923
		59*	(130)	Northamptonshire v. Sussex (Hastings) 1925
		38*	(102)	Northamptonshire v. Yorkshire (Bradford) 1929
Worrell, F. M.	............(1)	191*	(372)	West Indies v. England (Nottingham) 1957
Worthington, T. S.	.......(1)	156*	(376)	M.C.C. Australian Team v. Rest (Lord's) 1937
Wright, H.	..................(1)	26*	(63)	Leicestershire v. Hampshire (Southampton) 1914
Wright, L. G.	............(3)	59*	(112)	Derbyshire v. Essex (Leyton) 1899
		58*	(136)	Derbyshire v. Essex (Leyton) 1903
		50*	(104)	Derbyshire v. Leicestershire (Leicester) 1906
Wright, R. L.	...........(1)	96*	(201)	Northamptonshire v. Lancashire (Northampton) ...1923
Wright, W.	................(1)	127*	(371)	Nottinghamshire v. Gloucestershire (Nottingham) 1883
Zulch, J. W.	................(1)	43*	(103)	South Africa v. England (Cape Town) 1909 10

Fast Scoring

FAST FIFTIES

The following are the fastest times for reaching the fifty from the commencement of the innings:
min.

50*—11	C. I. J. Smith (66): Middx. v. Glos (Bristol) 1938
50*—14	S. J. Pegler (50): South Africans v. Tasmania (Launceston) 1910–11
52*—14	F. T. Mann (53): Middx. v. Notts. (Lord's) 1921
50*—14	H. B. Cameron (56): Transvaal v. O.F.S. (Johannesburg) 1934–35
50*—14	C. I. J. Smith (52) Middx. v. Kent (Maidstone) 1935
50*—15	G. L. Jessop (61): Glos. v. Somerset (Bristol) 1904
53*—15	G. L. Jessop (92): Glos. v. Hants. (Cheltenham) 1907
50*—15	F. R. Foster (63): Warwicks. v. Middx. (Birmingham) 1914
50*—15	H. R. Murrell (50): Middx. v. Hants. (Southampton) 1921
50*—15	C. C. Dacre (64): New Zealanders v. Glos. (Cheltenham) 1927
50*—15	G. F. Earle (59): Somerset v. Glos. (Taunton) 1929
50*—15	G. Cox (51): Sussex v. Cambridge U. (Hove) 1934
50*—15	J. Hardstaff jun. (77): Notts. v. Glos. (Bristol) 1937
53*—15	R. Smith (78): Essex v. Notts. (Brentwood) 1949

FAST CENTURIES

The following centuries have been reached when the batsman was at the wicket for an hour or less:
min.

100*—35	P. G. H. Fender (113*): Surrey v. Northants. (Northampton) 1920
101 —40	G. L. Jessop (101): Glos. v. Yorks. (Harrogate) 1897
100*—42	G. L. Jessop (191): Gentlemen of South v. Players of South (Hastings) 1907
100*—43	A. H. Hornby (106): Lancs. v. Somerset (Manchester) 1905
100*—45	E. M. Sprot (125*): Hants. v. Glos. (Bristol) 1911
100*—45	W. Voce (129): Notts. v. Glamorgan (Nottingham) 1931
100*—48	A. W. Carr (124): Notts. v. Sussex (Hove) 1925
100 —50	K. L. Hutchings (100): Kent v. Glos. (Catford) 1909
100*—50	D. R. A. Gehrs (119): South Australia v. Western Australia (Adelaide)............1912–13
100*—51	J. Hardstaff jun. (126): Notts. v. Kent (Canterbury) 1937
100 —52	L. N. Constantine (100): West Indians v. Tasmania (Launceston) 1930–31
100*—53	G. L. Jessop (139): Glos. v. Surrey (Bristol) 1911
100*—53	M. G. Francis (115*): O.F.S. v. Griqualand West (Bloemfontein) 1927–28
100*—54	J. E. Raphael (111): Oxford U. v. Worcs. (Worcester) 1904
100*—54	J. N. Crawford (114): M.C.C. v. South Australia (Adelaide) 1907–08
100*—55	F. G. J. Ford (112): Middx. v. Philadelphians (Lord's) 1897
100*—55	A. P. Day (100*): Kent v. Hants. (Southampton) 1911
100*—55	G. L. Tapscott (111): Rest v. Transvaal (Johannesburg) 1911–12
100*—55	G. L. Jessop (116): Londesborough's XI v. Kent (Scarborough) 1913
102*—55	Hon. L. H. Tennyson (102*): Hants. v. Glos. (Southampton) 1927
100*—57	G. L. Jessop (124): Glos. v. Middx. (Lord's) 1901
101 —57	V. T. Trumper (101): N.S.W. v. Victoria (Sydney) 1905–06
100*—57	H. T. Bartlett (157): Sussex v. Australians (Hove) 1938
100*—59	G. L. Jessop (139): Glos. v. Yorks. (Bradford) 1900
100*—60	E. C. Streatfeild (145): Cambridge U. P. & P. v. Australians (Leyton) 1890
100*—60	J. J. Lyons (149): Australians v. M.C.C. (Lord's) 1893
100*—60	G. L. Jessop (112*): Rest v. A. E. Stoddart's XI (Hastings) 1898
100*—60	G. L. Jessop (126): Glos. v. Notts. (Nottingham) 1899
100*—60	G. L. Jessop (109): Glos. v. Middx. (Lord's) 1900
100*—60	G. L. Jessop (169): M.C.C. v. Leics. (Lord's) 1901
100*—60	W. S. Lees (130): Surrey v. Hants. (Aldershot) 1905
100*—60	S. J. Snooke (121): Western Province v. Griqualand West (Johannesburg) 1906–07
100*—60	C. C. Page (164*): Middx. v. Somerset (Lord's) 1908
101 —60	G. N. Foster (101): Oxford U. v. Gentlemen of England (Eastbourne) 1908
101*—60	C. B. Llewellyn (101*): Hants. v. Sussex (Hove) 1909
100*—60	G. L. Jessop (165): Glos. v. Worcs. (Stourbridge) 1910
100*—60	P. J. Heather (109*): Transvaal v. Border (Durban) 1910–11
100*—60	H. L. Simms (126): Sussex v. Notts. (Hove) 1912
100*—60	K. O. Goldie (104): England XII v. Indian XII (Bombay) 1915–16
100*—60	W. V. S. Ling (187): Griqualand West v. O.F.S. (Pretoria) 1923–24
100*—60	A. W. Carr (100*): Notts. v. Northants. (Northampton)...........................1928
103 —60	L. N. Constantine (103): West Indians v. Middx. (Lord's) 1928
103 —60	C. R. Browne (103): West Indians v. Kent (Canterbury) 1928
100*—60	E. T. Killick (200*): Cambridge U. v. Glamorgan (Cambridge)....................1929
101 —60	C. J. Barnett (101): Glos. v. Hants. (Southampton) 1937
100*—60	G. Cox (142): Sussex v. Yorks. (Hove) 1938
100*—60	F. R. Brown (104*): South v. North (Scarborough) 1947
100*—60	C. J. Poole (154*): Notts. v. Leics. (Nottingham) 1949

FASTEST 150

150*—63	G. L. Jessop (191): Gentlemen of South v. Players of South (Hastings) 1907

FAST DOUBLE-CENTURIES

The following double-centuries have been scored within 2½ hours of the batsman reaching the wicket:
min.

200*—120	G. L. Jessop (286): Glos. v. Sussex (Hove) 1903
200*—130	G. L. Jessop (234): Glos. v. Somerset (Bristol) 1905
200*—131	V. T. Trumper (293): Australians v. Canterbury (Christchurch)....................1913–14
200*—135	S. M. J. Woods (215): Somerset v. Sussex (Hove) 1895
200*—135	G. L. Jessop (233): Rest v. Yorks. (Lord's) 1901
200*—135	C. R. Maxwell (268): Cahn's XI v. Leics. (Nottingham) 1935
200*—140	G. L. Jessop (206): Glos. v. Notts. (Nottingham) 1904
200*—144	D. C. S. Compton (300): M.C.C. v. N.E. Transvaal (Benoni) 1948–49
200*—145	J. S. F. Morrison (233*): Cambridge U. v. M.C.C. (Cambridge) 1914
200*—145	C. G. Macartney (345): Australians v. Notts. (Nottingham) 1921
200*—150	H. K. Foster (216): Worcs. v. Somerset (Worcester) 1903
200*—150	M. M. Walford (201*): Oxford U. v. M.C.C. (Lord's) 1938

FAST TRIPLE-CENTURIES

The following triple-centuries have been scored within the shortest time of reaching the wicket:
min.
300 —181   D. C. S. Compton (300): M.C.C. v. N.E. Transvaal (Benoni) 1948–49
300*—205   F. E. Woolley (305*): M.C.C. v. Tasmania (Hobart) 1911–12
300*—205   C. G. Macartney (345): Australians v. Notts. (Nottingham) 1921
300*—213   D. G. Bradman (369): South Australia v. Tasmania (Adelaide) 1935–36

FAST INNINGS

*The foregoing tables have given the fastest times for reaching the various milestones in an innings.
The fastest completed innings graded according to minutes batted have been as follows:*
min.
46 — 13   B. Sutcliffe: New Zealanders v. Hants. (Southampton).....................................1949
66 — 18   C. I. J. Smith: Middx. v. Glos. (Bristol) 1938
67*— 20   L. N. Constantine: West Indians v. Notts. (Nottingham) 1928
69 — 20   C. I. J. Smith: Middx. v. Sussex (Lord's) 1938
66*— 22   J. H. Sinclair: South Africans v. Tasmania (Launceston) 1910–11
68 — 24   G. Curgenven: Derby. v. Glos. (Gloucester) 1922
69 — 26   C. I. J. Smith: Middx. v. Somerset (Lord's) 1936
73 — 30   C. H. Knott: Kent v. Warwicks. (Tonbridge) 1930
75 — 30   R. T. D. Perks: Worcs. v. Notts. (Nottingham) 1938
78 — 32   R. Smith: Essex v. Notts. (Brentwood) 1949
74 — 35   F. Barratt: Notts. v. Glos. (Bristol) 1929
77 — 35   A. E. Watt: Over 30 v. Under 30 (Folkestone) 1937
83 — 40   F. R. Foster: Warwicks. v. Lancs. (Birmingham) 1914
101 — 40   G. L. Jessop: Glos. v. Yorks. (Harrogate) 1897
113*— 42   P. G. H. Fender: Surrey v. Northants. (Northampton) 1920
89 — 44   H. T. Bartlett: Sussex v. Worcs. (Eastbourne) 1939
106 — 45   A. H. Hornby: Lancs. v. Somerset (Manchester) 1905
90 — 45   H. C. Salmonson: Cahn's XI v. Essex (Nottingham) 1930
94 — 50   H. Martyn: Oxford U. v. Cambridge U. (Lord's) 1900
92 — 50   M. W. Payne: Cambridge U. v. Surrey (Oval)..1907
93 — 51   E. R. Dexter: Sussex v. Warwicks. (Birmingham) 1960
97 — 55   N. B. F. Mann: South Africans v. Glamorgan (Cardiff) 1947
96 — 57   H. A. Peach: Surrey v. Hants. (Oval) 1928
114 — 58   J. N. Crawford: M.C.C. v. South Australia (Adelaide) 1907–08
97 — 58   F. R. Brown: Northants. v. Somerset (Northampton) 1953
119 — 60   D. R. A. Gehrs: South Australia v. Western Australia (Adelaide) 1912–13
124 — 70   A. W. Carr: Notts. v. Sussex (Hove) 1925
129 — 75   W. Voce: Notts. v. Glamorgan (Nottingham) 1931
139 — 80   P. G. H. Fender: Surrey v. Somerset (Oval) 1931
139*— 84   F. Barratt: Notts. v. Warwicks. (Coventry) 1928
149 — 90   J. J. Lyons: Australians v. M.C.C. (Lord's) 1893
189 — 90   E. Alletson: Notts. v. Sussex (Hove) 1911
146 — 90   A. E. Lawton: Derby. v. Hants. (Derby) 1902
191 — 90   G. L. Jessop: Gentlemen of South v. Players of South (Hastings) 1907
161 — 95   G. L. Jessop: Glos. v. Hants. (Bristol) 1909
150*— 95   D. C. S. Compton: M.C.C. v. Griqualand West (Kimberley) 1948–49
154*— 97   C. J. Poole: Notts. v. Leics. (Nottingham) 1949
153 —100   C. B. Llewellyn: Hants. v. Somerset (Taunton) 1901
153 —103   C. K. Nayudu: Hindus v. M.C.C. (Bombay) 1926–27
179 —105   G. L. Jessop: Glos. v. Sussex (Hove) 1900
187 —120   W. V. S. Ling: Griqualand West v. O.F.S. (Pretoria) 1923–24
187 —125   D. G. Bradman: Australians v. Essex (Southend) 1948
206 —145   G. L. Jessop: Glos. v. Notts. (Nottingham) 1904
215 —150   S. M. J. Woods: Somerset v. Sussex (Hove) 1895
233 —150   G. L. Jessop: Rest v. Yorks. (Lord's) 1901
286 —175   G. L. Jessop: Glos. v. Sussex (Hove) 1903
293 —180   V. T. Trumper: Australians v. Canterbury (Christchurch) 1913–14
300 —181   D. C. S. Compton: M.C.C. v. N.E. Transvaal (Benoni) 1948–49
260 —185   A. P. F. Chapman: Kent v. Lancs. (Maidstone) 1927
305*—210   F. E. Woolley: M.C.C. v. Tasmania (Hobart) 1911–12
345 —235   C. G. Macartney: Australians v. Notts. (Nottingham) 1921
369 —253   D. G. Bradman: South Australia v. Tasmania (Adelaide) 1935–36
383 —345   C. W. Gregory: N.S.W. v. Queensland (Brisbane) 1906–07
452*—415   D. G. Bradman: N.S.W. v. Queensland (Sydney) 1929–30

FAST PARTNERSHIPS

The following table shows the fastest partnerships graded according to length in minutes that have been recorded:

runs	wkt.	min.	
113	9th	30	A. H. Hornby & W. Findlay: Lancs. v. Somerset (Manchester) 1905
104*	8th	30	C. R. Maxwell & J. W. A. Stephenson: M.C.C. v West Indians (Lord's) ...1939
109	6th	34	J. N. Crawford & L. C. Braund: M.C.C. v. South Australia (Adelaide) 1907–08
111	9th	35	C. H. B. Marsham & C. Blythe: Kent v. Sussex (Canterbury 1906
116	5th	35	C. J. Burnup & E. Humphreys: Kent v. Somerset (Taunton) 1906
108	4th	35	G. L. Jessop & C. P. McGahey: Gentlemen of South v. Players of South (Hastings) 1907
109	7th	35	E. Hendren & A. E. R. Gilligan: M.C.C. v. Tasmania (Launceston) 1924–25
105*	5th	35	D. C. S. Compton & J. H. A. Hulme: Middx. v. Worcs. (Lord's) 1937
147	10th	40	E. M. Sprot & A. E. Fielder: Hants. v. Glos. (Bristol) 1911
152	10th	40	E. Alletson & W. Riley: Notts. v. Sussex (Hove) 1911
124	10th	40	W. A. Oldfield & A. A. Mailey: Australians v. Warwicks. (Birmingham) ...1921
171*	6th	42	P. G. H. Fender & H. A. Peach: Surrey v. Northants. (Northampton) 1920
168	5th	50	H. L. Collins & V. T. Trumper: N.S.W. v. Tasmania (Hobart) 1912–13
152	8th	52	R. J. O. Meyer & S. A. Block: Free Foresters v. Cambridge U. (Cambridge) 1938
150	4th	55	A. Ducat & D. R. Jardine: Surrey v. Leics. (Oval) 1926
163*	3rd	60	N. S. Mitchell-Innes & R. C. M. Kimpton: Oxford U. v. Leics. (Oxford) ...1937
181	7th	65	G. N. Foster & W. B. Burns: Worcs. v. Hants. (Worcester) 1905
177	10th	65	J. H. Naumann & A. E. R. Gilligan: Cambridge U. v. Sussex (Hove) 1919
173	7th	65	E. Hendren & L. E. G. Ames: Rest v. Lancs. (Oval) 1928
166	6th	65	S. J. E. Loxton & R. A. Saggers: Australians v. Essex (Southend) 1948
202*	2nd	75	G. H. Hirst & W. Rhodes: Yorks. v. Somerset (Bath) 1906
188	3rd	75	W. Walker & W. Voce: Notts. v. Glamorgan (Nottingham) 1931
196*	4th	84	W. Walker & F. Barratt: Notts. v. Warwicks. (Coventry) 1928
236	6th	85	E. R. T. Holmes & R. E. C. Butterworth: Oxford U. v. Free Foresters(Oxford) 1927
255	3rd	90	J. S. F. Morrison & H. G. H. Mulholland: Cambridge U. v. M.C.C. (Cambridge)............1914
237	8th	90	W. V. D. Dickinson & R. St L. Fowler: Army v. M.C.C. (Lord's) 1920
243*	3rd	95	F. E. Woolley & E. Hendren: Rest v. Lancs. (Oval) 1926
251*	2nd	97	R. T. Simpson & C. J. Poole: Notts. v. Leics. (Nottingham) 1949
250	2nd	100	F. L. Bowley & H. K. Foster: Worcs. v. Somerset (Worcester) 1903
248	7th	100	E. Humphreys & A. P. Day: Kent v. Somerset (Taunton) 1908
254	5th	105	E. Smith & C. E. de Trafford: North v. South (Hastings) 1893
247	2nd	105	A. Sandham & A. Ducat: Surrey v. Northants. (Oval) 1921
291	4th	105	C. G. Macartney & C. E. Pellew: Australians v. Notts. (Nottingham) 1921
255	6th	105	K. S. Duleepsinhji & M. W. Tate: Sussex v. Northants. (Hove) 1930
269	6th	107	V. T. Trumper & C. Hill: Australians v. New Zealand XI (Wellington)...1904–05
247*	6th	110	J. F. Parker & E. R. T. Holmes: Surrey v. Notts. (Nottingham) 1947
259	4th	115	C. P. Mead & Hon. L. H. Tennyson: Hants. v. Leics. (Portsmouth) 1921
258	3rd	120	E. S. B. Williams & G. J. Bryan: Army v. Royal Navy (Lord's) 1928
295	2nd	130	A. Hartley & J. T. Tyldesley: Lancs. v. Somerset (Manchester)...............1910
277	2nd	130	W. J. Edrich & D. C. S. Compton: Middx. v. Leics (Leicester) 1947
276	2nd	130	J. B. Hobbs & R. J. Gregory: Surrey v. Hants. (Southampton)...............1926
288	5th	135	A. Ducat & H. A. Peach: Surrey v. Northants. (Northampton) 1920
336	5th	145	W. H. Ponsford & H. S. B. Love: Victoria v. Tasmania (Melbourne) ...1922–23
320	6th	150	G. L. Jessop & J. H. Board: Glos. v. Sussex (Hove) 1903
371	2nd	165	J. B. Hobbs & E. G. Hayes: Surrey v. Hants. (Oval) 1909
353	3rd	165	A. Ducat & E. G. Hayes: Surrey v. Hants. (Southampton) 1919
340*	3rd	170	F. M. Worrell & E. D. Weekes: West Indies v. Leics. (Leicester) 1950
363	3rd	172	D. G. Bradman & A. F. Kippax: N.S.W. v. Queensland (Sydney) 1933–34
433	8th	180	V. T. Trumper & A. Sims: Australians v. Canterbury (Christchurch)......1913–14
385	2nd	180	E. H. Bowley & M. W. Tate: Sussex v. Northants. (Hove) 1921
399	3rd	181	R. T. Simpson & D. C. S. Compton: M.C.C. v. N.E. Transvaal (Benoni) 1948–49
363	2nd	190	A. C. MacLaren & A. Paul: Lancs. v. Somerset (Taunton) 1895
338	5th	195	R. S. Lucas & T. C. O'Brien: Middx. v. Sussex (Hove) 1895
355	3rd	200	W. Bardsley & V. S. Ransford: Australians v. Essex (Leyton) 1909
346	1st	210	L. C. H. Palairet & H. T. Hewett: Somerset v. Yorks. (Taunton) 1892
368	1st	210	E. H. Bowley & J. H. Parks: Sussex v. Glos. (Hove) 1929
424*	3rd	240	W. J. Edrich & D. C. S. Compton: Middx. v. Somerset (Lord's) 1948
487*	6th	245	G. Headley & C. C. Passailaigue: Jamaican v. Tennyson's XI (Kimpton) 1931–32
445	3rd	268	P. E. Whitelaw & W. N. Carson: Auckland v. Otago (Dunedin) 1936–37
574*	4th	335	C. L. Walcott & F. M. Worrell: Barbados v. Trinidad (Trinidad) 1945–46
490	1st	350	E. H. Bowley & John Langridge: Sussex v. Middx. (Hove) 1933

Individual Innings of Fifty Reached
with the Least Scoring Strokes

A. E. Harragin (50) scored 50 with eleven scoring strokes—5 sixes, 4 fours, 2 twos—for West Indians v. W. G. Grace's XI (Crystal Palace) 1906.

D. A. Sparks (57*) scored 50* with eleven scoring strokes for Orange Free State v. M.C.C. (Bloemfontein) 1938–39. His full innings was scored in 27 minutes as follows: 6641461666461.

C. I. J. Smith (52) scored 50* with twelve scoring strokes for Middlesex v. Kent (Maidstone) 1935. He scored the first 49 runs off three overs from A. P. Freeman and completed his 50 with a single off C. S. Marriott, the 50 being reached after only 14 minutes' batting. His innings of 52 included 4 sixes, 6 fours, 1 two and 2 singles.

C. I. J. Smith (66) scored 50* with twelve scoring strokes for Middlesex v. Gloucestershire (Bristol) 1938, the fifty being reached in eleven minutes' batting—a record. He hit Sinfield for three sixes in succession and scored five sixes off G. M. Emmett in an innings which lasted only 18 minutes. His actual scoring strokes were: 2446166616266226.

G. L. Jessop (61) scored 50* in 15 minutes by 14 scoring strokes off 17 balls for Gloucestershire v. Somerset (Bristol) 1904. He altogether scored 61 out of 73 in 24 minutes as follows: 341040144644604420241102.

F. T. Mann scored 53 in 14 scoring strokes off the 20 balls bowled to him for Middlesex v. Nottinghamshire (Lord's) 1921. The balls bowled were scored off as follows: 60244164406610440010. He was caught by G. Gunn off the 20th ball he received.

K. M. Rangnekar (102) reached 50* off the first 17 balls he received by means of 11 fours and 2 threes, for Maharashtra v. Western India States (Poona) 1939–40.

H. R. Murrell (50) scored 50 in 15 minutes for Middlesex v. Hampshire (Southampton) 1921. He scored the runs by means of 1 six, 9 fours, 3 twos and 2 singles.

Batsmen to Reach the Century Before Lunch

The feat of a batsman reaching his century prior to the lunch interval on the first day of a match is a remarkable piece of fast scoring, as it is usually achieved by opening batsmen against a fresh bowling attack. It must be remembered, however, that the length of time between the start of the day's play and the stoppage for lunch may vary from 90 to 150 minutes, but for the purpose of this record the only qualification is the actual reaching of the century prior to lunch, irrespective of the time available.

W. G. Grace (134): Gentlemen of South v. Players of South (Oval) 1873
H. H. Massie (206): Australians v. Oxford U. (Oxford) 1882
   (*This was Massie's first innings in England.*)
R. Abel (152): Surrey v. Leicestershire (Oval) 1896
T. S. Fishwick (131): Warwickshire v. Gloucestershire (Bristol) 1900
V. T. Trumper (104): Australia v. England (Manchester) 1902
T. S. Fishwick (113): Warwickshire v. Leicestershire (Leicester) 1904
J. Douglas (114): Middlesex v. Somerset (Taunton) 1904
E. H. D. Sewell (107): Essex v. Warwickshire (Birmingham) 1904
   (*Scored out of 142 for first wicket in 80 minutes.*)
J. W. Rothery (118): Yorkshire v. Hampshire (Bournemouth) 1905
V. T. Trumper (108): Australians v. Gloucestershire (Bristol) 1905
W. H. B. Evans (139*): Oxford U. v. M.C.C. (Lord's) 1905
R. H. Spooner (164): Lancashire v. Nottinghamshire (Nottingham) 1905
H. K. Foster (180): Worcestershire v. Somerset (Worcester) 1905
J. B. Hobbs (125): Surrey v. Worcestershire (Worcester) 1906
T. Hayward (135): Surrey v. Leicestershire (Oval) 1906
   (*Scored 125* out of 184–0 at lunch on first day.*)
C. L. Townsend (214): Gloucestershire v. Worcestershire (Cheltenham) 1906
   (*Scored 130* out of 214–2 at lunch on first day.*)
R. H. Spooner (240): Lancashire v. Somerset (Bath) 1906
P. F. Warner (149): Middlesex v. Surrey (Oval) 1907
G. H. Simpson-Hayward (105): Worcestershire v. Oxford U. (Oxford) 1908
   (*Went in to bat at No. 6 and scored 105 out of 140 in 80 minutes.*)
J. B. Hobbs (205): Surrey v. Hampshire (Oval) 1909
T. Hayward (106): Surrey v. Warwickshire (Oval) 1910
A. O. Jones (103): Nottinghamshire v. Gloucestershire (Nottingham) 1911
J. B. Hobbs (107): Surrey v. Gloucestershire (Bristol) 1913
F. L. Bowley (177): Worcestershire v. Warwickshire (Birmingham) 1913
J. B. Hobbs (100): Surrey v. Yorkshire (Bradford) 1914
F. L. Bowley (276): Worcestershire v. Hampshire (Dudley) 1914

J. B. Hobbs (102): Surrey v. Lancashire (Manchester) 1919
J. B. Hobbs (134): Surrey v. Leicestershire (Leicester) 1920
P. V. Williams (146): Army v. Royal Navy (Lord's) 1920
F. L. Bowley (131): Worcestershire v. Essex (Leyton) 1920
J. W. Zulch (185): Transvaal v. Orange Free State (Bloemfontein) 1920–21
A. J. Richardson (280): South Australia v. M.C.C. (Adelaide)..........................1922–23
    (*The first time the feat had been achieved in Australia.*)
A. Ducat (115): Surrey v. Cambridge U. (Oval) 1923
J. B. Hobbs (104): Surrey v. Gloucestershire (Oval) 1925
J. S. Hiddleston (212): Wellington v. Canterbury (Wellington) 1925–26
C. G. Macartney (151): Australia v. England (Leeds) 1926
A. Sandham (150): M.C.C. v. Europeans (Rawalpindi) 1926–27
M. W. Tate (133): M.C.C. v. Parsis & Europeans (Bombay) 1926–27
J. B. Hobbs (131): Surrey v. Nottinghamshire (Oval) 1927
M. W. Tate (101): Sussex v. Hampshire (Portsmouth) 1927
    (*Scored out of 144 for first wicket in 68 minutes.*)
J. M. Gregory (152): New South Wales v. New Zealanders (Sydney) 1927–28
K. S. Duleepsinhji (121): Sussex v. Glamorgan (Eastbourne) 1928
    (*Scored 102* out of 137 in 65 minutes.*)
H. H. Gibbons (107): Worcestershire v. Hampshire (Southampton) 1928
H. T. W. Hardinge (114): Kent v. Hampshire (Dover) 1928
K. S. Duleepsinhji (115): Sussex v. Kent (Hastings) 1929
D. G. Bradman (334): Australia v. England (Leeds) 1930
F. E. Woolley (110): Kent v. Surrey (Blackheath) 1930
C. A. Roach (180): West Indians v. Surrey (Oval) 1933
W. W. Keeton (110): Nottinghamshire v. Yorkshire (Bradford) 1933
D. G. Bradman (132): Australians v. Leveson-Gower's XI (Scarborough) 1934
W. R. Hammond (116): M.C.C. v. Trinidad (Trinidad) 1934–35
W. G. L. F. Lowndes (118): Hampshire v. Kent (Portsmouth) 1935
W. R. Hammond (252): Gloucestershire v. Leicestershire (Leicester) 1935
H. Gimblett (106): Somerset v. Northamptonshire (Kettering) 1936
A. H. Dyson (104): Glamorgan v. Kent (Cardiff) 1937
    (*Achieved on first day of season.*)
R. H. Moore (316): Hampshire v. Warwickshire (Bournemouth) 1937
E. Paynter (322): Lancashire v. Sussex (Hove) 1937
J. H. Parks (104): Sussex v. Nottinghamshire (Hove) 1937
A. E. Fagg (244): Kent v. Essex (Colchester)..1938
F. E. Woolley (136): Kent v. Worcestershire (Tonbridge) 1938
J. D. Robertson (154): Middlesex v. Warwickshire (Lord's) 1939
H. Gimblett (114): Somerset v. Cambridge U. (Bath) 1946
S. M. Brown (118): Middlesex v. Essex (Westcliff) 1946
J. D. Robertson (118): Middlesex v. Nottinghamshire (Nottingham) 1947
R. G. Draper (122): Eastern Province v. Griqualand West (Kimberley) 1947–48
A. R. Morris (290): Australians v. Gloucestershire (Bristol) 1948
H. Gimblett (111): Commonwealth v. Governor's XI (Nagpur) 1950–51
E. A. B. Rowan (176): Transvaal v. Rhodesia (Salisbury) 1950–51
R. G. Draper (127): Griqualand West v. Orange Free State (Bloemfontein) 1951–52
Imtiaz Ahmed (103): Pakistan v. East Zone (Jamshedpur) 1952–53
R. G. Draper (145): Griqualand West v. Rhodesia (Salisbury) 1952–53
R. G. Draper (129): Griqualand West v. Border (Kimberley) 1952–53
R. T. Simpson (101): M.C.C. v. Yorkshire (Scarborough) 1953
L. Hutton (241): Players v. Gentlemen (Scarborough) 1953
R. T. Simpson (125): Commonwealth v. Holkar (Indore) 1953–54
F. M. Worrell (110): Commonwealth v. North Zone (Amritsar) 1953–54
R. T. Simpson (147): Nottinghamshire v. Somerset (Nottingham) 1954
W. R. Endean (235): Transvaal v. Orange Free State (Johannesburg) 1954–55
    (*Score 197* at lunch after three hours' play.*)
O. C. Dawson (139): Border v. Rhodesia (East London) 1954–55
K. N. Kirton (124): Border v. Rhodesia (East London) 1954–55
    (*The above two instances were on same day in same match.*)
L. B. Koch (111): Orange Free State v. Western Province (Bloemfontein) 1954–55
D. J. McGlew (121): Natal v. Orange Free State (Bloemfontein)....................1954–55
P. N. F. Mansell (111): Rhodesia v. Griqualand West (Kimberley) 1954–55
D. O'Connell-Jones (121): Rhodesia v. Orange Free State (Salisbury) 1955–56
F. Seyfried (144): North East Transvaal v. Orange Free State (Bloemfontein) 1955–56
K. N. Kirton (111): Border v. North East Transvaal (Benoni) 1955–56
E. R. Dexter (185): Cambridge U. v. Lancashire (Cambridge) 1957
J. D. Robertson (119): Middlesex v. Sussex (Lord's) 1957
P. E. Richardson (116): Worcestershire v. Derbyshire (Derby) 1957
W. J. Stewart (151): Warwickshire v. Combined Services (Birmingham) 1959
    (*Scored 131* out of 180—1 at lunch on first day.*)
G. Pullar (103): Rest of England v. Yorkshire (Oval) 1959

LEADING CASES ON OTHER DAYS

L. C. H. Palairet (181): Somerset v. Oxford U. (Oxford) 1894
  (Score taken from 80* to 181 on third day.)
R. Abel (193): Surrey v. Derbyshire (Oval) 1900
  (101* at lunch on second day of match.)
C. Hill (142): Australia v. South Africa (Johannesburg) 1902–03
  (Score taken from 28* to 138* on third morning.)
E. H. D. Sewell (106*): Essex v. Surrey (Oval) 1904
  (Achieved on second day of match.)
S. J. Snooke (157): South Africans v. Somerset (Bath) 1907
  (Innings started on third morning.)
F. A. Tarrant (250*): Middlesex v. Essex (Leyton) 1914
J. W. Hearne (106*): Middlesex v. Essex (Leyton) 1914
  (Achieved in same match, Tarrant taking his score from 140* to 250* on second morning, while the total was advanced from 245 to 464.)
J. L. Bryan (106): Kent v. Lancashire (Maidstone) 1921
  (Achieved on second morning of match.)
C. G. Macartney (120): New South Wales v. Wellington (Wellington) 1923–24
  (Innings started on third morning, 112* at lunch.)
C. G. Macartney (120): New South Wales v. Otago (Dunedin) 1923–24
  (Score taken from 19* to 120 on third morning.)
A. Punch (176): New South Wales v. Otago (Dunedin) 1923–24
  (Score taken from 59* to 175* on third morning.)
A. E. R. Gilligan (112): Gentlemen v. Players (Oval) 1924
  (Achieved on third morning of match.)
J. B. Hobbs (211): England v. South Africa (Lord's) 1924
  (Score taken from 12* to 114* on second morning.)
A. P. F. Chapman (136): Kent v. Hampshire (Canterbury) 1926
  (104 runs scored before lunch on second morning.)
C. C. Dacre (109): Auckland v. Otago (Dunedin) 1926–27
  (Achieved on third morning of match.)
N. E. Haig (104*): Middlesex v. Nottinghamshire (Nottingham) 1927
  (Achieved on third morning—only available play in match.)
W. R. Hammond (187): Gloucestershire v. Lancashire (Manchester) 1927
  (131 out of 186 scored on third morning of match.)
W. Vorath (103): Otago v. Wellington (Dunedin) 1927–28
  (Achieved on third morning of match.)
T. F. Shepherd (132): Surrey v. Warwickshire (Oval) 1928
  (109* in 85 minutes on second morning of match.)
F. E. Woolley (198): Kent v. Derbyshire (Maidstone) 1928
  (Score taken from 52* to 170* on third morning of match.)
R. C. Blunt (221): Otago v. Canterbury (Dunedin) 1928–29
  (Score taken from 104* to 210* on third morning of match.)
H. G. Owen-Smith (129): South Africa v. England (Leeds) 1929
  (Score taken from 27* to 129 on third morning of match.)
E. T. Killick (200*): Cambridge U. v. Glamorgan (Cambridge)...1929
  (Achieved on third morning of match.)
K. S. Duleepsinhji (202): Sussex v. Essex (Leyton) 1929
  (Achieved on third morning of match, score 122* at lunch.)
D. G. Bradman (452*): New South Wales v. Queensland (Sydney) 1929–30
  (Score taken from 205* to 310* on third morning of match.)
J. L. Powell (164): Canterbury v. Otago (Christchurch)...1929–30
  (Achieved on second morning of match.)
F. T. Badcock (105): Otago v. Canterbury (Christchurch) 1931–32
  (Achieved on third morning of match.)
W. R. Hammond (336*): England v. New Zealand (Auckland) 1932–33
  (Score taken from 41* to 152* on second morning of match.)
F. E. Woolley (161): Kent v. Derbyshire (Canterbury) 1933
  (Score taken from 21* to 131* on second morning of match.)
F. R. Santall (201*): Warwickshire v. Northamptonshire (Northampton) 1933
  (Score taken from 28* to 201* in 116 minutes on third morning.)
W. R. Hammond (163): Gloucestershire v. Kent (Canterbury) 1935
  (Achieved on second morning of match.)
S. J. McCabe (189*): Australia v. South Africa (Johannesburg) 1935–36
  (Score taken from 59* to 159* on fourth morning of match.)
J. N. Grover (121): Oxford U. v. Cambridge U. (Lord's) 1937
  (Score taken from 14* to 121* on second day.)
B. P. King (124): Worcestershire v. Hampshire (Worcester) 1938
  (Achieved on second morning of match.)
D. Tallon (152): Combined XI v. New South Wales (Brisbane) 1940–41
  (Achieved on third morning of match.)

V. S. Hazare (309): Rest v. Hindus (Bombay) 1943–44
   (*Achieved on third morning of match.*)
K. R. Miller (185): Dominions XI v. England XI (Lord's) 1945
   (*Score taken from 61* to 185 on third morning of match.*)
Mushtaq Ali (108): Prince's XI v. Australian Services (New Delhi) 1945–46
   (*Achieved on second morning of match.*)
A. P. Singleton (152): Worcestershire v. Hampshire (Southampton) 1946
   (*Achieved on second morning of match.*)
B. P. King (145): Lancashire v. Gloucestershire (Gloucester) 1946
   (*Score taken from 34* to 145 on third morning of match.*)
W. J. Edrich (128): Gentlemen v. Australians (Lord's) 1948
   (*Achieved on third morning of match, 104* at lunch.*)
A. R. Morris (108*): New South Wales v. Queensland (Sydney) 1948–49
   (*Achieved on third morning of match.*)
D. C. S. Compton (300): M.C.C. v. North Eastern Transvaal (Benoni) 1948–49
   (*Score taken from 120* to 300 in 90 minutes on second morning.*)
F. B. Smith (146): Canterbury v. Auckland (Auckland) 1948–49
   (*Score taken from 13* to 116* on second morning of match.*)
L. G. Berry (141): Leicestershire v. Sussex (Hove) 1949
   (*Score taken from 9* to 115* on second morning of match.*)
T. N. Pearce (111*): Essex v. Kent (Ilford) 1949
   (*Score taken from 4* to 111* on third morning of match.*)
A. E. G. Rhodes (126): Derbyshire v. Nottinghamshire (Ilkeston) 1949
   (*Achieved on third morning of match.*)
B. Sutcliffe (100*): New Zealanders v. Essex (Southend) 1949
   (*Achieved on third morning of match.*)
L. Hutton (141): Yorkshire v. Somerset (Huddersfield) 1950
   (*Score taken from 2* to 102* on second morning of match.*)
G. Dews (101*): Worcestershire v. Hampshire (Dudley) 1950
   (*Score taken from 1* to 101* on third morning of match.*)
J. R. Reid (283): Wellington v. Otago (Wellington) 1951–52
   (*Score taken from 80* to 180* on third morning of match.*)
G. M. Emmett (117): Gloucestershire v. Nottinghamshire (Bristol) 1952
   (*Achieved on second day of match, 106* at lunch.*)
R. G. Broadbent (108): Worcestershire v. Leicestershire (Leicester) 1952
   (*Achieved on third day of match.*)
W. H. H. Sutcliffe (171*): Yorkshire v. Worcestershire (Worcester) 1952
   (*Score taken from 70* to 171* on second day of match.*)
R. N. Harvey (180): Australians v. Glamorgan (Swansea) 1953
   (*Score taken from 20* to 152* on second morning of match.*)
D. J. Insole (114*): Essex v. Nottinghamshire (Southend) 1955
T. E. Bailey (114*): Essex v. Nottinghamshire (Southend) 1955
   (*These two instances were achieved on the third day, Insole 9* and Bailey 12* at the start
   of play.*)
A. C. Walton (116*): Oxford U. v. Sussex (Hove) 1956
   (*Achieved on second morning of match.*)
J. W. Burke (125*): Australians v. Somerset (Taunton) 1956
   (*Score taken from 10* to 125* on third morning of match.*)
P. E. Richardson (134): Worcestershire v. Nottinghamshire (Worcester) 1956
   (*Score taken from 12* to 122* on third morning of match.*)
R. E. Marshall (163): Hampshire v. Glamorgan (Portsmouth) 1957
   (*Achieved on second morning of match, score 104* at lunch.*)
D. C. S. Compton (109): Middlesex v. Essex (Leyton).....................................1957
   (*Score taken from 1* to 104* on second morning of match.*)
M. C. Cowdrey (165): Kent v. Nottinghamshire (Nottingham) 1957
   (*Achieved on second morning of match.*)
L. Favell (190): Australians v. Griqualand West (Kimberley) 1957–58
   (*Score taken from 53* to 167* on third morning of match.*)
R. A. Gale (106): Middlesex v. Kent (Gravesend) 1959
   (*Achieved on third morning of match.*)
W. J. Stewart (155): Warwickshire v. Lancashire (Blackpool) 1959
   (*Achieved on second morning of match, score 107* at lunch.*)
M. J. K. Smith (200*): Warwickshire v. Worcestershire (Birmingham)............1959
   (*Score taken from 77* to 200* on third morning of match.*)
M. J. K. Smith (182*): Warwickshire v. Gloucestershire (Stroud) 1959
   (*Score taken from 12* to 124* on third morning of match.*)
J. Pressdee (107*): Glamorgan v. Kent (Dartford) 1959
   (*Achieved on third morning of match.*)
E. R. Dexter (107): M.C.C. v. Leeward Islands (Antigua) 1959–60
   (*Achieved in 85 minutes on third morning of match.*)
E. R. Dexter (133): Sussex v. Somerset (Taunton) 1960
   (*Achieved on third morning of match.*)

R. E. Marshall (111): Hampshire v. Leicestershire (Bournemouth) 1960
  (*Score taken from 0* to 111 on third morning of match.*)
K. F. Barrington (111): Players v. Gentlemen (Scarborough) 1960
  (*Score taken from 8* to 111 on third morning of match.*)

MOST RUNS IN PRE-LUNCH SESSION

197 W. R. Endean (235): Transvaal v. Orange Free State (Johannesburg) 1954–55
  (*In three hours on first morning of match.*)
180 D. C. S. Compton (300): M.C.C. v. North East Transvaal (Benoni) 1948–49
  (*Score taken from 120* to 300 in 90 minutes on second day.*)
173 F. R. Santall (201*): Warwickshire v. Northamptonshire (Northampton) 1933
  (*Score taken from 28* to 201* in 116 minutes on third day.*)
164 J. L. Powell (164): Canterbury v. Otago (Christchurch) 1929–30
  (*In 130 minutes on second morning of match.*)
146 P. V. Williams (146): Army v. Royal Navy (Lord's) 1920
  (*In 100 minutes on first morning of match.*)
141* E. T. Killick (200*): Cambridge U. v. Glamorgan (Cambridge) 1929
  (*On third morning of match.*)

Batsmen Who Have Scored 300 Runs in a Day's Play

345 C. G. Macartney (345): Australians v. Nottinghamshire (Nottingham) 1921. The runs were scored out of 540 in 235 minutes on the first day, including 4 sixes and 47 fours. He completed 100* in 95 minutes, 200* in 145 minutes and 300* in 205 minutes. The highest score by a touring batsman. He was missed in the slips when 6.
334 W. H. Ponsford (352): Victoria v. New South Wales (Melbourne) 1926–27. He scored 334 out of 573—1 in 322 minutes on the second day. Altogether he hit 36 fours in a stay of six hours, reaching 100* in 125 minutes, 200* in 203 minutes and 300* in 285 minutes. The innings total reached 1107—the world record.
333 K. S. Duleepsinhji (333): Sussex v. Northamptonshire (Hove) 1930. Runs scored out of 513 in 5½ hours on the first day of the match, including 1 six and 34 fours. He reached 100* in 140 minutes, 200* in 245 minutes and 300* in 315 minutes.
331* J. D. Robertson (331*): Middlesex v. Worcestershire (Worcester) 1949. The runs, including 2 sixes and 39 fours, were scored in 6½ hours on the first day out of a total of 623 for five wickets.
322 E. Paynter (322): Lancashire v. Sussex (Hove) 1937. Runs scored out of 546 in 5 hours on the first day of the match, the century being reached before lunch, and altogether included 3 sixes and 39 fours.
318 C. W. Gregory (383): New South Wales v. Queensland (Brisbane) 1906–07. Runs scored in 345 minutes, including 55 fours, his score being taken from 48* to 366* on the second day.
316 R. H. Moore (316): Hampshire v. Warwickshire (Bournemouth) 1937. Runs scored out of 509 in 380 minutes on first day of match, including 3 sixes and 43 fours. This innings was scored on the same day as Paynter's above, and also included a century before lunch.
315 R. C. Blunt (338*): Otago v. Canterbury (Christchurch) 1931–32. Runs scored in 320 minutes on the third day, the innings ending on the fourth morning. The runs were scored out of 540 in 5½ hours and included 41 fours.
309 D. G. Bradman (334): Australia v. England (Leeds) 1930. Bradman batted 340 minutes on the first day to score 309 out of 456, completing his century (105) before lunch, and being 220* at tea. He took his score to 334 on the second morning, hitting 46 fours, and scoring in all 334 out of 506 in 375 minutes.
307 W. H. Ashdown (332): Kent v. Essex (Brentwood) 1934. Scored in 6 hours out of 623 runs on the first day of the match, the innings ending at 332 on the second morning. He hit 1 six and 45 fours.
306 A. Ducat (306*): Surrey v. Oxford U. (Oval) 1919. Scored in 280 minutes on first day of match, the first 100 taking 120 minutes, the remaining 206 taking 160 minutes. During the innings successive scoring strokes were: 4444454444, the complete innings including 3 fives and 47 fours.
305 F. R. Foster (305*): Warwickshire v. Worcestershire (Dudley) 1914. Runs scored in 260 minutes including 1 five and 44 fours out of 448 on the second day of the match.

Most Runs Scored by a Side in a Day's Play

721—10	Australians (721) v. Essex at Southend	1948
651—2	West Indians (682—2d) v. Leicestershire at Leicester	1950
649—8	New South Wales (752—8d) v. Otago at Dunedin	1923–24
645—4	Surrey (742) v. Hampshire at the Oval	1909
644—8	Oxford U. (644—8d) v. Leveson-Gower's XI at Eastbourne	1921
640—8	Lancashire (640—8d) v. Sussex at Hove	1937
636—7	Free Foresters (636—7d) v. Cambridge U. at Cambridge	1938
625—6	Gloucestershire (625—6d) v. Worcestershire at Dudley	1934
623—2	Kent (803—4d) v. Essex at Brentwood	1934
623—5	Middlesex (623—5d) v. Worcestershire at Worcester	1949
621—6	Lancashire (676—6d) v. Hampshire at Manchester	1911
621—8	Australians (658) v. Auckland at Auckland	1913–14
616—5	Surrey (616—5d) v. Northamptonshire at the Oval	1921
608—7	Australians (675) v. Nottinghamshire at Nottingham	1921
608—7	Players (651—7d) v. Gentlemen at the Oval	1934
607—3	Hampshire (672—7d) v. Somerset at Taunton	1899
607—6	Kent (607—6d) v. Gloucestershire at Cheltenham	1910
607—4	Surrey (619—5d) v. Northamptonshire at Northampton	1920
603—5	Rest of England (603—5d) v. Middlesex at the Oval	1920

The following matches have provided instances of over 600 runs being scored on one of the days.

666	Northamptonshire (59—2) v. Surrey (607—4 at Northampton	1920
663	Leicestershire (160—2) v. Middlesex (503—4) at Leicester	1947
649	Hampshire (570—8) v. Somerset (79—3) at Taunton	1901
647	Sussex (115) v. Surrey (532—6) at the Oval	1919
639	Hampshire (245—7 & 63—0) v. Gloucestershire (331—4) at Southampton	1919
626	Leicestershire (291) v. Nottinghamshire (335—4) at Nottingham	1919
626	Surrey (337—2) v. Hampshire (289) at Southampton	1919
622	Essex (99—2) v. Sussex (523) at Leyton	1919
619	Rest of England (603—5) v. Middlesex (16—2) at the Oval	1920
616	Transvaal (557) v. Orange Free State (59—6) at Johannesburg	1929–30
613	Worcestershire (6—1 & 47—1) v. Essex (560—5d) at Leyton	1921
610	Kent (544) v. Essex (66—3) at Gravesend	1938
608	Oxford U. (329—6) v. Somerset (279) at Oxford	1901
604	Natal (553) v. Orange Free State (51—3) at Bloemfontein	1954–55
602	Lancashire (408) v. Essex (194—3) at Manchester	1919
601	Surrey (361—5) v. Middlesex (240) at the Oval	1919

Owing to the longer hours of play in two-day matches in South Africa, there have been several cases of over 600 runs in a single day's play.

720—15 wkts	Orange Free State (412—5) v. Border (308) at Bloemfontein	1920–21
665—20 wkts	Transvaal (326) v. Rest of South Africa (339) at Johannesburg	1911–12
661—20 wkts	Griqualand West (460) v. Border (201) at Kimberley	1920–21
645—16 wkts	Transvaal (450—9) v. Orange Free State (195—7) at Johannesburg	1920–21
644—12 wkts	Natal (587) v. Eastern Province (57—2) at Durban	1939–40
641—12 wkts	Transvaal (499) v. Sherwell's XI (142—2) at Johannesburg	1913–14
606— 9 wkts	Griqualand West (378—5) v. Orange Free State (228—4) at Pretoria	1923–24

Fast Scoring by Sides

A list of the innings of over 200 in which the runs have been scored at the rate of 105 runs per 100 balls or more is given.

Runs per
100 balls

156	219—2	Kent v. Gloucestershire (Dover)	1937
132	279—1	Nottinghamshire v. Leicestershire (Nottingham)	1949
123	267—4d	Hampshire v. Essex (Bournemouth)	1919
121	460	Griqualand West v. Border (Kimberley)	1920–21
115	313	Gentlemen of South v. Players of South (Hastings)	1907
111	234—3	Kent v. Surrey (Oval)	1939
110	338—5d	Kent v. Somerset (Taunton)	1906
110	448	New South Wales v. Tasmania (Hobart)	1909–10
109	224—4	Transvaal v. Griqualand West (Kimberley)	1889–90
108	574—4d	M.C.C. v. Tasmania (Hobart)	1911–12
107	394—4d	Cambridge U. v. M.C.C. (Cambridge)	1914
105	463	Transvaal v. Orange Free State (Bloemfontein)	1920–21

Most Runs Scored in One Hit

The highest number of runs scored in one stroke is ten, but this hit was recorded under the 'net-system' of scoring that was in trial use during the 1900 season. Where known the name of the unfortunate bowler is given.

TEN

S. H. Hill-Wood off C. J. Burnup: Derby v. M.C.C. (Lord's) 1900

NINE

Hon. F. Ponsonby off name unknown: M.C.C. v. Cambridge U. (Cambridge) 1842
T. A. Raynes off name unknown: Gentlemen of Surrey & Sussex v. Gentlemen of England (Lord's) 1856
T. Hearne off name unknown: Middlesex v. Surrey (Oval) 1870
R. Daft off I. D. Walker: Players v. Gentlemen (Oval) 1872
C. Hill off T. Richardson: Australians v. Surrey (Oval) 1902
J. A. Cuffe off name unknown: Worcestershire v. Philadelphians (Worcester) 1903
R. A. Duff off W. Brearley: Australians v. Gentlemen (Crystal Palace) 1905
Hon. J. B. Coventry off C. W. L. Parker: Worcestershire v. Gloucestershire (Worcester) 1923
A. Ducat off J. H. Parks: Surrey v. Sussex (Oval) 1929
A. Staples off E. W. Clark: Nottinghamshire v. Northamptonshire (Kettering) 1932
J. D. Robertson off H. S. Squires: M.C.C. v. Surrey (Lord's) 1948
W. J. Edrich off V. H. Broderick: Middlesex v. Northamptonshire (Lord's) 1949

The hit for nine by Hon. F. Ponsonby in 1842 was made without the assistance of overthrows.
C. C. Case, playing for Somerset v. Surrey (Oval) 1925, hit a six all-run off a direct hit off the fourth ball of an over from P. G. H. Fender, and followed with a direct hit for five all-run off the last ball of the same over.
T. G. Evans, playing for Players v. Gentlemen (Lord's) 1949, straight drove a ball from T. E. Bailey to long on, six runs being added before the ball, which stopped on the edge of the boundary, was returned to the wicket.

Most Runs Scored off One Over

FOUR BALL OVERS

22 (6466) H. J. H. Scott off S. Wade: Australians v. Yorks. (Sheffield) 1886
20 (6446) C. I. Thornton off D. Buchanan: Cambridge U. v. Gentlemen (Cambridge).........1871
20 (6446) G. J. Bonnor off A. P. Lucas: Australians v. I. Zingari (Scarborough) 1882

FIVE BALL OVERS

21 (54444) E. Jones and W. P. Howell off E. R. Wilson: Australians v. Cambridge U.
(Cambridge).........1899
21 (66414) A. E. Trott and C. M. Wells off E. J. Tyler: Middx. v. Somerset (Taunton)...........1899

SIX BALL OVERS

34 (4664446) E. Alletson off E. H. Killick: Notts. v. Sussex (Hove) 1911
(The over included two no-balls)
32 (664664) C. Smart off G. Hill: Glamorgan v. Hants. (Cardiff)....................................1935
31 (666661) A. W. Wellard off F. E. Woolley: Somerset v. Kent (Wells) 1938
30 (466464) D. G. Bradman off A. P. Freeman: Australians v. England XI (Folkestone) ...1934
30 (444646) H. B. Cameron off H. Verity: South Africans v. Yorks (Sheffield) 1935
30 (066666) A. W. Wellard off T. R. Armstrong: Somerset v. Derby (Wells) 1936
30 (446646) P. L. Winslow off J. T. Ikin: South Africans v. Lancs. (Manchester) 1955
28 (444446) G. L. Jessop off L. C. Braund: Glos. v. Somerset (Bristol) 1904
28 (466246) G. L. Jessop off R. D. Burrows: Glos. v. Worcs. (Stourbridge) 1910
28 (666046) H. L. Hazell off H. Verity: Somerset v. Yorks . (Bath) 1936
28 (664444) H. T. Bartlett off T. P. B. Smith: Gentlemen v. Players (Lord's) 1938
28 (066646) J. H. de Courcy off W. T. Greensmith: Australians v. Essex (Southend) 1953
28 (644446) J. E. McConnon off N. I. Thomson: Glamorgan v. Sussex (Cardiff).............1955
28 (66664) D. W. White off J. D. Piachand: Hants. v. Oxford U. (Oxford) 1960
27 (664641) H. L. Simms off J. Gunn: Sussex v. Notts. (Hove) 1912

27 (466443)   J. M. Allan off V. E. Jackson: Oxford U. v. Leics. (Oxford) 1955
27 (346662)   D. E. V. Padgett and J. V. Wilson off J. M. Allan: Yorks v. Kent (Scarborough)...1956
26 (66644)   B. E. Gordon off name unknown: Border v. Eastern Province (Kingwilliamstown)
                                                                                     1903–04
26 (66644)   C. Hill off K. M. Ollivier: Australians v. New Zealand XI (Wellington) 1904–05
26 (646442)   A. Cotter off J. V. Saunders: N.S.W. v. Victoria (Melbourne) 1905–06
26 (444446)   G. L. Jessop off A. E. Relf: Gentlemen of South v. Players of South (Hastings)...1907
26 (66644)   G. L. Jessop off D. W. Carr: Londesborough's XI v. Kent (Scarborough) 1913
26 (444626)   G. F. Earle off F. E. Woolley: Somerset v. Kent (Gravesend) 1925
26 (644444)   A. H. H. Gilligan off J. T. Bell: Sussex v. Glamorgan (Eastbourne) 1928
26 (026666)   J. H. Parsons off O. C. Scott: Warwicks. v. West Indies (Birmingham) 1928
26 (666440)   A. M. Crawley off V. W. C. Jupp: Oxford U. v. Northants. (Wellingborough)...1929
26 (66644)   H. W. Stephenson off R. O. Jenkins: Somerset v. Worcs. (Kidderminster) 1954
26 (446046)   G. Cox off R. T. D. Perks: Sussex v. Worcs. (Dudley) 1955
26 (46444400) P. Burge off A. K. Walker: Australians v. Notts. (Nottingham) 1956
                   (*The over included two no-balls.*)
26 (626606)   J. Flavell off D. J. Shepherd: Worcs. v. Glamorgan (Swansea) 1956
26 (46664)   T. G. Evans off I. W. Johnson: Pearce's XI v. Australians (Scarborough) 1956

P. L. Winslow, playing for South Africans v. Lancashire (Manchester) 1955, hit 30 runs off an over by J. T. Ikin and then hit a 4 and 6 off F. Goodwin from the next two balls he received, thus scoring 40 runs off eight balls bowled to him.

EIGHT BALL OVERS

32 (34166066) D. K. Carmody (41) and I. D. Craig (366066) off I. W. Johnson: Morris's XI
                   v. Hassett's VI (Melbourne) 1953–54
31 (62460661) J. Mercer off R. Howorth: Glamorgan v. Worcs. (Cardiff) 1939
29 (1446644–) H. Jordaan (1) and P. G. Van der Byl (446644) off J. Buchanan: Western
                   Province v. Eastern Province (Cape Town) 1937–38

A. H. Bakewell hit T. F. Smailes for 444440, off the first over of the innings, Northamptonshire v. Yorkshire (Harrogate) 1935.
For Yorkshire v. Essex (Scarborough) 1932, H. Sutcliffe and M. Leyland scored 102 runs off 6 overs from both ends, four overs from K. Farnes being hit to the extent of 75 runs.

Most Sixes in an Innings

The increase in hits for six in the early years of this century is due to the change of scoring laws in 1910—prior to that date it was necessary to hit the ball out of the ground to score six, but in 1910 the law was amended and now it is only necessary to hit the ball out of the playing area.

ELEVEN

C. K. Nayudu (153): Hindus v. M.C.C. (Bombay) 1926–27
C. J. Barnett (194): Gloucestershire v. Somerset (Bath) 1934
R. Benaud (135): Australians v. Pearce's XI (Scarborough) 1953

TEN

H. L. Simms (126): Sussex v. Nottinghamshire (Hove) 1912
A. M. Crawley (204): Oxford U. v. Northamptonshire (Wellingborough) 1929
W. R. Hammond (336*): England v. New Zealand (Auckland) 1932–33
H. Sutcliffe (113): Yorkshire v. Northamptonshire (Kettering) 1933
W. J. Stewart (155): Warwickshire v. Lancashire (Blackpool) 1959

NINE

C. I. Thornton (124): Kent v. Sussex (Tunbridge Wells) 1869
P. J. Heather (109*): Transvaal v. Border (Durban) 1910–11
M. C. Bird (151): Surrey v. Sussex (Hove) 1911
H. Gimblett (141): Somerset v. Hampshire (Wells) 1937
E. Paynter (158): M.C.C. v. Griqualand West (Kimberley) 1938–39
G. J. Whittaker (148): Surrey v. Northamptonshire (Northampton) 1949
D. V. Smith (166): Sussex v. Gloucestershire (Hove) 1957

EIGHT

C. I. Thornton (107*): Gentlemen of England v. I Zingari (Scarborough) 1886
K. G. MacLeod (128): Lancashire v. Somerset (Bath) 1909
E. Alletson (189): Nottinghamshire v. Sussex (Hove) 1911
F. E. Woolley (215): Kent v. Somerset (Gravesend) 1925
A. W. Carr (206): Nottinghamshire v. Leicestershire (Leicester) 1925
G. F. Earle (130) M.C.C. v. Hindus (Bombay) 1926–27
C. C. Dacre (176): New Zealanders v. Derbyshire (Derby) 1927
E. R. T. Holmes (236): Oxford U. v. Free Foresters (Oxford) 1927
G. M. Lee (141*): Derbyshire v. Northamptonshire (Northampton).............................1931
H. Sutcliffe (132): Yorkshire v. Gloucestershire (Bradford).....................................1932
C. I. J. Smith (66): Middlesex v. Gloucestershire (Bristol) 1938
I. L. Bula (102): Fiji v. Canterbury (Christchurch) 1953–54
F. M. Worrell (101): A. E. R. Gilligan's XI v. New Zealanders (Hastings) 1958
P. Marner (95): Lancashire v. New Zealanders (Blackpool) 1958

Hits for Six off Consecutive Balls

FIVE SIXES OFF FIVE BALLS

A. W. Wellard off T. R. Armstrong: Somerset v. Derby (Wells) 1936
A. W. Wellard off F. E. Woolley: Somerset v. Kent (Wells) 1938

FOUR SIXES OFF FOUR BALLS

R. E. Foster off W. G. Grace: Oxford U. v. London County (Oxford) 1900
E. R. T. Holmes off J. C. Masterman and I. P. F. Campbell: Oxford U. v. Free Foresters
                                            (Oxford).............1927
J. H. Parsons off O. C. Scott: Warwicks. v. West Indians (Birmingham) 1928
A. Jepson off J. H. Wardle: Notts. v. Yorks. (Bradford)..1952
R. Benaud off R. Tattersall: Australians v. Pearce's XI (Scarborough) 1953

THREE SIXES OFF THREE BALLS

C. Hill off K. M. Ollivier: Australians v. New Zealand XI (Wellington) 1904–05
C. P. Carter off R. W. Sievwright: South Africans v. Scotland (Edinburgh) 1912
E. Alletson off W. Rhodes: Notts. v. Yorks. (Dewsbury) 1913
F. Barratt off W. Rhodes: Notts. v. Yorks. (Sheffield)...1919
F. T. Mann off M. W. Tate: Middx. v. Sussex (Hove) 1920
A. W. Carr off F. E. Woolley: Gentlemen v. Players (Scarborough) 1922
E. P. Hewetson off T. S. Jennings: Oxford U. v. Surrey (Oval) 1923
A. G. Liddell off R. W. V. Robins: Northants. v. Cambridge U. (Northampton) 1928
F. Barratt off V. W. C. Jupp: Notts. v. Northants. (Northampton) 1928
E. Hendren off J. Iddon: Rest of England v. Lancs. (Oval) 1928
L. N. Constantine off W. W. Whysall: West Indians v. Notts. (Nottingham) 1928
C. Wright off R. W. V. Robins: Kent v. Middx. (Dover) 1929
A. M. Crawley off V. W. C. Jupp: Oxford U. v. Northants. (Wellingborough) 1929
J. M. Hutchinson off C. F. Root: Derby v. Worcs. (Derby) 1931
G. M. Lee off V. W. C. Jupp: Derby v. Northants. (Northampton) 1931
E. T. Killick off T. W. Goddard: Middx. v. Glos. (Clifton) 1932
W. R. Hammond off J. Newman: England v. New Zealand (Auckland) 1932–33
G. Pearce off E. L. G. Hoad: Sussex v. West Indians (Hove) 1933
H. B. Cameron off R. Howorth: South Africans v. Worcs. (Worcester) 1935
H. B. Cameron off H. Verity: South Africans v. Yorks. (Sheffield) 1935
A. V. Pope off J. W. Lee: Derby v. Somerset (Derby) 1935
H. Larwood off G. S. Boyes: Notts. v. Hants. (Nottingham) 1935
A. E. Watt off R. A. Sinfield: Kent v. Glos. (Gravesend) 1936
W. Voce off T. W. Goddard: Notts. v. Glos. (Nottingham) 1936
H. Gimblett off P. F. Jackson: Somerset v. Worcs. (Yeovil) 1936
R. T. D. Perks off A. P. Freeman: Worcs. v. Kent (Worcester) 1936
R. T. D. Perks off W. Murray-Wood: Worcs. v. Oxford U. (Oxford) 1936
H. L. Hazell off H. Verity: Somerset v. Yorks. (Bath) 1936
J. C. Clay off James Langridge: Glamorgan v. Sussex (Hastings) 1937
D. G. Bradman off S. L. Putman: Australian XI v. Tasmania (Hobart)...................1937–38
C. I. J. Smith off R. A. Sinfield: Middx. v. Glos. (Bristol) 1938
L. L. Wilkinson off R. Howorth: Lancs. v. Worcs. (Manchester) 1938

I

A. E. Watt off S. H. Martin: Kent v. Worcs. (Gillingham)..1939
A. W. Wellard off D. V. P. Wright: Somerset v. Kent (Maidstone) 1939
H. T. Bartlett off E. P. Robinson: Sussex v. Yorks. (Bradford) 1947
K. R. Miller off C. J. Knott: Australians v. Hants. (Southampton)..............................1948
R. T. D. Perks off J. M. Sims: Worcs. v. Middx. (Lord's)..1948
K. Grieves off G. O. Rabone: Lancs. v. New Zealanders (Manchester)........................1949
G. J. Whittaker off V. H. Broderick: Surrey v. Northants. (Northampton) 1949
A. W. Wellard off W. E. Hollies: Somerset v. Warwicks. (Birmingham) 1949
G. Lambert off R. O. Jenkins: Glos. v. Worcs. (Dudley) 1949
H. Gimblett off J. E. McConnon: Somerset v. Glamorgan (Ebbw Vale) 1951
C. J. Scott off E. Smith: Glos. v. Derby (Buxton) 1952
W. S. Surridge off J. T. Ikin: South v. North (Kingston) 1952
R. T. Simpson off R. Illingworth: M.C.C. v. Yorks. (Scarborough)............................1953
J. H. de Courcy off W. T. Greensmith: Australians v. Essex (Southend) 1953
J. V. Wilson off J. M. Allan: Yorks. v. Kent (Scarborough) 1956
T. G. Evans off I. W. Johnson: Pearce's XI v. Australians (Scarborough)....................1956
T. W. Graveney off R. Maragh: Norfolk's XI v. Jamaica (Kingston) 1956–57
V. Mankad off R. R. Shelke: Rajasthan v. Vidarbha (Udaipur) 1957–58
D. B. Close off T. Greenhough: Yorks. v. M.C.C. (Lord's) 1959
J. B. Mortimore off J. S. Manning: England XI v. Commonwealth (Hastings) 1959

Other famous items of 'six-hitting' include:

G. M. Lee (141*), playing for Derbyshire v. Northamptonshire (Northampton) 1931, hit 8 sixes off the bowling of V. W. C. Jupp.

H. T. Bartlett (94), playing for Sussex v. Yorkshire (Leeds) 1938, hit the bowling of H. Verity for 7 sixes, six of them in the course of two consecutive overs as follows: 062660 and 006606.

H. Gimblett (70), playing for Somerset v. Glamorgan (Swansea) 1948, hit the bowling of B. L. Muncer for 6 sixes in 13 balls as follows: 6640060606006.

Most Sixes in a Match

W. J. Stewart, playing for Warwickshire v. Lancashire (Blackpool) 1959, hit 17 sixes—10 in a first innings of 155 and 7 in a second innings of 125.

A. W. Wellard, playing for Somerset v. Kent (Wells) 1938, hit 11 sixes—7 in a first innings of 57 and 4 in a second innings of 37.

G. J. Whittaker, playing for Surrey v. Northamptonshire (Northampton) 1949, hit 11 sixes—9 in a first innings of 148 and 2 in a second innings of 89*.

K. G. MacLeod, playing for Lancashire v. Somerset (Bath) 1909, hit 10 sixes—8 in a first innings of 128 and 2 in a second innings of 48.

A. W. Wellard, playing for Somerset v. Kent (Maidstone) 1935, hit 10 sixes—4 in a first innings of 74 and 6 in a second innings of 70.

A. E. Watt, playing for Kent v. Gloucestershire (Gravesend) 1936, hit 10 sixes—4 in a first innings of 24 and 6 in a second innings of 54. Watt hit 7 sixes off the first sixteen balls bowled to him in the match, four in the first innings and three in the second—all the sixes were off the bowling of R. A. Sinfield.

H. Gimblett, playing for Somerset v. Hampshire (Wells) 1937, hit 10 sixes—9 in a first innings of 141 and 1 in a second innings of 35.

G. J. Whittaker, playing for North v. South (Kingston) 1949, hit 10 sixes—4 in a first innings of 109 and 6 in a second innings of 84*.

Most Boundaries in an Innings

Some of the larger individual innings have contained a large number of strokes that reached the boundary, including hits for five. The following innings have contained the highest number of strokes to the boundary:

6s	5s	4s		
—	—	68	P. A. Perrin (343*): Essex v. Derby (Chesterfield)	1904
—	—	64	Hanif Mohammed (499): Karachi v. Bahawalpur (Karachi)	1958–59
1	—	62	A. C. MacLaren (424): Lancs. v. Somerset (Taunton)	1895
—	—	55	C. W. Gregory (383): N.S.W. v. Queensland (Brisbane)	1906–07
1	—	53	G. H. Hirst (341): Yorks. v. Leics. (Leicester)	1905
—	—	52	A. D. Nourse sen. (304*): Natal v. Transvaal (Johannesburg)	1919–20
4	—	48	D. G. Bradman (369): South Australia v. Tasmania (Adelaide)	1935–36
—	—	51	W. G. Grace (344): M.C.C. v. Kent (Canterbury)	1876

6s	5s	4s		
4	—	47	C. G. Macartney (345): Australians v. Notts. (Nottingham)	1921
1	—	49	B. B. Nimbalkar (443*): Maharashtra v. Western India States (Poona)	1948–49
3	—	46	B. Sutcliffe (385): Otago v. Canterbury (Christchurch)	1952–53
—	—	49	P. Holmes (275): Yorks. v. Warwicks. (Bradford)	1928
—	—	49	D. G. Bradman (452*): N.S.W. v. Queensland (Sydney)	1929–30
—	3	47	A. Ducat (306*): Surrey v. Oxford U. (Oval)	1919
4	—	44	C. R. Maxwell (268): Cahn's XI v. Leics. (Nottingham)	1935
—	—	48	J. T. Brown (300): Yorks. v. Derby (Chesterfield)	1898
—	—	48	J. Tunnicliffe (243): Yorks. v. Derby (Chesterfield)	1898
—	1	46	W. W. Read (338): Surrey v. Oxford U. (Oval)	1888
3	—	44	V. T. Trumper (293): Australians v. Canterbury (Christchurch)	1913–14
5	—	42	D. C. S. Compton (300): M.C.C. v. N.E. Transvaal (Benoni)	1948–49
2	—	45	D. P. B. Morkel (251): Cahn's XI v. South Americans (Nottingham)	1932
1	—	46	P. Holmes (277*): Yorks. v. Northants. (Harrogate)	1921
—	—	47	W. H. Ashdown (305*): Kent v. Derby (Dover)	1935
1	7	38	R. Abel (357*): Surrey v. Somerset (Oval)	1899
1	—	45	W. H. Ashdown (332): Kent v. Essex (Brentwood)	1934
—	—	46	D. G. Bradman (334): Australia v. England (Leeds)	1930
3	—	43	R. H. Moore (316): Hants. v. Warwicks. (Bournemouth)	1937
—	—	45	R. M. Poore (304): Hants. v. Somerset (Taunton)	1899
2	—	43	D. G. Bradman (304): Australia v. England (Leeds)	1934
2	—	43	F. E. Woolley (305*): M.C.C. v. Tasmania (Hobart)	1911–12
—	1	44	F. R. Foster (305*): Warwicks. v. Worcs. (Dudley)	1914
—	—	45	J. T. Brown (311): Yorks. v. Sussex (Sheffield)	1897

Innings in which a High Percentage of the Runs were Scored by Boundary Hits

Some innings by the famous hitters of the game have been scored by means of a very large percentage of hits to the boundary. The outstanding cases are as follows:

6s	4s		Inns.		
5	3	(42)	42	F. Barratt: Notts. v. Northants. (Northampton)	1928
5	3	(42)	42	A. E. Watt: Kent v. Notts. (Nottingham)	1933
1	9	(42)	42	H. L. Johnson: Derby v. Hants. (Southampton)	1960
1	10	(46)	51*	C. A. Rowland: Wales v. Minor Counties (Colwyn Bay)	1930
3	7	(46)	51*	P. G. Van der Byl: Western Province v. Eastern Province (Cape Town)	1937–38
—	12	(48)	52	P. G. H. Fender: Surrey v. Glamorgan (Oval)	1924
4	6	(48)	52	C. I. J. Smith: Middx. v. Kent (Maidstone)	1935
4	6	(48)	53	F. T. Mann: Middx. v. Notts. (Lord's)	1921
4	6	(48)	53	J. Oakes: Sussex v. Middx. (Lord's)	1949
1	11	(50)	54*	J. H. de Courcy: Australians v. Hants. (Southampton)	1953
—	13	(52)	55	V. W. C. Jupp: Northants. v. Notts. (Nottingham)	1928
7	13	(54)	57*	D. A. Sparks: O.F.S. v. M.C.C. (Bloemfontein)	1938–39
—	14	(56)	64	M. W. Payne: Cambridge U. v. Oxford U. (Lord's)	1906
4	8	(56)	61	O. W. Herman: Hants. v. Somerset (Wells)	1937
4	8	(56)	65*	F. Barratt: Notts. v. Kent (Nottingham)	1930
1	13	(58)	68	A. P. F. Chapman: Gentlemen v. Players (Folkestone)	1933
3	10	(58)	68	A. E. Watt: Kent v. Notts. (Nottingham)	1933
3	10	(58)	66	D. B. Close: Yorks. v. Surrey (Bradford)	1949
5	7	(58)	62	D. M. Sayer: Oxford U. v. Notts. (Oxford)	1959
4	9	(60)	67*	L. N. Constantine: West Indians v. Notts. (Nottingham)	1928
2	12	(60)	62	J. B. Statham: Lancs. v. Leics. (Manchester)	1955
—	16	(64)	73*	N. V. C. Turner: Notts. v. Middx. (Lord's)	1907
4	10	(64)	73	C. H. Knott: Kent v. Warwicks. (Tonbridge)	1930
6	7	(64)	74	J. H. Wardle: Yorks. v. South Africans (Sheffield)	1955
—	17	(68)	77	P. F. Warner: Middx. v. Somerset (Taunton)	1907
6	8	(68)	80	H. Larwood: Notts. v. Lancs. (Nottingham)	1934
6	9	(72)	79	O. G. Smith: West Indians v. Ames's XI (Hastings)	1957
7	8	(74)	81	C. G. Pepper: N.S.W. v. Queensland (Brisbane)	1939–40
—	19	(76)	82	A. E. Wilson: Glos. v. Worcs. (Cheltenham)	1953
5	12	(78)	86	L. C. Eastman: Essex v. Glamorgan (Westcliff)	1937
2	17	(80)	91*	P. G. H. Fender: Surrey v. Leics. (Leicester)	1922
—	21	(84)	99	E. R. Dexter: Sussex v. Kent (Tunbridge Wells)	1959
7	11	(86)	106	J. E. Walsh: Leics. v. Essex (Loughborough)	1948
—	22	(88)	102	R. C. M. Kimpton: Oxford U. v. Lancs. (Oxford)	1936

6s	4s		Inns.		
2	19	(88)	110	R. A. McLean: South Africans v. Gilligan's XI (Hastings)	1960
3	19	(94)	112	M. Leyland: Yorks. v. Kent (Gravesend)	1930
5	16	(94)	113*	P. G. H. Fender: Surrey v. Northants. (Northampton)	1920
8	12	(96)	107*	C. I. Thornton: Gentlemen v. I Zingari (Scarborough)	1886
—	24	(96)	114	A. J. Watkins: Glamorgan v. Worcs. (Swansea)	1953
—	25	(100)	115	G. J. Bonnor: Australians v. Yorks. (Bradford)	1888
4	20	(104)	125*	E. M. Sprot: Hants. v. Glos. (Bristol)	1911
1	25	(106)	120	K. J. Key: Leveson-Gower's XI v. Oxford U. (Oxford)	1902
7	17	(110)	143	H. Gimblett: Somerset v. Northants. (Bath)	1936
7	18	(114)	139*	F. Barratt: Notts. v. Warwicks. (Coventry)	1928
9	16	(118)	141	H. Gimblett: Somerset v. Hants. (Wells)	1937
3	26	(122)	137	R. W. Hooker: Middx. v. Kent (Gravesend)	1959
6	22	(124)	165	H. B. Hayman: Webbe's XI v. Oxford U. (Oxford)	1901
—	32	(128)	187	D. G. Bradman: Australians v. Essex (Southend)	1948
—	32	(128)	162	F. T. Delves: Victoria v. Tasmania (Launceston)	1908–09
1	31	(130)	176	M. R. Hallam: Leics. v. Kent (Leicester)	1957
8	21	(132)	176	C. C. Dacre: New Zealanders v. Derby (Derby)	1927
11	18	(138)	194	C. J. Barnett: Glos. v. Somerset (Bath)	1934
8	23	(140)	189	E. Alletson: Notts. v. Sussex (Hove)	1911
6	27	(144)	192	W. R. Hammond: Glos. v. Hants. (Southampton)	1927
10	22	(148)	204	A. M. Crawley: Oxford U. v. Northants. (Wellingborough)	1929
5	30	(150)	191	G. L. Jessop: Gentlemen of South v. Players of South (Hastings)	1907
5	30	(150)	204	P. R. Umrigar: Indians v. Kent (Canterbury)	1952
4	32	(152)	208*	W. J. Edrich: Middx. v. Derby (Chesterfield)	1956
8	27	(156)	215	F. E. Woolley: Kent v. Somerset (Gravesend)	1925
2	39	(168)	228	N. Kilner: Warwicks. v. Worcs. (Worcester)	1935
—	42	(168)	256	R. Kanhai: West Indies v. India (Calcutta)	1958–59
—	48	(192)	243	J. Tunnicliffe: Yorks. v. Derby (Chesterfield)	1898
—	49	(196)	275	P. Holmes: Yorks. v. Warwicks. (Bradford)	1928
5	42	(198)	300	D. C. S. Compton: M.C.C. v. N.E. Transvaal (Benoni)	1948–49
4	44	(200)	268	C. R. Maxwell: Cahn's XI v. Leics. (Nottingham)	1935
—	68	(272)	343*	P. A. Perrin: Essex v. Derby (Chesterfield)	1904

R. W. Hooker (137), playing for Middlesex v. Kent (Gravesend) 1959, included 1 six and 22 fours (94 by boundaries) in his first 103 runs.

W. J. Stewart (155 & 125), playing for Warwickshire v. Lancashire (Blackpool) 1959, hit 17 sixes and 24 fours (198 by boundaries) in the match—10 sixes and 12 fours in the first innings and 7 sixes and 12 fours in the second.

Slow Scoring

The following table gives the times for the slowest innings recorded, graded according to minutes batted.

Min.		
15*—120	A. C. Bannerman: Australia v. England (Sydney)	1886–87
6*—120	W. H. Scotton: Nottinghamshire v. Kent (Gravesend)	1890
4 —120	P. Corrall: Leicestershire v. Cambridge U. (Cambridge)	1930
15 —125	T. W. Graveney: England v. West Indies (Barbados)	1953–54
8 —125	T. E. Bailey: England v. South Africa (Leeds)	1955
16*—130	G. O. Rabone: New Zealanders v. Yorkshire (Bradford)	1949
13*—135	R. Subba Row: Northamptonshire v. Worcestershire (Worcester)	1959
14 —135	R. G. Barlow: Lancashire v. Nottinghamshire (Manchester)	1888
10*—135	T. G. Evans: England v. Australia (Adelaide)	1946–47
19 —144	G. A. S. Innes: Western Province v. Natal (Pietermaritzburg)	1955–56
17 —150	R. G. Barlow: Lancashire v. Yorkshire (Bradford)	1874
5 —150	R. G. Barlow: Lancashire v. Sussex (Manchester)	1876
5*—150	R. G. Barlow: Lancashire v. Nottinghamshire (Nottingham)	1882
19*—150	W. L. Murdoch: Australia v. England (Melbourne)	1882–83
14 —150	J. W. H. T. Douglas: Essex v. Worcestershire (Worcester)	1927
17 —155	W. H. Scotton: Nottinghamshire v. Yorkshire (Nottingham)	1884
12*—165	L. Hall: Yorkshire v. Kent (Canterbury)	1885
16*—180	W. E. Midwinter: Australians v. Nottinghamshire (Nottingham)	1878
19 —180	R. G. Barlow: Lancashire v. Nottinghamshire (Manchester)	1890
18 —180	G. O. Rabone: New Zealand v. England (Dunedin)	1954–55
18 —194	W. R. Playle: New Zealand v. England (Leeds)	1958
20 —197	Hanif Mohammed: Pakistan v. England (Lord's)	1954
17 —205	R. G. Barlow: Lancashire v. Nottinghamshire (Manchester)	1888

Min.

26 —205	R. Aird: Hampshire v. Yorkshire (Leeds)	1923
29 —210	L. Hall: Yorkshire v. Kent (Leeds)	1882
21 —210	P. G. Z. Harris: New Zealand v. Pakistan (Karachi)	1955–56
24 —210	C. B. Van Ryneveld: South Africa v. England (Port Elizabeth)	1956–57
22 —220	L. Hall: Yorkshire v. Nottinghamshire (Nottingham)	1888
36 —220	R. Reynolds: Queensland v. M.C.C. (Brisbane)	1958–59
34*—225	R. G. Barlow: Lancashire v. Nottinghamshire (Nottingham)	1876
34 —225	W. H. Scotton: England v. Australia (Oval)	1886
26 —240	A. Haygarth: Gentlemen v. Players (Lord's)	1846
45 —240	W. E. Midwinter: South v. North (Nottingham)	1878
41 —240	A. C. Bannerman: Australia v. England (Melbourne)	1891–92
44 —240	A. Mitchell: Yorkshire v. Nottinghamshire (Sheffield)	1939
36 —240	W. A. Hadlee: New Zealand v. Lancashire (Manchester)	1949
44 —245	J. W. H. T. Douglas: Essex v. Surrey (Oval)	1927
28*—250	J. W. Burke: Australia v. England (Brisbane)	1958–59
26 —251	T. E. Bailey: M.C.C. v. South African XI (Pretoria)	1956–57
38 —261	T. E. Bailey: England v. Australia (Leeds)	1953
40 —265	L. Hall: Yorkshire v. Nottinghamshire (Sheffield)	1887
31 —266	K. Mackay: Australia v. England (Lord's)	1956
42*—279	A. Dunn: Griqualand West v. Western Province (Kimberley)	1946–47
47 —280	L. Hall: Yorkshire v. Nottinghamshire (Nottingham)	1889
40 —285	N. Oldfield: Northamptonshire v. Lancashire (Liverpool)	1948
46 —290	W. H. Scotton: Nottinghamshire v. Gloucestershire (Nottingham)	1885
40 —295	H. L. Collins: Australia v. England (Manchester)	1921
34 —300	F. P. Fenner: England v. Kent (Canterbury)	1841
68 —306	D. J. McGlew: South Africa v. England (Nottingham)	1955
49 —315	R. G. Barlow: Lancashire v. Nottinghamshire (Liverpool)	1882
45 —318	Shujauddin: Pakistan v. Australia (Lahore)	1959–60
58 —320	G. Gunn: Nottinghamshire v. Yorkshire (Nottingham)	1929
64*—320	W. Watson: Yorkshire v. Warwickshire (Sheffield)	1955
45*—330	A. C. Bannerman: New South Wales v. Victoria (Melbourne)	1890–91
21 —332	V. J. Hazare: Rest v. Hindus (Bombay)	1943–44
94 —335	R. T. Simpson: England v. West Indies (Nottingham)	1950
97 —340	J. E. Barrett: Australians v. England XI (Manchester)	1890
90 —345	W. H. Scotton: England v. Australia (Oval)	1884
101*—356	Hanif Mohammed: Pakistan v. Australia (Karachi)	1959–60
101 —360	M. C. Cowdrey: England v. South Africa (Cape Town)	1956–57
82 —360	W. H. Scotton: England v. Australia (Adelaide)	1884–85
78 —360	P. R. Umrigar: India v. Australia (Bombay)	1956–57
79 —360	P. Roy: India v. Australia (Bombay)	1956–57
70 —360	D. J. McGlew: South Africa v. Australia (Johannesburg)	1957–58
91*—363	H. Jupp: Surrey v. Kent (Oval)	1877
103 —364	A. D. Nourse jun.: South Africa v. England (Durban)	1938–39
58 —367	Ijaz Butt: Pakistan v. Australia (Karachi)	1959–60
107 —367	W. Place: England v. West Indies (Kingston)	1947–48
89 —367	J. H. Ferrandi: Western Province v. Natal (Pietermaritzburg)	1955–56
84 —367	M. C. Cowdrey: M.C.C. v. Transvaal (Johannesburg)	1956–57
83 —370	J. D. Martin: Scotland v. Ireland (Dublin)	1929
110*—373	D. J. Insole: England v. South Africa (Durban)	1956–57
105 —375	A. Mitchell: Yorkshire v. Leicestershire (Leicester)	1927
99 —389	J. G. Leggat: Canterbury v. Auckland (Christchurch)	1951–52
115 —389	A. L. Hassett: Australia v. England (Nottingham)	1953
94 —390	L. A. Watt: Otago v. Auckland (Auckland)	1950–51
109 —390	K. Meuleman: Western Australia v. M.C.C. (Perth)	1954–55
62 —390	Waqar Hasan: Pakistan XI v. M.C.C. (Lahore)	1955–56
79*—390	W. Wooller: Glamorgan v. Sussex (Hove)	1956
99 —394	B. Mitchell: South Africa v. England (Port Elizabeth)	1948–49
80 —395	T. E. Bailey: England v. South Africa (Durban)	1956–57
103 —395	Hanif Mohammed: Pakistan v. West Indies (Karachi)	1958–59
114 —406	M. C. Cowdrey: England v. West Indies (Kingston)	1959–60
91 —410	E. Cooper: Worcestershire v. Glamorgan (Worcester)	1948
110 —415	L. Hall: Yorkshire v. Kent (Canterbury)	1887
104 —420	J. W. Burke: New South Wales v. M.C.C. (Sydney)	1958–59
102 —420	W. H. Denton: Northamptonshire v. Derbyshire (Derby)	1914
88 —420	B. Mitchell: South Africa v. England (Birmingham)	1929
120 —430	F. C. Gardner: Warwickshire v. Gloucestershire (Bristol)	1956
125 —438	P. G. Van der Byl: South Africa v. England (Durban)	1938–39
90 —444	P. Roy: India v. West Indies (Bombay)	1958–59
91 —448	A. C. Bannerman: Australia v. England (Sydney)	1891–92
31 —450	T. Pierpoint: Sussex v. Kent (Sevenoaks)	1827
120 —451	P. A. Gibb: England v. South Africa (Durban)	1938–39

Min.

181 —454	C. P. Mead: England v. South Africa (Durban) 1922–23
68 —458	T. E. Bailey: England v. Australia (Brisbane) 1958–59
152*—460	C. Hallows: Lancashire v. Yorkshire (Manchester) 1929
102 —465	J. W. Guy: New Zealand v. India (Hyderabad) 1955–56
100 —479	A. Dunn: Griqualand West v. Eastern Province (Kimberley) 1947–48
180 —490	W. Troup: Gloucestershire v. Nottinghamshire (Bristol) 1898
133*—500	K. Mackay: Queensland v. Western Australia (Brisbane) 1958–59
204 —510	G. Brown: Hampshire v. Yorkshire (Portsmouth) 1927
142 —510	Hanif Mohammed: Pakistan v. India (Bahawalpur) 1954–55
134 —513	J. H. B. Waite: South Africa v. Australia (Durban) 1957–58
152 —518	C. N. Frank: South Africa v. Australia (Johannesburg) 1921–22
117 —525	P. E. Richardson: England v. South Africa (Johannesburg) 1956–57
174 —534	D. J. McGlew: Natal v. Eastern Province (Port Elizabeth) 1955–56
138*—540	A. J. Watkins: England v. India (New Delhi) 1951–52
208 —550	A. D. Nourse jun.: South Africa v. England (Nottingham) 1951
228 —575	W. Gunn: Players v. Australians (Lord's) 1890
105 —575	D. J. McGlew: South Africa v. Australia (Durban) 1957–58
189 —578	J. W. Burke: Australia v. South Africa (Cape Town) 1957–58
223 —585	K. Mackay: Queensland v. Victoria (Brisbane) 1953–54
163*—587	M. L. Apte: India v. West Indies (Trinidad) 1952–53
142 —630	Hanif Mohammed: Pakistan XI v. M.C.C. (Lahore) 1955–56
234 —642	S. G. Barnes: Australia v. England (Sydney) 1946–47
197*—682	F. M. Worrell: West Indies v. England (Barbados) 1959–60

AN HOUR BEFORE SCORING FIRST RUN

The longest times that a batsman has been at the wicket before opening his score or without scoring a run are as follows:

Min.

97	T. G. Evans (10*): England v. Australia (Adelaide) 1946–47
75	J. Vine (57): Sussex v. Nottinghamshire (Hove) 1901
72	F. H. Vigar (3*): Essex v. Hampshire (Portsmouth) 1946
70	W. Humphreys (0*): Sussex v. Kent (Hove) 1892
68	D. Ward (0): Glamorgan v. Gloucestershire (Newport) 1956
67	J. W. Prodger (4): Kent v. Surrey (Blackheath).....................................1958
65	R. G. Barlow (0): A. Shrewsbury's XI v. New South Wales (Sydney) 1886–87
65	Shujauddin (45): Pakistan v. Australia (Lahore) 1959–60
64	R. McDonald (7): Western Province v. Natal (Pietermaritzburg) 1955–56
63	R. W. Barber (22): Lancashire v. Kent (Gravesend).....................................1959
62	D. J. McGlew (0): Natal v. Transvaal (Johannesburg) 1955–56
61	H. D. Davies (0*): Glamorgan v. Middlesex (Lord's) 1960
60	R. G. Barlow (34*): Lancashire v. Nottinghamshire (Nottingham) 1876
60	J. N. Fowke (19*): Auckland v. Canterbury (Christchurch) 1893–94
60	E. Smith (0*): Yorkshire v. Essex (Leyton) 1905
60	S. O'Linn (11): South Africans v. Kent (Canterbury) 1960

AN HOUR WITHOUT SCORING A RUN

The longest times that a batsman has been at the wicket without adding a run to his score are as follows:

Min.

90	B. Mitchell (58): South Africa v. Australia (Brisbane) 1931–32
80	R. G. Barlow (5*): Lancashire v. Nottinghamshire (Nottingham) 1882
80	Hanif Mohammed (142): Pakistan XI v. M.C.C. (Lahore) 1955–56
79	T. E. Bailey (8): England v. South Africa (Leeds).....................................1955
75	J. Vine (57): Sussex v. Nottinghamshire (Hove) 1901
72	T. E. Bailey (64*): M.C.C. v. Australians (Lord's) 1953
70	L. Hall (12*): Yorkshire v. Kent (Canterbury) 1885
70	A. C. Bannerman (45*): New South Wales v. Victoria (Melbourne) 1890–91
67	W. H. Scotton (34): England v. Australia (Oval) 1886
65	J. Vine (4): Sussex v. Gloucestershire (Hove) 1902
65	A. S. M. Oakman (40): Sussex v. Lancashire (Hastings) 1960
65	W. B. Stott (22): Yorkshire v. Surrey (Sheffield) 1960
63	W. R. Endean (18): South Africa v. England (Johannesburg) 1956–57
63	R. A. Evans (110): Griqualand West v. M.C.C. (Kimberley) 1956–57
63	W. R. Playle (18): New Zealand v. England (Leeds) 1958
62	R. Illingworth (53): Yorkshire v. Lancashire (Sheffield) 1955
60	A. P. Lucas (20): Gentlemen v. Players (Oval) 1882
60	W. H. Scotton (46): Nottinghamshire v. Gloucestershire (Nottingham) 1885

Min.
60 L. Hall (22): Yorkshire v. Nottinghamshire (Nottingham) 1888
60 S. Haigh (31): Yorkshire v. Leicestershire (Leicester) 1905
60 R. Aird (26): Hampshire v. Yorkshire (Leeds) 1923
60 D. R. Jardine (24): England v. Australia (Brisbane) 1932–33
60 B. Mitchell (73): South Africa v. England (Johannesburg) 1938–39
60 A. Tayfield (38): Transvaal v. M.C.C. (Johannesburg) 1956–57
60 T. E. Bailey (80): England v. South Africa (Durban) 1956–57
60 M. J. Horton (5*): Worcestershire v. Warwickshire (Dudley)............................1957

SLOW SCORING NOTES

Fourteen consecutive four-ball maiden overs were bowled to A. C. Bannerman and W. L. Murdoch at one stage of their second wicket partnership for Australia v. England (Melbourne) 1881–82.

A. C. Bannerman, playing for Australia v. England (Sydney) 1886–87, scored 19 runs in 200 minutes in his combined innings—15* in 120 minutes in the first and 4 in 80 minutes in the second.

R. G. Barlow, playing for Lancashire v. Nottinghamshire (Manchester) 1889, scored 31 runs in 350 minutes in his combined innings—17 in 215 minutes in the first and 14 in 135 minutes in the second.

Australia batted 325 minutes to total 175 v. England (Manchester) 1921, 58 maiden overs being included in the innings. The 100 took 200 minutes to reach.

L. A. Bates and R. E. S. Wyatt scored only one run in 35 minutes at one stage of their second wicket partnership for Warwickshire v. Yorkshire (Birmingham) 1926.

J. W. H. T. Douglas, playing for Essex v. Leicestershire (Leicester) 1927, scored 66 runs in 340 minutes in his combined innings—29 in 150 minutes in the first innings and 37 in 190 minutes in the second.

Yorkshire batted 435 minutes (167·3 overs) to score an innings total of 282 v. Leicestershire (Leicester) 1927.

Lancashire (76—2) batted 125 minutes to score 44 runs on the third day v. Nottinghamshire (Nottingham) 1927—rain then fell and stopped play.

B. Mitchell, making his debut in Test cricket for South Africa v. England (Birmingham) 1929, scored 149 runs in 575 minutes in his combined innings—88 in 420 minutes in the first innings and 61* in 155 minutes in the second.

England batted ten hours to total 356 v. Australia (Brisbane) 1932–33. D. R. Jardine did not score off 82 consecutive balls he received in the course of an hour.

England (341 all out) scored only 37 runs for the loss of four wickets before lunch on the first day v. Australia (Adelaide) 1932–33.

P. G. Van der Byl (125), playing for South Africa v. England (Durban) 1938–39, did not hit his first boundary until he had been batting for three hours. The first four of the innings (by A. Melville) was not scored for 130 minutes.

A. Mitchell (44), playing for Yorkshire v. Nottinghamshire (Sheffield) 1939, scored only 11 runs in 150 minutes between lunch and tea.

Lancashire (174 all out) batted for 40 minutes without scoring a run from the bat v. Surrey (Manchester) 1950—the only run added was a leg-bye.

Sussex scored only 36 runs for the loss of four wickets in two hours before lunch on the third day v. Warwickshire (Hove) 1952—the match ended in a tie.

England totalled 442 runs in 972 minutes off 1723 balls in their combined innings v. Australia (Leeds) 1953—167 in 386 minutes off 658 balls in the first innings and 275 in 586 minutes off 1065 balls in the second, at a scoring rate of 25 runs per 100 balls or 27 runs per hour.

England (181 all out) scored only 27 runs off 39 overs in 90 minutes before lunch on the third day v. West Indies (Barbados) 1953–54. The new ball became due after 65 overs with the score at 77, and in a five-hour day only 128 runs were scored (53—2 to 181—9).

Pakistan scored 208 runs in 373 minutes off 817 balls in their combined innings v. England (Lord's) 1954—87 in 233 minutes off 503 balls in the first innings. Hanif Mohammed scored 59 runs in 337 minutes in his combined innings—20 in 197 minutes in the first and 39 in 140 minutes in the second.

New Zealand (125 all out) were only 24 for one wicket after 90 minutes at lunch on the first day of the match v. England (Dunedin) 1954–55—they took the whole of the first day, 292 minutes, to total 125.

D. J. McGlew, playing for South Africa v. England (Nottingham) 1955, scored 119 runs in 555 minutes in his combined innings—68 in 306 minutes in the first and 51 in 249 minutes in the second.

New Zealand scored 69 for six wickets off 90 six-ball overs (56 maidens) in the second innings v. Pakistan (Dacca) 1955–56—in their two innings New Zealand scored 139 runs off 129·2 overs.

Glamorgan scored only 143 runs in 400 minutes on the second day of the match v. Sussex (Hove) 1956, 64 in the first innings and 79—0 in the follow-on. The score at lunch was only 39 after 140 minutes batting. On the last day only 121 runs (79—0 to 200—1) were scored in 180 minutes. On the two days 199 overs were bowled for 264 runs, 61 (64 runs) in the first innings and 138 (200 runs) in the second. W. Wooller (79* in 390 minutes) and W. G. A. Parkhouse (71 in 300 minutes) shared in a first wicket stand of 135 in 300 minutes in the second innings, the new ball being taken at 79 after 75 overs.

Leicestershire scored a first innings total of 131 off 108 overs v. Gloucestershire (Bristol) 1956.

Somerset scored a first innings total of 37 off 36·4 overs v. Hampshire (Bournemouth) 1956.

D. J. McGlew and T. L. Goddard, playing for Natal v. M.C.C. (Durban) 1956–57, batted for 183 minutes in compiling a first wicket stand of 82.

R. A. Evans (110), playing for Griqualand West v. M.C.C. (Kimberley) 1956–57, batted for 63 minutes with his score on 99—the last five minutes of the second day and the first 58 minutes of the third day, when only one run (off the 104th ball) was scored in the first hour of play.

Leicestershire scored a first innings total of 57 off 66 overs v. Derbyshire (Leicester) 1957.

Worcestershire ended their match v. Warwickshire at Dudley in 1957 by receiving 24 consecutive maiden overs—M. J. Horton then hit a 4 in the 25th over, the last of the match.

D. J. McGlew and J. H. B. Waite, playing for South Africa v. Australia (Durban) 1957–58, batted 515 minutes in adding 231 for the second wicket.

J. W. Burke and K. Mackay, playing for Australia v. South Africa (Cape Town) 1957–58, batted 228 minutes in adding 130 for the fourth wicket.

New Zealand twice failed to score 40 runs in a pre-lunch session v. England (Birmingham) 1958—they scored 32—6 before lunch on the second day and 37—3 on the fourth.

England scored only 19 runs before lunch on the fourth day v. Australia (Brisbane) 1958–59, an overnight score of 92—2 being carried to 114—4—T. E. Bailey scored 8 of the runs in the 90 minutes' play.

Queensland scored only 27 runs before lunch on the third day v. M.C.C. (Brisbane) 1958–59, an overnight score of 30—1 being carried to 57—2.

S. F. Bergin (31 & 23), playing for Ireland v. Leicestershire (Leicester) 1959, batted 402 minutes in scoring his 54 runs in the match.

Pakistan scored only 24 runs in the pre-lunch session of the fourth day v. Australia (Karachi) 1959–60. The innings of 194—8d lasted for eight hours (109·4 overs).

Ijaz Butt, playing for Pakistan v. Australia (Karachi) 1959–60, scored 66 runs in 483 minutes in his combined innings of the match—58 in 367 minutes in the first innings and 8 in 116 minutes in the second.

M. L. Jaisimha (74), playing for India v. Australia (Calcutta) 1959–60, batted right through the fourth day, taking an overnight score of 0* to 59*.

SLOWEST TIMES TO REACH CERTAIN TARGETS IN AN INNINGS

The following innings have been scored at a very slow rate and have taken the longest times for the batsmen to reach, fifties, centuries and double-centuries.

Slow fifties:

Min.

361	T. E. Bailey (68): England v. Australia (Brisbane)	1958–59
313	D. J. McGlew (70): South Africa v. Australia (Johannesburg)	1957–58
282	E. McMorris (73): West Indies v. England (Kingston)	1959–60
280	P. E. Richardson (117): England v. South Africa (Johannesburg)	1956–57
270	T. E. Bailey (134*): England v. New Zealand (Christchurch)	1950–51
268	Hanif Mohammed (142): Pakistan XI v. M.C.C. (Lahore)	1955–56
253	B. Mitchell (99): South Africa v. England (Port Elizabeth)	1948–49

Slow centuries:

Min.

545	D. J. McGlew (105): South Africa v. Australia (Durban)	1957–58
525	Hanif Mohammed (142): Pakistan XI v. M.C.C. (Lahore)	1955–56
488	P. E. Richardson (117): England v. South Africa (Johannesburg)	1956–57
479	A. Dunn (100): Griqualand West v. Eastern Province (Kimberley)	1947–48
468	Hanif Mohammed (142): Pakistan v. India (Bahawalpur)	1954–55
435	J. W. Guy (102): New Zealand v. India (Hyderabad)	1955–56
434	M. C. Cowdrey (154): England v. West Indies (Birmingham)	1957
420	W. H. Denton (102): Northamptonshire v. Derbyshire (Derby)	1914
414	J. H. B. Waite (134): South Africa v. Australia (Durban)	1957–58

Slow double-centuries:

Min.

570	S. G. Barnes (234): Australia v. England (Sydney)	1946–47

FEWEST RUNS SCORED IN A DAY'S PLAY

The following day's play have provided the fewest runs in a complete, or near complete, day:

95	Australia (80) v. Pakistan (15—2) at Karachi	1956–57
104	Pakistan (0—0 to 104—5) v. Australia at Karachi	1959–60

105   Queensland (30—1 to 135—5) v. M.C.C. at Brisbane 1958–59
106   England (92—2 to 198) v. Australia at Brisbane 1958–59
107   Pakistan XI (66—0 to 173—1) v. M.C.C. at Lahore.......................................1955–56
110   Combined XI (159—2 to 260) v. M.C.C. (9—1) at Perth...................................1958–59
112   Australia (138—6 to 187) v. Pakistan (63—1) at Karachi 1956–57
117   India (117—5) v. Australia at Madras 1956–57
119   South Africa (7—0 to 126—2) v. Australia at Johannesburg 1957–58
120   India (15—0 to 135—8) v. Australia at Calcutta 1956–57
122   England (110—9 to 110) v. South Africa (122—7) at Port Elizabeth 1956–57
122   Australia (156—6 to 186) v. England (92—2) at Brisbane 1958–59
122   Australia (282—6 to 306 & 9—0) v. England (87) at Melbourne 1958–59
124   Pakistan (74—4 to 134) v. Australia (64—1) at Dacca 1959–60
124   India (226—6 to 291) v. Australia (59—2) at Kanpur 1959–60
125   New Zealand (125) v. England at Dunedin 1954–55
127   India (162—3 to 245) v. Pakistan (44—1) at Peshawar..................................1954–55
128   England (53—2 to 181—9) v. West Indies at Barbados 1953–54
129   Pakistan (129—6) v. India at Peshawar 1954–55
129   India (46—1 to 149 & 26—2) v. Australia at Madras 1959–60
130   South Africa (200—7 to 243) v. New Zealand (79 & 8—1) at Johannesburg 1953–54
130   India (115—5 to 148) v. Pakistan (97—1) at Dacca 1954–55
130   West Indies (349–7 to 386) v. New Zealand (93–5) at Christchurch 1955–56
136   South Africa (138—5 to 164) v. England (110—9) at Port Elizabeth 1956–57
138   Australia (138—6) v. Pakistan at Karachi 1956–57
138   South Africa (138—5) v. England at Port Elizabeth 1956–57
140   New Zealand (8—1 to 148—6) v. South Africa at Johannesburg 1953–54

The lowest in England is 142—7 in 335 minutes (25 minutes lost for rain) by England on the first day of the Test match v. Australia at Leeds in 1953.

Glamorgan totalled only 143 runs in 400 minutes on the second day v. Sussex (Hove) 1956—64 all out in the first innings and 79—0 in the follow-on.

Australia scored only 121 runs for the loss of eight wickets in five hours (one hour lost through early finish) v. England (Manchester) 1956.

SLOW SCORING IN A MATCH

528 runs in four days—Pakistan v. Australia (Karachi) 1956–57—95 runs on first day, 184 on second, 138 on third and 112 on fourth.

538 runs in four days of complete match—South Africa v. England (Port Elizabeth) 1956–57—138 on first day, 136 on second, 122 on third, and 142 on fourth.

518 runs on first four days of match—Australia v. England (Brisbane) 1958–59—142 on first day, 148 on second, 122 on third and 106 on fourth.

Individual Innings of Long Duration

Min.
337 —973   Hanif Mohammed: Pakistan v. West Indies (Barbados) 1957–58
364 —800   L. Hutton: England v. Australia (Oval) 1938
262*—708   L. Wight: British Guiana v. Barbados (Georgetown) 1951–52
197*—682   F. M. Worrell: West Indies v. England (Barbados) 1959–60
226 —647   G. Sobers: West Indies v. England (Barbados) 1959–60
234 —642   S. G. Barnes: Australia v. England (Sydney) 1946–47
359*—640   V. M. Merchant: Bombay v. Maharashtra (Bombay) 1943–44
499 —640   Hanif Mohammed: Karachi v. Bahawalpur (Karachi) 1958–59
297*—630   H. Moses: N.S.W. v. Victoria (Sydney) 1887–88
275*—630   F. C. Thompson: Queensland v. N.S.W. (Brisbane) 1930–31
142 —630   Hanif Mohammed: Pakistan XI v. M.C.C. (Lahore) 1955–56
288 —628   V. S. Hazare: Baroda v. Holkar (Baroda) 1946–47
437 —621   W. H. Ponsford: Victoria v. N.S.W. (Melbourne) 1926–27
267 —615   A. Shrewsbury: Notts. v. Middx. (Nottingham) 1887
365*—608   G. Sobers: West Indies v. Pakistan (Kingston) 1957–58
325 —600   A. Sandham: England v. West Indies (Kingston) 1929–30

H. Sutcliffe batted for 810 minutes in scoring 176 (431 min.) and 127 (379 min.) for England v. Australia at Melbourne in 1924–25.

B. Mitchell batted for 801 minutes in scoring 120 (381 min.) and 189* (420 min.) for South Africa v. England at the Oval in 1947. He was on the field for all but eight minutes of actual play, during which only twelve balls were bowled—thus being on the field for 3222 of the 3234 balls during the match.

* I

Monopolizing the Scoring

On several occasions one batsman has provided a very large proportion of the innings total reached by his team, the record being established by V. S. Hazare in 1943–44 when he contributed no fewer than 309 out of his team's total of 387. A full list of all batsmen who have provided at least 70 per cent of their team's total is given, together with those batsmen who provided 65 per cent of the runs in a large innings. Several batsmen have been successful in providing over 50 per cent of their team's total in each innings—a great batting feat.

A list is also given of batsmen who have dominated the run-getting during their stay at the wicket, graduated according to the size of the innings.

All percentages are worked out ignoring decimal points, i.e. 60·9% is shown as 60%.

Lowest innings total to include an individual innings of fifty 66
Lowest innings total to include a century 144
Lowest innings total to include a double-century 315
Lowest innings total to include a treble-century 387

The following batsmen have scored 70% of their team's innings total:

%	Score	Inns.		
79	(309	—387)	V. S. Hazare: Rest v. Hindus (Bombay)	1943–44
79	(126	—159)	W. G. Grace: United South v. United North (Hull)	1876
78	(18	— 23)	J. Noel: South Australia v. Victoria (Melbourne)	1882–83
78	(45	— 57)	A. N. Hornby: M.C.C. v. Sussex (Lord's)	1890
78	(63*	— 80)	C. O. H. Sewell: Glos. v. Sussex (Hove)	1913
78	(52	— 66)	S. Nazir Ali: Indians v. Yorks. (Harrogate)	1932
77	(385	—500)	B. Sutcliffe: Otago v. Canterbury (Christchurch)	1952–53
75	(82	—109)	W. Beldham: Surrey v. England (Lord's)	1801
75	(55	— 73)	G. Wells: Sussex v. M.C.C. (Lord's)	1860
75	(69	— 92)	F. G. Rogers: Glos. v. Hants. (Southampton)	1924
75	(127*	—169)	W. J. Edrich: Middx. v. Glos. (Lord's)	1946
74	(20	— 27)	W. G. Grace: Sheffield's XI v. Australians (Sheffield Park)	1890
73	(50	— 68)	A. Morton: Derby v. Yorks. (Chesterfield)	1914
72	(150	—206)	D. C. S. Compton: Middx. v. Sussex (Lord's)	1955
71	(103*	—144)	F. E. Woolley: Kent v. Warwicks. (Folkestone)	1931
70	(122	—173)	W. G. Grace: South v. North (Sheffield)	1869
70	(70	—100)	E. Smith: Oxford U. v. M.C.C. (Oxford)	1891
70	(92	—131)	C. E. de. Trafford: Leics. v. Yorks. (Leicester)	1894
70	(67*	— 95)	W. Flowers: Notts. v. M.C.C. (Lord's)	1894
70	(97	—137)	F. H. B. Champain: Glos. v. Lancs. (Bristol)	1897
70	(161	—229)	F. E. Woolley: Kent v. Derby (Canterbury)	1933
70	(141	—199)	A. H. Bakewell: Northants. v. Worcs. (Northampton)	1935
70	(130	—184)	L. Amarnath: Indians v. Essex (Brentwood)	1936
70	(74*	—105)	R. E. S. Wyatt: Warwicks. v. Leics. (Birmingham)	1939

The following innings, although not providing 70% of the innings total, provided a high percentage of runs in a large innings total:

%	Score	Inns.		
69	(171*	—246)	G. L. Jessop: Cambridge U. v. Yorks. (Cambridge)	1899
69	(74*	—107)	R. A. Hamence: South Australia v. N.S.W. (Adelaide)	1945–46
68	(120*	—175)	A. E. Dipper: Glos. v. Warwicks. (Birmingham)	1920
68	(236	—345)	H. S. Squires: Surrey v. Lancs. (Oval)	1933
68	(117	—172)	M. P. Donnelly: Oxford U. v. Glos. (Bristol)	1946
67	(165*	—245)	C. Bannerman: Australia v. England (Melbourne)	1876–77
67	(159*	—237)	G. L. Jessop: South of England v. South Africans (Hastings)	1904
67	(100	—148)	R. P. Meherhomji: Parsis v. Europeans (Bombay)	1907–08
67	(257*	—383)	L. C. Braund: Somerset v. Worcs. (Worcester)	1913
67	(214	—315)	W. H. Ponsford: Victoria v. South Australia (Adelaide)	1926–27
67	(222*	—328)	S. Wazir Ali: South Punjab v. Bengal (Calcutta)	1938–39
67	(143	—211)	D. B. Carr: Oxford U. v. Sussex (Oxford)	1950
67	(200	—298)	T. W. Graveney: Glos. v. Glamorgan (Newport)	1956
66	(134*	—201)	W. G. Grace: Gentlemen v. Players (Lord's)	1868
66	(174	—263)	W. G. Grace: Gentlemen v. Players (Scarborough)	1885
66	(184	—276)	E. J. Diver: Warwicks. v. Leics. (Birmingham)	1899
66	(170*	—254)	C. B. Fry: Sussex v. Notts. (Nottingham)	1901
66	(341	—515)	G. H. Hirst: Yorks. v. Leics. (Leicester)	1905
66	(177	—266)	F. L. Bowley: Worcs. v. Warwicks. (Birmingham)	1913
66	(104*	—156)	G. M. Emmett: Glos. v. Oxford U. (Oxford)	1948
65	(106	—161)	W. Bates: Yorks. v. Derby (Leeds)	1886

65 (122 —185)   E. Smith: Thornton's XI v. Surrey (Scarborough) 1892
65 (113*—172)   L. C. H. Palairet: Somerset v. Middx. (Taunton) 1895
65 (131 —200)   W. R. Hammond: Glos. v. Northants. (Peterborough) 1928
65 (164 —252)   W. R. Hammond: Glos. v. Essex (Westcliff) 1934
65 (317 —485)   W. R. Hammond: Glos. v. Notts. (Gloucester) 1936
65 (230*—352)   R. T. Simpson: Notts. v. Glamorgan (Swansea) 1950
65 (172*—264)   D. J. Insole: Essex v. Surrey (Colchester) 1954
65 (100 —153)   T. W. Graveney: Glos. v. Essex (Romford) 1956
65 (163 —250)   M. T. Chandrubhan: Gujerat v. Bombay (Khadakvasla) 1957–58

On the following occasions one batsman has provided over 50% of his side's runs in each innings.
Score Total Score Total
62* (121)   92 (168)   James Broadbridge: Sussex v. Hants. (Petworth) 1825
80* (148)   79 (150)   Lord Harris: Kent v. Yorks. (Gravesend) 1883
56 (102)   42 (81)   J. T. Tyldesley: Lancs. v. Australians (Manchester) 1899
88 (159) 106 (212)   C. B. Fry: Sussex v. Hants. (Portsmouth) 1901
176 (336) 122 (197)   L. G. Wright: Derby v. Warwicks. (Birmingham) 1905
35 (63) 111 (205)   C. N. Woolley: Northants. v. Derby (Northampton) 1922
109* (196) 107 (205)   F. S. Lee: Somerset v. Worcs. (Worcester) 1938
129 (244) 112 (212)   L. B. Fishlock: Surrey v. Leics. (Leicester) 1946
97 (188) 175 (337)   P. B. H. May: Combined Services v. Worcs. (Worcester) 1949
154 (270)   34 (63)   M. C. Cowdrey: Oxford U. v. Surrey (Oval) 1953
100 (153)   67 (107)   T. W. Graveney: Glos. v. Essex (Romford) 1956
156* (257) 109 (191)   D. B. Carr: Derby v. Kent (Canterbury) 1959

The following are the leading cases of a batsman monopolizing the scoring during his stay at the wicket (the batsman's innings is given first, the number of runs scored during his stay at the wicket second).
39 — 39   J. N. Crawford: Surrey v. Somerset (Taunton) 1919
40 — 41   G. L. Jessop: Glos. v. Middx. (Lord's) 1907
43 — 44   A. B. Hipkin: Essex v. Yorks. (Leyton) 1929
45 — 46   P. S. McDonnell: Australians v. Shaw's XI (Leeds) 1882
50 — 51   E. A. McDonald: Lancs. v. Glos. (Manchester) 1926
53 — 54   M. Tompkin: Leics. v. Yorks. (Leicester) 1947
53 — 54   G. C. Gill: Somerset v. Hants. (Bath) 1902
56 — 57   C. I. J. Smith: Middx. v. Yorks. (Scarborough) 1936
61*— 63   P. G. H. Fender: Surrey v. Sussex (Eastbourne) 1926
63 — 65   G. L. Jessop: Glos. v. Yorks. (Cheltenham) 1895
66 — 66   G. L. Jessop: Glos. v. Sussex (Bristol) 1901
69 — 70   P. S. McDonnell: Australians v. Oxford & Cambridge U. P. & P. (Portsmouth)......1888
68 — 72   H. A. Peach: Surrey v. Glamorgan (Oval) 1928
72 — 75   V. T. Hill: Somerset v. Middx. (Lord's) 1900
70 — 76   E. Smith: Oxford U. v. M.C.C. (Oxford) 1891
73*— 80   A. W. Wellard: Somerset v. Glamorgan (Cardiff) 1938
76 — 82   G. L. Jessop: Glos. v. Notts. (Bristol) 1901
75 — 84   R. T. D. Perks: Worcs. v. Notts. (Nottingham) 1938
82 — 86   P. S. McDonnell: Australians v. North of England (Manchester) 1888
84 — 89   G. E. Winter: Cambridge U. v. Surrey (Oval) 1899
83 — 92   D. E. V. Padgett: Yorks. v. Derby (Leeds) 1956
93 —104   L. B. Fishlock: Surrey v. Australians (Oval) 1938
93 —108   E. R. Dexter: Sussex v. Warwicks. (Birmingham) 1960
88 —108   H. Gimblett: Somerset v. Sussex (Worthing) 1950
95 —109   W. P. Howell: N.S.W. v. Stoddart's XI (Sydney) 1897–98
96 —110   M. F. Tremlett: Somerset v. Glos. (Bristol) 1948
90 —113   D. C. S. Compton: Middx. v. Essex (Colchester) 1952
95 —114   V. W. C. Jupp: Northants. v. Essex (Kettering) 1933
103 —116   D. C. S. Compton: Rest v. England (Canterbury) 1946
97 —117   R. Benaud: Australia v. England (Lord's) 1956
101 —118   G. L. Jessop: Glos. v. Yorks. (Harrogate) 1897
103 —120   R. E. Marshall: Hants. v. Kent (Southampton) 1957
109 —120   G. L. Jessop: Glos. v. Middx. (Lord's) 1900
101*—121   C. I. J. Smith: Middx. v. Kent (Canterbury) 1939
108 —129   T. S. Worthington: Derby v. Notts. (Ilkeston) 1933
114*—129   K. G. Suttle: Sussex v. Worcs. (Eastbourne) 1952
106 —130   T. W. Graveney: Glos. v. Warwicks. (Birmingham) 1957
122 —131   F. R. Brown: Gentlemen v. Players (Lord's) 1950
112 —132   M. Leyland: Yorks. v. Kent (Gravesend) 1930
116 —137   W. Bates: Yorks. v. Notts. (Nottingham) 1884
130*—145   C. K. Nayudu: Indians v. Somerset (Taunton) 1932
143 —173   S. M. J. Woods: Somerset v. Sussex (Hove) 1898
134 —175   J. J. Lyons: Australia v. England (Sydney) 1891–92

137 —177   G. Brann: Sussex v. M.C.C. (Lord's) 1893
139 —181   P. G. H. Fender: Surrey v. Somerset (Oval) 1931
149 —181   J. J. Lyons: Australians v. M.C.C. (Lord's) 1893
144 —186   T. G. Evans: Kent v. Somerset (Taunton) 1952
153 —187   C. K. Nayudu: Hindus v. M.C.C. (Bombay) 1926–27
163 —201   W. Rashleigh: Kent v. Middx. (Tonbridge) 1896
164 —203   G. L. Jessop: Glos. v. Sussex (Gloucester) 1908
171*—206   G. L. Jessop: Cambridge U. v. Yorks. (Cambridge) 1899
170 —216   W. G. Grace: England v. Australia (Oval) 1886
174 —220   Hon. F. S. G. Calthorpe: Warwicks. v. Lancs. (Birmingham) 1925
183 —224   J. B. Hobbs: Surrey v. Warwicks. (Oval) 1914
189 —227   E. Alletson: Notts. v. Sussex (Hove) ...
192 —227   W. R. Hammond: Glos. v. Hants. (Southampton) 1927
191 —234   G. L. Jessop: Gentlemen of South v. Players of South (Hastings) 1907
200*—258   A. D. Nourse sen.: Natal v. Western Province (Cape Town) 1907–08
206 —265   H. H. Massie: Australians v. Oxford U. (Oxford) 1882
200 —279   T. W. Graveney: Glos. v. Glamorgan (Newport) 1956
201*—280   M. M. Walford: Oxford U. v. M.C.C. (Lord's) 1938
215 —282   S. M. J. Woods: Somerset v. Sussex (Hove) 1895
210*—289   M. Leyland: Yorks. v. Kent (Dover)...1933
220 —293   K. S. Ranjitsinhji: Sussex v. Kent (Hove) 1900
232 —300   S. J. McCabe: Australia v. England (Nottingham) 1938
239 —310   P. S. McDonnell: N.S.W. v. Victoria (Melbourne) 1886–87
217 —313   Hon. L. H. Tennyson: Hants. v. West Indians (Southampton) 1928
225 —315   J. H. Parsons: Warwicks. v. Glamorgan (Birmingham) 1927
286 —355   G. L. Jessop: Glos. v. Sussex (Hove) 1903
309 —373   V. S. Hazare: Rest v. Hindus (Bombay) 1943–44
300 —399   D. C. S. Compton: M.C.C. v. N. E. Transvaal (Benoni) 1948–49
305*—448   F. R. Foster: Warwicks. v. Worcs. (Dudley) 1914
317 —462   W. R. Hammond: Glos. v. Notts. (Gloucester) 1936
336*—492   W. R. Hammond: England v. New Zealand (Auckland) 1932–33
385 —500   B. Sutcliffe: Otago v. Canterbury (Christchurch) 1952–53
357 —502   D. G. Bradman: South Australia v. Victoria (Melbourne) 1935–36
369 —527   D. G. Bradman: South Australia v. Tasmania (Adelaide) 1935–36

In the following wicket-partnerships, the run-scoring was almost completely in the hands of one of the batsmen.

307 —10th   A. F. Kippax (238) & J. E. H. Hooker (62) (7 ex): N.S.W. v. Victoria (Sydney) 1928–29
300 — 6th   V. S. Hazare (266) & V. J. Hazare (21) (13 ex): Rest v. Hindus (Bombay)......1943–44
184 —10th   R. C. Blunt (146) & W. Hawkesworth (21) (17 ex): Otago v. Canterbury
(Christchurch).........1931–32
152 —10th   E. Alletson (142) & W. Riley (10): Notts. v. Sussex (Hove) 1911
128 — 9th   G. C. Cooper (109) & F. Pountain (16) (3 ex): Sussex v. Warwicks. (Birmingham)...1960
119*— 9th   K. G. Suttle (109) & P. A. Kelland (5) (5 ex): Sussex v. Worcs. (Eastbourne) 1952
116 —10th   C. I. J. Smith (98) & I. A. R. Peebles (14) (4 ex): Middx. v. Kent (Canterbury)......1939
107 —10th   H. J. Enthoven (102) & W. F. Price (3) (2 ex): Middx. v. Sussex (Lord's)..............1930
104 —10th   F. R. Brown (91) & J. F. Parker (12) (1 ex): Surrey v. Kent (Blackheath) 1932
101 —10th   W. W. Whysall (84) & W. Voce (17): Notts. v. Glos. (Nottingham) 1929
100*—10th   D. Tallon (91) & G. J. Noblet (9): Bradman's XI v. Hassett's XI (Melbourne)...1948–49
96 —10th   C. T. Ashton (91) & G. M. Louden (3) (2 ex): Essex v. Middx. (Leyton) 1922
88 — 7th   H. T. W. Hardinge (80) & W. H. Ashdown (4) (4 ex): Kent v. Leics. (Leicester)......1922
86 — 1st   P. S. McDonnell (82) & A. C. Bannerman (4): Australians v. North (Manchester)...1888
86 —10th   S. H. Day (82) & C. D. Dewe (4): Cambridge U. v. Sussex (Hove) 1901
84 —10th   H. A. Peach (78) & S. Fenley (5) (1 ex): Surrey v. Lancs. (Oval) 1928
80 —10th   J. N. Crawford (73) & T. Rushby (2) (5 ex): Surrey v. A.I.F. (Oval)..................1919
79 —10th   D. C. S. Compton (78) & L. H. Gray (1): Middx. v. Essex (Lord's) 1939
77 —10th   S. J. McCabe (72) & L. O'B. Fleetwood-Smith (5): Australia v. England (Nottingham) 1938
75 —10th   R. W. V. Robins (75) & J. A. Young (0): M.C.C. v. Yorks. (Scarborough).........1946
71 —10th   R. W. V. Robins (68) & L. H. Gray (1) (2 ex): Middx. v. Essex (Chelmsford) ...1937
69 —10th   H. J. Enthoven (61) & R. S. Machin (0) (8 ex): Cambridge U. v. Free Foresters
(Cambridge).........1926
69 —10th   A. H. Kardar (64) & W. E. Hollies (4) (1 ex): Warwicks. v. Middx. (Lord's).........1950
67 —10th   R. W. V. Robins (65) & N. F. Turner (0) (2 ex): Middx. v. Yorks. (Lord's) 1937
67*— 8th   M. J. Turnbull (64) & A. H. Fabian (3): Cambridge U. v. Yorks. (Cambridge) ...1929
57 —10th   C. I. J. Smith (56) & L. H. Gray (1): Middx. v. Yorks. (Scarborough) 1936
50 —10th   H. J. Enthoven (45) & L. G. Irvine (5): Cambridge U. v. Australians (Cambridge)...1926
50 —10th   W. J. Edrich (49) & L. H. Gray (1): Middx. v. Surrey (Lord's) 1939

Other interesting monopolies are as follows:

C. I. Thornton, playing for Kent v. Nottinghamshire (Tonbridge) 1869, scored an innings of 76 in a total of 114—66% of the runs. The next highest score was 9 by A. White.

Two brothers, G. McCanlis (60) and W. McCanlis (39), scored 99 runs out of the 107 from the bat in an innings total of 119 for Kent v. Surrey (Oval) 1873.

A. W. Ridley (64), playing for Oxford U. v. M.C.C. (Lord's) 1875, scored 45 runs at one stage of his innings while his partner (A. J. Webbe) did not score.

C. A. Absolom, playing for Kent v. Lancashire (Catford) 1875, opened the match by scoring all 21 runs on the board when he was first man out, his partner (W. Penn) still having to score his first run.

A. N. Hornby, playing for Lancashire v. Nottinghamshire (Nottingham) 1876, scored 44 out of the 45 runs scored for the first wicket. When Hornby was dismissed his partner (R..G. Barlow) still had to score, the other run being a bye.

A. G. Steel, playing for M.C.C. v. Yorkshire (Scarborough) 1881, went in to bat at the fall of the seventh wicket and scored 106* out of 140 in 80 minutes, the score changing from 48 for seven to 188 all out.

A. N. Hornby, playing for Lancashire v. Derbyshire (Manchester) 1881, scored 188 of the 251 runs on the board before he was dismissed, his main scoring strokes being 23 fours in an innings scored at a run a minute.

W. G. Grace (170), playing for England v. Australia (Oval) 1886, scored 62 runs at one stage of his innings while his partner (W. H. Scotton) did not score in a period of 67 minutes. Grace and Scotton scored 170 runs for the first wicket the latter's share being 34, and Grace was finally out for 170 out of 216 in 270 minutes' batting.

W. Bates (48), playing for A. Shrewsbury's XI v. New South Wales (Sydney) 1886–87, scored all the first 46 runs of the innings.

S. M. J. Woods (68), playing for Somerset v. Australians (Taunton) 1899, joined E. Robson at the wicket and scored his first 42 runs while Robson scored 5. By a strange coincidence the positions then changed completely Robson scoring his next 42 runs while Woods added 5.

G. L. Jessop, playing for Cambridge U. v. Yorkshire (Cambridge) 1899, scored 171* out of 206 runs added while he was at the wicket. Completing his century in only 64 minutes. Jessop at one time scored 52 runs out of 53 while in partnership with T. L. Taylor. Later in the innings A. M. Sullivan batted 80 minutes to score 3 runs, taking 45 minutes to open his score.

K. S. Ranjitsinhji (202), playing for Sussex v. Middlesex (Hove) 1900, scored 202 out of 272 in 180 minutes. At one stage of his innings he scored 164 out of 195 runs added, sharing in stands of 88 for the seventh wicket with C. L. A. Smith (2) and 79 for the eighth wicket with G. H. G. Bland (2).

C. E. de Trafford, playing for Leicestershire v. Australians (Leicester) 1905, scored all the first 56 runs from the bat. When he was dismissed with the score at 69, de Trafford had scored 63 runs, his partner (C. J. D. Wood) was 2 and there had been 4 extras.

W. V. Jephson (65), playing for Hampshire v. Sussex (Portsmouth) 1905, scored all the first 46 runs in the second innings.

M. W. Payne, playing for Cambridge U. v. Oxford U. (Lord's) 1906, scored 64 of the 73 runs put on for the first wicket in 30 minutes. Payne scored all the first 45 runs in 15 minutes and completed his 50 in 25 minutes.

G. L. Jessop, playing for Gloucestershire v. Nottinghamshire (Nottingham) 1908, scored 78 out of 86 in the first innings and 75 out of 80 in the second—153 out of 166 runs in the match.

J. B. Hobbs (54), playing for Players v. Gentlemen (Oval) 1912, scored all the first 41 runs from the bat, and completed 50 out of 55 in 21 minutes—he was caught at 72.

G. Gunn (109*), playing for Nottinghamshire v. Yorkshire (Nottingham) 1913, scored 93* out of the first 100 runs and completed his century with only 115 runs on the board.

L. C. Braund was responsible for the major portion of the runs in three consecutive innings for Somerset in 1913—257* out of a total of 383 and 50 out of 120 v. Worcestershire (Worcester) and 44* out of a total of 149 v. Yorkshire (Bradford).

J. B. Hobbs (169), playing for Surrey v. Hampshire (Southampton) 1920, scored 106 runs at one stage while his partner (H. S. Harrison) scored 7.

A. Morton (87), playing for Derbyshire v. Worcestershire (Derby) 1923, scored 50 runs while his partner (J. M. Hutchinson) scored a single at one point of their partnership.

F. J. Seabrook (107), playing for Gloucestershire v. Hampshire (Bristol) 1928, scored 36 runs at one stage while his partner (W. L. Neale) did not score.

A. F. Lane, playing for Worcestershire v. Essex (Leyton) 1929, scored 130 out of the 148 runs added during his combined innings of the match—70 out of 78 in 65 minutes (11 fours) in his first innings and 60 out of 70 in 50 minutes in his second.

P. Corrall (4), making his debut in first-class cricket for Leicestershire v. Cambridge U. (Cambridge) 1930, scored only 4 of the 112 runs added for the ninth wicket with G. Geary (99).

R. S. G. Scott (113), playing for Sussex v. Hampshire (Horsham) 1933, scored all the 44 runs added for the last wicket with J. Cornford (0*).

G. Cox (142), playing for Sussex v. Yorkshire (Hove) 1938, scored his first 100 runs out of only 114 added from the start of his innings.

V. S. Hazare scored 616 runs while his various colleagues scored only 299 runs in three consecutive completed innings played for the Rest in the 1943–44 Pentangular Tournament at Bombay—248 out of 395 (62%), 59 out of 133 (44%) and 309 out of 387 (79%).

R. W. V. Robins (116), playing for M.C.C. v. Yorkshire (Scarborough) 1946, scored 95 out of the last 96 runs from the bat during the innings. He scored all the last 75 runs added for the tenth wicket with J. A. Young (0*).

F. R. Brown, captain of Gentlemen v. Players (Lord's) 1950, scored 122 out of 131 in 110 minutes. The score was 194 for six wickets when Brown went in to bat and each of his partners held up one end while Brown did the scoring. The batsmen scored as follows: Doggart 6 in 55 minutes (while the score moved from 194 to 258 for the seventh wicket), Warr 2 in 5 minutes (258 to 260 for the eighth wicket), Brennan 0 in 35 minutes (260 to 295 for the ninth wicket) and Knott 1 in 15 minutes (295 to 325 all out). Brown was 93* when the last man joined him.

M. H. Stevenson (114* out of 146 in 120 minutes), playing for M.C.C. v. Oxford U. (Lord's) 1958, scored 95 while D. Eames scored 7 in a fifth wicket stand of 107.

R. Illingworth (150), playing for Yorkshire v. Essex (Colchester) 1959, hit the first 46 runs in a tenth wicket stand of 51 with C. Wood (4*).

Part III—Wicket Partnerships

Record Wicket Partnerships

WORLD RECORD FOR EACH WICKET

1st	555	P. Holmes & H. Sutcliffe: Yorks. v. Essex (Leyton)	1932
2nd	455	B. B. Nimbalkar & K. V. Bhandarkar: Maharashtra v. Western India States (Poona)	1948–49
3rd	445	P. E. Whitelaw & W. N. Carson: Auckland v. Otago (Dunedin)	1936–37
4th	577	Gul Mahomed & V. S. Hazare: Baroda v. Holkar (Baroda)	1946–47
5th	405	S. G. Barnes & D. G. Bradman: Australia v. England (Sydney)	1946–47
6th	487*	G. Headley & C. C. Passailaigue: Jamaica v. Tennyson's XI (Kingston)	1931–32
7th	347	D. Atkinson & C. Depeiza: West Indians v. Australia (Barbados)	1954–55
8th	433	V. T. Trumper & A. Sims: Australians v. Canterbury (Christchurch)	1913–14
9th	283	J. Chapman & A. R. Warren: Derby v. Warwicks. (Blackwell)	1910
10th	307	A. F. Kippax & J. E. H. Hooker: N.S.W. v. Victoria (Melbourne)	1928–29

Australian batsmen hold three records. English, West Indian and Indian batsmen two each and New Zealand batsmen one.

RECORDS BY ENGLISH BATSMEN

1st	555	P. Holmes & H. Sutcliffe: Yorks v Essex (Leyton)	1932
2nd	429*	J. G. Dewes & G. H. G. Doggart: Cambridge U. v. Essex (Cambridge)	1949
3rd	424*	W. J. Edrich & D. C. S. Compton: Middx. v. Somerset (Lord's)	1948
4th	448	R. Abel & T. Hayward: Surrey v. Yorks. (Oval)	1899
5th	393	E. G. Arnold & W. B. Burns: Worcs. v. Warwicks. (Birmingham)	1909
6th	411	R. M. Poore & E. G. Wynyard: Hants. v. Somerset (Taunton)	1899
7th	344	K. S. Ranjitsinhji & W. Newham: Sussex v. Essex (Leyton)	1902
8th	292	R. Peel & Lord Hawke: Yorks. v. Warwicks. (Birmingham)	1896
9th	283	J. Chapman & A. R. Warren: Derby v. Warwicks. (Blackwell)	1910
10th	235	F. E. Woolley & A. Fielder: Kent v. Worcs. (Stourbridge)	1909

RECORDS BY AUSTRALIAN BATSMEN

1st	456	E. R. Mayne & W. H. Ponsford: Victoria v. Queensland (Melbourne)	1923–24
2nd	451	W. H. Ponsford & D. G. Bradman: Australia v. England (Oval)	1934
3rd	389	W. H. Ponsford & S. J. McCabe: Australians v. M.C.C. (Lord's)	1934
4th	424	I. S. Lee & S. O. Quin: Victoria v. Tasmania (Melbourne)	1933–34
5th	405	S. G. Barnes & D. G. Bradman: Australia v. England (Sydney)	1946–47
6th	428	W. W. Armstrong & M. A. Noble: Australians v. Sussex (Hove)	1902
7th	335	C. W. Andrews & E. C. Bensted: Queensland v. N.S.W. (Sydney)	1934–35
8th	433	V. T. Trumper & A. Sims: Australians v. Canterbury (Christchurch)	1913–14
9th	232	C. Hill & E. Walkley: South Australia v. N.S.W. (Adelaide)	1900–01
10th	307	A. F. Kippax & J. E. H. Hooker: N.S.W. v. Victoria (Melbourne)	1928–29

RECORDS BY SOUTH AFRICAN BATSMEN

1st	424	J. F. W. Nicolson & I. J. Siedle: Natal v. O.F.S. (Bloemfontein)	1926–27
2nd	305	S. K. Coen & J. M. M. Commaille: O.F.S. v. Natal (Bloemfontein)	1926–27
3rd	319	A. Melville & A. D. Nourse jun.: South Africa v. England (Nottingham)	1947
4th	342	E. A. B. Rowan & P. J. M. Gibb: Transvaal v. N.E. Transvaal (Johannesburg)	1952–53
5th	327	H. B. Cameron & A. W. Briscoe: Transvaal v. Griqualand West (Johannesburg)	1934–35
6th	244*	J. M. M. Commaille & A. W. Palm: Western Province v. Griqualand West (Johannesburg)	1923–24
7th	299	B. Mitchell & A. Melville: Transvaal v. Griqualand West (Kimberley)	1946–47
8th	222	S. S. L. Steyn & D. P. B. Morkel: Western Province v. Border (Cape Town)	1929–30
9th	221	N. V. Lindsay & G. R. McCubbin: Transvaal v. Rhodesia (Bulawayo)	1922–23
10th	129	F. Caulfield & L. R. Tuckett: O.F.S. v. Western Province (Blemfontein)	1925–26

RECORDS BY WEST INDIAN BATSMEN

1st	390	L. Wight & G. Gibbs: British Guiana v. Barbados (Georgetown)...................1951–52
2nd	446	C. C. Hunte & G. Sobers: West Indies v. Pakistan (Kingston) 1957–58
3rd	434	J. B. Stollmeyer & G. E. Gomez: Trinidad v. British Guiana (Trinidad) 1946–47
4th	574*	C. L. Walcott & F. M. Worrell: Barbados v. Trinidad (Trinidad) 1945–46
5th	283	N. Bonitto & A. P. Binns: Jamaica v. British Guiana (Georgetown) 1952–53
6th	487*	G. Headley & C. C. Passailaigue: Jamaica v. Tennyson's XI (Kingston)............1931–32
7th	347	D. Atkinson & C. Depeiza: West Indies v. Australia (Barbados) 1954–55
8th	255	E. A. V. Williams & E. A. Martindale: Barbados v. Trinidad (Barbados) 1935–36
9th	125	A. M. Taylor & E. A. V. Williams: Barbados v. British Guiana (Georgetown) 1946–47
10th	138	E. L. G. Hoad & H. C. Griffith: West Indians v. Sussex (Hove) 1933

RECORDS BY NEW ZEALAND BATSMEN

1st	373	B. Sutcliffe & L. A. Watt: Otago v. Auckland (Auckland) 1950–51
2nd	301	C. S. Dempster & C. F. W. Allcott: New Zealanders v. Warwicks. (Birmingham) 1927
3rd	445	P. E. Whitelaw & W. N. Carson: Auckland v. Otago (Dunedin) 1936–37
4th	324	W. M. Wallace & J. R. Reid: New Zealanders v. Cambridge U. (Cambridge) ...1949
5th	266	B. Sutcliffe & W. S. Haig: Otago v. Auckland (Dunedin) 1949–50
6th	184	D. C. Collins & H. M. McGirr: Wellington v. Otago (Dunedin) 1923–24
7th	265	J. L. Powell & N. Dorreen: Canterbury v. Otago (Christchurch) 1929–30
8th	190*	J. W. E. Mills & C. F. W. Allcott: New Zealanders v. Civil Service (Chiswick) ...1927
9th	239	H. B. Cave & I. B. Leggat: Central Districts v. Otago (Dunedin) 1952–53
10th	184	R. C. Blunt & W. Hawkesworth: Otago v. Canterbury (Christchurch) 1931–32

RECORDS BY INDIAN BATSMEN

1st	413	V. Mankad & P. Roy: India v. New Zealand (Madras) 1955–56
2nd	455	B. B. Nimbalkar & K. V. Bhandarkar: Maharashtra v. Western India States (Poona) 1948–49
3rd	410	L. Amarnath & R. S. Modi: India in England v. Rest (Calcutta) 1946–47
4th	577	Gul Mahomed & V. S. Hazare: Baroda v. Holkar (Baroda) 1946–47
5th	360	U. M. Merchant & M. N. Raiji: Bombay v. Hyderabad (Bombay) 1947–48
6th	371	V. M. Merchant & R. S. Modi: Bombay v Maharashtra (Bombay) 1943–44
7th	274	K. C. Ibraham & K. M. Rangnekar: Bijapur XI v. Bengal XI (Bombay) 1942–43
8th	236	C. T. Sarwate & R. P. Singh: Holkar v. Delhi (New Delhi) 1949–50
9th	245	V. S. Hazare & N. D. Nagarwalla: Maharashtra v. Baroda (Poona) 1939–40
10th	249	C. T. Sarwate & S. N. Banerjee: Indians v. Surrey (Oval) 1946

RECORDS BY PAKISTAN BATSMEN

1st	277	Hanif Mohammed & Alimuddin: Karachi A. v. Sind A (Karachi) 1957–58
2nd	269	Nazar Mohammed & Murrawat Hussain: Pakistan v. Ceylon (Ceylon) 1948–49
3rd	273	Hanif Mohammed & V. L. Manjrekar: Hasan Mahmood's XI v. A. V. M. Cannon's XI (Karachi) 1953–54
4th	259	Hanif Mohammed & Wallis Mathias: Karachi v. Bahawalpur (Karachi) 1958–59
5th	192	Waqar Hasan & Wazir Mohammed: Pakistan v. Surrey (Oval) 1954
6th	171	Imtiaz Ahmed & Wazir Mohammed: Pakistan v. Central Zone (Indore).........1952–53
7th	308	Waqar Hasan & Imtiaz Ahmed: Pakistan v. New Zealand (Lahore) 1955–56
8th	136	S. F. Rehman & Humayun Zaman: Lahore v. Services (Lahore) 1958–59
9th	140	Mushtaq Mohammed & Abdul Dyer: Karachi Whites v. Hyderabad (Hyderabad) 1956–57
10th	109	Zulfiqar Ahmed & Amir Elahi: Pakistan v. India (Madras) 1952–53

Highest Score at the Fall of Each Wicket

The highest score reached at the fall of each wicket is as follows (Kent declared their innings closed after the fall of the 4th wicket):

1st	wicket	555	Yorks. (555—1d) v. Essex (Leyton) 1932
2nd	wicket	594	Victoria (1107) v. N.S.W. (Melbourne) 1926–27
3rd	wicket	667	Kent (803—4d) v. Essex (Brentwood) 1934
4th	wicket	801	Maharashtra (826—4) v. Western India States (Poona) 1948–49
5th	wicket	720	England (849) v. West Indies (Kingston) 1929–30
6th	wicket	834	Victoria (1107) v. N.S.W. (Melbourne) 1926–27
7th	wicket	956	Victoria (1059) v. Tasmania (Melbourne) 1922–23
8th	wicket	1043	Victoria (1107) v. N.S.W. (Melbourne) 1926–27
9th	wicket	1046	Victoria (1107) v. N.S.W. (Melbourne) 1926–27
10th	wicket	1107	Victoria (1107) v. N.S.W. (Melbourne) 1926–27

Wicket Partnerships of over 400

(Complete details of each partnership can be found in the appropriate wicket partnership section.)

577 —4th Gul Mahomed & V. S. Hazare for Holkar 1946–47
574*—4th C. L. Walcott & F. M. Worrell for Barbados 1945–46
555 —1st P. Holmes & H. Sutcliffe for Yorkshire 1932
554 —1st J. T. Brown & J. Tunnicliffe for Yorkshire 1898
502*—4th F. M. Worrell & J. D. C. Goddard for Barbados 1943–44
490 —1st E. H. Bowley & John Langridge for Sussex 1933
487*—6th G. Headley & C. C. Passailaigue for Jamaica 1931–32
456 —1st E. R. Mayne & W. H. Ponsford for Victoria 1923–24
455 —2nd B. B. Nimbalkar & K. V. Bhandarkar for Maharashtra 1948–49
451 —2nd W. H. Ponsford & D. G. Bradman for Australia 1934
448 —4th R. Abel & T. Hayward for Surrey 1899
446 —2nd C. C. Hunte & G. Sobers for West Indies 1957–58
445 —3rd P. E. Whitelaw & W. N. Carson for Auckland 1936–37
434 —3rd J. B. Stollmeyer & G. E. Gomez for Trinidad 1946–47
433 —8th V. T. Trumper & A. Sims for Australians 1913–14
429*—2nd J. G. Dewes & G. H. G. Doggart for Cambridge U. 1949
428 —1st J. B. Hobbs & A. Sandham for Surrey 1926
428 —6th W. W. Armstrong & M. A. Noble for Australians 1902
424 —1st J. F. W. Nicolson & I. J. Siedle for Natal 1926–27
424*—3rd W. J. Edrich & D. C. S. Compton for Middlesex 1948
424 —4th I. S. Lee & S. O. Quin for Victoria 1933–34
413 —1st V. Mankad & P. Roy for India 1955–56
411 —6th R. M. Poore & E. G. Wynyard for Hampshire 1899
411 —4th P. B. H. May & M. C. Cowdrey for England 1957
410 —3rd L. Amarnath & R. S. Modi for India in England 1946–47
410 —4th G. Abraham & B. Pandit for Kerala 1959–60
405 —5th S. G. Barnes & D. G. Bradman for Australia 1946–47
402 —4th W. Watson & T. W. Graveney for M.C.C. 1953–54

D. G. Bradman, W. H. Ponsford and F. M. Worrell are the only batsmen to appear twice in the above list—the latter is the only player to have shared in two stands of over 500.

Leading Wicket Partnerships

The following are the best partnerships for each wicket, the standard being 200 runs or over for the first to sixth wickets, 150 or over for the seventh to ninth, and 100 or over for the tenth.

FIRST WICKET

555 P. Holmes & H. Sutcliffe: Yorks v. Essex (Leyton) 1932
554 J. T. Brown & J. Tunnicliffe: Yorks. v. Derby (Chesterfield) 1898
490 E. H. Bowley & John Langridge: Sussex v. Middx. (Hove) 1933
456 E. R. Mayne & W. H. Ponsford: Victoria v. Queensland (Melbourne)........1923–24
428 J. B. Hobbs & A. Sandham: Surrey v. Oxford U. (Oval) 1926
424 J. F. W. Nicolson & I. J. Siedle: Natal v. O.F.S. (Bloemfontein) 1926–27
413 V. Mankad & P. Roy: India v. New Zealand (Madras) 1955–56
391 A. O. Jones & A. Shrewsbury: Notts. v. Glos. (Bristol) 1899
390 L. Wight & G. Gibbs: British Guiana v. Barbados (Georgetown) 1951–52
380 C. J. B. Wood & H. Whitehead: Leics. v. Worcs. (Worcester) 1906
379 R. Abel & W. Brockwell: Surrey v. Hants. (Oval) 1897
378 J. T. Brown & J. Tunnicliffe: Yorks. v. Sussex (Sheffield) 1897
377* N. F. Horner & K. Ibadulla: Warwicks. v. Surrey (Oval) 1960
375 W. M. Woodfull & W. H. Ponsford: Victoria v. N.S.W. (Melbourne) 1926–27
373 B. Sutcliffe & L. A. Watt: Otago v. Auckland (Auckland) 1950–51
368 A. C. MacLaren & R. H. Spooner: Lancs. v. Glos. (Liverpool) 1903
368 E. H. Bowley & J. H. Parks: Sussex v. Glos. (Hove) 1929
364 R. Abel & D. L. A. Jephson: Surrey v. Derby (Oval) 1900
361 N. Oldfield & V. H. Broderick: Northants. v. Scotland (Peterborough) 1953
359 L. Hutton & C. Washbrook: England v. South Africa (Johannesburg) 1948–49
355 A. F. Rae & J. B. Stollmeyer: West Indians v. Sussex (Hove) 1950
352 T. Hayward & J. B. Hobbs: Surrey v. Warwicks. (Oval) 1909
350* C. Washbrook & W. Place: Lancs. v. Sussex (Manchester) 1947
349 J. G. Dewes & D. S. Sheppard: Cambridge U. v. Sussex (Hove) 1950
347 P. Holmes & H. Sutcliffe: Yorks. v. Hants. (Portsmouth) 1920

346 L. C. H. Palairet & H. T. Hewett: Somerset v. Yorks. (Taunton) 1892
343 J. G. Dewes & D. S. Sheppard: Cambridge U. v. West Indians (Cambridge) 1950
340 J. H. Fingleton & W. A. Brown: N.S.W. v. Victoria (Sydney) 1933–34
338 T. Bowring & H. Teesdale: Oxford U. v. Gentlemen of England (Oxford) 1908
337 C. C. McDonald & K. Meuleman: Victoria v. South Australia (Adelaide) 1949–50
333 J. F. Byrne & S. P. Kinneir: Warwicks. v. Lancs. (Birmingham) 1905
330 B. Mitchell & E. A. B. Rowan: South Africans v. Surrey (Oval) 1935
323 J. B. Hobbs & W. Rhodes: England v. Australia (Melbourne) 1911–12
323 P. Holmes & H. Sutcliffe: Yorks. v. Lancs. (Sheffield) 1931
322 H. Storer & J. Bowden: Derby v. Essex (Derby)..................................1929
322 G. Gunn & A. Sandham: M.C.C. v. Jamaica (Kingston) 1929–30
318 W. W. Keeton & R. T. Simpson: Notts. v. Lancs. (Manchester) 1949
315 H. Sutcliffe & L. Hutton: Yorks. v. Leics. (Hull) 1937
315 H. Sutcliffe & L. Hutton: Yorks. v. Hants. (Sheffield) 1939
314 A. C. MacLaren & T. Hayward: MacLaren's XI v. N.S.W. (Sydney) 1901–02
313 T. Hayward & J. B. Hobbs: Surrey v. Worcs. (Worcester) 1913
313 A. J. Richardson & L. T. Gun: South Australia v. Western Australia (Adelaide) 1925–26
310 J. D. Robertson & S. M. Brown: Middx. v. Notts. (Lord's) 1947
309 F. L. Bowley & H. K. Foster: Worcs. v. Derby (Derby) 1901
309 P. Holmes & H. Sutcliffe: Yorks. v. Warwicks. (Birmingham) 1931
306 L. A. Cuff & J. D. Lawrence: Canterbury v. Auckland (Christchurch)............1893–94
306 P. F. Warner & J. Douglas: Middx. v. Notts. (Nottingham) 1904
306 F. L. Bowley & F. Pearson: Worcs. v. Glos. (Worcester) 1913
305 John Langridge & H. W. Greenwood: Sussex v. Essex (Hove)....................1935
303 G. L. Wilson & F. W. Marlow: Sussex v. Oxford U. (Hove) 1895
303 A. O. Jones & J. Iremonger: Notts. v. Glos. (Nottingham) 1904
299 D. V. Smith & M. J. K. Smith: M.C.C. v. Surrey (Lord's) 1958
298 V. T. Trumper & R. A. Duff: N.S.W. v. South Australia (Sydney) 1902–03
295 C. J. Barnett & A. E. Fagg: M.C.C. v. Queensland (Brisbane) 1936–37
295 John Langridge & J. H. Parks: Sussex v. Leics. (Hove) 1938
293 V. M. Merchant & V. Mankad: Indians v. Sussex (Hove) 1946
292 G. Challenor & P. H. Tarilton: Barbados v. Trinidad (Barbados) 1926–27
290 J. B. Hobbs & T. Hayward: Surrey v. Yorks. (Lord's) 1914
290 P. Holmes & H. Sutcliffe: Yorks. v. Middx. (Leeds) 1928
290 D. Kenyon & P. E. Richardson: Worcs. v. Glos. (Dudley) 1953
290 G. Pullar & M. C. Cowdrey: England v. South Africa (Oval) 1960
288 H. W. Bainbridge & W. G. Quaife: Warwicks. v. Hants. (Southampton) 1897
287 C. B. Fry & J. Vine: Sussex v. Hants. (Hove) 1904
286 R. E. H. Hudson & C. P. Hamilton: Army v. West Indians (Aldershot) 1933
286 B. Sutcliffe & D. D. Taylor: Auckland v. Canterbury (Auckland) 1948–49
286 J. B. Stollmeyer & A. G. Ganteaume: Trinidad v. Jamaica (Trinidad) 1949–50
286 L. Hutton & F. A. Lowson: Yorks. v. South Africans (Sheffield) 1951
285 I. J. Siedle & H. F. Wade: Natal v. Eastern Province (Pietermaritzburg) 1936–37
284 J. W. H. T. Douglas & A. E. Knight: England XI v. Australians (Blackpool) 1909
284 R. T. Simpson & R. J. Giles: Notts. v. Oxford U. (Oxford) 1951
283 W. G. Grace & B. B. Cooper: Gentlemen of South v. Players of South (Oval) 1869
283 J. B. Hobbs & H. Sutcliffe: England v. Australia (Melbourne) 1924–25
283 A. E. Fagg & P. R. Sunnucks: Kent v. Essex (Colchester) 1938
282* G. Wilson & W. W. Hill-Wood: M.C.C. v. Victoria (Melbourne) 1922–23
281 G. Pullar & M. C. Cowdrey: M.C.C. v. British Guiana (Georgetown) 1959–60
281* W. B. Stott & K. Taylor: Yorks. v. Sussex (Hove) 1960
279 P. Holmes & H. Sutcliffe: Yorks. v. Northants. (Northampton) 1919
279 C. F. Walters & H. H. Gibbons: Worcs. v. Essex (Chelmsford) 1934
278 A. A. Jackson & W. H. Ponsford: Ryder's XI v. Woodfull's XI (Sydney) 1929–30
278* C. F. Walters & H. H. Gibbons: Worcs. v. Leics. (Worcester)....................1934
278 A. M. Taylor & R. E. Marshall: Barbados v. Trinidad (Barbados) 1948–49
277 T. H. Fowler & H. Wrathall: Glos. v. London County (Crystal Palace) 1903
277 G. T. S. Stevens & E. T. Killick: Middx. v. Warwicks. (Lord's) 1931
277 W. W. Keeton & C. B. Harris: Notts. v. Middx. (Nottingham) 1933
277 D. Kenyon & L. Outschoorn: Worcs. v. Kent (Gravesend) 1954
277* Hanif Mohammed & Alimuddin: Karachi A v. Sind A (Karachi) 1957–58
277 M. R. Hallam & H. D. Bird: Leics. v. South Africans (Leicester) 1960
276 C. S. Dempster & J. W. E. Mills: New Zealand v. England (Wellington) 1929–30
274 F. L. Bowley & H. K. Foster: Worcs. v. Hants. (Portsmouth) 1907
274 P. Holmes & H. Sutcliffe: Yorks. v. Somerset (Hull) 1923
274 P. Holmes & H. Sutcliffe: Yorks. v. Glos. (Gloucester) 1927
274 A. H. Dyson & E. Davies: Glamorgan v. Leics. (Leicester) 1937
274 E. A. B. Rowan & A. I. Taylor: Transvaal v. Border (Johannesburg) 1952–53
273 Nazar Mohammed & Jagdish Lal: Northern India v. N.W.F.P. (Lahore) 1941–42
272 P. Holmes & H. Sutcliffe: Yorks. v. Leics. (Hull) 1925
272 A. J. Croom & N. Kilner: Warwicks. v. Worcs. (Birmingham) 1934
270* R. Abel & W. Brockwell: Surrey v. Kent (Oval) 1900

270   C. Hallows & H. Makepeace: Lancs. v. Worcs. (Worcester).....................................1922
270   A. V. Avery & T. C. Dodds: Essex v. Surrey (Oval) 1946
269* P. Holmes & H. Sutcliffe: North v. South (Sheffield) 1927
269   R. T. Simpson & W. W. Keeton: Notts. v. Kent (Nottingham) 1951
268   J. B. Hobbs & H. Sutcliffe: England v. South Africa (Lord's) 1924
268   P. Holmes & H. Sutcliffe: Yorks. v. Essex (Leyton) 1928
268   E. Paynter & C. Washbrook: Lancs. v. Sussex (Hove) 1937
268   P. C. Davies & F. Seyfried: N.E. Transvaal v. O.F.S. (Bloemfontein) 1955–56
267   V. T. Trumper & R. A. Duff: N.S.W. v. Victoria (Sydney) 1902–03
267   W. Barber & L. Hutton: Yorks. v. Kent (Leeds) 1934
266   A. Shrewsbury & A. E. Stoddart: England v. M.C.C. (Lord's) 1887
266   A. Sandham & A. Jeacocke: Surrey v. Northants. (Oval) 1921
266   N. Kilner & E. J. Smith: Warwicks. v. Middx. (Lord's) 1927
265   R. Abel & W. Brockwell: Surrey v. Warwicks. (Oval) 1898
265* P. Holmes & H. Sutcliffe: Yorks. v. Surrey (Oval) 1926
265   L. G. Berry & F. T. Prentice: Leics. v. New Zealanders (Leicester) 1937
265   W. A. Brown & G. G. Cook: Queensland v. N.S.W. (Sydney) 1938–39
264   J. B. Hobbs & A. Sandham: Surrey v. Somerset (Taunton) 1932
263   J. B. Hobbs & H. Sutcliffe: Players v. Gentlemen (Lord's) 1926
262   L. Hutton & W. J. Edrich: M.C.C. v. Griqualand West (Kimberley) 1938–39
262   F. G. Mann & J. R. Thompson: Cambridge U. v. Leics. (Cambridge) 1939
261   E. L. G. Hoad & P. H. Tarilton: Barbados v. M.C.C. (Barbados) 1929–30
261   D. J. McGlew & T. L. Goddard: Natal v. Rhodesia (Bulawayo) 1957–58
260   F. Watson & C. Hallows: Lancs. v. Hants. (Liverpool) 1927
260   B. Mitchell & I. J. Siedle: South Africa v. England (Cape Town) 1930–31
260   L. B. Fishlock & E. A. Bedser: Surrey v. Somerset (Oval) 1949
259   Hon. H. G. H. Mulholland & D. C. Collins: Cambridge U. v. Indians (Cambridge) 1911
259   A. R. Morris & J. A. R. Moroney: Australians v. Natal (Durban) 1949–50
258   A. E. Lewis & L. C. H. Palairet: Somerset v. Sussex (Taunton) 1901
258   John Langridge & J. H. Parks: Sussex v. Surrey (Horsham) 1934
258   E. A. B. Rowan & R. Connell: Eastern Province v. Griqualand West (Port Elizabeth)...1945–46
258   A. F. Rae & E. McMorris: Jamaica v. Trinidad (Georgetown) 1959–60
256   A. J. Richardson & V. Y. Richardson: South Australia v. M.C.C. (Adelaide) 1922–23
256   D. G. W. Fletcher, R. C. E. Pratt & M. J. Stewart: Surrey v. Cambridge U. (Guildford)...1956
       (*Fletcher retired hurt at 1, Pratt and Stewart added 255.*)
256   D. J. McGlew & T. L. Goddard: South Africans v. Glamorgan (Cardiff) 1960
255   C. F. Walters & H. H. Gibbons: Worcs. v. Lancs. (Worcester) 1933
255   V. Y. Richardson & H. C. Nitschke: South Australia v. Queensland (Adelaide) 1934–35
255   A. H. Dyson & E. Davies: Glamorgan v. Glos. (Newport) 1939
253   P. Holmes & H. Sutcliffe: Yorks. v. Lancs. (Sheffield) 1919
253* J. B. Hobbs & A. Sandham: Surrey v. West Indians (Oval) 1928
252   R. R. Relf & J. Vine: Sussex v. Notts. (Hove) 1912
252   G. Gunn & W. W. Whysall: Notts. v. Kent (Nottingham) 1924
252   B. Sutcliffe & V. J. Scott: New Zealand XI v. Rest (Christchurch) 1948–49
251   L. J. Todd & A. E. Fagg: Kent v. Leics. (Maidstone) 1949
251   P. Roy & S. Bose: Bengal v. Assam (Calcutta) 1951–52
250   R. A. Sinfield & C. J. Barnett: Glos. v. Glamorgan (Cardiff) 1935
249   F. L. Bowley & F. Pearson: Worcs. v. Warwicks. (Kidderminster) 1910
249   J. H. Fingleton & W. A. Brown: N.S.W. v. South Australia (Sydney) 1934–35
249   R. F. Marshall & J. R. Gray: Hants. v. Middx. (Portsmouth) 1960
248   P. F. Warner & L. J. Moon: Middx. v. Glos. (Lord's) 1903
247   H. T. W. Hardinge & James Seymour: Kent v. Derby (Derby) 1925
247   B. Sutcliffe & V. J. Scott: New Zealanders v. Combined Services (Gillingham) 1949
246   R. Abel & T. Hayward: Surrey v. Sussex (Hastings) 1902
246   M. Harvey & G. E. Tamblyn: Victoria v. South Australia (Adelaide) 1945–46
245   G. Gunn & W. W. Whysall: Notts. v. Warwicks. (Coventry) 1928
245   L. Hutton & F. A. Lowson: Yorks. v. Lancs. (Leeds) 1952
245   Nazar Mohammed & Hanif Mohammed: Pakistan v. South Zone (Hyderabad) 1952–53
244   J. R. M. Mackay & A. Diamond: N.S.W. v. Australian XI (Sydney) 1905–06
244   H. L. Collins & C. G. Macartney: N.S.W. v. M.C.C. (Sydney) 1920–21
244   J. B. Hobbs & A. Sandham: Surrey v. Middx. (Oval) 1923
243   K. J. Key & W. Rashleigh: Oxford U. v. Cambridge U. (Lord's) 1886
243   C. J. Burnup & E. W. Dillon: Kent v. Hants. (Tunbridge Wells) 1902
243   J. B. Hobbs & H. Sutcliffe: Leveson-Gower's XI v. New Zealanders (Scarborough) 1931
243   D. Brookes & P. Davis: Northants. v. Worcs. (Kidderminster) 1946
242   J. B. Hobbs & E. G. Hayes: Surrey v. Lancs. (Oval) 1911
241   P. F. Warner & H. W. Lee: Middx. v. Sussex (Lord's) 1920
241   P. Holmes & H. Sutcliffe: Yorks. v. Surrey (Oval) 1929
241   P. A. Gibb & J. R. Thompson: Cambridge U. v. Northants. (Cambridge) 1938
241   E. Davies & W. G. A. Parkhouse: Glamorgan v. Somerset (Cardiff) 1950
241   D. V. Smith & A. S. M. Oakman: Sussex v. Glamorgan (Hove) 1956
240   F. Watson & C. Hallows: Lancs. v. Derby (Blackpool) 1928

240 W. H. Ponsford & K. E. Rigg: Victoria v. South Australia (Adelaide)....................1933–34
240 L. Hutton & C. Washbrook: M.C.C. v. South Australia (Adelaide) 1946–47
239 C. S. Dempster & W. H. Dustin: Wellington v. Canterbury (Wellington) 1931–32
239 J. H. Parks & D. Smith: M.C.C. v. Otago (Dunedin) 1935–36
239 J. B. Stollmeyer & A. F. Rae: West Indies v. India (Madras) 1948–49
239 W. H. Ponsford & S. J. McCabe: Australians v. Surrey (Oval) 1934
238 W. G. Grace & T. G. Matthews: Glos. v. Yorks. (Sheffield) 1872
238 A. O. Jones & J. Iremonger: Notts. v. Essex (Leyton) 1901
238 C. B. Fry & J. Vine: Sussex v. Surrey (Hastings) 1902
238* P. Holmes & H. Sutcliffe: Yorks. v. Cambridge U. (Cambridge) 1923
238 H. T. W. Hardinge & W. H. Ashdown: Kent v. Leics. (Blackheath) 1925
238 John Langridge & D. S. Sheppard: Sussex v. Leics. (Hove) 1949
238* A. C. Shirreff & S. Smith: Combined Services v. Essex (Chelmsford) 1950
238 Hanif Mohammed & Alimuddin: Karachi A v. Sind B (Karachi) 1957–58
237 K. S. Ranjitsinhji & E. G. Wynyard: M.C.C. v. Cambridge U. (Lord's) 1904
237 H. Teesdale & Hon. C. N. Bruce: Oxford U. v. Leveson-Gower's XI (Eastbourne)........1908
237 C. Washbrook & W. Place: Lancs. v. Essex (Colchester) 1946
236* S. K. Coen & J. M. M. Commaille: O.F.S. v. Eastern Province (Port Elizabeth) 1926–27
236 W. M. Woodfull & W. H. Ponsford: Victoria v. South Australia (Melbourne) 1927–28
236 L. B. Fishlock, R. J. Gregory & H. S. Squires: Surrey v. Middx. (Lord's) 1938
          (*Fishlock retired hurt with the score at 68.*)
236 V. M. Merchant & V. Mankad: C.C. of India v. Nayudu's XI (Bombay) 1944–45
236 A. H. Dyson & E. Davies: Glamorgan v. Sussex (Hove) 1947
235 Hon. R. Anson & F. A. Tarrant: Middx. v. Essex (Leyton) 1914
235 E. H. Bowley & V. W. C. Jupp: Sussex v. Leics. (Leicester) 1921
235 P. Holmes & H. Sutcliffe: Yorks. v. Glamorgan (Sheffield) 1930
235 W. A. Hadlee & M. L. Page: Canterbury v. Wellington (Christchurch) 1936–37
235 W. R. Endean & A. I. Taylor: Transvaal v. O.F.S. (Johannesburg) 1954–55
234 T. Hayward & J. B. Hobbs: Surrey v. Kent (Blackheath) 1914
234 J. W. Lee & F. S. Lee: Somerset v. Essex (Leyton) 1932
234 L. P. O'Brien & K. E. Rigg: Victoria v. N.S.W. (Melbourne) 1934–35
233 P. F. Warner & C. J. Burnup: M.C.C. v. Cambridge U. (Lord's) 1902
233 J. B. Hobbs & A. Sandham: Surrey v. Glos. (Oval) 1922
233 W. E. Bates & A. H. Dyson: Glamorgan v. Yorks. (Sheffield) 1930
233 W. A. Brown & J. H. Fingleton: Australia v. South Africa (Cape Town) 1935–36
233 D. Smith & A. E. Alderman: Derby v. Leics. (Chesterfield) 1937
233* C. Washbrook & W. Place: Lancs. v. Sussex (Eastbourne) 1947
233 H. Halliday & W. Watson: Yorks. v. Northants. (Northampton) 1948
233 E. Davies & W. G. A. Parkhouse: Glamorgan v. Surrey (Swansea) 1950
233 J. D. Robertson & S. M. Brown: Middx. v. Hants. (Portsmouth) 1951
233 T. C. Dodds & A. V. Avery: Essex v. Somerset (Westcliff) 1952
232 P. F. Warner & J. Douglas: Middx. v. Surrey (Oval) 1907
232 R. H. Spooner & H. Makepeace: Lancs. v. Worcs. (Stourbridge) 1911
232 J. B. Hobbs & A. Sandham: Surrey v. Warwicks. (Oval) 1925
232 J. H. Edrich & D. G. W. Fletcher: Surrey v. Rhodesia (Salisbury) 1959–60
231 R. Abel & W. Brockwell: Surrey v. Sussex (Oval) 1897
231 G. E. V. Crutchley & H. W. Lee: Middx. v. Notts. (Lord's) 1921
231 J. B. Hobbs & A. Sandham: Surrey v. Somerset (Oval)......................................1931
231 W. W. Keeton & C. B. Harris: Notts. v. Lancs. (Nottingham) 1947
231 M. B. Hofmeyr & B. Boobbyer: Oxford U. v. Sussex (Chichester) 1950
231 D. Kenyon & L. Outschoorn: Worcs. v. Leics. (Worcester) 1954
230 B. H. Holloway & T. A. L. Whittington: M.C.C. v. British Guiana (Georgetown) ...1910–11
230 F. Watson & C. Hallows: Lancs. v. Worcs. (Worcester) 1928
230 H. Sutcliffe & L. Hutton: Yorks. v. Surrey (Leeds) 1936
230 A. E. Fagg & L. J. Todd: Kent v. Northants. (Tunbridge Wells) 1948
230 D. Brookes & P. Arnold: Northants. v. Somerset (Taunton) 1955
230 W. B. Stott & K. Taylor: Yorks. v. Notts. (Nottingham) 1957
229 B. Sutcliffe & V. J. Scott: New Zealanders v. Surrey (Oval) 1949
229 S. M. Brown & H. P. Sharp: Middx. v. Cambridge U. (Cambridge) 1949
228 A. E. Stoddart & T. C. O'Brien: Middx. v. Surrey (Lord's) 1893
228 H. Halliday & J. V. Wilson: Yorks. v. Scotland (Scarborough) 1951
227 W. M. Woodfull & W. H. Ponsford: Victoria v. N.S.W. (Melbourne) 1927–28
227 P. Holmes & H. Sutcliffe: Yorks. v. Leics. (Leicester) 1928
227 J. B. Hobbs & H. Sutcliffe: Players v. Gentlemen (Scarborough) 1931
227 F. C. Martin & S. K. Coen: Western Province v. Eastern Province (Pretoria) 1931–32
227 S. M. Brown & H. P. Sharp: Middx. v. Worcs. (Lord's) 1950
227 J. W. Burke & S. C. Carroll: N.S.W. v. South Australia (Adelaide) 1956–57
226 W. G. Grace & R. Abel: South v. North (Scarborough) 1889
226 E. H. Bowley & J. H. Parks: Sussex v. Notts. (Nottingham) 1928
226 R. D. Niehuus & R. J. Craig: South Australia v. Indians (Adelaide) 1947–48
226 C. J. Barnett & G. M. Emmett: Glos. v. Yorks. (Bristol) 1948
226 D. G. W. Fletcher & E. A. Bedser: Surrey v. Oxford U. (Guildford) 1948

226* W. A. Hadlee & J. G. Leggat: Canterbury v. Otago (Christchurch) 1948–49
226 N. Oldfield & T. L. Livingston: Commonwealth v. Indian XI (New Delhi)............1949–50
226 V. Mankad & P. L. Punjabi: Indians v. Karachi (Karachi) 1954–55
226 D. M. Young & C. A. Milton: Glos. v. Somerset (Bristol) 1959
225 L. C. H. Palairet & L. C. Braund: Somerset v. Lancs. (Bath) 1901
225 W. H. Ponsford & H. L. Hendry: Victoria v. Queensland (Brisbane) 1926–27
225 John Langridge & J. H. Parks: Sussex v. Kent (Hastings) 1937
225 L. Wight & B. H. Pairaudeau: British Guiana v. Jamaica (Georgetown) 1952–53
225* A. R. Morris & K. R. Miller: N.S.W. v. Queensland (Sydney) 1950–51
225 P. E. Richardson & W. Watson: M.C.C. v. Wellington (Wellington) 1958–59
224 A. Sandham & R. E. S. Wyatt: M.C.C. v. Bombay Presidency (Bombay) 1926–27
224 T. H. Barling & A. Ducat: Surrey v. Warwicks. (Oval) 1927
224 R. H. J. Brooke & C. B. Fordham: Minor Counties v. Oxford U. (Oxford) 1933
224 W. M. Woodfull & W. A. Brown: Australian XI v. Tasmania (Hobart) 1933–34
224 J. B. Stollmeyer & V. H. Stollmeyer: Trinidad v. Barbados (Trinidad) 1941–42
223 A. O. Jones & A. Shrewsbury: Notts. v. Kent (Nottingham) 1896
223 A. C. MacLaren & R. H. Spooner: Lancs. v. Sussex (Manchester) 1904
223 W. M. Woodfull & W. H. Ponsford: Australian XI v. Rest (Sydney) 1926–27
223 H. Sutcliffe & M. Leyland: M.C.C. v. South Australia (Adelaide) 1932–33
223 B. D. Carris & P. A. Gibb: Cambridge U. v. Glamorgan (Swansea) 1938
222 L. C. H. Palairet & L. C. Braund: Somerset v. Yorks. (Leeds) 1901
222 E. H. Bowley & J. H. Parks: Sussex v. Kent (Hastings) 1930
222 J. D. Robertson & S. M. Brown: Middx. v. Yorks. (Lord's) 1947
222 W. W. Keeton & R. T. Simpson: Notts. v. Warwicks. (Nottingham) 1950
222 W. B. Stott & K. Taylor: Yorks. v. Sussex (Bradford) 1958
221 J. B. Hobbs & W. Rhodes: England v. South Africa (Cape Town) 1909–10
221 J. L. Bryan & C. A. Fiddian-Green: Cambridge U. v. Leveson-Gower's XI (Eastbourne) 1921
221 P. Holmes & H. Sutcliffe: Yorks. v. Glamorgan (Huddersfield) 1925
221 N. Kilner & R. E. S. Wyatt: Warwicks. v. Worcs. (Birmingham) 1926
221 W. H. Ashdown & A. E. Fagg: Kent v. Indians (Canterbury) 1936
221 S. H. Curnow & E. A. B. Rowan: Transvaal v. Natal (Johannesburg) 1939–40
221 J. P. McNally & A. Dunn: Griqualand West v. Eastern Province (Kimberley) 1947–48
220 C. B. Fry & J. Vine: Sussex v. Cambridge U. (Hove) 1904
220 G. Gunn & W. W. Whysall: Notts. v. Worcs. (Nottingham) 1924
220 N. Kilner & W. A. Hill: Warwicks. v. Sussex (Birmingham) 1937
220 W. M. Woodfull & W. A. Brown: Australian XI v. Rest (Launceston) 1933–34
220 B. Sutcliffe & D. D. Taylor: Auckland v. Canterbury (Auckland) 1948–49
219 T. Hayward & J. B. Hobbs: Surrey v. Worcs. (Worcester) 1907
219 C. H. B. Marsham & H. T. W. Hardinge: Kent v. Derby (Derby) 1908
219* G. Challenor & P. H. Tarilton: West Indians v. Notts. (Nottingham) 1923
219 H. T. W. Hardinge & J. L. Bryan: Kent v. Somerset (Taunton) 1927
219 A. E. Dipper & D. N. Moore: Glos. v. Oxford U. (Oxford) 1930
219 P. Holmes & A. Mitchell: Yorks. v. Somerset (Bradford) 1930
219 A. J. Croom & N. Kilner: Warwicks. v. Northants. (Northampton) 1933
219 L. G. Berry & A. Shipman: Leics. v. Hants. (Portsmouth) 1935
219 L. Hutton & C. J. Barnett: England v. Australia (Nottingham) 1938
219 L. J. Todd & J. G. W. Davies: Kent v. Middx. (Lord's) 1946
218 A. E. Stoddart & H. B. Hayman: Middx. v. Yorks. (Lord's) 1896
218 P. F. Warner & J. Douglas: Middx. v. Lancs. (Lord's) 1901
218 G. Gunn & W. W. Whysall: Notts. v. Warwicks. (Nottingham) 1924
218 H. Sutcliffe & M. Leyland: Yorks. v. Middx. (Leeds) 1925
218 W. A. Hadlee & J. G. Leggat: Canterbury v. Wellington (Christchurch) 1947–48
217 G. Bean & G. L. Wilson: Sussex v. Glos. (Hove) 1893
217 K. J. Schneider & G. W. Harris: South Australia v. Victoria (Melbourne) 1927–28
217 W. H. Ashdown & C. Fairservice: Kent v. Worcs. (Gravesend) 1933
216 C. B. Fry & J. Vine: Sussex v. Kent (Hove) 1901
216 T. Hayward & A. Baker: Surrey v. Cambridge U. (Oval) 1904
216 W. Bardsley & C. Kelleway: N.S.W. v. Victoria (Melbourne) 1919–20
216 J. B. Hobbs & A. Sandham: Surrey v. Essex (Leyton) 1925
216 John Langridge & D. S. Sheppard: Sussex v. Kent (Hastings) 1952
215 L. A. Stricker & J. W. Zulch: Transvaal v. M.C.C. (Pretoria) 1909–10
215 E. H. Bowley & M. W. Tate: Sussex v. Kent (Dover) 1927
215 C. F. Walters & H. H. Gibbons: Worcs. v. Northants. (Northampton) 1934
215 W. A. Brown & J. H. Fingleton: Australians v. Natal (Durban) 1935–36
215* W. W. Keeton & C. B. Harris: Notts. v. Derby (Worksop) 1936
215 F. S. Lee & H. D. Burrough: Somerset v. Kent (Bath) 1937
215 C. Washbrook & E. Paynter: Lancs. v. Notts. (Nottingham) 1939
214 H. T. W. Hardinge & F. E. Woolley: Kent v. Sussex (Hove) 1907
214 W. M. Woodfull & W. H. Ponsford: Australians v. Otago (Dunedin) 1927–28
214* J. H. Parks & H. E. Hammond: Sussex v. Warwicks. (Birmingham) 1936
214 W. A. Brown & J. H. Fingleton: Australian XI v. Tasmania (Hobart)...............1937–38
214 A. R. Morris & J. A. R. Moroney: Australia v. South Africa (Johannesburg) 1949–50

214 R. E. Marshall & J. R. Gray: Hants. v. Glos. (Bristol) 1959
214 B. A. Bolton & G. T. Dowling: Canterbury v. Northern Districts (Christchurch) 1959–60
213 F. S. Lee & J. W. Lee: Somerset v. Surrey (Weston-super-Mare) 1934
213 C. Washbrook & E. Paynter: Lancs. v. Leics. (Leicester) 1939
213 M. H. Bushby & D. R. W. Silk: Cambridge U. v. M.C.C. (Cambridge) 1953
213 S. G. Barnes & J. W. Burke: N.S.W. v. Queensland (Sydney) 1951–52
212 P. F. Warner & L. J. Moon: Middx. v. Sussex (Lord's) 1908
212 C. D. McIver & A. C. Russell: Essex v. Leics. (Leyton) 1914
212 C. H. Titchmash & A. C. Russell: M.C.C. v. Scotland (Lord's) 1922
212 J. B. Hobbs & H. Sutcliffe: Rest of England v. Lancs. (Oval) 1928
212* C. Washbrook & W. Place: Lancs. v. Notts. (Nottingham) 1946
212 C. Washbrook & R. T. Simpson: England v. West Indies (Nottingham) 1950
212 D. Kenyon & P. E. Richardson: Worcs. v. Essex (Worcester) 1953
211 G. Bean & F. W. Marlow: Sussex v. Glos. (Hove) 1896
211* J. B. Hobbs & W. Rhodes: M.C.C. v. Transvaal (Johannesburg) 1913–14
211 E. J. Smith & A. J. Croom: Warwicks. v. Glamorgan (Swansea) 1930
211 H. W. Lee & J. W. Hearne: Middx. v. Glamorgan (Lord's) 1931
211* R. J. Gregory & L. B. Fishlock: Surrey v. Worcs. (Oval) 1939
211 J. D. Robertson & S. M. Brown: Middx. v. Surrey (Oval) 1947
211 D. Brookes & N. Oldfield: Northants. v. Glos. (Northampton) 1949
211 P. A. Gibb & K. Meuleman: Commonwealth v. Governor's XI (Jorhat) 1953–54
210 C. J. Burnup & E. W. Dillon: Kent v. Worcs. (Worcester) 1901
210 A. C. Russell & C. D. McIver: Essex v. Hants. (Leyton) 1913
210 H. O. Rock & H. L. Collins: N.S.W. v. Western Australia (Sydney) 1925–26
210* P. Holmes & H. Sutcliffe: Yorks. v. Notts. (Nottingham) 1928
210 J. B. Hobbs & A. Sandham: Surrey v. Glamorgan (Cardiff)...........................1929
210 C. F. Walters & H. H. Gibbons: Worcs. v. Warwicks. (Kidderminster) 1934
210 J. H. Parks & H. W. Greenwood: Sussex v. Glos. (Hove) 1935
210 R. A. Parker & C. L. Badcock: South Australia v. Victoria (Adelaide) 1935–36
210 A. R. Morris & J. A. R. Moroney: Australians v. Rhodesia (Bulawayo) 1949–50
210 S. G. Barnes & A. R. Morris: N.S.W. v. Victoria (Melbourne) 1951–52
210 M. C. Cowdrey & R. Subba Row: M.C.C. v. Leeward Islands (Antigua) 1959–60
209 W. W. Whysall & W. Walker: Notts. v. Glos. (Nottingham) 1926
209 A. E. Dipper & R. A. Sinfield: Glos. v. Worcs. (Bristol) 1927
209 J. B. Hobbs & A. Sandham: Surrey v. Glamorgan (Oval)..............................1931
209 H. Gimblett & M. M. Walford: Somerset v. Notts. (Nottingham) 1947
209 B. Sutcliffe & L. A. Watt: Otago v. Canterbury (Dunedin)........................1947–48
209 T. C. Dodds & A. V. Avery: Essex v. Derby (Derby) 1948
209 F. A. Lowson & D. E. V. Padgett: Yorks. v. Scotland (Hull) 1956
209 D. M. Young & C. A. Milton: Glos. v. Somerset (Taunton) 1956
209 J. D. Robertson & R. A. Gale: Middx. v. Sussex (Lord's) 1957
208 Lord Harris & Lord Throwley: Kent v. Sussex (Gravesend)..........................1882
208 C. W. Wright & F. Mitchell: M.C.C. v. Cambridge U. (Lord's) 1898
208 T. Hayward & J. B. Hobbs: Surrey v. Leics. (Oval) 1906
208 F. L. Fane & J. W. H. T. Douglas: Essex v. Middx. (Leyton) 1906
208 R. H. Spooner & A. Hartley: Lancs. v. Sussex (Eastbourne) 1909
208 J. Vine & R. R. Relf: Sussex v. Somerset (Bath)..................................1910
208 H. W. Lee & C. H. L. Skeet: Middx. v. Surrey (Lord's) 1920
208 R. C. Blunt & R. V. de W. Worker: Canterbury v. M.C.C. (Christchurch) 1922–23
208 F. Watson & C. Hallows: Lancs. v. Surrey (Manchester) 1927
208 A. Mitchell & E. Oldroyd: Yorks. v. Cambridge U. (Cambridge) 1929
208 F. Watson & J. L. Hopwood: Lancs. v. Kent (Manchester) 1935
208* D. Brookes & N. Oldfield: Northants. v. Yorks. (Wellingborough) 1949
207 F. L. Fane & J. W. H. T. Douglas: Essex v. Kent (Leyton) 1908
207 J. B. Hobbs & W. Rhodes: M.C.C. v. Natal (Durban) 1909–10
207 A. M. Crawley & P. V. F. Cazalet: Oxford U. v. Surrey (Oval) 1927
207 A. Mitchell & W. Barber: Yorks. v. Middx. (Lord's)...............................1935
207 L. Hutton & W. J. Edrich: M.C.C. v. Natal (Durban) 1938–39
207 J. D. Robertson & S. M. Brown: Middx. v. Lancs. (Manchester) 1949
207 W. G. A. Parkhouse & B. Hedges: Glamorgan v. Kent (Dartford) 1959
207 D. Kenyon & R. G. A. Headley: Worcs. v. Essex (Romford) 1960
206 W. W. Read & H. Jupp: Surrey v. Yorks. (Oval) 1877
206 R. W. Rice & C. L. Townsend: Glos. v. Sussex (Bristol) 1902
206 W. W. Hill-Wood & J. Bowden: Derby v. Somerset (Bath) 1923
206 A. C. Wilkinson & R. J. Shaw: Combined Services v. New Zealanders (Portsmouth) 1931
206 C. J. Barnett & C. C. Dacre: Glos. v. Worcs. (Worcester) 1933
206 C. L. Badcock & B. A. Barnett: Australians v. Surrey (Oval) 1938
206 S. H. Curnow & F. Warne: Rest of South Africa v. Air Force XI (Johannesburg) ...1942–43
205 A. J. Webbe & A. E. Stoddart: Middx. v. Kent (Gravesend) 1886
205 L. C. H. Palairet & G. Fowler: Somerset v. Glos. (Bristol) 1895
205 A. O. Jones & J. Iremonger: Notts. v. Lancs. (Nottingham) 1903
205 S. H. Curnow & E. A. B. Rowan: Transvaal v. Natal (Cape Town) 1932–33

205 A. W. Allen & G. W. Parker: Cambridge U. v. Oxford U. (Lord's) 1934
205 J. H. Fingleton & W. A. Brown: N.S.W. v. Western Australia (Perth) 1934–35
205 C. J. Barnett & G. W. Parker: Glos. v. Notts. (Bristol).....................1937
205 John Langridge & D. V. Smith: Sussex v. Kent (Hastings) 1950
205 D. G. W. Fletcher & E. A. Bedser: Surrey v. Essex (Ilford) 1952
204 R. Abel & W. Brockwell: Surrey v. Warwicks. (Birmingham) 1897
204 J. Vine & R. R. Relf: Sussex v. Somerset (Hove) 1919
204 A. Bowell & G. Brown: Hants. v. Worcs. (Portsmouth) 1920
204 S. H. Curnow & A. Langebrink: Transvaal v. O.F.S. (Johannesburg) 1929–30
204 C. J. Barnett & C. C. Dacre: Glos. v. Worcs. (Dudley) 1934
204 D. Smith & W. Barber: M.C.C. v. Queensland (Brisbane) 1935–36
204 F. E. Woolley & A. E. Fagg: Kent v. Worcs. (Tonbridge) 1938
204 K. V. Bhandarkar & S. W. Sohoni: Maharashtra v. Bombay (Poona) 1940–41
204 A. F. Rae & J. B. Stollmeyer: West Indians v. Lancs. (Manchester) 1950
204 E. Davies & W. G. A. Parkhouse: Glamorgan v. Glos. (Llanelly) 1950
204 E. A. B. Rowan & A. I. Taylor: Transvaal v. Griqualand West (Johannesburg) 1950–51
204 H. Furlonge & J. B. Stollmeyer: Trinidad v. Australians (Trinidad) 1954–55
204 M. J. Stewart & J. H. Edrich: Surrey v. Northants. (Oval) 1960
203 W. G. Grace & A. J. Webbe: Gentlemen v. Players (Lord's) 1875
203 C. B. Fry & J. Vine: Sussex v. Cambridge U. (Hove) 1901
203 P. F. Warner & F. A. Tarrant: Middx. v. Hants. (Lord's) 1908
203 W. Bardsley & C. G. Macartney: N.S.W. v. South Australia (Sydney).............1908–09
203 W. Bardsley & H. L. Collins: N.S.W. v. South Australia (Sydney) 1925–26
203 J. Kerr & I. T. Parker: Scotland v. Ireland (Greenock) 1926
203 J. B. Hobbs & A. Sandham: Surrey v. Notts. (Oval) 1927
203 P. Holmes & H. Sutcliffe: M.C.C. v. O.F.S. (Bloemfontein) 1927–28
203 J. B. Hobbs & H. Sutcliffe: Players v. Gentlemen (Oval) 1931
203 J. B. Hobbs & A. Sandham: Surrey v. Middx. (Lord's) 1932
203 V. M. Merchant & Mushtaq Ali: India v. England (Manchester) 1936
203 L. Hutton & C. Washbrook: Leveson-Gower's XI v. New Zealanders (Scarborough) ...1945
203 H. Gimblett & F. S. Lee: Somerset v. Notts. (Nottingham) 1946
203 D. Brookes & N. Oldfield: Northants. v. Middx. (Lord's) 1950
203 L. Hutton & F. A. Lowson: Yorks. v. Somerset (Huddersfield) 1952
203 F. C. Gardner & N. F. Horner: Warwicks. v. Glos. (Bristol) ,,,,,,,,,,1955
202 J. T. Brown & W. Chatterton: North v. South (Oval) 1894
202 J. H. Savigny & O. H. Douglas: Tasmania v. M.C.C. (Launceston) 1903–04
202 C. B. Fry & J. Vine: Sussex v. Surrey (Hove) 1904
202 C. J. B. Wood & A. E. Knight: Leics. v. Northants. (Leicester) 1908
202 H. O. Rock & J. G. Morgan: N.S.W. v. Victoria (Sydney).............1924–25
202 F. Watson & C. Hallows: Lancs. v. Glamorgan (Manchester) 1928
202 G. Lester & M. R. Hallam: Leics. v. Kent (Leicester) 1956
202 W. E. Russell & R. A. Gale: M.C.C. v. Oxford U. (Lord's).............1958
202 D. Kenyon & L. Outschoorn: Worcs. v. Notts. (Worcester) 1959
201 R. Abel & T. Hayward: Surrey v. Glos. (Oval) 1900
201 J. Devey & S. P. Kinneir: Warwicks. v. Hants. (Birmingham) 1906
201 L. Green & C. Hallows: Lancs. v. South Africans (Liverpool) 1924
201 E. Horspool & A. A. Anthony: Auckland v. Wellington (Auckland) 1924–25
201 V. Y. Richardson & G. W. Harris: South Australia v. Queensland (Adelaide) 1928–29
201* W. W. Keeton & C. B. Harris: Notts. v. Essex (Nottingham) 1936
201 W. W. Keeton & C. B. Harris: Notts. v. Northants. (Nottingham).............1946
201 A. H. Dyson & E. Davies: Glamorgan v. Hants. (Southampton) 1947
200 G. S. Patterson & F. H. Bohlen: Philadelphians v. F. Mitchell's XI (Haverford) 1895–96
200 P. F. Warner & H. B. Hayman: Middx. v. Glos. (Lord's) 1901
200 F. Watson & C. Hallows: Lancs. v. Northants. (Manchester) 1928
200 F. Watson & C. Hallows: Lancs. v. Kent (Maidstone) 1928
200* P. Holmes & H. Sutcliffe: Yorks. v. Oxford U. (Oxford) 1930
200 A. R. Morris & M. B. Cohen: N.S.W. v. Queensland (Sydney) 1940–41
200 T. C. Dodds & S. J. Cray: Essex v. Kent (Maidstone) 1947
200 A. F. Rae & G. Carew: West Indians v. Ceylon (Colombo) 1948–49

SECOND WICKET

455 B. B. Nimbalkar & K. V. Bhandarkar: Maharashtra v. Western India States (Poona) 1948–49
451 W. H. Ponsford & D. G. Bradman: Australia v. England (Oval) 1934
446 C. C. Hunte & G. Sobers: West Indies v. Pakistan (Kingston) 1957–58
429* J. G. Dewes & G. H. G. Doggart: Cambridge U. v. Essex (Cambridge) 1949
398 A. Shrewsbury & W. Gunn: Notts. v. Sussex (Nottingham) 1890
385 E. H. Bowley & M. W. Tate: Sussex v. Northants. (Hove) 1921
382 L. Hutton & M. Leyland: England v. Australia (Oval) 1938
380 F. A. Tarrant & J. W. Hearne: Middx. v. Lancs. (Lord's) 1914
371 J. B. Hobbs & E. G. Hayes: Surrey v. Hants. (Oval) 1909
371 F. Watson & E. Tyldesley: Lancs. v. Surrey (Manchester).............1928

368   W. Rhodes & A. C. Russell: M.C.C. v. South Australia (Adelaide) 1920–21
363   A. C. MacLaren & A. Paul: Lancs. v. Somerset (Taunton) 1895
358   B. J. Kortlang & C. McKenzie: Victoria v. Western Australia (Perth) 1909–10
352   W. H. Ashdown & F. E. Woolley: Kent v. Essex (Brentwood) 1934
349   C. B. Fry & E. H. Killick: Sussex v. Yorks. (Hove) 1901
349   C. S. Elliott & J. D. Eggar: Derby v. Notts. (Nottingham) 1947
346   W. Barber & M. Leyland: Yorks. v. Middx. (Sheffield) 1932
344   J. Devey & S. P. Kinneir: Warwicks. v. Derby (Birmingham) 1900
344   A. Sandham & R. J. Gregory: Surrey v. Glamorgan (Oval) 1937
343   F. A. Lowson & J. V. Wilson: Yorks. v. Oxford U. (Oxford) 1956
336   F. Watson & E. Tyldesley: Lancs. v. Worcs. (Worcester) 1929
334   A. A. Jackson & D. G. Bradman: N.S.W. v. South Australia (Adelaide) 1930–31
333   G. M. Lee & A. W. Carr: Notts. v. Leics. (Nottingham) 1913
333   P. Holmes & E. Oldroyd: Yorks. v. Warwicks. (Birmingham) 1922
331* W. K. Harbinson & E. T. Killick: Cambridge U. v. Glamorgan (Cambridge) 1929
327   F. Watson & E. Tyldesley: Lancs. v. Indians (Manchester) 1932
325   G. Brann & K. S. Ranjitsinhji: Sussex v. Surrey (Oval).....................................1899
324   I. D. Walker & Hon. A. Lyttelton: Middx. v. Glos. (Clifton) 1883
324   S. M. Brown & W. J. Edrich: Middx. v. Warwicks. (Birmingham) 1954
321   G. Brown & E. I. M. Barrett: Hants. v. Glos. (Southampton) 1920
319   H. W. Lee & G. O. Allen: Middx. v. Surrey (Oval) 1929
318   R. E. H. Hudson & C. P. Hamilton: Army v. Royal Air Force (Oval) 1932
318   M. C. Cowdrey & A. S. M. Oakman: M.C.C. v. O.F.S. (Bloemfontein) 1956–57
317   H. Sutcliffe & C. Hallows: England v. Rest (Bristol) 1927
316   J. L. Hopwood & E. Tyldesley: Lancs. v. Glos. (Bristol) 1934
315   A. Thompson & W. J. Edrich: Middx. v. Worcs. (Dudley) 1952
314   H. Sutcliffe & E. Oldroyd: Yorks. v. Essex (Southend) 1924
314   W. H. Ponsford & H. L. Hendry: Victoria v. Queensland (Melbourne) 1927–28
314   H. W. Lee & E. Hendren: Middx. v. Hants. (Lord's) 1928
312   A. Shrewsbury & W. Gunn: Notts. v. Sussex (Hove) 1891
307   H. T. W. Hardinge & James Seymour: Kent v. Worcs. (Kidderminster) 1922
307   John Langridge & H. W. Parks: Sussex v. Kent (Tonbridge) 1939
306   F. Watson & E. Tyldesley: Lancs. v. Sussex (Hove) 1928
306   C. L. Badcock & W. Horrocks: Combined XI v. M.C.C. (Perth) 1936–37
305   J. W. Rothery & D. Denton: Yorks. v. Derby (Chesterfield) 1910
305   S. K. Coen & J. M. M. Commaille: O.F.S. v. Natal (Bloemfontein)............1926–27
305   F. Watson & J. Iddon: Lancs. v. Somerset (Taunton) 1934
304   W. Bardsley & M. A. Noble: N.S.W. v. Victoria (Sydney) 1908–09
304   G. E. B. Abell & Agha Ahmed Raza: Northern India v. Army (Lahore)............1934–35
302   W. Watson & J. V. Wilson: Yorks. v. Derby (Scarborough) 1948
301   C. S. Dempster & C. F. W. Allcott: New Zealanders v. Warwicks. (Birmingham) 1927
301   A. R. Morris & D. G. Bradman: Australia v. England (Leeds) 1948
299   E. L. Bowley & J. T. Murray: South Australia v. Queensland (Adelaide) 1923–24
299   A. Sandham & A. Ducat: Surrey v. Lancs. (Manchester) 1928
299* T. L. Livingston & D. Barrick: Northants. v. Sussex (Northampton) 1953
296   E. J. Smith & L. A. Bates: Warwicks. v. Kent (Coventry) 1927
296   W. H. Ponsford & D. G. Bradman: Australian XI v. Tasmania (Hobart) 1929–30
295   A. Hartley & J. T. Tyldesley: Lancs. v. Somerset (Manchester) 1910
295   J. B. Stollmeyer & K. B. Trestrail: Trinidad v. Jamaica (Trinidad) 1949–50
294   W. A. Brown & D. G. Bradman: N.S.W. v. Queensland (Brisbane) 1933–34
294   A. V. Avery & P. A. Gibb: Essex v. Northants. (Northampton) 1952
293   L. Favell & R. B. Simpson: Australians v. Griqualand West (Kimberley) 1957–58
292* K. S. Ranjitsinhji & C. B. Fry: Sussex v. Somerset (Taunton) 1901
292   J. T. Ikin & G. A. Edrich: Lancs. v. Oxford U. (Oxford) 1951
291   A. Sandham & H. S. Squires: Surrey v. Yorks. (Oval) 1933
289   A. Shrewsbury & W. Barnes: Notts. v. Surrey (Oval) 1882
288   H. Sutcliffe & A. Mitchell: Yorks. v. Lancs. (Manchester) 1939
286   J. C. W. MacBryan & M. D. Lyon: Somerset v. Derby (Burton) 1924
284   P. J. Sharpe & F. R. Bailey: Minor Counties v. Indians (Stoke) 1959
283   A. J. Hopkins & M. A. Noble: N.S.W. v. South Australia (Adelaide) 1908–09
283   H. W. Taylor & R. A. Blake: Natal v. Griqualand West (Durban) 1910–11
283   I. J. Siedle & A. Melville: Natal v. Border (Durban) 1928–29
283   H. Sutcliffe & Nawab of Pataudi: M.C.C. v. Combined XI (Perth) 1932–33
283   V. Mehra & B. K. Kunderam: Railways v. Jammu & Kashmir (New Delhi) 1959–60
282   D. Brookes & T. L. Livingston: Northants. v. Kent (Maidstone) 1954
282   J. Rutherford & R. N. Harvey: Australians v. M.C.C. (Lord's) 1956
281   W. G. Grace & J. M. Cotterill: South v. North (Princes) 1877
281   A. Sandham & A. Ducat: Surrey v. Notts. (Nottingham) 1930
281   W. M. Woodfull & W. A. Brown: Australians v. Lancs. (Manchester) 1934
281   John Langridge & H. W. Parks: Sussex v. Glamorgan (Eastbourne) 1938
281   C. L. Walcott & F. M. Worrell: West Indians v. Tasmania (Hobart) 1951–52
280   L. Hall & F. Lee: Yorks. v. Lancs. (Bradford) 1887

280 G. Brown & E. I. M. Barrett: Hants. v. Warwicks. (Portsmouth) 1920
280 P. A. Gibb & W. J. Edrich: England v. South Africa (Durban)......................1938–39
280 J. W. Burke & R. N. Harvey: Australians v. Warwicks. (Birmingham) 1956
277 C. J. B. Wood & G. W. Beldam: London County v. Surrey (Oval) 1901
277 W. J. Edrich & D. C. S. Compton: Middx. v. Leics. (Leicester) 1947
276 W. Bardsley & C. G. Macartney: Australians v. Leics. (Leicester) 1921
276 J. B. Hobbs & R. J. Gregory: Surrey v. Hants. (Southampton) 1926
275 A. E. Fagg & F. G. H. Chalk: Kent v. Worcs. (Dudley) 1938
275 C. C. McDonald & A. L. Hassett: Australia v. South Africa (Adelaide) 1952–53
274 A. Shrewsbury & W. Gunn: Notts. v. Sussex (Hove) 1893
274 W. M. Woodfull & D. G. Bradman: Australia v. South Africa (Melbourne) 1931–32
274 H. H. Gibbons & Nawab of Pataudi: Worcs. v. Kent (Worcester) 1933
274 H. H. Gibbons & Nawab of Pataudi: Worcs. v. Glamorgan (Worcester) 1934
273 J. L. Hopwood & E. Tyldesley: Lancs. v. Glamorgan (Cardiff) 1934
273 L. J. Todd & L. E. G. Ames: Kent v. Essex (Maidstone) 1947
272 R. Abel & E. G. Hayes: Surrey v. Worcs. (Oval) 1900
271 M. Harvey & K. R. Miller: Victoria v. N.S.W. (Melbourne)......................1946–47
271 C. Washbrook & G. A. Edrich: Lancs. v. Sussex (Manchester) 1951
270 H. L. Collins & T. J. E. Andrews: N.S.W. v. M.C.C. (Sydney) 1924–25
270 W. M. Woodfull & C. G. Macartney: Australians v. Essex (Leyton) 1926
269 Nazar Mohammed & Murrawat Hussain: Pakistan v. Ceylon (Colombo) 1948–49
269 G. Sobers & C. L. Walcott: West Indies v. Pakistan (Georgetown) 1957–58
268 J. R. M. Mackay & M. A. Noble: N.S.W. v. Victoria (Melbourne) 1905–06
267 R. Surti & V. Mankad: Rajasthan v. Uttar Pradesh (Udaipur) 1959–60
266 P. E. Richardson & T. W. Graveney: England v. West Indies (Nottingham) 1957
265 A. Ward & J. T. Tyldesley: Lancs. v. Derby (Derby) 1901
265 G. Gunn & W. Walker: Notts. v. Hants. (Bournemouth) 1928
265 D. Brookes & W. Barron: Northants. v. Cambridge U. (Cambridge) 1948
265 A. R. Morris & K. R. Miller: N.S.W. v. M.C.C. (Sydney) 1950–51
263 G. B. Y. Cox & H. B. G. Austin: Barbados v. Trinidad (Barbados) 1897–98
262 J. M. Gregory & T. J. E. Andrews: N.S.W. v. New Zealanders (Sydney) 1927–28
262 H. T. W. Hardinge & F. E. Woolley: Kent v. Warwicks. (Tunbridge Wells)......................1928
262 W. P. J. Donaldson & K. R. Miller: N.S.W. v. Western Australia (Sydney) 1947–48
261 E. W. Dillon & James Seymour: Kent v. Somerset (Taunton) 1905
261 A. R. Morris & S. G. Barnes: N.S.W. v. Queensland (Sydney) 1940–41
261* L. Hutton & J. V. Wilson: Yorks. v. Scotland (Hull) 1949
261 N. Hill & J. D. Clay: Notts. v. Yorks. (Nottingham) 1959
260 A. E. Fagg & F. E. Woolley: Kent v. Northants. (Northampton) 1934
259 T. Hayward & E. G. Hayes: Surrey v. Yorks. (Oval) 1911
259 John Langridge & A. Melville: Sussex v. Indians (Hove) 1936
259 D. Brookes & T. L. Livingston: Northants. v. Leics. (Northampton) 1950
259* R. T. Spooner & T. W. Graveney: M.C.C. v. Pakistan (Lahore) 1951–52
258 H. Sutcliffe & E. Oldroyd: Yorks. v. Kent (Folkestone) 1931
256 W. G. Grace & W. Chatterton: M.C.C. v. Cambridge U. (Cambridge) 1894
256 W. W. Whysall & W. Walker: Notts. v. Hants. (Nottingham) 1930
256 H. F. Wade & E. A. B. Rowan: South Africans v. Glamorgan (Cardiff) 1935
256 S. G. Barnes, A. L. Hassett & R. N. Harvey: Australians v. Somerset (Taunton) 1948
256 C. T. M. Pugh & T. W. Graveney: Glos. v. Derby (Chesterfield) 1960
255 A. Ward & A. E. Stoddart: Stoddart's XI v. Queensland (Brisbane) 1894–95
255 V. Y. Richardson & D. E. Pritchard: South Australia v. M.C.C. (Adelaide) 1928–29
255 H. T. W. Hardinge & F. E. Woolley: Kent v. Derby (Chesterfield) 1929
254* L. G. Berry & N. F. Armstrong: Leics. v. Parkinson's XI (Blackpool) 1935
253 B. B. Wilson & D. Denton: Yorks. v. Warwicks. (Birmingham) 1912
253 C. T. Sarwate & L. Amarnath: Indians v. Tasmania (Launceston) 1947–48
253 J. W. Burke & K. Mackay: Australians v. Eastern Province (Port Elizabeth) 1957–58
253 J. W. Burke & R. N. Harvey: N.S.W. v. Queensland (Brisbane) 1958–59
252 G. Brann & K. S. Ranjitsinhji: Sussex v. Glos. (Bristol) 1899
252 W. Tyldesley & J. T. Tyldesley: Lancs. v. Derby (Derby) 1911
252 E. M. Beechey & W. A. Baker: Wellington v. Auckland (Wellington) 1918–19
251 J. C. W. MacBryan & A. Young: Somerset v. Glamorgan (Taunton)......................1923
251 C. J. Barnett & W. R. Hammond: Glos. v. Sussex (Cheltenham) 1934
251* R. T. Simpson & C. J. Poole: Notts. v. Leics. (Nottingham) 1949
250 F. L. Bowley & H. K. Foster: Worcs. v. Somerset (Worcester) 1903
250 A. C. Johnston & C. P. Mead: Hants. v. Warwicks. (Coventry) 1912
250 H. T. W. Hardinge & James Seymour: Kent v. Essex (Leyton) 1923
250 D. J. McGlew & M. K. Elgie: Natal v. Border (Durban) 1957–58
249 L. C. H. Palairet & R. C. N. Palairet: Somerset v. Sussex (Taunton) 1896
249 J. Vine & V. W. C. Jupp: Sussex v. Yorks. (Hove) 1914
248 H. Sutcliffe & M. Leyland: Yorks. v. Leics. (Leicester) 1926
248 J. B. Hobbs & A. Ducat: Surrey v. Warwicks. (Oval) 1931
247 T. Hayward & E. G. Hayes: Surrey v. Sussex (Oval) 1908
247 A. Sandham & A. Ducat: Surrey v Northants. (Oval) 1921

247 R. E. Marshall & F. M. Worrell: West Indians v. Leics. (Leicester) 1950
246 M. A. Noble & S. E. Gregory: Australian XI v. Rest (Sydney) 1908–09
246 John Langridge & J. H. Parks: Sussex v. Glamorgan (Hove) 1933
246 J. G. Dewes & G. H. G. Doggart: Cambridge U. v. Free Foresters (Cambridge) 1948
246 J. W. Burke & R. N. Harvey: N.S.W. v. M.C.C. (Sydney) 1958–59
245 A. Young & M. D. Lyon: Somerset v. Hants. (Bath) 1924
245 R. K. Nunes & G. Headley: Jamaica v. Tennyson's XI (Kingston) 1931–32
245 D. Brookes & T. L. Livingston: Northants. v. Somerset (Weston-super-Mare) 1951
244 J. J. Lyons & G. Giffen: South Australia v. N.S.W. (Sydney) 1891–92
244 N. Kilner & L. A. Bates: Warwicks. v. Surrey (Birmingham) 1926
244 W. A. Hill & F. R. Santall: Warwicks. v. Lancs. (Birmingham) 1939
244 J. Rutherford & K. Mackay: Johnson's XI v. Lindwall's XI (Sydney) 1955–56
243 H. Donnen & V. T. Trumper: N.S.W. v. Queensland (Sydney) 1899–00
243* L. G. Berry & N. F. Armstrong: Leics. v. Northants. (Leicester) 1937
243 R. T. Simpson & H. Winrow: Notts. v. Sussex (Nottingham) 1950
243 R. Reynolds & J. McLaughlin: Queensland v. South Australia (Adelaide) 1957–58
242 A. Sandham & R. J. Gregory: Surrey v. Australians (Oval) 1934
242* J. H. Fingleton & D. G. Bradman: Australians v. Hants. (Southampton) 1938
242 D. Brookes & T. L. Livingston: Northants. v. Somerset (Northampton) 1956
241 W. G. Grace & G. F. Grace: Gentlemen v. Players (Brighton) 1871
241 K. J. Key & W. W. Read: Surrey v. Kent (Oval) 1887
241 A. Shrewsbury & W. Gunn: Notts. v. Sussex (Hove) 1898
241 A. E. Knight & J. H. King: Leics. v. Notts. (Nottingham) 1903
241 B. P. Talang & M. Shukla: United Provinces v. Assam (Dehra Dun) 1950–51
241 M. R. Barton & P. B. H. May: Surrey v. Essex (Southend) 1951
240 S. E. Gregory & C. G. Macartney: Australians v. Northants. (Northampton) 1912
240* A. L. Hassett & R. N. Harvey: Australians v. Sussex (Hove) 1953
239 J. J. Lyons & G. Giffen: South Australia v. N.S.W. (Sydney) 1891–92
239 C. J. B. Wood & H. Whitehead: Leics. v. Surrey (Oval) 1911
239 A. E. Dipper & H. Smith: Glos. v. Glamorgan (Swansea) 1921
239 H. T. W. Hardinge & F. E. Woolley: Kent v. Yorks. (Tonbridge) 1929
239 A. Shipman & N. F. Armstrong: Leics. v. Hants. (Southampton) 1933
239 R. T. Simpson & R. J. Giles: Notts. v. Kent (Nottingham) 1953
238 F. J. Bryant & W. M. McRae: Western Australia v. Victoria (Perth) 1927–28
238 P. H. Tarilton & E. L. G. Hoad: Barbados–Born v. Rest (Barbados) 1927–28
238 N. F. Horner & J. S. Ord: Warwicks. v. Oxford U. (Oxford) 1952
237 R. Abel & F. C. Holland: Surrey v. Lancs. (Manchester) 1898
237* H. Carpenter & A. C. Russell: Essex v. Worcs. (Worcester) 1914
237 H. Sutcliffe & D. Denton: Yorks. v. Glos. (Leeds) 1919
237 W. H. Ponsford & H. L. Hendry: Victoria v. Queensland (Melbourne) 1926–27
237 E. H. Bowley & K. S. Duleepsinhji: Sussex v. Essex (Hove) 1931
237 P. Roy & V. L. Manjrekar: India v. West Indies (Kingston) 1952–53
236 W. Troup & C. L. Townsend: Glos. v. Somerset (Bristol) 1898
236 S. G. Barnes & D. G. Bradman: Australia v. India (Adelaide) 1947–48
236 F. A. Lowson & J. V. Wilson: Yorks. v. Essex (Sheffield) 1950
235 F. L. Fane & P. A. Perrin: Essex v. Leics. (Leicester) 1899
235* F. L. Fane & P. A. Perrin: Essex v. Notts. (Leyton) 1901
235 A. O. Jones & W. Gunn: Notts. v. Glos. (Nottingham) 1903
235 W. M. Woodfull & C. G. Macartney: Australia v. England (Leeds) 1926
235 E. H. Bowley & K. S. Duleepsinhji: Sussex v. Surrey (Hove) 1932
235* M. J. Stewart & K. F. Barrington: Surrey v. Combined Services (Oval) 1957
234 W. G. Grace & F. Townsend: Glos. v. Surrey (Oval) 1870
234 G. Giffen & J. J. Lyons: South Australia v. N.S.W. (Sydney) 1891–92
234 I. J. Siedle & B. Mitchell: South Africans v. Yorks. (Sheffield) 1929
234* H. W. Parks & C. Oakes: Sussex v. Surrey (Oval) 1946
233* G. Gunn & J. Gunn: Notts. v. Surrey (Nottingham) 1919
233 A. E. Dipper & H. Smith: Glos. v. Glamorgan (Swansea) 1921
232 A. Shrewsbury & W. Gunn: Notts. v. Kent (Nottingham) 1891
232 H. Carpenter & P. A. Perrin: Essex v. Kent (Leyton) 1901
232 H. W. Lee & J. W. Hearne: Middx. v. Surrey (Oval) 1924
232* J. B. Hobbs & R. J. Gregory: Surrey v. Essex (Oval) 1932
232 R. J. Craig & R. James: South Australia v. Queensland (Adelaide) 1947–48
232 A. F. Rae & K. Rickard: West Indians v. C.C. of India (Bombay) 1948–49
232* J. W. Burke & I. D. Craig: Australians v. Somerset (Taunton) 1956
231 H. T. W. Hardinge & James Seymour: Kent v. Hants. (Portsmouth) 1913
231 A. Sandham & R. J. Gregory: Surrey v. Oxford U. (Oval) 1928
231 A. A. Jackson & D. G. Bradman: Australians v. Somerset (Taunton) 1930
231 W. M. Woodfull & D. G. Bradman: Australia v. England (Lord's) 1930
231 E. Paynter & E. Tyldesley: Lancs. v. Cambridge U. (Cambridge) 1933
231 O. E. Wynne & G. M. Fullerton: Transvaal v. Eastern Province & Griqualand West
                                                              (Johannesburg)......1945–46
231 A. L. Hassett & D. G. Bradman: Australians v. Surrey (Oval) 1948

231   F. C. Gardner & A. V. Wolton: Warwicks. v. Essex (Westcliff) 1954
230   A. O. Jones & W. Gunn: Notts. v. Leics. (Nottingham) 1895
230   C. G. Macartney & A. Punch: N.S.W. v. Otago (Dunedin) 1923–24
230   H. Sutcliffe & E. Tyldesley: England v. South Africa (Johannesburg) 1927–28
230   D. N. Moore & W. R. Hammond: Glos. v. Oxford U. (Oxford).......................1930
230   E. H. Bowley & K. S. Duleepsinhji: Sussex v. Hants. (Portsmouth) 1930
230   L. Hutton & A. Mitchell: Yorks. v. Cambridge U. (Cambridge) 1938
229   E. G. Hayes & F. C. Holland: Surrey v. Worcs. (Worcester) 1905
229* F. A. Tarrant & J. W. Hearne: Middx. v. Essex (Leyton) 1914
229   L. G. Hemus & F. A. Midlane: Auckland v. Wellington (Wellington) 1918–19
229   R. H. Twining & J. W. Hearne: Middx. v. Surrey (Lord's) 1921
229   E. L. Bowley & J. T. Murray: South Australia v. Queensland (Adelaide) 1923–24
229   F. Watson & E. Tyldesley: Lancs. v. Warwicks. (Birmingham) 1929
229   W. H. Ponsford & D. G. Bradman: Australia v. West Indies (Brisbane) 1930–31
229   J. H. Parks & A. Melville: Sussex v. Somerset (Taunton) 1934
229   I. J. Siedle & L. T. H. Trotter: Natal v. Griqualand West (Durban) 1934–35
228   J. E. Barrett & W. L. Murdoch: Australians v. Sussex (Hove) 1890
228   H. T. W. Hardinge & F. E. Woolley: Kent v. Hants. (Folkestone) 1929
228   R. K. Nunes & G. Headley: West Indies v. England (Kingston) 1929–30
228   A. E. Fagg & L. E. G. Ames: Kent v. Sussex (Hastings) 1948
227   W. A. Baker & B. J. Kortlang: Wellington v. Otago (Dunedin) 1923–24
226   F. Hearne & G. G. Hearne: Kent v. Middx. (Gravesend) 1886
226   G. Bean & W. L. Murdoch: Sussex v. Lancs. (Manchester) 1893
226   F. W. Marlow & K. S. Ranjitsinhji: Sussex v. Somerset (Hove) 1895
226   W. L. Murdoch & C. J. B. Wood: London County v. Lancs. (Manchester) 1903
226   H. W. Lee & J. W. Hearne: Middx. v. Surrey (Oval).........................1919
226* C. B. Harris & J. Knowles: Notts. v. Glamorgan (Nottingham) 1936
226   W. G. Keighley & H. A. Pawson: Oxford U. v. Cambridge U. (Lord's) 1947
225   T. Hayward & J. T. Tyldesley: Thornton's XI v. South Africans (Scarborough) 1907
225   A. Hartley & J. T. Tyldesley: Lancs. v. Leics. (Leicester) 1908
225   T. Hayward & E. G. Hayes: Surrey v. Worcs. (Dudley) 1912
225   J. B. Hobbs & J. W. Hearne: M.C.C. v. Griqualand West (Kimberley) 1913–14
225   H. Sutcliffe & E. Oldroyd: Yorks. v. Derby (Dewsbury) 1928
225   F. Watson & J. Iddon: Lancs. v. Glamorgan (Manchester) 1929
225   B. W. Hone & F. G. H. Chalk: Oxford U. v. Surrey (Oval)....................1932
225* C. C. Dacre & W. R Hammond: Glos. v. Worcs. (Worcester) 1933
225   J. L. Hopwood & J. Iddon: Lancs. v. Surrey (Oval) 1934
225   N. S. Mitchell-Innes & M. R. Barton: Oxford U. v. Leics. (Oxford) 1937
225   S. G. Barnes & D. G. Bradman: Australians v. Leveson-Gower's XI (Scarborough) 1948
224   R. G. Barlow & C. F. H. Leslie: Bligh's XI v. N.S.W. (Sydney) 1882–83
224   E. Humphreys & James Seymour: Kent v. Glos. (Catford) 1909
224   W. Bardsley & C. Hill: Australia v. South Africa (Sydney) 1910–11
224   P. Holmes & E. Oldroyd: Yorks. v. Glamorgan (Cardiff) 1922
224   W. H. Ashdown & F. E. Woolley: Kent v. Yorks. (Bradford) 1931
224   D. J. McGlew & H. J. Keith: South Africans v. Leics. (Leicester) 1955
224   R. Reynolds & J. McLaughlin: Queensland v. Western Australia (Brisbane) 1959–60
223   R. H. Spooner & J. T. Tyldesley: Lancs. v. Yorks. (Manchester) 1905
223   John Langridge & C. Oakes: Sussex v. Oxford U. (Oxford) 1950
222   P. F. Warner & F. L. Fane: Hawke's XI v. Otago (Dunedin) 1902–03
222   P. F. Warner & J. T. Tyldesley: Rest of England v. Notts. (Oval) 1907
222   H. Sutcliffe & D. Denton: Yorks. v. Kent (Dover)...........................1919
222   S. M. Brown & W. J. Edrich: Middx. v. Northants. (Lord's) 1949
222   J. K. Holt & F. M. Worrell: West Indies v. England (Barbados) 1953–54
221   J. W. H. T. Douglas & P. A. Perrin: Essex v. Notts. (Nottingham) 1911
221   C. Kelleway & C. G. Macartney: N.S.W. v. Victoria (Sydney) 1913–14
221   H. Sutcliffe & W. R. Hammond: England v. South Africa (Birmingham) 1929
221   D. R. Wilcox & M. S. Nichols: Essex v. Hants. (Southend) 1936
221   R. E. S. Wyatt & W. R. Hammond: M.C.C. v. Western Australia (Perth) 1936–37
221   L. B. Fishlock & E. A. Bedser: Surrey v. Hants. (Oval) 1949
221   J. C. Marshall & C. C. P. Williams: Oxford U. v. Free Foresters (Oxford) ...1953
221   J. H. Edrich & K. F. Barrington: Surrey v. Notts. (Nottingham) 1959
220   R. Abel & F. C. Holland: Surrey v. Leics. (Oval) 1896
220   A. Hearne & W. H. Patterson: Kent v. Somerset (Tonbridge) 1898
220   G. T. S. Stevens & J. W. Hearne: Middx. v. Essex (Leyton) 1925
220   W. H. Ashdown & A. J. Evans: Kent v. Lancs. (Maidstone) 1927
220* N. Kilner & L. A. Bates: Warwicks. v. Lancs. (Birmingham) 1928
220   C. Boy & G. Headley: Jamaica v. Yorks. (Kingston) 1935–36
220   A. M. Taylor & C. L. Walcott: Barbados v. M.C.C. (Barbados) 1947–48
219   F. S. Jackson & D. Denton: Yorks. v. Middx. (Bradford) 1899
219   G. T. S. Stevens & M. D. Lyon: Gentlemen v. Players (Lord's) 1923
219   W. H. Ponsford & H. L. Hendry: Victoria v. N.S.W. (Melbourne) 1926–27
219   J. A. Cutmore & J. O'Connor: Essex v. Derby (Derby) 1930

219   F. E. Woolley & A. E. Fagg: Kent v. Surrey (Blackheath) 1934
219   E. A. B. Rowan & K. G. Viljoen: South Africans v. Minor Counties (Skegness) 1935
219   W. A. Brown & D. G. Bradman: Australians v. Essex (Southend) 1948
219   R. T. Simpson & C. J. Poole: Notts. v. Sussex (Hastings) 1949
219   W. G. A. Parkhouse & B. Hedges: Glamorgan v. Warwicks. (Llanelly) 1954
218   J. Devey & W. Quaife: Warwicks. v. Hants. (Bournemouth) 1899
218   W. Bardsley & C. G. Macartney: Australians v. Glos. (Cheltenham) 1921
218   R. A. Farquharson & H. G. Deane: Transvaal v. O.F.S. (Benoni) 1923–24
218   A. E. Fagg & F. E. Woolley: Kent v. Somerset (Taunton) 1934
218   R. P. Nelson & M. Tindall: Cambridge U. v. Somerset (Cambridge) 1935
218   L. B. Fishlock & R. J. Gregory: Surrey v. Yorks. (Bradford) 1937
218   R. S. Whitington & J. Pettiford: Australian Services v. Indian XI (Calcutta) 1945–46
218   E. Cooper & R. Howorth: Worcs. v. Northants. (Kidderminster) 1946
218   L. Hutton & W. J. Edrich: England v. New Zealand (Oval)...............................1949
217   R. H. Spooner & J. T. Tyldesley: Lancs. v. Essex (Leyton) 1909
217   W. H. Ponsford & H. L. Hendry: Victoria v. Queensland (Melbourne) 1926–27
217   D. D. Hindlekar & Mushtaq Ali: Indians v. Surrey (Oval) 1936
217   R. A. Westmass & R. J. Christiani: British Guiana v. Barbados (Georgetown) 1946–47
217*   A. S. M. Oakman & E. R. Dexter: Sussex v. Glamorgan (Hove) 1960
216   J. B. Hobbs & E. G. Hayes: Surrey v. Essex (Leyton) 1905
216   R. A. Haywood & S. G. Smith: Northants. v. Glos. (Bristol) 1913
216   F. A. Tarrant & J. W. Hearne: Middx. v. Worcs. (Lord's) 1914
216*   E. J. Smith & Hon. F. S. G. Calthorpe: Warwicks. v. Sussex (Birmingham) 1925
216   J. B. Hobbs & A. Jeacocke: Surrey v. Glamorgan (Oval) 1925
216   H. Sutcliffe & E. Tyldesley: M.C.C. v. Griqualand West (Kimberley) 1927–28
216   A. E. Dipper & W. R. Hammond: Glos. v. Middx. (Lord's) 1929
216   J. H. Fingleton & D. G. Bradman: N.S.W. v. South Africans (Sydney) 1931–32
216   F. T. Prentice & N. F. Armstrong: Leics. v. Northants. (Leicester) 1938
216   J. B. Stollmeyer & G. Headley: West Indians v. Middx. (Lord's) 1939
216   K. C. Ibrahim & P. J. Dickinson: Bombay v. Maharashtra (Bombay) 1947–48
216   F. C. Gardner & J. S. Ord: Warwicks. v. Cambridge U. (Birmingham) 1952
215   F. L. Fane & P. A. Perrin: Essex v. Lancs. (Leyton) 1911
215   James Seymour & A. F. Bickmore: Kent v. Essex (Tonbridge) 1922
215   E. H. Bowley & W. R. Hammond: Tennyson's XI v. Gilligan's XI (Folkestone) 1925
215   C. M. Morales & G. Headley: Jamaica v. Tennyson's XI (Kingston) 1927–28
215   W. M. Woodfull & H. L. Hendry: Australia v. England (Sydney) 1928–29
215   V. M. Merchant & Mushtaq Ali: Indians v. Minor Counties (Lord's) 1936
215   R. W. Currer &. R. C. Hicks: N.E. Transvaal v. O.F.S. (Bloemfontein) 1937–38
215   J. H. Fingleton & D. G. Bradman: Australians v. Cambridge U. (Cambridge)............1938
215   D. S. Sheppard & P. B. H. May: Cambridge U. v. Middx. (Cambridge) 1951
214   R. H. Spooner & J. T. Tyldesley: Lancs. v. Hants. (Manchester) 1911
214   C. Hallows & E. Tyldesley: Lancs. v. Sussex (Liverpool) 1925
214   W. Walker & W. Payton: Notts. v. Glamorgan (Nottingham) 1926
214   E. H. Bowley & K. S. Duleepsinhji: Sussex v. Middx. (Hove) 1928
214*   J. T. Ikin & G. A. Edrich: Lancs. v. Northants. (Northampton) 1953
214   C. C. McDonald & R. N. Harvey: Victoria v. N.S.W. (Sydney) 1955–56
214   R. Reynolds & K. Mackay: Queensland v. South Australia (Brisbane) 1958–59
213   J. Darling & G. Giffen: Australians v. South (Eastbourne) 1896
213   E. R. Mayne & R. L. Park: Victoria v. N.S.W. (Melbourne) 1919–20
213   H. T. W. Hardinge & F. E. Woolley: Kent v. Glos. (Gloucester) 1928
213   L. G. Berry & F. T. Prentice: Leics. v. Derby (Derby) 1949
212   W. W. Timms & R. A. Haywood: Northants. v. Essex (Northampton) 1921
212   E. Horspool & N. C. Snedden: Auckland v. Victoria (Auckland) 1924–25
212   C. L. Badcock & S. G. Barnes: McCabe's XI v. Bradman's XI (Melbourne) 1940–41
212   W. Lawry & I. Huntingdon: Victoria v. Western Australia (Melbourne) 1959–60
211   W. G. Grace & R. W. Rice: Glos. v. Sussex (Bristol) 1896
211   H. Makepeace & E. Tyldesley: Lancs. v. West Indians (Manchester) 1923
211   D. F. Pope & J. O'Connor: Essex v. Warwicks. (Leyton) 1930
211   R. A. Sinfield & W. R. Hammond: Glos. v. Glamorgan (Cardiff) 1931
211   A. E. Fagg & F. E. Woolley: Kent v. Hants. (Southampton) 1936
211   R. E. S. Wyatt & W. R. Hammond: M.C.C. v. Western Australia (Perth) 1936–37
211   N. Crompton & J. Shaw: Victoria v. N.S.W. (Sydney) 1957–58
210   C. J. Burnup & S. H. Day: Kent v. Hants. (Tonbridge) 1901
210   T. Hayward & E. G. Hayes: Surrey v. Oxford U. (Oval) 1906
210   J. W. H. T. Douglas & J. R. Freeman: Essex v. Worcs. (Worcester) 1920
210   W. A. Hadlee & F. P. O'Brien: Canterbury v. Otago (Christchurch) 1940–41
209   H. Makepeace & J. T. Tyldesley: Lancs. v. Kent (Canterbury) 1914
209   A. C. Russell & J. W. Hearne: M.C.C. v. South Australia (Adelaide) 1920–21
209   N. Kilner & L. A. Bates: Warwicks. v. Sussex (Birmingham) 1934
209   E. A. B. Rowan & R. E. Grieveson: Transvaal v. O.F.S. (Bloemfontein) 1934–35
209   D. Smith & T. S. Worthington: Derby v. Leics. (Oakham) 1936
209   G. E. Hart & W. J. Edrich: Middx. v. Somerset (Lord's) 1937

209 A. E. Alderman & D. Smith: Derby v. Leics. (Ashby-de-la-Zouch) 1948
209 J. G. Dewes & P. B. H. May: Cambridge U. v. Hants. (Cambridge) 1950
209 F. C. Gardner & E. Leadbeater: Warwicks. v. Glamorgan (Coventry) 1958
209 I. D. Craig & B. Booth: N.S.W. v. Queensland (Brisbane) 1959–60
209 M. J. Stewart & D. G. W. Fletcher: Surrey v. Notts. (Oval) 1960
208 A. E. Stoddart & R. C. N. Palairet: Gentlemen v. Notts. (Nottingham) 1894
208 A. Shrewsbury & W. Gunn: Notts. v. Sussex (Hove) 1899
208* H. Carpenter & P. A. Perrin: Essex v. Sussex (Leyton) 1905
208 W. W. Whysall & J. Gunn: Notts. v. Hants. (Southampton) 1925
208 W. M. Woodfull & D. G. Bradman: Australians v. Worcs. (Worcester) 1930
208 R. E. S. Wyatt & L. E. G. Ames: M.C.C. Australian Team v. Rest (Folkestone) 1932
208 E. Paynter & J. Iddon: Lancs. v. Leics. (Manchester) 1936
208 B. B. Irani & M. K. Mantri: Bombay v. Madras (Madras) 1948–49
207 S. Coe & H. Whitehead: Leics. v. Essex (Leyton) 1914
207 J. W. E. Mills & R. C. Blunt: New Zealanders v. Leveson-Gower's XI (Scarborough).........1927
207 C. Hallows & E. Tyldesley: Lancs. v. Kent (Manchester) 1928
207 H. H. Gibbons & M. Nichol: Worcs. v. West Indians (Worcester) 1928
207 A. G. Ganteaume & K. B. Trestrail: Trinidad v. Barbados (Trinidad) 1945–46
207 S. G. Barnes & D. G. Bradman: Australians v. Surrey (Oval) 1948
207 L. Favell & N. Dansie: South Australia v. Western Australia (Adelaide)...............1958–59
206 J. Tunnicliffe & F. S. Jackson: Yorks. v. Lancs. (Sheffield) 1898
206 D. Sutherland & W. H. McCormack: Victoria v. Tasmania (Launceston) 1900–01
206 R. H. Spooner & J. T. Tyldesley: Lancs. v. Notts. (Nottingham) 1903
206 W. Rhodes & F. E. Woolley: M.C.C. v. Tasmania (Hobart) 1911–12
206 J. B. Hobbs & H. S. Harrison: Surrey v. Lancs. (Oval) 1914
206 J. A. Cutmore & J. O'Connor: Essex v. Surrey (Oval) 1929
206 F. Watson & E. Tyldesley: Lancs. v. Kent (Manchester) 1930
206 H. Sutcliffe & M. Leyland: Yorks. v. Leics. (Leicester) 1931
206 W. A. Brown & D. G. Bradman: Australians v. Warwicks. (Birmingham) 1938
206 E. Davies & T. L. Brierley: Glamorgan v. Notts. (Swansea)...............1939
206 L. J. Todd & L. E. G. Ames: Kent v. Leics. (Dover) 1947
206 L. Hutton & R. T. Simpson: M.C.C. v. Transvaal (Johannesburg) 1948–49
205 E. Humphreys & James Seymour: Kent v. Hants. (Dover) 1910
205 H. T. W. Hardinge & James Seymour: Kent v. Surrey (Oval) 1922
205 G. W. Harris & J. T. Murray: South Australia v. Victoria (Adelaide) 1924–25
205 A. Ducat & T. F. Shepherd: Surrey v. Oxford U. (Oval) 1930
205 B. W. Hone & Nawab of Pataudi: Oxford U. v. Army (Folkestone) 1931
205 H. Sutcliffe & A. Mitchell: Yorks. v. Leics. (Leicester) 1933
205 John Langridge & A. Melville: Sussex v. Middx. (Hove) 1935
205* I. J. Siedle & E. A. B. Rowan: South Africans v. Oxford U. (Oxford) 1935
205 Imtiaz Ahmed & Mohammed Saaed: Pakistan v. West Indians (Lahore)...............1948–49
205 B. H. Pairaudeau & C. L. Walcott: West Indians v. Cambridge U. (Cambridge) 1957
205 N. Asgarali & R. Kanhai: West Indians v. Notts. (Nottingham) 1957
205 R. Reynolds & S. Trimble: Queensland v. South Australia (Adelaide) 1959–60
204 P. S. McDonnell & W. L. Murdoch: Australian XI v. Rest (Melbourne) 1883–84
204* P. V. F. Cazalet & F. E. Woolley: Kent v. Oxford U. (Oxford) 1928
204 A. T. Barber & E. Oldroyd: Yorks. v. England XI (Sheffield) 1929
204* D. C. H. Townsend & W. R. Hammond: M.C.C. v. British Guiana (Georgetown) ...1934–35
204 L. G. Berry & F. T. Prentice: Leics. v. Oxford U. (Oxford) 1936
204 C. Washbrook & J. Iddon: Lancs. v. Sussex (Hove) 1938
204 J. D. Robertson & W. J. Edrich: Middx. v. Hants. (Bournemouth) 1949
204 J. W. Burke & R. N. Harvey: Australia v. India (Bombay) 1956–57
204 R. E. Marshall & A. C. D. Ingleby-Mackenzie: Hants. v. Kent (Southampton) 1958
203 R. J. Howson & D. G. Paton: Tasmania v. Victoria (Hobart) 1911–12
203 T. Hayward & E. G. Hayes: Surrey v. Lancs. (Oval) 1912
203 W. Bardsley & J. Bogle: N.S.W. v. South Australia (Adelaide) 1919–20
203 J. O'Connor & C. Bray: Essex v. Middx. (Leyton) 1928
203 C. N. Woolley & B. Bellamy: Northants. v. Glos. (Bristol) 1928
203 John Langridge & H. W. Parks: Sussex v. Notts. (Nottingham) 1939
203 J. D. Robertson & W. J. Edrich: Middx. v. Northants. (Northampton)...............1954
202 F. Mitchell & J. T. Tyldesley: Hawke's XI v. Transvaal (Johannesburg) 1898–99
202* W. Rhodes & G. H. Hirst: Yorks. v. Somerset (Bath) 1906
202 J. B. Hobbs & A. Ducat: Surrey v. Sussex (Oval) 1920
202 A. Sandham & F. E. Woolley: M.C.C. v. N.S.W. (Sydney) 1924–25
202 A. J. Richardson & L. T. Gun: South Australia v. Queensland (Adelaide) 1926–27
202 J. W. Hearne & F. E. Woolley: England XI v. South Africans (Folkestone) 1929
202 C. L. Badcock & D. G. Bradman: South Australia v. N.S.W. (Adelaide) 1935–36
202 E. A. B. Rowan & J. H. Ward: Transvaal v. Griqualand West (Johannesburg) 1950–51
202 F. C. Gardner & W. J. Stewart: Warwicks. v. Northants. (Northampton)...............1960
201 R. Abel & T. Hayward: Surrey v. Hants. (Oval)...............1899
201 E. G. Wynyard & E. E. Steel: I Zingari v. Gentlemen (Lord's) 1904
201 F. A. Tarrant & J. W. Hearne: Middx. v. Somerset (Lord's) 1911

201 E. H. Bowley & K. S. Duleepsinhji: Sussex v. Essex (Hove)..................................1930
201 R. A. Sinfield & W. R. Hammond: Glos. v. Surrey (Bristol) 1933
201 C. J. Barnett & B. H. Lyon: Glos. v. Surrey (Cheltenham) 1934
201 L. B. Fishlock & R. J. Gregory: Surrey v. Yorks. (Oval) 1937
201 A. R. Morris & D. G. Bradman: Australian XI v. Western Australia (Perth) 1947–48
200 F. L. Bowley & E. G. Arnold: Worcs. v. Leics. (Worcester)..................................1906
200 A. C. Russell & J. Freeman: Essex v. Hants. (Bournemouth) 1921
200 I. Barrow & G. Headley: West Indies v. England (Manchester) 1933
200 H. Gimblett & G. G. Tordoff: Somerset v. Derby (Taunton) 1952

THIRD WICKET

445 P. E. Whitelaw & W. N. Carson: Auckland v. Otago (Dunedin) 1936–37
434 J. B. Stollmeyer & G. E. Gomez: Trinidad v. British Guiana (Trinidad) 1946–47
424* W. J. Edrich & D. C. S. Compton: Middx. v. Somerset (Lord's)........................1948
410 L. Amarnath & R. S. Modi: India in England v. Rest (Calcutta) 1946–47
399 R. T. Simpson & D. C. S. Compton: M.C.C. v. N.-E. Transvaal (Benoni) 1948–49
389 W. H. Ponsford & S. J. McCabe: Australians v. M.C.C. (Lord's) 1934
375 J. W. Hearne & E. Hendren: Middx. v. Hants. (Southampton) 1923
373 V. M. Merchant & R. S. Modi: Bombay v. Western India States (Bombay) 1944–45
370 W. J. Edrich & D. C. S. Compton: England v. South Africa (Lord's) 1947
369 W. Gunn & J. Gunn: Notts. v. Leics. (Nottingham) 1903
363 D. G. Bradman & A. F. Kippax: N.S.W. v. Queensland (Sydney) 1933–34
362 W. Bardsley & C. G. Macartney: Australians v. Essex (Leyton) 1912
356 D. G. Bradman & R. A. Hamence: South Australia v. Tasmania (Adelaide) 1935–36
355 W. Bardsley & V. S. Ransford: Australians v. Essex (Leyton) 1909
353 A. Ducat & E. G. Hayes: Surrey v. Hants. (Southampton) 1919
350 F. M. Worrell & E. D. Weekes: West Indians v. Cambridge U. (Cambridge) 1950
345 W. Bardsley & J. M. Taylor: N.S.W. v. South Australia (Adelaide) 1920–21
345 V. M. Merchant & H. R. Adhikari: Hindus v. Rest (Bombay) 1943–44
344 G. Brown & C. P. Mead: Hants. v. Yorks. (Portsmouth) 1927
343 P. A. Gibb & R. Horsfall: Essex v. Kent (Blackheath) 1951
340* F. M. Worrell & E. D. Weekes: West Indians v. Leics. (Leicester) 1950
338 E. D. Weekes & F. M. Worrell: West Indies v. England (Trinidad) 1953–54
336 W. R. Hammond & B. H. Lyon: Glos. v. Leics. (Leicester) 1933
335 D. K. Gaekwad & C. G. Borde: Baroda v. Maharashtra (Poona) 1959–60
333 R. M. Taylor & J. O'Connor: Essex v. Northants. (Colchester) 1937
330 A. E. Dipper & W. R. Hammond: Glos. v. Lancs. (Manchester) 1925
328 H. Carpenter & C. P. McGahey: Essex. v. Surrey (Oval) 1904
327 S. P. Kinneir & W. G. Quaife: Warwicks. v. Lancs. (Birmingham)....................1901
323 C. P. McGahey & P. A. Perrin: Essex v. Kent (Leyton) 1900
323* H. Sutcliffe & M. Leyland: Yorks. v. Glamorgan (Huddersfield) 1928
321* A. Hearne & J. R. Mason: Kent v. Notts. (Nottingham) 1899
320 W. W. Armstrong & M. A. Noble: Australians v. Somerset (Bath) 1905
320 T. L. Livingston & F. Jakeman: Northants. v. South Africans (Northampton) 1951
319 A. Melville & A. D. Nourse jun.: South Africa v. England (Nottingham)..............1947
318 G. A. Faulkner & A. D. Nourse sen.: South Africans v. N.S.W. (Sydney) 1910–11
318 T. W. Graveney & J. F. Crapp: Glos. v. Kent (Gillingham)............................1953
317 A. Ducat & T. F. Shepherd: Surrey v. Essex (Leyton) 1928
315 L. G. Crawley & W. V. Fox: Worcs. v. Northants. (Worcester) 1923
315 C. L. Badcock & A. L. Hassett: Australians v. Leics. (Leicester)....................1938
315 K. M. Tewari & V. L. Manjrekar: Uttar Pradesh v. Madhya Pradesh (Indore) 1957–58
313 Umer Khan & Prithviraj: Western India v. Bombay (Rajkot) 1943–44
313 E. Davies & W. E. Jones: Glamorgan v. Essex (Brentwood) 1948
312 P. A. Perrin & C. P. McGahey: Essex v. Derby (Leyton) 1912
310 A. Shrewsbury & W. Gunn: Non-Smokers v. Smokers (East Melbourne) 1886–87
309* C. B. Fry & A. C. MacLaren: Gentlemen v. Players (Lord's) 1903
306 R. Abel & F. C. Holland: Surrey v. Cambridge U. (Oval) 1895
306 E. Paynter & N. Oldfield: Lancs. v. Hants. (Southampton) 1938
306 S. Nurse & G. Sobers: Barbados v. M.C.C. (Barbados) 1959–60
305 W. E. Roller & W. W. Read: Surrey v. Lancs. (Manchester) 1887
304 W. J. Edrich & D. C. S. Compton: Middx. v. Glos. (Lord's) 1938
304 A. H. Phebey & R. C. Wilson: Kent v. Glamorgan (Blackheath) 1960
303 H. K. Foster & R. E. Foster: Worcs. v. Kent (Worcester) 1907
301 E. T. Killick & E. Hendren: Middx. v. Sussex (Hove) 1928
301 H. Sutcliffe & M. Leyland: Yorks. v. Middx. (Lord's) 1939
301* Atma Singh & H. T. Dani: Services v. Bengal (New Delhi) 1957–58
300 G. G. Atkinson & P. B. Wight: Somerset v. Glamorgan (Bath) 1960
298 K. S. Ranjitsinhji & E. H. Killick: Sussex v. Lancs. (Hove) 1901
298 J. B. Hobbs & E. Hendren: Players v. Gentlemen (Scarborough) 1925
296 R. H. Spooner & J. Hallows: Lancs. v. Essex (Leyton) 1904

296 W. J. Edrich & E. Hendren: M.C.C. v. Surrey (Lord's) 1936
296 W. J. Edrich & D. C. S. Compton: Middx. v. Surrey (Lord's) 1946
295 C. C. McDonald & R. N. Harvey: Australia v. West Indies (Kingston) 1954–55
294 J. M. Parks & James Langridge: Sussex v. Kent (Tunbridge Wells) 1951
292 A. C. Johnston & C. P. Mead: Hants. v. Warwicks. (Southampton) 1911
291 A. E. Knight & J. H. King: Leics. v. M.C.C. (Lord's) 1904
291 P. A. Perrin & F. H. Gillingham: Essex v. Cambridge U. (Cambridge) 1910
290* J. Solomon & B. F. Butcher: Berbice v. M.C.C. (Blairmont) 1959–60
287* W. J. Edrich & D. C. S. Compton: Middx. v. Surrey (Oval) 1947
286 J. W. Hearne & E. Hendren: Middx. v. Somerset (Taunton) 1928
284 E. T. Killick & G. C. Grant: Cambridge U. v. Essex (Cambridge) 1929
283 H. T. W. Hardinge & F. E. Woolley: Kent v. South Africans (Canterbury) 1924
283 J. M. Parks & K. F. Barrington: M.C.C. v. Berbice (Blairmont) 1959–60
281 W. G. Grace & L. Walker: London County v. M.C.C. (Crystal Palace) 1901
281 K. E. Rigg & L. S. Darling: Victoria v. South Australia (Adelaide) 1932–33
281 T. L. Livingston & R. Subba Row: Northants. v. Notts. (Nottingham) 1955
280 James Seymour & F. E. Woolley: Kent v. Lancs. (Dover) 1922
280 O. W. Bill & A. F. Kippax: N.S.W. v. Queensland (Brisbane) 1930–31
280 C. Richardson & D. Schonegevel: O.F.S. v. Transvaal B (Johannesburg) 1959–60
280 T. L. Goddard & R. A. McLean: South Africans v. Northants. (Northampton) 1960
279 H. Makepeace & E. Tyldesley: Lancs. v. Notts. (Manchester) 1926
279* E. Tyldesley & J. Iddon: Lancs. v. Worcs. (Worcester) 1932
279 H. H. Gibbons & S. H. Martin: Worcs. v. Northants. (Stourbridge) 1934
279 D. S. Sheppard & G. Cox: Sussex v. Yorks. (Hastings) 1953
278 A. Ward & F. H. Sugg: Lancs. v. Somerset (Taunton) 1898
278 C. J. B. Wood & A. E. Knight: Leics. v. Hants. (Southampton) 1905
278 T. N. Pearce & M. P. Donnelly: M.C.C. v. Yorks. (Scarborough) 1948
277 W. A. Hill & R. E. S. Wyatt: Warwicks. v. Northants. (Northampton) 1939
276 W. L. Murdoch & G. H. S. Trott: Australians v. Cambridge U. P. & P. (Leyton) 1890
276 M. N. Harbottle & R. E. H. Hudson: Army v. Oxford U. (Camberley) 1938
276 D. G. Bradman & A. L. Hassett: Australia v. England (Brisbane) 1946–47
273 F. L. Fane & G. J. V. Weigall: M.C.C. v. Cambridge U. (Lord's) 1901
273 H. T. W. Hardinge & F. E. Woolley: Kent v. Hants. (Southampton) 1922
273 F. C. de Saram & N. S. Mitchell Innes: Oxford U. v. Glos. (Oxford) 1934
273 W. R. Hammond & B. O. Allen: Glos. v. Leics. (Leicester) 1935
273 W. Place & G. A. Edrich: Lancs. v. Essex (Clacton) 1947
273 V. L. Manjrekar & B. R. Irani: Bombay v. Pakistan (Bombay) 1952–53
273 Hanif Mohammed & V. L. Manjrekar: Mahmood's XI v. Cannon's XI (Karachi) ...1953–54
272 C. P. Mead & E. Hendren: M.C.C. Australian XI v. Hawke's XI (Scarborough) 1929
272 D. G. Bradman & A. F. Kippax: N.S.W. v. Queensland (Brisbane) 1929–30
271 E. Paynter & N. Oldfield: Lancs. v. Sussex (Hove) 1937
269* G. Brown & C. P. Mead: Hants. v. Yorks. (Leeds) 1920
269 B. O. Allen & W. R. Hammond: Glos. v. Worcs. (Cheltenham) 1937
268 H. O. Rock & A. F. Kippax: N.S.W. v. Victoria (Sydney) 1924–25
268 N. F. Armstrong & C. S. Dempster: Leics. v. Glos. (Gloucester) 1937
268 V. S. Hazare & R. S. Modi: West Zone v. North Zone (Bombay) 1946–47
267 R. J. Gregory & T. H. Barling: Surrey v. Notts. (Oval) 1946
267 W. J. Edrich & S. M. Brown: Middx. v. Oxford U. (Oxford) 1952
266 R. Aird & C. P. Mead: Hants. v. Sussex (Hastings) 1924
266 C. B. Harris & J. Hardstaff jun.: Notts. v. Glos. (Nottingham) 1936
266 C. C. Hunte & G. Sobers: West Indies v. Universities XI (Nagpur) 1958–59
264 F. E. Woolley & J. W. Hearne: M.C.C. v. Tasmania (Hobart) 1911–12
264* C. B. Fry & E. I. M. Barrett: Hants. v. Oxford U. (Southampton) 1912
264 J. Vine & R. R. Relf: Sussex v. Oxford U. (Hove) 1913
264 L. Hutton & W. R. Hammond: England v. West Indies (Oval) 1939
263 D. F. Pope & A. C. Russell: Essex v. Sussex (Hove) 1930
263 D. G. W. Fletcher & H. S. Squires: Surrey v. Notts. (Nottingham) 1947
262 L. C. H. Palairet & C. A. Bernard: Somerset v. Hants. (Southampton) 1900
262 W. R. Hammond & D. R. Jardine: England v. Australia (Adelaide) 1928–29
261 A. Ducat & T. F. Shepherd: Surrey v. Leics. (Oval) 1926
261 B. Constable & P. B. H. May: Surrey v. Notts. (Nottingham) 1958
260 W. W. Keeton & J. Hardstaff jun.: Notts. v. Yorks. (Sheffield) 1949
259 C. L. Townsend & W. Troup: Glos. v. Essex (Clifton) 1899
259 L. E. G. Ames & L. J. Todd: Kent v. Glos. (Folkestone) 1933
259 J. Arnold & C. P. Mead: Hants. v. Derby (Portsmouth) 1934
258* J. T. Brown & F. Mitchell: Yorks. v. Warwicks. (Bradford) 1901
258 E. S. B. Williams & G. J. Bryan: Army v. Royal Navy (Lord's) 1928
258* E. D. Weekes & C. L. Walcott: West Indians v. Ceylon (Colombo) 1948–49
258 D. S. Sheppard & G. Cox: Sussex v. Glamorgan (Eastbourne) 1949
256 W. W. Whysall & A. W. Carr: Notts. v. Leics. (Leicester) 1928
255* W. G. Grace & E. M. Knapp: Glos. v. Surrey (Clifton) 1873
255 C. B. Fry & K. S. Ranjitsinhji: Sussex v. Yorks. (Sheffield) 1904

255   J. S. F. Morrison & Hon. H. G. H. Mulholland: Cambridge U. v. M.C.C. (Cambridge) 1914
255   J. W. Hearne & E. Hendren: Middx. v. Somerset (Taunton) 1934
255   L. Amarnath & V. S. Hazare: Indians v. Tasmania (Hobart) 1947–48
255   O. C. Dawson & K. N. Kirton: Border v. Rhodesia (East London) 1954–55
253   C. Hill & D. R. A. Gehrs: South Australia v. N.S.W. (Adelaide) 1909–10
253   H. T. W. Hardinge & F. E. Woolley: Kent v. Lancs. (Dover) 1926
252   C. L. Townsend & C. O. H. Sewell: Glos. v. Worcs. (Cheltenham) 1906
252   D. G. Bradman & K. R. Miller: Australian XI v. Indians (Sydney) 1947–48
252   D. E. V. Padgett & D. B. Close: Yorks. v. Notts. (Nottingham) 1959
252   G. E. Barker & J. Milner: Essex v. Leics. (Leicester) 1959
250* H. T. W. Hardinge & James Seymour: Kent v. Worcs. (Tonbridge) 1921
250   J. O'Connor & A. C. Russell: Essex v. Leics. (Leyton) 1927
250   E. H. Bowley & K. S. Duleepsinhji: Sussex v. Surrey (Oval) 1931
250   C. H. Bull & H. H. Gibbons: Worcs. v. Northants. (Kidderminster) 1937
250   R. J. Christiani & J. L. Thomas: British Guiana v. Barbados (Georgetown) 1946–47
250   M. K. Mantri & U. M. Merchant: Bombay v. Maharashtra (Poona) 1948–49
249   W. H. Ponsford & K. E. Rigg: Victoria v. South Australia (Melbourne) 1928–29
249   D. G. Bradman & S. J. McCabe: Australia v. England (Melbourne) 1936–37
249   M. J. Stewart & K. F. Barrington: Surrey v. Kent (Oval) 1960
249   D. E. V. Padgett & D. B. Close: Yorks. v. Notts. (Scarborough) 1960
248   Mushtaq Ali & C. T. Sarwate: Holkar v. West Bengal (Indore) 1949–50
247   W. W. Whysall & A. W. Carr: Notts. v. Leics. (Nottingham) 1922
247   P. Holmes & M. Leyland:Yorks. v. New Zealanders (Bradford) 1927
247   Hanif Mohammed & Wajir Mohammed: Karachi Whites v. Karachi Blues (Karachi) 1956–57
246   C. P. Mead & C. B. Fry: Hants. v. Kent (Southampton) 1912
246   G. O. Rabone & J. R. Reid: New Zealanders v. Notts. (Nottingham) 1949
246   J. Kelly & D. B. Carr: Derby v. Leics. (Chesterfield) 1957
246   P. Roy & V. L. Manjrekar: Indians v. Oxford U. (Oxford) 1959
245   F. E. Woolley & R. E. S. Wyatt: England v. South Africa (Manchester) 1929
245   W. A. Ashdown & L. E. G. Ames: Kent v. Essex (Brentwood) 1934
245   J. Hardstaff & W. R. Hammond: England v. New Zealand (Lord's) 1937
244   A. Sandham & T. H. Barling: Surrey v. Glamorgan (Cardiff) 1936
244   C. Washbrook & J. T. Ikin: Lancs. v. Yorks. (Manchester) 1948
244   T. W. Graveney & J. F. Crapp: Glos. v. Notts. (Bristol) 1950
244   D. E. V. Padgett & D. B. Close: Yorks. v. Oxford U. (Oxford) 1959
243* F. E. Woolley & E. Hendren: Rest of England v. Lancs. (Oval) 1926
243   M. L. Apte & R. B. Kenny: Bombay v. Bengal (Bombay) 1958–59
243   E. McMorris, G. Sobers & S. Nurse: West Indies v. England (Kingston) 1959–60
      (*McMorris retired hurt after the first 133 runs had been scored*).
242   N. F. Druce & C. E. M. Wilson: Cambridge U. v. M.C.C. (Lord's) 1896
242   A. Hearne & L. C. Braund: Grace's XI v. Australians (Crystal Palace) 1899
242   L. A. Stricker & A. D. Nourse sen.: South Africans v. South Australia (Adelaide) ...1910–11
242   C. Kelleway & W. Bardsley: Australia v. South Africa (Lord's) 1912
242   E. Paynter & W. R. Hammond: England v. South Africa (Durban) 1938–39
242   R. B. Nimbalkar & S. D. Deodhar: Maharashtra v. Kathiwar (Poona) 1948–49
242   Lalchand & Swaranjit Singh: East Punjab v. Delhi (New Delhi) 1951–52
242   C. L. Walcott & E. D. Weekes: West Indies v. Australia (Trinidad) 1954–55
241   C. L. Badcock & D. G. Bradman: Australian XI v. Tasmania (Hobart) 1937–38
241   A. Jabber & N. Chatterjee: Bengal v. Bihar (Calcutta) 1938–39
241   L. Outschoorn & C. H. Palmer: Worcs. v. Northants. (Worcester) 1949
240   James Seymour & K. L. Hutchings: Kent v. Derby (Derby) 1908
240   F. H. Gillingham & P. A. Perrin: Essex v. Surrey (Leyton) 1913
240   L. Hutton & M. Leyland: Yorks. v. Surrey (Leeds) 1939
239   J. B. Hobbs & A. Marshal: Surrey v. Kent (Oval) 1908
239   H. T. W. Hardinge & L. E. G. Ames: Kent v. Surrey (Blackheath) 1929
239   K. S. Duleepsinhji & H. W. Parks: Sussex v. Essex (Chelmsford) 1931
238   R. E. Foster & W. H. B. Evans: Worcs. v. Glos. (Worcester) 1901
238   A. R. Lonergan & C. L. Badcock: South Australia v. Queensland (Adelaide) 1934–35
238   F. S. Lee & H. T. F. Buse: Somerset v. Northants. (Kettering) 1938
238   P. R. Umrigar & V. L. Manjrekar: India v. New Zealand (Hyderabad) 1955–56
237   J. T. Tyldesley & J. Sharp: Lancs. v. Worcs. (Stourbridge) 1909
237   E. Tyldesley & J. Iddon: Lancs. v. Worcs. (Blackpool) 1929
237   John Langridge & G. Cox: Sussex v. Somerset (Worthing) 1950
237   W. Reilly & D. Schonegeval: O.F.S. v. Natal (Bloemfontein) 1957–58
236   J. Painter & W. Troup: Glos. v. Middx. (Lord's) 1888
236   C. Charlesworth & W. G. Quaife: Warwicks. v. Worcs. (Dewsbury) 1914
236   H. Sutcliffe & R. Kilner: Yorks. v. Notts. (Nottingham) 1920
236   W. W. Keeton & J. Hardstaff jun.: Notts. v. Essex (Nottingham) 1947
236   F. A. Lowson & J. V. Wilson: Yorks. v. Essex (Sheffield) 1950
236   L. Hutton & R. T. Simpson: M.C.C. v. N.S.W. (Sydney) 1950–51
236   M. Tompkin & C. H. Palmer: Leics. v. Surrey (Oval) 1951
236   A. K. Chaturvedi & N. S. Dutta: Uttar Pradesh v. Vidarbha (Nagpur) 1959–60

235 H. Carpenter & C. P. McGahey: Essex v. Sussex (Leyton) 1900
235 S. P. Kinneir & W. G. Quaife: Warwicks. v. Surrey (Oval) 1913
235 A. C. Russell & P. A. Perrin: Essex v. Kent (Leyton) 1919
235 A. Sandham & T. F. Shepherd: Surrey v. Leics. (Oval) 1924
235 D. Smith & L. F. Townsend: Derby v. Hants. (Chesterfield) 1935
234 A. O. Jones & G. Gunn: Notts. v. Essex (Leyton) 1904
234 W. W. Keeton & J. Hardstaff jun.: Notts. v. Glamorgan (Nottingham)...............1949
233 A. C. MacLaren & F. H. Hollins: Lancs. v. Worcs. (Worcester) 1903
233 P. A. Perrin & C. P. McGahey: Essex v. Middx. (Lord's) 1905
233 J. Gunn & A. W. Carr: Notts. v. Warwicks. (Nottingham) 1922
233 J. O'Connor & A. C. Russell: Essex v. Glos. (Chelmsford) 1928
233 L. Hutton & M. Leyland: Yorks. v. Worcs. (Stourbridge) 1937
233 P. B. H. May & M. H. Stevenson: Cambridge U. v. Hants. (Cambridge) 1950
233 D. M. Young & C. A. Milton: Glos. v. Warwicks. (Bristol)..........................1954
233* R. Kanhai & O. G. Smith: West Indians v. Bihar Governor's XI (Jamshedpur) 1958–59
232 C. H. B. Blount & G. J. Bryan: Combined Services v. South Africans (Portsmouth) 1924
232 H. C. Steele & A. F. Kippax: N.S.W. v. Queensland (Brisbane) 1926–27
232 J. O'Connor & A. C. Russell: Essex v. Worcs. (Worcester) 1928
232 D. S. Sheppard & G. Cox: Sussex v. Lancs. (Eastbourne) 1951
231 G. M. Lee & J. Gunn: Notts. v. Sussex (Hove) 1913
231 D. J. McGlew & J. H. B. Waite: South Africa v. Australia (Durban) 1957–58
230 C. B. Llewellyn & G. J. Thompson: M.C.C. v. Worcs. (Lord's) 1908
230 H. L. Dales & E. Hendren: Middx. v. Hants. (Portsmouth) 1922
230 E. Tyldesley & J. Iddon: Lancs. v. Kent (Tonbridge)..............................1931
230 G. Headley & J. E. D. Sealey: West Indians v. Notts. (Nottingham) 1939
230 V. M. Merchant & V. Mankad: Hindus v. Parsis (Bombay) 1944–45
230 D. Brookes & F. Jakeman: Northants. v. Essex (Chelmsford) 1951
229 L. Hall & R. Peel: Yorks. v. Middx. (Lord's) 1889
229 N. Kilner & R. E. S. Wyatt: Warwicks. v. Surrey (Birmingham).....................1929
229 D. G. Bradman & A. F. Kippax: Australia v. England (Leeds) 1930
229 L. S. M. Miller & B. Sutcliffe: New Zealanders v. South Australia (Adelaide) 1953–54
228 V. T. Trumper & B. W. Farquhar: N.S.W. v. New Zealanders (Sydney) 1898–99
228 J. W. Hearne & N. Haig: Middx. v. Sussex (Lord's) 1920
228 H. T. Hardinge & W. H. Ashdown: Kent v. Somerset (Taunton) 1927
228 L. G. Crawley & A. C. Russell: Essex v. Glamorgan (Swansea) 1928
228 A. Mitchell & M. Leyland: Yorks. v. Worcs. (Sheffield) 1933
228 W. J. Edrich & E. Hendren: Middx. v. Somerset (Weston-super-Mare) 1937
228 W. Barber & M. Leyland: Yorks. v. Surrey (Oval)................................1939
228 W. J. Edrich & D. C. S. Compton: England v. South Africa (Manchester) 1947
228 J. V. Wilson & D. E. V. Padgett: Yorks. v. Warwicks. (Birmingham) 1955
227 V. F. S. Crawford & R. Abel: Surrey v. Worcs. (Oval) 1901
227 L. J. Moon & B. J. T. Bosanquet: Middx. v. Somerset (Lord's) 1908
227 J. W. Hearne & N. Haig: Middx. v. Sussex (Lord's) 1920
227 C. F. Walters & H. H. Gibbons: Worcs. v. Northants. (Northampton) 1931
227 R. T. Simpson & F. W. Stocks: Notts. v. Northants. (Nottingham) 1948
226 A. E. Dipper & W. R. Hammond: Glos. v. Surrey (Oval) 1927
226 G. Headley & G. C. Grant: West Indians v. England XI (Folkestone) 1933
226 R. S. Modi & V. M. Merchant: Bombay v. Holkar (Bombay) 1944–45
226 James Langridge & G. Cox: Sussex v. Cambridge U. (Cambridge) 1947
226 R. J. Giles & J. Hardstaff jun.: Notts. v. Northants. (Nottingham) 1951
226 D. E. V. Padgett & D. B. Close: Yorks. v. Surrey (Oval) 1960
225 M. A. Noble & C. W. Gregory: N.S.W. v. Victoria (Melbourne) 1905–06
225 C. N. Woolley & R. L. Wright: Northants. v. Warwicks. (Kettering)...............1925
225 T. H. Barling & D. R. Jardine: Surrey v. Sussex (Oval) 1933
225 A. V. Avery & J. O'Connor: Essex v. Middx. (Lord's) 1939
225 F. H. Vigar & R. Horsfall: Essex v. Hants. (Bournemouth) 1947
225 T. D. Robertson & D. C. S. Compton: Middx. v. Worcs. (Lord's) 1957
224 W. Walker & A. W. Carr: Notts. v. Northants. (Nottingham)......................1931
224 P. B. H. May & B. Constable: Surrey v. Cambridge U. (Oval) 1954
224 R. N. Harvey & K. R. Miller: Australia v. West Indies (Kingston) 1954–55
224 J. V. Wilson & D. B. Close: Yorks. v. Cambridge U. (Cambridge) 1955
224 K. G. Suttle & E. R. Dexter: Sussex v. Notts. (Nottingham) 1959
224 N. O'Neill & G. Stevens: Australians v. President's XI (Ahmedabad) 1959–60
223 W. G. Grace & C. L. Townsend: Glos. v. Somerset (Bristol) 1895
223 L. C. Eastman & A. C. Russell: Essex v. Derby (Derby) 1929
223 E. Tyldesley & J. Iddon: Lancs. v. Warwicks. (Manchester) 1930
223 I. J. Siedle & A. D. Nourse jun.: Natal v. Western Province (Durban) 1936–37
223 J. Iddon & N. Oldfield: Lancs. v. Essex (Ilford) 1938
223 J. Arnold & N. McCorkell: Hants. v. Glos. (Bournemouth).......................1947
223 W. J. Edrich & D. C. S. Compton: Middx. v. Sussex (Lord's) 1947
223 J. Shaw & I. Huntington: Victoria v. Western Australia (Melbourne) 1957–58
223 A. Wharton & K. Grieves: Lancs. v. Cambridge U. (Manchester) 1960

K

222   N. C. Snedden & S. G. Smith: Auckland v. Hawke's Bay (Auckland) 1920–21
222   H. Elliott & L. F. Townsend: Derby v. Leics. (Loughborough) 1933
222* B. Sutcliffe & J. R. Reid: New Zealand v. India (New Delhi) 1955–56
222   E. R. Dexter & J. M. Parks: Sussex v. Surrey (Hove) 1960
221   T. Hayward & C. Baldwin: Surrey v. Yorks. (Oval) 1896
221   F. L. Bowley & E. G. Arnold: Worcs. v. Cambridge U. (Cambridge) 1903
221   H. K. Foster & J. A. Cuffe: Worcs. v. Warwicks. (Worcester) 1908
221   R. C. Blunt & J. McMillan: Otago v. Canterbury (Dunedin) 1928–29
221   A. A. Jackson & A. F. Kippax: N.S.W. v. South Australia (Adelaide) 1928–29
221   A. Mitchell & M. Leyland: Yorks. v. Notts. (Bradford) 1933
220   E. G. Hayes & J. E. Raphael: Surrey v. Derby (Derby) 1905
220   R. A. Haywood & W. W. Timms: Northants. v. Sussex (Northampton) 1921
220* A. E. Dipper & W. R. Hammond: Glos. v. Essex (Bristol) 1927
220   D. Davies & M. J. Turnbull: Glamorgan v. Notts. (Cardiff) 1932
220   F. E. Woolley & B. H. Valentine: Kent v. Sussex (Tunbridge Wells) 1938
220   E. Cooper & H. H. Gibbons: Worcs. v. Leics. (Leicester) 1939
219   L. Hall & W. Bates: Yorks. v. Cambridge U. (Cambridge) 1884
219* W. L. Foster & R. E. Foster: Worcs. v. Hants. (Worcester) 1899
219   D. G. Bradman & A. F. Kippax: N.S.W. v. South Australia (Sydney)................1930–31
219   K. E. Rigg & J. Ryder: Victoria v. Queensland (Melbourne) 1930–31
219   F. Watson & J. Iddon: Lancs. v. Middx. (Lord's) 1933
219   J. W. Seamer & N. S. Mitchell-Innes: Oxford U. v. Minor Counties (Oxford) 1934
219   L. P. O'Brien & W. A. Oldfield: Australians v. Griqualand West (Kimberley) 1935–36
219   John Langridge & G. Cox: Sussex v. Northants. (Kettering) 1939
219   L. Amarnath & Nawab of Pataudi: Indians v. Sussex (Hove) 1946
219   G. Stevens & C. Pinch: South Australia v. Western Australia (Adelaide)................1956–57
218   J. T. Tyldesley & E. Tyldesley: Lancs. v. Glos. (Manchester) 1919
218   W. M. Woodfull & K. J. Schneider: Australians v. New Zealand XI (Auckland)   ...1927–28
218   D. G. Bradman & A. F. Kippax: Woodfull's XI v. Ryder's XI (Sydney) 1929–30
218* G. T. S. Stevens & E. Hendren: Middx. v. Warwicks. (Birmingham) 1931
218   G. Headley & J. E. D. Sealey: West Indies v. Middx. (Lord's) 1939
218   W. R. Endean & K. J. Funston: Transvaal v. Rhodesia (Johannesburg) 1956–57
218   P. R. Umrigar & R. S. Modi: Bombay v. Gujerat (Khadakvasla) 1957–58
218* J. van Geloven & L. R. Gardner: Leics. v. Somerset (Leicester) 1960
217   K. G. Viljoen & J. F. W. Nicolson: Griqualand West v. Western Province (Kimberley) 1929–30
216   W. L. Murdoch & W. Newham: Sussex v. Somerset (Hove) 1896
216   S. P. Kinneir & W. G. Quaife: Warwicks. v. Worcs. (Worcester) 1909
216   L. G. Hemus & S. G. Smith: Auckland v. Canterbury (Auckland) 1919–20
216   J. W. Hearne & W. W. Whysall: M.C.C. v. Victoria (Melbourne) 1924–25
216   J. O'Connor & J. A. Cutmore: Essex v. Surrey (Leyton) 1932
216   D. G. Bradman & A. L. Hassett: Australians v. Notts. (Nottingham) 1938
215   C. Wilson & G. G. Hearne: Kent v. Yorks. (Canterbury)................................1886
215* A. Ward & J. Briggs: Lancs. v. Sussex (Manchester) 1890
215   A. Ward & A. C. MacLaren: Lancs. v. Kent (Gravesend) 1891
215   M. C. Bird & J. W. Hearne: M.C.C. v. O.F.S. (Bloemfontein) 1913–14
215   W. E. Astill & J. H. King: Leics. v. Hants. (Leicester) 1923
215   A. Ducat & T. F. Shepherd: Surrey v. Sussex (Hastings) 1923
215   A. Mitchell & M. Leyland: Yorks. v. Surrey (Bradford) 1928
215   D. Smith & G. M. Lee: Derby v. Essex (Leyton) 1931
215   D. Smith & A. F. Skinner: Derby v. Glos. (Gloucester) 1934
215   A. E. Alderman & L. F. Townsend: Derby v. Sussex (Eastbourne)................1938
215   F. G. H. Chalk & B. H. Valentine: Kent v. Sussex (Hastings) 1939
215   P. B. Wight & C. L. McCool: Somerset v. Worcs. (Stourbridge) 1958
214   A. Shrewsbury & W. Barnes: Notts. v. Middx. (Nottingham) 1887
214   Hon. F. S. G. Calthorpe & W. G. Quaife: Warwicks. v. Hants. (Birmingham) 1921
214* J. W. Hearne & E. Hendren: Middx. v. Warwicks. (Birmingham) 1924
214   A. J. Richardson & V. Y. Richardson: South Australia v. M.C.C. (Adelaide) 1924–25
214* H. H. Gibbons & W. V. Fox: Worcs. v. West Indians (Worcester) 1928
214   A. A. Anthony & H. D. Gillespie: Auckland v. Canterbury (Auckland) 1929–30
213   J. R. Mason & W. H. Patterson: Kent v. Glos. (Gravesend) 1898
213   E. Oldroyd & W. Barber: Yorks. v. Glamorgan (Hull) 1929
213   W. A. Hill & H. E. Dollery: Warwicks. v. Derby (Derby) 1937
213   John Langridge & G. Cox: Sussex v. Northants. (Northampton) 1938
213   P. Davis & J. E. Timms: Northants. v. Somerset (Northampton) 1947
213   F. M. Worrell & C. L. Walcott: West Indians v. Somerset (Taunton) 1950
213   L. Duldig & L. Flavell: South Australia v. N.S.W. (Adelaide) 1951–52
213   D. G. W. Fletcher & P. B. H. May: Surrey v. Kent (Blackheath) 1953
212   R. Carpenter & Thomas Hayward: Cambridgeshire v. Surrey (Oval) 1861
212   J. T. Tyldesley & J. Sharp: Lancs. v. Warwicks. (Birmingham) 1908
212   J. Hardstaff sen. & W. Payton: Notts. v. Leics. (Leicester) 1911
212   J. Sharp & E. Tyldesley: Lancs. v. Warwicks. (Birmingham) 1920
212   K. G. Viljoen & F. Nicholson: Griqualand West v. Western Province (Kimberley) ...1929–30

212 W. W. Keeton & G. V. Gunn: Notts. v. Northants. (Nottingham) 1938
212* M. Tompkin & C. H. Palmer: Leics. v. Northants. (Leicester)................1953
212 J. M. Allan & M. C. Cowdrey: Oxford U. v. Sussex (Oxford) 1954
211 V. T. Trumper & S. E. Gregory: Australians v. Sussex (Hove) 1899
211 S. H. Martin & B. W. Quaife: Worcs. v. Surrey (Oval) 1935
211 W. J. Edrich & D. C. S. Compton: Middx. v. Northants. (Northampton)........1947
211 P. R. Shyamsunder & L. T. Addisesh: Mysore v. Hyderabad (Bangalore) 1951–52
211 V. M. Merchant & V. S. Hazare: India v. England (New Delhi) 1951–52
211 V. Mankad & V. S. Hazare: India v. England (Lord's) 1952
211 J. Dell & D. J. Lewis: Rhodesia v. Border (East London) 1952–53
210 A. Ward & J. T. Brown: England v. Australia (Melbourne) 1894–95
210 James Seymour & F. E. Woolley: Kent v. Oxford U. (Oxford) 1913
210 J. W. H. T. Douglas & J. Freeman: Essex & Worcs. (Worcester) 1920
210 H. W. Lee & E. Hendren: Middx. v. Sussex (Lord's)........................1921
210* J. Sharp & J. T. Tyldesley: Lancs. v. Essex (Leyton) 1921
210 H. W. Lee & E. Hendren: Middx. v. Glamorgan (Swansea) 1933
210* F. T. Prentice & M. Tompkin: Leics. v. Essex (Leicester)   1947
210 K. C. Ibrahim & U. M. Merchant: Bombay v. Sind (Bombay) 1947–48
210 B. Constable & P. B. H. May: Surrey v. Cambridge U. (Cambridge) 1953
210 A. H. Phebey & M. C. Cowdrey: Kent v. Notts. (Blackheath)................1958
209 R. Abel & W. H. Lockwood: Surrey v. Kent (Oval) 1898
209 C. B. Fry & E. H. Killick: Sussex v. Australians (Hove) 1899
209 D. C. Robinson & G. L. Jessop: Glos. v. Worcs. (Worcester) 1912
209 H. D. Kanga & J. S. Warden: Parsis v. Muslims (Bombay) 1912–13
209 H. L. Collins & J. M. Gregory: Australia v. South Africa (Johannesburg) 1921–22
209 M. S. Nichols & J. O'Connor: Essex v Kent (Southend) 1936
209 C. J. Barnett & W. R. Hammond: Glos. v. Glamorgan (Bristol) 1937
209* G. F. H. Heane & J. Hardstaff jun.: Notts. v. Leics. (Leicester) 1939
209 D. C. S. Compton & Mushtaq Ali: Holkar v. Bombay (Bombay) 1944–45
209 G. A. Smithson & C. H. Palmer: Leics. v. Northants. (Northampton) 1953
208 A. C. MacLaren & A. Smith: Lancs. v. Sussex (Hove) 1892
208 W. Chatterton & G. Davidson: Derby v. Lancs. (Manchester) 1896
208 J. B. Hobbs & J. I. Piggott: Surrey v. Oxford U. (Oval) 1910
208 R. H. Spooner & P. F. Warner: Gentlemen v. Players (Oval) 1911
208 F. R. Santall & R. E. S. Wyatt: Warwicks. v. Leics. (Birmingham) 1937
208 B. O. Allen & W. R. Hammond: Glos. v. Essex (Brentwood) 1937
208 Ali Hussain & E. B. Aibara: Hyderabad v. C. P. & Berar (Nagpur) 1945–46
208 J. V. Wilson & E. Lester: Yorks. v. Sussex (Leeds) 1949
207 W. B. Money & H. A. Richardson: Cambridge U v. Surrey (Oval) 1868
207 W. L. Murdoch & H. J. H. Scott: Australia v. England (Oval) 1884
207 J. T. Tyldesley & D. Denton: Players v. Gentlemen (Scarborough)......1910
207 A. C. Russell & P. A. Perrin: Essex v. Northants. (Northampton) 1922
207 E. Cooper & H. H. Gibbons: Worcs. v. Lancs. (Dudley) 1938
207 E. Cooper & R. O. Jenkins: Worcs. v. Glos. (Dudley) 1949
207 J. C. Watkins & A. D. Nourse jun.: Natal v. O.F.S. (Durban) 1950–51
207 E. J. Martin & J. Hardstaff jun.: Notts. v. Derby (Nottingham) 1952
207 T. W. Graveney & P. B. H. May: England v. West Indies (Nottingham) ..1957
207 R. N. Harvey & N. O'Neill: Australia v. India (Bombay) 1959–60
206 W. Troup & W. H. Hale: Glos. v. Notts. (Bristol) 1902
206 H. Carpenter & C. P. McGahey: Essex v. Middx. (Lord's) 1906
206 J. W. Hearne & P. F. Warner: Middx. v. Sussex (Eastbourne) 1913
206 R. L. Harvey & A. D. Nourse jun.: Natal v. Border (Durban) 1936–37
206 V. Mankad & R. B. Kenny: Bombay v. Madras (Bombay) 1953–54
206 A. H. Preston & J. E. F. Beck: Wellington v. Canterbury (Christchurch) ..1955–56
206 K. F. Barrington & T. H. Clark: Surrey v. Middx. (Lord's) 1959
206 P. Burge & L. Favell: Australians v. Indian Universities (Bangalore) ...1959–60
205 F. S. Jackson & D. Denton: Yorks. v. Somerset (Taunton) 1897
205 C. Hill & M. A. Noble: Australians v. Glos. (Bristol) 1902
205 James Seymour & K. L. Hutchings: Kent v. Derby (Derby) 1910
205 H. S. B. Love & H. L. Collins: N.S.W. v. Victoria (Melbourne) .1921–22
205* E. Oldroyd & M. Leyland: Yorks. v. Hants. (Harrogate).............1924
205* C. J. Barnett & W. R. Hammond: Glos. v. Yorks. (Sheffield)........1936
205 R. E. S. Wyatt & H. E. Dollery: Warwicks. v. Yorks. (Birmingham)..1937
205 R. S. Modi & V. M. Merchant: Bombay v. Sind (Karachi) 1944–45
205 F. W. Freer & F. M. Worrell: Commonwealth v. West Zone (Poona) ..1949–50
205 D. E. V. Padgett & D. B. Close: Yorks. v. Somerset (Bath) 1959
204 A. P. Lucas & C. T. Studd: Gentlemen v. Players (Lord's) 1882
204 C. B. Fry & K. O. Goldie: Sussex v. Cambridge U. (Hove) 1901
204 B. O. Allen & W. R. Hammond: Glos. v. Warwicks. (Gloucester) ..1937
204 H. S. Squires & B. Constable: Surrey v. Essex (Southend) 1949
204 D. K. Gaekwad & V. S. Hazare: Baroda v. Services (Bardoda) ...1957–58
204 N. S. Harford & J. R. Reid: New Zealanders v. Oxford U. (Oxford) ...1958

203   D. Denton & J. Tunnicliffe: Yorks. v. Warwicks. (Birmingham) 1905
203   C. Bray & J. O'Connor: Essex v. Middx. (Leyton)......................................1928
203   J. A. Cutmore & J. O'Connor: Essex v. Hants. (Bournemouth) 1933
203   P. L. Ridings & R. A. Hamence: South Australia v. M.C.C. (Adelaide) 1946–47
203   H. W. Parks & James Langridge: Sussex v. Leics. (Hastings) 1947
203   D. M. Green & Javed Burki: Oxford U. v. Essex (Brentwood) 1960
202   J. Darling & G. Giffen: South Australia v. Queensland (Brisbane) 1898–99
202   L. G. Wright & E. M. Ashcroft: Derby v. Sussex (Derby) 1905
202   C. Kelleway & W. Bardsley: Australia v. South Africa (Manchester) 1912
202   J. B. Hobbs & D. J. Knight: Surrey v. Notts. (Oval) 1914
202   V. Y. Richardson & D. E. Pritchard: South Australia v. N.S.W. (Sydney) 1924–25
202   E. Hendren & F. T. Mann: Middx. v. Yorks. (Leeds) 1928
202   G. Headley & J. E. D. Sealey: West Indies v. England (Kingston) 1934–35
202   C. L. Badcock & D. G. Bradman: South Australia v. Queensland (Adelaide)........1938–39
202   L. E. G. Ames & B. H. Valentine: Kent v. Worcs. (Worcester) 1939
202   M. C. Cowdrey & N. C. F. Bloy: Free Foresters v. Oxford U. (Oxford) 1951
202   D. S. Sheppard & R. Subba Row: Cambridge U. v. Worcs. (Worcester) 1952
202   A. R. Morris & R. N. Harvey: Australia v. England (Brisbane) 1954–55
202   R. Raghunath & Balan Pandit: Kerala v. Andhra (Venkatagiri) 1958–59
201   J. Tunnicliffe & T. L. Taylor: Yorks. v. Surrey (Oval) 1900
201   C. J. B. Wood & A. E. Knight: Leics. v. Hants. (Leicester) 1905
201   E. G. McLeod & J. R. Lamason: Wellington v. Auckland (Wellington) 1935–36
201   K. E. Rigg & J. W. Scaife: Victoria v. Queensland (Melbourne) 1935–36
201   H. Sutcliffe & W. Barber: Yorks. v. Leics. (Leicester) 1938
201   C. L. Badcock & R. A. Hamence: South Australia v. Victoria (Melbourne) 1940–41
201   G. Lester & M. Tompkin: Leics. v. Oxford U. (Oxford) 1949
201   M. C. Cowdrey, C. H. Palmer & D. J. Insole: Gentlemen v. Players (Lord's) 1955
         (*Cowdrey retired hurt after the first six runs had been scored.*)
200   H. J. H. Scott & J. McIlwraith: Australian XI v. Victoria (Melbourne) 1885–86
200   W. G. Grace & K. S. Ranjitsinhji: M.C.C. v. Cambridge U. (Lord's) 1894
200   F. B. Wilson & E. M. Dowson: Cambridge U. v. Sussex (Hove)................1903
200   E. M. Sprot & A. J. L. Hill: Hants. v. Derby (Southampton) 1903
200   V. Y. Richardson & D. E. Pritchard: South Australia v. Victoria (Melbourne) 1919–20
200   H. L. Dales & E. Hendren: Middx. v. Somerset (Taunton) 1923
200   E. H. Bowley & T. E. Cook: Sussex v. Warwicks. (Horsham) 1927
200* E. Tyldesley & J. Iddon: Lancs. v. Glamorgan (Manchester) 1930

FOURTH WICKET

577   Gul Mahomed & V. S. Hazare: Baroda v. Holkar (Baroda) 1946–47
574* C. L. Walcott & F. M. Worrell: Barbados v. Trinidad (Trinidad) 1945–46
502* F. M. Worrell & J. D. C. Goddard: Barbados v. Trinidad (Barbados)....................1943–44
448   R. Abel & T. Hayward: Surrey v. Yorks. (Oval) 1899
424   I. S. Lee & S. O. Quin: Victoria v. Tasmania (Melbourne) 1933–34
411   P. B. H. May & M. C. Cowdrey: England v. West Indies (Birmingham) 1957
410   G. Abraham & B. Pandit: Kerala v. Andhra (Pulghat) 1959–60
402   W. Watson &. T. W. Graveney: M.C.C. v. British Guiana (Georgetown) 1953–54
399   G. Sobers & F. M. Worrell: West Indies v. England (Barbados) 1959–60
388   W. H. Ponsford & D. G. Bradman: Australia v. England (Leeds) 1934
382   V. M. Merchant & V. S. Hazare: C.C. of India v. Services XI (Bombay) 1944–45
381   H. P. Bayley & C. S. Persaud: British Guiana v. Barbados (Georgetown) 1937–38
377   K. R. Miller & J. H. de Courcy: Australians v. Combined Services (Kingston) 1953
366* P. R. Umrigar & V. S. Hazare: Indians v. Oxford U. (Oxford) 1952
361   A. O. Jones & J. Gunn: Notts. v. Essex (Leyton) 1905
342* S. W. Sohoni & V. S. Hazare: Maharashtra v. Western India States (Rajkot) 1940–41
342   E. A. B. Rowan & P. J. M. Gibb: Transvaal v. N.-E. Transvaal (Johannesburg) 1952–53
334   R. Abel & T. Hayward: Surrey v. Somerset (Oval) 1899
333   W. R. Hammond & E. Hendren: M.C.C. v. N.S.W. (Sydney) 1928–29
330   W. Barnes & W. Gunn: M.C.C. v. Yorks. (Lord's) 1885
328   P. Vaulkhard & D. Smith: Derby v. Notts. (Nottingham) 1946
326* James Langridge & G. Cox: Sussex v. Yorks. (Leeds) 1949
325   J. W. Hearne & E. Hendren: Middx. v. Hants. (Lord's) 1919
324   J. T. Tyldesley & A. C. MacLaren: Lancs. v. Notts. (Nottingham) 1904
324   J. R. Reid & W. M. Wallace: New Zealanders v. Cambridge U. (Cambridge) 1949
323   A. W. Carr & W. Payton: Notts. v. Kent (Nottingham) 1923
323   N. O'Neill & B. Booth: N.S.W. v. Victoria (Sydney) 1957–58
322   V. S. Hazare & V. Mankad: Indians v. Yorks. (Sheffield) 1946
322   D. K. Gaekwad & V. S. Hazare: Baroda v. Bombay (Sholapur) 1957–58
321   W. R. Hammond & W. L. Neale: Glos. v. Leics. (Gloucester) 1937
319   R. E. S. Wyatt & H. E. Dollery: Warwicks. v. Lancs. (Birmingham) 1937
315   M. A. Noble & S. E. Gregory: N.S.W. v. Victoria (Sydney) 1907–08

315 W. G. Quaife & J. H. Parsons: Warwicks. v. Glamorgan (Birmingham) 1927
312 D. Denton & G. H. Hirst: Yorks. v. Hants. (Southampton) 1914
308 G. Davidson & W. Storer: Derby v. Lancs. (Manchester)...............................1896
304 D. C. S. Compton & F. G. Mann: Middx. v. Surrey (Lord's) 1947
303* V. S. Hazare & H. R. Adhikari: Baroda v. Maharashtra (Poona) 1944–45
302 V. S. Hazare & Gul Mohamed: Bengal Cyclone XI v. Bijapur Famine XI (Bombay) ...1942–43
302 U. M. Merchant & D. G. Phadkar: Bombay v. Maharashtra (Poona) 1948–49
301 L. P. O'Brien & L. S. Darling: Victoria v. Queensland (Brisbane)...................1932–33
301 T. E. Bailey & P. B. H. May: M.C.C. v. Rhodesia (Salisbury) 1956–57
300 E. Tyldesley & J. Iddon: Lancs. v. Leics. (Leicester) 1928
299 P. Holmes & R. Kilner: Yorks. v. Northants. (Harrogate) 1921
299 W. M. Wallace & M. P. Donnelly: New Zealanders v. Leics. (Leicester) 1949
298 A. V. Avery & R. Horsfall: Essex v. Worcs. (Clacton) 1948
297 H. T. W. Hardinge & A. P. F. Chapman: Kent v. Hants. (Southampton) 1926
296 K. L. Hutchings & F. E. Woolley: Kent v. Northants. (Gravesend) 1908
294 I. D. Walker & G. F. Grace: Gentlemen of South v. Gentlemen of North (Beeston) ...1870
293 R. A. Duff & M. A. Noble: N.S.W. v. South Australia (Sydney) 1903–04
293 T. H. Barling & H. S. Squires: Surrey v. Oxford U. (Oval) 1932
293 P. R. Umrigar & G. Kishenchand: Gujerat v. Maharashtra (Kolhapur) 1951–52
291 C. G. Macartney & C. E. Pellew: Australians v. Notts. (Nottingham) 1921
289 A. Ducat & T. F. Shepherd: Surrey v. Glos. (Oval) 1927
283 F. M. Worrell & E. D. Weekes: West Indies v. England (Nottingham) 1950
282 A. P. F. Chapman & A. C. Wilkinson: M.C.C. v. Canterbury (Christchurch) 1922–23
282 D. C. S. Compton & J. Hardstaff jun.: M.C.C. v. Tasmania (Launceston) 1946–47
281 T. E. Cook & James Langridge: Sussex v. Surrey (Oval) 1930
279 R. E. Marshall & C. L. Walcott: West Indians v. Surrey (Oval) 1950
278 E. Hendren & L. E. G. Ames: M.C.C. v. British Guiana (Georgetown) 1929–30
278 A. W. Roberts & M. L. Page: Canterbury v. Wellington (Wellington) 1931–32
277 H. H. Gibbons & B. W. Quaife: Worcs. v. Middx. (Worcester) 1931
277 D. G. Bradman & C. L. Badcock: Australians v. Worcs. (Worcester)..................1938
276 P. G. T. Kingsley & N. M. Ford: Oxford U. v. Surrey (Oval) 1930
275 R. de W. K. Winlaw & J. H. Human: Cambridge U. v. Essex (Cambridge) 1934
275 C. L. Badcock & A. L. Hassett: Australians v. Cambridge U. (Cambridge) 1938
275 F. C. Gardner & H. E. Dollery: Warwicks. v. Somerset (Coventry) 1953
274* R. Flockton & G. Thomas: N.S.W. v. South Australia (Sydney) 1959–60
271 B. B. Wilson & W. Rhodes: Yorks. v. Sussex (Bradford) 1914
271 J. O'Connor & T. N. Pearce: Essex v. Lancs. (Clacton) 1931
270 J. B. Hobbs & D. R. Jardine: Surrey v. Middx. (Lord's) 1926
270 C. S. Dempster & G. S. Watson: Leics. v. Yorks. (Hull) 1937
268 H. Carpenter & T. M. Russell: Essex v. Derby (Derby) 1900
268* E. Tyldesley & J. Iddon: Lancs. v. Glamorgan (Swansea) 1933
267 C. L. Walcott & G. E. Gomez: West Indies v. India (New Delhi)....................1948–49
266* W. Payton & J. Gunn: Notts. v. Glos. (Nottingham) 1911
266 W. R. Hammond & T. S. Worthington: England v. India (Oval) 1936
266 G. Cox & James Langridge: Sussex v. Lancs. (Hove) 1939
265 Q. McMillan & H. B. Cameron: Transvaal v. O.F.S. (Cape Town) 1928–29
265 F. E. Woolley & M. J. Turnbull: M.C.C. v. N.S.W. (Sydney) 1929–30
265 P. A. Gibb & J. R. Thompson: Cambridge U. v. Free Foresters (Cambridge) 1938
264 I. D. Craig & W. Watson: N.S.W. v. Western Australia (Perth) 1956–57
263 G. Lavis & C. Smart: Glamorgan v. Worcs. (Cardiff) 1934
263 J. Hardstaff jun. & F. W. Stocks: Notts. v. Northants. (Nottingham) 1951
262 I. S. Lee & R. G. Gregory: Victoria v. M.C.C. (Melbourne) 1936–37
260 C. F. Walters & C. H. Bull: Worcs. v. Kent (Gravesend) 1933
259 A. Drake & G. H. Hirst: Yorks. v. Sussex (Hastings) 1911
259 C. P. Mead & Hon. L. H. Tennyson: Hants. v. Leics. (Portsmouth) 1921
259* D. V. Smith & James Langridge: Sussex v. Notts. (Nottingham)......................1950
259 Hanif Mohammed & Wallis Mathias: Karachi v. Bahawalpur (Karachi) 1958–59
258 J. Tunnicliffe & G. H. Hirst: Yorks. v. Hants. (Portsmouth) 1904
258 M. C. Datar & M. R. Rege: Maharashtra v. Bombay (Poona) 1948–49
256 R. Abel & F. C. Holland: Surrey v. Essex (Oval) 1895
256 A. E. Knight & H. Whitehead: Leics. v. Sussex (Leicester) 1900
256 E. Hendren & F. T. Mann: Middx. v. Essex (Leyton) 1923
256 A. C. Russell & P. A. Perrin: Essex v. Worcs. (Worcester) 1923
256 C. F. Walters & M. Nichol: Worcs. v. Hants. (Bournemouth) 1933
256 G. Cox & C. Oakes: Sussex v. Northants. (Northampton) 1950
256 H. R. Adhikari & H. T. Dani: Services v. Southern Punjab (Patiala) 1959–60
255 Hanif Mohammed & Raees Mohammed: Karachi v. Sind (Karachi) 1954–55
254 F. Chester & G. N. Foster: Worcs. v. Middx. (Lord's) 1913
254 K. G. Viljoen & J. C. Newton: O.F.S. v. Transvaal (Bloemfontein) 1933–34
254 J. R. Reid & L. S. M. Miller: New Zealanders v. Natal (Durban) 1953–54
253 R. E. S. Wyatt & H. E. Dollery: Warwicks. v. Derby (Birmingham) 1937
251* G. A. Edrich & K. Grieves: Lancs. v. Notts. (Manchester) 1951

250 H. H. Gibbons & M. Nichol: Worcs. v. Warwicks. (Dudley) 1929
250 T. H. Clark & R. C. E. Pratt: Surrey v. Kent (Oval) 1953
249 G. G. Hearne & F. Marchant: Kent v. Sussex (Gravesend) 1889
249 J. H. King & S. Coe: Leics. v. Northants. (Northampton) 1908
249* A. F. Kippax & D. G. Bradman: N.S.W. v. M.C.C. (Sydney) 1928–29
249 A. Sandham & L. E. G. Ames: England v. West Indies (Kingston) 1929–30
248 W. L. Knowles & J. R. Mason: Kent v. Surrey (Oval) 1900
248 A. Bowell & C. P. Mead: Hants. v. Worcs. (Worcester) 1926
248 L. Hutton & D. C. S. Compton: England v. West Indies (Lord's) 1939
248 J. T. Ikin & K. Grieves: Lancs. v. New Zealanders (Manchester) 1949
248 G. Dews & R. G. Broadbent: Worcs. v. Combined Services (Worcester) 1951
247 C. P. Mead & W. G. L. F. Lowndes: Hants. v. Australians (Southampton) 1934
247 M. Leyland & L. Hutton: Yorks. v. Essex (Hull) 1936
247 E. D. Weekes & C. L. Walcott: West Indians v. Surrey (Oval) 1950
246 C. B. Fry & G. Brown: Hants. v. Glos. (Southampton) 1911
246 C. B. Fry & E. I. M. Barrett: Hants. v. Yorks. (Southampton) 1912
246 V. M. Merchant & R. S. Cooper: Bombay v. Holkar (Bombay) 1944–45
246 A. W. H. Rayment & C. Walker: Hants. v. Glos. (Bristol) 1953
245 W. L. Murdoch & S. P. Jones: N.S.W. v. Victoria (Sydney) 1881–82
245 W. Gunn & A. Shrewsbury: Notts. v. Derby (Derby) 1901
245 A. F. Kippax & J. G. Morgan: N.S.W. v. Victoria (Sydney) 1927–28
245 E. Cooper & S. H. Martin: Worcs. v. Warwicks. (Dudley) 1938
244 G. E. Gomez & R. Tang Choon: Trinidad v. M.C.C. (Trinidad) 1947–48
244 L. B. Fishlock & M. R. Barton: Surrey v. Leics. (Leicester) 1948
243 L. G. Wright & W. Chatterton: Derby v. Glos. (Bristol) 1901
243 D. G. Bradman & A. A. Jackson: Australia v. England (Oval) 1930
243 M. Nichol & S. H. Martin: Worcs. v. Yorks. (Worcester) 1933
243 F. M. Worrell & C. L. Walcott: West Indies v. India (Kingston) 1952–53
242 J. T. Tyldesley & A. H. Hornby: Lancs. v. Worcs. (Liverpool) 1903
242 J. Sharp & H. Makepeace: Lancs. v. Hants. (Southampton) 1910
242 N. F. Armstrong & F. T. Prentice: Leics. v. Cambridge U. (Cambridge) 1939
242 M. C. Cowdrey & J. F. Pretlove: Kent v. Essex (Blackheath) 1959
241 R. Abel & J. M. Read: Surrey v. Australians (Oval) 1886
241 A. Melville & H. W. Parks: Sussex v. Oxford U. (Worthing) 1936
240 C. P. Mead & A. L. Hosie: Hants. v. Yorks. (Southampton) 1928
239* D. J. Insole & T. E. Bailey: Essex v. Notts. (Southend) 1955
238 John Langridge & James Langridge: Sussex v. Northants. (Peterborough) 1934
238 E. A. B. Rowan & J. E. Cheetham: South Africans v. Oxford U. (Oxford) 1951
238 R. G. Nadkarni & Y. P. Sidhaye: Maharashtra v. Baroda (Nasik) 1956–57
237 W. Robinson & F. Taylor: Lancs. v. Oxford U. (Manchester) 1883
237 L. E. G. Ames & A. P. F. Chapman: Kent v. Somerset (Taunton) 1928
237 E. Hendren & L. E. G. Ames: England v. West Indies (Trinidad)..........1929–30
237 M. F. Mistri & R. S. Modi: Parsis v. Europeans (Bombay) 1941–42
236 C. P. McGahey & A. J. Turner: Essex v. Northants. (Northampton) 1908
236 A. Sandham & A. Jeacocke: Surrey v. Sussex (Oval) 1922
236 E. Tyldesley & E. Paynter: Lancs. v. Sussex (Manchester) 1935
236 A. E. Fagg & R. Mayes: Kent v. Notts. (Nottingham) 1953
236 L. H. Savill & T. E. Bailey: Essex v. Cambridge U. (Cambridge) 1959
235 A. L. Hassett & K. R. Miller: Australia v. West Indies (Sydney) 1951–52
235 N. O'Neill & L. Favell: Australians v. President's XI (Ahmedabad) 1959–60
234 H. S. Squires & J. F. Parker: Surrey v. Hants. (Bournemouth) 1948
234 R. T. Simpson & D. C. S. Compton: M.C.C. v. Queensland (Brisbane) 1954–55
234 A. J. Pithey, R. A. McLean & C. Wesley: South Africans v. Worcs. (Worcester) 1960
     (*McLean retired hurt after 201 runs had been added.*)
233 K. L. Hutchings & F. E. Woolley: Kent v. Sussex (Hastings) 1910
233 J. M. Taylor & W. H. Ponsford: Australian XI v. Western Australia (Perth) 1925–26
233 A. C. Russell & H. M. Morris: Essex v. Hants. (Southampton) 1927
232 G. J. Thompson & S. G. Smith: Northants. v. Hants. (Portsmouth) 1910
232* A. Ducat & H. O. Bloomfield: Surrey v. Northants. (Northampton) 1921
231 W. E. Alley & T. L. Livingston: Commonwealth v. Services (New Delhi) 1949–50
231 K. Mackay & R. G. Archer: Queensland v. Victoria (Brisbane) 1953–54
230 C. Baldwin & D. L. A. Jephson: Surrey v. Kent (Oval) 1897
230 C. W. Gregory & E. L. Waddy: N.S.W. v. Queensland (Brisbane) 1906–07
230 L. E. G. Ames & L. J. Todd: Kent v. Surrey (Blackheath) 1933
230 D. C. H. Townsend & F. G. H. Chalk: Oxford U. v. Cambridge U. (Lord's) 1934
230 J. D. Robertson & G. O. Allen: Middx. v. Worcs. (Worcester) 1949
229 A. C. Russell & P. A. Perrin: Essex. v. Somerset (Leyton) 1925
229 A. D. Ratcliffe & W. G. F. Brown: N.S.W. v. New Zealanders (Sydney) 1925–26
229 J. Hardstaff jun. & G. V. Gunn: Notts. v. Kent (Nottingham) 1937
229 D. W. Begbie & K. G. Viljoen: Transvaal v. Natal (Johannesburg) 1948–49
228 M. Tompkin & G. J. Whittaker: North v. South (Kingston) 1949
228 R. T. Simpson & W. G. A. Parkhouse: M.C.C. v. N.S.W. (Sydney).......................1950–51

227 P. A. Perrin & F. H. Gillingham: Essex v. Middx. (Lord's) 1904
227 E. Tyldesley & E. Paynter: Lancs. v. Northants. (Peterborough) 1934
227 C. L. Walcott & E. D. Weekes: Barbados v. British Guiana (Barbados) 1949–50
227 F. M. Worrell & K. B. Trestrail: West Indians v. Lancs. (Liverpool) 1950
227 R. Horsfall & D. J. Insole: Essex v. Worcs. (Worcester) 1953
227 R. Surti & Hanumant Singh: Rajasthan v. Uttar Pradesh (Udaipur) 1959–60
226 G. Brann & F. M. Lucas: Sussex v. Hants. (Hove) 1886
226 W. H. Wilkinson & G. H. Hirst: Yorks. v. Northants. (Hull) 1909
226 W. R. Hammond & E. Hendren: Players v. Gentlemen (Folkestone) 1927
226* M. Nichol & C. H. Bull: Worcs. v. Northants. (Worcester) 1933
226 K. Mackay & R. G. Archer: Australians v. Glamorgan (Swansea) 1956
225 W. Troup & C. L. Townsend: Glos. v. Notts. (Bristol) 1898
225 A. I. Paine & T. E. Etlinger: Western Province v. Griqualand West (Johannesburg) 1896–97
225 C. H. Grimshaw & G. H. Hirst: Yorks. v. Oxford U. (Oxford) 1906
225 R. H. Spooner & G. L. Jessop: Londesborough's XI v. M.C.C. Australian Team
　　　　　　　　　　　　　　　　　　　　　　　(Scarborough)..................1911
225 H. T. Bartlett & J. H. Human: Cambridge U. v. Glamorgan (Cambridge) 1934
225 J. Hardstaff jun. & N. W. D. Yardley: North v. South (Scarborough) 1949
225 P. R. Umrigar & V. M. Merchant: Bombay v. Commonwealth (Bombay) 1949–50
225 V. S. Hazare & D. G. Phadkar: Indian XI v. Commonwealth (Bombay)..................1950–51
224 F. A. Tarrant & W. W. Armstrong: Victoria v. South Australia (Melbourne) 1907–08
224 P. Holmes & G. B. Legge: M.C.C. v. O.F.S. (Bloemfontein) 1927–28
224 D. R. Jardine & C. P. Mead: M.C.C. v. Tasmania (Launceston) 1928–29
224 K. R. Miller & A. L. Hassett: Victoria v. South Australia (Adelaide) 1946–47
223 F. C. Thompson & L. E. Oxenham: Queensland v. N.S.W. (Sydney) 1925–26
223 W. M. Woodfull & J. Ryder: Victoria v. South Australia (Melbourne) 1925–26
223 E. Hendren & D. C. S. Compton: Middx. v. Notts. (Nottingham) 1937
223 W. J. Edrich & F. G. Mann: Middx. v. Sussex (Hove) 1939
222 W. Andrew & A. J. L. Hill: Hants. v. Warwicks. (Southampton) 1897
222 W. R. Hammond & E. Paynter: England v. Australia (Lord's) 1938
222 G. E. Gomez & L. Harbin: Trinidad v. Jamaica (Trinidad) 1938–39
222 N. Oldfield & J. Iddon: Lancs. v. Worcs. (Manchester)......................................1939
222 V. S. Hazare & V. L. Marjrekar: India v. England (Leeds) 1952
221 G. H. S. Trott & S. E. Gregory: Australia v. England (Lord's) 1896
221* H. H. Gibbons & S. H. Martin: Worcs. v. Glamorgan (Worcester) 1938
221* R. N. Harvey & S. J. E. Loxton: Australians v. O.F.S. (Bloemfontein) 1949–50
220 W. H. Patterson & Lord Harris: Kent v. Somerset (Taunton) 1896
220 J. T. Tyldesley & J. Sharp: Lancs. v. Warwicks. (Birmingham) 1907
220 James Seymour & D. W. Jennings: Kent v. Essex (Tunbridge Wells) 1914
220 S. G. Smith & G. J. Thompson: Northants. v. Sussex (Hove) 1914
220 W. G. Quaife & Hon. F. S. G. Calthorpe: Warwicks. v. Lancs (Birmingham) 1925
220 E. Tyldesley & E. Paynter: Lancs. v. Leics. (Leicester) 1934
220 R. S. Modi & Nawab of Pataudi: Indians v. Cambridge U. (Cambridge) 1946
220 R. E. Hitchcock & H. E. Dollery: Warwicks. v. Leics. (Hinckley) 1955
219 H. G. Vivian & M. L. Page: New Zealanders v. Oxford U. (Oxford) 1931
219 K. G. Viljoen & D. W. Begbie: Transvaal v. Griqualand West (Kimberley) 1936–37
219 K. G. Viljoen & R. E. S. Vine: Transvaal v. Rhodesia (Bulawayo) 1945–46
219 H. W. Parks & G. Cox: Sussex v. Glamorgan (Hove) 1947
218 J. E. K. Studd & C. T. Studd: Cambridge U. v. Gentlemen (Cambridge) 1881
218 W. G. L. F. Lowndes & H. P. Ward: Oxford U. v. Leveson-Gower's XI (Eastbourne) ...1921
218 M. P. Donnelly & R. H. Maudsley: Oxford U. v. Lancs. (Oxford) 1946
218* P. B. H. May & K. F. Barrington: Surrey v. Lancs. (Oval) 1955
218 D. J. Insole & P. B. H. May: M.C.C. v. Eastern Province (Port Elizabeth)...............1956–57
217 G. Brann & A. Shrewsbury: Shrewsbury's XI v. N.S.W. (Sydney) 1887–88
217 C. Hill & S. E. Gregory: Australians v. Cambridge U. (Cambridge) 1899
217 W. E. Bates & J. J. Hills: Glamorgan v. Surrey (Oval) 1930
217 J. S. Ord & H. E. Dollery: Warwicks. v. Hants. (Bournemouth) 1949
217 R. Kanhai & B. F. Butcher: West Indies v. India (Calcutta) 1958–59
216 F. L. Bowley & E. G. Arnold: Worcs. v. Leics. (Stourbridge) 1905
216 K. G. Viljoen & X. C. Balaskas: Griqualand West v. Western Province (Kimberley) 1929–30
216* J. Hardstaff jun. & G. V. Gunn: Notts. v. Surrey (Nottingham) 1939
216 S. M. Brown & A. Thompson: Middx. v. Hants. (Southampton) 1953
216 G. Pullar & C. Washbrook: Lancs. v. Glamorgan (Manchester) 1958
215 A. Ward & W. R. Cuttell: Lancs. v. Notts. (Manchester) 1899
215 M. C. Bird & J. W. Hearne: M.C.C. v. O.F.S. (Bloemfontein) 1913–14
215 J. S. Ord & H. E. Dollery: Warwicks. v. Hants. (Birmingham) 1939
215 Mushtaq Ali & C. K. Nayudu: Holkar v. United Provinces (Indore) 1947–48
215 A. V. Avery & D. J. Insole: Essex v. Sussex (Hove) 1951
215 A. G. Kripal Singh & C. D. Gopinath: Madras v. Bengal (Madras).......................1954–55
215 J. W. Burke & K. R. Miller: N.S.W. v. Western Australia (Perth) 1955–56
214 G. McGregor & C. P. Foley: Cambridge U. v. Sussex (Hove) 1890
214 N. V. H. Riches & F. W. Matthias: Wales v. Ireland (Belfast) 1926

214	E. Hendren & C. D. Gray: Middx. v. Warwicks. (Lord's)	1927
214	H. W. Taylor & H. G. Deane: South Africa v. England (Oval)	1929
213	T. Hayward & E. G. Goatley: Surrey v. Warwicks. (Oval)	1906
213	E. Hendren & G. E. V. Crutchley: Middx. v. Somerset (Lord's)	1922
213	E. D. Weekes & C. B. Williams: Barbados v. Indians (Barbados)	1952–53
213	F. M. Worrell & C. L. Walcott: West Indies v. India (Kingston)	1952–53
212	B. B. Wilson & G. H. Hirst: Yorks. v. Sussex (Hastings)	1913
212	A. W. Lampard & V. S. Ransford: Australians v. New Zealand XI (Auckland)	1920–21
212	F. T. Prentice & V. E. Jackson: Leics. v. Notts. (Loughborough)	1949
211	F. E. Woolley & A. F. Bickmore: Kent v. Hants. (Southampton)	1920
211	T. F. Shepherd & T. H. Barling: Surrey v. Warwicks. (Oval)	1931
211	M. J. Turnbull & D. Davies: Glamorgan v. Northants. (Northampton)	1933
211	S. H. Martin & B. W. Quaife: Worcs. v. Surrey (Oval)	1935
211	A. H. Bakewell & D. Brookes: Northants. v. Derby (Chesterfield)	1936
211	J. V. Wilson & W. Watson: Yorks. v. Derby (Harrogate)	1951
210	R. V. Minnett & E. P. Barbour: N.S.W. v. Queensland (Sydney)	1910–11
210	C. P. Mead & H. L. V. Day: Hants. v. Middx. (Bournemouth)	1926
210	J. O'Connor & M. S. Nichols: Essex v. Hants. (Leyton)	1929
210	E. Hendren & J. Sims: Middx. v. Notts. (Nottingham)	1931
210*	A. Mitchell & M. Leyland: Yorks. v. Worcs. (Worcester)	1933
210	T. N. Pearce & M. S. Nichols: Essex v. Worcs. (Chelmsford)	1937
210	A. Sandham & E. W. Whitfield: Surrey v. Oxford U. (Oval)	1934
210	W. J. Edrich & D. C. S. Compton: Middx. v. Rest of England (Oval)	1944
210	D. C. S. Compton & J. G. Dewes: Middx. v. New Zealanders (Lord's)	1949
210	E. Lester & W. Watson: Yorks. v. Notts. (Nottingham)	1952
210	A. G. Kripal Singh & C. D. Gopinath: Madras v. Andhra (Madras)	1955–56
209	G. F. Grace & C. S. Gordon: Glos. v. Sussex (Clifton)	1874
209	G. R. R. Colman & I. P. F. Campbell: Oxford U. v. Hants. (Southampton)	1913
209	A. W. Carr & W. Payton: Notts. v. Essex (Worksop)	1924
209	T. E. Cook & James Langridge: Sussex v. Glos. (Cheltenham)	1927
209	H. Storer & D. Smith: Derby v. Middx. (Derby)	1932
208	W. R. Hammond & W. L. Neale: Glos. v. Glamorgan (Gloucester)	1933
208	P. B. H. May & M. H. Stevenson: Cambridge U. v. Lancs. (Cambridge)	1952
207	G. E. Bromley-Martin & H. K. Foster: Worcs. v. Derby (Worcester)	1899
207	C. A. Richardson & F. A. Midlane: Wellington v. Otago (Wellington)	1899–00
207	W. W. Armstrong & V. S. Ransford: N.S.W. v. Victoria (Sydney)	1908–09
207	F. T. Badcock & T. C. Lowry: Wellington v. Auckland (Wellington)	1927–28
207	R. H. Moore & C. G. A. Paris: Hants. v. Warwicks. (Bournemouth)	1937
207	K. R. Miller & C. I. Gunasekara: Commonwealth v. M.C.C. (Colombo)	1951–52
207	M. R. Hallam & W. Watson: Leics. v. Derby (Leicester)	1959
206	T. Hayward & R. Abel: Surrey v. Glos. (Oval)	1901
206	W. W. Armstrong & V. S. Ransford: Victoria v. Queensland (Melbourne)	1904–05
206	C. N. Frank & A. D. Nourse sen.: South Africa v. Australia (Johannesburg)	1921–22
206	H. Storer & J. M. Hutchinson: Derby v. Somerset (Derby)	1926
206	C. P. Mead & A. E. Pothecary: Hants. v. Kent (Canterbury)	1933
206*	K. R. Miller & K. Meuleman: Victoria v. N.S.W. (Sydney)	1946–47
205	H. Charlwood & G. F. Grace: South v. North (Huddersfield)	1875
205	W. Gunn & W. Barnes: Notts. v. Sussex (Nottingham)	1887
205	G. Higgins & J. Burns: Essex v. Warwicks. (Birmingham)	1895
205	E. Oldroyd & R. Kilner: Yorks. v. Worcs. (Dudley)	1922
205	W. Walker & W. Payton: Notts. v. Middx. (Lord's)	1930
205	H. H. Gibbons & C. A. Fiddian-Green: Worcs. v. Leics. (Hinckley)	1932
205	L. E. G. Ames & B. H. Valentine: Kent v. Northants. (Dover)	1933
205	E. Lester & W. Watson: Yorks. v. Somerset (Leeds)	1953
205	P. B. H. May & M. C. Cowdrey: Gentlemen v. Players (Scarborough)	1953
205	K. R. Miller & A. L. Hassett: Hassett's XI v. Morris's XI (Melbourne)	1953–54
205	M. J. K. Smith & G. P. S. Delisle: Oxford U. v. Glos. (Bristol)	1956
204	G. L. Jessop & C. B. Fry: England v. Yorks. (Lord's)	1901
204	R. S. Martin & K. J. Funston: N.E. Transvaal v. Border (Pretoria)	1946–47
204	A. L. Hassett & R. N. Harvey: Hassett's XI v. Morris's XI (Sydney)	1948–49
204*	D. Brookes & G. Tribe: Northants. v. Somerset (Taunton)	1956
204	R. N. Harvey & R. B. Simpson: Australians v. Otago (Dunedin)	1956–57
203	G. J. Bryan & L. P. Hedges: Kent v. Hants. (Canterbury)	1921
203	H. L. Higgins & J. W. Turner: Worcs. v. Northants. (Northampton)	1921
203	J. A. Cutmore & M. S. Nichols: Essex v. Worcs. (Leyton)	1930
203	C. L. Badcock & R. A. Hamence: South Australia v. N.S.W. (Adelaide)	1938–39
203	H. W. Parks & James Langridge: Sussex v. Glamorgan (Hove)	1939
202	G. E. V. Crutchley & R. H. Twining: Free Foresters v. Cambridge U. (Cambridge)	1919
202	A. C. Russell & J. W. H. T. Douglas: Essex v. Northants. (Leyton)	1921
202	E. Hendren & F. T. Mann: Middx. v. Yorks. (Leeds)	1928
202	E. Hendren & J. O'Connor: M.C.C. v. British Guiana (Georgetown)	1929–30
202	J. L. Hopwood & C. Hawkswood: Lancs. v. Yorks. (Leeds)	1933

202   D. Smith & E. Carrington: Derby v. Yorks. (Chesterfield) 1935
202   W. R. Hammond & J. F. Crapp: Glos. v. Yorks. (Gloucester) 1938
201   K. L. Hutchings & J. R. Mason: Kent v. Lancs. (Canterbury) 1906
201   E. Hendren & H. W. Lee: Middx. v. Warwicks. (Birmingham) 1931
201   N. W. D. Yardley & M. Tindall: Cambridge U. v. Sussex (Worthing) 1937
201   Prithviraj & J. H. Shodhan: Gujerat v. Kathiwar (Rajkot) 1946–47
201   W. H. H. Sutcliffe & L. Hutton: Yorks. v. Kent (Canterbury)...........................1952
201   M. C. Cowdrey & S. E. Leary: Kent v. Sussex (Tunbridge Wells) 1960
200   R. Carpenter & Thomas Hayward: All England XI v. Yorks. (Sheffield) 1865
200   F. E. Woolley & S. H. Day: Kent v. Worcs. (Canterbury) 1914
200   F. E. Woolley & J. C. Hubble: Kent v. Warwicks. (Birmingham) 1921
200   N. M. Ford & P. G. T. Kingsley: Oxford U. v. Leveson-Gower's XI (Eastbourne) ...1928
200   W. H. Ponsford & K. E. Rigg: Victoria v. West Indians (Melbourne) 1930–31
200   L. E. G. Ames & L. J. Todd: Kent v. Hants. (Portsmouth) 1934
200   H. Gimblett & G. E. S. Woodhouse: Somerset v. Middx. (Taunton) 1946
200   D. R. Fell & A. D. Nourse jun.: Natal v. Western Province (Cape Town) 1947–48
200   J. V. Wilson & W. Watson: Yorks. v. Somerset (Taunton) 1950
200   D. C. S. Compton & C. Washbrook: M.C.C. v. Combined XI (Launceston) 1950–51
200   R. Subba Row & A. F. Brazier: Surrey v. Northants. (Northampton) 1953
200   C. C. P. Williams & D. J. Insole: Essex v. Leics. (Leicester) 1955

FIFTH WICKET

405   S. G. Barnes & D. G. Bradman: Australia v. England (Sydney) 1946–47
397   W. Bardsley & C. Kelleway: N.S.W. v. South Australia (Sydney) 1920–21
393   E. G. Arnold & W. B. Burns: Worcs. v. Warwicks. (Birmingham) 1909
360   U. M. Merchant & M. N. Raiji: Bombay v. Hyderabad (Bombay) 1947–48
347   D. Brookes & D. Barrick: Northants. v. Essex (Northampton) 1952
343   R. Maddocks & J. Hallebone: Victoria v. Tasmania (Melbourne) 1951–52
340   E. Wainwright & G. H. Hirst: Yorks. v. Surrey (Oval) 1899
338   R. S. Lucas & T. C. O'Brien: Middx. v. Sussex (Hove) 1895
336   W. H. Ponsford & H. S. B. Love: Victoria v. Tasmania (Melbourne) 1922–23
332   E. Hendren & W. F. Price: Middx. v. Worcs. (Dudley) 1933
329   F. Mitchell & E. Wainwright: Yorks. v. Leics. (Leicester) 1899
327   P. Holmes & W. E. Astill: M.C.C. v. Jamaica (Kingston) 1925–26
327   H. B. Cameron & A. W. Briscoe: Transvaal v. Griqualand West (Johannesburg) 1934–35
325   V. M. Merchant & K. M. Rangnekar: Bombay v. Sind (Bombay) 1945–46
308   J. N. Crawford & F. C. Holland: Surrey v. Somerset (Oval) 1908
301* C. E. Pellew & C. B. Willis: A.I.F. v. Worcs. (Worcester) 1919
301   F. M. Worrell & W. H. H. Sutcliffe: Commonwealth v. Ceylon (Colombo) 1950–51
301   R. B. Simpson & K. Meuleman: Western Australia v. N.S.W. (Perth) 1959–60
300   D. W. Begbie & A. W. Briscoe: Transvaal v. O.F.S. (Johannesburg) 1937–38
297   J. H. Parks & H. W. Parks: Sussex v. Hants. (Portsmouth) 1937
291   A. D. Nourse sen. & J. M. Blanckenberg: Natal v. Western Province (Johannesburg) 1923–24
289* Nawab of Pataudi & L. E. G. Ames: England v. Rest (Lord's) 1934
288   H. A. Peach & A. Ducat: Surrey v. Northants. (Northampton) 1920
287   R. Abel & W. H. Lockwood: Surrey v. Lancs. (Oval) 1899
287   J. O'Connor & C. T. Ashton: Essex v. Surrey (Brentwood) 1934
286   M. A. Noble & S. E. Gregory: N.S.W. v. South Australia (Adelaide) 1899–00
285   E. Hendren & J. H. Human: Middx. v. Surrey (Oval) 1935
283   N. Bonitto & A. P. Binns: Jamaica v. British Guiana (Georgetown) 1952–53
281   C. L. Badcock & M. G. Waite: South Australia v. Queensland (Adelaide) 1939–40
277   F. E. Woolley & L. E. G. Ames: Kent v. New Zealanders (Canterbury) 1931
276   W. Rhodes & R. Kilner: Yorks. v. Northants. (Northampton) 1921
276   A. G. Kripal Singh & R. B. Alaganan: Madras v. Travancore-Cochin (Ernakulam) ...1954–55
275   M. A. Noble & J. Darling: Australians v. Sussex (Hove) 1905
273   L. Hutton & N. W. D. Yardley: Yorks. v. Hants. (Bournemouth) 1947
270   L. C. Braund & J. Hardstaff sen.: M.C.C. v. South Australia (Adelaide) 1907–08
268   W. G. Quaife & W. Quaife: Warwicks. v. Essex (Leyton) 1900
266   A. Shrewsbury & W. Gunn: Notts. v. Sussex (Hove) 1884
266   C. E. Pellew & C. B. Willis: A.I.F. v. Leics. (Leicester)...........................1919
266   R. E. S. Wyatt & A. J. Croom: Warwicks. v. Somerset (Birmingham) 1928
266   B. Sutcliffe & W. S. Haig: Otago v. Auckland (Dunedin) 1949–50
264   M. Robinson & S. W. Montgomery: Glamorgan v. Hants. (Bournemouth) 1949
264   A. R. Morris & R. Benaud: N.S.W. v. Queensland (Brisbane) 1953–54
263   J. M. Taylor & A. F. Kippax: N.S.W. v. South Australia (Adelaide) 1922–23
262   A. Jeacocke & W. J. Abel: Surrey v. Cambridge U. (Oval) 1923
262   W. H. Ponsford & W. A. Brown: Australians v. Cambridge U. (Cambridge) 1934
262   K. G. Viljoen & H. B. Cameron: South Africans v. Derby (Ilkeston)..........1935
261   W. G. Grace & W. O. Moberley: Glos. v. Yorks. (Cheltenham) 1876
261   H. H. Gibbons & C. H. Palmer: Worcs. v. Northants. (Dudley) 1939

* K

256* R. Abel & D. L. A. Jephson: Surrey v. Glos. (Oval) 1898
256 C. G. Macartney & N. Callaway: N.S.W. v. Queensland (Sydney) 1914–15
256* A. A. Baig & C. A. Fry: Oxford U. v. Free Foresters (Oxford) 1959
255 G. E. Healy & F. Vaughan: Victoria v. Tasmania (Melbourne) 1909–10
254 E. Humphreys & A. P. Day: Kent v. Lancs. (Tunbridge Wells) 1910
251 R. Kanhai & J. Solomon: British Guiana v. Barbados (Georgetown) 1956–57
250 T. Hayward & D. L. A. Jephson: Surrey v. Derby (Oval) 1901
249 R. A. McLean & A. L. Upton: Natal v. O.F.S. (Pietermaritzburg) 1954–55
247 J. Hardstaff jun. & A. Staples: Notts. v. Middx. (Nottingham) 1937
247* J. F. Parker & E. R. T. Holmes: Surrey v. Notts. (Nottingham) 1947
247 P. R. Umrigar & M. S. Hardikar: Bombay v. Sausashtra (Poona) 1957–58
246 K. S. Ranjitsinhji & A. Collins: Sussex v. Kent (Hove) 1900
245* H. Sutcliffe & W. Barber: Yorks. v. Northants. (Northampton) 1939
245 J. F. Crapp & A. E. Wilson: Glos. v. Worcs. (Dudley) 1953
244 H. Winrow & T. B. Reddick: Notts. v. Kent (Nottingham) 1947
243 F. W. Freer & W. E. Alley: Commonwealth v. C.C. of India (Bombay) 1949–50
242 W. R. Hammond & L. E. G. Ames: England v. New Zealand (Christchurch) 1932–33
242 W. R. Hammond & B. O. Allen: Glos. v. Somerset (Bristol) 1946
241* F. E. Woolley & D. W. Jennings: Kent v. Somerset (Tunbridge Wells) 1911
240 J. C. White & C. C. Case: Somerset v. Glos. (Taunton) 1927
239 M. M. Naidu & C. S. Nayudu: Baroda v. Rajputana (Baroda) 1942–43
237 L. O. S. Poidevin & L. W. Pye: N.S.W. v. Queensland (Sydney) 1904–05
237 D. C. S. Compton & N. W. D. Yardley: England v. South Africa (Nottingham)..1947
236 G. J. Thompson & R. Haywood: Northants. v. Yorks. (Dewsbury) 1911
236 W. W. Keeton & A. W. Carr: Notts. v. Essex (Nottingham) 1932
236 D. C. H. Townsend & F. G. H. Chalk: Oxford U. v. Free Foresters (Oxford) ...1933
235 B. J. T. Bosanquet & F. A. Tarrant: Rest of England v. Yorks. (Oval) 1908
235* W. M. Woodfull & V. S. Ransford: Victoria v. New Zealand XI (Christchurch) ...1924–25
235 G. Hill & D. F. Walker: Hants. v. Sussex (Portsmouth) 1937
235* N. Oldfield & A. E. Nutter: Lancs. v. Notts. (Manchester) 1939
234 P. F. Warner & C. B. Fry: Rest of England v. Warwicks. (Oval) 1911
234 D. G. Bradman & O. W. Bill: N.S.W. v. Victoria (Sydney) 1930–31
234* V. J. Scott & J. B. Morris: Auckland v. Central Districts (Auckland) 1951–52
233 D. A. R. Moloney & J. L. Kerr: New Zealanders v. England XI (Folkestone) ...1937
232 H. W. Taylor & R. H. Catterall: South Africans v. Combined Services (Portsmouth)......1924
232 A. D. Nourse jun. & D. F. Dowling: Natal v. Griqualand West (Durban) ...1947–48
231 C. B. Llewellyn & E. I. M. Barrett: Hants. v. Derby (Southampton) 1903
231 K. Mackay & R. G. Archer: Queensland v. Victoria (Brisbane) 1953–54
230 C. Baldwin & D. L. A. Jephson: Surrey v. Kent (Oval) 1897
230 James Seymour & J. R. Mason: Kent v. Somerset (Taunton) 1907
230 J. Iddon & M. Halliday: Lancs. v. Surrey (Oval) 1928
230 K. R. Miller & P. Burge: Australians v. Leics. (Leicester) 1956
228 C. S. Baker & A. A. Lilley: Warwicks. v. Worcs. (Worcester) 1907
228 G. Headley & C. A. Merry: West Indians v. Warwicks. (Birmingham) 1933
228 J. Hardstaff jun. & F. W. Stocks: Notts. v. Northants. (Northampton) 1952
227 W. G. Grace & P. C. Crutchley: M.C.C. v. Kent (Canterbury) 1876
227 A. D. Nourse sen. & S. S. L. Steyn: Western Province v. Natal (Cape Town) ...1932–33
227 R. C. Wilson & M. C. Cowdrey: Kent v. Northants (Tunbridge Wells) 1955
226* R. McDonald & F. Geeson: Leics. v. Derby (Glossop) 1901
226 R. T. Dick & C. W. Travers: O.F.S. v. Griqualand West (Bloemfontein) 1934–35
226* T. E. Cook & A. J. Holmes: Sussex v. Leics. (Leicester) 1937
225 V. M. Merchant & K. M. Rangnekar: Hindus v. Parsis (Bombay) 1941–42
224 O. G. Smith & A. P. Binns: Jamaica v. British Guiana (Georgetown) 1956–57
223* A. R. Morris & D. G. Bradman: Australia v. India (Melbourne) 1947–48
223 D. C. S. Compton & D. J. Insole: M.C.C. v. Transvaal (Johannesburg) 1956–57
222 C. L. Walcott & D. Atkinson: Barbados v. Trinidad (Barbados) 1950–51
221 C. J. Burnup & T. N. Perkins: Kent v. Lancs. (Manchester) 1900
221 W. J. Edrich & A. Thompson: Middx. v. Northants. (Northampton).........1946
221 P. B. Datta & A. Bhattacharjee: Bengal v. Bihar (Calcutta) 1954–55
220 G. S. Grimston & C. W. C. Packe: Army v. Cambridge U. (Cambridge) 1939
220 R. Subba Row & F. C. M. Alexander: Cambridge U. v. Notts. (Nottingham) ...1953
220 K. R. Miller & R. G. Archer: Australia v. West Indies (Kingston) 1954–55
219 J. G. Greig & C. B. Llewellyn: Hants. v. South Africans (Southampton) 1901
219 C. H. M. Ebden & K. R. B. Fry: Cambridge U. v. Leveson-Gower's XI (Cambridge) ...1902
219 C. P. Mead & H. L. V. Day: Hants. v. Kent (Southampton) 1922
219 J. M. Taylor & A. F. Kippax: N.S.W. v. Australian XI (Sydney) 1924–25
219 C. Washbrook & J. L. Hopwood: Lancs. v. Oxford U. (Oxford) 1935
219 E. D. Weekes & B. H. Pairaudeau: West Indies v. India (Trinidad) 1952–53
218 L. E. G. Ames & B. H. Valentine: Kent v. Glos. (Folkestone) 1933
218 C. K. Nayudu & C. T. Sarwate: Holkar v. Bengal (Indore) 1944–45
217 Mahomed Sharif & Ram Prakash: Northern India v. Maharashtra (Poona) ...1940–41
217 O. E. Wynne & D. E. Dimbleby: Western Province v. Border (Cape Town) ...1947–48

217 B. F. Butcher & J. Solomon: British Guiana v. Pakistan (Georgetown) 1957–58
216 L. A. Bates & N. Kilner: Warwicks. v. Worcs. (Birmingham) 1930
216 M. M. Dalvi & M. N. Raiji: Bombay v. Maharashtra (Bombay) 1947–48
216 D. G. Greasley & F. R. Brown: Northants. v. Notts. (Northampton) 1952
216 D. J. Insole & T. E. Bailey: Essex v. Hants. (Bournemouth) 1959
215 James Langridge & H. W. Parks: Sussex v. Kent (Hastings) 1932
215 A. F. Kippax & L. S. Darling: Australians v. Sussex (Hove) 1934
215 D. M. Young & J. B. Mortimore: Glos. v. Oxford U. (Oxford) 1955
214 S. E. Gregory & R. A. Duff: N.S.W. v. South Australia (Sydney) 1900–01
214 G. W. Parker & R. A. Sinfield: Glos. v. Kent (Dover) 1937
214 W. R. Hammond & J. F. Crapp: Glos. v. Glamorgan (Newport) 1939
214 K. G. Viljoen & A. Melville: South Africans v. Sussex (Hove) 1947
214 D. G. W. Fletcher & T. H. Clark: Surrey v. Cambridge U. (Oval) 1952
213* H. Van der Spry & B. Wallace: Western Province v. Transvaal (Cape Town)...........1936–37
213 E. Davis & F. R. Brown: Northants. v. Glos. (Gloucester) 1952
211 G. H. S. Trott & H. Donnan: Australians v. Derby (Derby) 1896
211 J. Potter & S. J. E. Loxton: Victoria v. South Australia (Melbourne) 1957–58
211 J. Maile & M. Richardson: Western Province v. Rhodesia (Cape Town) 1958–59
211 S. E. Leary & P. H. Jones: Kent v. Essex (Gravesend) 1960
210 B. Mitchell & H. B. Cameron: Transvaal v. Natal (Durban) 1934–35
210 G. G. Cooke & G. Baker: Queensland v. N.S.W. (Brisbane).........................1938–39
210 H. Gimblett & M. Coope: Somerset v. Sussex (Eastbourne)........................1948
209* J. Darling & M. A. Noble: Australians v. Oxford U. (Oxford) 1899
209* P. J. Beames & I. W. Johnson: Victoria v. Tasmania (Melbourne) 1938–39
209 J. Bailey & N. H. Rogers: Hants. v. Worcs. (Southampton)........................1946
208 D. L. A. Jephson & W. H. Lockwood: Surrey v. Yorks. (Oval) 1900
208 J. Douglas & C. M. Wells: Middx. v. Essex (Leyton) 1902
208 A. R. Morris & J. W. Burke: N.S.W. v. Victoria (Melbourne) 1948–49
208 A. K. Khanna & P. G. Joshi: Services v. Delhi (New Delhi) 1952–53
208 B. L. Reynolds & G. E. Tribe: Northants. v. Essex (Brentwood) 1956
207 J. Vine & K. S. Ranjitsinhji: Sussex v. Middx. (Lord's) 1908
207 A. J. Croom & J. H. Parsons: Warwicks. v. West Indians (Birmingham) 1928
207* H. H. Gibbons & S. H. Martin: Worcs. v. Hants. (Worcester) 1939
207 J. O'Connor & R. M. Taylor: Essex v. Notts. (Nottingham) 1939
206 C. Hill & J. C. Reedman: South Australia v. N.S.W. (Adelaide) 1900–01
206 E. Paynter & D. C. S. Compton: England v. Australia (Nottingham) 1938
206 C. L. Walcott & N. Asgarali: West Indies v. Kent (Canterbury) 1957
205 M. W. Payne & R. P. Keigwin: Cambridge U. v. Surrey (Cambridge) 1905
205 A. E. Dipper & W. R. Hammond: Glos. v. Somerset (Taunton) 1924
205 T. W. Graveney & J. F. Crapp: Glos. v. Derby (Chesterfield) 1954
205 R. G. Nadkarni & R. S. Bhosle: Maharashtra v. Gujerat (Poona) 1958–59
204 D. Davies & C. Smart: Glamorgan v. Somerset (Newport) 1939
203 P. N. F. Mansell & M. W. Davies: Rhodesia v. Griqualand West (Bulawayo) 1955–56
203 M. J. Horton & G. Dews: Worcs. v. Essex (Leyton) 1959
202 H. T. W. Hardinge & L. P. Hedges: Kent v. Surrey (Blackheath) 1921
202 H. E. Carris & F. R. Brown: Cambridge U. v. Leveson-Gower's XI (Eastbourne) 1930
202 L. E. G. Ames & B. H. Valentine: Kent v. Essex (Gravesend) 1938
202 H. V. Feltham & S. A. Thwaites: Eastern Province v. O.F.S. (Port Elizabeth) 1946–47
202 D. J. Insole & T. E. Bailey: Essex v. Somerset (Chelmsford) 1953
201* C. J. B. Wood & J. H. Board: London County v. Derby (Derby) 1902
201 G. W. Beldham & E. A. Beldham: Middx. v. Somerset (Lord's) 1904
201* H. Smith & B. A. Clarke: Glos. v. Hants. (Southampton) 1919
201 W. V. S. Ling & P. Rigal: Griqualand West v. O.F.S. (Pretoria) 1923–24
201 V. Y. Richardson & W. C. Alexander: Australians v. Auckland (Auckland) 1927–28
201 James Langridge & A. E. R. Gilligan: Sussex v. Worcs. (Worcester) 1928
201 C. Washbrook & N. Oldfield: Lancs. v. Indians (Manchester) 1936
201 A. J. McIntyre & G. J. Whittaker: Surrey v. Kent (Oval) 1946
201* T. W. Graveney & A. E. Wilson: Glos. v. Leics. (Bristol)........................1953
200 J. Freeman & P. A. Perrin: Essex v. Oxford U. (Chelmsford) 1925
200 E. Hendren & N. Haig: Middx. v. Notts. (Nottingham) 1931
200 X. C. Balaskas & O. N. Flemmer: Rest of South Africa v. Western Province
                                                            (Cape Town).........1932–33
200 J. W. Seamer & J. G. Halliday: Oxford U. v. Free Foresters (Oxford) 1934
200 G. Cox & H. T. Bartlett: Sussex v. Kent (Tunbridge Wells) 1949

SIXTH WICKET

487* G. Headley & C. C. Passailaigue: Jamaica v. Tennyson's XI (Kingston) 1931–32
428 W. W. Armstrong & M. A. Noble: Australians v. Sussex (Hove) 1902
411 R. M. Poore & E. G. Wynyard: Hants. v. Somerset (Taunton) 1899
376 R. Subba Row & A. Lightfoot: Northants. v. Surrey (Oval) 1958

371 V. M. Merchant & R. S. Modi: Bombay v. Maharashtra (Bombay) 1943–44
346 J. H. Fingleton & D. G. Bradman: Australia v. England (Melbourne) 1936–37
332 N. Marks & G. Thomas: N.S.W. v. South Australia (Sydney) 1958–59
323 E. Hendren & J. W. H. T. Douglas: M.C.C. v. Victoria (Melbourne) 1920–21
320 J. H. Board & G. L. Jessop: Glos. v. Sussex (Hove) 1903
316* H. R. Adhikari & A. K. Khanna: Services v. Rajasthan (Ajmer) 1951–52
313 J. A. Newman & Hon. L. H. Tennyson: Hants. v. West Indians (Southampton) 1928
303* H. Winrow & P. F. Harvey: Notts. v. Derby (Nottingham) 1947
300 V. S. Hazare & V. J. Hazare: Rest v. Hindus (Bombay) 1943–44
298 A. Sandham & H. S. Harrison: Surrey v. Sussex (Oval) 1913
294 D. R. Jardine & P. G. H. Fender: Surrey v. Yorks. (Bradford) 1928
289 S. J. E. Loxton & D. T. Ring: Victoria v. Queensland (Melbourne) 1946–47
285 W. R. Hammond & B. H. Lyon: Glos. v. Surrey (Oval) 1928
284 A. P. F. Chapman & G. B. Legge: Kent v. Lancs. (Maidstone) 1927
280* B. F. Butcher & J. Solomon: British Guiana v. Jamaica (Georgetown) 1956–57
279 A. L. Hassett & E. A. Williams: Australian Services v. Prince's XI (Delhi)...1945–46
278 J. Iddon & H. R. W. Butterworth: Lancs. v. Sussex (Manchester) 1932
277 O. G. Smith & A. P. Binns: Jamaica v. Australians (Kingston) 1954–55
276 M. Leyland & E. Robinson: Yorks. v. Glamorgan (Swansea) 1926
270 R. T. Simpson & A. Jepson: Notts. v. Worcs. (Nottingham) 1950
269 V. T. Trumper & C. Hill: Australians v. New Zealand XI (Wellington) 1904–05
262 A. Kenny & B. J. Kortlang: Victoria v. Queensland (Brisbane) 1909–10
262 A. T. Sharp & G. H. S. Fowke: Leics. v. Derby (Chesterfield) 1911
260 J. N. Crawford & Lord Dalmeny: Surrey v. Leics. (Oval)..............................1905
260 A. C. MacLaren & R. Whitehead: Lancs. v. Worcs. (Worcester) 1910
260 A. Wharton & K. Cranston: Lancs. v. Warwicks. (Birmingham)..........................1948
259 D. Brookes & E. Davis: Northants. v. Leics. (Leicester) 1947
258 V. T. Trumper & F. A. Iredale: N.S.W. v. Tasmania (Sydney) 1898–99
255 K. S. Duleepsinhji & M. W. Tate: Sussex v. Northants. (Hove) 1930
254 E. Smith & C. E. de Trafford: North v. South (Hastings) 1893
253 A. F. Kippax & J. G. Morgan: N.S.W. v. Queensland (Sydney) 1927–28
251 C. P. Mead & J. A. Newman: Hants. v. Warwicks. (Bournemouth) 1928
248 T. J. E. Andrews & W. W. Armstrong: Australians v. South (Hastings) 1921
247* W. Payton & W. A. Flint: Notts. v. Northants. (Nottingham).........................1927
245 J. L. Bryan & C. T. Ashton: Cambridge U. v. Surrey (Oval) 1921
244* J. M. M. Commaille & A. W. Palm: Western Province v. Griqualand West
                                              (Johannesburg)............1923–24
244 R. Benaud & A. K. Davidson: Australians v. Natal (Pietermaritzburg) 1957–58
243 W. R. Hammond & James Langridge: M.C.C. v. South Australia (Adelaide)............1946–47
241 A. A. Lilley & W. Smith: London County v. Cambridge U. (Crystal Palace) 1901
241 N. J. Contractor & D. H. Shodhan: Gujerat v. Baroda (Baroda) 1952–53
238 R. McDonald & O. Cowley: Queensland v. Hawke's Bay (Napier) 1896–97
236 E. R. T. Holmes & R. E. C. Butterworth: Oxford U. v. Free Foresters (Oxford)...........1927
234 D. C. S. Compton & P. B. H. May: M.C.C. v. South Australia (Adelaide).............1954–55
233 M. W. Booth & G. H. Hirst: Yorks. v. Worcs. (Worcester) 1911
233 J. N. Crawford & W. W. Armstrong: Australians v. New Zealand XI (Auckland).........1913–14
233 C. H. Knott & R. H. Bettington: Harlequins v. West Indians (Eastbourne) 1928
233 R. Mayes & W. Murray-Wood: Kent v. Sussex (Tunbridge Wells) 1952
231 V. F. S. Crawford & T. Jayes: Leics. v. Hants. (Leicester) 1908
230 W. E. Jones & B. L. Muncer: Glamorgan v. Worcs. (Worcester) 1953
229 W. Rhodes & N. Kilner: Yorks. v. Leics. (Leeds) 1921
228 M. J. Turnbull & F. J. Seabrook: Cambridge U. v. Sussex (Cambridge) 1928
227 N. W. D. Yardley & H. T. Bartlett: M.C.C. v. O.F.S. (Bloemfontein) 1938–39
226 K. C. Ibraham & J. B. Khot: Bombay v. Western India States (Bombay) 1941–42
226* V. S. Hazare & V. Mankad: Indians v. Middx. (Lord's) 1946
226* W. R. Hammond & G. M. Emmett: Glos. v. Notts. (Bristol) 1946
226 G. Cox & G. Potter: Sussex v. Worcs. (Worcester) 1954
225 E. Wainwright & Lord Hawke: Yorks. v. Hants. (Southampton) 1899
225 V. M. Merchant & H. R. Adhikari: Hindus v. Rest (Bombay) 1943–44
224* E. Tyldesley & James Tyldesley: Lancs. v. Warwicks. (Manchester) 1919
222 E. R. T. Holmes & F. R. Brown: Surrey v. Yorks. (Oval) 1936
221 C. W. Gregory & M. H. Blaxland: N.S.W. v. Queensland (Brisbane) 1906–07
221 R. Mayes & B. R. Edrich: Kent v. Glamorgan (Gravesend)............................1952
220 H. E. Dollery & J. Buckingham: Warwicks. v. Derby (Derby).........................1938
219 A. Diamond & C. G. Macartney: N.S.W. v. Victoria (Sydney) 1906–07
219 E. R. T. Holmes & J. F. Parker: Surrey v. Cambridge U. (Oval) 1937
218 J. W. Hearne & J. W. H. T. Douglas: M.C.C. v. Victoria (Melbourne) 1911–12
218 W. R. Hammond & T. O. Jameson: M.C.C. v. West Indian XI (Barbados) 1925–26
217 H. S. B. Love & A. E. V. Hartkopf: Victoria v. South Australia (Melbourne) 1926–27
217* H. Sutcliffe & A. Wood: Yorks. v. Worcs. (Sheffield) 1935
217 D. Davies & C. Smart: Glamorgan v. Lancs. (Cardiff) 1936
217 D. Watt & I. W. Johnson: Combined XI v. M.C.C. (Perth) 1946–47

217   M. Balakrishnan & C. D. Gopinath: Madras v. Mysore (Madras) 1956–57
216   J. W. Hearne & J. W. H. T. Douglas: M.C.C. v. Victoria (Melbourne) 1911–12
216   V. S. Ransford & A. E. Liddicut: Victoria v. M.C.C. (Melbourne) 1922–23
216   D. R. Jardine & B. H. Valentine: M.C.C. v. Viceroy's XI (New Delhi) 1933–34
216   V. S. Hazare & R. S. Cooper: C. C. of India v. C. K. Nayudu's XI (Bombay) 1944–45
215   L. Hutton & J. Hardstaff jun.: England v. Australia (Oval) 1938
214   C. W. Gregory & S. E. Gregory: N.S.W. v. South Australia (Adelaide) 1901–02
214   J. T. Morgan & T. C. Longfield: Cambridge U. v. Leics. (Leicester) 1928
214   W. Watson & N. W. D. Yardley: Yorks. v. Worcs. (Worcester) 1955
214   R. Subba Row & A. Lightfoot: Northants. v. Surrey (Oval) 1960
213* K. S. Ranjitsinhji & A. E. Relf: Sussex v. Lancs. (Hove) 1904
213   B. C. Alva & K. S. Khannan: Madras v. Mysore: (Madras) 1949–50
213* M. M. Dalvi & R. B. Kenny: Bombay v. Maharashtra (Sholapur) 1955–56
213   N. O'Neill & G. Thomas: N.S.W. v. Victoria (Sydney) 1958–59
212   G. M. Lee & T. S. Worthington: Derby v. Essex (Chesterfield) 1932
212   G. O. Allen & J. H. A. Hulme: Middx. v. Glamorgan (Lord's) 1934
211   R. Abel & V. F. S. Crawford: Surrey v. Somerset (Oval) 1899
211   A. Ward & C. R. Hartley: Lancs. v. Glos (Bristol) 1900
211   A. W. Carr & W. Walker: Notts. v. Leics. (Leicester) 1925
211   T. H. Barling & H. S. Squires: Surrey v. Leics. (Leicester) 1933
211   G. O. Allen & J. H. A. Hulme: Middx. v. Worcs. (Lord's) 1936
211   C. L. Walcott & G. E. Gomez: West Indies v. England (Lord's) 1950
211   T. Veivers & J. Bratchford: Queensland v. South Australia (Brisbane) 1959–60
210   J. Hardstaff sen. & W. Rhodes: M.C.C. v. Tasmania (Hobart) 1907–08
210   F. G. H. Chalk & R. G. Stainton: Oxford U. v. West Indians (Oxford) 1933
208   V. S. Hazare & S. R. Arolkar: Rest v. Muslims (Bombay) 1943–44
207   J. Hallows & J. J. Broughton: Lancs. v. Essex (Leyton) 1901
207   M. J. Susskind & H. B. Cameron: Transvaal v. Eastern Province (Johannesburg).........1926–27
206   J. O'Connor & J. W. H. T. Douglas: Essex v. Glos. (Cheltenham) 1923
206   K. R. Miller & R. G. Archer: Australians v. West Indies (Barbados) 1954–55
205   G. H. Hirst & S. Haigh: Yorks. v. Notts. (Sheffield) 1901
204   P. A. Perrin & C. P. McGahey: Essex v. Kent (Tunbridge Wells) 1906
204   W. G. Quaife & A. C. S. Glover: Warwicks. v. Worcs. (Worcester) 1908
204   H. L. Hendry & A. J. Lansdown: Victoria v. New Zealanders (Melbourne) 1925–26
204   L. E. G. Ames & W. H. Ashdown: Players v. Gentlemen (Folkestone) 1933
204   H. E. Dollery & R. E. Hitchcock: Warwicks. v. Leics. (Birmingham) 1952
204   K. R. Miller & R. G. Archer: Australians v. Leics. (Leicester) 1956
203   G. Gunn & S. F. Barnes: M.C.C. v. Western Australia (Perth) 1907–08
202   M. A. Noble & S. E. Gregory: N.S.W. v. South Australia (Adelaide) 1903–04
202   J. R. Gray & G. Hill: Hants. v. Essex (Southampton) 1952
201   J. Darling & F. A. Iredale: Australians v. Middx. (Lord's) 1899
201   C. P. Mead & G. J. Thompson: Players v. Gentlemen (Scarborough) 1911
201   J. E. Timms & A. D. G. Matthews: Northants. v. Essex (Clacton) 1934
200   D. Denton & G. H. Hirst: Yorks. v. Essex (Bradford) 1902
200   W. Payton & S. J. Staples: Notts. v. Surrey (Oval) 1923

SEVENTH WICKET

347   D. Atkinson & C. Depeiza: West Indies v. Australia (Barbados) 1954–55
344   K. S. Ranjitsinhji & W. Newham: Sussex v. Essex (Leyton) 1902
340   K. J. Key & H. Philipson: Oxford U. v. Middx. (Chiswick Park) 1887
336   F. C. W. Newman & C. R. Maxwell: Cahn's XI v. Leics. (Nottingham) 1935
335   C. W. Andrews & E. C. Bensted: Queensland v. N.S.W. (Sydney) 1934–35
325   G. Brown & C. H. Abercrombie: Hants. v. Essex (Leyton) 1913
323   E. Hendren & L. F. Townsend: M.C.C. v. Barbados (Barbados) 1929–30
308   Waqar Hasan & Imtiaz Ahmed: Pakistan v. New Zealand (Lahore)....................1955–56
299   B. Mitchell & A. Melville: Transvaal v. Griqualand West (Kimberley) 1946–47
289   G. Goonesena & G. W. Cook: Cambridge U. v. Oxford U. (Lord's) 1957
274   K. C. Ibrahim & K. M. Rangnekar: Bijapur XI v. Bengal XI (Bombay) 1942–43
273* W. W. Armstrong & J. Darling: Australians v. Gentlemen of England (Lord's) ...1905
271* E. Hendren & F. T. Mann: Middx. v. Notts. (Nottingham) 1925
270   C. P. Mead & J. P. Parker: Hants. v. Kent (Canterbury) 1926
268   A. H. Kardar & Imtiaz Ahmed: North Zone v. Australian Services (Lahore) 1945–46
265   J. L. Powell & N. Dorreen: Canterbury v. Otago (Christchurch) 1929–30
262* D. P. B. Morkel & A. W. Palm: Western Province v. Natal (Cape Town) 1929–30
261   J. W. H. T. Douglas & J. R. Freeman: Essex v. Lancs. (Leyton) 1914
257   J. T. Morgan & F. R. Brown: Cambridge U. v. Surrey (Oval) 1930
255   C. H. Knott & A. J. Evans: Harlequins v. West Indians (Eastbourne) 1928
254   D. C. F. Burton & W. Rhodes: Yorks. v. Hants. (Dewsbury) 1919
252   S. K. Girdhari & A. G. Roy: Assam v. Orissa (Cuttack) 1957–58
250   H. E. Dollery & J. S. Ord: Warwicks. v. Kent (Maidstone) 1953

249 W. L. Murdoch & J. H. Hunt: Gentlemen v. Players (Oval) 1904
248 W. G. Grace & E. L. Thomas: Glos. v. Sussex (Hove) 1896
248 A. P. Day & E. Humphreys: Kent v. Somerset (Taunton) 1908
247 P. Holmes & W. Rhodes: Yorks. v. Notts. (Nottingham) 1929
246 J. F. Ireland & K. G. McLeod: Cambridge U. v. Gentlemen (Eastbourne) 1908
246 D. J. McGlew & A. R. A. Murray: South Africa v. New Zealand (Wellington) 1952–53
245 J. Sharp & A. H. Hornby: Lancs. v. Leics. (Manchester) 1912
244 W. R. Patrick & C. F. W. Allcott: New Zealanders v. N.S.W. (Sydney) 1925–26
241* G. H. Pope & A. E. G. Rhodes: Derby v. Hants. (Portsmouth) 1948
240 S. M. J. Woods & V. T. Hill: Somerset v. Kent (Taunton) 1898
240 A. D. Nourse jun. & L. W. Payn: Natal v. Transvaal (Johannesburg) 1936–37
232 W. Bruce & H. Trumble: Australians v. Oxford & Cambridge Us. P. & P. (Portsmouth) 1893
229 W. W. Timms & F. A. Walden: Northants. v. Warwicks. (Northampton)...................1926
229 K. J. Schneider & W. A. Oldfield: Australians v. Canterbury (Christchurch) 1927–28
224 C. F. Browne & K. Mason: Barbados v. Trinidad (Barbados) 1919–20
224 V. J. Scott & A. M. Matheson: Auckland v. Canterbury (Auckland) 1937–38
222 G. J. Thompson & R. Haywood: Northants. v. Glos. (Northampton) 1911
218 T. E. Cook & A. F. Wensley: Sussex v. Worcs. (Eastbourne) 1933
218 J. H. Cameron & E. A. V. Williams: West Indians v. Oxford U. (Oxford) 1939
216 D. B. Deodhar & M. N. Paranjpye: Maharashtra v. Nawanaja (Poona) 1944–45
215 E. Robinson & D. C. F. Burton: Yorks. v. Leics. (Leicester) 1921
213* K. Vasudevamurthy & D. Gupta: Mysore v. Kerada (Mangalore) 1959–60
212 W. A. Tester & J. Jones: Players of South v. Gentlemen of South (Oval) 1885
208 C. G. Macartney & A. J. Hopkins: N.S.W. v. Queensland (Sydney) 1906–07
207 G. Kishenchand & Fazal Mahmood: North Zone v. South Zone (Bombay) 1946–47
206 A. H. Hornby & W. R. Cuttell: Lancs. v. Somerset (Manchester) 1904
203 M. E. Z. Ghazali & Qamar Yusuf: Services v. Karachi (Karachi) 1953–54
202 A. E. Lawton & R. T. Crawford: Gentlemen v. Oxford U. (Eastbourne) 1910
202 S. J. E. Loxton & B. A. Barnett: Commonwealth v. Bombay (Bombay) 1953–54
201 R. H. Howitt & R. Bagguley: Notts. v. Sussex (Nottingham) 1895
200 T. F. Shepherd & J. W. Hitch: Surrey v. Kent (Blackheath) 1921
200 F. Watson & M. L. Taylor: Lancs. v. Oxford U. (Oxford) 1930
199 E. C. Bensted & K. L. Mossop: Queensland v. South Australia (Brisbane) 1931–32
199 H. E. Dollery & T. Collin: Warwicks. v. Glos. (Birmingham) 1935
199 Mohammed Sharif & Jahanghir Khan: Northern India v. N.W.F.P. (Lahore) 1941–42
198 J. I'Anson & A. Eccles: Lancs. v. Surrey (Manchester) 1902
197 H. H. Gibbons & R. Howorth: Worcs. v. Surrey (Oval) 1938
197 M. J. K. Smith & J. M. Parks: England v. West Indies (Trinidad) 1959–60
196 A. C. Shirreff & B. Constable: Combined Services v. Surrey (Oval) 1946
195 W. R. Hammond & C. C. Dacre: Glos. v. Kent (Tunbridge Wells) 1934
195* W. Wooller & W. E. Jones: Glamorgan v. Lancs. (Liverpool) 1947
194* W. G. Quaife & A. C. S. Glover: Warwicks. v Hants. (Birmingham) 1899
194 H. Whitehead & W. W. Odell: Leics. v. Essex (Leicester) 1905
194 L. E. G. Ames & T. A. Pearce: Kent v. Northants. (Tunbridge Wells) 1932
193 W. C. Bridgeman & L. Martineau: Cambridge U. v. Sussex (Hove) 1887
192 K. S. Ranjitsinhji & G. R. Cox: Sussex v. Surrey (Hastings) 1902
192 M. A. Noble & S. E. Gregory: Australian XI v. Rest (Sydney) 1907–08
191 J. Kelly & G. Dawkes: Derby v. Hants. (Burton-on-Trent) 1954
191 J. S. Manning & K. V. Andrew: Northants. v. Yorks. (Harrogate).................1957
190 R. E. S. Wyatt & R. O. Jenkins: Worcs. v. Leics. (Worcester) 1949
189 J. C. White & R. A. Ingle: Somerset v. Hants. (Southampton) 1935
189 M. B. Hofmeyr & J. Blewitt: N.E. Transvaal v. Border (Pretoria) 1951–52
189 T. W. Graveney & G. Lambert: Glos. v. Leics. (Bristol) 1956
188 A. H. Hornby & R. Whitehead: Lancs. v. Notts. (Manchester) 1908
187 P. A. McAlister & A. W. Murray: Victoria v. New Zealanders (Melbourne) 1898–99
187 Abdus Salaam & M. H. Vishram: Muslims v. Europeans (Bombay)..................1927–28
186 J. N. Crawford & W. S. Lees: Surrey v. Sussex (Oval) 1906
185 E. H. D. Sewell & J. W. H. T. Douglas: London County v. Surrey (Crystal Palace) 1904
185 B. B. Nimbalkar & Raja of Jath: Maharashtra v. Bombay (Bombay) 1950–51
184 C. Turner & A. Wood: Yorks. v. Somerset (Sheffield) 1936
184 D. B. Close & R. Illingworth: Players v. Gentlemen (Lord's) 1959
183 F. Mitchell & P. W. Sherwell: Transvaal v. Griqualand West (Port Elizabeth) 1902–03
183 G. H. Hirst & H. Myers: Yorks. v. Leics. (Leicester) 1905
183 F. Chancellor & J. L. Hudson: Tasmania v. Victoria (Hobart) 1908–09
183 J. W. Rymill & W. C. Alexander: South Australia v. Victoria (Melbourne) 1925–26
183 A. D. Nourse jun. & R. J. Williams: Natal v. Griqualand West (Kimberley) 1946–47
182 W. Newham & G. Bean: Sussex v. Yorks. (Hove) 1897
182 S. S. Rogers & H. W. Stephenson: Somerset v. Northants. (Frome) 1950
182 B. Sutcliffe & A. W. Gilbertson: Otago v. Canterbury (Christchurch) 1952–53
182 K. Garapathy Rao & T. D. Krishnan: Mysore v. Kerala (Mangalore)................1957–58
181 G. N. Foster & W. B. Burns: Worcs. v. Hants. (Worcester) 1905
180 A. Ducat & J. W. Hitch: Surrey v. Somerset (Taunton) 1911

180 M. W. Tate & A. E. Relf: Sussex v. Hants. (Horsham) 1921
180 H. L. Hendry & W. A. Oldfield: N.S.W. v. South Australia (Adelaide) 1922–23
180 F. G. H. Chalk & B. H. Valentine: Kent v. Hants. (Canterbury) 1937
179 F. C. Holland & K. J. Key: Surrey v. Derby (Derby) 1897
179 A. E. Knight & S. Coe: Leics. v. London County (Leicester) 1902
179 A. C. S. Glover & H. J. Goodwin: Warwicks. v. Sussex (Hove) 1908
178 C. B. Fry & H. R. Butt: Sussex v. Glos. (Bristol) 1894
178 E. M. Ashcroft & G. Davidson: Derby v. Notts. (Nottingham) 1897
178 W. Walker & W. A. Flint: Notts. v. Surrey (Oval) 1924
177 A. Shrewsbury & W. Attewell: Notts. v. Middx. (Lord's) 1885
177 E. J. Diver & A. C. S. Glover: Warwicks. v. Leics. (Leicester) 1897
177 J. Sharp & A. H. Hornby: Lancs. v. Essex (Manchester) 1904
177* T. J. E. Andrews & J. Ryder: Australians v. South (Bristol) 1926
177 W. R. Hammond & W. J. Edrich: England XI v. Dominions XI (Lord's)...............1945
177* R. Benaud & A. K. Davidson: Australians v. Rhodesia (Salisbury) 1957–58
176 G. Baker & G. Yates: Lancs. v. Kent (Tonbridge) 1892
176 A. L. Hosie & F. G. Rogers: Europeans v. Hindus (Bombay) 1924–25
176 L. Amarnath & C. T. Sarwate: Indians v. South Australia (Adelaide) 1947–48
176 G. O. Rabone & F. L. H. Mooney: New Zealanders v. M.C.C. (Lord's) 1949
176 J. D. Henderson & W. A. Edward: Scotland v. Ireland (Perth) 1950
176 B. Das Gupta & B. Chanda: Bengal v. Madhya Pradesh (Calcutta) 1955–56
176 R. B. Simpson & A. K. Davidson: Australians v. Transvaal (Johannesburg) 1957–58
175 E. Wainwright & G. H. Hirst: Yorks. v. Glos. (Bristol) 1897
175 E. L. Kidd & Hon. F. S. G. Calthorpe: Cambridge U. v. Sussex (Cambridge) 1912
175 A. E. Relf & H. S. Malik: Sussex v. Leics. (Horsham) 1921
174 A. Anthony & C. A. Snedden: Auckland v. Canterbury (Christchurch) 1920–21
174 M. C. Cowdrey & T. G. Evans: England v. West Indies (Lord's) 1957
173 C. R. Browne & C. V. Wight: West Indian XI v. M.C.C. (Georgetown) 1925–26
173 E. Hendren & L. E. G. Ames: Rest v. Lancs. (Oval) 1928
172 J. R. Mason & E. Humphreys: Kent v. Somerset (Dover) 1908
172 E. L. D. Bartley & T. E. Halsey: Royal Navy v. Army (Lord's) 1927
172 T. P. B. Smith & A. V. Avery: Essex v. Hants. (Brentwood) 1938
171 V. F. S. Crawford & W. W. Odell: Leics. v. Sussex (Eastbourne) 1908
171 J. H. Human & E. Cawston: Cambridge U. v. Leveson-Gower's XI (Eastbourne) 1932
171 Y. N. Gokhale & D. B. Deodhar: Maharashtra v. Northern India (Poona) 1940–41
171 K. G. Suttle & J. M. Parks: Sussex v. Derby (Hove) 1953
171 K. R. Miller & R. G. Archer: Australians v. Worcs. (Worcester) 1953
171 T. E. Bailey & B. R. Knight: Essex v. Worcs. (Leyton) 1959
170 W. Rhodes & J. Iremonger: England v. Rest (Lord's) 1911
170 A. W. Lampard & C. E. Pellew: Australians v. Surrey (Oval) 1919
170 J. L. Bryan & G. C. Collins: Kent v. Hants. (Canterbury) 1923
170 F. C. Thompson & F. Taaffe: Australian XI v. M.C.C. (Brisbane) 1924–25
170 G. M. Lee & A. V. Pope: Derby v. Leics. (Chesterfield) 1933
170 C. G. Pepper & J. A. Workman: Australian Services v. Indian XI (Bombay) 1945–46
170 W. R. Playle & T. S. Hambrook: Auckland v. Central Districts (Auckland) 1957–58
169* F. G. J. Ford & W. H. Lockwood: Stoddart's XI v. Rest (Hastings) 1895
169 E. Russell & J. W. H. T. Douglas: Essex v. Derby (Chesterfield) 1901
169 A. E. Lawton & B. S. Foster: M.C.C. v. South Africans (Lord's) 1907
169 J. W. Hearne & J. M. Sims: Middx. v. Kent (Gravesend)........................1933
169* C. H. Moodie & A. A. Fuller: Jamaica v. M.C.C. (Kingston) 1934–35
169 C. J. Poole & B. Dooland: Notts. v. Somerset (Nottingham) 1953
168 A. F. Kippax & H. L. Hendry: N.S.W. v. Victoria (Sydney) 1922–23
168 K. C. James & H. M. McGirr: Wellington v. Canterbury (Wellington) 1927–28
167* A. C. Bannerman & G. J. Bonnor: Australians v. I Zingari (Scarborough) 1882
167 A. J. Webbe & W. P. Robertson: Middx. v. Worcs. (Worcester) 1900
167 D. Reese & T. A. Carlton: Canterbury v. Australians (Christchurch) 1909–10
167 C. Oakes & H. E. Hammond: Sussex v. Surrey (Horsham) 1938
167 R. Benaud & A. K. Davidson: Australian XI v. Combined XI (Launceston) 1952–53
167 D. Kenyon & L. N. Devereux: Worcs. v. Yorks. (Worcester) 1953
166 W. H. Lockwood & W. Brockwell: Surrey v. Glos. (Oval) 1894
166 A. E. Relf & H. L. Simms: Sussex v. Hants. (Portsmouth) 1906
166 F. R. Foster & E. J. Smith: Warwicks. v. Worcs (Dudley) 1914
166 A. J. Richardson & P. D. Rundell: South Australia v. M.C.C. (Adelaide) 1920–21
166 J. W. Seamer & R. G. Tindall: Oxford U. v. M.C.C. (Lord's) 1934
166 J. Hardstaff jun. & B. Lilley: Notts. v. Warwicks. (Nottingham)..............1936
166 W. Pearson & J. Ledward: Victoria v. Queensland (Brisbane) 1936–37
166 A. L. Hassett & D. T. Ring: Victoria v. M.C.C. (Melbourne) 1950–51
166 G. S. Ramchand & V. Mankad: Bombay v. Holkar (Bombay) 1951–52
165 C. Hill & H. Trumble: Australia v. England (Melbourne) 1897–98
165 A. Reid & J. H. Anderson: Western Province v. Border (Cape Town) 1903–04
165 S. E. Gregory & D. R. A. Gehrs: Australians v. Hants. (Southampton) 1905
165 A. Ducat & H. Strudwick: Surrey v. Essex (Leyton) 1921

164   E. Wainwright & S. Haigh: Yorks. v. Somerset (Taunton) 1900
164   W. H. Ponsford & K. J. Schneider: Victoria v. Tasmania (Melbourne) 1922–23
164   A. Galland & A. R. Knight: Otago v. Auckland (Auckland) 1925–26
164   E. Tyldesley & J. Iddon: Lancs. v. Yorks. (Leeds) 1927
164   H. M. McGirr & K. C. James: Wellington v. Otago (Dunedin) 1927–28
164   A. C. Revill & C. Gladwin: Derby v. Notts. (Nottingham) 1949
164   K. M. Rangnekar & M. M. Jagdale: Holkar v. Services (Indore) 1951–52
163* W. G. Quaife & S. P. Kinneir: Warwicks. v. Hants. (Birmingham)..........................1898
163   E. M. Ashcroft & S. Cadman: Derby v. Leics. (Leicester) 1904
163   T. S. Worthington & H. Elliott: Derby v. Worcs. (Chesterfield) 1933
163   A. L. Apte & N. S. Tamhane: Bombay v. Baroda (Bombay) 1958–59
162   W. W. Read & G. A. Lohmann: Surrey v. Cambridge U. (Oval) 1886
162   P. W. Sherwell & A. E. E. Vogler: South Africans v. Scotland (Edinburgh) 1907
162   A. Smith & E. A. Loveridge: South Australia v. Victoria (Melbourne) 1921–22
162   H. S. Squires & H. A. Peach: Surrey v. Kent (Blackheath) 1930
162   J. Iddon & P. T. Eckerley: Lancs. v. Warwicks. (Birmingham) 1933
162   F. R. Santall & J. H. Parsons: Warwicks. v. Northants. (Northampton) 1933
162* M. M. Walford & H. T. F. Buse: Somerset v. Indians (Taunton) 1946
162   R. B. Kenny & H. D. Amroliwalla: Bombay v. Madras (Bombay) 1956–57
161   V. S. Ransford & E. L. Waddy: Australians v. Hawke's Bay (Napier) 1920–21
161   G. W. Parker & W. L. Neale: Glos. v. Hants. (Bournemouth) 1933
161   C. Walker & R. O. Prouton: Hants. v. Leics. (Portsmouth) 1953
161   S. L. Hanson & P. R. Carlstein: O.F.S. v. Natal (Bloemfontein) 1954–55
160   J. Tunnicliffe & D. Hunter: Yorks. v. Worcs. (Worcester) 1900
160   A. G. Slater & J. M. Hutchinson: Derby v. Somerset (Burton-on-Trent) 1929
160   C. H. Knott & A. C. Wright: Kent v. Sussex (Hastings) 1929
160   R. R. Lindwall & R. A. Saggers: Hassett's XI v. Bradman's XI (Melbourne)...........1948–49
159   W. Gunn & W. Attewell: Notts. v. Middx. (Nottingham)................................1884
159   L. C. Braund & W. H. Lockwood: Players v. Gentlemen (Lord's) 1902
159   C. B. Fry & E. M. Sprot: Hants. v. Worcs. (Bournemouth) 1910
159   C. S. Hurst & J. C. Hubble: Kent v. Lancs. (Manchester) 1922
159   C. H. Taylor & G. Geary: Leics. v. Hants. (Southampton) 1924
159   R. de W. K. Winlaw & J. H. Human: Cambridge U. v. Free Foresters (Cambridge) 1933
159   D. C. S. Compton & W. F. Price: Middx. v. Essex (Lord's).................................1938
159   I. D. Craig & K. R. Miller: N.S.W. v. South Africans (Sydney) 1952–53
159   R. N. Harvey & J. H. de Courcy: Australians v. Glos. (Bristol) 1953
159   P. Burge & A. W. Grout: Queensland v. Victoria (Brisbane).......................1956–57
158   K. S. Ranjitsinhji & F. W. Marlow: Sussex v. Glos. (Hove)...............................1900
158   A. E. Knight & T. Jayes: Leics. v. Warwicks. (Birmingham) 1906
158* F. T. Mann & N. E. Haig: Middx. v. Kent (Maidstone) 1912
158   A. Deb & S. Mustafi: Bengal v. United Provinces (Benares) 1941–42
157   W. Mortlock & J. W. Noble: Surrey v. Middx. (Oval) 1866
157   James Seymour & E. Humphreys: Kent v. Hants. (Tonbridge) 1907
157   E. Hendren & G. T. S. Stevens: Middx. v. Notts. (Lord's) 1920
157   W. Rhodes & Biart: Europeans v. Parsis (Bombay) 1921–22
157   J. H. Human & Jahangir Khan: Cambridge U. v. Sussex (Hove) 1934
157* M. F. Tremlett & J. Lawrence: Somerset v. Glos (Bristol) 1950
157   C. H. Palmer & J. Firth: Leics. v. Somerset (Leicester) 1951
157* F. A. Lowson & R. Booth: Yorks. v. Worcs. (Worcester) 1953
156   H. Moses & F. A. Iredale: N.S.W. v. South Australia (Sydney) 1893–94
156   W. W. Armstrong & T. J. Matthews: Victoria v. N.S.W. (Sydney) 1912–13
156   Saeed Ahmed & Amir Elahi: Muslims v. Hindus (Bombay) 1938–39
156   D. Brookes & A. W. Childs-Clarke: Northants. v. Essex (Northampton) 1947
156   K. Carmody & B. Shepherd: Western Australia v. Queensland (Perth) 1955–56
156   J. E. McConnon & J. Pressdee: Glamorgan v. Middx. (Cardiff) 1958
155   P. F. Warner & Hon. R. Anson: Middx. v. Worcs. (Worcester) 1910
155   F. L. le Roux & E. P. Nupen: Transvaal v. O.F.S. (Johannesburg) 1920–21
155   W. M. Woodfull & A. E. Liddicut: Victoria v. South Australia (Melbourne) 1922–23
155   R. M. Levy & R. K. Oxenham: Queensland v. South Australia (Adelaide) 1933–34
155   A. K. Khanna & Inderjit: Services v. Delhi (New Delhi) 1952–53
155* G. Goonesena & K. J. Poole: Notts. v. Northants. (Nottingham) 1955
154   J. M. Dowson & H. R. B. Davenport: Lucas's XI v. Barbados (Barbados) 1894–95
154* G. H. Hirst & J. T. Newstead: Yorks. v. Notts. (Nottingham) 1908
154   C. E. Winn & P. J. Whitcombe: Oxford U. v. M.C.C. (Lord's) 1950
154   O. G. Smith & J. D. C. Goddard: West Indies v. England (Nottingham) 1957
154   P. J. Sainsbury & L. Harrison: Hants. v. Worcs. (Worcester) 1957
154   K. F. Barrington & A. J. McIntyre: Surrey v. Leics. (Leicester) 1958
153* A. J. Croom & F. R. Santall: Warwicks. v. Sussex (Birmingham) 1928
153   A. L. Hosie & W. H. Livsey: Hants. v. Middx. (Portsmouth) 1928
153   J. H. Pawle & D. C. Rought-Rought: Cambridge U. v. Hants. (Basingstoke) 1937
153   B. Hedges & W. Wooller: Glamorgan v. Sussex (Chichester) 1950
153   M. L. Apte & V. Mankad: India v. West Indies (Trinidad) 1952–53

152 E. F. Waddy & A. J. Bowden: N.S.W. v. M.C.C. (Sydney) 1907–08
152 J. P. Duminy & A. H. C. Cooper: Transvaal v. M.C.C. (Pretoria) 1927–28
152 V. W. C. Jupp & A. H. Bakewell: Northants. v. Essex (Leyton) 1928
152 W. F. Farrimond & W. J. Edrich: Minor Counties v. Oxford U. (Oxford) 1934
152 C. G. Pepper & S. G. Sismey: Australian Services v. Leveson-Gower's XI (Scarborough) 1945
151 F. C. Holland & K. J. Key: Surrey v. Middx. (Lord's) 1897
151 R. P. Keigwin & A. J. Turner: Essex v. Lancs. (Leyton) 1904
151 H. W. Parks & L. Williams: Sussex v. Essex (Hove) 1930
151 B. O. Allen & G. W. Parker: Glos. v. Hants. (Gloucester) 1932
151 D. Hansen & R. K. Oxenham: Queensland v. South Australia (Brisbane) 1934–35
151 R. A. Sinfield & E. J. Stephens: Glos. v. Warwicks. (Birmingham) 1935
151* A. L. Dixon & D. G. Ufton: Kent v. Glos. (Maidstone) 1960
150 J. H. Stuckey & F. Laver: Victoria v. South Australia (Melbourne) 1901–02
150 G. A. T. Vials & John Seymour: Northants. v. Kent (Tunbridge Wells) 1912
150 J. A. Newman & P. E. Lawrie: Hants. v. Glamorgan (Southampton) 1921
150 G. Brown & J. A. Newman: Hants. v. Kent (Canterbury) 1923
150 C. Hallows & R. Tyldesley: Lancs. v. Essex (Southend) 1923
150 M. S. Nichols & L. C. Eastman: Essex v. Worcs. (Leyton) 1933
150 K. R. Miller & I. W. Johnson: Australia v. England (Sydney) 1950–51

EIGHTH WICKET

433 V. T. Trumper & A. Sims: Australians v. Canterbury (Christchurch) 1913–14
292 R. Peel & Lord Hawke: Yorks. v. Warwicks. (Birmingham) 1896
270 V. T. Trumper & E. P. Barbour: N.S.W. v. Victoria (Sydney) 1912–13
263 D. R. Wilcox & R. M. Taylor: Essex v. Warwicks. (Southend) 1946
255 E. A. V. Williams & E. A. Martindale: Barbados v. Trinidad (Barbados) 1935–36
246 L. E. G. Ames & G. O. Allen: England v. New Zealand (Lord's) 1931
243 C. Hill & R. J. Hartigan: Australia v. England (Adelaide) 1907–08
239 W. R. Hammond & A. E. Wilson: Glos. v. Lancs. (Bristol) 1938
237 W. V. D. Dickinson & R. St L. Fowler: Army v. M.C.C. (Lord's) 1920
236 R. A. Duff & A. J. Hopkins: N.S.W. v. Hawke's XI (Sydney) 1902–03
236 C. T. Sarwate & R. P. Singh: Holkar v. Delhi (Delhi)..1949–50
229* C. L. A. Smith & G. Brann: Sussex v. Kent (Hove) 1902
228 A. J. Croom & R. E. S. Wyatt: Warwicks. v. Worcs. (Dudley) 1925
222 S. S. L. Steyn & D. P. B. Morkel: Western Province v. Border (Cape Town) 1929–30
220 G. F. H. Heane & R. Winrow: Notts. v. Somerset (Nottingham) 1935
218 C. G. Macartney & J. D. Scott: N.S.W. v. Queensland (Sydney) 1913–14
217 C. K. Nayudu & N. D. Marshall: Indians v. Warwicks. (Birmingham) 1932
216 C. A. Browne & E. L. Bartlett: Barbados v. British Guiana (Barbados) 1926–27
215 W. W. Armstrong & R. L. Park: Victoria v. South Australia (Melbourne) 1919–20
214 J. A. Cutmore & T. P. B. Smith: Essex v. Indians (Brentwood) 1936
210 V. M. Merchant & R. S. Cooper: Bombay v. Maharashtra (Bombay) 1943–44
210 M. M. Dalvi & V. R. Amladi: Bombay v. Sind (Bombay) 1947–48
209 G. Stannard & H. E. Roberts: Sussex v. Worcs. (Hove) 1920
209 K. M. Rangnekar & J. N. Bhaya: Holkar v. Hyderabad (Indore) 1950–51
204 T. Hayward & L. C. Braund: Surrey v. Lancs. (Oval) 1898
204 W. A. Oldfield & C. O. Nicholls: N.S.W. v. Victoria (Sydney) 1927–28
203 G. Kishenchand & V. Desai: Gujerat v. Services (Ahmedabad) 1950–51
202 D. Davies & J. J. Hills: Glamorgan v. Sussex (Eastbourne) 1928
198 R. W. McLeod & F. Laver: Victoria v. South Australia (Adelaide) 1892–93
198 K. F. Barrington & J. C. Laker: Surrey v. Glos. (Oval) 1954
197 T. H. Barling & A. V. Bedser: Surrey v. Somerset (Taunton) 1947
195 W. Payton & T. W. Oates: Notts. v. Kent (Nottingham) 1920
193 W. W. Armstrong & A. E. Liddicut: Victoria v. South Australia (Melbourne) 1920–21
192 C. Hill & W. F. Giffen: South Australia v. Stoddart's XI (Adelaide) 1894–95
192 W. L. Neale & A. E. Wilson: Glos. v. Middx. (Lord's) 1938
191* W. Rhodes & G. G. Macaulay: Yorks. v. Essex (Harrogate) 1922
190* J. W. E. Mills & C. F. W. Allcott: New Zealanders v. Civil Services (Chiswick) .1927
189 W. N. Carson & A. M. Matheson: Auckland v. Wellington (Auckland) 1938–39
188 H. S. Bush & V. F. S. Crawford: Surrey v. Lancs. (Manchester) 1902
188 R. L. Holdsworth & A. E. R. Gilligan: Sussex v. Lancs. (Eastbourne) 1927
187 J. D. Henderson & W. A. Edward: Scotland v. Ireland (Paisley) 1954
185* J. D. Nel & J. H. Ferrandi: Western Province v. Eastern Province (Port Elizabeth) ...1952–53
184 M. S. Nichols & T. P. B. Smith: Essex v. Kent (Gravesend) 1938
183 D. J. Insole & R. Smith: Essex v. Worcs. (Worcester) 1951
183 T. E. Bailey & C. Griffiths: Essex v. Kent (Tunbridge Wells) 1952
182 R. Abel & W. E. Roller: Surrey v. Kent (Oval) 1883
182 G. N. Wyatt & H. Phillips: Sussex v. Australians (Hove) 1884
182* M. H. C. Doll & H. R. Murrell: Middx. v. Notts. (Lord's) 1913
182 A. H. M. Jackson & W. Carter: Derby v. Leics. (Leicester) 1922

180   W. Barber & T. F. Smailes: Yorks. v. Sussex (Leeds) 1935
179* G. Leach & C. L. A. Smith: Sussex v. Derby (Hove)................................1909
179   L. D. Kemp & S. O. Quin: Victoria v. Tasmania (Hobart)..............................1932–33
178   C. P. Mead & C. P. Brutton: Hants. v. Worcs. (Bournemouth) 1925
177   W. G. Quaife & A. Whittle: Warwicks. v. Essex (Birmingham) 1904
176   H. W. Parks & A. F. Wensley: Sussex v. Cambridge U. (Cambridge) 1936
175   E. Pooley & J. Southerton: Surrey v. M.C.C. (Oval) 1871
175   A. J. Bowden & A. D. Fisher: N.S.W. v. Queensland (Sydney) 1907–08
174   W. E. Jones & G. Lavis: Glamorgan v. Essex (Cardiff) 1947
174   O. C. Dawson & L. A. Markham: Natal v. O.F.S. (Durban) 1947–48
173   J. M. Gregory & C. E. Pellew: Australia v. England (Melbourne) 1920–21
173   B. Constable & J. C. Laker: Surrey v. Cambridge U. (Guildford) 1949
172   V. T. Trumper & J. J. Kelly: N.S.W. v. Tasmania (Sydney)................1898–99
172   W. E. Astill & A. E. R. Gilligan: M.C.C. v. Yorks. (Scarborough) 1923
172   J. F. Crapp & L. M. Cranfield: Glos. v. Cambridge U. (Cambridge) 1947
171   R. James & R. R. Lindwall: N.S.W. v. Queensland (Sydney)................1945–46
171   A. J. McIntyre & E. R. T. Holmes: Surrey v. Hants. (Guildford) 1948
170   H. Moses & J. R. Wood: N.S.W. v. Victoria (Sydney) 1887–88
169   S. E. Gregory & A. L. Newell: N.S.W. v. Stoddart's XI (Sydney)................1897–98
168   P. Cartwright & C. L. A. Smith: Sussex v. Leics. (Leicester) 1909
168   E. H. Bowley & T. O. Jameson: Tennyson's XI v. Rhodesia (Bulawayo)................1924–25
167   F. Barratt & A. Staples: Notts. v. Surrey (Oval) 1928
167   J. L. Ellis & H. I. Ebeling: Victoria v. South Australia (Adelaide) 1928–29
166   J. Pettiford & F. W. Freer: Commonwealth v. Indian XI (Bombay) 1949–50
165   S. Haigh & Lord Hawke: Yorks. v. Surrey (Oval) 1902
165* J. N. Crawford & A. Eckhold: Otago v. Wellington (Wellington) 1914–15
163   W. Reeves & C. P. Buckenham: Essex v. Sussex (Leyton) 1906
163   G. G. Macaulay & A. Waddington: Yorks. v. Worcs. (Leeds) 1927
162   C. P. Mead & W. K. Pearce: Hants. v. Glamorgan (Southampton) 1923
161   F. M. Lucas & G. Brann: Sussex v. Australians (Hove) 1886
161   H. Moses & T. W. Garrett: N.S.W. v. Victoria (Sydney) 1890–91
161   E. Smith & W. Rhodes: Yorks. v. M.C.C. (Scarborough)................1901
161   H. S. Squires & G. S. Mobey: Surrey v. Cambridge U. (Oval) 1932
161   D. G. Bradman & M. G. Waite: South Australia v. Queensland (Adelaide) 1937–38
161   S. S. Grewal & Inderjit: Services v. Southern Punjab (Patiala) 1950–51
160   H. Philipson & A. C. M. Croome: Oxford U. v. M.C.C. (Lord's) 1889
160   K. S. Ranjitsinhji & F. W. Tate: Sussex v. Surrey (Hastings) 1902
160   H. W. Parks & A. E. R. Gilligan: Sussex v. Kent (Hastings) 1928
160   C. R. Browne & R. L. Hunte: British Guiana v. Barbados (Georgetown) 1929–30
158   J. Pettiford & R. A. Saggers: N.S.W. v. Queensland (Brisbane)................1947–48
157   P. A. Turner & A. D. Nourse sen.: Natal v. Eastern Province (Johannesburg) 1896–97
157   A. C. McLaren & J. F. McLean: M.C.C. v. New Zealand XI (Wellington) 1922–23
157   A. L. Hilder & C. Wright: Kent v. Essex (Gravesend) 1924
157   A. Hamer & E. Smith: Derby v. Notts. (Nottingham) 1955
156   T. Langdon & J. H. Board: Glos. v. Middx. (Bristol) 1903
156   G. C. White & R. O. Schwarz: South Africans v. Glos. (Bristol) 1907
156   S. F. Hird & C. J. Hill: N.S.W. v. Queensland (Sydney) 1932–33
156   W. T. Greensmith & F. Rist: Essex v. Kent (Blackheath) 1953
155   A. Morton & W. Horsley: Derby v. Essex (Leyton) 1924
155   F. R. Brown & A. E. Nutter: Northants. v. Glamorgan (Northampton) 1952
154   G. J. Bonnor & S. P. Jones: Australia v. England (Sydney) 1884–85
154   C. W. Wright & H. R. B. Davenport: England v. South Africa (Johannesburg)............1895–96
154   F. T. Badcock & K. C. James: Wellington v. Canterbury (Christchurch)................1926–27
154   D. Tallon & R. R. Lindwall: Australia v. England (Melbourne) 1946–47
153   L. Amarnath & C. S. Nayudu: Indians v. Victoria (Melbourne) 1947–48
152   W. Rhodes & J. W. Rothery: Yorks. v. Hants. (Portsmouth) 1904
152* R. J. O. Meyer & S. A. Block: Free Foresters v. Cambridge U. (Cambridge) 1938
152   F. H. Vigar & R. Smith: Essex v. Derby (Colchester) 1948
151   W. Rhodes & Lord Hawke: Yorks. v. Somerset (Taunton) 1905
151   W. Payton & H. Larwood: Notts. v. Northants. (Nottingham) 1925
151   K. Grieves & K. C. Gulliver: N.S.W. v. Australian Services (Sydney) 1945–46
150   A. Ward & C. R. Hartley: Lancs. v. Leics. (Leicester) 1900
150   E. A. Halliwell & G. C. White: South Africans v. Leics. (Leicester) 1904
150   H. L. Wilson & G. Stannard: Sussex v. Warwicks. (Hove) 1920
150   G. Geary & T. E. Sidwell: Leics. v. Surrey (Oval) 1926

NINTH WICKET

283   J. Chapman & A. R. Warren: Derby v. Warwicks. (Blackwell) 1910
251   J. W. H. T. Douglas & S. N. Hare: Essex v. Derby (Leyton) 1921
245   V. S. Hazare & N. D. Nagarwalla: Maharashtra v. Baroda (Poona) 1939–40

239 H. B. Cave & I. B. Leggat: Central Districts v. Otago (Dunedin) 1952–53
232 C. Hill & E. Walkley: South Australia v. N.S.W. (Adelaide) 1900–01
231 P. Sen & J. Mitter: Bengal v. Bihar (Jamshedpur) 1950–51
226 C. Kelleway & W. A. Oldfield: N.S.W. v. Victoria (Melbourne) 1925–26
225 W. W. Armstrong & E. A. Windsor: Australian XI v. Rest (Sydney) 1907–08
221 E. F. Waddy & W. P. Howell: N.S.W. v. South Australia (Adelaide) 1904–05
221 N. V. Lindsay & G. R. McCubbin: Transvaal v. Rhodesia (Bulawayo) 1922–23
217 A. D. Nourse sen. & B. C. Cooley: Natal v. Western Province (Johannesburg) ...1906–07
203* J. J. Hills & J. C. Clay: Glamorgan v. Worcs. (Swansea) 1929
200 E. B. Forssberg & H. S. B. Love: N.S.W. v. Queensland (Sydney) 1920–21
200 G. W. Cook & C. S. Smith: Cambridge U. v. Lancs. (Liverpool) 1957
197 C. P. Mead & W. R. Shirley: Hants. v. Warwicks. (Birmingham) 1923
193 W. G. Grace & S. A. P. Kitcat: Glos. v. Sussex (Bristol) 1896
193 G. O. Allen & N. E. Haig: Gentlemen v. Players (Oval) 1925
192 G. H. Hirst & S. Haigh: Yorks. v. Surrey (Bradford) 1898
184 A. C. Russell & L. C. Eastman: Essex v. Middx. (Lord's) 1920
181 J. A. Cuffe & R. D. Burrows: Worcs. v. Glos. (Worcester) 1907
179 C. P. McGahey & C. P. Buckenham: Essex v. Notts. (Leyton) 1904
178 H. W. Parks & A. F. Wensley: Sussex v. Derby (Horsham) 1930
177 G. Brown & W. H. Livsey: Hants. v. Warwicks. (Birmingham) 1922
176* R. Moorhouse & G. H. Hirst: Yorks. v. Glos. (Bristol) 1894
173 S. Haigh & W. Rhodes: Yorks. v. Sussex (Hove) 1902
173 P. Roy & S. K. Girdhari: Bengal Governor's XI v. West Indians (Calcutta) 1948–49
172 R. G. Barlow & W. Flowers: Players v. Australians (Nottingham) 1886
171 D. P. B. Morkel & N. A. Quinn: South Africans v. Western Australia (Perth) 1931–32
170 T. W. Garrett & T. R. McKibbin: N.S.W. v. South Australia (Sydney) 1896–97
169 C. B. Willis & W. A. Oldfield: Australians v. Notts. (Nottingham)..................1919
168 L. G. Crawley & F. Watson: M.C.C. v. Jamaica (Kingston) 1925–26
168 E. R. T. Holmes & E. W. Brookes: Surrey v. Hants. (Oval)..........................1936
167 W. McIntyre & G. Wootton: Notts. v. Kent (Nottingham) 1869
167 H. Verity & T. F. Smailes: Yorks. v. Somerset (Hull) 1936
164 W. A. Oldfield & E. S. White: N.S.W. v. South Australia (Sydney) 1936–37
162 W. Rhodes & S. Haigh: Yorks. v. Lancs. (Manchester) 1904
161 E. Smith & W. Rhodes: Yorks. v. Sussex (Sheffield) 1900
161 B. R. Edrich & F. Ridgway: Kent v. Sussex (Tunbridge Wells) 1949
161 G. J. Whittaker & W. S. Surridge: Surrey v. Glamorgan (Oval) 1951
160 R. T. Crawford & W. W. Odell: Leics. v. Worcs. (Leicester) 1902
160* K. S. Ranjitsinhji & F. W. Tate: Sussex v. Surrey (Hastings) 1902
160 P. S. Arnott & C. V. Single: N.S.W. v. Western Australia (Sydney) 1912–13
160 J. W. H. T. Douglas & H. W. F. Franklin: Essex v. Middx. (Leyton) 1923
160* E. Hendren & T. J. Durston: Middx. v. Essex (Leyton) 1927
160 D. R. Wilcox & R. Smith: Essex v. Yorks. (Southend) 1947
159 H. V. Page & W. O. Vizard: Glos. v. Notts. (Cheltenham) 1883
159 Saeed Ahmed & Rathod: Western India States v. Sind (Karachi) 1939–40
158 F. Marchant & E. B. Shine: Kent v. Warwicks. (Tonbridge) 1897
157 C. P. Mead & W. H. Livsey: Hants. v. Notts. (Southampton) 1921
157 H. M. Garland-Wells & C. K. Hill-Wood: Oxford U. v. Kent (Oxford) 1928
157 H. G. Gaekwad & K. Bhatnagar: Holkar v. Bihar (Jamshedpur) 1948–49
156 A. Street & F. E. Smith: Surrey v. Leics. (Leicester) 1895
156 T. Hayward & J. T. Hearne: Players v. Gentlemen (Lord's) 1896
156 H. Wrathall & W. S. A. Brown: Glos. v. Warwicks. (Birmingham) 1898
156 M. W. Payne & G. H. M. Cartwright: Free Foresters v. Cambridge U. (Cambridge) ...1927
156 R. Subba Row & S. Starkie: Northants. v. Lancs. (Northampton) 1955
155 F. R. Brown & M. J. C. Allom: Surrey v. Middx. (Oval) 1932
154 S. E. Gregory & J. McC. Blackham: Australia v. England (Sydney) 1894–95
154 G. W. Stephens & A. J. Croom: Warwicks. v. Derby (Birmingham) 1925
153 J. S. Shepherd & R. M. Rutherford: Otago v. Southland (Dunedin) 1913–14
152 E. Martin & H. R. Murrell: Middx. v. Essex (Leyton) 1919
152* A. W. Grout & W. Walmsley: Queensland v. N.S.W. (Sydney) 1956–57
151 W. H. Scotton & W. W. Read: England v. Australia (Oval) 1884
150 A. E. Relf & S. Haigh: Londesborough's XI v. Australians (Scarborough) 1912

TENTH WICKET

307 A. F. Kippax & J. E. H. Hooker: N.S.W. v. Victoria (Melbourne) 1928–29
249 C. T. Sarwate & S. N. Banerjee: Indians v. Surrey (Oval) 1946
235 F. E. Woolley & A. Fielder: Kent v. Worcs. (Stourbridge) 1909
230 R. W. Nicholls & W. Roche: Middx. v. Kent (Lord's) 1899
218 F. H. Vigar & T. P. B. Smith: Essex v. Derby (Chesterfield) 1947
211 M. Ellis & T. Hastings: Victoria v. South Australia (Melbourne) 1902–03
192 A. Bowell & W. H. Livsey: Hants. v. Worcs. (Bournemouth) 1921

184   R. C. Blunt & W. Hawkesworth: Otago v. Canterbury (Christchurch) 1931–32
177   J. H. Naumann & A. E. R. Gilligan: Cambridge U. v. Sussex (Hove) 1919
173   J. Briggs & R. Pilling: Lancs. v. Surrey (Liverpool) 1885
173   A. Ducat & A. Sandham: Surrey v. Essex (Leyton) 1921
169   R. B. Minnett & C. McKew: N.S.W. v. Victoria (Sydney) 1911–12
167   A. F. Somerset & W. C. Smith: M.C.C. v. Barbados (Barbados) 1912–13
157   J. Parnham & J. White: North v. South (Lord's) 1886
157   A. C. Russell & A. B. Hipkin: Essex v. Somerset (Taunton) 1926
157   W. E. Astill & W. H. Marlow: Leics. v. Glos. (Cheltenham) 1933
156   H. R. Butt & G. R. Cox: Sussex v. Cambridge U. (Cambridge) 1908
154   F. Buttesworth & J. Lanigan: Western Australia v. Victoria (Perth) 1921–22
152   E. Alletson & W. Riley: Notts. v. Sussex (Hove) 1911
149   F. H. Hollins & B. A. Collins: Oxford U. v. M.C.C. (Oxford) 1901
149   K. Farnes & T. H. Wade: Essex v. Somerset (Taunton) 1936
148   Lord Hawke & D. Hunter: Yorks. v. Kent (Sheffield) 1898
148   B. Bellamy & V. Murdin: Northants. v. Glamorgan (Northampton) 1925
147   E. M. Sprot & A. E. Fielder: Hants. v. Glos. (Bristol) 1911
147   C. G. Macartney & S. C. Everett: Australian XI v. Tasmania (Hobart) 1925–26
145   G. A. Rotherham & J. H. Naumann: Cambridge U. v. A.I.F. (Cambridge) 1919
144   S. Wazir Ali & J. G. Navle: Indians v. Scotland (Dundee) 1932
143   H. Gibbs & J. J. Bridges: Somerset v. Essex (Weston-super-Mare) 1919
141   J. T. Tyldesley & W. Worsley: Lancs. v. Notts. (Nottingham) 1905
141   J. R. Mason & C. Blythe: Kent v. Surrey (Oval) 1909
140   S. J. Staples & L. B. Richmond: Notts. v. Derby (Worksop) 1922
140* G. S. Boyes & A. E. Thomas: Players v. Gentlemen (Folkestone) 1930
139   P. R. Johnson & R. C. Robertson-Glasgow: Somerset v. Surrey (Oval) 1926
138   K. C. James & W. S. Brice: Wellington v. Otago (Wellington) 1926–27
138   E. L. G. Hoad & H. C. Griffith: West Indians v. Sussex (Hove) 1933
138   Yadvendrasinhji & Mubarak Ali: Nawanagar v. Bengal (Bombay) 1936–37
136   J. O'Halloran & A. E. Johns: Victoria v. South Australia (Melbourne) 1896–97
136   K. S. Ranjitsinhji & P. R. May: London County v. M.C.C. (Crystal Palace) 1903
136   G. Challenor & G. N. Francis: West Indians v. Surrey (Oval) 1923
136   H. Larwood & W. Voce: Notts. v. Sussex (Nottingham) 1931
136   J. S. Patel & H. A. Nakhuda: Gujerat v. Holkar (Indore) 1950–51
135   T. Hayward & H. Young: Players v. Gentlemen (Oval) 1899
135   W. A. Oldfield & A. A. Mailey: N.S.W. v. South Australia (Adelaide) 1923–24
134   A. E. R. Gilligan & M. Falcon: Gentlemen v. Players (Oval) 1924
134   H. G. Gaekwad & M. Salim Khan: Holkar v. Delhi (New Delhi) 1949–50
133* A. Sandham & W. J. Abel: Surrey v. Middx. (Oval) 1919
133   G. A. Bartlett & I. A. Colquhoun: Northern Districts v. Auckland (Auckland) 1959–60
132   R. W. McLeod & C. H. Ross: Victoria v. South Australia (Adelaide) 1899–00
132   V. A. Valentine & H. G. Griffith: West Indians v. Middx. (Lord's) 1933
131   D. L. A. Jephson & F. Stedman: Surrey v. Lancs. (Oval) 1900
131   E. Tyldesley & R. Whitehead: Lancs. v. Warwicks. (Birmingham) 1914
131   W. R. Gouldsworthy & J. G. Bessant: Glos. v. Somerset (Bristol) 1923
131* C. Smart & W. D. Hughes: Glamorgan v. South Africans (Cardiff) 1935
130   G. W. Beldham & C. Headlam: Middx. v. Surrey (Lord's) 1902
130   R. E. Foster & W. Rhodes: England v. Australia (Sydney) 1903–04
130   H. Strudwick & J. W. Hitch: Surrey v. Warwicks. (Birmingham) 1911
130   G. R. Cox & G. Stannard: Sussex v. Essex (Hove) 1919
130   N. J. Venkartsen & C. R. Rangachari: Madras v. Madhya Pradesh (Madras) 1951–52
129   E. G. Goatly & F. Stedman: Surrey v. South Africans (Oval) 1904
129   F. Caulfield & L. R. Tuckett: O.F.S. v. Western Province (Bloemfontein) 1925–26
128   W. Mudie & T. Sewell: Surrey v. Kent & Sussex (Oval) 1859
128   H. D. G. Leveson-Gower & G. K. Molineux: Gentlemen v. Oxford U. (Eastbourne) ...1908
128   F. R. Santall & W. Sanders: Warwicks. v. Yorks. (Birmingham) 1930
127   C. P. Mead & G. S. Boyes: Hants. v. Worcs. (Worcester) 1922
127   J. M. Taylor & A. A. Mailey: Australia v. England (Sydney) 1924–25
126   J. W. Hearne & H. Strudwick: Jessop's XI v. Warner's XI (Sheffield) 1911
126   R. E. S. Wyatt & J. H. Mayer: Warwicks. v. Surrey (Oval) 1927
125   A. L. Hosie & W. L. Budd: Hants. v. Glamorgan (Bournemouth) 1935
124   W. A. Oldfield & A. A. Mailey: Australians v. Warwicks. (Birmingham) 1921
123   H. B. Massey & L. Beard: Wellington v. Otago (Wellington)........................1927–28
123   R. Duckfield & J. C. Clay: Glamorgan v. Leics. (Cardiff)............................1933
123   B. Dooland & A. K. Walker: Notts. v. Somerset (Nottingham) 1956
122   W. G. Ward & N. Dodds: Tasmania v. Victoria (Hobart) 1898–99
122   J. W. Hitch & H. Strudwick: Players v. Gentlemen (Oval) 1914
122   W. Reeves & G. M. Louden: Essex v. Surrey (Leyton) 1919
122   W. R. Hammond & C. I. J. Smith: M.C.C. v. Barbados (Barbados) 1934–35
121   W. Bates & E. Peate: Under 30 v. Over 30 (Lord's) 1882
121   J. T. Brown & D. Hunter: Yorks. v. Liverpool & District (Liverpool) 1894
121   W. L. Murdoch & J. Gilman: London County v. Cambridge U. (Crystal Palace) 1900

120 R. A. Duff & W. W. Armstrong: Australia v. England (Melbourne) 1901–02
120 A. J. Hopkins & W. McIntyre: N.S.W. v. Queensland (Sydney) 1906–07
120 G. Lavis & J. Mercer: Glamorgan v. Surrey (Oval) 1934
119 W. B. Burns & G. A. Wilson: Worcs. v. Somerset (Worcester) 1906
119 C. D. McIver & C. U. Peat: Leveson-Gower's XI v. Cambridge U. (Eastbourne) 1921
119* W. H. Ponsford & A. J. Richardson: Australians v. M.C.C. (Lord's)......................1926
119* E. A. Watts & J. V. Daley: Surrey v. Hants. (Bournemouth) 1936
119 W. N. Carson & J. A. Cowie: Auckland v. Otago (Auckland) 1937–38
118 C. T. Calvert & T. Sewell: Surrey v. Sussex (Brighton) 1868
118 Lord Hawke & D. Hunter: Yorks. v. Kent (Leeds) 1896
118 C. H. Abercrombie & H. A. H. Smith: Hants. v. Worcs. (Dudley) 1913
118 A. Hurwood & P. M. Hornibrook: Australians v. Sussex (Hove) 1930
118 R. J. L. Hammond & J. H. G. Deighton: Combined Services v. Essex (Chelmsford) ...1950
117* R. Dare & R. O. Prouton: Hants. v. Worcs. (Bournemouth) 1952
116 C. I. J. Smith & I. A. R. Peebles: Middx. v. Kent (Canterbury) 1939
115 W. Drysdale & Tandy: Europeans v. Parsis (Poona) 1900–01
115 L. G. Fuller & L. R. Tuckett: O.F.S. v. Western Province (Bloemfontein) 1925–26
115 B. W. Malcolm & T. Bhattacharjee: Bengal v. Madras (Calcutta) 1938–39
115 A. J. Watkins & D. J. Shepherd: Glamorgan v. Northants. (Northampton) 1958
113 J. G. Greig & C. Robson: Hants. v. Lancs. (Liverpool) 1901
113 G. R. Cox & H. R. Butt: Sussex v. Hants. (Chichester) 1906
113* E. W. Whitfield & J. F. Parker: Surrey v. Indians (Oval) 1932
113 F. L. H. Mooney & D. Knapp: Wellington v. Auckland (Wellington) 1943–44
112 J. J. Kelly & F. Laver: Australians v. Glos. (Bristol) 1905
112 A. E. Dipper & G. Dennett: Glos. v. Sussex (Gloucester)......................................1908
112 A. E. Relf & H. E. Roberts: Sussex v. Lancs. (Hove) 1914
112 C. Kellaway & H. Carter: N.S.W. v. South Australia (Adelaide) 1920–21
112 J. W. Lee & W. T. Luckes: Somerset v. Kent (Taunton) 1934
111 A. Ward & A. Mold: Lancs. v. Leics. (Manchester) 1895
111 M. A. Noble & W. P. Howell: N.S.W. v. Victoria (Sydney) 1896–97
111 J. Gunn & W. A. Flint: Notts. v. Middx. (Nottingham) 1919
111* A. P. F. Chapman & F. T. Mann: South v. North (Folkestone) 1927
111 J. F. Parker & A. R. Gover: Surrey v. Indians (Oval) 1936
110 J. S. E. Hood & C. E. Green: Cambridge U. v. M.C.C. (Lord's) 1867
110 J. R. Sheffield & T. H. Wade: Essex v. Warwicks. (Chelmsford) 1929
110* A. G. Marshall & G. Hunt: Somerset v. Hants. (Taunton) 1930
110* F. W. Stocks & E. A. Meads: Notts. v. Worcs. (Nottingham) 1946
109 W. Gunn & R. G. Hardstaff: Notts. v. Derby (Derby) 1896
109 A. L. Newell & W. P. Howell: N.S.W. v. Stoddart's XI (Sydney) 1897–98
109 G. Dewhurst & C. Fraser: Trinidad v. Barbados (Georgetown) 1922–23
109 D. C. S. Compton & O. P. Rawal: Holkar v. Bombay (Bombay) 1944–45
109 H. R. Adhikari & Ghulam Ahmed: India v. Pakistan (New Delhi) 1952–53
108 Lord Hawke & L. Whitehead: Yorks. v. Lancs. (Manchester) 1903
108 R. G. Nadkarni & S. R. Patil: Maharashtra v. Bombay (Bombay) 1953–54
107 A. Jaques & W. H. Livsey: Hants. v. Worcs. (Southampton) 1914
107 J. A. Small & G. N. Francis: West Indians v. Harlequins (Eastbourne) 1928
107 H. J. Enthoven & W. F. Price: Middx. v. Sussex (Lord's) 1930
106 G. Wootton & R. S. Forster: M.C.C. v. Sussex (Brighton) 1863
106 H. Wrathall & J. H. Board: Glos. v. Surrey (Oval) 1899
106 E. R. Wilson & C. E. Hatfeild: M.C.C. v. Argentine (Hurlingham) 1911–12
106 G. Brown & A. S. Kennedy: Hants. v. Worcs. (Bournemouth) 1913
106 R. C. Robertson-Glasgow & V. R. Price: Oxford U. v. Somerset (Oxford) 1922
106 F. W. Gilligan & M. S. Nichols: Essex v. Kent (Canterbury) 1926
106 E. S. Sim & H. J. O'Reilly: Rhodesia v. Griqualand West (Kimberley) 1929–30
106 E. Hendren & G. E. Hart: Middx. v. Somerset (Taunton) 1935
106 A. B. Sellers & D. V. Brennan: Yorks. v. Worcs. (Worcester) 1948
106 D. Bennett & H. W. Tilly: M.C.C. v. Oxford U. (Lord's)....................................1955
105 W. Brockwell & T. Richardson: Surrey v. Glos. (Oval) 1893
105 L. W. Pye & A. J. Bowden: N.S.W. v. Queensland (Sydney) 1899–00
105* W. Walmsley & J. Freeman: Queensland v. N.S.W. (Brisbane) 1957–58
105 A. Wilson & R. Tattersall: Lancs. v. Leics. (Manchester) 1958
104 W. O. Reid & J. T. Hings: Transvaal v. Natal (Pietermaritzburg) 1894–95
104 W. S. A. Brown & F. G. Roberts: Glos. v. Sussex (Bristol) 1903
104 G. Brown & J. Mercer: M.C.C. v. Hindus-Muslims XI (Calcutta) 1926–27
104 K. C. James & H. B. Murray: Wellington v. Australians (Wellington) 1927–28
104 F. R. Brown & J. F. Parker: Surrey v. Kent (Blackheath) 1932
104 L. Michael & E. Pynor: South Australia v. Victoria (Adelaide)...........................1949–50
104 Zulfiqar Ahmed & Amir Elahi: Pakistan v. India (Madras) 1952–53
103 L. S. D'Ade & S. Rudder: Trinidad v. Priestley's XI (Trinidad) 1896–97
103 P. A. McAlister & F. A. Tarrant: Victoria v. New Zealanders (Melbourne) 1898–99
103 James Seymour & A. Fielder: Kent v. Worcs. (Maidstone) 1904
103 A. Dolphin & E. Smith: Yorks. v. Essex (Leyton) 1919

103 W. Voce & S. J. Staples: Notts. v. Leics. (Leicester) 1933
103 H. G. Owen-Smith & A. J. Bell: South Africa v. England (Leeds) 1929
102 D. Denton & D. Hunter: Yorks. v. Cambridge U. (Cambridge) 1895
102 James Seymour & A. Fielder: Kent v. Essex (Leyton) 1911
102 P. T. Eckersley & W. E. Phillipson: Lancs. v. Sussex (Manchester) 1933
102 H. G. Gaekwad & O. P. Rawal: Holkar v. Baroda (Indore) 1945–46
102 K. Salahuddin & Salimuddin: Punjab B. v. Peshawar (Peshawar) 1956–57
101 A. J. L. Hill & E. C. Streatfeild: Cambridge U. v. Yorks. (Cambridge) 1890
101 C. R. Hartley & A. Mold: Lancs. v. Glos. (Gloucester) 1901
101 G. Giffen & J. F. Travers: South Australia v. Victoria (Adelaide)..........1902–03
101 H. D. G. Leveson-Gower & R. H. Fox: Leveson-Gower's XI v. Oxford U. (Oxford) ...1904
101* J. W. H. T. Douglas & B. Tremlin: Essex v. Derby (Leyton) 1914
101 W. W. Armstrong & G. Truman: Victoria v. South Australia (Melbourne) 1918–19
101 F. G. Travers & B. Howlett: Europeans v. Muslims (Bombay) 1925–26
101 W. W. Whysall & W. Voce: Notts. v. Glos. (Nottingham) 1929
101 A. E. Wilson & T. W. Goddard: Glos. v. Somerset (Bristol) 1939
100 G. E. Palmer & W. H. Cooper: Victoria v. N.S.W. (Sydney).............1881–82
100 P. H. Tarilton & H. W. Ince: Barbados v. M.C.C. (Barbados) 1912–13
100 E. L. Dalton & A. L. Ochse: South Africans v. Kent (Canterbury) 1929
100 A. Hurwood & P. M. Hornibrook: Australians v. Sussex (Hove) 1930
100 S. N. Banerjee & C. S. Nayudu: Indians v. Hants. (Bournemouth) 1936
100 W. A. Sime & W. Voce: Notts. v. Cambridge U. (Cambridge) 1935
100* D. Tallon & G. J. Noblet: Bradman's XI v. Hassett's XI (Melbourne) 1948–49

ELEVENTH WICKET

80 H. Whitfield & P. H. Morton: Cambridge U. v. Surrey (Oval) 1878

A Century First-wicket Partnership in each Innings

123 108 L. Hall & G. Ulyett: Yorks. v. Sussex (Hove) 1885
139 147* J. T. Brown & J. Tunnicliffe: Yorks. v. Middx. (Lord's) 1896
135 148 C. B. Fry & G. Brann: Sussex v. Middx. (Lord's) 1899
131 142 W. G. Grace & C. J. B. Wood: London County v. Surrey (Crystal Palace) 1901
108 100 C. J. Burnup & E. Humphreys: Kent v. South Africans (Beckenham) 1901
114 109 R. Abel & D. L. A. Jephson: Surrey v. Sussex (Hove) 1901
134 144* A. O. Jones & J. Iremonger: Notts. v. Surrey (Oval) 1901
170 179 C. B. Fry & J. Vine: Sussex v. Leics. (Hove) 1903
113 119* V. T. Trumper & R. A. Duff: N.S.W. v. Victoria (Sydney) 1903–04
102 303 A. O. Jones & J. Iremonger: Notts. v. Glos. (Nottingham) 1904
106 125 T. Hayward & J. B. Hobbs: Surrey v. Cambridge U. (Oval) 1907
147 105 T. Hayward & J. B. Hobbs: Surrey v. Middx. (Lord's) 1907
              (These two instances were recorded in the same week.)
105 118 T. Hayward & J. B. Hobbs: Surrey v. Oxford U. (Oval) 1908
103 100 A. Hartley & W. Tyldesley: Lancs. v. Hants. (Southampton) 1910
122 121 V. T. Trumper & W. Bardsley: N.S.W. v. South Africans (Sydney) 1910–11
141 193 A. H. Hornby & H. Makepeace: Lancs. v. Notts. (Nottingham) 1912
127 136 A. E. Dipper & C. S. Barnett: Glos. v. Somerset (Bristol) 1913
191 104 A. C. Russell & F. Loveday: Essex v. Lancs. (Leyton) 1921
122 140 F. H. Gillingham & A. C. Russell: Essex v. Surrey (Oval) 1922
154 155 J. S. Shepherd & R. V. de R. Worker: Otago v. Wellington (Dunedin) 1923–24
157 110 J. B. Hobbs & H. Sutcliffe: England v. Australia (Sydney) 1924–25
114 116 H. Makepeace & C. Hallows: Lancs. v. Australians (Liverpool) 1926
105 265* P. Holmes & H. Sutcliffe: Yorks. v. Surrey (Oval) 1926
109 100 J. A. Newman & H. L. Dales: Calthorpe's XI v. Tennyson's XI (Folkestone) 1926
202 107* F. Watson & C. Hallows: Lancs. v. Glamorgan (Manchester) 1928
184 210* P. Holmes & H. Sutcliffe: Yorks. v. Notts. (Nottingham) 1928
106 368 E. H. Bowley & J. H. Parks: Sussex v. Glos. (Hove) 1929
119 171 R. H. Catterall & B. Mitchell: South Africa v. England (Birmingham) 1929
129 109 N. E. Haig & H. W. Lee: Middx. v. Leics. (Lord's) 1930
102 113 D. Ayling & A. L. S. Jackson: South Americans v. Cahn's XI (Nottingham) 1932
125 128 W. W. Keeton & C. B. Harris: Notts. v. Kent (Nottingham) 1933
119 121 A. W. Snowden & A. H. Bakewell: Northants. v. Warwicks. (Birmingham) 1934
              (Both stands were made on the same day.)
119 146 J. W. Lee & F. S. Lee: Somerset v. Sussex (Eastbourne) 1934

101	127	W. H. Ashdown & A. E. Fagg: Kent v. Glamorgan (Cardiff) 1935	
111	109	J. H. Parks & H. E. Hammond: Sussex v. Hants. (Portsmouth) 1936	
109	102	N. Kilner & A. J. Croom: Warwicks. v. Worcs. (Worcester) 1937	
108	126*	E. Paynter & C. Washbrook: Lancs. v. Notts. (Nottingham) 1937	
102	100	N. McCorkell & J. Arnold: Hants. v. Kent (Southampton) 1938	
116	105	F. S. Lee & H. Gimblett: Somerset v. Sussex (Taunton) 1939	
152	169	I. S. Lee & B. A. Barnett: Victoria v. Queensland (Brisbane) 1939–40	
123	136	D. Brookes & P. Davis: Northants. v. Lancs. (Northampton) 1946	
137	100	L. Hutton & C. Washbrook: England v. Australia (Adelaide) 1946–47	
110	117	L. Hutton & W. Watson: Yorks. v. Lancs. (Manchester) 1947	
121	116	A. H. Dyson & E. Davies: Glamorgan v. Sussex (Cardiff) 1947	
121	176	J. D. Robertson & S. M. Brown: Middx. v. Essex (Colchester) 1947	
124	139	L. G. Berry & G. Lester: Leics. v. Middx. (Leicester) 1948	
168	129	L. Hutton & C. Washbrook: England v. Australia (Leeds) 1948	
220	286	B. Sutcliffe & D. D. Taylor: Auckland v. Canterbury (Auckland) 1948–49	
122	151*	W. W. Keeton & C. B. Harris: Notts. v. Northants. (Northampton) 1950	
199	109	J. D. Robertson & S. M. Brown: Middx. v. Somerset (Lord's) 1951	
166	108	B. C. Khanna & R. Balasundaram: Uttar Pradesh v. Madhya Pradesh (Nagpur)...1952–53	
101	118	C. Washbrook & J. T. Ikin: Lancs. v. Hants. (Manchester) 1953	
107	132	A. E. Fagg & A. H. Phebey: Kent v. Glos. (Gloucester) 1954	
106	104	D. V. Smith & A. S. M. Oakman: M.C.C. v. Oxford U. (Lord's) 1956	
122	230	W. B. Stott & K. Taylor: Yorks. v. Notts (Nottingham)...............................1957	
172	112	G. G. Atkinson & R. Virgin: Somerset v. Cambridge U. (Taunton) 1960	
198	137	R. M. Prideaux & A. R. Lewis: Cambridge U. v. Somerset (Taunton)..................1960	
152	110	M. J. Stewart & J. H. Edrich: Surrey v. Somerset (Taunton) 1960	

A. Sandham, playing for Surrey v. Essex (Leyton) 1925, shared in opening stands of 216 with J. B. Hobbs in the first innings and 181 with A. Jeacocke in the second.

F. W. Shipston, playing for Nottinghamshire v. Gloucestershire (Bristol) 1932, shared in two century stands—113 with G. Gunn in the first innings and 139 with C. B. Harris in the second.

A. S. M. Oakman, playing for Sussex v. Oxford U. (Oxford) 1956, shared in two century stands—109 with D. V. Smith in the first innings and 100 with A. A. K. Lawrence in the second.

Part IV—Bowling

Most Wickets in a Season

	Season	Balls in an over	Overs	Mdns.	Runs	Wkts.	Avge.
A. P. Freeman	1928	(6-ball)	1976·1	423	5489	304	18·05
A. P. Freeman	1933	(6-ball)	2039	651	4549	298	15·26
T. Richardson	1895	(5-ball)	1690·1	463	4170	290	14·37
C. T. B. Turner	1888	(4-ball)	2427·2	1127	3307	283	11·68
A. P. Freeman	1931	(6-ball)	1618	360	4307	276	15·60
A. P. Freeman	1930	(6-ball)	1914·3	472	4632	275	16·84
T. Richardson	1897	(5-ball)	1603·4	495	3945	273	14·45
A. P. Freeman	1929	(6-ball)	1670·5	381	4879	267	18·27
W. Rhodes	1900	(6-ball)	1553	455	3606	261	13·81
J. T. Hearne	1896	(5-ball)	2003·1	818	3670	257	14·28
A. P. Freeman	1932	(6-ball)	1565·5	404	4149	253	16·39
W. Rhodes	1901	(6-ball)	1565	505	3797	251	15·12

150 WICKETS IN AN ENGLISH SEASON

	Season	Overs	Mdns.	Runs	Wkts.	Avge.
Appleyard, R. (Yorks.) ....(2)	1951	1323·1	391	2829	200	14·14
	1954	1026·3	315	2221	154	14·42
Astill, W. E. (Leics.) ....(1)	1921	1226·3	316	3212	153	20·99
Attewell, W. (Notts.) ....(2)	1890	1581·2	820	1874	151	12·41
	1891	1514·3	706	2132	153	13·93
Bedser, A. V. (Surrey) ....(2)	1952	1184·4	296	2530	154	16·42
	1953	1253	340	2702	162	16·67
Blythe, C. (Kent) ....(7)	1907	1136·1	291	2822	183	15·42
	1908	1366·4	386	3326	197	16·88
	1909	1273·5	343	3128	215	14·54
	1910	1041·3	274	2497	175	14·26
	1912	919·3	241	2183	178	12·26
	1913	1120·2	289	2729	167	16·34
	1914	1008·4	280	2583	170	15·19
Booth, M. W. (Yorks.) ....(2)	1913	1156·2	185	3342	181	18·46
	1914	983·5	178	2803	157	17·85
Bowes, W. E. (Yorks.) ....(3)	1932	1194·2	271	2877	190	15·14
	1933	1010·4	226	2828	159	17·78
	1935	1286·5	342	2981	193	15·44
Bradley, W. M. (Kent) ....(1)	1899	1257	414	2981	156	19·10
Braund, L. C. (Somerset) ....(1)	1902	1100	250	3407	172	19·80
Brearley, W. (Lancs.) ....(2)	1905	1049·4	191	3486	181	19·25
	1908	856·2	165	2636	163	16·17
Briggs, J. (Lancs.) ....(5)	1888	1450·2	763	1679	160	10·49
	1890	1113·2	456	1950	158	12·34
	1893	1364	488	2639	166	15·89
	1896	1741·4	592	3253	165	19·71
	1897	1288	387	2560	155	16·51
Clay, J. C. (Glamorgan)........................(1)	1937	1103·3	229	3052	176	17·34
Cook, L. (Lancs.)................................(2)	1920	1069·4	275	2322	156	14·88
	1921	1402	293	3472	151	22·99
Copson, W. H. (Derby) ....(1)	1936	946·4	239	2135	160	13·34
Cox, G. R. (Sussex) ....(2)	1905	1557·3	456	3719	170	21·87
	1907	1218·2	359	2900	164	17·68
Dean, H. (Lancs.) ....(2)	1911	1295·5	324	3191	183	17·43
	1912	1060	356	2216	162	13·67
Dennett, G. (Glos.) ....(6)	1905	1161·3	280	3421	163	20·98
	1906	1145·5	256	3093	175	17·69
	1907	1216·2	305	3227	201	16·05
	1908	1317·1	409	3148	153	20·57
	1909	1039·5	242	2977	156	19·08
	1913	1175·1	289	3139	153	20·51
Dooland, B. (Notts.) ....(3)	1953	1332·3	461	2852	172	16·58

	Season	Overs	Mdns.	Runs	Wkts.	Avge.
Dooland, B. (*cont.*)	1954	1287·1	408	3035	196	15·48
	1955	1245·3	327	3452	150	23·01
Drake, A. (Yorks.) ....(1)	1914	1017·2	283	2428	158	15·36
Faulkner, G. A. (South Africans)............(1)	1912	1015·1	207	2514	163	15·42
Ferris, J. J. (Australians) ....(2)	1888	2085·1	937	2934	199	14·74
	1890	1545·1	628	2657	186	14·28
Fender, P. G. H. (Surrey) ....(2)	1922	1116	208	3329	157	21·20
	1923	1324·2	307	3558	178	19·98
Fielder, A. (Kent) ....(2)	1906	1159·3	234	3756	186	20·19
	1907	977·3	197	2773	172	16·12
Freeman, A. P. (Kent) ....(14)	1921	1017·2	217	3086	166	18·59
	1923	990	262	2642	157	16·82
	1922	1101·1	270	2839	194	14·63
	1924	1035·2	250	2518	167	15·07
	1926	1353·5	327	3740	180	20·77
	1927	1220·1	269	3330	181	18·39
	1928	1976·1	423	5489	304	18·05
	1929	1670·5	381	4879	267	18·27
	1930	1914·3	472	4632	275	16·84
	1931	1618	360	4307	276	15·60
	1932	1565·5	404	4149	253	16·39
	1933	2039	651	4549	298	15·26
	1934	1744·4	440	4753	205	23·18
	1935	1503·2	320	4562	212	21·51
Geary, G. (Leics.) ....(1)	1929	1495·2	500	2980	152	19·60
Giffen, G. (Australians) ....(1)	1886	1673·2	710	2674	154	17·36
Gilligan, A. E. R. (Sussex) ....(1)	1923	1075·4	235	2853	163	17·50
Gladwin, C. (Derby) ....(1)	1952	1258·2	402	2917	152	19·19
Goddard, T. W. (Glos.) ....(10)	1929	1285·1	357	3015	184	16·38
	1932	1316	343	3258	170	19·16
	1933	1371·5	414	3187	183	17·41
	1935	1553	384	4073	200	20·36
	1936	1425·2	323	3106	153	20·30
	1937	1478·1	359	4158	248	16·76
	1939	819	139	2973	200	14·86
	1946	1310·2	358	3095	177	17·48
	1947	1451·2	344	4119	238	17·30
	1949	1187·2	326	3069	160	19·18
Gover, A. R. (Surrey).............................(2)	1936	1159·2	185	3547	200	17·73
	1937	1219·4	191	3816	201	18·98
Grace, W. G. (Glos.) ....(2)	1875	1689·1	698	2468	191	12·92
	1877	1801	772	2291	179	12·79
Haigh, S. (Yorks.) ....(3)	1900	958·3	259	2416	163	14·82
	1902	799	219	1984	158	12·55
	1906	971·3	209	2540	174	14·59
Hallam, A. W. (Notts.) ....(1)	1907	937·1	302	2133	168	12·69
Hearne, J. T. (Middx.) ....(6)	1892	1360·3	527	2510	163	15·39
	1893	1741·4	667	3492	212	16·47
	1894	1486	600	2739	195	14·04
	1896	2003·1	818	3670	257	14·28
	1897	1619·3	647	3066	173	17·72
	1898	1802·2	781	3120	222	14·05
Hilton, M. J. (Lancs.).............................(1)	1956	1199·5	558	2207	158	13·96
Hirst, G. H. (Yorks.) ....(6)	1895	1262·1	429	2560	150	17·06
	1901	1135·3	261	2999	183	16·38
	1906	1306·1	271	3434	208	16·50
	1907	1167·4	269	2859	188	15·20
	1908	1121·5	290	2445	174	14·05
	1910	1021·2	252	2426	164	14·79
Hitch, J. W. (Surrey) ....(3)	1911	965·1	160	3477	151	23·02
	1913	958·4	169	3228	174	18·55
	1919	1052	207	3430	161	21·30
Hollies, W. E. (Warwicks.) ....(2)	1946	1528	433	2871	184	15·60
	1949	1627·4	484	3413	166	20·56
Howell, H. (Warwicks.) ....(2)	1920	1050·3	222	2885	161	17·91
	1923	1090·4	197	3126	152	20·56
Howorth, R. (Worcs.) ....(1)	1947	1254	375	2929	164	17·85
Humphreys, W. (Sussex) ....(1)	1893	813·4	122	2598	150	17·32
Jackson, L. (Derby) ....(1)	1960	1082·2	310	2179	160	13·61
Jenkins, R. O. (Worcs.) ....(1)	1949	1146·1	187	3879	183	21·19
Jupp, V. W. C. (Northants.) ....(1)	1928	1023	192	3345	166	20·15

	Season	Overs	Mdns.	Runs	Wkts.	Avge.
Kennedy, A. S. (Hants.)..........................(6)	1914	1289·4	331	3243	162	20·01
	1920	1179·4	279	3093	169	18·30
	1921	1427	316	4009	186	21·55
	1922	1346·4	366	3444	205	16·80
	1923	1376·5	370	3599	184	19·55
	1929	1178·5	344	2773	154	18·00
Kilner, R. (Yorks.) ....(1)	1923	1259·5	507	2040	158	12·91
Laker, J. C. (Surrey) ....(1)	1950	1409·5	522	2544	166	15·32
Langridge, James (Sussex) ....(1)	1933	1228·3	355	2617	158	16·56
Larwood, H. (Notts.) ....(1)	1932	866·4	203	2084	162	12·86
Lees, W. S. (Surrey) ....(2)	1905	1388·2	387	3476	193	18·01
	1906	1258·5	321	3402	168	20·25
Llewellyn, C. B. (Hants.) ....(2)	1902	1129·4	314	3164	170	18·61
	1910	951·3	161	2930	152	19·27
Lock, G. A. R. (Surrey) ....(4)	1955	1407·4	497	3109	216	14·39
	1956	1058·2	437	1932	155	12·46
	1957	1194·1	449	2550	212	12·02
	1958	1014·4	382	2055	170	12·08
Lockwood, W. H. (Surrey) ....(3)	1892	890·2	292	2052	151	13·58
	1893	931·2	267	2517	150	16·78
	1894	894·2	244	2233	150	14·88
Lohmann, G. A. (Surrey) ....(7)	1886	1715	809	2425	160	15·15
	1887	1634·2	737	2404	154	15·61
	1888	1649·1	783	2280	209	10·90
	1889	1614·1	646	2714	202	13·83
	1890	1759·1	737	2998	220	13·62
	1891	1189·3	445	2065	177	11·66
	1892	1213·4	431	2316	151	15·33
Macaulay, G. G. (Yorks.) ....(3)	1923	1042·4	245	2297	166	13·83
	1924	1220·4	343	2514	190	13·23
	1925	1338·2	307	3268	211	15·48
Martin, F. (Kent) ....(1)	1890	1702·2	711	2481	190	13·05
McDonald, E. A. (Lancs.) ....(4)	1925	1249·4	282	3828	205	18·67
	1926	1177·4	222	3541	175	20·23
	1927	1137·3	223	3586	150	23·90
	1928	1254·1	266	3754	190	19·75
Mead, W. (Essex) ....(1)	1895	1206	390	2605	179	14·50
Mitchell, T. B. (Derby) ....(2)	1934	986·1	202	3064	159	19·27
	1935	919·5	142	3448	171	20·16
Mold, A. (Lancs.) ....(4)	1893	1282·4	426	2817	166	16·97
	1894	1288·3	456	2548	207	12·30
	1895	1629	598	3400	213	15·96
	1896	1116·1	373	2719	150	18·12
Morley, F. (Notts.) ....(2)	1878	1916·1	1017	2265	190	11·92
	1880	1712·1	872	2077	174	11·93
Muncer, B. L. (Glamorgan) ....(1)	1948	1289·2	381	2748	159	17·28
Newman, J. A. (Hants.) ....(3)	1910	1012·1	192	2879	156	18·45
	1921	1234·1	260	3817	177	21·56
	1926	1277	267	3904	154	24·70
Nichols, M. S. (Essex) ....(2)	1935	972·3	196	2610	157	16·62
	1938	1228·1	264	3408	171	19·92
Paine, G. A. E. (Warwicks.) ....(1)	1934	1285·5	463	2664	156	17·07
Parker, C. W. L. (Glos.) ....(10)	1921	1178·5	381	2893	164	17·64
	1922	1294·5	445	2712	206	13·16
	1923	1420·2	520	3229	172	18·77
	1924	1303·5	411	2913	204	14·27
	1925	1512·3	478	3311	222	14·91
	1926	1739·5	556	3920	213	18·40
	1927	1727·4	540	3849	193	19·94
	1928	1474·2	470	3602	162	22·23
	1930	1016·3	301	2299	179	12·84
	1931	1320·4	386	3125	219	14·26
Parkin, C. H. (Lancs.) ....(4)	1922	1309·3	348	3300	189	17·46
	1923	1356·2	356	3543	209	16·94
	1924	1162·5	357	2735	200	13·67
	1925	1075·1	281	2935	152	19·30
Peate, E. (Yorks.) ....(2)	1881	1712	731	2195	173	12·68
	1882	1562·1	864	2466	214	11·52
Peel, R. (Yorks.) ....(3)	1888	1648·1	830	2091	171	12·23
	1890	1552·4	714	2239	172	13·01
	1895	1691·1	714	2695	180	14·96

		Season	Overs	Mdns.	Runs	Wkts.	Avge.
Pegler, S. J. (South Africans)	...............(1)	1912	1286·5	352	2885	189	15·26
Perks, R. T. D. (Worcs.)	....................(1)	1939	828	112	3057	159	19·22
Pritchard, T. L. (Warwicks.)	..............(1)	1948	1271·3	276	3225	172	18·75
Relf, A. E. (Sussex)	.............................(2)	1908	1301·3	428	2648	151	17·53
		1910	1360·3	448	3108	158	19·67
Rhodes, W. (Yorks.)	...........................(10)	1898	1240	482	2249	154	14·60
		1899	1518·4	543	3062	179	17·10
		1900	1553	455	3606	261	13·81
		1901	1565	505	3797	251	15·12
		1902	1306·3	405	2801	213	13·15
		1903	1378	425	2813	193	14·57
		1905	1241·3	310	3085	182	16·95
		1907	1067·1	231	2757	177	15·57
		1919	1048·3	305	2365	164	14·42
		1920	1028·4	291	2123	161	13·18
Richardson, T. (Surrey	.........................(7)	1893	993·4	288	2680	174	15·40
		1894	936·3	293	2024	196	10·32
		1895	1690·1	463	4170	290	14·37
		1896	1656·2	526	4015	246	16·32
		1897	1603·4	495	3945	273	14·48
		1898	1223·4	342	3147	161	19·54
		1901	1301·4	271	3697	159	23·25
Richmond, L. B. (Notts.)	....................(2)	1920	949·4	162	2981	150	19·87
		1922	862·2	209	2279	169	13·48
Robins, R. W. V. (Middx.)	...................(1)	1929	1154·4	159	3489	162	21·53
Robinson, E. P. (Yorks.)	.....................(1)	1946	1138·2	354	2498	167	14·95
Root, C. F. (Worcs.)	............................(3)	1923	1263·3	353	3498	170	20·52
		1924	1007·3	281	2508	153	16·39
		1925	1493·2	416	3770	219	17·21
Shackleton, D. (Hants.)	.........................(4)	1953	1219·4	328	3070	150	20·46
		1955	1220·2	438	2138	159	13·72
		1957	1217·3	446	2429	155	15·67
		1958	1320·2	505	2549	165	15·44
Shaw, A. (Notts.)	...............................(4)	1875	1755·1	1023	1495	160	9·34
		1876	2631·2	1528	2601	190	13·68
		1878	2465	1468	2044	189	10·81
		1880	1995	1251	1512	177	8·54
Shepherd, D. J. (Glamorgan)	...............(1)	1956	1226·5	433	2719	177	15·36
Sims, J. M. (Middx.)	............................(1)	1939	775·4	72	3228	159	20·30
Sinfield, R. A. (Glos.)	..........................(1)	1936	1501	461	3082	161	19·14
Smith, C. I. J. (Middx.)	........................(1)	1934	1398	346	3248	172	18·88
Smith, H. A. (Leics.)	............................(1)	1935	1103·2	230	2950	150	19·66
Smith, T. P. B. (Essex)	.........................(2)	1937	995·3	186	3039	155	19·60
		1947	1606	287	4667	172	27·13
Smith, W. C. (Surrey)	..........................(2)	1910	1423·3	420	3225	247	13·05
		1911	1283·4	368	3223	160	20·14
Southerton, J. (Surrey)	.........................(4)	1868	1096·2	238	2093	150	13·95
		1870	1876·1	709	3074	210	14·63
		1871	1633·1	643	2375	151	15·72
		1872	1570·1	629	2209	169	13·07
Spofforth, F. R. (Australians)	..............(1)	1884	1577	653	2744	207	13·25
Steel, A. G. (Lancs.)	............................(1)	1878	1223	447	1547	164	9·43
Tarrant, F. A. (Middx.)	.......................(2)	1907	1085·5	244	2874	183	15·70
		1908	1124·2	297	2819	169	16·68
Tate, F. W. (Sussex)	.............................(1)	1902	1183·2	359	2828	180	15·71
Tate, M. W. (Sussex)	...........................(6)	1923	1608·5	331	3061	219	13·97
		1924	1469·5	465	2818	205	13·74
		1925	1694·3	472	3415	228	14·97
		1928	1584·2	491	3184	165	19·29
		1929	1420·1	393	2903	156	18·60
		1932	1380·1	440	2494	160	15·58
Tattersall, R. (Lancs.)	..........................(2)	1950	1404·4	502	2623	193	13·59
		1953	1186	345	2974	164	18·13
Thompson, G. J. (Northants.)	...............(1)	1909	905·5	228	2392	163	14·67
Titmus, F. J. (Middx.)	.........................(1)	1955	1449·5	522	3117	191	16·31
Tribe, G. E. (Northants.)	......................(1)	1955	1289	342	3366	176	19·12
Trott, A. E. (Middx.)	...........................(3)	1899	1772·4	587	4086	239	17·09
		1900	1547·1	363	4923	211	23·33
		1901	1289·1	289	3835	176	21·78
Trueman, F. S. (Yorks.)	........................(2)	1955	996·5	214	2454	153	16·03
		1960	1068·4	274	2447	175	13·98

	Season	Overs	Mdns.	Runs	Wkts.	Avge.
Turner, C. T. B. (Australians) ....(2)	1888	2427·2	1127	3307	283	11·68
	1890	1501·1	655	2544	179	14·21
Tyldesley, R. (Lancs.) ....(2)	1924	1075·3	346	2574	184	13·98
	1929	1114·3	350	2399	154	15·57
Verity, H. (Yorks.) ....(9)	1931	1137·3	356	2542	188	13·52
	1932	1117·5	401	2250	162	13·88
	1933	1195·4	428	2553	190	13·43
	1934	1282·1	500	2645	150	17·63
	1935	1279·2	453	3032	211	14·36
	1936	1289·3	463	2847	216	13·18
	1937	1386·2	487	3168	202	15·68
	1938	1191·4	424	2476	158	15·67
	1939	936·3	270	2509	191	13·13
Wainwright, E. (Yorks.).........................(1)	1894	1087·3	413	2114	166	12·73
Walsh, J. E. (Leics.) ....(2)	1947	1032·1	135	3477	152	22·87
	1948	1175·3	193	3405	174	19·56
Wardle, J. H. (Yorks.) ....(6)	1948	1283·4	483	2923	150	19·48
	1950	1627·1	741	2909	174	16·71
	1952	1857	810	3460	177	19·54
	1954	1262	520	2449	155	15·80
	1955	1486·4	572	3149	195	16·14
	1956	1230·2	464	2482	153	16·22
Wass, T. (Notts.) ....(1)	1907	885	218	2328	163	14·28
Wellard, A. W. (Somerset) ....(2)	1937	1276·1	220	3675	156	23·55
	1938	1233·4	241	3491	172	20·29
White, J. C. (Somerset) ....(1)	1929	1556·1	631	2648	168	15·76
Wilkinson, L. L. (Lancs.) ....(1)	1938	1251·2	240	3531	151	23·38
Woods, S. M. J. (Somerset) ....(1)	1892	1055·4	319	2576	153	16·83
Woolley, F. E. (Kent).............................(3)	1920	1135·4	315	2633	185	14·23
	1921	1163·1	367	2697	167	16·14
	1922	1233·1	370	2995	163	18·37
Wright, D. V. P. (Kent) ....(2)	1947	1175·5	252	3739	177	21·12
	1950	929·3	187	3140	151	20·79
Young, J. A. (Middx.) ....(4)	1947	1291·1	416	2765	159	17·38
	1949	1453·3	526	2948	150	19·65
	1951	1680·2	741	2976	157	18·95
	1952	1448·1	511	3241	163	19·88

Overseas Bowlers

Owing to the limited fixture list in overseas countries, it is rare for a bowler to take 100 wickets, so the best seasonal aggregates are listed under each country.

AUSTRALIA

	Season	Overs	Mdns.	Runs	Wkts.	Avge.
C. T. B. Turner (N.S.W.)............................1887–88	1066·3	473	1441	106	13·59
G. Giffen (South Australia) 1894–95	808·5	195	2097	93	22·54
C. V. Grimmett (South Australia) 1929–30	471·7	52	1943	82	23·69
R. Benaud (N.S.W.) 1958–59	559·5	146	1579	82	19·25
A. A. Mailey (N.S.W. 1920–21	2986*	45	1825	81	22·53
M. W. Tate (M.C.C.) 1924–25	502·2	93	1464	77	19·01
C. V. Grimmett (South Australia) 1931–32	588·4	166	1535	77	19·93
E. Jones (South Australia) 1897–98	575·1	121	1653	76	21·75
C. V. Grimmett (South Australia) 1930–31	449·9	99	1417	74	19·14
C. V. Grimmett (South Australia) 1939–40	442·7	57	1654	73	22·65
C. V. Grimmett (South Australia) 1928–29	5252*	134	2432	71	34·25
C. T. B. Turner (N.S.W.)............................1886–87	536·1	273	538	70	7·68
W. J. Whitty (South Australia) 1910–11	493·3	99	1419	70	20·27
H. J. Tayfield (South Africans) 1952–53	608·4	123	1954	70	27·91
T. Richardson (Stoddart's XI) 1894–95	592·2	148	1616	69	23·42
H. Ironmonger (Victoria)..........................1930–31	379·5	112	972	68	14·29
J. N. Crawford (M.C.C.) 1907–08	566	115	1663	66	25·19
J. V. Saunders (Victoria) 1907–08	555·4	113	1587	66	24·04
C. V. Grimmett (South Australia) 1933–34	420·5	68	1441	66	21·83
W. Rhodes (M.C.C.) 1903–04	423·3	112	1055	65	16·23
J. C. White (M.C.C.) 1928–29	5213*	223	1471	65	22·63

* Number of balls bowled given as both six and eight-ball overs bowled.

	Season	Overs	Mdns.	Runs	Wkts.	Avge.
L. O'B. Fleetwood-Smith (Victoria)	1937–38	395·1	29	1436	64	22·43
W. J. O'Reilly (N.S.W.)	1937–38	310·7	91	784	64	12·25
G. A. Lohmann (Shrewsbury's XI)	1887–88	659·1	354	755	63	11·98
H. Ironmonger (Victoria)	1931–32	491·5	178	1168	63	18·53
F. R. Foster (M.C.C.)	1911–12	485·1	110	1252	62	20·19
W. J. O'Reilly (N.S.W.)	1932–33	642·5	237	1237	62	19·95
L. C. Braund (MacLaren's XI)	1901–02	623·5	147	1779	61	29·16
V. Mankad (Indians)	1947–48	494·3	76	1595	61	26·14

SOUTH AFRICA

	Season	Overs	Mdns.	Runs	Wkts.	Avge.
R. Benaud (Australians)	1957–58	743·6	185	2057	106	19·40
S. F. Barnes (M.C.C.)	1913–14	460·2	129	1117	104	10·74
W. J. O'Reilly (Australians)	1935–36	662·5	250	1289	95	13·56
C. V. Grimmett (Australians)	1935–36	663·1	229	1362	92	14·80
J. H. Wardle (M.C.C.)	1956–57	380·3	94	1103	90	12·25
I. W. Johnson (Australians)	1949–50	414·6	77	1280	77	16·62
A. K. Davidson (Australians)	1957–58	430·5	101	1090	72	15·12
R. O. Jenkins (M.C.C.)	1948–49	406·7	64	1508	71	21·23
I. A. R. Peebles (M.C.C.)	1930–31	444·4	80	1274	66	19·30
A. S. Kennedy (Tennyson's XI)	1924–25	480·2	121	1287	65	19·80
J. T. Botten (N.E. Transvaal)	1958–59	261·3	68	667	63	10·58
A. S. Kennedy (M.C.C.)	1922–23	478·5	168	1024	61	16·78
G. Geary (Tennyson's XI)	1924–25	408	104	955	59	16·18
A. E. E. Vogler (Transvaal)	1909–10	317·3	50	1109	58	19·12
P. G. H. Fender (M.C.C.)	1922–23	380·1	81	1136	58	19·58
C. Blythe (M.C.C.)	1905–06	481·2	167	1046	57	18·35
W. A. Johnston (Australians)	1949–50	335·2	77	770	56	13·75
G. A. R. Lock (M.C.C.)	1956–57	352·7	120	833	56	14·87
H. J. Tayfield (Natal)	1956–57	450·1	153	1036	56	18·50
A. E. E. Vogler (Eastern Province)	1906–07	190·1	40	580	55	10·54
J. J. Kotze (Western Province)	1906–07	196·1	38	585	54	10·83
H. J. Tayfield (Natal)	1953–54	401·7	160	850	54	15·74
L. Kline (Australians)	1957–58	423	122	1103	54	20·42
C. Blythe (M.C.C.)	1909–10	404·1	129	820	53	15·47
J. E. Waddington (Griqualand West)	1952–53	303·6	59	893	53	16·84
A. E. Hall (Transvaal)	1926–27	277·4	60	650	52	12·50
P. N. F. Mansell (Rhodesia)	1951–52	295·5	49	917	52	17·63
D. V. P. Wright (M.C.C.)	1938–39	343·4	35	1453	51	28·49
D. V. P. Wright (M.C.C.)	1948–49	378·1	53	1544	51	30·27
C. L. McCool (Australians)	1949–50	314·2	56	976	51	19·13
J. R. Reid (New Zealanders)	1953–54	350·4	89	986	51	19·33
A. P. Freeman (M.C.C.)	1927–28	325·3	73	965	50	19·30
R. R. Lindwall (Australians)	1949–50	292·4	53	729	50	14·58
H. J. Tayfield (Natal)	1951–52	387·2	121	889	50	17·78
V. I. Smith (Natal)	1952–53	335·5	63	892	50	17·84
A. R. MacGibbon (New Zealanders)	1953–54	343·6	70	983	50	19·66
J. C. Laker (M.C.C.)	1956–57	388·7	121	875	50	17·50

WEST INDIES

	Season	Overs	Mdns.	Runs	Wkts.	Avge.
E. M. Dowson (Bennett's XI)	1901–02	404·5	121	997	80	12·46
G. J. Thompson (Brackley's XI)	1904–05	353·5	81	1048	75	13·97
E. R. Wilson (Bennett's XI)	1901–02	414·1	144	767	67	11·44
J. W. Hearne (M.C.C.)	1910–11	398·4	62	1450	67	21·64
C. E. Goodman (Barbados)	1896–97	304·2	71	676	57	11·85
H. R. B. Davenport (Lucas's XI)	1894–95	317·2	95	561	56	10·01
B. J. T. Bosanquet (Bennett's XI)	1901–02	338·3	92	906	55	16·47
A. E. Stoddart (Priestley's XI)	1896–97	303·4	128	520	53	9·81
F. W. Bush (Lucas's XI)	1894–95	284·4	90	610	51	11·96
S. P. Gupte (Indians)	1952–53	510	147	1182	50	23·64
S. G. Smith (Trinidad)	1901–02	220·5	36	568	48	11·83
S. G. Smith (M.C.C.)	1910–11	300·2	57	845	47	17·97
A. Cumberbatch (Trinidad)	1896–97	223·3	74	529	45	11·75
W. Voce (M.C.C.)	1929–30	387·2	68	1188	44	27·00
W. Williams (Priestley's XI)	1896–97	202·3	55	464	43	10·79
C. R. Browne (Barbados)	1910–11	220·2	51	555	41	13·53
E. Humphreys (M.C.C.)	1912–13	249·1	57	660	40	16·73
G. A. E. Paine (M.C.C.)	1934–35	369	103	957	40	23·92

	Season	Overs	Mdns.	Runs	Wkts.	Avge.
W. Rhodes (M.C.C.)	1929–30	501·1	172	947	39	24·28
A. L. Valentine (Jamaica)	1952–53	580·5	220	1202	38	31·63
W. E. Astill (M.C.C.)	1929–30	494·1	131	1171	37	31·64
F. S. Trueman (M.C.C.)	1959–60	342·3	86	883	37	23·86
J. Woods (Trinidad)	1896–97	173	53	349	36	9·69
J. C. Laker (M.C.C.)	1947–48	388·5	116	971	36	26·97
S. M. J. Woods (Priestley's XI)	1896–97	226·2	75	501	35	14·31

NEW ZEALAND

	Season	Overs	Mdns.	Runs	Wkts.	Avge.
G. J. Thompson (Hawke's XI)	1902–03	297	104	668	57	11·71
S. T. Callaway (Canterbury)	1903–04	224·5	73	474	54	8·77
R. W. Blair (Wellington)	1956–57	325·1	105	784	53	14·79
W. W. Armstrong (Australians)	1913–14	307·4	81	789	52	15·17
S. Austin (New South Wales)	1893–94	291·5	86	612	52	11·76
J. W. H. T. Douglas (M.C.C.)	1906–07	239·3	51	663	50	13·26
J. V. Saunders (Wellington)	1913–14	267	65	893	49	18·22
R. W. Blair (Wellington)	1957–58	302·2	103	606	49	12·36
J. A. Hayes (Auckland)	1957–58	244·3	49	568	48	11·83
W. Lankham (Auckland)	1882–83	257·2	128	294	48	6·12
W. Robertson (Canterbury)	1893–94	261·2	66	570	47	12·12
P. M. Hornibrook (Australians)	1920–21	170	33	573	47	12·19
C. V. Grimmett (Australians)	1927–28	319·4	65	795	47	16·91
R. W. Blair (Central Districts)	1955–56	280·5	54	882	47	18·76
J. C. Alabaster (Otago)	1959–60	313	78	824	47	17·53
K. W. Hough (Auckland)	1958–59	414·3	151	701	46	15·23
P. R. May (M.C.C.)	1906–07	248·4	47	719	45	15·97
H. Ironmonger (Australians)	1920–21	198·3	40	593	45	13·17

INDIA, PAKISTAN AND CEYLON

	Season	Overs	Mdns.	Runs	Wkts.	Avge.
M. W. Tate (M.C.C.)	1926–27	727·1	211	1599	116	13·78
G. Tribe (Commonwealth)	1949–50	787·2	215	1805	99	18·23
W. Hall (West Indians)	1958–59	519·2	167	1312	87	15·08
R. K. Oxenham (Australians)	1935–36	323·3	149	586	86	6·81
G. Geary (M.C.C.)	1926–27	528·1	148	1162	81	14·34
G. A. R. Lock (M.C.C.)	1955–56	557	296	869	81	10·79
K. T. Ramadhin (Commonwealth)	1950–51	754·3	261	1553	79	19·65
H. Verity (M.C.C.)	1933–34	482·2	179	1180	78	15·12
G. Tribe (Commonwealth)	1950–51	592	127	1619	76	21·30
W. E. Astill (M.C.C.)	1926–27	567·4	151	1556	71	21·91
G. E. Gomez (West Indians)	1949–49	729	238	1328	71	18·70
R. Gilchrist (West Indians)	1958–59	386·5	117	964	71	13·57
S. P. Gupte	1954–55	571·2	201	1095	69	15·86
R. B. Desai	1958–59	324·1	88	940	63	14·92
B. Dooland (Commonwealth)	1950–51	545·4	131	1480	60	24·66
F. Mair (Australians)	1935–36	309	44	1186	58	20·44
G. H. Pope (Tennyson's XI)	1937–38	341·4	71	924	58	15·93
G. S. Boyes (M.C.C.)	1926–27	457·3	127	1047	56	18·69
E. W. Clark (M.C.C.)	1933–34	381·1	111	890	56	15·89
M. S. Nichols (M.C.C.)	1933–34	344·2	70	989	55	17·98
P. E. Jones (West Indians)	1948–49	389·3	101	946	51	18·54
D. Shackleton (M.C.C.)	1951–52	484·2	125	1184	51	23·21
H. G. Gaekwad (Holkar)	1949–50	549	188	1167	50	23·34

Outstanding Bowling Averages

In the years before 1900 a large number of bowlers who took 100 wickets in a season returned an average of less than 13, but since that date so few bowlers have achieved such a low average that the complete list is given, a lower figure being taken for the years before 1900.

PRIOR TO 1900

	Seasons	Overs	Mdns.	Runs	Wkts.	Avge.
A. Shaw (Notts.)	1880	1995	1251	1512	177	8·54
A. Shaw (Notts.)	1875	1755·1	1023	1495	160	9·34
A. G. Steel (Lancs.)	1878	1223	447	1547	164	9·43

	Season	Overs	Mdns.	Runs	Wkts.	Avge.
A. Shaw (Notts.)	1879	1501	870	1232	129	9·55
E. Willsher (Kent)	1868	979·2	529	1128	113	9·98
T. Richardson (Surrey)	1894	936·3	293	2024	196	10·32
J. Briggs (Lancs.)	1888	1450·2	763	1679	160	10·49
A. Shaw (Notts.)	1878	2465	1486	2044	189	10·81
G. A. Lohmann (Surrey)	1888	1649·1	783	2280	209	10·90

SINCE 1900

	Season	Overs	Mdns.	Runs	Wkts.	Avge.
L. Jackson (Derby)	1958	829	295	1572	143	10·99
W. Rhodes (Yorks.)	1923	929	345	1547	134	11·54
A. Booth (Yorks.)	1946	917·2	423	1289	111	11·61
R. O. Schwarz (South Africans)	1907	711·3	153	1616	137	11·79
G. A. R. Lock (Surrey)	1957	1194·1	449	2550	212	12·02
H. Larwood (Notts.)	1931	651·3	142	1553	129	12·03
G. A. R. Lock (Surrey)	1958	1014·4	382	2055	170	12·08
W. Rhodes (Yorks.)	1922	814·1	312	1451	119	12·19
C. Blythe (Kent)	1912	919·3	241	2183	178	12·26
J. B. Statham (Lancs.)	1958	894·2	275	1648	134	12·29
J. B. Statham (Lancs.)	1960	844·1	274	1662	135	12·31
S. Haigh (Yorks.)	1912	813·4	245	1541	125	12·32
G. A. R. Lock (Surrey)	1956	1058·2	437	1932	155	12·46
S. Haigh (Yorks.)	1902	799	219	1984	158	12·55
A. W. Hallam (Notts.)	1907	937·1	302	2133	168	12·69
S. G. Smith (Northants.)	1912	559	165	1269	100	12·69
J. T. Hearne (Middx.)	1910	752	253	1523	119	12·79
S. Haigh (Yorks.)	1907	591·3	146	1308	102	12·82
C. W. L. Parker (Glos.)	1930	1016·3	301	2299	179	12·84
H. Larwood (Notts.)	1932	866·4	203	2084	162	12·86
R. Kilner (Yorks.)	1923	1259·5	507	2040	158	12·91
H. Larwood (Notts.)	1936	679·1	165	1544	119	12·97

Leading Bowler of a Season

With a few exceptions slow bowlers have usually had the best record in an English season—the qualification being the taking of at least 100 wickets at the lowest cost.

Season		Overs	Mdns.	Runs	Wkts.	Avge.
1894	T. Richardson (Surrey)	936·3	293	2024	196	10·32
1895	C. L. Townsend (Glos.)	746·1	178	1827	131	13·94
1896	J. T. Hearne (Middx.)	2003·1	818	3670	257	14·28
1897	T. Richardson (Surrey)	1603·4	495	3945	273	14·45
1898	J. T. Hearne (Middx.)	1802·2	781	3120	222	14·05
1899	A. E. Trott (Middx.)	1772·4	587	4086	239	17·09
1900	W. Rhodes (Yorks.)	1553	455	3606	261	13·81
1901	W. Rhodes (Yorks.)	1565	505	3797	251	15·12
1902	S. Haigh (Yorks.)	799	219	1984	158	12·55
1903	W. Mead (Essex)	971·3	355	1791	131	13·67
1904	J. T. Hearne (Middx.)	1153·3	330	2732	145	18·84
1905	S. Haigh (Yorks.)	831·5	220	1983	120	15·37
1906	S. Haigh (Yorks.)	971·3	209	2540	174	14·59
1907	A. W. Hallam (Notts.)	937·1	302	2133	168	12·69
1908	S. Haigh (Yorks.)	623·2	176	1380	103	13·39
1909	S. Haigh (Yorks.)	844·2	205	1702	122	13·95
1910	J. T. Hearne (Middx.)	752	253	1523	119	12·79
1911	G. J. Thompson (Northants.)	735·5	199	1889	113	16·71
1912	C. Blythe (Kent)	919·3	241	2183	178	12·26
1913	C. Blythe (Kent)	1120·2	289	2729	167	16·34
1914	C. Blythe (Kent)	1008·4	280	2583	170	15·19
1919	W. Rhodes (Yorks.)	1048·3	305	2365	164	14·42
1920	W. Rhodes (Yorks.)	1028·4	291	2123	161	13·18
1921	W. Rhodes (Yorks.)	963	316	1872	141	13·27
1922	W. Rhodes (Yorks.)	814·1	312	1451	119	12·19
1923	W. Rhodes (Yorks.)	929	345	1547	134	11·54
1924	G. G. Macaulay (Yorks.)	1220·4	343	2514	190	13·23
1925	C. W. L. Parker (Glos.)	1512·3	478	3311	222	14·91

		Overs	Mdns.	Runs	Wkts.	Avge.
1926	W. Rhodes (Yorks.)	892·4	315	1709	115	14·86
1927	H. Larwood (Notts.)	629·2	147	1695	100	16·95
1928	H. Larwood (Notts.)	834·5	204	2003	138	14·51
1929	R. Tyldesley (Lancs.)	1114·3	350	2399	154	15·57
1930	C. W. L. Parker (Glos.)	1016·3	301	2299	179	12·84
1931	H. Larwood (Notts.)	651·3	142	1553	129	12·03
1932	H. Larwood (Notts.)	866·4	203	2084	162	12·86
1933	H. Verity (Yorks.)	1195·4	428	2553	190	13·43
1934	G. A. E. Paine (Warwicks.)	1285·5	463	2664	156	17·07
1935	H. Verity (Yorks.)	1279·2	453	3032	211	14·36
1936	H. Larwood (Notts.)	679·1	165	1544	119	12·97
1937	H. Verity (Yorks.)	1386·2	487	3168	202	15·68
1938	W. E. Bowes (Yorks.)	932·3	294	1844	121	15·23
1939	H. Verity (Yorks.)	936·3	270	2509	191	13·13
1946	A. Booth (Yorks.)	917·2	423	1289	111	11·61
1947	T. W. Goddard (Glos.)	1451·2	344	4119	238	17·30
1948	C. Gladwin (Derby)	954·5	266	2174	128	16·98
1949	T. W. Goddard (Glos.)	1187·2	326	3069	160	19·18
1950	R. Tattersall (Lancs.)	1404·4	502	2623	193	13·59
1951	R. Appleyard (Yorks.)	1323·1	391	2829	200	14·14
1952	A. V. Bedser (Surrey)	1184·4	296	2530	154	16·42
1953	L. Jackson (Derby)	741·4	229	1574	103	15·28
1954	R. Appleyard (Yorks.)	1026·3	315	2221	154	14·42
1955	D. Shackleton (Hants.)	1220·2	438	2183	159	13·72
1956	G. A. R. Lock (Surrey)	1058·2	437	1932	155	12·46
1957	G. A. R. Lock (Surrey)	1194·1	449	2550	212	12·02
1958	L. Jackson (Derby)	829	295	1572	143	10·99
1959	J. B. Statham (Lancs.)	977·4	267	2087	139	15·01
1960	J. B. Statham (Lancs.)	844·1	274	1662	135	12·31

In the following seasons bowlers of the touring team finished with a better average than the leading English bowler:

		Overs	Mdns.	Runs	Wkts.	Avge.
1896	T. R. McKibbin (Australians)	647·1	198	1441	101	14·26
1907	R. O. Schwarz (South Africans)	711·3	153	1616	137	11·79
1934	W. J. O'Reilly (Australians)	870	320	1858	109	17·04
1948	W. A. Johnston (Australians)	850·1	279	1675	102	16·42

Most Balls Bowled by a Bowler in a Season

	Balls	Season	Overs	Mdns.	Runs	Wkts.	Avge.
A. P. Freeman (Kent)	12234	1933	2039	651	4549	298	15·26
A. P. Freeman (Kent)	11857	1928	1976·1	423	5489	304	18·05
A. P. Freeman (Kent)	11487	1930	1914·3	472	4632	275	16·84
J. H. Wardle (Yorks.)	11142	1952	1857	810	3460	177	19·54
A. Shaw (Notts.)	10526	1876	2631·2	1528	2601	190	13·68
A. P. Freeman (Kent)	10468	1934	1744·4	440	4753	205	23·18
C. W. L. Parker (Glos.)	10439	1926	1739·5	556	3920	213	18·40
C. W. L. Parker (Glos.)	10366	1927	1727·4	540	3849	193	19·94
M. W. Tate (Sussex)	10167	1925	1694·3	472	3415	228	14·97
J. A. Young (Middx.)	10082	1951	1680·2	741	2976	157	18·95
A. P. Freeman (Kent)	10025	1929	1670·5	381	4879	267	18·27
J. T. Hearne (Middx.)	10016	1896	2003·1	818	3670	257	14·28

Most Runs off a Bowler in a Season

	Season	Overs	Mdns.	Runs	Wkts.	Avge.
A. P. Freeman (Kent)	1928	1976·1	423	5489	304	18·05
A. E. Trott (Middx.)	1900	1547·1	363	4923	211	23·33
A. P. Freeman (Kent)	1929	1670·5	381	4879	267	18·27
A. P. Freeman (Kent)	1934	1744·4	440	4753	205	23·18
T. P. B. Smith (Essex)	1947	1606	287	4667	172	27·13
R. Smith (Essex)	1947	1557	324	4658	125	37·26

	Season	Overs	Mdns.	Runs	Wkts.	Avge.
A. P. Freeman (Kent)	1930	1914·3	472	4632	275	16·84
A. P. Freeman (Kent)	1935	1503·2	320	4562	212	21·51
A. P. Freeman (Kent)	1933	2039	651	4549	298	15·26
A. P. Freeman (Kent)	1931	1618	360	4307	276	15·60
T. Richardson (Surrey)	1895	1690·1	463	4170	290	14·37
T. W. Goddard (Glos.)	1937	1478·1	359	4158	248	16·76
A. P. Freeman (Kent)	1932	1565·5	404	4149	253	16·39
T. W. Goddard (Glos.)	1947	1451·2	344	4119	238	17·30
A. E. Trott (Middx.)	1899	1772·4	587	4086	239	17·09
T. W. Goddard (Glos.)	1935	1553	384	4073	200	20·36
T. Richardson (Surrey)	1896	1656·2	526	4015	246	16·79
A. S. Kennedy (Hants.)	1921	1427	316	4009	186	21·55

The Most Expensive 100 Wickets in a Season

The following bowlers have taken over 100 wickets in a season, but at the high cost of over 30 runs each:

	Season	Overs	Mdns.	Runs	Wkts.	Avge.
R. Smith (Essex)	1947	1557	324	4658	125	37·26
R. Smith (Essex)	1950	1267	298	3547	102	34·77
O. W. Herman (Hants.)	1938	1098	198	3263	101	32·30
C. W. L. Parker (Glos.)	1934	1417·2	344	3724	117	31·82
R. Smith (Essex)	1949	1185·5	252	3290	104	31·62
L. C. Braund (Somerset)	1901	988·3	161	3675	120	30·62
J. K. Nye (Sussex)	1939	769·1	56	3367	110	30·60
R. Smith (Essex)	1948	1241	316	3157	104	30·35
J. A. Newman (Hants.)	1928	1118	199	3394	112	30·30

Four Wickets with Consecutive Balls

The feat of taking four wickets with four successive balls has been performed as follows:

J. Wells	Kent v. Sussex (Brighton)	1862
G. Ulyett	Lord Harris' XI v. N.S.W. (Sydney)	1878–79
J. B. Hide	Sussex v. M.C.C. (Lord's)	1890
F. Shacklock	Notts. v. Somerset (Nottingham)	1893
A. Downes	Otago v. Auckland (Dunedin)	1893–94
F. Martin	M.C.C. v. Derby (Lord's)	1895
A. Mold	Lancs. v. Notts. (Nottingham)	1895
W. Brearley	Lancs. v. Somerset (Manchester)	(a) 1905
S. Haigh	M.C.C. v. Army XI (Pretoria)	1905–06
A. E. Trott	Middx. v. Somerset (Lord's)	(b) 1907
F. A. Tarrant	Middx. v. Glos. (Bristol)	1907
A. Drake	Yorks. v. Derby (Chesterfield)	1914
S. G. Smith	Northants. v. Warwicks. (Birmingham)	1914
H. A. Peach	Surrey v. Sussex (Oval)	1924
A. F. Borland	Natal v. Griqualand West (Kimberley)	1926–27
J. E. H. Hooker	N.S.W. v. Victoria (Sydney)	(a) 1928–29
R. Tyldesley	Lancs. v. Derby (Derby)	(a) 1929
R. J. Crisp	Western Province v. Griqualand West (Johannesburg)	1931–32
R. J. Crisp	Western Province v. Natal (Durban)	1933–34
A. R. Gover	Surrey v. Worcs. (Worcester)	1935
W. H. Copson	Derby v. Warwicks. (Derby)	1937
W. A. Henderson	N.E. Transvaal v. O.F.S. (Bloemfontein)	1937–38
F. Ridgway	Kent v. Derby (Folkestone)	1951
A. K. Walker	Notts. v. Leics. (Leicester)	(c) 1956

(a) Not all in the same innings.
(b) Hat-trick performed in same innings—Trott's benefit match.
(c) Wicket with last ball of first innings and hat-trick with first three balls in second innings.

Surrey lost four wickets in the course of a four-ball over from G. Bennett in a match with England at the Oval in 1862. The four batsmen dismissed were H. H. Stephenson (st.), W. Caffyn (run out), E. Dowson (bowled) and G. Griffiths (caught).

'Hat-Tricks'

The following bowlers have performed the 'hat-trick' in each innings of the same match:

A. Shaw ....Notts. v. Glos. (Nottingham) 1884
T. J. Matthews....................Australia v. South Africa (Manchester) 1912
C. W. L. Parker ....Glos. v. Middx. (Bristol) 1924
R. O. Jenkins ....Worcs. v. Surrey (Worcester) 1949

The following strange 'hat-tricks' have been performed:

All stumped W. H. Brain ......C. L. Townsend: Glos. v. Somerset (Cheltenham) 1893
All caught G. J. Thompson ...S. G. Smith: Northants. v. Warwicks. (Birmingham)...............1914
(Smith then took another wicket to perform the four in four balls feat.)
All l.b.w. ....H. Fisher: Yorks. v. Somerset (Sheffield) 1932
All caught wicket G. Dawkes...L. Jackson: Derby v. Worcs. (Kidderminster) 1958

The following bowlers have performed four or more hat-tricks in a career:

7—D. V. P. Wright.
6—T. W. Goddard, C. W. L. Parker.
5—S. Haigh, V. W. C. Jupp, A. E. G. Rhodes, F. A. Tarrant.
4—J. T. Hearne, J. C. Laker, G. G. Macaulay, T. J. Matthews, T. Richardson.

The following is the complete list of hat-tricks:

Abdul Wahab ....(1)	Karachi v. Services (Karachi) 1954–55
Allom, M. J. C. ....(1)	England v. New Zealand (Christchurch) 1929–30
Anderson, I. D. E. ....(1)	Natal v. Griqualand West (Durban) 1934–35
Andrews, W. H. R. ....(1)	Somerset v. Surrey (Oval) 1937
Appleyard, R. ....(1)	Yorks. v. Glos. (Sheffield) 1956
Armstrong, W. W. ....(1)	Victoria v. N.S.W. (Melbourne) 1902–03
Arnott, T. ....(1)	Glamorgan v. Somerset (Cardiff) 1926
Arshad ....(1)	Dacca U. v. East Pakistan B. (Dacca) 1957–58
Bailey, T. E. ....(1)	Essex v. Glamorgan (Newport) 1950
Baird, H. H. C. ....(1)	Navy & Army v. Oxford & Cambridge Us. (Aldershot) ...1910
Banerjee, S. N. ....(1)	East Zone v. West Zone (Bombay) 1948–49
Banerjee, Shute ....(1)	Bihar v. Delhi & District (Jamshedpur) 1948–49
Bannister, J. D. ....(1)	Warwicks. v. Yorks. (Sheffield) 1955
Baqa Jilani, M. ....(1)	Northern India v. Southern Punjab (Amritsar)............1934–35
Barclay, F. ....(1)	Auckland v. Canterbury (Auckland) 1903–04
Barlow, R. G. ....(3)	Lancs. v. Derby (Derby) 1881
	Players v. Gentlemen (Oval) 1884
	Lancs. v. Notts. (Manchester) 1886
Barnes, S. F. ....(1)	England v. Rest (Oval) 1912
Barratt, E. ....(1)	North v. South (Princes) 1872
Bates, W. ....(1)	England v. Australia (Melbourne) 1882–83
Beaumont, J. ....(1)	South v. North (Hastings) 1889
Bedser, A. V. ....(1)	Surrey v. Essex (Oval) 1953
Beesley, R. ....(1)	Border v. Griqualand West (Queenstown) 1946–47
Benskin, W. E...................(2)	Leics. v. Essex (Southend) 1906
	Scotland v. Oxford U. (Oxford) 1913
Bennett, J. H. ....(1)	Canterbury v. Wellington (Wellington) 1911–12
Bettington, R. H. B. ....(1)	Oxford U. v. Essex (Oxford) 1920
Best, W. F. ....(1)	Kent v. Somerset (Taunton) 1891
Blackman, W. ....(1)	Sussex v. Surrey (Hove) 1881
Blythe, C. ....(2)	Kent v. Surrey (Blackheath) 1910
	Kent v. Derby (Gravesend) 1910
Booth, M. W. ....(2)	Yorks. v. Worcs. (Bradford) 1911
	Yorks. v. Essex (Leyton)...................................1912
Borland, A. F. ....(2)	Natal v. Griqualand West (Kimberley) (4 in 4) 1926–27
	Natal v. Transvaal (Johannesburg) 1931–32
Bosanquet, B. J. T. ....(1)	Bennett's XI v. Barbados (Barbados) 1901–02
Bowes, W. E. ....(1)	M.C.C. v. Cambridge U. (Lord's) 1928
Boyes, G. S. ....(2)	Hants. v. Surrey (Portsmouth) 1925
	Hants. v. Warwicks. (Birmingham) 1926
Bradley, W. M. ....(3)	Kent v. Essex (Leyton) 1899
	Kent v. Yorks. (Tonbridge) 1899
	Kent v. Somerset (Blackheath) 1900
Braund, L. C. ....(1)	Somerset v. Worcs. (Worcester) 1906
Brearley, W. ....(1)	Lancs. v. Somerset (Manchester) (4 in 4) 1905
Bridges, J. J.....................(1)	Somerset v. Derby (Burton upon Trent) 1924
Briggs, J. ....(2)	North v. South (Scarborough) 1891
	England v. Australia (Sydney) 1891–92

Brockwell, W. ....(1)	Surrey v. Yorks. (Sheffield) 1900	
Bromley-Davenport, H. R. ...(1)	Lucas's XI v. British Guiana (Georgetown) 1894–95	
Brown, J. T. ....(1)	Yorks. v. Derby (Derby)..............................1896	
Browne, C. R. ....(1)	British Guiana v. Barbados (Georgetown)..................1937–38	
Buchanan, D. ....(1)	Gentlemen v. Cambridge U. (Cambridge) 1874	
Budgen, E. A. ....(1)	O.F.S. v. Griqualand West (Kimberley)..................1921–22	
Bullough, J. ....(1)	Lancs. v. Derby (Derby) 1914	
Burns, W. B. ....(1)	Worcs. v. Glos. (Worcester) 1913	
Butler, H. J. ....(3)	Notts. v. Surrey (Nottingham) 1937	
	Notts. v. Leics. (Worksop) 1937	
	Notts. v. Hants. (Nottingham) 1939	
Carey, P. A. D. ....(1)	Sussex v. Glamorgan (Hove) 1947	
Cartwright, G. H. M. ....(1)	Free Foresters v. Cambridge U. (Cambridge) 1920	
Chowdhury, N. R. ....(1)	Gen. Stewart's XI v. Gov. Bengal's XI (Calcutta) 1944–45	
Clark, E. W..........................(1)	Northants. v. West Indians (Northampton)..................1923	
Cobden, F. C. ....(1)	Cambridge U. v. Oxford U. (Lord's) 1870	
Coldwell, L. J. ....(1)	Worcs. v. Leics. (Stourbridge) 1957	
Constantine, L. N. ....(1)	West Indians v. Northants. (Northampton) 1928	
Cooke, R. ....(1)	Warwicks. v. Kent (Tunbridge Wells) 1925	
Copson, W. H. ....(3)	Derby v. Lancs. (Burton upon Trent) 1937	
	Derby v. Warwicks. (Derby) (4 in 4) 1937	
	Derby v. Oxford U. (Oxford)..............................1939	
Cousens, P. ....(1)	Essex v. Combined Services (Chelmsford) 1950	
Cox, A. L. ....(1)	Northants. v. Lancs. (Northampton) 1930	
Coxon, A. ....(1)	Yorks. v. Worcs. (Leeds) 1946	
Crisp, R. J. ....(3)	Western Province v. Griqualand West (Johannesburg)	
	(4 in 4) 1931–32	
	Western Province v. Transvaal (Johannesburg) 1931–32	
	Western Province v. Natal (Durban) (4 in 4) 1933–34	
Crossland, J. ....(1)	Lancs. v. Surrey (Oval) 1881	
Cuffe, J. A. ....(1)	Worcs. v. Hants. (Bournemouth) 1910	
Davidson, F. ....(1)	Derby v. Notts. (Derby) 1898	
Davidson, G. ....(2)	Derby v. Lancs. (Derby) 1895	
	Derby v. M.C.C. (Lord's) 1898	
Davies, E. ....(1)	Glamorgan v. Leics. (Leicester) 1937	
Davies, P. H. ....(1)	Oxford U. v. Middx. (Oxford) 1914	
Davies, R. E. ....(1)	Natal v. Western Province (Cape Town) 1934–35	
Dawson, O. C. ....(1)	South Africans v. Northants. (Northampton) 1947	
Dean, T. A. ....(1)	Hants. v. Worcs. (Bournemouth) 1939	
Dench, C. E. ....(1)	Notts. v. Glos. (Bristol) 1899	
Dennett, G. ....(2)	Glos. v. Northants. (Gloucester) 1907	
	Glos. v. Surrey (Bristol) 1913	
Dewdney, T. ....(1)	West Indians v. Hants. (Southampton) 1957	
Deyes, G. ....(1)	Yorks. v. Gentlemen of Ireland (Bray)..................1907	
Divecha, R. V. ....(1)	Indians v. Surrey (Oval) 1952	
Dixon, J. A. ....(1)	Notts. v. Lancs. (Nottingham) 1887	
Dollery, K. R. ....(2)	Warwicks. v. Glos. (Bristol) 1953	
	Warwicks. v. Kent (Coventry) 1956	
Dooland, B. ....(1)	South Australia v. Victoria (Melbourne) 1945–46	
Douglas, J. W. H. T. ....(3)	Essex v. Yorks. (Leyton)..............................1905	
	M.C.C. v. N.S.W. (Sydney) 1920–21	
	Essex v. Sussex (Leyton) 1923	
Downes, A. ....(1)	Otago v. Auckland (Dunedin) (4 in 4) 1893–94	
Drake, A. ....(2)	Yorks. v. Essex (Huddersfield) 1912	
	Yorks. v. Derby (Chesterfield) (4 in 4) 1914	
Durston, T. J. ....(2)	Middx. v. Cambridge U. (Cambridge) 1922	
	Middx. v. Oxford U. (Oxford) 1923	
Ebeling, H. I. ....(1)	Victoria v. Queensland (Melbourne) 1928–29	
Enthoven, H. J. ....(2)	Gentlemen v. Players (Lord's) 1926	
	Middx. v. Australians (Lord's) 1934	
Evans, H. ....(1)	Derby v. Sussex (Hove) 1881	
Evans, W. H. B. ....(1)	Oxford U. v. Notts. (Oxford)..............................1905	
Fannin, H. A. ....,.....................(1)	Hawke's Bay v. Taranaki (Napier) 1897–98	
Farnes, K. ....(1)	Essex v. Notts. (Clacton) 1939	
Farrands, F. H. ....(1)	M.C.C. v. Cambridge U. (Cambridge) 1872	
Faulkner, G. A. ....(2)	Transvaal v. Western Province (Cape Town) 1906–07	
	Transvaal v. Border (Cape Town) 1908–09	
Fender, P. G. H. ....(2)	Surrey v. Somerset (Oval) 1914	
	Surrey v. Glos. (Oval) 1924	
Field, F. E. ....(1)	Warwicks. v. Hants. (Birmingham) 1911	
Fisher, H. ....(1)	Yorks. v. Somerset (Sheffield) 1932	
Flanagan, M. ....(1)	M.C.C. v. Surrey (Lord's) 1876	

Flavell, J. ....(2) Worcs. v. Kent (Kidderminster) 1951
                                     Worcs. v. Cambridge U. (Cambridge) 1953
Fletcher, A. ....(1) Yorks. v. M.C.C. (Lord's) 1892
Flowers, W. ....(2) Notts. v. Kent (Maidstone) 1888
                                     M.C.C. v. Oxford U. (Oxford) 1892
Foster, D. G. ....(1) Warwicks. v. Hants. (Birmingham) 1929
Freeman, A. P. ....(3) Kent v. Middx. (Canterbury) 1920
                                     M.C.C. v. South Australia (Adelaide) 1922–23
                                     Kent v. Surrey (Blackheath) 1934
Freeman, G. ....(1) Yorks. v. Lancs. (Holbeck, Leeds) 1868
Frith, C. ....(1) Otago v. Canterbury (Dunedin) 1884–85
Fry, C. B. ....(1) Oxford U. v. M.C.C. (Lord's) 1894
Fulljames, R. E. G...............(1) R.A.F. v. Royal Navy (Oval)..................................1928
Geary, G. ....(1) Leics. v. Glos. (Bristol) 1922
Gibbs, K. ....(1) O.F.S. v. Eastern Province (Bloemfontein) 1952–53
Giffen, G. ....(3) Australians v. Lancs. (Manchester) 1884
                                     South Australia v. Vernon's XI (Adelaide) 1887–88
                                     Australians v. England XI (Wembley Park) 1896
Gilbert, G. H. B. ....(1) N.S.W. v. Victoria (Melbourne) 1857–58
Gilligan, A. E. R. ....(1) Sussex v. Surrey (Oval) 1923
Gladwin, C. ....(2) M.C.C. v. N.E. Transvaal (Benoni) 1948–49
                                     Derby v. New Zealanders (Derby) 1958
Goddard, T. L. ....(1) Natal v. Border (East London) 1959–60
Goddard, T. W. ....(6) Glos. v. Sussex (Eastbourne) 1924
                                     Glos. v. Glamorgan (Swansea) 1930
                                     England v. South Africa (Johannesburg) 1938–39
                                     M.C.C. v. Rhodesia (Salisbury) 1938–39
                                     Glos. v. Glamorgan (Swansea) 1947
                                     Glos. v. Somerset (Bristol) 1947
Gordon, N. ....(1) Transvaal v. Border (East London) 1937–38
Gothard, E. J. ....(1) Derby v. Middx. (Derby) 1947
Gover, A. R. ....(1) Surrey v. Worcs. (Worcester) (4 in 4) 1935
Grace, W. G. ....(1) M.C.C. v. Kent (Canterbury)..............................1874
Gregson, W. R. ....(1) Lancs. v. Leics. (Blackpool) 1906
Griffin, G. ....(1) South Africa v. England (Lord's) 1960
Grimmett, C. V. ....(1) South Australia v. Queensland (Brisbane) 1928–29
Grove, C. W. ....(1) Warwicks. v. Somerset (Taunton) 1947
Gunn, J. ....(2) Notts. v. Middx. (Lord's) 1899
                                     Notts. v. Derby (Chesterfield) 1904
Haigh, S. ....(5) Yorks. v. Derby (Bradford) 1897
                                     Hawke's XI v. Cape Province (Cape Town) 1898–99
                                     Yorks. v. Somerset (Sheffield) 1902
                                     M.C.C. v. Army XI (Pretoria) (4 in 4) 1905–06
                                     Yorks. v. Lancs. (Manchester) 1909
Halfyard, D. J. ....(2) Kent v. Worcs. (Folkestone) 1957
                                     Kent v. Leics. (Gillingham) 1958
Hall, W. ....(1) West Indies v. Pakistan (Lahore) 1958–59
Hallam, A. W. ....(1) Notts. v. Leics. (Nottingham) 1907
Hammersley, W. J. ....(1) M.C.C. v. Surrey (Oval) 1848
Hammond, H. E. ....(1) Sussex v. Warwicks. (Hove) 1946
Harvey, E. ....(1) Cambridge U. v. M.C.C. (Lord's) 1872
Haslip, S. M. ....(1) Middx. v. Notts. (Nottingham) 1919
Hay, H. ....(1) South Australia v. Hawke's XI (Adelaide) 1902–03
Hayward, T. ....(2) Surrey v. Glos. (Oval) 1899
                                     Surrey v. Derby (Chesterfield) 1899
Hayward, Thomas ....(1) Players v. Gentlemen (Lord's) 1870
Hazare, V. S. ....(1) Baroda v. Maharashtra (Poona) 1941–42
Hearne, A. ....(1) Kent v. Glos. (Clifton) 1900
Hearne, G. G. ....(2) Kent v. Lancs. (Manchester) 1875
                                     M.C.C. v. Yorks. (Lord's) 1888
Hearne, J. T. ....(4) Middx. v. Kent (Tonbridge) 1896
                                     England v. Australia (Leeds) 1899
                                     Middx. v. Essex (Lord's) 1902
                                     Middx. v. Warwicks. (Lord's) 1912
Hearne, J. W. ....(3) Middx. v. Essex (Lord's)....................................1911
                                     Middx. v. Kent (Lord's) 1914
                                     Middx. v. Essex (Leyton) 1922
Hearne, T. ....(1) Middx. v. Kent (Islington) 1868
Hearne, W. ....(1) Kent v. Lancs. (Tonbridge) 1894
Henderson, W. A. ....(1) N.E. Transvaal v. O.F.S. (Bloemfontein) (4 in 4) 1937–38
Herman, O. W. ....(1) Hants. v. Glamorgan (Portsmouth) 1938
Hesketh-Prichard, H. ....(1) M.C.C. v. Philadelphians (Haverford) 1907–08

Hide, J. B.	........................(1)	Sussex v. M.C.C. (Lord's) (4 in 4) 1890
Higgs, K.	...........................(1)	Lancs. v. Essex (Blackpool) 1960
Hill, A.	...............................(3)	Yorks. v. United South XI (Bradford) 1874
		Players v. Gentlemen (Lord's) 1874
		Yorks. v. Surrey (Oval) 1880
Hilton, J.	..............................(1)	Somerset v. Hants. (Weston-super-Mare)..................1955
Hipkin, A. B.	..........................(1)	Essex v. Lancs. (Blackpool) 1924
Hirst, G. H.	............................(2)	Yorks. v. Leics. (Leicester) 1895
		Yorks. v. Leics. (Hull)...1907
Hitch, J. W.	............................(2)	Surrey v. Cambridge U. (Oval) 1911
		Surrey v. Warwicks. (Oval) 1914
Hooker, J. E. H.	...................(1)	N.S.W. v. Victoria (Sydney) (4 in 4) 1928–29
Hopkins, A. J.	..................(2)	Australians v. Cambridge U. (Cambridge) 1902
		N.S.W. v. South Australia (Sydney) 1903–04
Horsley, W.	...........................(1)	Derby v. A.I.F. (Derby) 1919
Horton, M. J.	.......................(1)	Worcs. v. Somerset (Bath) 1956
Howard, T. H.	......................(1)	N.S.W. v. Queensland (Sydney) 1902–03
Howell, W. P.	......................(2)	Australians v. Western Province (Cape Town) 1902–03
		Australians v. New Zealand XI (Wellington) 1904–05
Howorth, R.	...........................(1)	Worcs. v. Warwicks. (Birmingham) 1950
Huggins, J. H.	.......................(1)	Glos. v. Notts (Nottingham) 1903
Humphreys, W.	...................(2)	Sussex v. Australians (Hove) 1880
		Sussex v. Australians (Hove) 1884
Ikin, J. T.	.............................(1)	Lancs. v. Somerset (Taunton) 1949
Ireland, J. F.	..........................(1)	Cambridge U. v. Oxford U. (Lord's) 1911
Ironmonger, H.	......................(1)	Victoria v. M.C.C. (Melbourne) 1924–25
Jackson, L.	..........................(2)	Derby v. Worcs. (Kidderminster) 1958
		Derby v. Worcs. (Derby) 1960
Jackson, P. F.	.......................(1)	Worcs. v. Glamorgan (Neath) 1936
Jackson, V. E.	......................(2)	Leics. v. Derby (Derby) 1946
		Leics. v. Surrey (Leicester) 1950
Jayes, T.	...........................(2)	Leics. v. Northants. (Leicester) 1906
		Leics. v. Kent (Maidstone) 1907
Jenkins, R. O.	.....................(3)	Worcs. v. Surrey (Oval) 1948
		Worcs. v. Surrey (Worcester) 1st inns. 1949
		Worcs. v. Surrey (Worcester) 2nd inns. 1949
Jephson, D. L. A.	...............(1)	Surrey v. Middx. (Oval) 1904
Jones, J. F.	........................(1)	Wellington v. Central Districts (Wellington) 1953–54
Jupp, V. W. C.	.................(5)	Sussex v. Surrey (Hove) 1911
		Sussex v. Essex (Leyton) 1919
		Sussex v. Essex (Colchester) 1921
		Northants. v. Glamorgan (Swansea) 1925
		Northants. v. Glos. (Bristol) 1931
Kennedy, A. S.	..................(3)	Hants. v. Glos. (Southampton) 1920
		Hants. v. Somerset (Bournemouth) 1920
		Hants. v. Glos. (Southampton) 1924
Kermode, A.	......................(1)	Lancs. v. Leics. (Leicester) 1906
Khot, J. B.	..........................(1)	Bombay v. Baroda (Bombay) 1943–44
King, J. H.	..........................(2)	Leics. v. Sussex (Hove) 1903
		Leics. v. Somerset (Weston-super-Mare) 1920
Kline, L.	...............................(1)	Australia v. South Africa (Cape Town) 1957–58
Knott, C. J.	..........................(1)	Gentlemen v. Players (Lord's) 1950
Kotze, J. J.	..........................(2)	Transvaal v. Griqualand West (Port Elizabeth) 1902–03
		Western Province v. Eastern Province (Cape Town) ...1904–05
Laker, J. C.	........................(4)	Warner's XI v. South of England (Hastings) 1947
		Surrey v. Glos. (Gloucester) 1951
		Surrey v. Warwicks. (Oval) 1953
		Surrey v. Cambridge U. (Guildford)...........................1953
Langridge, James	................(1)	Sussex v. Derby (Derby) 1939
Larwood, H.	.....................(2)	Notts. v. Cambridge U. (Cambridge) 1926
		Notts. v. Glamorgan (Nottingham) 1931
Lawrence, J.	......................(1)	Somerset v. Yorks. (Taunton) 1948
Lees, W. S.	.........................(1)	Surrey v. Hants. (Southampton) 1897
Lewis, C.	...........................(1)	Kent v. Notts. (Nottingham) 1939
Leyland, M.	.........................(1)	Yorks. v. Surrey (Sheffield) 1935
Loader, P. J.	.......................(1)	England v. West Indies (Leeds)..................................1957
Lock, G. A. R.	..................(3)	Surrey v. Somerset (Weston-super-Mare) 1955
		M.C.C. v. Bahawalpur XI (Bahawalpur) 1955–56
		M.C.C. v. Combined XI (Multan) 1955–56
Lockwood, W. H.	..............(3)	Surrey v. Cambridge U. (Cambridge) 1893
		Surrey v. Derby (Oval) 1901
		Surrey v. Yorks. (Sheffield) 1903

Lohmann, G. A. ....(1)	England v. South Africa (Port Elizabeth) 1895–96	
Lomax, J. G. ....(1)	Somerset v. Notts. (Weston-super-Mare).................1958	
Longfield, T. C. ....(1)	Bengal v. Bihar (Calcutta) 1937–38	
Louden, G. M. ....(1)	Essex v. Somerset (Southend).................1921	
Lowe, R. G. H. ....(1)	Cambridge U. v. Oxford U. (Lord's) 1926	
Macaulay, G. G. ....(4)	Yorks. v. Warwicks. (Birmingham) 1923	
	Yorks. v. Leics. (Hull).................1930	
	Yorks. v. Glamorgan (Cardiff) 1933	
	Yorks. v. Lancs. (Manchester) 1933	
Maile, J. H. ....(1)	Western Province v. Rhodesia (Salisbury) 1958–59	
Marlar, R. G. ....(1)	Cambridge U. v. Essex (Cambridge).................1952	
Marlow, J. ....(1)	Derby v. Kent (Derby) 1884	
Marriott, C. S. ....(1)	M.C.C. v. Madras (Madras) 1933–34	
Martin, F.................(2)	Kent v. Surrey (Oval) 1890	
	M.C.C. v. Derby (Lord's) (4 in 4) 1895	
Matthews, T. J. ....(4)	Victoria v. Tasmania (Launceston) 1908–09	
	Australia v. South Africa (Manchester) 1st inns 1912	
	Australia v. South Africa (Manchester) 2nd inns 1912	
	Australians v. Philadelphians (Germantown) 1912–13	
McCarthy, C. N. ....(1)	South Africans v. Sussex (Hove) 1951	
McConnon, J. E.................(1)	Glamorgan v. South Africans (Swansea) 1951	
McDonald, E. A. ....(3)	Lancs. v. Sussex (Hove) 1925	
	Lancs. v. Kent (Dover) 1926	
	Lancs. v. Warwicks. (Birmingham) 1930	
McKibbin, T. R. ....(1)	Australians v. Lancs. (Liverpool) 1896	
Melle, B. G. ....(1)	Oxford U. v. Scotland (Oxford) 1913	
Melville, A. ....(1)	Oxford U. v. Leveson-Gower's XI (Eastbourne) 1932	
Mercer, J. ....(1)	Glamorgan v. Surrey (Oval) 1932	
Merchant, V. M. ....(1)	Pereira's XI v. Mehta's XI (Bombay) 1946–47	
Middleton, F. S. ....(1)	Wellington v. Hawke's Bay (Wellington) 1919–20	
Mills, P. T. ....(1)	Glos. v. Hants. (Clifton) 1920	
Moir, A. M. ....(1)	Otago v. Canterbury (Christchurch) 1950–51	
Mold, A. ....(2)	Lancs. v. Somerset (Manchester) 1894	
	Lancs. v. Notts. (Nottingham) (4 in 4).................1895	
Moore, F. W. ....(1)	Lancs. v. Essex (Chelmsford) 1956	
More, R. E. ....(1)	Bosanquet's XI v. Philadelphians (Philadelphia) 1901–02	
Morton, F. L. ....(1)	Victoria v. Tasmania (Melbourne) 1931–32	
Morton, P. H. ....(1)	Cambridge U. v. Oxford U. (Lord's) 1880	
Moss, A. E. ....(1)	Middx. v. Glos. (Lord's) 1956	
Mubarak Ali ....(1)	Nawanagar v. Western India States (Poona) 1936–37	
Muddiah, V. M. ....(1)	Services v. East Punjab (New Delhi) 1955–56	
Mulcock, E. T. ....(1)	Canterbury v. Otago (Christchurch) 1937–38	
Munden, V. S. ....(1)	Leics. v. Derby (Ashby-de-la-Zouch) 1953	
Murdin, V. ....(1)	Northants. v. Kent (Northampton) 1920	
Murray, R. McK. ....(1)	Wellington v. Otago (Wellington) 1949–50	
Narottam, D. ....(1)	Kathiwar v. Baroda (Dhrol).................1947–48	
Nayudu, C. S. ....(1)	Indians v. Surrey (Oval) 1946	
Needham, P. G. ....(1)	Transvaal v. Eastern Province (Johannesburg) 1951–52	
Newman, J. A.................(1)	Hants. v. Australians (Southampton) 1909	
Newstead, J. T. ....(1)	Yorks. v. Worcs. (Bradford) 1907	
Nichols, M. S. ....(1)	Essex v. Yorks. (Leeds) 1931	
Noble, M. A. ....(1)	N.S.W. v. Tasmania (Sydney) 1898–99	
Oakman, A. S. M. ....(1)	Sussex v. Somerset (Hove) 1952	
O'Connor, J. ....(1)	Essex v. Worcs. (Worcester) 1925	
Odell, W. W. ....(2)	London County v. M.C.C. (Lord's) 1904	
	Leics. v. Northants. (Leicester) 1908	
Oliff, C. ....(1)	Auckland v. Wellington (Auckland) 1912–13	
Orchard, S. A. ....(1)	Canterbury v. Auckland (Auckland) 1909–10	
Orton, C. T. ....(1)	Europeans v. Muslims (Bombay) 1938–39	
Overton, G. W. F. ....(1)	Otago v. Canterbury (Christchurch) 1946–47	
Owen-Smith, H. G. ....(2)	Oxford U. v. Leveson-Gower's XI (Folkestone) 1931	
	Gentlemen v. Players (Folkestone) 1935	
Oxenham, R. K. ....(1)	Australians v. Ceylon (Colombo) 1935–36	
Paine, G. A. E. ....(2)	Warwicks. v. Middx. (Lord's) 1932	
	Warwicks. v. Glamorgan (Cardiff) 1933	
Palmer, G. E. ....(2)	Australians v. Sussex (Hove) 1882	
	Victoria v. South Australia (Melbourne) 1882–83	
Parakh, M. D. ....(1)	Parsis v. Hindus (Bombay) 1912–13	
Parker, C. W. L. ....(6)	Glos. v. Yorks. (Bristol) 1922	
	Glos. v. Middx. (Bristol) 1st inns 1924	
	Glos. v. Middx. (Bristol) 2nd inns 1924	
	Glos. v. Surrey (Oval) 1924	

Parker, C. W. L. (*cont.*)	Glos. v. Yorks. (Hull)	1926
	Glos. v. Essex (Chelmsford)	1930
Partridge, R. J. ....(1)	Northants. v. Notts. (Nottingham)	1946
Peach, H. A. ....(1)	Surrey v. Sussex (Oval) (4 in 4)	1924
Pearson, F. ....(1)	Worcs. v. Surrey (Worcester)	1914
Peate, E. ....(2)	Yorks. v. Kent (Sheffield)	1882
	Yorks. v. Glos. (Moreton-in-the-Marsh)	1884
Peebles, I. A. R. ....(1)	Middx. v. Glos. (Lord's)	1932
Peel, R. ....(1)	Yorks. v. Kent (Halifax)	1897
Pegler, S. J. ....(1)	South Africans v. Yorks. (Huddersfield)	1912
Pepper, C. G. ....(1)	Commonwealth v. Holkar (Indore)	1949–50
Perks, R. T. D. ....(2)	Worcs. v. Kent (Stourbridge)	1931
	Worcs. v. Warwicks. (Birmingham)	1933
Phillips, R. R. ....(1)	Border v. Eastern Province (Port Elizabeth)	1939–40
Pieris, P. L. ....(1)	Cambridge U. v. Jardine's XI (Eastbourne)	1958
Platts, J. ....(1)	Derby v. Yorks. (Derby)	1880
Plowden, H. M. ....(1)	Cambridge U. v. M.C.C. (Cambridge)	1862
Pollard, R. ....(2)	Lancs. v. Glamorgan (Preston)	1939
	Lancs. v. Warwicks. (Blackpool)	1947
Pope, G. H. ....(1)	Derby v. Notts. (Ilkeston)	1947
Pougher, A. D. ....(1)	M.C.C. v. Cambridge U. (Lord's)	1887
Preece, C. A. ....(1)	Worcs. v. Warwicks. (Birmingham)	1924
Pritchard, T. L. ....(3)	Warwicks. v. Leics. (Birmingham)	1948
	Warwicks. v. Kent (Maidstone)	1949
	Warwicks. v. Glamorgan (Birmingham)	1951
Ramadhin, K. T. ....(1)	West Indians v. Hyderabad (Hyderabad)	1958–59
Rangachari, C. R. ....(1)	Indians v. Tasmania (Hobart)	1947–48
Ranjane, V. R. ....(1)	Maharashtra v. Saurashtra (Khadakvasla)	1956–57
Read, H. D. ....(1)	Essex v. Glos. (Bristol)	1935
Read, W. W. ....(1)	Gentlemen v. Sherwin's Notts. XI (Scarborough)	1891
Reid, R. ....(1)	Wellington v. Otago (Dunedin)	1958–59
Relf, A. E. ....(1)	Sussex v. Worcs. (Hove)	1902
Rhodes, A. E. G. ....(5)	Derby v. Ireland (Buxton)	1947
	M.C.C. v. Surrey (Lord's)	1948
	Derby v. Essex (Colchester)	1948
	Derby v. Oxford U. (Oxford)	1950
	Derby v. Sussex (Derby)	1951
Rhodes, W. ....(1)	Yorks. v. Derby (Derby)	1920
Richardson, T. ....(4)	Surrey v. Glos. (Oval)	1893
	Surrey v. Leics. (Oval)	1896
	Surrey v. Warwicks. (Oval)	1898
	Surrey v. Sussex (Hove)	1898
Richmond, L. B. ....(1)	Notts. v. Lancs. (Nottingham)	1926
Ridgway, F. ....(2)	Kent v. Derby (Folkestone) (4 in 4)	1951
	Kent v. Oxford U. (Oxford)	1958
Robins, R. W. V. ....(2)	Middx. v. Leics. (Lord's)	1929
	Middx. v. Somerset (Lord's)	1937
Robinson, E. ....(2)	Yorks. v. Sussex (Hull)	1928
	Yorks. v. Kent (Gravesend)	1930
Robinson, E. P. ....(1)	Yorks. v. Kent (Leeds)	1939
Robson, E. ....(2)	Somerset v. Hants. (Bath)	1898
	Somerset v. Yorks. (Taunton)	1902
Roller, W. E. ....(1)	Surrey v. Sussex (Oval)	1885
Rorke, G. ....(1)	N.S.W. v. Queensland (Sydney)	1958–59
Rought-Rought, R. C. ....(1)	Cambridge U. v. Sussex (Hove)	1932
Rylott, A. ....(1)	M.C.C. v. Derby (Lord's)	1884
Sadler, W. ....(1)	Surrey v. Cambridge U. (Oval)	1923
Sarwate, C. T. ....(1)	Holkar v. Bihar (Jamshedpur)	1948–49
Sayer, D. M. ....(1)	Oxford U. v. Kent (Oxford)	1958
Sedgwick, H. ....(1)	Yorks. v. Worcs. (Hull)	1906
Sen, P. ....(1)	Bengal v. Orissa (Cuttack)	1954–55
Shacklock, F. ....(1)	Notts. v. Somerset (Nottingham) (4 in 4)	1893
Shaw, A. ....(3)	Notts. v. Derby (Derby)	1875
	Notts. v. Glos. (Nottingham) 1st inns	1884
	Notts. v. Glos. (Nottingham) 2nd inns	1884
Shepherd, T. F. ....(1)	Surrey v. Glos. (Oval)	1926
Shepstone, G. H. ....(1)	Transvaal v. Border (Port Elizabeth)	1902–03
Shipman, W. ....(1)	Leics. v. Derby (Leicester)	1909
Simms, H. L. ....(1)	Europeans v. Muslims (Poona)	1915–16
Sims, J. M. ....(1)	Middx. v. South Africans (Lord's)	1947
Smales, K. ....(1)	Notts. v. Lancs. (Nottingham)	1955
Smith, C. I. J. ....(1)	Middx. v. Lancs. (Manchester)	1939

Smith, D. V. ....(2) M.C.C. v. Oxford U. (Lord's) 1956
                                     Sussex v. Cambridge U. (Cambridge) 1958
Smith, S. G. ....(2) Northants. v. Leics. (Leicester) 1912
                                     Northants. v. Warwicks. (Birmingham) (4 in 4) 1914
Smith, V. I. ....(2) Natal v. Border (Pietermaritzburg) 1946–47
                                     South Africans v. Derby (Derby) 1947
Smith, W. C. ....(2) Surrey v. Hants. (Oval) 1908
                                     Surrey v. Northants. (Oval) 1910
Somers-Cox, A. ....(1) Barbados v. Priestley's XI (Barbados) 1896–97
Southerton, J. ....(1) South v. North (Sheffield) 1869
Spofforth, F. R. ....(3) Australians v. M.C.C. (Lord's) 1878
                                     Australia v. England (Melbourne) 1878–79
                                     Australians v. South (Oval) 1884
Statham, J. B. ....(3) Lancs. v. Sussex (Manchester) 1956
                                     M.C.C. v. Transvaal (Johannesburg) 1956–57
                                     Lancs. v. Leics. (Manchester) 1958
Steel, A. G. ....(1) Cambridge U. v. Oxford U. (Lord's) 1879
Stephenson, H. H. ....(1) England v. Kent (Lord's) 1858
Tarrant, F. A. ....(5) Middx. v. Glos. (Bristol) (4 in 4) 1907
                                     M.C.C. v. Cambridge U. (Cambridge) 1908
                                     Middx. v. Surrey (Lord's) 1909
                                     Middx. v. Glos. (Bristol)..............................1909
                                     Middx. v. Somerset (Bath) 1911
Tate, F. W. ....(1) Sussex v. Surrey (Oval) 1901
Tate, M. W. ....(3) Sussex v. Middx. (Lord's) 1926
                                     Rest of England v. Lancs. (Oval) 1926
                                     Sussex v. Northants. (Peterborough) 1934
Tattersall, R. ....(1) Lancs. v. Notts. (Manchester) 1953
Tayfield, H. J. ....(2) Natal v. Transvaal (Durban) 1946–47
                                     South Africans v. Victoria (Melbourne) 1952–53
Thomas, A. E. ....(1) Northants. v. Leics. (Northampton) 1927
Thompson, G. J. ....(1) Northants. v. Lancs. (Manchester) 1907
Thompson, R. G. ....(1) Warwicks. v. Sussex (Horsham) 1956
Thorbourn, D. ....(1) Jamaica v. Leeward Islands (Kingston) 1958–59
Toone, P. ....(1) Essex v. Kent (Leyton) 1920
Townsend, C. L. ....(1) Glos. v. Somerset (Cheltenham) 1893
Townsend, L. F. ....(1) Derby v. Northants. (Northampton) 1931
Treanor, J. ....(1) N.S.W. v. Queensland (Brisbane) 1954–55
Tremlin, B. ....(1) Essex v. Derby (Derby) 1914
Trott, A. E. ....(2) Middx. v. Somerset (Lord's) (4 in 4) 1907
                                     Middx. v. Somerset (Lord's) same inns 1907
Trueman, F. S. ....(3) Yorks. v. Notts. (Nottingham) 1951
                                     Yorks. v. Notts. (Scarborough) 1955
                                     Yorks. v. M.C.C. (Lord's) 1958
Trumble, H. ....(3) Australians v. Glos. (Cheltenham) 1896
                                     Australia v. England (Melbourne) 1901–02
                                     Australia v. England (Melbourne) 1903–04
Turner, C. T. B. ....(1) N.S.W. v. Victoria (Melbourne) 1886–87
Tyldesley, James ....(2) Lancs. v. Derby (Manchester) 1920
                                     Lancs. v. Worcs. (Manchester) 1922
Tyldesley, R. ....(1) Lancs. v. Derby (Derby) (4 in 4) 1929
Tyler, E. J. ....(1) Somerset v. Yorks. (Taunton) 1895
Ulyett, G. ....(2) Lord Harris' XI v. N.S.W. (Sydney) (4 in 4)..........1878–79
                                     Yorks. v. Lancs. (Sheffield) 1883
Verity, H. ....(2) Yorks. v. Notts. (Leeds) 1932
                                     M.C.C. Australian XI v. Leveson-Gower's XI (Scarborough) 1937
Waddington, A. ....(1) Yorks. v. Northants. (Northampton) 1920
Wainwright, E. ....(1) Yorks. v. Sussex (Dewsbury) 1894
Waite, M. G. ....(1) South Australia v. M.C.C. (Adelaide) 1935–36
Walker, A. K. ....(2) N.S.W. v. Queensland (Sydney) 1948–49
                                     Notts. v. Leics. (Leicester) (4 in 4) 1956
Walker, Ashley ....(1) Cambridge U. v. Surrey (Oval)..........................1865
Walsh, J. E. ....(1) Leics. v. Notts. (Loughborough) 1949
Ward, A. S. ....(1) Griqualand West v. O.F.S. (Kimberley)..............1926–27
Warr, J. J. ....(1) Middx. v. Leics. (Loughborough) 1956
Wass, T. ....(1) Notts. v. Essex (Nottingham)...........................1908
Weighell, W. B. ....(1) Cambridge U. v. M.C.C. (Lord's) 1866
Wellard, A. W. ....(1) Somerset v. Leics. (Leicester) 1929
Wells, Joseph ....(1) Kent v. Sussex (Brighton) (4 in 4) 1862
Wells, W. ....(1) Northants. v. Notts. (Northampton) 1910
Wensley, A. F. ....(1) Sussex v. Middx. (Lord's) 1935
Whateley, E. G. ....(1) Oxford U. v. Philadelphians (Oxford) 1903

White, G. C. ...(1)	South Africans v. Kent (Canterbury) ...1904	
White, J. C. ...(1)	Somerset v. Middx. (Lord's) ...1923	
Whitehead, R. ...(1)	Lancs. v. Surrey (Manchester) ...1912	
Wilkinson, L. L. ...(1)	Lancs. v. Sussex (Hove) ...1938	
Willsher, E. ...(1)	Players of South v. Gentlemen of South (Oval) ...1868	
Wilson, D. ...(1)	Yorks. v. Notts. (Middlesbrough) ...1959	
Wilson, E. R. ...(1)	Gentlemen v. Players (Scarborough)...1919	
Wilson, G. A. ...(3)	Worcs. v. London Co. (Worcester) ...1900	
	Worcs. v. Surrey (Worcester) ...1901	
	Worcs. v. Australians (Worcester)...1905	
Wiltshire, G. G. M. ...(1)	Glos. v. Yorks. (Leeds) ...1958	
Woods, S. M. J. ...(1)	Cambridge U. v. Thornton's XI (Cambridge) ...1888	
Woolley, C. N. ...(1)	Northants. v. Essex (Northampton) ...1920	
Woolley, F. E. ...(1)	Kent v. Surrey (Blackheath) ...1919	
Wooster, G. ...(1)	Northants. v. Dublin U. (Northampton) ...1925	
Wootton, G....(1)	M.C.C. v. Sussex (Lord's) ...1863	
Wright, A. C. ...(1)	Kent v. Warwicks. (Tunbridge Wells) ...1925	
Wright, D. V. P. ...(7)	Kent v. Worcs. (Worcester) ...1937	
	Kent v. Notts. (Nottingham) ...1937	
	Kent v. Glos. (Gillingham) ...1938	
	M.C.C. v. Border (East London) ...1938–39	
	Kent v. Glos. (Bristol)...1939	
	Kent v. Sussex (Hastings) ...1947	
	Kent v. Hants. (Canterbury) ...1949	
Wyatt, R. E. S. ...(1)	M.C.C. v. Ceylon (Colombo) ...1926–27	
Young, H. ...(1)	Essex v. Leics. (Leyton) ...1907	
Young, J. A. ...(2)	Middx. v. Northants. (Northampton) ...1946	
	Middx. v. Lancs. (Lord's) ...1951	

Four Wickets with Five Successive Balls

J. Southerton	Surrey v. Lancashire (Oval)	1869
S. E. Butler	Oxford U. v. M.C.C. (Oxford)	1871
W. F. Neilson	Canterbury v. Otago (Christchurch)	1876–77
W. Flowers	A. Shaw's XI v. T. Emmett's XI (Bradford)	1881
G. A. Lohmann	Surrey v. Lancashire (Manchester)	1888
A. Downes	Otago v. Canterbury (Dunedin)	1891–92
J. T. Hearne	Middlesex v. Essex (Lord's)	1902
F. S. Jackson	Yorkshire v. Australians (Leeds)	1902
T. H. Howard	New South Wales v. Queensland (Sydney)	1902–03
W. P. Howell	Australians v. Western Province (Cape Town)	1902–03
G. A. Wilson	Worcestershire v. Gloucestershire (Cheltenham)	1903
G. J. Thompson	Northamptonshire v. Leicestershire (Leicester)	1905
W. R. Gregson	Lancashire v. Leicestershire (Blackpool)	1906
C. Blythe	Kent v. Surrey (Blackheath)	1910
J. W. Hitch	Surrey v. Cambridge U. (Oval)	1911
S. J. Pegler	South Africans v. M.C.C. (Lord's)	1912
H. B. Fawcus	Army v. Royal Navy (Lord's)	1913
M. F. S. Jewell	Worcestershire v. Gloucestershire (Cheltenham)	1919
C. W. L. Parker	Gloucestershire v. Warwickshire (Bristol)	1920
A. Waddington	Yorkshire v. Northamptonshire (Northampton)	1920
W. E. Benskin	Leicestershire v. Derbyshire (Leicester)	1921
C. W. L. Parker	Gloucestershire v. Yorkshire (Bristol)	1922
M. W. Tate	England v. Rest—Trial match (Lord's)	1923
L. Cook	Sharp's XI v. Tennyson's XI (Blackpool)	1923
R. Cooke	Warwickshire v. Kent (Tunbridge Wells)	1925
P. G. H. Fender	Surrey v. Middlesex (Lord's)	1927
G. O. Allen	Middlesex v. Lancashire (Lord's)	1929
M. J. C. Allom	England v. New Zealand (Christchurch)	1929–30
A. L. Cox	Northamptonshire v. Lancashire (Northampton)	1930
R. J. Crisp	Western Province v. Transvaal (Johannesburg)	1931–32
G. G. Macaulay	Yorkshire v. Lancashire (Manchester)	1933
T. A. Dean	Hampshire v. Worcestershire (Bournemouth)	1939
W. H. Copson	Derbyshire v. Oxford U. (Oxford)	1939
James Langridge	Sussex v. Somerset (Weston-super-Mare)	1948
J. Lawrence	Somerset v. Yorkshire (Taunton)	1948
C. Gladwin	M.C.C. v. North Eastern Transvaal (Benoni)	1948–49
A. J. Watkins	Glamorgan v. Derbyshire (Chesterfield)	1954
A. Brown	Kent v. Nottinghamshire (Folkestone)	1959

* L

Good Bowling Spells

A number of bowlers have succeeded in taking several wickets very quickly with a small number of deliveries, the leading cases being given.

Wkts. Balls

10 in 42	A. Drake: Yorks. v. Somerset (Weston-super-Mare) 1914
10 in 52	H. Verity: Yorks. v. Notts. (Leeds) 1932
9 in 38	A. Drake: Yorks. v. Somerset (Weston-super-Mare) 1914
9 in 39	H. Verity: Yorks. v. Notts (Leeds) 1932
9 in 39	H. Verity: Yorks. v. Kent (Sheffield) 1936
9 in 44	T. W. Wall: South Australia v. N.S.W. (Sydney) 1932–33
9 in 47	A. P. Freeman: Kent v. Sussex (Hove) 1922
8 in 23	A. Drake: Yorks. v. Somerset (Weston-super-Mare) 1914
8 in 24	G. E. Tribe: Northants. v. Yorks. (Northampton) 1958
8 in 32	K. T. Ramadhin: West Indians v. Glos. (Cheltenham) 1950
8 in 34	H. Verity: Yorks. v. Notts (Leeds) 1932
8 in 34	J. E. D. Sealey: Barbados v. Trinidad (Barbados) 1941–42
8 in 36	G. Dennett: Glos. v. Northants. (Gloucester) 1907
8 in 36	T. B. Mitchell: Derby v. Worcs. (Stourbridge) 1934
8 in 36	H. Verity: Yorks. v. Kent (Sheffield) 1936
8 in 39	A. P. Freeman: Kent v. Sussex (Hove) 1922
8 in 39	W. H. R. Andrews: Somerset v. Surrey (Oval) 1937
8 in 40	W. G. Grace: Glos. v. Yorks. (Clifton) 1877
7 in 15	H. Verity: Yorks. v. Notts. (Leeds) 1932
7 in 17	W. G. Grace: Glos. v. Notts. (Cheltenham) 1877
7 in 19	R. Tattersall: Lancs. v. Notts. (Manchester) 1953
7 in 20	A. Mold: Lancs. v. Somerset (Manchester) 1894
7 in 20	J. H. King: Leics. v. Yorks. (Leicester) 1911
7 in 20	A. Drake: Yorks. v. Somerset (Weston-super-Mare) 1914
7 in 20	P. G. H. Fender: Surrey v. Middlesex (Oval) 1927
7 in 22	R. Appleyard: Yorks. v. Somerset (Taunton) 1954
7 in 22	J. C. Laker: England v. Australia (Manchester) 1956
7 in 23	W. H. Copson: Derby v. Warwicks. (Derby) 1937
7 in 24	W. Rhodes: Thornton's XI v. Australians (Scarborough) 1899
7 in 24	F. E. Woolley: Kent v. Surrey (Oval) 1911
7 in 24	H. Verity: Yorks. v. Kent (Sheffield) 1936
7 in 25	J. W. Hearne: Middx. v. Essex (Lord's) 1910
7 in 25	V. W. C. Jupp: Northants. v. Glamorgan (Swansea) 1925
7 in 25	T. W. Durnell: Warwicks. v. Northants. (Birmingham) 1927
7 in 25	R. J. Crisp: Western Province v. Griqualand West (Johannesburg)............1931–32
7 in 25	A. P. Freeman: Kent v. Somerset (Taunton) 1935
7 in 26	K. T. Ramadhin: West Indians v. Glos. (Cheltenham) 1950
7 in 26	M. G. Melle: Transvaal v. Griqualand West (Johannesburg) 1950–51
7 in 28	A. Cotter: Australians v. Worcs. (Worcester) 1905
7 in 28	W. Rhodes: Yorks. v. Essex (Leyton) 1929
7 in 29	J. E. D. Sealey: Barbados v. Trinidad (Barbados) 1941–42
7 in 29	T. E. Bailey: Essex v. Glamorgan (Brentwood) 1950
7 in 30	T. Wass: Notts. v. Sussex (Hove)..1902
6 in 12	P. G. H. Fender: Surrey v. Middx. (Lord's) 1927
6 in 12	R. J. Crisp: Western Province v. Griqualand West (Johannesburg)............1931–32
6 in 13	T. B. Mitchell: Derby v. Middx. (Derby) 1934
6 in 13	H. Verity: Yorks. v. Kent (Sheffield) 1936
6 in 13	W. H. Copson: Derby v. Warwicks. (Derby) 1937
6 in 14	S. E. Butler: Oxford U. v. Cambridge U. (Lord's) 1871
6 in 14	A. S. Kennedy: Hants. v. Warwicks. (Portsmouth) 1927
6 in 14	H. Verity: Yorks. v. Notts. (Leeds) 1932
6 in 15	P. G. H. Fender: Surrey v. Middx. (Lord's) 1927
5 in 6	W. H. Copson: Derby v. Warwicks. (Derby) 1937
5 in 6	W. A. Henderson: N.E. Transvaal v. O.F.S. (Bloemfontein) 1937–38
5 in 7	J. Briggs: Lancs. v. Sussex (Manchester) 1890
5 in 7	E. Wainwright: Yorks. v. Sussex (Dewsbury) 1894
5 in 7	P. H. Clark: Philadelphians v. Bosanquet's XI (Philadelphia) 1901–02
5 in 7	P. G. H. Fender: Surrey v. Middx. (Lord's) 1927
5 in 7	T. W. Goddard: Glos. v. Glamorgan (Swansea) 1930
5 in 7	T. W. Goddard: Glos. v. Somerset (Bristol) 1947
5 in 8	J. W. H. T. Douglas: Essex v. Yorks. (Leyton) 1905

Wkts. Balls
| | | |
5 in 8 R. J. Crisp: Western Province v. Griqualand West (Johannesburg)................1931–32
5 in 9 C. F. Root: Worcs. v. Glos. (Cheltenham)..1924
5 in 9 V. W. C. Jupp: Northants. v. Worcs. (Dudley)....................................1928
5 in 9 J. E. Walsh: Leics. v. Notts (Nottingham) 1946
5 in 9 D. Shackleton: Hants. v. Leics. (Leicester)....................................1950
5 in 9 T. E. Bailey: Pearce's XI v. Indians (Scarborough) 1952
5 in 10 S. Haigh: Yorks. v. Derby (Bradford)...1897
5 in 10 C. Blythe: Kent v. Surrey (Blackheath) 1910
5 in 10 J. N. Fraser: Oxford U. v. Leveson-Gower's XI (Eastbourne) 1912
5 in 10 C. W. L. Parker: Glos. v. Warwicks. (Bristol) 1920
5 in 10 H. Verity: Yorks. v. Kent (Sheffield) 1936

All Ten Wickets in an Innings

O.	M.	R.		
			E. Hinkly: Kent v. England (Lord's)	1848
			J. Wisden: North v. South (Lord's)	1850
43	—17—	74	V. E. Walker: England v. Surrey (Oval)	1859
32·2—	7—	69	E. M. Grace: M.C.C. v. Gentlemen of Kent (Canterbury)..............	1862
44·2—	—104		V. E. Walker: Middx. v. Lancs. (Manchester)	1865
			G. Wootton: All England XI v. Yorks. (Sheffield)	1865
24·1—11—	38		S. E. Butler: Oxford U. v. Cambridge U. (Lord's)	1871
60·2—22—129			James Lillywhite: South v. North (Canterbury)	1872
36·2—	8—	73	A. Shaw: M.C.C. v. North (Lord's)	1874
29	—11—	43	E. Barratt: Players v. Australians (Oval)	1878
26	—10—	66	G. Giffen: Australian XI v. Rest (Sydney)	1883–84
36·2—17—	49		W. G. Grace: M.C.C. v. Oxford U. (Oxford)	1886
52·3—25—	59		G. Burton: Middx. v. Surrey (Oval)	1888
21 3—10—	28		A. E. Moss: Canterbury v. Wellington (Christchurch)	1889–90
31	— 6—	69	S. M. J. Woods: Cambridge U. v. Thornton's XI (Cambridge)	1890
15·3—	3—	45	T. Richardson: Surrey v. Essex (Oval)	1894
27	—11—	32	H. Pickett: Essex v. Leics. (Leyton)	1895
34·3—15—	49		E. J. Tyler: Somerset v. Surrey (Taunton)	1895
23·2—14—	28		W. P. Howell: Australians v. Surrey (Oval)	1899
25·2—	0—	48	C. H. G. Bland: Sussex v. Kent (Tonbridge)........................	1899
14·2—	5—	42	A. E. Trott: Middx. v. Somerset (Taunton)	1900
28·5—	7—	55	J. Briggs: Lancs. v. Worcs. (Manchester)	1900
24·5—	1—	90	A. Fielder: Players v. Gentlemen (Lord's)	1906
19·4—	7—	40	G. Dennett: Glos. v. Essex (Bristol)	1906
12	— 2—	26	A. E. E. Vogler: Eastern Province v. Griqualand West (Johannesburg) ...	1906–07
16	— 7—	30	C. Blythe: Kent v. Northants. (Northampton)	1907
8·5—	0—	35	A. Drake: Yorks. v. Somerset (Weston-super-Mare)	1914
19	— 2—	40	W. Bestwick: Derby v. Glamorgan (Cardiff)..........................	1921
28·4—	5—	66	A. A. Mailey: Australians v. Glos. (Cheltenham)	1921
42·2—11—	76		J. C. White: Somerset v. Worcs. (Worcester)	1921
17·5—	4—	43	T. Rushby: Surrey v. Somereset (Taunton)	1921
40·3—13—	79		C. W. L. Parker: Glos. v. Somerset (Bristol)	1921
19·3—	4—	65	G. G. Collins: Kent v. Notts. (Dover)	1922
25·1—	5—	51	H. Howell: Warwicks. v. Yorks. (Birmingham)	1923
22·4—10—	37		A. S. Kennedy: Players v. Gentlemen (Oval)	1927
25·3—10—	40		G. O. Allen: Middx. v. Lancs. (Lord's)	1929
42	— 9—131		A. P. Freeman: Kent v. Lancs. (Maidstone)	1929
16·2—	8—	18	G. Geary: Leics. v. Glamorgan (Pontypridd)	1929
22·3—	8—	37	C. V. Grimmett: Australians v. Yorks. (Sheffield)	1930
30·4—	8—	53	A. P. Freeman: Kent v. Essex (Southend)	1930
18·4—	6—	36	H. Verity: Yorks. v. Warwicks. (Leeds)	1931
36·1—	9—	79	A. P. Freeman: Kent v. Lancs. (Manchester)	1931
39	— 6—127		V. W. C. Jupp: Northants. v. Kent (Tunbridge Wells)	1932
19·4—16—	10		H. Verity: Yorks. v. Notts. (Leeds)	1932
12·4—	2—	36	T. W. Wall: South Australia v. N.S.W. (Sydney)	1932–33
19·1—	4—	64	T. B. Mitchell: Derby v. Leics. (Leicester)	1935
26	—10—	51	J. Mercer: Glamorgan v. Worcs. (Worcester)	1936
28·4—	4—113		T. W. Goddard: Glos. v. Worcs. (Cheltenham)	1937
17·1—	5—	47	T. F. Smailes: Yorks. v. Derby (Sheffield).........................	1939
24·1—	8—	67	E. A. Watts: Surrey v. Warwicks. (Birmingham)	1939
20·4—	4—	49	W. E. Hollies: Warwicks. v. Notts. (Birmingham)	1946
18·4—	2—	90	J. M. Sims: East v. West (Kingston)	1948

O.   M.   R.

18·4—	2—	66	J. K. Graveney: Glos. v. Derby (Chesterfield)	....	1949
39·4—	9—	90	T. E. Bailey: Essex v. Lancs. (Clacton)	....	1949
36·2—	9—	102	R. Berry: Lancs. v. Worcs. (Blackpool)	....	1953
24·2—	7—	78	S. P. Gupte: Bombay v. Pakistan Services (Bombay)	....	1954–55
46 —	18—	88	J. C. Laker: Surrey v. Australians (Oval)	....	1956
41·3—	20—	66	K. Smales: Notts. v. Glos. (Stroud)	....	1956
29·1—	18—	54	G. A. R. Lock: Surrey v. Kent (Blackheath)	....	1956
51·2—	23—	53	J. C. Laker: England v. Australia (Manchester)	....	1956
19 —	11—	20	P. Chatterjee: Bengal v. Assam (Jorhat)	....	1956–57
23·3—	11—	41	J. D. Bannister: Warwicks. v. Combined Services (Birmingham)	....	1959

Only one bowler went on to take 17 wickets in a match, C. Blythe taking 17 wickets in a day at a personal cost of 48 runs, for Kent v. Northamptonshire (Northampton) 1907.

E. M. Grace (1862) took all ten wickets in an innings in a twelve-a-side match, one batsman being absent.

W. P. Howell achieved the feat against Surrey in 1899 in his first match in England.

W. G. Grace, playing for M.C.C. v. Kent (Canterbury), 1873, took 10 wickets at a cost of 92 runs (46·1 overs) in an innings in a twelve-a-side match.

Nine or Ten Wickets in an Innings

Allen, G. O.	(1)	10—40	Middx. v. Lancs. (Lord's) 1929
Allom, M. J. C.	(1)	9—55	Cambridge U. v. Army (Cambridge) 1927
Appleby, A.	(1)	9—25	Lancs. v. Sussex (Hove) 1877
Arkwright, H. A.	(3)	9—43 ⎱	M.C.C. v. Gentlemen of Kent (Canterbury) 1861
		9—54 ⎰	
		9—79	M.C.C. v. Gentlemen of Kent (Canterbury) 1864
Arnold, E. G.	(1)	9—64	Worcs. v. Oxford U. (Oxford) 1905
Astill, W. E.	(1)	9—41	Leics. v. Warwicks. (Birmingham) 1923
Attewell, W.	(1)	9—23	Notts. v. Sussex (Nottingham) 1886
Bailey, T. E.	(1)	10—90	Essex v. Lancs. (Clacton) 1949
Bannister, J. D.	(2)	9—35	Warwicks. v. Yorks. (Sheffield) 1955
		10—41	Warwicks. v. Combined Services (Birmingham) ...1959
Baring, A. E. G.	(1)	9—26	Hants. v. Essex (Colchester) 1931
Barlow, R. G.	(1)	9—39	Lancs. v. Sussex (Manchester) 1886
Barnes, S. F.	(1)	9—103	England v. South Africa (Johannesburg) 1913–14
Barratt, E.	(1)	10—43	Players v. Australians (Oval) 1878
Bennett, G.	(1)	9—113	Kent v. Sussex (Brighton) 1871
Berry, R.	(1)	10—102	Lancs. v. Worcs. (Blackpool) 1953
Bestwick, W.	(2)	10—40	Derby v. Glamorgan (Cardiff) 1921
		9—65	Derby v. Warwicks. (Birmingham) 1921
Blair, R. W.	(2)	9—75	Wellington v. Canterbury (Wellington) 1956–57
		9—72	Wellington v. Auckland (Wellington) 1956–57
Blanckenberg, J. M.	(1)	9—78	Western Province v. Transvaal (Johannesburg) 1920–21
Bland, C. H. G.	(1)	10—48	Sussex v. Kent (Tonbridge) 1899
Blythe, C.	(6)	9—67	Kent v. Essex (Canterbury) 1903
		9—30	Kent v. Hants. (Tonbridge) 1904
		10—30	Kent v. Northants. (Northampton) 1907
		9—42	Kent v. Leics. (Leicester) 1909
		9—44	Kent v. Northants. (Northampton) 1909
		9—97	Kent v. Surrey (Lord's) 1914
Bosanquet, B. J. T.	(2)	9—31	Oxford U. v. Sussex (Oxford) 1900
		9—107	M.C.C. v. South Africans (Lord's) 1904
Botten, J.	(1)	9—23	N.E. Transvaal v. Griqualand West (Pretoria) 1958–59
Bowes, W. E.	(1)	9—121	Yorks. v. Essex (Scarborough) 1932
Bowley, E. H.	(1)	9—114	Sussex v. Derby (Hove) 1929
Boyes, G. S.	(1)	9—57	Hants. v. Somerset (Yeovil) 1938
Bradley, W. M.	(1)	9—87	Kent v. Hants. (Tonbridge) 1901
Braund, L. C.	(1)	9—41	Somerset v. Yorks. (Sheffield) 1902
Brearley, W.	(2)	9—47	Lancs. v. Somerset (Manchester) 1905
		9—80	Lancs. v. Yorks. (Manchester) 1909
Brice, W. S.	(1)	9—67	Wellington v. Auckland (Wellington) 1918–19
Briggs, J.	(4)	9—29	Lancs. v. Derby (Derby) 1885
		9—88	Lancs. v. Sussex (Manchester) 1888
		9—31	Londesborough's XI v. Australians (Scarborough) 1890
		10—55	Lancs. v. Worcs. (Manchester) 1900
Broderick, V. H.	(1)	9—35	Northants. v. Sussex (Horsham) 1948

Buchanan, D.	(1)	9—82	Gentlemen v. Players (Oval)	1868
Bull, F. G.	(1)	9—93	Essex v. Surrey (Oval)	1897
Burton, G.	(1)	10—59	Middx. v. Surrey (Oval)	1888
Butler, S. E.	(1)	10—38	Oxford U. v. Cambridge U. (Lord's)	1871
Caffyn, W.	(1)	9—29	Surrey & Sussex v. England (Oval)	1857
Chatterjee, P.	(1)	10—20	Bengal v. Assam (Jorhat)	1956—57
Chester, J.	(1)	9—	M.C.C. v. Cambridge U. (Cambridge)	1850
Clarke, W.	(2)	9—	Notts. v. Kent (Town Malling)	1840
		9—29	Notts. v. Kent (Nottingham)	1845
Clay, J. C.	(3)	9—54	Glamorgan v. Northants. (Llanelly)	1935
		9—59	Glamorgan v. Essex (Westcliff)	1937
		9—66	Glamorgan v. Worcs. (Swansea)	1937
Collins, G. G.	(1)	10—65	Kent v. Notts. (Dover)	1922
Conway, A. J.	(1)	9—38	Worcs. v. Glos. (Moreton-in-the-Marsh)	1914
Cook, C.	(1)	9—42	Glos. v. Yorks. (Bristol)	1947
Cooke, F. H.	(1)	9—73	Otago v. Canterbury (Christchurch)	1884—85
Cornford, J.	(1)	9—53	Sussex v. Northants. (Rushden)	1949
Cowan, M. J.	(1)	9—43	Yorks. v. Warwicks. (Birmingham)	1960
Cox, G. R.	(1)	9—50	Sussex v. Warwicks. (Horsham)	1926
Crisp, R. J.	(1)	9—64	Western Province v. Natal (Durban)	1933—34
Cuffe, J. A.	(1)	9—38	Worcs. v. Yorks. (Bradford)	1907
Davidson, G.	(2)	9—42	Derby v. Glos. (Derby)	1886
		9—39	Derby v. Warwicks. (Derby)	1895
Dean, H.	(6)	9—46	Lancs. v. Derby (Chesterfield)	1907
		9—35	Lancs. v. Warwicks. (Liverpool)	1909
		9—31	Lancs. v. Somereset (Manchester)	1909
		9—77	Lancs. v. Somerset (Bath)	1910
		9—109	Lancs. v Leics. (Leicester)	1911
		9—62	Lancs. v. Yorks. (Liverpool)	1913
Dean, J.	(1)	9—34	M.C.C. v. Notts. (Nottingham)	1843
Deas, L. M.	(1)	9—91	Europeans v. Hindus (Bombay)	1905—06
Dennett, G.	(2)	10—40	Glos. v. Essex (Bristol)	1906
		9—63	Glos. v. Surrey (Bristol)	1913
Dent, T. H.	(1)	9—47	Hawke's Bay v. Wellington (Napier)	1900—01
Douglas, J. W. H. T.	(2)	9—105	Gentlemen v. Players (Lord's)	1914
		9—47	Essex v. Derby (Leyton)	1921
Drake, A.	(1)	10—35	Yorks. v. Somerset (Weston-super-Mare)	1914
Dwyer, E. B.	(2)	9—35	Sussex v. Derby (Hove)	1906
		9—44	Sussex v. Middx. (Hove)	1906
Eden, T.	(1)	9—43	Nelson v. Wellington (Wellington)	1875—76
Emmett, T.	(2)	9—34	Yorks. v. Notts. (Dewsbury)	1868
		9—23	Yorks. v. Cambridgeshire (Hunslet, Leeds)	1869
Evans, A. H.	(1)	9—59	England XI v. Daft's XI (Lord's)	1880
Fazal Mahmood	(1)	9—43	Punjab v. Services (Lahore)	1956—57
Fee, F.	(1)	9—26	Ireland v. Scotland (Dublin)	1957
Field, F. E.	(1)	9—104	Warwicks. v. Leics. (Leicester)	1899
Fielder, A.	(2)	10—90	Players v. Gentlemen (Lord's)	1906
		9—108	Kent v. Lancs. (Canterbury)	1907
Fisher, A. H.	(1)	9—50	Otago v. Queensland (Dunedin)	1896—97
Flanagan, M.	(1)	9—78	M.C.C. v. Surrey (Lord's)	1876
Flavell, J.	(2)	9—122	Worcs. v. Sussex (Hastings)	1954
		9—30	Worcs. v. Kent (Dover)	1955
Fleetwood-Smith, L. O'B.	(2)	9—36	Victoria v. Tasmania (Melbourne)	1932—33
		9—135	Victoria v. South Australia (Melbourne)	1937—38
Foster, F. R.	(1)	9—118	Warwicks. v. Yorks. (Birmingham)	1911
Foster, T.	(1)	9—59	Yorks. v. M.C.C. (Lord's)	1894
Freeman, A. P.	(8)	9—87	Kent v. Sussex (Hastings)	1921
		9—11	Kent v. Sussex (Hove)	1922
		9—104	Kent v. West Indians (Canterbury)	1928
		10—131	Kent v. Lancs. (Maidstone)	1929
		9—50	Kent v. Derby (Ilkeston)	1930
		10—53	Kent v. Essex (Southend)	1930
		10—79	Kent v. Lancs. (Manchester)	1931
		9—61	Kent v. Warwicks. (Folkestone)	1932
Geary, G.	(2)	9—33	Leics. v. Lancs. (Ashby-de-la-Zouch)	1926
		10—18	Leics. v. Glamorgan (Pontypridd)	1929
Ghulam Ahmed	(1)	9—53	Hyderabad v. Madras (Secunderabad)	1947—48
Giffen, G.	(5)	10—66	Australian XI v. Rest (Sydney)	1883—84
		9—91	South Australia v. Victoria (Adelaide)	1885—86
		9—60	Australians v. Derby (Derby)	1886
		9—96	South Australia v. Victoria (Adelaide)	1891—92
		9—147	South Australia v. Victoria (Adelaide)	1892—93

Gill, G. ....(1)	9—89	Leics. v. Warwicks. (Birmingham) 1905	
Gladwin, C. ....(3)	9—119	Derby v. Lancs. (Buxton) 1947	
	9—64	North v. South (Kingston) 1951	
	9—41	Derby v. Worcs. (Stourbridge) 1952	
Goddard, T. W. ....(9)	9—21	Glos. v. Cambridge U. (Cheltenham) 1929	
	9—37	Glos. v. Leics. (Bristol) 1934	
	10—113	Glos. v. Worcs. (Cheltenham) 1937	
	9—55	Glos. v. Worcs. (Bristol) 1939	
	9—38	Glos. v. Kent (Bristol) 1939	
	9—44	Glos. v. Somerset (Bristol) 1939	
	9—82	Glos. v. Surrey (Cheltenham) 1946	
	9—41	Glos. v. Notts. (Bristol) 1947	
	9—61	Glos. v. Derby (Bristol) 1949	
Gomez, G. E. ....(1)	9—24	West Indians v. South Zone (Madras) ....1948—49	
Grace, E. M. ....(1)	10—69	M.C.C. v. Gentlemen of Kent (Canterbury) 1862	
Grace, W. G. ....(5)	10—92	M.C.C. v. Kent (Canterbury) 1873	
	9—48	South v. North (Loughborough) 1875	
	9—55	Glos. v. Notts. (Cheltenham) 1877	
	9—20	M.C.C. v. Notts. (Lord's) 1885	
	10—49	M.C.C. v. Oxford U. (Oxford) 1886	
Graveney, J. K. ....(1)	10—66	Glos. v. Derby (Chesterfield) 1949	
Gregory, J. M. ....(1)	9—32	A.I.F. v. Natal (Durban) ....1919—20	
Greswell, W. T. ....(1)	9—62	Somerset v. Hants. (Weston-super-Mare) 1928	
Griffith, G. ....(1)	9—130	Surrey v. Lancs. (Oval) 1867	
Grimmett, C. V. ....(3)	10—37	Australians v. Yorks (Sheffield) 1930	
	9—74	Australians v. Cambridge U (Cambridge) 1934	
	9—180	South Australia v. Queensland (Adelaide) ......1934—35	
Grove, C. W. ....(1)	9—39	Warwicks. v. Sussex (Birmingham) 1952	
Grundy, J. ....(1)	9—19	Notts. v. Kent (Nottingham) 1864	
Gupte, S. P.......................(2)	10—78	Bombay v. Pakistan Services (Bombay) ....1954—55	
	9—102	India v. West Indies (Kanpur) ....1958—59	
Haigh, S. ....(1)	9—25	Yorks. v. Glos. (Leeds) 1912	
Halfyard, D. J. ....(2)	9—39	Kent v. Glamorgan (Neath) 1957	
	9—61	Kent v. Worcs. (Maidstone) 1959	
Hallows, J. ....(1)	9—37	Lancs. v. Glos. (Gloucester) 1904	
Hammond, W. R. ....(1)	9—23	Glos. v. Worcs. (Cheltenham) 1928	
Hargreave, S. ....(1)	9—35	Warwicks. v. Surrey (Oval) 1903	
Harry, F. ....(1)	9—44	Lancs. v. Warwicks. (Manchester) 1906	
Hay, H. ....(1)	9—67	South Australia v. Hawke's XI (Adelaide) ......1902—03	
Heap, J. S. ....(1)	9—43	Lancs. v. Northants. (Northampton) 1910	
Hearne, J. T. ....(8)	9—32	Middx. v. Notts. (Nottingham) 1891	
	9—41	M.C.C. v. Notts. (Lord's) 1892	
	9—43	M.C.C. v. Lancs. (Lord's) 1894	
	9—73	M.C.C. v. Australians (Lord's)...........................1896	
	9—54	M.C.C. v. Oxford U. (Oxford) 1897	
	9—68	Middx. v. Lancs. (Manchester)...........................1898	
	9—71	Middx. v. Yorks. (Leeds) 1900	
	9—78	Middx. v. Yorks. (Bradford)...........................1908	
Hearne, J. W. ....(3)	9—82	Middx. v. Surrey (Lord's) 1911	
	9—65	Middx. v. Somerset (Lord's) 1920	
	9—61	Middx. v. Derby (Chesterfield) 1933	
Hinkly, E. ....(1)	10—	Kent v. England (Lord's) 1848	
Hirst, G. H. ....(4)	9—45	Yorks. v. Middx. (Sheffield) 1907	
	9—23	Yorks. v. Lancs. (Leeds) 1910	
	9—41	Yorks. v. Worcs. (Worcester) 1911	
	9—69	Yorks. v. M.C.C. (Lord's) 1912	
Hollies, W. E. ....(3)	9—93	Warwicks. v. Glamorgan (Birmingham) 1939	
	10—49	Warwicks. v. Notts. (Birmingham) 1946	
	9—56	Warwicks. v. Northants. (Birmingham) 1950	
Hopwood, J. L. ....(2)	9—33	Lancs. v. Leics. (Manchester) 1933	
	9—69	Lancs. v. Worcs. (Blackpool) 1934	
Horton, M. J. ....(1)	9—56	Worcs. v. South Africans (Worcester) 1955	
Howell, H. ....(3)	10—51	Warwicks. v. Yorks. (Birmingham) 1923	
	9—35	Warwicks. v. Somerset (Taunton) 1924	
	9—32	Warwicks. v. Hants. (Birmingham) 1925	
Howell, W. P. ....(3)	10—28	Australians v. Surrey (Oval) 1899	
	9—23	Australians v. Western Province (Cape Town) 1902—03	
	9—52	N.S.W. v. Victoria (Melbourne) ....1902—03	
Huddleston, W. ....(1)	9—36	Lancs. v. Notts. (Liverpool) 1906	
Huggins, J. H. ....(1)	9—34	Glos. v. Sussex (Bristol)...................................1904	
Hulme, J. ....(1)	9—27	Derby v. Yorks. (Sheffield) 1894	
Iddon, J. ....(1)	9—42	Lancs. v. Yorks. (Sheffield) 1937	

Illingworth, R.	.............(1)	9—42	Yorks. v. Worcs. (Worcester) 1957
Israr Ali	..................(1)	9—58	Bahawalpur v. Punjab A (Bahawalpur) 1957–58
Jackson, J.	....................(3)	9—27	Kent v. England (Lord's) 1858
		9—35	Kent v. England (Canterbury) 1858
		9—49	Notts. v. Surrey (Oval) 1860
Jackson, L.	....................(2)	9—60	Derby v. Lancs. (Manchester) 1952
		9—17	Derby v. Cambridge U. (Cambridge) 1959
Jackson, P. F.	................(1)	9—45	Worcs. v. Somerset (Dudley) 1935
James, A. E.	................(1)	9—60	Sussex v. Yorks. (Hove) 1955
Jayes, T.	....................(1)	9—78	Leics. v. Derby (Leicester)..........................1905
Jupp, V. W. C.	..............(1)	10—127	Northants. v. Kent (Tunbridge Wells) 1932
Kannan, K. S.	................(1)	9—50	Madras v. Hyderabad (Secunderabad) 1947–48
Kennedy, A. S.	..............(3)	9—33	Hants. v. Lancs. (Liverpool) 1920
		10—37	Players v. Gentlemen (Oval) 1927
		9—46	Hants. v. Derby (Portsmouth) 1929
King, J. B.	....................(2)	9—25	Philadelphians v. Warner's XI (Belmont) 1897–98
		9—62	Philadelphians v. Lancs. (Manchester) 1903
Knutton, H. J.	..............(1)	9—100	England XI v. Australians (Bradford) 1902
Laker, J. C.	....................(3)	10—88	Surrey v. Australians (Oval) 1956
		9—37	England v. Australia (Manchester) 1st innings ...1956
		10—53	England v. Australia (Manchester) 2nd innings ...1956
Lampard, A. W.	..............(1)	9—42	A.I.F. v. Lancs. (Manchester) 1919
Langford, B. A.	..............(1)	9—26	Somerset v. Lancs. (Weston-super-Mare) 1958
Langridge, James	.............(1)	9—34	Sussex v. Yorks. (Sheffield) 1934
Larwood, H.	..................(1)	9—41	Notts. v. Kent (Nottingham) 1931
Lees, W. S.	....................(1)	9—81	Surrey v. Sussex (Eastbourne) 1905
Lillywhite, James	.........(3)	9—29	Sussex v. M.C.C. (Lord's) 1862
		9—73	Sussex v. Kent (Folkestone) 1863
		10—129	South v. North (Canterbury) 1872
Lillywhite, W.	..................(4)	9—	Sussex v. Hants. & Surrey (Bramshill) 1826
		9—	Players v. Gentlemen (Lord's) 1837
		9—	Slow Bowlers v. Fast Bowlers (Lord's) 1841
		9—	M.C.C. v. Cambridge U. (Cambridge) 1846
Lipscombe, R.	................(1)	9—88	Kent v. M.C.C. (Lord's) 1871
Llewelyn, C. B.	..............(1)	9—55	London County v. Cambridge U. (Crystal Palace) 1902
Loader, P. J.	..................(2)	9—28	Surrey v. Kent (Blackheath) 1953
		9—17	Surrey v. Warwicks. (Oval) 1958
Lock, G. A. R.	..............(2)	10—54	Surrey v. Kent (Blackheath) 1956
		9—77	Surrey v. Oxford U. (Guildford) 1960
Lockwood, W. H.	............(3)	9—105	Surrey v. Glos. (Cheltenham) 1899
		9—94	Surrey v. Essex (Oval) 1900
		9—59	Surrey v. Essex (Leyton) 1902
Lohmann, G. A.	..............(2)	9—67	Surrey v. Sussex (Hove) 1889
		9—28	England v. South Africa (Johannesburg) 1895–96
Mailey, A. A.	..................(3)	9—121	Australia v. England (Melbourne) 1920–21
		10—66	Australians v. Glos. (Cheltenham) 1921
		9—86	Australians v. Lancs. (Liverpool) 1926
Marchant, J. W.	..............(1)	9—21	Wellington v. Hawke's Bay (Wellington) 1873–74
Marlar, R. G.	..................(1)	9—46	Sussex v. Lancs. (Hove) 1955
Marsham, C. D.	..............(1)	9—64	Gents of England v. Gents of M.C.C. (Lord's) ...1855
Matthews, F. C. L.	.........(1)	9—50	Notts. v. Northants. (Nottingham) 1923
McBeath, D. J.	..............(1)	9—56	Canterbury v. Auckland (Christchurch) 1918–19
McCormick, E. L.	............(1)	9—40	Victoria v. South Australia (Adelaide) 1936–37
McIntyre, M.	..................(1)	9—33	Notts. v. Surrey (Oval) 1872
McKibbin, T. R.	..............(1)	9—68	N.S.W. v. Queensland (Brisbane) 1894–95
McMillan, Q.	..................(1)	9—53	South Africans v. South Australia (Adelaide) ...1931–32
McNally, J. P.	................(1)	9—91	Griqualand West v. Border (Kimberley) 1951–52
McShane, P. G.	..............(1)	9—45	Rest v. Australian XI (Sydney) 1880–81
Mead, W.	....................(3)	9—52	Essex v. Hants. (Southampton) 1895
		9—75	Essex v. Leics. (Leyton) 1896
		9—40	Essex v. Hants. (Southampton) 1900
Mee, R. J.	....................(1)	9—54	Notts. v. Sussex (Nottingham) 1893
Melle, M. G.	..................(1)	9—22	South Africans v. Tasmania (Launceston) 1952–53
Mercer, J.	....................(2)	9—24	Wales v. Scotland (Perth) 1923
		10—51	Glamorgan v. Worcs. (Worcester) 1936
Meyer, R. J. O.	..............(1)	9—160	Europeans v. Muslims (Bombay) 1927–28
Mistri, K. B.	..................(1)	9—81	Parsis v. Europeans (Poona) 1906–07
Mitchell, T. B.	................(1)	10—64	Derby v. Leics. (Leicester) 1935
Mold, A.	........................(4)	9—41	Lancs. v. Yorks. (Huddersfield) 1890
		9—43	Thornton's XI v. Australians (Barnes) 1890
		9—29	Lancs. v. Kent (Tonbridge) 1892
		9—62	Lancs. v. Kent (Manchester)..........................1895

Morton, A. ....(1)	9—71	Derby v. Notts. (Blackwell) 1911
Moss, A. E. ....(1)	10—28	Canterbury v. Wellington (Christchurch) ....1889—90
Muncer, B. L. ....(2)	9—97	Glamorgan v. Surrey (Cardiff) 1947
	9—62	Glamorgan v. Essex (Brentwood) 1948
Mycroft, W. ....(1)	9—80	Derby v. Lancs. (Derby) 1875
Mynn, A. ....(1)	9—	Gents of Kent v. Gents of M.C.C. (Lord's) 1842
Napier, G. G. ....(1)	9—17	Europeans v. Parsis (Poona) ....1909—10
Nash, J. ....(1)	9—93	Glamorgan v. Sussex (Swansea) 1922
Neill, R. ....(2)	9—75	Auckland v. Canterbury (Auckland) ....1891—92
	9—86	Auckland v. Canterbury (Auckland) ....1897—98
Newman, J. A....................(1)	9—131	Hants. v. Essex (Bournemouth) 1921
Nichols, M. S...................(4)	9—59	Essex v. Hants. (Chelmsford) 1927
	9—116	Essex v. Middx. (Leyton) 1930
	9—32	Essex v. Notts. (Nottingham) 1936
	9—37	Essex v. Glos. (Gloucester) 1938
Nixon, T. ....(1)	9—	M.C.C. v. Middx. (Lord's) 1851
Nupen, E. P. ....(1)	9—48	Transvaal v. Griqualand West (Johannesburg) 1931—32
O'Reilly, W. J. ....(3)	9—50	N.S.W. v. Victoria (Melbourne) ....1933—34
	9—38	Australians v. Somerset (Taunton) 1934
	9—41	N.S.W. v. South Australia (Adelaide) ....1937—38
Oxenham, R. K................(1)	9—18	Australians v. Ceylon (Colombo) ....1935—36
Pallett, H. J. ....(1)	9—55	Warwicks. v. Essex (Leyton) 1894
Parker, C. W. L...............(9)	9—35	Glos. v. Leics. (Cheltenham)............................1920
	10—79	Glos. v. Somerset (Bristol) 1921
	9—87	Glos. v. Derby (Gloucester) 1922
	9—36	Glos. v. Yorks. (Bristol) 1922
	9—44	Glos. v. Essex (Gloucester) 1925
	9—118	Glos. v. Surrey (Gloucester) 1925
	9—103	Glos. v. Somerset (Bristol) 1927
	9—46	Glos. v. Northants. (Northampton)...................1927
	9—44	Glos. Warwicks. (Cheltenham) 1930
Parkin, C. H. ....(2)	9—85	Players v. Gentlemen (Oval) 1920
	9—32	Lancs. v. Leics. (Ashby-de-la-Zouch) 1924
Partridge, R. J. ....(1)	9—66	Northants. v. Warwicks. (Kettering) 1934
Patel, J. S. ....(1)	9—69	India v. Australia (Kanpur) ....1959—60
Pearson, F. ....(1)	9—41	H. K. Foster's XI v. Oxford U. (Oxford) 1913
Peel, R. ....(1)	9—22	Yorks. v. Somerset (Leeds) 1895
Perks, R. T. D. ....(2)	9—40	Worcs. v. Glamorgan (Stourbridge) 1939
	9—42	Worcs. v. Glos. (Cheltenham) 1946
Pickett, H. ....(1)	10—32	Essex v. Leics. (Leyton) 1895
Pougher, A. D. ....(1)	9—34	England XI v. Surrey (Oval) 1895
Powys, W. N. ....(1)	9—42	Cambridge U. v. M.C.C. (Cambridge) 1871
Preston, J. M. ....(1)	9—28	Yorks. v. M.C.C. (Scarborough) 1888
Quilty, J. ....(1)	9—55	South Australia v. Victoria (Adelaide) ....1881—82
Raikes, T. B. ....(1)	9—38	Oxford U. v. Army (Oxford) 1924
Ranjane, V. R...................(1)	9—35	Maharashtra v. Saurashtra (Khadakvasla) ......1956—57
Relf, A. E. ....(1)	9—95	Sussex v. Warwicks. (Hove) 1910
Rhodes, W. ....(3)	9—28	Yorks. v. Essex (Leyton) 1899
	9—24	Thornton's XI v. Australians (Scarborough) 1899
	9—39	Yorks. v. Essex (Leyton) 1929
Richardson, T. ....(4)	9—47	Surrey v. Yorks. (Sheffield) 1893
	10—45	Surrey v. Essex (Oval) 1894
	9—49	Surrey v. Sussex (Oval) 1895
	9—70	Surrey v. Hants. (Oval) 1895
Richmond, L. B. ....(2)	9—21	Notts. v. Hants. (Nottingham) 1922
	9—55	Notts. v. Northants. (Nottingham) 1925
Ringrose, W. ....(1)	9—76	Yorks. v. Australians (Bradford) 1905
Robertson, W. ....(1)	9—98	Canterbury v. Wellington (Christchurch) ....1894—95
Robertson-Glasgow, R. C....(1)	9—38	Somerset v. Middx. (Lord's) 1924
Robinson, E. ....(1)	9—36	Yorks. v. Lancs. (Bradford) 1920
Root, C. F. ....(3)	9—40	Worcs. v. Essex (Worcester) 1924
	9—81	Worcs. v. Kent (Tunbridge Wells) 1930
	9—23	Worcs. v. Lancs. (Worcester) 1931
Rowan, A. M. B. ....(1)	9—19	Transvaal v. Australians (Johannesburg) ....1949—50
Rushby, T. ....(1)	10—43	Surrey v. Somerset (Taunton) 1921
Rylott, A. ....(1)	9—30	M.C.C. v. Cambridge U. (Cambridge) 1873
Sajjad ....(1)	9—80	Peshawar v. Services (Peshawar) ....1958—59
Sarwate, C. T..................(1)	9—61	Holkar v. Mysore (Indore) ....1945—46
Shackleton, D. ....(4)	9—77	Hants. v. Glamorgan (Newport) 1953
	9—59	Hants. v. Glos. (Bristol) 1958
	9—81	Hants. v. Glos. (Bristol) 1959
	9—30	Hants. v. Warwicks. (Portsmouth) 1960

Sharp, J.	(1)	9—77	Lancs. v. Worcs. (Worcester) 1901
Sharpe, J. W.	(1)	9—47	Surrey v. Middx. (Oval)....................................1891
Shaw, A.	(1)	10—73	M.C.C. v. North (Lord's) 1874
Shaw, J. C.	(1)	9—84	Notts. v. Glos. (Nottingham) 1871
Shepherd, D. J.	(1)	9—77	Glamorgan v. Northants. (Cardiff) 1954
Shipman, W.	(1)	9—83	Leics. v. Surrey (Oval) 1910
Sims, J. M.	(2)	9—92	Middx. v. Lancs. (Manchester)........................1934
		10—90	East v. West (Kingston)...................................1948
Sinfield, R. A.	(1)	9—111	Glos. v. Middx. (Lord's) 1936
Smailes, T. F.	(1)	10—47	Yorks. v. Derby (Sheffield) 1939
Smales, K.	(1)	10—66	Notts. v. Glos. (Stroud) 1956
Smith, E.	(1)	9—64	Derby v. Scotland (Edinburgh) 1955
Smith, S. G.	(1)	9—34	West Indian XI v. Bennett's XI (Trinidad) 1901–02
Smith, T. P. B.	(4)	9—121	M.C.C. v. N.S.W. (Sydney) 1946–47
		9—77	Essex v. Middx. (Colchester) 1947
		9—117	Essex v. Notts. (Southend) 1948
		9—108	Essex v. Kent (Maidstone) 1948
Smith, V. I.	(1)	9—88	Natal v. Border (Pietermaritzburg) 1946–47
Smith, W. C.	(1)	9—31	Surrey v. Hants. (Oval) 1904
Southerton, J.	(1)	9—30	South v. North (Lord's) 1875
Spencer, C. T.	(1)	9—63	Leics. v. Yorks. (Huddersfield) 1954
Spofforth, F. R.	(2)	9—53	Australians v. Lancs. (Manchester) 1878
		9—18	Australians v. Oxford U. (Oxford) 1886
Staples, S. J.	(1)	9—141	Notts. v. Kent (Canterbury) 1927
Steel, A. G.	(1)	9—63	Lancs. v. Yorks. (Manchester) 1878
Stephenson , J. W. A.	(1)	9—46	Gentlemen v. Players (Lord's) 1936
Tarrant, F. A.	(6)	9—57	Middx. v. Yorks. (Leeds) 1906
		9—54	Middx. v. Lancs. (Manchester).........................1906
		9—41	Middx. v. Glos. (Bristol) 1907
		9—59	Middx. v. Notts. (Lord's) 1907
		9—105	Middx. v. Lancs. (Manchester).........................1914
		9—35	England XII v. Indian XII (Bombay) 1915–16
		9—99	Europeans v. Parsis (Bombay) 1916–17
Tate, F. W.	(1)	9—73	Sussex v. Leics. (Leicester) 1902
Tate, M. W.	(1)	9—71	Sussex v. Middx. (Lord's) 1926
Tattersall, R.	(1)	9—40	Lancs. v. Notts. (Manchester) 1953
Tayfield, H. J.	(1)	9—113	South Africa v. England (Johannesburg) 1956–57
Thomas, A. E.	(1)	9—30	Northants. v. Yorks. (Bradford) 1920
Thompson, G. J.	(2)	9—85	Hawke's XI v. South Australia (Adelaide) 1902–03
		9 64	Northants. v. Derby (Northampton) 1906
Thompson, R. G.	(1)	9—65	Warwicks. v. Notts. (Birmingham) 1952
Townsend, C. L.	(2)	9—48	Glos. v. Middx. (Lord's) 1898
		9—128	Glos. v. Warwicks. (Cheltenham) 1898
Travers, J. F.	(1)	9—30	South Australia v. Victoria (Melbourne) 1900–01
Tremlin, B.	(1)	9—126	Essex v. Derby (Leyton) 1905
Tribe, G. E.	(4)	9—45	Queensland v. Victoria (Brisbane) 1945–46
		9—50	Commonwealth v. Governor's XI (Calcutta) ...1949–50
		9—45	Northants. v. Yorks. (Bradford) 1955
		9—43	Northants. v. Worcs. (Northampton) 1958
Trott, A. E.	(1)	10—42	Middx. v. Somerset (Taunton) 1900
Trumble, H.	(1)	9—39	Australians v. South of England (Bournemouth) ...1902
Turner, C. T. B.	(2)	9—15	Australians v. England XI (Stoke) 1888
		9—37	Australians v. England XI (Hastings) 1888
Tyler, E. J.	(3)	9—33	Somerset v. Notts. (Taunton) 1892
		10—49	Somerset v. Surrey (Taunton) 1895
		9—83	Somerset v. Sussex (Hastings) 1907
Verity, H.	(9)	9—60	Yorks. v. Glamorgan (Swansea) 1930
		10—36	Yorks. v. Warwicks. (Leeds) 1931
		10—10	Yorks. v. Notts. (Leeds) 1932
		9—44	Yorks. v. Essex (Leyton) 1933
		9—59	Yorks. v. Kent (Dover) 1933
		9—12	Yorks. v. Kent (Sheffield) 1936
		9—48	Yorks. v. Essex (Westcliff) 1936
		9—43	Yorks. v. Warwicks. (Leeds) 1937
		9—62	Yorks. v. M.C.C. (Lord's)...............................1939
Vogler, A. E. E.	(2)	9—44	M.C.C. v. West Indians (Lord's) 1906
		10—26	Eastern Province v. Griqualand West (Johannesburg) 1906–07
Waddington, J. E.	(1)	9—105	Griqualand West v. Eastern Province (Port Elizabeth) 1954–55
Wadkar, R. D.	(1)	9—38	Bombay v. Western India States (Jamnagar) ...1937–38
Wainwright, E.	(1)	9—66	Yorks. v. Middx. (Sheffield) 1894

Walker, G. G.	...............(1)	9—68	Derby v. Leics. (Leicester)	....	1895
Walker, V. E.	...............(3)	10—74	England v. Surrey (Oval)	....	1859
		9—62	Middx. v. Sussex (Islington)	....	1864
		10—104	Middx. v. Lancs. (Manchester)	....	1865
Wall, T. W.	...............(1)	10—36	South Australia v. N.S.W. (Sydney)	....	1932–33
Walsh, J. E.	...............(1)	9—101	Cahn's XI v. Glamorgan (Newport)	....	1938
Wardle, J. H.	...............(2)	9—48	Yorks. v. Sussex (Hove)	....	1954
		9—25	Yorks. v. Lancs. (Manchester)	....	1954
Warr, J. J.	...............(1)	9—65	Middx. v. Kent (Lord's)	....	1956
Wass, T.	...............(2)	9—91	Notts. v. Surrey (Oval)	....	1902
		9—67	Notts. v. Derby (Blackwell)	....	1911
Watson, A.	...............(1)	9—117	Lancs. v. Derby (Manchester)	....	1874
Watts, E. A.	...............(1)	10—67	Surrey v. Warwicks. (Birmingham)	....	1939
Wells, G.	...............(1)	9—105	Sussex v. Surrey (Brighton)	....	1860
Wensley, A. F.	...............(1)	9—36	Auckland v. Otago (Auckland)	....	1929–30
White, J. C.	...............(5)	9—46	Somerset v. Glos. (Bristol)	....	1914
		10—76	Somerset v. Worcs. (Worcester)	....	1921
		9—58	Somerset v. Warwicks. (Birmingham)	....	1922
		9—71	Somerset v. Sussex (Eastbourne)	....	1931
		9—51	Somerset v. Glamorgan (Bath)	....	1932
Williams, A. C.	...............(1)	9—29	Yorks. v. Hants. (Dewsbury)	....	1919
Wilson, G. A.	...............(1)	9—75	Worcs. v. Oxford U. (Oxford)	....	1904
Wisden, J.	...............(2)	10—	North v. South (Lord's)	....	1850
		9—	Under 36 v. Over 36 (Lord's)	....	1850
Woodcock, A.	...............(1)	9—28	Leics. v. M.C.C. (Lord's)	....	1899
Woods, S. M. J.	...............(1)	10—69	Cambridge U. v. Thorton's XI (Cambridge)	....	1890
Wootton, G.	...............(3)	9—37	M.C.C. v. Oxford U. (Lord's)	....	1865
		10—	All England XI v. Yorks. (Sheffield)	....	1865
		9—45	M.C.C. v. England (Lord's)	....	1868
Wright, D. V. P.	...............(2)	9—47	Kent v. Glos. (Bristol)	....	1939
		9—51	Kent v. Leics. (Maidstone)	....	1949
Wright, W.	...............(1)	9—72	Kent v. M.C.C. (Lord's)	....	1889
Young, J. A.	...............(1)	9—55	England XI v. Commonwealth (Hastings)	....	1952

Seventeen or More Wickets in a Match

NINETEEN WICKETS

O.   M.   R.   W.
68 —27— 90—19   J. C. Laker: England v. Australia (Manchester)................................1956

EIGHTEEN WICKETS

O.   M.   R.   W.
48 — — 96—18   H. A. Arkwright: M.C.C. v. Gentlemen of Kent (Canterbury) 1861
                        (*This was a twelve-a-side match.*)

SEVENTEEN WICKETS

O.   M.   R.   W.
76·1—36— 89—17   W. G. Grace: Glos. v. Notts. (Cheltenham) 1877
116·2—41—201—17   G. Giffen: South Australia v. Victoria (Adelaide) 1885–86
69 —37— 50—17   C. T. B. Turner: Australians v. England XI (Hastings) 1888
77·3—32—119—17   W. Mead: Essex v. Hants. (Southampton) 1895
26·3— 6— 54—17   W. P. Howell: Australians v. Western Province (Cape Town) 1902–03
35·2— 7—137—17   W. Brearley: Lancs. v. Somerset (Manchester) 1905
31·1—14— 48—17   C. Blythe: Kent v. Northants. (Northampton) 1907
47·4—10— 91—17   H. Dean: Lancs. v. Yorks. (Liverpool) 1913
65·3—16—159—17   S. F. Barnes: England v. South Africa (Johannesburg) 1913–14
33·5—10— 67—17   A. P. Freeman: Kent v. Sussex (Hove) 1922
30 — 6— 89—17   F. C. L. Matthews: Notts. v. Northants. (Nottingham) 1923
48·3—23— 56—17   C. W. L. Parker: Glos. v. Essex (Gloucester) 1925
75·3—36—106—17   G. R. Cox: Sussex v. Warwicks. (Horsham) 1926
41·4—12— 92—17   A. P. Freeman: Kent v. Warwicks. (Folkestone) 1932
41·1—13— 91—17   H. Verity: Yorks. v. Essex (Leyton) 1933
62·5—11—212—17   J. C. Clay: Glamorgan v. Worcs. (Swansea) 1937
31·6— 3—106—17   T. W. Goddard: Glos. v. Kent (Bristol) 1939

Sixteen or More Wickets in a Day's Play

17—48	C. Blythe: Kent v. Northants. (Northampton)		1907
17—91	H. Verity: Yorks. v. Essex (Leyton)		1933
17—106	T. W. Goddard: Glos. v. Kent (Bristol)		1939
16—38	T. Emmett: Yorks. v. Cambridgeshire (Hunslet)		1869
16—38	A. E. E. Vogler: Eastern Province v. Griqualand West (Johannesburg)		1906–07
16—52	J. Southerton: South v. North (Lord's)		1875
16—69	T. Wass: Notts. v. Lancs. (Liverpool)		1906
16—83	J. C. White: Somerset v. Worcs. (Bath)		1919
16—103	T. Wass: Notts. v. Essex (Nottingham)		1908

Fifteen or More Wickets in a Match

Arkwright, H. A.	(1)	18—96	M.C.C. v. Gentlemen of Kent (Canterbury)	1861
Baldwin, H.	(1)	15—142	Hants. v. Sussex (Hove)	1898
Barnes, S. F.	(1)	17—159	England v. South Africa (Johannesburg)	1913–14
Blythe, C.	(5)	15—76	Kent v. Hants. (Tonbridge)	1904
		15—99	England v. South Africa (Leeds)	1907
		17—48	Kent v. Northants. (Northampton)	1907
		16—102	Kent v. Leics. (Leicester)	1909
		15—45	Kent v. Leics. (Leicester)	1912
Bosanquet, B. J. T.	(1)	15—65	Oxford U. v. Sussex (Oxford)	1900
Botten, J.	(1)	15—49	N.E. Transvaal v. Griqualand West (Pretoria)	1958–59
Bowes, W. E.	(1)	16—35	Yorks. v. Northants. (Kettering)	1935
Braund, L. C.	(1)	15—71	Somerset v. Yorks. (Sheffield)	1902
Brearley, W.	(1)	17—137	Lancs. v. Somerset (Manchester)	1905
Briggs, J.	(2)	15—28	England v. South Africa (Cape Town)	1888–89
		15—57	Londesborough's XI v. Australians (Scarborough)	1890
Burton, G.	(1)	16—114	Middx. v. Yorks. (Sheffield)	1888
Butler, S. E.	(1)	15—95	Oxford U. v. Cambridge U. (Lord's)	1871
Callaway, S. T.	(2)	15—175	N.S.W. v. New Zealand XI (Christchurch)	1895–96
		15—60	Canterbury v. Hawke's Bay (Napier)	1903–04
Chatterjee, P.	(1)	15—109	Bengal v. Madhya Pradesh (Calcutta)	1955–56
Chester, J.	(1)	15—	M.C.C. v. Cambridge U. (Cambridge)	1850
Clarke, W.	(2)	16—	Notts. v. Kent (Nottingham)	1845
		15—98	North v. South (Oval)	1851
Clay, J. C.	(2)	15—86	Glamorgan v. Northants. (Llanelly)	1935
		17—212	Glamorgan v. Worcs. (Swansea)	1937
Collins, G. G.	(1)	16—83	Kent v. Notts. (Dover)	1922
Conway, A. J.	(1)	15—87	Worcs. v. Glos. (Moreton-in-the-Marsh)	1914
Cooke, F. H.	(1)	15—94	Otago v. Canterbury (Christchurch)	1882–83
Cox, G. R.	(1)	17—106	Sussex v. Warwicks. (Horsham)	1926
Davidson, G.	(1)	15—116	Derby v. Essex (Leyton)	1898
Dean, H.	(3)	16—103	Lancs. v. Somerset (Bath)	1910
		15—108	Lancs. v. Kent (Manchester)	1912
		17—91	Lancs. v. Yorks. (Liverpool)	1913
Deas, L. M.	(1)	16—166	Europeans v. Hindus (Bombay)	1905–06
Dennett, G.	(7)	15—96	Glos. v. Middx. (Bristol)	1904
		15—88	Glos. v. Essex (Bristol)	1906
		15—140	Glos. v. Worcs. (Cheltenham)	1906
		15—21	Glos. v. Northants. (Gloucester)	1907
		15—97	Glos. v. Northants. (Northampton)	1907
		16—146	Glos. v. Hants. (Bristol)	1912
		15—195	Glos. v. Surrey (Bristol)	1913
Dooland, B.	(2)	16—83	Notts. v. Essex (Nottingham)	1954
		15—193	Notts. v. Kent (Gravesend)	1956
Dowson, E. M.	(1)	16—58	Bennett's XI v. Jamaica (Kingston)	1901–02
Drake, A.	(1)	15—51	Yorks. v. Somerset (Weston-super-Mare)	1914
Dwyer, E. B.	(1)	16—100	Sussex v. Notts. (Hove)	1906
Ellis, C. H.	(1)	15—297	Sussex v. Surrey (Brighton)	1863
Emmett, T.	(1)	16—38	Yorks. v. Cambridgeshire (Hunslet)	1869
Farnes, K.	(1)	15—113	Essex v. Glamorgan (Clacton)	1938
Fazal Mahmood	(1)	15—76	Punjab v. Services (Lahore)	1956–57
Fleetwood-Smith, L. O'B.	(2)	15—226	Victoria v. N.S.W. (Sydney)	1934–35
		15—96	Victoria v. Queensland (Melbourne)	1936–37
Freeman, A. P.	(9)	17—67	Kent v. Sussex (Hove)	1922
		15—224	Kent v. Leics. (Tonbridge)	1928

Freeman, A. P. (cont.)

16—94	Kent v. Essex (Southend)	1930
15—142	Kent v. Essex (Gravesend)	1931
15—144	Kent v. Leics. (Maidstone)	1931
15—94	Kent v. Somerset (Canterbury)	1931
17—92	Kent v. Warwicks. (Folkestone)	1932
16—82	Kent v. Northants. (Tunbridge Wells)	1932
15—122	Kent v. Middx. (Lord's)	1933

Geary, G.	(1)	16—96	Leics. v. Glamorgan (Pontypridd) ... 1929
Giffen, G.	(6)	17—201	South Australia v. Victoria (Adelaide) ... 1885–86
		16—101	Australians v. Derby (Derby) ... 1886
		16—65	Australians v. Lancs. (Manchester) ... 1886
		16—166	South Australia v. Victoria (Adelaide) ... 1891–92
		16—186	South Australia v. N.S.W. (Adelaide) ... 1894–95
		15—185	South Australia v. Victoria (Adelaide) ... 1902–03
Gladwin, C.	(1)	16—84	Derby v. Worcs. (Stourbridge) ... 1952
Glover, G. K.	(1)	15—68	Griqualand West v. Eastern Province (Cape Town) ... 1893–94
Goddard, T. W.	(7)	16—181	Glos. v. Worcs. (Cheltenham) ... 1937
		16—99	Glos. v. Worcs. (Bristol) ... 1939
		17—106	Glos. v. Kent (Bristol) ... 1939
		15—81	Glos. v. Notts. (Bristol) ... 1947
		15—134	Glos. v. Leics. (Gloucester) ... 1947
		15—156	Glos. v. Middx. (Cheltenham) ... 1947
		15—107	Glos. v. Derby (Bristol) ... 1949
Grace, E. M.	(1)	15—	Gents of M.C.C. v. Gents of Kent (Canterbury) 1862
Grace, W. G.	(5)	15—79	Glos. v. Yorks. (Sheffield) ... 1872
		15—147	M.C.C. v. Kent (Canterbury) ... 1873
		17—89	Glos. v. Notts. (Cheltenham) ... 1877
		15—116	Glos. v. Surrey (Cheltenham) ... 1879
		16—60	M.C.C. v. Notts. (Lord's) ... 1885
Grimmett, C. V.	(1)	16—289	South Australia v. Queensland (Adelaide) ... 1934–35
Halfyard, D. J.	(1)	15—117	Kent v. Worcs. (Maidstone) ... 1959
Hammond, W. R.	(1)	15—128	Glos. v. Worcs. (Cheltenham) ... 1928
Hargreave, S.	(1)	15—76	Warwicks. v. Surrey (Oval) ... 1903
Harry, F.	(1)	15—70	Lancs. v. Warwicks. (Manchester) ... 1906
Hearne, J. T.	(4)	15—154	Middx. v. Notts. (Nottingham) ... 1893
		15—110	M.C.C. v. Oxford U. (Oxford) ... 1897
		16—114	Middx. v. Lancs. (Manchester) ... 1898
		15—93	Middx. v. Somerset (Lord's) ... 1904
Hearne, W.	(1)	15—114	Kent v. Lancs. (Manchester) ... 1893
Henderson, R.	(1)	15—98	Gents. of England v. Oxford U. (Oxford) ... 1877
Hinkly, W.	(1)	16—	Kent v. England (Lord's) ... 1848
Hirst, G. H.	(1)	15—63	Yorks. v. Leics. (Hull) ... 1907
Hopwood, J. L.	(1)	15—112	Lancs. v. Worcs. (Blackpool) ... 1934
Howell, W. P.	(2)	15—57	Australians v. Surrey (Oval) ... 1899
		17—54	Australians v. Western Province (Cape Town) 1902–03
Humphreys, W.	(1)	15—193	Sussex v. Somerset (Taunton) ... 1893
Illingworth, R.	(1)	15—123	Yorks. v. Glamorgan (Swansea) ... 1960
Jackson, J.	(2)	15—91	North v. South (Lord's) ... 1857
		15—73	Notts. v. Surrey (Oval) ... 1860
Jenkins, R. O.	(1)	15—122	Worcs. v. Sussex (Dudley) ... 1953
Jupp, V. W. C.	(1)	15—52	Northants. v. Glamorgan (Swansea) ... 1925
Kennedy, A. S.	(1)	15—116	Hants. v. Somerset (Bath) ... 1922
Laker, J. C.	(2)	15—97	Surrey v. M.C.C. (Lord's) ... 1954
		19—90	England v. Australia (Manchester) ... 1956
Langford, B. A.	(1)	15—54	Somerset v. Lancs. (Weston-super-Mare) ... 1958
Lillywhite, W.	(2)	16—	Sussex v. Hants. & Surrey (Bramshill) ... 1826
		15—	England v. Kent (Lord's) ... 1840
Litteljohn, A. R.	(1)	15—189	Middx. v. Lancs. (Lord's) ... 1911
Lock, G. A. R.	(2)	16—83	Surrey v. Kent (Blackheath) ... 1956
		15—182	Surrey v. Kent (Blackheath) ... 1958
Lockwood, W. H.	(1)	15—184	Surrey v. Glos. (Cheltenham) ... 1899
Lohmann, G. A.	(2)	15—98	Surrey v. Sussex (Hove) ... 1889
		15—45	England v. South Africa (Port Elizabeth) ... 1895–96
Mailey, A. A.	(1)	15—193	Australians v. Notts. (Nottingham) ... 1926
Marlar, R. G.	(2)	15—133	Sussex v. Glamorgan (Swansea) ... 1952
		15—119	Sussex v. Lancs. (Hove) ... 1955
Marsham, C. D.	(1)	16—93	Gents of England v. Gents of M.C.C. (Lord's) ... 1855
Matthews, F. C. L.	(1)	17—89	Notts. v. Northants. (Nottingham) ... 1923
McBeath, D. J.	(1)	15—168	Canterbury v. Auckland (Christchurch) ... 1918–19
McDonald, E. A.	(1)	15—154	Lancs. v. Kent (Manchester) ... 1928
McDonell, H. C.	(1)	15—138	Cambridge U. v. Surrey (Cambridge) ... 1904

McIntyre, W.	...............(1)	15—47	Lancs. v. Derby (Derby) 1877
McKibbin, T. R.	............(1)	15—125	N.S.W. v. South Australia (Adelaide) 1896–97
Mead, W.	........................(2)	17—119	Essex v. Hants. (Southampton) 1895
		15—115	Essex v. Leics. (Leyton) 1903
Meyer, R. J. O.	..............(1)	16—188	Europeans v. Muslims (Bombay) 1927–28
Moir, A. M.	..................(1)	15—203	Otago v. Central Districts (New Plymouth) ...1953–54
Mold, A.	........................(4)	15—131	Lancs. v. Somerset (Taunton) 1891
		15—87	Lancs. v. Sussex (Hove) 1894
		16—111	Lancs. v. Kent (Manchester) 1895
		15—85	Lancs. v. Notts. (Nottingham) 1895
Morley, F.	.......................(1)	15—35	Notts. v. Kent (Town Malling) 1878
Mortimore, G.	.................(1)	15—	Nelson v. Wellington (Nelson) 1862–63
Muncer, B. L.	.................(2)	15—161	Glamorgan v. Essex (Brentwood) 1948
		15—201	Glamorgan v. Sussex (Swansea) 1948
Mynn, A.	.......................(1)	15—73	Gents of Kent v. Gents of England (Canterbury)...1843
Nash, J.	..........................(1)	15—116	Glamorgan v. Worcs. (Swansea) 1921
Newman, J. A.	................(1)	16—88	Hants. v. Somerset (Weston-super-Mare) 1927
Nichols, M. S.	................(1)	15—165	Essex v. Glos. (Gloucester) 1938
Nupen, E. P.	...................(1)	16—136	Transvaal v. Griqualand West (Johannesburg) 1931–32
Parker, C. W. L.	..............(7)	15—109	Glos. v. Derby (Derby) 1924
		17—56	Glos. v. Essex (Gloucester) 1925
		16—154	Glos. v. Somerset (Bristol) 1927
		15—173	Glos. v. Northants. (Gloucester) 1927
		16—109	Glos. v. Middx. (Cheltenham) 1930
		15—91	Glos. v. Surrey (Cheltenham) 1930
		15—113	Glos. v. Notts. (Bristol) 1931
Parkin, C. H.	...................(1)	15—95	Lancs. v. Glamorgan (Blackpool) 1923
Parris, F. H.	.....................(1)	15—98	Sussex v. Glos. (Bristol) 1894
Peel, R.	.........................(1)	15—50	Yorks. v. Somerset (Leeds) 1895
Perks, R. T. D.	................(1)	15—106	Worcs. v. Essex (Worcester) 1937
Relf, A. E.	.....................(1)	15—77	Sussex v. Leics. (Hove) 1912
Rhodes, W.	....................(2)	15—56	Yorks. v. Essex (Leyton) 1899
		15—124	England v. Australia (Melbourne) 1903 04
Richardson, T	.............(5)	15—95	Surrey v. Essex (Oval) 1894
		15—155	Surrey v. Hants. (Oval) 1895
		15—113	Surrey v. Leics. (Oval) 1896
		15—154	Surrey v. Yorks. (Leeds) 1897
		15—83	Surrey v. Warwicks. (Oval) 1898
Roberts, F. G.	.............(1)	15—123	Glos. v. Kent (Maidstone) 1897
Robinson, E. P.	.............(1)	15—78	Somerset v. Sussex (Weston-super-Mare) 1952
Rowan, A. M. B.	............(1)	15—68	Transvaal v. Australians (Johannesburg) 1949–50
Smith, S. G.	...................(1)	16—85	West Indian XI v. Bennett's XI (Trinidad) ...1901–02
Smith, T. P. B.	...................(1)	16—215	Essex v. Middx. (Colchester) 1947
Southerton, J.	..................(1)	16—52	South v. North (Lord's) 1875
Spofforth, F. R.	..............(1)	15—36	Australians v. Oxford U. (Oxford) 1886
Statham, J. B.	..................(1)	15—89	Lancs. v. Warwicks. (Coventry) 1957
Tarrant, F. A.	.................(3)	15—47	Middx. v. Hants. (Lord's) 1913
		16—176	Middx. v. Lancs. (Manchester) 1914
		16—69	England XII v. India XII (Bombay) 1915–16
Tarrant, G.	.....................(1)	15—56	Cambridgeshire v. Kent (Chatham) 1862
Tate, F. W.	.....................(1)	15—68	Sussex v. Middx. (Lord's) 1902
Thompson, G. J.	............(1)	15—167	Northants. v. Leics. (Northampton) 1906
Tinley, R. C.	...................(1)	15—78	Notts. v. Cambridgeshire (Nottingham) 1862
Titmus, F. J.	...................(1)	15—95	Middx. v. Somerset (Bath) 1955
Townsend, C. L.	..............(5)	16—122	Glos. v. Notts. (Nottingham) 1895
		15—184	Glos. v. Yorks. (Cheltenham) 1895
		15—134	Glos. v. Middx. (Lord's) 1898
		15—141	Glos. v. Essex (Clifton) 1898
		15—205	Glos. v. Warwicks. (Cheltenham) 1898
Tribe, G. E.	.....................(2)	15—75	Northants. v. Yorks. (Bradford)......................1955
		15—31	Northants. v. Yorks. (Northampton) 1958
Trott, A. E.	.....................(1)	15—187	Middx. v. Sussex (Lord's) 1901
Trumble, H.	.................(2)	15—199	Victoria v. South Australia (Adelaide) 1888–89
		15—68	Australians v. South of England (Bournemouth) 1902
Turner, C. T. B.	..............(3)	16—79	N.S.W. v. Shrewsbury's XI (Sydney) 1887–88
		17—50	Australians v. England XI (Hastings) 1888
		15—174	N.S.W. v. Victoria (Sydney) 1890–91
Tyler, E. J.	.....................(2)	15—96	Somerset v. Notts. (Taunton) 1892
		15—95	Somerset v. Sussex (Taunton) 1895
Verity, H.	........................(5)	17—91	Yorks. v. Essex (Leyton) 1933
		15—104	England v. Australia (Lord's) 1934
		15—129	Yorks. v. Oxford U. (Oxford) 1936

Verity, H. (*cont.*)		15—38	Yorks. v. Kent (Sheffield)	1936
		15—100	Yorks. v. Essex (Westcliff)	1936
Vine, J.	(1)	15—161	Sussex v. Notts. (Nottingham)	1901
Vogler, A. E. E.	(1)	16—38	Eastern Province v. Griqualand West (Johannesburg)	1906—07
Walsh, J. E.	(3)	15—100	Leics. v. Sussex (Hove)	1948
		15—164	Leics. v. Notts. (Loughborough)	1949
		16—225	Leics. v. Oxford U. (Oxford)	1953
Wardle, J. H.	(1)	16—112	Yorks. v. Sussex (Hull)	1954
Warren, A. R.	(1)	15—112	Derby v. Notts. (Welbeck)	1904
Wass, T.	(2)	16—69	Notts. v. Lancs. (Liverpool)	1906
		16—103	Notts. v. Essex (Nottingham)	1908
Wellard, A. W.	(1)	15—101	Somerset v. Worcs. (Bath)	1947
White, J. C.	(3)	16—83	Somerset v. Worcs. (Bath)	1919
		15—175	Somerset v. Worcs. (Worcester)	1921
		15—96	Somerset v. Glamorgan (Bath)	1932
Wilson, G. A.	(1)	15—142	Worcs. v. Somerset (Taunton)	1905
Wisden, J.	(1)	15—	Sussex v. Kent (Brighton)	1848
Woodcock, A.	(1)	15—136	Leics. v. Notts. (Leicester)	1894
Woods, S. M. J.	(2)	15—88	Cambridge U. v. Thornton's XI (Cambridge)	1890
		15—86	Hawke's XI v. Philadelphians (Philadelphia)	1891—92
Wright, D. V. P.	(3)	16—80	Kent v. Somerset (Bath)	1939
		15—173	Kent v. Sussex (Hastings)	1947
		15—163	Kent v. Leics. (Maidstone)	1949
Young, H.	(1)	15—154	Essex v. Warwicks. (Birmingham)	1899

Outstanding Innings Bowling Analyses

TEN WICKETS

O. M. R. W.

19·4—16—10—10	H. Verity: Yorks. v. Notts. (Leeds)	1932
16·2— 8—18—10	G. Geary: Leics. v. Glamorgan (Pontypridd)	1929
19 —11—20—10	P. Chatterjee: Bengal v. Assam (Jorhat)	1956—57
12 — 2—26—10	A. E. E. Vogler: Eastern Province v. Griqualand West (Johannesburg)	1906—07
21·3—10—28—10	A. E. Moss: Canterbury v. Wellington (Christchurch)	1889—90
23·2—14—28—10	W. P. Howell: Australians v. Surrey (Oval)	1899
16 — 7—30—10	C. Blythe: Kent v. Northants. (Northampton)	1907

NINE WICKETS

O. M. R. W.

10 — 4—11—9	A. P. Freeman: Kent v. Sussex (Hove)	1922
6·3— 3—12—9	H. Verity: Yorks. v. Kent (Sheffield)	1936
17·1—10—15—9	C. T. B. Turner: Australians v. England XI (Stoke)	1888
14·5— 9—17—9	G. G. Napier: Europeans v. Parsis (Poona)	1909—10
15·5— 6—17—9	P. J. Loader: Surrey v. Warwicks. (Oval)	1958
17·3— 9—17—9	L. Jackson: Derby v. Cambridge U. (Cambridge)	1959
15·2— 7—18—9	F. R. Spofforth: Australians v. Oxford U. (Oxford)	1886
13 — 6—18—9	R. K. Oxenham: Australians v. Ceylon (Colombo)	1935—36
25 — —19—9	J. Grundy: Notts. v. Kent (Nottingham)	1864
15·4— 7—19—9	A. M. B. Rowan: Transvaal v. Australians (Johannesburg)	1949—50
35·1—25—20—9	W. G. Grace: M.C.C. v. Notts. (Lord's)	1885
19·3— 8—21—9	J. W. Marchant: Wellington v. Hawke's Bay (Wellington)	1873—74
15·1— 8—21—9	L. B. Richmond: Notts. v. Hants. (Nottingham)	1922
13·5— 8—21—9	T. W. Goddard: Glos. v. Cambridge U. (Cheltenham)	1929
21·3—10—22—9	R. Peel: Yorks. v. Somerset (Leeds)	1895
10·3— 2—22—9	M. G. Melle: South Africans v. Tasmania (Hobart)	1952—53

EIGHT WICKETS

O. M. R. W.

14 —12— 2—8	J. C. Laker: England v. Rest (Bradford)	1950
11·1— 7— 4—8	D. Shackleton: Hants. v. Somerset (Weston-super-Mare)	1955
16 —11— 5—8	E. Peate: Yorks. v. Surrey (Holbeck)	1883
14 — — 7—8	J. Bickley: England v. Kent & Sussex (Lord's)	1856
9·4— 5— 7—8	G. A. Lohmann: England v. South Africa (Port Elizabeth)	1895—96
12 — 2— 7—8	C. H. Palmer: Leics. v. Surrey (Leicester)	1955
6·7— 2— 8—8	J. E. D. Sealey: Barbados v. Trinidad (Barbados)	1941—42

O. M. R. W.

12	—	7—	8—8	M. G. Melle: Transvaal v. Griqualand West (Johannesburg)	1950–51
13·2—	—	9—8		G. Wootton: M.C.C. v. Sussex (Lord's)	1863
6	—	1—	9—8	G. Dennett: Glos. v. Northants. (Gloucester)	1907
14·2—10—		9—8		G. Tribe: Northants. v. Yorks. (Northampton)	1958
13	—	8—11—8		G. Freeman: Yorks. v. Lancs. (Holbeck)	1868
14·2—	5—11—8			J. Briggs: England v. South Africa (Cape Town)	1888–89
11·4—	6—11—8			B. M. Billimaria: Parsis v. Europeans (Poona)	1896–97
13	—	7—11—8		A. S. Kennedy: Hants. v. Glamorgan (Cardiff)	1921
8·2—	2—11—8			W. H. Copson: Derby v. Warwicks. (Derby)	1937
13·4—	—12—8			R. C. Tinley: Notts. v. Cambridgeshire (Nottingham)	1862
20·2—13—12—8				R. Peel: Yorks. v. Notts. (Sheffield)	1888
12	—	8—12—8		R. W. Norden: Transvaal v. Rhodesia (Johannesburg)	1904–05
17	—10—12—8			C. W. L. Parker: Glos. v. Essex (Gloucester)	1925
6·4—	2—12—8			W. H. R. Andrews: Somerset v. Surrey (Oval)	1937
9·4—	3—12—8			G. S. Ramchand: Bombay v. Saurashtra (Bombay)	1959–60
13	—	6—13—8		J. P. Firth: Wellington v. Hawke's Bay (Wellington)	1883–84
21·3—12—13—8				C. T. B. Turner: Australians v. England XI (Hastings)	1888
13·2—	5—13—8			E. Robinson: Yorks. v. Cambridge U. (Cambridge)	1928
8	—	2—13—8		D. P. B. Morkel: South Africans v. Western Australia (Perth)	1931–32
12	—	7—13—8		Zafar: Multan v. Quetta (Multan)	1958–59
27·1—17—14—8				A. Shaw: M.C.C. v. Derby (Lord's)	1881
19	—12—14—8			S. Austen: N.S.W. v. Hawke's Bay (Napier)	1893–94
7·5—	1—14—8			H. D. Kanga: Parsis v. Europeans (Poona)	1913–14
33·3—	—15—8			G. Wootton: M.C.C. v. Surrey (Lord's)	1867
11	—	7—15—8		A. Hearne: Kent v. Glos. (Tonbridge)	1903
14	—	8—15—8		H. J. Butler: Notts. v. Surrey (Nottingham)	1937
6·4—	2—15—8			K. T. Ramadhin: West Indians v. Glos. (Cheltenham)	1950

SEVEN WICKETS

O. M. R. W.

8·3—	6	3	7	Г. R. Spofforth: Australians v. England XI (Birmingham)	1884
9·3—	7—	4—7		W. A. Henderson: N.-E. Transvaal v. O.F.S. (Bloemfontein)	1937–38
21·2—18—	6—7			F. Morley: M.C.C. v. Oxford U. (Oxford)	1877
7	—	4—	6—7	A. Waddington: Yorks. v. Sussex (Hull)	1922
14	—12—	6—7		R. Tyldesley: Lancs. v. Northants. (Liverpool)	1924
24	—20—	7—7		W. Caffyn: Surrey v. Kent (Canterbury)	1862
41·2—38—	7—7			A. Shaw: Notts. v. M.C.C. (Lord's)	1875
10·2—	7—	7—7		F. Morley: Notts. v. Derby (Nottingham)	1879
6·4—	3—	7—7		L. T. Driffield: Cambridge U. v. M.C.C. (Cambridge)	1900
7	—	3—	7—7	J. Bailey: Hants. v. Notts. (Southampton)	1932
13·3—	8—	7—7		G. Geary: Leics. v. Warwicks. (Hinckley)	1936
14	—	9—	8—7	L. Cook: Lancs. v. Derby (Chesterfield)	1920
16	—	9—	8—7	G. R. Cox: Sussex v. Derby (Hove)	1920
10	—	7—	8—7	A. S. Kennedy: Hants. v. Warwicks. (Portsmouth)	1927
11·5—	7—	8—7		James Langridge: Sussex v. Glos. (Cheltenham)	1932
10	—	—	9—7	G. Bennett: Kent v. Sussex (Brighton)	1857
9·3—	6—	9—7		T. Emmett: Yorks. v. Sussex (Hove)	1878
22	—15—	9—7		F. Morley: Notts. v. Kent (Town Malling)	1878
19·2—12—	9—7			F. Morley: Notts. v. Surrey (Oval)	1880
6·3—	3—	9—7		F. E. Woolley: Kent v. Surrey (Oval)	1911
7·5—	3—	9—7		C. Blythe: Kent v. Leics. (Leicester)	1912
14	—	7—	9—7	G. G. Macaulay: Yorks. v. Northants. (Kettering)	1933
6	—	1—	9—7	H. Verity: Yorks. v. Sussex (Hove)	1939
12·1—	8—	9—7		J. T. Partridge: Rhodesia v. Border (Buawago)	1959–60
16	—	—10—7		H. Stubberfield: Sussex v. Kent (Brighton)	1859
9	—	7—10—7		A. Mold: Lancs. v. Somerset (Manchester)	1894
8	—	2—10—7		A. J. Hopkins: Australians v. Cambridge U. (Cambridge)	1902
6·2—	1—10—7			A. C. King: Natal v. Griqualand West (Johannesburg)	1906–07
8·2—	4—10—7			J. T. Newstead: Yorks. v. Worcs. (Bradford)	1907
9	—	4—10—7		J. C. White: Somerset v. Glos (Bristol)	1920
5·3—	2—10—7			P. G. H. Fender: Surrey v. Middx. (Lord's)	1927
20·4—13—10—7				F. M. Sibbles: Lancs. v. Yorks. (Bradford)	1932

SIX WICKETS

O. M. R. W.

21·1—20—1—6	S. Costick: Victoria v. Tasmania (Melbourne)	1868–69
4·5— 3—1—6	V. I. Smith: South Africans v. Derby (Derby)	1947

O. M. R. W.

11 —10—1—6	Israr Ali: Bahawalpur v. Dacca U. (Bahawalpur) 1957–58
8·4— 7—2—6	F. E. Field: Warwicks. v. Worcs. (Dudley) 1914
8·1— 6—3—6	H. F. Boyle: Australians v. M.C.C. (Lord's) 1878
13·3—11—3—6	A. Penn: Kent v. Sussex (Tunbridge Wells) 1878
10·1— 9—3—6	R. G. Barlow: Lancs. v. Derby (Derby) 1881
4·4— 3—3—6	T. Wass: Notts. v. M.C.C. (Lord's) 1907
7 — 4—3—6	G. G. Macaulay: Yorks. v. Derby (Hull) 1921
8 — 5—3—6	J. A. Cowie: New Zealanders v. Ireland (Dublin) 1937
11 — 9—3—6	T. L. Goddard: Natal v. Border (East London) 1959–60
5·3— 3—4—6	F. R. Spofforth: Australians v. M.C.C. (Lord's) 1878
7·5— 4—4—6	W. Rhodes: Yorks. v. Notts. (Nottingham) 1901
8 — 5—4—6	S. T. Callaway: Canterbury v. Wellington (Wellington) 1903–04
9·2— —5—6	C. Reid: Victoria v. Tasmania (Melbourne) 1870–71
9·2— 3—5—6	Bennett: Nelson v. Wellington (Nelson) 1885–86
9·1— 6—5—6	G. S. Boyes: Hants. v. Derby (Portsmouth) 1933
14 —11—5—6	J. C. Laker: Surrey v. Notts. (Oval) 1955
18·2—13—6—6	W. W. Robinson: Auckland v. Nelson (Nelson) 1873–74
8·4— 5—6—6	A. E. Bailey: Somerset v. Warwicks. (Taunton) 1906
8 — 5—6—6	C. H. Parkin: Lancs. v. Glamorgan (Liverpool).........................1924
9·4— 7—6—6	J. H. Wardle: Yorks. v. Glos. (Bristol) 1955

FIVE WICKETS

O. M. R. W.

3 — 3—0—5	A. D. Pougher: M.C.C. v. Australians (Lord's) 1896
6 — 6—0—5	G. R. Cox: Sussex v. Somerset (Weston-super-Mare) 1921
5 — 5—0—5	R. Tyldesley: Lancs. v. Leics. (Manchester) 1924
6·4— 6—0—5	P. T. Mills: Glos. v. Somerset (Bristol) 1928
4 — 3—1—5	F. W. Tate: Sussex v. Kent (Tonbridge) 1888
15·2—13—2—5	D. Ashby: Canterbury v. Auckland (Auckland) 1877–78
6·1— 4—2—5	E. H. Killick: Sussex v. Hants. (Chichester) 1907
5·2— 4—2—5	J. C. Clay: Glamorgan v. Somerset (Cardiff) 1922
2·3— 1—2—5	E. R. H. Toshack: Australia v. India (Brisbane) 1947–48
5·3— 4—2—5	G. A. R. Lock: Surrey v. Worcs. (Oval) 1954
2·2— 1—3—5	B. D. Hylton-Stewart: Somerset v. Worcs. (Stourbridge) 1912
5 — 3—3—5	C. F. W. Allcott: New Zealanders v. Somerset (Taunton) 1927
8·2— —4—5	R. Lang: Cambridge U. v. Oxford U. (Lord's) 1862
9 — 6—4—5	S. Haigh: Yorks. v. Worcs. (Huddersfield) 1903
4·4— 2—4—5	G. A. Rotherham: Warwicks. v. Northants. (Northampton) 1921
7·1— 4—4—5	V. Murdin: Northants. v. Worcs. (Northampton) 1921
3 — 1—4—5	T. W. Goddard: Glos. v. Somerset (Bristol) 1947
8 — 4—4—5	P. F. Jackson: Worcs. v. Warwicks. (Birmingham) 1950
21·5—18—5—5	J. W. Sharpe: Surrey v. Oxford U. (Oxford) 1889
14 —10—5—5	S. Rudder: Barbados v. Trinidad (Barbados) 1897–98
4·4— 2—5—5	W. Rhodes: Yorks. v. Derby (Bradford) 1910
7 — 3—5—5	P. A. Wright: Cambridge U. v. Lancs. (Cambridge) 1922
8 — 5—5—5	Firasat Hussain: United Provinces v. Delhi (Agra) 1934–35
7 — 4—5—5	C. J. Knott: Hants. v. Sussex (Eastbourne)............................1950
15·4—12—5—5	D. Shackleton: Hants. v. Somerset (Weston-super-Mare) 1956
11 — 7—5—5	S. P. Gupte: Bombay v. Gujerat (Bombay) 1958–59

FOUR WICKETS

O. M. R. W.

2 — 2—0—4	Sir F. Bathurst: England v. Kent (Lord's) 1843
3·2— 3—0—4	J. R. Napier: Lancs. v. Yorks. (Sheffield) 1888
5 — 5—0—4	A. Hearne: Kent v. Somerset (Taunton) 1893
0·5— 0—0—4	A. F. Borland: Natal v. Griqualand West (Kimberley) 1926–27
2·1— 2—0—4	L. C. Eastman: Essex v. Somerset (Weston-super-Mare) 1934
7 — 7—0—4	L. Amarnath: Railways v. Patiala (Patiala) 1958–59
6 — 5—1—4	R. C. W. Burn: Brackley's XI v. Barbados (Barbados)...............1904–05
3·3— 2—1—4	A. G. Slater: Derby v. Essex (Leyton) 1913
4 — 3—1—4	J. L. Hopwood: Lancs. v. Glos. (Manchester) 1931
10 — 9—1—4	R. G. Garlick: Northants. v. Middx. (Northampton) 1950
8·3— 6—2—4	D. N. Writer: Parsis v. Europeans (Bombay) 1894–95
3 — 2—2—4	E. H. Killick: Sussex v. Notts. (Nottingham) 1905
5 — 3—2—4	C. V. Grimmett: Australians v. Worcs. (Worcester) 1926
8 — 6—2—4	H. Larwood: Notts. v. Cambridge U. (Cambridge) 1926
7 — 5—2—4	L. Amarnath: Southern Punjab v. Sind (Patiala) 1938–39

O. M. R. W.

8·2— —3—4	S. Dakin: West of England v. M.C.C. (Bath)	1843
8 — —3—4	W. H. Anstead: Surrey v. Kent (Oval)	1870
6·3— 4—3—4	J. Young: Derby v. Notts. (Nottingham)	1900
10·2— 7—3—4	W. R. Cuttell: Lancs. v. Kent (Manchester)	1904
5 — 3—3—4	J. A. Newman: Hants. v. Glamorgan (Swansea)	1922
7·3— 5—3—4	G. S. Boyes: Hants. v. Somerset (Southampton)	1936
5·4— 4—3—4	R. A. Sinfield: Glos. v. Lancs. (Preston)	1936
8 — 5—3—4	B. L. Muncer: Glamorgan v. Kent (Swansea)	1949
7 — 5—3—4	C. S. Matthews: Notts. v. Somerset (Frome)	1957
5·5— 4—3—4	J. G. Lomax: Somerset v. Cambridge U. (Cambridge)	1959
4 — 2—3—4	Tahir Ali: Karachi v. Hyderabad (Hyderabad)	1959–60
10 — 6—4—4	H. H. Stephenson: Surrey v. Notts. (Nottingham)	1854
11 — 9—4—4	J. T. Hearne: M.C.C. v. Australians (Lord's)	1896
3·1— 1—4—4	J. H. Vincett: Sussex v. Glos. (Bristol)	1909
8 — 5—4—4	R. Tyldesley: Lancs. v. Scotland (Manchester)	1925
11 — 8—4—4	S. J. Staples: Notts. v. Hants. (Southampton)	1932

A. Drake returned analyses of 4·3—1—4—4 and 6·1—4—3—3 for Yorkshire v. Somerset (Bath) 1913.

T. Hayward returned analyses of 0·3—0—0—1 and 0·3—0—0—2 for Surrey v. Leicestershire (Leicester) 1895.

Outstanding Match Bowling Analyses

NINETEEN WICKETS

19—90 (9—37 & 10—53) J. C. Laker: England v. Australia (Manchester) 1956

EIGHTEEN WICKETS

18—97 (9—43 & 9—54) H. A. Arkwright: M.C.C. v. Gentlemen of Kent (Canterbury) 1861

SEVENTEEN WICKETS

17—48 (10—30 & 7—18)	C. Blythe: Kent v. Northants. (Northampton)	1907
17—50 (8—13 & 9—37)	C. T. B. Turner: Australians v. England XI (Hastings)	1888
17—54 (8—31 & 9—23)	W. P. Howell: Australians v. Western Province (Cape Town)	1902–03
17—56 (9—44 & 8—12)	C. W. L. Parker: Glos. v. Essex (Gloucester)	1925
17—67 (9—11 & 8—56)	A. P. Freeman: Kent v. Sussex (Hove)	1922
17—89 (9—55 & 8—34)	W. G. Grace: Glos. v. Notts. (Cheltenham)	1877
17—89 (8—39 & 9—50)	F. C. L. Matthews: Notts. v. Northants. (Nottingham)	1923
17—91 (9—62 & 8—29)	H. Dean: Lancs. v. Yorks. (Liverpool)	1913
17—91 (8—47 & 9—44)	H. Verity: Yorks. v. Essex (Leyton)	1933
17—92 (8—31 & 9—61)	A. P. Freeman: Kent v. Warwicks. (Folkestone)	1932

SIXTEEN WICKETS

16—35 (8—18 & 8—17)	W. E. Bowes: Yorks. v. Northants. (Kettering)	1935
16—38 (7—15 & 9—23)	T. Emmett: Yorks. v. Cambridgeshire (Hunslet)	1869
16—38 (6—12 & 10—26)	A. E. E. Vogler: Eastern Province v. Griqualand West (Johannesburg)	1906–07
16—52 (9—30 & 7—22)	J. Southerton: South v. North (Lord's)	1875
16—58 (8—21 & 8—37)	E. M. Dowson: Bennett's XI v. Jamaica (Kingston)	1901–02
16—60 (7—40 & 9—20)	W. G. Grace: M.C.C. v. Notts. (Lord's)	1885
16—65 (8—23 & 8—42)	G. Giffen: Australians v. Lancs. (Manchester)	1886
16—69 (8—25 & 8—44)	T. Wass: Notts. v. Lancs. (Liverpool)	1906
16—69 (9—35 & 7—34)	F. A. Tarrant: England XII v. Indian XII (Bombay)	1915–16
16—79 (8—39 & 8—40)	C. T. B. Turner: N.S.W. v. Shrewsbury's XI (Sydney)	1887–88
16—80 (8—35 & 8—45)	D. V. P. Wright: Kent v. Somerset (Bath)	1939
16—82 (8—38 & 8—44)	A. P. Freeman: Kent v. Northants. (Tunbridge Wells)	1932
16—83 (8—36 & 8 47)	J. C. White: Somerset v. Worcs. (Bath)	1919
16—83 (6—18 & 10—65)	G. G. Collins: Kent v. Notts. (Dover)	1922
16—83 (8—39 & 8—34)	B. Dooland: Notts. v. Essex (Nottingham)	1954
16—83 (6—29 & 10—54)	G. A. R. Lock: Surrey v. Kent (Blackheath)	1956
16—84 (7—43 & 9—41)	C. Gladwin: Derby v. Worcs. (Stourbridge)	1952

16—85   (9—34 & 7—51)   S. G. Smith: West Indian XI v. Bennett's XI (Trinidad) ....1901—02
16—88   (8—65 & 8—23)   J. A. Newman: Hants. v. Somerset (Weston-super-Mare) 1927

FIFTEEN WICKETS

15—21   (8— 9 & 7—12)   G. Dennett: Glos. v. Northants. (Gloucester) 1907
15—28   (7—17 & 8—11)   J. Briggs: England v. South Africa (Cape Town) ....1888—89
15—31   (7—22 & 8— 9)   G. Tribe: Northants. v. Yorks. (Northampton) 1958
15—35   (7— 9 & 8—26)   F. Morley: Notts. v. Kent (Town Malling) 1878
15—36   (9—18 & 6—18)   F. R. Spofforth: Australians v. Oxford U. (Oxford) 1886
15—38   (6—26 & 9—12)   H. Verity: Yorks. v. Kent (Sheffield) 1936
15—45   (7—38 & 8— 7)   G. A. Lohmann: England v. South Africa (Port Elizabeth) ......1895—96
15—45   (7— 9 & 8—36)   C. Blythe: Kent v. Leics. (Leicester) 1912
15—47   (8—31 & 7—16)   W. McIntyre: Lancs. v. Derby (Derby) 1877
15—47   (7—27 & 8—20)   F. A. Tarrant: Middx. v. Hants. (Lord's) 1913
15—49   (9—23 & 6—26)   J. Botten: N.E. Transvaal v. Griqualand West (Pretoria) ....1958—59
15—50   (9—22 & 6—28)   R. Peel: Yorks. v. Somerset (Leeds) 1895
15—51   (5—16 & 10—35)   A. Drake: Yorks. v. Somerset (Weston-super-Mare) 1914
15—52   (7—34 & 8—18)   V. W. C. Jupp: Northants. v. Glamorgan (Swansea) 1925
15—54   (9—26 & 6—28)   B. A. Langford: Somerset v. Lancs. (Weston-super-Mare) 1958
15—56   (7—40 & 8—16)   G. Tarrant: Cambridgeshire v. Kent (Chatham) 1862
15—56   (9—28 & 6—28)   W. Rhodes: Yorks. v. Essex (Leyton) 1899
15—57   (9—31 & 6—26)   J. Briggs: Londesborough's XI v. Australians (Scarborough) 1890
15—57   (10—28 & 5—29)   W. P. Howell: Australians v. Surrey (Oval) 1899
15—60   (8—33 & 7—27)   S. T. Callaway: Canterbury v. Hawke's Bay (Napier) ....1903—04

FOURTEEN WICKETS

14—29   (6— 7 & 8—22)   T. Emmett: Yorks. v. Surrey (Sheffield) 1867
14—29   (6—16 & 8—13)   W. C. Smith: Surrey v. Northants. (Oval) 1910
14—29   (8— 4 & 6—25)   D. Shackleton: Hants. v. Somerset (Weston-super-Mare) 1955
14—33   (8—12 & 6—21)   R. Peel: Yorks. v. Notts. (Sheffield) 1888
14—34   (8—15 & 6—19)   A. Rylott: M.C.C. v. Kent (Lord's) 1878
14—37   (7—34 & 7— 3)   F. R. Spofforth: Australians v. England XI (Birmingham) 1884
14—38   (6—18 & 8—20)   W. Mycroft: North v. South (Loughborough) 1875
14—43   (8—21 & 6—22)   S. Haigh: Yorks. v. Hants. (Southampton) 1898
14—43   (7—23 & 7—20)   W. Voce: Notts. v. Northants. (Nottingham) 1929
14—44   (7—31 & 7—13)   R. K. Oxenham: Australians v. Central India & Rajputana
                                                                        (Ajmer)............1935—36
14—45   (6—24 & 8—21)   G. G. Hearne: Kent v. M.C.C. (Lord's) 1879
14—45   (9—17 & 5—28)   G. G. Napier: Europeans v. Parsis (Poona)..........................1909—10
14—45   (8—23 & 6—22)   W. J. O'Reilly: N.S.W. v. Queensland (Sydney) ....1939—40

THIRTEEN WICKETS

13—14   (7— 6 & 6— 8)   F. Morley: M.C.C. v. Oxford U. (Oxford) 1877
13—25   (7—19 & 6— 6)   W. W. Robinson: Auckland v. Nelson (Nelson) ....1873—74
13—38   (6—18 & 7—20)   E. Wainwright: Yorks. v. Sussex (Dewsbury) 1894
13—38   (6—27 & 7—11)   T. R. McKibbin: Australians v. Lancs. (Liverpool) 1896
13—39   (7—35 & 6— 4)   J. Briggs: Lancs. v. Derby (Manchester) 1888
13—39   (6—22 & 7—17)   H. R. B. Davenport: Lucas's XI v. British Guiana (Georgetown) 1894—95
13—40   (6—22 & 7—18)   G. Howitt: U.N. England XI v. U.S. England XI (Lord's) 1870
13—40   (6—18 & 7—22)   J. Briggs: Londesborough's XI v. Australians (Scarborough).........1888
13—40   (8—17 & 5—23)   T. Wass: Notts. v. Derby (Nottingham) 1901
13—40   (6—27 & 7—13)   S. Haigh: Yorks. v. Warwicks. (Sheffield) 1907
13—41   (4— 5 & 9—36)   W. Huddleston: Lancs. v. Notts. (Liverpool) 1906
13—42   (6—24 & 7—18)   J. Jackson: North v. South (Tunbridge Wells) 1857
13—43   (6—36 & 7— 7)   G. Geary: Leics. v. Warwicks. (Hinckley) 1936
13—44   (5—16 & 8—28)   H. H Stephenson: England v. Kent (Lords) 1858
13—45   (7—33 & 6—12)   F. Morley: Notts. v. Yorks. (Sheffield) 1876
13—45   (7—24 & 6—21)   W. Rhodes: Yorks. v. Somerset (Bath) 1898

TWELVE WICKETS

12—18   (6—13 & 6— 5)   Bennett: Nelson v. Wellington (Nelson) ....1885—86
12—19   (6—12 & 6— 7)   G. H. Hirst: Yorks. v. Northants. (Northampton) 1908
12—20   (5— 6 & 7—14)   T. Richardson: Surrey v. Leics. (Leicester) 1897
12—23   (8—11 & 4—12)   G. Freeman: Yorks. v. Lancs. (Holbeck) 1868

12—28	(6—19 & 6— 9)	E. Willsher: Kent v. Yorks. (Sheffield) 1865
12—29	(7—12 & 5—17)	G. H. Hirst: Yorks. v. Essex (Leyton) 1901
12—30	(6—11 & 6—19)	T. B. Mitchell: Derby v. Sussex (Chesterfield) 1931
12—33	(4—21 & 8—12)	R. W. Norden: Transvaal v. Rhodesia (Johannesburg) 1904–05
12—33	(3—16 & 9—17)	L. Jackson: Derby v. Cambridge U. (Cambridge) 1959
12—34	(7—15 & 5—19)	A. Cotter: Australians v. Worcs. (Worcester) 1905
12—34	(6—20 & 6—14)	G. A. R. Lock: Surrey v. Glamorgan (Oval) 1957
12—35	(6—22 & 6—13)	J. C. Shaw: Notts. v. Kent (Crystal Palace) 1870
12—35	(7— 7 & 5—28)	F. Morley: Notts. v. Derby (Nottingham) 1879
12—35	(8—18 & 4—17)	A. V. Bedser: Surrey v. Warwicks. (Oval) 1953
12—39	(5—12 & 7—27)	Munir: Rawalpindi v. Peshawar (Rawalpindi) 1958–59
12—40	(7—12 & 5—28)	A. Downes: Otago v. Canterbury (Dunedin) 1896–97
12—40	(5—19 & 7—21)	G. G. Macaulay: Yorks. v. Glos. (Gloucester) 1924

ELEVEN WICKETS

11—17	(8—17 & 3— 0)	G. A. R. Lock: M.C.C. v. East Pakistan (Dacca) 1955–56
11—24	(5— 6 & 6—18)	H. Ironmonger: Australia v. South Africa (Melbourne) 1931–32
11—25	(6— 9 & 5—16)	G. Fowler: Nelson v. Wellington (Nelson) 1887–88
11—27	(8— 9 & 3—18)	G. Wootton: M.C.C. v. Sussex (Lord's) 1863
11—29	(7—12 & 4—17)	F. Martin: M.C.C. v. Sussex (Lord's) 1894
11—30	(8— 5 & 3—25)	E. Peate: Yorks. v. Surrey (Holbeck) 1883
11—31	(4—18 & 7—13)	A. E. Trott: Middx. v. Somerset (Lord's) 1899
11—31	(6— 8 & 5— 23)	G. G. Macaulay: Yorks. v. Northants. (Northampton) 1922
11—31	(3— 1 & 8—30)	J. A. Newman: Hants. v. Northants. (Northampton) 1926
11—31	(5— 2 & 6—29)	E. R. H. Toshack: Australia v. India (Brisbane)............1947–48
11—32	(6— 7 & 5—25)	J. J. Ferris: M.C.C. v. Notts. (Lord's) 1891
11—34	(7— 9 & 4—25)	G. G. Macaulay: Yorks. v. Northants. (Kettering) 1933
11—34	(7—17 & 4—17)	L. H. Gray: Middx. v. Hants. (Lord's) 1946

TEN WICKETS

10—15	(5—6 & 5— 9)	F. A. Tarrant: Europeans v. Muslims (Poona) 1915–16
10—20	(6—4 & 4—16)	F. R. Spofforth: Australians v. M.C.C. (Lord's) 1878
10—21	(3—12 & 7—9)	T. Emmett: Yorks. v. Sussex (Hove) 1878
10—21	(6—17 & 4—4)	S. J. Staples: Notts. v. Hants. (Southampton) 1932
10—21	(5—12 & 5—9)	W. H. Copson: Derby v. Oxford U. (Oxford) 1939
10—22	(6—8 & 4—14)	A. Shaw: Notts. v. Surrey (Nottingham) 1875
10—23	(6—8 & 4—15)	W. F. Downes: Otago v. Canterbury (Christchurch) 1866–67
10—23	(5—10 & 5—13)	G. Fowler: Nelson v. Wellington (Nelson) 1883–84
10—24	(4—11 & 6—13)	G. F. Grace: U.S.E.E. v. U.N.E.E. (Northampton) 1872
10—25	(6—12 & 4—13)	G. H. Pope: Derby v. Yorks. (Chesterfield) 1948
10—29	(3—11 & 7—18)	J. T. Newstead: Yorks. v. Leics. (Leicester) 1908
10—30	(5—13 & 5—17)	Lawson: Wellington v. Nelson (Nelson) 1883–84
10—30	(5— 8 & 5—22)	F. Martin: M.C.C. v. Notts. (Lord's) 1894
10—30	(2—22 & 8— 8)	M. G. Melle: Transvaal v. Griqualand West (Johannesburg) ...1950–51

Inexpensive Bowling Analyses

FOUR-BALL OVERS

O.	M.	R.	W.		
24	—20—	5—3		W. Attewell: Notts. v. Glos. (Cheltenham) 1888
25·2	—24—	3—1		W. Clark: Middx. v. Notts. (Nottingham) 1882
26	—23—	3—0		J. Beaumont: Surrey v. Oxford U. (Oxford) 1888
29	—25—	5—3		A. Shaw: A. Shaw's XI v. N.S.W. (Sydney)............................1881–82
35	—29—	8—3		W. Flowers: Notts. v. Sussex (Hove) 1885
40	—35—	7—0		A. Shaw: Notts. v. M.C.C. (Lord's) 1882
41·2	—36—	7—7		A. Shaw: Notts. v. M.C.C. (Lord's) 1875
48	—40—	12—3		A. Shaw: Players v. Gentlemen (Princes)............................1876
53	—43—	14—2		E. Lockwood: Yorks. v. Notts. (Sheffield) 1876
53	—42—	15—3		A. Shaw: Notts. v. Kent (Nottingham) 1878
60	—47—	14—4		James Lillywhite: Sussex v. Kent (Hove) 1879
65·3	—45—	28—5		W. Attewell: Vernon's XI v. Victoria (Melbourne) 1887–88
79·3	—56—	34—4		A. Shaw: M.C.C. v. Cambridge U. (Lord's) 1880
81	—65—	28—3		W. Attewell: Notts. v. Kent (Maidstone) 1888
89	—62—	46—1		W. Attewell: Notts. v. Kent (Nottingham) 1888
98	—69—	58—3		E. Peate: Yorks. v. Sussex (Hove) 1884

O.   M.   R.   W.
```
99 —66—64—3  A. Shaw: North v. South (Nottingham) ...........................................1878
114 —72—85—3  A. Watson: Lancs. v. M.C.C. (Lord's).............................................1884
120 —81—90—3  W. G. Grace: Glos. v. Notts. (Nottingham) ..................................1885
122·1—81—87—2  J. T. Rawlin: Vernon's XI v. South Australia (Adelaide) ..................1887–88
```

FIVE-BALL OVERS

O.   M.   R.   W.
```
25 —21— 7—4  W. Attewell: Notts. v. Kent (Beckenham) ......................................1889
30·4—22—17—5  J. Briggs: Lancs. v. Oxford U. (Oxford) .......................................1894
42·2—32—21—4  W. Attewell: Notts. v. Australians (Nottingham)............................1890
45 —32—19—5  W. Attewell: North v. South (Oval) ...............................................1889
53 —34—34—4  W. Attewell: Notts. v. Sussex (Nottingham) ...................................1889
64 —35—52—6  W. Attewell: Notts. v. Glos. (Cheltenham) .....................................1895
69 —42—57—3  W. Attewell: Notts. v. Lancs. (Manchester) ...................................1892
76 —43—71—4  W. Attewell: Notts. v. Lancs. (Nottingham) ...................................1889
```

SIX-BALL OVERS

O.   M.   R.   W.
```
25 —19— 18—0  Fazal Mahmood: Pakistan v. India (Dacca) ...............................1954–55
27 —16— 21—4  W. Rhodes: Yorks. v. Glos. (Bristol) .............................................1930
27 —15— 22—0  A. H. Kardar: Pakistan v. New Zealand (Karachi) ......................1955–56
27 —14— 22—6  A. E. Relf: Auckland v. Otago (Auckland) ..................................1907–08
27·3—17— 22—4  H. B. Cave: New Zealand v. West Indies (Auckland) .................1955–56
27·3—16— 26—7  W. Rhodes: Europeans v. Hindus (Bombay) .............................1921–22
28 —18— 15—1  E. Robinson: Yorks. v. Middx. (Sheffield) ...................................1927
28 —17— 21—2  A. H. Kardar: Pakistan v. New Zealand (Dacca) .........................1955–56
29 —24— 14—0  C. Cook: Glos. v. Sussex (Bristol) ...............................................1954
29·3—18— 20—5  H. C. Snary: Leics. v. Hants. (Leicester) ..................................1930
30 —25— 19—0  V. Mankad: Indians v. Karachi (Karachi) .................................1954–55
30 —19— 20—4  M. W. Tate: Sussex v. Essex (Hove) ..........................................1923
30 —19— 20—2  Khan Mohammed: Pakistan v. New Zealand (Dacca) ...............1955–56
31 —25— 12—0  J. A. Young: Middx. v. Glamorgan (Lord's) ..............................1950
31 —12— 21—1  W. B. Roberts: Lancs. v. Northants. (Peterborough) ..................1949
32 —23— 24—4  J. H. Wardle: England v. South Africa (Nottingham) ...............1955
32 —20— 21—0  A. F. Wensley: Sussex v. Derby (Chesterfield) ..........................1928
32 —26— 14—5  J. B. Mortimore: Glos. v. Leics. (Leicester) ...............................1958
33 —26— 19—3  W. Rhodes: Yorks. v. Glos. (Gloucester) ....................................1921
34 —23— 17—3  A. E. Thomas: Northants. v. Leics. (Leicester) .........................1930
35 —29— 11—0  W. Rhodes: Yorks. v. Notts. (Nottingham) ...............................1929
36 —23— 27—3  J. C. Laker: England v. New Zealand (Leeds) ...........................1958
40 —25— 34—6  J. A. Young: Middx. v. Essex (Lord's) ......................................1946
42 —31— 22—6  R. Kilner: Yorks. v. Essex (Harrogate) .....................................1922
43 —18— 35—3  W. E. Hollies: Warwicks. v. Notts. (Nottingham) .....................1957
43·2—28— 31—6  W. B. Roberts: Lancs. v. Northants. (Liverpool) ....................1948
43·2—27— 31—5  A. S. Player: Auckland v. Otago (Dunedin) ...........................1928–29
44 —32— 19—1  W. Rhodes: Yorks. v. Lancs. (Leeds) .........................................1930
45 —30— 44—2  R. T. Weeks: Warwicks. v. Glamorgan (Birmingham) .............1952
45 —28— 48—4  A. L. Valentine: West Indies v. England (Lord's) .....................1950
45 —26— 42—6  K. Mackay: Australia v. Pakistan (Dacca) ...............................1959–60
46 —24— 43—1  W. Attewell: England v. Australia (Sydney) ............................1891–92
46·1—20— 42—1  G. E. Gomez: West Indies v. India (Trinidad) ........................1952–53
46·3—24— 42—6  Zulfiqar Ahmed: Pakistan v. New Zealand (Karachi) .............1955–56
47 —29— 43—4  J. H. Wardle: Yorks. v. Glos. (Huddersfield) ...........................1949
47 —29— 42—5  H. Ironmonger: Australia v. South Africa (Brisbane) ...............1931–32
47 —28— 39—3  C. V. Grimmett: Australia v. England (Nottingham) ...............1934
47 —29— 30—6  C. Cook: Glos. v. Leics. (Bristol) ..............................................1956
47·4—31— 34—4  R. Kilner: Yorks. v. Leics. (Leicester) ....................................1923
48 —26— 44—3  R. A. Sinfield: Glos. v. Warwicks. (Bristol) ............................1936
51 —32— 49—3  G. R. Cox: Sussex v. Lancs. (Hove) ..........................................1926
53 —31— 47—2  A. E. Thomas: Northants. v. Yorks. (Sheffield) .......................1925
53 —28— 46—3  R. Kilner: Yorks. v. Lancs. (Manchester) .................................1927
53 —30— 50—4  K. T. Ramadhin: West Indies v. England (Barbados) ..............1953–54
54 —29— 49—4  A. E. Relf: Sussex v. Yorks. (Bradford) ....................................1906
56·4—30— 62—7  J. C. White: Somerset v. Warwicks. (Birmingham) ................1926
57 —30— 64—1  J. C. White: England v. Australia (Melbourne) ......................1928–29
60 —39— 65—0  E. A. Bedser: Surrey v. Northants. (Oval) ...............................1958
61 —34— 71—1  V. Mankad: India v. Pakistan (Peshawar) ................................1954–55
```

O.	M.	R.	W.		
61	—32—	51	—3	W. Attewell: England v. Australia (Melbourne)	1891–92
62	—37—	69	—5	T. L. Goddard: South Africa v. England (Leeds)	1955
62	—35—	61	—1	D. Atkinson: West Indies v. Pakistan (Barbados)	1957–58
62	—35—	71	—3	V. H. Broderick: Northants. v. Notts. (Nottingham)	1948
62	—34—	71	—3	C. W. L. Parker: Glos. v. Somerset (Taunton)	1927
62	—35—	61	—1	D. Atkinson: West Indies v. Pakistan (Barbados)	1957–58
63·2	—38—	57	—4	Saeed Ahmed: Western India States v. Bombay (Rajkot)	1943–44
64	—20—	63	—3	W. E. Hollies: Warwicks. v. Glamorgan (Birmingham)	1951
66	—28—	81	—3	J. Iremonger: Notts. v. Hants. (Southampton)	1914
68	—31—	83	—5	C. S. Marriott: Kent v. Lancs. (Dover)	1934
71	—47—	79	—3	A. L. Valentine: West Indies v. England (Lord's)	1950
72	—43—	86	—6	K. T. Ramadhin: West Indies v. England (Lord's)	1950
72	—34—	105	—5	J. C. White: Somerset v. Glos. (Bristol)	1928
73	—28—	110	—3	W. E. Hollies: Warwicks. v. Worcs. (Worcester)	1949
76	—47—	58	—4	V. Mankad: India v. England (New Delhi)	1951–52
77	—44—	99	—3	G. A. R. Lock: M.C.C. v. Pakistan XI (Lahore)	1955–56
79	—43—	106	—5	J. C. White: Somerset v. Hants. (Taunton)	1930
80	—35—	113	—4	L. Gibbs: British Guiana v. Jamaica (Georgetown)	1956–57
81	—36—	105	—5	G. Geary: England v. Australia (Melbourne)	1928–29
83	—42—	98	—5	R. W. McLeod: Victoria v. N.S.W. (Melbourne)	1892–93

C. Cook, playing for Gloucestershire v. Surrey (Gloucester) 1956, had match bowling figures of 85–37–94–7 (six-ball overs).

J. B. Mortimore, playing for Gloucestershire v. Cambridge U. (Stroud) 1958, had match bowling figures of 17–15–2–2 (six-ball overs)—8–7–1–1 in the first innings and 9–8–1–1 in the second.

R. G. Nadkarni, playing for Indians v. Middlesex (Lord's) 1959, had match figures of 67–39–75–8 (six-ball overs).

EIGHT-BALL OVERS

O.	M.	R.	W.		
26	—17—	19	—4	L. W. Payn: Natal v. O.F.S. (Bloemfontein)	1946–47
26	16—	28	—2	E. S. White: N.S.W. v. Queensland (Sydney)	1935–36
29·7	—12—	36	—3	C. G. Macartney: N.S.W. v. Victoria (Sydney)	1923–24
34	—18—	29	—2	N. B. F. Mann: Eastern Province v. Griqualand West (Port Elizabeth)	1946–47
34	—17—	36	—4	R. K. Oxenham: Queensland v. Victoria (Melbourne)	1933–34
40·3	—16—	46	—6	H. J. Tayfield: Natal v. Transvaal (Durban)	1946–47
57	—26—	55	—3	L. Heaney: Transvaal v. Griqualand West (Johannesburg)	1947–48
67·6	—38—	69	—6	N. B. F. Mann: Eastern Province v. Transvaal (Johannesburg)	1946–47

Expensive Bowling Analyses

FIVE-BALL OVERS

O.	M.	R.	W.		
5	—0—	50	—5	W. G. Grace: South v. North (Hastings)	1893
13	—1—	76	—0	W. H. Lockwood: C. I. Thornton's XI v. Australians (Scarborough)	1893
14	—0—	94	—0	K. S. Ranjitsinhji: Sussex v. Notts. (Nottingham)	1895
19	—2—	127	—2	J. B. Wood: Oxford U. v. M.C.C. (Lord's)	1893
22	—3—	114	—1	S. Coe: Leics. v. Yorks. (Leicester)	1896
26	—5—	138	—5	E. J. Tyler: Somerset v. Lancs. (Taunton)	1899
30	—1—	154	—1	A. C. S. Glover: Warwicks. v. Yorks. (Birmingham)	1896

SIX-BALL OVERS

O.	M.	R.	W.		
4	—0—	53	—0	W. Knightley-Smith: Middx. v. Notts. (Nottingham)	1922
6	—0—	66	—0	E. H. Bowley: Rest v. Lord Cowdray's XI (Hastings)	1923
7	—0—	64	—0	D. Shackleton: Hants. v. Yorks. (Bradford)	1958
8·2	—0—	98	—0	T. W. Goddard: Glos. v. Kent (Dover)	1937
9	—0—	81	—0	E. L. G. Hoad: West Indians v. Harlequins (Eastbourne)	1928
9	—0—	81	—0	R. Haywood: Northants. v. Sussex (Hove)	1921
9	—0—	89	—2	H. Verity: Yorks. v. Somerset (Bath)	1936
10	—0—	87	—1	N. I. Thomson: Sussex v. Yorks. (Hove)	1959
11	—0—	100	—2	T. E. S. Francis: Cambridge U. v. Surrey (Oval)	1923
14	—0—	109	—0	E. O. Blamires: Otago v. N.S.W. (Dunedin)	1923–24

O.	M.	R.	W.		
14	—0	—153	—3	J. Gunn: Notts. v. Sussex (Hove)	1912
15	—0	—120	—0	J. W. H. T. Douglas: Essex v. Hants. (Bournemouth)	1919
15	—2	—131	—2	F. E. Woolley: Rest v. Lord Cowdray's XI (Hastings)	1924
19	—0	—132	—0	D. A. R. Moloney: Otago v. Canterbury (Christchurch)	1929–30
19	—0	—144	—2	L. C. Braund: Somerset v. Hants. (Taunton)	1901
20	—0	—138	—0	C. V. Tarbox: Worcs. v. Kent (Kidderminster)	1922
20	—0	—156	—0	E. Price: Essex v. Australians (Southend)	1948
20·2	—0	—142	—6	A. E. Trott: Players v. Gentlemen (Lord's)	1900
21	—1	—156	—1	V. R. Price: Surrey v. Middx. (Oval)	1919
22	—0	—188	—3	A. Bailey: Somerset v. Kent (Taunton)	1906
22·4	—0	—162	—1	V. Murdin: Northants. v. Surrey (Northampton)	1920
23	—0	—142	—1	A. E. Thomas: Northants. v. Surrey (Northampton)	1920
28	—1	—175	—3	W. R. Rees-Davies: Cambridge U. v. Free Foresters (Cambridge)	1938
30	—1	—184	—2	V. Murdin: Northants. v. Surrey (Oval)	1921
33	—0	—185	—3	P. Toone: Essex v. Kent (Leyton)	1921
34	—0	—195	—2	P. T. Mills: Glos. v. Australians (Bristol)	1921
36	—2	—208	—0	T. P. B. Smith: Essex v. Kent (Brentwood)	1934
40·2	—2	—227	—5	L. C. Braund: Somerset v. Lancs. (Manchester)	1905
54	—5	—259	—0	Khan Mohammed: Pakistan v. West Indies (Kingston)	1957–58

EIGHT-BALL OVERS

O.	M.	R.	W.		
2·7	—0	— 50	—0	J. Buchanan: Eastern Province v. Western Province (Cape Town)	1937–38
6	—0	— 71	—2	E. D. R. Eagar: Oxford U. v. M.C.C. (Lord's)	1939
8	—0	— 71	—4	E. W. Dempster: New Zealanders v. Natal (Pietermaritzburg)	1953–54
8	—0	— 87	—5	A. A. Mailey: N.S.W. v. South Australia (Adelaide)	1919–20
9	—0	— 90	—1	A. Davis: Tasmania v. M.C.C. (Launceston)	1924–25
12·7	—0	—149	—5	W. E. Merritt: Northants. v. Somerset (Taunton)	1939
20·4	—0	—174	—6	N. L. Williams: Rest v. Australian XI (Sydney)	1926–27
23·2	—0	—218	—5	W. E. Merritt: New Zealanders v. N.S.W. (Sydney)	1927–28
23·6	—0	—206	—4	N. L. Williams: South Australia v. N.S.W. (Sydney)	1922–23
64	—0	—362	—4	A. A. Mailey: N.S.W. v. Victoria (Melbourne)	1926–27

Most Expensive Bowling in an Innings

O.	M.	R.	W.		
64	— 0	—362	—4	A. A. Mailey: N.S.W. v. Victoria (Melbourne)	1926–27
87	—12	—309	—5	G. Giffen: South Australia v. Stoddart's XI (Adelaide)	1894–95
69	— 7	—301	—4	B. K. Garudachar: Mysore v. Holkar (Indore)	1945–46
87	—11	—298	—1	L. O'B. Fleetwood-Smith: Australia v. England (Oval)	1938
77·1	— 7	—287	—8	G. Giffen: South Australia v. N.S.W. (Sydney)	1899–00
88	—15	—275	—5	C. S. Nayudu: Holkar v. Bombay (Bombay)	1944–45
80·2	—13	—266	—5	O. C. Scott: West Indies v. England (Kingston)	1929–30
54	— 5	—259	—0	Khan Mohammed: Pakistan v. West Indies (Kingston)	1957–58
83	—17	—249	—6	J. A. O'Connor: South Australia v. Victoria (Melbourne)	1907–08
85·2	—20	—247	—2	Fazal Mahmood: Pakistan v. West Indies (Kingston)	1957–58
55	— 3	—245	—4	A. P. Freeman: M.C.C. v. Victoria (Melbourne)	1928–29
92·3	—21	—245	—4	Ghulam Ahmed: Hyderabad v. Holkar (Indore)	1950–51
52	— 8	—236	—3	J. H. Wardle: North v. South (Scarborough)	1947
56	— 7	—232	—3	C. J. Eady: Tasmania v. N.S.W. (Sydney)	1898–99
63	—10	—231	—6	C. W. L. Parker: Glos. v. Somerset (Bristol)	1923
38	— 1	—228	—2	A. C. Facy: Tasmania v. Victoria (Melbourne)	1922–23
82	—17	—228	—5	V. Mankad: India v. West Indies (Kingston)	1952–53
40·2	— 2	—227	—5	L. C. Braund: Somerset v. Lancs. (Manchester)	1905
59	—11	—226	—6	E. B. Shine: Kent v. Surrey (Oval)	1897
49	— 7	—225	—2	F. Jarvis: South Australia v. N.S.W. (Sydney)	1900–01

Most Expensive Bowling in a Match

Runs			
428	(6—153 & 5—275)	C. S. Nayudu: Holkar v. Bombay (Bombay)	1944–45
394	(4—192 & 6—202)	C. V. Grimmett: South Australia v. N.S.W. (Sydney)	1925–26
374	(5—266 & 4—108)	O. C. Scott: West Indies v. England (Kingston)	1929–30

Runs

362	(4—362)	A. A. Mailey: N.S.W. v. Victoria (Melbourne)	1926–27
359	(3—149 & 4—210)	D. G. Chaudhari: Maharashtra v. Bombay (Poona)	1948–49
345	(3—190 & 0—155)	J. D. Scott: South Australia v. N.S.W. (Sydney)	1925–26
331	(6—199 & 2—132)	A. P. Freeman: Kent v. M.C.C. (Folkestone)	1934
326	(6—134 & 5—192)	N. L. Williams: South Australia v. Victoria (Adelaide)	1928–29
322	(5—309 & 0— 13)	G. Giffen: South Australia v. Stoddart's XI (Adelaide)	1894–95
321	(3—195 & 1—126)	S. D. Dhanwade: Maharashtra v. Bombay (Poona)	1948–49
320	(3—142 & 3—178)	D. G. Phadkar: Bombay v. Maharashtra (Poona)	1948–49
309	(2—122 & 2—187)	Amir Elahi: Prince's XI v. Australian Services (New Delhi)	1945–46
308	(4—129 & 3—179)	A A. Mailey: Australia v. England (Sydney)	1924–25
306	(2—174 & 2—132)	J. Briggs: Lancs. v. Sussex (Manchester)	1897
304	(2—173 & 0—131)	G. R. Dickinson: Otago v. Wellington (Dunedin)	1923–24
302	(5—160 & 5—142)	A. A. Mailey: Australia v. England (Adelaide)	1920–21
301	(4—301)	B. K. Garudachar: Mysore v. Holkar (Indore)	1945–46
300	(6—172 & 4—128)	S. G. Smith: Auckland v. Wellington (Wellington)	1923–24

Most Balls Bowled in an Innings

Balls	O.	M.	R.	W.		
588—	98	—35	—179	—2	K. T. Ramadhin: West Indies v. England (Birmingham)	1957
555—	92·3	—21	—245	—4	Ghulam Ahmed: Hyderabad v. Holkar (Indore)	1950–51
552—	92	—49	—140	—3	A. L. Valentine: West Indies v. England (Nottingham)	1950
545—	90·5	—32	—165	—2	A. L. Valentine: Jamaica v. British Guiana (Georgetown)	1956–57
542—	67·6	—38	— 69	—6	N. B. F. Mann: Eastern Province v. Transvaal (Johannesburg)	1946–47
536—	67	—27	— 90	1	A. Tayfield: Natal v. Transvaal (Johannesburg)	1948–49
528—	88	—15	—275	—5	C. S. Nayudu: Holkar v. Bombay (Bombay)	1944–45
522—	87	—12	—309	—5	G. Giffen: South Australia v. A. E. Stoddart's XI (Adelaide)	1894–95
522—	87	—11	—298	—1	L. O'B. Fleetwood-Smith: Australia v. England (Oval)	1938
512 —64		0	—362	—4	A. A. Mailey: N.S.W. v. Victoria (Melbourne)	1926–27
512—	85·2	—20	—247	—2	Fazal Mahmood: Pakistan v. West Indies (Kingston)	1957–58
510—	85	—26	—178	—3	W. J. O'Reilly: Australia v. England (Oval)	1938
510—	85	—11	—209	—3	Ghulam Ahmed: Hyderabad v. Bombay (Bombay)	1947–48
504—	84	—18	—168	—4	I. Madray: British Guiana v. Jamaica (Georgetown)	1956–57
501—	100·1	—31	—168	—4	A. Shaw: Sussex v. Notts. (Nottingham)	1895
501—	83·3	—35	—150	—6	G. Giffen: South Australia v. N.S.W. (Adelaide)	1890–91
498—	83	—42	— 98	—5	R. W. McLeod: Victoria v. N.S.W. (Melbourne)	1892–93
498—	83	—17	—249	—6	J. A. O'Connor: South Australia v. Victoria (Melbourne)	1907–08
496—	62	—15	—157	—3	L. W. Payn: Natal v. Transvaal (Johannesburg)	1948–49
492—	123	—56	—146	—5	D. Buchanan: Gents of England v. Cambridge U. (Cambridge)	1880
492—	82	—17	—228	—5	V. Mankad: India v. West Indies (Kingston)	1952–53
490—	98	—34	—151	—4	F. Martin: Kent v. Notts. (Nottingham)	1891
489—	122·1	—81	— 87	—2	J. T. Rawlin: G. F. Vernon's XI v. South Australia (Adelaide)	1887–88
488—	61	—20	—152	—2	W. Douglas: N.E. Transvaal v. Transvaal (Benoni)	1947–48
488—	81·2	—25	—135	—5	K. T. Ramadhin: West Indies v. England (Nottingham)	1950
488—	61	—18	—126	—5	L. Kline: Victoria v. N.S.W. (Sydney)	1956–57
486—	81	—36	—105	—5	G. Geary: England v. Australia (Melbourne)	1928–29
486—	81	—37	—172	—3	J. H. Wardle: Yorks. v. Derby (Bradford)	1949
482—	80·2	—13	—266	—5	O. C. Scott: West Indies v. England (Kingston)	1929–30
480—	120	—81	— 90	—3	W. G. Grace: Glos. v. Notts. (Nottingham)	1885
480—	80	—22	—187	—3	W. Huddleston: Lancs. v. Warwick. (Birmingham)	1901
480—	80	—28	—138	—3	G. S. Boyes: Hants. v. Notts. (Southampton)	1934
480—	80	—13	—178	—4	C. S. Nayudu: Holkar v. Baroda (Baroda)	1946–47
480—	60	— 9	—167	—5	A. M. B. Rowan: South Africa v. England (Port Elizabeth)	1948–49
480—	80	—21	—174	—2	Maqsood Ahmed: Karachi Blues v. Karachi Whites (Karachi)	1956–57
480—	80	—35	—113	—4	L. Gibbs: British Guiana v. Jamaica (Georgetown)	1956–57
476—	119	—40	—152	—5	J. Southerton: Surrey v. Glos. (Clifton)	1871
474—	79	—43	—106	—5	J. C. White: Somerset v. Hants. (Taunton)	1930
474—	79	—19	—184	—3	Nasimul Ghani: Karachi Blues v. Karachi Whites (Karachi)	1956–57
472—	59	—24	— 94	—3	H. J. Tayfield: South Africa v. Australia (Durban)	1957–58
470—	78·2	—21	—156	—6	G. Giffen: Australia v. England (Melbourne)	1894–95
465—	93	—33	—134	—3	J. J. Ferris: Australians v. Players (Lord's)	1890
464—	58	—14	—138	—6	J. E. Waddington: Griqualand West v. Transvaal (Kimberley)	1946 47
463—	77·1	— 7	—287	—8	G. Giffen: South Australia v. N.S.W. (Adelaide)	1899–00
462—	77	—44	— 99	—3	G. A. R. Lock: M.C.C. v. Pakistan XI (Lahore)	1955–56
460—	76·4	—35	—128	—7	S. P. Gupte: India v. New Zealand (Hyderabad)	1955–56
456—	114	—71	—101	—5	W. A. Woof: Glos. v. Notts. (Nottingham)	1885
456—	114	—72	— 85	—3	A. Watson: Lancs. v. M.C.C. (Lord's)	1884

Balls O.   M.   R.   W.
456— 57 — 6—139—3   J. Waller: N.E. Transvaal v. Transvaal (Benoni) 1947–48
456— 57 —26— 55—3   L. Heaney: Transvaal v. Griqualand West (Johannesburg) 1947–48
456— 76 —47— 58—4   V. Mankad: India v. England (New Delhi) 1951–52
456— 76 —29—136—5   J. H. Wardle: Yorks. v. Worcs. (Worcester) 1953
456— 57 —25— 93—1   A. R. A. Murray: Eastern Province v. Natal (Port Elizabeth) ...1955–56
455— 75·5—10—186—5   S. G. Shinde: Maharashtra v. Bombay (Bombay) 1943–44
454—113·2—71—118—4   A. Watson: Lancs. v. Yorks. (Bradford) 1887
453— 75·3—22—136—2   J. C. White: England v. Australia (Melbourne) 1928–29
452—113 —66—108—6   W. Flowers: Notts. v. Lancs. (Manchester) 1886
451— 75·1—16—190—7   A. Newell: N.S.W. v. South Australia (Adelaide) 1893–94
450— 75 —25—164—4   G. Giffen: Australia v. England (Sydney) 1894–95
450— 90 —32—185—6   J. Briggs: Lancs. v. Derby (Manchester) 1896
450— 75 —16—166—7   C. S. Nayudu: Baroda v. Bombay (Bombay) 1943–44
450— 75 —16—202—3   V. Mankad: India v. West Indies (Bombay) 1948–49

Most Balls Bowled in a Match

Balls O.   M.   R.   W.
917—152·5—25—428—11   C. S. Nayudu: Holkar v. Bombay (Bombay) 1944–45
848—106 —14—394—10   C. V. Grimmett: South Australia v. N.S.W. (Sydney) 1925–26
805—161 —71—204—13   J. H. Piton: Transvaal v. Griqualand West (Johannesburg) ...1890–91
774—129 —51—228— 9   K. T. Ramadhin: West Indies v. England (Birmingham) 1957
766— 95·6—23—184— 4   H. Verity: England v. South Africa (Durban) 1938–39
749—124·5—37—256—13   J. C. White: England v. Australia (Adelaide) 1928–29
748— 92·7—22—255—10   D. D. J. Blackie: Victoria v. South Australia (Adelaide) 1926–27
738— 92·2—17—256— 1   N. Gordon: South Africa v. England (Durban) 1938–39
736— 92 —16—267— 9   C. V. Grimmett: South Australia v. Victoria (Adelaide) 1924–25
730— 91·2—33—190—10   N. B. F. Mann: Eastern Province v. Western Province
                                                    (Cape Town) 1947–48
728— 91 —24—203— 4   A. B. C. Langton: South Africa v. England (Durban) 1938–39
726—121 —30—299— 9   K. K. Tarapore: Bombay v. Maharashtra (Poona) 1948–49
725—120·5—58—152—11   R. W. McLeod: Victoria v. N.S.W. (Melbourne) 1892–93
712— 89 —19—228—11   M. W. Tate: England v. Australia (Sydney) 1924–25
708—118 —42—239— 8   G. Giffen: Australia v. England (Sydney) 1894–95
696—116 —75—127— 7   A. L. Valentine: West Indies v. England (Lord's) 1950
695—115·5—50—191—11   G. Giffen: South Australia v. N.S.W. (Adelaide) 1892–93
691—115·1—60—135— 6   V. Mankad: India v. Pakistan (Peshawar) 1954–55
690—115 —70—152—11   K. T. Ramadhin: West Indies v. England (Lord's) 1950
688— 86 —15—258— 5   A. P. Freeman: England v. Australia (Sydney) 1924–25
686— 85·6—44—123— 9   N. B. F. Mann: Eastern Province v. Transvaal (Johannesburg) 1946–47
683—113·5—50—171— 6   J. C. White: England v. Australia (Melbourne) 1928–29
672— 84 —15—266— 7   W. A. Johnson: Australia v. South Africa (Melbourne) 1952–53
666— 83·2— 9—281— 8   A. A. Mailey: N.S.W. v. South Australia (Adelaide) 1926–27
664— 83 —19—191— 9   J. E. Waddington: Griqualand West v. N.E. Transvaal (Pretoria) 1955–56
662—110·2—37—184— 7   K. T. Ramadhin: West Indies v. England (Nottingham) 1950
662—110·2—44—167— 7   S. P. Gupte: India v. Pakistan (Lahore) 1954–55
660—110 —55—183— 5   A. L. Valentine: West Indies v. England (Nottingham) 1950
659—109·5—29—267—10   V. Mankad: Gujerat v. Holkar (Indore) 1950–51
656—109·2—30—225— 5   C. V. Grimmett: Australia v. England (Oval) 1930
656— 82 —19—240— 8   F. Ward: Australia v. England (Brisbane) 1936–37
655—109·1—43—192—14   J. J. Ferris: N.S.W. v. South Australia (Adelaide) 1890–91
654—109 —37—192— 8   C. V. Grimmett: Australia v. South Africa (Melbourne) 1931–32
654—109 —17—294— 2   C. T. Sarwate: Holkar v. Bombay (Bombay) 1944–45
654—109 —62—111— 7   V. Mankad: India v. England (New Delhi) 1951–52
651—108·3—56—253— 2   S. G. Shinde: India v. England (New Delhi) 1951–52
648—108 —30—245— 9   G. Giffen: South Australia v. Victoria (Adelaide) 1899–00
640— 80 —31—135— 3   H. J. Tayfield: South Africa v. Australia (Durban) 1957–58
636—106 —36—204—11   A. L. Valentine: West Indies v. England (Manchester) 1950
633—105·3—52—120— 8   C. V. Grimmett: Australia v. England (Nottingham) 1934
632— 79 —12—207— 8   M. W. Tate: England v. Australia (Sydney) 1924–25
632—105·2—13—374— 9   O. C. Scott: West Indies v. England (Kingston)...................1929–30
630—105 —45—165— 8   J. W. Sharpe: England v. Australia (Melbourne) 1891–92
630—126 —33—306— 4   J. Briggs: Lancs. v. Sussex (Manchester) 1897
630—105 —41—199— 4   J. C. Laker: England v. West Indies (Nottingham) 1957
629—104·5—44—178— 9   F. T. Badcock: Otago v. Canterbury (Christchurch) 1923–24
629— 78·5—26—166— 8   L. Drury: Griqualand West v. N.E. Transvaal (Pretoria) 1955–56
627— 78·3—18—241— 9   M. W. Tate: England v. Australia (Melbourne) 1924–25

Balls	O.	M.	R.	W.	
626—	78·2—	3—	326—	11	N. L. Williams: South Australia v. Victoria (Adelaide) 1928–29
625—	104·1—	27—	219—	6	C. V. Grimmett: Australia v. England (Adelaide) 1928–29
625—	78·1—	14—	178—	8	R. Kilner: England v. Australia (Adelaide) 1924–25
624—	156	—86—	184—	8	W. G. Grace: Gentlemen v. Players (Oval) 1876
624—	78	—11—	222—	5	A. A. Mailey: N.S.W. v. South Australia (Adelaide) 1927–28
624—	104	—55—	132—	3	C. S. Marriott: Kent v. Northants. (Dover) 1934
624—	104	—28—	254—	6	V. Mankad: India v. West Indies (Kingston) 1952–53
612—	102	—16—	260—	9	E. Jones: South Australia v. Victoria (Adelaide) 1898–99
611—	101·5—	38—	206—	14	A. P. Freeman: Kent v. Northants. (Dover) 1934
610—	101·4—	41—	158—	10	G. Dennett: Glos. v. Notts. (Nottingham) 1908
608—	76	—18—	173—	4	R. L. A. McNamee: N.S.W. v. Queensland (Sydney) 1926–27
607—	101·1—	26—	233—	10	A. Newell: N.S.W. v. South Australia (Adelaide) 1893–94
606—	101	—34—	203—	6	J. Briggs: Lancs. v. Kent (Manchester) 1900
606—	101	—41—	136—	6	G. Geary: England v. Australia (Melbourne) 1928–29
606—	75·6—	28—	161—	5	W. J. O'Reilly: Australia v. England (Brisbane)..................1936–37
606—	101	—45—	165—	6	Fazal Mahmood: Pakistan v. West Indies (Trinidad) 1957–58
604—	75·4—	15—	244—	7	F. Ward: South Australia v. N.S.W. (Adelaide) 1935–36
603—	100·3—	40—	161—	6	W. J. O'Reilly: Australia v. England (Adelaide) 1932–33
601—	100·1—	44—	171—	13	A. P. Freeman: Kent v. Lancs. (Tonbridge) 1933
600—	75	—23—	161—	5	C. F. W. Allcott: Auckland v. Canterbury (Christchurch) 1924–25
600—	100	—39—	180—	0	M. W. Tate: England v. Australia (Melbourne) 1928–29

Bowlers Unchanged Through a Completed Match

During the early years of cricket history, when innings totals were small, it was comparatively common for two bowlers to bowl unchanged through both completed innings of a match, but through the years this feat has become rarer and nowadays it is hardly ever seen.

SEASON 1852

J. Wisden (10—57) & J. Dean (10—92) ....Sussex v. Kent (Brighton

SEASON 1853

W. Hillyer (10—75) & E. Hinkly (10—38) ....South v. North (Oval)
W. Hillyer (12—57) & W. Clarke (6—49) ....M.C.C. v. England (Lord's)
Sir F. Bathurst (11—50) & M. Kempson (9—54) ....Gentlemen v. Players (Lord's)
W. Clarke (7—106) & J. Wisden (8—36) ....England v. Kent (Canterbury)

SEASON 1854

J. Dean (8—89) & J. Grundy (11—76) ...........................M.C.C. v. Cambridge U. (Cambridge)
J. Grundy (6—39) & T. Nixon (11—46) ....M.C.C. v. Surrey (Lord's)

SEASON 1855

J. Wisden (12—92) & J. Dean (6—77) ....Sussex v. M.C.C. (Lord's)
T. Sherman (8—71) & John Lillywhite (11—70) ....South v. North (Tunbridge Wells)
J. Grundy (10—73) & J. Dean (9—76) ....M.C.C. v. Surrey (Lord's)

SEASON 1856

E. Willsher (10—54) & F. Hollands (9—54) ....Kent v. M.C.C. (Lord's)
W. Martingell (10—69) & T. Sherman (7—82) ....Surrey v. Sussex (Oval)
W. Martingell (10—67) & G. Griffith (9—35) ....Surrey v. Kent (Tunbridge Wells)

SEASON 1857

W. Caffyn (9—28) & G. Griffith (10—34) ....Surrey v. Sussex (Oval)
J. Wisden (11—45) & G. Griffith (8—35) ....Surrey & Sussex v. England (Brighton)
J. Jackson (13—42) & W. Martingell (7—64) ....North v. South (Tunbridge Wells)
W. Caffyn (8—71) & G. Griffith (7—56) ....North v. South (Sheffield)
John Lillywhite (9—59) & G. Hooker (10—65) ....Sussex v. M.C.C. (St Leonard's)

SEASON 1858

C. D. Marsham (7—27) & H. H. Stephenson (13—44) ....England v. Kent (Lord's)

SEASON 1859

W. Caffyn (12—68) & H. H. Stephenson (5—70) ....Surrey v. M.C.C. (Oval)
W. Caffyn (11—63) & G. Atkinson (8—46) ..............................U.N.E.E. v. England XI (Lord's)
V. E. Walker (8—89) & G. Wells (9—79) ....Middx. v. Kent (Canterbury)
J. Jackson (12—74) & J. Grundy (8—96) ....North v. South (Canterbury)

SEASON 1860

J. Grundy (9—51) & A. Haygarth (11—56) ......................................M.C.C. v. Sussex (Lord's)
J. Jackson (7—57) & R. C. Tinley (12—93) ....North v. South (Oval)
A. B. Rowley (10—48) & J. B. Payne (8—75).........Gents. of North v. Gents. of South (Manchester)
C. Brampton (12—38) & J. Grundy (8—52) ......................................M.C.C. v. Sussex (Lewes)

SEASON 1861

J. Jackson (11—99) & E. Willsher (6—70) ....Players v. Gentlemen (Lord's)
I. Hodgson (9—88) & G. Atkinson (10—115) ....Yorks. v. Surrey (Sheffield)
C. Lawrence (10—86) & V. E. Walker (9—104) ....Middx. v. M.C.C. (Lord's)

SEASON 1862

H. Stubberfield (6—40) & James Lillywhite (14—57)...........................Sussex v. M.C.C. (Lord's)

SEASON 1863

G. Wootton (11—55) & J. Grundy (8—94)........................M.C.C. v. Cambridge U. (Cambridge)
G. Wootton (11—27) & J. Grundy (9—50)......................................M.C.C. v. Sussex (Lord's)
J. Jackson (12—43) & J. Grundy (8—48)......................................Notts. v. Kent (Canterbury)

SEASON 1864

V. E. Walker (14—103) & T. Hearne (5—94)....................................Middx. v. Sussex (Islington)
E. Willsher (9—55) & G. Tarrant (11—49)....................................Players v. Gentlemen (Lord's)
T. Hearne (7—91) & V. E. Walker (12—85)....................................Middx. v. M.C.C. (Lord's)

SEASON 1865

W. G. Grace (13—84) & I. D. Walker (6—86) ....Gentlemen of South v. Players of South (Oval)
G. Bennett (7—58) & E. Willsher (12—28)..Kent v. Yorks. (Sheffield)

SEASON 1866

G. Tarrant (13—77) & F. Reynolds (6—75)...........................Cambridgeshire v. Yorks. (Bradford)
T. Hearne (12—76) & R. D. Walker (7—73)................................Middx. v. Notts. (Nottingham)
G. Tarrant (12—84) & Thomas Hayward (8—76) ....Cambridgeshire v. Middx. (Islington)

SEASON 1867

G. Wootton (8—131) & A. Shaw (10—47)....................................M.C.C. v. Oxford U. (Oxford)
James Lillywhite (6—41) & J. Southerton (13—68) ....Sussex v. Kent (Gravesend)
L. Greenwood (11—71) & G. Freeman (8—73)....................................Yorks. v. Surrey (Oval)
L. Greenwood (7—76) & G. Freeman (12—51)....................................Yorks. v. Lancs. (Blackburn)
G. Tarrant (9—108) & G. Freeman (9—90)....................................North v. Notts. (Nottingham)

SEASON 1868

R. F. Miles (9—45) & E. L. Fellowes (9—29) ....Oxford U. v. M.C.C. (Oxford)
F. Silcock (7—75) & E. Willsher (12—103)................................England v. M.C.C. (Lord's)
G. Freeman (12—23) & T. Emmett (8—24)..Yorks. v. Lancs. (Leeds)
G. Freeman (12—61) & T. Emmett (6—58)....................................Yorks. v. Middx. (Sheffield)

SEASON 1869

G. Freeman (13—61) & T. Emmett (5—53) ....Yorks. v. Surrey (Sheffield)
G. Freeman (4—31) & T. Emmett (16—38).............................Yorks. v. Cambridgeshire (Leeds)

SEASON 1870

A. Shaw (13—58) & G. Wootton (6—71)...M.C.C. v. Surrey (Oval)
J. C. Shaw (12—35) & G. Howitt (5—63)....................................Notts. v. Kent (Crystal Palace)
G. Freeman (10—43) & T. Emmett (9—92) ....Yorks. v. Surrey (Oval)

SEASON 1871

J. Southerton (14—67) & James Lillywhite (6—64)............................Sussex v. Kent (Brighton)
G. Freeman (7—81) & T. Emmett (11—86)......................Yorks. v. Lancs. (Manchester)
J. Southerton (11—67) & James Lillywhite (8—44)..........................Sussex v. Kent (Maidstone)
T. Emmett (8—113) & A. Hill (12—57)...Yorks. v. Surrey (Oval)
J. Southerton (14—99) & James Lillywhite (5—84) ....Sussex v. Surrey (Oval)

SEASON 1872

J. Southerton (13—69) & James Lillywhite (6—35)..............................South v. North (Liverpool)
W. McIntyre (11—38) & A. Watson (7—72).....................................Lancs. v. Derby (Derby)
J. Southerton (12—100) & James Lillywhite (6—71) ....Sussex v. Kent (Hove)
J. Southerton (9—108) & J. Street (11—61)....................................Surrey v. Kent (Maidstone)
J. C. Shaw (4—49) & E. Lockwood (13—82) .................U.N.E.E. v. U.S.E.E. (Bishops Stortford)

SEASON 1873

A. Shaw (7—49) & A. Rylott (9—75)...M.C.C. v. Yorks. (Lord's)
T. Emmett (11—82) & A. Hill (8—47) ....Yorks. v. Lancs. (Manchester)
T. Emmett (12—84) & A. Hill (8—55)..................................Yorks. v. Surrey (Sheffield)
W. McIntyre (11—70) & A. Watson (8—79) ....Lancs. v. Surrey (Manchester)
W. McIntyre (11—53) & A. Watson (8—48).............................Lancs. v. Surrey (Oval)
James Lillywhite (7—101) & R. Fillery (13—123)..............................Sussex v. Surrey (Oval)
James Lillywhite (11—86) & R. Fillery (9—96) ....Sussex v. Kent (Lord's)
James Lillywhite (11—99) & R. Fillery (8—110) ....Sussex v. Glos. (Hove)
James Lillywhite (8—84) & R. Fillery (10—105)...........................Sussex v. Kent (Eastbourne)

SEASON 1874

T. Emmett (9—87) & A. Hill (10—96) ....Yorks. v. Notts. (Nottingham)
A. Hill (9—67) & G. Ulyett (10—104) ....Yorks. v. U.S.E.E. (Bradford)
A. Hill (10—38) & T. Emmett (8—74)..Yorks. v. Lancs. (Manchester)
James Lillywhite (11—84) & R. Fillery (7—71) ....Sussex v. Notts. (Hove)

SEASON 1876

W. McIntyre (14—72) & A. Watson (5—63)..............................Lancs. v. Derby (Manchester)
W. McIntyre (9—96) & A. Watson (10—83)...Lancs. v. Derby (Derby)

SEASON 1877

W. McIntyre (12—63) & A. Watson (8—63)................................Lancs. v. Notts. (Manchester)

SEASON 1878

A. Shaw (11—55) & F. Morley (8—72) ....Notts. v. Australians (Nottingham)
A. Shaw (7—56) & F. Morley (12—70).................................Notts. v. Surrey (Nottingham)
A. Shaw (3—69) & F. Morley (14—94) ....Notts. v. Yorks. (Nottingham)
W. G. Grace (12—109) & W. R. Gilbert (8—106)..............................Glos. v. Lancs. (Clifton)
A. Shaw (5—49) & F. Morley (15—35)...............................Notts. v. Kent (Town Malling)
W. Bates (9—34) & T. Emmett (10—21)..Yorks. v. Sussex (Hove)

SEASON 1879

A. Shaw (8—25) & F. Morley (12—35)................................Notts. v. Derby (Nottingham)
A. G. Steel (9—43) & A. H. Evans (10—74)...........................Gentlemen v. Players (Oval)
A. Shaw (5—35) & F. Morley (14—53)..Notts. v. Derby (Derby)

SEASON 1880

A. Shaw (12—53) & F. Morley (8—62).......................................M.C.C. v. Oxford U. (Oxford)
A. Shaw (7—54) & F. Morley (11—43) ....M.C.C. v. Derby (Lord's)
H. F. Boyle (7—80) & G. E. Palmer (11—89)....................Australians v. Players (Crystal Palace)

SEASON 1881

A. Hill (6—85) & E. Peate (14—77)..Yorks. v. Surrey (Huddersfield)
E. Peate (8—57) & W. Bates (11—47)..Yorks. v. Notts. (Nottingham)
A. Penn (13—69) & G. Wootton (7—41) ....Kent v. Sussex (Maidstone)

SEASON 1882

G. E. Palmer (9—133) & H. F. Boyle (11—107) ....Australians v. Liverpool Club (Liverpool)

SEASON 1883

E. Peate (8—59) & G. P. Harrison (11—76)...................................Yorks. v. Kent (Dewsbury)
R. G. Barlow (6—88) & A. Watson (12—67)....................................Lancs. v. Derby (Derby)

SEASON 1884

A. Shaw (14—65) & W. Attewell (6—46) ....Notts. v. Glos. (Nottingham)
G. Giffen (10—121) & G. E. Palmer (10—72) ....Australians v. Sheffeld's XI (Sheffield Park)
F. R. Spofforth (9—61) & G. E. Palmer (11—54) ....Australians v. Yorks. (Bradford)
F. R. Spofforth (12—43) & G. E. Palmer (7—72) ....Australians v. Middx. (Lord's)

SEASON 1886

F. R. Spofforth (15—36) & T. W. Garrett (5—34) ....Australians v. Oxford U. (Oxford)
E. Peate (12—50) & A. Watson (7—34) ....North v. Australians (Manchester)

SEASON 1888

J. Briggs (12—45) & R. G. Barlow (6—42) ....Lancs. v. Glos. (Liverpool)
C. T. B. Turner (11—59) & J. J. Ferris (7—63) ....Australians v. Middx. (Lord's)
C. T. B. Turner (13—48) & J. J. Ferris (6—48) ....Australians v. England XI (Stoke)

SEASON 1889

J. Beaumont (10—49) & G. A. Lohmann (10—49)..................................Surrey v. Kent (Oval)
W. Wright (9—51) & F. Martin (10—65)..Kent v. Yorks. (Maidstone)

SEASON 1890

G. A. Lohmann (13—54) & J. W. Sharpe (7—50) ....Surrey v. Lancs. (Manchester)
A. Watson (9—13) & J. Briggs (10—41) ....Lancs. v. Sussex (Manchester)
F. Martin (11—72) & W. Wright (9—81)....................................Kent v. Sussex (Town Malling)
A. Watson (6—66) & A. Mold (13—76).......................................Lancs. v. Yorks. (Huddersfield)

SEASON 1891

G. A. Lohmann (11—40) & J. W. Sharpe (9—31) ....Surrey v. Somerset (Oval)
F. Martin (13—48) & W. Wright (6—59)...Kent v. Middx. (Lord's)
J. Briggs (8—54) & A. Mold (11—65)..Lancs. v. Sussex (Hove)

SEASON 1892

A. Mold (13—91) & J. Briggs (5—54) ....Lancs. v. Kent (Tonbridge)
A. Mold (14—159) & A. Watson (4—67)...Lancs. v. Sussex (Hove)
J. T. Hearne (12—91) & J. T. Rawlin (7—85) ....Middx. v. Sussex (Hove)
J. T. Hearne (7—61) & F. Martin (13—51) ....M.C.C. v. Sussex (Lord's)

SEASON 1893

A. Coningham (9—100) & R. W. McLeod (10—56)...Australians v. Liverpool and District (Liverpool)

SEASON 1894

T. Richardson (9—99) & F. Smith (10—71) ....Surrey v. Glos. (Oval)
E. Wainwright (13—38) & R. Peel (7—60) ....Yorks. v. Sussex (Dewsbury)
G. Davidson (9—54) & J. Hulme (10—70) ....Derby v. Yorks. (Sheffield)
W. Hearne (13—98) & F. Martin (6—65) ....Kent v. Surrey (Catford)
S. M. J. Woods (6—124) & F. S. Jackson (12—77) ....Gentlemen v. Players (Lord's)
J. T. Hearne (14—66) & A. D. Pougher (5—60) ...............................M.C.C. v. Kent (Lord's)

SEASON 1895

J. Briggs (8—78) & A. Mold (9—72) ....Lancs. v. Middx. (Lord's)
J. Briggs (12—51) & A. Mold (8—97) ....Lancs. v. Leics. (Leicester)
J. Briggs (4—62) & A. Mold (15—85) ....Lancs. v. Notts. (Nottingham)
T. Richardson (11—60) & G. A. Lohmann (8—59) ....Surrey v. Derby (Derby)
T. Soar (11—113) & H. Baldwin (8—93) ....Hants. v. Derby (Southampton)

SEASON 1896

J. T. Hearne (12—90) & J. T. Rawlin (7—69) ....Middx. v. Surrey (Oval)
H. Trumble (6—46) & T. R. McKibbin (13—38) ....Australians v. Lancs. (Liverpool)
J. T. Hearne (13—107) & A. D. Pougher (7—103) ...Earl de la Warr's XI v. Australians (Bexhill)

SEASON 1897

T. Richardson (12—20) & T. Hayward (7—43) ....Surrey v. Leics. (Leicester)
C. H. G. Bland (14—72) & F. W. Tate (6—113) ....Sussex v. Cambridge U. (Cambridge)

SEASON 1899

J. T. Hearne (8—44) & A. E. Trott (11—31) ....Middx. v. Somerset (Lord's)
E. Jones (10—125) & C. E. McLeod (10—84) ....Australians v. Middx. (Lord's)

SEASON 1900

W. Rhodes (11—36) & S. Haigh (7—49) ....Yorks. v. Worcs. (Bradford)
W. R. Cuttell (8—46) & S. Webb (11—41) ....Lancs. v. Hants. (Manchester)

SEASON 1901

J. Sharp (11—105) & S. Webb (8—68) ....Lancs. v. Kent (Manchester)
G. A. Rowe (6—53) & J. H. Sinclair (13—73) ....South Africans v. Glos. (Clifton)
C. Blythe (6—85) & J. R. Mason (12—55) ....Kent v. Somerset (Taunton)
G. H. Hirst (12—29) & W. Rhodes (6—37) ....Yorks. v. Essex (Leyton)

SEASON 1902

J. Hallows (13—71) & W. R. Cuttell (7—50) ....Lancs. v. Kent (Tonbridge)
F. W. Tate (8—109) & E. G. Arnold (12—87)......South of England v. Australians (Bournemouth)

SEASON 1903

S. Haigh (12—52) & W. Rhodes (7—55) ....Yorks. v. Cambridge U. (Sheffield)
S. Hargreave (15—76) & S. Santall (5—66) ....Warwicks. v. Surrey (Oval)
G. H. Hirst (10—67) & W. Rhodes (10—81) ....Yorks. v. Surrey (Oval)
C. Blythe (12—67) & A. Hearne (7—61) ....Kent v. Surrey (Oval)
B. Cranfield (13—102) & L. C. Braund (7—77) ....Somerset v. Glos. (Gloucester)
F. G. Roberts (11—93) & G. Dennett (9—99) ....Glos. v. Surrey (Bristol)

SEASON 1904

W. Rhodes (10—39) & S. Haigh (10—49) ....Yorks. v. Hants. (Leeds)
J. N. Crawford (10—78) & H. C. McDonell (10—89) ....Surrey v. Glos. (Cheltenham)

SEASON 1905

G. J. Thompson (13—105) & H. B. Simpson (6—66) ....Northants. v. Leics. (Leicester)

SEASON 1906

W. Mead (10—73) & A. E. E. Vogler (10—90) ....................................M.C.C. v. Leics. (Lord's)
G. Dennett (15—88) & F. G. Roberts (5—111) ....Glos. v. Essex (Bristol)
G. Dennett (9—109) & P. H. Ford (11—113)................................Glos. v. Sussex (Cheltenham)
G. G. Napier (7—88) & P. R. May (12—66) ....Cambridge U. v. Yorks. (Cambridge)

SEASON 1907

E. G. Arnold (7—66) & J. A. Cuffe (13—76) ....Worcs. v. Yorks. (Bradford)
J. N. Crawford (11—63) & T. Rushby (6—67) ....Surrey v. Sussex (Oval)
J. N. Crawford (6—52) & W. C. Smith (11—65) ....Surrey v. Derby (Derby)
H. Dean (7—84) & W. Huddleston (12—82) ....Lancs. v. Surrey (Manchester)
W. Mead (12—73) & W. Reeves (8—98) ....Essex v. Notts. (Leyton)
S. Hargreave (8—82) & S. Santall (11—91) ....Warwicks. v. Leics. (Coventry)
G. J. Thompson (8—72) & W. East (12—62) ....Northants. v. Glos. (Gloucester)
T. Wass (9—69) & A. W. Hallam (9—65) ....Notts. v. Northants. (Northampton)
T. Wass (10—67) & A. W. Hallam (8—84) ....Notts. v. Derby (Chesterfield)
G. H. Hirst (11—44) & W. Rhodes (8—71) ....Yorks. v. Derby (Glossop)

SEASON 1908

W. S. Lees (8—104) & T. Rushby (9—90) ....Surrey v. Lancs. (Manchester)
T. Wass (16—103) & A. W. Hallam (4—44) ....Notts. v. Essex (Nottingham)
G. H. Hirst (12—19) & S. Haigh (6—19) ....Yorks. v. Northants. (Northampton)
F. A. Tarrant (10—46) & A. E. Trott (9—59) ....Middx. v. Philadelphians (Lord's)

SEASON 1909

T. Wass (10—107) & A. W. Hallam (10—63) ....Notts. v. Derby (Nottingham)
W. Huddleston (8—101) & H. Dean (11—102) ....Lancs. v. Essex (Liverpool)

SEASON 1910

J. T. Hearne (12—70) & F. A. Tarrant (8—59) ....Middx. v. Glos. (Lord's)
H. Dean (11—67) & W. Huddleston (9—38) ....Lancs. v. Worcs. (Manchester)
C. Blythe (11—95) & F. E. Woolley (8—91) ....Kent v. Yorks. (Maidstone)

SEASON 1912

G. J. Thompson (9—55) & S. G. Smith (10—72) ....Northants. v. Essex (Northampton)
C. Blythe (11—56) & F. E. Woolley (9—58)................................Kent v. Notts. (Canterbury)
C. Blythe (7—81) & D. W. Carr (13—74) ....Kent v. Glos. (Dover)
H. Dean (10—66) & W. Huddleston (10—83)................................Lancs. v. Leics. (Leicester)

SEASON 1913

G. J. Thompson (10—104) & S. G. Smith (10—95) ....Northants. v. Sussex (Horsham
T. Wass (10—123) & J. Iremonger (10—73) ....Notts. v. Derby (Chesterfield)

SEASON 1914

J. W. H. T. Douglas (11—98) & B. Tremlin (9—115) ....Essex v. Surrey (Oval)
J. W. H. T. Douglas (9—62) & B. Tremlin (10—52) ....Essex v. Derby (Derby)
A. Jaques (14—54) & A. S. Kennedy (6—64) ....Hants. v. Somerset (Bath)
M. W. Booth (5—77) & A. Drake (15—51) ....Yorks. v. Somerset (Weston-super-Mare)
M. W. Booth (12—89) & A. Drake (8—81)...Yorks. v. Glos. (Bristol)

SEASON 1919

E. Robson (8—107) & J. C. White (11—114) ....Somerset v. Derby (Derby)
H. L. Collins (12—69) & C. E. Winning (8—63) ...........................A.I.F. v. Somerset (Taunton)

SEASON 1920

A. Waddington (13—48) & E. Robinson (6—34) ....Yorks. v. Northants. (Northampton)

SEASON 1921

A. Waddington (9—61) & E. Robinson (10—70) ....Yorks. v. Northants. (Harrogate)
A. S. Kennedy (11—86) & J. A. Newman (9—103) ....Hants. v. Sussex (Portsmouth)

SEASON 1922

P. T. Mills (9—43) & C. W. L. Parker (11—50) ....Glos. v. Worcs. (Gloucester)
W. E. Astill (10—65) & G. Geary (10—68) ....Leics. v. Glos. (Bristol)

SEASON 1923

A. S. Kennedy (12—72) & J. A. Newman (7—62) ....Hants. v. Somerset (Portsmouth)

SEASON 1924

C. H. Parkin (10—78) & R. Tyldesley (10—103) ....Lancs. v. Warwicks. (Manchester)

SEASON 1925

W. E. Astill (8—35) & G. Geary (11—61) ....Leics. v. Glamorgan (Leicester)
M. W. Tate (14—58) & A. F. Wensley (4—52) ....Sussex v. Glamorgan (Hove)

SEASON 1927

G. G. Macaulay (12—50) & E. Robinson (8—65) ....Yorks. v. Worcs. (Leeds)

SEASON 1932

H. Larwood (10—88) & W. Voce (10—35) ....Notts. v. Leics. (Nottingham)

SEASON 1935

H. A. Smith (11—91) & G. Geary (9—62) ....Leics. v. Northants. (Northampton

SEASON 1952

D. Shackleton (12—67) & V. H. D. Cannings (8—55) ....Hants. v. Kent (Southampton)

SEASON 1958

D. Shackleton (7—88) & M. Heath (13—87) ....Hants. v. Derby (Burton upon Trent)

The feat has been performed very rarely in overseas cricket, the following being the leading cases:

F. R. Spofforth (9—72) & E. Evans (10—52) ...............N.S.W. v. Victoria (Sydney)   1875–76
F. R. Spofforth (12—105) & G. E. Palmer (7—65)...Australian XI v. Rest (Melbourne)   1880–81
H. F. Boyle (8—46) & G. E. Palmer (9—61) ....Victoria v. N.S.W. (Sydney)   1882–83
F. H. Cooke (6—30) & Bennett (12—18) ....Nelson v. Wellington (Nelson)   1885–86
D. Dunlop (10—36) & R. Halley (9—52) ....Canterbury v. Wellington (Wellington)   1886–87
G. A. Lohmann (9—67) & J. Briggs (11—58)...Shrewsbury's XI v. Australian XI (Sydney)   1887–88
S. T. Callaway (12—58) & W. McGlinchy (8—41) ...............N.S.W. v. Otago (Dunedin)   1889–90
F. W. Bush (7—70) & H. R. B. Davenport (13—39)............Lucas's XI v. British Guiana
                                                                              (Georgetown)   1894–95
F. W. Bush (14—71) & H. R. B. Davenport (7—35).........Lucas's XI v. Jamaica (Kingston)   1894–95
F. W. Bush (11—91) & H. R. B. Davenport (9—68).........Lucas's XI v. Jamaica (Kingston)   1894–95
G. A. Lohmann (9—88) & G. A. Rowe (10—48)...Western Province v. Griqualand West
                                                                              (Johannesburg)   1896–97
A. H. Fisher (5—31) & A. Downes (12—40)..................Otago v. Canterbury (Dunedin)   1896–97
E. Upham (8—72) & K. Tucker (10—89)...............Wellington v. Auckland (Auckland)   1899–00
A. Downes (12—108) & A. H. Fisher (7—55)..............Otago v. Wellington (Dunedin)   1900–01
J. J. Kotze (11—37) & J. H. Sinclair (8—49) Transvaal v. Griqualand West (Port Elizabeth)   1902–03
A. H. Metha (9—36) & M. D. Bulsara (8—43)...............Parsis v. Europeans (Bombay)   1904–05
A. W. Alloo (10—50) & Holdeness (10—39)...............Otago v. Southland (Invercargill)   1918–19
N. Gordon (9—50) & E. J. Wickham (10—44) Transvaal v. Eastern Province (Port Elizabeth)   1937–38

Most Maiden Overs in Succession

FOUR-BALL OVERS

23 A. Shaw: North v. South (Nottingham) 1876
20 A. Shaw: Notts. v. M.C.C. (Lord's) 1875
20 C. F. Tufnell: Kent v. Notts. (Nottingham) 1878
18 W. Flowers: Notts. v. Sussex (Hove) 1885
15 E. Willsher: South v. North (Canterbury) 1871
15 A. Shaw: M.C.C. v. Yorks. (Scarborough) 1878
14 A. Appleby: Gentlemen v. Players (Lord's) 1870
14 A. Shaw: Players v. Gentlemen (Lord's) 1880

FIVE-BALL OVERS

19 J. W. Trumble: Victoria v. N.S.W. (Melbourne) 1885–86
10 E. Robson: Somerset v. Sussex (Hove) 1897

SIX-BALL OVERS

17 H. L. Hazell: Somerset v. Glos. (Taunton) 1949
      (*Spell of 105 balls without conceding a run.*)
17 G. A. R. Lock: M.C.C. v. Governor-General's XI (Karachi) 1955–56
      (*First 104 balls of innings bowled without conceding a run.*)
15 W. S. Haig: Otago v. Wellington (Dunedin) 1956–57
14 J. A. Young: Middx. v. Glos. (Bristol) 1949
14 W. E. Alley: Somerset v. Essex (Yeovil) 1960
13 J. C. White: Somerset v. Yorks. (Bradford) 1927
13 J. A. Young: Middx. v. Glamorgan (Lord's) 1950
13 G. A. R. Lock: Surrey v. Leics. (Leicester) 1954
13 J. H. Wardle: England v. South Africa (Nottingham) 1955
13 C. H. Palmer: Leics. v. Somerset (Taunton) 1956
12 A. E. Relf: Sussex v. Leics. (Leicester) 1908
12 E. Smith: Yorks. v. Hants. (Bournemouth) 1926
12 C. H. Palmer: Leics. v. Surrey (Leicester) 1st inns 1955
12 T. L. Goddard: South Africans v. Middx. (Lord's) 1955
12 W. E. Hollies: Warwicks. v. Leics. (Hinckley) 1957
11 J. C. White: Somerset v. Worcs. (Stourbridge) 1927
11 J. C. White: Somerset v. Northants. (Northampton) 1929
11 J. A. Young: England v. Australia (Nottingham) 1948
11 M. J. Hilton: Lancs. v. Sussex (Horsham) 1948
11 K. T. Ramadhin: West Indies v. England (Lord's) 1950
11 M. J. Hilton: M.C.C. v. Maharashtra (Poona) 1951–52
11 R. Berry: Lancs. v. Glos. (Manchester) 1952
11 C. H. Palmer: Leics. v. Surrey (Leicester) 2nd inns 1955
11 C. Gladwin: Derby v. Yorks. (Leeds) 1956
11 W. E. Hollies: Warwicks. v. Worcs. (Dudley) 1957
11 N. I. Thomson: Sussex v. Glos. (Worthing) 1960
10 J. H. Hunt: Middx. v. Somerset (Lord's) 1908
10 M. A. Noble: N.S.W. v. Victoria (Sydney) 1908–09
10 W. Huddleston: Lancs. v. Notts. (Nottingham) 1914
10 C. W. L. Parker: Glos. v. Kent (Cheltenham) 1922
10 A. E. Thomas: Northants. v. Glamorgan (Kettering) 1924
10 J. C. White: Somerset v. Worcs. (Stourbridge) 1927
10 J. C. White: Somerset v. Yorks. (Bath) 1930
10 C. S. Marriott: Kent v. Lancs. (Dover) 1934
10 D. C. S. Compton: Middx. v. Hants. (Lord's) 1948
10 C. Gladwin: Derby v. Glos. (Chesterfield) 1949
10 K. T. Ramadhin: West Indies v. England (Lord's) 1950
10 J. H. Wardle: Yorks. v. Kent (Canterbury) 1952
10 C. Gladwin: Derby v. Essex (Ilford) 1955
10 G. A. R. Lock: M.C.C. v. Pakistan XI (Lahore) 1955–56
10 C. Cook: Glos. v. Surrey (Gloucester) 1956
10 R. Benaud: Australians v. Warwicks. (Birmingham) 1956
10 J. H. Wardle: Players v. Gentlemen (Lord's) 1958
10 D. N. F. Slade: Worcs. v. Indians (Worcester) 1959
10 B. D. Wells: Notts. v. Middx. (Lord's) 1960

EIGHT-BALL OVERS

16 H. J. Tayfield: South Africa v. England (Durban) 1956–57
      (137 balls without conceding a run, 20000000, then 14 maidens to end innings, 2 maidens at
      start of second innings, and then 00200100).
9 H. J. Tayfield: South Africa v. Australia (Melbourne) 1952–53
9 P. J. Loader: M.C.C. v. Griqualand West (Kimberley) 1956–57

Sequences of Successful Bowling

Several bowlers have been highly successful during the course of several innings and a list of the leading performers is given.

3 INNINGS

26	C. W. L. Parker (Glos.)	1925	(9—44, 8—12, 9—118)
25	A. P. Freeman (Kent)	1932	(8—56, 8—31, 9—61)
25	G. Giffen (Australians)	1886	(9—60, 8—56, 8—23)
24	H. Dean (Lancs.)	1913	(7—70, 9—62, 8—29)
24	T. W. Goddard (Glos.)	1939	(7—38, 9—38, 8—68)
24	G. A. Lohmann (Hawke's XI)	...1895–96	(7—38, 8—7, 9—28)
24	W. Mead (Essex)	1895	(8—67, 9—52, 7—73)
24	C. W. L. Parker (Glos.)	1930	(9—44, 8—38, 7—53)
24	G. J. Thompson (Northants.)	...1906	(9—64, 7—72, 8—95)
24	J. C. White (Somerset)	1921	(7—52, 7—58, 10—76)
24	J. Wisden (Sussex)	1850	(10, 9 and 5)

4 INNINGS

33	G. Giffen (Australians)	1886	(9—60, 8—56, 8—23, 8—42)
32	C. W. L. Parker (Glos.)	1925	(6—61, 9—44, 8—12, 9—118)
30	A. P. Freeman (Kent)	1932	(5—88, 8—56, 8—31, 9—61)
30	A. P. Freeman (Kent)	1932	(8—56, 8—31, 9—61, 5—143)
30	T. W. Goddard (Glos.)	1939	(6—61, 7—38, 9—38, 8—68)
30	C. L. Townsend (Glos.)	1895	(8—67, 8—130, 7—54, 7—80)
30	H. Verity (Yorks.)	1933	(7—34, 6—67, 8—47, 9—44)

5 INNINGS

40	G. Giffen (Australians)	1886	(7—41, 9—60, 8—56, 8—23, 8—42)
38	C. L. Townsend (Glos.)	1898	(8—66, 9—128, 6—77, 8—64, 7—77)
38	A. P. Freeman (Kent)	1932	(8—56, 8—31, 9—61, 5—143, 8—44)
37	C. W. L. Parker (Glos.)	1925	(5—19, 6—61, 9—44, 8—12, 9—118)
37	H. Verity (Yorks.)	1933	(7—54, 7—34, 6—67, 8—47, 9—44)

6 INNINGS

46	G. Giffen (Australians)	1886	(6—71, 7—41, 9—60, 8—56, 8—23, 8—42)
46	A. P. Freeman (Kent)	1932	(8—56, 8—31, 9—61, 5—143, 8—44, 8—38)
44	H. Verity (Yorks.)	1933	(7—29, 7—54, 7—34, 6—67, 8—47, 9—44)
42	C. L. Townsend (Glos.)	1895	(8—67, 8—130, 7—54, 7—80, 5—95, 7—122)
41	A. P. Freeman (Kent)	1930	(6—97, 8—101, 8—70, 5—40, 8—71, 6—72)

7 INNINGS

51	A. P. Freeman (Kent)	1932	(5—88, 8—56, 8—31, 9—61, 5—143, 8—44, 8—38)
50	H. Verity (Yorks.)	1933	(7—29, 7—54, 7—34, 6—67, 8—47, 9—44, 6—103)
50	C. L. Townsend (Glos.)	1898	(8—66, 9—128, 6—77, 8—64, 7—77, 5—51, 7—66)
47	C. L. Townsend (Glos.)	1895	(5—43, 8—67, 8—130, 7—54, 7—80, 5—95, 7—122)

*M

Eight Wickets Before Lunch

Few bowlers have succeeded in taking eight or more wickets in the pre-lunch session of the first day of a match, a feat considerably more difficult than that of a batsman scoring a century. The bowling figures for the complete innings are given, as in some cases it is not possible to give the actual lunch-time figures. The innings total is given in parentheses.

8—48	(80)	E. Barratt: Surrey v. Sussex (Oval)	1883
8—12	(24)	R. Peel: Yorks. v. Notts. (Sheffield)	1888
8—13	(35)	G. A. Lohmann: Surrey v. Lancs. (Manchester)	1888
8—29	(59)	G. Bean: Sussex v. M.C.C. (Lord's)	1889
8—33	(78)	A. Mold: Lancs. v. Surrey (Manchester)	1896
8—22	(43)	F. W. Stocks: Oxford v. Webbe's XI (Oxford)	1899
8—23	(47)	S. Santall: Warwicks. v. Leics. (Birmingham)	1900
8—30	(70)	G. A. Wilson: Worcs. v. Somerset (Taunton)	1905
9—47	(65)	W. Brearley: Lancs. v. Somerset (Manchester)	1905
8—80	(153)	G. H. Hirst: Yorks. v. Somerset (Sheffield)	1910
9—41	(113)	G. H. Hirst: Yorks. v. Worcs. (Worcester)	1911
8—35	(85)	W. Wells: Northants. v. Yorks. (Sheffield)	1919
8—11	(37)	A. S. Kennedy: Hants. v. Glamorgan (Cardiff)	1921
8—33	(67)	F. C. L. Matthews: Notts. v. Kent (Canterbury)	1924
9—23	(35)	W. R. Hammond: Glos. v. Worcs. (Cheltenham)	1928
8—38	(79)	C. W. L. Parker: Glos. v. Surrey (Cheltenham)	1930
8—44	(85)	H. A. Smith: Leics. v. Northants. (Northampton)	1935
8—18	(62)	W. E. Bowes: Yorks. v. Northants. (Kettering)	1935
8—11	(28)	W. H. Copson: Derby v. Warwicks. (Derby)	1937
8— 2	(27)	J. C. Laker: England v. Rest (Bradford—Test Trial)	1950
9—39	(79)	C. W. Grove: Warwicks. v. Sussex (Birmingham)	1952
		(First eight wickets before lunch).	
8—28	(76)	F. S. Trueman: Yorks. v. Kent (Dover)	1954
9—39	(89)	D. J. Halfyard: Kent v. Glamorgan (Neath)	1957

[Eight Batsmen Cleaned Bowled in an Innings

J. Wisden, playing for North v. South (Lord's) 1850, clean bowled all his victims when taking ten wickets in an innings.

A number of bowlers have succeeded in clean bowling eight batsmen in an innings:

S. E. Butler (10—38): Oxford U. v. Cambridge U. (Lord's) 1871
James Lillywhite (8—55): Sussex v. M.C.C. (Brighton) 1871
W. Frith (8—18): Canterbury v. Otago (Christchurch) 1880–81
J. Briggs (8—11): England v. South Africa (Cape Town) 1888–89
J. T. Hearne (8—22): Middlesex v. Lancashire (Lord's) 1891
A. Mold (8—49): Lancashire v. Sussex (Hove) 1893
H. Fannin (8—19): Hawke's Bay v. Auckland (Auckland) 1897–98
S. Haigh (8—34): Hawke's XI v. Cape Province (Cape Town) 1898–99
W. P. Howell (10—28): Australians v. Surrey (Oval) 1899
A. Woodcock (9—28): Leicestershire v. M.C.C. (Lord's) 1899
A. E. Trott (8—47): Middlesex v. Gloucestershire (Clifton) 1900
J. J. Kotze (8—18): Transvaal v. Griqualand West (Port Elizabeth) 1902–03
J. B. King (9—62): Philadelphians v. Lancashire (Manchester) 1903
A. E. E. Vogler (8—24): Eastern Province v. O.F.S. (Johannesburg) 1906–07
G. H. Hirst (9—23): Yorkshire v. Lancashire (Leeds) 1910
G. H. Hirst (9—41): Yorkshire v. Worcestershire (Bradford) 1911
H. Howell (8—31): Warwickshire v. Northamptonshire (Northampton) 1922
C. W. L. Parker (9—87): Gloucestershire v. Derbyshire (Gloucester) 1922
J. M. Blanckenberg (8—97): South Africans v. Glamorgan (Cardiff) 1924
G. O. Allen (10—40): Middlesex v. Lancashire (Lord's) 1929
A. J. Bell (8—34): Western Province v. Eastern Province (Cape Town) 1929–30

Long Distance for a Bail

The distances which a bail has travelled after a bowler has clean bowled a batsman are sometimes almost incredible, and there are a number of cases of over 50 yards. The longest distances are:

yds in.
67 6 by R. D. Burrows in bowling W. Huddleston: Worcestershire v. Lancashire (Manchester) 1911
66   by H. Larwood in bowling G. W. Martin: M.C.C. v. Tasmania (Launceston)............1928–29
64 6 by R. D. Burrows in bowling A. C. MacLaren: Worcestershire v. Lancashire (Manchester) 1901
63 6 by A. Mold in bowling G. A. Lohmann: Lancashire v. Surrey (Oval)............................1896

Earliest Dates for Reaching Certain Wicket Aggregates

The following are the earliest dates for reaching certain wicket aggregates in an English season (in 1928 A. P. Freeman took his 300th wicket on September 14th—the only time that aggregate has been reached):

100 WICKETS		200 WICKETS	
June 12 1896	J. T. Hearne	July 27 1928	A. P. Freeman
June 12 1931	C. W. L. Parker	August 1 1931	A. P. Freeman
June 13 1931	A. P. Freeman	August 6 1930	A. P. Freeman
June 14 1930	A. P. Freeman	August 7 1929	A. P. Freeman
June 17 1925	M. W. Tate	August 14 1933	A. P. Freeman
June 17 1932	A. P. Freeman		

Good Bowling on Début in First-Class Cricket

Several bowlers have succeeded in returning a very good bowling analysis on the occasion of their first match in first-class cricket, equivalent to a batsman scoring a century on debut, and a list of the outstanding cases is given.

GOOD FIGURES IN A MATCH

14—57   James Lillywhite: Sussex v. M.C.C. (Lord's) 1862
14—100 F. Fee: Ireland v. M.C.C. (Dublin) 1956
14—171 F. G. Gloucestershire v. Yorkshire (Dewsbury) 1887
14—112 V. R. Price: Oxford U. v. Gentlemen of England (Oxford) 1919
13—84   W. G. Grace: Gentlemen of South v. Players of South (Oval) 1865
12—87   A. H. C. Fargus: Gloucestershire v. Middlesex (Lord's) 1900
12—97   V. M. Muddiah: Services v. Southern Punjab (Patiala) 1949–50
11—43   E. T. A. Fuller: Canterbury v. Otago (Christchurch) 1872–73
11—95   B. Mitchell: Transvaal v. Border (East London) 1925–26
11—209 L. W. Payn: Natal v. Orange Free State (Bloemfontein) 1936–37
10—100 T. A. Carlton: Canterbury v. Otago (Christchurch) 1909–10
10—101 S. Webb: Middlesex v. Nottinghamshire (Nottingham) 1897
10—115 J. Hewitson: Lancashire v. Oxford U. (Manchester) 1890
10—136 G. T. S. Stevens: Middlesex v. Hampshire (Lord's) 1919
10—137 A. J. Jessup: Oxford U. v. Free Foresters (Oxford) 1950
10—141 R. Rees: South Australia v. Victoria (Melbourne) 1903–04
10—145 L. O'B. Fleetwood-Smith: Victoria v. Tasmania (Hobart) 1931–32
10—149 J. I'Anson: Lancashire v. M.C.C. (Lord's) 1896

GOOD FIGURES IN AN INNINGS

The following bowlers had good analyses in one innings of their first match (bowlers appearing in the above list are excluded from this):
8—54 V. M. Muddiah: Services v. Southern Punjab (Patiala) 1949–50
8—64 W. B. Gadsden: Natal v. Transvaal (Durban) 1928–29
8—70 G. A. Wilson: Worcestershire v. Yorkshire (Worcester) 1899
8—88 M. H. J. Allen: Northamptonshire v. Nottinghamshire (Nottingham) 1956
       (This was his second match, he did not bowl in the first.)

8—91 F. Barratt: Nottinghamshire v. M.C.C. (Lord's) 1914
7—10 A. C. King: Natal v. Griqualand West (Johannesburg) 1906–07
7—28 C. E. Dench: Nottinghamshire v. M.C.C. (Lord's) 1897
7—32 J. A. Bailey: Essex v. Nottinghamshire (Southend)...............................1953
7—49 H. Hunt: Somerset v. Derbyshire (Ilkeston) 1935
7—50 L. G. Robinson: Natal v. Griqualand West (Cape Town) 1893–94
7—54 R. F. Delport: Western Province v. Rhodesia (Cape Town) 1950–51
7—70 W. K. Laidlaw: Scotland v. Yorkshire (Harrogate) 1938
7—76 B. Stead: Yorkshire v. Indians (Bradford) 1959
7—77 L. R. Tuckett: Natal v. M.C.C. (Durban) 1909–10
7—91 G. Anderson: Rhodesia v. Transvaal (Johannesburg) 1904–05
7—95 W. H. Ashley: South Africa v. England (Cape Town) 1888–89
6—19 G. W. Youngson: Scotland v. Ireland (Cork) 1947
6—31 A. Shaw: Nottinghamshire v. Kent (Nottingham) 1864
6—32 S. C. Adams: Northamptonshire v. Dublin U. (Northampton) 1926
6—44 E. A. Barlow: Oxford U. v. Yorkshire (Oxford) 1932
6—47 J. Iverson: Victoria v. Western Australia (Perth) 1949–50
6—53 W. Flint: Nottinghamshire v. Middlesex (Lord's) 1919
6—111 T. Sutherland: Hampshire v. Warwickshire (Southampton) 1898
5—5   J. W. Sharpe: Surrey v. Oxford U. (Oxford) 1889
5—7   J. Smurthwaite: Yorkshire v. Derbyshire (Sheffield) 1939

WICKET WITH FIRST BALL IN FIRST-CLASS CRICKET

H. Stubberfield: Sussex v. Surrey (Brighton) 1857
R. G. Barlow: Lancashire v. Yorkshire (Sheffield) 1871
G. McCanlis: Kent v. Surrey (Oval) 1873
J. J. Parfitt: Surrey v. Yorkshire (Oval) 1881
E. C. Streatfeild: Surrey v. Lancashire (Oval) 1890
M. Berkley: Essex v. Yorkshire (Halifax) 1894
L. C. V. Bathurst: Middlesex v. Sussex (Lord's) 1894
T. Lancaster: Lancashire v. Nottinghamshire (Manchester) 1894
H. G. Curgenven: Derbyshire v. Essex (Leyton) 1896
C. Blythe: Kent v. Yorkshire (Tonbridge) 1899
H. J. Hodgkins: Gloucestershire v. Somerset (Bristol) 1900
J. H. Hunt: Middlesex v. Somerset (Lord's) 1902
C. Thorneycroft: Northamptonshire v. Kent (Catford) 1907
L. Cook: Lancashire v. Essex (Manchester) 1907
G. de L. Hough: Kent v. Essex (Leyton) 1919
T. Collins: Nottinghamshire v. Leicestershire (Nottingham) 1921
J. John: Glamorgan v. Somerset (Cardiff) 1922
A. E. Waters: Gloucestershire v. Glamorgan (Cheltenham) 1923
R. H. Sharp: Essex v. Gloucestershire (Leyton) 1925
S. C. Adams: Northamptonshire v. Dublin U. (Northampton) 1926
J. G. O'Gorman: Surrey v. Glamorgan (Oval) 1927
W. H. Copson: Derbyshire v. Surrey (Oval) 1932
F. W. Stocks: Nottinghamshire v. Lancashire (Manchester) 1946
C. Cook: Gloucestershire v. Oxford U. (Oxford) 1946
T. C. Dodds: Essex v. Middlesex (Westcliff) (first ball in England) 1946
E. Tilley: Leicestershire v. Derbyshire (Derby) 1946
J. Lee: Leicestershire v. Glamorgan (Cardiff) 1947
R. Hiern: South Australia v. Victoria (Melbourne) 1949–50
G. A. Robertson: Cambridge U. v. Hampshire (Cambridge) 1950
R. Flockton: New South Wales v. Queensland (Brisbane) 1951–52
D. H. Mitchell: Transvaal v. Natal (Durban) 1954–55
F. C. Brailsford: Derbyshire v. Sussex (Derby) 1958
W. G. Davies: Glamorgan v. Surrey (Oval) 1958

S. C. Adams, playing for Northamptonshire v. Dublin U. (Northampton) 1925, took two wickets with his first two balls, and three wickets at the cost of a single in his first over.

C. G. Fynn, playing for Hampshire v. Lancashire (Bournemouth) 1930, took two wickets in his first over.

R. R. Phillips, playing for Border v. Eastern Province (Port Elizabeth) 1939–40, performed the 'hat-trick' in his first over in first-class cricket. He had previously played in four matches without bowling.

A. Tayfield, making his debut in first-class cricket for Natal v. Transvaal (Johannesburg) 1948–49, returned the following analysis 67–27–90–1 (eight-ball overs).

R. Roxley (5–84), playing for New South Wales v. South Australia (Adelaide) 1952–53, took the first five wickets to fall in his first match.

J. M. Allan (Oxford U.) bowled seven consecutive maidens v. Yorkshire (Oxford) 1953, in his first match, and three more for the wickets of K. R. Miller and I. D. Craig in his second match v. Australians (Oxford), before conceding his first first-class run in his 11th over.

Successful First Season—Bowling

The following bowlers have achieved the feat of taking 100 wickets in their début first-class season. The age given is that at the start of the season.

	Age	Season	Overs	Mdns.	Runs	Wkts.	Avge.
G. P. Harrison (Yorks.)	21	1883	786	328	1326	100	13·26
A. Mold (Lancs.)	23	1889	679	262	1207	102	11·83
C. H. G. Bland (Sussex)	24	1897	1140·2	337	2798	129	21·68
W. Rhodes (Yorks.)	20	1898	1240	482	2249	154	14·60
F. Barratt (Notts.)	20	1914	920	192	2507	115	21·80
A. Waddington (Yorks.)	26	1919	718·1	186	1874	100	18·74
J. M. Gregory† (Australians)	23	1919	830	124	2383	131	18·19
G. W. Brook (Worcs.)	34	1930	974·4	165	2889	132	21·88
C. Cook (Glos.)	24	1946	1123·1	327	2477	133	18·62
D. B. Close (Yorks.)	18	1949	1245	324	3150	113	27·87

† *Gregory did not make his debut in Australia until 1919–20.*

A. G. Steel (Lancashire) took 164 wickets (av. 9·40) in 1878, after playing only one match in 1877.

W. Rhodes (Yorkshire) took 154 wickets in 1898, 179 in 1899 and 261 in 1900—his first three seasons in first-class cricket.

N. A. Knox (Surrey) took 129 wickets (av. 21·44) in 1905, after taking 12 wickets (av. 29·66) in two matches in 1904.

D. W. Carr (Kent) took 95 wickets (av. 18·27) in 1909, his debut season in first-class cricket. His first match was for Kent v. Oxford U. (Oxford), his second for Gentlemen at the Oval and his third for Gentlemen at Lord's. His eighth match was for England v. Australia at the Oval.

P. Jeeves (Warwickshire) took 106 wickets (av. 20·88) in 1913, after playing only two matches in 1912, while qualifying for the county.

T. J. Durston (Middlesex) took 113 wickets (av. 21·88) in 1920, after playing in only four matches in 1919.

A. W. Wellard (Somerset) took 131 wickets (av. 21·38) in 1929, after playing only two matches in 1927 and 1928.

C. I. J. Smith (Middlesex) took 172 wickets (av. 18·88) in 1934, his first full season for the county, after taking only 29 wickets in odd matches in the four seasons 1930 to 1933.

H. Verity (Yorkshire) took 188 wickets (av. 13·52) in 1931, his first full season, after taking 64 wickets (av. 12·42) in twelve matches in 1930.

L. L. Wilkinson (Lancashire) took 151 wickets (av. 23·38) in 1938, after taking 22 wickets (av. 28·18) in seven matches in 1937.

A. V. Bedser (Surrey) took 128 wickets (av. 20·13) in 1946, after having failed to take a wicket in the two matches in which he played in 1939.

C. Gladwin (Derbyshire) took 109 wickets (av. 18·36) in 1946, after having failed to take a wicket in the four matches in which he played in 1939.

R. Appleyard (Yorkshire) took 200 wickets (av. 14·14) in 1951, after taking 11 wickets (av. 16·09) in three matches in 1950.

K. T. Ramadhin took 135 wickets (av. 14·28) and A. L. Valentine 123 wickets (av. 17·94) for the 1950 West Indies team in England, although each player had appeared in only two first-class matches before the start of the tour.

Part V—All-Round Cricket
The Cricketer's 'Double'

The cricketer's 'double'—the scoring of 1000 runs and taking of 100 wickets in the course of a season—was first performed in 1873 by W. G. Grace. He repeated this feat in each season up to 1878, but his record remained unequalled until C. T. Studd achieved the 'double' in 1882. With the extension of the first-class fixture list in 1894 it became easier to reach the coveted all-rounder's honour.

The following outstanding 'doubles' have been recorded:

2000 runs and 200 wickets.....................G. H. Hirst in 1906.
3000 runs and 100 wickets.....................J. H. Parks in 1937.
2000 runs and 100 wickets.....................W. G. Grace in 1876.
              C. L. Townsend in 1899.
              G. L. Jessop in 1900.
              G. H. Hirst in 1904 and 1905.
              W. Rhodes in 1909 and 1911.
              F. A. Tarrant in 1911.
              J. W. Hearne in 1913, 1914 and 1920.
              F. E. Woolley in 1914, 1921, 1922 and 1923.
              V. W. C. Jupp in 1921.
              L. F. Townsend in 1933.
              E. Davies in 1937.
              James Langridge in 1937.
              T. E. Bailey in 1959.
1000 runs and 200 wickets.....................A. E. Trott in 1899 and 1900.
              A. S. Kennedy in 1922.
              M. W. Tate in 1923, 1924 and 1925.

The cricketers who have performed the 'double' on the most occasions are:

16 times W. Rhodes.
14 times G. H. Hirst.
10 times V. W. C. Jupp.
9 times W. E. Astill.
8 times M. S. Nichols, A. E. Relf, F. A. Tarrant, M. W. Tate and F. E. Woolley.

The cricketers who have performed the 'double' the most times in successive seasons are:

11 times G. H. Hirst (1903–1913).
8 times F. A. Tarrant (1907–1914) and M. W. Tate (1922–1929).
7 times W. Rhodes, twice (1903–1909 & 1914–1924).
6 times W. E. Astill (1921–1926), G. Tribe (1952–1957), and F. E. Woolley (1914–1923).

The complete list of cricketers to achieve the 'double' are as follows:

	Season	Runs	H.S.	Avge.	100s		Wkts.	Avge.
Andrews, W. H. R. (Somerset) ....(2)	1937	1141	80	20·74	—	...	143	20·53
	1938	1001	77*	22·24	—	...	124	21·80
Armstrong, W. W. (Australians) ....(3)	1905	1902	303*	50·05	4	...	122	18·20
	1909	1451	110*	43·96	3	...	113	16·38
	1921	1213	182*	41·82	3	...	100	14·44
Arnold, E. G. (Worcs.) ....(4)	1902	1067	92	26·02	—	...	113	18·88
	1903	1157	128	30·44	2	...	143	17·44
	1904	1039	111	25·97	1	...	114	24·48
	1905	1148	134	37·03	—	...	115	22·32
Astill, W. E. (Leics.) ....(9)	1921	1380	115	27·05	2	...	153	20·99
	1922	1210	78	23·72	—	...	144	19·23
	1923	1307	106	27·80	2	...	114	23·50
	1924	1126	88	25·59	—	...	103	20·84
	1925	1601	109	32·02	1	...	105	20·99
	1926	1291	158*	30·02	1	...	107	24·48
	1928	1127	89	24·50	—	...	130	22·33
	1929	1004	127	25·10	2	...	121	20·94
	1930	1022	84	24·92	—	...	111	22·25

	Season	Runs	H.S.	Avge.	100s		Wkts.	Avge.
Bailey, J. (Hants.) ....(1)	1948	1399	88	31·79	—	...	121	18·13
Bailey, T. E. (Essex) ....(6)	1949	1380	93	35·38	—	...	130	24·20
	1952	1513	155*	36·90	1	...	103	29·09
	1954	1344	108*	32·78	1	...	101	21·39
	1957	1322	132	38·88	2	...	104	17·02
	1959	2011	146	46·76	6	...	100	24·69
	1960	1639	118	39·02	1	...	117	20·25
Barratt, F. (Notts.) ....(1)	1928	1167	139*	29·17	2	...	114	25·18
Booth, M. W. (Yorks.) ....(1)	1913	1228	107*	27·28	1	...	181	18·46
Bosanquet, B. J. T. (Middx.)...............(1)	1904	1405	145	36·02	4	...	132	21·62
Braund, L. C. (Somerset) ....(3)	1901	1587	115*	36·06	4	...	120	30·62
	1902	1432	141	27·53	2	...	172	19·80
	1903	1425	132	32·38	3	...	134	21·01
Brockwell, W. (Surrey) ....(1)	1899	1542	167	33·52	3	...	105	25·26
Broderick, V. H. (Northants.) ....(1)	1948	1066	135	26·65	2	...	100	22·77
Brown, F. R. (Surrey & Northants.) ...(2)	1932	1135	212	32·42	3	...	120	20·46
	1949	1077	94	24·47	—	...	111	27·00
Calthorpe, Hon. F. S. G. (Warwicks.)...(1)	1920	1025	102	22·77	1	...	100	24·26
Close, D. B. (Yorks.) ....(2)	1949	1098	88*	27·45	—	...	113	27·87
	1952	1192	87*	33·11	—	...	114	24·08
Collins, H. L. (Australians) ....(1)	1919	1615	127	38·45	5	...	106	16·55
Constantine, L. N. (West Indians) ......(1)	1928	1381	130	34·52	3	...	107	22·95
Crawford, J. N. (Surrey) ....(2)	1906	1174	148	30·10	1	...	118	20·28
	1907	1158	103	30·47	1	...	124	16·95
Cuffe, J. A. (Worcs.) ....(1)	1911	1054	78	25·70	—	...	110	23·56
Cuttell, W. R. (Lancs.) ....(1)	1898	1003	85*	25·71	—	...	114	21·21
Davidson, G. (Derby)........................(1)	1895	1296	80	28·07	—	...	138	16·79
Davies, E. (Glamorgan) ....(2)	1935	1326	155*	28·21	2	...	100	21·07
	1937	2012	140	40·24	3	...	103	23·03
Dooland, B. (Notts.) ....(2)	1954	1012	88	28·11	—	...	196	15·48
	1957	1604	115*	28·64	1	...	141	23·21
Douglas, J. W. H. T. (Essex) ....(5)	1914	1288	146	35·77	2	...	138	19·10
	1919	1178	144	34·64	2	...	136	25·14
	1920	1328	147	32·39	2	...	147	21·38
	1921	1547	210*	37·73	3	...	130	20·32
	1923	1110	147*	29·21	2	...	146	22·35
Drake, A. (Yorks.) ....(1)	1913	1056	108	23·46	1	...	116	16·93
Faulkner, G. A. (South Africans)........(1)	1912	1075	145*	23·88	2	...	163	15·42
Fender, P. G. H. (Surrey) ....(6)	1921	1152	101	21·33	1	...	134	26·58
	1922	1169	185	34·38	2	...	157	21·20
	1923	1427	124*	29·12	2	...	178	19·98
	1925	1042	81*	28·16	—	...	137	21·08
	1926	1043	104	30·67	1	...	112	24·54
	1928	1376	177	37·18	3	...	110	28·17
Flowers, W. (Notts.) ....(1)	1883	1144	131	24·86	1	...	113	14·95
Foster, F. R. ....(2)	1911	1614	200	42·47	3	...	141	20·31
	1914	1460	305*	34·76	1	...	122	18·62
Giffen, G. (Australians) ....(3)	1886	1424	119	26·86	1	...	154	17·36
	1893	1133	180	23·12	2	...	118	19·04
	1896	1208	130	25·17	2	...	117	19·29
Gilligan, A. E. R. (Sussex) ....(1)	1923	1183	114*	21·12	2	...	163	17·50
Goonesena, G. (Notts.) ....(2)	1955	1380	118	28·75	2	...	134	21·05
	1957	1156	211	26·88	1	...	110	23·26
Grace, W. G. (Glos.) ....(7)	1874	1664	179	52·00	8	...	140	12·71
	1875	1498	152	32·56	3	...	191	12·92
	1876	2622	344	62·42	7	...	129	19·05
	1877	1474	261	39·83	2	...	179	12·79
	1878	1116	116	29·36	1	...	147	14·36
	1885	1614	221*	44·83	4	...	109	18·07
	1886	1846	170	35·50	4	...	122	19·99
Gregory, J. M. (Australians) ....(1)	1921	1135	107	36·61	3	...	116	16·58
Gunn, J. (Notts.) ....(4)	1903	1665	294	42·69	3	...	118	19·34
	1904	1225	100	30·62	1	...	123	25·27
	1905	1366	178	35·94	3	...	111	25·46
	1906	1395	130	35·76	2	...	112	21·66
Haig, N. E. (Middx.) ....(3)	1921	1009	108	22·95	1	...	111	23·10
	1927	1059	104*	22·53	1	...	109	27·45
	1929	1552	130	25·02	2	...	129	24·17
Haigh, S. (Yorks.) ....(1)	1904	1055	138	26·37	2	...	121	19·85
Hallows, J. (Lancs.) ....(1)	1904	1071	137*	39·66	3	...	108	19·37
Hayward, T. (Surrey) ....(1)	1897	1368	130	38·00	1	...	114	18·18

	Season	Runs	H.S.	Avge.	100s		Wkts.	Avge.
Hearne, J. W. (Middx.) ....(5)	1911	1627	234*	42·81	4	...	102	22·00
	1913	2036	189	44·26	6	...	124	22·26
	1914	2116	204	60·45	8	...	123	22·69
	1920	2148	215*	55·07	6	...	142	17·83
	1923	1519	232	47·46	5	...	113	20·03
Hirst, G. H. (Yorks.) ....(14)	1896	1122	107	28·05	1	...	104	21·61
	1897	1535	134	35·69	1	...	101	23·22
	1901	1950	214	42·39	3	...	183	16·38
	1903	1844	153	47·28	5	...	128	14·94
	1904	2501	157	54·36	9	...	132	21·09
	1905	2266	341	53·95	6	...	110	19·94
	1906	2385	169	45·86	6	...	208	16·50
	1907	1334	91*	28·38	—	...	188	15·20
	1908	1598	128*	38·97	1	...	174	14·05
	1909	1256	140	27·30	1	...	115	20·05
	1910	1840	158	32·85	3	...	164	14·79
	1911	1789	218	33·12	3	...	137	20·40
	1912	1133	109	25·75	1	...	118	17·37
	1913	1540	166*	35·81	3	...	101	20·13
Hopwood, J. L. (Lancs.) ....(2)	1934	1672	220	38·00	3	...	111	20·69
	1935	1538	104	33·43	2	...	103	20·55
Horton, M. J. (Worcs.) ....(1)	1955	1296	103	22·73	1	...	103	27·38
Howorth, R. (Worcs.) ....(3)	1939	1019	69	21·22	—	...	100	24·34
	1946	1201	114	24·51	2	...	114	19·35
	1947	1510	95	26·03	—	...	164	17·85
Illingworth, R. (Yorks.) ....(3)	1957	1213	97	28·20	—	...	106	18·40
	1959	1726	162	46·64	5	...	110	21·46
	1960	1006	86	25·79	—	...	109	17·55
Jackson, F. S. (Yorks.) ....(1)	1898	1566	160	41·21	5	...	104	15·67
Jackson, V. E. (Leics.) ....(1)	1955	1582	121	29·29	4	...	112	21·71
Jenkins, R. O. (Worcs.) ....(2)	1949	1183	91*	28·16	—	...	183	21·19
	1952	1087	85	24·70	—	...	136	25·65
Jessop, G. L. (Glos.) ....(2)	1897	1219	140	29·73	4	...	116	17·85
	1900	2210	179	40·18	6	...	104	21·00
Jupp, V. W. C. (Sussex & Northants.) (10)	1920	1444	151	28·31	3	...	111	18·56
	1921	2169	179	38·73	7	...	121	22·78
	1925	1306	144	27·78	1	...	116	20·68
	1926	1560	197	35·45	2	...	113	19·95
	1927	1519	116	38·94	3	...	121	20·42
	1928	1574	113	34·97	2	...	166	20·15
	1930	1037	142*	28·02	1	...	106	20·96
	1931	1540	128	28·00	2	...	131	24·91
	1932	1712	163	31·70	2	...	130	22·61
	1933	1155	121	28·17	1	...	108	29·46
Kennedy, A. S. (Hants.)...............(5)	1921	1305	152*	26·10	2	...	186	21·55
	1922	1129	110*	22·13	1	...	205	16·80
	1923	1327	163*	25·51	2	...	184	19·55
	1928	1437	128	26·61	2	...	105	28·38
	1930	1006	94*	20·53	—	...	120	25·72
Killick, E. H. (Sussex) ....(1)	1905	1392	104	26·26	1	...	108	21·93
Kilner, R. (Yorks.) ....(4)	1922	1198	124	27·22	2	...	122	14·73
	1923	1404	79	34·24	—	...	158	12·91
	1925	1068	124	30·51	2	...	131	17·92
	1926	1187	150	37·09	1	...	107	22·52
King, J. H. (Leics.) ....(1)	1912	1074	104*	22·85	1	...	130	17·63
Langridge, James (Sussex) ....(6)	1930	1386	159*	30·13	2	...	112	20·60
	1931	1007	92*	28·77	—	...	102	18·60
	1932	1192	128	32·21	2	...	115	17·66
	1933	1578	159*	37·57	5	...	158	16·56
	1935	1375	114*	33·53	2	...	102	19·67
	1937	2082	150*	40·82	1	...	101	22·92
Llewellyn, C. B. (Hants.) ....(3)	1901	1025	216	31·06	2	...	134	22·53
	1908	1347	154	28·06	3	...	102	25·13
	1910	1232	107	29·33	2	...	152	19·27
Lockwood, W. H. (Surrey) ....(2)	1899	1272	131	37·14	3	...	117	19·52
	1900	1367	165	32·54	2	...	125	19·99
Mankad, V. (Indians) ....(1)	1946	1120	132	28·00	3	...	129	20·76
Martin, S. H. (Worcs.) ....(2)	1937	1130	92	21·73	—	...	114	20·25
	1939	1262	102*	25·24	1	...	106	25·00
Mason, J. R. (Kent) ....(1)	1901	1561	145	36·30	3	...	118	20·44
Mortimore, J. B. (Glos.)...............(1)	1959	1060	76	20·78	—	...	113	18·28

	Season	Runs	H.S.	Avge.	100s		Wkts.	Avge.
Muncer, B. L. (Glamorgan) ....(1)	1952	1097	135	24·37	1	...	105	17·29
Newman, J. A. (Hants.) ....(5)	1921	1065	166*	30·42	1	...	177	21·56
	1923	1006	130	22·86	1	...	148	25·35
	1926	1468	134	30·58	1	...	154	24·70
	1927	1448	102*	32·17	2	...	115	23·19
	1928	1474	118	29·48	3	...	112	30·32
Nichols, M. S. (Essex) ....(8)	1929	1301	138	28·91	1	...	104	25·59
	1932	1430	105	31·77	1	...	115	24·92
	1933	1406	135	28·69	3	...	145	20·97
	1935	1249	146	23·56	1	...	157	16·62
	1936	1315	205	29·22	3	...	114	19·42
	1937	1247	120	25·44	2	...	148	18·52
	1938	1452	163	35·41	3	...	171	19·92
	1939	1387	146	35·56	2	...	121	18·87
Parks, J. H. (Sussex) ....(2)	1935	1633	156	33·32	4	...	103	19·57
	1937	3003	168	50·89	11	...	101	25·83
Pearson, F. (Worcs.) ....(1)	1923	1052	103*	25·04	1	...	111	22·89
Peel, R. (Yorks.) ....(1)	1896	1206	210*	30·15	3	...	128	17·50
Pope, G. H. (Derby) ....(2)	1938	1040	85	29·71	—	...	103	24·13
	1948	1152	207*	38·40	3	...	100	17·24
Relf, A. E. (Sussex)............................(8)	1904	1214	154	28·23	2	...	102	26·04
	1905	1386	120	29·48	1	...	111	23·45
	1906	1256	189*	25·63	2	...	106	23·24
	1908	1335	138	28·40	1	...	151	17·53
	1910	1296	87	23·56	—	...	158	19·67
	1911	1691	101*	29·66	1	...	142	21·44
	1912	1312	104	23·85	2	...	133	19·44
	1913	1846	130	31·82	4	...	141	18·09
Rhodes, W. (Yorks.)........................(16)	1903	1137	98*	27·07	—	...	193	14·57
	1904	1537	196	35·74	2	...	131	21·59
	1905	1581	201	35·93	2	...	182	16·95
	1906	1721	119	29·16	3	...	128	23·57
	1907	1055	112	22·93	1	...	177	15·57
	1908	1673	146	31·56	3	...	115	16·13
	1909	2094	199	40·26	5	...	141	15·89
	1911	2261	128	38·32	5	...	117	24·07
	1914	1377	113	29·29	2	...	118	18·27
	1919	1237	135	34·36	1	...	164	14·42
	1920	1123	167*	28·07	1	...	161	13·18
	1921	1474	267*	39·83	3	...	141	13·27
	1922	1511	110	39·76	4	...	119	12·19
	1923	1321	126	33·02	2	...	134	11·54
	1924	1126	100	26·18	1	...	109	14·46
	1926	1132	132	34·30	1	...	115	14·86
Robins, R. W. V. (Middx.) ....(1)	1929	1134	106	26·37	1	...	162	21·53
Root, C. F. (Worcs.) ....(1)	1928	1044	107	20·88	1	...	118	29·66
Simms, H. L. (Sussex) ....(1)	1912	1099	126	20·73	1	...	107	23·12
Sinfield, R. A. (Glos.)........................(2)	1934	1228	83	31·48	—	...	122	23·40
	1937	1001	74*	24·41	—	...	129	22·92
Smailes, T. F. (Yorks.) ....(1)	1938	1002	117	25·05	2	...	113	20·84
Smith, R. (Essex)..............................(3)	1947	1386	86*	28·87	—	...	125	37·26
	1950	1149	80	23·93	—	...	102	34·77
	1952	1044	107*	24·27	1	...	136	28·87
Smith, S. G. (Northants.) ....(3)	1909	1091	126	30·30	1	...	115	19·51
	1913	1522	133	37·12	4	...	111	17·25
	1914	1373	177	42·90	1	...	105	16·25
Smith, T. P. B. (Essex) ....(1)	1947	1065	163	23·66	1	...	172	27·13
Studd, C. T. (Middx.)........................(2)	1882	1249	126*	32·86	4	...	131	16·01
	1883	1193	175*	41·13	2	...	112	17·46
Tarrant, F. A. (Middx.) ....(8)	1907	1552	147	32·33	2	...	183	15·70
	1908	1724	157	41·04	5	...	169	16·68
	1909	1643	138	32·86	2	...	125	19·26
	1910	1425	142	36·53	3	...	134	16·18
	1911	2030	207*	46·13	5	...	111	19·23
	1912	1492	140	30·44	2	...	140	14·78
	1913	1630	142	40·75	3	...	136	17·08
	1914	1879	250*	45·82	5	...	138	18·84
Tate, M. W. (Sussex) ....(8)	1922	1050	88	19·44	—	...	119	17·42
	1923	1168	97	22·03	—	...	219	13·97
	1924	1419	164	29·56	2	...	205	13·74
	1925	1290	121	23·45	2	...	228	14·97

	Season	Runs	H.S.	Avge.	100s		Wkts.	Avge.
Tate, M. W. (*cont.*)	1926	1347	93	32·07	—	...	147	17·51
	1927	1713	146	36·44	3	...	147	20·53
	1928	1469	126	30·60	3	...	165	19·29
	1929	1161	100*	25·80	1	...	156	18·60
Thompson, G. J. (Northants.) ....(2)	1906	1014	103*	25·35	1	...	136	22·20
	1910	1021	101	23·74	2	...	129	17·86
Titmus, F. J. (Middx.) ....(5)	1955	1235	104	24·70	1	...	191	16·31
	1956	1227	96	28·53	—	...	105	20·84
	1957	1056	70	19·92	—	...	106	19·74
	1959	1273	90	25·75	—	...	104	24·83
	1960	1205	105	27·38	1	...	117	19·83
Todd, L. J. (Kent) ....(1)	1936	1320	113	28·08	1	...	103	21·93
Townsend, C. L. (Glos.) ....(2)	1898	1270	159	34·32	5	...	145	20·60
	1899	2440	224*	51·91	9	...	101	29·06
Townsend, L. F. (Derby) ....(3)	1928	1001	98	29·44	—	...	104	23·56
	1932	1497	153*	31·18	1	...	117	18·45
	1933	2268	233	44·47	6	...	100	18·71
Tribe, G. E. (Northants.) ....(7)	1952	1039	78	29·68	—	...	126	25·61
	1953	1260	121	36·00	2	...	108	22·22
	1954	1117	136*	27·92	1	...	149	19·79
	1955	1127	80*	25·04	—	...	176	19·12
	1956	1204	116	32·54	1	...	126	19·02
	1957	1181	101	25·12	1	...	140	18·71
	1959	1082	105*	26·39	1	...	122	23·95
Trott, A. E. (Middx.) ....(2)	1899	1175	164	23·03	2	...	239	17·09
	1900	1357	112	23·87	2	...	211	23·33
Trumble, H. (Australians) ....(1)	1899	1183	100	27·51	1	...	142	18·43
Vine, J. (Sussex) ....(1)	1901	1190	94	28·33	—	...	113	29·72
Wainwright, E. (Yorks.)....................(1)	1897	1612	171	35·82	5	...	101	23·06
Walsh, J. E. (Leics.) ....(1)	1952	1106	102	24·04	1	...	122	25·87
Watkins, A. J. (Glamorgan) ....(2)	1954	1640	170*	34·89	2	...	103	15·82
	1955	1160	111	24·16	2	...	114	20·49
Wellard, A. W. (Somerset) ....(3)	1933	1085	77	27·12	—	...	104	25·57
	1935	1347	112	31·32	1	...	114	20·68
	1937	1049	91*	18·73	—	...	156	23·55
Wensley, A. F. (Sussex) ....(1)	1929	1057	91	21·14	—	...	113	25·22
White, J. C. (Somerset) ....(2)	1929	1179	192	27·41	1	...	168	15·76
	1930	1050	97	26·25	—	...	123	19·51
Wooller, W. (Glamorgan) ....(1)	1954	1059	71	24·06	—	...	107	18·42
Woolley, F. E. (Kent)........................(8)	1910	1101	120	24·46	3	...	136	14·50
	1912	1827	117	41·52	2	...	126	14·30
	1914	2272	160*	45·44	6	...	125	19·45
	1919	1082	164	41·61	3	...	128	17·15
	1920	1924	158	40·93	5	...	185	14·23
	1921	2101	174	42·87	6	...	167	16·14
	1922	2022	188	45·95	5	...	163	18·37
	1923	2091	270	41·00	5	...	101	19·18

J. W. Hearne (Middlesex) missed the 'double' by only one wicket in 1922, totalling 1835 runs (av. 48·28) and 99 wickets (av. 22·28).

V. W. C. Jupp was the first player to achieve the 'double' for two counties—for Sussex in 1920 and Northamptonshire between 1925 and 1933.

R. W. V. Robins (Middlesex) missed the 'double' by only one wicket in 1937, totalling 1076 runs (av. 29·08) and 99 wickets (av. 20·00).

R. Howorth (Worcestershire) missed the 'double' by only three runs in 1938, totalling 997 runs (av. 20·34) and 108 wickets (av. 25·63).

M. S. Nichols (Essex) was the first player to complete the 'double' in each of five consecutive seasons from 1935 to 1939.

D. B. Close (Yorkshire) set up two records in 1949, becoming the youngest player (aged 18) to achieve the 'double' and the first to do so in a debut season.

F. R. Brown was the second player to achieve the 'double' for two counties—for Surrey in 1932 and for Northamptonshire in 1949.

Not one player achieved the 'double' in 1951, the first time since the fixture list had been extended in 1895 that the feat had been missed. The season of 1958 was also without a single 'double'.

F. R. Brown (Northamptonshire) missed the 'double' by only one wicket in 1952, totalling 1118 runs (av. 28·66) and 99 wickets (av. 24·31).

B. R. Knight (Essex) missed the 'double' by only five runs in 1959, totalling 995 runs (av. 27·63) and 101 wickets (av. 23·56).

Earliest Dates for Reaching 'Double'

The following are the earliest dates for achieving the 'double' in an English season. In establishing the record in 1906, G. H. Hirst completed the 'double' in his 16th match of the season.

June 28 1906 G. H. Hirst (Yorkshire)	July 26 1920 F. E. Woolley (Kent)
July 12 1901 G. H. Hirst (Yorkshire)	July 27 1905 W. Rhodes (Yorkshire)
July 15 1907 F. A. Tarrant (Middlesex)	July 28 1922 F. E. Woolley (Kent)
July 17 1928 V. W. C. Jupp (Northamptonshire)	July 30 1928 M. W. Tate (Sussex)
July 24 1908 F. A. Tarrant (Middlesex)	July 31 1914 J. W. H. T. Douglas (Essex)
July 25 1933 James Langridge (Sussex)	July 31 1926 J. A. Newman (Hampshire)

All-Round Cricket in a Match

The feat of scoring 100 runs and taking 10 wickets in the course of a match is a very great performance, usually a match-winning one, and is a great deal less common than is generally supposed. The perfect 'double' was recorded by G. H. Hirst in 1906, when he scored a century in each innings and took five wickets in each Somerset innings during a match at Bath. W. R. Hammond performed a unique feat by scoring a century in each innings and holding ten catches in a match, but this does not really come into consideration as it was not an all-round performance with the bat and ball.

The following players have scored 150 runs and taken 15 wickets in a match:

Grace, E. M.:	192*	& 15 wkts	M.C.C. v. Gentlemen of Kent (Canterbury)	1862
Grace, W. G.:	150	& 15—79	Glos. v. Yorks. (Sheffield)	1872
Giffen, G.:	271	& 16—166	South Australia v. Victoria (Adelaide)	1891–92
Giffen, G.:	81* 97	& 15—185	South Australia v. Victoria (Adelaide)	1901–02
Nichols, M. S.:	159	& 15—165	Essex v. Glos. (Gloucester)	1938

The following players have scored 100 runs and taken 10 wickets in a match, including the above:

Allen, G. O. (1)
38 & 104*,   7—120 & 3—36   M.C.C. v. New Zealanders (Lord's) 1927

Amarnath, L. (1)
83 & 63,   7—60 & 3—56   Southern Punjab v. United Provinces (Delhi).........1935–36

Amar Singh (1)
103 & 55,   6—48 & 4—35   Nawanagar v. Sind (Ahmedabad) 1936–37

Armstrong, W. W. (2)
126*   5—27 & 5—25   Australians v. New Zealand XI (Christchurch) 1904–05
55 & 50*,   3—20 & 8—50   Australians v. Middx. (Lord's) 1905

Arnold, E. G. (1)
200*   3—70 & 7—44   Worcs. v. Warwicks. (Birmingham) 1909

Ashton, C. T. (1)
10 & 98,   7—91 & 3—60   Cambridge U. v. Army (Cambridge) 1923

Bailey, J. (1)
63 & 88,   6—51 & 5—19   Hants. v. Leics. (Southampton) 1948

Bailey, T. E. (2)
59 & 71*,   6—32 & 8—49   Essex v. Hants. (Romford) 1957
60* & 46,   7—40 & 5—61   Essex v. Yorks. (Leeds) 1960

Balaskas, X. C. (2)
132   5—87 & 6—43   Griqualand West v. Eastern Province (Kimberley)...1929–30
101   6—142 & 6—93   Griqualand West v. Western Province (Kimberley) 1929–30

Barlow, R. G. (2)
71 & 39*,   5—27 & 5—92   Lancs. v. Surrey (Manchester) 1883
10* & 101,   4—6 & 6—42   North v. Australians (Nottingham) 1884

Barnett, C. J. (1)
168   5—63 & 6—40   Glos. v. Lancs. (Manchester) 1938

Bates, W. (1)
106 & 14,   5—30 & 5—45   Yorks. v. Derby (Leeds) 1886

Bedser, E. A. (1)
71 & 30,   7—142 & 3—89   Surrey v. Glos. (Oval) 1951

Bettington, R. H. B. (1)
28 & 95,   4—87 & 6—78   Middx. v. Sussex (Lord's) 1928

Bosanquet, B. J. T. (4)
86 & 82*, 7—61 & 3—119   Leveson-Gower's XI v. Oxford U. (Oxford) 1902
71 & 41*, 6—109 & 4—61   Middx. v. Kent (Tunbridge Wells)......................1903
141   5—112 & 5—136   Middx. v. Yorks. (Sheffield).............................1904
103 & 100*, 3—75 & 8—53   Middx. v. Sussex (Lord's) 1905

Briggs, J. (3)
129*   5—25 & 5—16   Lancs. v. Sussex (Manchester) 1890
115   8—113 & 5—96   Lancs. v. Yorks. (Manchester) 1892
112   5—51 & 6—64   Lancs. v. Surrey (Oval) 1893

Brown, L. S. (1)
63 & 37,   6—89 & 4—54   N.E. Transvaal v. Transvaal (Springs) 1937–38

Browne, C. R. (2)
102   5—77 & 8—58   British Guiana v. Barbados (Trinidad) 1925–26
83 & 24*, 5—56 & 6—134   British Guiana v. Trinidad (Georgetown)............1929–30

Buckland, F. M. (1)
104   4—14 & 6—53   Oxford U. v. Middx. (Lord's)................................1877

Christian, A. H. (1)
73 & 57,   7—144 & 4—56   Western Australia v. South Australia (Fremantle)...1908–09

Clark, P. H. (1)
67 & 52,   4—148 & 8—91   Philadelphians v. Worcs. (Worcester) 1903

Compton, D. C. S. (1)
137*   6—94 & 6—80   Middx. v. Surrey (Oval) 1947

Constantine, L. N. (1)
107   7—45 & 6—67   West Indians v. Northants. (Northampton) 1928

Crawford, J. N. (3)
148   7—85 & 4—63   Surrey v. Glos. (Bristol) 1906
91 & 40,   5—89 & 5—71   South Australia v. N.S.W. (Sydney) 1913–14
110   5—90 & 5—53   Wellington v. Auckland (Auckland) 1917–18

Dooland, B. (1)
115* & 11, 4—54 & 6—48   Notts. v. Sussex (Worthing) 1957

Douglas, J. W. H. T. (2)
8 & 123*, 7—91 & 7—65   Essex v. Worcs. (Leyton) 1921
210*   9—47 & 2—0   Essex v. Derby (Leyton) 1921

Faulkner, G. A. (2)
42 & 68*, 6—72 & 4—94   Transvaal v. Western Province (Cape Town) 1908–09
54 & 73,   5—32 & 5—106   South Africans v. Queensland (Brisbane) 1910–11

Fender, P. G. H. (1)
104   3—48 & 7—76   Surrey v. Essex (Leyton) 1926

Flowers, W. (3)
131   4—43 & 6—44   M.C.C. v. Derby (Lord's) 1883
122   6—20 & 8—60   †M.C.C. v. Cambridge U. (Lord's) 1884
107   6—44 & 5—84   Notts. v. Lancs. (Manchester) 1893

Foster, F. R. (1)
105 & 18, 9—118 & 3—84   Warwicks. v. Yorks. (Birmingham) 1911

Geeson, F. (1)
104*   6—128 & 6—111   Leics. v. Derby (Glossop) 1901

Giffen, G. (9)

20 & 82,	9—91 & 8—110	South Australia v. Victoria (Adelaide)	1885–86
166	8—65 & 6—60	South Australia v. Victoria (Adelaide)	1887–88
135 & 19,	6—82 & 7—77	South Australia v. Victoria (Melbourne)	1888–89
237	5—89 & 7—103	South Australia v. Victoria (Melbourne)	1890–91
271	9—96 & 7—70	South Australia v. Victoria (Adelaide)	1891–92
120	7—122 & 5—28	South Australia v. N.S.W. (Sydney)	1891–92
43 & 181,	9—147 & 2—88	South Australia v. Victoria (Adelaide)	1892–93
64 & 58*,	5—175 & 6—49	South Australia v. Stoddart's XI (Adelaide)	1894–95
81 & 97*,	7—75 & 8—110	South Australia v. Victoria (Adelaide)	1902–03

Grace, E. M. (1)

192*	15 wkts (5—10)	M.C.C. v. Gentlemen of Kent (Canterbury)	1862

Grace, W. G. (16)

134*	6—50 & 4—31	Gentlemen v. Players (Lord's)	1868
81 & 42*,	6—68 & 4—83	W. G. Grace's XI v. Kent (Maidstone)	1871
117	7—67 & 5—79	†M.C.C. v. Kent (Canterbury)	1871
114	7—78 & 4—48	South v. North (Oval)	1872
150	8—33 & 7—46	Glos. v. Yorks. (Sheffield)	1872
179	5—76 & 7—82	Glos. v. Sussex (Hove)	1874
23 & 110,	3—61 & 7—58	Gentlemen v. Players (Prince's)	1874
167	4—57 & 7—44	Glos. v. Yorks. (Sheffield)	1874
94 & 121,	6—92 & 4—68	Glos. & Kent v. England (Canterbury)	1874
123	5—82 & 6—47	†M.C.C. v. Kent (Canterbury)	1874
127	5—44 & 5—77	Glos. v. Yorks. (Clifton)	1874
7 & 152,	7—64 & 5—61	Gentlemen v. Players (Lord's)	1875
261	5—62 & 6—77	South v. North (Prince's)	1877
89 & 35,	5—64 & 7—92	Glos. v. Middx. (Lord's)	1883
221*	6—45 & 5—75	Glos. v. Middx. (Clifton)	1885
104	2—60 & 10—49	M.C.C. v. Oxford U. (Oxford)	1886

Gregory, R. J. (1)

171	5—36 & 5—66	Surrey v. Middx. (Lord's)	1930

Gunn, J. (2)

95 & 39*,	7—77 & 4—66	Notts. v. Glos. (Gloucester)	1904
148 & 6*,	8—80 & 2—31	Notts. v. Lancs. (Nottingham)	1921

Hartkopf, A. E. V. (1)

86 & 14*,	5—23 & 8—105	Victoria v. M.C.C. (Melbourne)	1922–23

Hearne, J. W. (6)

54 & 88,	7—83 & 4—104	Middx. v. Worcs. (Worcester)	1913
106*	7—54 & 7—92	Middx. v. Essex (Leyton)	1914
88 & 37*,	5—78 & 5—91	Middx. v. Essex (Lord's)	1914
79 & 28,	6—74 & 4—73	Middx. v. Notts. (Lord's)	1922
140 & 57*,	6—83 & 6—45	Middx. v. Sussex (Lord's)	1923
14 & 93,	5—38 & 6—36	Middx. v. Glos. (Lord's)	1924

Hill, C. J. (1)

17 & 91,	7—18 & 5 49	N.S.W. v. Queensland (Sydney)	1932–33

Hirst, G. H. (4)

86 & 18*,	7—55 & 4—28	Yorks. v. M.C.C. (Lord's)	1901
101 & 4,	4—46 & 7—33	Yorks. v. Kent (Catford)	1906
111 & 117*,	6—70 & 5—45	Yorks. v. Somerset (Bath)	1906
100	9—41 & 2—89	Yorks. v. Worcs. (Worcester)	1911

Hopwood, J. L. (1)

110 & 45,	1—20 & 9—33	Lancs. v. Leics. (Manchester)	1933

Ikin, J. T. (1)

67 & 85*,	5—98 & 6—21	Lancs. v. Notts. (Manchester)	1947

Jackson, V. E. (1)

108 & 13,	6—46 & 4—53	Leics. v. Kent (Gillingham)	1954

Jupp, V. W. V. (3)

102 & 33*,	6—61 & 6—78	Sussex v. Essex (Colchester)	1921
56 & 70,	5—34 & 7—71	Northants. v. Essex (Colchester)	1925
113	7—42 & 5—79	Northants. v. Essex (Leyton)	1928

Langridge, James (1)

13 & 103,	7—58 & 4—66	Sussex v. Glamorgan (Swansea)	1929

Le Couteur, P. R. (1)
160   6—20 & 5—46 Oxford U. v. Cambridge U. (Lord's) 1910

Lee, G. M. (1)
100*   5—65 & 7—78 Derby v. Northants. (Northampton) 1927

Lee, H. W. (1)
119   5—21 & 6—47 Middx. v. Sussex (Lord's) 1920

Lewis, A. E. (1)
93 & 20, 6—43 & 4—15 Somerset v. Hants. (Bath) 1911

Llewellyn, C. B. (1)
153   5—115 & 5—68 Hants. v. Somerset (Taunton)................................1901

Lockwood, W. H. (1)
63 & 37, 6—48 & 6—48 Surrey v. Lancs. (Oval) 1902

Mansell, P. N. F. (1)
94* & 13*, 7—71 & 3—79 Rhodesia v. N.E. Transvaal (Pretoria) 1951–52

Mason, J. R. (5)
72 & 46*, 4—23 & 6—34 Kent v. Middx. (Tonbridge) 1900
145   4—26 & 8—29 Kent v. Somerset (Taunton) 1901
126   7—120 & 3—60 Kent v. Somerset (Beckenham) 1904
1 & 100, 6—71 & 4—60 Kent v. Somerset (Taunton) 1904
133   5—102 & 5—120 Kent v. Somerset (Taunton) 1905

McGahey, C. P. (2)
66 & 91, 6—86 & 6—71 Essex v. Glos. (Clifton) 1901
89 & 14, 7—27 & 3—37 Essex v. Notts. (Leyton) 1906

Muncer, L. B. (1)
107*   5—34 & 5—23 Glamorgan v. Derby (Chesterfield) 1951

Murray, A. R. A. (1)
78 & 44*, 5—77 & 5—54 Eastern Province v. Border (East London)............1953–54

Nayudu, C. S. (1)
127   5—20 & 7—36 Baroda v. Rajputana (Baroda) 1942–43

Neill, R. (1)
94 & 13 4—54 & 6—43 Auckland v. Wellington (Wellington) 1896–97

Newman, J. A. (1)
66 & 42*, 8—61 & 6—87 Hants. v. Glos. (Bournemouth) 1926

Nichols, M. S. (3)
73 & 33, 5—67 & 5—37 Essex v. Sussex (Horsham) 1933
146   4—17 & 7—37 Essex v. Yorks. (Huddersfield) 1935
159   9—37 & 6—126 Essex v. Glos. (Gloucester) 1938

Pougher, A. D. (1)
5 & 109*, 6—29 & 8—60 Leics. v. Essex (Leyton) 1894

Quaife, W. G. (1)
104*   5—51 & 7—76 Warwicks. v. Worcs. (Birmingham) 1901

Ram Singh, A. G. (2)
74 & 70, 5—88 & 6—71 Madras v. Hyderabad (Hyderabad) 1934–35
55 & 91, 5—35 & 5—45 Madras v. Mysore (Madras) 1939–40

Ramchandra (1)
97* & 5, 7—52 & 3—53 Bengal v. Mysore (Calcutta) 1941–42

Relf, A. E. (2)
42 & 83, 6—22 & 6—25 Auckland v. Otago (Auckland) 1907–08
103*   8—41 & 7—36 Sussex v. Leics. (Hove) 1912

Rhodes, W. (1)
183   5—26 & 7—33 Europeans v. Parsis (Bombay) 1921–22

Robinson, E. (1)
108   7—25 & 4—60 Yorks. v. Hants. (Bradford) 1930

Smith, S. G. (2)
5 & 136, 2—3 & 8—39 Northants. v. Somerset (Bath) 1912
82 & 20, 6—82 & 4—25 Northants. v. Derby (Northampton) 1913

Smith, T. P. B. (1)
1 & 101, 2—69 & 8—99 Essex v. Middx. (Chelmsford) 1938

Stoddart A. E. (1)
143 7—67 & 3—10 Priestley's XI v. Jamaica (Kingston) 1896–97

Studd, C. T. (1)
105* 6—79 & 4—45 Middx. v. Kent (Canterbury) 1883

Tarrant, F. A. (3)
152 & 11, 7—93 & 5—56 Middx. v. Glos. (Bristol) 1908
14 & 101*, 9—105 & 7—71 Middx. v. Lancs. (Manchester) 1914
68* & 80, 6—82 & 5—67 Europeans v. Hindus (Bombay) 1916–17

Tate, M. W. (2)
90 & 35, 5—48 & 6—42 Sussex v. Oxford U. (Hove) 1920
101 6—52 & 4—43 Sussex v. Hants. (Portsmouth) 1927

Townsend, L. F. (2)
106* 6—66 & 5—64 Derby v. Somerset (Weston-super-Mare) 1934
44 & 90*, 5—89 & 7—25 Auckland v. Wellington (Auckland) 1934–35

Trott, A. E. (5)
101* 7—74 & 6—66 Hawke's XI v. Transvaal (Johannesburg) 1898–99
64 & 69, 6—57 & 5—56 M.C.C. v. Sussex (Lord's) 1899
123 & 35*, 6—132 & 6—68 Middx. v. Sussex (Lord's) 1899
112 8—54 & 3—84 Middx. v. Essex (Lord's) 1901
68 & 80*, 7—58 & 4—93 Hawke's Bay v. Canterbury (Christchurch) 1901–02

Vine, J. (1)
86 & 54, 2—45 & 8—68 Sussex v. Oxford U. (Eastbourne) 1906

Wainwright, E. (1)
10 & 104, 7—66 & 4—57 Yorks. v. Sussex (Sheffield) 1892

Walker, V. E. (1)
20* & 108, 10—74 & 4—17 England v. Surrey (Oval) 1859

Wellard, A. W. (2)
75 & 55, 6—82 & 5—93 Somerset v. Glos. (Taunton) 1929
77 & 60, 7—43 & 3—66 Somerset v. Hants. (Portsmouth) 1933

Woolley, F. E. (6)
77 & 111*, 7—66 & 5—56 Kent v. Glos. (Gloucester) 1914
20 & 139*, 6—52 & 4—80 Kent v. Sussex (Horsham) 1920
174 8—22 & 3—44 Kent v. Glos. (Maidstone) 1921
15 & 109, 7—40 & 3—76 Kent v. Notts. (Nottingham) 1921
156 4—26 & 6—52 Kent v. Warwicks. (Tunbridge Wells) 1928
132 6—50 & 4—38 M.C.C. v. Otago (Dunedin) 1929–30

Young, A. (1)
63 & 70, 3—47 & 8—30 Somerset v. Derby (Taunton) 1930

† *These matches were played twelve-a-side, but are regarded as first-class matches.*

Century and 'Hat-Trick' in the Same Match

The following players have achieved the unusual double of scoring a century and performing a 'hat-trick' in the same match:

W. G. Grace (123): M.C.C. v. Kent (Canterbury) 1874
G. Giffen (113): Australians v. Lancashire (Manchester) 1884
W. E. Roller (204): Surrey v. Sussex (Oval) 1885
W. B. Burns (102*): Worcestershire v. Gloucestershire (Worcester) 1913
V. W. C. Jupp (102): Sussex v. Essex (Colchester) 1921
R. E. S. Wyatt (124): M.C.C. v. Ceylon (Colombo) 1926–27
L. N. Constantine (107): West Indians v. Northamptonshire (Northampton) 1928
E. Davies (139): Glamorgan v. Leicestershire (Leicester) 1937

Part VI—Fielding and Wicket-keeping

In dealing with fielding records it is only possible to go into the records of catches held, but of course this is not a true guide to a fielder's quality. Many fielders have saved thousands of runs, but as they are not in a position in which catches come regularly they cannot figure in these records. A typical example of this is the work by J. B. Hobbs on the 1911–12 M.C.C. Australian tour, when he caught seven batsmen and ran out fifteen more—all from cover point.

Fielders—Most Catches in an Innings

SEVEN

Stewart, M. J.: Surrey v. Northamptonshire (Northampton) 1957

SIX

Broadbent, R. G.: Worcestershire v. Glamorgan (Stourbridge) 1960
Clay, J. D.: Nottinghamshire v. Derbyshire (Nottingham) 1957
Deas, L. M.: Europeans v. Parsis (Poona) 1898–99
Grieves, K.: Lancashire v. Sussex (Manchester) 1951
Griffith, G.: Surrey v. Gentlemen of South (Oval) 1863
Hammond, W. R.: Gloucestershire v. Surrey (Cheltenham) 1928
Hammond, W. R.: Gloucestershire v. Nottinghamshire (Bristol) 1933
Leary, S. E.: Kent v. Cambridge U. (Cambridge) 1958
Robinson, E. P.: Yorkshire v. Leicestershire (Bradford) 1938
Seymour, James: Kent v. South Africans (Canterbury) 1904
Sheppard, J. F.: Queensland v. New South Wales (Brisbane) 1914–15
Tarrant, F. A.: Middlesex v. Essex (Leyton) 1906
Tyldesley, R.: Lancashire v. Hampshire (Liverpool)..1921
Webbe, A. J.: Gentlemen v. Players (Lord's) 1877

FIVE

Abel, R.: Surrey v. Hampshire (Portsmouth)...1898
Ashton, H.: Cambridge U. v. Surrey (Oval) 1922
Astill, W. E.: Leicestershire v. Somerset (Weston-super-Mare) 1920
Atkinson, J.: Tasmania v. Victoria (Melbourne) 1928–29
Bakewell, A. H.: Northamptonshire v. Essex (Leyton) 1928
Barton, M. R.: Oxford U. v. Minor Counties (Oxford) 1937
Bates, W. E.: Glamorgan v. Warwickshire (Birmingham) 1928
Boyle, H. F.: Australians v. Yorkshire (Dewsbury) 1880
Braund, L. C.: Somerset v. Worcestershire (Taunton) 1909
Brown, G.: Hampshire v. Somerset (Bath)..1914
Brown, G.: Hampshire v. Kent (Portsmouth) 1932
Burbidge, F.: Gentlemen v. Players (Oval) 1858
Carr, A. W.: Nottinghamshire v. Leicestershire (Nottingham) 1933
Crapp, J. F.: Gloucestershire v. Lancashire (Manchester) 1949
Daniell, J.: Somerset v. Kent (Taunton) 1901
Eyre, C. H.: Cambridge U. v. G. J. V. Weigall's XI (Cambridge) 1904
Fagg, A. E.: Kent v. Hampshire (Southampton) 1952
Fishwick, T. S.: Warwickshire v. South Africans (Birmingham) 1904
Ford, F. G. J.: Cambridge U. v. M.C.C. (Lord's) 1888
Foster, R. F.: Oxford U. v. A. J. Webbe's XI (Oxford) 1898
Gillingham, F. H.: Essex v. Surrey (Oval) 1919
Grace, E. M.: Gentlemen of M.C.C. v. Gentlemen of Kent (Canterbury) 1866
Grieves, K.: Lancashire v. Glamorgan (Blackpool) 1950
Grieves, K.: Lancashire v. Gloucestershire (Bristol) 1954
Gunn, G.: Nottinghamshire v. Surrey (Nottingham) 1909
Haig, N. E.: Middlesex v. Nottinghamshire (Lord's) 1928
Hammond, W. R.: M.C.C. West Indies XI v. Leveson-Gower's XI (Scarborough) 1935
Hayes, E. G.: Surrey v. London County (Oval) 1901

376

Hunt, G.: Somerset v. Hampshire (Weston-super-Mare) 1928
Hutton, L.: Players v. Gentlemen (Lord's) 1952
Ikin, J. T.: M.C.C. v. Auckland (Auckland) 1946–47
Insole, D. J.: Essex v. Lancashire (Blackpool) 1958
Jones, A. O.: Nottinghamshire v. Sussex (Hove) 1907
Lamason, J. R.: Wellington v. Otago (Dunedin)..............................1937–38
Langridge, John: Sussex v. Somerset (Taunton) 1950
Lee, C.: Derbyshire v. Lancashire (Chesterfield) 1960
Lee, G. M.: Nottinghamshire v. Hampshire (Southampton) 1913
Lock, G. A. R.: Surrey v. Lancashire (Manchester) 1953
Lyon, B. H.: Gloucestershire v. Leicestershire (Cheltenham) 1933
McAlister, P. A.: Victoria v. South Australia (Melbourne) 1901–02
McCool, C. L.: New South Wales v. Rest of Australia (Sydney) 1939–40
Mead, C. P.: Hampshire v. Middlesex (Portsmouth) 1912
Milton, C. A.: Gloucestershire v. Pakistan (Cheltenham) 1954
Morgan, D. C.: Derbyshire v. Glamorgan (Chesterfield) 1960
Nicholls, B. E.: Oxford U. v. Australians (Oxford) 1884
Nichols, M. S.: Essex v. Sussex (Hove) 1926
Nicholson, J. H.: Northamptonshire v. Worcestershire (Dudley) 1928
Nourse, A. D., jun.: Natal v. Border (Durban) 1933–34
Oakman, A. S. M.: Sussex v. Glamorgan (Worthing) 1958
Outschoorn, L.: Worcestershire v. Derbyshire (Kidderminster) 1948
Painter, J.: Gloucestershire v. Sussex (Hove) 1891
Paul, A.: Lancashire v. Derbyshire (Derby) 1897
Pierce, T. N.: Barbados v. Trinidad (Barbados) 1941–42
Pollock, J. S.: Ireland v. M.C.C. (Dublin) 1956
Quinton, F. W. D.: Hampshire v. Yorkshire (Harrogate) 1896
Rabone, G. O.: New Zealanders v. Oxford U. (Oxford) 1949
Reid, J. R.: New Zealanders v. South Zone (Bangalore) 1955–56
Richardson, V. Y.: Australia v. South Africa (Durban) 1935–36
Ryder, J.: Victoria v. M.C.C. (Melbourne) 1922–23
Sellers, A. B.: Yorkshire v. Essex (Leyton) 1933
Surridge, W. S.: Surrey v. Lancashire (Oval) 1955
Trumble, H.: Australians v. Cambridge U. (Cambridge) 1890
Trumble, H.: Australians v. Oxford U. (Oxford) 1893
Trumble, H.: Victoria v. South Australia (Melbourne) 1900–01
Tunnicliffe, J.: Yorkshire v. Leicestershire (Leeds) 1897
Tunnicliffe, J.: Yorkshire v. Leicestershire (Leicester) 1900
Tunnicliffe, J.: Yorkshire v. Leicestershire (Scarborough) 1901
Upton, Hon. A.: Gentlemen v. Players (Lord's) 1806
Vigar, F. H.: Essex v. Middlesex (Westcliff) 1946
Vigar, F. H.: Essex v. Northamptonshire (Brentwood) 1946
Vigar, F. H.: Essex v. Surrey (Oval) 1951
Walker, P. M.: Glamorgan v. Leicestershire (Swansea) 1960
Walker, V. E.: Middlesex v. Surrey (Oval) 1865
Watkins, A. J.: M.C.C. v. South Zone (Bangalore) 1951–52
Wensley, A. F.: Sussex v. Warwickshire (Birmingham) 1932
Wensley, A. F.: Sussex v. Surrey (Horsham) 1934
White, C.: Border v. Griqualand West (Queenstown) 1946–47
Williams, N.: Auckland v. Hawkes Bay (Napier) 1894–95
Wood, C. J. B.: Leicestershire v. Warwickshire (Hinckley) 1919
Woolley, F. E.: Kent v. Middlesex (Blackheath) 1926
Woolley, F. E.: Kent v. Hampshire (Canterbury) 1936
Wright, F. W.: Oxford U. v. Surrey (Oval) 1865

Fielders—Most Catches in a Match

TEN

Hammond, W. R.: Gloucestershire v. Surrey (Cheltenham) 1928

EIGHT

Bakewell, A. H.: Northamptonshire v. Essex (Leyton)........................1928
Burns, W. B.: Worcestershire v. Yorkshire (Bradford).......................1907
Grieves, K.: Lancashire v. Sussex (Manchester) 1951
Hammond, W. R.: Gloucestershire v. Worcestershire (Cheltenham) 1932
Lock, G. A. R.: Surrey v. Warwickshire (Oval) 1957
Milton, C. A.: Gloucestershire v. Sussex (Hove) 1952

SEVEN

Ashton, H.: Cambridge U. v. Surrey (Oval) 1922
Atkinson, J.: Tasmania v. Victoria (Melbourne) 1928–29
Broadbent, R. G.: Worcestershire v. Glamorgan (Stourbridge) 1960
Crapp, J. F.: Gloucestershire v. Derbyshire (Bristol) 1950
Dean, T. A.: Hampshire v. Essex (Colchester) 1947
Deas, L. M.: Europeans v. Parsis (Poona) 1898–99
De Vigne, S. P.: North-Eastern Transvaal v. Orange Free State (Benoni) 1950–51
Dollery, H. E.: Warwickshire v. Hampshire (Portsmouth) 1953
Fagg, A. E.: Kent v. Hampshire (Southampton) 1952
Felix, N.: Kent v. England (Canterbury) 1847
Ford, A. F. J.: Middlesex v. Gloucestershire (Lord's) 1882
Jones, A. O.: Nottinghamshire v. Gloucestershire (Nottingham) 1908
Langridge, John: Sussex v. Somerset (Taunton) 1950
Leary, S. E.: Kent v. Cambridge U. (Cambridge) 1958
Lock, G. A. R.: Surrey v. Lancashire (Manchester) 1953
Mason, J. R.: Kent v. Surrey (Oval) 1905
Nicholls, B. E.: Oxford U. v. Australians (Oxford) 1884
Oakman, A. S. M.: Sussex v. Glamorgan (Worthing) 1958
Parker, J. F.: Surrey v. Kent (Blackheath) 1952
Pierce, T. N.: Barbados v. Trinidad (Barbados) 1941–42
Poidevin, L. O. S.: Lancashire v. Yorkshire (Manchester) 1906
Robinson, E. P.: Yorkshire v. Leicestershire (Bradford) 1938
Sellers, A. B.: Yorkshire v. Essex (Leyton) 1933
Stanning, J.: Cambridge U. v. M.C.C. (Cambridge)............1900
Stewart, M. J.: Surrey v. Northamptonshire (Northampton) 1957
Surridge, W. S.: South v. North (Kingston) 1952
Tarrant, F. A.: Middlesex v. Essex (Leyton) 1906
Trumble, H.: Victoria v. South Australia (Melbourne) 1900–01
Tunnicliffe, J.: Yorkshire v. Leicestershire (Leeds) 1897
Tunnicliffe, J.: Yorkshire v. Leicestershire (Leicester) 1900
Voce, W.: Nottinghamshire v. Glamorgan (Pontypridd) 1929
Walker, P. M.: Glamorgan v. Northamptonshire (Northampton) 1960
Wensley, A. F.: Sussex v. Surrey (Horsham) 1934
Woolley, F. E.: Kent v. Warwickshire (Birmingham) 1920

SIX

Abel, R.: Surrey v. Derbyshire (Derby) 1884
Abel, R.: Surrey v. Hampshire (Portsmouth)............1898
Allen, B. O.: Gloucestershire v. Glarmorgan (Bristol) 1938
Bakewell, A. H.: Northamptonshire v. Sussex (Peterborough) 1929
Belton, C.: Kent v. Surrey (Aylesford) 1847
Benaud, R.: New South Wales v. Victoria (Melbourne) 1954–55
Bird, R. E.: M.C.C. v. Ireland (Dublin) 1956
Brown, G.: Hampshire v. Kent (Portsmouth) 1932
Carr, A. W.: Nottinghamshire v. Leicestershire (Nottingham) 1933
Chapman, A. P. F.: Rest of England v. Lancashire (Oval) 1930
Chatterton, W.: Derbyshire v. M.C.C. (Lord's) 1896
Chatterton, W.: Derbyshire v. Nottinghamshire (Chesterfield) 1900
Clarke, R. W.: Northamptonshire v. Surrey (Oval) 1950
Clay, J. D.: Nottinghamshire v. Derbyshire (Nottingham) 1957
Clift, P. B.: Glamorgan v. Sussex (Swansea) 1948
Constantine, E.: Trinidad v. Barbados (Trinidad) 1931–32
Constantine, L. N.: West Indies XI v. J. Cahn's XI (Kingston) 1928–29
Cox, G. R.: Sussex v. Kent (Hove) 1919
Cuffe, J. A.: Worcestershire v. Hampshire (Portsmouth) 1907
Doggart, G. H. G.: Sussex v. Somerset (Weston-super-Mare) 1948
Douglas, J.: Middlesex v. Gloucestershire (Bristol) 1906
Duleepsinhji, K. S.: Sussex v. Kent (Hastings) 1929
Eckersley, P. T.: Lancashire v. Sussex (Manchester) 1930
Edrich, G. A.: Lancashire v. Essex (Colchester) 1946
Edrich, W. J.: Middlesex v. Surrey (Lord's) 1949
Evans, A. J.: Oxford U. v. Leveson-Gower's XI (Eastbourne) 1912
Fender, P. G. H.: Surrey v. Leicestershire (Leicester) 1928
Fillery, R.: Sussex v. Gloucestershire (Hove) 1873
Foster, R. E.: Oxford U. v. A. J. Webbe's XI (Oxford) 1898
Foster, R. E.: Oxford U. v. M.C.C. (Lord's) 1898
Freeman, J. R.: Essex v. Somerset (Taunton) 1926
Gibbons, H. H.: Worcestershire v. Middlesex (Worcester) 1930

Gilbert, W. R.: Gloucestershire v. Surrey (Oval) 1876
Gimblett, H.: Somerset v. Leicestershire (Bath) 1953
Grace, E. M.: Gloucestershire v. Surrey (Cheltenham) 1874
Grace, E. M.: Gloucestershire v. Surrey (Clifton) 1877
Grace, E. M.: Gloucestershire v. Lancashire (Clifton) 1878
Grace, W. G.: M.C.C. v. Yorkshire (Lord's) 1873
Grace, W. G.: Gloucestershire v. Sussex (Cheltenham) 1878
Gregory, J. M.: Australia v. England (Sydney) 1920–21
Grieves, K.: Lancashire v. Glamorgan (Blackpool) 1950
Grieves, K.: Lancashire v. Hampshire (Liverpool) 1954
Grieves, K.: Lancashire v. Gloucestershire (Bristol) 1954
Griffith, G.: Surrey v. Gentlemen of South (Oval) 1863
Hammond, W. R.: Gloucestershire v. Essex (Gloucester) 1925
Hammond, W. R.: Gloucestershire v. Nottinghamshire (Bristol) 1933
Hayes, E. G.: Surrey v. Leicestershire (Leicester) 1906
Hazell, H. L.: Somerset v. Surrey (Oval) 1937
Hill, N.: Nottinghamshire v. Northamptonshire (Nottingham) 1958
Hillyard, G. W.: Leicestershire v. Yorkshire (Leicester) 1895
Holland, F. C.: Surrey v. Leicestershire (Leicester) 1908
Iddison, R.: England XI v. Nottinghamshire (Newark) 1856
Ikin, J. T.: M.C.C. v. Auckland (Auckland) 1946–47
Ikin, J. T.: Lancashire v. Oxford U. (Oxford) 1949
Jones, A. O.: Nottinghamshire v. Northamptonshire (Northampton) 1906
Jones, A. O.: Nottinghamshire v. Sussex (Hove) 1907
Jones, A. O.: Nottinghamshire v. Yorkshire (Nottingham) 1908
Jones, A. O.: Nottinghamshire v. Philadelphians (Nottingham) 1908
Kortright, C. J.: Essex v. Leicestershire (Leicester) 1901
Langridge, John: Sussex v. Nottinghamshire (Hove) 1933
Langridge, John: Sussex v. Surrey (Oval) 1947
Lee, G. M.: Nottinghamshire v. Hampshire (Southampton) 1913
Lyon, B. H.: Gloucestershire v. Leicestershire (Cheltenham) 1933
Macaulay, G. G.: Yorkshire v. Leicestershire (Bradford) 1933
Marchant, J. W.: Wellington v. Nelson (Nelson) 1873–74
Marner, P.: Lancashire v. Derbyshire (Manchester) 1960
Mason, J. R.: Kent v. Surrey (Oval) 1895
Mason, J. R.: Kent v. Surrey (Canterbury) 1904
Merchant, U. M.: Bombay v. Halkar (Bombay) 1944–45
Milton, C. A.: Gloucestershire v. Middlesex (Lord's) 1953
Milton, C. A.: Gloucestershire v. Glamorgan (Cheltenham) 1955
Milton, C. A.: Gloucestershire v. Nottinghamshire (Nottingham) 1956
Milton, C. A.: Gloucestershire v. Glamorgan (Swansea) 1959
Milton, C. A.: Gloucestershire v. Kent (Dover) 1959
Mitchell, A.: Yorkshire v. Northamptonshire (Leeds) 1933
Mitchell, A.: Yorkshire v. Hampshire (Bournemouth) 1939
Mitchell, B.: South Africans v. Sussex (Hove) 1929
Mitchell, B.: South Africans v. Australia (Melbourne) 1931–32
Mordaunt, G. J.: Oxford U. v. Gentlemen of England (Oxford) 1893
Morgan, D. C.: Derbyshire v. Glamorgan (Pontypridd) 1953
Nichols, M. S.: Essex v. Sussex (Hove) 1926
Nourse, A. D., jun.: Natal v. Border (Durban) 1933–34
Oakman, A. S. M.: Sussex v. Essex (Hove) 1958
Outschoorn, L.: Worcestershire v. Essex (Worcester) 1948
Partridge, N. E.: Warwickshire v. Cambridge U. (Cambridge) 1921
Pollock, J. S.: Ireland v. M.C.C. (Dublin) 1956
Pratt, R. C. E.: Surrey v. Sussex (Hastings) 1956
Reid, J. R.: New Zealanders v. South Zone (Bangalore) 1955–56
Richardson, V. Y.: Australia v. South Africa (Durban) 1935–36
Seymour, James: Kent v. South Africans (Canterbury) 1904
Seymour, James: Kent v. Yorkshire (Hull) 1905
Sharpe, P. J.: Yorkshire v. Warwickshire (Sheffield) 1959
Shaw, A.: Nottinghamshire v. Sussex (Nottingham) 1885
Shepherd, T. F.: Surrey v. Kent (Oval) 1929
Sheppard, D. S.: Sussex v. Hampshire (Worthing) 1953
Sheppard, J. F.: Queensland v. New South Wales (Brisbane) 1914–15
Shrewsbury, A.: Nottinghamshire v. Middlesex (Nottingham) 1880
Shrewsbury, A.: England v. Australia (Sydney) 1887–88
Simpson, R. B.: New South Wales v. M.C.C. (Sydney) 1954–55
Smith, H. A.: Leicestershire v. Oxford U. (Oxford) 1935
Smith, M. J. K.: Warwickshire v. Somerset (Weston-super-Mare) 1959
Subba Row, R.: Northamptonshire v. Surrey (Northampton) 1955
Surridge, W. S.: Surrey v. Leicestershire (Oval) 1955
Surridge, W. S.: Surrey v. Glamorgan (Cardiff) 1956

Trumble, H.: Australians v. Cambridge U. (Cambridge) 1890
Trumble, H.: Victoria v. South Australia (Melbourne) 1900–01
Tunnicliffe, J.: Yorkshire v. Lancashire (Manchester) 1893
Tunnicliffe, J.: Yorkshire v. Surrey (Sheffield) 1893
Tunnicliffe, J.: Yorkshire v. Nottinghamshire (Sheffield) 1895
Tunnicliffe, J.: Yorkshire v. Warwickshire (Bradford) 1895
Tunnicliffe, J.: Yorkshire v. Hampshire (Portsmouth) 1900
Tunnicliffe, J.: Yorkshire v. Derbyshire (Glossop) 1901
Tunnicliffe, J.: Yorkshire v. Hampshire (Harrogate) 1901
Turner, W. M.: Essex v. Leicestershire (Leicester) 1914
Tyldesley, J. D.: Lancashire v. Gloucestershire (Bristol) 1919
Tyldesley, R.: Lancashire v. Hampshire (Liverpool)..1921
Tyldesley, R.: Lancashire v. Oxford U. (Oxford) 1924
Upton, Hon. A.: Gentlemen v. Players (Lord's) 1806
Vernon, G. F.: Middlesex v. Nottinghamshire (Lord's) 1888
Vigar, F. H.: Essex v. Nottinghamshire (Ilford) 1950
Vogler, A. E. E.: South Africa v. England (Durban) 1909–10
Waddington, A.: Yorkshire v. Warwickshire (Sheffield) 1924
Walker, P. M.: Glamorgan v. Kent (Dartford) 1959
Walker, V. E.: Middlesex v. Surrey (Oval) 1865
Watkins, A. J.: M.C.C. v. South Zone (Bangalore) 1951–52
Webbe, A. J.: Gentlemen v. Players (Lord's) 1877
Wells, G.: Single v. Married (Oval) 1858
Wheldon, F.: Worcestershire v. Hampshire (Southampton) 1904
Wheldon, F.: Worcestershire v. Oxford U. (Oxford) 1904
Wheldon, F.: Worcestershire v. Oxford U. (Oxford) 1905
White, C.: Border v. Griqualand West (Queensland) 1946–47
White, J. C.: Somerset v. Glamorgan (Bath) 1925
Whysall, W. W.: Nottinghamshire v. Worcestershire (Nottingham) 1929
Williams, N.: Auckland v. Hawke's Bay (Napier) 1894–95
Willsher, E.: Kent v. Surrey (Oval) 1866
Wilson, J. V.: Yorkshire v. Glamorgan (Leeds) 1951
Wilson, J. V.: Yorkshire v. Somerset (Leeds) 1957
Woolley, F. E.: England v. Australia (Sydney) 1911–12
Woolley, F. E.: Kent v. Middlesex (Blackheath) 1926
Wright, D. V. P.: Kent v. Lancashire (Canterbury) 1938

Wicket-keepers—Most Dismissals in an Innings

N.B. The figures in brackets denote the number of catches and stumpings respectively.

EIGHT

Grout, A. W. ....(8—0)   Queensland v. Western Australia (Brisbane) 1959–60

SEVEN

Brown, J. ....(4—3)   Scotland v. Ireland (Dublin) 1957
Farrimond, W. F. ......(6—1)   Lancashire v. Kent (Manchester) 1930
Kirsten, N. ....(6—1)   Border v. Rhodesia (East London) 1959–60
Price, W. F. ....(7—0)   Middlesex v. Yorkshire (Lord's) 1937
Saggers, R. A. ....(7—0)   New South Wales v. Combined XI (Brisbane) 1940–41
Smith, E. J. ....(4—3)   Warwickshire v. Derbyshire (Birmingham) 1926
Smith, M. ....(7—0)   Natal v. Border (East London) 1959–60
Tallon, D. ....(3—4)   Queensland v. Victoria (Brisbane) 1938–39
Yarnold, H. ....(1—6)   Worcestershire v. Scotland (Dundee) 1951

SIX

Allen, R. ....(2—4)   Yorkshire v. Sussex (Hove) 1921
Ames, L. E. G. ....(4—2)   Kent v. Sussex (Maidstone) 1929
Ames, L. E. G. ....(5—1)   Kent v. Sussex (Folkestone) 1930
Baker, E. A. ....(6—0)   Victoria v. New South Wales (Melbourne) 1946–47
Baker, E. A. ....(1—5)   Victoria v. New South Wales (Sydney) 1946–47
Bale, E. ....(2—4)   Worcestershire v. Australians (Worcester) 1909

Bhandarkar, K. V. ......(5—1)	Holkar v. Ceylon (Colombo)	1948—49
Binns, A. P. ....(3—3)	Jamaica v. British Guiana (Georgetown)	1952—53
Bromham, C. ....(6—0)	North Eastern Transvaal v. Western Province (Cape Town) 1939—40	
Brooks, E. W. ....(6—0)	Surrey v. Kent (Blackheath)	1935
Buckingham, J. ....(5—1)	Warwickshire v. Sussex (Birmingham)	1939
Butt, H. R. ....(6—0)	Sussex v. Gloucestershire (Bristol)	1899
Butt, H. R. ....(6—0)	Sussex v. Hampshire (Hove)	1901
Butt, H. R. ....(6—0)	Sussex v. Leicestershire (Hove)	1909
Compton, L. H. ....(4—2)	Middlesex v. Essex (Lord's)	1953
Corrall, P. ....(4—2)	Leicestershire v. Sussex (Hove)	1936
Corrall, P. ....(3—3)	Leicestershire v. Middlesex (Leicester)	1949
Duckworth, G............(5—1)	Lancashire v. Kent (Dover)	1926
Duckworth, G............(5—1)	Lancashire v. Worcestershire (Worcester)	1936
Elliott, H. ....(4—2)	Derbyshire v. Worcestershire (Worcester)	1931
Elliott, H. ....(5—1)	Derbyshire v. Middlesex (Derby)	1932
Elliott, H. ....(4—2)	Derbyshire v. Lancashire (Manchester)	1935
Endean, W. R. ....(6—0)	Transvaal v. Rhodesia (Salisbury)	1950—51
Foster, T. ....(6—0)	Derbyshire v. Surrey (Oval)	1883
Garnett, H. G. ....(6—0)	Lancashire v. Warwickshire (Birmingham)	1914
Gaukrodger, G. ....(4—2)	Worcestershire v. Kent (Tunbridge Wells)	1907
Gibb, P. A. ....(6—0)	Lord Tennyson's XI v. Indian XI (Bombay)	1937—38
Gibson, K. L. ....(5—1)	Essex v. Derbyshire (Leyton)	1911
Gilligan, F. W. ....(2—4)	Essex v. Gloucestershire (Cheltenham)	1928
Griffith, S. C. ....(6—0)	England v. Australian Services (Manchester)	1945
Grout, A. W. ....(6—0)	Queensland v. New South Wales (Sydney)	1955—56
Grout, A. W. ....(6—0)	Australia v. South Africa (Johannesburg)	1957—58
Guillen, S. C. ....(3—3)	West Indians v. Tasmania (Launceston)	1951—52
Hubble, J. C. ....(5—1)	Kent v. Gloucestershire (Cheltenham)	1923
Huish, F. H...............(1—5)	Kent v. Surrey (Oval)	1911
Hunter, D. ....(5—1)	Yorkshire v. Surrey (Sheffield)	1891
Hunter, D. ....(6—0)	Yorkshire v. Middlesex (Leeds)	1909
Hunter, J. ....(6—0)	Yorkshire v. Gloucestershire (Gloucester)	1887
Inkster, G. B. ....(4—2)	South Australia v. Victoria (Melbourne)	1926—27
James, K. C. ....(6—0)	Northamptonshire v. Glamorgan (Swansea)	1937
Jarvis, A. H. ....(2—4)	Australian XI v. Victoria (Melbourne)	1885—86
Kirby, G. N. G. ....(6—0)	Surrey v. Cambridge U. (Guildford)	1949
Lambert, W...............(3—3)	M.C.C. v. Hampshire (Lord's)	1816
Langley, G. R. ....(5—1)	South Australia v. Queensland (Brisbane)	1947—48
Levett, W. V. H. ....(4—2)	Kent v. Northamptonshire (Northampton)	1934
Levett, W. H. V. ....(5—1)	Kent v. Glamorgan (Neath)	1939
Lewis, E. B. ....(6—0)	Warwickshire v. Cambridge U. (Cambridge)	1956
Lilley, A. A. ....(4—2)	Warwickshire v. Worcestershire (Birmingham)	1906
Lilley, B. ....(6—0)	Nottinghamshire v. Somerset (Taunton)	1932
Matthews, M. H..........(4—2)	Oxford U. v. Surrey (Oval)	1937
Meads, E. A. ....(5—1)	Nottinghamshire v. Derbyshire (Ilkeston)	1948
Meads, E. A. ....(5—1)	Nottinghamshire v. Kent (Nottingham)	1949
Millman, G. ....(6—0)	Nottinghamshire v. Northamptonshire (Nottingham)	1959
Mooney, F. L. H. ....(4—2)	New Zealanders v. Worcestershire (Worcester)	1949
Murrell, H. R. ....(4—2)	Middlesex v. Gloucestershire (Bristol)	1926
Oates, T. W...............(6—0)	Nottinghamshire v. Middlesex (Nottingham)	1906
Oates, T. W...............(6—0)	Nottinghamshire v. Leicestershire (Leicester)	1907
Oldfield, W. A. ....(3—3)	New South Wales v. West Indians (Sydney)	1930—31
Parks, J. M. ....(6—0)	Sussex v. Worcestershire (Dudley)	1959
Phillips, H. ....(3—3)	Sussex v. Surrey (Oval)	1872
Pooley, E. ....(5—1)	Surrey v. Sussex (Oval) (1st inns)	1868
Pooley, E. ....(3—3)	Surrey v. Sussex (Oval) (2nd inns)	1868
Pooley, E. ....(1—5)	Surrey v. Kent (Oval)	1878
Price, W. F. ....(3—3)	M.C.C. v. Kent (Folkestone)	1934
Price, W. F. ....(6—0)	Middlesex v. Warwickshire (Lord's)	1938
Russell, T. M. ....(3—3)	Essex v. Lancashire (Manchester)	1898
Russell, T. M. ....(2—4)	Essex v. Kent (Canterbury)	1901
Saggers, R. A............(4—2)	New South Wales v. Queensland (Sydney)	1946—47
Scattergood, J. H. ......(5—1)	Philadelphians v. Warner's XI (Philadelphia)	1897—98
Shaw, A. A...............(3—3)	Sussex v. Cambridge U. (Hove)	1927
Sismey, S. G. ....(6—0)	New South Wales v. Victoria (Sydney)	1949—50
Smith, H. ....(3—3)	Gloucestershire v. Sussex (Bristol)	1923
Spooner, R. T...........(6—0)	Warwickshire v. Nottinghamshire (Birmingham)	1957
Strudwick, H. ....(6—0)	Surrey v. Sussex (Oval)	1914
Swetman, R. ....(6—0)	Surrey v. Kent (Oval)	1960
Swetman, R. ....(6—0)	Surrey v. Somerset (Taunton)	1960
Tallon, D. ....(1—5)	Queensland v. M.C.C. (Brisbane)	1935—36
Tallon, D. ....(3—3)	Queensland v. New South Wales (Brisbane)	1938—39

Tallon, D.	...(5—1)	Queensland v. New South Wales (Sydney) (1st innings)	...1938–39
Tallon, D.	...(4—2)	Queensland v. New South Wales (Sydney) (2nd innings)	...1938–39
Taylor, B.	...(6—0)	Essex v. Lancashire (Blackpool)	...1958
Trueman, G.	...(5—1)	New South Wales v. Queensland (Sydney)	...1952–53
Turner, M.	...(3—3)	Gentlemen of England v. Oxford U. (Oxford)	...1871
Turner, M.	...(3—3)	Gentlemen of England v. Cambridge U. (Cambridge)	...1876
Wade, T. H.	...(4—2)	Essex v. Lancashire (Clacton)	...1947
Walker, C. W.	...(2—4)	South Australia v. New South Wales (Sydney)	...1939–40
Webb, R. T.	...(3—3)	Sussex v. Nottinghamshire (Hove)	...1955
Webb, R. T.	...(6—0)	Sussex v. Somerset (Hove)	...1960
Wilson, A. E.	...(6—0)	Gloucestershire v. Hampshire (Portsmouth)	...1953
Yarnold, H.	...(3—3)	Worcestershire v. Hampshire (Worcester)	...1949

Wicket-keepers—Most Dismissals in a Match

TWELVE

| Pooley, E. | ...(8—4) | Surrey v. Sussex (Oval) | ...1868 |
| Tallon, D. | ...(9—3) | Queensland v. New South Wales (Sydney) | ...1938–39 |

TEN

Corrall, P.	...(7—3)	Leicestershire v. Sussex (Hove)	...1936
Elliott, H.	...(8—2)	Derbyshire v. Lancashire (Manchester)	...1935
Hubble, J. C.	...(9—1)	Kent v. Gloucestershire (Cheltenham)	...1923
Huish, F. H.	...(1—9)	Kent v. Surrey (Oval)	...1911
Oates, T. W.	...(9—1)	Nottinghamshire v. Middlesex (Nottingham)	...1906
Phillips, H.	...(5—5)	Sussex v. Surrey (Oval)	...1872
Pooley, E.	...(2—8)	Surrey v. Kent (Oval)	...1878
Saggers, R. A.	...(9—1)	New South Wales v. Combined XI (Brisbane)	...1940–41
Wilson, A. E.	...(10—0)	Gloucestershire v. Hampshire (Portsmouth)	...1953

NINE

Ames, L. E. G.	...(9—0)	Kent v. Oxford U. (Oxford)	...1928
Ames, L. E. G.	...(5—4)	Kent v. Sussex (Maidstone)	...1929
Baker, E. A.	...(2—7)	Victoria v. New South Wales (Sydney)	...1946–47
Baker, E. A.	...(9—0)	Victoria v. New South Wales (Melbourne)	...1946–47
Broadbridge, W.	...(2—7)	Sussex v. Hampshire & Surrey (Bramshill)	...1826
Brown, J.	...(4—5)	Scotland v. Ireland (Dublin)	...1957
Clayton, G.	...(8—1)	Lancashire v. Gloucestershire (Gloucester)	...1959
Davidson, H.	...(6—3)	New South Wales v. South Australia (Sydney)	...1928–29
Dolphin, A.	...(8—1)	Yorkshire v. Derbyshire (Bradford)	...1919
Evans, T. G.	...(8—1)	Kent v. New Zealanders (Canterbury)	...1949
Ferrandi, J.	...(7—2)	Western Province v. Transvaal (Johannesburg)	...1958–59
Gamsy, D.	...(8—1)	Natal v. Transvaal (Johannesburg)	...1959–60
Gibson, K. L.	...(7—2)	Essex v. Derbyshire (Leyton)	...1911
Hunter, J.	...(9—0)	Yorkshire v. Gloucestershire (Gloucester)	...1887
Inkster, G. B.	...(4—5)	South Australia v. Victoria (Melbourne)	...1926–27
Joshi, P. G.	...(6—3)	Maharashtra v. Gujerat (Ahmednagar)	...1959–60
Kirsten, N.	...(7—2)	Border v. Rhodesia (East London)	...1959–60
Langley, G. L.	...(8—1)	Australia v. England (Lord's)	...1956
Levett, W. H. V.	...(5—4)	Kent v. Nottinghamshire (Maidstone)	...1933
Levett, W. H. V.	...(7—2)	Kent v. Northamptonshire (Northampton)	...1934
Levett, W. H. V.	...(5—4)	Kent v. Sussex (Tunbridge Wells)	...1935
Lewis, E. B.	...(8—1)	Warwickshire v. Oxford U. (Birmingham)	...1949
Lilley, B.	...(9—0)	Nottinghamshire v. Somerset (Taunton)	...1932
Livsey, W. H.	...(4—5)	Hampshire v. Warwickshire (Southampton)	...1914
Mantri, M. K.	...(4—5)	Bombay v. Northern India (Lahore)	...1941–42
Newton, A. E.	...(6—3)	Somerset v. Middlesex (Lord's)	...1901
Oldfield, W. A.	...(4—5)	New South Wales v. West Indians (Sydney)	...1930–31
Tallon, D.	...(4—5)	Queensland v. Victoria (Brisbane)	...1938–39
Turner, M.	...(4—5)	Gentlemen of England v. Oxford U. (Oxford)	...1871
Turner, M.	...(6—3)	Middlesex v. Nottinghamshire (Princes)	...1875
Walker, C. W.	...(3—6)	South Australia v. New South Wales (Sydney)	...1939–40
Yarnold, H.	...(5—4)	Worcestershire v. Hampshire (Worcester)	...1949

EIGHT

Ames, L. E. G.	.........(4—4)	Kent v. Gloucestershire (Bristol)	1929
Ames, L. E. G.	.........(4—4)	Kent v. Derbyshire (Chesterfield)	1929
Ames, L. E. G.	.........(6—2)	Kent v. Hampshire (Folkestone)	1929
Ames, L. E. G.	.........(1—7)	Kent v. Warwickshire (Tonbridge)	1930
Ames, L. E. G.	.........(6—2)	England v. West Indies (Oval)	1933
Ames, L. E. G.	.........(6—2)	Players v. Gentlemen (Lord's)	1937
Bairstow, A. L.	.........(7—1)	Yorkshire v. Cambridge U. (Cambridge)	1899
Bale, E.	.........(7—1)	Worcestershire v. Gloucestershire (Cheltenham)	1913
Board, J. H.	.............(7—1)	Gloucestershire v. Somerset (Bristol)	1895
Board, J. H.	.............(2—6)	Gloucestershire v. Northamptonshire (Bristol)	1910
Brooks, E. W.	.............(7—1)	Surrey v. Somerset (Oval)	1933
Butt, H. R.	.............(8—0)	Sussex v. Somerset (Hove)	1900
Butt, H. R.	.............(6—2)	Sussex v. Hampshire (Hove)	1903
Catt, A. W.	.............(7—1)	Kent v. Warwickshire (Birmingham)	1958
Cornford, W. F.	.............(4—4)	Sussex v. Worcestershire (Worcester)	1928
Curtis, W. M.	.............(8—0)	North Island v. South Island (Wellington)	1957–58
Davies, H. G.	.............(6—2)	Glamorgan v. South Africans (Swansea)	1955
Dawkes, G.	.............(8—0)	Derbyshire v. Essex (Westcliff)	1958
Ducker, J.	.............(5—3)	South Australia v. Queensland (Adelaide)	1952–53
Duckworth, G.	.........(5—3)	Lancashire v. Kent (Maidstone)	1928
Duckworth, G.	.........(3—5)	Lancashire v. Warwickshire (Manchester)	1936
Easton, A.	.............(3—5)	New South Wales v. Queensland (Sydney)	1933–34
Elliott, H.	.............(5—3)	Derbyshire v. Worcestershire (Derby)	1931
Elliott, H.	.............(6—2)	Derbyshire v. Essex (Derby)	1933
Ellis, J. L.	.............(3—5)	Australians v. Lancashire (Liverpool)	1926
Evans, T. G.	.............(5—3)	Kent v. Derbyshire (Canterbury)	1947
Firth, J.	.............(3—5)	Leicestershire v. Kent (Folkestone)	1952
Firth, J.	.............(7—1)	Leicestershire v. Essex (Colchester)	1953
Gibb, P. A.	.............(7—1)	Essex v. Kent (Tunbridge Wells)	1952
Grout, A. W.	.............(8—0)	Queensland v. New South Wales (Sydney)	1955–56
Grout, A. W.	.............(3—5)	Queensland v. South Australia (Brisbane)	1956–57
Grout, A. W.	.............(8—0)	Queensland v. Western Australia (Brisbane)	1959–60
Guillen, S. C.	.............(3—5)	West Indians v. Tasmania (Launceston)	1951–52
Harris, C.	.............(7—1)	Rhodesia v. North-Eastern Transvaal (Pretoria)	1951–52
Harrison, L.	.............(8—0)	Hampshire v. Sussex (Hove)	1959
Harty, J.	.............(5—3)	Border v. Eastern Province (East London)	1957–58
Hubble, J. C.	.............(6—2)	Kent v. Leicestershire (Leicester)	1925
Hubble, J. C.	.............(2—6)	Kent v. Gloucestershire (Gravesend)	1926
Huish, F. H.	.............(8—0)	Kent v. Nottinghamshire (Nottingham)	1899
Huish, F. H.	.............(7—1)	Kent v. Gloucestershire (Catford)	1905
Huish, F. H.	.............(6—2)	Kent v. Somerset (Taunton)	1908
Huish, F. H.	.............(4—4)	Kent v. Northamptonshire (Northampton)	1911
Huish, F. H.	.............(7—1)	Kent v. Leicestershire (Leicester)	1913
Huish, F. H.	.............(6—2)	Kent v. Middlesex (Lord's)	1913
Huish, F. H.	.............(7—1)	Kent v. Londesborough's XI (Scarborough)	1913
Hunter, D.	.............(2—6)	Yorkshire v. Surrey (Bradford)	1898
Imtiaz Ahmed	.............(4—4)	Pakistan v. Oxford U. (Oxford)	1954
Jackman, C. K.	.........(1—7)	Canterbury v. Wellington (Wellington)	1935–36
James, K. C.	.............(3—5)	New Zealanders v. Derbyshire (Derby)	1927
Kelly, J. J.	.............(8—0)	Australia v. England (Sydney)	1901–02
Kent, L. A. W.	.........(2—6)	Auckland v. Wellington (Wellington)	1944–45
Khanna, S. K.	.........(4—4)	Bengal v. Bihar (Patna)	1957–58
Kingscote, H. B.	.........(5—3)	M.C.C. v. Kent (Canterbury)	1877
Langley, G. R.	.............(3—5)	South Australia v. Victoria (Melbourne)	1950–51
Levett, W. H. V.	.........(3—5)	Kent v. Lancashire (Dover)	1930
Levett, W. H. V.	.........(6—2)	Kent v. Gloucestershire (Gloucester)	1938
Lilley, A. A.	.............(8—0)	Warwickshire v. M.C.C. (Lord's)	1896
Lilley, A. A.	.............(8—0)	Warwickshire v. Kent (Birmingham)	1897
Lilley, A. A.	.............(7—1)	Players v. Gentlemen (Lord's)	1904
Lilley, A. A.	.............(7—1)	England XI v. West Indians (Blackpool)	1906
Luckes, W. T.	.............(6—2)	Somerset v. Worcestershire (Worcester)	1948
Lyttelton, Hon. A.	......(6—2)	Gentlemen v. Players (Oval)	1877
Maddocks, L.	.............(7—1)	Victoria v. New South Wales (Sydney)	1956–57
Maddocks, L.	.............(8—0)	Victoria v. Western Australia (Perth)	1956–57
Meyer, B. J.	.............(8—0)	Gloucestershire v. Worcestershire (Worcester)	1960
Murray, J. T.	.............(3—5)	Ames's XI v. West Indians (Hastings)	1957
Murray, J. T.	.............(8—0)	Middlesex v. Glamorgan (Lord's)	1960
Nayle, J. G.	.............(7—1)	Hindus v. Europeans (Poona)	1926–27
Oates, T. W.	.............(7—1)	Nottinghamshire v. Leicestershire (Leicester)	1907
Oates, T. W.	.............(8—0)	Nottinghamshire v. Kent (Dover)	1923

Pearce, R. W.	(7—1)	Natal v. Western Province (Durban)	1956–57
Petrie, E. C.	(8—0)	New Zealanders v. Sussex (Hove)	1958
Phillips, H.	(3—5)	Sussex v. Kent (Hove)	1884
Pinder, G.	(2—6)	Yorkshire v. Lancashire (Sheffield)	1872
Pooley, E.	(4—4)	Surrey v. Kent (Gravesend)	1868
Pooley, E.	(6—2)	Surrey v. Middlesex (Oval)	1875
Pooley, E.	(4—4)	Surrey v. M.C.C. (Lord's)	1876
Popplewell, O. B.	(7—1)	Cambridge U. v. Sussex (Hove)	1950
Price, W. F.	(5—3)	M.C.C. v. Kent (Folkestone)	1934
Price, W. F.	(3—5)	Middlesex v. South Africans (Lord's)	1935
Russell, T. M.	(8—0)	Essex v. Kent (Leyton)	1899
Saggers, R. A.	(6—2)	New South Wales v. Queensland (Sydney)	1946–47
Sherwin, M.	(5—3)	Nottinghamshire v. Gloucestershire (Nottingham)	1889
Smith, E. J.	(5—3)	Warwickshire v. Derbyshire (Birmingham)	1926
Smith, E. J.	(7—1)	Warwickshire v. Worcestershire (Birmingham)	1930
Smith, H.	(6—2)	Gloucestershire v. Glamorgan (Cheltenham)	1924
Smith, H.	(7—1)	Gloucestershire v. Kent (Folkestone)	1928
Spooner, R. T.	(8—0)	Warwickshire v. Leicestershire (Birmingham)	1959
Stephenson, H. W.	(6—2)	Somerset v. Sussex (Eastbourne)	1949
Stephenson, H. W.	(5—3)	Somerset v. Gloucestershire (Taunton)	1954
Stephenson, H. W.	(8—0)	Somerset v. Worcestershire (Taunton)	1955
Stewart, W. A.	(6—2)	Oxford U. v. Cambridge U. (Lord's)	1869
Street, G.	(7—1)	Sussex v. Worcestershire (Hastings)	1923
Strudwick, H.	(7—1)	Surrey v. Essex (Leyton)	1904
Tallon, D.	(4—4)	Queensland v. New South Wales (Brisbane)	1938–39
Tallon, D.	(6—2)	Queensland v. Western Australia (Perth)	1950–51
Travers, F. G.	(8—0)	Europeans v. Parsis (Bombay)	1923–24
Tufnell, N. C.	(1—7)	Cambridge U. v. Yorkshire (Cambridge)	1909
Turner, M.	(3—5)	Gentlemen of England v. Cambridge U. (Cambridge)	1876
Wade, W. W.	(1—7)	Natal v. Griqualand West (Durban)	1947–48
Walker, C. W.	(3—5)	South Australia v. New South Wales (Sydney)	1928–29
Webb, R. T.	(8—0)	Sussex v. Somerset (Hove)	1960
Wilson, A.	(8—0)	Lancashire v. Hampshire (Portsmouth)	1955
Wood, A.	(8—0)	Yorkshire v. Northamptonshire (Huddersfield)	1932
Yarnold, H.	(4—4)	Worcestershire v. Kent (Dover)	1949
Yarnold, H.	(3—5)	Worcestershire v. Cambridge U. (Worcester)	1950
Yarnold, H.	(1—7)	Worcestershire v. Scotland (Dundee)	1951

Most Catches in a Season by a Fielder

When W. R. Hammond took 78 catches at first slip in 1928, he established yet another record that may stand for ever, only one fielder having come close to that total in the years that have followed.

The following cases of over 50 catches in a season have been recorded:

78	W. R. Hammond	Gloucestershire	1928
77	M. J. Stewart	Surrey	1957
70	J. Tunnicliffe	Yorkshire	1901
70	P. M. Walker	Glamorgan	1960
69	John Langridge	Sussex	1955
65	J. Tunnicliffe	Yorkshire	1895
65	W. R. Hammond	Gloucestershire	1925
65	P. M. Walker	Glamorgan	1959
64	J. Tunnicliffe	Yorkshire	1904
64	K. F. Barrington	Surrey	1957
64	G. A. R. Lock	Surrey	1957
63	K. Grieves	Lancashire	1950
63	C. A. Milton	Gloucestershire	1956
61	J. V. Wilson	Yorkshire	1955
61	M. J. Stewart	Surrey	1958
59	John Langridge	Sussex	1933
58	John Langridge	Sussex	1950
58	W. S. Surridge	Surrey	1952
57	A. S. M. Oakman	Sussex	1958
56	W. S. Surridge	Surrey	1955
56	P. J. Sainsbury	Hampshire	1957
56	C. A. Milton	Gloucestershire	1959
55	J. T. Ikin	Lancashire	1946

55	J. V. Wilson	Yorkshire	1951
55	C. A. Milton	Gloucestershire	1952
55	K. F. Barrington	Surrey	1958
54	E. G. Hayes	Surrey	1906
54	W. R. Hammond	Gloucestershire	1933
54	W. R. Hammond	Gloucestershire	1935
54	L. Outschoorn	Worcestershire	1949
54	G. A. R. Lock	Surrey	1952
54	K. Grieves	Lancashire	1953
54	W. S. Surridge	Surrey	1956
53	J. V. Wilson	Yorkshire	1957
52	H. Trumble	Australians	1893
52	P. G. H. Fender	Surrey	1921
52	W. J. Edrich	Middlesex	1949
52	M. J. Stewart	Surrey	1955
52	A. S. M. Oakman	Sussex	1959
52	M. J. Stewart	Surrey	1959
51	John Langridge	Sussex	1934
50	J. Tunnicliffe	Yorkshire	1900
50	James Seymour	Kent	1913

Most Dismissals by a Wicket-Keeper in a Season

Only five wicket-keepers have succeeded in reaching a season's total of 100 victims in one season. The two Kent wicket-keepers, F. H. Huish and L. E. G. Ames, were both helped by great Kent slow bowlers—Huish by C. Blythe and Ames by A. P. Freeman.

		Season	Total	Caught	St.
L. E. G. Ames	Kent	1929	127	79	48
L. E. G. Ames	Kent	1928	121	69	52
H. Yarnold	Worcestershire	1949	110	63	47
J. G. Binks	Yorkshire	1960	108	97	11
G. Duckworth	Lancashire	1928	107	77	30
J. T. Murray	Middlesex	1957	104	82	22
F. H. Huish	Kent	1913	102	70	32
J. T. Murray	Middlesex	1960	102	95	7
R. Booth	Worcestershire	1960	101	85	16
F. H. Huish	Kent	1911	100	62	38
L. E. G. Ames	Kent	1932	100	36	64
G. Street	Sussex	1923	97	71	26
L. E. G. Ames	Kent	1930	97	49	48
W. F. Price	Middlesex	1937	97	68	29
H. Yarnold	Worcestershire	1951	95	58	37
G. Duckworth	Lancashire	1929	95	58	37
A. J. McIntyre	Surrey	1949	95	72	23
H. Yarnold	Worcestershire	1950	94	62	32
J. M. Parks	Sussex	1959	93	86	7
T. G. Evans	Kent	1947	93	69	24
A. Wood	Yorkshire	1934	93	76	17
H. Strudwick	Surrey	1903	91	71	20
H. Elliott	Derbyshire	1935	90	69	21

The Wicket-Keeper's 'Double'

Only two players, L. E. G. Ames and J. T. Murray, have achieved the wicket-keeper's 'double' of 1000 runs and 100 dismissals in a season.

	Season	Runs	H.S.	Avge.	100s		Total	Ct.	St.
Ames, L. E. G. (Kent) ......(3)	1928	1919	200	35·53	4	...	121	69	52
	1929	1795	145	35·90	5	...	127	79	48
	1932	2482	180	57·72	9	...	100	36	64
Murray, J. T. (Middx.) ......(1)	1957	1025	120	19·71	1	...	104	82	22

N

Innings Without Byes

672—7d	A. P. Wickham: Somerset v. Hants. (Taunton)	1899
659—8d	T. G. Evans: England v. Australia (Sydney)	1946–47
594—6d	J. H. Board: Glos. v. Hants. (Southampton)	1911
577—4	A. E. Wilson: Glos. v. Glamorgan (Newport)	1939
574—4	W. T. Luckes: Somerset v. Glamorgan (Newport)	1939
570—8d	E. W. Brookes: Surrey v. Essex (Brentwood)	1934
569	S. O. Quin: Victoria v. South Australia (Melbourne)	1935–36
559—9d	W. W. Wade: South Africa v. England (Cape Town)	1938–39
557—7d	H. Smith: Glos. v. Surrey (Oval)	1927
555—6d	S. C. Griffith: Sussex v. South Africans (Hove)	1947
551—7d	D. Hunter: Yorks. v. Surrey (Oval)	1899
551	J. J. Kelly: Australia v. England (Sydney)	1894–95
546	S. C. Griffith: Sussex v. New Zealanders (Hove)	1937
535—8d	N. McCorkell: Hants. v. Leics. (Leicester)	1938
533—5d	R. Swetman: M.C.C. v. Barbados (Barbados)	1959–60
521—7d	B. Bellamy: Northants. v. Sussex (Hove)	1930
521	W. A. Oldfield: Australia v. England (Brisbane)	1928–29
520—8d	M. Patten: Free Foresters v. Oxford U. (Oxford)	1927
520	J. H. B. Waite: South Africa v. Australia (Melbourne)	1952–53
512	J. D. P. Tanner: Oxford U. v. Lancs. (Oxford)	1947

J. D. P. Tanner was making his debut in first-class cricket.

512	W. T. Luckes: Somerset v. Surrey (Oval)	1936
507—6d	E. A. Meads: Notts. v. Kent (Nottingham)	1953
501—6d	B. Bellamy: Northants. v. Worcs. (Northampton)	1930
501—8d	A. B. Wheat: Notts. v. Glamorgan (Swansea)	1939
500	J. P. Whiteside: Leics. v. Surrey (Leicester)	1900

Innings Productive of Extras

Inns	Exs.	B.	L.B.	W.	N.B.		
529	74					British Guiana v. W. Shepherd's XI (Georgetown)	1909–10
374	73	48	23	2	—	Northants. v. Kent (Northampton)	1955
287	70	24	—	46	—	Cambridge U. v. Oxford U. (Lord's)	1839
539	68	57	6	5	—	Yorks. v. Cambridge U. (Cambridge)	1884
197	66	49	—	17	—	M.C.C. v. Cambridge U. (Cambridge)	1842
200	63	36	—	21	6	Oxford U. v. Cambridge U. (Lord's)	1836
405	62	45	11	3	3	A.I.F. v. H. K. Foster's XI (Hereford)	1919
532	62	44	11	7	—	M.C.C. v. Wales (Lord's)	1925
400	59	46	13	—	—	Army v. Cambridge U. (Cambridge)	1920
423	58	38	18	—	2	M.C.C. v. Notts. (Lord's)	1899
343—9d	58	29	28	1	—	Cambridge U. v. Free Foresters (Cambridge)	1929
380—5	58	41	14	—	3	Wellington v. Auckland (Wellington)	1929–30
387	57	31	16	—	10	New Zealand v. England (Auckland)	1929–30
468—7d	57	27	12	14	4	England v. Australian Services (Lord's)	1945
468	57	39	4	8	6	Yorks. v. Essex (Southend)	1947
266	56	29	5	21	1	Cambridge U. v. Oxford U. (Lord's)	1851
555	56	34	14	8	—	Kent v. Worcs. (Stourbridge)	1909
127	55	45	—	9	1	Cambridge U. v. Oxford U. (Lord's)	1836
409	55	49	4	2	—	Glos. v. Middx. (Lord's)	1888
519	55					Jamaica v. Tennyson's XI (Kingston)	1926–27
188	55	46	2	—	7	Oxford U. v. Harlequins (Oxford)	1927
505—9d	54	32	19	2	1	Somerset v. Middx. (Weston-super-Mare)	1933
204	53	37	—	13	3	M.C.C. v. Oxford U. (Lord's)	1837
388	53	36	12	4	1	Northants. v. Leics. (Northampton)	1906
441	53					M.C.C. v. West Indian XI (Georgetown)	1912–13
407	53	29	22	—	2	Essex v. Worcs. (Worcester)	1923
305	53	37	5	4	7	Leveson-Gower's XI v. Oxford U. (Eastbourne)	1923
473—6	53	26	10	—	17	Canterbury v. Auckland (Christchurch)	1930–31
359—7d	52	43	8	1	—	Lancs. v. Middx. (Lord's)	1901
370	52					Wellington v. Canterbury (Christchurch)	1922–23
503—9d	52	39	10	3	—	M.C.C. v. Sussex (Lord's)	1905
611	52	41	9	1	1	Sussex v. Essex (Leyton)	1905
592—4d	51	47	3	1	—	Lancs. v. Worcs. (Worcester)	1929
308	51					Baroda v. Maharashtra (Baroda)	1942–43
403	50	37	10	3	—	Eastern Province v. Griqualand West (Johannesburg)	1906–07

Inns	Exs.	B.	L.B.	W.	N.B.		
246	50	42	5	—	3	Free Foresters v. Oxford U. (Oxford)	1920
480—9d	50	33	11	3	3	Kent v. Hants. (Canterbury)	1923
464—9d	50					Scotland v. Ireland (Greenock)	1926
602—8d	50					Otago v. Canterbury (Dunedin)	1928–29
327	50	37	8	1	4	Australia v. England (Oval)	1934
443—9d	50					Western Province v. Border (Cape Town)	1934–35
903—7d	50	22	19	1	8	England v. Australia (Oval)	1938

Part VII—Career Records
Batting

A date in italics denotes the first part of an overseas season, for example *1959* means 1959-60. The number of times a batsman has completed 1000 runs in a season is also given, for example, J. B. Hobbs's figures of 24+2 means 24 times in England and twice overseas.

The following batsmen have scored over 30,000 runs during a first-class cricket career.

	Career	Inns.	N.O.	Runs	H.S.	Avge.	100s	1000s
J. B. Hobbs	1905–1934	1315	106	61237	316*	50·65	197	24+2
F. E. Woolley	1906–1938	1532	85	58969	305*	40·75	145	28
E. Hendren	1907–1938	1300	166	57611	301*	50·81	170	21+4
C. P. Mead	1905–1936	1340	185	55061	280*	47·67	153	27
W. G. Grace †	1865–1908	1493	105	54896	344	39·55	126	28
W. G. Grace 'corrected' †	1865–1908	1468	103	53856	344	39·45	124	28
W. R. Hammond	1920–1951	1004	104	50493	336*	56·10	167	17+5
H. Sutcliffe	1919–1945	1087	123	50135	313	52·00	149	21+3
T. Hayward	1893–1914	1138	96	43551	315*	41·79	104	20
A. Sandham	1911–*1937*	1000	79	41283	325	44·82	107	18+2
L. Hutton	1934–1960	814	91	40140	364	55·51	129	12+5
W. Rhodes	1898–1930	1528	237	39802	267*	30·83	58	20+1
R. E. S. Wyatt	1923–1957	1141	157	39404	232	40·04	85	17+1
E. Tyldesley	1909–1936	961	106	38874	256*	45·46	102	18+1
D. C. S. Compton	1936–*1959*	831	88	38635	300	51·99	122	14+3
J. T. Tyldesley	1895–1923	994	62	37897	295*	40·66	86	19
J. W. Hearne	1909–1936	1025	116	37252	285*	40·98	96	19
L. E. G. Ames	1926–1951	950	95	37245	295	43·56	102	17
W. J. Edrich	1934–1958	964	92	36965	267*	42·39	86	15
D. Denton	1894–1920	1163	70	36479	221	33·37	69	21
G. H. Hirst	1891–1929	1215	151	36323	341	34·13	60	19
W. G. Quaife	1894–1928	1203	186	36021	255*	35·41	72	24
G. Gunn	1902–1932	1062	82	35234	220	35·95	62	20
John Langridge	1928–1955	984	66	34380	250*	37·45	76	17
C. Washbrook	1933–1959	902	107	33944	251*	42·69	76	17+3
M. Leyland	1920–1948	932	101	33660	263	40·50	80	17
H. T. W. Hardinge	1902–1933	1021	103	33519	263*	36·51	75	18
R. Abel	1881–1904	994	73	32669	357*	35·47	74	14
J. D. Robertson	1937–1959	897	46	31914	331*	37·50	67	14+1
J. Hardstaff jun.	1930–1955	812	94	31847	266	44·35	83	13+1
James Langridge	1924–1953	1058	157	31716	167	35·20	42	20
C. B. Fry	1892–*1921*	658	43	30886	258*	50·22	94	12
D. Brookes	1934–1959	925	70	30874	257	36·10	71	17
P. Holmes	1913–1935	810	84	30574	315*	42·11	67	14+1
L. G. Berry	1924–1951	1048	57	30188	232	30·46	45	18

† Two sets of career figures are given for W. G. Grace—the first the 'accepted' figures and the second the 'corrected' figures in which all minor matches have been excluded.

The following batsmen have recorded a career aggregate of over 10,000 runs.

Abel, R.	1881–1904	994	73	32669	357*	35·47	74	14
Alderman, A. E.	1928–1948	529	51	12376	175	25·89	12	6
Allen, B. O.	1932–1951	512	20	14195	220	28·85	14	6
Ames, L. E. G.	1926–1951	950	95	37245	295	43·56	102	17
Armstrong, N. F.	1919–1939	637	61	19002	186	32·98	36	13
Armstrong, W. W.	*1898–1921*	407	61	16177	303*	46·75	45	4+2
Arnold, E. G.	1899–1913	592	62	15853	215	29·91	24	10
Arnold, J.	1929–1950	710	45	21831	227	32·82	37	14
Ashdown, W. H.	1914–1947	812	77	22589	332	30·73	39	11
Astill, W. E.	1906–1939	1153	145	22726	164*	22·54	15	11
Avery, A. V.	1935–1954	455	35	14137	224	33·65	25	7
Bailey, T. E.	1945–1960	745	141	21025	205	34·80	25	12
Bakewell, A. H.	1928–1936	453	24	14570	257	33·98	31	8
Barber, W.	1926–1947	526	49	16402	255	34·38	29	8
Bardsley, W.	*1903–1927*	376	35	17031	264	49·94	53	4+1
Barling, T. H.	1927–1948	609	54	19209	269	34·61	34	9
Barlow, R. G.	1871–1891	598	63	10762	117	20·11	4	1

	Career	Inns.	N.O.	Runs	H.S.	Avge.	100s	1000s
Barnes, W.	1875–1894	716	56	15242	160	23·09	21	5
Barnett, C. J.	1927–1953	821	45	25389	259	32·71	48	12+1
Barrick, D.	1949–1960	490	62	13970	211	32·64	20	7
Barrington, K. F.	1953–1960	391	60	12732	186	38·46	26	6
Bartlett, H. T.	1933–1951	350	34	10098	183	31·95	16	4
Bates, L. A.	1913–1935	749	53	19380	211	27·84	21	12
Bates, W.	1877–1887	494	20	10214	144*	21·54	10	5
Bates, W. E.	1907–1931	685	30	15884	200*	24·25	12	7
Bedser, E. A.	1939–1960	651	64	14247	163	24·27	10	6
Berry, L. G.	1924–1951	1048	57	30188	232	30·46	45	18
Board, J. H.	1891–1914	906	97	15672	214	19·37	9	6
Bosanquet, B. J. T.	1898–1919	381	32	11694	214	33·50	21	6
Bowell, A.	1902–1927	810	43	18510	204	24·13	25	8
Bowley, E. H.	1912–1934	853	46	28163	283	34·89	52	15
Bowley, F. L.	1899–1923	738	25	21121	276	29·62	38	14
Bradman, D. G.	1927–1948	338	43	28067	452*	95·14	117	4+12
Brann, G.	1885–1905	475	43	11201	161	25·92	25	2
Braund, L. C.	1896–1920	752	57	17801	257*	25·61	25	7
Broadbent, R. G.	1950–1960	414	44	10442	155	28·22	11	6
Brockwell, W.	1886–1903	539	47	13285	225	27·00	22	6
Briggs, J.	1879–1900	821	54	14002	186	18·25	10	—
Brookes, D.	1934–1959	925	70	30874	257	36·10	71	17
Brown, F. R.	1930–1959	533	49	13275	212	27·42	22	4
Brown, G.	1908–1933	1012	52	25649	232*	26·71	37	11
Brown, J. T.	1889–1904	633	47	17850	311	30·46	29	10
Brown, S. M.	1937–1955	580	40	15756	232*	29·17	22	9
Brown, W. A.	1932–1949	284	15	13840	265*	51·44	39	3+2
Burnup, C. J.	1895–1907	395	25	13614	200	36·79	26	8
Buse, H. T. F.	1929–1953	523	54	10623	132	22·65	7	5
Cadman, S.	1900–1926	690	34	14068	126	21·44	8	2
Calthorpe, Hon. F. S. G.	1911–1935	576	52	12596	209	24·03	13	5
Carpenter, H.	1893–1920	551	26	14939	199	28·45	25	7
Carr, A. W.	1910–1935	710	42	21100	206	31·58	45	11
Carr, D. B.	1945–1960	629	62	16104	170	28·40	20	9
Chapman, A. P. F.	1920–1939	554	44	16309	260	31·97	27	3+1
Charlesworth, C.	1898–1921	632	27	14289	216	23·61	15	5
Chatterton, W.	1882–1902	507	39	10863	169	23·21	8	3
Clark, T. H.	1947–1959	426	35	11490	191	29·38	12	6
Close, D. B.	1949–1960	503	59	14109	198	31·77	20	8
Coe, S.	1896–1923	775	70	17438	252*	24·73	19	7
Compton, D. C. S.	1936–1959	831	88	38635	300	51·99	122	14+3
Constable, B.	1939–1960	556	55	14957	205*	29·85	21	10
Cook, T. E.	1922–1937	730	65	20198	278	30·37	32	10
Cooper, E.	1936–1951	444	28	13304	216*	31·98	18	9
Cowdrey, M. C.	1950–1960	535	44	19913	250	40·55	47	10+4
Cox, G.	1931–1960	752	57	22912	234*	32·96	50	13
Cox, G. R.	1895–1928	978	197	14643	167*	18·74	2	1
Crapp, J. F.	1936–1956	754	80	23615	175	35·03	38	14
Crawford, V. F. S.	1896–1910	479	32	11909	172*	26·64	16	5
Croom, A. J.	1922–1939	628	65	17689	211	31·41	24	12
Cutmore, J. A.	1924–1936	595	36	15975	238*	28·58	15	11
Dacre, C. C.	1914–1936	437	20	12166	223	29·17	24	7
Daniell, J.	1898–1927	531	54	10468	174*	21·94	9	—
Darling, J.	1893–1907	334	25	10637	210	34·42	21	4
Davies, D.	1923–1939	698	62	15458	216	24·30	16	7
Davies, E.	1924–1954	1033	79	26566	287*	27·84	32	16
Dawkes, G.	1937–1960	716	103	11042	143	18·01	1	—
Dawson, E. W.	1922–1934	483	17	12662	146	27·17	14	6
Dempster, C. S.	1921–1947	305	36	12098	212	44·97	35	5
Denton, D.	1894–1920	1163	70	36479	221	33·37	69	21
Dews, G.	1946–1960	582	46	15282	145	28·51	19	10
Dillon, E. W.	1900–1923	414	25	11006	143	28·29	15	3
Dipper, A. E.	1908–1932	865	69	28075	252*	35·27	53	15
Dodds, T. C.	1943–1960	691	18	19384	157	28·80	17	13
Dollery, H. E.	1933–1955	717	66	24413	212	37·50	50	15
Douglas, J. W. H. T.	1901–1930	1035	156	24530	210*	27·90	26	10
Ducat, A.	1906–1931	669	59	23373	306*	38·31	52	14
Duleepsinhji, K. S.	1924–1932	333	23	15485	333	49·95	50	7
Dyson, A. H.	1926–1948	697	37	17922	208	27·15	24	10
Eagar, E. D. R.	1935–1958	599	42	12178	158*	21·86	10	6
Eastman, L. C.	1920–1939	696	50	13438	161	20·80	7	5

	Career	Inns.	N.O.	Runs	H.S.	Avge.	100s	1000s
Edrich, G. A.	1946–1958	508	60	15600	167*	34·82	26	8
Edrich, W. J.	1934–1958	964	92	36965	267*	42·39	86	15
Elliott, C. S.	1932–1953	468	29	11965	215	27·25	9	6
Emmett, G. M.	1936–1959	865	50	25602	188	31·41	37	13+1
Evans, T. G.	1939–1960	742	48	14689	144	21·17	7	4
Fagg, A. E.	1932–1957	803	46	27291	269*	36·05	58	13
Fane, F. L.	1895–1924	715	42	18527	217	27·52	25	5
Fender, P. G. H.	1910–1936	783	69	19034	185	26·65	21	9
Fishlock, L. B.	1931–1952	699	54	25376	253	39·34	56	12+1
Fletcher, D. G. W.	1946–1960	511	40	14305	194	30·37	22	4
Flowers, W.	1877–1896	683	53	12691	173	20·34	9	2
Foster, H. K.	1894–1925	523	21	17154	216	34·17	29	8
Freeman, J. R.	1905–1928	579	55	14604	286	27·88	26	7
Fry, C. B.	1892–*1921*	658	43	30886	258*	50·22	94	12
Gardner, F. C.	1947–1960	593	65	17822	215*	33·75	29	10
Geary, G.	1912–1938	819	138	13498	122	19·82	8	—
Gibb, P. A.	1934–1956	479	33	12520	204	28·07	19	5
Gibbons, H. H.	1927–1946	671	57	21087	212*	34·34	44	12
Giffen, G.	*1877–1903*	421	24	11757	271	29·61	18	4
Gillingham, F. H.	1903–1928	352	24	10050	201	30·64	19	1
Gimblett, H.	1935–1954	673	37	23007	310	36·17	50	12+1
Grace, W. G.	1865–1908	1493	105	54896	344	39·55	126	28
Grace, W. G. 'corrected'	1865–1908	1468	103	53856	344	39·45	124	28
Graveney, T. W.	1948–1960	751	79	29216	258	43·47	77	12+2
Gray, J. R.	1948–1960	588	59	16247	176*	30·71	21	10
Gregory, R. J.	1925–1947	646	78	19495	243	34·32	39	9
Gregory, S. E.	*1889–1912*	592	55	15303	201	28·49	25	4
Grieves, K.	*1945*–1960	570	67	17514	224	34·81	23	10+1
Gunn, G.	1902–1932	1062	82	35234	220	35·95	62	20
Gunn, G. V.	1928–1950	395	42	10337	184	29·28	11	5
Gunn, J.	1896–1932	847	105	24740	294	33·34	41	11
Gunn, W.	1880–1904	846	71	25457	273	32·84	47	12
Haig, N. E.	1912–1936	779	49	15208	131	20·83	12	6
Haigh, S.	1895–1913	747	119	11715	159	18·65	4	1
Hall, L.	1873–1894	538	63	10853	160	22·84	11	4
Hallam, M. R.	1950–1960	452	16	12026	210*	27·58	16	7
Hallows, C.	1914–1932	586	66	20926	233*	40·24	55	11
Hamer, A.	1938–1960	515	19	15465	227	31·17	19	10
Hammond, W. R.	1920–1951	1004	104	50493	336*	56·10	167	17+5
Hardinge, H. T. W.	1902–1933	1021	103	33519	263*	36·51	75	18
Hardstaff, J. sen.	1902–1926	620	73	17146	213*	31·34	26	7+1
Hardstaff, J. jun.	1930–1955	812	94	31847	266	44·35	83	13+1
Harris, C. B.	1928–1951	601	64	18823	239*	35·05	30	11
Harvey, R. N.	*1946–1959*	373	31	17866	255	52·23	56	2+4
Hassett, A. L.	*1932–1953*	322	32	16890	232	58·24	59	3+2
Hawke, Lord	1881–1911	920	105	16506	166	20·25	13	1
Hayes, E. G.	1896–1926	896	48	27318	276	32·21	48	16
Hayward, T.	1893–1914	1138	96	43551	315*	41·80	104	20
Hazare, V. S.	*1934–1959*	347	42	17659	316*	57·90	57	2+5
Hearne, A.	1884–1910	825	76	16287	194	21·74	15	4
Hearne, J. W.	1909–1936	1025	116	37252	285*	40·98	96	19
Hendren, E.	1907–1938	1300	166	57611	301*	50·81	170	21+4
Hill, A. J. L.	1890–1921	389	26	10141	199	27·93	18	—
Hill, C.	*1892–1925*	417	21	17216	365*	43·47	45	3+2
Hirst, G. H.	1891–1929	1215	151	36323	341	34·13	60	19
Hobbs, J. B.	1905–1934	1315	106	61237	316*	50·65	197	24+2
Holland, F. C.	1894–1908	429	29	10384	171	25·96	12	4
Holmes, E. R. T.	1924–1955	465	51	13598	236	32·84	24	6
Holmes, P.	1913–1935	810	84	30574	315*	42·11	67	14+1
Hopwood, J. L.	1923–1939	575	55	15548	220	29·90	27	8
Hornby, A. N.	1867–1899	698	39	15763	188	23·91	15	2
Horner, N. F.	1950–1960	458	24	12756	203*	29·39	17	8
Horton, H.	1946–1960	388	44	10976	140*	31·90	18	6
Howorth, R.	1933–1951	611	56	11479	114	20·68	4	4
Hubble, J. C.	1904–1929	528	65	10935	189	23·61	5	1
Humphreys, E.	1899–1920	639	45	16603	208	27·95	21	8
Hutchings, K. L.	1902–1912	311	12	10054	176	33·62	22	6
Hutton, L.	1934–1960	814	91	40140	364	55·51	129	12+5
Iddon, J.	1924–1945	712	95	22681	222	36·76	46	13
Ikin, J. T.	1938–1960	550	66	17813	192	36·80	27	10+1
Insole, D. J.	1947–1960	708	70	24506	219*	38·41	54	13

	Career	Inns.	N.O.	Runs	H.S.	Avge.	100s	1000s
Iremonger, J.	1899–1914	534	60	16622	272	35·06	31	9
Jackson, F. S.	1890–1907	500	35	15824	160	34·03	31	10
Jackson, G. R.	1919–1936	468	22	10288	140	23·06	9	4
Jackson, V. E.	1936–1958	605	53	15698	170	28·43	21	11
Jardine, D. R.	1920–1948	377	61	14823	214*	46·90	35	8+1
Jenkins, R. O.	1938–1958	573	120	10073	109	22·23	1	4
Jessop, G. L.	1894–1914	855	37	26698	286	32·63	53	14
Johnson, P. R.	1900–1927	488	24	11931	164	25·71	18	1
Jones, A. O.	1892–1914	774	47	22935	296	31·54	34	9
Jones, W. E.	1937–1958	563	64	13535	212*	27·12	11	7
Jupp, H.	1862–1881	677	45	14817	165	23·44	11	6
Jupp, V. W. C.	1909–1938	876	84	23278	217	29·39	30	13
Keeton, W. W.	1926–1952	657	43	24276	312*	39·53	54	12
Kennedy, A. S.	1907–1936	1025	130	16586	163*	18·53	10	5
Kenyon, D.	1946–1960	814	45	27868	259	36·23	63	13
Key, K. J.	1882–1909	560	69	12925	281	26·32	13	3
Killick, E. H.	1893–1913	770	53	18768	200	26·17	22	11
Kilner, N.	1919–1937	619	42	17522	228	30·36	25	12
Kilner, R.	1911–1926	540	55	14422	206*	29·73	17	10
King, J. H.	1895–1926	988	69	25121	227*	27·33	34	14
Kinneir, S. P.	1898–1914	525	47	15641	268*	32·72	26	8
Kippax, A. F.	1918–1936	254	33	12747	315*	57·69	43	1+2
Knight, A. E.	1895–1912	702	40	19357	229*	29·24	34	10
Langdon, T.	1900–1914	519	14	10723	156	21·23	6	3
Langridge, James	1924–1953	1058	157	31716	167	35·20	42	20
Langridge, John	1928–1955	984	66	34380	250*	37·45	76	17
Lee, F. S.	1925–1947	586	38	15310	169	27·93	23	8
Lee, G. M.	1910–1933	622	47	14858	200*	25·84	22	7
Lee, H. W.	1911–1934	716	51	20069	243*	30·17	37	13
Lester, E.	1945–1956	347	28	10912	186	34·20	25	6
Lester, G.	1937–1958	649	54	12857	143	21·60	9	5
Leyland, M.	1920–1948	932	101	33660	263	40·50	80	17
Lilley, A. A.	1891–1911	639	46	15597	171	26·30	16	3
Lilley, B.	1921–1937	512	79	10496	124	24·24	7	2
Livingston, T. L.	1941–1958	382	44	15229	210	45·05	34	7+1
Llewellyn, C. B.	1894–1912	461	34	11425	216	26·75	18	6
Lockwood, W. H.	1886–1904	531	44	10673	163	21·91	15	2
Lowson, F. A.	1949–1958	449	37	15321	259*	37·18	31	8+1
Lyon, B. H.	1921–1948	448	20	10694	189	24·98	16	4
Macartney, C. G.	1905–1935	360	32	15050	345	45·88	49	3
MacBryan, J. C. W.	1911–1936	362	12	10322	164	29·52	18	4
MacLaren, A. C.	1890–1922	699	52	22022	424	34·03	47	8+1
Makepeace, H.	1906–1930	778	66	25799	203	36·23	43	13
Mann, F. T.	1908–1933	608	47	13154	194	23·44	9	3
Marshall, R. E.	1945–1960	465	22	16256	193	36·69	31	7
Martin, S. H.	1925–1949	457	31	11511	191*	27·02	13	7
Mason, J. R.	1893–1919	557	36	17337	183	33·27	34	8
May, P. B. H.	1948–1959	541	67	24651	285*	52·00	80	9+3
McCabe, S. J.	1928–1941	262	20	11951	240	49·39	29	3
McCool, C. L.	1939–1960	413	36	12420	172	32·94	18	5
McCorkell, N.	1932–1951	696	67	16108	203	25·60	17	9
McGahey, C. P.	1894–1921	751	65	20723	277	30·20	31	10
McIntyre, A. J.	1938–1960	566	78	11095	143*	22·73	7	3
Mead, C. P.	1905–1936	1340	185	55061	280*	47·67	153	27
Melville, A.	1928–1948	295	15	10598	189	37·85	25	3
Merchant, V. M.	1929–1951	221	44	12876	359*	72·74	43	2+1
Milton, C. A.	1948–1960	582	75	17486	163	34·48	29	8
Miller, K. R.	1937–1959	326	36	14183	281*	48·90	41	2+2
Mitchell, A.	1922–1947	593	72	19523	189	37·47	44	10
Mitchell, B.	1925–1949	281	30	11395	195	45·39	30	3+1
Morris, A. R.	1940–1954	242	15	12489	290	55·01	46	2+4
Morton, A.	1901–1926	625	56	10933	131	19·21	6	1
Murdoch, W. L.	1876–1904	684	48	17070	321	26·83	20	3
Mushtaq Ali	1932–1959	357	18	12397	233	36·56	30	1
Nayudu, C. K.	1916–1958	303	14	10148	200	35·11	21	2
Ncale, W. L.	1923–1948	700	79	14752	145*	23·75	14	6
Newham, W.	1881–1905	633	43	14318	201*	24·26	18	4
Newman, J. A.	1906–1930	837	129	15333	166*	21·65	10	6
Nichols, M. S.	1924–1939	758	85	17843	205	26·51	20	9
Noble, M. A.	1893–1919	378	34	14034	284	40·80	37	4+1
Nourse, A. D. sen.	1896–1935	371	39	14216	304*	42·82	38	3+1

	Career	Inns.	N.O.	Runs	H.S.	Avge.	100s	1000s
Nourse, A. D. jun.	1931–1952	269	27	12472	260*	51·53	41	2
Oakes, C.	1935–1954	474	40	10893	160	25·09	14	5
Oakman, A. S. M.	1947–1960	517	40	12231	178	25·64	12	6
O'Brien, T. C.	1881–1914	452	30	11399	202	27·01	15	2
O'Connor, J.	1921–1939	906	80	28875	248	34·95	72	16
Oldfield, N.	1935–1954	521	51	17811	168	37·89	38	11
Oldroyd, E.	1910–1931	511	58	15929	194	35·16	37	10
Ord, J. S.	1933–1953	459	35	11788	187*	27·80	16	6
Outschoorn, L.	1946–1959	595	53	15496	215*	28·59	25	9
Palairet, L. C. H.	1890–1909	488	19	15777	292	33·63	27	7
Palmer, C. H.	1938–1959	588	38	17458	201	31·74	33	8
Parker, J. F.	1932–1952	523	71	14272	255	31·57	20	9
Parkhouse, W. G. A.	1948–1960	670	45	20346	201	32·55	29	13
Parks, H. W.	1926–1949	745	98	21725	200*	33·57	42	14
Parks, J. H.	1924–1952	758	63	21369	197	30·74	41	12
Parks, J. M.	1949–1960	525	64	17106	205*	37·10	35	8
Parsons, J. H.	1910–1936	553	51	17909	225	35·67	38	10+1
Paynter, E.	1926–1950	532	58	20023	322	42·24	45	9+1
Payton, W.	1905–1931	770	126	22132	169	34·36	39	9
Pearce, T. N.	1929–1952	406	54	12060	211*	34·26	22	6
Pearson, F.	1900–1926	811	38	18735	167	24·23	22	8
Peel, R.	1882–1899	689	66	12135	210*	19·46	7	1
Perrin, P. A.	1896–1928	918	91	29709	343*	35·92	66	18
Phebey, A. H.	1946–1960	555	28	13654	157	25·90	12	9
Place, W.	1937–1955	487	49	15609	266*	35·63	36	8
Ponsford, W. H.	1920–1934	235	23	13819	437	65·18	47	2+2
Poole, C. J.	1948–1960	551	40	16936	222*	33·14	23	11
Prentice, F. T.	1934–1951	421	24	10997	191	27·70	17	5
Quaife, W. G.	1894–1928	1203	186	36021	255*	35·41	72	24
Ranjitsinhji, K. S.	1893–1920	500	62	24692	285*	56·37	72	11+1
Read, J. M.	1880–1895	599	41	13570	186*	24·31	10	2
Read, W. W.	1873–1897	738	50	21568	338	31·62	37	9
Reid, J. R.	1947–1959	277	23	10317	283	40·61	24	2+2
Relf, A. E.	1900–1921	900	69	22176	189*	26·68	26	11
Relf, R. R.	1905–1933	527	18	14441	272*	28·37	24	6
Revill, A. C.	1946–1960	654	53	15917	156*	26·48	16	9
Rhodes, W.	1898–1930	1528	237	39802	267*	30·83	58	20+1
Richardson, P. E.	1949–1960	490	29	15635	185	33·91	24	7
Richardson, V. Y.	1918–1937	297	12	10714	231	37·59	27	—
Robertson, J. D.	1937–1959	897	46	31914	331*	37·50	67	14+1
Robins, R. W. V.	1925–1958	566	39	13940	140	26·45	11	4
Robson, E.	1895–1923	761	46	12620	163*	17·65	5	1
Rogers, N. H.	1946–1955	529	28	16056	186	32·04	28	9
Rowan, E. A. B.	1929–1953	258	17	11710	306*	48·58	30	2
Russell, A. C.	1908–1930	719	59	27546	273	41·73	71	13
Ryder, J.	1912–1935	274	37	10494	295	44·28	24	0+1
Sandham, A.	1911–1937	1000	79	41283	325	44·82	107	18+2
Santall, F. R.	1919–1939	797	86	17730	201*	24·93	21	7
Seymour, James	1900–1926	911	62	27238	218*	32·08	53	16
Sharp, J.	1899–1925	805	75	22715	211	31·11	38	10
Shepherd, T. F.	1919–1932	531	61	18715	277*	39·81	42	12
Sheppard, D. S.	1947–1960	341	28	13747	239*	43·92	41	5
Shipman, A.	1920–1936	661	72	13682	226	23·22	15	8
Shrewsbury, A.	1875–1902	801	88	26306	267	36·89	59	13
Simpson, R. T.	1944–1960	795	48	28647	259	38·34	61	13+1
Sinfield, R. A.	1921–1939	696	86	15674	209*	25·69	16	10
Smith, D.	1927–1952	753	63	21843	225	31·65	32	12
Smith, D. V.	1946–1960	534	41	14590	206*	29·59	16	7
Smith, E. J.	1904–1930	814	55	16997	177	22·42	20	6
Smith, H.	1912–1935	656	56	13413	149	22·35	10	5
Smith, M. J. K.	1951–1960	400	36	15144	201*	41·60	28	7
Smith, R.	1934–1956	682	88	12042	147	20·27	8	4
Smith, S. G.	1899–1925	379	30	10918	256	31·28	14	4
Smith, T. P. B.	1929–1952	692	126	10170	163	17·98	8	1
Spooner, R. H.	1899–1923	393	16	13681	247	36·28	31	6
Spooner, R. T.	1948–1959	580	72	13874	168*	27·31	12	6
Sprot, E. M.	1898–1914	458	28	12328	147	28·66	13	4
Squires, H. S.	1928–1949	658	44	19186	236	31·24	37	11
Staples, A.	1924–1938	512	60	12762	153*	28·23	12	7
Stephenson, H. W.	1948–1960	602	70	10844	114	20·38	5	5
Stevens, G. T. S.	1919–1933	381	36	10288	182	29·82	12	2

	Career	Inns.	N.O.	Runs	H.S.	Avge.	100s	1000s
Stewart, M. J.	1954–1960	343	29	10327	169*	32·69	22	6
Stocks, F. W.	1946–1957	430	45	11397	171	29·60	13	5
Stoddart, A. E.	1885–1900	537	16	16738	221	32·12	26	6
Stone, J.	1900–1923	526	63	10362	174	22·38	6	3
Storer, H.	1920–1936	517	29	13515	232	27·69	18	6
Storer, W.	1887–1905	490	41	12966	216*	28·87	17	7
Subba Row, R.	1951–1960	350	60	12299	300	42·41	27	5
Sugg, F. H.	1883–1899	510	29	11653	220	24·22	15	5
Sutcliffe, B.	1941–1959	314	25	14508	385	50·20	40	2+2
Sutcliffe, H.	1919–1945	1087	123	50135	313	52·00	149	21+3
Suttle, K. G.	1949–1960	499	53	13630	186	30·56	21	8
Tarrant, F. A.	1898–1936	535	46	17629	250	36·04	32	9
Tate, M. W.	1912–1937	969	102	21698	203	25·02	23	11+1
Taylor, H. W.	1909–1935	340	27	13105	250*	41·87	30	3
Tennyson, Lord	1913–1937	759	38	16828	217	23·33	19	7
Thompson, G. J.	1897–1922	606	59	12018	131*	21·97	9	3
Timms, J. E.	1925–1949	847	30	20457	213	25·03	31	11
Todd, L. J.	1927–1950	727	94	20087	174	31·73	38	10
Tompkin, M.	1938–1956	655	29	19927	186	31·83	31	10
Townsend, A.	1948–1960	553	70	12054	154	24·95	6	5
Townsend, L. F.	1922–1939	786	76	19555	233	27·54	22	9
Tremlett, M. F.	1947–1960	681	49	16038	185	25·37	16	10
Tribe, G.	1945–1959	454	82	10177	136*	27·35	7	7
Trott, A. E.	1892–1911	601	52	10696	164	19·48	8	2
Trumper, V. T.	1894–1913	401	21	16939	300*	44·57	42	4+1
Tunnicliffe, J.	1891–1907	806	59	20268	243	27·13	23	12
Turnbull, M. J.	1924–1939	626	37	17543	233	29·78	29	10
Tyldesley, E.	1909–1936	961	106	38874	256*	45·46	102	18+1
Tyldesley, J. T.	1895–1923	994	62	37897	295*	40·66	86	19
Ulyett, G.	1873–1893	912	39	20484	199*	23·46	18	9
Umrigar, P. R.	1944–1959	271	33	12322	252*	51·77	36	2+1
Valentine, B. H.	1927–1950	645	38	18306	242	30·15	35	9
Vine, J.	1896–1922	920	79	25171	202	29·94	34	14
Wainwright, E.	1888–1902	603	31	12485	228	21·82	19	3
Walcott, C. L.	1941–1959	222	27	11289	314*	57·89	38	2+2
Walker, I. D.	1862–1884	491	39	11098	179	24·55	7	—
Walker, W.	1913–1937	624	60	18259	165*	32·37	31	10
Walters, C. F.	1923–1935	427	32	12145	226	30·74	21	5
Ward, A.	1886–1904	642	51	17783	219	30·08	29	9
Warner, P. F.	1894–1929	875	75	29028	244	36·28	60	14
Washbrook, C.	1933–1959	902	107	33944	251*	42·69	76	17+3
Watkins, A. J.	1939–1960	738	86	20035	170*	30·72	32	13
Watson, F.	1920–1937	688	50	23596	300*	36·98	50	12
Watson, W.	1939–1960	656	100	22293	257	40·09	46	12
Webbe, A. J.	1875–1900	634	58	14236	243*	24·71	14	1
Weekes, E. D.	1944–1959	206	21	11034	304*	59·64	35	2+1
Wellard, A. W.	1927–1950	679	45	12515	112	19·73	2	4
Wensley, A. F.	1922–1939	590	64	10735	154	20·40	9	3
Wharton, A.	1946–1960	606	56	18248	199	33·17	25	9
White, J. C.	1909–1937	765	102	12202	192	18·40	6	2
Whitehead, H.	1898–1922	680	25	15112	174	23·07	14	4
Whysall, W. W.	1910–1930	601	44	21592	248	38·74	51	10
Wight, P. B.	1950–1960	371	26	11640	222*	33·73	19	7
Wilson, A. E.	1932–1955	502	77	10744	188	25·28	7	6
Wilson, J. V.	1946–1960	661	68	19366	230	32·65	28	12
Wilson, R. C.	1952–1960	352	20	10113	159	30·46	14	7
Wolton, A. V.	1947–1960	478	61	12907	165	30·95	12	7
Wood, C. J. B.	1896–1923	823	54	23879	255	31·05	37	13
Woodfull, W. M.	1921–1934	245	39	13392	284	65·00	49	3
Woods, S. M. J.	1886–1910	690	35	15352	215	23·43	19	4
Wooller, W.	1935–1960	677	77	13586	128	22·64	5	5
Woolley, C. N.	1909–1931	658	34	15395	204*	24·67	13	7
Woolley, F. E.	1906–1938	1532	85	58969	305*	40·75	145	28
Worrell, F. M.	1941–1959	258	39	12972	308*	59·23	39	2+2
Worthington, T. S.	1924–1947	720	59	19221	238*	29·07	31	10
Wrathall, H.	1894–1907	509	20	11023	176	22·54	9	4
Wright, L. G.	1883–1909	593	12	15166	195	26·10	20	6
Wyatt, R. E. S.	1923–1957	1141	157	39404	232	40·04	85	17+1
Yardley, N. W. D.	1935–1955	658	75	18173	183*	31·17	27	8
Young, A.	1911–1933	537	22	13159	198	25·55	11	5
Young, D. M.	1946–1960	647	39	19090	194	31·39	34	10

*N

Most Centuries Scored in a Career

The number of centuries scored by all the leading batsmen is included in the total of runs section, so only those batsmen who have scored 50 or more are included in this list.

	Career	100s	First	Date of 100th	Last	Inns. for 100 cents.
J. B. Hobbs	1905–1934	197	1905	1923	1934	821
E. Hendren	1907–1938	170	1911	1928	1937	740
W. R. Hammond	1920–1951	167	1923	1935	1947	679
C. P. Mead	1905–1936	153	1906	1927	1936	892
H. Sutcliffe	1919–1945	149	1919	1932	1939	700
F. E. Woolley	1906–1938	145	1906	1929	1938	1031
L. Hutton	1934–1960	129	1934	1951	1955	619
W. G. Grace †	1865–1908	126	1866	1895	1904	1113
W. G. Grace 'corrected'	1865–1908	124	1866	1895	1904	1093
D. C. S. Compton	1936–1959	122	1936	1952	1957	552
D. G. Bradman	1927–1948	117	1927	1947	1948	295
A. Sandham	1911–1937	107	1913	1935	1937	871
T. Hayward	1893–1914	104	1893	1913	1914	1076
L. E. G. Ames	1926–1951	102	1926	1950	1951	915
E. Tyldesley	1909–1936	102	1912	1934	1935	919

The following batsmen scored 50 or more centuries in their career. (The centuries scored by all leading batsmen can be referred to in the Career Averages Section.)

J. W. Hearne (1909–1936) 96
C. B. Fry (1892–1921) 94
W. J. Edrich (1934–1958) 86
J. T. Tyldesley (1895–1923) 86
R. E. S. Wyatt (1923–1957) 85
J. Hardstaff jun. (1930–1955) 83
M. Leyland (1920–1948) 80
P. B. H. May (1948–1959) 80
T. W. Graveney (1948–1960) 77
John Langridge (1928–1955) 76
C. Washbrook (1933–1959) 76
H. T. W. Hardinge (1902–1933) 75
R. Abel (1881–1904) 74
J. O'Connor (1921–1939) 72
W. G. Quaife (1894–1928) 72
K. S. Ranjitsinhji (1893–1920) 72
D. Brookes (1934–1959) 71
A. C. Russell (1908–1930) 71
D. Denton (1894–1920) 69
P. Holmes (1913–1935) 67
J. D. Robertson (1937–1959) 67
P. A. Perrin (1896–1928) 66
D. Kenyon (1946–1960) 63
G. Gunn (1902–1932) 62
R. T. Simpson (1944–1960) 61

G. H. Hirst (1891–1929) 60
P. F. Warner (1894–1929) 60
A. L. Hassett (1932–1953) 59
A. Shrewsbury (1875–1902) 59
A. E. Fagg (1932–1957) 58
W. Rhodes (1898–1930) 58
V. S. Hazare (1934–1959) 57
L. B. Fishlock (1931–1952) 56
R. N. Harvey (1946–1959) 56
C. Hallows (1914–1932) 55
D. J. Insole (1947–1960) 54
W. W. Keeton (1926–(1952) 54
W. Bardsley (1903–1927) 53
A. E. Dipper (1908–1932) 53
G. L. Jessop (1894–1914) 53
James Seymour (1900–1926) 53
E. H. Bowley (1912–1934) 52
A. Ducat (1906–1931) 52
W. W. Whysall (1910–1930) 51
G. Cox (1931–1960) 50
H. E. Dollery (1933–1955) 50
K. S. Duleepsinhji (1924–1932) 50
H. Gimblett (1935–1954) 50
F. Watson (1920–1937) 50

1000 Runs in a Season 20 or more times

The number of times each batsman has passed the 1000 runs aggregate in a season is included in the career section, so only those with 20 or more cases are shown here.

The dates shown are both inclusive, i.e., 1869 to 1878 means that 1000 runs were scored in each of the seasons from 1869 to 1878.

28 W. G. Grace (Gloucestershire): 1869–1878, 1883–1890, 1892–1898, 1900–1902.
28 F. E. Woolley (Kent): 1907–1938.
27 C. P. Mead (Hampshire): 1906–1936.
24 W. G. Quaife (Warwickshire): 1896–1906, 1908–1914, 1920–1923, 1925–1926.
24 J. B. Hobbs (Surrey): 1905–1920, 1922–1933.
21 D. Denton (Yorkshire): 1895–1897, 1899–1920.
21 E. Hendren (Middlesex): 1911, 1913, 1919–1937.
21 H. Sutcliffe (Yorkshire): 1919–1939.

20 G. Gunn (Nottinghamshire): 1905, 1908–1911, 1913–1931.
20 T. Hayward (Surrey): 1895–1914.
20 James Langridge (Sussex): 1927–1939, 1946–1952.
20 W. Rhodes (Yorkshire): 1903–1926.

Bowling

The following bowlers have taken over 2000 wickets during a first-class cricket career:

	Career	Runs	Wkts.	Avge.	100 wkts.
W. Rhodes	1898–1930	69993	4187	16·71	23
A. P. Freeman	1914–1936	69577	3776	18·42	17
C. W. L. Parker	1903–1935	63821	3278	19·47	16
J. T. Hearne	1888–1923	54342	3061	17·75	15
T. W. Goddard	1922–1952	59116	2979	19·84	16
W. G. Grace †	1865–1908	51545	2876	17·99	10
A. S. Kennedy	1907–1936	61044	2874	21·24	15
M. W. Tate	1912–1937	50544	2783	18·16	13+1
W. G. Grace 'corrected'	1865–1908	50250	2763	18·18	7
G. H. Hirst	1891–1929	51300	2739	18·72	15
C. Blythe	1899–1914	42136	2506	16·81	14
W. E. Astill	1906–1939	57784	2431	23·76	9
J. C. White	1909–1937	43759	2356	18·57	14
W. E. Hollies	1932–1957	48656	2323	20·94	14
R. T. D. Perks	1930–1955	53770	2233	24·07	16
J. Briggs	1879–1900	35289	2212	15·95	12
G. Dennett	1903–1926	42568	2147	19·82	12
T. Richardson	1892–1905	38794	2105	18·42	10
F. E. Woolley	1906–1938	41066	2068	19·85	8
G. Geary	1912–1938	41339	2063	20·03	11
D. V. P. Wright	1932–1957	49305	2056	23·98	10
J. A. Newman	1906–1930	51211	2032	25·20	9
S. Haigh	1895–1913	32091	2012	15·94	11
A. Shaw	1864–1897	24179	2001	12·08	9

The following bowlers have recorded a career aggregate of over 1000 wickets:

Arnold, E. G.	1899–1913	24745	1069	23·14	4
Astill, W. E.	1906–1939	57784	2431	23·76	9
Attewell, W.	1881–1900	29745	1932	15·39	10
Bailey, T. E.	1945–1960	34987	1513	23·12	7
Barrett, F.	1914–1931	27803	1224	22·71	5
Bedser, A. V.	1939–1960	39281	1924	20·41	11
Bestwick, W.	1898–1925	31003	1458	21·33	4
Blythe, C.	1899–1914	42136	2506	16·81	14
Bowes, W. E.	1928–1947	27446	1638	16·75	9
Boyes, G. S.	1921–1939	34610	1472	23·51	3
Braund, L. C.	1896–1920	30388	1113	27·30	4
Briggs, J.	1879–1900	35289	2212	15·95	12
Brown, F. R.	1930–1959	31917	1219	26·18	3
Buckenham, C. P.	1899–1914	29157	1152	25·31	6
Clark, E. W.	1922–1947	25919	1203	21·54	2
Clay, J. C.	1921–1949	26003	1315	19·77	3
Cook, C.	1946–1960	32505	1587	20·48	9
Copson, W. H.	1932–1950	20752	1094	18·96	3
Cornford, J.	1931–1952	26999	1019	26·49	—
Cox, G. R.	1895–1928	42138	1843	22·86	5
Dean, H.	1906–1921	23606	1301	18·14	8
Dennett, G.	1903–1926	42568	2147	19·82	12
Dooland, B.	*1945–1957*	22332	1016	21·98	5
Douglas, J. W. H. T.	1901–1930	44176	1894	23·32	7
Durston, T. J.	1919–1933	23279	1329	22·03	6
Eastman, L. C.	1920–1939	26980	1006	26·81	—
Emmett, T.	1866–1888	21147	1582	13·36	4
Fender, P. G. H.	1910–1936	47457	1894	25·05	7
Field, F. E.	1897–1920	24094	1026	23·48	3
Fielder, A.	1900–1914	26852	1277	21·02	5
Flowers, W.	1877–1896	18687	1169	15·98	2
Freeman, A. P.	1914–1936	69577	3776	18·42	17
Geary, G.	1912–1938	41339	2063	20·03	11

	Career	Runs	Wkts.	Avge.	100 wkts.
Giffen, G.	1877–1903	21782	1022	21·31	3
Gladwin, C.	1939–1958	30265	1653	18·30	12
Goddard, T. W.	1922–1952	59116	2979	19·84	16
Gover, A. R.	1928–1948	36753	1555	23·63	8
Grace, W. G.†	1865–1908	51545	2876	17·99	10
Grace, W. G. 'corrected'.	1865–1908	50250	2763	18·18	7
Grimmett, C. V.	1911–1940	31740	1424	22·28	3
Grundy, J.	1850–1869	10355	1045	13·05	1
Gunn, J.	1896–1932	30659	1245	24·62	5
Haig, N. E.	1912–1936	30666	1116	27·47	5
Haigh, S.	1895–1913	32091	2012	15·94	11
Hallam, A. W.	1895–1910	19256	1012	19·02	3
Hearne, A.	1884–1910	22925	1144	20·03	—
Hearne, J. T.	1888–1923	54342	3061	17·75	15
Hearne, J. W.	1909–1936	44927	1839	24·43	5
Herman, O. W.	1929–1948	28222	1045	27·00	5
Hilton, M. J.	1946–1959	19402	1001	19·38	4
Hirst, G. H.	1891–1929	51300	2739	18·72	15
Hitch, J. W.	1907–1925	30041	1398	21·48	7
Hollies, W. E.	1932–1957	48656	2323	20·94	14
Howorth, R.	1933–1951	29427	1345	21·87	9
Jackson, L.	1947–1960	24855	1473	16·87	9
Jackson, P. F.	1929–1950	30521	1159	26·33	4
Jenkins, R. O.	1938–1958	30925	1309	23·62	5
Jepson, A.	1938–1959	30567	1051	29·08	1
Jupp, V. W. C.	1909–1938	38166	1658	23·01	10
Kennedy, A. S.	1907–1936	61044	2874	21·24	15
King, J. H.	1895–1925	30289	1204	25·15	2
Laker, J. C.	1946–1959	32767	1814	18·06	11
Langridge, James	1924–1953	34524	1530	22·56	6
Larwood, H.	1924–1938	24998	1427	17·51	8
Lees, W. S.	1896–1911	29998	1402	21·39	7
Lillywhite, James	1862–1881	17535	1140	15·38	1
Llewellyn, C. B.	1894–1912	23715	1013	23·41	3
Loader, P. J.	1951–1960	18574	1029	18·05	5
Lock, G. A. R.	1946–1960	31232	1857	16·81	10
Lockwood, W. H.	1886–1904	25245	1376	18·34	7
Lohmann, G. A.	1884–1897	25110	1805	13·91	8
Macaulay, G. G.	1920–1935	32440	1837	17·65	10
Martin, F.	1885–1900	22903	1317	17·38	6
Mayer, J. H.	1926–1939	25404	1144	22·20	2
McDonald, E. A.	1909–1935	28966	1395	20·76	7
Mead, W.	1892–1913	36387	1916	18·99	10
Mercer, J.	1919–1947	37302	1593	23·41	9
Mitchell, T. B.	1928–1939	30526	1483	20·58	10
Mold, A.	1889–1901	26012	1673	15·54	9
Morley, F.	1872–1883	16475	1231	13·38	7
Moss, A. E.	1950–1960	21280	1021	20·84	4
Newman, J. A.	1906–1930	51211	2032	25·20	9
Nichols, M. S.	1924–1939	39738	1834	21·66	11
Paine, G. A. E.	1926–1947	23334	1021	22·85	5
Parker, C. W. L.	1903–1935	63821	3278	19·47	16
Parkin, C. H.	1906–1926	18434	1048	17·58	4
Peate, E.	1879–1890	14511	1076	13·48	6
Peel, R.	1882–1899	28446	1754	16·21	8
Perks, R. T. D.	1930–1955	53770	2233	24·07	16
Pollard, R.	1933–1952	25314	1122	22·56	7
Relf, A. E.	1900–1921	39724	1897	20·94	11
Rhodes, W.	1898–1930	69993	4187	16·71	23
Richardson, T.	1892–1905	38794	2105	18·42	10
Richmond, T. L.	1912–1932	24959	1176	21·22	7
Ridgway, F.	1946–1960	25317	1067	23·72	1
Robinson, E. P.	1934–1952	22784	1009	22·58	5
Robson, E.	1895–1923	30334	1147	26·44	—
Root, C. F.	1910–1933	31933	1512	21·11	9
Ryan, F. B.	1919–1931	21314	1008	21·14	5
Santall, S.	1894–1914	29250	1219	23·99	1
Shackleton, D.	1948–1960	33169	1748	18·97	12
Shaw, A.	1864–1897	24179	2001	12·08	9
Shepherd, D. J.	1950–1960	22846	1048	21·79	5
Sims, J. M.	1929–1953	39401	1582	24·90	8

	Career	Runs	Wkts.	Avge.	100 wkts.
Sinfield, R. A.	1921–1939	28734	1173	24·49	4
Smith, H. A.	1925–1939	27968	1076	25·99	5
Smith, R.	1934–1956	41265	1350	30·56	7
Smith, T. P. B.	1929–1952	45193	1697	26·63	6
Smith, W. C.	1900–1914	18910	1077	17·55	3
Southerton, J.	1854–1879	23268	1626	14·30	10
Staples, S. J.	1920–1934	30421	1331	22·85	5
Statham, J. B.	1950–1960	21363	1376	15·52	7
Tarrant, F. A.	1898–1936	26104	1470	17·75	8
Tate, F. W.	1887–1905	28690	1331	21·55	5
Tate, M. W.	1912–1937	50544	2783	18·16	13+1
Tattersall, R.	1948–1960	24614	1363	18·05	8
Thompson, G. J.	1897–1922	30060	1591	18·89	8
Titmus, F. J.	1949–1960	21546	1025	21·02	7
Townsend, L. F.	1922–1939	22985	1088	21·12	4
Tribe, G.	1945–1959	28321	1378	20·55	8
Trott, A. E.	1892–1911	35316	1674	21·09	7
Trueman, F. S.	1949–1960	23578	1288	18·30	6
Tyldesley, R.	1919–1935	25980	1509	17·21	10
Verity, H.	1930–1939	29099	1956	14·87	9
Voce, W.	1927–1952	35961	1558	23·08	6
Wainwright, E.	1888–1902	19331	1062	18·20	5
Walsh, J. E.	1936–1956	29225	1190	24·55	7
Wardle, J. H.	1946–1958	34910	1842	18·95	10
Wass, T.	1896–1920	34091	1666	20·46	10
Watson, A.	1872–1893	18123	1351	13·41	1
Wellard, A. W.	1927–1950	39302	1614	24·35	8
Wensley, A. F.	1922–1939	29989	1135	26·42	5
White, J. C.	1909–1937	43759	2356	18·57	14
Willsher, E.	1850–1874	14921	1188	13·07	1
Woods, S. M. J.	1886–1910	21653	1040	20·82	2
Woolley, F. E.	1906–1938	41066	2068	19·85	8
Wright, D. V. P.	1932–1957	49305	2056	23·98	10
Young, J. A.	1933–1956	26795	1361	19·68	8

100 Wickets in a Season 12 or more times

The number of times each bowler has taken 100 wickets in an English season is included in the career section, so only those with 12 or more cases are shown here.

23 W. Rhodes (Yorkshire): 1898–1909, 1911, 1914–1924, 1926, 1928–1929.
17 A. P. Freeman (Kent): 1920–1936.
16 C. W. L. Parker (Gloucestershire): 1920–1935.
16 T. W. Goddard (Gloucestershire): 1929–1939, 1946–1950.
16 R. T. D. Perks (Worcestershire): 1934–1939, 1946–1955.
15 J. T. Hearne (Middlesex): 1891–1895, 1897, 1899–1900, 1902–1904, 1906, 1908, 1910–1911.
15 G. H. Hirst (Yorkshire): 1895–1897, 1901, 1903–1913.
15 A. S. Kennedy (Hampshire): 1912, 1914–1925, 1927–1932.
14 C. Blythe (Kent): 1900, 1902–1914.
14 W. E. Hollies (Warwickshire): 1935, 1937–1939, 1946–1952, 1954–1955, 1957.
14 J. C. White (Somerset): 1919–1932.
13 M. W. Tate (Sussex): 1922–1932, 1934–1935 (also in India in 1926–27).
12 J. Briggs (Lancashire): 1887–1897, 1900.
12 G. Dennett (Gloucestershire): 1904–1914, 1921.
12 C. Gladwin (Derbyshire): 1946–1949, 1951–1958.
12 D. Shackleton (Hampshire): 1949–1960.

All-Round Cricket

The following cricketers have scored 10,000 runs and taken over 1000 wickets during their career.

	Career	Runs	Avge.	100s		Wkts.	Avge.	'Doubles'
Arnold, E. G.	1899–1913	15853	29·91	24	...	1069	23·14	... 4
Astill, W. E.	1906–1939	22726	22·54	15	...	2431	23·76	... 9
Bailey, T. E.	1945–1960	21025	34·80	25	...	1513	23·12	... 6
Braund, L. C.	1896–1920	17801	25·61	25	...	1113	27·30	... 3

	Career	Runs	Avge.	100s		Wkts.	Avge.	'Doubles'
Briggs, J.	1879–1900	14002	18·25	10	...	2212	15·95	... —
Brown, F. R.	1930–1959	13275	27·42	22	...	1219	26·18	... 2
Cox, G. R.	1895–1928	14643	18·74	2	...	1843	22·86	... —
Douglas, J. W. H. T.	1901–1930	24530	27·90	26	...	1894	23·32	... 5
Eastman, L. C.	1920–1939	13438	20·80	7	...	1006	26·80	... —
Fender, P. G. H.	1910–1936	19034	26·65	21	...	1894	25·05	... 6
Flowers, W.	1877–1896	12691	20·34	9	...	1169	15·98	... 1
Geary, G.	1912–1938	13498	19·82	8	...	2063	20·03	... —
Giffen, G.	1877–1903	11757	29·61	18	...	1022	21·31	... 3
Grace, W. G.†	1865–1908	54896	39·55	126	...	2876	17·99	... 8
Grace, W. G. 'corrected'	1865–1908	53856	39·45	124	...	2763	18·18	... 7
Gunn, J.	1896–1932	24740	33·34	41	...	1245	24·62	... 4
Haig, N. E.	1912–1936	15208	20·83	12	...	1116	27·47	... 3
Haigh, S.	1895–1913	11715	18·65	4	...	2012	15·94	... 1
Hearne, A.	1884–1910	16287	21·74	15	...	1144	20·03	... —
Hearne, J. W.	1909–1936	37252	40·98	96	...	1839	24·43	... 5
Hirst, G. H.	1891–1929	36323	34·13	60	...	2739	18·72	... 14
Howorth, R.	1933–1951	11479	20·68	4	...	1345	21·87	... 3
Jenkins, R. O.	1938–1958	10073	22·23	1	...	1309	23·62	... 2
Jupp, V. W. C.	1909–1938	23278	29·39	30	...	1658	23·01	... 10
Kennedy, A. S.	1907–1936	16586	18·53	10	...	2874	21·24	... 5
King, J. H.	1895–1925	25121	27·33	34	...	1204	25·15	... 1
Langridge, James	1924–1953	31716	35·20	42	...	1530	22·56	... 6
Llewellyn, C. B.	1894–1912	11425	26·75	18	...	1013	23·41	... 3
Lockwood, W. H.	1886–1904	10673	21·91	15	...	1376	18·34	... 2
Newman, J. A.	1906–1930	15333	21·65	10	...	2032	25·20	... 5
Nichols, M. S.	1924–1939	17843	26·51	20	...	1834	21·66	... 8
Peel, R.	1882–1899	12135	19·46	7	...	1754	16·21	... 1
Relf, A. E.	1900–1921	22176	26·68	26	...	1897	20·94	... 8
Rhodes, W.	1898–1930	39802	30·83	58	...	4187	16·71	... 16
Robson, E.	1895–1923	12620	17·65	5	...	1147	26·44	... —
Sinfield, R. A.	1921–1939	15674	25·69	16	...	1173	24·49	... 2
Smith, R.	1934–1956	12042	20·27	8	...	1350	30·56	... 3
Smith, T. P. B.	1929–1952	10170	17·98	8	...	1697	26·63	... 1
Tarrant, F. A.	1898–1936	17629	36·04	32	...	1470	17·75	... 8
Tate, M. W.	1912–1937	21698	25·02	23	...	2783	18·16	... 8
Thompson, G. J.	1897–1922	12018	21·97	9	...	1591	18·89	... 2
Townsend, L. F.	1922–1939	19555	27·54	22	...	1088	21·12	... 3
Tribe, G.	1945–1959	10177	27·35	7	...	1378	20·55	... 7
Trott, A. E.	1892–1911	10696	19·48	8	...	1674	21·09	... 2
Wainwright, E.	1888–1902	12485	21·82	19	...	1062	18·20	... 1
Wellard, A. W.	1927–1950	12515	19·73	2	...	1614	24·35	... 3
Wensley, A. F.	1922–1939	10735	20·40	9	...	1135	26·42	... 1
White, J. C.	1909–1937	12202	18·40	6	...	2356	18·57	... 2
Woods, S. M. J.	1886–1910	15352	23·43	19	...	1040	20·82	... —
Woolley, F. E.	1906–1938	58969	40·75	145	...	2068	19·85	... 8

Fielding and Wicket-Keeping

The number of victims that fieldsmen and wicket-keepers collect in a first-class career is not really a guide to their proficiency, as certain types of bowling assist in a higher percentage of catches, and fielders near the wicket have more opportunities for catches than those in the outfield.

For mainly interest purposes, therefore, the leaders are as follows:

Fielders	Career	Catches
F. E. Woolley (Kent)	1906–1938	913
W. G. Grace (Gloucestershire)	1865–1908	871
W. R. Hammond (Gloucestershire)	1920–1951	819
John Langridge (Sussex)	1928–1955	786
E. Hendren (Middlesex)	1907–1938	722
W. Rhodes (Yorkshire)	1898–1930	708
J. Tunnicliffe (Yorkshire)	1891–1907	691
C. P. Mead (Hampshire)	1905–1936	668
James Seymour (Kent)	1900–1926	622
A. O. Jones (Nottinghamshire)	1892–1914	575
P. G. H. Fender (Sussex & Surrey)	1910–1936	558

Fielders	Career	Catches
G. H. Hirst (Yorkshire)	1891–1929	550
G. A. R. Lock (Surrey)	1946–1960	542
E. G. Hayes (Surrey & Leicestershire)	1896–1926	533
A. S. Kennedy (Hampshire)	1907–1936	523
W. J. Edrich (Middlesex)	1934–1958	522
K. Grieves (New South Wales & Lancashire)	1945–1960	518
G. R. Cox (Sussex)	1895–1928	510
L. C. Braund (Surrey & Somerset)	1896–1920	508

Wicket-keepers	Career	Total	Ct.	St.
H. Strudwick (Surrey)	1902–1927	1468	1215	253
F. H. Huish (Kent)	1895–1914	1328	952	376
D. Hunter (Yorkshire)	1889–1909	1327	995	372
H. R. Butt (Sussex)	1890–1912	1262	971	291
H. Elliott (Derbyshire)	1920–1947	1195	895	300
J. H. Board (Gloucestershire)	1891–1914	1132	797	335
L. E. G. Ames (Kent)	1926–1951	1113	698	415
G. Duckworth (Lancashire)	1923–1947	1090	751	339
T. G. Evans (Kent)	1939–1960	1038	799	239
T. W. Oates (Nottinghamshire)	1897–1925	1005	766	239
G. Dawkes (Leicestershire & Derbyshire)	1937–1960	1002	857	145
W. F. Cornford (Sussex)	1921–1947	1000	656	344
W. F. Price (Middlesex)	1926–1947	964	648	316
A. A. Lilley (Warwickshire)	1891–1911	883	679	204
A. Wood (Yorkshire)	1928–1947	848	603	245
H. W. Stephenson (Somerset)	1948–1960	843	537	306
W. T. Luckes (Somerset)	1924–1949	820	586	234
E. W. Brookes (Surrey)	1925–1939	819	724	95
E. J. Smith (Warwickshire)	1904–1930	819	676	143
M. Sherwin (Nottinghamshire)	1876–1896	800	579	221
A. J. McIntyre (Surrey)	1938–1960	791	634	157
H. G. Davies (Glamorgan)	1935–1958	788	584	204
B. Lilley (Nottinghamshire)	1921–1937	777	645	132
R. T. Spooner (Warwickshire)	1948–1959	768	589	179

Career Records for Overseas Players

Owing to the shortened fixture lists in overseas countries, it is difficult for an overseas batsman to complete 10,000 runs in first-class cricket and, with one or two exceptions, virtually impossible to reach 1,000 wickets. Where such players have done so, their complete career figures are included in the foregoing sections, but the following tables are of interest. The standard for inclusion is a large aggregate of either runs or wickets, and the tables are given in descending order of runs and wickets.

Overseas players whose career was mainly for English counties are omitted in the tables, unless sufficient cricket in their native land was played to justify their 'overseas players' qualification.

BATTING

AUSTRALIA

	Career	Inns.	N.O.	Runs	H.S.	Avge.	100s	1000s
D. G. Bradman	1927–1948	338	43	28067	452*	95·14	117	4+12
R. N. Harvey	1946–1959	373	31	17866	225	52·23	56	2+4
C. Hill	1892–1925	417	21	17216	365*	43·47	45	3+2
W. L. Murdoch	1876–1904	684	48	17070	321	26·83	20	3
W. Bardsley	1903–1927	376	35	17031	264	49·94	53	4+1
V. T. Trumper	1894–1914	401	21	16939	300*	44·57	42	4+1
A. L. Hassett	1932–1953	322	32	16890	232	58·24	59	3+2
W. W. Armstrong	1898–1921	407	61	16177	303*	46·75	45	4+2
S. E. Gregory	1889–1912	592	55	15303	201	28·49	25	4
C. G. Macartney	1905–1935	360	32	15050	345	45·88	49	3
K. R. Miller	1937–1959	326	36	14183	281*	48·90	41	2+2
M. A. Noble	1893–1919	378	34	14034	284	40·80	37	4+1
W. A. Brown	1932–1949	284	15	13840	265*	51·44	39	3+2
W. H. Ponsford	1920–1934	235	23	13819	437	65·18	47	2+2
W. M. Woodfull	1921–1934	245	39	13392	284	65·00	49	3

	Career	Inns.	N.O.	Runs	H.S.	Avge.	100s	1000s
A. F. Kippax	1918–1935	254	33	12747	315*	57·69	43	1+2
A. R. Morris	1940–1954	242	15	12489	290	55·01	46	2+4
C. L. McCool	1939–1960	413	36	12420	172	32·94	18	5
S. J. McCabe	1928–1941	262	20	11951	240	49·39	29	3
G. Giffen	1877–1903	421	24	11757	271	28·61	18	4
J. Darling	1893–1908	334	25	10637	210	34·42	21	4
J. Ryder	1912–1935	274	37	10494	295	44·28	24	0+1
H. L. Collins	1909–1926	256	10	9921	282	40·33	32	1
C. C. McDonald	1947–1959	252	18	9526	229	40·70	19	1

SOUTH AFRICA

	Career	Inns.	N.O.	Runs	H.S.	Avge.	100s	1000s
A. D. Nourse sen.	1896–1935	371	39	14216	304*	42·82	38	3+1
H. W. Taylor	1909–1935	340	27	13105	250*	41·87	30	3
A. D. Nourse jun.	1931–1952	269	27	12472	260*	51·53	41	2
E. A. B. Rowan	1929–1953	258	17	11710	306*	48·58	30	2
C. B. Llewellyn	1894–1912	461	34	11425	216	26·75	18	6
B. Mitchell	1925–1949	281	30	11395	195	45·39	30	3+1
A. Melville	1928–1948	295	15	10598	189	37·85	25	3
D. J. McGlew	1947–1960	237	27	9924	255*	47·23	22	3+1
R. A. McLean	1949–1960	256	17	8373	207	35·03	16	2
K. G. Viljoen	1926–1948	209	25	7964	215	43·28	23	2
J. H. B. Waite	1948–1960	244	26	7909	219	36·27	19	1
I. J. Siedle	1922–1936	204	11	7730	265*	40·05	17	2
W. R. Endean	1945–1959	214	23	7282	247	38·12	13	1+1
T. L. Goddard	1952–1960	174	11	6153	200	37·74	15	2

WEST INDIANS

	Career	Inns.	N.O.	Runs	H.S.	Avge.	100s	1000s
F. M. Worrell	1941–1959	258	39	12972	308*	59·23	39	2+2
C. L. Walcott	1941–1959	222	27	11289	314*	57·89	38	2+2
E. D. Weekes	1944–1959	206	21	11034	304*	59·64	35	2+1
S. G. Smith	1899–1925	379	30	10918	256	31·28	14	4
G. Headley	1927–1954	164	22	9921	344*	69·86	33	2+1
J. B. Stollmeyer	1938–1956	194	16	7942	324	44·61	14	1+1
G. E. Gomez	1937–1957	182	27	6764	216*	43·63	14	1
G. Sobers	1952–1959	127	22	6261	365*	59·62	17	1+2
G. Challenor	1905–1929	160	9	5822	237*	38·55	15	2
R. J. Christiani	1938–1953	142	16	5103	181	40·50	12	1
C. A. Roach	1925–1934	177	4	4851	209	28·04	4	2
A. F. Rae	1946–1959	128	7	4798	179	39·65	17	1+1
L. N. Constantine	1921–1945	194	11	4451	133	24·32	5	1
J. K. Holt jun.	1946–1959	114	12	4253	172	41·69	9	0+1
O. G. Smith	1954–1958	112	12	4031	169	40·31	10	1

NEW ZEALAND

	Career	Inns.	N.O.	Runs	H.S.	Avge.	100s	1000s
B. Sutcliffe	1941–1959	314	25	14508	385	50·20	40	2+2
C. C. Dacre	1914–1936	437	20	12166	223	29·17	24	7
C. S. Dempster	1921–1947	305	36	12098	212	44·97	35	5
J. R. Reid	1947–1959	277	23	10320	283	40·63	24	2+2
T. C. Lowry	1917–1937	322	20	9421	181	31·19	18	3
M. P. Donnelly	1936–1950	219	26	9210	208*	47·72	23	5
R. C. Blunt	1917–1931	204	14	7769	338*	40·88	14	2
W. M. Wallace	1933–1957	188	16	7536	211	43·81	16	2
W. A. Hadlee	1933–1951	202	17	7421	198	40·11	17	2
M. L. Page	1921–1942	213	17	5857	206	29·88	9	1
V. J. Scott	1937–1952	128	16	5575	204	49·77	16	1
J. W. E. Mills	1925–1937	161	8	5025	185	32·84	11	2
G. L. Weir	1928–1946	172	16	5022	191	32·19	10	1

INDIA

	Career	Inns.	N.O.	Runs	H.S.	Avge.	100s	1000s
V. S. Hazare	1934–1959	347	42	17659	316*	57·90	57	2+5
V. M. Merchant	1929–1951	221	44	12876	359*	72·74	43	2+1
P. R. Umrigar	1944–1959	271	33	12322	252*	51·77	36	2+1
Mushtaq Ali	1932–1959	357	18	12397	233	36·56	30	1
C. K. Nayudu	1916–1958	303	14	10148	200	35·11	21	2

PAKISTAN

	Career	Inns.	N.O.	Runs	H.S.	Avge.	100s	1000s
Hanif Mohammed	1951–1959	157	21	7975	499	58·62	26	1
Imtiaz Ahmed	1944–1959	188	20	6461	300*	38·45	15	1

BOWLING

AUSTRALIA

	Career	Runs	Wkts.	Avge.	100s
C. V. Grimmett	1911–1940	31740	1424	22·19	3
E. A. McDonald	1909–1935	28966	1395	20·76	7
G. Giffen	1877–1903	21782	1022	21·31	3
C. T. B. Turner	1882–1909	14154	992	14·27	3+1
H. Trumble	1887–1903	17134	929	18·44	4
F. R. Spofforth	1874–1897	12646	840	15·05	2
W. W. Armstrong	1898–1921	16367	828	19·77	3
J. J. Ferris	1886–1897	14249	813	17·52	2
R. R. Lindwall	1941–1959	16656	789	21·11	—
A. A. Mailey	1912–1930	18775	779	24·10	2
W. J. O'Reilly	1927–1945	12850	774	16·60	2
R. Benaud	1948–1959	15741	653	22·57	0+1
E. Jones	1892–1907	14676	645	22·75	2
M. A. Noble	1893–1919	14492	628	23·08	—
I. W. Johnson	1935–1956	14419	619	23·29	—
G. E. Palmer	1878–1896	10686	614	17·40	3
C. L. McCool	1939–1960	16543	602	27·47	—
L. O'B. Fleetwood-Smith	1931–1939	13519	597	22·64	1
W. A. Johnston	1945–1954	12934	554	23·34	1
J. V. Saunders	1899–1913	12072	553	21·83	1
W. P. Howell	1894–1905	11171	521	21·44	1
J. M. Gregory	1919–1928	10579	504	20·99	2
K. R. Miller	1937–1959	11080	497	22·29	—
W. J. Whitty	1907–1925	11488	491	23·40	1
A. K. Davidson	1949–1959	10068	473	21·28	—
H. Ironmonger	1909–1935	9992	464	21·53	—
D. T. Ring	1938–1953	12855	451	28·50	—
T. W. Garrett	1876–1896	8366	445	18·80	2
A. Cotter	1901–1913	10739	441	24·35	1
C. G. Macartney	1905–1935	8781	419	20·96	—
F. Laver	1891–1913	9987	404	24·72	1

SOUTH AFRICA

	Career	Runs	Wkts.	Avge.	100s
C. B. Llewellyn	1894–1912	23715	1013	23·41	3
H. J. Tayfield	1945–1960	17335	806	21·50	2
J. H. Sinclair	1892–1911	10527	491	21·43	—
G. A. Faulkner	1902–1924	7825	449	17·42	1
S. J. Pegler	1908–1930	8324	425	19·58	2
A. E. E. Vogler	1903–1912	7275	401	18·14	1
R. O. Schwarz	1901–1914	7000	398	17·58	1
J. E. Waddington	1934–1958	9155	375	24·41	—
C. P. Carter	1897–1924	6849	366	18·71	—
V. I. Smith	1945–1959	8244	365	21·58	—
J. J. Kotze	1901–1910	6217	348	17·86	1
E. P. Nupen	1920–1936	6077	334	18·19	—
N. A. T. Adcock	1952–1960	5926	334	17·74	1
T. L. Goddard	1952–1960	6814	316	21·56	—
A. D. Nourse sen.	1896–1935	7125	305	23·36	—
P. N. F. Mansell	1936–1959	7724	295	26·18	—
J. M. Blanckenberg	1912–1924	6230	293	21·26	1
C. L. Vincent	1920–1942	7006	293	23·91	—
X. C. Balaskas	1926–1946	6656	276	24·11	—
R. J. Crisp	1929–1938	5487	276	19·88	1
A. M. B. Rowan	1939–1951	6408	273	23·47	1
N. B. F. Mann	1939–1951	5952	251	23·71	—
B. Mitchell	1925–1949	6382	249	25·63	—
P. S. Heine	1951–1958	5388	249	21·63	—
A. E. Hall	1920–1930	4501	234	19·23	—
A. J. Bell	1925–1938	5312	228	23·29	—
A. H. McKinnon	1952–1960	4414	227	19·44	—
L. Tuckett	1934–1954	5191	225	23·07	—
C. B. Van Ryneveld	1946–1958	6200	206	30·09	—

WEST INDIES

	Career	Runs	Wkts.	Avge.	100s
S. G. Smith	1898–1925	17277	955	18·09	4
K. T. Ramadhin	1949–1959	11500	608	18·91	2
L. N. Constantine	1921–1945	8738	424	20·60	2
A. L. Valentine	1949–1959	9187	376	24·43	1
C. B. Clarke	1937–1960	8694	331	26·26	—
C. R. Browne	1919–1936	6557	290	22·61	—
F. M. Worrell	1941–1959	8153	288	28·30	—
H. C. Griffith	1922–1934	7092	254	27·92	—

NEW ZEALAND

	Career	Runs	Wkts.	Avge.	100s
W. E. Merritt	1926–1947	13669	536	25·50	1
T. B. Burtt	1943–1954	9054	408	22·19	1
R. W. Blair	1951–1959	7183	370	19·41	—
H. B. Cave	1945–1958	8664	362	23·93	—
J. A. Cowie	1932–1949	7972	359	22·20	1
A. R. MacGibbon	1947–1959	8591	324	26·51	—
A. M. Moir	1949–1959	7909	318	24·87	—
A. D. Downes	1888–1913	4564	311	14·67	—
J. R. Reid	1947–1959	6787	306	22·17	—
J. A. Hayes	1946–1958	6698	289	23·17	—
E. F. Upham	1892–1909	4414	265	16·27	—

Part VIII—Competition Records, etc.

The County Championship

The first rules of qualification for playing for the counties were laid down in the winter of 1872–73, and it is from 1873 that the County Championship is always considered to date, although a kind of Championship had been decided before that date. In 1873 nine counties—Derbyshire, Gloucestershire, Kent, Lancashire, Middlesex, Nottinghamshire, Surrey, Sussex and Yorkshire—competed for the honour and until 1887 the composition of the first-class counties remained unchanged. In 1888 Derbyshire fell out and joined the second-class counties, but the form of several of them was such that in 1891 Somerset were promoted to first-class status. In 1894 a further expansion took place, Derbyshire re-entering the competition and Essex, Hampshire, Leicestershire and Warwickshire being promoted. These five counties were all given first-class status in 1894 (Hampshire after the season ended), but they did not compete in the Championship for the first time until 1895, mainly due to the fact that the fixtures for the 1894 season had already been decided. The fifteenth county (Worcestershire) was added in 1899, the sixteenth (Northamptonshire) in 1905 and the 'youngest' (Glamorgan) in 1921.

METHODS OF DECIDING THE CHAMPIONSHIP

Numerous changes have been made to the method of deciding the Championship. In most years a minimum number of matches has been fixed for inclusion in the Championship, but all inter-county matches have been counted except in the seasons stated.

1873 to 1886—The smallest number of lost matches decided the order of merit.

1887 to 1889—A win counted one point, drawn matches half a point. County with most points adjudged Champions for the season.

1890 to 1894—Losses were deducted from wins, drawn games being ignored. The county with the highest number of points adjudged Champions.

1895 to 1909—One point for each win, one point deducted for each loss, unfinished games ignored. Championship decided by the greatest proportionate number of points in finished games.

1910—Result determined by percentage of wins to matches played.

1911 to 1914—The order decided by the greatest proportionate number of points obtained to points possible: 5 points to the county winning the match; 3 points to the county leading on first innings; 1 point to the county behind on first innings.

1919—In this season, when each match was restricted to two days of longer playing hours than hitherto, the order was decided by the greatest percentage of wins to matches played.

1920 to 1923—Order decided by percentage of points obtained to maximum points possible. Games in which 'no result' was obtained on the first innings were ignored: 5 points to the county winning the match; 2 points to the county winning on first innings in a drawn match.

1924 to 1926—The method for 1920 to 1923 was followed, except for changes in the points, as follows: 5 points to the county winning the match; 3 points to the county winning on first innings in a drawn match; 1 point to the county behind on first innings in a drawn match.

1927 to 1928—Order decided by percentage of points gained to maximum points possible. Matches in which six hours had not actually been played—provided no result had been reached—were not counted in the Championship: 8 points to the county winning the match; 5 points to the county winning on first innings in a drawn match; 3 points to the county behind on first innings in a drawn match; 4 points to each side in a tie match, for games in which a result had not been reached in first innings if six hours actual play had taken place, or for a tie on first innings.

1929 to 1930—Each county to play 28 matches, and 28 only, with other counties. The county gaining the most points to be the winner of the Championship: 8 points to the county winning the match; 5 points to the county winning on first innings in a drawn match; 3 points to the county behind on first innings in a drawn match; 4 points to each side for a tie on first innings or in the match, or if no result has been reached on first innings, or for games in which play had not taken place.

1931 to 1932—Each county to play 28 matches. The county gaining the most points to be winner of the Championship: 15 points for the county winning the match; 7½ points to each side in a match finished with scores level; 5 points to the county winning on first innings in a drawn match; 3 points to the county behind on first innings in a drawn match; 4 points to each side if scores are level on first innings in a drawn match, where no result is obtained on first innings or when no play has taken place.

1933 to 1937—Each county to play 24 matches to qualify for the Championship. Counties allowed to play more matches, but all must be reckoned in the competition. No county to play another county more than twice in the season. The county obtaining the greatest proportionate number of points on a percentage basis to be adjudged winner of the Championship. For the purpose of calculating the result, the unit of 100 per cent in all matches was the equivalent of 15 points; 15 points to the county winning the match; 7½ points to each side in a match ending with scores level; 5 points to the county winning on first innings in a drawn match; 3 points to the county behind on first innings in a drawn match; 4 points to each side in a match in which no result on first innings was reached, or if scores on first innings were level, or if no play had taken place; 10 points to the side winning on first innings and 3 points to their opponents in a match restricted to play on the third day only.

1938 to 1939—Each county to play a minimum of 24 matches to qualify for the Championship. In deciding the Championship the points gained were divided by the number of matches played, the county with the highest average being adjudged Champions. 'Matches played' were exclusive of those in which there was no play or no result reached on first innings: 12 points to the county winning the match; 6 points to each side if the match ended with scores level; 4 points to the county winning on first innings, these points to be retained if the county eventually lost the match, but 12 points only to be counted for a win; 2 points to each side if scores are level on first innings in a drawn match, these points also to be retained by a defeated side; 8 points to the side winning on first innings in a match restricted to play on the third day only.

1946 to date—With the exception of a few minor adjustments, the points scoring method in all seasons since the war has been constant. For the four seasons from 1946 to 1949 each county played 26 matches. Between 1950 and 1959 each county played 28 matches, but in 1960 counties were allowed to play either 28 or 32 matches and the table order decided on average points per match. The points scoring has been as follows: 12 points to the county winning the match; 4 points for the county leading on first innings in a drawn match: if the county eventually lost the match, but won on first innings, the 4 points gained to be retained; 2 points to each side in a drawn match where scores are level on first innings, these points to be retained if the county eventually lost the match; 8 points to the side leading on first innings in a drawn match restricted to play on the third day only.

The main changes have been those for points in tie matches. In 1946 it was ruled that each side scored 6 points for a tie, but in 1949 an amendment stated that in future the points for a tie match would be 8 points to the county which had gained a lead on first innings and 4 points to the county behind on first innings. In 1953 the scoring reverted to 6 points for each side in a tie match (or a game which ended with scores level where both sides had batted twice).

A change in points for first innings lead was made in 1957, the 4 points being reduced to 2 points and bonus points (2) being introduced—these were given to the side leading on first innings if they also scored faster, based on a rate of runs per over.

CHAMPION COUNTY EACH SEASON

1873	Gloucestershire and Notting-hamshire	1909	Kent .
		1910	Kent
1874	Derbyshire	1911	Warwickshire
1875	Lancashire, Nottinghamshire and Sussex	1912	Yorkshire
		1913	Kent
1876	Gloucestershire	1914	Surrey
1877	Gloucestershire	1919	Yorkshire
1878	Middlesex	1920	Middlesex
1879	Lancashire and Nottingham-shire	1921	Middlesex
		1922	Yorkshire
1880	Gloucestershire and Notting-hamshire	1923	Yorkshire
		1924	Yorkshire
1881	Lancashire	1925	Yorkshire
1882	Lancashire and Nottingham-shire	1926	Lancashire
		1927	Lancashire
1883	Nottinghamshire	1928	Lancashire
1884	Nottinghamshire	1929	Nottinghamshire
1885	Nottinghamshire	1930	Lancashire
1886	Nottinghamshire	1931	Yorkshire
1887	Surrey	1932	Yorkshire
1888	Surrey	1933	Yorkshire
1889	Lancashire, Nottinghamshire and Surrey	1934	Lancashire
		1935	Yorkshire
1890	Surrey	1936	Derbyshire
1891	Surrey	1937	Yorkshire
1892	Surrey	1938	Yorkshire
1893	Yorkshire	1939	Yorkshire
1894	Surrey	1946	Yorkshire
1895	Surrey	1947	Middlesex
1896	Yorkshire	1948	Glamorgan
1897	Lancashire	1949	Middlesex and Yorkshire
1898	Yorkshire	1950	Lancashire and Surrey
1899	Surrey	1951	Warwickshire
1900	Yorkshire	1952	Surrey
1901	Yorkshire	1953	Surrey
1902	Yorkshire	1954	Surrey
1903	Middlesex	1955	Surrey
1904	Lancashire	1956	Surrey
1905	Yorkshire	1957	Surrey
1906	Kent	1958	Surrey
1907	Nottinghamshire	1959	Yorkshire
1908	Yorkshire	1960	Yorkshire

Surrey were outright County Champions for seven consecutive seasons between 1952 and 1958.

Surrey were County Champions for six consecutive seasons between 1887 and 1892—the title was shared in 1889.

Nottinghamshire were County Champions for five consecutive seasons between 1882 and 1886, but shared the title in the first season (1882).

Yorkshire have twice been County Champions for four consecutive seasons—1922 to 1925 and 1937 to 1946.

Note.—The above table is compiled strictly in accordance with the 'least matches lost' principle before 1886. *Wisden*'s list differs slightly, giving Nottinghamshire only in 1875 and 1880.

CHAMPION COUNTY v. REST OF ENGLAND

Yorkshire, Champion county in 1901, met the Rest of England in a benefit match for W. Yardley's widow and children at Lord's at the end of that season. This was the first of a series of matches that have been played at the end of the season between the Champion County and a side representing the Rest of England. The second match was played at the Oval in 1903, and all subsequent matches have been played on that ground except that of 1957 which was played at Scarborough. The proceeds have normally gone to charity, those in recent years being devoted to the Umpires' Testimonial Fund. The results of the matches played to date have been:

1901	Yorkshire	Rest won by an innings and 115 runs.
1903	Middlesex	Match drawn.
1904	Lancashire	Match drawn.
1905	Yorkshire	Yorkshire won by 65 runs.
1906	Kent	Rest won by 251 runs.
1907	Nottinghamshire	Match drawn.
1908	Yorkshire	Match drawn.
1909	Kent	Match drawn.
1910	Kent	Rest won by 244 runs.
1911	Warwickshire	Rest won by an innings and 365 runs.
1912	Yorkshire	Rest won by an innings and 122 runs.
1913	Kent and Yorkshire	Rest won by an innings and 45 runs.
1919	Yorkshire	Rest won by ten wickets.
1920	Middlesex	Match drawn.
1921	Middlesex	Rest won by nine wickets.
1922	Yorkshire	Match drawn.
1923	Yorkshire	Match drawn.
1924	Yorkshire	Rest won by an innings and 124 runs.
1925	Yorkshire	Match drawn.
1926	Lancashire	Rest won by 374 runs.
1927	Lancashire	Match drawn.
1928	Lancashire	Rest won by an innings and 91 runs.
1929	Nottinghamshire	Rest won by 8 runs.
1930	Lancashire	Rest won by ten wickets.
1931	Yorkshire	Match drawn.
1932	Yorkshire	Match drawn.
1933	Yorkshire	Rest won by an innings and 23 runs.
1934	Lancashire	Rest won by eight wickets.
1935	Yorkshire	Yorkshire won by 149 runs.
1947	Middlesex	Middlesex won by nine wickets.
1955	Surrey	Rest won by two wickets
1956	Surrey	Rest won by 128 runs.
1957	Surrey	Surrey won by six wickets.
1959	Yorkshire	Yorkshire won by 66 runs.
1960	Yorkshire	Yorkshire won by 137 runs.

ORDER OF MERIT EACH SEASON

Since the County Championship started in 1873 the counties have finished in the following positions each season (in the case of counties finishing equal they are given equal ranking, the next position in the table being omitted—e.g. in 1894 Kent and Lancashire finished joint fourth, fifth place is omitted and Somerset shown as sixth):

Season	DERBYSHIRE	ESSEX	GLAMORGAN	GLOUCESTERSHIRE	HAMPSHIRE	KENT	LANCASHIRE	LEICESTERSHIRE	MIDDLESEX	NORTHAMPTONSHIRE	NOTTINGHAMSHIRE	SOMERSET	SURREY	SUSSEX	WARWICKSHIRE	WORCESTERSHIRE	YORKSHIRE
1873	4	—	—	1	—	4	6	—	3	—	1	—	9	8	—	—	7
1874	1	—	—	2	—	3	4	—	7	—	4	—	9	8	—	—	4
1875	4	—	—	6	—	9	1	—	6	—	1	—	8	1	—	—	4
1876	4	—	—	1	—	6	8	—	2	—	4	—	9	6	—	—	3
1877	2	—	—	1	—	4	4	—	4	—	7	—	3	9	—	—	7
1878	7	—	—	2	—	5	3	—	1	—	3	—	7	9	—	—	6
1879	6	—	—	5	—	9	1	—	3	—	1	—	6	3	—	—	6
1880	8	—	—	1	—	3	3	—	5	—	1	—	9	5	—	—	5
1881	6	—	—	2	—	7	1	—	3	—	5	—	9	8	—	—	3
1882	3	—	—	6	—	6	1	—	3	—	1	—	8	8	—	—	3
1883	4	—	—	7	—	7	4	—	2	—	1	—	4	7	—	—	2
1884	9	—	—	8	—	7	3	—	2	—	1	—	3	6	—	—	3
1885	6	—	—	7	—	3	3	—	7	—	1	—	5	9	—	—	2
1886	9	—	—	6	—	6	4	—	3	—	1	—	2	6	—	—	4
1887	9	—	—	7	—	6	2	—	5	—	3	—	1	7	—	—	3
1888	—	—	—	4	—	2	5	—	7	—	6	—	1	8	—	—	2
1889	—	—	—	5	—	4	1	—	6	—	1	—	1	8	—	—	7
1890	—	—	—	6	—	3	2	—	7	—	5	—	1	8	—	—	3
1891	—	—	—	9	—	5	2	—	3	—	4	5	1	7	—	—	8
1892	—	—	—	7	—	7	4	—	5	—	2	3	1	9	—	—	6
1893	—	—	—	9	—	4	2	—	3	—	6	8	5	7	—	—	1
1894	—	—	—	9	—	4	4	—	3	—	7	6	1	8	—	—	2
1895	5	9	—	4	10	14	2	12	6	—	12	8	1	11	6	—	3
1896	7	5	—	10	8	9	2	13	3	—	6	11	4	14	12	—	1
1897	14	3	—	5	9	12	1	13	8	—	10	11	2	6	7	—	4
1898	9	5	—	3	12	7	6	13	2	—	8	13	4	9	9	—	1
1899	15	6	—	9	10	8	4	13	2	—	10	13	1	5	7	12	3
1900	13	10	—	7	15	3	2	14	7	—	5	11	7	3	6	12	1
1901	15	10	—	14	7	7	3	12	2	—	9	12	6	4	5	11	1
1902	10	13	—	14	15	7	5	11	12	—	3	7	4	2	6	9	1
1903	12	8	—	13	14	8	4	14	1	—	5	10	11	2	7	6	3
1904	10	14	—	9	15	3	1	7	4	—	5	12	11	6	7	13	2
1905	14	12	—	8	16	6	2	5	11	13	10	15	4	3	7	8	1
1906	16	7	—	9	8	1	4	15	11	11	5	11	3	10	6	14	2
1907	16	7	—	10	12	8	6	11	5	15	1	14	4	13	9	2	2
1908	14	11	—	10	9	2	7	13	4	15	8	16	3	5	12	6	1
1909	15	14	—	16	8	1	2	13	6	7	10	11	5	4	12	8	3
1910	15	11	—	12	6	1	4	10	3	9	5	16	2	7	14	13	8
1911	14	6	—	12	11	2	4	15	3	10	8	16	5	13	1	9	7
1912	12	15	—	11	6	3	4	13	5	2	8	14	7	10	9	16	1
1913	13	15	—	9	10	1	8	14	6	4	5	16	3	7	11	12	2
1914	12	8	—	16	5	3	11	13	2	9	10	15	1	6	7	14	4
1919	9	14	—	8	7	2	5	9	13	12	3	5	4	11	15	—	1
1920	16	9	—	8	11	5	2	13	1	14	7	10	3	6	12	15	4
1921	12	15	17	7	6	4	5	11	1	13	8	10	2	9	16	14	3
1922	11	8	16	13	6	4	5	14	7	15	2	10	3	9	12	17	1
1923	10	13	16	11	7	5	3	14	8	17	2	9	4	6	12	15	1
1924	17	15	13	6	12	5	4	11	2	16	6	8	3	10	9	14	1
1925	14	7	17	10	9	5	3	12	6	11	4	15	2	13	8	16	1
1926	11	9	8	15	7	3	1	13	6	16	4	14	5	10	12	17	2
1927	5	8	15	12	13	4	1	7	9	16	2	14	6	10	11	17	3
1928	10	16	15	5	12	2	1	9	8	13	3	14	6	7	11	17	4
1929	7	12	17	4	11	8	2	9	6	13	1	15	10	4	14	16	2

Season	DERBYSHIRE	ESSEX	GLAMORGAN	GLOUCESTERSHIRE	HAMPSHIRE	KENT	LANCASHIRE	LEICESTERSHIRE	MIDDLESEX	NORTHAMPTONSHIRE	NOTTINGHAMSHIRE	SOMERSET	SURREY	SUSSEX	WARWICKSHIRE	WORCESTERSHIRE	YORKSHIRE
1930	9	6	11	2	13	5	1	12	16	17	4	13	8	7	15	10	3
1931	7	10	15	2	12	3	6	16	11	17	5	13	8	4	9	14	1
1932	10	14	15	13	8	3	6	12	10	16	4	7	5	2	9	17	1
1933	6	4	16	10	14	3	5	17	12	13	8	11	9	2	7	15	1
1934	3	8	13	7	14	5	1	12	10	17	9	15	11	2	4	16	5
1935	2	9	13	15	16	10	4	6	3	17	5	14	11	7	8	12	1
1936	1	9	16	4	10	8	11	15	2	17	5	7	6	14	13	12	3
1937	3	6	7	4	14	12	9	16	2	17	10	13	8	5	11	15	1
1938	5	6	16	10	14	9	4	15	2	17	12	7	3	8	13	11	1
1939	9	4	13	3	15	5	6	17	2	16	12	14	8	10	11	7	1
1946	15	8	6	5	10	6	3	11	2	16	13	4	11	17	14	8	1
1947	5	11	9	2	16	4	3	14	1	17	11	11	6	9	15	7	7
1948	6	13	1	8	9	15	5	11	3	17	14	12	2	16	7	10	4
1949	15	9	8	7	16	13	11	17	1	6	11	9	5	13	4	3	1
1950	5	17	11	7	12	9	1	16	14	10	15	7	1	13	4	6	3
1951	11	8	5	12	9	16	3	15	7	13	17	14	6	10	1	4	2
1952	4	10	7	9	12	15	3	6	5	8	16	17	1	13	10	14	2
1953	6	12	10	6	14	16	3	3	5	11	8	17	1	2	9	15	12
1954	3	15	4	13	14	11	10	16	7	7	5	17	1	9	6	11	2
1955	8	14	16	12	3	13	9	6	5	7	11	17	1	4	9	15	2
1956	12	11	13	3	6	16	2	17	5	4	8	15	1	9	14	9	7
1957	4	5	9	12	13	14	6	17	7	2	15	8	1	9	11	16	3
1958	5	6	15	14	2	8	7	12	10	4	17	3	1	13	16	9	11
1959	7	9	6	2	8	13	5	16	10	11	17	12	3	15	4	14	1
1960	5	6	11	8	12	10	2	17	3	9	16	14	7	4	15	13	1

COMPLETE PLAYING RECORD FOR ALL CHAMPIONSHIP MATCHES

(*Note.*—Derbyshire did not compete in the Championship for seven season, 1888 to 1894, both seasons inclusive.)

	Seasons	Played	Won	Drawn	Lost	Tie	Aban'd
Derbyshire	1873–1960	1409	371	453	570	—	15
Essex	1895–1960	1376	370	547	445	4	10
Glamorgan	1921–1960	896	197	357	337	—	5
Gloucestershire	1873–1960	1648	515	484	641	1	7
Hampshire	1895–1960	1414	364	509	531	3	7
Kent	1873–1960	1695	664	467	550	2	12
Lancashire	1873–1960	1815	788	681	325	3	18
Leicestershire	1895–1960	1342	260	491	581	1	9
Middlesex	1873–1960	1517	595	506	405	2	9
Northamptonshire	1905–1960	1105	239	396	464	2	4
Nottinghamshire	1873–1960	1627	550	674	394	—	9
Somerset	1891–1960	1347	303	392	644	3	5
Surrey	1873–1960	1822	796	619	388	3	16
Sussex	1873–1960	1747	518	612	606	3	8
Warwickshire	1895–1960	1348	355	567	417	1	8
Worcestershire	1899–1960	1284	276	457	545	1	5
Yorkshire	1873–1960	1892	954	650	272	1	15
Total		25284	8115	8862	8115	30	162

Aggregate Records for Each County

The following are the highest aggregates of runs and wickets that have been registered for each county in a season and in a career. The figures are for all matches for the county, not just county championship matches alone.

HIGHEST AGGREGATE OF RUNS IN A SEASON

	Season	Inns.	N.O.	Runs	H.S.	Avge.	100s
Derbyshire—D. B. Carr	1959	52	7	2165	156*	48·11	5
Essex—J. O'Connor	1934	47	6	2308	248	56·29	9
Glamorgan—W. G. A. Parkhouse	1959	45	3	2071	154	49·30	6
Gloucestershire—W. R. Hammond	1933	46	5	2860	264	69·75	11
Hampshire—C. P. Mead	1928	45	9	2854	180	79·55	12
Kent—F. E. Woolley	1928	52	3	2894	198	59·06	10
Lancashire—J. T. Tyldesley	1901	51	4	2633	221	56·02	8
Leicestershire—L. G. Berry	1937	51	4	2246	184*	52·04	7
Middlesex—W. J. Edrich	1947	38	7	2650	267*	85·48	10
Northamptonshire—D. Brookes	1952	50	7	2198	204*	51·11	6
Nottinghamshire—W. W. Whysall	1929	52	3	2620	244	53·46	7
Somerset—P. B. Wight	1960	61	5	2316	155*	41·35	7
Surrey—T. Hayward	1906	53	8	3246	219	72·13	13
Sussex—John Langridge	1949	49	5	2850	234*	64·77	12
Warwickshire—M. J. K. Smith	1959	50	10	2417	200*	60·42	6
Worcestershire—H. H. Gibbons	1934	57	6	2654	157	52·03	8
Yorkshire—H. Sutcliffe	1932	41	5	2883	313	80·08	12

MOST CENTURIES IN A SEASON

Derbyshire	6	L. F. Townsend in 1933.
Essex	9	J. O'Connor in 1934 and D. J. Insole in 1955.
Glamorgan	7	W. G. A. Parkhouse in 1950.
Gloucestershire	13	W. R. Hammond in 1938.
Hampshire	12	C. P. Mead in 1928.
Kent	10	F. E. Woolley in 1928 and 1934.
Lancashire	11	C. Hallows in 1928.
Leicestershire	7	L. G. Berry in 1937 and W. Watson in 1959.
Middlesex	13	D. C. S. Compton in 1947.
Northamptonshire	8	R. Haywood in 1921.
Nottinghamshire	9	W. W. Whysall in 1928.
Somerset	7	F. S. Lee in 1938, H. Gimblett in 1946 and P. B. Wight in 1960.
Surrey	13	T. Hayward in 1906 and J. B. Hobbs in 1925.
Sussex	12	John Langridge in 1949.
Warwickshire	8	R. E. S. Wyatt in 1937.
Worcestershire	9	C. F. Walters in 1933.
Yorkshire	12	H. Sutcliffe in 1932.

HIGHEST AGGREGATE OF WICKETS IN A SEASON

	Season	Overs	Mdns.	Runs	Wkts.	Avge.
Derbyshire—T. B. Mitchell	1935	866·5	134	3284	168	19·54
Essex—T. P. B. Smith	1947	1606	287	4667	172	27·13
Glamorgan—J. C. Clay	1937	1103·3	229	3052	176	17·34
Gloucestershire—T. W. Goddard	1937	1335	325	3730	222	16·80
	1947	1327·1	323	3636	222	16·37
Hampshire—A. S. Kennedy	1922	1190·3	322	2967	190	15·61
Kent—A. P. Freeman	1933	1829·2	610	3862	262	14·74
Lancashire—E. A. McDonald	1925	1204·4	277	3674	198	18·55
Leicestershire—J. E. Walsh	1948	1124·3	185	3224	170	18·96
Middlesex—F. J. Titmus	1955	1179	443	2312	158	14·63
Northamptonshire—G. E. Tribe	1955	1272	341	3273	175	18·70
Nottinghamshire—B. Dooland	1954	1197·4	393	2708	181	14·96
Somerset—A. W. Wellard	1938	1168·4	233	3152	169	19·24
Surrey—T. Richardson	1895	1444·4	394	3515	250	14·06
Sussex—M. W. Tate	1925	1440	416	2669	198	13·45
Warwickshire—W. E. Hollies	1946	1470	432	2725	180	15·13
Worcestershire—C. F. Root	1925	1440·5	404	3627	207	17·52
Yorkshire—W. Rhodes	1900	1366·4	411	3054	240	12·72

HIGHEST AGGREGATE OF RUNS IN A CAREER

	Career	Runs	H.S.	Avge.	100s
Derbyshire—D. Smith	1927–1952	20516	225	31·41	30
Essex—P. A. Perrin	1896–1928	29162	343*	27·13	65
Glamorgan—E. Davies	1924–1954	26104	287*	27·82	31
Gloucestershire—W. R. Hammond	1920–1951	33664	317	57·05	113
Hampshire—C. P. Mead	1905–1936	48892	280*	48·84	138
Kent—F. E. Woolley	1906–1938	48483	270	42·05	112
Lancashire—J. T. Tyldesley	1895–1923	32267	295*	41·68	73
Leicestershire—L. G. Berry	1924–1951	30106	232	30·53	45
Middlesex—E. Hendren	1907–1937	40302	301*	49·81	119
Northamptonshire—D. Brookes	1934–1959	28980	257	36·13	67
Nottinghamshire—G. Gunn	1902–1932	31327	220	36·71	56
Somerset—H. Gimblett	1935–1954	21108	310	37·09	49
Surrey—J. B. Hobbs	1905–1934	43703	316*	49·77	144
Sussex—John Langridge	1928–1955	34152	250*	37·69	76
Warwickshire—W. G. Quaife	1894–1928	34172	255*	35·31	71
Worcestershire—D. Kenyon	1946–1960	25418	259	37·26	59
Yorkshire—H. Sutcliffe	1919–1945	38561	313	50·21	112

MOST CENTURIES IN A CAREER

With a few exceptions the batsman scoring the most runs for a county has also scored the most centuries, the three different records being as follows:

Essex	71	by J. O'Connor	1921–1939
Lancashire	91	by E. Tyldesley	1909–1936
Nottinghamshire	62	by J. Hardstaff jun.	1930–1955

First-class County Cricket Clubs

DERBYSHIRE

Formed—1870
Colours—Chocolate, amber and pale blue
Badge—Rose and Crown
County Championship—1873 to 1887, re-entered 1895
Champions (2)—1874, 1936

ESSEX

Formed—1864–65, dissolved in 1866 and re-formed in 1876 and 1886
Colours—Blue, gold and red
Badge—Three Scimitars with word 'Essex' underneath
Promoted to first-class status—1894 (1895 in Championship)
Best final position in Championship—Third in 1897

GLAMORGAN

Formed—1888–89
Colours—Blue and gold
Badge—Gold Daffodil
Promoted to first-class status—1921
Champions—1948

GLOUCESTERSHIRE

Formed—1870
Colours—Blue, gold, brown, sky-blue, green and red
Badge—Coat of arms of the City and County of Bristol
Champions (2)—1876, 1877
Joint Champions (2)—1873, 1880

HAMPSHIRE

Formed—1863
Colours—Blue, gold and white
Badge—Tudor Rose and Crown
Promoted to first-class status—1895
Best final position in Championship—Runners-up in 1958

KENT

Formed—1859, re-formed 1870
Colours—Red and white
Badge—White Horse on a red background
Champions (4)—1906, 1909, 1910, 1913

LANCASHIRE

Formed—1864
Colours—Red, green and blue
Badge—Red Rose
Champions (8)—1881, 1897, 1904, 1926, 1927, 1928, 1930, 1934
Joint Champions (5)—1875, 1879, 1882, 1889, 1950

LEICESTERSHIRE

Formed—1873
Colours—Scarlet and dark green
Badge—Running Fox (gold) on green background
Promoted to first-class status—1894 (1895 in Championship)
Best final position in Championship—Third in 1953

MIDDLESEX

Formed—1864
Colours—Blue
Badge—Three Seaxes
Champions (5)—1878, 1903, 1920, 1921, 1947
Joint Champions—1949

NORTHAMPTONSHIRE

Formed—About 1843, re-formed 1878
Colours—Maroon
Badge—Tudor Rose
Promoted to first-class status—1905
Best final position in Championship—Runners-up in 1912 and 1957

NOTTINGHAMSHIRE

Formed—1859
Colours—Green and gold
Badge—County badge of Nottinghamshire
Champions (6)—1883, 1884, 1885, 1886, 1907, 1929
Joint Champions (6)—1873, 1875, 1879, 1880, 1882, 1889

SOMERSET

Formed—1875, reorganized 1885
Colours—Black, white and maroon
Badge—Wessex Wyvern
Promoted to first-class status—1891
Best final position in Championship—Third in 1892 and 1958

SURREY

Formed—1845
Colours—Chocolate
Badge—Prince of Wales' Feathers
Champions (16)—1887, 1888, 1890, 1891, 1892, 1894, 1895, 1899, 1914, 1952, 1953, 1954, 1955, 1956, 1957, 1958
Joint Champions (2)—1889, 1950

SUSSEX

Formed—1836, re-formed 1839 and 1857
Colours—Dark blue, light blue and gold
Badge—County arms of Six Martlets (in shape of inverted pyramid)
Joint Champions—1875
Runners-up (6)—1902, 1903, 1932, 1933, 1934, 1953

WARWICKSHIRE

Formed—1863–64, re-formed 1882
Colours—Blue, yellow and white
Badge—Bear and Ragged Staff
Promoted to first-class status—1894 (1895 in Championship)
Champions (2)—1911, 1951

WORCESTERSHIRE

Formed—1865
Colours—Dark green and black
Badge—Shield, *Argent* bearing *Fess* between three *Pears Sable*
Promoted to first-class status—1899
Best final position in Championship—Joint Runners-up in 1907, Third in 1949

YORKSHIRE

Formed—1863
Colours—Oxford blue, Cambridge blue and gold
Badge—White Rose
Champions (24)—1893, 1896, 1898, 1900, 1901, 1902, 1905, 1908, 1912, 1919, 1922, 1923, 1924, 1925, 1931, 1932, 1933, 1935, 1937, 1938, 1939, 1946, 1959, 1960
Joint Champions—1949

Captains of the Counties

The full list of players officially appointed as county captains for each county is as follows: (*Note:* Professional captains are given in italics.)

DERBYSHIRE

1894–1898	S. H. Evershed
1899–1901	S. H. Hill-Wood
1902–1903	A. E. Lawton
1904–1905	A. E. Lawton and E. M. Ashcroft
1906	A. E. Lawton and L. G. Wright
1907	L. G. Wright
1908	A. E. Lawton and L. G. Wright
1909	A. E. Lawton
1910–1912	J. Chapman
1913–14	R. R. C. Baggallay
1919–1920	L. Oliver
1921	G. M. Buckston
1922–1930	G. R. Jackson
1931–1936	A. W. Richardson
1937–1939	R. H. R. Buckston
1946	G. F. Hodgkinson
1947–1948	E. J. Gothard
1949	D. A. Skinner
1950	P. Vaulkhard
1951–1954	G. L. Willatt
1955–1960	D. B. Carr

ESSEX

1894	A. P. Lucas
1895–1900	H. G. Owen
1901	H. G. Owen and A. P. Lucas
1902	H. G. Owen
1903	C. J. Kortright
1904–1906	F. L. Fane
1907–1910	C. P. McGahey
1911–1928	J. W. H. T. Douglas
1929–1932	H. M. Morris
1933–1938	T. N. Pearce and D. R. Wilcox
1939	D. R. Wilcox, F. St G. Unwin and J. W. A. Stephenson
1946–1949	T. N. Pearce
1950	T. N. Pearce and D. J. Insole
1951–1960	D. J. Insole

GLAMORGAN

1921	N. V. H. Riches
1922–1923	T. A. L. Whittington
1924–1927	J. C. Clay
1928	T. Arnott
1929	J. C. Clay and N. V. H. Riches
1930–1939	M. J. Turnbull
1946	J. C. Clay
1947–1960	W. Wooller

GLOUCESTERSHIRE

1871–1898	W. G. Grace
1899	W. Troup
1900–1911	G. L. Jessop
1912–1914	C. O. H. Sewell
1919–1921	F. G. Robinson
1922–1923	P. F. C. Williams
1924–1926	D. C. Robinson
1927–1928	W. H. Rowlands
1929–1934	B. H. Lyon
1935–1936	D. A. C. Page
1937–1938	B. O. Allen

1939–1946	W. R. Hammond
1947–1950	B. O. Allen
1951–1952	Sir D. Bailey
1953–1954	*J. F. Crapp*
1955–1958	*G. M. Emmett*
1959–1960	*T. W. Graveney*

HAMPSHIRE

1895	R. Bencraft
1896–1899	E. G. Wynyard
1900–1902	C. Robson
1903–1914	E. M. Sprot
1919–1933	Lord (Hon. L. H.) Tennyson
1934–1935	W. G. L. F. Lowndes
1936–1937	R. H. Moore
1938	C. G. A. Paris
1939	G. R. Taylor
1946–1957	E. D. R. Eagar
1958–1960	A. C. D. Ingleby-Mackenzie

KENT

1859–1870	W. S. Norton
1871–1874	No official appointment
1875–1889	Lord Harris
1890–1893	F. Marchant and W. H. Patterson
1894–1897	F. Marchant
1898–1902	J. R. Mason
1903	C. J. Burnup
1904–1908	C. H. B. Marsham
1909–1913	E. W. Dillon
1914–1923	L. H. W. Troughton
1924–1926	W. S. Cornwallis
1927	A. J. Evans
1928–1930	G. B. Legge
1931–1936	A. P. F. Chapman
1937	R. T. Bryan and B. H. Valentine
1938–1939	F. G. H. Chalk
1946–1948	B. H. Valentine
1949–1951	D. G. Clark
1952–1953	W. Murray-Wood
1954–1956	*D. V. P. Wright*
1957–1960	M. C. Cowdrey

LANCASHIRE

1870–1879	E. B. Rowley
1880–1891	A. N. Hornby
1892–1893	A. N. Hornby and S. M. Crosfield
1894–1896	A. C. MacLaren
1897–1898	A. N. Hornby
1899	A. C. MacLaren and G. R. Bardswell
1900–1907	A. C. MacLaren
1908–1914	A. H. Hornby
1919–1922	M. N. Kenyon
1923–1925	J. Sharp
1926–1928	L. Green
1929–1935	P. T. Eckersley
1936–1939	W. H. L. Lister
1946	J. Fallows
1947–1948	K. Cranston
1949–1953	N. D. Howard
1954–1959	*C. Washbrook*
1960	R. W. Barber

LEICESTERSHIRE

1894–1906	C. E. de Trafford
1907–1910	Sir A. Hazlerigg
1911–1913	J. Shields
1914–1920	C. J. B. Wood
1921	A. T. Sharp
1922–1927	G. H. S. Fowke
1928–1929	E. W. Dawson
1930	J. A. de Lisle
1931	E. W. Dawson
1932	Shared between six amateurs
1933	E. W. Dawson
1934	A. G. Hazlerigg
1935	*W. E. Astill*
1936–1938	C. S. Dempster
1939	M. St J. Packe
1946–1948	*L. G. Berry*
1949	S. J. Symington
1950–1957	C. H. Palmer
1958–1960	*W. Watson*

MIDDLESEX

1864–1872	V. E. Walker
1873–1884	I. D. Walker
1885–1897	A. J. Webbe
1898	A. J. Webbe and A. E. Stoddart
1899–1907	G. MacGregor
1908–1920	P. F. Warner
1921–1928	F. T. Mann
1929–1932	N. E. Haig
1933–1934	N. E. Haig and H. J. Enthoven
1935–1938	R. W. V. Robins
1939	I. A. R. Peebles
1946–1947	R. W. V. Robins
1948–1949	F. G. Mann
1950	R. W. V. Robins
1951–1952	W. J. Edrich and *D. C. S. Compton*
1953–1957	W. J. Edrich
1958–1960	J. J. Warr

NORTHAMPTONSHIRE

1905–1906	T. Horton
1907	E. M. Crosse
1908–1910	T. E. Manning
1911–1912	G. A. T. Vials
1913	G. A. T. Vials and S. G. Smith
1914	S. G. Smith
1919	J. N. Beasley
1920–1921	R. O. Raven
1922	C. H. Tyler
1923–1924	A. H. Bull
1925–1926	J. M. Fitzroy
1927	J. M. Fitzroy and V. W. C. Jupp
1928–1931	V. W. C. Jupp
1932–1935	W. C. Brown
1936–1937	G. B. Cuthbertson
1938–1939	R. P. Nelson
1946	P. E. Murray-Willis
1947–1948	A. W. Childs-Clarke
1949–1953	F. R. Brown
1954–1957	*D. Brookes*
1958–1960	R. Subba Row

NOTTINGHAMSHIRE

1835–1855	*W. Clarke*
1856–1870	*G. Parr*
1871–1880	*R. Daft*
1881–1882	*W. Oscroft*
1883–1886	*A. Shaw*
1887–1888	*M. Sherwin*
1889–1899	J. A. Dixon
1900–1912	A. O. Jones
1913	A. O. Jones and G. O. Gauld
1914	A. O. Jones
1919–1934	A. W. Carr
1935	G. F. H. Heane and S. D. Rhodes
1936–1946	G. F. H. Heane
1947–1950	W. A. Sime
1951–1960	R. T. Simpson

SOMERSET

1891–1893	H. T. Hewett
1894–1906	S. M. J. Woods
1907	L. C. H. Palairet
1908–1912	J. Daniell
1913–1914	E. S. M. Poyntz
1919–1926	J. Daniell
1927–1931	J. C. White
1932–1937	R. A. Ingle
1938–1946	E. F. Longrigg
1947	R. J. O. Meyer
1948	N. S. Mitchell-Innes, G. E. S. Woodhouse and J. W. Seamer
1949	G. E. S. Woodhouse
1950–1952	S. S. Rogers
1953–1954	B. G. Brocklehurst
1955	G. G. Tordoff
1956–1959	*M. F. Tremlett*
1960	*H. W. Stephenson*

SURREY

1846–1850	C. H. Hoare
1851–1857	F. P. Miller
1858–1865	F. Burbidge
1866	E. Dowson
1867	W. J. Collyer
1868	C. Calvert
1869–1870	S. H. Akroyd
1871	J. C. Gregory
1872–1875	G. Strachan
1876	A. Chandler
1877–1879	G. Strachan
1880–1893	J. Shuter
1894–1899	K. J. Key
1900–1902	D. L. A. Jephson
1903	L. Walker
1904	No official appointment
1905–1907	Lord Dalmeny
1908–1909	H. D. G. Leveson-Gower
1910	H. D. G. Leveson-Gower and M. C. Bird
1911–1913	M. C. Bird
1914–1919	C. T. A. Wilkinson
1920	C. T. A. Wilkinson and P. G. H. Fender
1921–1931	P. G. H. Fender
1932–1933	D. R. Jardine
1934–1938	E. R. T. Holmes
1939	H. M. Garland-Wells
1946	N. H. Bennett
1947–1948	E. R. T. Holmes
1949–1951	M. R. Barton
1952–1956	W. S. Surridge
1957–1960	P. B. H. May

SUSSEX

1839–1846	C. G. Taylor
1847–1862	E. Napper
1863	J. H. Hale
1864	J. H. Hale and C. H. Smith
1865–1873	C. H. Smith
1874	C. H. Smith and J. M. Cotterill
1875	J. M. Cotterill
1876–1878	F. F. J. Greenfield
1879	C. Sharp
1880	R. T. Ellis
1881–1882	F. F. J. Greenfield
1883–1884	H. Whitfield
1885	G. N. Wyatt
1886	F. M. Lucas
1887–1888	C. A. Smith
1889	W. Newham
1890	C. A. Smith
1891–1892	W. Newham
1893–1898	W. L. Murdoch
1899	W. L. Murdoch and K. S. Ranjit-sinhji
1900–1903	K. S. Ranjitsinhji
1904–1905	C. B. Fry
1906	C. B. Fry and C. L. A. Smith
1907–1908	C. B. Fry
1909	C. L. A. Smith
1910–1914	H. P. Chaplin
1919–1921	H. L. Wilson
1922–1929	A. E. R. Gilligan
1930	A. H. H. Gilligan
1931–1932	K. S. Duleepsinhji
1933	R. S. G. Scott
1934–1935	A. Melville
1936–1939	A. J. Holmes
1946	S. C. Griffith
1947–1949	H. T. Bartlett
1950–1952	*James Langridge*
1953	D. S. Sheppard
1954	G. H. G. Doggart
1955–1959	R. G. Marlar
1960	E. R. Dexter

WARWICKSHIRE

1894–1901	H. W. Bainbridge
1902	H. W. Bainbridge and T. S. Fishwick
1903–1906	J. F. Byrne
1907	J. F. Byrne and T. S. Fishwick
1908–1909	A. C. S. Glover
1910	H. J. Goodwin
1911–1914	F. R. Foster
1919	G. W. Stephens
1920–1929	Hon. F. G. S. Calthorpe

1930–1937	R. E. S. Wyatt
1938–1947	P. Cranmer
1948	R. H. Maudsley and *H. E. Dollery*
1949–1955	*H. E. Dollery*
1956	*W. E. Hollies*
1957–1960	M. J. K. Smith

WORCESTERSHIRE

1899–1900	H. K. Foster
1901	R. E. Foster
1902–1910	H. K. Foster
1911–1912	G. H. Simpson-Hayward
1913	H. K. Foster
1914	W. H. Taylor
1920–1921	M. F. S. Jewell
1922	W. H. Taylor
1923–1925	M. K. Foster
1926	M. F. S. Jewell
1927	Hon. C. B. Ponsonby
1928	M. F. S. Jewell
1929	M. F. S. Jewell and Hon. J. B. Coventry
1930	Hon. J. B. Coventry
1931–1935	C. F. Walters
1936–1939	Hon. C. J. Lyttelton
1946	A. P. Singleton
1947–1948	A. F. T. White
1949	R. E. S. Wyatt and A. F. T. White
1950–1951	R. E. S. Wyatt
1952–1954	R. E. Bird
1955	*R. T. D. Perks*
1956–1958	P. E. Richardson
1959–1960	*D. Kenyon*

YORKSHIRE

1863–1870	*R. Iddison*
1871–1875	*J. Rowbotham*
1876–1877	*E. Lockwood*
1878–1882	*T. Emmett*
1883–1910	Lord Hawke
1911	E. J. Radcliffe
1912–1914	Sir A. W. White
1919–1921	D. C. F. Burton
1922–1924	G. Wilson
1925–1927	A. W. Lupton
1928–1929	W. A. Worsley
1930	A. T. Barber
1931–1932	F. E. Greenwood
1933–1947	A. B. Sellers
1948–1955	N. W. D. Yardley
1956–1957	W. H. H. Sutcliffe
1958–1959	J. R. Burnet
1960	*J. V. Wilson*

County Caps Awarded since 1946

The award of a county cap is the highest honour that a county can bestow on one of their players. It is impossible to compile a complete list of caps awarded before the war, but the following have been given since the war:

DERBYSHIRE

1946 J. D. Eggar, C. Gladwin, G. F. Hodkinson, P. Vaulkhard
1947 G. Dawkes, E. J. Gothard, E. A. Marsh, A. C. Revill
1949 L. Jackson, D. A. Skinner
1950 A. Hamer, G. L. Willatt
1951 D. B. Carr, J. Kelly, D. C. Morgan, R. Sale
1954 E. Smith
1956 C. Lee
1958 H. L. Johnson, H. J. Rhodes

ESSEX

1946 H. P. Crabtree, T. C. Dodds, R. F. T. Paterson, F. H. Vigar
1947 T. E. Bailey, L. S. Clark, S. J. Cray
1948 R. Horsfall, F. Rist
1949 D. J. Insole, G. R. Pullinger
1951 P. A. Gibb, K. C. Preston
1952 W. T. Greensmith
1954 J. A. Bailey
1955 G. E. Barker
1956 B. Taylor
1957 L. H. R. Ralph
1958 M. J. Bear
1959 B. R. Knight, L. H. Savill
1960 G. J. Smith

GLAMORGAN

1946 W. E. Jones, A. Porter, M. Robinson
1947 B. L. Muncer, A. J. Watkins
1948 P. B. Clift, J. Eaglestone, N. G. Hever, W. G. A. Parkhouse
1951 J. E. McConnon
1952 J. Pleass, D. J. Shepherd
1954 B. Hedges
1955 J. Pressdee
1956 L. N. Devereux
1958 P. M. Walker
1959 D. L. Evans
1960 J. B. Evans, A. R. Lewis

GLOUCESTERSHIRE

1946 C. Cook
1948 T. W. Graveney
1949 Sir D. Bailey, J. K. Graveney, C. A. Milton
1950 D. M. Young
1954 F. P. McHugh, J. B. Mortimore, B. D. Wells
1955 P. Rochford

1957 A. S. Brown, D. Hawkins, R. B. Nicholls, D. R. Smith
1958 B. J. Meyer
1959 D. A. Allen

HAMPSHIRE

1946 E. D. R. Eagar, A. G. Holt
1947 N. H. Rogers
1948 G. Dawson
1949 V. J. Ransom, D. Shackleton, C. Walker
1950 V. H. D. Cannings
1951 J. R. Gray, L. Harrison
1952 A. W. H. Rayment
1953 D. E. Blake
1954 J. R. Bridger, R. Dare
1955 H. M. Barnard, M. D. Burden, H. Horton, R. E. Marshall, P. J. Sainsbury
1957 M. Heath, A. C. D. Ingleby-Mackenzie
1959 D. O. Baldry
1960 D. W. White

KENT

1946 T. G. Evans, R. R. Dovey, J. W. Martin, H. A. Pawson
1947 N. W. Harding, P. Hearn, F. Ridgway
1948 E. E. Crush
1949 D. G. Clark, B. R. Edrich, A. W. H. Mallett
1951 M. C. Cowdrey, W. Murray-Wood
1952 R. Mayes, A. H. Phebey, A. C. Shirreff
1953 G. Smith
1954 J. Pettiford, R. C. Wilson
1955 J. M. Allan
1956 D. G. Ufton
1957 D. J. Halfyard, S. E. Leary, J. C. T. Page, J. F. Pretlove
1960 A. L. Dixon

LANCASHIRE

1946 T. L. Brierley, G. A. Edrich, J. A. Fallows, J. T. Ikin, B. P. King, E. Price, A. Wharton
1947 K. Cranston, R. G. Garlick, B. J. Howard
1948 E. H. Edrich, N. D. Howard
1949 P. Greenwood, K. Grieves
1950 A. T. Barlow, R. Berry, M. J. Hilton, J. B. Statham, R. Tattersall
1951 A. Wilson
1952 J. G. Lomax
1953 F. D. Parr
1956 J. Dyson, T. Greenough, J. Jordan, C. S. Smith
1958 R. W. Barber, P. Marner, G. Pullar
1959 K. Higgs
1960 G. Clayton

LEICESTERSHIRE

1946 V. E. Jackson, G. Lester, M. Tompkin, J. E. Walsh
1949 G. Evans, S. J. Symington
1950 C. H. Palmer
1951 J. Firth, V. S. Munden, G. A. Smithson
1952 C. T. Spencer
1953 T. J. Goodwin
1954 M. R. Hallam
1955 M. J. K. Smith
1958 B. Boshier, A. C. Revill, J. Savage, W. Watson
1959 J. Van Geloven
1960 H. D. Bird

MIDDLESEX

1946 J. P. Mann, A. Thompson, J. A. Young
1947 L. H. Compton, A. Fairbairn
1948 P. I. Bedford, J. G. Dewes, E. A. Ingram, H. P. Sharp
1949 J. J. Warr
1951 R. Routledge
1952 D. Bennett, W. Knightley-Smith, A. E. Moss
1953 F. J. Titmus
1955 G. P. S. Delisle
1956 J. T. Murray
1957 R. A. Gale, R. J. Hurst, A. C. Walton
1959 R. W. Hooker, W. E. Russell
1960 P. H. Parfitt

NORTHAMPTONSHIRE

1946 W. Barron, P. E. Murray-Willis
1947 V. H. Broderick, A. W. Childs-Clarke, C. B. Clarke, K. Fiddling, J. Webster
1948 A. E. Nutter, N. Oldfield
1949 F. R. Brown, R. W. Clarke, R. G. Garlick
1950 T. L. Livingston
1951 F. Jakeman
1952 D. Barrick, G. Tribe
1953 E. Davis
1954 K. V. Andrew, S. Starkie, F. H. Tyson
1955 P. Arnold R. Subba Row
1956 J. S. Manning, B. G. Reynolds
1957 M. J. H. Allen
1960 L. A. Johnson, M. E. J. C. Norman

NOTTINGHAMSHIRE

1946 E. A. Meads, T. B. Reddick, R. T. Simpson, F. W. Stocks
1947 W. A. Sime, H. Winrow
1949 P. F. Harvey, C. J. Poole
1951 R. J. Giles
1952 J. D. Clay
1953 B. Dooland
1954 E. J. Martin, E. J. Rowe
1955 G. Goonesena, K. Smales
1956 A. K. Walker
1957 G. Millman
1959 N. Hill
1960 J. Cotton, J. D. Springall, B. D. Wells

SOMERSET

1946 F. Castle, G. R. Langdale, J. Lawrence, M. M. Walford
1947 M. Coope, M. F. Tremlett, G. E. S. Woodhouse
1949 E. Hill, S. S. Rogers, H. W. Stephenson
1950 F. L. Angell, E. P. Robinson
1951 J. Redman
1952 G. G. Tordoff
1953 B. G. Brocklehurst, T. A. Hall, C. G. Mitchell, Roy Smith
1954 J. G. Lomax, J. W. McMahon, P. B. Wight, Yawar Saeed
1955 B. Lobb
1956 C. L. McCool, L. Pickles
1957 W. E. Alley, B. A. Langford, D. R. W. Silk
1958 G. G. Atkinson, K. Palmer
1959 K. Biddulph
1960 R. Virgin

SURREY

1946 A. V. Bedser, N. H. Bennett, A. J. McIntyre
1947 E. A. Bedser, D. G. W. Fletcher, J. C. Laker
1948 M. R. Barton, J. W. McMahon, W. S. Surridge
1949 G. J. Whittaker
1950 B. Constable, G. A. R. Lock, P. B. H. May
1952 T. H. Clark
1953 P. J. Loader, R. Subba Row
1955 K. F. Barrington, M. J. Stewart
1958 R. Swetman
1959 J. H. Edrich
1960 D. Gibson

SUSSEX

1948 P. D. S. Blake
1949 G. H. G. Doggart, J. Oakes, D. S. Sheppard
1950 A. E. James, D. V. Smith, R. T. Webb
1951 A. S. M. Oakman, J. M. Parks
1952 R. G. Marlar, K. G. Suttle
1953 N. I. Thomson
1957 D. L. Bates, L. J. Lenham
1959 E. R. Dexter

WARWICKSHIRE

1946 W. E. Fantham, J. J. Hossell, J. M. A. Marshall, R. H. Maudsley, R. Sale, N. A. Shortland, K. A. Taylor
1947 V. H. D. Cannings, C. W. Grove, T. L. Pritchard, J. R. Thompson
1948 M. P. Donnelly, R. T. Spooner, A. Townsend
1949 F. C. Gardner, A. H. Kardar, A. V. Wolton
1951 R. E. Hitchcock, E. B. Lewis, R. T. Weeks
1953 N. F. Horner
1954 J. D. Bannister, K. R. Dollery
1955 R. G. Thompson
1957 K. Ibadulla, M. J. K. Smith, W. J. Stewart
1958 R. G. Carter, T. W. Cartwright
1959 O. S. Wheatley

WORCESTERSHIRE

1946 R. E. Bird, A. F. T. White, R. E. S. Wyatt
1947 D. Kenyon, H. Yarnold
1948 L. Outschoorn
1949 M. L. Y. Ainsworth
1950 G. H. Chesterton, G. Dews
1951 R. G. Broadbent
1952 P. E. Richardson
1955 J. Flavell, M. J. Horton
1956 R. Booth, D. W. Richardson
1957 R. Berry
1959 K. J. Aldridge, L. J. Coldwell, D. B. Pearson
1960 D. N. F. Slade

YORKSHIRE

1946 A. Booth
1947 D. V. Brennan, A. Coxon, G. A. Smithson, J. H. Wardle, W. Watson
1948 R. Aspinall, H. Halliday, E. Lester, J. V. Wilson
1949 D. B. Close, F. A. Lowson
1951 R. Appleyard, F. S. Trueman
1952 W. H. H. Sutcliffe
1955 R. Illingworth
1957 J. G. Binks, W. B. Stott, K. Taylor
1958 J. R. Burnet, D. E. V. Padgett
1959 R. K. Platt
1960 J. B. Bolus, M. J. Cowan, P. J. Sharpe, D. Wilson

o

The Sheffield Shield

The first matches between Victoria and New South Wales were played in the 1850's and shortly afterwards matches with South Australia and Tasmania were added. It was not until 1892–93 that Championship cricket was started in Australia. In the winter of 1891–92 the Earl of Sheffield took a team to Australia, under the captaincy of W. G. Grace, and the tour aroused so much enthusiasm that the Earl, before leaving Australia, gave the sum of 150 guineas to be used for the promotion of cricket in Australia. The newly formed Cricket Council had the disposal of the gift and decided on a Shield to be competed for by the leading cricket colonies (now States).

Starting in 1892–93 the competition included New South Wales, South Australia and Victoria, Queensland being added in 1926–27 and Western Australia in 1947–48. Until the entry of Queensland all matches were played to a finish, resulting in heavy scoring in the 1920's, but with an extension of fixtures it was decided to play all future matches on a time limit basis. Western Australia won the Shield during their first season in the competition, but their programme was curtailed because of heavy travelling, each State being met once only, and they did not in every case meet the full strength of the other States owing to Test calls. Western Australia received full membership of the competition for the 1956–57 seasons.

SHIELD WINNERS EACH SEASON

1892–93	Victoria	1912–13	South Australia	1935–36	South Australia
1893–94	South Australia	1913–14	New South Wales	1936–37	Victoria
1894–95	Victoria	1914–15	Victoria	1937–38	New South Wales
1895–96	New South Wales	1915–19	No competition	1938–39	South Australia
1896–97	New South Wales	1919–20	New South Wales	1930–40	New South Wales
1897–98	Victoria	1920–21	New South Wales	1940–46	No competition
1898–99	Victoria	1921–22	Victoria	1946–47	Victoria
1899–90	New South Wales	1922–23	New South Wales	1947–48	Western Australia
1900–01	Victoria	1923–24	Victoria	1948–49	New South Wales
1901–02	New South Wales	1924–25	Victoria	1949–50	New South Wales
1902–03	New South Wales	1925–26	New South Wales	1950–51	Victoria
1903–04	New South Wales	1926–27	South Australia	1951–52	New South Wales
1904–05	New South Wales	1927–28	Victoria	1952–53	South Australia
1905–06	New South Wales	1928–29	New South Wales	1953–54	New South Wales
1906–07	New South Wales	1929–30	Victoria	1954–55	New South Wales
1907–08	Victoria	1930–31	Victoria	1955–56	New South Wales
1908–09	New South Wales	1931–32	New South Wales	1956–57	New South Wales
1909–10	South Australia	1932–33	New South Wales	1957–58	New South Wales
1910–11	New South Wales	1933–34	Victoria	1958–59	New South Wales
1911–12	New South Wales	1934–35	Victoria	1959–60	New South Wales

PLAYING RECORD OF EACH TEAM

	Début Season	Played	Won	Drawn	Lost	Tie	Aban'd
New South Wales	1892–93	300	165	65	69	1	—
Victoria	1892–93	299	140	66	91	1	1
South Australia	1892–93	296	82	57	157	—	—
Queensland	1926–27	181	32	62	86	—	1
Western Australia	1947–48	66	13	24	29	—	—
Total		1142	432	274	432	2	2

1920–21—New South Wales v. South Australia match at Sydney abandoned as a draw owing to heavy rain—awarded to New South Wales as a win for competition purposes.

1930–31—Queensland v. Victoria match at Brisbane abandoned without a ball being bowled.

1935–36—New South Wales v. South Australia match at Sydney abandoned as a draw through the death of King George V.

The Currie Cup Tournament

This trophy was presented by Sir Donald Currie in 1888–89 for competition between the South African provinces. The first tournament was held in 1889–90 and has been held periodically ever since. It is not normally held when a touring team is visiting South Africa.

The various competitions have been won as follows:

1st	1889–90	Transvaal	16th	1921–22	Transvaal, Natal and Western Province (Equal)
2nd	1890–91	Griqualand West			
3rd	1892–93	Western Province	17th	1923–24	Transvaal
4th	1893–94	Western Province	18th	1925–26	Transvaal
5th	1894–95	Transvaal	19th	1926–27	Transvaal
6th	1896–97	Western Province	20th	1929–30	Transvaal
7th	1897–98	Western Province	21st	1931–32	Western Province
8th	1902–03	Transvaal	22nd	1933–34	Natal
9th	1903–04	Transvaal	23rd	1934–35	Transvaal
10th	1904–05	Transvaal	24th	1936–37	Natal
11th	1906–07	Transvaal	25th	1937–38	Transvaal and Natal (Equal)
12th	1908–09	Western Province	26th	1946–47	Natal
13th	1910–11	Natal	27th	1947–48	Natal
14th	1912–13	Natal	28th	1950–51	Transvaal
15th	1920–21	Western Province			

A new system was introduced for the 1951–52 season, the nine competing teams being divided into two sections, each playing home and away matches against the other teams, instead of only one meeting per season as had previously been the case. The leader of A section was the winner of the Currie Cup, the side finishing bottom of A section was relegated to B section, and the leader of B section was promoted to A section. The split of the nine teams for the 1951–52 season was as follows:

A—Eastern Province, Natal, Transvaal, Western Province.

B—Border, Griqualand West, North-Eastern Transvaal, Orange Free State, Rhodesia.

Season	Winner of Currie Cup	Relegated to B	Leader of B Section
1951–52	Natal	Transvaal	Orange Free State
1952–53	Western Province	Eastern Province	Transvaal
1954–55	Natal	Orange Free State	Eastern Province
1955–56	Western Province	Eastern Province	Rhodesia
1958–59	Transvaal	Western Province*	Border
1959–60	Natal	Border	{ Eastern Province { Transvaal B

Western Province was not relegated in 1958–59, as a tenth team—Transvaal B—entered the tournament B section in 1959–60.

PLAYING RECORD OF EACH TEAM

	Début Season	Played	Won	Drawn	Lost	Tie
Transvaal	1889–90	157	101	30	26	—
Griqualand West	1889–90	138	31	27	80	—
Western Province	1892–93	148	72	32	44	—
Natal	1893–94	143	86	36	21	—
Eastern Province	1893–94	127	33	22	71	1
Border	1897–98	122	40	16	66	—
Orange Free State	1903–04	130	33	26	70	1
Rhodesia	1904–05	63	25	13	25	—
South-West Districts	1904–05	1	0	0	1	—
North-Eastern Transvaal	1937–38	57	13	11	33	—
Transvaal B	1959–60	6	4	1	1	—
Total		1092	438	214	438	2

The West Indies Inter-Colonial Tournament

The Inter-Colonial Tournament was first competed for in 1891–92, Barbados winning on their own ground, but as British Guiana failed to send a team this tournament has not been regarded as one of the regular series. Barbados, British Guiana and Trinidad have played in the Tournament, the matches being played on each ground in turn, but because of the problems of distance Jamaica never competed. The last tournament was held in 1938–39 and it was not resumed after the war.

1st	1892–93	Barbados (Trinidad)	15th	1923–24	Barbados (Barbados)
2nd	1895–96	British Guiana (Georgetown)	16th	1924–25	Trinidad (Trinidad)
3rd	1897–98	Barbados (Barbados)	17th	1925–26	Trinidad (Georgetown)
4th	1899–00	Barbados (Trinidad)	18th	1926–27	Barbados (Barbados)
5th	1901–02	Trinidad (Georgetown)	19th	1928–29	Trinidad (Trinidad)
6th	1903–04	Trinidad (Barbados)	20th	1929–30	British Guiana (Georgetown
7th	1905–06	Barbados (Trinidad)	21st	1931–32	Trinidad (Barbados)
8th	1907–08	Trinidad (Georgetown)	22nd	1933–34	Trinidad (Trinidad)
9th	1908–09	Barbados (Barbados)	23rd	1934–35	British Guiana (Georgetown)
10th	1909–10	Trinidad (Trinidad)	24th	1935–36	British Guiana (Barbados)
11th	1910–11	Barbados (Georgetown)	25th	1936–37	Trinidad (Trinidad)
12th	1911–12	Barbados (Barbados)	26th	1937–38	British Guiana (Georgetown)
13th	1921–22	No result (Trinidad)	27th	1938–39	Trinidad (Barbados)
14th	1922–23	Barbados (Georgetown)			

In October 1956 a quadrangular tournament was held at Georgetown, all four colonies meeting for the first time. The results of three matches were as follows:

Barbados (433) beat Trinidad (115 & 170) by an innings and 148 runs.
British Guiana (601—5d & 60—1) drew with Jamaica (469).
Final: British Guiana (581) drew with Barbados (211 & 67—4).

The Plunket Shield

The Plunket Shield, which is the New Zealand equivalent of the County Championship, was presented by Lord Plunket, Governor-General of New Zealand, in 1906–07. It was originally awarded by the New Zealand Cricket Council to Canterbury and for the first few years it was competed for on a 'challenge match' system. The holders of the Shield from the initial award until the change to a competition basis in 1921–22 were as follows (the number of challenges resisted is shown in brackets):

Canterbury	1906–07 to December 1907
Auckland	December 1907 to February 1911 (7)
Canterbury	February 1911 to February 1912 (2)
Auckland	February 1912 to January 1913 (1)
Canterbury	January 1913 to December 1918 (9)
Wellington	December 1918 to January 1919 (0)
Canterbury	January 1919 to January 1920 (2)
Auckland	January 1920 to January 1921 (3)
Wellington	January 1921—challenge system ended.

Apart from two matches by Hawkes Bay, in 1914–15 and in 1920–21, the competition was played between Auckland, Canterbury, Otago and Wellington until 1949–50. In the last few years two new teams have entered the tournament, Central Districts in 1950–51 and Northern Districts in 1956–57.

The winners of the Shield for each season since 1921–22 have been as follows:

1921–22	Auckland	1933–34	Auckland	1950–51	Otago
1922–23	Canterbury	1934–35	Canterbury	1951–52	Canterbury
1923–24	Wellington	1935–36	Wellington	1952–53	Otago
1924–25	Otago	1936–37	Auckland	1953–54	Central Districts
1925–26	Wellington	1937–38	Auckland	1954–55	Wellington
1926–27	Auckland	1938–39	Auckland	1955–56	Canterbury
1927–28	Wellington	1939–40	Auckland	1956–57	Wellington
1928–29	Auckland	1945–46	Canterbury	1957–58	Canterbury
1929–30	Wellington	1946–47	Auckland	1958–59	Auckland
1930–31	Canterbury	1947–48	Otago	1959–60	Canterbury
1931–32	Wellington	1948–49	Canterbury		
1932–33	Otago	1949–50	Wellington		

The Bombay Pentangular Tournament

This tournament grew from very small beginnings. In 1892 a series of Presidency matches was begun between Europeans and Parsis and played at Bombay and Poona. In 1907 the Hindus entered the tournament, which then became Triangular. At first the Muslims played with the Hindus, but in 1912 they entered their own team and the tournament became Quadrangular. The last change came in 1937 when a fifth side, The Rest, was added, the competition then becoming Pentangular. It was contested up to the 1945–46 season, but then the tournament lapsed.

The annual competition resulted as follows:

PRESIDENCY MATCHES

1892–93   Match drawn (Bombay).
1893–94   Match drawn (Bombay).
1894–95   Parsis won by 120 runs (Bombay).
1895–96   Europeans won by 9 wickets (Bombay). Parsis won by an innings & 10 runs (Poona).
1896–97   Europeans won by 10 wickets (Bombay) and 2 wickets (Poona).
1897–98   Match drawn (Bombay), Parsis won by 308 runs (Poona).
1898–99   Europeans won by an innings & 16 runs (Bombay) and an innings & 36 runs (Poona).
1899–00   Match drawn (Bombay). Not played at Poona owing to plague.
1900–01   Parsis won by 135 runs (Bombay). Match drawn (Poona).
1901–02   Parsis won by 8 wickets (Bombay). Europeans won by 192 runs (Poona).
1902–03   Parsis won by 44 runs (Bombay). Europeans won by 4 wickets (Poona).
1903–04   Parsis won by 149 runs (Bombay) and an innings & 6 runs (Poona).
1904–05   Parsis won by 180 runs (Bombay). Abandoned owing to rain (Poona).
1905–06   Parsis won by an innings & 226 runs (Poona). Not played at Bombay.
1906–07   Europeans won by 6 wickets (Poona). Not played at Bombay.

TRIANGULAR TOURNAMENT (final match results)

1907–08   Parsis beat Europeans by 143 runs (Bombay)
1908–09   Europeans beat Parsis by 176 runs (Bombay)—Hindus did not compete.
1909–10   Match drawn (Europeans v. Parsis at Bombay).
1910–11   Match drawn (Europeans v. Hindus at Bombay).
1911–12   Parsis beat Europeans by 2 wickets (Bombay).

QUADRANGULAR TOURNAMENT

1912–13   Parsis beat Muslims by an innings & 177 runs (Bombay).
1913–14   Match drawn (Hindus v. Muslims at Bombay).
1914–15   Abandoned without a ball being bowled (Hindus v. Parsis at Bombay).
1915–16   Europeans beat Hindus by 10 wickets (Poona).
1916–17   Match drawn (Europeans v. Parsis at Bombay).
1917–18   Match drawn (Hindus v. Parsis at Bombay).
1918–19   Europeans beat Parsis by 91 runs (Poona).
1919–20   Hindus beat Muslims by an innings & 13 runs (Bombay).
1920–21   Match drawn (Hindus v. Parsis at Bombay).
1921–22   Europeans beat Parsis by an innings & 297 runs (Bombay).
1922–23   Parsis beat Hindus by 121 runs (Poona).
1923–24   Hindus beat Europeans by 9 wickets (Bombay).
1924–25   Muslims beat Hindus by 5 wickets (Bombay).
1925–26   Hindus beat Europeans by 4 wickets (Bombay).
1926–27   Hindus beat Europeans by 11 runs (Poona).
1927–28   Europeans beat Muslims by 4 wickets (Bombay).
1928–29   Parsis beat Europeans by 134 runs (Bombay).
1929–30   Hindus beat Parsis by 5 wickets (Bombay).
1934–35   Muslims beat Hindus by 91 runs (Bombay).
1935–36   Muslims beat Hindus by 221 runs (Bombay).
1936–37   Hindus beat Europeans by 257 runs (Bombay).

PENTANGULAR TOURNAMENT

1937–38   Muslims beat Europeans by an innings & 91 runs (Bombay). Hindus did not compete.
1938–39   Muslims beat Hindus by 6 wickets (Bombay).
1939–40   Hindus beat Muslims by 5 wickets (Bombay).
1940–41   Muslims beat Rest by 7 wickets (Bombay). Hindus did not compete.
1941–42   Hindus beat Parsis by 10 wickets (Bombay).
1943–44   Hindus beat Rest by an innings & 61 runs (Bombay).
1944–45   Muslims beat Hindus by 1 wicket (Bombay).
1945–46   Hindus beat Parsis by 310 runs (Bombay).

The 'Ranji' Trophy

The 'Ranji' Trophy tournament was established in India in the summer of 1934, in memory of the greatest of all Indian cricketers, K. S. Ranjitsinhji, who died in 1933.

The competition is decided on knock-out lines, and owing to the vastness of India, the country was divided into four Zones. The winners of the knock-out competition in each Zone met in the semi-finals and the two winners in the final. The semi-finals and finals were played to a finish, the other matches being of four days duration.

In 1948–49 the competition was decided on a 'knock-out basis on an open draw', but a return was made to the zonal basis for 1949–50. In recent years a fifth zone (Central Zone) has been added, and the number of competing teams increased. In 1957–58 the Zone's operated on a league basis, with the five leading teams then meeting on a knock-out basis.

The winners of the trophy each year have been as follows:

1934–35   Bombay beat Northern India at Bombay by 208 runs.
1935–36   Bombay beat Madras at Delhi by 190 runs.
1936–37   Nawanagar beat Bengal at Bombay by 256 runs.
1937–38   Hyderabad beat Nawanagar at Bombay by 1 wicket.
1938–39   Bengal beat Southern Punjab at Calcutta by 178 runs.
1939–40   Maharashtra beat United Provinces at Poona by 10 wickets.
1940–41   Maharashtra beat Madras at Madras by 6 wickets.
1941–42   Bombay beat Mysore at Bombay by an innings and 281 runs.
1942–43   Baroda beat Hyderabad at Secunderabad by 307 runs.
1943–44   Western India States beat Bengal at Bombay by an innings and 23 runs.
1944–45   Bombay beat Holkar at Bombay by 374 runs.
1945–46   Holkar beat Baroda at Indore by 374 runs.
1946–47   Baroda beat Holkar at Baroda by an innings and 409 runs.
1947–48   Holkar beat Bombay at Indore by 9 wickets.
1948–49   Bombay beat Baroda at Bombay by 468 runs.
1949–50   Baroda beat Holkar at Baroda by 4 wickets.
1950–51   Holkar beat Gujerat at Indore by 189 runs.
1951–52   Bombay beat Holkar at Bombay by 531 runs.
1952–53   Holkar beat Bengal at Calcutta on first innings (match drawn).
1953–54   Bombay beat Holkar at Indore by 8 wickets.
1954–55   Madras beat Holkar at Indore by 46 runs.
1955–56   Bombay beat Bengal at Calcutta by 8 wickets.
1956–57   Bombay beat Services at New Delhi by an innings and 38 runs.
1957–58   Baroda beat Services at Baroda by an innings and 51 runs.
1958–59   Bombay beat Bengal at Bombay by 420 runs.
1959–60   Bombay beat Mysore at Bombay by an innings and 22 runs.

The Quaid-I-Azam Trophy

Instituted in 1953–54 as Pakistan's national championship, it is played on a knock-out principle in the final stages, although early rounds are sometimes played on a league basis in regions.

The winners of the trophy each season have been as follows:

1953–54   Bahawalpur beat Punjab at Karachi by 8 wickets.
1954–55   Karachi beat Services at Karachi by 9 wickets.
1955–56   Not held.
1956–57   Punjab beat Karachi Whites at Lahore by 43 runs.
1957–58   Bahawalpur beat Karachi 'C' at Bahawalpur by 211 runs.
1958–59   Karachi beat Services at Karachi by 279 runs.
1959–60   Karachi beat Lahore at Karachi by 99 runs.

Cricket at the Universities

The first University match was played at Lord's in 1827, and regularly since the 1830's, when it was first established as a regular feature. In the early years some University players actually appeared in five fixtures, but after some discussion in the 1860's it was decided that a player was only qualified to play for his University for the first four seasons after he had taken up residence. 'Blues' are awarded to those appearing in the match at Lord's.

The complete list of Blues awarded since 1827 is as follows:
The actual years of appearance are given: 1935–38 means played in 1935 and 1938. 1935–36–37–38 means played in all four years.

OXFORD UNIVERSITY BLUES

Abell, G. E. B. (Marlborough)—1924–26–27
Ainslie, M. M. (Eton)—1843–44–45 (Captain 1844–45)
Aitken, H. M. (Eton)—1853
Aitken, J. (Eton)—1848–49–50 (Captain 1850)
Alington, H. G. (Rugby)—1859
Allan, J. M. (Edinburgh Academy)—1953–54–55–56
Altham, H. S. (Repton)—1911–12
Arenhold, J. A. (Diocesan College, S.A.)—1954
Arkwright, H. A. (Eton)—1895
Armistead, W. G. (Westminster)—1853–54–56–57
Arnall-Thompson, H. T. (Rugby)—1886
Asher, A. G. G. (Loretto)—1883
Awdry, R. W. (Winchester)—1904

Baig, A. A. (Osmania U.)—1959–60
Bailey, J. A. (Christ's Hospital)—1956–57–58 (Captain 1958)
Balfour, E. (Westminster)—1852–53–54
Ballance, T. G. L. (Uppingham)—1935–37
Bannon, B. D. (Tonbridge)—1898
Barber, A. T. (Shrewsbury)—1927–28–29 (Captain 1929)
Bardsley, R. V. (Shrewsbury) 1911–12–13
Bardswell, G. R. (Uppingham)—1894–96–97 (Captain 1897)
Barlow, E. A. (Shrewsbury)—1932–33–34
Barnard, F. H. (Charterhouse)—1922–24
Barnes, R. G. (Harrow)—1906–07
Bartholomew, A. C. (Marlborough)—1868
Bartlett, J. N. (Chichester)—1946–51
Barton, M. R. (Winchester)—1936–37
Bassett, H. (Bedford House, Oxford)—1889–90–91
Bastard, E. W. (Sherborne)—1883–84–85
Bateman, E. L. (Repton & Marlborough)—1854–55
Bathurst, F. (Winchester)—1848
Bathurst, L. C. V. (Radley)—1893–94
Bathurst, R. A. (Winchester)—1838–39
Bathurst, S. E. (Winchester)—1836
Bayly, C. H. (Winchester)—1827–29
Beauclerk, C. W. (Charterhouse)—1836
Belcher, T. H. (Magdalen College School)—1870
Bell, G. F. (Repton)—1919
Belle, B. H. (Forest School)—1936
Benn, A. (Harrow)—1935
Bennett, G. (Winchester)—1856
Benson, E. T. (Blundell's)—1928–29
Bere, C. S. (Rugby) 1851
Berkeley, G. F. H. (Wellington)—1890–91–92–93
Bettington, R. H. B. (King's School, Parramatta)—1920–21–22–23 (Captain 1923)
Bickmore, A. F. (Clifton)—1920–21

Bird, J. W. (Winchester)—1827–29
Bird, W. S. (Malvern)—1904–05–06 (Captain 1906)
Birrell, H. B. (St Andrew's, S.A.)—1953–54
Blagg, P. H. (Shrewsbury)—1939
Blaikie, K. G. (Maritzburg)—1924
Blake, P. D. S. (Eton)—1950–51–52 (Captain 1952)
Bligh, E. V. (Eton)—1850
Bloy, N. C. F. (Dover)—1946–47
Boger, A. J. (Winchester)—1891
Bolitho, W. E. T. (Harrow)—1883–85
Bonham-Carter, M. (Winchester)—1902
Boobbyer, B. (Uppingham)—1949–50–51–52
Bosanquet, B. J. T. (Eton)—1898–99–1900
Boswell, W. G. K. (Eton)—1913–14
Bowden-Smith, F. H. (Rugby)—1861
Bowman, R. C. (Fettes)—1957
Bowring, T. (Rugby)—1907–08
Boyle, C. E. (Charterhouse)—1865–66–67
Boyle, C. W. (Clifton)—1873
Bradby, H. C. (Rugby)—1890
Braddell, R. L. (Charterhouse)—1910–11
Bradshaw, W. H. (Malvern)—1930–31
Brain, J. H. (Clifton)—1884–85–86–87 (Captain 1887)
Brain, W. H. (Clifton)—1891–92–93
Brandt, D. R. (Harrow)—1907
Brandt, F. (Cheltenham)—1859–60–61 (Captain 1861)
Branston, G. T. (Charterhouse)—1904–05–06
Brett, P. J. (Winchester)—1929
Briggs, R. (Winchester)—1875–76
Bristowe, O. C. (Eton)—1914
Bromley Martin, G. E. (Eton)—1897–98
Brooke, R. H. J. (St Edward's, Oxford)—1932
Brougham, H. (Wellington)—1911
Brownlee, L. D. (Clifton)—1904
Bruce, Hon. C. N. (later Lord Aberdare) (Winchester)—1907–08
Buckland, E. H. (Marlborough)—1884–85–86–87
Buckland, F. M. (Eton)—1875–76–77
Bull, H. E. (Westminster)—1863
Bullock-Hall, W. H. (Rugby)—1857–58–60
Burki, J. (Punjab U.)—1958–59–60
Burn, R. C. W. (Winchester)—1902–03–04–05
Bush, J. E. (Magdalen School, Oxford)—1952
Butler, S. E. (Eton)—1870–71–72–73
Butterworth, R. E. C. (Harrow)—1927
Buxton, R. V. (Eton)—1906

Campbell, D. (Melbourne U.)—1874–75–76
Campbell, I. P. (Canford)—1949–50
Campbell, I. P. F. (Repton)—1911–12–13 (Captain 1913)

Carlisle, K. M. (Harrow)—1903–04–05 (Captain 1905)

Carpenter-Garnier, J. (Harrow)—1858

Carr, D. B. (Repton)—1949–50–51 (Captain 1950)

Carter, E. S. (Durham Grammar School)—1866–67

Case, T. (Rugby)—1864–65–67

Case, T. B. (Winchester)—1891–92
Case came into the game by permission of the Cambridge captain in 1891, after the Hon. F. J. N. Thesiger had retired shortly after the start of the match.

Cassan, E. J. P. (Bruton)—1859

Cator, W. (Bromsgrove Grammar School)—1860

Cazalet, P. V. F. (Eton)—1927

Cazenove, A. (Private)—1851–52

Chalk, F. G. H. (Uppingham)—1931–32–33–34 (Captain 1934)

Champain, F. H. B. (Cheltenham)—1897–98–99–1900 (Captain 1899)

Cherry, G. C. (Harrow)—1841–42–43

Chesterton, G. H. (Malvern)—1949

Chitty, J. W. (Eton)—1848–49

Clarke, W. G. (Winchester)—1840

Clement, R. (Rugby)—1853

Clube, S. V. M. (St John's, Leatherhead)—1956

Cobb, A. R. (Winchester)—1886

Cochrane, A. H. J. (Repton)—1885–86–88

Coker, J. (Winchester)—1840–42–43–44 (Captain 1842–43)

Colebrooke, E. L. (Charterhouse)—1880

Coleridge, C. E. (Eton)—1849–50

Coleridge, F. J. (Eton)—1847–50

Colley, R. H. (Bridgnorth Grammar School)—1853–54–55

Collins, L. P. (Marlborough)—1899

Colman, G. R. R. (Eton)—1913–14

Commerell, W. A. (Harrow)—1843

Cooke, J. (Winchester)—1829

Coote, A. (Eton)—1838–39–40 (Captain 1838)

Corran, A. J. (Gresham's)—1958–59–60

Coutts, I. D. F. (Dulwich)—1952

Cowburn, A. (Winchester)—1841

Cowdrey, M. C. (Tonbridge)—1952–53–54 (Captain 1954)

Coxon, A. J. (Harrow C.G.S.)—1952

Crawfurd, J. W. F. (Merchant Taylors')—1900–01

Crawley, A. M. (Harrow)—1927–28–29–30

Croome, A. C. M. (Wellington)—1888–89

Crutchley, G. E. V. (Harrow)—1912

Cunliffe, F. H. E. (Eton)—1895–96–97–98 (Captain 1898)

Currer, C. S. (Harrow)—1847

Curteis, H. M. (Westminster)—1841–42

Curwen, W. J. H. (Charterhouse)—1906

Darnell, N. (Winchester)—1838–39–40

Darwall-Smith, R. F. H. (Charterhouse)—1935–36–37–38

Daubeny, E. T. (Bromsgrove Grammar School)—1861–62

Dauglish, M. J. (Harrow)—1889–90

Davenport, E. (Rugby)—1866

Davidson, W. W. (Brighton)—1947–48

Davies, P. H. (Brighton)—1913–14

Davies, W. H. (Charterhouse)—1846–47–48

Delisle, G. P. S. (Stonyhurst)—1955–56

De Montmorency, R. H. (Cheltenham & St Paul's)—1899

Denison, H. (Eton)—1829

Denne, T. (Private)—1827

de Saram, F. C. (Royal College, Colombo)—1934–35

Des Vœux, H. D. (Harrow)—1844

Digby, K. E. (Harrow)—1857–58–59

Digby, R. (Harrow)—1867–68–69

Dillon, E. W. (Rugby)—1901–02

Divecha, R. V. (Bombay U.)—1950–51

Dixon, E. J. H. (St Edward's, Oxford)—1937–38–39 (Captain 1939)

Dolphin, J. M. (Marlborough)—1860

Donnelly, M. P. (Canterbury U., New Zealand)—1946–47 (Captain 1947)

Dowding, A. L. (St Peter's, Adelaide)—1952–53 (Captain 1953)

Drybrough, C. D. (Highgate)—1960

Dryden, A. E. (Winchester)—1841–42–43

Duff, A. R. (Radley)—1960

Durell, J. D. (Westminster)—1838

Dury, T. S. (Harrow)—1876

Dyson, E. M. (Queen Elizabeth G.S., Wakefield)—1958

Dyson, J. H. (Charterhouse)—1936

Eagar, E. D. R. (Cheltenham)—1939

Eagar, M. A. (Rugby)—1956–57–58–59

Eccles, A. (Repton)—1897–98–99

Eden, F. M. (Rugby)—1850–51

Eggar, J. D. (Winchester)—1938

Ellis, W. W. (Rugby)—1827

Evans, A. H. (Rossall & Clifton)—1878–79–80–81 (Captain 1881)

Evans, A. J. (Winchester)—1909–10–11–12 (Captain 1911)

Evans, E. N. (Haileybury)—1932

Evans, F. R. (Cheltenham & Rugby)—1863–64–65

Evans, G. (St Asaph)—1939

Evans, W. H. B. (Malvern)—1902–03–04–05 (Captain 1904)

Evelyn, F. L. (Rugby)—1880

Evetts, W. (Harrow)—1868–69

Fane, F. L. (Charterhouse)—1897–98

Fasken, D. K. (Wellington)—1953–54–55

Fellowes, E. L. (Marlborough)—1865–66–68 (Captain 1868)

Fellows, W. (Westminster)—1854–55–56–57

Fellows-Smith, J. P. (Durban H.S., S.A.)—1953–54–55

Fiennes, W. S. T. W. (Winchester)—1856–57–58

Findlay, W. (Eton)—1901–02–03—(Captain 1903)

Fisher, C. D. (Westminster)—1900

Foord-Kelcey, W. (Chatham House, Ramsgate)—1874–75

Forbes, D. H. (Eton)—1894

Ford, G. J. (King's College, London)—1839–40

Ford, N. M. (Harrow)—1928–29–30

Forster, H. W. (Eton)—1887–88–89

Fortescue, A. T. (Marlborough)—1868–69–70

Foster, G. N. (Malvern)—1905–06–07–08

Foster, H. K. (Malvern)—1894–95–96

Foster, R. E. (Malvern)—1897–98–99–1900 (Captain 1900)

Fowler, G. (Clifton)—1888

Fowler, H. (Clifton)—1877–79–80

Fox, R. W. (Wellington)—1897–98

Francis, C. K. (Rugby)—1870–71–72–73

Franklin, H. W. F. (Christ's Hospital)—1924

Fraser, J. N. (Church of England G.S., Melbourne)—1912–13

Frazer, J. E. (Winchester)—1924

Frederick, J. St J. (Eton)—1864–67
Fry, C. A. (Repton)—1959–60
Fry, C. B. (Repton)—1892–93–94–95 (Captain 1894)
Fuller, G. P. (Winchester)—1854–55

Game, W. H. (Sherborne)—1873–74–75–76 (Captain 1876)
Garland-Wells, H. M. (St Paul's)—1928–29–30
Garnett, C. A. (Cheltenham & Eton)—1860–61–62
Garnier, E. S. (Marlborough)—1873
Garnier, T. P. (Winchester)—1861–62–63
Garth, R. (Eton)—1839–40–41–42 (Captain 1840–41)
Garthwaite, P. F. (Wellington)—1929
Gibbon, J. H. (Harrow)—1869
Gibson, I. (Manchester G.S.)—1955–56–57–58
Gilbert, H. A. (Charterhouse)—1907–08–09
Gillett, H. H. (Winchester)—1857–58
Gilliatt, I. A. W. (Charterhouse)—1925
Gilligan, F. W. (Dulwich)—1919–20 (Captain 1920)
Gordon, J. H. (Winchester)—1906–07
Goring, C. (Winchester)—1836
Green, D. M. (Manchester G.S.)—1959–60
Greene, A. D. (Clifton)—1877–78–79–80 (Captain 1880)
Greenstock, J. W. (Malvern)—1925–26–27
Gresson, F. H. (Winchester)—1887–88–89
Grimston, Hon. E. H. (Harrow)—1836
Grimston, Hon. R. (Harrow)—1838
Grover, J. N. (Winchester)—1936–37–38 (Captain 1938)
Guise, J. L. (Winchester)—1924–25 (Captain 1925)

Hadow, W. H. (Harrow)—1870–71–72
Hale, T. W. (Rugby)—1851–52
Halliday, J. G. (City of Oxford High School)—1935
Hamilton, W. D. (Haileybury)—1882
Hanbury, O. R. (Rugby)—1849
Hankey, R. (Harrow)—1853–55 (Captain 1855)
Hare, J. H. M. (Uppingham)—1879
Harris, Hon. G. R. C. (later Lord Harris) (Eton)—1871–72–74
Harrison, G. C. (Malvern & Clifton)—1880–81
Hart, T. M. (Strathallan)—1931–32
Hartley, J. C. (Marlborough & Tonbridge)—1896–97
Haskett-Smith, A. (Eton)—1879
Hatfeild, C. E. (Eton)—1908
Haygarth, J. W. (Winchester)—1862–63–64
Heath, A. H. (Clifton)—1876–77–78–79
Hedges, L. P. (Tonbridge)—1920–21–22
Henderson, D. (St Edward's School, Oxford)—1950
Henley, D. F. (later Henley-Welch) (Harrow)—1947
Henley, F. A. H. (Forest School)—1905
Hewetson, E. P. (Shrewsbury)—1923–24–25
Hewett, H. T. (Harrow)—1886
Hildyard, H. C. T. (Eton)—1845–46
Hildyard, L. D'arcy (Private)—1884–85–86
Hill, F. H. (Bradfield)—1867–69–70
Hill, V. T. (Winchester)—1892
Hill-Wood, C. K. (Eton)—1928–29–30
Hill-Wood, D. J. (Eton)—1928
Hine-Haycock, T. R. (Wellington)—1883–84
Hirst, E. T. (Rugby)—1878–79–80
Hobbs, J. A. D. (Liverpool College)—1957

Hodgkinson, G. L. (Harrow)—1857–58–59
Hofmeyr, M. B. (Pretoria, S.A.)—1949–50–51 (Captain 1951)
Holdsworth, R. L. (Repton)—1919–20–21–22
Hollins, A. M. (Eton)—1899
Hollins, F. H. (Eton)—1901
Holmes, E. R. T. (Malvern)—1925–26–27 (Captain 1927)
Hone, B. W. (Adelaide U.)—1931–32–33 (Captain 1933)
Honywood, R. (Eton)—1845–46–47
Hooman, C. V. L. (Charterhouse)—1909–10
Hopkins, H. O. (St Peter's College, Adelaide)—1923
Hore, A. H. (Tonbridge)—1851
Howell, M. (Repton)—1914–19 (Captain 1919)
Hughes, G. E. (Rugby)—1845
Hughes, T. (Rugby)—1842
Hume, E. (Marlborough)—1861–62
Hurst, C. S. (Uppingham)—1907–08–09 (Captain 1909)

Inge, F. G. (Rossall & Charterhouse)—1861–62–63
Inge, W. (Shrewsbury)—1853
Isherwood, F. W. (Rugby)—1872

Jackson, K. L. T. (Rugby)—1934
Jardine, D. R. (Winchester)—1920–21–23
Jardine, M. R. (Fettes)—1889–90–91–92 (Captain 1891)
Jellicoe, F. G. G. (Haileybury)—1877–79
Jenkins, V. G. J. (Llandovery)—1933
Jones, M. (Harrow)—1849–50
Jones, R. T. (Eton)—1892
Jones, T. B. (Christ College, Brecon & Trinity College, Dublin)—1874
Jones-Bateman, R. L. (Winchester)—1846–48
Jose, A. D. (Adelaide U.)—1950–51
Jowett, D. C. P. R. (Sherborne)—1952–53–54–55
Jowett, R. L. (Bradford G.S.)—1957–58–59

Kamm, A. (Chaterhouse)—1954
Kardar, A. H. (Punjab U.)—1947–48–49
Keighley, W. G. (Eton)—1947–48
Kelly, G. W. F. (Stonyhurst)—1901–02
Kemp, C. W. M. (Harrow)—1878
Kemp, M. C. (Harrow)—1881–82–83–84 (Captain 1883–84)
Kenney, E. M. (later Kenney-Herbert) (Rugby)—1866–67–68
Kentish, E. S. M. (Cornwall College, Jamaica)—1956
Ker, R. J. C. R. (Eton)—1842
Key, K. J. (Clifton)—1884–85–86–87
Kimpton, R. C. M. (Melbourne U.)—1935–37–38
Kingsley, P. G. T. (Winchester)—1928–29–30 (Captain 1930)
Knatchbull, H. E. (Winchester)—1827–29
Knight, D. J. (Malvern)—1914–19
Knight, N. S. (Uppingham)—1934
Knight, R. L. (Clifton)—1878
Knott, C. H. (Tonbridge)—1922–23–24 (Captain 1924)
Knott, F. H. (Tonbridge)—1912–13–14 (Captain 1914)
Knox, F. P. (Dulwich)—1899–1900–01 (Captain 1901)

Lagden, R. O. (Marlborough)—1909–10–11–12
Lane, C. G. (Westminster)—1856–58–59–60 (Captain 1859–60)

*o

Lang, T. W. (Edinburgh Academy & Clifton)—
1874–75
Law, A. P. (Rugby)—1857
Law, W. (Harrow)—1871–72–73–74 (Captain 1874)
Lear, F. (Winchester)—1843–44
Le Couteur, P. R. (Warrnambool Academy & Melbourne U.)—1909–10–11
Lee, E. C. (Winchester)—1898
Lee, G. B. (Winchester)—1838–39 (Captain 1838)
Legard, A. R. (Winchester)—1932–35
Legge, G. B. (Malvern)—1925–26 (Captain 1926)
Leigh, E. C. (Harrow)—1852–53–54
Leslie, C. F. H. (Rugby)—1881–82–83
Leslie, J. (Harrow)—1843
Leveson-Gower, H. D. G. (Winchester)—1893–94–95–96 (Captain 1896)
Lewis, C. P. (Llandovery & King's College, Gloucester)—1876
Lewis, D. J. (Cape Town U.)—1951
Lewis, R. P. (Winchester)—1894–95–96
Lewis, W. H. (Harrow)—1827
Lindsay, W. O'B. (Harrow)—1931
Linton, H. (Harrow)—1858–59
Linton, S. (Rugby)—1861–62
Lipscombe, W. H. (Marlborough)—1868
Llewelyn, W. D. (Eton)—1890–91
Loch, C. R. F. (Edinburgh Academy & Rugby)—1846–48
Loftus, Lord H. Y. A. (Harrow)—1841
Lomas, J. M. (Charterhouse)—1938–39
Longe, F. D. (Harrow)—1851–52
Lowe, J. C. M. (Uppingham)—1907–08–09
Lowndes, R. (Winchester)—1841
Lowndes, W. G. L. F. (Eton)—1921
Lowth, A. J. (Eton & Winchester)—1838–40–41
Lyon, B. H. (Rugby)—1922–23
Lyon, G. W. F. (Brighton)—1925

Macindoe, D. H. (Eton)—1937–38–39–46 (Captain 1946)
Maitland, W. F. (Brighton & Harrow)—1864–65–66–67 (Captain 1867)
Mallett, A. W. H. (Dulwich)—1947–48
Marcon, W. (Eton)—1844
Marriott, C. (Winchester)—1871
Marriott, G. S. (Winchester)—1878
Marshall, J. C. (Rugby)—1953
Marsham, A. J. B. (Eton)—1939
Marsham, C. D. B. (Private)—1854–55–56–57–58 (Captain 1857–58)
Marsham, C. H. B. (Eton)—1900–01–02 (Captain 1902)
Marsham, C. J. B. (Private)—1851
Marsham, R. H. B. (Private)—1856
Marsland, G. P. (Rossall)—1954
Martin, E. G. (Eton)—1903–04–05–06
Martyn, H. (Exeter G.S.)—1899–1900
Mathews, E. (Harrow)—1868–69
Matthews, M. H. (Westminster)—1936–37
Maude, J. (Eton)—1873
Maudsley, R. H. (Malvern)—1946–47
Mayhew, J. F. N. (Eton)—1930
McBride, W. N. (Westminster)—1926
McCanlis, M. A. (Cranleigh)—1926–27–28 (Captain 1928)
McIntosh, R. I. F. (Uppingham)—1927–28
McIver, C. D. (Forest School)—1903–04
McKinna, G. H. (Manchester G.S.)—1953
McLachlan, N. (Loretto)—1879–80–81–82 (Captain 1882)
Medlicott, W. S. (Harrow)—1902

Melle, B. G. (S.A. College School & S.A. College, Cape Town)—1913–14
Melville, A. (Michaelhouse, S.A.)—1930–31–32–33 (Captain 1931–32)
Melville, C. D. (Michaelhouse, S.A.)—1957
Metcalfe, S. G. (Leeds G.S.)—1956
Miles, R. F. (Marlborough)—1867–68–69
Mills, B. S. T. (Harrow)—1841–42–43
Mitchell, R. A. H. (Eton)—1862–63–64–65 (Captain 1863–64–65)
Mitchell, W. M. (Dulwich)—1951–52
Mitchell-Innes, N. S. (Sedbergh)—1934–35–36–37 (Captain 1936)
Moberley, H. E. (Winchester)—1842–43–44–45
Monro, R. W. (Harrow)—1860
Moore, D. N. (Shrewsbury)—1930
Moore was the appointed captain in 1931, but was unable to play owing to illness.
Mordaunt, G. J. (Wellington)—1893–94–95–96 (Captain 1895)
More, R. E. (Westminster)—1900–01
Morley, J. W. (Marlborough)—1859–60
Morres, E. J. (Winchester)—1850
Moss, R. H. (Radley)—1889
Munn, J. S. (Forest School)—1901
Murray-Wood, W. (Mill Hill)—1936
Musters, W. M. (Eton)—1829

Napier, C. W. A. (Harrow)—1838–39
Naumann, F. C. G. (Malvern)—1914–19
Nepean, C. E. B. (Charterhouse)—1873
Nepean, E. A. (Sherborne)—1887–88
Neser, V. H. (S.A. College, Cape Town)—1921
Nethercote, H. O. (Charterhouse & Harrow)—1840–41
Newman, G. C. (Eton)—1926–27
Newton, A. E. (Eton)—1885
Newton-Thompson, J. O. (Diocesan College, S.A.)—1946
Nicholls, B. E. (Winchester)—1884
Nunn, J. A. (Sherborne)—1926–27

O'Brien, T. C. (St Charles' College, Notting Hill)—1884–85
Oldfield, P. C. (Repton)—1932–33
Oliver, F. W. (Westminster)—1856–57
Ottaway, C. J. (Eton)—1870–71–72–73 (Captain 1873)
Owen-Smith, H. G. (Diocesan College, S.A.)—1931–32–33

Page, H. V. (Cheltenham)—1883–84–85–86 (Captain 1885–86)
Palairet, L. C. H. (Repton)—1890–91–92–93 (Captain 1892–93)
Palairet, R. C. N. (Repton)—1893–94
Papillon, J. (Winchester)—1827
Parker, W. W. (Rugby)—1852–53–55
Pataudi, Nawab of (Chief's College, Lahore)—1929–30–31
Pataudi, Nawab of (Winchester)—1960
Patten, M. (Winchester)—1922–23
Patterson, J. I. (Chatham House, Ramsgate)—1882
Patterson, W. H. (Chatham House & Harrow)—1880–81
Patteson, J. C. (Eton)—1843
Pauncefoot, B. (Rugby)—1868–69–70–71 (Captain 1869–70)
Pawson, A. C. (Winchester)—1903
Pawson, A. G. (Winchester)—1908–09–10–11 (Captain 1910)

Pawson, H. A. (Winchester)—1947–48 (Captain 1948)
Payne, A. (Private)—1852–54–55–56 (Captain 1856)
Payne, A. F. (Private)—1855
Payne, C. A. L. (Charterhouse)—1906–07
Peake, E. (Marlborough)—1881–82–83
Pearse, G. V. (Maritzburg College, Natal)—1919
Pearson, A. (Loretto & Rugby)—1876–77
Peat, C. U. (Sedbergh)—1913
Peebles, I. A. R. (Glasgow Academy)—1930
Peel, H. R. (Eton)—1851–52
Pepys, J. A. (Eton)—1861
Pershke, W. J. (Uppingham)—1938
Pether, S. (Magdalen College School)—1939
Philipson, H. (Eton)—1887–88–89 (Captain 1889)
Phillips, F. A. (Rossall)—1892–94–95
Phillips, J. B. (King's, Canterbury)—1955
Piachaud, J. D. (St Thomas's, Colombo)—1958–59–60
Pilkington, C. C. (Eton)—1896
Pilkington, H. C. (Eton)—1899–1900
Pilkington, W. (Midhurst)—1827
Pole, E. (Winchester)—1827
Popham, F. L. (Harrow)—1829
Potts, H. J. (Stand G.S.)—1950
Price, R. (Winchester)—1827–29
Price, V. R. (Bishop's Stortford)—1919–20–21–22 (Captain 1921)
Proud, R. B. (Winchester)—1939
Pulman, W. W. (Marlborough)—1874–75
Pycroft, J. (Bath)—1836

Raikes, D. C. G. (Shrewsbury)—1931
Raikes, G. B. (Shrewsbury)—1894–95
Raikes, T. B. (Winchester)—1922–23–24
Randolph, B. M. (Charterhouse)—1855–56
Randolph, C. (Eton)—1844–45
Randolph, J. (Westminster)—1843
Randolph, L. C. (Westminster)—1845
Ranken, R. B. (Edinburgh Academy)—1860
Raphael, J. E. (Merchant Taylors')—1903–04–05
Rashleigh, J. (Harrow)—1842
Rashleigh fielded substitute for R. Garth in the 1842 match and was allowed to bowl. R. Garth batted.
Rashleigh, W. (Tonbridge)—1886–87–88–89 (Captain 1888)
Rawlinson, G. (Ealing)—1836
Raybould, J. G. (Leeds G.S.)—1959
Reade, H. St John (Tonbridge)—1861–62 (Captain 1862)
Reid, R. T. (Cheltenham)—1866–67–68
Rice, R. W. (Cardiff)—1893
Richardson, J. V. (Uppingham)—1925
Ricketts, G. W. (Winchester)—1887
Ridding, A. (Winchester)—1846–47–48–49–50 (Captain 1849)
Ridding, C. H. (Winchester)—1845–46–47–48–49
Ridding, W. (Winchester)—1849–50–52–53 (Captain 1852)
Ridding was also appointed captain in 1851, but was unable to play owing to illness.
Ridley, A. W. (Eton)—1872–73–74–75 (Captain 1875)
Ridsdale, S. O. B. (Tonbridge)—1862
Robertson, G. P. (Rugby)—1866
Robertson, J. C. (Winchester)—1829
Robertson-Glasgow, R. C. (Charterhouse)—1920–21–22–23

Robinson, G. E. (Burton)—1881–82–83
Robinson, H. B. (North Shore, Vancouver, B.C.)—1947–48
Robinson, R. L. (St Peter's College, Adelaide & Adelaide U.)—1908–09
Royle, V. P. F. A. (Rossall)—1875–76
Rucker, C. E. S. (Charterhouse)—1914
Rucker, P. W. (Charterhouse)—1919
Rudd, C. R. D. (Eton)—1949
Ruggles-Brise, H. G. (Winchester)—1883
Rumbold, J. S. (St Andrew's College, N.Z.)—1946
Russell, H. S. (Harrow)—1839
Ryle, J. C. (Eton)—1836–38

Sale, R., sen. (Repton)—1910
Sale, R., jun. (Repton)—1939–46
Salter, M. G. (Cheltenham)—1909–10
Samson, O. M. (Cheltenham)—1903
Sandford, E. G. (Rugby)—1859–61
Sankey, P. M. (King's School, Canterbury)—1852
Savory, J. H. (Winchester)—1877–78
Sayer, D. M. (Maidstone G.S.)—1958–59–60
Schwann, H. S. (Clifton)—1890
Scott, Lord George (Eton)—1887–88–89
Scott, J. (Bruce Castle)—1863
Scott, K. B. (Winchester)—1937
Scott, M. D. (Winchester)—1957
Scott, R. S. G. (Winchester)—1931
Seamer, J. W. (Marlborough)—1934–35–36
Seitz, J. A. (Geelong & Melbourne U.)—1909
Shaw, E. A. (Marlborough)—1912–14
Shaw, E. D. (Forest School)—1882
Sibthorpe, G. T. W. (Harrow)—1836
Simpson, E. T. B. (Harrow)—1888
Sinclair, E. H. (Winchester)—1924
Singleton, A. P. (Shrewsbury)—1934–35–36–37 (Captain 1937)
Skeet, C. H. L. (St Paul's)—1920
Skene, R. W. (Sedbergh)—1928
Smith, A. C. (King Edward's, Birmingham)—1958–59–60 (Captain 1959–60)
Smith, E. (Clifton)—1890–91
Smith, G. O. (Charterhouse)—1895–96
Smith, M. J. K. (Stamford)—1954–55–56 (Captain 1956)
Smith, V. S. C. (Winchester)—1844–45–46–47 (Captain 1846–47)
Soames, S. (Rugby)—1846–47
Spencer-Smith, O. (Eton)—1866
Spinks, T. (Merchant Taylors')—1840
Stainton, R. G. (Malvern)—1933
Stanning, J. (Winchester)—1939
Stephenson, J. S. (Shrewsbury)—1925–26
Stevens, G. T. S. (U.C.S.)—1920–21–22–23 (Captain 1922)
Stewart, W. A. (Winchester)—1869–70
Stewart-Brown, P. H. (Harrow)—1925–26
Stocks, F. W. (Lancing & Denstone)—1898–99
Sutton, M. A. (Ampleforth)—1946

Taswell, H. J. (Rugby)—1851
Taylor, C. H. (Westminster)—1923–24–25–26
Teape, A. S. (Eton)—1863–64–65
Teesdale, H. (Winchester)—1908
Thesiger, Hon. F. J. N. (Winchester)—1888–90 (Captain 1890)
Thesiger (1st Viscount Chelmsford) retired hurt in the 1891 match, his place being taken by T. B. Case.
Thornton, W. A. (Winchester)—1879–80–81–82

Tindall, R. G. (Winchester)—1933–34
Torre, H. J. (Harrow)—1839–40
Townsend, D. C. H. (Winchester)—1933–34
Townsend, W. H. (Rugby)—1842–43
Townshend, W. (Rossall)—1870–71–72
Traill, W. F. (Merchant Taylors')—1858–59–60
Travers, B. H. (Sydney U., N.S.W.)—1946–48
Trevor, A. H. (Winchester)—1880–81
Tritton, E. W. (Eton)—1864–65–66–67 (Captain 1866)
Trower, C. F. (Winchester)—1838
Tuff, F. N. (Malvern)—1910
Twining, R. H. (Eton)—1910–11–12–13 (Captain 1912)
Tylecote, E. F. S. (Clifton)—1869–70–71–72 (Captain 1871–72)
Tylecote, H. G. (Clifton)—1874–75–76–77

Udal, N. R. (Winchester)—1905–06

Vance, G. (Eton)—1836–38
Van der Byl, P. G. (Diocesan College, S.A.)—1932
Van Ryneveld, C. B. (Diocesan College, S.A.)—1948–49–50 (Captain 1949)
Veitch, H. G. J. (Twyford)—1854–55–56
Vidler, J. L. S. (Repton)—1910–11–12
Von Ernsthausen, A. C. (Uppingham)—1902–03–04
Voules, S. C. (Marlborough)—1863–64–65–66

Waddy, P. S. (King's School, Parramatta, N.S.W.)—1896–97
Waldock, F. A. (Uppingham)—1919–20
Walford, M. M. (Rugby)—1936–38
Walker, D. F. (Uppingham)—1933–34–35 (Captain 1935)
Walker, J. G. (Loretto)—1882–83
Walker, R. D. (Harrow)—1861–62–63–64–65
Wallace, A. (Winchester)—1851
Wallington, E. W. (Sherborne)—1877
Wallroth, C. A. (Harrow)—1872–73–74
Walshe, A. P. (Milton, Rhodesia)—1953–55–56
Walter, A. F. (Eton)—1869
Walton, A. C. (Radley)—1955–56–57 (Captain 1957)
Ward, H. P. (Shrewsbury)—1919–21
Ward, Lord (later Earl of Dudley) (Eton)—1841–42
Warner, P. F. (Rugby)—1895–96
Watson, A. K. (Harrow)—1889
Watson, H. D. (Harrow)—1891

Waud, B. W. (Eton)—1857–58–59–60
Webb, H. E. (Winchester)—1948
Webbe, A. J. (Harrow)—1875–76–77–78—(Captain 1877–78)
Webbe, H. R. (Winchester)—1877–78–79 (Captain 1879)
Wellings, E. M. (Cheltenham)—1929–31
Wheatley, G. A. (Uppingham)—1946
Whitby, H. O. (Leamington)—1884–85–86–87
Whitcombe, P. A. (Winchester)—1947–48–49
Whitcombe, P. J. (Worcester R.G.S.)—1951–52
White, H. (Denstone)—1900
Whitehouse, P. M. (Marlborough)—1938
Whiting, A. O. (Charterhouse & Sherborne)—1881–82
Wickham, A. P. (Marlborough)—1878
Wiley, W. G. E. (Diocesan College, S.A.)—1952
Wilkinson, W. A. C. (Eton)—1913
Willes, E. H. L. (Winchester)—1852–53–54 (Captain 1853–54)
Williams, C. C. P. (Westminster)—1953–54–55 (Captain 1955)
Williams, P. (Winchester)—1844–45–46–47
Williams, R. A. (Winchester)—1901–02
Willis, C. F. (Tonbridge)—1847–48–49
Wilson, A. (Rugby)—1848–49–50
Wilson, G. L. (Repton & Brighton)—1890–91
Wilson, R. W. (Warwick)—1957
Wilson, T. S. B. (Bath College)—1892–93
Winn, C. E. (K.C.S., Wimbledon)—1948–49–50–51
Wood, J. B. (Marlborough)—1892–93
Woodcock, R. G. (Worcester R.G.S.)—1957–58
Wordsworth, Charles (Harrow)—1827–29 (Captain 1827–29)
Worthington, G. (Tonbridge)—1844
Wright, E. C. (Clergy Orphan School, Canterbury)—1897
Wright, E. L. (Winchester)—1905–06–07–08 (Captain 1907–08)
Wright, F. B. (Winchester)—1829
Wright, F. W. (Rossall)—1863–64–65
Wrigley, M. H. (Harrow)—1949
Wyatt, M. T. H. (Private)—1850–51 (Acting Captain 1851)
Wyld, H. J. (Harrow)—1901–02–03
Wynne, J. H. G. (Eton)—1839–40
Wynne-Finch, C. G. (Eton)—1836

Yonge, C. D. (Eton)—1836
Yonge, G. E. (Eton)—1844–45–46–47–48 (Captain 1848)
Young, D. E. (K.C.S., Wimbledon)—1938

CAMBRIDGE UNIVERSITY BLUES

Abercrombie, J. (Tonbridge)—1838
Absolom, C. A. (Private)—1866–67–68–69
Aird, R. (Eton)—1923
Alexander, F. C. M. (Wolmer's College, Jamaica)—1952–53
Allen, A. W. (Eton)—1933–34
Allen, B. O. (Clifton)—1933
Allen, G. O. (Eton)—1922–23
Allom, M. J. C. (Wellington)—1927–28
Allsopp, H. T. (Cheltenham)—1876
Anson, T. A. (Eton)—1839–40–41–42 (Captain 1840–41–42)
Arkwright, H. A. (Harrow)—1858
Arnold, A. C. P. (Malvern)—1914
Ash, E. P. (Rugby)—1865

Ashton, C. T. (Winchester)—1921–22–23 (Captain 1923)
Ashton, G. (Winchester)—1919–20–21 (Captain 1921)
Ashton, H. (Winchester)—1920–21–22 (Captain 1922)
Atkins, G. (Challenor's G. S., Amersham)—1960
Austin, H. M. (Melbourne)—1924

Baggallay, M. E. C. (Eton)—1911
Bagge, T. E. (Eton)—1859–60–61 (Captain 1861)
Bagnall, H. F. (Harrow)—1923
Bailey, T. E. (Dulwich)—1947–48
Baily, E. P. (Harrow)—1872–74
Baily, R. E. H. (Harrow)—1908

Bainbridge, H. W. (Eton)—1884–85–86 (Captain 1886)

Baker, E. C. (Brighton)—1912–14

Balfour, R. D. (Bradfield & Westminster)—1863–64–65–66

Barber, R. W. (Ruthin)—1956–57

Barchard, E. (Winchester)—1846–47–48

Barker, G. (Bury St Edmunds)—1840

Barnett, W. E. (Eton)—1849–50

Bartlett, H. T. (Dulwich)—1934–35–36 (Captain 1936)

Bastard, J. H. (Winchester)—1838–40

Bateman, A. (Brighton)—1859–60–61

Bayford, R. A. (Kensington G.S.)—1857–58–59 (Captain 1859)

Bennett, C. T. (Harrow)—1923–25 (Captain 1925)

Benthall, W. H. (Westminster & Marlborough)—1858–59–60

Bernard, J. R. (Clifton)—1958–59–60

Blacker, W. (Harrow)—1873–74–75–76

Blake, J. P. (Aldenham)—1939

Blaker, R. N. (Elizabeth College, Guernsey)—1842–43

Blaker, R. N. R. (Westminster)—1900–01–02

Blayds, E. (Harrow)—1846–47–48–49

Bligh, Hon. Ivo F. W. (later Earl of Darnley) (Eton)—1878–79–80–81 (Captain 1881)

Block, S. A. (Marlborough)—1929

Blofeld, H. C. (Eton)—1959

Blore, E. W. (Eton)—1848–49–50–51 (Captain 1851)

Blundell, E. D. (Waitaki, N.Z.)—1928–29

Bodkin, P. E. (Bradfield)—1946 (Captain 1946)

Boldero, H. K. (Harrow)—1851–52–53

Booth, C. (Rugby)—1862–63–64–65 (Captain 1864)

Booth, H. W. (Eton)—1836 (Captain 1836)

Boudier, G. J. (Eton)—1841–43 (Joint-captain with T. L. French 1843)

Bourne, A. A. (Rugby)—1870

Bray, E. (Westminster)—1871–72

Bray, E. H. (Charterhouse)—1896–97

Brereton, C. J. (Marlborough)—1858

Bridgeman, W. C. (Eton)—1887

Brocklebank, J. M. (Eton)—1936

Brodhurst, A. H. (Malvern)—1939

Brodie, J. B. (Union H.S., South Africa)—1960

Bromley-Davenport, H. R. (Eton)—1892–93

Brooke-Taylor, G. P. (Cheltenham)—1919–20

Broughton, R. J. P. (Harrow)—1836–38–39

Brown, F. R. (Leys)—1930–31

Browne, F. B. R. (Aldro School & Eastbourne)—1922

Brune, C. J. (Godolphin School, Hammersmith)—1867–68–69

Brunton, J. du V. (Lancaster G.S.)—1894

Bryan, J. L. (Rugby)—1921

Buchanan, D. (Rugby)—1850

Buchanan, J. N. (Charterhouse)—1906–07–08–09 (Captain 1909)

Buckston, G. M. (Eton)—1903

Bulwer, J. B. R. (King's College, London)—1841

Burghley, Lord (later Marquess of Exeter) (Eton)—1847

Burnett, A. C. (Lancing)—1949

Burnup, C. J. (Malvern)—1896–97–98

Burr, G. F. (Maidstone)—1840

Burrough, J. (King's School, Bruton & Shrewsbury)—1895

Bury, L. (Eton)—1877

Bury, T. W. (Winchester)—1855

Bury, W. (Private)—1861–62

Bushby, M. H. (Dulwich)—1952–53–54 (Captain 1954)

Butler, E. M. (Harrow)—1888–89

Butterworth, H. R. W. (Rydal Mount)—1929

Buxton, C. D. (Harrow)—1885–86–87–88 (Captain 1888)

Calthorpe, Hon. F. S. G. (Repton)—1912–13–14–19

Calvert, C. T. (Shrewsbury)—1848

Cameron, J. H. (Taunton)—1935–36–37

Campbell, S. C. (Bury St Edmunds)—1845

Cangley, B. G. M. (Felsted)—1947

Carris, B. D. (Harrow)—1938–39

Carris, H. E. (Mill Hill)—1930

Cawston, E. (Lancing)—1932

Chapman, A. P. F. (Oakham & Uppingham)—1920–21–22

Christopher, A. W. M. (Private)—1843

Christopherson, J. C. (Uppingham)—1931

Clement, R. A. (Rugby)—1854

Clissold, S. T. (Eton)—1844–46

Cobbold, P. W. (Eton)—1896

Cobbold, R. H. (Eton)—1927

Cobden, F. C. (Harrow)—1870–71–72

Cockburn-Hood, J. S. E. (Rugby)—1865–67

Cockett, J. A. (Aldenham)—1951

Coghlan, T. B. L. (Rugby)—1960

Colbeck, L. G. (Marlborough)—1905–06

Collins, D. C. (Wellington College, N.Z.)—1910–11

Collins, T. (Bury St Edmunds)—1863

Comber, J. T. H. (Marlborough)—1931–32–33

Conradi, E. R. (Oundle)—1946

Coode, A. T. (Fauconberge School, Beccles)—1898

Cook, G. W. (Dulwich)—1957–58

Cooke, C. R. (Eton & Ipswich)—1858

Cookesley, W. G. (Eton)—1827

Cotterill, G. E. (Brighton)—1858–59–60

Cowie, A. G. (Charterhouse)—1910

Crawley, E. (Harrow)—1887–88–89

Crawley, L. G. (Harrow)—1923–24–25

Croft, P. D. (Gresham's)—1955

Crofts, C. D. (Winchester)—1843

Crookes, D. V. (Michaelhouse, S.A.)—1953

Cumberlege, B. S. (Durham)—1913

Currie, F. L. (Rugby)—1845

Curteis, T. S. (Felsted & Bury St Edmunds)—1864–65

Dale, J. W. (Tonbridge)—1868–69–70

Daniel, A. W. T. (Harrow)—1861–62–63–64

Daniell, J. (Clifton)—1899–1900–01

Datta, P. B. (Asutosh College, Calcutta)—1947

Davies, G. B. (Rossall)—1913–14

Davies, J. G. W. (Tonbridge)—1933–34

Dawson, E. W. (Eton)—1924–25–26–27 (Captain 1927)

Day, S. H. (Malvern)—1899–1900–01–02 (Captain 1901)

de Gray, T. (later Lord Walsingham) (Eton)—1862–63

de Little, E. R. (Geelong Grammar School)—1889

de Paravicini, P. J. (Eton)—1882–83–84–85

de St Croix W. (Eton)—1839–40–41–42

de Zoete, H. W. (Eton)—1897–98

Deacon, W. S. (Eton)—1848–49–50 (Captain 1850)

Dewes, J. G. (Aldenham)—1948–49–50

Dewing, E. M. (Harrow)—1842–43–44–45 (Captain 1844–45)
Dexter, E. R. (Radley)—1956–57–58 (Captain 1958)
Dickinson, D. C. (Clifton)—1953
Dickinson, P. J. (K.C.S., Wimbledon)—1939
Doggart, A. G. (Bishop's Stortford)—1921–22
Doggart, G. H. G. (Winchester)—1948–49–50 (Captain 1950)
Dolphin, J. (Eton)—1827
Dorman, A. W. (Dulwich)—1886
Douglas, J. (Dulwich)—1892–93–94
Douglas, R. N. (Dulwich)—1890–91–92
Douglas-Hamilton, H. A. (Wellington)—1873–75
Douglas-Pennant, S. (Eton)—1959
Downes, K. D. (Rydal)—1939
Dowson, E. M. (Harrow)—1900–01–02–03 (Captain 1903)
Drake, E. T. (Westminster)—1852–53–54
Driffield, L. T. (Leatherhead)—1902
Druce, N. F. (Marlborough)—1894–95–96–97 (Captain 1897)
Druce, W. G. (Marlborough)—1894–95 (Captain 1895)
Du Cane, A. R. (Harrow)—1854–55
Duleepsinhji, K. S. (Cheltenham)—1925–26–28
Dupuis, G. R. (Eton)—1857
Dyke, E. F. (Eton)—1865
Dykes, T. (Kingston College, Hull)—1844

Ebden, C. H. M. (Eton)—1902–03
Edwards, R. S. (Huntingdon G.S. & Christ's Hospital)—1850
Elgood, B. C. (Bradfield)—1948
Ellis, E. C. (Private)—1829
Enthoven, H. J. (Harrow)—1923–24–25–26 (Captain 1926)
Estcourt, N. S. D. (Plumtree, Southern Rhodesia) —1954
Evans, R. G. (King Edward's, Bury St Edmunds) —1921
Eyre, C. H. (Harrow)—1904–05–06 (Captain 1906)

Fabian, A. H. (Highgate)—1929–30–31
Fairbairn, G. A. (Church of England G.S., Geelong)—1913–14–19
Falcon, M. (Harrow)—1908–09–10–11 (Captain 1910)
Fargus, A. H. C. (Clifton & Haileybury)— 1900–01
Farmer, A. A. (Winchester)—1836
Farnes, K. (R.L.S., Romford)—1931–32–33
Fawcett, E. B. (Brighton)—1859–60
Fenn, S. (Blackheath Proprietary)—1851
Fenn, W. M. (Blackheath Proprietary)—1848–50–51
Fernie, A. E. (Wellingborough)—1897–1900
Fiddian-Green, C. A. (Leys)—1921–22
Field, E. (Clifton)—1894
FitzGerald, R. A. (Harrow)—1854–56
Foley, C. P. (Eton)—1889–90–91
Foley, C. W. (Eton)—1880
Ford, A. F. J. (Repton)—1878–79–80–81
Ford, F. G. J. (Repton)—1887–88–89–90 (Captain 1889)
Ford, W. J. (Repton)—1873
Fowler, T. F. (Uppingham)—1864
Francis, T. E. S. (Tonbridge)—1925
Franklin, W. B. (Repton)—1912
Fraser, T. W. (Jeppe, S.A.)—1937

Freeman-Thomas, F. (later Lord Willingdon) (Eton)—1886–87–88–89
French, T. L. (Winchester)—1842–43–44 (Joint-captain with G. J. Boudier 1843)
Frere, J. (Eton)—1827
Fry, K. R. B. (Cheltenham)—1904
Fryer, C. W. H. (Rugby)—1854
Fryer, F. E. R. (Harrow)—1870–71–72–73 (Captain 1873)
Fuller, E. A. (Rugby)—1852
Fuller, J. M. (Marlborough)—1855–56–57–58 (Captain 1857–58)

Gaddum, F. D. (Uppingham & Rugby)—1882
Gay, L. H. (Marlborough & Brighton)—1892–93
Gibb, P. A. (St Edward's, Oxford)—1935–36–37–38
Gibson, C. H. (Eton)—1920–21
Gibson, J. S. (Harrow)—1855
Gillespie, D. W. (Uppingham)—1939
Gilligan, A. E. R. (Dulwich)—1919-20
Gilman, J. (St Paul's)—1902
Godsell, R. T. (Clifton)—1903
Goldie, C. D. (Kensington G.S.)—1846
Goodwin, H. J. (Marlborough)—1907–08
Goonesena, G. (Royal College, Colombo)— 1954–55–56–57 (Captain 1957)
Gordon, Hon. F. A. (later Lord Francis Gordon) (Charterhouse)—1829
Gosling, R. C. (Eton)—1888–89–90
Grace, W. G., jun. (Clifton)—1895–96
Grant, G. C. (Trinidad)—1929–30
Grant, R. S. (Trinidad)—1933
Gray, H. (Perse)—1894–95
Grazebrook, H. G. (Winchester)—1829
Green, C. E. (Uppingham)—1865–66–67–68 (Captain 1868)
Green, D. J. (Burton G.S.)—1957–58–59 (Captain 1959)
Greenfield, F. F. J. (Hurstpierpoint)—1874–75–76 (Captain 1876)
Grierson, H. (Bedford G.S.)—1911
Griffith, S. C. (Dulwich)—1935
Griffiths, W. H. (Charterhouse)—1946–47–48
Grimshaw, J. W. T. (King William's School, Isle of Man)—1934–35
Grimston, Hon. S. (Harrow)—1843–44–45
Grout, J. (Private)—1838–39

Hadingham, A. W. G. (St Paul's)—1932
Hale, H. (Hutchin's School, Hobart, Tasmania) —1887–89–90
Hales, J. (Rugby)—1855–56
Hall, P. J. (Geelong)—1949
Hammersley, W. J. (Private)—1847
Hammond, O. (Uppingham)—1855–56–57
Harbinson, W. K. (Marlborough)—1929
Hardy, J. R. (Charterhouse)—1829
Harenc, E. A. F. (Naval College, Portsmouth)— 1841
Harper, L. V. (Rossall)—1901–02–03
Harris, J. E. (Sheffield Collegiate)—1859
Harrison, W. P. (Rugby)—1907
Hartopp, E. S. E. (Eton)—1841–42
Hawke, Hon. M. B. (later Lord Hawke) (Eton)— 1882–83–85 (Captain 1885)
Hawkins, H. H. B. (Whitgift)—1898–99
Hayward, W. I. D. (St Peter's, Adelaide)— 1950–51–53
Hazlerigg, A. G. (Eton)—1930–31–32 (Captain 1932)

Helm, G. F. (Marlborough)—1862–63
Hemingway, W. McG. (Uppingham)—1895–96
Henery, P. J. T. (Harrow)—1882–83
Hewan, G. E. (Marlborough)—1938
Hill, A. J. L. (Marlborough)—1890–91–92–93
Hill-Wood, W. W. (Eton)—1922
Hind, A. E. (Uppingham)—1898–99–1900–01
Hoare, A. M. (Private)—1844
    Hoare was appointed captain in 1846, but did not play owing to illness.
Hobson, B. S. (Taunton)—1946
Hodgson, E. F. (Eton)—1836
Holloway, N. J. (Leys)—1910–11–12
Hone, N. T. (Rugby)—1881
Hone-Goldney, G. H. (Eton)—1873
Hope-Grant, F. C. (Harrow)—1863
Hopley, F. J. V. (Harrow)—1904
Hopley, G. W. V. (Harrow)—1912
Horne, E. L. (Shrewsbury)—1855–57–58
Horsman, E. (Rugby)—1827–29
Hotchkin, N. S. (Eton)—1935
Howard-Smith, G. (Eton)—1903
Howland, C. B. (Dulwich)—1958–59–60 (Captain 1960)
Hughes, O. (Malvern)—1910
Hughes, T. F. (Private)—1845
Human, J. H. (Repton)—1932–33–34 (Captain 1934)
Human, R. H. C. (Repton)—1930–31
Hume, A. (Eton)—1841–42
Hunt, R. G. (Aldenham)—1937
Hurd, A. (Chigwell)—1958–59–60

Imlay, A. D. (Clifton)—1907
Ingram, C. P. (Westminster)—1854
Insole, D. J. (Monoux, Walthamstow)—1947–48–49 (Captain 1949)
Ireland, J. F. (Marlborough)—1908–09–10–11 (Captain 1911)
Irvine, L. G. (Taunton)—1926–27

Jackson, F. S. (Harrow)—1890–91–92–93 (Captain 1892–93)
Jagger, S. T. (Malvern)—1925–26
Jahangir Khan, M. (Lahore)—1933–34–35–36
James, R. M. (St John's, Leatherhead)—1956–57–58
Jarvis, L. K. (Harrow)—1877–78–79
Jeffery, G. E. (Rugby)—1873–74
Jenner, C. H. (Eton)—1829
Jenner, Herbert (Eton)—1827 (Captain 1827)
Jenner, H. L. (Harrow)—1841
Jenyns, G. F. G. (Private)—1849–50
Jephson, D. L. A. (Manor House, Clapham)—1890–91–92
Jessop, G. L. (Cheltenham G.S.)—1896–97–98–99 (Captain 1899)
Johnson, G. R. (Bury St Edmunds)—1855–56–57 (Captain 1855)
Johnson, P. R. (Eton)—1901
Jones, A. O. (Bedford Modern)—1893
Jones, R. S. (Chatham House, Ramsgate)—1879–80
Jones-Bateman, J. B. (Winchester)—1848
Judd, A. K. (St Paul's)—1927

Kaye, M. A. C. P. (Harrow)—1938
Keigwin, R. P. (Clifton)—1903–04–05–06
Kelland, P. A. (Repton)—1950
Kemp, G. M. (later Lord Rochdale) (Mill Hill & Shrewsbury)—1885–86–88

Kempson, S. M. E. (Cheltenham)—1851–53
Kempson, W. J. (Rugby)—1855
Kemp-Welch, G. D. (Charterhouse)—1929–30–31 (Captain 1931)
Kenny, C. J. M. (Ampleforth)—1952
Khanna, B. C. (Lahore)—1937
Kidd, E. L. (Wellington)—1910–11–12–13 (Captain 1912)
Killick, E. T. (St Paul's)—1928–29–30
King, F. (Dulwich)—1934
King, R. T. (Oakham)—1846–47–48–49 (Captain 1849)
Kingdon, S. N. (Eton)—1827
Kingston, F. W. (Abingdon House, Northampton)—1878
Kirby, D. (St Peter's, York)—1959–60
Kirwan, J. H. (Eton)—1839
Knatchbull-Hugessen, C. M. (later Lord Brabourne) (Eton)—1886
Knightley-Smith, W. (Highgate)—1953
Koe, B. D. (Eton)—1838

Lacey, F. E. (Sherborne)—1882
Lucy-Scott, D. G. (Marlborough)—1946
Lagden, R. B. (Marlborough)—1912–13–14
Lancashire, O. P. (Lancing)—1880
Lang, A. H. (Harrow)—1913
Lang, R. (Harrow)—1860–61–62
Langley, J. D. A. (Stowe)—1938
Latham, P. H. (Malvern)—1892–93–94 (Captain 1894)
Latham, T. (Winchester)—1873–74
Lawrence, A. S. (Harrow)—1933
Leake, W. M. (Rugby)—1851–52–53–54
Lee, F. (Rugby)—1860
Lee, J. M. (Blackheath Proprietary & Oundle)—1846–47–48
Leith, J. (Private)—1848
Lewis, A. R. (Neath G.S.)—1960
Lewis, L. K. (Taunton)—1953
Lockhart, J. H. B. (Sedbergh)—1909–10
Long, F. E. (Eton)—1836
Long, R. P. (Harrow)—1845–46
Longfield, T. C. (Aldenham)—1927–28
Longman, G. H. (Eton)—1872–73–74–75 (Captain 1874–75)
Longman, H. K. (Eton)—1901
Longrigg, E. F. (Rugby)—1927–28
Lowe, R. G. H. (Westminster)—1925–26–27
Lowe, W. W. (Malvern)—1895
Lowry, T. C. (Christ's College, N.Z.)—1923–24 (Captain 1924)
Lucas, A. P. (Uppingham)—1875–76–77–78
Luddington, H. T. (Uppingham)—1876–77
Lumsden, V. R. (Munro College, Jamaica)—1953–54–55
Lyon, M. D. (Rugby)—1921–22
Lyon, W. J. (Highstead, Torquay)—1861
Lyttelton, 4th Lord (Eton)—1838
Lyttelton, Hon. Alfred (Eton)—1876–77–78–79 (Captain 1879)
Lyttelton, Hon. C. F. (Eton)—1908–09
Lyttelton, Hon. C. G. (later Lord Cobham) (Eton)—1861–62–63–64
Lyttelton, Hon. Edward (Eton)—1875–76–77–78 (Captain 1878)
Lyttelton, Hon. G. W. S. (Eton)—1866–67

Macan, G. (Harrow)—1874–75
MacBryan, J. C. W. (Exeter)—1920
MacGregor, G. (Uppingham)—1888–89–90–91 (Captain 1891)

Machin, R. S. (Lancing)—1927
Mackinnon, F. A. (Harrow)—1870
MacLeod, K. G. (Fettes)—1908–09
MacNiven, E. (Eton)—1846
Mainprice, H. (Blundell's)—1906
Makinson, J. (Huddersfield & Owen's College)—1856–57–58
Mann, E. W. (Harrow)—1903–04–05 (Captain 1905)
Mann, F. G. (Eton)—1938–39
Mann, F. T. (Malvern)—1909–10–11
Mann, J. E. F. (Geelong)—1924
Manners-Sutton, Hon. J. H. T. (later Viscount Canterbury) (Eton)—1836
Mansfield, J. W. (Winchester)—1883–84
Maples, W. (Haileybury & Winchester)—1839
Marchant, F. (Rugby & Eton)—1884–85–86–87 (Captain 1887)
Marlar, R. G. (Harrow)—1951–52–53 (Captain 1953)
Marriott, C. S. (St Columba's)—1920–21
Marriott, H. H. (Malvern)—1895–96–97–98
Marsh, J. F. (Amersham Hall)—1904
Marshall, H. M. (Westminster)—1861–62–63–64
Marshall, J. H. (King Edward VI School, Birmingham)—1859
Marshall, J. W. (King Edward VI School, Birmingham)—1855–56–57
Martin, M. T. (Rugby)—1862–64
Martineau, L. (Uppingham)—1887
Massey, W. (Harrow)—1838–39
Mathews, K. P. A. (Felsted)—1951
Maule, W. (Tonbridge)—1853
May, P. B. H. (Charterhouse)—1950–51–52
May, P. R. (Private)—1905–06
McCarthy, C. N. (Pietermaritzburg College, S.A.)—1952
McCormick, J. (Liverpool College & Bingley)—1854–56 (Captain 1856)
McDonell, H. C. (Winchester)—1903–04–05
McLachlan, I. M. (St Peter's, Adelaide)—1957–58
Meetkerke, A. (Eton)—1840
Mellor, F. H. (Cheltenham)—1877
Melluish, M. E. L. (Rossall)—1954–55–56 (Captain 1956)
Meryweather, W. S. T. M. (Charterhouse)—1829
Meyer, R. J. O. (Haileybury)—1924–25–26
Meyrick-Jones, F. (Marlborough)—1888
Micklethwaite, F. N. (Eton)—1836
Micklethwaite, S. N. (Shrewsbury)—1843
Mills, J. M. (Oundle)—1946–47–48 (Captain 1948)
Mills, W. (Harrow)—1840–41–42–43
Mischler, N. M. (St Paul's)—1946–47
Mitchell, F. (St Peter's School, York)—1894–95–96–97 (Captain 1896)
Money, W. B. (Harrow)—1868–69–70–71 (Captain 1870)
Moon, L. J. (Westminster)—1899–1900
Morcom, A. F. (Repton)—1905–06–07
Mordaunt, H. J. (Eton)—1888–89
Morgan, J. T. (Charterhouse)—1928–29–30 (Captain 1930)
Morgan, M. N. (Marlborough)—1954
Morris, R. J. (Blundell's)—1949
Morrison, J. S. F. (Charterhouse)—1912–14–19 (Captain 1919)
Morse, C. (Dedham)—1842–43–44
Morton, P. H. (Rossall)—1878–79–80
Mugliston, F. H. (Rossall)—1907–08
Mulholland, Hon. H. G. H. (Eton)—1911–12–13 (Captain 1913)

Napier, G. G. (Marlborough)—1904–05–06–07
Nason, J. W. W. (University School, Hastings)—1909–10
Naumann, J. H. (Malvern)—1913–19
Nelson, R. P. (St George's, Harpenden)—1936
Newton, S. C. (Victoria College, Jersey)—1876
Nicholson, J. (Rugby & Harrow)—1845
Norman, C. L. (Eton)—1852–53
Norman, F. H. (Eton)—1858–59–60 (Captain 1860)
Norris, W. A. (Eton)—1851
Northey, A. E. (Harrow)—1859–60
Nunn, F. (Bury St Edmunds)—1859

O'Brien, R. P. (Wellington)—1955–56
Oddie, H. H. (Eton)—1836
Olivier, E. (Repton)—1908–09
Onslow, D. R. (Brighton)—1860–61
Orford, L. A. (Uppingham)—1886–87
Ottey, G. P. (Rugby)—1844–45–46–47

Page, C. C. (Malvern)—1905–06
Palmer, C. (Uppingham)—1907
Parker, G. W. (Crypt, Gloucester)—1934–35 (Captain 1935)
Parker, H. (Maidstone)—1839
Parry, D. M. (Merchant Taylors')—1931
Parsons, A. B. D. (Brighton)—1954–55
Partridge, N. E. (Malvern)—1920
Patterson, W. S. (Uppingham)—1875–76–77 (Captain 1877)
Pawle, J. H. (Harrow)—1936–37
Payne, A. U. (St Edmund's, Canterbury)—1925
Payne, M. W. (Wellington)—1904–05–06–07 (Captain 1907)
Payton, W. E. G. (Nottingham H.S.)—1937
Pelham, A. G. (Eton)—1934
Pelham, Hon. F. G. (later Earl of Chichester) (Eton)—1864–65–66–67 (Captain 1866–67)
Pell, O. C. (Rugby)—1844–45–46–47 (Captain 1847)
Penn, E. F. (Eton)—1899–1902
Pepper, J. (Leys)—1946–47–48
Perkins, H. (Bury St Edmunds)—1854
Perkins, T. T. N. (Leatherhead)—1893–94
Phillips, E. S. (Marlborough)—1904
Pickering, E. H. (Eton)—1827–29 (Captain 1829)
Pickering, W. P. (Eton)—1840–42
Pieris, P. I. (St Thomas's, Colombo)—1957–58
Pigg, H. (Abingdon House, Northampton)—1877
Plowden, H. M. (Harrow)—1860–61–62–63 (Captain 1862–63)
Ponsonby, Hon. F. G. B. (Harrow) (later Lord Bessborough)—1836
Pontifex, C. (K.C.S., London)—1851–53
Pope, C. G. (Harrow)—1894
Popplewell, O. B. (Charterhouse)—1949–50–51
Potter, A. (Private)—1849
Powell, A. G. (Charterhouse)—1934
Powys, W. N. (Private)—1871–72–74
Prest, E. B. (Eton)—1850
Prest, H. E. W. (Malvern)—1909–11
Preston, B. (Westminster)—1869
Pretlove, J. F. (Alleyn's)—1954–55–56
Prideaux, R. M. (Tonbridge)—1958–59–60
Pryer, B. J. K. (City of London)—1948

Ramsay, R. C. (Harrow)—1882
Ranjitsinhji, K. S. (Rajkumar College, India)—1893
Ratcliffe, A. (Rydal)—1930–31–32
Raymond-Barker, H. B. (Winchester)—1844

Raynor, G. S. (Winchester)—1872
Reddy, N. S. K. (Doon School, Dehra Dun, India)—1959–60
Rees-Davies, W. R. (Eton)—1938
Reynolds, E. M. (Royal Institution, Liverpool)—1853–54
Richardson, H. A. (Tonbridge)—1867–68–69
Richardson, J. M. (Harrow)—1866–67–68
Riddell, V. H. (Clifton)—1926
Riley, W. N. (R.G.S., Worcester)—1912
Rimell, A. G. J. (Charterhouse)—1949–50
Rippingall, S. F. (Rugby)—1845
Roberts, F. B. (Rossall)—1903
Robertson, W. P. (Harrow)—1901
Robins, R. W. V. (Highgate)—1926–27–28
Robinson, J. J. (Appleby)—1894
Rock, C. W. (Launceston G.S., Tasmania)—1884–85–86
Roe, W. N. (Clergy Orphan School, Canterbury)—1883
Romilly, E. (Bury St Edmunds)—1827
Rotherham, G. A. (Rugby)—1919
Rought-Rought, D. C. (Private)—1937
Rought-Rought, R. C. (Private)—1930–32.
Rowe, F. C. C. (Harrow)—1881
Rowell, W. I. (Marlborough)—1891
Royston, Viscount (Harrow)—1857

St John, E. (Private)—1829
Salter, H. W. (Private)—1861–62
Savile, Hon. A. (Eton)—1840
Savile, G. (Eton & Rossall)—1868
Saville, S. H. (Marlborough)—1911–12–13–14 (Captain 1914)
Sayres, E. (Midhurst)—1838–39–40–41
Schultz, S. S. (later Storey) (Uppingham)—1877
Scott, A. T. (Brighton)—1870–71
Seabrook, F. J. (Haileybury)—1926–27–28 (Captain 1928)
Seddon, R. (Bridgnorth G.S.)—1846–47
Sharpe, C. M. (Private)—1875
Shaw, V. K. (Haileybury)—1876
Shelmerdine, G. O. (Cheltenham)—1922
Sheppard, D. S. (Sherborne)—1950–51–52 (Captain 1952)
Sherwell, N. B. (Tonbridge)—1923–24–25
Shine, E. B. (King Edward School, Saffron Walden)—1896–97
Shirley, W. R. (Eton)—1924
Shirreff, A. C. (Dulwich)—1939
Shuttleworth, G. M. (Blackburn G.S.)—1946–47–48
Silk, D. R. W. (Christ's Hospital)—1953–54–55 (Captain 1955)
Simonds, H. J. (Eton)—1850
Sims, H. M. (St Peter's, York)—1873–74–75
Singh, S. (Khalsa & Punjab U.)—1955–56
Sivewright, E. (Eton)—1829
Slack, J. K. E. (U.C.S., London)—1954
Smith, A. F. (Harrow & Wellington)—1875
Smith, C. A. (Charterhouse)—1882–83–84–85
Smith, C. S. (William Hulme's G.S.)—1954–55–56–57
Smith, D. J. (Stockport G.S.)—1955–56
Southwell, H. G. (Harrow)—1852–53
Spencer, R. (Harrow)—1881
Spiro, D. G. (Harrow)—1884
Stacey, F. E. (Eton)—1853
Stanning, J. (Rugby)—1900
Stedman, H. C. P. (Private)—1871
Steel, A. G. (Marlborough)—1878–79–80–81 (Captain 1880)

Steel, D. Q. (Uppingham)—1876–77–78–79
Stevenson, M. H. (Rydal)—1949–50–51–52
Stogdon, J. H. (Harrow)—1897–98–99
Stow, M. H. (Harrow)—1867–68–69 (Captain 1869)
Streatfeild, E. C. (Charterhouse)—1890–91–92–93
Studd, C. T. (Eton)—1880–81–82–83 (Captain 1883)
Studd, G. B. (Eton)—1879–80–81–82 (Captain 1882)
Studd, J. E. K. (Eton)—1881–82–83–84 (Captain 1884)
Studd, P. M. (Harrow)—1937–38–39 (Captain 1939)
Studd, R. A. (Eton)—1895
Subba Row, R. (Whitgift)—1951–52–53
Sutthery, A. M. (Uppingham & Oundle)—1887
Swift, B. T. (St Peter's, Adelaide)—1957
Sykes, W. (Private)—1844

Tabor, A. S. (Eton)—1872–73–74
Taylor, C. G. (Eton)—1836–38–39 (Captain 1838–39)
Taylor, T. L. (Uppingham)—1898–99–1900 (Captain 1900)
Templeton, C. H. (Winchester)—1827
Thackeray, F. (Eton)—1838–39–40
Thomas, A. (Winchester)—1838
Thompson, J. R. (Tonbridge)—1938–39
Thompson, W. T. (Ruthin)—1836
Thornewill, E. J. (Harrow)—1856
Thornton, C. I. (Eton)—1869–70–71–72 (Captain 1872)
Tillard, C. (Repton)—1873–74
Tindall, M. (Harrow)—1935–36–37 (Captain 1937)
Tobin, F. (Rugby)—1870–71–72
Tomblin, A. C. (Uppingham)—1857
Tomlinson, W. J. V. (Felsted)—1923
Topham, H. G. (Repton)—1883–84
Toppin, C. (Sedbergh)—1885–86–87
Tordoff, G. G. (Normanton G.S.)—1952
Townley, T. M. (Eton)—1847–48
Trapnell, B. M. W. (U.C.S., London)—1946
Tremlett, T. D. (Eton)—1854
Trevelyan, W. B. (Edinburgh Academy & Harrow)—1842–43
Tuck, G. H. (Eton)—1863–64–65–66 (Captain 1865)
Tufnell, N. C. (Eton)—1909–10
Turnbull, M. J. (Downside)—1926–28–29 (Captain 1929)
Turner, J. A. (Uppingham)—1883–84–85–86
Turner, J. B. (Blackheath Proprietary)—1841

Urquhart, J. R. (King Edward VI School, Chelmsford)—1948

Valentine, B. H. (Repton)—1929
Vernon, H. (Harrow)—1850–51–52 (Captain 1852)
Vincent, H. G. (Haileybury)—1914

Wait, O. J. (Dulwich)—1949–51
Walker, Ashley (Westminster)—1864–65–66
Walker, F. (Private)—1849–50–51–52
Walker, John (Private)—1847–48–49 (Captain 1848)
Ward, A. R. (Private)—1853
Ward was appointed captain in 1854 but did not play owing to illness.

Ward, E. E. (Bury St Edmunds)—1870–71
Warner, W. S. O. (Torquay)—1867–68
Warr, J. J. (Ealing C.G.S.)—1949–50–51–52 (Captain 1951)
Warren, C. (Oakham)—1866
Watts, H. E. (Downside)—1947
Webb, R. H. (Eton)—1827
Webster, J. (Bradford G.S.)—1939
Webster, W. H. (Highgate)—1932
Weigall, G. J. V. (Wellington)—1891–92
Weighell, W. B. (Bedford Grammar)—1866–68–69
Wells, C. M. (Dulwich)—1891–92–93
Wells, T. U. (Kings, Auckland)—1950
Weston, J. S. (Rugby)—1851–52
Wheatley, O. S. (King Edward's, Birmingham)—1957–58
Wheelhouse, A. (Nottingham H.S.)—1959
White, A. F. T. (Uppingham)—1936
White, A. H. (Geelong)—1924
White, H. S. (Bury St Edmunds & Brighton)—1852
Whitfield, H. (Eton)—1878–79–80–81
Whymper, F. H. (Eton)—1849
Wilcox, D. R. (Dulwich)—1931–32–33 (Captain 1933)
Wild, J. V. (Taunton)—1938
Wilenkin, B. C. G. (Harrow)—1956
Willard, M. J. L. (Judd, Tonbridge)—1959–60
Wilkins-Leir, E. J. P. (Marlborough)—1858
Willatt, G. L. (Repton)—1946–47 (Captain 1947)
Wills, T. W. (Rugby)—1856
Wills had been entered at Cambridge and played as Cambridge were one short, but had never actually been in residence.

Wilson, C. E. M. (Uppingham)—1895–96–97–98 (Captain 1898)
Wilson, C. P. (Uppingham & Marlborough)—1880–81
Wilson, E. R. (Rugby)—1899–1900–01–02 (Captain 1902)
Wilson, F. B. (Harrow)—1902–03–04 (Captain 1904)
Wilson, G. (Harrow)—1919
Wilson, T. W. (Repton)—1869
Wingfield, W. (Rossall)—1855–56–57
Winlaw, R. de W. K. (Winchester)—1932–33–34
Winter, A. H. (Westminster)—1865–66–67
Winter, C. E. (Uppingham)—1902
Winter, G. E. (Winchester)—1898–99
Winthrop, S. (Rugby)—1829
Wood, G. E. C. (Cheltenham)—1914–19–20 (Captain 1920)
Wood, H. (Sheffield Collegiate School)—1879
Woodroffe, K. H. C. (Marlborough)—1913–14
Woods, S. M. J. (Brighton)—1888–89–90–91 (Captain 1890)
Wooller, W. (Rydal)—1935–36
Wright, C. C. G. (Tonbridge)—1907–08
Wright, C. W. (Charterhouse)—1882–83–84–85
Wright, P. A. (Wellingborough)—1922–23–24
Wroth, H. T. (Uppingham)—1845
Wykes, N. G. (Oundle)—1928

Yardley, N. W. D. (St Peter's, York)—1935–36–37–38 (Captain 1938)
Yardley, W. (Rugby)—1869–70–71–72 (Captain 1871)
Young, R. A. (Repton)—1905–06–07–08 (Captain 1908)

UNIVERSITY MATCH RESULTS

With a few exceptions the matches have been played at Lord's, the others are denoted as follows—(*a*) at Magdalen Ground, (*b*) at Bullingdon Green, (*c*) at Cowley Marsh, all at Oxford. The results of the University matches have been as follows:

1827	Drawn	1863	Oxford—8 wickets
1829	Oxford—115 runs (*a*)	1864	Oxford—4 wickets
1836	Oxford—121 runs	1865	Oxford—114 runs
1838	Oxford—98 runs	1866	Oxford—12 runs
1839	Cambridge—Innings & 125 runs	1867	Cambridge—5 wickets
1840	Cambridge—63 runs	1868	Cambridge—168 runs
1841	Cambridge—8 runs	1869	Cambridge—58 runs
1842	Cambridge—162 runs	1870	Cambridge—2 runs
1843	Cambridge—54 runs (*b*)	1871	Oxford—8 wickets
1844	Drawn	1872	Cambridge—Innings & 166 runs
1845	Cambridge—6 wickets	1873	Oxford—3 wickets
1846	Oxford—3 wickets (*a*)	1874	Oxford—Innings & 92 runs
1847	Cambridge—138 runs	1875	Oxford—6 runs
1848	Oxford—23 runs (*a*)	1876	Cambridge—9 wickets
1849	Cambridge—3 wickets	1877	Oxford—10 wickets
1850	Oxford—127 runs (*c*)	1878	Cambridge—238 runs
1851	Cambridge—Innings & 4 runs	1879	Cambridge—9 wickets
1852	Oxford—Innings & 77 runs	1880	Cambridge—115 runs
1853	Oxford—Innings & 19 runs	1881	Oxford—135 runs
1854	Oxford—Innings & 8 runs	1882	Cambridge—7 wickets
1855	Oxford—3 wickets	1883	Cambridge—7 wickets
1856	Cambridge—3 wickets	1884	Oxford—7 wickets
1857	Oxford—81 runs	1885	Cambridge—7 wickets
1858	Oxford—Innings & 38 runs	1886	Oxford—133 runs
1859	Cambridge—28 runs	1887	Oxford—7 wickets
1860	Cambridge—3 wickets	1888	Drawn
1861	Cambridge—133 runs	1889	Cambridge—Innings & 105 runs
1862	Cambridge—8 wickets	1890	Cambridge—7 wickets

1891	Cambridge—2 wickets		1925	Drawn
1892	Oxford—5 wickets		1926	Cambridge—34 runs
1893	Cambridge—266 runs		1927	Cambridge—116 runs
1894	Oxford—8 wickets		1928	Drawn
1895	Cambridge—134 runs		1929	Drawn
1896	Oxford—4 wickets		1930	Cambridge—205 runs
1897	Cambridge—179 runs		1931	Oxford—8 wickets
1898	Oxford –9 wickets		1932	Drawn
1899	Drawn		1933	Drawn
1900	Drawn		1934	Drawn
1901	Drawn		1935	Cambridge—195 runs
1902	Cambridge—5 wickets		1936	Cambridge—8 wickets
1903	Oxford—268 runs		1937	Oxford—7 wickets
1904	Drawn		1938	Drawn
1905	Cambridge—40 runs		1939	Oxford—45 runs
1906	Cambridge—94 runs		1946	Oxford—6 wickets
1907	Cambridge—5 wickets		1947	Drawn
1908	Oxford—2 wickets		1948	Oxford—Innings & 8 runs
1909	Drawn		1949	Cambridge—7 wickets
1910	Oxford—Innings & 126 runs		1950	Drawn
1911	Oxford—74 runs		1951	Oxford—21 runs
1912	Cambridge—3 wickets		1952	Drawn
1913	Cambridge—4 wickets		1953	Cambridge—2 wickets
1914	Oxford—194 runs		1954	Drawn
1919	Oxford—45 runs		1955	Drawn
1920	Drawn		1956	Drawn
1921	Cambridge—Innings & 24 runs		1957	Cambridge—Innings & 186 runs
1922	Cambridge—Innings & 100 runs		1958	Cambridge—99 runs
1923	Oxford—Innings & 227 runs		1959	Oxford—85 runs
1924	Cambridge—9 wickets		1960	Drawn

Of the 116 matches played to date, Oxford has won 43 matches, Cambridge 50 matches, and 23 have been drawn.

CENTURIES IN THE UNIVERSITY MATCH

M. J. K. Smith (Oxford 1954 to 1956) is the only batsman to have scored three centuries in the series of matches. The following batsmen have scored two centuries —W. Yardley (1870 and 1872), H. J. Enthoven (1924 and 1925), Nawab of Pataudi (1929 and 1931), A. Ratcliffe (1931 and 1932) and D. R. W. Silk (1953 and 1954).

Oxford (33):

109	W. H. Game	1876	109	C. H. Taylor	1923
117*	F. M. Buckland	1877	113	E. R. T. Holmes	1927
107*	W. H. Patterson	1881	106	Nawab of Pataudi	1929
143	K. J. Key	1886	238*	Nawab of Pataudi	1931
107	W. Rashleigh	1886	167	B. W. Hone	1932
100	Lord George Scott	1887	193	D. C. H. Townsend	1934
140	M. R. Jardine	1892	108	F. G. H. Chalk	1934
114	V. T. Hill	1892	121	J. N. Grover	1937
100*	C. B. Fry	1894	142	M. P. Donnelly	1946
121	H. K. Foster	1895	135	H. A. Pawson	1947
132	G. O. Smith	1896	145*	H. E. Webb	1948
109	A. Eccles	1898	116	M. C. Cowdrey	1953
171	R. E. Foster	1900	201	M. J. K. Smith	1954
100*	C. H. B. Marsham	1901	104	M. J. K. Smith	1955
130	J. E. Raphael	1903	117	M. J. K. Smith	1956
160	P. R. Le Couteur	1910	131	Nawab of Pataudi	1960
170	M. Howell	1919			

Cambridge (37):

100	W. Yardley	1870	127	H. J. Mordaunt	1889
130	W. Yardley	1872	116	E. C. Streatfeild	1892
105*	W. S. Patterson	1876	115	C. E. M. Wilson	1898
120	G. B. Studd	1882	118	E. R. Wilson	1901
102	C. W. Wright	1883	117*	S. H. Day	1902
101	H. W. Bainbridge	1885	172*	J. F. Marsh	1904
103*	E. Crawley	1887	107	L. G. Colbeck	1905

150	R. A. Young	1906
118	H. Ashton	1921
102*	A. P. F. Chapman	1922
104	H. J. Enthoven	1924
129	H. J. Enthoven	1925
124	A. K. Judd	1927
101*	R. W. V. Robins	1928
149	J. T. Morgan	1929
136	E. T. Killick	1930
201	A. Ratcliffe	1931
157	D. R. Wilcox	1932
124	A. Ratcliffe	1932
115	A. W. Allen	1934
101	N. W. D. Yardley	1937
122	P. A. Gibb	1938
100	P. J. Dickinson	1939
127	D. S. Sheppard	1952
116*	D. R. W. Silk	1953
118	D. R. W. Silk	1954
114	J. F. Pretlove	1955
146	R. P. O'Brien	1956
211	G. Goonesena	1957
111*	G. W. Cook	1957

HIGHEST INNINGS TOTALS IN THE UNIVERSITY MATCH

503	Oxford	1900
457	Oxford	1947
453—8d	Oxford	1931
432—9d	Cambridge	1936
431	Cambridge	1932
425	Cambridge	1938
424—7d	Cambridge	1957
422	Oxford	1923
415—8d	Cambridge	1921
415	Oxford	1934
409	Cambridge	1925
408—9d	Cambridge	1952
403—4d	Cambridge	1922
401—3d	Oxford	1954
400	Cambridge	1934

RECORD WICKET PARTNERSHIPS IN UNIVERSITY MATCH

1st	243	K. J. Key & W. Rashleigh	Oxford	1886
2nd	226	W. G. Keighley & H. A. Pawson	Oxford	1947
3rd	183	A. T. Barber & E. R. T. Holmes	Oxford	1927
4th	230	D. C. H. Townsend & F. G. H. Chalk	Oxford	1934
5th	191	J. E. Raphael & E. L. Wright	Oxford	1905
6th	178	M. R. Jardine & V. T. Hill	Oxford	1892
7th	289	G. Goonesena & G. W. Cook	Cambridge	1957
8th	112	H. E. Webb & A. W. H. Mallett	Oxford	1948
9th	97*	J. F. Marsh & F. J. V. Hopley	Cambridge	1904
10th	90	W. J. H. Curwen & E. G. Martin	Oxford	1906

1,000 RUNS IN A UNIVERSITY SEASON

		Season	Inns.	N.O.	Runs	H.S.	Avge.	100s
D. S. Sheppard	Cambridge	1952	23	3	1581	239*	79·05	7
R. M. Prideaux	Cambridge	1960	34	0	1311	140	38·55	4
Nawab of Pataudi	Oxford	1931	16	2	1307	238*	93·35	6
A. R. Lewis	Cambridge	1960	32	2	1307	125	43·56	2
P. B. H. May	Cambridge	1951	24	6	1286	178*	71·44	4
G. H. G. Doggart	Cambridge	1949	24	5	1280	219*	67·36	3
J. G. Dewes	Cambridge	1950	20	4	1262	212	78·87	5
M. P. Donnelly	Oxford	1946	22	2	1256	142	62·80	6
E. R. Dexter	Cambridge	1958	32	2	1256	114	41·86	3
E. R. Dexter	Cambridge	1957	32	1	1209	185	39·00	2
J. G. Dewes	Cambridge	1949	22	2	1175	204*	58·75	1
J. H. Human	Cambridge	1934	21	3	1160	146*	64·44	5
A. A. Baig	Oxford	1959	29	4	1148	221*	45·92	3
M. P. Donnelly	Oxford	1947	21	4	1144	154*	67·29	3
A. M. Crawley	Oxford	1928	21	0	1137	167	54·14	5
A. C. Walton	Oxford	1956	29	4	1128	152	41·77	3
M. C. Cowdrey	Oxford	1953	24	2	1124	154	51·09	3
F. C. de Saram	Oxford	1934	23	1	1119	208	50·86	3
G. D. Kemp-Welch	Cambridge	1931	24	1	1111	126	48·30	3
P. A. Gibb	Cambridge	1938	17	1	1075	204	67·18	4
T. C. Lowry	Cambridge	1923	24	2	1077	161	48·95	4
D. S. Sheppard	Cambridge	1950	20	1	1072	227	56·42	4
M. J. K. Smith	Oxford	1954	26	4	1065	201*	48·40	2
M. B. Hofmeyr	Oxford	1950	21	2	1063	162	55·94	4
M. J. Turnbull	Cambridge	1929	24	4	1001	167*	50·05	3
M. J. K. Smith	Oxford	1956	27	2	1001	126	40·04	3

HIGHEST RUN AGGREGATES IN A UNIVERSITY CAREER

		Seasons	Inns.	N.O.	Runs	H.S.	Avge.	100s
D. S. Sheppard	Cambridge	1950–1952	62	5	3545	239*	62·19	14
N. S. Mitchell-Innes	Oxford	1934–1937	78	8	3319	207	47·41	9
E. R. Dexter	Cambridge	1956–1958	92	5	3298	185	37·90	7
J. G. Dewes	Cambridge	1948–1950	62	8	3247	212	60·12	7
M. J. K. Smith	Oxford	1954–1956	80	7	3049	201*	41·76	8
A. M. Crawley	Oxford	1927–1930	63	3	2914	204	48·56	9
P. B. H. May	Cambridge	1950–1952	58	12	2861	227*	62·19	9
M. C. Cowdrey	Oxford	1952–1954	70	5	2848	154	43·81	5
Nawab of Pataudi	Oxford	1928–1931	59	5	2744	238*	50·81	9
R. M. Prideaux	Cambridge	1958–1960	92	5	2684	143	30·85	6
G. H. G. Doggart	Cambridge	1948–1950	56	9	2599	219*	55·29	7
E. W. Dawson	Cambridge	1924–1927	87	4	2581	140	31·09	4
E. T. Killick	Cambridge	1927–1930	59	3	2534	201	45·25	8
M. B. Hofmeyr	Oxford	1949–1951	65	8	2495	161	43·77	5
G. T. S. Stevens	Oxford	1920–1923	72	8	2484	182	38·81	2
R. C. M. Kimpton	Oxford	1935–1938	68	7	2412	160	39·54	5
M. P. Donnelly	Oxford	1946–1947	43	6	2400	154*	64·86	9
K. S. Duleepsinhji	Cambridge	1925–1928	57	4	2333	254*	44·02	5
G. Goonesena	Cambridge	1954–1957	87	8	2309	211	29·22	2
C. C. P. Williams	Oxford	1952–1955	75	4	2301	139*	32·40	4
M. A. Eagar	Oxford	1956–1959	93	8	2298	125	27·03	1
J. Burki	Oxford	1958–1960	78	9	2272	144*	32·92	5
H. Ashton	Cambridge	1920–1922	43	8	2258	236	64·51	7
A. C. Walton	Oxford	1955–1957	80	2	2254	152	28·89	3
J. H. Human	Cambridge	1932–1934	48	8	2205	158*	55·12	10
D. B. Carr	Oxford	1948–1951	67	4	2200	170	34·92	5
P. A. Gibb	Cambridge	1935–1938	73	8	2199	204	33·83	5
F. G. H. Chalk	Oxford	1931–1934	77	7	2141	149	30·58	6
N. F. Druce	Cambridge	1894–1897	51	4	2121	227*	45·12	7
N. W. D. Yardley	Cambridge	1935–1938	77	5	2099	116*	29·15	4
H. J. Enthoven	Cambridge	1923–1926	68	8	2024	129	33·73	2
N. M. Ford	Oxford	1928–1930	62	8	2016	183	37·33	5

MOST WICKETS IN A UNIVERSITY SEASON

		Season	Overs	Mdns.	Runs	Wkts.	Avge.
O. S. Wheatley	Cambridge	1959	578·1	149	1411	80	17·63
A. G. Steel	Cambridge	1878	456	212	557	75	7·42
I. A. R. Peebles	Oxford	1930	442·2	77	1271	70	18·15
C. M. Sharpe	Cambridge	1875	546·3	168	848	66	12·84
F. R. Brown	Cambridge	1931	499·2	104	1461	66	22·13
C. W. Rock	Cambridge	1886	696·2	326	868	65	13·35
E. M. Dowson	Cambridge	1902	420·3	95	1174	65	18·06
D. M. Sayer	Oxford	1959	509·2	103	1470	64	22·96
D. M. Sayer	Oxford	1958	408·4	129	831	62	13·40
R. H. B. Bettington	Oxford	1923	303·4	60	1010	61	16·55
R. G. Marlar	Cambridge	1953	610·1	172	1619	61	26·54
S. M. J. Woods	Cambridge	1888	500	176	990	60	16·50
F. H. E. Cunliffe	Oxford	1896	471·4	168	984	60	16·40
M. J. C. Allom	Cambridge	1927	465·5	95	1345	60	22·41
G. Goonesena	Cambridge	1955	520·2	140	1290	60	21·50
P. R. le Couteur	Oxford	1910	243·4	39	845	59	14·32
A. Hurd	Cambridge	1960	723·2	214	1883	59	31·91
R. C. Ramsay	Cambridge	1882	534	215	856	58	14·75
A. Hurd	Cambridge	1959	714·2	217	1888	58	32·58
F. S. Jackson	Cambridge	1892	327·2	98	829	57	14·54
H. A. Gilbert	Oxford	1909	350·5	112	756	57	13·26
C. S. Marriott	Cambridge	1921	443·3	128	1064	57	18·66
G. Goonesena	Cambridge	1954	587·3	170	1336	57	23·43
G. G. Napier	Cambridge	1905	338·1	75	973	56	17·37
R. H. B. Bettington	Oxford	1920	292·3	65	847	56	15·12
P. A. Wright	Cambridge	1924	394·2	127	888	56	15·85
R. F. H. Darwall-Smith	Oxford	1937	394·3	77	1102	56	19·67

Gentlemen v. Players

The first match between the Gentlemen and the Players took place at Lord's in 1806 and since that date it has normally been a regular fixture. For many years a match was played at the Oval each season, but in the 1930's the match was abandoned in view of the congestion of the fixture list and the consequent difficulty in selecting a representative team. For the Lord's match the elevens are selected by M.C.C. and an invitation to play is looked upon in the same light as an invitation for England, but in the last few years the Oval teams—selected by the Surrey committee—were restricted to players whose counties were without a fixture on the days involved. This led to some very weak teams being fielded, the fixture eventually being cancelled in view of the ever-increasing difficulties.

In most years the Scarborough Festival has included a Gentlemen v. Players match and other official matches have been played at Brighton, Hastings and Princes. The matches played at Folkestone and Bournemouth are not regarded as part of the official series.

CENTURIES SCORED IN THE SERIES OF MATCHES

Gentlemen

Players

At Lord's

	Gentlemen			Players	
102*	W. Ward	1825	113*	T. Beagley	1821
134*	W. G. Grace	1868	100	J. Saunders	1827
109	W. G. Grace	1870	132	Thomas Hayward	1860
112	W. G. Grace	1872	112*	Thomas Hayward	1863
163	W. G. Grace	1873	122*	Thomas Hearne	1866
152	W. G. Grace	1875	102	R. Daft	1872
169	W. G. Grace	1876	111	A. Shrewsbury	1887
103	A. W. Ridley	1876	130*	W. Barnes	1889
107	A. P. Lucas	1882	103	W. Gunn	1892
100	C. T. Studd	1882	116*	T. Hayward	1896
107	E. F. S. Tylecote	1883	125	A. Shrewsbury	1897
118	W. G. Grace	1895	139	W. Gunn	1898
104	C. B. Fry	1899	163	J. T. Brown	1900
102* 136 }	R. E. Foster	1900	111	T. Hayward	1900
			140	J. T. Tyldesley	1901
126	C. B. Fry	1901	141	L. C. Braund	1902
232*	C. B. Fry	1903	100	W. H. Lockwood	1902
168*	A. C. MacLaren	1903	139	A. E. Knight	1903
121	K. S. Ranjitsinhji	1904	104 109* }	J. H. King	1904
114	R. H. Spooner	1906			
124	D. J. Knight	1919	123*	T. Hayward	1905
101	P. G. H. Fender	1921	146*	T. Hayward	1907
160	A. P. F. Chapman	1922	154*	J. B. Hobbs	1911
122	G. T. S. Stevens	1923	113	J. B. Hobbs	1919
120	M. D. Lyon	1923	108	C. P. Mead	1921
129	G. T. S. Stevens	1925	140	J. B. Hobbs	1922
108	A. P. F. Chapman	1926	162	A. C. Russell	1922
123	D. R. Jardine	1927	118	J. B. Hobbs	1924
125 103* }	K. S. Duleepsinhji	1930	113	R. Kilner	1924
			140	J. B. Hobbs	1925
165	Nawab of Pataudi	1932	163	J. B. Hobbs	1926
132	K. S. Duleepsinhji	1932	107	H. Sutcliffe	1926
104*	R. E. S. Wyatt	1934	131	E. Tyldesley	1926
175*	H. T. Bartlett	1938	161*	J. B. Hobbs	1932
162*	M. P. Donnelly	1947	110	W. R. Hammond	1932
122	F. R. Brown	1950	120	A. Mitchell	1934
119*	P. B. H. May	1951	105	C. Washbrook	1946
127	C. H. Palmer	1952	101	C. Washbrook	1947
117	R. T. Simpson	1953	132*	L. Hutton	1948
154	C. H. Palmer	1955	123	H. E. Dollery	1950
102*	R. Subba Row	1958	150	D. C. S. Compton	1951
166	M. J. K. Smith	1959	115	M. Tompkin	1955
			102	D. V. Smith	1957
			101	C. A. Milton	1958
			112	D. B. Close	1959
			100	R. Illingworth	1959

Gentlemen | Players

At the Oval

Gentlemen			Players		
107*	A. Lubbock	1867	119	R. Carpenter	1860
165	I. D. Walker	1868	106	R. Carpenter	1861
215	W. G. Grace	1870	117	H. H. Stephenson	1864
109*	W. B. Money	1870	134	G. Ulyett	1884
117	W. G. Grace	1872	127	A. Shrewsbury	1886
158	W. G. Grace	1873	151*	A. Shrewsbury	1892
144	A. N. Hornby	1877	168*	R. Abel	1894
100	W. G. Grace	1881	100	F. W. Marlow	1895
159	W. W. Read	1885	195	R. Abel	1899
112*	C. L. Townsend	1899	134*	T. Hayward	1899
123	C. J. Burnup	1900	153*	R. Abel	1900
145	B. J. T. Bosanquet	1904	247	R. Abel	1901
140	W. L. Murdoch	1904	177	T. Hayward	1902
128	J. H. Hunt	1904	203	T. Hayward	1904
190	R. H. Spooner	1911	104	J. Hardstaff sen.	1906
101	C. B. Fry	1912	158	S. P. Kinneir	1911
107	G. L. Jessop	1913	123*	J. W. Hearne	1912
127	Hon. C. N. Bruce	1921	126	J. W. Hearne	1913
112	A. E. R. Gilligan	1924	156	J. B. Hobbs	1914
130	G. O. Allen	1925	120*	J. B. Hobbs	1919
193	D. R. Jardine	1928	127	H. T. W. Hardinge	1921
115	R. E. S. Wyatt	1929	126	T. F. Shepherd	1923
123*	D. R. Jardine	1932	124	A. Sandham	1924
112	Lord Tennyson	1932	103	J. W. Hearne	1925
			125	A. Sandham	1926
			150	E. Hendren	1927
			110	J. B. Hobbs	1931
			120	H. Sutcliffe	1931
			194*	E. Hendren	1932
			125	J. Arnold	1934
			119	H. S. Squires	1934
			106	R. Duckfield	1934

At Prince's

Gentlemen			Players		
104	A. N. Hornby	1873	118	G. Ulyett	1877
110	W. G. Grace	1874			
134	G. F. Grace	1877			

At Brighton

217	W. G. Grace	1871

At Hastings

Gentlemen			Players		
131	W. G. Grace	1894	169	W. Gunn	1891
105	A. O. Jones	1901	117	R. Abel	1892
			108	A. Ward	1897
			124*	G. H. Hirst	1903

At Bournemouth

117	C. P. Mead	1928

At Scarborough

Gentlemen			Players		
174	W. G. Grace	1885	125	G. J. Thompson	1900
134	F. S. Jackson	1900	157*	D. Denton	1906
102	T. L. Taylor	1902	122*	E. G. Hayes	1906
102	C. J. Burnup	1902	105	J. T. Tyldesley	1910
137	E. G. Wynyard	1906	223	C. P. Mead	1911
120	K. L. Hutchings	1908	116	J. B. Hobbs	1919
103	B. J. T. Bosanquet	1911	146	J. W. Hearne	1919
119	G. L. Jessop	1913	138	J. B. Hobbs	1920
101	G. A. Faulkner	1913	105	J. B. Hobbs	1923
101	A. P. F. Chapman	1920	100*	E. Hendren	1923
100	F. T. Mann	1922	266*	J. B. Hobbs	1925
101	A. W. Carr	1925	129	E. Hendren	1925
101*	V. W. C. Jupp	1927	119	J. B. Hobbs	1927

Gentlemen			Players		
106	M. C. Cowdrey	1951	127	P. Holmes	1927
157	P. B. H. May	1953	116	E. Tyldesley	1927
100	M. C. Cowdrey	1953	144	J. B. Hobbs	1931
133	W. J. Edrich	1953	100	J. Hardstaff jun.	1938
112*	P. B. H. May	1954	241	L. Hutton	1953
133	W. J. Edrich	1955	143*	W. Watson	1953
133	W. J. Edrich	1956	122	J. V. Wilson	1954
104	A. C. D. Ingleby-Mackenzie	1959	124	T. W. Graveney	1956
119	D. R. W. Silk	1960	111	K. F. Barrington	1960

At Folkestone

Gentlemen			Players		
101	Hon. F. S. G. Calthorpe	1927	103	E. Hendren	1927
136	B. W. Hone	1932	138	W. R. Hammond	1927
128	C. P. Johnstone	1933	141*	F. E. Woolley	1928
115	R. C. M. Kimpton	1936	118	A. Sandham	1931
			129	T. S. Worthington	1932
			201	L. E. G. Ames	1933
			117	W. H. Ashdown	1933
			109	G. Geary	1934
			106	W. R. Hammond	1935

HIGHEST INDIVIDUAL INNINGS

266*	J. B. Hobbs (Players)	Scarborough	1925
247	R. Abel (Players)	Oval	1901
241	L. Hutton (Players)	Scarborough	1951
232*	C. B. Fry (Gentlemen)	Lord's	1901
223	C. P. Mead (Players)	Scarborough	1913
217	W. G. Grace (Gentlemen)	Brighton	1873
215	W. G. Grace (Gentlemen)	Oval	1870
203	T. Hayward (Players)	Oval	1904
201	L. E. G. Ames (Players)	Folkestone	1933

HIGHEST INNINGS TOTALS

651—7d	Players	Oval	1934
647	Players	Oval	1899
608—8d	Players	Oval	1921
579	Players	Lord's	1926
578	Gentlemen	Oval	1904
561—6d	Players	Folkestone	1927
552—8d	Players	Folkestone	1933

LOWEST INNINGS TOTALS

24	Players	Lord's	1829
31	Gentlemen	Lord's	1848
35	Gentlemen	Lord's	1837
36	Gentlemen	Lord's	1831
37	Players	Lord's	1829
37	Gentlemen	Lord's	1853
39	Gentlemen	Lord's	1840

RECORD WICKET PARTNERSHIPS—GENTLEMEN

1st	203	W. G. Grace & A. J. Webbe at Lord's	1875
2nd	241	W. G. Grace & G. F. Grace at Brighton	1871
3rd	309*	C. B. Fry & A. C. MacLaren at Lord's	1903
4th	205	P. B. H. May & M. C. Cowdrey at Scarborough	1953
5th	172	A. P. F. Chapman & D. R. Jardine at Lord's	1926
6th	164	K. L. Hutchings & F. L. Fane at Scarborough	1908
7th	249	W. L. Murdoch & J. H. Hunt at the Oval	1904
8th	129	T. L. Taylor & E. Smith at Scarborough	1902
9th	193	G. O. Allen & N. E. Haig at the Oval	1925
10th	134	A. E. R. Gilligan & M. Falcon at the Oval	1924

RECORD WICKET PARTNERSHIPS—PLAYERS

1st	263	J. B. Hobbs & H. Sutcliffe at Lord's	1926
2nd	181	J. B. Hobbs & P. Holmes at Scarborough	1927
3rd	298	J. B. Hobbs & E. Hendren at Scarborough	1925
4th	226	E. Hendren & W. R. Hammond at Folkestone	1927
5th	160	J. W. Hearne & F. A. Tarrant at the Oval	1912
6th	204	L. E. G. Ames & W. H. Ashdown at Folkestone	1933
7th	184	D. B. Close & R. Illingworth at Lord's	1959
8th	118	A. E. Knight & S. F. Barnes at Lord's	1903
9th	156	T. Hayward & J. T. Hearne at Lord's	1896
10th	140*	G. S. Boyes & A. E. Thomas at Folkestone	1930

BOWLING UNCHANGED THROUGH MATCH

There are nine cases of bowlers bowling unchanged through both innings (both bowlers were given men in 1829):

W. Lillywhite (14 wickets) & James Broadbridge (5 wickets) for Gentlemen at Lord's 1829
W. Lillywhite & James Broadbridge for Players at Lord's 1832
W. Lillywhite (13 wickets) & S. Redgate (5 wickets) for Players at Lord's 1837
J. Wisden (8 wickets) & W. Clarke (12 wickets) for Players at Lord's 1850
Sir F. Bathurst (11—50) & M. Kempson (9—54) for Gentlemen at Lord's 1853
J. Jackson (11—99) & E. Willsher (6—70) for Players at Lord's 1861
G. Tarrant (11—49) & E. Willsher (9—55) for Players at Lord's 1864
A. H. Evans (10—74) & A. G. Steel (9—43) for Gentlemen at the Oval 1879
F. S. Jackson (12—77) & S. M. J. Woods (6—124) for Gentlemen at Lord's 1894

RESULTS OF MATCHES AT LORD'S SINCE 1919

In the seasons before Test matches became annual events, the match between the Gentlemen and Players at Lord's was regarded as the high-spot of the season. In those days the players were selected for their services to the game and their clubs during that season and in previous years. With the widening of Test cricket the match has come to be looked upon as more of an unofficial Test trial, but selection for the matches is just as high an honour.

To be asked to captain one of the teams in the annual Lord's match is a high honour, in the case of a professional the highest honour with which he could be rewarded until 1952, when L. Hutton was made captain of England.

		Captain	
Season	*Result*	*Gentlemen*	*Players*
1919	Match drawn	P. F. Warner	G. H. Hirst
1920	Players—7 wickets	J. W. H. T. Douglas	W. Rhodes
1921	Players—9 wickets	J. W. H. T. Douglas	W. Rhodes
1922	Match drawn	F. T. Mann	J. B. Hobbs
1923	Match drawn	F. T. Mann	J. B. Hobbs
1924	Players—Innings & 231 runs	A. E. R. Gilligan	J. B. Hobbs
1925	Match drawn	A. W. Carr	J. B. Hobbs
1926	Match drawn	A. W. Carr	J. B. Hobbs
1927	Match drawn	A. P. F. Chapman	F. E. Woolley
1928	Players—9 wickets	A. P. F. Chapman	F. E. Woolley
1929	Players—7 wickets	A. W. Carr	F. E. Woolley
1930	Match drawn	A. P. F. Chapman	J. B. Hobbs
1931	Match drawn	D. R. Jardine	H. Sutcliffe
1932	Match drawn	D. R. Jardine	J. B. Hobbs
1933	Players—10 wickets	D. R. Jardine	H. Sutcliffe
1934	Gentlemen—7 wickets	R. E. S. Wyatt	E. Hendren
1935	Players—9 wickets	R. E. S. Wyatt	W. R. Hammond
1936	Match drawn	G. O. Allen	W. R. Hammond
1937	Players—8 wickets	A. B. Sellers	W. R. Hammond
1938	Gentlemen—133 runs	W. R. Hammond	F. E. Woolley
1939	Players—160 runs	W. R. Hammond	E. Paynter
1946	Players—Innings & 140 runs	W. R. Hammond	J. Hardstaff jun.
1947	Match drawn	N. W. D. Yardley	L. E. G. Ames
1948	Players—7 wickets	N. W. D. Yardley	L. Hutton
1949	Players—4 wickets	F. G. Mann	D. C. S. Compton
1950	Match drawn	F. R. Brown	H. E. Dollery
1951	Players—21 runs	N. D. Howard	D. C. S. Compton
1952	Players—2 runs	F. R. Brown	L. Hutton

Season	Result	Gentlemen	Captain	Players
1953	Gentlemen—95 runs	F. R. Brown		C. Washbrook
1954	Players—49 runs	D. S. Sheppard		D. C. S. Compton
1955	Players—20 runs	D. J. Insole		A. V. Bedser
1956	Match drawn	C. H. Palmer		C. Washbrook
1957	Match drawn	P. B. H. May		D. C. S. Compton
1958	Match drawn	D. J. Insole		T. G. Evans
1959	Match drawn	P. B. H. May		D. Brookes
1960	Match drawn	M. C. Cowdrey		J. B. Statham

APPEARANCES AT LORD'S SINCE 1919

Gentlemen

Allan, J. M. (1) 1956
Allen, B. O. (1) 1938
Allen, G. O. (6) 1925–29–30–32–34–36
Allom, M. J. C. (2) 1930–32
Ashton, H. (3) 1920–21–22
Bailey, T. E. (8) 1947–49–50–52–53–54–56–59
Barber, R. W. (2) 1959–60
Barnett, B. A. (2) 1954–55
Bartlett, H. T. (2) 1938–39
Bartlett, J. N. (1) 1946
Baxter, A. D. (1) 1934
Benson, E. T. (1) 1929
Bettington, R. H. B. (2) 1920–25
Brennan, D. V. (4) 1950–51–52–53
Brocklebank, J. M. (1) 1939
Brown, F. R. (13) 1931–32–34–35–36–37–38–39–47–49–50–52–53
Bruce, Hon. C. N. (2) 1919–21
Bryan, J. L. (3) 1923–24–25
Calthorpe, Hon. F. S. G. (1) 1925
Carr, A. W. (7) 1919–22–23–24–25–26–29
Carr, D. B. (3) 1950–59–60
Chalk, F. G. H. (1) 1939
Chapman, A. P. F. (9) 1920–21–22–23–26–27–28–30–32
Clay, J. C. (1) 1935
Corran, A. J. (1) 1960
Cowdrey, M. C. (6) 1954–55–56–57–58–60
Cranston, K. (2) 1947–48
Crawley, A. M. (3) 1928–29–31
Davies, J. G. W. (1) 1946
Dawson, E. W. (2) 1925–27
Dempster, C. S. (1) 1937
Dewes, J. G. (3) 1948–49–50
Dexter, E. R. (4) 1957–58–59–60
Divecha, R. V. (1) 1951
Doggart, G. H. G. (2) 1949–50
Donnelly, M. P. (3) 1946–47–48
Douglas, J. W. H. T. (4) 1919–20–21–24
Duleepsinhji, K. S. (4) 1925–30–31–32
Edrich, W. J. (6) 1947–48–49–51–53–54
Enthoven, H. J. (2) 1925–26
Evans, A. J. (2) 1919–27
Falcon, M. (1) 1919
Farnes, K. (5) 1933–36–37–38–39
Fellows-Smith, J. P. (1) 1955
Foster, D. G. (1) 1931
Foster, M. K. (1) 1924
Fender, P. G. H. (10) 1920–21–22–23–24–25–26–28–29–33
Fiddian-Green, C. A. (1) 1922
Franklin, W. B. (3) 1926–27–28
Gibb, P. A. (1) 1938
Gilligan, A. E. R. (3) 1922–23–24
Gillingham, F. H. (1) 1919

Goonesena, G. (4) 1954–55–57–58
Griffith, S. C. (5) 1939–46–47–48–49
Haig, N. E. (5) 1921–26–27–28–29
Hammond, W. R. (3) 1938–39–46
Hazlerigg, A. G. (1) 1932
Heane, G. F. H. (2) 1935–39
Holmes, E. R. T. (4) 1927–34–35–36
Howard, N. D. (1) 1951
Howland, C. B. (1) 1959
Human, J. H. (1) 1934
Hurd, A. (2) 1959–60
Ingleby-Mackenzie, A. C. D. (1) 1958
Insole, D. J. (8) 1950–51–52–53–55–56–57–58
Jardine, D. R. (6) 1926–27–28–31–32–33
Jupp, V. W. C. (4) 1920–21–27–28
Kardar, A. H. (1) 1949
Kemp-Welch, G. D. (1) 1931
Killick, E. T. (1) 1929
Kimpton, R. C. M. (1) 1937
Knight, D. J. (2) 1919–20
Knott, C. J. (2) 1946–50
Levett, W. H. V. (4) 1931–32–34–36
Lewis, E. B. (1) 1957
Louden, G. M. (4) 1919–20–22–23
Lowry, T. C. (1) 1923
Lyon, B. H. (2) 1929–30
Lyon, M. D. (5) 1923–24–26–28–30
MacBryan, J. C. W. (1) 1924
Macindoe, D. H. (1) 1937
Mallett, A. W. H. (2) 1946–47
Mann, F. G. (2) 1948–49
Mann, F. T. (2) 1922–23
Marlar, R. G. (8) 1951–52–53–54–55–56–57–58
Marriott, C. S. (3) 1921–31–33
Maxwell, C. R. (2) 1935–37
May, P. B. H. (6) 1951–52–53–54–57–59
McCarthy, C. N. (1) 1952
Melluish, M. E. L. (1) 1956
Melville, A. (3) 1934–35–36
Meyer, R. J. O. (1) 1938
Mitchell-Innes, N. S. (3) 1935–36–37
Moore, R. H. (1) 1938
Oldfield, P. C. (1) 1933
Owen-Smith, H. G. (2) 1933–37
Palmer, C. H. (5) 1948–52–53–55–56
Parsons, J. H. (1) 1930
Pataudi, Nawab of (3) 1931–32–33
Pawson, H. A. (1) 1947
Pearce, T. N. (2) 1936–48
Peebles, I. A. R. (3) 1930–32–35
Pretlove, J. F. (1) 1955
Prideaux, R. M. (1) 1960
Read, H. D. (1) 1935
Richardson, P. E. (3) 1956–57–58
Robertson-Glasgow, R. C. (1) 1924

Robins, R. W. V. (4) 1928–29–30–31
Robinson, D. C. (1) 1919
Sayer, D. M. (2) 1959–60
Sellers, A. B. (1) 1937
Sheppard, D. S. (5) 1951–52–53–54–57
Sherwell, N. B. (1) 1925
Simpson, R. T. (8) 1947–49–50–51–52–53–54–56
Singleton, A. P. (1) 1946
Smith, A. C. (1) 1960
Smith, C. S. (1) 1957
Smith, H. T. O. (1) 1933
Smith, M. J. K. (5) 1955–56–58–59–60
Stephenson, J. W. A. (3) 1936–38–39
Stevens, G. T. S. (8) 1919–20–22–23–24–25–26–27
Subba Row, R. (3) 1958–59–60
Tennyson, Hon. L. H. (2) 1920–21
Tordoff, G. G. (1) 1955

Trapnell, B. M. W. (1) 1946
Turnbull, M. J. (4) 1933–34–35–36
Valentine, B. H. (3) 1934–39–46
Van Ryneveld, C. B. (1) 1949
Walters, C. F. (2) 1933–34
Warner, P. F. (1) 1919
Warr, J. J. (7) 1950–51–54–55–56–57–58
Wheatley, O. S. (2) 1958–59
Whitcombe, P. A. (1) 1948
White, J. C. (9) 1921–22–23–24–26–27–28–29–30
Willatt, G. L. (2) 1947–52
Wood, G. E. C. (3) 1920–21–22
Wooller, W. (2) 1948–53
Wyatt, R. E. S. (14) 1926–27–28–29–30–31–32
  33–34–35–36–37–38–39
Yardley, N. W. D. (9) 1937–38–46–47–48–49–
  50–51–54

Players

Allen, D. A. (1) 1960
Ames, L. E. G. (5) 1931–33–34–37–47
Appleyard, R. (1) 1954
Arnold, J. (2) 1931–35
Bakewell, A. H. (1) 1931
Barber, W. (1) 1935
Barnett, C. J. (4) 1933–36–37–47
Barrington, K. F. (3) 1955–59–60
Barrick, D. (1) 1953
Bedser, A. V. (6) 1948–50–51–52–53–55
Bestwick, W. (1) 1919
Bowes, W. E. (3) 1931–35–39
Bowley, E. H. (1) 1929
Brookes, D. (1) 1959
Brown, G. (2) 1920–21
Butler, H. J. (1) 1947
Cartwright, T. W. (1) 1959
Clark, E. W. (1) 1933
Clark, T. H. (1) 1957
Close, D. B. (2) 1949–59
Compton, D. C. S. (13) 1937–38–39–46–47–48
  49–51–52–53–54–56–57
Cook, L. (1) 1921
Copson, W. H. (2) 1936–39
Crapp, J. F. (1) 1948
Dollery, H. E. (5) 1939–46–48–50–55
Dolphin, A. (1) 1919
Dooland, B. (2) 1953–54
Ducat, A. (1) 1921
Duckworth, G. (7) 1924–27–28–29–30–32–35
Durston, T. J. (1) 1921
Edrich, J. H. (2) 1959–60
Edrich, W. J. (1) 1938
Emmett, G. M. (1) 1953
Evans, T. G. (12) 1946–47–48–49–50–51–52–53
  54–56–57–58
Fishlock, L. B. (2) 1936–46
Fletcher, D. G. W. (2) 1947–52
Freeman, A. P. (5) 1924–28–29–30–32
Gardner, F. C. (1) 1957
Geary, G. (2) 1926–30
Gimblett, H. (3) 1936–39–50
Gladwin, C. (1) 1947
Goddard, T. W. (2) 1929–37
Gover, A. R. (1) 1936
Graveney, T. W. (7) 1949–51–53–54–56–57–58
Gray, L. H. (1) 1946
Gunn, G. (1) 1919
Hallows, C. (1) 1927
Hammond, W. R. (11) 1927–28–29–30–31–32–
  33–34–35–36–37

Hardinge, H. T. W. (2) 1921–22
Hardstaff, J. jun. (6) 1935–36–37–38–39–46
Harrison, L. (1) 1955
Hearne, J. W. (8) 1919–20–21–22–23–24–25–27
Hendren, E. (13) 1919–20–21–23–24–25–26–27–
  28–29–30–32–34
Hilton, M. J. (1) 1951
Hirst, G. H. (1) 1919
Hobbs, J. B. (9) 1919–20–22–23–24–25–26–30–32
Hollies, W. E. (4) 1946–49–50–57
Holmes, P. (4) 1925–26–27–28
Horton, H. (1) 1960
Howell, H. (3) 1920–23–24
Hutton, L. (7) 1937–38–39–48–49–51–52
Iddon, J. (1) 1931
Ikin, J. T. (2) 1946–51
Illingworth, R. (1) 1959
Jackson, L. (3) 1949–59–60
Jenkins, R. O. (1) 1949
Kennedy, A. S. (2) 1919–??
Kenyon, D. (3) 1950–54–55
Kilner, R. (4) 1923–24–25–26
Laker, J. C. (3) 1952–56–57
Langridge, James (3) 1933–35–37
Langridge, John (1) 1949
Larwood, H. (3) 1927–30–32
Leyland, M. (7) 1928–29–30–33–34–35–36
Livsey, W. H. (1) 1922
Loader, P. J. (1) 1954
Lock, G. A. R. (3) 1954–55–56
Lowson, F. A. (1) 1954
Macaulay, G. G. (2) 1922–25
Marshall, R. E. (1) 1958
McCorkell, N. (1) 1936
Mead, C. P. (6) 1919–20–21–22–23–28
Milton, C. A. (1) 1958
Mitchell, A. (1) 1934
Mitchell, T. B. (2) 1931–34
Moss, A. E. (2) 1953–60
Muncer, B. L. (1) 1948
Murray, J. T. (2) 1959–60
Nichol, M. (1) 1931
Nichols, M. S. (3) 1933–34–38
Oakman, A. S. M. (1) 1956
O'Connor, J. (1) 1934
Padgett, D. E. V. (1) 1960
Parkhouse, W. G. A. (2) 1950–59
Parkin, C. H. (5) 1919–20–21–22–23
Parks, J. H. (1) 1935
Parks, J. M. (3) 1954–55–58
Paynter, E. (4) 1932–37–38–39

Perks, R. T. D. (2) 1931–49
Pollard, R. (2) 1938–46
Pope, G. H. (1) 1939
Price, W. F. (2) 1938–39
Pritchard, T. L. (1) 1948
Pullar, G. (1) 1959
Rhodes, W. (2) 1920–21
Richardson, D. W. (1) 1957
Robertson, J. D. (5) 1947–48–49–51–52
Robinson, E. P. (1) 1946
Root, C. F. (1) 1926
Russell, A. C. (2) 1920–22
Russell, W. E. (1) 1960
Shackleton, D. (2) 1950–52
Sibbles, F. M. (1) 1927
Sims, J. M (1) 1935
Sinfield, R. A. (1) 1936
Smailes, T. F. (1) 1938
Smith, C. I. J. (2) 1934–37
Smith, D. (1) 1935
Smith, D. V. (3) 1956–57–58
Smith, H. (1) 1923
Smith, T. P. B. (1) 1938
Statham, J. B. (4) 1951–54–58–60
Strudwick, H. (3) 1920–25–26
Stewart, M. J. (1) 1960

Sutcliffe, H. (11) 1923–24–25–26–27–29–30–31–32–33–34
Tate, M. W. (9) 1923–24–25–26–27–28–29–30–32
Tattersall, R. (3) 1950–51–53
Thomas, A. E. (1) 1928
Titmus, F. J. (1) 1955
Tompkin, M. (1) 1955
Townsend, L. F. (2) 1929–33
Tribe, G. E. (1) 1958
Trueman, F. S. (4) 1956–57–58–59
Tyldesley, E. (4) 1922–24–26–28
Tyldesley, R. (1) 1925
Tyson, F. H. (3) 1955–56–57
Verity, H. (4) 1931–33–34–36
Voce, W. (1) 1932
Walsh, J. E. (1) 1947
Wardle, J. H. (3) 1948–52–58
Washbrook, C. (6) 1946–47–48–50–53–56
Watkins, A. J. (1) 1952
Watson, F. (1) 1933
Watson, W. (5) 1951–52–53–55–58
Wellard, A. W. (1) 1937
Wharton, A. (1) 1956
Woolley, F. E. (14) 1919–20–21–22–23–24–25–26–27–28–29–30–32–38
Wright, D. V. P. (3) 1939–47–50

Two players—W. R. Hammond and W. J. Edrich—appeared for both the Gentlemen and the Players. W. R. Hammond made his début in the series in 1927 and appeared in every match (14) until his retirement after the 1946–47 tour of Australia.

Other players who appeared for both Gentlemen and Players in the complete series of matches are: R. Daft, E. J. Diver and J. H. Parsons.

Match Record of Touring Teams

The playing records of all the important touring teams in first-class and all matches since the first-ever tour in 1859 are as follows:

* Official M.C.C. touring team.
† Played matches in both Australia and New Zealand.
J. Played matches in Jamaica only.
P. Played matches in Pakistan only.

ENGLAND TEAMS IN AUSTRALIA

Season	Captain	First-class matches						All matches				
		P.	W.	D.	L.	T.		P.	W.	D.	L.	T.
1861–62	H. H. Stephenson	—	—	—	—	—	...	12	6	4	2	—
1863–64†	G. Parr	—	—	—	—	—	...	12	7	5	0	—
1873–74	W. G. Grace	—	—	—	—	—	...	15	10	2	3	—
1876–77†	James Lillywhite	3	1	1	1	—	...	15	5	6	4	—
1878–79	Lord Harris	5	2	0	3	—	...	13	5	5	3	—
1881–82†	A. Shaw	7	3	2	2	—	...	18	8	7	3	—
1882–83	Hon. Ivo Bligh	7	4	0	3	—	...	17	9	5	3	—
1884–85	A. Shrewsbury	8	6	0	2	—	...	33	16	15	2	—
1886–87	A. Shrewsbury	10	6	2	2	—	...	29	12	15	2	—
1887–88	G. F. Vernon	8	6	1	1	—	...	25	10	14	1	—
1887–88†	A. Shrewsbury	7	5	0	2	—	...	22	14	6	2	—
1887–88	Combined team	1	1	0	0	—	...	1	1	0	0	—
1891–92	W. G. Grace	8	6	0	2	—	...	27	12	13	2	—
1894–95	A. E. Stoddart	12	8	0	4	—	...	23	9	10	4	—
1897–98	A. E. Stoddart	12	4	3	5	—	...	22	6	11	5	—
1901–02	A. C. MacLaren	11	5	0	6	—	...	22	8	8	6	—
1902–03†	P. F. Warner	3	0	1	2	—	...	3	0	1	2	—
1903–04	P. F. Warner*	14	9	3	2	—	...	20	10	8	2	—
1907–08	A. O. Jones*	18	7	7	4	—	...	19	7	8	4	—
1911–12	J. W. H. T. Douglas*	14	11	2	1	—	...	18	12	5	1	—
1920–21	J. W. H. T. Douglas*	13	5	2	6	—	...	22	9	7	6	—
1922–23†	A. C. MacLaren*	7	0	4	3	—	...	8	0	5	3	—
1924–25	A. E. R. Gilligan*	17	7	4	6	—	...	23	8	9	6	—
1928–29	A. P. F. Chapman*	17	8	8	1	—	...	24	10	13	1	—
1929–30†	A. H. H. Gilligan*	5	2	1	2	—	...	5	2	1	2	—
1932–33†	D. R. Jardine*	17	10	5	1	1	...	22	10	10	1	1
1935–36†	E. R. T. Holmes*	6	3	2	1	—	...	6	3	2	1	—
1936–37†	G. O. Allen*	17	5	7	5	—	...	24	7	12	5	—
1946–47†	W. R. Hammond*	17	1	13	3	—	...	25	4	18	3	—
1950–51†	F. R. Brown*	16	5	7	4	—	...	25	7	14	4	—
1954–55†	L. Hutton*	17	8	7	2	—	...	23	13	8	2	—
1958–59†	P. B. H. May*	17	4	9	4	—	...	20	7	9	4	—
	TOTAL	314	142	91	80	1	...	593	247	256	89	1

ENGLAND TEAMS IN SOUTH AFRICA

Season	Captain	First-class matches						All matches				
		P.	W.	D.	L.	T.		P.	W.	D.	L.	T.
1888–89	C. A. Smith	2	2	0	0	—	...	19	13	2	4	—
1891–92	W. W. Read	1	1	0	0	—	...	20	13	7	0	—
1895–96	Lord Hawke	4	3	1	0	—	...	16	7	7	2	—
1898–99	Lord Hawke	5	5	0	0	—	...	17	15	2	0	—
1905–06	P. F. Warner*	12	7	0	5	—	...	26	17	4	5	—
1909–10	H. D. G. Leveson-Gower*	14	7	3	4	—	...	18	10	4	4	—
1913–14	J. W. H. T. Douglas*	18	9	8	1	—	...	22	12	9	1	—
1922–23	F. T. Mann*	14	10	3	1	—	...	22	14	7	1	—
1924–25	Hon. L. H. Tennyson	14	5	7	2	—	...	21	8	11	2	—
1927–28	R. T. Stanyforth*	16	7	7	2	—	...	18	7	9	2	—
1930–31	A. P. F. Chapman*	16	5	10	1	—	...	18	5	12	1	—
1938–39	W. R. Hammond*	17	8	9	0	—	...	18	9	9	0	—
1948–49	F. G. Mann*	20	9	11	0	—	...	23	11	12	0	—
1956–57	P. B. H. May*	20	11	6	3	—	...	22	13	6	3	—
1959–60	W. S. Surridge (Surrey C.C.C.)	2	0	1	1	—	...	2	0	1	1	—
1959–60	D. C. S. Compton (Commonwealth)	3	1	2	0	—	...	5	2	3	0	—
	TOTAL	178	90	68	20	—	...	287	156	105	26	—

ENGLAND TEAMS IN WEST INDIES

Season	Captain	First-class matches P.	W.	D.	L.	T.		All matches P.	W.	D.	L.	T.
1894–95	R. S. Lucas	8	4	1	3	—	...	16	10	2	4	—
1896–97	Lord Hawke	7	3	2	2	—	...	14	9	3	2	—
1896–97	A. Priestley	9	4	0	5	—	...	16	10	1	5	—
1901–02	R. A. Bennett	11	6	0	5	—	...	19	13	1	5	—
1904–05	Lord Brackley	10	6	1	3	—	...	20	11	6	3	—
1910–11	A. F. Somerset*	11	3	3	4	1	...	12	4	3	4	1
1912–13	A. F. Somerset*	9	5	1	3	—	...	9	5	1	3	—
1925–26	Hon. F. S. G. Calthorpe*	12	2	9	1	—	...	13	2	10	1	—
1926–27J	Hon. L. H. Tennyson	3	0	3	0	—	...	7	1	6	0	—
1927–28J	Hon. L. H. Tennyson	3	0	1	2	—	...	5	1	2	2	—
1928–29J	Sir J. Cahn	3	0	1	2	—	...	5	0	3	2	—
1929–30	Hon. F. S. G. Calthorpe*	12	4	6	2	—	...	13	4	7	2	—
1931–32J	Lord Tennyson	3	0	0	3	—	...	6	1	2	3	—
1934–35	R. E. S. Wyatt*	12	2	8	2	—	...	12	2	8	2	—
1935–36J	P. A. Gibb (Yorkshire C.C.C.)	3	1	2	0	—	...	6	1	5	0	—
1938–39J	E. J. H. Dixon (Comb. Us.)	2	0	1	1	—	...	7	2	4	1	—
1947–48	G. O. Allen*	11	0	9	2	—	...	11	0	9	2	—
1953–54	L. Hutton*	10	6	2	2	—	...	17	8	7	2	—
1955–56	M. C. Cowdrey	4	1	1	2	—	...	6	2	2	2	—
1956–57J	E. D. R. Eagar	3	2	1	0	—	...	10	4	6	0	—
1959–60	P. B. H. May*	13	4	8	1	—	...	15	4	10	1	—
	TOTAL	159	53	60	45	1	...	239	94	98	46	1

ENGLAND TEAMS IN NEW ZEALAND

Season	Captain	First-class matches P.	W.	D.	L.	T.		All matches P.	W.	D.	L.	T.
1863–64†	G. Parr	—	—	—	—	—	...	4	3	1	0	—
1876–77†	James Lillywhite	—	—	—	—	—	...	8	6	2	0	—
1881–82†	A. Shaw	—	—	—	—	—	...	7	5	2	0	—
1887–88†	A. Shrewsbury	—	—	—	—	—	...	3	0	3	0	—
1902–03†	P. F. Warner	7	7	0	0	—	...	18	18	0	0	—
1906–07	E. G. Wynyard*	11	6	3	2	—	...	16	10	4	2	—
1922–23†	A. C. MacLaren*	8	6	2	0	—	...	14	11	3	0	—
1929–30†	A. H. H. Gilligan*	8	2	6	0	—	...	17	9	8	0	—
1932–33†	D. R. Jardine*	2	0	2	0	—	...	3	0	3	0	—
1935–36†	E. R. T. Holmes*	8	2	5	1	—	...	18	5	12	1	—
1936–37†	G. O. Allen*	3	1	2	0	—	...	3	1	2	0	—
1938–39	Sir J. Cahn	1	0	1	0	—	...	10	2	8	0	—
1946–47†	W. R. Hammond*	4	2	2	0	—	...	4	2	2	0	—
1950–51†	F. R. Brown*	4	3	1	0	—	...	4	3	1	0	—
1954–55†	L. Hutton*	4	4	0	0	—	...	4	4	0	0	—
1958–59†	P. B. H. May*	5	3	2	0	—	...	5	3	2	0	—
	TOTAL	65	36	26	3	—	...	138	82	53	3	—

ENGLAND TEAMS IN INDIA, CEYLON AND PAKISTAN

Season	Captain	First-class matches P.	W.	D.	L.	T.		All matches P.	W.	D.	L.	T.
1926–27	A. E. R. Gilligan*	30	10	20	0	—	...	34	11	23	0	—
1933–34	D. R. Jardine*	18	10	7	1	—	...	34	17	16	1	—
1936–37	Sir J. Cahn	1	1	0	0	—	...	9	3	6	0	—
1937–38	Lord Tennyson	15	4	6	5	—	...	24	8	11	5	—
1949–50	T. L. Livingston (Commonwealth)	21	10	9	2	—	...	28	12	14	2	—
1950–51	L. E. G. Ames (Commonwealth)	27	13	14	0	—	...	29	14	15	0	—
1951–52	N. D. Howard*	23	7	13	3	—	...	27	10	14	3	—
1953–54	B. A. Barnett (Commonwealth)	21	3	13	5	—	...	21	3	13	5	—
1955–56P	D. B. Carr*	14	7	5	2	—	...	16	7	7	2	—
1956–57	W. J. Edrich	2	1	0	1	—	...	2	1	0	1	—
	TOTAL	172	66	87	19	—	...	224	86	119	19	—

ENGLAND TEAMS IN NORTH AMERICA

Season	Captain	First-class matches P.	W.	D.	L.	T.	All matches P.	W.	D.	L.	T.
1859–60	G. Parr	—	—	—	—	— ...	5	5	0	0	—
1868–69	E. Willsher	—	—	—	—	— ...	6	5	1	0	—
1872–73	R. A. Fitzgerald	—	—	—	—	— ...	8	7	1	0	—
1879–80	R. Daft	—	—	—	—	— ...	12	9	3	0	—
1885–86	E. J. Sanders	2	1	0	1	— ...	8	6	1	1	—
1886–87	E. J. Sanders	2	2	0	0	— ...	9	8	1	0	—
1891–92	Lord Hawke	2	1	0	1	— ...	8	6	1	1	—
1894–95	Lord Hawke	2	2	0	0	— ...	5	3	2	0	—
1895–96	F. Mitchell	2	1	0	1	— ...	5	2	1	2	—
1897–98	P. F. Warner	2	1	0	1	— ...	5	2	2	1	—
1898–99	P. F. Warner	2	2	0	0	— ...	8	6	2	0	—
1899–00	K. S. Ranjitsinhji	2	2	0	0	— ...	5	3	2	0	—
1901–02	B. J. T. Bosanquet	2	1	0	1	— ...	5	3	0	2	—
1903–04	C. J. Burnup (Kent C.C.C.)	2	2	0	0	— ...	4	4	0	0	—
1905–06	E. W. Mann*	2	1	0	1	— ...	8	5	2	1	—
1907–08	H. Hesketh-Prichard*	2	0	2	0	— ...	5	1	4	0	—
1937–38	G. C. Newman*	—	—	—	—	— ...	19	12	6	1	—
1951–52	R. W. V. Robins*	1	1	0	0	— ...	22	18	2	2	—
1959–60	D. R. W. Silk*	—	—	—	—	— ...	23	19	4	0	—
	TOTAL	25	17	2	6	— ...	170	124	35	11	—

ENGLAND TEAMS IN SOUTH AMERICA

Season	Captain	First-class matches P.	W.	D.	L.	T.	All matches P.	W.	D.	L.	T.
1911–12	Lord Hawke*	3	2	0	1	— ...	9	6	2	1	—
1926–27	P. F. Warner*	4	2	1	1	— ...	10	6	3	1	—
1929–30	Sir J. Cahn	3	1	2	0	— ...	6	2	3	1	—
1937–38	Sir T. E. W. Brinckman	3	1	1	1	— ...	11	4	6	1	—
1958–59	G. H. G. Doggart*	—	—	—	—	— ...	10	9	1	0	—
	TOTAL	13	6	4	3	— ...	46	27	15	4	—

AUSTRALIAN TEAMS IN ENGLAND

Season	Captain	First-class matches P.	W.	D.	L.	T.	All matches P.	W.	D.	L.	T.
1878	D. W. Gregory	15	7	4	4	— ...	37	18	12	7	—
1880	W. L. Murdoch	10	5	3	2	— ...	37	21	12	4	—
1882	W. L. Murdoch	32	17	11	4	— ...	38	23	11	4	—
1884	W. L. Murdoch	31	17	7	7	— ...	32	18	7	7	—
1886	H. J. H. Scott	37	9	21	7	— ...	39	9	22	8	—
1888	P. S. McDonnell	37	17	7	13	— ...	40	19	7	14	—
1890	W. L. Murdoch	34	10	8	16	— ...	38	13	9	16	—
1893	J. McC. Blackham	31	14	7	10	— ...	36	18	8	10	—
1896	G. H. S. Trott	34	19	9	6	— ...	34	19	9	6	—
1899	J. Darling	35	16	16	3	— ...	35	16	16	3	—
1902	J. Darling	38	22	14	2	— ...	39	23	14	2	—
1905	J. Darling	35	15	17	3	— ...	38	16	19	3	—
1909	M. A. Noble	37	11	22	4	— ...	39	13	22	4	—
1912	S. E. Gregory	36	9	19	8	— ...	37	9	20	8	—
1919	H. L. Collins (A.I.F.)	28	12	12	4	— ...	32	13	15	4	—
1921	W. W. Armstrong	34	21	11	2	— ...	38	22	14	2	—
1926	H. L. Collins	33	9	23	1	— ...	40	12	27	1	—
1930	W. M. Woodfull	31	11	18	1	1 ...	33	12	19	1	1
1934	W. M. Woodfull	30	13	16	1	— ...	34	15	18	1	—
1938	D. G. Bradman	29	15	12	2	— ...	35	20	13	2	—
1948	D. G. Bradman	31	23	8	0	— ...	34	25	9	0	—
1953	A. L. Hassett	33	16	16	1	— ...	35	16	18	1	—
1956	I. W. Johnson	31	9	19	3	— ...	34	11	20	3	—
	TOTAL	722	317	300	104	1 ...	834	381	341	111	1

AUSTRALIAN TEAMS IN SOUTH AFRICA

Season	Captain	First-class matches					All matches				
		P.	W.	D.	L.	T.	P.	W.	D.	L.	T.
1902–03	J. Darling	4	3	1	0	— ...	6	3	3	0	—
1919–20	H. L. Collins (A.I.F.)	8	6	2	0	— ...	9	7	2	0	—
1921–22	H. L. Collins	6	4	2	0	— ...	6	4	2	0	—
1935–36	V. Y. Richardson	16	13	3	0	— ...	16	13	3	0	—
1949–50	A. L. Hassett	21	14	7	0	— ...	25	18	7	0	—
1957–58	I. D. Craig	20	11	9	0	— ...	22	11	11	0	—
	TOTAL	75	51	24	0	— ...	84	56	28	0	—

AUSTRALIAN TEAMS IN NEW ZEALAND

Season	Captain	First-class matches					All matches				
		P.	W.	D.	L.	T.	P.	W.	D.	L.	T.
1877–78	D. W. Gregory	—	—	—	—	— ...	7	5	1	1	—
1880–81	W. L. Murdoch	—	—	—	—	— ...	10	6	3	1	—
1883–84	J. G. Davis (Tasmania)	4	0	1	3	— ...	7	2	2	3	—
1886–87	H. J. H. Scott	—	—	—	—	— ...	5	2	3	0	—
1889–90	J. Davis (N.S.W.)	5	4	1	0	— ...	7	6	1	0	—
1893–94	J. Davis (N.S.W.)	7	4	2	1	— ...	8	4	3	1	—
1895–96	L. T. Cobcroft (N.S.W.)	5	3	1	1	— ...	5	3	1	1	—
1896–97	G. H. S. Trott	—	—	—	—	— ...	5	3	2	0	—
1896–97	O. Hitchcock (Queensland)	5	3	1	1	— ...	8	4	3	1	—
1904–05	M. A. Noble	4	3	1	0	— ...	6	4	2	0	—
1909–10	W. W. Armstrong	6	5	1	0	— ...	9	7	2	0	—
1913–14	A. Sims	9	6	3	0	— ...	16	8	8	0	—
1920–21	V. S. Ransford	9	6	3	0	— ...	14	11	3	0	—
1923–24	C. G. Macartney (N.S.W.)	6	5	1	0	— ...	12	8	4	0	—
1924–25	E. R. Mayne (Victoria)	6	1	4	1	— ...	12	4	7	1	—
1927–28	V. Y. Richardson	6	4	2	0	— ...	13	6	7	0	—
1945–46	W. A. Brown	5	5	0	0	— ...	5	5	0	0	—
1949–50	W. A. Brown	5	3	2	0	— ...	14	9	5	0	—
1956–57	I. D. Craig	7	5	2	0	— ...	12	7	5	0	—
1959–60	I. D. Craig	6	2	4	0	— ...	9	4	5	0	—
	TOTAL	95	59	29	7	— ...	184	108	67	9	—

AUSTRALIAN TEAMS IN INDIA AND PAKISTAN

Season	Captain	First-class matches					All matches				
		P.	W.	D.	L.	T.	P.	W.	D.	L.	T.
1935–36	J. Ryder (F. A. Tarrant)	17	11	3	3	— ...	23	11	9	3	—
1945–46	A. L. Hassett (Services)	9	2	5	2	— ...	10	2	6	2	—
1956–57	I. W. Johnson	4	2	1	1	— ...	4	2	1	1	—
1959–60	R. Benaud	11	5	5	1	— ...	11	5	5	1	—
	TOTAL	41	20	14	7	— ...	48	20	21	7	—

AUSTRALIAN TEAMS IN NORTH AMERICA

Season	Captain	First-class matches					All matches				
		P.	W.	D.	L.	T.	P.	W.	D.	L.	T.
1878–79	D. W. Gregory	1	0	1	0	— ...	6	4	2	0	—
1893–94	J. McC. Blackham	2	1	0	1	— ...	6	4	1	1	—
1896–97	G. H. S. Trott	3	2	0	1	— ...	6	4	1	1	—
1912–13	S. E. Gregory	2	1	0	1	— ...	7	5	1	1	—
1913–14	A. Diamond	5	4	1	0	— ...	53	49	3	1	—
1932–33	V. Y. Richardson	—	—	—	—	— ...	51	44	6	1	—
	TOTAL	13	8	2	3	— ...	129	110	14	5	—

SOUTH AFRICAN TEAMS IN ENGLAND

Season	Captain	First-class matches					All matches				
		P.	*W.*	*D.*	*L.*	*T.*	*P.*	*W.*	*D.*	*L.*	*T.*
1894	H. H. Castens	—	—	—	—	—	24	12	7	5	—
1901	M. Bisset	15	5	0	9	1	25	13	2	9	1
1904	F. Mitchell	22	10	9	2	1	26	13	9	3	1
1907	P. W. Sherwell	27	17	6	4	—	31	21	6	4	—
1912	F. Mitchell	37	13	16	8	—	37	13	16	8	—
1924	H. W. Taylor	35	8	18	9	—	38	8	21	9	—
1929	H. G. Deane	34	9	18	7	—	37	11	19	7	—
1935	H. F. Wade	31	17	12	2	—	39	22	15	2	—
1947	A. Melville	28	14	9	5	—	33	16	12	5	—
1951	A. D. Nourse jun.	30	5	20	5	—	34	8	21	5	—
1955	J. E. Cheetham	28	15	9	4	—	31	16	11	4	—
1960	D. J. McGlew	30	14	11	5	—	31	15	11	5	—
	TOTAL	317	127	128	60	2	386	168	150	66	2

SOUTH AFRICAN TEAMS IN AUSTRALIA

Season	Captain	First-class matches					All matches				
		P.	*W.*	*D.*	*L.*	*T.*	*P.*	*W.*	*D.*	*L.*	*T.*
1910–11	P. W. Sherwell	15	6	2	7	—	22	12	3	7	—
1931–32†	H. B. Cameron	16	4	6	6	—	18	6	6	6	—
1952–53†	J. E. Cheetham	16	4	9	3	—	21	7	11	3	—
	TOTAL	47	14	17	16	—	61	25	20	16	—

SOUTH AFRICAN TEAMS IN NEW ZEALAND

Season	Captain	First-class matches					All matches				
		P.	*W.*	*D.*	*L.*	*T.*	*P.*	*W.*	*D.*	*L.*	*T.*
1931–32†	H. B. Cameron	3	3	0	0	—	3	3	0	0	—
1952–53†	J. E. Cheetham	4	1	3	0	—	5	1	4	0	—
	TOTAL	7	4	3	0	—	8	4	4	0	—

WEST INDIAN TEAMS IN ENGLAND

Season	Captain	First-class matches					All matches				
		P.	*W.*	*D.*	*L.*	*T.*	*P.*	*W.*	*D.*	*L.*	*T.*
1900	R. S. A. Warner	—	—	—	—	—	17	5	4	8	—
1906	H. B. G. Austin	13	3	2	8	—	19	7	2	10	—
1923	H. B. G. Austin	20	6	7	7	—	26	12	7	7	—
1928	R. K. Nunes	30	5	13	12	—	36	7	17	12	—
1933	G. C. Grant	30	5	16	9	—	38	8	21	9	—
1939	R. S. Grant	25	8	11	6	—	31	9	16	6	—
1950	J. D. C. Goddard	31	17	11	3	—	33	19	11	3	—
1957	J. D. C. Goddard	30	14	13	3	—	34	16	15	3	—
	TOTAL	179	58	73	48	—	234	83	93	58	—

WEST INDIAN TEAMS IN AUSTRALIA

Season	Captain	First-class matches					All matches				
		P.	*W.*	*D.*	*L.*	*T.*	*P.*	*W.*	*D.*	*L.*	*T.*
1930–31	G. C. Grant	14	4	2	8	—	16	5	3	8	—
1951–52†	J. D. C. Goddard	13	4	1	8	—	15	5	2	8	—
	TOTAL	27	8	3	16	—	31	10	5	16	—

WEST INDIAN TEAMS IN NEW ZEALAND

Season	Captain	First-class matches					All matches				
		P.	*W.*	*D.*	*L.*	*T.*	*P.*	*W.*	*D.*	*L.*	*T.*
1951–52†	J. D. C. Goddard	4	2	2	0	—	5	3	2	0	—
1955–56	D. Atkinson	8	6	1	1	—	15	11	3	1	—
	TOTAL	12	8	3	1	—	20	14	5	1	—

P

WEST INDIAN TEAMS IN INDIA AND PAKISTAN

Season	Captain	First-class matches						All matches			
		P.	W.	D.	L.	T.	P.	W.	D.	L.	T.
1948–49	J. D. C. Goddard	19	6	12	1	—	23	7	15	1	—
1958–59	F. C. M. Alexander	23	13	8	2	—	23	13	8	2	—
	TOTAL	42	19	20	3	—	46	20	23	3	—

NEW ZEALAND TEAMS IN ENGLAND

Season	Captain	First-class matches						All matches			
		P.	W.	D.	L.	T.	P.	W.	D.	L.	T.
1927	T. C. Lowry	26	7	14	5	—	38	13	20	5	—
1931	T. C. Lowry	32	6	23	3	—	36	7	26	3	—
1937	M. L. Page	32	9	14	9	—	37	13	15	9	—
1949	W. A. Hadlee	32	13	18	1	—	35	14	20	1	—
1958	J. R. Reid	31	7	17	6	1	35	7	21	6	1
	TOTAL	153	42	86	24	1	181	54	102	24	1

NEW ZEALAND TEAMS IN AUSTRALIA

Season	Captain	First-class matches						All matches			
		P.	W.	D.	L.	T.	P.	W.	D.	L.	T.
1898–99	L. T. Cobcroft	2	0	0	2	—	4	1	1	2	—
1913–14	D. Reese	4	1	1	2	—	9	5	2	2	—
1925–26	W. R. Patrick	4	0	3	1	—	9	3	5	1	—
1927–28	T. C. Lowry	1	0	0	1	—	1	0	0	1	—
1937–38	M. L. Page	3	0	0	3	—	3	0	0	3	—
1953–54	B. Sutcliffe	3	2	1	0	—	3	2	1	0	—
	TOTAL	17	3	5	9	—	29	11	9	9	—

NEW ZEALAND TEAM IN SOUTH AFRICA

Season	Captain	First-class matches						All matches			
		P.	W.	D.	L.	T.	P.	W.	D.	L.	T.
1953–54	G. O. Rabone	16	3	9	4	—	17	3	10	4	—

NEW ZEALAND TEAM IN INDIA AND PAKISTAN

Season	Captain	First-class matches						All matches			
		P.	W.	D.	L.	T.	P.	W.	D.	L.	T.
1955–56	H. B. Cave	16	3	7	6	—	16	3	7	6	—

INDIAN TEAMS IN ENGLAND

Season	Captain	First-class matches						All matches			
		P.	W.	D.	L.	T.	P.	W.	D.	L.	T.
1911	Maharajah of Patiala	14	2	2	10	—	23	6	2	15	—
1932	Maharajah of Porbandar	26	9	9	8	—	36	13	14	9	—
1936	Maharajah of Vizianagram	28	4	12	12	—	31	5	13	13	—
1946	Nawab of Pataudi	29	11	14	4	—	33	13	16	4	—
1952	V. S. Hazare	29	4	20	5	—	34	6	23	5	—
1959	D. K. Gaekwad	33	6	16	11	—	35	7	17	11	—
	TOTAL	159	36	73	50	—	192	50	85	57	—

INDIAN TEAM IN AUSTRALIA

Season	Captain	First-class matches						All matches			
		P.	W.	D.	L.	T.	P.	W.	D.	L.	T.
1947–48	L. Amarnath	14	2	5	7	—	20	5	8	7	—

INDIAN TEAM IN WEST INDIES

Season	Captain	First-class matches					All matches				
		P.	W.	D.	L.	T.	P.	W.	D.	L.	T.
1952–53	V. S. Hazare	9	1	7	1	—	10	1	8	1	—

INDIAN TEAM IN PAKISTAN

Season	Captain	First-class matches					All matches				
		P.	W.	D.	L.	T.	P.	W.	D.	L.	T.
1954–55	V. Mankad	14	5	9	0	—	14	5	9	0	—

PAKISTAN TEAM IN ENGLAND

Season	Captain	First-class matches					All matches				
		P.	W.	D.	L.	T.	P.	W.	D.	L.	T.
1954	A. H. Kardar	30	9	18	3	—	32	10	19	3	—

PAKISTAN TEAM IN WEST INDIES

Season	Captain	First-class matches					All matches				
		P.	W.	D.	L.	T.	P.	W.	D.	L.	T.
1957–58	A. H. Kardar	9	1	5	3	—	16	3	10	3	—

PAKISTAN TEAM IN INDIA

Season	Captain	First-class matches					All matches				
		P.	W.	D.	L.	T.	P.	W.	D.	L.	T.
1952–53	A. H. Kardar	12	1	9	2	—	12	1	9	2	—

PHILADELPHIAN TEAMS IN ENGLAND

Season	Captain	First-class matches					All matches				
		P.	W.	D.	L.	T.	P.	W.	D.	L.	T.
1884	R. S. Newhall	—	—	—	—	—	18	8	5	5	—
1889	D. S. Newhall	—	—	—	—	—	12	4	5	3	—
1897	G. S. Patterson	15	2	4	9	—	15	2	4	9	—
1903	J. A. Lester	14	6	2	6	—	16	7	3	6	—
1908	J. B. King	10	4	0	6	—	14	7	1	6	—
	TOTAL	39	12	6	21	—	75	28	18	29	—

CANADIAN TEAM IN ENGLAND

Season	Captain	First-class matches					All matches				
		P.	W.	D.	L.	T.	P.	W.	D.	L.	T.
1954	H. B. Robinson	4	0	2	2	—	15	4	8	3	—

SOUTH AMERICAN TEAM IN ENGLAND

Season	Captain	First-class matches					All matches				
		P.	W.	D.	L.	T.	P.	W.	D.	L.	T.
1932	C. H. Gibson	6	2	1	3	—	18	2	17	5	—

Laws of Cricket

The first Laws of Cricket of which we have a printed record were formulated in 1744, but it is probable that these were in fact a revision of an earlier set of laws. They have been the subject of continual amendment, addition and revision, the main changes being given in the following tables. The exact date of amendment is not known in all cases in the early years, but by far the most reliable dates are those given by R. S. Rait-Kerr in his book *The Laws of Cricket* published in 1950.

THE WICKET

The terms 'wicket' and 'stumps' seem to have derived from the very early years, when the bowler's target was either a wicket gate or a tree stump. In the early years the wicket was one foot high and two feet wide, but a different shape was adopted in 1744, changes being made in the year given.

1744 22 inches high and 6 inches wide.
1775 Third stump added but still only one bail.
*c.*1786 Second bail added to wicket.
1798 Two inches added to height and one inch to width (24″ × 7″).
*c.*1821 Two inches added to height (26″ × 7″).
*c.*1823 One inch added to both height and width (27″ × 8″).
1931 One inch added to both height and width (28″ × 9″) for first-class matches, but the earlier size was still optional until 1947 for minor matches. The bail was allowed to project not more than half an inch above the top of the stumps. Change made after experiment in 1929 and 1930.

THE BALL

1744 No size given, but the weight to be between 5 and 6 ounces.
1774 Weight reduced to finer limits, to be between $5\frac{1}{2}$ and $5\frac{3}{4}$ ounces.
1798 A new ball may be demanded by either side at the start of an innings.
1838 Circumference of the ball to be between 9 and $9\frac{1}{4}$ inches.
1907 New ball rule after 200 runs adopted in England, the Australians having experimented for some years with this amendment.
1927 Circumference reduced to be between $8\frac{13}{16}$ and 9 inches.
1946 Trial of new ball after 55 overs rule.
1949 Experimental margin increased from 55 to 65 overs.
1955 A return to the 200 runs new ball rule for one season only.
1956 Further experiment, new ball now available after 200 runs or 75 overs, whichever comes first.

BALLS TO AN OVER

1744 Four balls to the over in earliest laws.
1887 Australia adopt the six-ball over.
1889 Five-ball over adopted in England and in laws.
1900 Six-ball over adopted in England and in laws.
1918 Australia adopt the eight-ball over. The 1920–21 M.C.C. team used the six-ball over, the 1924–25 the eight-ball over, the 1928–29 and 1932–33 teams the eight-ball over in State matches and six-ball in Tests. The latter conditions also applied to the 1930–31 West Indies and 1931–32 South African teams. The eight-ball over became universal in Australia in 1935–36.
1924 New Zealand adopt the eight-ball over in May 1924, but revert to the six-ball over in November 1927.
1937 South Africa adopt the eight-ball over for their 1937–38 season.
1939 Eight-ball over tried experimentally in England, but return made to six-ball over after the war.
1947 Final over of the match to be played out at the request of either captain.

NO-BALLS

1744 Only no-ball if bowler overstepped the crease.
*c.*1811 A striker allowed to play at a no-ball and score any resulting runs. The ball to be bowled with hand below the elbow.
1829 The one-run penalty for a no-ball introduced.

1835 Law amended to allow the ball up to the level of the shoulder, and mention of 'thrown or jerked' for the first time.
1845 Umpires to call 'no-ball' unless *absolutely satisfied* that the hand is below the shoulder in delivery.
1864 Overarm bowling legalized.
1899 *Either* umpire may call 'no-ball' if not satisfied with the absolute fairness of a delivery.
1947 The law no longer required a bowler to have his back foot on the ground at the moment of delivery, although his foot must be behind the line.

MEASUREMENTS OF THE PITCH

1744 Length of pitch laid down as 22 yards, no limit for the bowling crease, but the popping crease to be 46 inches in front of the wicket.
1774 Bowling crease limited to 36 inches each side of the wicket.
c.1821 Distance of popping crease increased to 48 inches in front of the wicket.
c.1823 Bowling crease increased to 6 feet 7 inches with return crease each end at right angles.
c.1825 Bowling crease increased to 6 feet 8 inches to conform with size of wicket.
1902 Bowling crease increased to 8 feet 8 inches (4 feet each side of the wicket, but now 3 feet 11½ inches since the 1931 increase in the size of the wicket).

CARE OF THE PITCH

1744 Pitch to be untouched during the course of a match.
1788 Rolling, watering, covering and mowing of pitch allowed during a match by mutual consent.
c.1823 After rain the pitch may be changed by mutual consent.
1831 Proviso allowing a bowler to water his run up deleted.
1849 Pitch may be swept and rolled between innings subject to request by either side.
1860 Rolling of pitch to be at the request of the side next to bat.
1883 Pitch may be rolled for ten minutes before the start of play each day.
1913 Covering of each end of wicket authorized for first time.
1931 Period of rolling cut from ten to seven minutes.
1959 Covering of wicket allowed outside agreed playing hours, and wicket to be covered directly play is abandoned for the day.

THE BAT

1771 Width of bat limited to 4¼ inches.
1835 Length of bat limited to 38 inches.

DECLARATION OF INNINGS

1889 Allowed at any time on the third day of the match.
1900 Allowed after the start of lunch on the second day.
1906 Declaration on the first day of a two-day match allowed provided 100 minutes remain for play.
1910 Declaration allowed at any time on the second day of a three-day match.
1946 Experiment in England allowing declaration on first day after batting side has scored 300 runs.
1951 Experiment extended to allow declaration at any time on first day of match.
1957 Experiment incorporated into the laws.

FOLLOW-ON OF INNINGS

1835 Compulsory if team batting second 100 runs behind on first innings.
1854 Limit reduced to 80 runs (60 runs in a one-day match).
1894 Limit increased to 120 runs for a three-day match, but still compulsory.
1900 Follow-on to be optional, limits 150 runs for a three-day match, 100 runs for a two-day match and 75 runs for a one-day match.

LEG BEFORE WICKET

1774 First l.b.w. law—'Striker to be out if he puts his *leg* before the wicket with a *design* to stop the ball, and actually prevents the ball by hitting his wicket by it.'
1788 Restricted to a ball which pitched between wicket and wicket.
c.1823 Amended to require the ball to pitch straight and to strike any part of the batsman's person.
1839 Amended back to 1788 law, requiring the ball to pitch straight irrespective of the line of of delivery.
1937 After experiment in 1935 and 1936, law amended to allow a dismissal when the ball pitched outside the off-stump, provided that the point of impact was between wicket and wicket.

SCORING

1774   'Short runs' referred to in the laws for the first time.
c.1809 'Lost ball' law allowed striker to score all the runs he had made, with a minimum of four runs.
c.1811 Striker may play at a 'no-ball' and score any resulting runs.
c.1811 One-run penalty for a wide introduced, but to be scored as byes.
c.1823 'Lost ball' allowance increased from four to six runs.
1828   The allowance for a 'wide' to be scored as wides, and no longer as byes.
1829   One-run penalty for a no-ball introduced.
1835   Ball to be called 'dead' after a wide, so that only one run can be scored.
1836   Bowlers to be given credit for all wickets caught or stumped off their bowling.
1840   Bowling analyses kept for the first time.
1844   Batting side may count all runs resulting from a wide.
1884   Boundaries officially mentioned for the first time, but they had been general in first-class cricket for many years.
1884   Byes and leg-byes separated for the first time in the laws, although they had been scored separately since 1848.
1910   Allowance of six for a hit out of the playing area introduced for the first time, until this date only hits right out of the ground had counted six.

MISCELLANEOUS

1744   The side winning the toss had choice of both pitch and innings.
1744   The bowler could change ends only once in an innings.
1774   The visiting team to have choice of both pitch and innings.
1798   Penalty of five runs if a fielder stops the ball with his hat introduced.
c.1811 The toss to decide the choice of innings, the pitch to be selected by the umpires within 30 yards of a centre chosen by the visiting team.
c.1823 Selection of pitch left to the umpires.
1840   Interval between innings reverts to ten minutes, since 1774 it had been fifteen minutes.

Part IX—Miscellaneous Records

Attendance Records for County Cricket

Gate	Receipts		
80,000	£2,300	Surrey v. Yorkshire (Oval) (W. S. Lees's benefit)	1906
78,792	£3,703	Yorkshire v. Lancashire (Leeds) (G. H. Hirst's benefit)	1904
78,617		Lancashire v. Yorkshire (Manchester)..	1926
76,000		Surrey v. Kent (Oval)	1920
71,000		Yorkshire v. Middlesex (Leeds) (R. Kilner's benefit)	1925
70,000		Surrey v. Yorkshire (Oval)	1922

The crowd totalled 46,000 (38,906 paid) on the August Bank Holiday Monday for the match between Lancashire and Yorkshire at Manchester in 1926.

Awards at Cricket

THE LAWRENCE TROPHY

In 1934 Sir Walter Lawrence presented a trophy, together with a prize of £100, for presentation each year to the batsman scoring the fastest century of the season. The award came to an end in 1939.

The winners each year were:

1934	F. E. Woolley (104): Kent v. Northamptonshire (Dover)....................................	63 mins.
1935	H. Gimblett (123): Somerset v. Essex (Frome)...................................	63 mins.
	(Gimblett was making his debut in first-class cricket.)	
1936	L. E. G. Ames (107): England XI v. Indians (Folkestone)...................	68 mins.
1937	J. Hardstaff jun. (126): Nottinghamshire v. Kent (Canterbury)...............	51 mins.
1938	H. T. Bartlett (157): Sussex v. Australians (Hove)..........................	57 mins.
1939	L. E. G. Ames (136*): Kent v. Surrey (Oval)	67 mins.

THE 'DAILY MAIL' AWARD

This award was also for the fastest century of the season, but was discontinued after only one year. The winner was:

1950	E. D. Weekes (200*): West Indians v. Leics. (Leicester).....................................| 65 mins.

'NEWS CHRONICLE' BRIGHTER CRICKET AWARD

Started in 1952, this award was made to the county who scored their runs in championship matches at the fastest rate, based on runs scored for every 100 balls received by the batsmen. The award was ended after the 1953 season:

1952 Essex—scored 11,546 runs at 50·44 runs per 100 balls.
1953 Essex—scored 10,017 runs at 49·13 runs per 100 balls.

YOUNG CRICKETER OF THE YEAR

At the end of each season the members of the Cricket Writers' Club select by ballot the player whom they consider to be the best young cricketer of that season. The award, a suitable trophy, is presented to the player at the clubs' annual dinner. The winner each season since the institution of the trophy in 1950 has been as follows:

1950	R. Tattersall (Lancashire).	1956	B. Taylor (Essex).
1951	P. B. H. May (Surrey).	1957	M. J. Stewart (Surrey).
1952	F. S. Trueman (Yorkshire).	1958	A. C. D. Ingleby-Mackenzie (Hampshire)
1953	M. C. Cowdrey (Kent).	1959	G. Pullar (Lancashire).
1954	P. J. Loader (Surrey).	1960	D. A. Allen (Gloucestershire).
1955	K. F. Barrington (Surrey).		

THE COUNTY CUPS

The most recent awards for first-class cricketers in England are the 'County' cups, instituted in 1954. They are awarded annually for the fastest century, the best bowling performance in figures, the fielder taking the most catches, the leading wicket-keeper and a special award for the best performance of the season. An extra 'Visitor's Award' was added in 1958. Performances in festival matches, games outside England and Wales, and some Champion County v. Rest of England matches are ignored when calculating the award. The winners each season have been as follows:

BATTING—FASTEST CENTURY

1954   G. M. Emmett (172): Gloucestershire v. Somerset (Taunton)............................84 mins.
1955   R. Smith (101*): Essex v. Northamptonshire (Wellingborough)..........................73 mins.
1956   A. C. Walton (116*): Oxford U. v. Sussex (Oxford) ....61 mins.
1957   R. E. Marshall (103): Hampshire v. Kent (Southampton)...............................66 mins.
1958   A. C. D. Ingleby-Mackenzie (113*): Hampshire v. Somerset (Bournemouth)............61 mins.
1959   J. M. Parks (108*): Sussex v. Lancashire (Manchester)...............................61 mins.
1960   E. R. Dexter (133): Sussex v. Somerset (Taunton).....................................85 mins.

BOWLING—BEST FIGURES IN AN INNINGS

1954   J. H. Wardle: Yorkshire v. Lancashire (Manchester) ....9—25
1955   J. Flavell: Worcestershire v. Kent (Dover) ....9—30
1956   J. C. Laker: England v. Australia (Manchester) ....10—53
1957   D. J. Halfyard: Kent v. Glamorgan (Neath) ....9—39
1958   P. J. Loader: Surrey v. Warwickshire (Oval) ....9—17
1959   J. D. Bannister: Warwickshire v. Combined Services (Birmingham) ....10—41
1960   D. Shackleton: Hampshire v. Warwickshire (Portsmouth) ....9—30

FIELDING—MOST CATCHES IN A SEASON

1954   C. A. Milton (Gloucestershire) ....44 ct.
1955   John Langridge (Sussex) ....69 ct.
1956   C. A. Milton (Gloucestershire) ....60 ct.
1957   M. J. Stewart (Surrey) ....75 ct.
1958   M. J. Stewart (Surrey) ....61 ct.
1959   P. M. Walker (Glamorgan) ....64 ct.
1960   P. M. Walker (Glamorgan) ....69 ct.

WICKET-KEEPING—MOST VICTIMS IN A SEASON

1954   H. W. Stephenson (Somerset) .... 86 (50 ct. 36 st.)
1955   A. J. McIntyre (Surrey) .... 85 (65 ct. 20 st.)
1956   J. T. Murray (Middlesex) .... 77 (63 ct. 13 st.)
1957   J. T. Murray (Middlesex) .... 94 (79 ct. 15 st.)
1958   J. T. Murray (Middlesex) .... 81 (74 ct. 7 st.)
1959   J. M. Parks (Sussex) .... 91 (85 ct. 6 st.)
1960   J. T. Murray (Middlesex) ....102 (95 ct. 7 st.)

SPECIAL AWARD FOR BEST PERFORMANCE OF SEASON

1954   Fazal Mahmood, for taking 12—99 for Pakistan v. England (Oval) in fourth Test.
1955   South African cricket team, for their cricket during the season.
1956   Surrey and W. S. Surridge, their captain, for winning County Championship for five consecutive seasons.
1957   P. B. H. May (285*) and M. C. Cowdrey (154), for their fourth wicket stand of 411 v. West Indies (Birmingham)—the highest-ever partnership for England.
1958   D. Shackleton, whose 165 wickets played a large part in the Hampshire challenge to Surrey's supremacy (Hampshire finished runners-up, their best-ever final position).
1959   M. J. K. Smith (Warwickshire), the first batsman to score 3,000 runs in a season for ten years.
1960   T. E. Bailey (Essex), for consistent all-round form.

VISITOR'S AWARD

1958   J. R. Reid of New Zealand (Captain of touring team).
1959   A. A. Baig of India (century—112—on début in Test cricket).
1960   N. A. T. Adcock of South Africa (108 wickets with average of 14·02).

Benefit Matches

A professional cricketer is usually awarded a benefit match by his county after a number of years of good service (usually about ten) to the club. It should be remembered, however, that not every county can afford to do this, and in some instances a county awards a 'testimonial' of either a fixed amount or by members' contributions instead of setting aside a particular match for his benefit. There are other instances of a player retiring after having played for the county for a number of years, but not long enough to qualify for a benefit. In these cases the county sometimes gives the player a fixed sum as a testimonial.

As a result of a High Court action and appeal by the Inland Revenue authorities against James Seymour (Kent) in the 1920's, it was ruled that a cricketer's benefit is not subject to income tax—unlike a footballer who pays income tax on his benefit as this is part of the terms of service and agreed in the contract.

Owing to the difference of valuation in the £ over the years, the leading benefit figures are given in three tables; before the 1914 war, the period between the wars and since 1946.

The following benefit receipts are among the largest that have been recorded (in some cases only the approximate amount is available).

BEFORE 1914

£3,703	G. H. Hirst: Yorkshire v. Lancashire (Leeds)	1904
£3,111	J. T. Tyldesley: Lancashire v. Yorkshire (Manchester)	1906
£2,282	J. T. Brown: Yorkshire v. Lancashire (Leeds)	1901
£2,202	W. Rhodes: Yorkshire v. Lancashire (Sheffield)	1911
£2,120	W. S. Lees: Surrey v. Yorkshire (Oval)	1906
£2,071	S. Haigh: Yorkshire v. Lancashire (Bradford)	1909
£2,000	R. Peel: Yorkshire v. Lancashire (Bradford)	1894

1919 TO 1939

£4,016	R. Kilner: Yorkshire v. Middlesex (Leeds)	1925
£3,648	M. Leyland: Yorkshire v. Nottinghamshire (Leeds)	1934
£3,059	H. Sutcliffe: Yorkshire v. Surrey (Leeds)	1929
£2,906	C. Hallows: Lancashire v. Surrey (Manchester)	1928
£2,620	P. Holmes: Yorkshire v. Middlesex (Leeds)	1928
£2,620	W. R. Hammond: Gloucestershire v. Hampshire (Bristol)	1934
£2,563	A. Wood: Yorkshire v. Middlesex (Bradford)	1939

SINCE 1946

£14,000	C. Washbrook: Lancashire v. Australians (Manchester)	1948
£12,866	A. V. Bedser: Surrey v. Yorkshire (Oval)	1953
£12,200	D. C. S. Compton: Middlesex v. Sussex (Lord's)	1949
£11,000	J. C. Laker: Surrey v. Yorkshire (Oval)	1956
£9,713	L. Hutton: Yorkshire v. Middlesex (Leeds)	1950
£8,500	R. Pollard: Lancashire v. Derbyshire (Manchester)	1949
£8,500	A. J. McIntyre: Surrey v. Yorkshire (Oval)	1955
£8,233	H. Verity: Yorkshire—Memorial Fund	1946
£8,129	J. H. Wardle: Yorkshire v. Surrey (Bradford)	1957
£8,083	W. E. Bowes: Yorkshire v. Middlesex (Leeds)	1947
£7,700	E. A. Bedser: Surrey v. Yorkshire (Oval)	1958
£7,600	D. G. W. Fletcher: Surrey v. Middlesex (Oval)	1957
£7,437	H. P. Sharp & A. Thompson: Middlesex joint-benefit	1955
£7,175	J. T. Ikin: Lancashire v. Surrey (Manchester)	1953
£6,650	G. Cox: Sussex v. Middlesex (Hove)	1951
£6,515	B. Constable: Surrey v. Yorkshire (Oval)	1959
£6,363	H. E. Dollery: Warwickshire v. Middlesex (Birmingham)	1949
£6,297	W. Place: Lancashire v. Middlesex (Manchester)	1952
£6,187	L. H. Compton: Middlesex v. Sussex (Lord's)	1954
£6,000	L. H. Gray: Middlesex v. Sussex (Lord's)	1948
£5,757	J. V. Wilson: Yorkshire v. Surrey (Sheffield)	1958
£5,756	K. Grieves: Lancashire v. Northamptonshire (Blackpool)	1956
£5,696	S. M. Brown: Middlesex v. Sussex (Lord's)	1953
£5,400	T. W. Graveney: Gloucestershire v. Middlesex (Cheltenham)	1959
£5,356	W. Watson: Yorkshire v. Surrey (Sheffield)	1956
£5,259	T. G. Evans: Kent v. Hampshire (Canterbury)	1953

*P

£5,254   D. V. P. Wright: Kent v. Hampshire (Canterbury) 1950
£5,250   L. B. Fishlock: Surrey v. Middlesex (Oval) 1950
£5,104   T. F. Smailes: Yorkshire v. Surrey (Sheffield) 1948
£5,000   E. A. Watts: Surrey v. Middlesex (Oval) 1949
£5,000   J. A. Young: Middlesex v. Sussex (Lord's) 1952
£5,000   D. Shackleton: Hampshire v. Lancashire (Bournemouth) 1958

The records for counties not already mentioned are:
£4,750   A. J. Watkins: Glamorgan v. Gloucestershire (Swansea) 1955
£4,030   H. W. Stephenson: Somerset v. Surrey (Weston-super-Mare) 1957
£3,900   T. H. Wade: Essex v. Surrey (Ilford) 1948
£3,840   D. Kenyon: Worcestershire v. Gloucestershire (Worcester) 1957
£3,500   C. B. Harris: Nottinghamshire v. Yorkshire (Nottingham) 1949
£3,300   C. Gladwin: Derbyshire—Testimonial Fund...1953
£3,280   D. Brookes: Northamptonshire v. Worcestershire (Northampton) 1958
£3,157   M. Tompkin: Leicestershire v. Lancashire (Leicester) 1954

W. G. Grace, although an amateur, received several testimonials during his career, three of them in 1895 which totalled £8,835 (£1,458, £2,377 and £5,000).

The record for an Australian from his Testimonial match is £A10,000 by D. G. Bradman—the match, D. G. Bradman's XI v. A. L. Hassett's XI, was played at Melbourne in 1948–49.

Centuries Scored by Number Eleven Batsmen

It is rare for the last man in to score a century, the feat having been performed only six times during the history of cricket.

T. Hastings (106*): Victoria v. South Australia (Melbourne) 1902–03
He joined M. Ellis (No. 9—118) when nine wickets had fallen for 261 and helped to add 211 runs for the last wicket.
A. Fielder (112*): Kent v. Worcestershire (Stourbridge) 1909
He joined F. E. Woolley (No. 5—185) when nine wickets had fallen for 320 and helped to add 235 runs for the last wicket in 140 minutes.
W. C. Smith (126): M.C.C. v. Barbados (Barbados) 1912–13
He joined A. F. Somerset (No. 9—55) when nine wickets had fallen for 205 runs and helped to add 167 for the last wicket.*
A. E. R. Gilligan (101): Cambridge U. v. Sussex (Hove)..1919
He joined J. H. Naumann (No. 7—134) and together they added 177 runs for the last wicket in 65 minutes, taking the score from 434 for 9 to 611 all out.*
S. N. Banerjee (121): Indians v. Surrey (Oval) 1946
He joined C. T. Sarwate (No. 10—124) and together they added 249 for the last wicket, taking the score from 205 for 9 to 454 all out. This is the only case of both Nos. 10 and 11 scoring centuries in the same innings.*
T. P. B. Smith (163): Essex v. Derbyshire (Chesterfield) 1947
He joined F. H. Vigar (No. 5—114) after nine wickets had fallen for 199 and helped to add 218 for the last wicket.*

J. J. Bridges (99*) was one run short of this feat when he lost his partner (H. Gibbs), when playing for Somerset v. Essex (Weston-super-Mare) 1919, after they had added 143 in 70 minutes for the last wicket.

Eleven Bowlers in One Innings

Twelve bowlers, including the wicket-keeper, were used by the Gentlemen in an innings of 593 by Cambridge U. at Cambridge in 1880, the game being played twelve-a-side.

There have been a number of instances of all eleven players of the fielding team going on to bowl during the course of a single innings. The details are as follows (the fielding side is given first, the side scoring the runs second):

455   Surrey v. Middlesex (Oval) 1866
370   Gentlemen of England v. Cambridge University (Cambridge) 1881
551   England v. Australia (Oval) 1884
464   Kent v. Sussex (Hove) 1884
698   Sussex v. Surrey (Oval) 1888
445   Natal v. Kimberley (Kimberley) 1889–90

475	Hampshire v. Warwickshire (Southampton)	1897
579	Hampshire v. Surrey (Oval)	1897
310—8	Lancashire v. Leicestershire (Leicester)	1900
609—8d	Sussex v. Leicestershire (Leicester)	1900
463—7	Derbyshire v. Worcestershire (Worcester)	1902
585—7	Surrey v. Warwickshire (Oval)	1905
627	Nottinghamshire v. Lancashire (Nottingham)	1905
591	Queensland v. New South Wales (Brisbane)	1907–08
426—8d	Sussex v. Middlesex (Eastbourne)	1910
495—5d	Warwickshire v. Yorkshire (Huddersfield)	1922
535—6d	Warwickshire v. Middlesex (Birmingham)	1922
257—5	M.C.C. v. Australian XI (Brisbane)	1924–25
355	Gloucestershire v. Warwickshire (Bristol)	1933
385—7	Lancashire v. Somerset (Taunton)	1936
260—7	Glamorgan v. Nottinghamshire (Nottingham)	1951
345—9	Derbyshire v. Leicestershire (Ashby-de-la-Zouch)	1955
200—1	Sussex v. Glamorgan (Hove)	1956
295—3d	Somerset v. Leicestershire (Taunton)	1957

F.A. Cup Winners' Medals

The following players who have appeared in first-class cricket have gained F.A. Cup winners' medals at Association Football:

E. Lubbock (Kent): Wanderers in 1871–72 and Old Etonians in 1878–79.
W. S. Kenyon-Slaney (M.C.C.): Wanderers in 1872–73.
C. E. B. Nepean (Middlesex): Oxford U. in 1873–74.
F. H. Birley (Lancashire & Surrey): Oxford U. in 1873–74.
C. J. Ottoway (Kent & Middlesex): Oxford U. in 1873–74.
H. W. Renny-Tailyour (Kent): Royal Engineers in 1874–75.
H. Whitfield (Sussex): Old Etonians in 1878–79.
E. G. Wynyard (Hampshire): Old Carthusians in 1880–81.
P. J. Paravicini (Middlesex): Old Etonians in 1881–82.
H. B. Daft (Nottinghamshire): Notts County in 1893–94.
J. Devey (Warwickshire): Aston Villa in 1896–97.
E. Needham (Derbyshire): Sheffield United in 1898–99 and 1901–02.
W. George (Warwickshire): Aston Villa in 1904–05.
J. Sharp (Lancashire): Everton in 1905–06.
H. Makepeace (Lancashire): Everton in 1905–06.
A. Ducat (Surrey): Aston Villa in 1919–20.
J. H. A. Hulme (Middlesex): Arsenal in 1929–30 and 1935–36.
E. J. Drake (Hampshire): Arsenal in 1935–36.
H. Carter (Derbyshire): Derby County in 1945–46.
D. C. S. Compton (Middlesex): Arsenal in 1949–50.
L. H. Compton (Middlesex): Arsenal in 1949–50.
J. Dyson (Lancashire): Manchester City in 1955–56.

H. Makepeace holds a unique record: (a) F.A. Cup winners' medal with Everton in 1905–06, (b) League Championship medal with Everton in 1914–15, (c) Football international 'caps' v. Scotland in 1905–06, 1909–10 and 1911–12 and v. Wales in 1911–12, (d) four Test appearances against Australia in 1920–21, and (e) member of Lancashire team which won the County Championship in 1926, 1927 and 1928.

Four Bowlers only in an Innings

During the course of the following large innings only four bowlers were used by the fielding captain:

Gloucestershire while Warwickshire scored 484—9d (Birmingham)		1899
Lancashire while Yorkshire scored 489 (Leeds)		1921
Gloucestershire while Lancashire scored 469 (Bristol)		1927
Somerset while Leicestershire scored 490 (Frome)		1937
Essex while Lancashire scored 510 (Clacton)		1947
Warwickshire while Middlesex scored 452—5d (Birmingham)		1947
Essex while Somerset scored 488 (Clacton)		1949
New Zealand while England scored 482 (Oval)		1949
Essex while Kent scored 532 (Maidstone)		1950

Honorary Life Membership of M.C.C.

At a Committee meeting of the M.C.C., held in July 1949, it was decided to add an amendment to the rules which would allow honorary life membership of the club to be granted to ex-professional cricketers. The stipulation was made that such membership would be restricted to the 'really great'. The first list of players to receive election, on July 28th, 1949, were:

S. F. Barnes (Lancs.)
C. J. Barnett (Glos.)
W. E. Bowes (Yorks.)
L. C. Braund (Somerset)
G. Duckworth (Lancs.)
A. P. Freeman (Kent)
G. Geary (Leics.)
G. Gunn (Notts.)
J. W. Hearne (Middx.)

E. Hendren (Middx.)
G. H. Hirst (Yorks.)
J. B. Hobbs (Surrey)
H. Larwood (Notts.)
M. Leyland (Yorks.)
C. P. Mead (Hants.)
E. Paynter (Lancs.)
W. Rhodes (Yorks.)
A. C. Russell (Essex)

A. Sandham (Surrey)
E. J. Smith (Warwicks.)
H. Strudwick (Surrey)
H. Sutcliffe (Yorks.)
M. W. Tate (Sussex)
E. Tyldesley (Lancs.)
W. Voce (Notts.)
F. E. Woolley (Kent)

Since then the following have been elected:
1951 L. E. G. Ames (Kent)
1955 L. Hutton (Yorks.)
1958 D. C. S. Compton (Middx.), D. V. P. Wright (Kent)
1959 J. T. Ikin (Lancs.)
1960 T. G. Evans (Kent, J. C. Laker* (Surrey), C. Washbrook (Lancs.)
 * *Laker's membership was terminated in June 1960.*

Innings with few Boundaries

On a few occasions a large innings has been scored with the minimum of help from strokes which reached the boundary, the following being the leading examples:

INNINGS WITHOUT BOUNDARIES

84* A. V. Avery: Essex v. Derbyshire (Southend) 1939
74* H. A. Pawson: Oxford U. v. Somerset (Bath) 1948
72 R. A. Sinfield: Gloucestershire v. Sussex (Cheltenham) 1937
67 E. A. B. Rowan: South Africa v. England (Durban) 1938–39
56 W. Bardsley: Australia v. South Africa (Nottingham) 1912
51 J. L. Hopwood: Lancashire v. Gloucestershire (Gloucester) 1935

INNINGS WITH ONLY ONE FOUR

118 W. M. Woodfull: Australians v. Surrey (Oval) 1926
102 A. Shipman: Leicestershire v. Essex (Leyton) 1925
97* T. N. Pearce: Essex v. Northamptonshire (Colchester) 1935

INNINGS WITH ONLY TWO FOURS

120 P. A. Gibb: England v. South Africa (Durban)...1938–39
116 C. A. Milton: M.C.C. v. Victoria (Melbourne) 1958–59
115 A. R. Morris: Australian XI v. M.C.C. (Melbourne) 1946–47
112 G. Gunn: Nottinghamshire v. Essex (Leyton) 1924
97* W. L. Neale: Gloucestershire v. Glamorgan (Newport) 1936
92 J. Iddon: Lancashire v. Gloucestershire (Bristol) 1936

Knighthoods

The number of Knighthoods conferred in sporting circles are very few, the following being awarded to cricket personalities for their share in the administration of cricket. (Note— A number of Knighthoods have been conferred on cricketers for their work in other spheres, but they do not come within the scope of this note.)

Sir Francis (F. E.) Lacey—on retirement from the position of Secretary to the M.C.C. in 1926, his appointment having taken effect in 1898.

Sir Frederick (F. C.) Toone—on his return from Australia in 1929 with the third M.C.C. team he had managed in Australia. (The three tours were 1920–21, 1924–25 and 1928–29.)

Sir Pelham (P. F.) Warner—conferred in the 1937 Coronation Honours List in recognition of his work over a large number of years.

Sir Donald (D. G.) Bradman—conferred January 1st, 1949 on his retirement from first-class cricket.

Sir Henry (H. D. G.) Leveson-Gower—conferred on January 1st, 1953, in recognition of 60 years' service to the game.

Sir John (J. B.) Hobbs—conferred in the 1953 Coronation Honours List.

Sir Leonard Hutton—conferred in the 1956 Birthday Honours.

Long Overs—No-balls and Wides

W. N. Powys, playing for Cambridge University v. M.C.C. (Lord's) 1872, bowled a strange opening over. Two wides were conceded off the first ball, the second was a no-ball, the third conceded a bye, the fourth was another no-ball, the fifth resulted in a leg-bye and then two more balls completed the over.

A. H. Heath, playing for M.C.C. v. Surrey (Lord's) 1876, was another bowler to send down a strange over. The first ball was a wide, the second went over long-stop's head for five byes, the third clean bowled G. Elliott, the fourth nearly clean bowled R. Humphrey, the fifth was a wide from which two runs were scored and the sixth was played by the batsman.

Some bowlers in the 1870's and 1880's were very prolific with their concession of wides. R. F. Miles (Gloucestershire) delivered no fewer than 46 wides in the eight county matches in which he appeared during the 1878 season. T. Emmett (Yorkshire) set up a highly undesirable record by bowling no fewer than 85 wides during the 1885 season, a figure he had approached in the previous summer.

G. Bean, playing for Sussex v. Surrey (Oval) 1887, bowled eight no-balls in one over in an attempt to keep Surrey batting and leave less time for Sussex to be dismissed, declaration of innings not being allowed by the Laws at that time. T. Bowley and E. Mills, the last pair of Surrey batsmen, had received orders to get out, as the wicket was becoming increasingly difficult, and Bowley kept running down the pitch, but the Sussex wicket-keeper (W. H. Dudley) made no attempt to stump him. Bowley eventually trod on his own wicket to a legitimate delivery by A. Hide, but why the batsman had not taken that step earlier is a mystery. Sussex were finally left with 85 minutes' batting, and lost seven wickets for 61 runs in poor light on an impossible wicket, the match being left drawn.

W. Attewell, playing for Nottinghamshire v. Kent (Canterbury) 1892, bowled a wide ball to the boundary, conceding four runs, in order that Kent should be prevented from following-on and allow Nottinghamshire to take their second innings. This was one of the earliest incidents that led to the change in the follow-on law, making such decisions optional instead of compulsory.

C. M. Wells, playing for Cambridge in the University match at Lord's in 1893, bowled two balls to the boundary (a wide and a no-ball) conceding eight runs, in order to prevent Oxford from following-on, a step then compulsory in the event of a first innings deficit of 80 runs.

T. Richardson, who made his début in first-class cricket for Surrey in 1892, was one of the fast bowlers who rarely overstepped the crease, but in the match against Kent at the Oval in 1894 he overstepped the line and delivered his first no-ball. It clean bowled F. Marchant, the Kent batsman.

E. B. Shine, playing for Cambridge in the University match at Lord's in 1896, bowled three balls to the boundary, conceding twelve runs, in order that Oxford should not have to follow their innings. The final outcome of this match, however, was a four wickets victory for the Dark Blues, Oxford winning with a fourth innings of 330 for six wickets (G. O. Smith 132).

H. Trumble, playing for Victoria v. South Australia (Melbourne) 1896–97, bowled no-balls in order to prevent the visitors from following-on. Victoria eventually won the match by 49 runs.

F. C. Liggins, playing for Otago v. Wellington (Wellington) 1899–1900, was the next bowler to send down a strange over: one all the more curious as the question of a follow-on was not involved. Liggins bowled only two overs, one of them a maiden, conceding four runs, but during this time no fewer than three wides and twenty-three byes were added to the Wellington score.

L. B. Braund, playing for Somerset v. Middlesex (Lord's) 1900, provided a no-ball oddity. Braund was no-balled by the umpire (H. Pickett) but, realizing that he had overstepped the line, the bowler did not release the ball. It was decided officially, however, that the one-run penalty for the no-ball should be added to the score.

F. W. Tate, playing for Sussex v. Lancashire (Hastings) 1900, conceded 16 runs in byes in the course of five balls, the batsman being A. C. MacLaren. The last three balls of one over from Tate went straight through to the boundary, being followed by the second ball of Tate's next over. It must be added that these byes were not deliberate.

S. Santall, playing for Warwickshire v. Derbyshire (Birmingham) 1912, clean bowled A. G Slater with the last ball of an over, but when the next batsman arrived at the wicket the umpire allowed five more balls—making an eleven-ball over.

G. G. Collins, playing for Kent v. Middlesex (Lord's) 1922, bowled four consecutive wides in the middle of one over. The first three balls of the over conceded two singles to the batsmen, then came the four wides, and finally three more balls to complete what was a rather unusual over.

R. C. Robertson-Glasgow, playing for Somerset v. Yorkshire (Taunton) 1926, bowled one over consisting of fourteen balls, four wides and four no-balls being included, in order to hasten the taking of the new ball.

There was a fourteen-ball over in each of the Wellington innings in their Plunket Shield match against Auckland at Auckland in 1926–27—the eight-ball over law was in force in New Zealand at that time.

T. W. Wall, playing for South Australia v. Queensland (Brisbane) 1929–30, was no-balled twelve times in the course of the match.

H. Verity, playing for Yorkshire v. Surrey (Oval) 1933, sent down a lob, but as the batsman had not been informed and this was unexpected, F. Chester promptly called 'no-ball.'

K. Farnes, playing for Cambridge in the University match at Lord's in 1934, sent down no fewer than twenty-one no-balls in Oxford's innings of 368.

G. O. Allen, playing for England v. Australia (Manchester) 1934, opened the England attack with a thirteen-ball over that included three wides and four no-balls.

F. Warne, making his début for Worcestershire v. Sussex (Hastings) 1934, bowled three consecutive wides in his second over and a further wide with his second ball of his third over.

J. H. Human, playing for M.C.C. v. New Zealand XI (Dunedin) 1935–36, conceded 24 runs by means of wides and byes in order to gain the new ball with the view to forcing victory. New Zealand were nearly 300 runs behind with only three second innings wickets in hand at this point, but the game was then stopped by bad light and rain, the ruse failing.

W. R. Rees-Davies, playing for Cambridge University v. Sussex at Cambridge in 1936, was another bowler who had a spell of overstepping the crease, being no-balled for this offence sixteen times in one innings.

A. B. Sellers, playing for Yorkshire v. Surrey (Leeds) 1936, bowled one over conceding four byes and nine wides in order to hurry the arrival of the new ball. T. F. Smailes then rushed Surrey to defeat, the score changing from 200—5 to 207 all out.

In the following season A. B. Sellers again tried the same plan, but this time it did not lead to success. Playing for Yorkshire v. New Zealanders (Leeds) 1937, Sellers bowled four balls to the boundary, conceding 16 runs in byes, to obtain the new ball. Once obtained, M. L. Page and J. A Dunning fell immediate victims, but the last pair of batsmen, E. W. Tindill and J. A. Cowie, safely played out the last twenty minutes of the match and ensured a draw.

E. R. T. Holmes, playing for Surrey v. Middlesex (Lord's) 1937, started to bowl a long over in order to obtain the new ball. After four legitimate balls had been bowled, conceding 24 runs in wides and byes, the new ball was available, but before it could be brought into use a successful appeal against the light was upheld and the match ended in a draw. The sun was shining at the time of the appeal, but a position that was fast becoming farcical was brought to an end.

E. L. McCormick, the opening fast bowler with the 1938 Australian team in England, must have suffered nightmares with umpires yelling 'no-ball' in his ear in the early days of the tour. In the opening match, against Worcestershire (Worcester), McCormick's first three overs consisted of 37 balls: eight no-balls in the first over, nine in the second and two in the third. In the match McCormick bowled the record number of thirty-five no-balls, and, although he was not so prolific in the third match against Leicestershire (Leicester), he conceded a further fifteen no-balls.

J. M. A. Marshall, making his début in first-class cricket for Warwickshire v. Worcestershire (Dudley) 1946, delivered an over of eleven legitimate balls. Marshall took a wicket with the last ball of one over, but he was allowed, inadvertently, by the umpire to bowl five more balls in order to complete an over that had actually been completed with the dismissal of the batsman.

M. F. Tremlett (Somerset) had two spells of 'wide' bowling during the 1950 season. Playing against Northamptonshire (Rushden), he included four wides in his opening over, while shortly afterwards, against Essex (Westcliff), Tremlett included five wides in his opening over.

W. J. Edrich, playing for Middlesex v. Nottinghamshire (Lord's) 1956, bowled two balls to the boundary, conceding eight byes, in order to gain the new ball.

E. A. Bedser, playing for Surrey v. Hampshire (Guildford) 1956, bowled a ball for four wides in order to claim the new ball.

J. M. Allan (Kent) and C. H. Palmer (Leicetershire), the latter twice, were no-balled for having more than five fielders on the leg-side in the match at Hinckley in 1957. They were the first bowlers to be penalized under the experimental fielding law introduced that season.

W. Wooller, playing for Glamorgan v. Sussex (Hastings) 1957, bowled five consecutive lobs to R. G. Marlar as a protest against the home county's slow scoring.

Hampshire won the match v. Sussex at Hove in 1959 by a no-ball bowled by L. J. Lenham, called because he had three men behind the popping crease on the leg-side.

M.C.C. Presidents

The full record of all Presidents of the M.C.C. since 1821 is given, but unfortunately the list of Presidents before that date is not in existence. It is interesting to note that few first-class players have achieved the honour. The office of President is the gift of the retiring President, who names his successor.

Until 1951 it was the custom for the President to take over his duties at the A.G.M. in May, subsequent Presidents taking over office on 1st October, although nominated in May. W. Findlay held the office of President from May 1951 to October 1952.

1821	Lord Strathavon	1880	Sir William Hart-Dyke
1822	H. T. Lloyd	1881	Lord George Hamilton
1823	B. Aislabie	1882	2nd Lord Belper
1824	H. T. Lane	1883	Hon. Robert Grimston
1825	C. J. Barnett	1884	5th Earl of Winterton
1826	Lord Frederick Beauclerk, D.D.	1885	3rd Baron Wenlock
1827	H. R. Kingscote	1886	5th Baron Lyttelton
1828	A. F. Greville	1887	Hon. Edward Chandos Leigh
1829	J. Barnard	1888	6th Duke of Buccleuch
1830	Hon. G. Ponsonby	1889	Sir Henry James
1831	W. Deedes	1890	22nd Baron Willoughby de Eresby
1832	H. Howard	1891	V. E. Walker
1833	H. Jenner	1892	W. E. Denison
1834	Hon. A. H. Ashley	1893	6th Earl of Dartmouth
1835	Lord Charles Russell	1894	7th Earl of Jersey
1836	4th Baron Suffield	1895	4th Baron Harris
1837	4th Viscount Grimston	1896	14th Earl of Pembroke
1838	2nd Marquess of Exeter	1897	3rd Earl of Lichfield
1839	6th Earl of Chesterfield	1898	Hon. Alfred Lyttelton
1840	1st Earl of Verulam	1899	Sir Archibald L. Smith
1841	2nd Earl of Craven	1900	Hon. Ivo Bligh
1842	Earl of March	1901	4th Earl Howe
1843	2nd Earl of Dulcie	1902	A. G. Steel
1844	Sir John Bayley	1903	1st Baron Alverstone
1845	T. Chamberlayne	1904	Marquess of Granby
1846	4th Earl of Winterton	1905	C. E. Green
1847	12th Earl of Strathmore	1906	W. H. Long
1848	2nd Earl of Leicester	1907	1st Baron Loreburn
1849	6th Earl of Darnley	1908	3rd Earl of Cawdor
1850	Lord Guernsey	1909	10th Earl of Chesterfield
1851	7th Earl of Stamford	1910	2nd Earl of Londesborough
1852	Viscount Dupplin	1911	1st Baron Desborough
1853	Marquess of Worcester	1912	9th Duke of Devonshire
1854	Earl Vane	1913	Earl of Dalkeith
1855	Earl of Uxbridge	1914	7th Baron Hawke
1856	Viscount Milton	1919	1st Lord Forster
1857	Sir F. H. Hervey-Bathurst	1920	4th Earl of Ellesmere
1858	Lord Garlies	1921	Hon. Sir Stanley (F. S.) Jackson
1859	9th Earl of Coventry	1922	1st Viscount Chelmsford (F. J. N. Thesiger)
1860	2nd Earl of Skelmersdale		
1861	5th Earl of Spencer	1923	1st Viscount Ullswater
1862	4th Earl of Sefton	1924	1st Baron Ernle
1863	5th Baron Suffield	1925	Admiral of the Fleet Sir John de Robeck
1864	1st Earl of Dudley	1926	3rd Viscount Hampden
1865	1st Earl of Ebury	1927	3rd Baron Leconfield
1866	7th Earl of Sandwich	1928	5th Earl of Lucan
1867	2nd Earl of Verulam	1929	Field Marshal Baron Plumer
1868	2nd Baron Methuen	1930	Sir Kynaston Studd
1869	5th Marquess of Lansdowne	1931	1st Viscount Bridgeman
1870	J. H. Scourfield	1932	Viscount Lewisham
1871	5th Earl of Clarendon	1933	1st Viscount Hailsham
1872	8th Viscount Downe	1934	2nd Earl of Cromer
1873	Viscount Chelsea	1935	9th Viscount Cobham
1874	Marquess of Hamilton	1936	6th Baron Somers
1875	Sir Charles Legard	1937	Col. Hon. J. J. Astor
1876	2nd Earl of Londesborough	1938	1st Earl of Baldwin of Bewdley
1877	8th Duke of Beaufort	1939	S. Christopherson
1878	2nd Lord Fitzhardinge	1946	General Sir Ronald Adam
1879	W. Nicholson	1947	Lord Cornwallis

1948	Earl of Gowrie	1955	Field Marshal Earl Alexander of Tunis
1949	H.R.H. Duke of Edinburgh	1956	Viscount Monckton
1950	Sir Pelham Warner	1957	16th Duke of Norfolk
1951	W. Findlay	1958	Marshal of the R.A.F. Viscount Portal
1952	10th Duke of Beaufort	1959	H. S. Altham
1953	6th Earl of Rosebery	1960	Sir Hubert Ashton
1954	10th Viscount Cobham		

M.C.C. Secretaries

Secretaries

1822–1842	B. Aislabie
1842–1858	R. Kynaston
1858–1863	A. Baillie
1863–1876	R. A. Fitzgerald
1876–1897	H. Perkins
1898–1926	Sir Francis Lacey
1926–1936	W. Findlay
1936–1952	Col. R. S. Rait-Kerr
1952—	R. Aird

Assistant Secretaries

1878–1907	J. A. Murdoch
1919–1926	W. Findlay
1926–1952	R. Aird
1949—	J. G. Dunbar
1952—	S. C. Griffith

A. Cornwell Legh acted as Clerk to the Committee from 1907 to 1926.

During the war of 1939–1945, Sir Pelham Warner acted as Secretary when Col. R. S. Rait-Kerr and R. Aird were absent on active service, W. Findlay also giving his assistance.

'Mosts' in a Season

The following table of 'mosts' in a season is of interest.

Most 3000 run aggregates	5 in 1928
Most 2000 run aggregates	23 in 1959
Most 1000 run aggregates	101 in 1959
Most 300 wicket aggregates	1 in 1928
Most 200 wicket aggregates	5 in 1925
Most 100 wicket aggregates	30 in 1955 and 1957
Most 'doubles'	12 in 1923
Most 300's in a season	3 in 1899 and 1934
Most 200's in a season	34 in 1933
Most centuries in a season	414 in 1928

No-balled for Throwing

The following bowlers provide the leading instances of a bowler being 'called' for throwing:

E. Jones: Australia v. England (Melbourne)	1897–98
C. B. Fry: Sussex v. Nottinghamshire (Nottingham)	1898
C. B. Fry: Sussex v. Oxford U. (Hove)	1898
C. B. Fry: Sussex v. Middlesex (Lord's)	1898
F. J. Hopkins: Warwickshire v. Kent (Tonbridge)	1898
E. R. Bradford: Hampshire v. Leicestershire (Leicester)	1899
E. R. Bradford: Hampshire v. Australians (Southampton)	1899
(No-balled by both umpires.)	
R. G. Hardstaff: Nottinghamshire v. Australians (Nottingham)	1899
C. B. Fry: Sussex v. Gloucestershire (Hove)	1900
A. Mold: Lancashire v. Nottinghamshire (Nottingham)	1900
E. J. Tyler: Somerset v. Surrey (Taunton)	1900
(No-balled twice in one over by J. Phillips.)	
J. J. Marsh: New South Wales v. Victoria (Melbourne)	1900–01
(No-balled twice by R. W. Crockett.)	
J. J. Marsh: New South Wales v. Victoria (Sydney)	1900–01
(No-balled 19 times by R. W. Crockett.)	
A. Mold: Lancashire v. Somerset (Manchester)	1901
(No-balled 16 times in 10 overs by J. Phillips.)	

A. Paish: Gloucestershire v. Nottinghamshire (Bristol) 1903
A. Paish: Gloucestershire v. Yorkshire (Bristol) 1903
    (*No-balled by W. A. J. West in consecutive matches, on four occasions in second match.*)
R. Whitehead: Lancashire v. Nottinghamshire (Manchester) 1908
    (*His debut match in first-class cricket, he also scored a century—131*.*)
G. John: West Indian XI v. M.C.C. (Georgetown) 1910–11
R. Halcombe: Western Australia v. Victoria (Melbourne) 1929–30
    (*No-balled 8 times in succession in the only over he bowled.*)
E. Gilbert: Queensland v. Victoria (Melbourne) 1931–32
    (*No-balled 8 times in 2 overs.*)
Mabarak Ali: Trinidad v. Barbados (Barbados) 1941–42
    (*No-balled 30 times in one innings.*)
R. R. Frankish: Western Australia v. Victoria (Melbourne) 1950–51
M. R. Rege: Maharashtra v. M.C.C. (Poona) 1951–52
    (*No-balled twice in the only over he bowled.*)
C. N. McCarthy: Cambridge U. v. Worcestershire (Worcester) 1952
G. A. R. Lock: Surrey v. Indians (Oval) 1952
    (*No-balled 3 times by W. F. Price, twice in one over.*)
G. A. R. Lock: England v. West Indies (Kingston) 1953–54
G. A. R. Lock: M.C.C. v. Barbados (Barbados) 1953–54
    (*No-balled by both umpires, once by one and twice in three balls by the other.*)
D. B. Pearson: Worcestershire v. Gloucestershire (Bristol) 1954
K. Slater: Western Australia v. Victoria (Melbourne) 1957–58
C. Stayers: British Guiana v. Barbados (Barbados) 1958–59
G. Griffin: Natal v. Transvaal (Durban) 1958–59
G. Griffin: Natal v. Border & Eastern Province (East London) 1958–59
D. B. Pearson: Worcestershire v. Indians (Worcester) 1959
    (*No-balled 5 times by J. S. Buller.*)
D. B. Pearson: Worcestershire v. Essex (Worcester) 1959
G. A. R. Lock: Surrey v. Glamorgan (Cardiff) 1959
K. J. Aldridge: Worcestershire v. Leicestershire (Kidderminster) 1959
    (*No-balled twice by J. S. Buller.*)
J. McLaughlin: Queensland v. New South Wales (Sydney) 1959–60
G. A. R. Lock: Surrey v. Cambridge U. (Cambridge) 1960
K. J. Aldridge: Worcestershire v. Glamorgan (Pontypridd) 1960
H. J. Rhodes: Derbyshire v. South Africans (Derby) 1960
    (*No-balled 6 times by P. A. Gibb.*)
G. Griffin: South Africans v. M.C.C. (Lord's) 1960
    (*No-balled once by F. S. Lee and twice by John Langridge. He was also called for dragging by F. S. Lee each time John Langridge no-balled him for throwing.*)
D. B. Pearson: Worcestershire v. Northamptonshire (Dudley) 1960
    (*No-balled twice by T. J. Bartley.*)
G. Griffin: South Africans v. Nottinghamshire (Nottingham) 1960
    (*No-balled 11 times in the first innings, 5 times for throwing and 6 times for dragging. He was called 3 times for throwing by T. J. Bartley and twice by W. H. Copson. No-balled for throwing 3 times in the second innings.*)
E. Bryant: Somerset v. Gloucestershire (Bath) 1960
    (*No-balled 5 times by H. Yarnold, 4 times in one over.*)
G. Griffin: South Africans v. Hampshire (Southampton) 1960
    (*No-balled by both umpires once each in first innings and 4 times in the second innings, 3 times by J. H. Parks and once by H. Elliott.*)
G. Griffin: South Africa v. England (Lord's) 1960
    (*No-balled 11 times by F. S. Lee in England's only innings.*)
D. W. White: Hampshire v. Sussex (Hove) 1960
    (*No-balled 3 times by P. A. Gibb, twice in first innings and once in the second.*)
R. T. Simpson: Nottinghamshire v. Derbyshire (Nottingham) 1960
    (*No-balled once by H. Yarnold.*)

Oldest First-Class Cricketers

J. Wheatley, who played for Canterbury between 1882–83 and 1903–04, was 100 on January 8th, 1960, the first first-class cricketer to reach the century of years, although three players have lived to be 98. The following players all lived to the age of 94 or more:

Years Months			Born	Died
98	11	G. C. Attfield (Surrey)	27-1-1826	16- 1-1925
98	10	F. A. Mackinnon (Cambridge U. & Kent)	9-4-1848	27- 2-1947
98	5	H. Jenner (Cambridge U. & Kent)	23-2-1806	30- 7-1904
96	0	W. Beldham (Surrey)	5-2-1766	20- 2-1862
95	11	A. C. Walthen (Kent)	27-3-1841	14- 3-1937
95	5	G. Moore (New South Wales)	17-4-1821	29- 9-1916
94	11	R. J. P. Broughton (Cambridge U.)	11-7-1816	15- 6-1911
94	6	E. Bayley (later Laurie) (Kent)	16-5-1823	3-12-1917
94	3	G. P. Fuller (Oxford U.)	8-1-1833	2- 4-1927
94	1	A. C. Bartholomew (Oxford U.)	21-2-1846	29- 3-1940

It is more difficult still when trying to list cricketers born before 1867, as several for whom no date of death is known are quite obviously no longer with us. The following list of living first-class cricketers who have already reached 94 seems reasonably accurate if not complete: the date of birth is given.

J. Wheatley (Canterbury)	8- 1-1860
R. C. Ramsay (Cambridge U.)	20-12-1861
A. Daffen (Kent)	30-12-1862
E. Coupe (Derbyshire)	9- 6-1863
F. Dunkley (Middlesex)	9- 9-1863
E. A. English (Hampshire)	1- 1-1864
F. Bolus (Somerset)	2-11-1864
H. Donnan (New South Wales)	12-11-1864
F. Ward (Lancashire)	9- 1-1865
H. J. Tinsley (Yorkshire & Lancashire)	20- 2-1865
T. Robinson (Somerset)	16- 2-1866
H. Tebay (Sussex)	5-10-1866

Penalties, etc.

I. D. Walker, playing for Middlesex v. Nottinghamshire (Nottingham) 1884, bowled a ball to W. H. Scotton which the batsman drove straight back down the wicket. Walker's cap, which had slipped from his head in the action of bowling, stopped the ball and the batsman was credited with five runs. As the Laws are framed, a ball has to be stopped *wilfully* for the five runs penalty to come into effect, so that the award of runs to Scotton appears to be incorrect.

R. Peel, playing for Yorkshire v. Middlesex (Sheffield) 1897, was sent off the field by Lord Hawke for 'going into the field when not in a fit condition to play.'

The Hampshire captain, Hon. L. H. Tennyson, sent J. A. Newman off the field during the course of the match between Hampshire and Nottinghamshire at Nottingham in 1922. There is no Law to cover this action.

T. W. Goddard, playing for Gloucestershire v. Sussex (Cheltenham) 1932, stopped with his cap a ball that had been hit by A. Melville, conceding five runs to the batsman. Melville had actually run a single off the ball, but the umpires ruled that only five runs in all should be scored. A later amendment to the Laws made it clear that the five runs penalty should be added to the runs already made, if any runs had been completed before the offence.

L. Hutton, playing for England v. Australia (Oval) 1938, conceded four runs to Australia: a present he could well afford as he had set up a new Test record earlier in the match with an individual innings of 364. In the closing stages of Australia's first innings, W. A. Brown, the opening batsman, was trying to farm the bowling and, hitting a ball close to the boundary, took a single off the last ball of an over. Hutton kicked the ball over the boundary, apparently with the thought that this would mean the lesser batsman keeping the strike, but under the Laws four runs were added to the single already run and Brown retained the strike.

Public Schoolboy Cricketers

Several players have made their début in first-class cricket while still at a public school, with one more summer term to come a year later. A few boys, however, have actually made their first-class début with two more summer terms to come, as follows:

H. S. Critchley-Salmonson (Winchester) ....Somerset 1910
D. J. Knight (Malvern) ....Surrey 1911
E. P. Hewetson (Shrewsbury) ....Warwickshire 1919
H. C. A. Gaunt (Tonbridge) ....Warwickshire 1919
T. G. B. Welch (Malvern) ....Northamptonshire 1922
N. S. Mitchell-Innes (Sedbergh) ....Somerset 1931
Nawab of Pataudi (Winchester) ....Sussex 1957

Similarity of Dismissal

On several occasions the same combination of field and bowler has disposed of several batsmen in the course of an innings, the following being the leading cases (in each case the fielding team is given first):

HAT-TRICKS

st W. H. Brain b C. L. Townsend: Glos. v. Somerset (Cheltenham) 1895
c G. J. Thompson b S. G. Smith: Northants. v. Warwicks. (Birmingham) 1914
lbw b H. Fisher: Yorks. v. Somerset (Sheffield) 1932
c G. Dawkes b L. Jackson: Derby v. Worcs. (Kidderminster) 1958

FIRST FIVE WICKETS TO FALL IN AN INNINGS

c or st H. R. Butt: Sussex v. Notts. (Hove) 1905
c G. M. Lee: Notts. v. Hants. (Southampton) 1913
c or st H. Elliott: Derby v. Sussex (Buxton) 1934
c or st K. C. James: Northants v. Cambridge U. (Cambridge) 1939
c R. T. Spooner: Warwicks. v. Notts. (Birmingham) 1957

FIRST FOUR WICKETS TO FALL IN AN INNINGS

st M. Turner b J. Buchanan: Gentlemen of England v. Oxford U. (Oxford) 1870
c V. E. Walker b E. Rutter: Middx. v. Surrey (Prince's) 1873
st J. P. Whiteside b F. Geeson: Leics. v. Essex (Leicester) 1901
c T. W. Oates: Notts. v. Kent (Catford) 1901
c H. L. Simms b A. E. Relf: Sussex v. Derby (Hove) 1908
c H. R. Murrell: Middx. v. Notts. (Nottingham) 1921
All clean bowled for 1: Lancs. v. Essex (Colchester) 1928
c or st W. F. Cornford: Sussex v. Surrey (Oval) 1930
c W. R. Hammond b C. W. L. Parker: Glos. v. Notts. (Bristol) 1933
c A. F. Wensley: Sussex v. Surrey (Horsham) 1934
c F. E. Woolley: Kent v. Notts. (Canterbury) 1934
c or st D. D. Hindlekar: Indians v. Oxford U. (Oxford) 1936
c J. Firth: Leics. v. Essex (Colchester) 1953
c B. T. Swift: Cambridge U. v. Hants. (Bournemouth) 1957
c or st G. Millman: Notts. v. Surrey (Oval) 1957
c A. Wilson: Lancs. v. Hants. (Manchester) 1958
c M. F. Tremlett: Somerset v. Lancs. (Weston-super-Mare) 1958

FIRST THREE WICKETS TO FALL IN AN INNINGS

run out: South Australia v. G. F. Vernon's XI (Adelaide) 1887–88
st N. C. Tufnell b J. H. B. Lockhart: Cambridge U. v. Australians (Cambridge) 1909
c H. L. V. Day b G. S. Boyes: Hants. v. Glos. (Southampton) 1922
c G. B. Legge b M. A. McCanlis: Oxford U. v. Cambridge U. (Lord's) 1926
c or st W. H. Livsey b G. Brown: Hants. v. Kent (Southampton) 1926
st W. F. Price b J. W. Hearne: Middx. v. Yorks. (Lord's) 1927
c C. F. Root b C. V. Tarbox, 0: Worcs. v. Essex (Worcester) 1927
st F. L. H. Mooney b T. B. Burtt: New Zealanders v. Leveson-Gower's XI (Scarborough) ...1949

FIVE BATSMEN IN SUCCESSION IN COURSE OF AN INNINGS

c T. W. Oates b A. W. Hallam: Notts. v. Middx. (Nottingham) 1906
c W. R. Hammond b C. W. L. Parker: Glos. v. Surrey (Cheltenham) 1928
c or st P. Corrall: Leics. v. Sussex (Hove) 1936

FOUR BATSMEN IN SUCCESSION IN COURSE OF AN INNINGS

c or st W. F. Farrimond: Lancs. v. Kent (Manchester) 1930
c V. Y. Richardson: Australia v. South Africa (Durban) 1935–36
c John Langridge b James Langridge: Sussex v. Lancs. (Manchester) 1936

SEVEN OUT OF FIRST EIGHT WICKETS TO FALL

c or st W. F. Farrimond (www.wwww): Lancs. v. Kent (Manchester) 1930

SEVEN OUT OF NINE WICKETS TO FALL

c W. F. Price (.www.w.www): Middx. v. Yorks. (Lord's) 1937

SIX OUT OF EIGHT SUCCESSIVE WICKETS TO FALL

c or st W. H. V. Levett: Kent v. Northants. (Northampton) 1934
c or st P. Corrall: Leics. v. Sussex (Hove) 1936
c or st M. H. Matthews: Oxford U. v. Surrey (Oval) 1937
c K. C. James: Northants. v. Glamorgan (Swansea) 1937

SIX OUT OF SEVEN SUCCESSIVE WICKETS TO FALL, INCLUDING FIVE IN FIVE

c W. R. Hammond (wwwww.w): Glos. v. Surrey (Cheltenham)...................................1928
c or st H. Elliott (wwwww.w): Derby v. Lancs. (Manchester) 1935

FIVE DISMISSALS IN ONE INNINGS (OUTSTANDING CASES)

c F. G. J. Ford (only 7 wkts fell): Cambridge U. v. M.C.C. (Lord's) 1888
c or st D. Hunter b W. Rhodes (last 5 wkts): Yorks. v. Surrey (Bradford) 1898
c T. W. Oates b. A. W. Hallam (in 34 balls): Notts. v. Middx. (Nottingham) 1906
st N. C. Tufnell b J. H. B. Lockhart: Cambridge U. v. Yorks. (Cambridge) 1909
c G. Brown b A. Jaques: Hants. v. Somerset (Bath) 1914
c J. F. Sheppard b D. MacAndrews: Queensland v. N.S.W. (Brisbane) 1914–15
c J. H. Nicholson b V. W. C. Jupp: Northants. v. Worcs. (Dudley) 1928
c V. Y. Richardson (....w.wwww): Australia v. South Africa (Durban) 1935–36
c T. N. Pierce b J. E. D. Sealey: Trinidad v. Barbados (Barbados) 1941–42

Spells of Good Batting

On several occasions batsmen have retained their best form over a series of consecutive innings. The leading cases are as follows:

2 innings	639	W. H. Ponsford	1927–28	437	202			
	591	W. H. Ponsford	1921–23	162	429			
	590	D. G. Bradman	1935–36	233	357			
	581	D. G. Bradman	1935–37	369	212			
3 innings	839	W. G. Grace	1876	344	177	318*		
	772	W. H. Ponsford	1927–28	133	437	202		
	750	V. M. Merchant	1943–44	250*	141	359*		
	707	D. G. Bradman	1935–36	117	233	357		
4 innings	1013	W. H. Ponsford	1927–28	437	202	38	336	
	917	W. G. Grace	1876	344	177	318*	78	
	812	V. M. Merchant	1943–44	62	250*	141	359*	
	789	H. Sutcliffe	1932	313	96	110*	270	
5 innings	1146	W. H. Ponsford	1927–28	133	437	202	38	336
	940	V. S. Hazare	1943–44	248	59	309	101	222
	934	W. G. Grace	1876	17	344	177	318*	78

Unusual Dismissals

There are nine ways in which a batsman can be dismissed, six of which occur regularly and three which are very unusual. The complete list of these dismissals, together with two other unusual ways of getting out, is given.

HANDLED BALL

There have been few recorded instances of a batsman being dismissed 'handled ball', several of them being recorded before the passing of Law 33b in 1899. Before this date a batsman could be dismissed 'handled ball' for removing a ball which lodged in his clothing, but the amendment ruled that in future cases the ball became dead. The cases in 1872, 1893 and 1894–95 came under the earlier rule:

J. Grundy (15): M.C.C. v. Kent (Lord's) 1857
The first recorded case in first-class cricket. After playing the ball to his feet he hit the ball away with his hand. The bowler (E. Willsher) was given credit for the dismissal in the score sheet
G. Bennett (0): Kent v. Sussex (Hove) 1872
W. H. Scotton (18): Smokers v. Non-Smokers (East Melbourne) 1886–87
This match was played between combined England and Australian teams. Scotton played the last ball of the match to his feet, his intention being to retain it as a souvenir. On bending to pick it up he was given out by the umpire.
C. W. Wright (4): Nottinghamshire v. Gloucestershire (Bristol)..................................1893
E. Jones (9): South Australia v. Victoria (Melbourne) 1894–95
A. D. Nourse sen. (1): South Africans v. Sussex (Hove) 1907
Nourse stopped with his hand a ball which seemed likely to roll into his wicket.
E. T. Benson (29): M.C.C. v. Auckland (Auckland) 1929–30
Benson was given out after stooping to pick up the ball, but it is doubtful if he did actually touch it.
A. W. Gilbertson (7): Otago v. Auckland (Auckland) 1952–53
Gilbertson played the ball, which came to rest about a foot outside the off-stump. It could not possibly have hit the wicket, but the batsman picked it up and was given out on appeal.
W. R. Endean (3): South Africa v. England (Cape Town) 1956–57
P. Burge (11): Queensland v. New South Wales (Sydney) 1958–59
Dildar Awan (8): Services v. Lahore (Lahore) 1959–60

HIT THE BALL TWICE

H. E. Bull (29): M.C.C. v. Oxford U. (Lord's) 1864
H. Charlwood (73): Sussex v. Surrey (Hove) 1872
The batsman played the ball, but seeing it roll towards his wicket hit it again while standing out of his crease. His partner (A. A. Reed) was backing-up half way down the wicket, and on appeal by the wicket-keeper (E. Pooley), Charlwood was given out by the square-leg umpire.
I. J. Salmon (13): Wellington v. Hawke's Bay (Wellington) 1873–74
R. G. Barlow (20): North v. South (Lord's) 1878
P. S. Wimble (0): Transvaal v. Griqualand West (Kimberley) 1892–93
The batsman responded to his partner's call for a run after playing the ball twice.
G. B. Nicholls (10): Somerset v. Gloucestershire (Bristol) 1896
Nicholls attempted to run after hitting the ball twice.
A. A. Lilley (13): Warwickshire v. Yorkshire (Birmingham) 1897
J. H. King (13): Leicestershire v. Surrey (Oval)..1906
King hit the ball so hard the second time that he attempted a run.
A. P. Binns (151): Jamaica v. British Guiana (Georgetown) 1956–57

OBSTRUCTING THE FIELD

C. A. Absolom (38): Cambridge U. v. Surrey (Oval) 1868
Absolom was running between wickets when the ball hit his bat on being returned from the outfield, a rather unlucky and perhaps incorrect dismissal.
T. Straw (8): Worcestershire v. Warwickshire (Worcester) 1899
T. Straw (3): Worcestershire v. Warwickshire (Birmingham) 1901
J. P. Whiteside (0): Leicestershire v. Lancashire (Leicester) 1901
L. Hutton (27): England v. South Africa (Oval) 1951
J. A. Hayes (0): Canterbury v. Central Districts (Christchurch) 1954–55
The batsman (A. R. MacGibbon) played the ball to the on side and sent Hayes, who was backing-up, back. Two fielders went for the ball and Hayes slipped as he turned, hitting the ball, and colliding with a fieldsman.
D. D. Deshpande (6): Madhya Pradesh v. Uttar Pradesh (Benares) 1956–57

RUN OUT BY THE BOWLER

The following cases have been recorded of a batsman being run out by the bowler whilst backing up before the ball had been bowled:

G. Jones (6) by (name unknown): Surrey v. Australians (Oval) 1878
C. W. Wright (13) by G. P. Harrison: Cambridge U. v. Yorks. (Cambridge) 1883
E. J. Tyler (25) by A. Hearne: Somerset v. Kent (Taunton) 1894
T. W. Reese (15) by A. Downes: Canterbury v. Otago (Christchurch) 1894–95
J. Hardstaff jun. (2) by Khadim Hussain: Lord Tennyson's XI v. Sind (Karachi) 1937–38
W. A. Brown (30) by V. Mankad: Australian XI v. Indians (Sydney) 1947–48
W. A. Brown (18) by V. Mankad: Australia v. India (Sydney) 1947–48
R. Routledge (1) by J. P. Fellows-Smith: Middlesex v. Oxford U. (Oxford) 1953
G. E. Barker (33) by W. Wooller: Essex v. Glamorgan (Cardiff) 1956

STUMPED BY A SUBSTITUTE

N. C. Tufnell (sub for H. Strudwick) st S. J. Snooke: England v. South Africa (Durban) 1909–10
N. C. Tufnell (sub for W. Findlay) st G. C. Drysdale: M.C.C. v. Argentine (Buenos Aires)...1911–12
L. E. G. Ames (sub for R. T. Stanyforth) st J. S. Mackenzie: M.C.C. v. British Guiana
(Georgetown)......1929–30
R. T. Spooner (sub for J. T. Kendall) st I. J. M. Lumsden: Warwicks. v. Scotland (Birmingham)...1948
H. W. Stephenson (sub for A. T. Barlow) st M. D. Mohoni: Commonwealth v. Governor's XI
(Nagpur)......1950–51
P. Rochford (sub for D. V. Brennan) st T. E. Bailey: Yorks. v. M.C.C. (Scarborough)............1951
M. Fitchett (sub for I. H. McDonald) st J. Grove: Victoria v. South Australia (Adelaide)......1952–53
L. A. Johnson (sub for K. V. Andrew) st P. M. Walker: Northants. v. Glamorgan (Northampton) 1959

Envoi

The records included in this book are complete to the end of the 1960 cricket season, but while it was being prepared for publication a number of records were set up during the 1960–61 season. For that reason I have added the following brief envoi, listing the major records set up between the end of the 1960 season and the date of going to press.

TIE IN TEST CRICKET

The first Test match at Brisbane between Australia (505 & 232) and West Indies (453 & 284) resulted in the first-ever tie in Test cricket. It was, incidentally, the 498th Test match.

MATCH DOUBLE IN TEST CRICKET

A. K. Davidson, playing for Australia v. West Indies at Brisbane, became the first player to score 100 runs and take ten wickets in a Test match, by scoring 44 & 80 and taking eleven wickets (5—135 & 6—87).

RECORD ATTENDANCE FIGURES IN TEST CRICKET

A crowd of 90,800 people watched play on the second day (11th February) of the first Test at Melbourne between Australia and West Indies, setting up a new gate record for Test cricket. The total attendance for the match was 274,404 (receipts £39,000).

OPPONENTS SENT IN TO BAT

R. Benaud sent West Indies in to bat in the fifth Test at Melbourne, and won the game by two wickets. This is the forty-third time that a Test captain has chosen to field first, but only the thirteenth time the game has been won. Benaud, incidentally, has now taken this step three times and been successful each time.

First-Class Cricket Records

LARGE INNINGS TOTAL

633   Lahore v. Punjab University (Lahore).

SMALL INNINGS TOTALS

23 & 28   Jammu & Kashmir v. Delhi (Srinagar).

DOUBLE-CENTURIES

283* R. G. Nadkarni: Bombay v. Delhi (Bombay).
266   W. Lawry: Victoria v. New South Wales (Sydney).
252   R. Kanhai: West Indians v. Victoria (Melbourne).
240   P. Burge: Queensland v. South Australia (Adelaide).
229   R. N. Harvey: New South Wales v. Queensland (Sydney).
222   Hanif Mohammed: Pakistan v. Combined Universities (Poona).
221* R. B. Simpson: Western Australia v. West Indians (Perth).
204   M. J. K. Smith: Commonwealth v. Natal (Durban).
203* I. A. Bokhari: Lahore v. Punjab University (Lahore).
201   B. Sutcliffe: Otago v. Northern Districts (Hamilton).

CENTURY ON DÉBUT FOR WEST INDIAN TEAM IN AUSTRALIA

119   G. Sobers: West Indians v. Western Australia (Perth).
103   R. Kanhai: West Indians v. Australia XI (Perth).

A CENTURY IN EACH INNINGS

117 & 115   R. Kanhai: West Indies v. Australia (Adelaide).

CENTURY BEFORE LUNCH ON FIRST DAY OF MATCH

Hanif Mohammed (222): Pakistan v. Combined Universities (Poona).

LARGE WICKET PARTNERSHIPS

323	2nd	I. D. Craig & R. N. Harvey: N.S.W. v. Queensland (Sydney).
295	3rd	K. Mackay & P. Burge: Queensland v. South Australia (Adelaide).
290	5th	M. M. Sood & Ramesh Saxena: Delhi v. Southern Punjab (New Delhi).
277	2nd	S. G. Adhikari & H. Amroliwalla: Bombay v. Maharashtra (Bombay).
268	5th	R. Lloyd & I. M. McLachlan: South Australia v. Queensland (Adelaide).
252	2nd	W. Lawry & J. Potter: Victoria v. N.S.W. (Sydney).
246	2nd	Hanif Mohammed & Saeed Ahmed: Pakistan v. India (Bombay).
237	2nd	W. Lawry & J. Potter: Victoria v. Queensland (Brisbane).
236*	1st	V. Mehra & B. K. Kunderam: Railways v. Jammu & Kashmir (Srinagar).
227	4th	E. Brotherton & K. C. Bland: S.A. Universities v. Western Province (Cape Town).
223*	2nd	Imtiaz Ahmed & Saeed Ahmed: Pakistan v. Baroda (Baroda).
222	2nd	I. A. Bokhari & Mohammed Iqbal: Lahore v. Punjab U. (Lahore).
213	4th	M. Sargent & R. Lloyd: South Australia v. Queensland (Brisbane).
209*	5th	Mushtaq Mohammed & Wallis Mathias: Pakistan v. Combined Universities (Poona).
208	3rd	I. D. Craig & B. Booth: N.S.W. v. Western Australia (Perth).
202	3rd	P. R. Umrigar & R. G. Nadkarni: Bombay v. Saurashtra (Rajkot).
191	6th	B. Booth & R. Flockton: N.S.W. v. South Australia (Sydney).
160	7th	K. Venkataranamamurthi & R. P. Gupta: Andhra v. Mysore (Bangalore).
158*	7th	Viswanath & Kasturirangan: Mysore v. Andhra (Bangalore).
154	7th	Rajendran & V. Sreedhar: Madras v. Kerala (Trivandrum).

HAT-TRICK

G. Gibbs: West Indies v. Australia (Adelaide).

THREE WICKETS IN FOUR BALLS (TEST MATCHES)

G. Gibbs: West Indies v. Australia (Sydney).
J. Martin: Australia v. West Indies (Melbourne).

NINE WICKETS IN AN INNINGS

9—28	Khalid Qureshi: Lahore v. Board of Education (Lahore).
9—32	A. F. Hagemann: Border v. Griqualand West (Kimberley).
9—122	G. Hall: S.A. Universities v. Western Province (Cape Town).

MOST MAIDEN OVERS IN SUCCESSION (EIGHT-BALL OVERS)

8   R. Benaud: Australia v. West Indies (Sydney).

BOWLERS UNCHANGED IN A MATCH

Rajindernath (9—20) & Sitaram (11–30): Delhi v. Jammu & Kashmir (Srinagar).

'NO-BALLED FOR THROWING'

B. Quigley: South Australia v. Victoria (Adelaide): twice on first day.
B. K. Bose: East Zone v. Pakistan (Jamshedpur): three times.

MEMORABILIA

Mahmood-ul-Hasan (50) was dismissed 'handled ball': Karachi U. v. Railways & Quetta (Karachi).

New South Wales won the Sheffield Shield for the eighth season in succession.

Pakistan drew all fourteen matches on their tour of India, the first time that a touring team has not taken one match to a definite result.

Index

The following detailed list of contents is more suitable to this work than the more conventional type of alphabetical index. The arrangement of the records throughout this book have followed a set pattern, and a short perusal of this index will enable readers to find their way more easily through the pages.

TEST CRICKET RECORDS—1876-77 TO 1960

Results and Scores of all Test matches:

England v. Australia	12
England v. South Africa	15
England v. West Indies	17
England v. New Zealand	18
England v. India	19
England v. Pakistan	19
Australia v. South Africa	19
Australia v. West Indies	20
Australia v. New Zealand	20
Australia v. India	21
Australia v. Pakistan	21
South Africa v. New Zealand	21
West Indies v. New Zealand	21
West Indies v. India	21
West Indies v. Pakistan	22
New Zealand v. India	22
New Zealand v. Pakistan	22
India v. Pakistan	22

PART I—THE SIDES

Highest innings totals	23
Highest second innings totals	24
Lowest innings totals	24
Highest fourth innings totals	24
Record innings totals for each Test ground	25
Highest match aggregates	25
Lowest match aggregates—completed matches	26
Greatest victories	26
Closest victories	26
Longest matches	27
Matches completed in two days	27
Complete side dismissed twice in a day's play	27
Most runs scored in a day's play by one side	27
Most runs scored in a day's play by both sides	27
Matches dominated by batting	28
Eclectic score card	28
Five centuries in one innings	28
Four centuries in one innings	28
Three centuries in one innings	28
Most centuries scored in one Test match	29
Most centuries scored in one Test rubber	29
Most centuries scored by one side in a Test rubber	29
Test team unchanged for complete Test rubber	29
Most players engaged by one side in complete rubber	29
Most consecutive victories in all Test cricket	30
Most consecutive matches without defeat	30
Most consecutive matches without victory	30
Most consecutive defeats in all Test cricket	30
Most consecutive victories in a series	30
Most consecutive matches without defeat in a series	30
Double figures by all eleven batsmen in an innings	30
Complete innings without a score of double figures	31
Outstanding collapses	31
Outstanding recoveries	31

PART II—BATTING

Highest individual innings 33
A century on début in Test cricket 34
A century in each innings of a match 35
Five centuries in consecutive innings 36
Four centuries in consecutive innings 36
Three centuries in consecutive innings 36
Most fifties in consecutive innings 36
Highest run aggregates in a Test rubber 36
Five centuries in one Test rubber 37
Four centuries in one Test rubber 37
Highest individual innings scored on each Test ground 37
Most runs scored by a batsman in a day's play 38
Most runs added during a batsman's innings 38
Batsmen scoring a high percentage of innings total 38
Opening batsman carrying bat through innings 38
Batsmen who scored maiden century in a Test match 39
A century and 'duck' in the same Test 39
Batsmen registering a 'pair of spectacles' 39
Fastest times to certain scores 40
Fast scoring in a complete innings 41
Fast partnerships 41
Most runs scored off a single over 42
Most boundary strokes in an innings 43
Monopoly of run scoring during innings 43

PART III—WICKET PARTNERSHIPS

Record Wicket Partnerships:
    All Test cricket 45
    England, Australia, South Africa and West Indies 45
    New Zealand, India and Pakistan 46
Highest score reached at the fall of each wicket 46
Lowest score reached at the fall of each wicket 46
Wicket partnerships of over 300 47
Four century stands in one innings.. 47
Three century stands in one innings.. 47
Century stand for same wicket in each innings 47
Batsmen with most century stands 48

PART IV—BOWLING

'Hat-tricks' 49
Three wickets with four consecutive balls 49
Eight or more wickets in an innings 49
Fourteen or more wickets in a match 50
Outstanding innings bowling analyses 50
Outstanding match bowling analyses 50
Most wickets taken by a bowler in a day 50
Bowlers taking ten or more wickets on début 50
Bowlers taking a wicket with first ball in Test cricket 51
Highest wicket aggregates in a Test rubber 51
Most runs conceded in an innings 51
Most runs conceded in a match 52
Bowlers unchanged in a completed innings 52

PART V—ALL-ROUND CRICKET

All-round performances—100 runs and 8 wickets in a match 53
Best all-round records in a Test rubber 53

PART VI—FIELDING AND WICKET-KEEPING

Fielders:
    Most catches in an innings 54
    Most catches in a match 54
    Most catches in a Test rubber 54

Wicket-keepers:
    Most dismissals in an innings 54
    Most dismissals in a match 54
    Most dismissals in a Test rubber 54
No byes conceded in a high innings total 55

PART VII—CAREER RECORDS

Highest run aggregates 56
Best batting averages—qualification 15 innings 56
Batsmen scoring most centuries 57
Highest wicket aggregates 57
Best bowling averages—qualification 25 wickets 58
Most frequent wicket-takers—qualification 25 wickets 58
Most economical bowling figures—qualification 1800 balls 58
Most dismissals by a wicket-keeper 59
Most catches by a fielder 59
Best all-round records 59

PART VIII—MEMORABILIA

Abandoned without a ball bowled 61
Accidents 61
Attendance records in England 61
Attendance records in Australia 61
Attendance records in South Africa 62
Batting curiosities 62
Batting through a complete day's play 62
Benefits and collections 63
Boundaries 63
Bowling aggregates 63
Bowling curiosities 63
Bowling milestones reached quickly 64
Bowling spells 64
Captaincy curiosities 64
Centuries and fifties 65
Century before lunch on first day.. 65
Century before lunch on other days.. 65
Centuries by batsman lower than No. 8 in order 65
Début in Test cricket 65
Declarations 65
Dismissals 66
Dismissal—escapes from 66
Dismissals—unusual 66
Disputes 67
'Ducks' 67
England Test selectors 67
Extras 68
Family relationships in Test cricket 68
Favourite grounds of batsmen 69
Fielding 69
Figure curiosities 69
Four bowlers only in a long innings 69
Good batting sequences 70
Good bowling sequences 70
Good bowling spells 70
Innings totals 71
Most consecutive Test appearances 71
Most Test appearances 72
Oldest players to make début in Test cricket 72
On field for whole of match 72
Partnership memorabilia 73
Players who have represented two countries 73
Umpires 73
Weather 73
Youngest players to make début in Test cricket 74
Youngest players to score a century in Test cricket 74
Miscellaneous 74

APPENDICES

'A'—Test Career Records, 1876–77 to 1960

Batting and Fielding:
England.. 75
Australia 80
South Africa.. 84
West Indies 87
New Zealand 88
India 90
Pakistan 91

Bowling:
England.. 92
Australia 95
South Africa.. 97
West Indies 99
New Zealand 101
India 102
Pakistan 103

Consolidated record of players who have appeared for two countries 103
Summary of Averages 104

'B'—Centuries in Test Cricket:
England.. 105
Australia 109
South Africa.. 112
West Indies 113
New Zealand 114
India 115
Pakistan 115

'C'—Bowlers taking Ten Wickets in a Test Match 117

'D'—Century Wicket Partnerships:
England.. 120
Australia 125
South Africa.. 128
West Indies 130
New Zealand 132
India 133
Pakistan 134
Summary 135

'E'—Test Match Captains, 1876–1960 136

'F'—Records of Individual Test Series 141
Highest run aggregates in each series 144
Highest wicket aggregates in each series 146
Records for individual Test series 148

'G'—Counties Providing England Players 156

FIRST-CLASS CRICKET RECORDS

PART I—THE SIDES

Large innings totals 162
Innings totals of over 600 162
Large second innings totals 167
Small innings totals.. 168
Large fourth innings totals 172
Variation of innings totals 173
Victories by vast margins 173
Highest match aggregates 174
Lowest match aggregates 175
Tie matches 176
First-class matches completed in one day 177
Teams scoring four or more centuries in an innings 178
Matches dominated by batting 179
Collapses and recoveries 180

PART II—BATTING

Highest individual innings 183
Highest individual innings for and against each team 184
Highest maiden centuries 185
Double Centuries:
    Four or more in a season 186
    Two in successive innings 186
    Nearest to three in successive innings 186
    Complete list 186
A century on début in first-class cricket 204
A century on début for first-class county 206
A century on début for a touring team 207
A century in each innings of a match 209
Batsmen scoring over 350 runs in a match 214
Three or more centuries in successive innings 214
Sequences of centuries in successive innings 218
Most fifties in successive innings 219
Most runs before being dismissed 220
High Aggregate of Runs in a Season:
    3000 in England 220
    2000 in England 221
    1000 in Australia 227
    1000 in South Africa 228
      700 in West Indies 229
      600 in New Zealand 229
    1000 in India, Pakistan and Ceylon 230
Twelve or more centuries in a season 230
Leading batsmen of the season 231
Outstanding batting averages 232
1000 runs with average of less than 20 233
Batsmen scoring 1000 runs in a month 233
1000 runs during May 234
Earliest dates for reaching run aggregates 234
Most runs added during a batsman's innings 234
Successful first season's batting 235
Carrying bat through completed innings 235
Fast Scoring:
    Fast fifties 245
    Fast centuries 246
    Fastest 150 246
    Fast double-centuries 246
    Fast triple-centuries 247
    Fast innings 247
    Fast partnerships 248
    Individual innings of fifty with least scoring strokes 249
    Batsmen to reach the century before lunch 249
    Batsmen who have scored 300 runs in a day's play 253
    Most runs scored by a side in a day's play 254
    Fast scoring by sides 254
    Most runs scored in one hit 255
    Most runs scored off one over 255
    Most sixes in an innings 256
    Hits for six off consecutive balls 257
    Most sixes in a match 258
    Most boundaries in an innings 258
    High percentage of runs scored by boundary hits 259
Slow Scoring:
    Slowest innings 260
    An hour before scoring first run 262
    An hour without scoring a run 262
    Slow scoring notes 263
    Slowest times to reach certain targets in an innings 264
    Fewest runs scored in a day's play 264
    Slow scoring in a match 265
Individual innings of long duration 265
Monopolizing the scoring 266

PART III—WICKET PARTNERSHIPS

World record for each wicket	271
Records by English, Australian and South African batsmen	271
Records by West Indian, New Zealand, Indian and Pakistan batsmen	272
Highest score at the fall of each wicket	272
Wicket partnerships of over 400	273

Leading Wicket Partnerships:

First wicket (200 and over)	273
Second wicket (200 and over)	279
Third wicket (200 and over)	286
Fourth wicket (200 and over)	292
Fifth wicket (200 and over)	297
Sixth wicket (200 and over)	299
Seventh wicket (150 and over)	301
Eighth wicket (150 and over)	305
Ninth wicket (150 and over)	306
Tenth wicket (100 and over)	307
Eleventh wicket	310
A century first-wicket partnership in each innings	310

PART IV—BOWLING

Most wickets in a season	312
Overseas bowlers	316
Outstanding bowling averages	318
Leading bowler of a season	319
Most balls bowled by a bowler in a season	320
Most runs off a bowler in a season	320
The most expensive 100 wickets in a season	321
Four wickets with consecutive balls	321
'Hat-tricks'	322
Four wickets with five successive balls	329
Good bowling spells	330
All ten wickets in an innings	331
Nine or ten wickets in an innings	332
Seventeen or more wickets in a match	338
Sixteen or more wickets in a day's play	339
Fifteen or more wickets in a match	339
Outstanding innings bowling analyses	342
Outstanding match bowling analyses	345
Inexpensive bowling analyses	347
Expensive bowling analyses	349
Most expensive bowling in an innings	350
Most expensive bowling in a match	350
Most balls bowled in an innings	351
Most balls bowled in a match	352
Bowlers unchanged through a completed match	353
Most maiden overs in succession	360
Sequences of successful bowling	361
Eight wickets before lunch	362
Eight batsmen clean bowled in an innings	362
Long distance for a bail	363
Earliest dates for reaching certain wicket aggregates	363
Good bowling on début in first-class cricket	363
Wicket with first ball in first-class cricket	364
Successful first season—bowling	365

PART V—ALL-ROUND CRICKET

The Cricketer's 'Double'—1000 runs and 100 wickets	366
Earliest dates for reaching 'double'	371
All-round cricket in a match	371
Century and 'hat-trick' in the same match	375

PART VI—FIELDING AND WICKET-KEEPING

Fielders:
Most catches in an innings 376
Most catches in a match 377
Wicket-keepers:
Most dismissals in an innings 380
Most dismissals in a match 382
Most catches in a season by a fielder 384
Most dismissals by a wicket-keeper in a season 385
The wicket-keeper's 'double' 385
Innings without byes 386
Innings productive of extras 386

PART VII—CAREER RECORDS

Batting:
30,000 runs in a career 388
10,000 runs in a career 388
Most centuries scored in a career 394
1000 runs in a season 20 or more times 394
Bowling:
2000 wickets in a career 395
1000 wickets in a career 395
100 wickets in a season 12 or more times 397
All-round cricket—10,000 runs and 1000 wickets 397
Fielding and wicket-keeping 398
Career records for overseas players 399

PART VIII—COMPETITION RECORDS, ETC.

The County Championship 403
Methods of deciding the Championship 403
Champion County each season 405
Champion County v. Rest of England 406
Order of merit each season 407
Complete playing record for all Championship matches 408
Aggregate records for each county 409
First-class county cricket clubs 410
Captains of the counties.. 412
County caps awarded since 1946 415
The Sheffield Shield 418
The Currie Cup Tournament 419
The West Indies Inter-Colonial Tournament 420
The Plunket Shield 420
The Bombay Pentangular Tournament 421
The 'Ranji' Trophy 422
The Quaid-I-Azam Trophy 422
Cricket at the Universities:
Oxford University Blues.. 423
Cambridge University Blues 428
University match results... 434
Centuries in the University match 435
Highest innings totals in the University match 436
Record wicket partnerships in University match 436
1000 runs in a University season 436
Highest run aggregates in a University career 437
Most wickets in a University season 437
Gentlemen v. Players 438
Centuries scored in the series of matches 438
Highest individual innings 440
Highest and lowest innings totals 440
Record wicket partnerships 440
Bowling unchanged through match 441
Results of matches at Lord's since 1919 441
Appearances at Lord's since 1919 442
Match record of Touring teams 445
Laws of Cricket 452

PART IX—MISCELLANEOUS

Attendance records for county cricket 455
Awards at cricket 455
Benefit matches 457
Centuries scored by Number Eleven batsmen 458
Eleven bowlers in one innings 458
F.A. cup winners' medals 459
Four bowlers only in an innings 459
Honorary life membership of M.C.C. 460
Innings with few boundaries 460
Knighthoods 461
Long overs—no-balls and wides 461
M.C.C. Presidents 463
M.C.C. Secretaries 464
'Mosts' in a season... 464
No-balled for throwing 464
Oldest first-class cricketers 466
Penalties, etc. 466
Public schoolboy cricketers 467
Similarity of dismissal 467
Spells of good batting.. 468
Unusual dismissals 469

Envoi 471